STRATEGIC MARKETING PROBLEMS

STRATEGIC MARKETING PROBLEMS

Cases and Comments

NINTH EDITION

Roger A. Kerin
Southern Methodist University

Robert A. Peterson
University of Texas

PRENTICE HALL, Upper Saddle River, New Jersey 07458

Acquisitions Editor: Whitney Blake
Editorial Assistant: Anthony Palmiotto
Editor-in-Chief: Natalie E. Anderson
Marketing Manager: Shannon More
Managing Editor (Editorial): Bruce Kaplan
Senior Production Editor: Mary Ellen McCourt
Managing Editor (Production): John Roberts
Production Manager: Arnold Vila
Associate Director, Manufacturing: Vincent Scelta
Electronic Artist: Rainbow Graphics, LLC.
Design Manager: Pat Smythe
Image Permission Supervisor: Kay Dellosa
Cover Design: Marjory Dressler
Composition: Rainbow Graphics, LLC.

Library of Congress Cataloging-in-Publication Data
Kerin, Roger A.
Strategic marketing problems : cases and comments / Roger A. Kerin, Robert A. Peterson. — 9th ed.
p. cm.
Includes bibliographical references and indexes.
ISBN 0-13-027661-8
1. Marketing—Decision making—Case studies. 2. Marketing—Management—Case studies. I. Peterson, Robert A. (Robert Allen), 1944- . II. Title.
HF5415.135.K47 2000
658.8′02—dc21 00-022379
CIP

Credits and acknowledgments for materials borrowed from other sources and reproduced, with permission, in this textbook appear on pages 78, 79, 89, 90, 99, 101, 109, 123–127, 143, 174, 175, 177–180, 182, 183, 187, 190, 202, 237, 238, 241, 257, 268, 271, 274, 288–292, 295–297, 317, 318, 321–323, 325, 327, 328, 331, 332, 335, 336, 338–340, 343, 344, 347, 348, 351, 352, 354, 357–359, 361, 363–365, 370, 371, 376, 379, 384, 394, 396, 397, 399, 401, 402, 405, 406, 408, 412, 416–418, 420, 423, 426, 427, 430, 449, 450, 453, 454, 475, 476, 478, 481, 489, 497, 498, 501, 502, 505, 507, 512, 520, 522, 529–531, 535, 536, 539–542, 564, 567, 570, 578, 579, 581, 584, 585, 589, 590, 592, 594–596, 615, 616, 632, 633, 637, 641, 646–648, 650, 651, 657, 658, 664, and 698.

Printed in the United States of America
10 9 8 7 6 5 4 3 2 1
ISBN 0-13-027661-8

To Our Families

Contents

Preface

Decision making in marketing is first and foremost a skill. Like most skills, it requires tools and terminology. Like all skills, it is best learned through practice. This book is dedicated to the development of decision-making skills in marketing. Textual material introduces concepts and tools useful in structuring and solving marketing problems. Case studies describing actual marketing problems provide an opportunity for those concepts and tools to be employed in practice. In every case study, the decision maker must develop a strategy consistent with the underlying factors existing in the situation presented and must consider the implications of that strategy for the organization and its environment.

The ninth edition of *Strategic Marketing Problems: Cases and Comments* seeks a balance between marketing management content and process. The book consists of 11 chapters and 42 cases.

Chapter 1, "Foundations of Strategic Marketing Management," provides an overview of the strategic marketing management process. The principal emphasis is on defining an organization's business, mission, and goals, identifying and framing organizational opportunities, formulating product-market strategies, budgeting, and controlling the marketing effort. The Appendix to Chapter 1 contains a marketing plan for an actual company, Paradise Kitchens®, Inc. The plan is annotated to focus attention on substantive elements of the plan as well as style and layout elements.

Chapter 2, "Financial Aspects of Marketing Management," reviews basic concepts from managerial accounting and managerial finance that are useful in marketing management. Primary emphasis is placed on such concepts as cost structure, relevant versus sunk costs, margins, contribution analysis, liquidity, discounted cash flow, operating leverage, and preparing *pro forma* income statements.

Chapter 3, "Marketing Decision Making and Case Analysis," introduces a systematic process for decision making and provides an overview of various aspects of case and decision analysis. A sample case and written student analysis are presented in the Appendix at the end of the book. The student analysis illustrates the nature and scope of a written case presentation, including the qualitative and quantitative analyses essential to a good presentation.

Chapter 4, "Opportunity Analysis and Market Targeting," focuses on the identification and evaluation of marketing opportunities. Market segmentation, market targeting, and market potential and profitability issues are considered in some depth.

Chapter 5, "Product and Service Strategy and Brand Management," focuses on the management of the organization's offering. New-offering development, life-cycle management, product or service positioning, branding decisions, brand growth strategies, and brand valuation are emphasized.

Chapter 6, "Integrated Marketing Communication Strategy and Management," raises issues in the design, execution, and evaluation of an integrated communication mix. Decisions concerned with communications objectives, strategy, budgeting, programming, and effectiveness, as well as sales management, are addressed.

Chapter 7, "Marketing Channel Strategy and Management," introduces a variety of considerations affecting channel selection and modification as well as trade relations. Specific decision areas covered include direct versus indirect distribution, dual distribution, cost-benefit analysis of channel choice and management, and marketing channel conflict and coordination.

Chapter 8, "Pricing Strategy and Management," highlights concepts and applications in price determination and modification. Emphasis is placed on evaluating demand, cost, and competitive influences when selecting or modifying pricing strategies for products and services and product-line pricing.

Chapter 9, "Interactive Marketing and Electronic Commerce," introduces strategic marketing management issues encountered by companies engaged in electronic commerce. Attention is placed on marketing opportunity analysis, different Internet business models, formulating a customer value proposition, and strategic and operational challenges facing incumbent and new entrant companies in the new marketspace.

Chapter 10, "Marketing Strategy Reformulation: The Control Process," focuses on the appraisal of marketing actions for the purpose of developing reformulation and recovery strategies. Considerations and techniques applicable to strategic and operations control are introduced.

Chapter 11, "Comprehensive Marketing Programs," raises issues in developing integrated marketing strategies. Emphasis is placed on marketing program decisions for new and existing products and services, including issues related to marketing-mix interactions, marketing program implementation, and marketing organization.

The case selection in this book reflects a broad overview of contemporary marketing problems and applications. Seventy-six percent of the cases are dated since 1995; 40 percent are dated since 1998. Of the 42 cases included, 30 deal with consumer products and services and 12 have a business-to-business marketing orientation. Nine cases introduce marketing issues in the international arena. Marketing of services is addressed in four cases, and four cases deal with electronic commerce. Sixty-one percent of the cases are new, revised, or updated for this edition, and many have spreadsheet applications embedded in the case analysis. All text and case material has been classroom tested.

Computer-assisted programs and a student manual are available for use with 17 of the cases in the book. The manual contains all the material necessary to use spreadsheets. It includes a sample case demonstration, instructions for use with specific cases, and input and output forms. If this material is not available from your instructor or bookstore, please write to the publisher.

The efforts of many people are reflected here. First, we thank those institutions and individuals who have kindly granted us permission to include their cases in this edition. The cases contribute significantly to the overall quality of the book, and each individual is prominently acknowledged in the Contents and at the bottom of the page on which the case begins. We specifically wish to thank the Harvard Business School and The University of Western Ontario for granting permission to reproduce cases authored by their faculties. Second, we wish to thank our numerous collaborators, whose efforts made the difference between good cases and excellent cases. Third, we thank the adopters of the previous eight editions of the book for their many comments and suggestions for improvements. Finally, we wish to thank the numerous reviewers of this and previous editions for their conscientious reviews of our material: David Berkowitz, University of Alabama in Huntsville; Lynne Payne, Livingston University; Michael Laric, University of Baltimore; Charles Brooks, Quinnipiac College; Michael Messina, Gannon University; Avery Abernethy, Auburn University; Richard Kolbe, Kent State University; Dwight Scherban, Central Connecticut State

University; David E. Griffith, University of Oklahoma; Tammy Pappas, Eastern Michigan University; Audrey Guskey, Duquesne University; and John Barnes, University of Texas at El Paso. Naturally, we bear full responsibility for any errors of omission and commission in the final product.

Roger A. Kerin

Robert A. Peterson

CHAPTER 1

Foundations of Strategic Marketing Management

The primary purpose of marketing is to create long-term and mutually beneficial exchange relationships between an entity and the publics (individuals and organizations) with which it interacts. Though this fundamental purpose of marketing is timeless, the manner in which organizations undertake it continues to evolve. No longer do marketing managers function solely to direct day-to-day operations; they must make strategic decisions as well. This elevation of marketing perspectives to a strategic position in organizations has resulted in expanded responsibilities for marketing managers. Increasingly, they find themselves involved in charting the direction of the organization and contributing to decisions that will create and sustain a competitive advantage and affect long-term organizational performance. According to a senior strategic-planning manager at General Electric:

> [T]he marketing manager is the most significant functional contributor to the strategic-planning process, with leadership roles in defining the business mission; analysis of the environmental, competitive, and business situations; developing objectives, goals, and strategies; and defining product, market distribution, and quality plans to implement the business's strategies. This involvement extends to the development of programs and operational plans that are fully linked with the strategic plan.[1]

The transition of the marketing manager from being only an implementer to being a maker of organization strategy has prompted the emergence of strategic marketing management as a course of study and practice. *Strategic marketing management* consists of five complex and interrelated analytical processes.

1. Defining the organization's business, mission, and goals
2. Identifying and framing organizational growth opportunities
3. Formulating product-market strategies
4. Budgeting marketing, financial, and production resources
5. Developing reformulation and recovery strategies

The remainder of this chapter discusses each of these processes and their relationships to one another.

DEFINING THE ORGANIZATION'S BUSINESS, MISSION, AND GOALS

The practice of strategic marketing management begins with a clearly stated business definition, mission, and set of goals or objectives. A business definition outlines the scope of a particular organization's operations. Its mission is a written statement of organizational purpose. Goals or objectives specify what an organization intends to achieve. Each plays an important role in describing the character of an organization and what it seeks to accomplish.

Business Definition

Determining what business an organization is in is neither obvious nor easy. In many instances, a single organization may operate several businesses, as is the case with large *Fortune* 500 companies. Defining each of these businesses is a necessary first step in strategic marketing management.

Contemporary strategic marketing perspectives indicate that an organization should define a business by the type of customers it wishes to serve, the particular needs of those customer groups it wishes to satisfy, and the means or technology by which the organization will satisfy these customer needs.[2] By defining a business from a customer or market perspective, an organization is appropriately viewed as a customer-satisfying endeavor, not a product-producing or service-delivery enterprise. Products and services are transient, as is often the technology or means used to produce or deliver them. Basic customer needs and customer groups are more enduring. For example, the means for delivering prerecorded music has undergone significant change over the past 25 years. During this period, the dominant prerecorded music technologies and products evolved from plastic records, to eight-track tapes, to cassettes, and most recently, to compact discs. By comparison, the principal consumer buying segment(s) and needs satisfied have varied little.

Much of the recent corporate restructuring and refocusing has resulted from senior company executives asking the question, "What business are we in?" The experience of *Encyclopaedia Britannica* is a case in point.[3] The venerable publishing company is best known for its comprehensive and authoritative 32-volume, leather-bound book reference series first printed in 1768. In the late 1990s, however, the company found itself in a precarious competitive environment. CD-ROMs and the Internet had become the study tools of choice for students and Microsoft's Encarta CD-ROM and IBM's CD-ROM joint venture with *World Book* were attracting Britannica's core customers. The result? Book sales fell 83 percent between 1990 and 1997. Britannica's senior management was confident that the need for dependable and trustworthy information among curious and intelligent customers remained. However, the technology for satisfying these needs had changed. This realization prompted Britannica to redefine its business. According to a company official: "We're reinventing our business. We're not in the book business. We're in the information business." By early 2000, the company was on its way to becoming the premier information site on the Internet. Britannica's subscription service (www.eb.com) markets archival information to schools and public and business libraries. Its consumer Web site (www.britannica.com) is a source of information and search engine leading to some 150,000 Web sites selected by Britannica staffers for information quality and accuracy.

Business Mission

An organization's business mission complements its business definition. As a written statement, a mission underscores the scope of an organization's operations apparent in its business definition and reflects management's vision of what the organization seeks to do. Although there is no overall definition for all mission statements, most statements describe an organization's purpose with reference to its customers, products or services, markets, philosophy, and technology.[4] Some mission statements are generally stated such as that for Saturn Corporation, a division of General Motors. Saturn's mission is to:

> Market vehicles developed and manufactured in the United States that are world leaders in quality, cost, and customer satisfaction through the integration of people, technology, and business systems and to transfer knowledge, technology, and experience throughout General Motors.

Others are more specifically written, like that for Hendison Electronics Corporation. Hendison Electronics Corporation aspires

> to serve the discriminating purchasers of home entertainment products who approach their purchase in a deliberate manner with heavy consideration of long-term benefits. We will emphasize home entertainment products with superior performance, style, reliability, and value that require representative display, professional selling, trained service, and brand acceptance—retailed through reputable electronic specialists to those consumers whom the company can most effectively service.

Mission statements also apply to not-for-profit organizations. For instance, the mission of the American Red Cross is

> to improve the quality of human life; to enhance self-reliance and concern for others; and to help people avoid, prepare for, and cope with emergencies.

A carefully crafted mission statement that succinctly conveys organizational purpose can provide numerous benefits to an organization including focus to its marketing effort. It can (1) crystallize management's vision of the organization's long-term direction and character; (2) provide guidance in identifying, pursuing, and evaluating market and product opportunities; and (3) inspire and challenge employees to do those things that are valued by the organization and its customers. It also provides direction for setting business goals or objectives.

Business Goals

Goals or objectives convert the organization's mission into tangible actions and results that are to be achieved, often within a specific time frame. For example, the 3M Company emphasizes research and development and innovation in its business mission. This view is made tangible in one of the company's goals: 30 percent of 3M's annual revenues must come from company products that are less than four years old.[5]

Goals or objectives divide into three major categories: production, financial, and marketing. Production goals or objectives apply to the use of manufacturing and service capacity and to product and service quality. Financial goals or objectives focus on return on investment, return on sales, profit, cash flow, and shareholder wealth. Marketing goals or objectives emphasize market share, marketing productivity, sales volume, profit, customer satisfaction, and customer value creation. When production, financial, and marketing goals or objectives are combined, they represent a composite picture of organizational purpose within a specific time frame; accordingly, they must complement one another.

Goal or objective setting should be problem-centered and future-oriented. Because goals or objectives represent statements of what the organization wishes to achieve in a specific time frame, they implicitly arise from an understanding of the current situation. Therefore, managers need an appraisal of operations or a *situation analysis* to determine reasons for the gap between what was or is expected and what has happened or will happen. If performance has met expectations, the question arises as to future directions. If performance has not met expectations, managers must diagnose the reasons for this difference and enact a remedial program. Chapter 3 provides an expanded discussion on performing a situation analysis.

IDENTIFYING AND FRAMING ORGANIZATIONAL GROWTH OPPORTUNITIES

Once the character and direction of the organization have been outlined in its business definition, mission, and goals or objectives, the practice of strategic marketing management enters an entrepreneurial phase. Using business definition, mission, and goals as a guide, the search for and evaluation of organizational growth opportunities can begin.

Converting Environmental Opportunities into Organizational Opportunities

Three questions help marketing managers decide whether certain environmental opportunities represent viable organizational growth opportunities:

- What might we do?
- What do we do best?
- What must we do?

Each of these questions assists in identifying and framing organizational growth opportunities. They also highlight major concepts in strategic marketing management.

The *what might we do* question introduces the concept of *environmental opportunity*. Unmet or changing consumer needs, unsatisfied buyer groups, and new means or technology for delivering value to prospective buyers represent sources of environmental opportunities for organizations. In this regard, environmental opportunities are boundless. However, the mere presence of an environmental opportunity does not mean that an organizational growth opportunity exists. Two additional questions must be asked.

The *what do we do best* question introduces the concept of organizational capability, or distinctive competency. *Distinctive competency* describes an organization's unique strengths or qualities, including skills, technologies, or resources that distinguish it from other organizations.[6] In order for any of an organization's strengths or qualities to be considered truly distinctive and a source of competitive advantage, two criteria must be satisfied. First, the strength must be imperfectly imitable by competitors. That is, competitors cannot replicate a skill (such as the direct-marketing competency of Dell Computer) easily or without a sizable investment of time, effort, and money. Second, the strength should make a significant contribution to the benefits perceived by customers and, by doing so, provide superior value to them. For example, the ability to engage in technological innovation that is wanted and provides value to customers is a distinctive competency. Consider the Safety Razor Division of the Gillette Company.[7] Its distinctive competencies lie in three areas: (1) shaving technology and development, (2) high-volume manufacturing of precision metal and plastic products, and (3) marketing of mass-distributed consumer package goods. These competencies were responsible for the Mach 3 razor, a technological innovation, which sustained Gillette's dominance of the wet-shaving market.

Finally, the *what must we do* question introduces the concept of success requirements in an industry or market. *Success requirements* are basic tasks that an organization must perform in a market or industry to compete successfully. These requirements are subtle in nature and often overlooked. For example, distribution and inventory control are critical success factors in the cosmetics industry. Firms competing in the personal computer industry recognize that the requirements for success include low-cost production capabilities, access to distribution channels, and continuous innovation in software development.

The linkage among environmental opportunity, distinctive competency, and success requirements will determine whether an organizational opportunity exists. A clearly defined statement of success requirements serves as a device for matching an environmental opportunity with an organization's distinctive competencies. If *what must be done* is inconsistent with *what can be done* to capitalize on an environmental opportunity, an organizational growth opportunity will fail to materialize. Too often, organizations ignore this linkage and pursue seemingly lucrative environmental opportunities that are doomed from the start. Exxon Corporation learned this lesson painfully after investing $500 million in the office products market over a ten-year period only to see the venture fail. After the company abandoned this venture, a former Exxon executive summed up what had been learned: "Don't get involved where you don't have the skills. It's hard enough to make money at what you're good at."[8] By clearly establishing the linkages necessary for success before taking any action, an organization can minimize its risk of failure. An executive for L'eggs hosiery illustrates this point when specifying his new-venture criteria:

> [P]roducts that can be sold through food and drugstore outlets, are purchased by women, . . . can be easily and distinctly packaged, and comprise at least a $500 million retail market not already dominated by one or two major producers.[9]

When one considers L'eggs' past successes, it is apparent that whatever environmental opportunities are pursued will be consistent with what L'eggs does best, as illustrated by past achievements in markets whose success requirements are similar. An expanded discussion of these points is found in chapter 4.

SWOT Analysis

SWOT analysis is a formal framework for identifying and framing organizational growth opportunities. SWOT is an acronym for an organization's *S*trengths and *W*eaknesses and external *O*pportunities and *T*hreats. It is an easy-to-use framework for focusing attention on the fact that an organizational growth opportunity results from a good fit between an organization's internal capabilities (apparent in its strengths and weaknesses) and its external environment reflected in the presence of environmental opportunities and threats. Many organizations also perform a SWOT analysis as part of their goal- or objective-setting process.

Exhibit 1.1 (page 6) displays a SWOT analysis framework depicting representative entries for internal strengths and weaknesses and external opportunities and threats. A strength is something that an organization is good at doing or some characteristic that gives the organization an important capability. Something an organization lacks or does poorly relative to other organizations is a weakness. Opportunities represent external developments or conditions in the environment that have favorable implications for the organization. Threats, on the other hand, pose dangers to the welfare of the organization.

A properly conducted SWOT analysis goes beyond the simple preparation of lists. Attention needs to be placed on evaluating strengths, weaknesses, opportunities, and threats and drawing conclusions about how each might affect the organization. The following questions might be asked once strengths, weaknesses, opportunities, and threats have been identified:

1. Which internal strengths represent distinctive competencies? Do these strengths compare favorably with what are believed to be market or industry success requirements? Looking at Exhibit 1.1, for example, does "proven innovation skill" strength represent a distinctive competency and a market success requirement?
2. Which internal weaknesses disqualify the organization from pursuing certain opportunities? Look again at Exhibit 1.1, and note that the organization acknowledges that it has a "weak distribution network and a subpar salesforce." How might this organizational weakness affect the opportunity described as

EXHIBIT 1.1

Sample SWOT Analysis Framework and Representative Examples

Selected Internal Factors	***Representative***		***Selected External Factors***	***Representative***	
	Strengths	*Weaknesses*		*Opportunities*	*Threats*
Management	Experienced management talent	Lack of management depth	Economic	Upturn in the business cycle; evidence of growing personal disposable income	Adverse shifts in foreign exchange rates
Marketing	Well thought of by buyers; effective advertising program	Weak distribution network; subpar salesforce	Competition	Complacency among domestic competitors	Entry of lower-cost foreign competitors
Manufacturing	Available manufacturing capacity	Higher overall production costs relative to key competitors	Consumer trends	Unfulfilled customer needs on high and low end of product category suggesting a product line expansion possibility	Growing preference for private-label products
R & D	Proven innovation skills	Poor track record in bringing innovations to the marketplace	Technology	Patent protection of complementary technology ending	Newer substitute technologies imminent
Finance	Little debt relative to industry average	Weak cash flow position	Legal/ regulatory	Falling trade barriers in attractive foreign markets	Increased U.S. regulation of product-testing procedures and labeling
Offerings	Unique, high-quality products	Too narrow a product line	Industry/ market structure	New distribution channels evolving that reach a broader customer population	Low-entry barriers for new competitors

"new distribution channels evolving that reach a broader customer population"?

3. Does a pattern emerge from the listing of strengths, weaknesses, opportunities, and threats? Inspection of Exhibit 1.1 reveals that low-entry barriers into the market/industry may contribute to the entry of lower-cost foreign competitors. This does not bode well for domestic competitors labeled as "complacent" and the organization's acknowledged high production costs.

FORMULATING PRODUCT-MARKET STRATEGIES

In practice, organizational opportunities frequently emerge from an organization's existing markets or from newly identified markets. Opportunities also arise for existing, improved, or new products and services. Matching products and markets to form product-market strategies is the subject of the next set of decision processes.

Product-market strategies consist of plans for matching an organization's existing or potential offerings with the needs of markets, informing markets that the offerings exist, having offerings available at the right time and place to facilitate exchange, and assigning prices to offerings. In short, a product-market strategy involves selecting specific markets and profitably reaching them through an integrated program called a *marketing mix.*

Exhibit 1.2 classifies product-market strategies according to the match between offerings and markets.[10] The operational implications and requirements of each strategy are briefly described in the following subsections.

Market-Penetration Strategy

A *market-penetration strategy* dictates that an organization seek to gain greater dominance in a market in which it already has an offering. This strategy involves attempts to increase present buyers' usage or consumption rates of the offering, attract buyers of competing offerings, or stimulate product trial among potential customers. The mix of marketing activities might include lower prices for the offerings, expanded distribution to provide wider coverage of an existing market, and heavier promotional efforts extolling the "unique" advantages of an organization's offering over competing offerings. The Coca-Cola Company used all of these activities in attempting to achieve its announced goal of increasing its market share from 42 percent to 50 percent of the U.S. soft drink market by the year 2000.[11]

Several organizations have attempted to gain dominance by promoting more frequent and varied usage of their offering. For example, the Florida Orange Growers Association advocates drinking orange juice throughout the day rather than for breakfast only. Airlines stimulate usage through a variety of reduced-fare programs and various family-travel packages, designed to reach the primary traveler's spouse and children.

Marketing managers should consider a number of factors before adopting a penetration strategy. First, they must examine market growth. A penetration strategy is usually more effective in a growth market. Attempts to increase market share when volume is stable often result in aggressive retaliatory actions by competitors. Second, they must consider competitive reaction. Procter & Gamble implemented a penetration strategy for its Folger's coffee in selected East Coast cities, only to run

EXHIBIT 1.2

Product-Market Strategies

		Markets	
		Existing	*New*
Offerings	*Existing*	Market penetration	Market development
	New	New offering development	Diversification

head-on into an equally aggressive reaction from Kraft Foods' Maxwell House Division. According to one observer of the competitive situation:

> When Folger's mailed millions of coupons offering consumers 45 cents off on a one-pound can of coffee, Maxwell House countered with newspaper coupons of its own. When Folger's gave retailers 15 percent discounts from the list price . . . , Maxwell House met them head-on. [Maxwell House] let Folger's lead off with a TV blitz. . . . Then [Maxwell House] saturated the airwaves.[12]

The result of this struggle was no change in market share for either firm. Third, marketing managers must consider the capacity of the market to increase usage or consumption rates and the availability of new buyers. Both are particularly relevant when viewed from the perspective of the conversion costs involved in capturing buyers from competitors, stimulating usage, and attracting new users.

Market-Development Strategy

A *market-development strategy* dictates that an organization introduce its existing offerings to markets other than those it is currently serving. Examples include introducing existing products to different geographical areas (including international expansion) or different buying publics. For example, Harley-Davidson engaged in a market-development strategy when it entered Japan, Germany, and France. O. M. Scott and Sons Company employed this strategy when it moved from the home lawn-improvement market to large users of lawn-care products, such as golf courses and home construction contractors.

The mix of marketing activities used must often be varied to reach different markets with differing buying patterns and requirements. Reaching new markets often requires modification of the basic offering, different distribution outlets, or a change in sales effort and advertising.

Like the market-penetration strategy, market development involves a careful consideration of competitor strengths and weaknesses and competitor retaliation potential. Moreover, because the firm seeks new buyers, it must understand their number, motivation, and buying patterns in order to develop marketing activities successfully. Finally, the firm must consider its strengths, in terms of adaptability to new markets, in order to evaluate the potential success of the venture.

Market development in the international arena has grown in importance and usually takes one of four forms: (1) exporting, (2) licensing, (3) joint venture, or (4) direct investment.[13] Each option has advantages and disadvantages. Exporting involves marketing the same offering in another country either directly (through sales offices) or through intermediaries in a foreign country. Because this approach typically requires minimal capital investment and is easy to initiate, it is a popular option for developing foreign markets. Procter & Gamble, for instance, exports its deodorants, soaps, fragrances, shampoos, and other health and beauty products to Eastern Europe and Russia. Licensing is a contractual arrangement whereby one firm (licensee) is given the rights to patents, trademarks, know-how, and other intangible assets by its owner (licensor) in return for a royalty (usually 5 percent of gross sales) or a fee. For example, Cadbury Schweppes PLC, a London-based multinational firm, has licensed Hershey Foods to sell its candies in the United States for a fee of $300 million. Licensing provides a low-risk, quick, and capital-free entry into a foreign market. However, the licensor usually has no control over production and marketing by the licensee. A joint venture, often called a strategic alliance, involves investment by both a foreign firm and a local company to create a new entity in the host country. The two companies share ownership, control, and profits of the entity. Joint ventures are popular because one company may not have the necessary financial, technical, or managerial resources to enter a market alone. This approach also often ensures against trade barriers being imposed on the foreign firm by the government of the host company. Japanese companies frequently engage in joint ventures with American and European firms to gain access to foreign markets. A problem frequently arising from joint ventures is that the partners do not always agree on how the new entity should be run. Direct investment in a manufacturing and/or assembly facility in a foreign market is the most risky option and requires the greatest commitment. However, it brings the firm closer to its customers and may be the most profitable approach for developing foreign markets. For these reasons, direct investment must be evaluated closely in terms of benefits and costs. Direct investment often follows one of the three other approaches to foreign-market entry. For example, Mars, Inc. originally exported its M&Ms, Snickers, and Mars bars to Russia and recently opened a $200 million candy factory outside Moscow.[14]

Product-Development Strategy

A *product-development strategy* dictates that the organization create new offerings for existing markets. The approach taken may be to develop totally new offerings (product innovation) to enhance the value to customers of existing offerings (product augmentation), or to broaden the existing line of offerings by adding different sizes, forms, flavors, and so forth (product line extension). Personal digital assistants, such as Palm Pilot, are an example of product innovation, as is the introduction of the "Cash Management Account" by Merrill Lynch in the financial services industry. Product augmentation can be achieved in numerous ways. One is to bundle complementary items or services with an existing offering. For example, programming services, application aids, and training programs for buyers enhance the value of personal computers. Another way is to improve the functional performance of the offering. Producers of facsimile machines have done this by improving print quality. Many types of product-line extensions are possible. Personal-care companies market deodorants in powder, spray, and liquid forms; Quaker Oats produces 30 flavors of Gatorade; and Frito-Lay offers its Lay's potato chips in a number of package sizes.

Companies successful at developing and commercializing new offerings lead their industries in sales growth and profitability. The likelihood of success is increased if the development effort results in offerings that satisfy a clearly understood buyer need. In the toy industry, for instance, these needs translate into products with three qualities: (1) lasting play value, (2) the ability to be shared with other children, and (3) the ability to stimulate a child's imagination.[15] Successful commercialization occurs when the offering can be communicated and delivered to a well-defined buyer group at a price it is willing and able to pay.

Important considerations in planning a product-development strategy concern the market size and volume necessary for the effort to be profitable, the magnitude and timing of competitive response, the impact of the new product on existing offerings, and the capacity (in terms of human and financial investment and technology) of the organization to deliver the offerings to the market(s). More importantly, successful new offerings must have a significant "point of difference" reflected in superior product or service characteristics that deliver unique and wanted benefits to consumers. Two examples from the cereal industry illustrate this view.[16] In 1995, General Mills introduced Fringos, a sweetened cereal flake about the size of a corn chip. Consumers were supposed to snack on them, but they didn't. The point of difference was not significant enough to get consumers to switch from competing snacks such as popcorn, potato chips, or tortilla chips. On the other hand, Nabisco's fat-free Snackwell Cereal Bars became the number one brand in the $700-million snack-bar category in 1996 by delivering a unique and wanted benefit.

The potential for cannibalism must be considered with a product-development strategy. *Cannibalism* occurs when sales of a new product or service come at the expense of sales of existing products or services already marketed by the firm. For example, it is estimated that 75 percent of Gillette's Mach 3 razor volume came from the company's other razors and shaving systems. Cannibalism of this degree is likely to occur in many product-development programs. The issue faced by the manager is whether it detracts from the overall profitability of the organization's total mix of offerings. At Gillette, the cannibalism rate for Mach 3 is viewed favorably since its gross profit margin is three times higher than the company's other razors.[17]

Diversification

Diversification involves the development or acquisition of offerings new to the organization and the introduction of those offerings to publics not previously served by the organization. Many firms have adopted this strategy in recent years to take advantage of perceived growth opportunities. Yet diversification is often a high-risk strategy because both the offerings (and often their underlying technology) and the public or market served are new to the organization.

Consider the following examples of failed diversification.[18] Anheuser-Busch recorded 17 years of losses with its Eagle Snacks Division and incurred a $206 million write-off when the division was finally shut down. Rohr Industries, a subcontractor in the aerospace industry, reported a $59.9 million write-off on a mass-transit diversification. Singer's effort to develop a business-machines venture over a 10-year period was abandoned while still unprofitable. Gerber Products Company, which holds 70 percent of the U.S. baby-food market, has been mostly unsuccessful in diversifying into child-care centers, toys, furniture, and adult food and beverages. Coca-Cola's many attempts at diversification—acquiring wine companies, a movie studio, and a pasta manufacturer, and producing television game shows—have also proven to be largely unsuccessful. These examples highlight the importance of understanding the link between market success requirements and an organization's distinctive competency. In each of these cases, a bridge was not made between these two concepts and thus an organizational opportunity was not realized.

Still, diversifications can be successful. Successful diversifications typically result from an organization's attempt to apply its distinctive competency in reaching new markets with new offerings. By relying on its marketing expertise and extensive distribution system, Procter & Gamble has had success with offerings ranging from cake mixes to disposable diapers.

Strategy Selection

A recurrent issue in strategic marketing management is determining the consistency of product-market strategies with the organization's definition, mission and capabilities, market capacity and behavior, environmental forces, and competitive activities. Proper analysis of these factors depends on the availability and evaluation of relevant information. Information on markets should include data on size, buying behavior, and requirements. Information on environmental forces such as social, legal, political, and economic changes is necessary to determine the future viability of the organization's offerings and the markets served. In recent years, for example, organizations have had to alter or adapt their product-market strategies because of political actions (deregulation), social changes (increase in the number of employed women), economic fluctuations (income shifts and changes in disposable personal income), attitudes (value consciousness), technological advances (the growth of the Internet/World Wide Web), and population shifts (city to suburb and northern to southern United States)—to name just a few of the environmental changes. Competitive activities must be monitored to ascertain their existing or possible strategies and performance in satisfying buyer needs.

In practice, the strategy selection decision is based on an analysis of the costs and benefits of alternative strategies and their probabilities of success. For example, a manager may compare the costs and benefits involved in further penetrating an existing

EXHIBIT 1.3

Decision-Tree Format

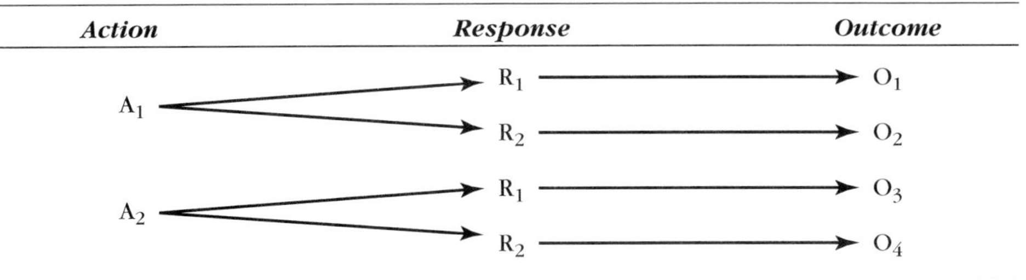

market to those associated with introducing the existing product to a new market. It is important to make a careful analysis of competitive structure; market growth, decline, or shifts; and opportunity costs (potential benefits not obtained). The product or service itself may dictate a strategy change. If the product has been purchased by all of the buyers it is going to attract in an existing market, opportunities for growth beyond replacement purchases are reduced. This situation would indicate a need to search out new buyers (markets) or to develop new products or services for present markets.

The probabilities of success of the various strategies must then be considered. A. T. Kearney, a management consulting firm, has provided rough probability estimates of success for each of the four basic strategies.[19] The probability of a successful diversification is 1 in 20. The probability of successfully introducing an existing product into a new market (market-development strategy) is 1 in 4. There is a 50–50 chance of success for a new product being introduced into an existing market (product-development strategy). Finally, minor modification of an offering directed toward its existing market (market-penetration strategy) has the highest probability of success.

A useful technique for gauging potential outcomes of alternative marketing strategies is to array possible actions, the responses to these actions, and the outcomes in the form of a decision tree, so named because of the branching out of responses from action taken. This implies that for any action taken, certain responses can be anticipated, each with its own specific outcomes. Exhibit 1.3 shows a decision tree.

As an example, consider a situation in which a marketing manager must decide between a market-penetration strategy and a market-development strategy. Suppose the manager recognizes that competitors may react aggressively or passively to either strategy. This situation can be displayed vividly using the decision-tree scheme, as shown in Exhibit 1.4. This representation allows the manager to consider actions,

EXHIBIT 1.4

Sample Decision Tree

Action	*Response*	*Outcome*
Market-penetration strategy	Aggressive competition →	Estimated profit of $2 million
	Passive competition →	Estimated profit of $3 million
Market-development strategy	Aggressive competition →	Estimated profit of $1 million
	Passive competition →	Estimated profit of $4 million

responses, and outcomes simultaneously. The decision tree shows that the highest profits will result if a market-development strategy is enacted and competitors react passively. The manager must resolve the question of competitive reaction because an aggressive response will plunge the profit to $1 million, which is less than either outcome under the market-penetration strategy. The manager must rely on informed judgment to assess subjectively the likelihood of competitive response. Chapter 3 provides a more detailed description of decision analysis and its application.

The Marketing Mix

Matching offerings and markets requires recognition of the other marketing activities available to the marketing manager. Combined with the offering, program of activities form the marketing mix.

A marketing mix typically encompasses activities controllable by the organization. These include the kind of product, service, or idea offered (product strategy), how it will be communicated to buyers (communication strategy), the method for distributing the offering to buyers (channel strategy), and the amount buyers will pay for the offering (price strategy). Each of these individual strategies is described later in this book. Here it is sufficient to note that each element of the marketing mix plays a role in stimulating a market's (buyers') willingness and ability to buy and creating customer value. For example, communications—personal selling, advertising, sales promotion, and public relations—informs and assures buyers that the offering will meet their needs. Marketing channels satisfy buyers' shopping patterns and purchase requirements in terms of point-of-purchase information and offering availability. Price represents the value or benefits provided by the offering.

The appropriate marketing mix for a product or service depends on the success requirements of the markets at which it is directed. The "rightness" of a product, communication, channel, or price strategy can be interpreted only in the context of markets served. Recognition of this fact has prompted the use of regional marketing, whereby different marketing mixes are employed to accommodate unique consumer preferences and competitive conditions in different geographical areas. For instance, Frito-Lay's Tostitos brand of tortilla chips is marketed as a specialty product sold mostly through delicatessens in some northeastern states. The brand's communication and price policies are not aggressive in these states because of fragmented competition. Tortilla chips in southwestern states are a commodity-type product sold by many competitors through supermarkets. The Tostitos brand is therefore supported in that geographic area by more aggressive price and communication programs. Firms that market products and services worldwide often "glocalize" their marketing mixes. That is, global decisions are made in such areas as product development, but decisions related to advertising, pricing, and distribution are arrived at by local (country-specific) marketing managers. A prime example of glocalization is found in the marketing of Swatch watches. In developed countries, Swatch watches are marketed as a fashion item; in less developed countries, the marketing mix emphasizes simple design, affordable cost, and functional qualities.

Internet/Web-based technologies have created another market setting, called the market*space*. As described in Chapter 9, companies that succeed in the marketspace deliver customer value through the interactive capabilities of these technologies, which allow for greater flexibility in managing marketing mix elements. For example, on-line sellers routinely adjust prices and advertisements to changing environmental conditions, purchase situations, and purchase behaviors of on-line buyers. Also, interactive two-way Internet/Web-based capabilities in marketspace allow a customer to tell a seller exactly what his or her buying interests and requirements are, making possible the transformation of a product or service into a customized solution for the individual. In addition, the purpose and role of channel intermediaries in marketspace changes (described in greater detail in chapter 9).

In addition to being consistent with the needs of markets served, a marketing mix must be consistent with the organization's capacity, and the individual activities must complement one another. Several questions offer direction in evaluating an organization's marketing mix. First, is the marketing mix internally consistent? Do the individual activities complement one another to form a whole, as opposed to fragmented pieces? Does the mix fit the organization, the market, and the environment into which it will be introduced? Second, are buyers more sensitive to some marketing mix activities than to others? For example, are they more likely to respond favorably to a decrease in price or an increase in advertising? Third, what are the costs of performing marketing mix activities and the costs of attracting and retaining buyers? Do these costs exceed their benefits? Can the organization afford the marketing mix expenditures? Finally, is the marketing mix properly timed? For example, are communications scheduled to coincide with product availability? Is the entire marketing mix timely with respect to the buying cycle of consumers, competitor actions, and the ebb and flow of environmental forces?

Implementation of the marketing mix is as much an art as a science. Successful implementation requires an understanding of markets, environmental forces, organizational capacity, and marketing mix activities with a healthy respect for competitor reactions. These topics are raised again in Chapter 11. An example of an implementation with less than successful results is that of A&P's WEO (Where Economy Originates) program. Prior to implementing the program, A&P had watched its sales volume plateau with shrinking profits, while other supermarket chains continued to increase sales volume and profits. When the WEO program was initiated, it emphasized discount pricing (price strategy) with heavy promotional expenditures (communication strategy). The program increased sales volume by $800 million but produced a profit loss of over $50 million. In the words of one industry observer at the time:

> Its competitors are convinced that A&P's assault with WEO was doomed from the start. Too many of its stores are relics of a bygone era. Many are in poor locations [distribution strategy]. . . . They are just not big enough to support the tremendous volume that is necessary to make a discounting operation profitable [capacity] . . . stores lack shelf space for stocking general merchandise items, such as housewares and children's clothing [product strategy].[20]

The product-market strategy employed by A&P could be classified as a market-penetration strategy. Its implementation, however, could be questioned in terms of internal consistency, costs of the marketing mix activities, and fit with organizational capacity. Moreover, the retail grocery industry was plagued at the time by rising food costs, an environmental force that had a destructive effect on strategy success.

■ BUDGETING MARKETING, FINANCIAL, AND PRODUCTION RESOURCES

The fourth phase in the strategic marketing management process is budgeting. A budget is a formal, quantitative expression of an organization's planning and strategy initiatives expressed in financial terms. A well-prepared budget meshes and balances an organization's financial, production, and marketing resources so that overall organizational goals or objectives are attained.

An organization's master budget consists of two parts: (1) an operating budget and (2) a financial budget. The operating budget focuses on an organization's income statement. Since the operating budget projects future revenues and expenses, it is sometimes referred to as a *pro forma* income statement or profit plan. The financial budget focuses on the effect that the operating budget and other initiatives (such as capital expenditures) will have on the organization's cash position. For example, the 1999 master budget for Saturn Corporation included an income statement that detailed revenues, expenses, and profit for its three existing models—a small sedan, a station wagon, and a coupe—and its planned midsize car code-named *Innovate.* Its financial budget included the $900 million Saturn expected to invest in capital expenditures to manufacture the planned midsize car.[21]

In addition to the operating and financial budget, many organizations prepare supplemental special budgets such as an advertising and sales budget, and related reports tied to the master budget. For example, a report showing how revenues, costs, and profits change under different marketing decisions and competitive and economic conditions is often prepared. As indicated, budgeting is more than an accounting function. It is an essential element of strategic marketing management.

A complete description of the budgetary process is beyond the scope of this section. However, Chapter 2, "Financial Aspects of Marketing Management," provides an overview of cost concepts and behavior. It also describes useful analytical tools for dealing with the financial dimensions of strategic marketing management, including cost-volume-profit analysis, discounted cash flow, and the preparation of *pro forma* income statements.

■ DEVELOPING REFORMULATION AND RECOVERY STRATEGIES

Reformulation and recovery strategies form the cornerstone of adaptive behavior in organizations. Strategies are rarely timeless. Changing markets, economic conditions, and competitive behavior require periodic, if not sudden, adjustments in strategy.

Marketing audit and control procedures are fundamental to the development of reformulation and recovery strategies. The *marketing audit* has been defined as follows:

> A marketing audit is a comprehensive, systematic, independent, and periodic examination of a company's—or business unit's—marketing environment, objectives, strategies and activities with a view of determining problem areas and opportunities and recommending a plan of action to improve the company's marketing performance.[22]

The audit process directs the manager's attention to both the strategic fit of the organization with its environment and the operational aspects of the marketing program. Strategic aspects of the marketing audit address the synoptic question "Are we doing the right things?" Operational aspects address an equally synoptic question—"Are we doing things right?"

The distinction between strategic and operational perspectives, as well as the implementation of each, is examined in Chapter 10. Suffice it to say here that marketing audit and control procedures underlie the processes of defining the organization's business, mission, and goals or objectives, identifying external opportunities and threats and internal strengths and weaknesses, formulating product-market strategies and marketing mix activities, and budgeting resources. The intellectual process of developing reformulation and recovery strategies during the planning process serves two important purposes. First, it forces the manager to consider the "what if" questions. For example, "What if an unexpected environmental threat arises that renders a strategy obsolete?" or "What if competitive and market response to a strategy is inconsistent with what was originally expected?" Such questions focus the manager's attention on the sensitivity of results to assumptions made in the strategy-development process. Second, preplanning of reformulation and recovery strategies, or *contingency plans,* leads to a faster reaction time in implementing remedial action. Marshaling and reorienting resources is a time-consuming process itself without additional time lost in planning.

DRAFTING A MARKETING PLAN

A marketing plan embodies the strategic marketing management process. It is a formal, written document that describes the context and scope of an organization's marketing effort to achieve defined goals or objectives within a specific future time period. Marketing plans go by a variety of names depending on their particular focus. For example, there are business marketing plans, product marketing plans, and brand marketing plans. At Frito-Lay, Inc., for instance, a marketing plan is drafted for a particular business (snack chips), for a product class (potato chips, tortilla chips), and for specific brands (Lay's potato chips, Ruffles potato chips). Marketing plans also have a time dimension. Short-run marketing plans typically focus on a one-year period and are called annual marketing plans. Long-run marketing plans often have a three- to five-year planning horizon.

A formal, written marketing plan represents a distillation of and the attention and thought given the five interrelated analytical processes in this chapter. It is the tangible result of an intellectual effort. As a written document, a marketing plan also exhibits certain stylistic elements. Although there is no "generic" marketing plan that applies to all organizations and all situations, marketing plans follow a general format. The appendix at the end of this chapter provides an actual example of a condensed marketing plan for Paradise Kitchens®, Inc., a company that produces and markets a unique line of single-serve and microwaveable Southwestern/Mexican-style frozen chili products. This example illustrates both the substance and style of a five-year marketing plan.

MARKETING ETHICS AND SOCIAL RESPONSIBILITY

On a final note, it must be emphasized that matters of ethics and social responsibility permeate every aspect of the strategic marketing management process. Indeed, most marketing decisions involve some degree of moral judgment and reflect an organization's orientation toward the publics with which it interacts. Enlightened marketing executives no longer subscribe to the view that if an action is legal, then it is also ethical and socially responsible. These executives are sensitive to the fact that the marketplace is populated by individuals and groups with diverse value systems. Moreover, they recognize that their actions will be judged publicly by others with different values and interests.

Enlightened ethical and socially responsible decisions arise from the ability of marketers to discern the precise issues involved and their willingness to take action even when the outcome may negatively affect their standing in an organization or the company's financial interests. Although the moral foundations on which marketing decisions are made will vary among individuals and organizations, failure to recognize issues and take appropriate action is the least ethical and most socially irresponsible approach. A positive approach to ethical and socially responsible behavior is evident by Anheuser-Busch, which spends $40 million annually to promote responsible drinking of alcoholic beverages. Anheuser-Busch executives acknowledge the potential for alcohol abuse and are willing to forgo business generated by misuse of the company's products. These executives have discerned the issues and have recognized an ethical obligation to present and potential customers. They have also recognized the company's social responsibility to the general public by encouraging safe driving and responsible drinking habits.[23]

NOTES

1. Steve Harrell, strategic planner at General Electric, quoted in Philip Kotler, *Marketing Management,* 10th ed. (Upper Saddle River, NJ: Prentice Hall, 2000): 64.

2. Derek F. Abell, *Defining the Business: The Starting Point of Strategic Planning* (Upper Saddle River, NJ: Prentice Hall, 1980); Roger A. Kerin, Vijay Mahajan, and P. Rajan Varadarajan, *Contemporary Perspective on Strategic Market Planning* (Boston: Allyn and Bacon, 1990).

3. "Brittannica.com Arrives, Belatedly," *Advertising Age* (May 10, 1999): 24; "Dusting Off the Brittannica," *Business Week* (October 20, 1997): 141, 147.

4. Jeffrey Abraham, *The Mission Statement Book* (Berkeley, CA: Ten Speed Press, 1995). For examples of mission statements, see Patricia Jones and Larry Kahaner, *Say It and Live It: The 50 Corporate Mission Statements That Hit the Mark* (New York: Currency/Doubleday, 1995); and Christopher K. Bart, "Sex, Lies, and Mission Statements," *Business Horizons* (November-December 1997): 9-18.

5. Eric von Hippel, Stephan Thomke, and Mary Sonnack, "Creating Breakthroughs at 3M," *Harvard Business Review* (September-October 1999): 47-56.

6. Robert A. Pitts and David Lei, *Strategic Management: Building and Sustaining Competitive Advantage* (St. Paul, MN: West Publishing Company, 2000): 6.

7. "Gillette Safety Razor Division: The Blank Cassette Project," Harvard Business School case #9-574-058; Glenn Rifkin, "Mach 3: Anatomy of Gillette's Latest Global Launch," *Strategy & Business* (2nd quarter, 1999): 34-41.

8. "Exxon's Flop in Field of Office Gear Shows Diversification Perils," *Wall Street Journal* (September 3, 1985): 1*ff*.

9. "Hanes Expands L'eggs to the Entire Family," *Business Week* (June 14, 1975): 57*ff.*

10. This classification is adapted from H. Igor Ansoff, *Corporate Strategy* (New York: McGraw-Hill, 1964): chapter 6. For an extended discussion on product-market strategies, see Roger A. Kerin, Vijay Mahajan, and P. Rajan Varadarajan, *Contemporary Perspectives on Strategic Market Planning* (Boston: Allyn and Bacon, 1990): Chapter 6.

11. Robert Frank, "Soft-Drink Prices May Be Softening on Shelves," *Wall Street Journal* (September 12, 1996): B10.

12. H. Menzies, "Why Folger's Is Getting Creamed Back East," *Fortune* (July 17, 1978): 69.

13. Warren J. Keegan, *Global Marketing Management,* 6th ed. (Upper Saddle River, NJ: Prentice Hall, 1998).

14. "We Will Buy You . . . With a Snickers," *U.S. News & World Report* (January 26, 1998): 50-51.

15. "Hasbro, Inc.," in Eric N. Berkowitz, Roger A. Kerin, Steven N. Hartley, and William Rudelius, *Marketing,* 5th ed. (Chicago, IL: Richard D. Irwin, 1997): 656-57.

16. Greg Burns, "Has General Mills Had Its Wheaties?" *Business Week* (May 8, 1995): 68-69; and "1995 Edison Best New Products Awards Winners," *Marketing News* (May 6, 1996): supplement.

17. "Gillette Co. Sees Strong Early Sales For Its New Razor," *Wall Street Journal* (July 17, 1998): B3.

18. These examples are from "How Eagle Became Extinct," *Business Week* (March 4, 1996): 68-69; "Some Things Don't Go Better with Coke," *Forbes* (March 21, 1988): 34-35; and "Gerber Goes Global with 'Superbrand' Concept," *Marketing News* (September 16, 1991): 21.

19. These estimates were reported in "The Breakdown of U.S. Innovation," *Business Week* (February 16, 1976): 56*ff.*

20. Robert F. Hartley, *Marketing Mistakes,* 5th ed. (New York: John Wiley & Sons, 1992). Items in brackets added for illustrative purposes.

21. "GM's Saturn Division Plans to Build a Midsize Car to Keep Customers Loyal," *Wall Street Journal* (August 6, 1996): A4.

22. Philip Kotler, *Marketing Management,* 10th ed. (Upper Saddle River, NJ: Prentice Hall, 2000): 708.

23. *Fighting Alcohol Abuse Through Awareness & Education* (St. Louis: Anheuser-Busch Companies, 1999); and "Know When to Change Ads," *Advertising Age* (September 13, 1999): 24.

APPENDIX

A Sample Marketing Plan

Crafting a marketing plan is hard, but satisfying, work. When completed, a marketing plan serves as a roadmap that details the context and scope of marketing activities including, but not limited to, a mission statement, goals and objectives, a situation analysis, growth opportunities, target market(s) and marketing (mix) program, a budget, and an implementation schedule.

As a written document, the plan conveys in words the analysis, ideas, and aspirations of its author pertaining to a business, product, and/or brand marketing effort. How a marketing plan is written communicates not only the substance of the marketing effort, but also the professionalism of the author. Writing style will not overcome limitations in substance. However, a poorly written marketing plan can detract from the perceived substance of the plan.

■ WRITING AND STYLE CONSIDERATIONS

Given the importance of a carefully crafted marketing plan, authors of marketing plans adhere to certain guidelines. The following writing and style guidelines generally apply:

- Use a direct, professional writing style. Use appropriate business and marketing terms without jargon. Present and future tenses with active voice are generally better than past tense and passive voice.
- Be positive and specific. At the same time, avoid superlatives ("terrific," "wonderful"). Specifics are better than glittering generalities. Use numbers for impact, justifying computations and projections with facts or reasonable quantitative assumptions where possible.
- Use bullet points for succinctness and emphasis. As with the list you are reading, bullets enable key points to be highlighted effectively and with great efficiency.
- Use "A-level" (the first level) and "B-level" (the second level) headings under major section headings to help readers make easy transitions from one topic to another. This also forces the writer to organize the plan more carefully. Use these headings liberally, at least once every 200 to 300 words.
- Use visuals where appropriate. Illustrations, graphs, and charts enable large amounts of information to be presented succinctly.
- Shoot for a plan 15 to 35 pages in length, not including financial projections and appendices. An uncomplicated small business may require only 15 pages, while a new business startup may require more than 35 pages.
- Use care in layout, design, and presentation. Laser or ink-jet printers give a more professional look than do dot matrix printers or typewriters. A bound report with a cover and clear title page adds professionalism.

This appendix is adapted from Eric N. Berkowitz, Roger A. Kerin, Steven W. Hartley, and William Rudelius, *Marketing*, 6th ed. (Burr Ridge, IL: Irwin/McGraw Hill, 2000). Used with permission.

■ SAMPLE FIVE-YEAR ANNOTATED MARKETING PLAN FOR PARADISE KITCHENS®, INC.

The marketing plan that follows for Paradise Kitchens®, Inc. is based on an actual plan developed by the company. The company was founded in 1989, and its products entered distribution in 1990. To protect proprietary information about the company, a number of details and certain data have been altered, but the basic logic of the plan has been preserved. Various appendices are omitted due to space limitations.

Notes in the margins next to the Paradise Kitchens®, Inc. marketing plan fall into two categories:

1. *Substantive notes* elaborate on the rationale or significance of an element in the marketing plan.
2. *Writing style, format, and layout notes* explain the editorial or visual rationale for the element.

As you read the marketing plan, you might consider adding your own notes in the margins related to the discussion in the text. For example, you may wish to compare the application of SWOT analysis and reference to "points of difference" in the Paradise Kitchens®, Inc. marketing plan with the discussion in Chapter 1. As you read additional chapters in the text, you may return to the marketing plan and insert additional notes pertaining to terminology used and techniques employed.

The Table of Contents provides quick access to the topics in the plan, usually organized by section and subsection headings.

Seen by many experts as the single most important element in the plan, the Executive Summary, with a maximum of two pages, "sells" the document to readers through its clarity and brevity.

The Company Description highlights the recent history and recent successes of the organization.

The Strategic Focus and Plan sets the strategic direction for the entire organization, a direction with which proposed actions of the marketing plan must be consistent. This section is not included in all marketing plans.

The Mission Statement focuses the activities of Paradise Kitchens for the stakeholder groups to be served.

FIVE-YEAR MARKETING PLAN

Paradise Kitchens®, Inc.

Table of Contents

2. Company Description

Paradise Kitchens®, Inc. was started in 1989 by cofounders Randall F. Peters and Leah E. Peters to develop and market Howlin' Coyote® Chili, a unique line of single-serve and microwaveable Southwestern/Mexican style frozen chili products. The Howlin' Coyote® line of chili was introduced into the Minneapolis-St. Paul market in 1990. The line was subsequently expanded to Denver in 1992 and Phoenix in 1994.

To the Company's knowledge, Howlin' Coyote® is the only premium-quality, authentic Southwestern/Mexican style, frozen chili sold in U.S. grocery stores. Its high quality has gained fast, widespread acceptance in these markets. In fact, same-store sales doubled in the last year for which data are available. The Company believes the Howlin' Coyote® brand can be extended to other categories of Southwestern/Mexican food products.

Paradise Kitchens believes its high-quality, high-price strategy has proven successful. This marketing plan outlines how the Company will extend its geographic coverage from 3 markets to 20 markets by the year 2003.

3. Strategic Focus and Plan

This section covers three aspects of corporate strategy that influence the marketing plan: (1) the mission, (2) goals, and (3) core competence/sustainable competitive advantage of Paradise Kitchens.

MISSION

The mission and vision of Paradise Kitchens is to market lines of high-quality Southwestern/Mexican food products at premium prices that satisfy consumers in this fast-growing food segment while providing challenging career opportunities for employees and above-average returns to stockholders.

The Goals section sets both the financial and nonfinancial targets—where possible in quantitative terms—against which the company's performance will be measured.

Lists use parallel construction to improve readability—in this case a series of infinitives starting with "To . . .".

The Situation Analysis is a snapshot to answer the question, "Where are we now?"

GOALS

For the coming five years Paradise Kitchens seeks to achieve the following goals:

- Nonfinancial goals
  1. To retain its present image as the highest-quality line of Southwestern/Mexican products in the food categories in which it competes.
  2. To enter 17 new metropolitan markets.
  3. To achieve national distribution in two convenience store or supermarket chains by 2001 and five by 2003.
  4. To add a new product line every third year.
  5. To be among the top three chili lines—regardless of packaging (frozen, canned) in one third of the metro markets in which it competes by 2001 and two thirds by 2003.
- Financial goals
  1. To obtain a real (inflation adjusted) growth in earnings per share of 8 percent per year over time.
  2. To obtain a return on equity of at least 20 percent.
  3. To have a public stock offering by the year 2001.

CORE COMPETENCY AND SUSTAINABLE COMPETITIVE ADVANTAGE

In terms of core competency, Paradise Kitchens seeks to achieve a unique ability (1) to provide distinctive, high-quality chilies and related products using Southwestern/Mexican recipes that appeal to and excite contemporary tastes for these products and (2) to deliver these products to the customer's table using effective manufacturing and distribution systems that maintain the Company's quality standards.

To translate these core competencies into a sustainable competitive advantage, the Company will work closely with key suppliers and distributors to build the relationships and alliances necessary to satisfy the high taste standards of our customers.

4. Situation Analysis

This situation analysis starts with a snapshot of the current environment in which Paradise Kitchens finds itself by providing a brief SWOT (strengths, weaknesses, opportunities, threats) analysis. After this overview, the analysis probes ever-finer levels of detail: industry, competitors, company, and consumers.

The SWOT Analysis identifies strengths, weaknesses, opportunities, and threats to provide a solid foundation as a springboard to identify subsequent *actions* in the marketing plan.

SWOT ANALYSIS

Figure 1 shows the internal and external factors affecting the market opportunities for Paradise Kitchens. Stated briefly, this SWOT analysis highlights the great strides taken by the Company in the eight years since its products first appeared on grocers' shelves. In the Company's favor internally are its strengths of an experienced management team and board of directors, excellent acceptance of its lines in the three metropolitan markets in which it competes, and a strong manufacturing and distribution system to serve these limited markets. Favorable external factors (opportunities) include the increasing appeal of Southwestern/Mexican foods, the strength of the upscale market for the Company's products, and food-processing technological breakthroughs that make it easier for smaller food producers to compete.

Each long table, graph, or photo is given a figure number and title. It then appears as soon as possible after the first reference in the text, accommodating necessary page breaks. This also avoids breaking long tables like this one in the middle. Short tables or graphs that are less than 1½ inches are often inserted in the text without figure numbers because they don't cause serious problems with page breaks.

Figure 1. SWOT Analysis for Paradise Kitchens

Internal Factors	*Strengths*	*Weaknesses*
Management	Experienced and entrepreneurial management and board	Small size can restrict options
Offerings	Unique, high-quality, high-price products	Many lower-quality, lower-price competitors
Marketing	Distribution in 3 markets with excellent acceptance	No national awareness or distribution
Personnel	Good work force, though small; little turnover	Big gap if key employee leaves
Finance	Excellent growth in sales revenues	Limited resources may restrict growth opportunities when compared to giant competitors
Manufacturing	Sole supplier ensures high quality	Lack economies of scale of huge competitors
R&D	Continuing efforts to ensure quality in delivered products	

Figure 1. SWOT Analysis for Paradise Kitchens (continued)

External Factors	*Opportunities*	*Threats*
Consumer/Social	Upscale market, likely to be stable; Southwestern/Mexican food category is fast-growing segment	Premium price may limit access to mass markets
Competitive	Distinctive name and packaging in its markets	Not patentable; competitors can attempt to duplicate product
Technological	Technical breakthroughs enable smaller food producers to achieve many economies available to large competitors	
Economic	Consumer income is high; convenience important to U.S. households	Many households "eating out," and bringing prepared take-out into home
Legal/Regulatory	High U.S. Food & Drug Admin. standards eliminate fly-by-night competitors	

Among unfavorable factors, the main weakness is the limited size of Paradise Kitchens relative to its competitors in terms of the depth of the management team, available financial resources, and national awareness and distribution of product lines. Threats include the danger that the Company's premium prices may limit access to mass markets and competition from the "eating-out" and "take-out" markets.

The Industry Analysis section provides the backdrop for the subsequent, more detailed analysis of competition, the company, and the company's customers. Without an in-depth understanding of the industry, the remaining analysis may be misdirected.

Industry Analysis: Trends in Spicy and Mexican Foods

Total spice consumption increased 50 percent from 1985 to 1995, and consumption of spices jumped from an annual average of 2 pounds per American in 1988 to 2.7 pounds in 1994. Currently, Mexican food and ingredients are used in 64 percent of American households. Burritos, enchiladas, and taco dinner kits, which had insignificant numbers in 1981, reached between 4 percent and 11 percent of American households in 1996. Age Wave, Inc.'s *1998 Boomer Report* also stated that Baby Boomers consumed 84 percent more Mexican food in 1995 than they did in 1986.

Even though relatively brief, this in-depth treatment of the Spicy Southwestern/Mexican food industry in the United States demonstrates to the plan's readers the company's understanding of the industry in which it competes. It gives readers confidence that the company thoroughly understands its own industry.

This summary of sales in the Southwestern/Mexican product category shows it is significant and provides a variety of future opportunities for Paradise Kitchens.

According to *Grocery Marketing,* as the general population becomes more accustomed to different ethnic cuisines and styles of eating, spicy foods and unusual flavors are turning up on the dinner tables of middle America and the aisles of supermarkets, as well. As Baby Boomers grow older, their taste buds will become less sensitive, and they will want stronger-tasting foods. In addition to age, growth in population, incomes, and tastes in the American diet should continue to fuel the trend for spicy foods in the United States. Retail sales of fiery food could top $1.8 billion in the year 2000, according to *Packaged Facts,* up from $1 billion in 1994.

These trends reflect a generally more favorable attitude toward spicy foods on the part of Americans. The Southwestern/Mexican market includes the foods shown in Figure 2.

Figure 2. Some Foods Included in the Southwestern/Mexican Product Category 1996

Item	*Percentage of Sales*	*Sales in Millions*
Salsa	39	$624
Cheese/bean dips	13	208
Refried beans	9	144
Seasoning mix	8	128
Chilies	7	112
Taco shells	7	112
Dinner kits	5	80
Taco sauce	3	48
Enchilada sauce	2	32
Other	7	112
Total	100	$1,600

As with the Industry Analysis, the Competitor Analysis demonstrates that the company has a realistic understanding of who its major competitors are and what their marketing strategies are. Again, a realistic assessment gives confidence to readers that subsequent marketing actions in the plan rest on a solid foundation.

Competitors in Southwestern/Mexican Market

The chili market represents $495 million in annual sales. The products fall primarily into two groups: canned chili (62 percent of sales) and dry chili (16 percent of sales). The remaining 22 percent of sales go to frozen chili products. Besides Howlin' Coyote®, Stouffers and Marie Callender's offer frozen chilies as part of their broad lines of frozen dinners and entrees. Major canned chili brands include Hormel, Wolf, Dennison, Stagg, Chili Man, Chili Magic, and Castleberry's. Their retail prices range from $.99 to $1.79.

Bluntly put, the major disadvantage of the segment's dominant product, canned chili, is that it does not taste very good. A taste test described in the October 1990 issue of *Consumer Reports* magazine ranked 26 canned chili products "poor" to "fair" in overall sensory quality. The study concluded, "Chili doesn't have to be hot to be good. But really good chili, hot or mild, doesn't come out of a can."

Dry mix brands include such familiar spice brands as Lawry's, McCormick, French's, and Durkee, along with smaller offerings such as Wick Fowler's and Carroll Shelby's. Their retail prices range from \$.99 to \$1.99. The *Consumer Reports* study was more favorable about dry chili mixes, ranking them from "fair" to "very good." The magazine recommended, "If you want good chili, make it with fresh ingredients and one of the seasoning mixes we tested." A major drawback of dry mixes is that they require the preparers to add their own meat, beans, and tomatoes and take more preparation time than canned or frozen chilies.

The *Consumer Reports* study did not include the frozen chili entrees from Stouffer's or Marie Callender's (Howlin' Coyote® was not yet on the market at the time of the test). However, it is fair to say that these products—consisting of ground beef, chili beans, and tomato sauce—are of average quality. Furthermore, they are not singled out for special marketing or promotional programs by their manufacturers. Marie Callender's (including cornbread) retails for \$3.09, and Stouffer's retails for \$2.99.

The Company Analysis provides details of the company's strengths and marketing strategies that will enable it to achieve the mission and goals identified earlier.

COMPANY ANALYSIS

The husband-and-wife team that cofounded Paradise Kitchens®, Inc. in 1989 has 44 years of experience between them in the food-processing business. Both have played key roles in the management of the Pillsbury Company. They are being advised by a highly seasoned group of business professionals, who have extensive understanding of the requirements for new product development.

Currently, Howlin' Coyote® products compete in the chili and Mexican frozen entree segments of the Southwestern/Mexican food market. While the chili obviously competes as a stand-alone product, its exceptional quality means it can complement such dishes as burritos, nachos, and enchiladas and can be readily used as a smothering sauce for pasta, rice, or potatoes. This flexibility of use is relatively rare in the prepared food marketplace. With Howlin' Coyote®, Paradise Kitchens is broadening the position of frozen chili in a way that can lead to impressive market share for the new product category.

This "introductory overview" sentence tells the reader the topics covered in the section—in this case customer characteristics and health and nutrition concerns. While this sentence may be omitted in short memos or plans, it helps readers see where the text is leading. These sentences are used throughout this plan.

The higher-level "A heading" of Customer Analysis has a more dominant typeface and position than the lower-level "B heading" of Customer Characteristics. These headings introduce the reader to the sequence and level of topics covered.

Satisfying customers and providing genuine value to them is why organizations exist in a market economy. This section addresses the question of "Who are the customers for Paradise Kitchens's products?"

The Company now uses a single outside producer with which it works closely to maintain the consistently high quality required in its products. The greater volume has increased production efficiencies, resulting in a steady decrease in the cost of goods sold.

CUSTOMER ANALYSIS

In terms of customer analysis, this section describes (1) the characteristics of customers expected to buy Howlin' Coyote® products and (2) health and nutrition concerns of Americans today.

Customer Characteristics. Demographically, chili products in general are purchased by consumers representing a broad range of socioeconomic backgrounds. Howlin' Coyote® chili is purchased chiefly by consumers who have achieved higher levels of education and whose income is $30,000 and higher. These consumers represent 57 percent of canned and dry mix chili users.

The household buying Howlin' Coyote® has one to three people in it. Among married couples, Howlin' Coyote® is predominantly bought by households in which both spouses work. While women are a majority of the buyers, single men represent a significant segment. Anecdotally, Howlin' Coyote® has heard from fathers of teenaged boys who say they keep a freezer stocked with the chili because the boys devour it.

Because the chili offers a quick way to make a tasty meal, the product's biggest users tend to be those most pressed for time. Howlin' Coyote®'s premium pricing also means that its purchasers are skewed toward the higher end of the income range. Buyers range in age from 25 to 55. Because consumers in the western United States have adopted spicy foods more readily than the rest of the country, Howlin' Coyote®'s initial marketing expansion efforts will be concentrated in that region.

This section demonstrates the company's insights into a major trend that has a potentially large impact.

Health and Nutrition Concerns. Coverage of food issues in the U.S. media is often erratic and occasionally alarmist. Because Americans are concerned about their diets, studies from organizations of widely varying credibility frequently receive significant attention from the major news organizations. For instance, a study of fat levels of movie popcorn was reported in all the major media. Similarly, studies on the healthfulness of Mexican food have received prominent "play" in print and broadcast reports. The high caloric levels of much Mexican and Southwestern-style food had been widely reported and often exaggerated.

Less certain is the link between these reports and consumer buying behavior. Most indications are that while Americans are well-versed in dietary matters, they are not significantly changing their eating patterns. The experience of other food manufacturers is that Americans expect certain foods to be high in calories and are not drawn to those that claim to be low-calorie versions. Low-fat frozen pizza was a flop. Therefore, while Howlin' Coyote® is already lower in calories, fat, and sodium than its competitors, those qualities are not being stressed in its promotions. Instead, in the space and time available for promotions, Howlin' Coyote®'s taste, convenience, and flexibility are stressed.

5. Product-Market Focus

This section describes the five-year marketing and product objectives for Paradise Kitchens and the target markets, points of difference, and positioning of its lines of Howlin' Coyote® chilies.

MARKETING AND PRODUCT OBJECTIVES

The chances of success for a new product are significantly increased if objectives are set for the product itself and if target market segments are identified for it. This section makes these explicit for Paradise Kitchens. The objectives also serve as the planned targets against which marketing activities are measured in program implementation and control.

Howlin' Coyote®'s marketing intent is to take full advantage of its brand potential while building a base from which other revenue sources can be mined—both in and out of the retail grocery business. These are detailed in four areas below:

- Current markets. Current markets will be grown by expanding brand and flavor distribution at the retail level. In addition, same-store sales will be grown by increasing consumer awareness and repeat purchases. With this increase in same-store sales, the more desirable broker/warehouse distribution channel will become available, increasing efficiency and saving costs.

- New markets. By the end of Year 5, the chili and salsa business will be expanded to a total of 20 metropolitan areas. This will represent 72 percent of U.S. food store sales.
- Food service. Food service sales will include chili products and smothering sauces. Sales are expected to reach $693,000 by the end of Year 3 and $1.5 million by the end of Year 5.
- New products. Howlin' Coyote®'s brand presence will be expanded at the retail level through the addition of new products in the frozen-foods section. This will be accomplished through new product concept screening in Year 1 to identify new potential products. These products will be brought to market in Years 2 and 3. Additionally, the brand may be licensed in select categories.

This section identifies the specific niches or target markets toward which the company's products are directed. When appropriate and when space permits, this section often includes a product-market matrix.

TARGET MARKETS

The primary target market for Howlin' Coyote® products is households with one to three people, where often both adults work, with household income typically above $30,000 per year. These households contain more experienced, adventurous consumers of Southwestern/Mexican food and want premium quality products.

POINTS OF DIFFERENCE

The "points of difference"—characteristics that make Howlin' Coyote® chilies unique relative to competitors—fall into three important areas:

An organization cannot grow by offering only "me-too products." The greatest single factor in a new product's failure is the lack of significant "points of difference" that set it apart from competitors' substitutes. This section makes these points of difference explicit.

- Unique taste and convenience. No known competitor offers a high-quality, "authentic" frozen chili in a range of flavors. And no existing chili has the same combination of quick preparation and home-style taste.
- Taste trends. The American palate is increasingly intrigued by hot spices, and Howlin' Coyote® brands offer more "kick" than most other prepared chilies.
- Premium packaging. Howlin' Coyote®'s high-value packaging graphics convey the unique, high-quality product contained inside and the product's nontraditional positioning.

A positioning strategy helps communicate the company's unique points of difference of its products to prospective customers in a simple, clear way. This section describes this positioning.

Everything that has gone before in the marketing plan sets the stage for the marketing mix actions covered in the marketing program.

This section describes in detail three key elements of the company's product strategy: the product line, its quality and how this is achieved, and its "cutting edge" packaging.

Using parallel structure, this bulleted list presents the product line efficiently and crisply.

Positioning

In the past chili products have been either convenient or tasty, but not both. Howlin' Coyote® pairs these two desirable characteristics to obtain a positioning in consumers' minds as very high-quality "authentic Southwestern/Mexican tasting" chilies that can be prepared easily and quickly.

6. Marketing Program

The four marketing mix elements of the Howlin' Coyote® chili marketing program are detailed below. Note that "chile" is the vegetable and "chili" is the dish.

Product Strategy

After first summarizing the product line, the approach to product quality and packaging is covered.

Product Line. Howlin' Coyote® chili, retailing for $2.99 for a 10- or 11.5-ounce serving, is available in five flavors. The five are:

- Green Chile Chili: braised extra-lean pork with fire-roasted green chilies, onions, tomato chunks, bold spices, and jalapeno peppers, based on a Southwestern favorite.
- Red Chile Chili: extra-lean cubed pork, deep-red acho chilies, and sweet onions; known as the "Texas Bowl of Red."
- Beef and Black Bean Chili: lean braised beef with black beans, tomato chunks, and Howlin' Coyote®'s own blend of red chilies and authentic spicing.
- Chicken Chunk Chili: hearty chunks of tender chicken, fire-roasted green chilies, black beans, pinto beans, diced onions, and zesty spices.
- Mean Bean Chili: vegetarian, with nine distinctive bean varieties and fire-roasted green chilies, tomato chunks, onion, and a robust blend of spices and rich red chilies.

Unique Product Quality. The flavoring systems of the Howlin' Coyote® chilies are proprietary. The products' tastiness is due to extra care lavished upon the ingredients during production. The ingredients used are of unusually high quality. Meats are low-fat cuts and are fresh, not frozen, to preserve cell structure and moistness. Chilies are fire-roasted for fresher taste, not the canned variety used by more mainstream products. Tomatoes and vegetables are select quality. No preservatives or artificial flavors are used.

Packaging. Reflecting the "cutting edge" marketing strategy of its producers, Howlin' Coyote® bucks conventional wisdom in packaging. It avoids placing predictable photographs of the product on its containers. (Head to any grocer's freezer and you will be hardpressed to find a product that does not feature a heavily stylized photograph of the contents.) Instead, Howlin' Coyote®'s package shows a Southwestern motif that communicates the product's out-of-the-ordinary positioning. This approach signals the product's nontraditional qualities: "adventurous" eating with minimal fuss—a frozen meal for people who do not normally enjoy frozen meals.

This Price Strategy section makes the company's price point very clear, along with its price position relative to potential substitutes. When appropriate and when space permits, this section might contain a break-even analysis.

PRICE STRATEGY

Howlin' Coyote® Chili is, at $2.99 for a 10- to 11.5-ounce package, priced comparably to the other frozen offerings and higher than the canned and dried chili varieties. However, the significant taste advantages it has over canned chilies and the convenience advantages over dried chilies justify this pricing strategy.

PROMOTION STRATEGY

Key promotion programs feature in-store demonstrations, recipes, and cents-off coupons.

Elements of the Promotion Strategy are highlighted here with B-headings in terms of the three key promotional activities the company is emphasizing for its product line: in-store demonstrations, recipes featuring its Howlin' Coyote® chilies, and cents-off coupons.

In-Store Demonstrations. In-store demonstrations will be conducted to give consumers a chance to try Howlin' Coyote® products and learn about their unique qualities. Demos will be conducted regularly in all markets to increase awareness and trial purchases.

Recipes. Because the products' flexibility of use is a key selling point, recipes will be offered to consumers to stimulate use. The recipes will be given at all in-store demonstrations, on the back of packages, and through a mail-in recipe book offer. In addition, recipes will be included in coupons sent by direct-mail or free-standing inserts. For new markets, recipes will be included on in-pack coupon inserts.

Cents-Off Coupons. To generate trial and repeat-purchase of Howlin' Coyote® products, coupons will be distributed in four ways:

- In Sunday newspaper inserts. Inserts are highly read and will help generate awareness. Coupled with in-store

Another bulleted list adds many details for the reader, including methods of gaining customer awareness, trial, and repeat purchases as Howlin' Coyote® enters new metropolitan areas.

demonstrations, this has been a very successful technique so far.

- In-pack coupons. Inside each box of Howlin' Coyote® chili will be coupons for $1 off two more packages of the chili. These coupons will be included for the first three months the product is shipped to a new market. Doing so encourages repeat purchases by new users.
- Direct-mail chili coupons. Those households that fit the Howlin' Coyote® demographics described above will be mailed coupons. This is likely to be an efficient promotion due to its greater audience selectivity.
- In-store demonstrations. Coupons will be passed out at in-store demonstrations to give an additional incentive to purchase.

The Distribution Strategy is described here in terms of both (1) the present method and (2) the new one to be used when the increased sales volume makes it feasible.

DISTRIBUTION STRATEGY

Howlin' Coyote® is distributed in its present markets through a food distributor. The distributor buys the product, warehouses it, and then resells and delivers it to grocery retailers on a store-by-store basis. This is typical for products that have moderate sales—compared with, say, staples like milk or bread. As sales grow, we will shift to a more efficient system using a broker who sells the products to retail chains and grocery wholesalers.

All the marketing mix decisions covered in the marketing program have both revenue and expense effects. These are summarized in this section of the marketing plan.

7. Financial Data and Projections

PAST SALES REVENUES

Historically, Howlin' Coyote® has had a steady increase in sales revenues since its introduction in 1990. In 1994, sales jumped, due largely to new promotion strategies. Sales have continued to rise during the last four years, but at a less dramatic rate. The trend in sales revenues appears in Figure 3.

Figure 3. Sales Revenues for Paradise Kitchens®, Inc.

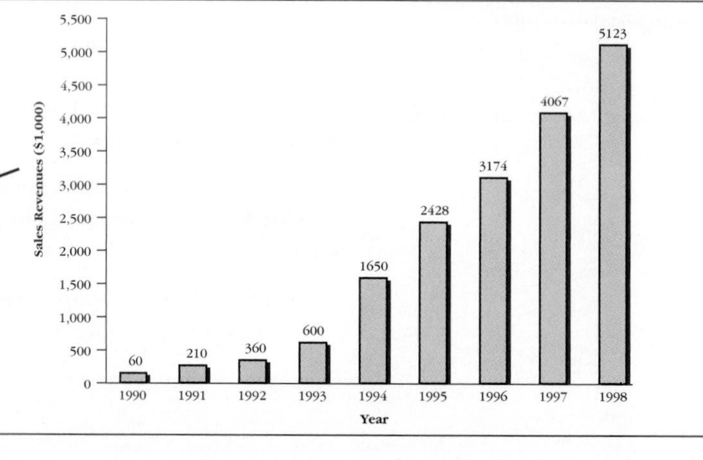

The graph shows more clearly the dramatic growth of sales revenue than data in a table would do.

Because this table is very short, it is woven into the text, rather than given a table number and title.

The Five-Year Financial Projections section starts with the judgment forecast of cases sold and the resulting net sales. Gross profit and then operating profit—critical for the company's survival—are projected. An actual plan often contains many pages of computer-generated spreadsheet projections, usually shown in an appendix to the plan.

FIVE-YEAR PROJECTIONS

Five-year financial projections for Paradise Kitchens appear below:

			Projections				
Financial Element	*Units*	*Actual 1998*	*Year 1 1999*	*Year 2 2000*	*Year 3 2001*	*Year 4 2002*	*Year 5 2003*
Cases sold	1,000	353	684	889	1,249	1,499	1,799
Net sales	$1,000	5,123	9,913	12,884	18,111	21,733	26,080
Gross profit	$1,000	2,545	4,820	6,527	8,831	10,597	12,717
Selling and general and admin. expenses	$1,000	2,206	3,835	3,621	6,026	7,231	8,678
Operating profit (loss)	$1,000	339	985	2,906	2,805	3,366	4,039

These projections reflect the continuing growth in number of cases sold (with 8 packages of Howlin' Coyote® chili per case) and increasing production and distribution economies of scale as sales volume increases.

The Implementation Plan shows how the company will turn plans into results. Gantt charts are often used to set deadlines and assign responsibilities for the many tactical marketing decisions needed to enter a new market.

8. Implementation Plan

Introducing Howlin' Coyote® chilies to new metropolitan areas is a complex task and requires that creative promotional activities gain consumer awareness and initial trial among the target market households identified earlier. The anticipated rollout schedule to enter these metropolitan markets appears in Figure 4.

Figure 4. Rollout Schedule to Enter New U.S. Markets

Year	*New Markets Added*	*Cumulative Markets*	*Cumulative Percentage of U.S. Market*
Today (1998)	2	5	16
Year 1 (1999)	3	8	21
Year 2 (2000)	4	12	29
Year 3 (2001)	2	14	37
Year 4 (2002)	3	17	45
Year 5 (2003)	3	20	53

The essence of Evaluation and Control is comparing actual sales with the targeted values set in the plan and taking appropriate actions. Note that the section briefly describes a contingency plan for alternative actions, depending on how successful the entry into a new market turns out to be.

The diverse regional tastes in chili will be monitored carefully to assess whether minor modifications may be required in the chili recipes. For example, what is seen as "hot" in Boston may not be seen as "hot" in Dallas. As the rollout to new metropolitan areas continues, Paradise Kitchens will assess manufacturing and distribution trade-offs. This is important in determining whether to start new production with selected high-quality regional contract packers.

9. Evaluation and Control

Monthly sales targets in cases have been set for Howlin' Coyote® chili for each metropolitan area. Actual case sales will be compared with these targets and tactical marketing programs modified to reflect the unique sets of factors in each metropolitan area. The speed of the roll-out program may increase or decrease, depending on Paradise Kitchens' performance in the successive metropolitan markets it enters. Similarly, as described above in the section on the implementation plan, Paradise Kitchens may elect to respond to variations in regional tastes by using contract packers, which will reduce transportation and warehousing costs but will require special efforts to monitor production quality.

Various appendices may appear at the end of the plan, depending on the purpose and audience for them. For example, detailed financial spreadsheets often appear in an appendix.

10. Appendices

CHAPTER 2

Financial Aspects of Marketing Management

Marketing managers are accountable for the impact of their actions on profits. Therefore, they need a working knowledge of basic accounting and finance. This chapter provides an overview of several concepts from managerial accounting and managerial finance that are useful in marketing management: (1) variable and fixed costs, (2) relevant and sunk costs, (3) margins, (4) contribution analysis, (5) liquidity, (6) operating leverage, and (7) discounted cash flow. In addition, considerations when preparing *pro forma* income statements are described.

■ VARIABLE AND FIXED COSTS

An organization's costs divide into two broad categories: variable costs and fixed costs.

Variable Costs

Variable costs are expenses that are uniform per unit of output within a relevant time period (usually defined as a budget year); yet total variable costs fluctuate in direct proportion to the output volume of units produced. In other words, as volume increases, total variable costs increase.

Variable costs are divided into two categories, one of which is *cost of goods sold.* For a manufacturer or a provider of a service, cost of goods sold covers materials, labor, and factory overhead applied directly to production. For a reseller (wholesaler or retailer), cost of goods sold consists primarily of the cost of merchandise. The second category of variable costs consists of expenses that are not directly tied to production but that nevertheless vary directly with volume. Examples include sales commissions, discounts, and delivery expenses.

Fixed Costs

Fixed costs are expenses that do not fluctuate with output volume within a relevant time period (the budget year) but become progressively smaller per unit of output as volume increases. The decrease in per-unit fixed cost results from the increase in the number of output units over which fixed costs are allocated. Note, however, that no matter how large volume becomes, the absolute size of fixed costs remains unchanged.

Fixed costs divide into two categories: programmed costs and committed costs. *Programmed costs* result from attempts to generate sales volume. *Marketing expenditures are generally classified as programmed costs.* Examples include advertising, sales promotion, and sales salaries. *Committed costs* are those required to maintain the organization. They are usually nonmarketing expenditures such as rent and administrative and clerical salaries.

It is important to understand the concept of fixed cost. Remember that total fixed costs do not change during a budget year, regardless of changes in volume. Once fixed expenditures for a marketing program have been made, they remain the same whether or not the program causes unit volume to change.

Despite the clear-cut classification of costs into variable and fixed categories suggested here, cost classification is not always apparent in actual practice. Many times costs have a fixed and a variable component. For example, selling expenses often have a fixed component (such as salary) and a variable component (such as commissions or bonus) that are not always evident at first glance.

■ RELEVANT AND SUNK COSTS

Relevant Costs

Relevant costs are expenditures that (1) are expected to occur in the future as a result of some marketing action and (2) differ among marketing alternatives being considered. In short, relevant costs are future expenditures unique to the decision alternatives under consideration.

The concept of relevant cost can best be illustrated by an example. Suppose a manager considers adding a new product to the product mix. Relevant costs include potential expenditures for manufacturing and marketing the product, plus salary costs arising from the time sales personnel give to the new products at the expense of other products. If this additional product does not affect the salary costs of sales personnel, salaries are not a relevant cost.

As a general rule, opportunity costs are also a relevant cost. Opportunity costs are the forgone benefits from an alternative not chosen.

Sunk Costs

Sunk costs are the direct opposite of relevant costs. Sunk costs are past expenditures for a given activity and are typically irrelevant in whole or in part to future decisions. In a marketing context, sunk costs include past research and development expenditures (including test marketing) and last year's advertising expense. These expenditures, although real, will neither recur in the future nor influence future expenditures. When marketing managers attempt to incorporate sunk costs into future decisions affecting new expenditures, they often fall prey to the *sunk cost fallacy*—that is, they attempt to recoup spent dollars by spending still more dollars in the future.

■ MARGINS

Another useful concept for marketing managers is that of *margin*, which refers to the difference between the selling price and the "cost" of a product or service. Margins are expressed on a total volume basis or on an individual unit basis, in dollar terms or as percentages. The three described here are gross, trade, and net profit margins.

Gross Margin

Gross margin, or gross profit, is the difference between total sales revenue and total cost of goods sold, or, on a per-unit basis, the difference between unit selling price and unit cost of goods sold. Gross margin may be expressed in dollar terms or as a percentage.

Total Gross Margin	*Dollar Amount*	*Percentage*
Net sales	$100	100%
Cost of goods sold	–40	–40
Gross profit margin	$ 60	60%
Unit Gross Margin		
Unit sales price	$1.00	100%
Unit cost of goods sold	–0.40	–40
Unit gross profit margin	$0.60	60%

Gross margin analysis is a useful tool because it implicitly includes unit selling prices of products or services, unit costs, and unit volume. A decrease in gross margin is of immediate concern to a marketing manager, because such a change has a direct impact on profits, providing that other expenditures remain unchanged. Changes in total gross margin should be examined in depth to determine whether the change was brought about by fluctuations in unit volume, changes in unit price or unit cost of goods sold, or a modification in the sales mix of the firm's products or services.

Trade Margin

Trade margin is the difference between unit sales price and unit cost at each level of a marketing channel (for example, manufacturer → wholesaler → retailer). A trade margin is frequently referred to as a *markup* or *mark-on* by channel members, and it is often expressed as a percentage.

Trade margins are occasionally confusing, since the margin percentage can be computed on the basis of cost or selling price. Consider the following example. Suppose a retailer purchases an item for $10 and sells it at a price of $20—that is, a $10 margin. What is the retailer's margin percentage?

Retailer margin as a percentage of cost is

$$\frac{\$10}{\$10} \times 100 = 100 \text{ percent}$$

Retailer margin as a percentage of selling price is

$$\frac{\$10}{\$20} \times 100 = 50 \text{ percent}$$

Differences in margin percentages show the importance of knowing the base (cost or selling price) on which the margin percentage is determined. *Trade margin percentages are usually determined on the basis of selling price,* but practices do vary among firms and industries.

Trade margins affect the pricing of individual items in two ways. First, suppose a wholesaler purchases an item for $2.00 and seeks to achieve a 30 percent margin on this item based on selling price. What would be the selling price?

$2.00 = 70 percent of selling price

or

Selling price = $2.00/0.70 = $2.86

Second, suppose a manufacturer suggests a retail list price of \$6.00 on an item for ultimate resale to the consumer. The item will be sold through retailers whose policy is to obtain a 40 percent margin based on selling price. For what price must the manufacturer sell the item to the retailer?

$$\frac{x}{\$6.00} = 40 \text{ percent of selling price}$$

where x is the retailer margin. Solving for x indicates that the retailer must obtain \$2.40 for this item. Therefore, the manufacturer must set the price to the retailer at \$3.60 (\$6.00 – \$2.40).

The manufacturer's problem of suggesting a price for ultimate resale to the consumer becomes more complex as the number of intermediaries between the manufacturer and the final consumer increases. This complexity can be illustrated by expanding the above example to include a wholesaler between the manufacturer and retailer. The retailer receives a 40 percent margin on the sales price. If the retailer must receive \$2.40 per unit, the wholesaler must sell the item for \$3.60 per unit. In order for the wholesaler to receive a 20 percent margin, for what price must the manufacturer sell the unit to the wholesaler?

$$\frac{x}{\$3.60} = 20 \text{ percent wholesaler margin on selling price}$$

where x is the wholesaler margin. Solving for x shows that the wholesaler's margin is \$0.72 for this item. Therefore, the manufacturer must set the price to the wholesaler at \$2.88.

This example shows that a manager must work backward from the ultimate price to the consumer through the marketing channel to arrive at a product's selling price. Assuming that the manufacturer's cost of goods sold is \$2.00, we can calculate the following margins, which incidentally show the manufacturer's gross margin of 30.6 percent.

	Unit Cost of Goods Sold	*Unit Selling Price*	*Gross Margin as a Percentage of Selling Price*
Manufacturer	\$2.00	\$2.88	30.6%
Wholesaler	2.88	3.60	20.0
Retailer	3.60	6.00	40.0
Consumer	6.00		

Net Profit Margin (Before Taxes)

The last margin to be considered is the net profit margin before taxes. This margin is expressed as a dollar figure or a percentage. *Net profit margin* is the remainder after cost of goods sold, other variable costs, and fixed costs have been subtracted from sales revenue. The place of net profit margin in an organization's income statement is illustrated by the following:

	Dollar Amount	*Percentage*
Net sales	\$100,000	100%
Cost of goods sold	–30,000	–30
Gross profit margin	\$70,000	70%
Selling expenses	–20,000	–20
Fixed expenses	–40,000	–40
Net profit margin	\$10,000	10%

Net profit margin dollars represent a major source of funding for the organization. As will be shown later, net profit influences the working capital position of the organization; hence, the dollar amount ultimately affects the organization's ability to pay its cost of goods sold plus its selling and administrative expenses. Furthermore, net profit also affects the organization's cash flow position.

■ CONTRIBUTION ANALYSIS

Contribution analysis is an important concept in marketing management. *Contribution* is the difference between total sales revenue and total variable costs, or, on a per-unit basis, the difference between unit selling price and unit variable cost. Contribution analysis is particularly useful in assessing relationships among costs, prices, and volumes of products and services.

Break-Even Analysis

Break-even analysis is one of the simplest applications of contribution analysis. *Break-even analysis* identifies the unit or dollar sales volume at which an organization neither makes a profit nor incurs a loss. Stated in equation form:

$$\text{Total revenue} = \text{total variable costs} + \text{total fixed costs}$$

Since break-even analysis identifies the level of sales volume at which total costs (fixed and variable) and total revenue are equal, it is a valuable tool for evaluating an organization's profit goals and assessing the riskiness of actions.

Break-even analysis requires three pieces of information: (1) an estimate of unit variable costs, (2) an estimate of the total dollar fixed costs to produce and market the product or service unit (note that only relevant costs apply), and (3) the selling price for each product or service unit.

The formula for determining the number of units required to break even is as follows:

$$\text{Unit break-even volume} = \frac{\text{total dollar fixed costs}}{\text{unit selling price} - \text{unit variable cost}}$$

The denominator in this formula (unit selling price minus unit variable costs) is called *contribution per unit*. Contribution per unit is the dollar amount that each unit sold "contributes" to the payment of fixed costs.

Consider the following example. A manufacturer plans to sell a product for \$5.00. The unit variable costs are \$2.00, and total fixed costs assigned to the product are \$30,000. How many units must be sold to break even?

$$\begin{aligned}
\text{Fixed costs} &= \$30{,}000 \\
\text{Contribution per unit} &= \text{unit selling price} - \text{unit variable cost} \\
&= \$5 - \$2 = \$3 \\
\text{Unit break-even volume} &= \$30{,}000/\$3 = 10{,}000 \text{ units}
\end{aligned}$$

This example shows that for every unit sold at \$5.00, \$2.00 is used to pay variable costs. The balance of \$3.00 "contributes" to fixed costs.

A related question is what the manufacturer's dollar sales volume must be to break even. The manager need only multiply unit break-even volume by the unit selling price to determine the dollar break-even volume: 10,000 units × \$5 = \$50,000.

A manager can calculate a dollar break-even point directly without first computing unit break-even volume. First the *contribution margin* must be determined from the formula:

$$\text{Contribution margin} = \frac{\text{unit selling price} - \text{unit variable cost}}{\text{unit selling price}}$$

EXHIBIT 2.1

Break-Even Analysis Chart

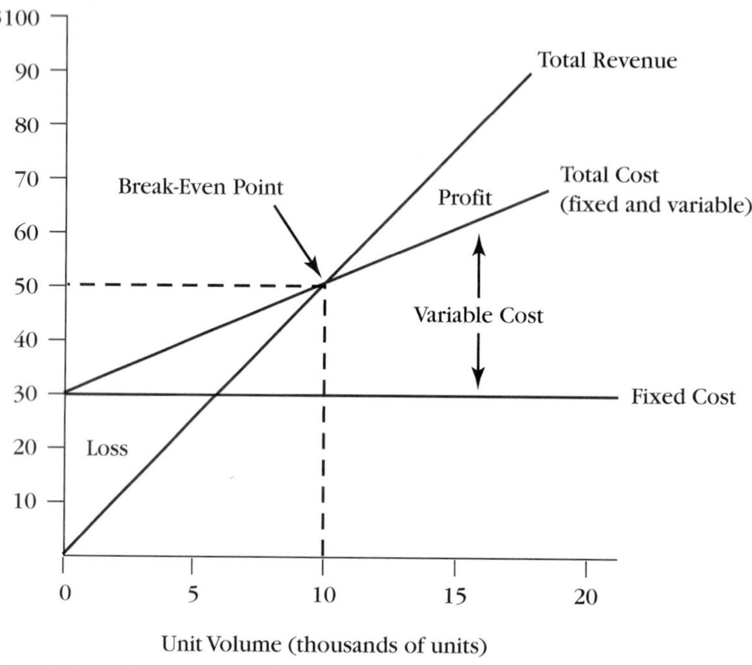

Using the figures from our example, we find that the contribution margin is 60 percent:

$$\text{Contribution margin} = \frac{\$5 - \$2}{\$5} = 60 \text{ percent}$$

Then the dollar break-even point is computed as follows:

$$\text{Dollar volume} = \frac{\text{total fixed costs}}{\text{contribution margin}} = \frac{\$30{,}000}{0.60} = \$50{,}000$$

In many cases it is useful to develop a graphic representation of a break-even analysis. Exhibit 2.1 provides a visual solution to the problem posed above. The horizontal line at $30,000 represents fixed costs. The upward-sloping line beginning at $30,000 represents the total cost, which is equal to the sum of fixed plus variable costs. This line has a slope equal to $2.00—each unit increase in volume results in a $2.00 increase in the total cost. The upward-sloping line beginning at zero represents revenue and has a slope of $5.00—each unit increase in sales produces a $5.00 increase in revenue. The distance between the revenue line and the total cost line represents dollars of profit (above the break-even point) or loss (below the break-even point).

Sensitivity Analysis

Contribution analysis can be applied in a number of different ways, depending on the manager's needs. The following illustrations show how the break-even points in our example can be varied by changing selling price, variable costs, and fixed costs.

1. What would break-even volume be if fixed costs were increased to \$40,000 while the selling price and variable costs remained unchanged?

$$\begin{aligned} \text{Fixed costs} &= \$40{,}000 \\ \text{Contribution per unit} &= \$3 \\ \text{Unit break-even volume} &= \$40{,}000/\$3 = 13{,}333 \text{ units} \\ \text{Dollar break-even volume} &= \$40{,}000/0.60 = \$66{,}667 \end{aligned}$$

Note that the difference between the dollar break-even volume calculated from the contribution margin and the result of simply multiplying unit selling price by unit break-even volume (13,333 × \$5 = \$66,665) is due to rounding.

2. What would break-even volume be if selling price were dropped from \$5.00 to \$4.00 while fixed and variable costs remained unchanged?

$$\begin{aligned} \text{Fixed costs} &= \$30{,}000 \\ \text{Contribution per unit} &= \$2 \\ \text{Unit break-even volume} &= \$30{,}000/\$2 = 15{,}000 \text{ units} \\ \text{Dollar break-even volume} &= \$30{,}000/0.50 = \$60{,}000 \end{aligned}$$

3. Finally, what would break-even volume be if unit variable cost per unit were reduced to \$1.50, selling price remained at \$5.00, and fixed costs were \$30,000?

$$\begin{aligned} \text{Fixed costs} &= \$30{,}000 \\ \text{Contribution per unit} &= \$3.50 \\ \text{Unit break-even volume} &= \$30{,}000/\$3.50 = 8{,}571 \text{ units} \\ \text{Dollar break-even volume} &= \$30{,}000/0.70 = \$42{,}857 \end{aligned}$$

Contribution Analysis and Profit Impact

No manager is content to operate at the break-even point in unit or dollar sales volume. Profits are necessary for the continued operation of an organization. A modified break-even analysis is used to incorporate a profit goal.

In simple break-even analysis, contribution per unit is the dollar amount available to pay fixed costs. To modify the break-even formula to incorporate the dollar profit goal, we need only regard the profit goal as an additional fixed cost, as follows:

$$\text{Unit volume to achieve profit goal} = \frac{\text{total dollar fixed costs} + \text{dollar profit goal}}{\text{contribution per unit}}$$

Suppose a firm has fixed costs of \$200,000 budgeted for a product or service, the unit selling price is \$25.00, and the unit variable costs are \$10.00. How many units must be sold to achieve a profit goal of \$20,000?

$$\begin{aligned} \text{Fixed costs} + \text{profit goal} &= \$200{,}000 + \$20{,}000 = \$220{,}000 \\ \text{Contribution per unit} &= \$25 - \$10 = \$15 \\ \text{Unit volume to achieve profit goal} &= \$220{,}000/\$15 \\ &= 14{,}667 \text{ units} \end{aligned}$$

Many firms specify their profit goal as a percentage of sales rather than as a dollar amount ("Our profit goal is a 20 percent profit on sales"). This objective can be incorporated into the break-even formula by including the profit goal in the contribution-per-unit calculation. If the goal is to achieve a 20 percent profit on sales, each dollar of sales must "contribute" \$0.20 to profit. In our example, each unit sold for \$25.00 must contribute \$5.00 to profit. The break-even formula incorporating a percent profit on sales goal is as follows:

$$\text{Unit volume to achieve profit goal} = \frac{\text{total dollar fixed costs}}{\text{unit selling price} - \text{unit variable costs}}$$

The unit volume break-even point to achieve a 20 percent profit goal is 20,000 units:

$$\begin{aligned} \text{Fixed costs} &= \$200{,}000 \\ \text{Contribution per unit} &= \$25 - \$10 - \$5 = \$10 \\ \text{Unit volume to achieve profit goal} &= \$200{,}000/\$10 \\ &= 20{,}000 \text{ units} \end{aligned}$$

Contribution Analysis and Market Size

An important consideration in contribution analysis is the relationship of break-even unit or dollar volume to market size. Consider the situation in which a manager has conducted a break-even analysis and found the unit volume break-even point to be 50,000 units. This number has meaning only when compared with the potential size of the market segment sought. If the market potential is 100,000 units, the manager's product or service must capture 50 percent of the market sought to break even. An important question to be resolved is whether such a percentage can be achieved. A manager can assess the feasibility of a venture by comparing the break-even volume with market size and market-capture percentage.

Contribution Analysis and Performance Measurement

A second application of contribution analysis lies in performance measurement. For example, a marketing manager may wish to examine the performance of products. Consider an organization with two products, X and Y. A description of each product's financial performance follows:

	Product X (10,000 volume)	***Product Y (20,000 volume)***	***Total (30,000 volume)***
Unit price	$ 10	$ 3	
Sales revenue	100,000	60,000	$160,000
Unit variable costs	4	1.50	
Total variable costs	40,000	30,000	70,000
Unit contribution	6	1.50	
Total contribution	60,000	30,000	90,000
Fixed costs	45,000	10,000	55,000
Net profit	$15,000	$20,000	$35,000

The net profit figure shows that Product Y is more profitable than Product X. Product X is four times more profitable than Product Y on a unit-contribution basis, however, and generates twice the contribution dollars to overhead. The difference in profitability comes from the allocation of fixed costs to the products. In measuring performance, it is important to consider which products contribute most heavily to the organization's total fixed costs ($55,000 in this example) and then to total profit.

Should a manager look only at net profit, a decision might be made to drop Product X. Product Y would then have to cover total fixed costs, however. If the fixed costs remain at $55,000 and only Product Y is sold, this organization will experience a *net loss* of $25,000, assuming no change in Product Y volume.

Assessment of Cannibalization

A third application of contribution analysis is in the assessment of cannibalization effects. Cannibalization is the process by which one product or service sold by a firm gains a portion of its revenue by diverting sales from another product or service also sold by the firm. For example, sales of Brand X's new gel toothpaste may be at the expense of sales of Brand X's existing opaque white toothpaste. The problem facing a marketing manager is to assess the financial effect of cannibalization.

Consider the following data:

	Existing Opaque White Toothpaste	***New Gel Toothpaste***
Unit selling price	\$1.00	\$1.10
Unit variable costs	−0.20	−0.40
Unit contribution	\$0.80	\$0.70

The gel toothpaste can be sold at a slightly higher price, given its formulation and taste, but the variable costs are also higher. Hence the gel toothpaste has a lower contribution per unit. Therefore, for every unit of the gel toothpaste sold instead of a unit of the opaque white toothpaste, the firm "loses" \$0.10. Suppose further that the company expects to sell 1 million units of the new gel toothpaste in the first year after introduction and that, of that amount, 500,000 units will be diverted from the opaque white toothpaste, of which the company had expected to sell 1 million units. The task of the marketing manager is to determine how the introduction of the new gel toothpaste will affect Brand X's total contribution dollars.

One approach to assessing the financial impact of cannibalization is shown below:

1. Brand X expects to lose \$0.10 for each unit diverted from the opaque white toothpaste to the gel toothpaste.
2. Given that 500,000 units will be cannibalized from the opaque white toothpaste, the total contribution *lost* is \$50,000 (\$0.10 × 500,000 units).
3. However, the new gel toothpaste will sell an additional 500,000 units at a contribution per unit of \$0.70, which means that \$350,000 (\$0.70 × 500,000 units) in additional contribution will be generated.
4. Therefore, the net financial effect is a positive increase in contribution dollars of \$300,000 (\$350,000 – \$50,000).

Another approach to assessing the cannibalization effect is as follows:

1. The opaque white toothpaste alone had been expected to sell 1 million units with a unit contribution of \$0.80. Therefore, contribution dollars without the gel would equal \$800,000 (\$0.80 × 1,000,000 units).
2. The gel toothpaste is expected to sell 1 million units with a unit contribution of \$0.70.
3. Given the cannibalism rate of 50 percent (that is, one-half of the gel's volume is diverted from the opaque white toothpaste), the combined contribution can be calculated as follows:

Product	***Unit Volume***	***Unit Contribution***	***Contribution Dollars***
Opaque white toothpaste	500,000	\$0.80	\$400,000
Gel toothpaste:			
Cannibalized volume	500,000	0.70	350,000
Incremental volume	500,000	0.70	350,000
Total	1,500,000		\$1,100,000
Less original forecast volume for opaque white toothpaste	1,000,000	0.80	800,000
Total	+500,000		+\$300,000

Both approaches arrive at the same conclusion: Brand X will benefit by $300,000 from the introduction of the gel toothpaste. The manager should use whichever approach he or she is more comfortable with in an analytic sense.

It should be emphasized, however, that the incremental fixed costs associated with advertising and sales promotion or any additions or changes in manufacturing capacity must be considered to complete the analysis. If the fixed costs approximate or exceed $300,000, the new product should be viewed in a very different light.

■ LIQUIDITY

Liquidity refers to an organization's ability to meet short-term (usually within a budget year) financial obligations. A key measure of an organization's liquidity position is its working capital. *Working capital* is the dollar value of an organization's *current assets* (such as cash, accounts receivable, prepaid expenses, inventory) ***minus*** the dollar value of *current liabilities* (such as short-term accounts payable for goods and services, income taxes).

A manager should be aware of the impact of marketing actions on working capital. Marketing expenditures precede sales volume; therefore, cash outlays for marketing efforts reduce current assets. If marketing expenditures cannot be met out of cash, accounts payable are incurred. In either case, working capital is reduced. In a positive vein, a marketing manager's creation of sales volume, with corresponding increases in net profit, contributes to working capital. Since the timing of marketing expenditures and sales volume is often lagged, a marketing manager must be wary of marketing efforts that unnecessarily deplete working capital and must assess the likelihood of potential sales, given a specified expenditure level.

■ OPERATING LEVERAGE

A financial concept closely akin to break-even analysis is operating leverage. *Operating leverage* refers to the extent to which fixed costs and variable costs are used in the production and marketing of products and services. Firms that have high total fixed costs relative to total variable costs are defined as having high operating leverage. Examples of firms with high operating leverage include airlines and heavy-equipment manufacturers. Firms with low total fixed costs relative to total variable costs are defined as having low operating leverage. Firms typically having low operating leverage include residential contractors and wholesale distributors.

The higher a firm's operating leverage, the faster its total profits will increase once sales exceed break-even volume. By the same token, however, those firms with high operating leverage will incur losses at a faster rate once sales volume falls below the break-even point.

Exhibit 2.2 illustrates the effect of operating leverage on profit. The base case shows two firms that have identical break-even sales volumes. The cost structures of the two firms differ, however, with one having high fixed and low variable costs and the other having low fixed and high variable costs. Note that when sales volume is increased 10 percent, the firm with high fixed and low variable costs achieves a much higher profit than the firm with low fixed and high variable costs. When sales volume declines, however, just the opposite is true. That is, the firm with high fixed and low variable costs incurs losses at a faster rate than the firm with high variable and low fixed costs once sales fall below the break-even point.

The message of operating leverage should be clear from this example. Firms with high operating leverage benefit more from sales gains than do firms with low

EXHIBIT 2.2

Effect of Operating Leverage on Profit

	Base Case		*10% Increase in Sales*		*10% Decrease in Sales*	
	High-Fixed-Cost Firm	*High-Variable-Cost Firm*	*High-Fixed-Cost Firm*	*High-Variable-Cost Firm*	*High-Fixed-Cost Firm*	*High-Variable-Cost Firm*
Sales	$100,000	$100,000	$110,000	$110,000	$90,000	$90,000
Variable costs	20,000	80,000	22,000	88,000	18,000	72,000
Fixed costs	80,000	20,000	80,000	20,000	80,000	20,000
Profit	$0	$0	$8,000	$2,000	($8,000)	($2,000)

operating leverage. At the same time, firms with high operating leverage are more sensitive to sales-volume declines, since losses will be incurred at a faster rate. Knowledge of a firm's cost structure will therefore prove valuable in assessing the gains and losses from changes in sales volume brought about by marketing efforts.

■ DISCOUNTED CASH FLOW

Another useful concept from finance is discounted cash flow. Discounted cash flow incorporates the theory of the time value of money, or present-value analysis. The idea behind the present value of money is that a dollar received next year is not equivalent to a dollar received today because the use of money has a value reflected by risk, inflation, and opportunity cost. To illustrate, if $500 can be invested today at 10 percent, $550 will be received a year later ($500 + 10% of $500). In other words, $550 to be received next year has a present value of $500 if 10 percent can be earned ($550/110% = $500). Following this line of reasoning, the estimated results of an investment (e.g., a business) can be stated as a cash equivalent at the present time (i.e., its present value). *Discounted cash flows* are future cash flows expressed in terms of their present value.

The discounted cash flow technique employs this reasoning by evaluating the present value of a business's net *cash flows* (cash inflows minus cash outflows). A simplified view of cash flow is "cash flow from operations," which is net income plus depreciation charges, because depreciation is a noncash charge against sales to determine net income. The present value of a stream of cash flows is obtained by selecting an interest or discount rate at which these flows are to be valued, or discounted, and the timing of each. The interest or discount rate is often defined by the opportunity *cost of capital*—the cost of earnings opportunities forgone by investing in a business with its attendant risk as opposed to investing in risk-free securities such as U.S. Treasury Bills.

A simple application of discounted cash flow analysis illustrates the mechanics involved. Suppose, for example, that a firm is considering investing $105,000 in one of two businesses. The firm has forecast cash flows for each business over the next five years. The discount rate adopted by the firm is 15 percent. Given the discount rate of 15 percent, the cash flow when the investment is made is a negative $105,000 (no cash inflows, only outflows). The first-year cash flow for Business A is discounted by the factor $1/(1 + 0.15)^1$, or $25,000 × 0.879 = $21,700. The second-year cash flow for Business A is discounted by the factor $1/(1 + 0.15)^2$, or $35,000 × 0.756 = $26,460, and so forth. Exhibit 2.3 shows the complete analysis for Businesses A and B for the five-year planning horizon.

EXHIBIT 2.3

Application of Discounted Cash Flow Analysis with a 15 Percent Discount Factor

		Business A			*Business B*		
Year	*Discount Factor*	*Cash Flow*	*Cumulative Cash Flow*	*Discounted Cash Flow*	*Cash Flow*	*Cumulative Cash Flow*	*Discounted Cash Flow*
0	1.000	($105,000)	($105,000)	($105,000)	($105,000)	($ 105,000)	($105,000)
1	0.870	25,000	(80,000)	21,750	50,000	(55,000)	43,500
2	0.756	35,000	(45,000)	26,460	55,000	0	41,580
3	0.658	50,000	5,000	32,900	60,000	60,000	39,480
4	0.572	70,000	75,000	40,040	65,000	125,000	37,180
5	0.497	90,000	165,000	44,730	70,000	195,000	34,790
Totals			$270,000	$ 17,380		$300,000	$ 44,010

Three points are of particular interest. First, an important series of numbers is the *cumulative cash flow.* This series shows that the cumulative cash flows from Business B are greater than from Business A. Second, the *payback period* is two years for Business B, as opposed to about three years for Business A. In other words, Business B will recover its investment sooner than will Business A. Finally, the discounted cash flows incorporating the time value of money is clearly indicated. Business A will produce a higher cash flow in later years than will Business B. However, the present value of these cash flows five years in the future, when discounted, is less than the value of the cash flows in the near future that Business B will produce.

From a decision-making perspective, both businesses produce a positive net present value. This is important given the decision rule when interpreting net present value: An investment should be accepted if the net present value is positive and rejected if it is negative. In which business should the firm invest its capital? Assuming that the firm wishes to create value for its shareholders, the option with the higher net present value (Business B) is preferred.

A valuable characteristic of present-value analysis is that the discount factors and discounted cash are additive. If the projected cash flows from an investment are equal over a specified time period, summing the discount factors for each of the time periods (say three years) and multiplying this figure by the annual cash flow estimate will give the present value.

Suppose, for example, that a firm can expect a constant cash flow of $10 million per year for three years, and the discount rate is 15 percent. The present value of this cash flow can be computed as follows (in millions of dollars):

$$0.870 \times \$10 = \$8.70$$
$$0.756 \times \$10 = \$7.56$$
$$\underline{0.658} \times \underline{\$10 = \$6.58}$$
$$2.284 \times \$10 = \$22.84$$

Any basic finance textbook covers discounted cash flow in depth and should be consulted for further study. As a word of caution, the application of discounted cash flow analysis is deceptively simple. Determining appropriate discount rates and projecting future cash flows is not an easy task. Conservative estimates and the use of several "what if" scenarios will ensure that the discounted cash flow technique will highlight investment opportunities that create value for the firm and its shareholders.

PREPARING A PRO FORMA INCOME STATEMENT

Because marketing managers are accountable for the profit impact of their actions, they must translate their strategies and tactics into *pro forma*, or projected, income statements. A *pro forma* income statement displays projected revenues, budgeted expenses, and estimated net profit for an organization, product, or service during a specific planning period, usually a year. *Pro forma* income statements include a sales forecast and a listing of variable and fixed costs that can be programmed or committed.

Pro forma income statements can be prepared in different ways and reflect varying levels of specificity. Exhibit 2.4 shows a typical layout for a *pro forma* income statement consisting of six major categories or line items:

1. *Sales*—forecasted unit volume times unit selling price.
2. *Cost of goods sold*—costs incurred in buying or producing products and services. Generally speaking, these costs are constant per unit within certain volume ranges and vary with total unit volume.
3. *Gross margin* (sometimes called *gross profit*)—represents the remainder after cost of goods sold has been subtracted from sales.
4. *Marketing expenses*—generally, programmed expenses budgeted to produce sales. Advertising expenses are typically fixed. Sales expenses can be fixed, such as a salesperson's salary, or variable, such as sales commissions. Freight or delivery expenses are typically constant per unit and vary with total unit volume.
5. *General and administrative expenses*—generally, committed fixed costs for the planning period, which cannot be avoided if the organization is to operate. These costs are frequently called overhead.
6. *Net income before (income) taxes* (often called *net profit before taxes*)—the remainder after all costs have been subtracted from sales.

A *pro forma* income statement reflects a marketing manager's expectations (sales) given certain inputs (costs). This means that a manager must think specifi-

EXHIBIT 2.4

Pro Forma Income Statement for the 12-Month Period Ended December 31, 2000

Sales		$1,000,000
Cost of goods sold		500,000
Gross margin		$500,000
Marketing expenses		
Sales expenses	$170,000	
Advertising expenses	90,000	
Freight or delivery expenses	40,000	300,000
General and administrative expenses		
Administrative salaries	$120,000	
Depreciation on buildings and equipment	20,000	
Interest expense	5,000	
Property taxes and insurance	5,000	
Other administrative expenses	5,000	155,000
Net profit before (income) tax		$45,000

cally about customer response to strategies and tactics and focus attention on the organization's financial objectives of profitability and growth when preparing a *pro forma* income statement.

■ SUMMARY

This chapter provides an overview of basic accounting and financial concepts. A word of caution is necessary, however. Financial analysis of marketing actions is a necessary but insufficient criterion for justifying marketing programs. A careful analysis of other variables impinging on the decision at hand is required. Thus, judgment enters the picture. "Numbers" serve only to complement general marketing analysis skills and are not an end in themselves. In this regard, it is wise to consider some words of Albert Einstein: "Not everything that counts can be counted, and not everything that can be counted counts."

■ EXERCISES

1. Executives of Studio Recordings, Inc., produced the latest compact disc by the Starshine Sisters Band, titled *Sunshine/Moonshine*. The following cost information pertains to the new CD:

CD package and disc (direct material and labor)	$1.25/CD
Songwriters' royalties	$0.35/CD
Recording artists' royalties	$1.00/CD
Advertising and promotion	$275,000
Studio Recordings, Inc., overhead	$250,000
Selling price to CD distributor	$9.00

   Calculate the following:

   a. Contribution per CD unit

   b. Break-even volume in CD units and dollars

   c. Net profit if 1 million CDs are sold

   d. Necessary CD unit volume to achieve a $200,000 profit

2. Video Concepts, Inc. (VCI) markets video equipment and film through a variety of retail outlets. Presently, VCI is faced with a decision as to whether it should obtain the distribution rights to an unreleased film entitled *Touch of Orange*. If this film is distributed by VCI directly to large retailers, VCI's investment in the project would be $150,000. VCI estimates the total market for the film to be 100,000 units. Other data available are as follows:

Cost of distribution rights for film	$125,000
Label design	5,000
Package design	10,000
Advertising	35,000
Reproduction of copies (per 1,000)	4,000
Manufacture of labels and packaging (per 1,000)	500
Royalties (per 1,000)	500

   VCI's suggested retail price for the file is $20 per unit. The retailer's margin is 40 percent.

a. What is VCI's unit contribution and contribution margin?

b. What is the breakeven point in units? In dollars?

c. What share of the market would the film have to achieve to earn a 20 percent return on VCI's investment the first year?

3. The group product manager for ointments at American Therapeutic Corporation was reviewing price and promotion alternatives for two products: Rash-Away and Red-Away. Both products were designed to reduce skin irritation, but Red-Away was primarily a cosmetic treatment whereas Rash-Away also included a compound that eliminated the rash.

The price and promotion alternatives recommended for the two products by their respective brand managers included the possibility of using additional promotion or a price reduction to stimulate sales volume. A volume, price, and cost summary for the two products follows:

	Rash-Away	*Red-Away*
Unit price	$2.00	$1.00
Unit variable costs	1.40	0.25
Unit contribution	$0.60	$0.75
Unit volume	1,000,000 units	1,500,000 units

Both brand managers included a recommendation to either reduce price by 10 percent or invest an incremental $150,000 in advertising.

a. What absolute increase in unit sales and dollar sales will be necessary to recoup the incremental increase in advertising expenditures for Rash-Away? For Red-Away?

b. How many additional sales dollars must be produced to cover each $1.00 of incremental advertising for Rash-Away? For Red-Away?

c. What absolute increase in unit sales and dollar sales will be necessary to maintain the level of total contribution dollars if the price of each product is reduced by 10 percent?

4. After spending $300,000 for research and development, chemists at Diversified Citrus Industries have developed a new breakfast drink. The drink, called Zap, will provide the consumer with twice the amount of vitamin C currently available in breakfast drinks. Zap will be packaged in an eight-ounce can and will be introduced to the breakfast drink market, which is estimated to be equivalent to 21 million eight-ounce cans nationally.

One major management concern is the lack of funds available for marketing. Accordingly, management has decided to use newspapers (rather than television) to promote Zap in the introductory year and distribute Zap in major metropolitan areas that account for 65 percent of U.S. breakfast drink volume. Newspaper advertising will carry a coupon that will entitle the consumer to receive $0.20 off the price of the first can purchased. The retailer will receive the regular margin and be reimbursed by Diversified Citrus Industries. Past experience indicates that for every five cans sold during the introductory year, one coupon will be returned. The cost of the newspaper advertising campaign (excluding coupon returns) will be $250,000. Other fixed overhead costs are expected to be $90,000 per year.

Management has decided that the suggested retail price to the consumer for the eight-ounce can will be $0.50. The only unit variable costs for the product are $0.18 for materials and $0.06 for labor. The company intends to give retailers a margin of 20 percent off the suggested retail price and wholesalers a margin of 10 percent of the retailers' cost of the item.

a. At what price will Diversified Citrus Industries be selling its product to wholesalers?

b. What is the contribution per unit for Zap?

c. What is the break-even unit volume in the first year?

d. What is the first-year break-even share of market?

5. Video Concepts, Inc. (VCI) manufactures a line of videocassette recorders (VCRs) that are distributed to large retailers. The line consists of three models of VCRs. The following data are available regarding the models:

Model	*VCR Selling Price per Unit*	*Variable Cost per Unit*	*Demand/Year (units)*
Model LX1	$175	$100	2,000
Model LX2	250	125	1,000
Model LX3	300	140	500

VCI is considering the addition of a fourth model to its line of VCRs. This model would be sold to retailers for $375. The variable cost of this unit is $225. The demand for the new Model LX4 is estimated to be 300 units per year. Sixty percent of these unit sales of the new model is expected to come from other models already being manufactured by VCI (10 percent from Model LX1, 30 percent from Model LX2, and 60 percent from Model LX3). VCI will incur a fixed cost of $20,000 to add the new model to the line. Based on the above data, should VCI add the new Model LX4 to its line of VCRs? Why?

6. Max Leonard, Vice President of Marketing for Dysk Computer, Inc., must decide whether to introduce a mid-priced version of the firm's DC6900 personal computer product line—the DC6900-X. The DC6900-X would sell for $3,900, with unit variable costs of $1,800. Projections made by an independent marketing research firm indicate that the DC6900-X would achieve a sales volume of 500,000 units next year, in its first year of commercialization. One-half of the first year's volume would come from competitors' personal computers and market growth. However, a consumer research study indicates that 30 percent of the DC6900-X sales volume would come from the higher-priced DC6900-Omega personal computer, which sells for $5,900 (with unit variable costs of $2,200). Another 20 percent of the DC6900-X sales volume would come from the economy-priced DC6900-Alpha personal computer, priced at $2,500 (with unit variable costs of $1,200). The DC6900-Omega unit volume is expected to be 400,000 units next year, and the DC6900-Alpha is expected to achieve a 600,000-unit sales level. The fixed costs of launching the DC6900-X have been forecast to be $2 million during the first year of commercialization. Should Mr. Leonard add the DC6900-X model to the line of personal computers? Why?

7. A sports nutrition company is examining whether a new high-performance sports drink should be added to its product line. A preliminary feasibility analysis indicated that the company would need to invest $17.5 million in a new manufacturing facility to produce and package the product. A financial analysis using sales and cost data supplied by marketing and production personnel indicated that the net cash flow (cash inflows minus cash outflows) would be $6.1 million in the first year of commercialization, $7.4 million in year two, $7.0 million in year three, and $5.5 million in year 4.

Senior company executives were undecided whether to move forward with the development of the new product. They requested that a discounted cash flow analysis be performed using two different discount rates: 20 percent and 15 percent.

a. Should the company proceed with development of the product if the discount rate is 20 percent? Why?

b. Does the decision to proceed with development of the product change if the discount rate is 15 percent? Why?

8. The annual planning process at Century Office Systems, Inc., had been arduous but produced a number of important marketing initiatives for the next year. Most notably, company executives had decided to restructure its product-marketing team into two separate groups: (1) Corporate Office Systems and (2) Home Office Systems. Angela Blake was assigned responsibility for the Home Office Systems group, which would market the company's word-processing hardware and software for home and office-at-home use by individuals. Her marketing plan, which included a sales forecast for next year of $25 million, was the result of a detailed market analysis and negotiations with individuals both inside and outside the company. Discussions with the sales director indicated that 40 percent of the company sales force would be dedicated to selling products of the Home Office Systems group. Sales representatives would receive a 15 percent commission on sales of home office systems. Under the new organizational structure, the Home Office Systems group would be charged with 40 percent of the budgeted sales force expenditure. The sales director's budget for salaries and fringe benefits of the sales force and noncommission selling costs for both the Corporate and Home Office Systems groups was $7.5 million.

The advertising and promotion budget contained three elements: trade magazine advertising, cooperative newspaper advertising with Century Office Systems, Inc., dealers, and sales promotion materials including product brochures, technical manuals, catalogs, and point-of-purchase displays. Trade magazine ads and sales promotion materials were to be developed by the company's advertising and public relations agency. Production and media placement costs were budgeted at $300,000. Cooperative advertising copy for both newspaper and radio use had budgeted production costs of $100,000. Century Office Systems, Inc.'s, cooperative advertising allowance policy stated that the company would allocate 5 percent of company sales to dealers to promote its office systems. Dealers always used their complete cooperative advertising allowances.

Meetings with manufacturing and operations personnel indicated that the direct costs of material and labor and direct factory overhead to produce the Home Office System product line represented 50 percent of sales. The accounting department would assign $600,000 in indirect manufacturing overhead (for example, depreciation, maintenance) to the product line and $300,000 for administrative overhead (clerical, telephone, office space, and so forth). Freight for the product line would average 8 percent of sales.

Blake's staff consisted of two product managers and a marketing assistant. Salaries and fringe benefits for Ms. Blake and her staff were $250,000 per year.

a. Prepare a *pro forma* income statement for the Home Office Systems group given the information provided.

b. Prepare a *pro forma* income statement for the Home Office Systems group given annual sales of only $20 million.

c. At what level of dollar sales will the Home Office Systems group break even?

CHAPTER 3

Marketing Decision Making and Case Analysis

Skill in decision making is a prerequisite to being an effective marketing manager. Indeed, Nobel laureate Herbert Simon viewed managing and decision making as being one and the same.[1] Another management theorist, Peter Drucker, has said that the burden of decision making can be lessened and better decisions can result if a manager recognizes that "decision making is a rational and systematic process and that its organization is a definite sequence of steps, each of them in turn rational and systematic."[2]

One objective of this chapter is to introduce a systematic process for decision making; another is to introduce basic considerations in case analysis. Just as decision making and managing can be viewed as being identical in scope, so the decision-making process and case analysis go hand in hand. For this reason, many companies today use case studies when interviewing an applicant to assess his or her decision-making skill. They have found that the applicant's approach to the case demonstrates strategic thinking, analytical ability and judgment, along with a variety of communication skills, including listening, questioning, and dealing with confrontation.[3]

■ DECISION-MAKING PROCESS

Although no simple formula exists that can assure a correct solution to all problems at all times, use of a systematic decision-making process can increase the likelihood of arriving at better solutions.[4] The decision-making process described here is called DECIDE:[5]

Define the problem.
Enumerate the decision factors.
Consider relevant information.
Identify the best alternative.
Develop a plan for implementing the chosen alternative.
Evaluate the decision and the decision process.

A definition and a discussion of the implications of each step follow.

Define the Problem

The philosopher John Dewey observed that "a problem well defined is half solved." What this statement means in a marketing setting is that a well-defined problem outlines the framework within which a solution can be derived. This framework includes the *objectives* of the decision maker, a recognition of *constraints,* and a clearly articulated *success measure*, or goal, for assessing progress toward solving the problem.

Consider the situation faced by El Nacho Foods, a marketer of Mexican foods. The company had positioned its line of Mexican foods as a high-quality brand and used advertising effectively to convey that message. Shortly after the company's introduction of frozen dinners, two of its competitors began cutting the price of their frozen dinner entrees. The firm lost market share and sales as a result of these price reductions; this loss led to reductions in the contribution dollars available for advertising and sales promotion. How might the problem be defined in this situation? One definition of the problem leads to the question: "Should we reduce our price?" A much better definition of the problem leads one to ask: "How can we maintain our quality brand image (objective) and regain our lost market share (success measure), given limited funds for advertising and sales promotion (constraint)?"

The first problem definition asks for a response to an immediate issue facing the company. It does not articulate the broader and more important considerations of competitive positioning. Hence, the problem statement fails to capture the significance of the issue raised. The second definition provides a broader perspective on the immediate issue posed and allows the manager greater latitude in seeking solutions.

In a case study, the analyst is frequently given alternative courses of action to consider. The narrow approach to case analysis is simply to compare these different options. Such an approach often leads to the selection of alternative A or alternative B without regard to the significance of the choice in the broader context of the situation facing the company or the decision maker.

Enumerate the Decision Factors

Two sets of decision factors must be enumerated in the decision-making process: (1) *alternative courses of action,* and (2) *uncertainties* in the competitive environment. Alternative courses of action are controllable decision factors because the decision maker has complete command of them. Alternatives are typically product-market strategies or changes in the various elements of the organization's marketing mix (described in Chapter 1). Uncertainties, on the other hand, are uncontrollable factors that the manager cannot influence. In a marketing context, they often include actions of competitors, market size, and buyer response to marketing action. Assumptions often have to be made concerning these factors. These assumptions need to be spelled out, particularly if they will influence the evaluation of alternative courses of action.

The experience of Cluett Peabody and Company, the maker of Arrow shirts, illustrates how the combination of an action and uncertainties can spell disaster. Arrow departed from its normal practice of selling classic men's shirts to offer a new line featuring bolder colors, busier patterns, and higher prices (action). The firm soon realized that men's tastes had changed to more conservative styles (environmental uncertainties). The result? The company posted a $4.5 million loss. According to the company president, "We tried to be exciting, and we really didn't look at the market."[6]

Case analysis provides an opportunity to relate alternatives to uncertainties, and these factors *must* be related if decision making is to be effective. No expected outcome, financial or otherwise, of a chosen course of action can realistically be considered apart from the environment into which it is introduced.

Consider Relevant Information

The third step in the decision-making process is the consideration of relevant information. *Relevant information*, like the relevant costs discussed in Chapter 2, consists of information that relates to the alternatives identified by the manager as being likely to affect future events. More specifically, relevant information might include characteristics of the industry or competitive environment, characteristics of the organization (such as competitive strengths and position), and characteristics of the alternatives themselves.

Identifying relevant information is difficult both for the practicing manager and for the case analyst. There is frequently an overabundance of facts, figures, and viewpoints available in any decision-making setting. In fact, it has been said that "The truly successful managers and leaders of the next century will . . . be characterized not by how they can access information, but how they can access the most relevant information and differentiate it from the exponentially multiplying masses of nonrelevant information."[7] Determining what matters and what does not is a skill that is best gained through experience. Analyzing many and varied cases is one way to develop this skill.

Two notes of caution are necessary. First, the case analyst must resist the temptation to consider *everything* in a case as "fact." Many cases, including actual marketing situations, contain conflicting data. Part of the task in any case analysis is to exercise judgment in assessing the validity of the data presented. Second, in many instances relevant information must be created. An example of creating relevant information is the blending together of several pieces of data, as in the calculation of a simple break-even point.

It should be clear at this point that even though the consideration of relevant information is the third step in the decision-making process, relevant information will also affect the two previous steps. As the manager or case analyst becomes more deeply involved in considering and evaluating information, the problem definition may be modified or the decision factors may change.[8]

Upon the conclusion of the first three steps, the manager or case analyst has completed a *situation analysis*. The situation analysis should produce an answer to the synoptic question "Where are we now?" (Specific questions relating to situation analysis are found in Exhibit 3.4 later in this chapter.)

Identify the Best Alternative

Identifying the best alternative is the fourth step in the decision-making process. The selection of a course of action is not simply a matter of choosing Alternative A over other alternatives but, rather, of evaluating identified alternatives and the uncertainties apparent in the problem setting.

A framework for identifying the best alternative is *decision analysis*, which was introduced in Chapter 1. In its simplest form, decision analysis matches each alternative identified by the manager with the uncertainties existing in the environment and assigns a quantitative value to the outcome associated with each match. Managers implicitly use a decision tree and a payoff table to describe the relationship among alternatives, uncertainties, and potential outcomes. The use of decision analysis and the application of decision trees and payoff tables can be illustrated by referring back to the situation faced by El Nacho Foods.

Suppose that at the conclusion of Step 2 in the DECIDE process (that is, enumerating decision factors), El Nacho executives identified two alternatives: (1) reduce the price on frozen dinners, or (2) maintain the price. They also recognized two uncertainties: (1) competitors could maintain the lower price, or (2) competitors could reduce the price further. Suppose further that at the conclusion of Step 3 in the DECIDE process (considering relevant information), El Nacho executives examined the changes in market share and sales volume that would be brought about by the

EXHIBIT 3.1

Decision Tree for El Nacho Foods

Company Action	*Competitive Response*	*Financial Outcome*
Reduce price	Maintain price →	$150,000
	Reduce price further →	$110,000
Maintain price	Maintain price →	$175,000
	Reduce price further →	$90,000

pricing actions. They also calculated the contribution per unit of frozen dinners for each alternative for each competitor response. They performed a contribution analysis because the problem was defined in terms of contribution to advertising and sales promotion in Step 1 of the DECIDE process (defining the problem).

Given two alternatives, two competitive responses, and a calculated contribution per unit for each combination, they identified four unique financial outcomes. These outcomes are displayed in the decision tree shown in Exhibit 3.1.

It is apparent from the decision tree that the largest contribution will be generated if El Nacho maintains its price on frozen dinners *and* competitors maintain their lower price. If El Nacho maintains its price and competitors reduce their price further, however, the lowest contribution among the four outcomes identified will be generated. The choice of an alternative obviously depends on the likelihood of occurrence of uncertainties in the environment.

A *payoff table* is a useful tool for displaying the alternatives, uncertainties, and outcomes facing a firm. In addition, a payoff table includes another dimension—management's subjective determination of the probability of the occurrence of an uncertainty. Suppose, for example, that El Nacho management believes that competitors are also operating with slim contribution margins and hence are most likely to maintain the lower price regardless of El Nacho's action. They believe that there is a 10 percent chance that competitors will reduce the price of frozen dinners even further.[9] Since only two uncertainties have been identified, the subjective probability of competitors' maintaining their price is 90 percent (note that the probabilities assigned to the uncertainties must total 1.0, or 100 percent). Given these probabilities, the payoff table for El Nacho Foods is as shown in Exhibit 3.2.

EXHIBIT 3.2

Payoff Table for El Nacho Foods

		Uncertainties	
		Competitors Maintain Price (Probability = 0.9)	*Competitors Reduce Price (Probability = 0.1)*
Alternatives	*Reduce price*	$150,000	$110,000
	Maintain price	$175,000	$90,000

The payoff table allows the manager or case analyst to compute the "expected monetary value" for each alternative. The expected monetary value is calculated by multiplying the outcome for each uncertainty by its probability of occurrence and then totaling across the uncertainties for each alternative. The expected monetary value of an alternative can be viewed as the value that would be obtained if the manager were to choose the same alternative many times under the same conditions.

The expected monetary value of the price-reduction alternative equals the probability that competitors will maintain prices, multiplied by the financial contribution if competitors maintain prices, plus the probability that competitors will further reduce prices, multiplied by the financial contribution if competitors further reduce prices. The calculation is

$$(0.9)(\$150{,}000) + (0.1)(\$110{,}000) = \$135{,}000 + \$11{,}000 = \$146{,}000$$

The expected monetary value of maintaining the price is

$$(0.9)(\$175{,}000) + (0.1)(\$90{,}000) = \$157{,}500 + \$9{,}000 = \$166{,}500$$

The higher average contribution of $166,500 for maintaining the price indicates that El Nacho's management should maintain the price. The contribution is higher because competitors are expected to maintain their prices nine times out of ten. Under the same conditions (same outcomes, same probability estimates), El Nacho would achieve an average contribution of $146,000 if the price-reduction alternative were chosen. A rational management would therefore select the price-maintenance alternative.

Familiarity with decision analysis is important for four reasons. First, decision analysis is a fundamental tool for considering "what if" situations. By organizing alternatives, uncertainties, and outcomes in this manner, a manager or case analyst becomes sensitive to the dynamic processes present in a competitive environment. Second, decision analysis forces the case analyst to quantify outcomes associated with specific actions. Third, decision analysis is useful in a variety of settings. For example, Warner-Lambert Canada, Ltd. applied decision analysis when deciding to manufacture and distribute Listerine throat lozenges in Canada; Ford Motor Company used decision analysis in deciding whether to produce its own tires, and Pillsbury used it in determining whether to switch from a box to a bag for a certain grocery product.[10] Fourth, an extension of decision analysis can be used in determining the value of "perfect" information.

Exhibit 3.3 (page 56) shows how the expected monetary value of "perfect" information (EMVPI) can be calculated using the El Nacho Foods example. Simply speaking, EMVPI is the difference between what El Nacho would achieve in contribution dollars if its management knew for certain what competitors would do and the average contribution dollars realized without such information. In other words, if El Nacho knew for certain that competitors would maintain their price, the "maintain price" alternative would be selected. If El Nacho management knew for certain that competitors would reduce their price, however, the "reduce price" alternative would be chosen. Assuming El Nacho management faced this decision ten times and knew what competitor reaction would be each time, El Nacho management would make the appropriate decision each time. The result would be an expected monetary value of $168,500. The difference of $2,000 between $168,500 and $166,500 (the best alternative without such information) is viewed as the upper limit to pay for "perfect" information. EMVPI is a useful guide for determining how much money should be spent for marketing research information to identify the best alternative or course of action.

Develop a Plan for Implementing the Chosen Alternative

The selection of a course of action must be followed by development of a plan for its implementation. Simply deciding what to do will not make it happen. The execution phase is critical, and planning for it forces the case analyst to consider resource

EXHIBIT 3.3

Decision Analysis and the Value of Information

		Payoff Table Uncertainties	
		Competitors Maintain Price (Probability = 0.9)	*Competitors Reduce Price (Probability = 0.1)*
Alternatives	A_1: Reduce price	$150,000	$110,000
	A_2: Maintain price	$175,000	$90,000

Calculation of Expected Monetary Value (EMV):

EMV_{A_1} = 0.9($150,000) + 0.1($110,000) = $146,000
EMV_{A_2} = 0.9($175,000) + 0.1($90,000) = $166,500

Calculation of Expected Monetary Value of Perfect Information (EMVPI):

$EMV_{certainty}$ = 0.9($175,000) + 0.1($110,000) = $168,500
EMVPI = $EMV_{certainty} - EMV_{best\ alternative}$
EMVPI = $168,500 – $166,500 = $2,000

allocation and timing questions. For example, if a new product launch is recommended, it is important to consider how managerial, financial, and manufacturing resources will be allocated to this course of action. If a price reduction is recommended, it will be important to monitor whether the reduced prices are reaching the final consumer and not being absorbed by resellers in the marketing channel. Timing is crucial, since a marketing plan takes time to develop and implement.

As a final note, it is important to recognize that strategy formulation and implementation are not necessarily separate sequential processes. Rather, an interactive give-and-take occurs between formulation and implementation until the case analyst realizes that "what might be done can be done," given organizational strengths and market requirements. Another reading of the discussion on the marketing mix in Chapter 1 will highlight these points.

Evaluate the Decision and the Decision Process

The last step in the decision-making process is evaluating the decision made and the decision process itself. With respect to the decision itself, two questions should be asked. First, *Was a decision made*? This seemingly odd question addresses a common shortcoming of case analyses, whereby a case analyst does not make a decision but, rather, "talks about" the situation facing the organization.

The second question is, *Was the decision appropriate, given the situation identified in the case setting*? This question speaks to the issue of insufficient information on the one hand and the failure to consider and interpret information on the other. In many marketing cases, and indeed in some actual business situations, some of the information needed to make a decision is simply not available. When information is incomplete, assumptions must be made. A case analyst is often expected to make assumptions to fill in gaps, but such assumptions should be logically developed and articulated. Merely making assumptions to make the "solution" fit a preconceived notion of the correct answer is a death knell in case analysis and business practice.

The case analyst should constantly monitor how he or she applies the decision-making process.[11] The mere fact that one's decision was right is not sufficient reason to think that the decision process was appropriate. For example, we have all found ourselves lost while trying to locate a home or business from an address. Eventually we somehow find it, but are again at a loss when later asked to direct someone else to the same address. Analogously, the case analyst may arrive at the "correct" solution but be unable to outline (map) the process involved.

After completing a class discussion of a case, a written case assignment, or a group presentation, the case analyst should critically examine his or her performance by answering the following questions:

1. Did I define the problem adequately?
2. Did I identify all pertinent alternatives and uncertainties? Were my assumptions realistic?
3. Did I consider all information relevant to the case?
4. Did I recommend the appropriate course of action? If so, was my logic consistent with the recommendation? If not, were my assumptions different from the assumptions made by others? Did I overlook an important piece of information?
5. Did I consider how my recommendation could be implemented?

Honest answers to these questions will improve the chances of making better decisions in the future.

■ CASE ANALYSIS

How do I prepare a case? This question is voiced by virtually every student exposed to the case method for the first time. One of the most difficult tasks in preparing a case for presentation—or, more generally, resolving an actual marketing problem—is structuring your thinking process to address relevant forces confronting the organization in question. The previous discussion of the decision-making process should be of help in this regard. The remainder of this chapter provides some useful hints to assist you in preparing a marketing case.

Approaching the Case

On your first reading of a marketing case, you should concentrate on becoming acquainted with the situation in which the organization finds itself. This first reading should provide some insights into the problem requiring resolution, as well as background information on the environment and organization.

Then read the case again, paying particular attention to key facts and assumptions. At this point, you should determine the relevance and reliability of the quantitative data provided in the context of what you see as the issues or problems facing the organization. Valuable insights often arise from analyzing two or more bits of quantitative information concurrently. It is essential that extensive note taking occurs during the second reading. Working by writing is very important; simply highlighting statements or numbers in the case is not sufficient. Behavioral scientists estimate that the human mind can focus on only eight facts at a time and that our mental ability to link these facts in a meaningful way is limited without assistance.[12] Experienced analysts and managers always work out ideas on paper—whether they are working alone or in a group.

There are three pitfalls you should avoid during the second reading. First, *do not rush to a conclusion*. If you do so, information is likely to be overlooked or possibly distorted to fit a preconceived notion of the answer. Second, *do not "work the numbers"* until you understand their meaning and derivation. Third, *do not confuse supposition with fact.* Many statements are made in a case, such as "Our firm subscribes to the marketing concept." Is this a fact, based on an appraisal of the firm's actions and performance, or a supposition?

Formulating the Analysis

The previous remarks should provide some direction in approaching a marketing case. The marketing case analysis worksheet shown in Exhibit 3.4 provides a framework for organizing information. Four analytical categories are shown, with illustrative questions pertaining to each. You will find it useful to consider each analytical category when preparing a case.

Nature of the Industry, Market, and Buying Behavior The first analytical category focuses on the organization's environment—the context in which the organization operates. Specific topics of interest include (1) an assessment of the structure, conduct, and performance of the industry and competition, and (2) an understanding of who the buyers are and why, where, when, how, what, and how much they buy.

The Organization It is important to develop an understanding of the organization's financial, human, and material resources, its strengths and weaknesses, and the reasons for its success or failure. Of particular importance is an understanding of what the organization wishes to do. The "fit" between the organization and its environment represents the first major link drawn in case analysis. This link is the essence of the situation analysis, since it is an interpretation of where the organization currently stands. A SWOT analysis like that described in Chapter 1 might be helpful in organizing your thoughts at this point.

EXHIBIT 3.4

Marketing Case Analysis Worksheet

	Specific Points of Inquiry
Nature of the industry, market, and buyer behavior	1. What is the nature of industry structure, conduct, and performance? 2. Who are the competitors, and what are their strengths and weaknesses? 3. How do consumers buy in this industry or market? 4. Can the market be segmented? How? Can the segments be quantified? 5. What are the requirements for success in this industry?
The organization	1. What are the organization's mission, objectives, and distinctive competency? 2. What is its offering to the market? How can its past and present performance be characterized? What is its potential? 3. What is the situation in which the manager or organization finds itself? 4. What factors have contributed to the present situation?
A plan of action	1. What actions are available to the organization? 2. What are the costs and benefits of action in both qualitative and quantitative terms? 3. Is there a disparity between what the organization wants to do, should do, can do, and must do?
Potential outcomes	1. What will be the buyer, trade, and competitive response to each course of action? 2. How will each course of action satisfy buyer, trade, and organization requirements? 3. What is the potential profitability of each course of action? 4. Will the action enhance or reduce the organization's ability to compete in the future?

A Plan of Action You should be prepared to identify possible courses of action on the basis of the situation analysis. More often than not, several alternatives are possible, and each should be fully articulated. Each course of action typically has associated costs and revenues. These should be carefully calculated on the basis of realistic estimates of the magnitude of effort expected in their pursuit.

Potential Outcomes Finally, the potential outcomes of all courses of action identified should be evaluated. On the basis of the appraisal of outcomes, one course of action or strategy should be recommended. The evaluation, however, must indicate not only why the recommendation was preferred, but also why other actions were dismissed.

Though it is always useful to consider each of the analytical categories just described, the method in which they are arranged may vary. There is no one way to analyze a case, just as there is no single correct way to attack a marketing problem. Just be sure to cover the bases.

Communicating the Analysis

Three means exist for communicating case analyses: (1) class discussion, (2) group presentation, and (3) written report.

Class Discussion Discussing case studies in the classroom setting can be an exciting experience, provided that each student actively prepares for and participates in the discussion. Preparation involves more than simply reading the case prior to the scheduled class period—the case should be carefully analyzed, using the four analytical categories described earlier. Four to five hours of preparation are usually required for each assigned case. The notes developed during the preparation should be brought to class.

Similarly, participation involves more than talking. Other students should be carefully watched and listened to during a class discussion. Attentiveness to the views of others is necessary in order to build on previous comments and analyses. Most class discussions follow a similar format. Class analysis begins with a discussion of the organization and its environment. This discussion is followed first by a discussion of the alternative courses of action and then by a consideration of possible implementation strategies. Knowing where the class is in the discussion is important both for organizing the multitude of ideas and analyses presented and for preparing remarks for the subsequent steps in the class discussion.

Immediately after the class discussion, you should prepare a short summary of the analysis developed in class. This summary, which should include the specific facts, ideas, analyses, and generalizations developed, will be useful in comparing and contrasting case situations.

Group Presentation Group presentation of a case requires a slightly different set of skills. Usually, a group of three to five students conducts a rigorous analysis of a case and presents it to classmates. Role-playing may be featured: Class members may serve as an executive committee witnessing the presentation of a task force or project team.

If the instructor asks you to form your own groups, do not form groups solely on the basis of friendship. Rather, try to develop a balanced team where various skills complement one another (financial skills, oral presentation skills, and so on). Seek out individuals who are committed and dependable. Finally, organize the efforts of the group around individual interests and skills.

A polished presentation is very important. Thus, the group should rehearse its presentation, with group members seriously critiquing one another's performance. At the very least, the group should prepare an outline of the presentation (including important exhibits) and distribute it to the class. It is a good idea to use transparencies, electronic slides, or other visual aids to highlight important points and unique analyses, but *don't* read transparencies or electronic slides to your audience. For further information, consult a text on oral presentations or guidelines for effective speaking.

Written Report What you need to do to generate a written analysis of a case assignment is similar to what you should do to prepare for class discussion. The only difference is in the submission of the analysis; a written report should be carefully organized, legible (preferably typed), and grammatically correct.

There is no one correct approach to organizing a written case analysis. However, it is usually wise to think about the report as having three major sections: (1) identification of the strategic issues and problems, (2) analysis and evaluation, and (3) recommendations. The first section should contain a focused paragraph that defines the problem and specifies the constraints and options available to the organization. Material in the second section should provide a carefully developed assessment of the industry, market and buyer behavior, the organization, and the alternative courses of action. *Analysis and evaluation should represent the bulk of the written report.* This section should not contain a restatement of case information; it should contain an assessment of the facts, quantitative data, and management views. The last section should consist of a set of recommendations. These recommendations should be documented with references to the previous section and should be operational given the case situation. By all means, commit to a decision!

A case and a written student analysis of it are presented in the appendix at the end of the book. It is recommended that you carefully analyze the case before reading the student analysis.

NOTES

1. Herbert A. Simon, *The New Science of Management Decision* (New York: Harper & Row, 1960).

2. Peter Drucker, "How to Make a Business Decision," *Nation's Business* (April 1956): 38-39.

3. Melissa Raffoni, "Use Case Interviewing to Improve Your Hiring," *Harvard Management Update* (July 1999): 10.

4. There are a variety of systematic approaches to the decision-making process. See, for example, Max Bazerman, *Judgement in Managerial Decision Making,* 4th ed. (New York: John Wiley & Sons, 1998); and James R. Evans, *Creative Thinking in the Decision and Management Sciences* (Cincinnati, OH: South-Western Publishing, 1991).

5. DECIDE acronym copyright © by William Rudelius. Used with permission.

6. "Cluett Peabody & Co. Loses Shirt Trying to Jazz Up the Arrow Man," *Wall Street Journal* (July 28, 1988): 24.

7. Mark David Nevins and Stephen A. Stumpf, "21st-Century Leadership: Redefining Management Education," *Strategy & Business* (Third Quarter, 1999): 41-51.

8. Lawrence D. Gibson, "Defining Marketing Problems," *Marketing Research* (Spring 1998): 5-12.

9. An issue that frequently arises in developing these subjective probabilities is how to select them. One source is past experience, in the form of statistics such as A. T. Kearney's probabilities of success for alternative strategies, presented in Chapter 1. Alternatively, case information can be used to develop probability estimates. At the very least, when two possible uncertainties exist, a subjective probability of .5 can be assigned to each. This means that the two uncertainties have an equal chance of occurring. These probabilities can then be revised up or down, depending on case information.

10. These examples and a further reading on decision analysis can be found in Peter C. Bell, *Management Science/Operations Research: A Strategic Perspective* (Cincinnati, OH: South-Western Publishing, 1999): Chapter 3; and "Special Issue: Decision and Risk Analysis," *Interfaces* (November-December 1992).

11. For an interesting description of how eight psychological "traps" influence the decision-making process, see John S. Hammond, Ralph L. Keeny, and Howard Raiffa, "The Hidden Traps in Decision Making," *Harvard Business Review* (September–October 1998): 47–58.

12. Amitai Etzioni, "Humble Decision Making," *Harvard Business Review* (July–August 1989): 122–26.

CHAPTER 4

Opportunity Analysis and Market Targeting

The development and implementation of marketing strategy are complicated and challenging tasks. At its pinnacle, marketing strategy involves the selection of markets and the development of programs to reach these markets. This process is carried out in a manner that simultaneously benefits both the markets selected (satisfying the needs or wants of buyers) and the organization (typically in dollar-profit terms).

Within this framework, a necessary first task is opportunity analysis and market targeting. This chapter describes analytical concepts and tools that marketing managers find useful in performing opportunity analyses, selecting market targets, and estimating market and sales potential.

■ OPPORTUNITY ANALYSIS

Opportunity analysis consists of three interrelated activities:

- Opportunity identification
- Opportunity-organization matching
- Opportunity evaluation

Opportunities arise from identifying new types or classes of buyers, uncovering unsatisfied needs of buyers, or creating new ways or means for satisfying buyer needs. Opportunity analysis focuses on finding markets that an organization can profitably serve.

The case of Reebok International, Ltd., highlights the value of careful *opportunity identification.* In 1981, Reebok was known primarily for its custom running shoes. Consumer interest in running had plateaued, however, and new opportunities had to be identified for the company to grow. Careful investigation revealed that there existed numerous opportunities for product development based on buyer types and needs. In quick succession, Reebok introduced an aerobic dance shoe in 1982; a tennis shoe, a basketball shoe, and a children's shoe in 1984; a walking shoe in 1986; an all-purpose shoe in 1988; step-trainers in 1991; hiking shoes in 1994; special track and field shoes for 1996 U.S. Olympians; and a golf shoe in 1997. Reebok

EXHIBIT 4.1

Opportunity Evaluation Matrix: Attractiveness Criteria

Market Niche Criterion	*Competitive Activity*	*Buyer Requirements*	*Demand/ Supply*	*Political, Technological, and Socioeconomic Forces*	*Organizational Capabilities*
Buyer type	How many and which firms are competing for this user group?	What affects the willingness and ability to buy?	Do different buyer types have different levels of effective demand? How important are adequate sources of supply?	How sensitive are different buyers to these forces?	Can we gain access to buyers through marketing-mix variables? Can we supply these buyers?
Buyer needs	Which firms are satisfying which buyer needs?	Are there buyer needs that are not being satisfied? What are they?	Are buyer needs likely to be long term? Do we have or can we acquire resources to satisfy buyer needs?	How sensitive are buyer needs to these forces?	Which buyer needs can our organization satisfy?
Means for satisfying buyer needs	What are the strategies being employed to satisfy buyer needs?	Is the technology for satisfying buyer needs changing?	To what extent are the means for satisfying buyer needs affected by supply sources? Is the demand for the means for satisfying buyer needs changing?	How sensitive are the means for satisfying buyer needs to these forces?	Do we have the financial, human, technological, and marketing expertise to satisfy buyer needs?

had identified buyer needs based on athletic activities (tennis, basketball, walking, track and field) and buyer types (men, women, and children). By doing so, Reebok increased sales from $1 million to more than $3.2 billion in 17 years. In the late 1990s, Reebok's attention turned to opportunities in the global marketplace. The company quickly learned that the English want white cricket shoes only and the Japanese want ultralight running shoes.[1]

Opportunity-organization matching determines whether an identified market opportunity is consistent with the definition of the organization's business, mission statement, and distinctive competencies. This determination usually involves an assessment of the organization's strengths and weaknesses and an identification of the success requirements for operating profitably in a market. A SWOT analysis like that described in Chapter 1 is often employed to assess the match between identified market opportunities and the organization.

For some companies, market opportunities that promise sizable sales and profit gains are not pursued because they do not conform to an organization's character. Starbucks is a case in point. The company has built a thriving business serving freshly brewed, specialty, gourmet coffee. However, the company refuses to use artifically flavored coffee despite its growth potential. According to company chairman Howard Schultz, "The largest growth segment in our category is artificially flavored coffee; it would give us maybe 40 percent incremental volume, but we won't do it." He adds, "It's not in our DNA."[2]

Opportunity evaluation typically has two distinct phases—qualitative and quantitative. The qualitative phase focuses on matching the attractiveness of an opportunity with the potential for uncovering a market niche. Attractiveness is dependent on (1) competitive activity; (2) buyer requirements; (3) market demand and supplier sources; (4) social, political, economic, and technological forces; and (5) organizational capabilities. Each of these factors in turn must be tied to its impact on the types of buyers sought, the needs of buyers, and the means for satisfying these needs. Exhibit 4.1 is an opportunity evaluation matrix containing illustrative questions useful in the qualitative analysis of a market opportunity. The quantitative phase yields estimates of market sales potential and sales forecasts. It also produces budgets for financial, human, marketing, and production resources, which are necessary to assess the profitability of a market opportunity.

Opportunity identification, matching, and evaluation are challenging assignments, because subjective factors play a large role and managerial insight and foresight are necessary. These activities are even more difficult in the global arena, where social and political forces and uncertainties related to organizational capabilities in unfamiliar economic environments assume a significant role.

WHAT IS A MARKET?

The fact that an opportunity has been identified does not necessarily imply that a market exists for the organization. Although definitions vary, a *market* may be considered to be the prospective buyers (individuals or organizations) willing and able to purchase the existing or potential offering (product or service) of an organization.

This definition of a market has several managerial implications. First, the definition focuses on buyers, not on products or services. People and organizations whose idiosyncrasies dictate whether and how products and services will be acquired, consumed, or used make up markets. Second, by highlighting the buyer's willingness and ability to purchase a product or service, this definition introduces the concept of *effective demand.* Even if buyers are willing to purchase a product or service, exchange cannot occur unless they are able to do so. Likewise, if buyers are able to purchase a product or service but are unwilling to do so, exchange will not occur. These relationships are important to grasp because a marketing strategist must ascertain the extent of effective demand for an offering in order to determine whether a market exists. To a large degree, the extent of effective demand will depend on the marketing-mix activities of the organization. Third, use of the term *offering*, rather than *product* or *service*, expands the definition of what organizations provide for buyers. Products and services are not purchased for the sake of purchase; they are purchased for the values or benefits that buyers expect to derive from them. It is for this reason that the late Charles Revson of Revlon Cosmetics continually reiterated that his company did not sell cosmetics but, rather, hope. This expanded definition of an offering requires strategists to consider benefits provided by a product or service apart from its tangible nature.

Frequently, one hears or reads about the automobile market, the soft drink market, or the health care market. These terms can be misleading because each refers to a composite of multiple minimarkets. Viewing a market as composed of minimarkets allows a marketer to better gauge opportunities. Consider, for example, the "coffee

EXHIBIT 4.2

Market Structure for Coffee

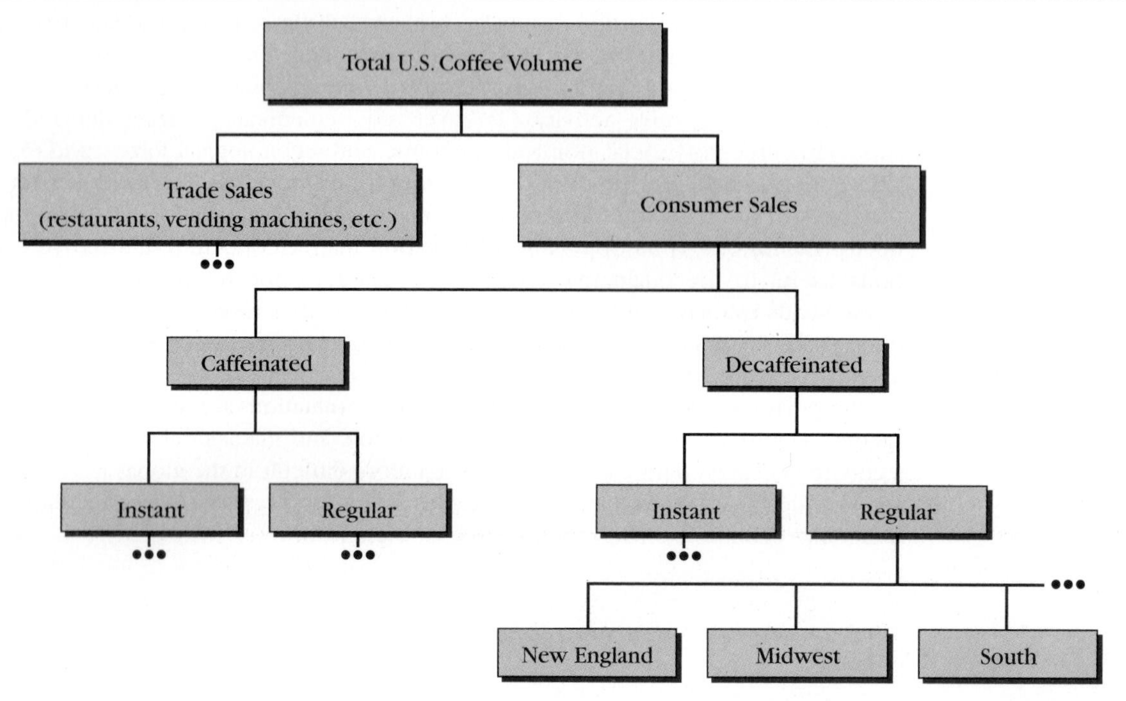

market." Exhibit 4.2 shows how the U.S. coffee market might be broken down into multiple markets by a marketing manager for Maxwell House or Folgers. With this breakdown, the manager can more effectively identify who is competing in the caffeinated versus the decaffeinated markets and how they are competing, monitor changes in sales volume for instant decaffeinated coffee, and appreciate differences between buyer taste preferences and competition in the South and in New England. For these reasons, among others, regional marketing has become popular. For example, Folgers' management observed that vacuum brick-packs of coffee were relatively more popular than cans in the South. They repackaged their Folgers brand coffee for those markets and developed a new advertising campaign. Sales of Folgers coffee increased 32 percent in targeted markets.[3]

Finally, how a market is defined has a crucial effect on the concept of market share. *Market share* can be defined as the sales of a firm, product, or brand divided by the sales of the "market." Obviously, market definition is critical in calculating this percentage. For example, consider the market share of Brand X, an instant, decaffeinated coffee brand with annual sales of $1 billion. Depending on the definition of the market, the brand's share will range from 12.5 percent to 50 percent, as shown in the following table.

Market Definition	*Dollar Sales*	*Brand X Sales*	*Market Share*
U.S. coffee market	$8 billion	$1 billion	12.5%
U.S. decaffeinated coffee market	$4 billion	$1 billion	25.0%
U.S. instant decaffeinated coffee market	$2 billion	$1 billion	50.0%

■ MARKET SEGMENTATION

A useful technique for structuring markets is *market segmentation*—the breaking down or building up of potential buyers into groups. These groups are typically termed *market segments*. Each segment is thought of as possessing some sort of homogeneous characteristic relating to its purchasing or consumption behavior, which is ultimately reflected in its responsiveness to marketing programs. Market segmentation grew out of the recognition that, in general, an organization cannot be all things to all people.[4]

Although Henry Ford is reputed to have said that buyers of his automobiles could have any color they desired as long as it was black, most marketers today agree that such an undifferentiated marketing strategy is no longer appropriate. The idea that an organization can effectively apply one marketing strategy to all possible buyers is not viable in today's marketing environment.

At the other extreme, unless the organization is highly specialized and sells only to, say, one buyer, it is often not feasible to treat each potential buyer as unique. Thus, as Ben Enis has so aptly written, market segmentation "is a compromise between the ineffectiveness of treating all customers alike and the inefficiency of treating each one differently."[5]

Advances in information technology and flexible manufacturing and service delivery systems have made "segments of one" a reality in some settings. *Mass customization*—tailoring products and services to the tastes and preferences of individual buyers in high volumes and at a relatively low cost—combines the efficiencies of mass production and the effectiveness of designing offerings to a single buyer's unique wants.[6] Mass customization is an important element of the value proposition in Internet marketing, as described in Chapter 9.

Segmentation offers two principal benefits with regard to the development of marketing strategy. First, needs, wants, and behaviors of specific groups of buyers can be more precisely determined. More specifically, the following six fundamental buyer-related questions can be answered for each market segment:

1. Who are they?
2. What do they want to buy?
3. How do they want to buy?
4. When do they want to buy?
5. Where do they want to buy?
6. Why do they want to buy?

Second, resources can be more effectively allocated to marketing-mix activities designed to satisfy the needs, wants, and behaviors of buyer segments. For example, Procter & Gamble markets its Crest toothpaste with different advertising and promotion campaigns directed at six different market segments, including children, Hispanics, and senior citizens.[7]

These advantages, though, are not without their costs. There are research costs associated with identifying appropriate market segments. And designing more than one marketing strategy is likely to increase expenses for such items as offering design, salesperson training, and channel selection.

A variety of measures is useful for segmenting markets. A brief listing includes the following:

- Socioeconomic characteristics, such as gender, age, occupation, income, family life cycle, education, or geographic location
- Buying and usage characteristics, such as end use versus intermediate use, buying for another versus buying for self, size of purchase, or volume of consumption

- Benefits sought from products or services, such as status, economy, taste, convenience of use, or value for the money

Increasingly, marketers are complementing these measures with attitudinal and lifestyle measures to better understand why and how people buy, use, or consume their products and services. Segmentation research at Frito-Lay, Inc. is a case in point. In addition to studying consumer socioeconomic characteristics, buying and usage behavior, and product benefits sought, the company has identified two attitudinal and lifestyle market segments that consume snack chips. "Indulgers" are consumers who know they should limit their fat consumption but cannot and those who simply don't care. This segment represents 47 percent of snack chip consumers who are heavy users of snack chips. The other 53 percent of consumers are "compromisers," who restrict their snack chip intake because of nutrition concerns.[8]

In selecting the measures to use for segmenting a particular market, the manager must depend on his or her knowledge of their relative contributions to buyer behavior and effective demand. Whichever measures are selected must satisfy a number of important requirements. First, the measures should assist in the identification of distinct groups of prospective buyers. Second, the groups identified should be economically accessible to a product or service organization through existing or possible marketing programs. Finally, the groups should be large enough in terms of sales volume potential to support the costs of the organization serving them. Frito-Lay, Inc. executives believed the "compromiser" segment met all three requirements and targeted this group for innovative "better-for-you" products. Baked Lay's low-fat potato crisps were introduced in 1996 and posted sales of $250 million in their first full year on the market. This success was followed by the WOW! snack chip line, which included Ruffles, Doritos, and Tostitos made with Olean, a fat-free, calorie-free cooking oil. This line recorded first-year sales of $350 million in 1999 and was the most successful new food introduction of the 1990s.[9]

■ OFFERING-MARKET MATRIX

A useful procedure for investigating markets is to construct an *offering-market matrix*. Such a matrix relates offerings to selected groups of buyers. Exhibit 4.3 shows an illustrative matrix for handheld calculators marketed by Texas Instruments, Casio, Citizen Business Machines, and Hewlett-Packard, among others. Four possible user groups (or market segments) are business, scientific, home, and school. Displaying offerings and user groups in this manner facilitates identification of competitors and their offerings and possible gaps in the calculator market reflected in empty cells in the matrix. Knowing where competitors are active provides a basis for determining whether a market opportunity exists. Identification of gaps in the market and knowledge of competitive activities in specific offering-market cells should assist the marketing manager in gauging the effective demand for an organization's offering and the likelihood of developing a profitable marketing program. Regardless of whether the organization is investigating a potential or an existing market, development of an offering-market matrix is often a prerequisite for market targeting.

■ MARKET TARGETING

After a market has been segmented, it is necessary to select the segment(s) on which marketing efforts will be focused. *Market targeting* (or target marketing) is merely

EXHIBIT 4.3

Offering-Market Matrix for Handheld Calculators

Computational Characteristics	***Market Segments (User Groups)***			
	Business	*Scientific*	*Home*	*School*
Simple (arithmetic operations only)				
Moderate (arithmetic operations, squares, and square roots)				
Complex (all of the above plus business, scientific, and statistical functions)				
Very complex (all of the above plus programmable features)				

the specification of the segment(s) the organization wishes to pursue. Once the manager has selected the target market(s), the organization must decide which marketing strategies to employ.

For example, recognizing that Wal-Mart, Lowe's, and a host of regional competitors were targeting the home-improvement "do-it-yourselfer" segment for home repairs and remodeling, Home Depot decided to pursue the "professional" segment for growth alongside the "do-it-yourselfer" segment. This segment consisted of housing professionals, such as managers of major apartment and condominium complexes and hotel chains, and professional building contractors. Once decided, the company modified its merchandise assortment to meet the needs of the "professional" segment and broadened its services, including longer store hours, delivery, commercial credit, truck and equipment rental, and ordering via phone, fax, or the Internet.[10]

Two frequently used market targeting approaches are *differentiated marketing* and *concentrated marketing*. In a differentiated marketing approach, the organization simultaneously pursues several different market segments, usually with a unique marketing strategy for each. An example of this type of marketing is the strategy of *Time* magazine. It publishes more than 200 different U.S. editions and more than 100 international editions, each targeted at its own geographic and demographic segments.[11] In a concentrated approach, the organization focuses on a single market segment. An extreme case would be one in which an organization marketed a single product offering to a single market segment. More commonly, an organization will offer a product line to a single segment. For many years, Gerber proclaimed that "babies are our only business." Today, Gerber further segments the "baby" segment into developmental phases, ranging from newborn to head-up, sitter, crawler, and toddler, and provides specially prepared foods for each phase.[12]

■ MARKET SALES POTENTIAL AND PROFITABILITY

An essential activity in opportunity evaluation is the determination of market sales potential and profitability. Estimating a market's sales potential for offerings is a difficult task even for a seasoned marketing executive. Markets and offerings can be defined in numerous ways that can lead to different estimates of market size and dollar sales potential. This was illustrated earlier in the description of market structure and resulting market shares in the U.S. coffee industry. For innovative offerings or new markets, marketing analysts must often rely almost entirely on judgment and creativity when estimating market sales potential. Therefore, it is understandable that market sales potential estimates vary greatly for high-definition television (HDTV) and electric automobiles. The underlying technology for both offerings is still evolving as is the physical form. In such dynamic settings, measures for identifying prospective market segments are uncertain.

Estimating Market Sales Potential

Market sales potential is a quantitative approximation of effective demand. Specifically, *market sales potential* is the maximum level of sales that might be available to all organizations serving a defined market in a specific time period given (1) the marketing-mix activities and effort of all organizations, and (2) a set of environmental conditions. As this definition indicates, market sales potential is not a fixed amount. Rather, it is a function of a number of factors, some of which are controllable and others not controllable by organizations. For instance, controllable marketing-mix activities and marketing-related expenditures of organizations can influence market sales potential. On the other hand, consumer disposable income, government regulations, and other social, economic, and political conditions are not controllable by organizations, but do affect market sales potential. These uncontrollable factors are particularly relevant in estimating market sales potential in developing countries. For example, U.S., European, and Japanese passenger car manufacturers have come to realize that automobile market sales potential in China, the world's most populous country, is affected by obstacles outside their control. In China, sudden government policy shifts toward foreign manufacturers are common. There are less than 1,000 auto distributorships in the entire country. China is a cash-based society, and consumers have little access to financing or credit, making buying a car a formidable proposition. The bicycle is the preferred mode of transportation, which is understandable because China has limited navigable roads for cars outside its major cities, where 80 percent of the population lives.[13]

Three variables are commonly considered when estimating market sales potential.[14] These include: (1) the number of prospective buyers (B) who are willing and able to purchase an offering; (2) the quantity (Q) of an offering purchased by an average buyer in a specific time period, typically one calendar year; and (3) the price (P) of an average unit of the offering. Market sales potential is the product of these three variables:

$$\text{Market sales potential} = B \times Q \times P$$

Though simple, this expression contains the building blocks for developing a more complex formulation through what is called the *chain ratio method*, which involves multiplying a base number by several adjusting factors that are believed to influence market sales potential. An application of this method by Coca-Cola and Pepsi-Cola is shown in the following calculation of cola-flavored carbonated soft drink potential in a South American country:

Market sales potential for cola-flavored carbonated soft drinks in a country	=	Population aged 8 years and over × proportion of the population that consumes carbonated soft drinks on a daily basis × proportion of the population preferring cola-flavored carbonated soft drinks × the average number of carbonated soft drink occasions per day × the average amount consumed per consumption occasion (expressed in ounces) × 365 days in a calendar year × the average price per ounce of cola

The chain ratio method serves three important purposes. First, it yields a quantitative estimate of market sales potential. Second, it highlights factors that are controllable and not controllable by organizations. Clearly, a country's population aged 8 years and older is an uncontrollable factor. However, the other factors are controllable or can be influenced to some degree. For example, organizations can influence the proportion of a population that consumes carbonated soft drinks through primary demand advertising and the cost of cola drinks through pricing. If either of these two factors change, market sales potential changes, other things being equal. Finally, it affords a manager flexibility in estimating market sales potential for different buyer groups and different offerings. For example, by including another factor such as the proportion of the population preferring diet colas, the potential for this offering can be calculated.

Sales and Profit Forecasting

Sales and profit forecasting follow the estimation of market sales potential. A *sales forecast* is the level of sales a single organization expects to achieve based on a chosen marketing strategy and an assumed competitive environment. An organization's forecasted sales are typically some fraction of estimated market sales potential.

Forecasted sales reflect the size of the target market(s) chosen by the organization and the marketing mix chosen for these target market(s). Forecasted sales also reflect the assumed number of competitors and competitive intensity in the chosen target market(s). For example, suppose an organization's target market represents one-fourth of 1 million prospective buyers for a particular offering. The marketing channel chosen for the offering provides access to about three-fourths of these buyers and the communication program (advertising) reaches these same buyers. Suppose further that the average purchase rate is 20 units of an offering per year and the average offering unit price is $10.00. Using a version of the chain ratio method, forecasted sales might be calculated as follows:

Total estimated prospective buyers	1 million
times	
Target market (25% of total buyers)	× .25
times	
Distribution/Communication coverage (75% of target market)	× .75
times	
Annual purchase rate (20 units per year)	× 20
times	
Average offering unit price ($10.00)	× $10.00
Forecasted sales	$37.5 million

The $37.5 million sales forecast does not consider the number of competitors vying for the same market target nor does it consider competitive intensity. Therefore, this sales forecast should be adjusted downward to reflect these realities.

Forecasting sales, like estimating market sales potential, is not an easy task. Nevertheless, the task is central to opportunity evaluation and must be undertaken. For this reason, sales forecasting is addressed again in Chapter 5 in reference to product and service life cycles.

Finally, a *pro forma* income statement should be prepared showing forecasted sales, budgeted expenses, and estimated net profit (Chapter 2). When completed, the marketing analyst can review the identified opportunities and decide which can be most profitably pursued given organizational capabilities.

NOTES

1. Reebok's growth is detailed in Eric N. Berkowitz, Roger A. Kerin, Steven W. Hartley, and William Rudelius, *Marketing*, 6th ed. (Burr Ridge, IL: Irwin/McGraw Hill, 2000): 255–59.

2. Terry Lefton, "Schultz' Caffeinated Crusade," *Brandweek* (July 5, 1999): 20–25.

3. For additional examples of regional marketing, see S. McKenna, *The Complete Guide to Regional Marketing* (Homewood, IL: Richard D. Irwin, 1992).

4. For a comprehensive treatment of market segmentation, see James H. Myers, *Segmentation and Positioning for Strategic Marketing Decisions* (Chicago: American Marketing Association, 1996).

5. Ben M. Enis, *Marketing Principles: The Management Process*, 2nd ed. (Pacific Palisades, CA: Goodyear, 1977): 241.

6. For an extended disucssion of mass customization and its application, see Erick Schonfeld, "The Customized, Digitized, Have-It-Your-Way Economy, *Fortune* (September 28, 1998): 115–24; and James H. Gilmore and B. Joseph Pine III, "The Four Faces of Mass Customization," *Harvard Business Review* (January–February 1997): 91–101.

7. "Make It Simple," *Business Week* (September 9, 1996): 96–104.

8. "Salting Away Big Profits," *U.S. News & World Report* (September 16, 1996): 71–72.

9. "Frito-Lay Named New Product Marketer of 1995," *Marketing News* (May 6, 1996): special supplement; and "American Marketing Association Edison Best New Products," *Marketing News* (March 29, 1999): special supplement.

10. Roy S. Johnson, "Home Depot Renovates," *Fortune* (November 23, 1998): 200–12; and *www.homedepot.com/1998,* annual report.

11. "Split Decision," *Brandweek* (March 8, 1999): 8.

12. *www.gerber.com/phases,* December 15, 1999.

13. "Want to Sell Cars in China?" *Advertising Age* (January 15, 1999): 10; and Edward Tse, "The Right Way to Achieve Profitable Growth in the Chinese Consumer Market," *Strategy & Business* (Second Quarter, 1998): 10–21.

14. Portions of this discussion are based on Donald R. Lehmann and Russell S. Winer, *Analysis for Marketing Planning*, 4th ed. (Chicago: Richard D. Irwin, 1997): Chapter 6; and Philip Kotler, *Marketing Management*, 10th ed. (Upper Saddle River, NJ: Prentice Hall, 2000): Chapter 4.

CASE

Quetzal Collections, Inc.

Quetzal Collections, Inc. is an importer and distributor of a wide variety of South American and African artifacts. It is also a major source of southwestern Indian—especially Hopi and Navajo—authentic jewelry and pottery. Although the firm's headquarters is located in Phoenix, Arizona, there are currently branch offices in Los Angeles, Miami, and Boston.

Quetzal (named after the national bird of Guatemala) originated as a trading post operation near Tucson, Arizona, in the early 1900s. Through a series of judicious decisions, the firm established itself as one of the more reputable dealers in authentic southwestern jewelry and pottery. Over the years, Quetzal gradually expanded its product line to include pre-Columbian artifacts from Peru and Venezuela (see Exhibit 1) and tribal and burial artifacts from Africa. Through its careful verification of the authenticity of these South American and African artifacts, Quetzal developed a national reputation as one of the most respected importers of these types of artifacts.

In the early 1990s, Quetzal further expanded its product line to include items that were replicas of authentic artifacts. For example, African fertility gods and masks were made by craftspeople who took great pains to produce these items so that only the truly knowledgeable buyer—a collector—would know that they were replicas. Quetzal now has native craftspeople in Central America, South America, Africa, and the southwestern United States who provide these items. Replicas account for only a small portion of total Quetzal sales; the company agreed to enter this business only at the prodding of the firm's clients, who desired an expanded line. The replicas have found most favor among gift buyers and individuals looking for decorative items.

Quetzal's gross sales are about $20 million and have increased at a constant rate of 20 percent per year over the last decade, despite little price inflation. Myron Rangard, the firm's national sales manager, attributed the sales increase to the popularity of Quetzal's product line and to the expanded distribution of South American and African artifacts:

> For some reason, our South American and certainly our African artifacts have been gaining greater acceptance. Two of our department store customers featured examples of our African line in their Christmas catalogs last year. I personally think consumer tastes are changing from the modern and abstract to the more concrete, like our products.

Quetzal distributes its products exclusively through specialty dealers (including interior decorators), firm-sponsored showings, and a few exclusive department stores. Often, the company is the sole supplier to its clients. Rangard recently expressed the reasons for this highly limited distribution:

> Our limited distribution has been dictated to us because of the nature of our product line. As acceptance grew, we expanded our distribution to specialty dealers and some exclusive department stores. Previously, we had to push our products through

---

This case was prepared by Professors Roger A. Kerin, of the Edwin L. Cox School of Business, Southern Methodist University, and Robert A. Peterson, of the University of Texas, as a basis for class discussion and is not designed to illustrate effective or ineffective handling of an administrative situation. Names have been disguised.

EXHIBIT 1

Pre-Columbian Water Vessel from Peru

> our own showings. Furthermore, we just didn't have the product. These South American artifacts aren't always easy to get and the political situation in Africa is limiting our supply. Our perennial supply problem has become even more critical in recent years for several reasons. Not only must we search harder for new products, but the competition for authentic artifacts has increased tenfold. On top of this, we must now contend with governments' not allowing exportation of certain artifacts because of their "national significance."

The problem of supply has forced Quetzal to add three new buyers in the last two years. Whereas Quetzal identified five major competitors a decade ago, there are 11 today. "Our bargaining position has eroded," noted David Olsen, Director of Procurement. "We have watched our gross margin slip in recent years due to aggressive competitive bidding by others."

"And competition at the retail level has increased also," injected Rangard. "Not only are some of our specialty and exclusive department store customers sending out their own buyers to deal directly with some of our Hopi, Navajo, and African suppliers, but we are often faced with amateurs or fly-by-night competitors. These people move into a city and dump a bunch of inauthentic junk on the public at exorbitant prices. Such antics give the industry a bad name." Rangard acknowledged that high-quality decorative items were also now available on the Internet (see for example, authenticafrica.com).

A recent article in *U.S. News & World Report* supported Rangard's observation.[1] According to the article, which featured African artifacts:

> It's best to buy from a dealer you can trust since a growing number of fakes are turning up on the market. Throughout Africa, artisans in "craft centers" simply churn out copies of authentic items. And sometimes, "traditional" art is created in the absence of any tradition. In Kenya, for example, masks made by the Masai people sell for anywhere from \$50 to \$200. But the Masai have never carved masks.

In recent years, several mass-merchandise department store chains have begun to sell merchandise similar to that offered by Quetzal. Even though product quality was often mixed and most items were replicas, occasionally an authentic group of items was found in these stores, according to company sales representatives. Subsequent inquiries by both Rangard and Olsen revealed that other competing distributors had signed purchase contracts with these outlets. Moreover, the items were typically being sold at retail prices below those charged by Quetzal's dealers.

In early January 1999, Rangard was contacted by a mass-merchandise department store chain concerning the possibility of carrying a complete line of Quetzal products and particularly a full assortment of authentic items. The chain was currently selling a competitor's items but wished to add a more exclusive product line. A tentative contract submitted by the chain stated that it would buy at 10 percent below Quetzal's existing prices, and that its initial purchase would be for no less than \$750,000. Depending on consumer acceptance, purchases were estimated to be at least \$4 million annually. An important clause in the contract dealt with the supply of replicas. Inspection of this clause revealed that Quetzal would have to triple its replica production to satisfy the contractual obligation. Soon after Quetzal executives began discussing the contract, Quetzal's president, Andrew Smythe, mentioned that accepting the contract could have a dramatic effect on how Quetzal defined its business. Smythe added:

> The contract presents us with an opportunity to broaden our firm's position. The upside is that we have the potential to add \$4 million in additional sales over and above our annual growth. On the other hand, do we want to commit such a large percent of our business to replicas? Is that the direction that the market is going? What effect will this contract have on our current dealers, and, I might add, our current customers?
>
> I want you both (Rangard and Olsen) to consider this contract in light of your respective functions and the company as a whole. Let's meet in a few days to discuss this matter again.

[1]Kerry Hannon, "News You Can Use: Out of Africa," *U.S. News & World Report* (May 5, 1997): 71-73.

CASE

Jones•Blair Company

In early January 1997, Alexander Barrett, President of Jones•Blair Company, slumped back in his chair as his senior management executives filed out of the conference room. "Another meeting and still no resolution," he thought. After two lengthy meetings, the executive group still had not decided where and how to deploy corporate marketing efforts among the various architectural paint coatings markets served by the company in the southwestern United States. He asked his secretary to schedule another meeting for next week.

■ THE U.S. PAINT INDUSTRY

The U.S. paint industry is divided into three broad segments: (1) architectural coatings, (2) original equipment manufacturing (OEM) coatings, and (3) special-purpose coatings. Architectural coatings consist of general-purpose paints, varnishes, and lacquers used on residential, commercial, and institutional structures, sold through wholesalers and retailers, and purchased by do-it-yourself consumers, painting contractors, and professional painters. Architectural coatings are commonly called *shelf goods* and account for 43 percent total industry dollar sales. OEM coatings are formulated to industrial buyer specifications and are applied to original equipment during manufacturing. These coatings are used for durable goods such as automobiles, trucks, transportation equipment, appliances, furniture and fixtures, metal containers and building products, and industrial machinery and equipment. OEM coatings represent 35 percent of total industry dollar sales. Special-purpose coatings are formulated for special applications or environmental conditions, such as extreme temperatures, exposure to chemicals, or corrosive conditions. These coatings are used for automotive and machinery refinishing, industrial construction and maintenance (including factories, equipment, utilities, and railroads), bridges, marine applications (ship and offshore facilities such as oil rigs), highway and traffic markings, aerosol and metallic paints, and roof paints. Special-purpose coatings account for 22 percent of total industry dollar sales.

The U.S. paint industry is generally considered to be a maturing industry. Industry sales in 1996 were estimated to be slightly over $13 billion. Average annual dollar sales growth was forecasted to approximate the general rate of inflation through 2000.

Outlook for Architectural Paint Coatings and Sundries

Industry sources estimated U.S. sales of architectural paint coatings and sundries (brushes, rollers, paint removers and thinners, etc.) to be $10 billion-plus in 1996. Ar-

The cooperation of Jones•Blair Company in the preparation of this case is gratefully acknowledged. This case was prepared by Professor Roger A. Kerin, Edwin L. Cox School of Business, Southern Methodist University, as a basis for class discussion and is not designed to illustrate effective or ineffective handling of an administrative situation. Certain names and selected market and sales data have been disguised and are not useful for research purposes.

chitectural coatings are considered to be a mature market with long-term sales growth projected in the range of 1 to 2 percent per year. Demand for architectural coatings and sundries reflect the level of house redecorating, maintenance, and repair, as well as sales of existing homes, and to a lesser extent new home, commercial, and industrial construction. Industry sources also noted that the demand for architectural coatings and sundries is affected by two other factors. First, the architectural coating segment faced competition from alternative materials, such as aluminum and vinyl siding, interior wall coverings, and wood paneling. Second, paint companies had developed higher-quality products that reduced the amount of paint necessary per application and the frequency of repainting. Counteracting these factors, industry observers foresaw increasing demand for paint sundries due to a trend toward do-it-yourself painting by household consumers.

U.S. paint manufacturers are under growing pressure to reduce emissions of volatile organic compounds (VOCs) from paints and to limit the consumption of solvents. The Environmental Protection Agency (EPA) has proposed a three-step plan for the reduction of VOCs in architectural and industrial maintenance coatings. The first phase of the plan, which took effect in 1996, required a 25 percent reduction in VOC content from the base year of 1990. VOCs must be reduced by 35 percent (from the 1990 base year) in 2000 and 45 percent in the third phase in 2003. Compliance with EPA regulations has further eroded historically low profit margins in the paint industry.

Consolidation and Competition in the Architectural Coatings Segment

Slow sales growth, the necessity for ongoing research and development, and recent compliance with governmental regulations have fueled merger and acquisition activity in the U.S. paint industry since 1990. Companies seeking growth and a higher sales base to support increasing costs are making acquisitions. Companies that were unwilling or unable to make capital and research and development (R&D) commitments necessary to remain competitive sold their paint businesses. Industry sources estimate that the number of paint companies is currently 600, or about 40 percent fewer companies than in 1975. The number of paint companies is presently declining at a rate of 2 to 3 percent per year. Merger activity generally involved the purchase of small companies by larger firms to boost their specific market or geographic presence. Still, because of readily available technology and difference in paint formulations associated with regional climatic needs, a small number of regional paint manufacturers, such as Jones•Blair Company, have competed successfully against paint manufacturers that distribute their products nationally.

Major producers of paint for the architectural coatings segment include Sherwin-Williams, Benjamin Moore, the Glidden unit of Imperial Chemicals, PPG Industries, Valspar Corporation, Grow Group, and Pratt & Lambert. These producers account for upwards of 60 percent of sales in the architectural coatings segment. They market paint under their own brand names and for retailers under private, controlled, or store brand names. For example, Sherwin-Williams markets the Sherwin-Williams brand and produces paint for Sears.

About 50 percent of architectural coatings are sold under private, controlled, or store brands. Sears, Kmart, Wal-Mart, and Home Depot are major marketers of these brands. In addition, hardware store groups such as True Value and Ace Hardware market their own paint brands.

Specialty paint stores, lumberyards, and independent hardware stores that sell architectural paint and paint sundries have been able to compete in the paint business despite the presence of mass merchandisers (such as Sears) and home improvement centers (such as Lowe's and Home Depot). Industry sources estimate that specialty paint stores account for about 36 percent of paint and sundry sales; hardware and lumberyards account for 14 percent. Furthermore, specialty paint and hardware stores and lumberyards in nonmetropolitan areas have outdistanced mass merchandisers and home improvement centers as sources for paint and paint sundries. This is largely attributable to a lack of home improvement centers and mass-merchandiser distribution in these areas and paint store, hardware, and lumberyard customer relations and service. However, Wal-Mart has been an effective competitor in many nonmetropolitan areas.

Exhibit 1 shows store patronage by do-it-yourself painters and professional painters for 1991 and 1993. As indicated, home centers (including wholesale home

EXHIBIT 1

Store Patronage by Type of Buyer: Do-It-Yourselfer and Professional Painter

Where Do-It-Yourselfers Most Often Buy Paint and Sundries

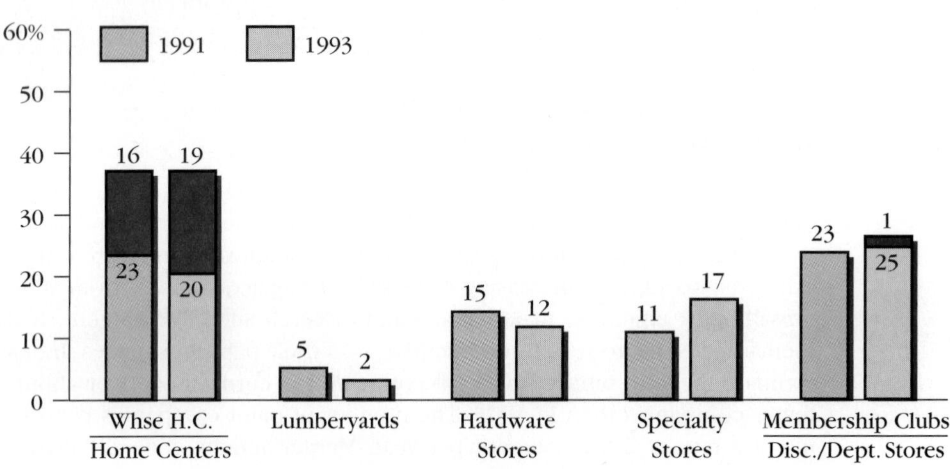

Where Professional Painters Purchased Majority of Paint/Varnish/Stain

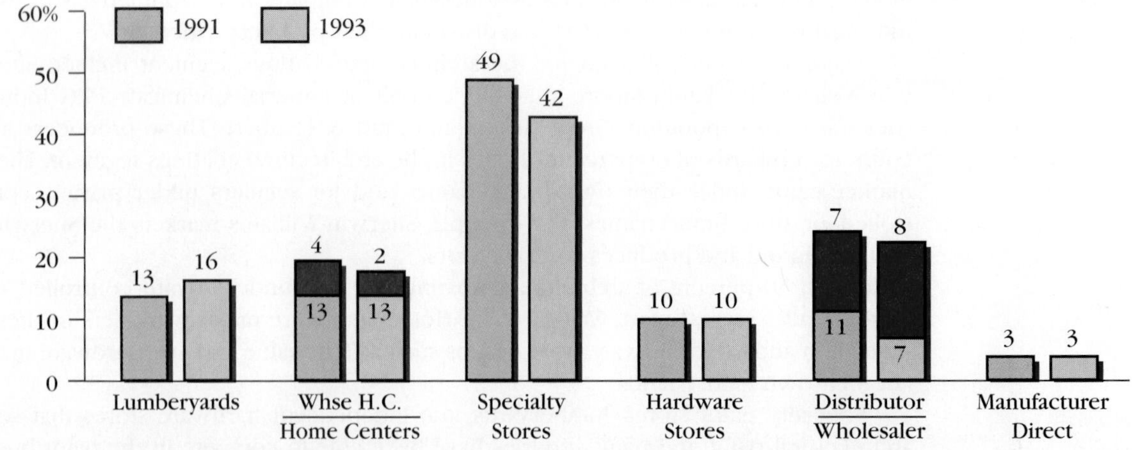

Source: Home Improvement Research Institute. Reprinted from *National Home Center News*, "10 Forces Reshaping the Retail Home Improvement Market," © 1996. Used with permission.

centers) and mass merchandisers (including membership clubs such as Sam's) represent the two most frequently patronized categories of retailers shopped by do-it-yourself painters for paint and sundry items. Specialty paint stores and lumberyards were the most frequently patronized retail stores by professional painters for paint products and sundry items.

Architectural Coatings Purchase Behavior

Approximately 50 percent of architectural coatings dollar sales are accounted for by do-it-yourselfer painters. Professional painter purchases account for 25 percent of dollar sales. The remainder of architectural coatings dollar sales result from government, export, and contractor sales.

Almost 60 percent of annual architectural coatings sales are for interior paints. Exterior paint represents 38 percent of sales. Lacquers and all other applications make up the balance of sales. Slightly less than one in four households purchase interior house paint in any given year. The percentage of households purchasing exterior house paint is considerably less than that for interior paint. The popularity of do-it-yourself painting, particularly for interior applications, has increased the paint and sundry item product line carried by retail outlets. Paint industry consumer research indicates that the average dollar paint purchase per purchase occasion is about $74.00. The average dollar sundry purchase per purchase occasion is about $12.00.

Recent research by the Home Improvement Research Institute indicates that do-it-yourself painters first choose a retail outlet for paint and paint sundries, then choose a paint brand. This research also identified four steps in the do-it-yourself decision process for home improvement products, including paint. The results of this research are summarized in Exhibit 2.

"Paint has become a commodity," commented Barrett. "Do-it-yourself purchasers all too often view paint as paint—a covering—and try to get the best price. But there are a significant number of people who desire service as well in the form of in-

EXHIBIT 2

Consumer Buying Decision Process for Home Improvement Products

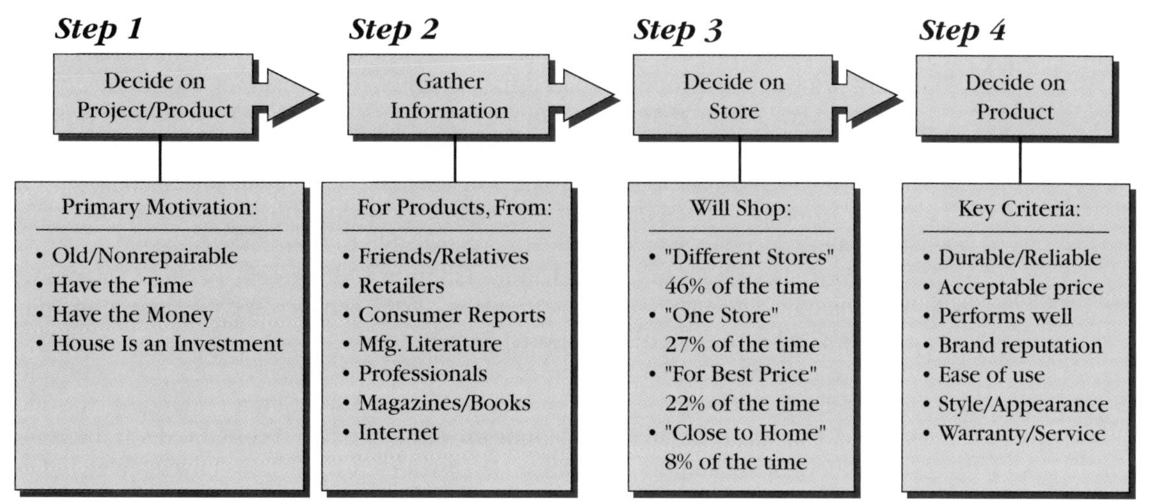

Source: Home Improvement Research Institute. Reprinted from *National Home Center News*, "10 Forces Reshaping the Retail Home Improvement Market," © 1996. Used with permission.

formation about application, color matching, surface preparation, and durability," he added. He conceded that "once paint is on the wall, you can't initially tell the difference between premium-priced and competitively priced paint."

"There is a difference between painting contractors and professional painters, however," he continued. "Pot and brush guys [professional painters] do seek out quality products, since their reputation is on the line and maintenance firms don't want to have to paint an office each time a mark appears on a wall. They want paint that is durable, washable, and will cover in a single coat. They also look to retailers who will go the extra mile to give them service. Many request and get credit from stores. They appreciate being able to get to stores early in the morning to pick up paint and supplies. They deal with stores that can mix large quantities of custom colors and expect to work with knowledgeable store employees who can give them what they want. It is not surprising to me that paint stores remain the preferred outlet for paint and sundries for professional painters. Contractors simply want a coating in many instances and strive for the lowest price, particularly on big jobs."

■ JONES•BLAIR COMPANY SERVICE AREA

Jones•Blair Company markets its paint and sundry items in over 50 counties in Texas, Oklahoma, New Mexico, and Louisiana from its plant and headquarters in Dallas, Texas. The eleven county Dallas–Fort Worth (DFW) metropolitan area is the major business and financial center in the company's southwestern service area.

Competition at the retail level has accelerated in recent years. Sears and Kmart have multiple outlets in DFW, as do Sherwin-Williams and Home Depot. Competition for retail selling space in paint stores, lumberyards, and hardware stores has also increased. "Our research indicates that 1,000 of these outlets now operate in the 50-county service area, and DFW houses 450 of them," noted Barrett. "When you consider that the typical lumberyard or hardware store gets 10 percent of its volume ($65,000) from paint and the typical paint store has annual sales of $400,000 with three brands, you can see that getting and keeping widespread distribution is a key success factor in this industry. Over 1,200 outlets were in operation in the area in 1990; about 600 were situated in the DFW area."

Competition at the paint manufacturing level has increased as well. The major change in competitive behavior has occurred among paint companies that sell to contractors serving the home construction industry. These companies have aggressively priced their products to capture a higher percentage of the home construction market. "Fortunately, these companies have not pursued the 400 or so professional painting firms in DFW and the 200 professional painters outside the DFW area or the do-it-yourselfer market as yet," said Barrett. "They have not been able to gain access to retail outlets, but they may buy their way in through free goods, promotional allowances, or whatever means are available to them in the future."

"We believe that mass merchandisers control 50 percent of the do-it-yourselfer paint market in the DFW metropolitan area. Price seems to be the attraction, but we can't quarrel with their quality," noted Barrett.

The estimated dollar volume of architectural paint and allied products sold in Jones•Blair's 50-county service area in 1996 was $80 million (excluding contractor sales). DFW was estimated to account for 60 percent of this figure, with the remaining volume being sold in other areas. Do-it-yourself household buyers were believed to account for 70 percent of non-contractor-related volume in DFW and 90 percent of non-contractor-related volume in other areas. A five-year summary of architectural paint and allied product sales in the Jones•Blair service area is shown in Exhibit 3.

EXHIBIT 3

Architectural Paint and Sundry Sales Volume, Excluding Contractor Sales (in Millions of Dollars)

Year	*Total Dollar Sales*	*DFW Area Sales*	*Non-DFW Area Sales*
1992	$75.7	$50.9	$24.8
1993	76.4	50.8	25.6
1994	77.6	50.5	27.1
1995	78.4	50.7	27.7
1996	80.0	48.0	32.0

JONES•BLAIR COMPANY

Jones•Blair Company is a privately held corporation that produces and markets architectural paint under the Jones•Blair brand name. In addition to producing a full line of architectural coatings, the company sells paint sundries (brushes, rollers, thinners, etc.) under the Jones•Blair name, even though these items are not manufactured by the company. The company also operates a very large OEM coatings division, which sells its products throughout the U.S. and worldwide.

Company architectural paint and allied products sales volume in 1996 was $12 million, and net profit before taxes was $1,140,000. Dollar sales had increased at an average annual rate of 4 percent per year over the past decade. Paint gallonage, however, had remained stable over the past five years. "We have been very successful in maintaining our margins even with increased research and development, material and labor costs, but I'm afraid we're approaching the threshold on our prices," Barrett said. "We are now the highest-priced paint in our service area." In 1996, paint cost-of-goods sold, including freight expenses, was 60 percent of net sales.

Distribution

The company distributes its products through 200 independent paint stores, lumberyards, and hardware outlets. Forty percent of its outlets are located in the 11-county DFW area. The remaining outlets are situated in the other 39 counties in the service area. Jones•Blair sales are distributed evenly between DFW and non-DFW accounts. Exhibit 4 shows the account and sales volume distribution by size of dollar purchase per year.

EXHIBIT 4

Account and Sales Volume Percentage Distribution by Dollar Purchase per Year

	Retail Accounts			*Dollar Sales Volume*		
Dollar Purchase/Year	*DFW*	*Non-DFW*	*Total*	*DFW*	*Non-DFW*	*Total*
$50,000+	7%	10%	17%	28%	28%	56%
$25,000–$50,000	14	20	34	13	13	26
Less than $25,000	19	30	49	9	9	18
Total	40%	60%	100%	50%	50%	100%

EXHIBIT 5

Jones•Blair Company Print Advertisement

Retail outlets outside the DFW area with paint and sundry purchases exceeding $50,000 annually carry only the Jones•Blair product line. However, except for 14 outlets in DFW (those with purchases greater than $50,000 annually), which carry the Jones•Blair line exclusively, DFW retailers carry two or three lines, with Jones•Blair's line being premium priced. "Our experience to date shows that in our DFW outlets, the effect of multiple lines has been to cause a decline in gallonage volume. The non-DFW outlets, by comparison, have grown in gallonage volume. When you combine the two, you have stable gallonage volume," remarked Barrett.

Promotional Efforts for Architectural Coating Sales

Jones•Blair employs eight sales representatives. They are responsible for monitoring inventories of Jones•Blair paint and sundry items in each retail outlet, as well as for order taking, assisting in store display, and coordinating cooperative advertising programs. A recent survey of Jones•Blair paint dealers indicated that the sales representatives were well liked, helpful, professional, and knowledgeable about paint. Commenting on the survey findings, Barrett said, "Our reps are on a first-name basis with their customers. It is common for our reps to discuss business and family over coffee during a sales call, and some of our people even 'mind the store' when the proprietor has to run an errand or two." Sales representatives are paid a salary and a 1 percent commission on sales.

The company spends approximately 3 percent of net sales on advertising and sales promotion efforts. Approximately 55 percent of advertising and sales promotion dollars are allocated to cooperative advertising programs with retail accounts. The cooperative program, whereby Jones•Blair pays a portion of an account's media costs based on the dollar amount of paint purchased from Jones•Blair, applies to newspaper advertising and seasonal catalogs distributed in a retailer's immediate trade area. Exhibit 5 shows an example of a Jones•Blair Company cooperative print advertisement. The remainder of the advertising and sales promotion budget is spent on in-store displays, corporate brand advertising, outdoor signs, regional magazines, premiums, and advertising production costs. The company also established a corporate Web site (*www.jones-blair.com*) in early 1997. The Web site provides information on Jones•Blair OEM coatings and architectural coatings.

■ PLANNING MEETING

Senior management executives of Jones•Blair Company assembled again to consider the question of where and how to deploy corporate marketing efforts among the various architectural paint coatings markets served by the company. Barrett opened the meeting with a statement that it was absolutely necessary to resolve this question at the meeting in order for the tactical plan to be developed. The peak painting season was soon approaching and decisions had to be made.

Vice President of Advertising: Alex, I still believe that we must direct our efforts toward bolstering our presence in the DFW do-it-yourselfer market. I just received the results of our DFW consumer advertising awareness study. As you can see [Exhibit 6 on page 84], awareness is related to paint purchase behavior. Industry research on paint purchase behavior indicates that a large number of do-it-yourselfers choose a store before selecting a brand. However, a brand name is also important to consumers because they do think about paint they have seen advertised when choosing a brand. This becomes very important in those stores carrying multiple brands. It seems to me that we need an awareness level of at least 30 percent among do-it-yourselfers to materially affect our sales.

Preliminary talks with our ad agency indicate that an increase of $350,000 in corporate brand advertising beyond what we are now spending, with an emphasis on television, will be necessary to achieve this awareness level. Furthermore, this television coverage will reach non-DFW consumers in some 15 counties as well.

Vice President of Operations: I don't agree. Advertising is not the way to go, and reference to the DFW area alone is too narrow a focus. We have to be competitive in the do-it-yourselfer paint market, period. Our shopper research program indi-

EXHIBIT 6

Percentage of DFW Population That Was Aware of Paint Brands and Purchased Paint in the Last 12 Months

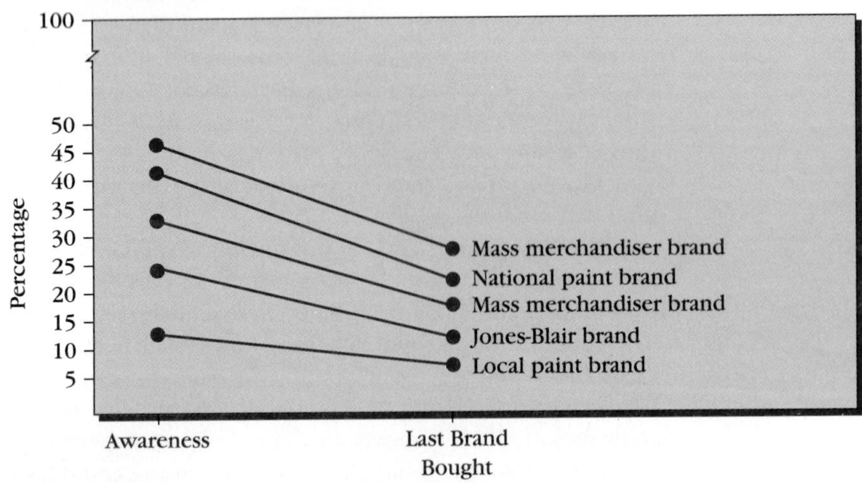

Awareness Question: "What brands come to mind when you think of paint?"

Last Brand Bought: "What paint brand did you purchase the last time you bought paint?"

Note: Sample size was N = 400. Percentages are subject to a 5 percent sampling error.

cated that dealers will quickly back off from our brand when the customer appears price-sensitive. We must cut our price by 20 percent on all paint products to achieve parity with national paint brands. Look here. In today's newspaper, we advertise a price-off special on our exterior paint, and our price is still noticeably higher than a mass merchandiser's everyday price. With both ads on the same page, a customer would have to be an idiot to patronize one of our dealers.

Vice President of Sales: Forget the DFW market. We ought to be putting our effort into non-DFW areas, where half of our sales and most of our dealers exist right now. I hate to admit it, but our sales representatives could be more aggressive. We have only added five new accounts in the last five years; our account penetration in non-DFW areas is only 16 percent. I'm partially at fault, but I'm ready to act. We should add one additional sales representative whose sole responsibility is to develop new retail account leads and presentations or call on professional painters to solicit their business through our dealers. I've figured the direct cost to keep one rep in the field at $60,000 per year, excluding commission.

Vice President of Finance: Everyone is proposing a change in our orientation. Let me be the devil's advocate and favor pursuing our current approach. We now sell to both the home owner and the professional painter in DFW and non-DFW markets through our dealers. We have been and will continue to be profitable by judiciously guarding our margins and controlling costs. Our contribution margin is 35 percent. Everyone suggests that increasing our costs will somehow result in greater sales volume. Let me remind you, Alex, we have said that it is our policy to recoup noncapital expenditures within a one-year time horizon. If we increase our advertising by an incremental amount of $350,000, then we had better see the incremental sales volume as well. The same goes for additional sales representatives and, I might add, any across-the-board cut in prices.

Mr. Barrett: We keep going over the same ground. All of you have valid arguments, but we must prioritize. Let's think about what's best for all of us.

Increased advertising seems reasonable, since national paint firms and mass merchandisers outspend us tenfold in absolute terms. You are right in saying people have to be aware of us before they will buy, or even consider, Jones•Blair. But I am not sure what advertising will do for us given that about 75 percent of the audience is not buying paint. Your reference to DFW as being our major market has been questioned by others. Can't we take that $350,000 of incremental advertising and apply it toward newspapers and catalogs in non-DFW areas?

The price cut is a more drastic action. We might have to do it just to keep our gallonage volume. It would appear from our sales representatives' forecast that gallonage demand for paint in our service area will not increase next year and we can't increase our prices this year. Any increases will have to come out of a competitor's hide. Moreover, since our costs are unlikely to decline, we must recoup gross profit dollars from an increase in volume. Is this possible?

The idea of hiring additional representatives has merit, but what do we do with them? Do they focus on the retail account side or on recruiting the professional painter? Our survey of retail outlets indicated that 70 percent of sales through our DFW dealers went to the professional painter, while 70 percent of our sales through our non-DFW outlets went to do-it-yourselfers. These figures are identical to the 1990 survey of retail outlets. Our contractor sales in DFW and other areas are minimal. We would need a 40 percent price cut to attract contractors, not to mention the increased costs, expertise, and headaches of competitive bidding for large jobs.

Now that I've had my say, let's think about your proposals again. We're not leaving until we agree on a course of action.

CASE

Tyler Pet Foods, Inc.

Executives of Tyler Pet Foods (TPF), Inc. looked forward to their meeting with representatives of Marketing Ventures Unlimited, a marketing and advertising consulting firm. The purpose of the meeting was to review the program for TPF's entry into the household dog food market in the Boston, Massachusetts, metropolitan area. TPF had sought out the consulting firm's services after discussions with food brokers who cited the tremendous potential for TPF in the household dog food market. These brokers had become aware that frozen dog food was being sold in the freezer section of selected supermarkets in a few cities in the southwestern United States. They believed these limited efforts represented a market opportunity for frozen dog food in Boston-area supermarkets.

■ THE COMPANY AND THE PRODUCT

Tyler Pet Foods, Inc. is a major distributor of dog food for show-dog kennels in the United States. TPF has prospered as a supplier of a unique dog food for show dogs called Show Circuit Frozen Dog Dinner. Show Circuit was originally formulated by a mink rancher as a means of improving the coats of his minks. After several years of research, he perfected the formula for a specially prepared food and began feeding his preparation to his stock on a regular basis. After a short period of time, he noticed that their coats showed a marked improvement. Shortly thereafter, a nearby kennel owner noticed the improvement and asked to use some of the food to feed his dogs. The dogs' coats improved dramatically, and a business was born.

Show Circuit contains federally inspected beef by-products, beef, liver, and chicken. Fresh meat constitutes 85 percent of the product's volume, and the highest-quality cereal accounts for the remaining 15 percent. The ingredients are packaged frozen to prevent spoilage of the fresh uncooked meat.

■ PACKAGING AND DISTRIBUTION MODIFICATIONS

TPF executives recognized that modifications in the packaging of Show Circuit would be necessary to make the transition from the kennel market to the household dog food market. After some discussion, it was decided that Show Circuit would be packaged in a 15-ounce plastic tub, with 12 tubs per case. The cost of production, freight, and packaging of the meal was $6.37 per case, which represented total variable costs.

The discussions with food brokers indicated that distribution through supermarkets would be best for Show Circuit because of the need for refrigeration. Food bro-

The cooperation of Tyler Pet Foods, Inc. in the preparation of this case is gratefully acknowledged. This case was prepared by Professor Roger A. Kerin, of the Edwin L. Cox School of Business, Southern Methodist University, as a basis for class discussion and is not designed to illustrate effective or ineffective handling of an administrative situation. Certain names have been disguised.

kers would represent Show Circuit to supermarkets and would receive for their services a 7 percent commission based on the suggested price to retailers, which had yet to be determined. Supermarkets typically receive a gross margin of 25 percent of their selling price for pet foods.

■ THE MEETING

TPF executives listened attentively to the presentation made by representatives from Marketing Ventures Unlimited. Excerpts from their presentation follow.

During the course of the meeting, TPF executives raised a number of questions. The questions were primarily designed to clarify certain aspects of the program. One question that was never asked but that plagued TPF executives was "Will this program establish a place in the market for Show Circuit?" This direct question implied several subissues:

1. Was the market itself adequately defined and segmented?
2. What position would Show Circuit seek in the market? Should the program be targeted toward all dog food buyers or toward specific segments?
3. Could the food brokers get distribution in supermarkets given the sales program?
4. What should be TPF's recommended selling list price to the consumer for Show Circuit?
5. Could TPF at least break even in the introductory year and achieve a 15 percent return on sales in subsequent years?

TPF executives realized that they had to answer these questions and others before they accepted the proposal. The cost of the proposed plan could be $400,000 to $600,000, exclusive of slotting fees, which TPF executives considered reasonable, although it would stretch their promotional budget.

■ PROPOSAL OF MARKETING VENTURES UNLIMITED

The following is an excerpted version of the proposal presented to TPF.

The Situation

Our goal is to introduce and promote effectively the sale of Show Circuit dog food in the Boston market area. Show Circuit is among the costliest dog foods to prepare and will be available through supermarkets.

Show Circuit is a completely balanced frozen dog food. It is of the finest quality and has been used and recommended by professional show-dog owners for years.

Yet, in spite of this history, Show Circuit is essentially a new product and is unknown to the general public. The fact that Show Circuit will be the only dog food located right next to "people food" in the frozen food section of the supermarket is an advantage that must be capitalized upon. Show Circuit's history of blue-ribbon winners is another plus. So, in essence, to market Show Circuit successfully, we must accomplish two objectives:

- Make the public aware of the brand name of Show Circuit, what the packaging looks like, and the fact that Show Circuit is a high-quality dog food.

- Direct dog owners to shop for dog food in the frozen food section of supermarkets.

The Environment

Sales of dog food will total about $5.6 billion this year at manufacturers' prices. Still, fewer than half of the dogs in the United States are regularly fed prepared dog food, which means the dog food industry has yet to tap its full potential.

Four trends indicate that this optimism is well founded. First, the dog food industry has benefited from increasing dog ownership. The U.S. dog population of 53 million, spurred on by the owners' desire for companionship or need for protection, is growing steadily and is expected to continue growing. Second, the trend toward using convenience foods in the household contributes to a lack of table scraps to be served to the dog, a fact that will only improve the prospects for selling prepared dog foods. A third important trend is that pet owners continue to invest their animal companions with human qualities and view them as members of the family. For example, a study conducted by the advertising agency, Bates USA, reported: "A person who owns a dog actually identifies with the pet, assigning human characteristics to the dog such as language, thoughts, feelings, and needs."[1] Not surprisingly, one-half of dog owners consider themselves "Mom and Dad" to their animal companions.[2] Therefore, it comes as no surprise that dog owners spend more than $10 billion annually for veterinarians' fees; medication for dogs; and dog toys, clothing, accessories, and furniture.

A fourth trend is the growth in premium and super-premium dog foods. According to an article in *U.S. News & World Report,* these dog foods have fueled the growth in dog food sales along with the increase in pet ownership.[3]

The choice of supermarket distribution focuses on the dominant retail channel for dog food. Supermarkets dispense 55 percent of all dog food sold in the United States, which represents $3.1 billion in sales at manufacturers' prices. The other 45 percent is sold by pet superstores such as Petco and PETsMART, discount and mass merchandisers, warehouse clubs, Internet companies, veterinarians, and pet stores. These percentages also apply to the Boston market.

Finally, the Boston market is an ideal area for launching a new dog food. We estimate that the greater Boston area has 1.5 percent of the U.S. population (and 1.5 percent of the dog population since dog and human populations are highly correlated). Also, expenditures for pet products in the greater Boston area approximate the national average.[4]

The Competition

There are about 50 dog food manufacturers and 350 dog food brands in the United States. However, five companies—Ralston Purina, Kal-Kan Foods (a subsidiary of Mars, Inc.), H. J. Heinz, Nestlé USA, and Nabisco—capture about 83 percent of supermarket dog food sales. Exhibit 1 shows the supermarket share of the major dog food manufacturers along with their most well-known brand.

In addition to market share, competitor advertising spending and forms of advertising used will be major considerations in planning Show Circuit's introductory marketing strategy. Total spending for advertising in the dog food industry is about 2 percent of sales. Ralston Purina is the leading national advertiser of dog food, spending about $80 million per year, exclusive of major new product launches.[5]

---

[1] *Pet Food Market Gets a Touch of the Good Life* (New York: Bates USA, 1995).

[2] "Looking Out for Fido," *American Demographics* (March 1998): 39.

[3] "Tail of the Pampered Pooch," *U.S. News & World Report* (May 17, 1999): 46–47.

[4] "Pet Places," *American Demographics* (September 1998): 38–39.

[5] "100 Leading National Advertisers," *Advertising Age* (September 28, 1998): S43.

EXHIBIT 1

Top Dog Food Manufacturers in the United States

Rank	*Company*	*Estimated Market Share*[a]	*Principal Brand*
1	Ralston Purina	30.0%	Purina
2	Kal-Kan Foods, Inc. (subsidiary of Mars, Inc.)	19.0	Kal-Kan
3	H. J. Heinz	17.9	Ken-L-Ration
4	Nestlé USA	12.0	Alpo
5	Nabisco	4.3	Milk-Bone
	Other (including private labels)	16.8	
		100.0%	

[a] Estimated market share in supermarkets.
Source: Informations Resources, Inc. Used with permission.

The Problems and Opportunities

Introducing a New Dog Food in a New Form This is an opportunity to educate the consumer. Until Show Circuit's program breaks, dog foods fall into four categories: canned, dry, semimoist, and snack-type (dog biscuits and treats), as shown in Exhibit 2 (page 90).

Canned dog foods average about 75 percent moisture and 25 percent solid materials. They are marketed either as complete foods or as supplementary foods.

Dry dog foods are usually produced as flakes, small pellets, or large chunks containing about 10 percent moisture and 90 percent solids. They are chewy, usually well rounded, and more economical than canned or moist foods.

Semimoist dog foods come in chunk or patty form and are about 25 percent moisture and 75 percent solids. They require no refrigeration and are made to look tempting to humans.

Dog food treats have a wide variety of ingredients and, while tasty, are not recommended as a complete food.

All these product forms are typically marketed in the same area of the store. The consumer must now be taught to shop for dog food in another part of the store—the frozen-food section. Fortunately, some of the pioneering work has been done already. A few Boston-area supermarkets carry a frozen dog treat called Frosty Paws, which sells for $1.89 for 14 fluid ounces. This product is often placed near ice cream.

Overcoming Objections to Frozen Dog Food An objection must be anticipated regarding the requirement for thawing time and freezer space. Therefore, we should state on the container the thawing time, suggestions for quick thawing, how long the food will keep in the refrigerator, plus a gentle reminder to pull that container out of the freezer in the morning. Microwave instructions are a possibility.

Lack of Appeal of Frozen Dog Food We can quickly turn this problem into an asset in our advertising ("the first dog food made to appeal only to dogs").

Pricing We have considerable latitude in pricing as shown in Exhibit 3 on page 90. Furthermore, while dog owners in general are price sensitive, they are also concerned about the health and welfare of their animal companion. Show Circuit's quality suggests a premium price. This view is supported by the food brokers who first recognized the opportunity for Show Circuit. They report that Bil Jac, a frozen dog

EXHIBIT 2

Top Five Brands in the Four Major Dog Food Categories

Category	*Share of Total Dog Food*	*Major Brands*	*Market Share*
Canned	23.7%	Kal-Kan	22.9%
		Skippy	18.5
		Alpo	18.2
		Pedigree	14.8
		Mighty Dog	10.2
Dry	58.6%	Pedigree Mealtime	13.5%
		Purina Dog Chow	12.6
		Purina O•N•E•	10.8
		Private label	9.3
		Kibbles 'n Bits	8.8
Semimoist	2.2%	Moist & Meaty	59.5%
		Private label	15.8
		Butchers Burgers	8.0
		Moist & Beefy	4.6
		Reward Special Cuts	4.3
Biscuits/Treats	15.5%	Milk-Bone	27.8%
		Private label	13.3
		Beggin Strips	9.3
		Pup-peroni	9.1
		Meaty Bone	6.4

Source: Information Resources, Inc. Chicago, IL. Used with permission.

food sold in selected supermarkets in Dallas, Texas, carried a retail price of $2.29 for a two-pound package and $4.19 for a five-pound package.

Summary of Opportunities We see Show Circuit seizing upon three opportunities:

1. The opportunity to be first to tap the vast market potential of a complete frozen dog food in supermarkets

EXHIBIT 3

Representative Dog Food Brand Prices and Package Sizes in Boston-Area Supermarkets by Product Form

Canned Foods		*Dry Foods*	
Mighty Dog	$.55/5.5 oz.	Dog Chow	$8.99/22 lbs.
Cycle	$.63/13.2 oz.	Gravy Train	$9.99/17.6 lbs.
Alpo	$.63/13.2 oz.	Purina O·N·E	$9.39/8 lbs.
Semimoist Foods		***Biscuits/Treats***	
Moist & Meaty	$9.99/13.5 lbs.	Milk Bone	$2.49/24 oz.
Gaines Burgers	$3.49/3.75 lbs.	Jerky Treats	$1.79/3 oz.

2. The opportunity to be among the first to claim to produce an organic dog food (Ralston Purina has introduced Nature's Course, a dry dog food positioned as "organic")
3. The opportunity to lay the groundwork for entering the frozen cat food business

Creative Strategies

Positioning Show Circuit will be positioned as the finest dog food available at any price and the only thing you will want to feed a dog that is truly a member of the family.

Target Market We believe Show Circuit advertising should be targeted at singles and marrieds between the ages of 21 and 50 with a household income greater than $25,000. The reason is that single adults and married couples, with and without children, and roommate households regard their dogs as part of the family. The dog sleeps on the bed and has free run of the house or apartment. Industry research indicates that 79 percent of parents with school-age children buy pet food and supplies, compared with 71 percent of parents with younger or older children, 72 percent of roommate households, and 73 percent of young, childless couples. Income also plays a role in pet spending. Only 48 percent of households with annual incomes of less than $12,000 spend money to keep a pet. However, over 63 percent of households with incomes greater than $25,000 invest in pet food, supplies, and care according to research by the American Veterinary Medical Association. We see little initial opportunity in targeting older households. Only 30 percent of older singles and 41 percent of retired couples spend money on pets.

Concepts Because Show Circuit is such a unique product, there are a variety of concepts that can easily be applied, each with adequate justification:

1. The luxurious fur coat
2. The world's finest dog food
3. The guilt concept (shouldn't your dog eat as well as you do?)
4. Now your dog can eat what show champions have been eating for years.

All these will be touched on as the campaign progresses.

Creative Directions Initially, the campaign will focus attention on product identification and an introductory coupon offer.

Newspapers will supply a smaller, more retentive audience with facts to justify all claims. They will also supply the coupon, proven crucial to a successful introduction in the pet food market. The container and coupon will be prominently displayed, and the copy will emphasize Show Circuit's quality. Special-interest ads will appear in the society, sports, television, and dining-out sections. This unusual media placement is warranted by the product's unique qualities. Also, placement in these sections will pull a relatively low promotional budget out of the mass of food-section advertising.

Radio and television will provide access to a mass audience. Prime objectives are to register the brand name and the package design in the viewer's or listener's memory. Because of the proven qualities of these media, an imaginative and all-important emotional approach will be taken.

Geographical Directions The entire campaign has been designed to accommodate product introduction outside the Boston market area. When the product goes national, the television spot will be ready, the introductory ads will be ready, the radio spots will be ready, and the immediate follow-up will be ready.

Sales Packet

The sales packet given to brokers should include, in the most persuasive form possible, the following categories of information:

1. Profits available in the dog food category
2. Chain store acceptance of dog food
3. Market potential
4. Suggested manufacturer's list price to consumers and quantity discount schedule
5. Information about Show Circuit
6. Information about the container
7. User endorsements
8. Promotional schedule
9. Order information
10. Reprint of ads and TV storyboard
11. Sample shelf strip

The packet should be designed to persuade the supermarket frozen-food buyer to provide freezer space to Show Circuit. Two major problems have to be overcome. Because of the organizational modes of supermarket buying departments, we will not be dealing with the regular pet food buyer. Instead, it will be necessary to persuade the frozen-food buyer to stock Show Circuit. The other major problem involves the usual higher margin for frozen foods. It will be necessary to persuade the buyer that greater product turnover will compensate for a potentially lower margin for Show Circuit.

The task will not be easy. Some 15 percent of new products introduced to supermarkets each year are aimed at the freezer case. Eighty percent of these products fail. It is highly likely Tyler Pet Foods will need to budget about $30,000 for slotting fees paid to supermarkets to buy freezer space.

Creative Strategy by Media

Creative strategies will differ by media. Print media will be utilized to position the product against its competition by comparing it to canned, dry, and semimoist categories. The print campaign will open with an attention-getting ad with a brief product history.

Television will carry the brunt of the attack. The most pressing problem is seen as the difficulty of finding the food in the supermarket, so the TV spot will emphasize location.

In order to give the campaign continuity, each ad will show the container. At the top of each of the ads designed to position the competition, the artwork reproduced on the container will be used.

No single breed of dog will be associated with the product. Both the container and the ads will show a variety of breeds from show dogs to mongrels.

The myth/fact format in newspapers will be utilized to take advantage of the current publicity dealing with the nutritional value of all-meat dog food and the continued trend toward more natural foods (see Exhibit 4).

The copy block dealing with Show Circuit will turn the problem of Show Circuit's being frozen into a product advantage.

Media Plan

Because dog food is heavily advertised, TPF must follow suit to compete.

EXHIBIT 4

Show Circuit Print Advertisement

Myth:

A diet of nothing but dry dog food is healthy for your dog.

Fact:

Dogs are not born vegetarians. Dry dog food contains little, if any, meat. Dry dog food is inexpensive. Dry dog food is good to chew. And just by adding water, dry dog food melts into gravy. Dry dog food must be cooked, which removes nutrition. It must be filled with additives and preservatives to keep it fresh. And because of the low meat content, it must be "fortified" with various supplements.

Show Circuit

It's the perfect marriage of meat and cereal. 85% is federally inspected beef by-products, beef, liver and chicken. The other 15% is the finest cereal made. It promotes and insures digestion of the meat, plus supplies the vitamins and minerals meat cannot. Show Circuit is uncooked, because cooking removes nutrition. And it's frozen for freshness—there's no need for additives or preservatives. Find Show Circuit in the frozen food section—right next to people food.

SHOW CIRCUIT.
Frozen Dog Dinner

Now your dog can eat what show dogs have eaten for years.

General Media Strategy Advertising objectives are as follows:

1. Create awareness of new brand
2. Obtain distribution through grocery outlets
3. Motivate trial through coupon redemption
4. Motivate trial through emotional impact of television

Collateral Advertising Accomplishment of objective 2, getting distribution in grocery stores, is the main purpose of collateral advertising. The sales packet, containing fact sheets, shelf strips, the TV storyboard, and testimonial letters, gives the food broker an impressive story to tell to the supermarket buyer. This is recognized as the critical stage of the campaign, for without sufficient distribution, consumer advertising will be delayed.

Newspaper/Magazine The primary purpose of newspaper advertising is distribution of coupons into the market. This will be accomplished by half-page ads in major Boston newspapers. As a secondary means of distribution, full-page ads will be placed in *Better Homes and Gardens* and *Dog Fancy* magazine for distribution throughout most of the Boston market area (see Exhibit 5 on page 94). We expect that one out of ten sales will involve a coupon redemption.

The second phase of coupon distribution will be effected through 30-inch ads in the same newspapers. A final coupon distribution will be made through a 30-inch ad midway through the campaign. Newspaper insertion will be coordinated with TV flights.

EXHIBIT 5

Show Circuit Print Advertisement

Television The bulk of the budget will be placed in TV production and time. A sizable portion of the time budget will be spent on "The Late Show with David Letterman." Fixed space will be purchased within the first half-hour of the program. The remainder of the budget will reach daytime and nighttime audiences. Each flight will begin on a Monday, and newspaper advertising will be placed on Thursday of the following week.

Two basic approaches can be used for 30-second TV spots. The first approach capitalizes on the love of pet owners for their dogs. A somewhat frowzy, middle-aged, semigreedy woman is shown enjoying a steak dinner—in contrast to an unappetizing cylinder of canned dog food. The spot ends on a close-up of the product. The storyboard for this spot is shown in Exhibit 6.

A second TV spot will emphasize location of the food in the supermarket. A description of the video and audio characteristics of this spot is as follows:

Video	*Audio*
Supermarket—long establishing shot of small boy with bulge under jacket	Announcer: There are many things to remember about new Show Circuit Frozen Dog Dinner.
Close-up of boy, as puppy pops out of top of jacket	Remember, although it's new to you, champion dogs have eaten it for years.
Manager walks by, boy hides dog, looks relieved	Remember, it contains all the vitamins your dog needs.
Close-up of sign indicating pet foods	Remember, Show Circuit is a perfectly balanced diet of meat and cereal. Remember, it doesn't come in a can.

EXHIBIT 6

Show Circuit Television Spot

SHOW CIRCUIT

Dog's Eye View

(A 30 second full color live-action commercial.)

HW: Ralphie, I don't understand you...

I buy you eighteen cent a can food

I come straight home and feed you

So why don't you eat, Ralphie?

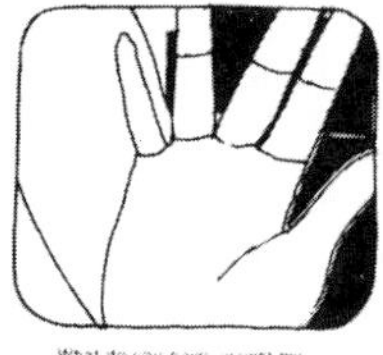

What do you have against my cooking?

Long down-shot of dog food. Cylinder of dog food is covered in runny white gravy.

VO: It's a crying shame what some people feed their dogs.

VO: Now your dog can eat what show dogs have eaten for years.
Show Circuit, a nutritious dog dinner so different it's found in the frozen food section... next to people food.

HW: Ralphie, think of all the hungry dogs in the world who would love to have your food.

Dolly shot of boy looking at competitive brands	
Close-up of boy and dog (sync)	Boy: I don't see it anywhere, Sparky.
Boy walks out of store past frozen-food compartment People turn to stare Tilt down and zoom in on product	Announcer: But most important, remember you find Show Circuit in the frozen (bark) food section, where you shop for other members of your family.

Program Budget The budget for the program described can be either $400,000 or $600,000 (Exhibit 7 on page 96). We see this expense and the $30,000 slotting fee as being the only incremental cost associated with the launch in the Boston market.

We believe that this expenditure is reasonable, since most major established brands are spending $7 million to $8 million annually for ongoing nationwide media promotion. For a new product, a higher initial expense is necessary. For instance, Heinz Pet Products spent $30 million to introduce Reward, a premium canned dog food. Ralston Purina spent $25 million to $30 million to introduce Nature's Course, a premium dry dog food. A line extension, Alpo Lite, with 25 fewer calories than regular Alpo, was launched with a $10 million advertising effort.

EXHIBIT 7

Alternative Advertising and Trade Promotion Expenditure Levels for Show Circuit Frozen Dog Dinner

	Budget Levels	
Item	*$400,000*	*$600,000*
Television[a]	$259,000	$429,000
Newspapers/Magazines[b]	100,500	130,500
Collateral (sales pack)	9,750	9,750
Miscellaneous	5,250	5,250
Agency fees	25,500	25,500
Total	$400,000	$600,000

[a] The difference in television cost is due to the production of a second commercial and larger television schedule.

[b] The difference in newspaper/magazine cost is due to a larger number of insertions in *Better Homes and Gardens* and *Dog Fancy* magazines.

CASE

Curtis Automotive Hoist

Market Opportunities in the European Union

In September 1998, Mark Curtis, President of Curtis Automotive Hoist (CAH), had just finished reading a feasibility report on entering the European market in 1999. CAH manufactured surface automotive hoists, a product used by garages, service stations, and other repair shops to lift cars for servicing (Exhibit 1 on page 98). The report, prepared by the company's marketing manager, Pierre Gagnon, outlined the opportunities in the European Union and the entry options available.

Mr. Curtis was not sure if his company was ready for this move. While the company had been successful in expanding sales into the U.S. market, Mr. Curtis wondered if this success could be repeated in Europe. He thought that, with more effort, sales could be increased in the United States. On the other hand, there were some positive aspects to the European idea. He began reviewing the information in preparation for the meeting the following day with Mr. Gagnon.

■ CURTIS AUTOMOTIVE HOIST

Mr. Curtis, a design engineer, had worked for eight years for the Canadian subsidiary of a U.S. automotive hoist manufacturer. During those years, he had spent considerable time designing an above-ground (or surface) automotive hoist. Although Mr. Curtis was very enthusiastic about the unique aspects of the hoist, including a scissor lift and wheel alignment pads, senior management expressed no interest in the idea. In 1988, Mr. Curtis left the company to start his own business with the express purpose of designing and manufacturing the hoist. He left with the good wishes of his previous employer, who had no objections to his plans to start a new business.

Over the next three years, Mr. Curtis obtained financing from a venture capital firm, opened a plant in Lachine, Quebec, and began manufacturing and marketing the hoist, called the Curtis Lift (Exhibit 1).

From the beginning, Mr. Curtis had taken considerable pride in the development and marketing of the Curtis Lift. The original design included a scissor lift and a safety locking mechanism that allowed the hoist to be raised to any level and locked in place. The scissor lift offered easy access for the mechanic to work on the raised vehicle as well. Because the hoist was fully hydraulic and had no chains or pulleys, it required little maintenance. Another key feature was the alignment turn plates that were an integral part of the lift. The turn plates meant that mechanics could accurately and easily perform wheel alignment jobs. Because it was a surface lift, it could be installed in a garage in less than a day.

This case was prepared by Professor Gordon H. G. McDougall, Wilfrid Laurier University, as the basis for class discussion rather than to illustrate either effective or ineffective handling of an administrative situation. Certain names and data have been disguised and are not useful for research purposes. Used by permission.

EXHIBIT 1

Examples of Automotive Hoists

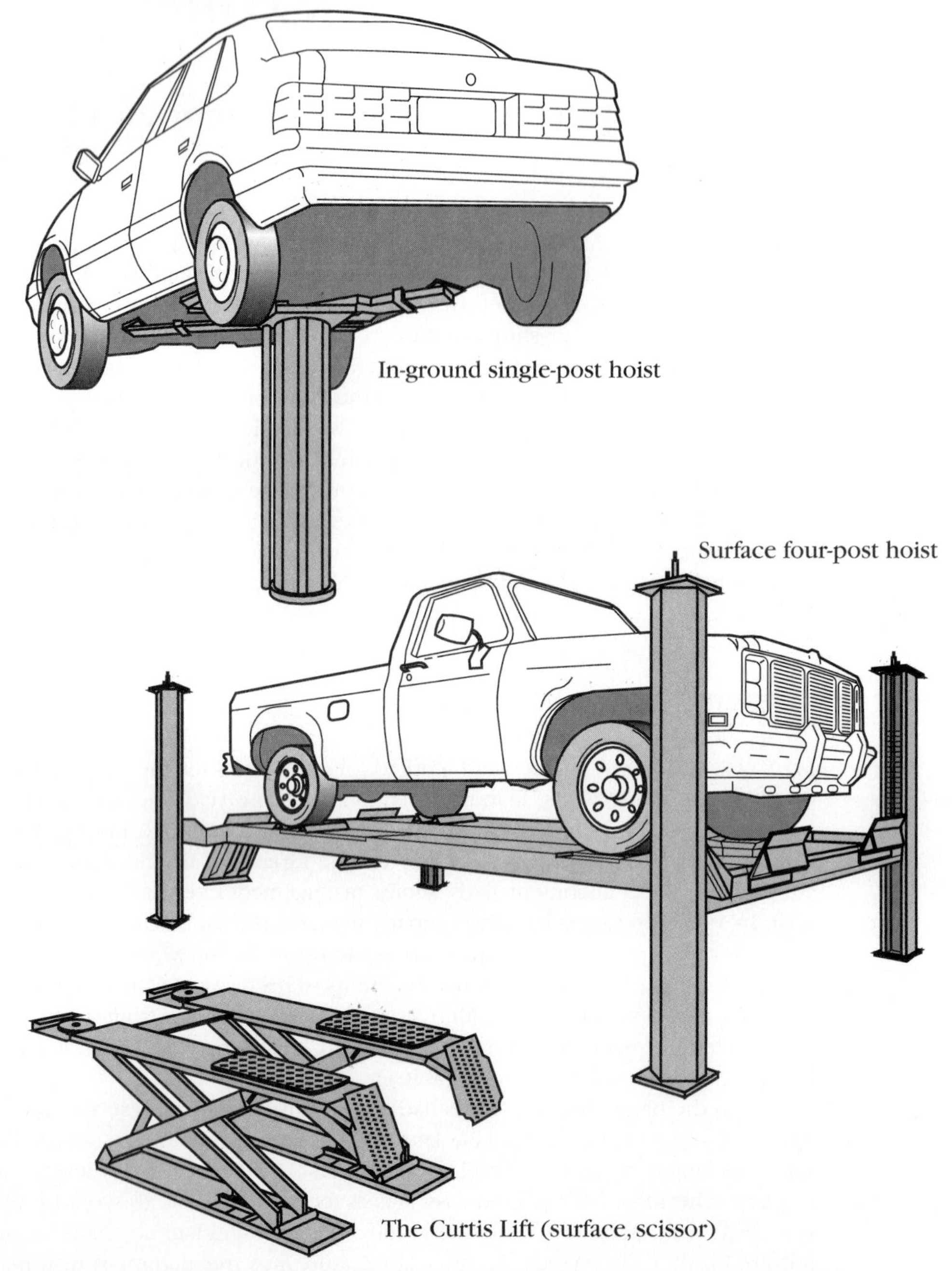

Mr. Curtis continually made improvements to the product, including adding more safety features. In fact, the Curtis Lift was considered a leader in automotive lift safety. Safety was an important factor in the automotive hoist market. Although hoists seldom malfunctioned, when they did, it often resulted in a serious accident.

The Curtis Lift developed a reputation in the industry as the "Cadillac" of hoists; the unit was judged by many as superior to competitive offerings because of its de-

EXHIBIT 2

Curtis Automotive Hoist Selected Financial Statistics (1995–1997)

	1995	*1996*	*1997*
Sales	$6,218,000	$7,454,000	$9,708,000
Cost of sales	4,540,000	5,541,000	6,990,000
Contribution	1,678,000	1,913,000	2,718,000
Marketing expenses[a]	507,000	510,000	530,000
Administrative expenses	810,000	820,000	840,000
Earnings before tax	361,000	583,000	1,348,000
Units sold	723	847	1,054

[a] Marketing expenses in 1997 included advertising ($70,000), four salespeople ($240,000), marketing manager and three sales support staff ($220,000).

Source: Company records.

sign, the quality of the workmanship, the safety features, the ease of installation, and the five-year warranty. Mr. Curtis held four patents on the Curtis Lift including the lifting mechanism on the scissor design and a safety locking mechanism. A number of versions of the product were designed that made the Curtis Lift suitable (depending on the model) for a variety of tasks, including rustproofing, muffler repairs, and general mechanical repairs.

In 1990, CAH sold 23 hoists and had sales of $172,500. During the early years the majority of sales were to independent service stations and garages specializing in wheel alignment in the Quebec and Ontario markets. Most of the units were sold by Mr. Gagnon, who was hired in 1990 to handle the marketing side of the operation. In 1992, Mr. Gagnon began using distributors to sell the hoist to a wider geographic market in Canada. In 1994, he signed an agreement with a large automotive wholesaler to represent CAH in the U.S. market. By 1997, the company sold 1,054 hoists and had sales of $9,708,000 (Exhibit 2). In 1997, about 60% of unit sales were to the U.S. with the remaining 40% to the Canadian market.

■ THE INDUSTRY

Approximately 49,000 hoists were sold each year in North America. Hoists were typically purchased by any automotive outlet that serviced or repaired cars including new car dealers, used car dealers, specialty shops (for example, muffler shops, transmission, wheel alignment), chains (for example, Firestone, Goodyear, Canadian Tire), and independent garages. It was estimated that new car dealers purchased 30% of all units sold in a given year. In general, the specialty shops focused on one type of repair, such as mufflers or rust proofing, while "nonspecialty" outlets handled a variety of repairs. While there was some crossover, in general CAH competed in the specialty shop segment and, in particular, those shops that dealt with wheel alignment. This included chains such as Firestone and Canadian Tire as well as new car dealers (for example, Ford) who devote a certain percentage of their lifts to the wheel alignment business and independent garages who specialized in wheel alignment.

The purpose of a hoist was to lift an automobile into a position where a mechanic or service person could easily work on the car. Because different repairs required different positions, a wide variety of hoists had been developed to meet specific needs. For example, a muffler repair shop required a hoist where the mechanic could gain easy access to the underside of the car. Similarly, a wheel alignment job required a hoist that offered a level platform where the wheels could be adjusted as well as providing easy access for the mechanic. Mr. Gagnon estimated that 85% of CAH sales were to the wheel alignment market to service centers like Firestone, Goodyear, and Canadian Tire and independent garages that specialized in wheel alignment. About 15 percent of sales were made to customers who used the hoist for general mechanical repairs.

Firms purchasing hoists were part of an industry called the automobile aftermarket. This industry was involved in supplying parts and service for new and used cars and was worth over $54 billion at retail in 1997 while servicing the approximately 14 million cars on the road in Canada. The industry was large and diverse; there were over 4,000 new car dealers in Canada, over 400 Canadian Tire stores, over 100 stores in each of the Firestone and Goodyear chains, and over 220 stores in the Rust Check chain.

The purchase of an automotive hoist was often an important decision for the service station owner or dealer. Because the price of hoists ranged from $3,000 to $15,000, it was a capital expense for most businesses.

For the owner/operator of a new service center or car dealership the decision involved determining what type of hoist was required, then what brand would best suit the company. Most new service centers or car dealerships had multiple bays for servicing cars. In these cases, the decision would involve what types of hoists were required (for example, in-ground, surface). Often, more than one type of hoist was purchased, depending on the service center/dealership needs.

Experienced garage owners seeking a replacement hoist (the typical hoist had a useful life of 10 to 13 years) would usually determine what products were available and then make a decision. If the garage owners were also mechanics, they would probably be aware of two or three types of hoists but not very knowledgeable about the brands or products currently available. Garage owners or dealers who were not mechanics probably knew very little about hoists. The owners of car or service dealerships often bought the product that was recommended and/or approved by the parent company.

Competition

Sixteen companies competed with CAH in the automotive lift market in North America: 4 Canadian and 12 U.S. firms. Hoists were subject to small import duties. In 1998, duties on hoists entering the U.S. market from Canada were 1.2% of the selling price; from the United States entering Canada the import duty was 3.4%. With the advent of the 1988 U.S.-Canada Free Trade Agreement, the duties between the two countries were soon to be phased out. For Mr. Curtis, the import duties had never played a part in any decisions—the fluctuating exchange rates between the two countries had a far greater impact on selling prices.

A wide variety of hoists were manufactured in the industry. The two basic types of hoists were in-ground and surface. As the names imply, in-ground hoists required a pit to be dug "in-ground" where the piston that raised the hoist was installed. In-ground hoists were either single post or multiple post, were permanent, and obviously could not be moved. In-ground lifts constituted approximately 21% of total lift sales in 1997 (Exhibit 3). Surface lifts were installed on a flat surface, usually concrete. Surface lifts came in two basic types, post lift hoists and scissor hoists. Surface lifts, compared to in-ground lifts, were easier to install and could be moved, if necessary. Surface lifts constituted 79% of total lift sales in 1997. Within each type of hoist (for example, post lift surface hoists), there were numerous variations in terms of size, shape, and lifting capacity.

EXHIBIT 3

North American Automotive Lift Unit Sales, by Type (1995–1997)

	1995	*1996*	*1997*
In-ground			
Single post	5,885	5,772	5,518
Multiple post	4,812	6,625	5,075
Surface			
Two post	27,019	28,757	28,923
Four post	3,862	3,162	3,745
Scissor	2,170	2,258	2,316
Other	4,486	3,613	3,695
Total	48,234	50,187	49,272

Source: Company records.

The industry was dominated by two large U.S. firms, AHV Lifts and Berne Manufacturing, who together held approximately 60% of the market. AHV Lifts, the largest firm with approximately 40% of the market and annual sales of about $60 million, offered a complete line of hoists (that is, in-ground, surface) but focused primarily on the in-ground market and the two-post surface market. AHV Lifts was the only company that had its own direct sales force; all other companies used (1) only wholesalers or (2) a combination of wholesalers and company sales force. AHV Lifts offered standard hoists with few extra features and competed primarily on price. Berne Manufacturing, with a market share of approximately 20%, also competed in the in-ground and two-post surface markets. It used a combination of wholesalers and company salespeople and, like AVH Lifts, competed primarily on price.

Most of the remaining firms in the industry were companies that operated in a regional market (for example, California, British Columbia) and/or who offered a limited product line (for example, four-post surface hoist).

CAH had two competitors that manufactured scissor lifts. AVH Lifts marketed a scissor hoist that had a different lifting mechanism and did not include the safety locking features of the Curtis Lift. On average, the AVH scissor lift was sold for about 20% less than the Curtis Lift. The second competitor, Mete Lift, was a small regional company with sales in California and Oregon. It had a design that was very similar to the Curtis Lift but lacked some of its safety features. The Mete Lift, regarded as a well-manufactured product, sold for about 5% less than the Curtis Lift.

■ MARKETING STRATEGY FOR CURTIS AUTOMOTIVE HOIST

As of early 1998, CAH had developed a reputation for a quality product backed by good service in the hoist lift market, primarily in the wheel alignment segment.

The distribution system employed by CAH reflected the need to engage in extensive personal selling. Three types of distributors were used: a company sales force, Canadian distributors, and a U.S. automotive wholesaler. The company sales force consisted of four salespeople and Mr. Gagnon. Their main task was to service large "direct" accounts. The initial step was to get the Curtis Lift approved by large chains and manufacturers and then, having received the approval, to sell to individual dealers or operators. For example, if General Motors approved the hoist, then

CAH could sell it to individual General Motors dealers. CAH sold directly to the individual dealers of a number of large accounts including General Motors, Ford, Chrysler, Petro-Canada, Firestone, and Goodyear. CAH had been successful in obtaining manufacturer approval from the big three automobile manufacturers in both Canada and the United States. CAH had also received approval from service companies such as Canadian Tire and Goodyear. To date, CAH had not been rejected by any major account but, in some cases, the approval process had taken over four years.

In total, the company sales force generated about 25 percent of the unit sales each year. Sales to the large "direct" accounts in the United States went through CAH's U.S. wholesaler.

The Canadian distributors sold, installed, and serviced units across Canada. These distributors handled the Curtis Lift and carried a line of noncompetitive automotive equipment products (for example, engine diagnostic equipment, wheel balancing equipment) and noncompetitive lifts. These distributors focused on the smaller chains and the independent service stations and garages.

The U.S. wholesaler sold a complete product line to service stations as well as manufacturing some equipment. The Curtis Lift was one of five different types of lifts that the wholesaler sold. Although the wholesaler provided CAH with extensive distribution in the United States, the Curtis Lift was a minor product within the wholesaler's total line. While Mr. Gagnon did not have any actual figures, he thought that the Curtis Lift probably accounted for less than 20 percent of the total lift sales of the U.S. wholesaler.

Both Mr. Curtis and Mr. Gagnon felt that the U.S. market had unrealized potential. With a population of 264 million people and over 146 million registered vehicles, the U.S. market was almost 10 times the size of the Canadian market (population of 30 million, approximately 14 million vehicles). Mr. Gagnon noted that the six New England states (population over 13 million), the three largest mid-Atlantic states (population over 38 million), and the three largest mideastern states (population over 32 million) were all within a day's drive of the factory in Lachine. Mr. Curtis and Mr. Gagnon had considered setting up a sales office in New York to service these states, but they were concerned that the U.S. wholesaler would not be willing to relinquish any of its territory. They had also considered working more closely with the wholesaler to encourage it to "push" the Curtis Lift. It appeared that the wholesaler's major objective was to sell a hoist, not necessarily the Curtis Lift.

CAH distributed a catalog-type package with products, uses, prices, and other required information for both distributors and users. In addition, CAH advertised in trade publications (for example, *Service Station & Garage Management*), and Mr. Gagnon traveled to trade shows in Canada and the United States to promote the Curtis Lift.

In 1997, Curtis Lifts sold for an average retail price of $10,990 and CAH received, on average, $9,210 for each unit sold. This average reflected the mix of sales through the three distribution channels: (1) direct (where CAH received 100 percent of the selling price), (2) Canadian distributors (where CAH received 80 percent of the selling price), and (3) the U.S. wholesaler (where CAH received 78 percent of the selling price).

Both Mr. Curtis and Mr. Gagnon felt that the company's success to date was based on a strategy of offering a superior product that was primarily targeted to the needs of specific customers. The strategy stressed continual product improvements, quality workmanship, and service. Personal selling was a key aspect of the strategy; salespeople could show customers the benefits of the Curtis Lift over competing products.

THE EUROPEAN UNION MARKET

Against this background, Mr. Curtis had been thinking of ways to continue the rapid growth of the company. One possibility that kept coming up was the promise and potential of markets in the European Union. The fact that Europe became a single market in 1993 suggested that it was an opportunity that should at least be explored. With this in mind, Mr. Curtis asked Mr. Gagnon to prepare a report on the possibility of CAH entering the European Union. The highlights of Mr. Gagnon's report follow.

History of the European Union

The European Union (EU) had its basis formed from the 1957 "Treaty of Rome" in which five countries decided it would be in their best interest to form an internal market. These countries were France, Spain, Italy, West Germany, and Luxembourg. By late 1998, the EU consisted of 15 countries (the additional 10 were Austria, Belgium, Denmark, Finland, Greece, Ireland, the Netherlands, Portugal, Sweden, and the United Kingdom) with a population of over 370 million people. Virtually all barriers (physical, technical, and fiscal) in the EU were scheduled to be removed for companies located within the EU. This allowed the free movement of goods, persons, services, and capital.

In the last 10 years, many North American and Japanese firms had established themselves in the EU. The reasoning for this was twofold. First, these companies regarded the community as an opportunity to increase global market share and profits. The market was attractive because of its sheer size and lack of internal barriers. Second, there was continuing concern that companies not established within the EU would have difficulty exporting to the EU due to changing standards and tariffs. To date, this concern had not materialized.

Market Potential

The key indicator of the potential market for the Curtis Lift hoist was the number of passenger cars and commercial vehicles in use in a particular country. Four European Union countries had more than 20 million vehicles in use with Germany having the largest domestic fleet of 41 million vehicles followed in order by Italy, France, and the United Kingdom (Exhibit 4). The number of vehicles was an important indicator since the more vehicles in use meant a greater number of service and repair facilities that needed vehicle hoists and potentially the Curtis Lift.

EXHIBIT 4

Number of Vehicles and Population in Five European Union Countries

Country	*Vehicles in Use (Thousands) in 1996*		*1997 New Vehicle Registrations (Thousands)*	*1997 Population (Thousands)*
	Passenger	*Commercial*		
Germany	38,325	2,842	3,209	81,500
France	24,385	4,890	1,973	58,000
Italy	29,600	2,746	1,610	57,200
United Kingdom	20,344	3,991	1,911	58,300
Spain	13,440	2,783	910	39,200

An indicator of the future vehicle repair and service market was the number of new vehicle registrations. The registration of new vehicles was important as this maintained the number of vehicles in use by replacing cars that had been retired. Again, Germany had the most new cars registered in 1997 and was followed in order by France, the United Kingdom, and Italy.

Based primarily on the fact that a large domestic market was important for initial growth, the selection of a European country should be limited to the "Big Four" industrialized nations: Germany, France, the United Kingdom, or Italy. In an international survey, companies from North America and Europe ranked European countries on a scale of 1 to 100 on market potential and investment site potential. The results showed that Germany was favored for both market potential and investment site opportunities, while France, the United Kingdom, and Spain placed second, third, and fourth, respectively. Italy did not place in the top four in either market or investment site potential. However, Italy had a large number of vehicles in use, had the fourth largest population in Europe, and was an acknowledged leader in car technology and production.

Little information was available on the competition within Europe. There was, as yet, no dominant manufacturer, as was the case in North America. At this time, there was one firm in Germany that manufactured a scissor-type lift. The firm sold most of its units within the German market. The only other available information was that 22 firms in Italy manufactured vehicle lifts.

■ INVESTMENT OPTIONS

Mr. Gagnon felt that CAH had three options for expansion into the European market: licensing, joint venture, or direct investment. The licensing option was a real possibility as a French firm had expressed an interest in manufacturing the Curtis Lift.

In June 1998, Mr. Gagnon had attended a trade show in Detroit to promote the Curtis Lift. At the show, he met Phillipe Beaupre, the marketing manager for Bar Maisse, a French manufacturer of wheel alignment equipment. The firm, located in Chelles, France, sold a range of wheel alignment equipment throughout Europe. The best-selling product was an electronic modular aligner that enabled a mechanic to utilize a sophisticated computer system to align the wheels of a car. Mr. Beaupre was seeking a North American distributor for the modular aligner and other products manufactured by Bar Maisse.

At the show, Mr. Gagnon and Mr. Beaupre had a casual conversation wherein both explained what their respective companies manufactured. They exchanged company brochures and business cards, and both went on to other exhibits. The next day, Mr. Beaupre sought out Mr. Gagnon and asked if he might be interested in having Bar Maisse manufacture and market the Curtis Lift in Europe. Mr. Beaupre believed the lift would complement Bar Maisse's product line and the licensing would be of mutual benefit to both parties. They agreed to pursue the idea. Upon his return, Mr. Gagnon told Mr. Curtis about these discussions and they agreed to explore this possibility.

Mr. Gagnon called a number of colleagues in the industry and asked them what they knew about Bar Maisse. About half had not heard of the company, but those who had commented favorably on the quality of its products. One colleague, with European experience, knew the company well and said that Bar Maisse's management had integrity and would make a good partner. In July 1998, Mr. Gagnon sent a fax to Mr. Beaupre stating that CAH was interested in further discussions and attaching various company brochures including price lists and technical information on the Curtis Lift. In late August 1998, Mr. Beaupre responded stating that Bar Maisse would like to enter a three-year licensing agreement with CAH to manufacture the Curtis Lift in Europe. In exchange for the manufacturing rights, Bar Maisse was prepared to pay a royalty rate of 5% of gross sales. Mr. Gagnon had not yet responded to this proposal.

A second possibility was a joint venture. Mr. Gagnon had wondered if it might not be better for CAH to offer a counterproposal to Bar Maisse for a joint venture. He had not worked out any details, but Mr. Gagnon felt that CAH would learn more about the European market and probably make more money if they were an active partner in Europe. Mr. Gagnon's idea was a 50–50 proposal where the two parties shared the investment and the profits. He envisaged a situation in which Bar Maisse would manufacture the Curtis Lift in its plant with technical assistance from CAH. Mr. Gagnon also thought that CAH could get involved in the marketing of the lift through the Bar Maisse distribution system. Further, he thought that the Curtis Lift, with proper marketing, could gain a reasonable share of the European market. If that happened Mr. Gagnon felt that CAH was likely to make greater returns with a joint venture.

The third option was direct investment where CAH would establish a manufacturing facility and set up a management group to market the lift. Mr. Gagnon had contacted a business acquaintance who had recently been involved in manufacturing fabricated steel sheds in Germany. On the basis of discussions with his acquaintance, Mr. Gagnon estimated the costs involved in setting up a plant in Europe at: (1) $250,000 for capital equipment (welding machines, cranes, other equipment), (2) $200,000 in incremental costs to set the plant up, and (3) carrying costs to cover $1,000,000 in inventory and accounts receivable. While the actual costs of renting a building for the factory would depend on the site location, he estimated that annual building rent including heat, light, and insurance would be about $80,000. Mr. Gagnon recognized these estimates were guidelines but he felt that the estimates were probably within 20% of actual costs.

THE DECISION

As Mr. Curtis considered the contents of the report, a number of thoughts crossed his mind. He began making notes concerning the European opportunity and the future of the company:

- If CAH decided to enter Europe, Mr. Gagnon would be the obvious choice to head up the "direct investment" option or the "joint venture" option. Mr. Curtis felt that Mr. Gagnon had been instrumental in the success of the company to date.
- While CAH had the financial resources to go ahead with the direct investment option, the joint venture would spread the risk (and the returns) over the two companies.
- CAH had built its reputation on designing and manufacturing a quality product. Regardless of the option, Mr. Curtis wanted the firm's reputation to be maintained.
- Either the licensing agreement or the joint venture appeared to build on the two companies' strengths; Bar Maisse had knowledge of the market and CAH had the product. What troubled Mr. Curtis was whether this apparent synergy would work or would Bar Maisse seek to control the operation.

- It was difficult to estimate sales under any of the options. With the first two (licensing and joint venture), it would depend on the effort and expertise of Bar Maisse; with the third, it would depend on Mr. Gagnon.
- CAH sales in the U.S. market could be increased if the U.S. wholesaler would "push" the Curtis Lift. Alternatively, the establishment of a sales office in New York to cover the eastern states could also increase sales.

As Mr. Curtis reflected on the situation he knew he should probably get additional information—but it wasn't obvious exactly what information would help him make a yes or no decision. He knew one thing for sure—he was going to keep this company on a "fast growth" track, and at tomorrow's meeting he and Mr. Gagnon would decide how to do it.

CASE

Frito-Lay's® Dips

In late 1986, Ben Ball, Marketing Director, and Ann Mirabito, Product Manager, had just completed the planning review for the line of dips sold by Frito-Lay, Inc. Frito-Lay's® Dips were a highly profitable product line and had shown phenomenal sales growth in the past five years. Sales in 1985 were $87 million, compared with $30 million in 1981.

A major issue raised at the planning meeting was where and how Frito-Lay's® Dips could be developed further. Two different viewpoints were expressed. One view was that the dip line should be more aggressively promoted in its present market segment. This segment was broadly defined as the "chip dip" category. The other view was that Frito-Lay should also actively pursue the "vegetable dip" category. The company had recently introduced a shelf-stable, sour cream–based French onion dip nationally, and 1986 sales were forecasted to be $10 million. The new dip was the first sour cream–based dip introduced by Frito-Lay. Some executives felt that this dip could provide a bridge to the vegetable dip category, which could be further developed.

Frito-Lay executives had yet to decide how much emphasis to place on each category in 1987. Furthermore, expense budgets would need special consideration. More aggressive marketing would require higher marketing investment or at least a reallocation of funds, while at the same time the gross margin and profit contribution of dips would have to be preserved.

DIP CATEGORY

Dips are typically used as an appetizer, snack, or accompaniment to a meal. Dip popularity has risen in recent years as a result of the convenience of use, multiple uses, and "grazing" trends in the United States. Dips can be served along with chips, crackers, or raw vegetables.

The market for dips is highly fragmented and difficult to measure; however, upward of 80 percent of dip sales are accounted for by supermarkets. According to industry estimates, total dip retail dollar sales volume through supermarkets was $620 million in 1985. Two-thirds of this dollar volume was captured by prepared dips; the remaining one-third was accounted for by dip mixes for at-home preparation. About 55 percent of the prepared dips sold in supermarkets required refrigeration. The major competitors in this segment were Kraft, Borden, a large number of regional dairies, and numerous store brands. Refrigerated dip retail prices were typically in the range of $0.07 to $0.15 per ounce. About 45 percent of prepared dips were "shelf stable" (that is, they were packaged in metal cans and required no refrigera-

This case was prepared by Jeanne Bertels, graduate student, under the supervision of Professor Roger A. Kerin, of the Edwin L. Cox School of Business, Southern Methodist University, as a basis for class discussion and is not designed to illustrate effective or ineffective handling of an administrative situation. The cooperation of Frito-Lay, Inc. is gratefully acknowledged. Selected financial and market data have been disguised or approximated and are not useful for research purposes.

tion). These dips could be displayed virtually anywhere in a supermarket, though they were typically located near snack foods. Frito-Lay was the major competitor in shelf-stable dips, followed by regional chip manufacturers. Shelf-stable dip retail prices were in the range from $0.13 to $0.20 per ounce. By comparison, prices of dip mix were typically $0.09 per ounce (including the cost of a sour cream mixer or base).

Exhibit 1 shows a breakdown of the $620 million sales of dips in supermarkets by product type. Industry research indicates that dip dollar sales are growing at 10 percent per year, but this growth has come about because of price (inflationary) increases. No real growth is evident. Virtually all of the growth in 1984 and 1985 was accounted for by cheese-based dips, which captured market share from other dip flavors.

Flavor Popularity and Usage

Sour cream-based dips are the most popular flavor. Sour cream-based prepared dips and dip mixes account for about 50 percent of total dip sales. Cheese-based dips are the second most popular segment and account for about 25 percent of total dip sales. Bean and picante dips account for about 10 percent of total dip sales, and cream cheese-based dips account for the remaining 15 percent.

Dips are most frequently used with salty snacks, such as potato chips and corn chips. Whereas about 67 percent of total dip sales are linked to salty snack usage, virtually all bean and picante dips are consumed with salty snacks. One-fourth of cream cheese-based dip volume and 85 percent of cheese-based volume are linked with chip usage. Shelf-stable dips and many dip mixes are located adjacent to salty snack foods in supermarkets. Dry soup mixes are typically shelved with canned soups. Approximately 33 percent of all dip sales ($207 million) are linked to vegetable usage, and most of this volume is sold through supermarkets. Vegetable dips are located throughout supermarkets, in produce, soup mix, salad dressing, and snack sections, because they are viewed as a complementary as opposed to a primary product. Two brands—Libby's Dip Mixes and Bennett's Toppings/Dips—are located in the produce section, but each is sold only on a regional basis. Numerous local brands are also shelved in the produce section.

The popularity of Mexican food, including nachos, has fueled the growth of cheese-based dips in particular. New product introductions and accompanying market expenditures have also stimulated trial and acceptance of Mexican-style dips. For instance, Kraft, a major competitor in cheese dips, added Mexican flavors to both new and existing product lines in 1984. New products included Kraft Nacho Cheese Dip and Kraft Premium Jalapeno Cheese Dip. Kraft also added a Mexican zest to two of its popular products: Velveeta Mexican process cheese spread features jalapeno peppers, and Kraft Cheese Whiz is offered in variations of hot salsa and mild salsa. Kraft competes primarily in the refrigerated segment of the dip market. In late 1985, however, Kraft entered the shelf-stable market with Kraft Nacho Dip and Kraft Hot Nacho Dip.

Dip Substitutes

Even though the market for dips is large, it is estimated that about 20 percent of all dip volume consumed by households in the United States is homemade. In addition, many consumers use refrigerated salad dressings for dips, especially for vegetables. It is estimated that 35 percent of refrigerated salad dressing volume is used for dips. These refrigerated salad dressings are typically located in the produce section of supermarkets and include such brands as Marie's, Bob's Big Boy, Marzetti's, and Walden Farms, as well as a few local brands in different areas of the country. Market research indicates that refrigerated salad dressings sold in the produce section of supermarkets account for $67 million in retail sales annually. Retail sales of refrigerated salad dressings have been growing at a compound annual rate of 18 percent since 1978.

EXHIBIT 1

Estimated 1985 Supermarket Dip Sales at Retail Prices

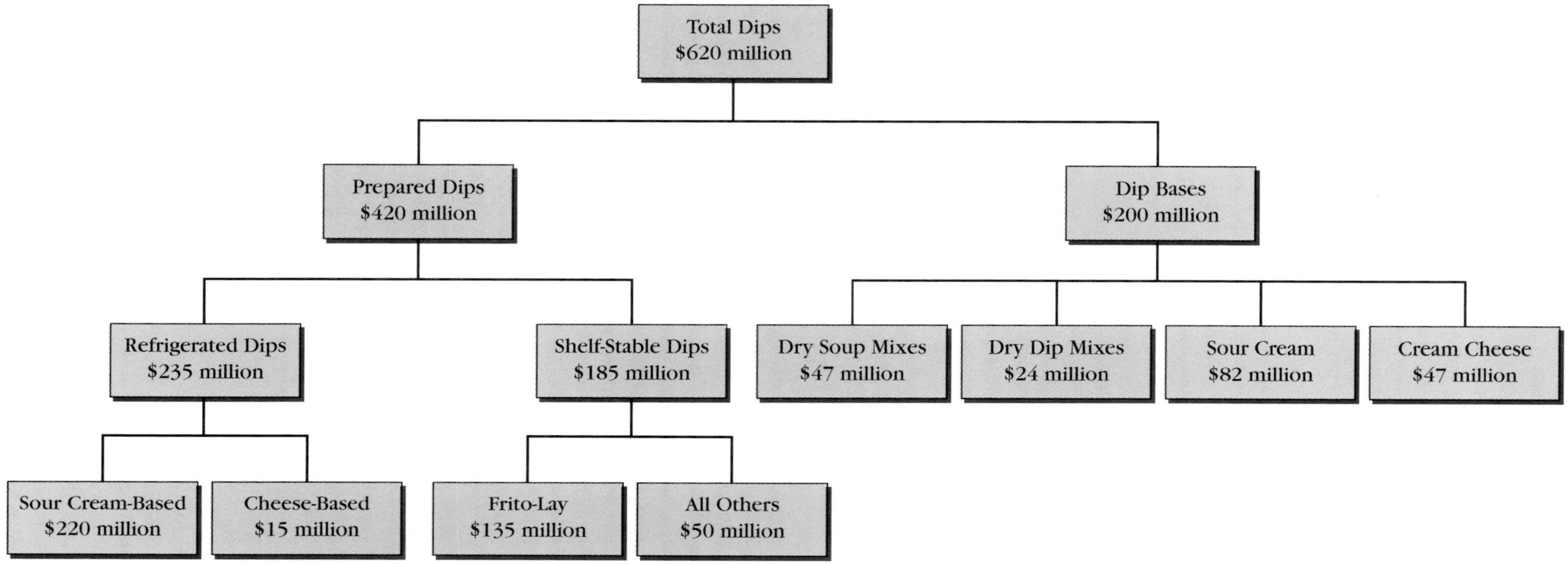

- Total Dips — $620 million
  - Prepared Dips — $420 million
    - Refrigerated Dips — $235 million
      - Sour Cream-Based — $220 million
      - Cheese-Based — $15 million
    - Shelf-Stable Dips — $185 million
      - Frito-Lay — $135 million
      - All Others — $50 million
  - Dip Bases — $200 million
    - Dry Soup Mixes — $47 million
    - Dry Dip Mixes — $24 million
    - Sour Cream — $82 million
    - Cream Cheese — $47 million

Source: Frito-Lay, Inc. company records.

Competitive Activity

Competitive activity in the dip market accelerated in 1984 and 1985. During these two years, numerous new products were introduced, and advertising expenditures increased. Industry sources estimated that dip competitors combined (excluding Frito-Lay) spent $58 million for consumer advertising alone in 1985. This figure was 25 percent higher than in 1984.

Equally noteworthy is the fact that large, well-financed companies began to aggressively pursue the dip market. For example, Campbell Soup introduced a nacho soup/dip and a line of vegetable dip mixes in 1985, and Lipton expanded its line of vegetable dip mixes and upgraded its packaging in 1985. According to Ann Mirabito, "These companies, coupled with Borden, Kraft, and regional chip manufacturers, have dramatically altered the competitive environment for chip dips in the past two years."

■ FRITO-LAY, INC.

Frito-Lay, Inc. is a division of PepsiCo, Inc., a New York-based diversified consumer goods and services firm. Other PepsiCo, Inc. divisions include Pizza Hut, Taco Bell, Pepsi Cola Bottling Group, Kentucky Fried Chicken, and PepsiCo Foods International. PepsiCo, Inc. recorded net sales of over $8 billion in 1985.

Frito-Lay is a nationally recognized leader in the manufacture and marketing of salty snack foods. The company's major salty snack products and brands include potato chips (Lay's®, O'Grady's®, Ruffles®, Delta Gold®), corn chips (Fritos®), tortilla chips (Doritos®, Tostitos®), cheese puffs (Cheetos®), and pretzels (Rold Gold®). Other well-known products include Baken-Ets® brand fried pork skins, Munchos® brand potato chips, and Funyuns® brand onion-flavored snacks. In addition, the company markets a line of nuts, peanut butter crackers, processed beef sticks, Grandma's® brand cookies and snack bars, and assorted other snacks. Frito-Lay's net sales in 1985 approached $3 billion.

Given the nature of its products, Frito-Lay competes primarily within what is termed the salty snack food segment of the snack food market. In 1985, Frito-Lay captured about 33 percent of the salty snack food tonnage sold in the United States.

The Dip Business

The first two dips introduced by Frito-Lay were Frito-Lay's® Jalapeno Bean Dip and Enchilada Bean Dip. These dips, marketed in the 1950s, were viewed as a logical complement to the company's Fritos® corn chips. A Picante Sauce Dip was introduced in 1978 to complement the newly introduced Tostitos® tortilla chips. These three dips were the only Frito-Lay dips sold until 1983.

Dip popularity accelerated extension of the dip product line in 1983. In late 1983 and early 1984, Frito-Lay introduced a number of cheese-based dips, including Mild Cheddar, Cheddar and Herb, Cheddar and Jalapeno, and Cheddar and Bacon, all of which were packaged in nine-ounce cans like the Mexican-style dips. According to Ben Ball, "Cheese dips were an extension of Frito-Lay's tortilla chip business and were a response to the Mexican food phenomenon sweeping the country." These new dips were shelf stable and were sold under the Frito-Lay's® brand name. Ball commented, "There was some discussion about whether or not we should use the Frito-Lay's® brand name with the cheese dips. However, we chose to stay with the Frito-Lay's® name to trade off the company's equity in salty snacks and capitalize on the company's strengths in marketing and distribution." The cheese dips, like their predecessors, were displayed in the salty snack section of supermarkets.

EXHIBIT 2

Dollar Sales of Frito-Lay's® Dips (in Millions of Dollars)

Year	*Mexican Dips*	*Cheese Dips*	*Sour Cream Dip*	*Total Dips*
1986 (forecast)	$41	$48	$10	$99
1985	39	48	—	87
1984	40	55	—	95
1983	38	5	—	43
1982	35	—	—	35
1981	30	—	—	30

In 1986, Frito-Lay introduced its first sour cream-based, shelf-stable dip. This dip carried the Frito-Lay's® brand name and was displayed in the salty snack section of supermarkets. Its French onion flavor was viewed as an ideal accent for the company's potato chips. Industry data indicated that about 50 percent of salty snack volume sold in the United States was accounted for by potato chips. In addition, this onion dip was also deemed suitable as a vegetable dip.

Frito-Lay's dip sales for the period 1981–1985 are shown in Exhibit 2. Jalapeno Bean Dip and Picante Sauce Dip showed consistent, although slow growth in these years. Enchilada Bean Dip was dropped from the Mexican dip line in mid-1985 as a result of falling sales. Sales trends indicated that Mexican dips would show a 4 percent increase in sales in 1986. Cheese dips, by comparison, represented a huge success and outsold Mexican dips in their introductory year. Nevertheless, total dollar sales of dips declined in 1985, and forecasted 1986 sales of cheese dips would be unchanged from the previous year. Ann Mirabito attributed the decline to three factors. First, the novelty of shelf-stable cheese dips had passed. Mirabito commented, "We had good initial penetration for the products; however, with the passage of time, we settled down to a core group of customers." Second, she believed that increased competitive activity had played a part in slowing Frito-Lay's dip volume growth. Third, discontinuance of Enchilada Bean Dip had had an unexpected effect. It had been expected that consumers would switch to Frito-Lay's other Mexican dips. "They didn't, and we lost customers," Mirabito noted. Nevertheless, dips were a highly profitable product line. Exhibit 3 on page 112 shows the 1985 income statement for the dip product line.

Dip Distribution and Sales Effort

Frito-Lay distributes its products through 350,000 outlets nationwide. In 1985, 34,000 outlets were supermarkets, 47,000 were convenience stores, and 20,000 were nonfood outlets. The remainder of Frito-Lay's 350,000 outlets were small grocery stores, liquor stores, service stations, and a variety of institutional customers. The great majority of Frito-Lay's® Dips, however, are sold through supermarkets.

Frito-Lay's distribution system is organized around four geographical zones that cover the entire United States. Each zone contains distribution centers that inventory products for the Frito-Lay sales force, which is composed of over 10,000 individuals who make 400,000 sales and delivery calls during an average workday. Each Frito-Lay salesperson follows a specific, assigned route and is responsible for selling company products to present and potential customers on his or her route.

Frito-Lay uses a "front-door store delivery system," in which one person performs the sales and delivery functions. During a visit to a store, the driver/salesperson takes orders, unloads the product, stocks and arranges the shelves, and handles in-store merchandising. This sales and delivery system is particularly suited to the

EXHIBIT 3

Income Statement for Frito-Lay's® Dips, 1985 (in Thousand of Dollars)

	Mexican Dip	*Cheese Dip*	*Total Dip*
Net sales	$39,040	$48,296	$87,336
Gross margin	19,146	21,876	41,022
Marketing expense:			
Selling	8,798	11,044	19,842
Freight	1,464	1,825	3,289
Consumer advertising	60	87	147
Consumer and trade promotion	851	1,352	2,203
Total marketing expense	11,173	14,308	25,481
General and administrative overhead	2,781	3,791	6,572
Profit contribution	$5,192	$3,777	$8,969

Note: Selling and freight expenses are variable costs, consumer advertising and consumer and trade promotion are fixed costs budgeted annually, and general and administrative overhead expenses are fixed costs.

270,000 nonchain outlets serviced by Frito-Lay. Experience has indicated, however, that sales calls on chain-store accounts, which include most supermarkets, virtually always require participation by a Frito-Lay Region or Division Manager. Such participation is necessary because chain-store snack buyers purchase for all outlets in the chain and approve in-store merchandising plans as well. Furthermore, the sales task and account servicing are more time-consuming and complex, although no less important, than those required for individual outlets (for example, "mom-and-pop" grocery stores and liquor stores).

Dip Marketing

Prior to 1983, the Frito-Lay's® Dips line was viewed as a nonpromoted profit producer. With the introduction of cheese dips in 1983, Frito-Lay began promoting dips, but virtually all marketing and promotion were directed toward retail-store snack food buyers in the form of trade-oriented promotions. In 1985, the emphasis shifted to consumer promotions such as product sampling and couponing to generate trial

EXHIBIT 4

Frito-Lay's® Dips Advertising and Merchandising Expenditures, 1983–1986

Year	*Consumer Advertising*[a]	*Consumer Promotion*[b]	*Trade Promotion*[c]	*Total*
1986	$1,170,000	$3,389,220	$169,290	$4,728,510
1985	147,045	1,459,050	744,101	2,350,196
1984	None	535,266	312,180	847,446
1983	None	22,322	425,478	447,800

[a] Television and radio advertising.

[b] Product sampling, cents-off coupons, etc.

[c] Trade discounts, advertising to store buyers, etc.

EXHIBIT 5

Frito-Lay's® Dips Consumer Promotion

of the new products, and television and radio advertising was used for the first time since the 1950s. Frito-Lay's new product effort, coupled with increased competitive activity, resulted in further planned increases in consumer advertising and promotion in 1986. Exhibit 4 summarizes the advertising and merchandising expenditures for dips for the period 1983–1986. Exhibit 5 illustrates a typical consumer promotion, and Exhibit 6 on page 114 shows a typical trade promotion. A Frito-Lay's® Dip television commercial is shown in Exhibit 7 on page 115.

Ann Mirabito provided the following rationale for the change in promotion emphasis:

> The phenomenal success of Frito-Lay's® Dips was due to two factors. First, we had the right products—cheese dips were novel, and our flavors were innovative. Second, we had the right merchandising location next to salty snacks. Prior to 1985, all of our advertising and merchandising spending was trade-oriented because our goal was to gain distribution in supermarkets and shelf space rapidly. Our consumer household penetration increased from 12 percent in 1983 to 20 percent in 1984, driven largely by placing cheese dips near salty snacks. In 1985, penetration flattened, indicating a need for consumer-pull marketing.

For the most part, dips were promoted jointly with Frito-Lay salty snacks, particularly Doritos® tortilla chips. According to Ben Ball, this approach was adopted because "dips are a complementary product." He added, "Growth occurred when our dips were displayed in conjunction with a natural carrier. That's how we built the chip dip business. This association was conveyed in our promotion and in our shelf placement with salty snacks."

EXHIBIT 6

Frito-Lay's® Dips Trade Promotions

4 COLUMN INCHES

6 COLUMN INCHES

EXHIBIT 7

Frito-Lay's® Dips Television Commercial

TRACY-LOCKE
CLIENT: Frito-Lay, Inc.
PRODUCT: Frito Lay's® Dips

TITLE: "Magnetism"
LENGTH: 15 Seconds
COMM'L. NO.: PECD 6193
FIRST AIR DATE: 2/21/86

SFX: LABORATORY SOUNDS
SCIENCE EDITOR: Do you forget Frito-Lay's® Dip?

Use the theory of magnetism,

so when you pick up the chips you automatically . . .

SFX: METALLIC CLINK
SCIENCE EDITOR: pick up the Dip.

ANNCR (VO) AND SCIENCE EDITOR EATING: The best way to remember Frito-Lay's® Dip is to taste [CRUNCH! Mmmmm!] what it does to our chips.

SCIENCE EDITOR: What an attractive concept!

FUTURE GROWTH OPPORTUNITIES

Two opportunities for the Frito-Lay's® Dips product line were raised at the planning review meeting. Frito-Lay could continue to develop the chip dip market, where it already had a strong foothold, or it could pursue the vegetable dip market as well, using the new sour cream–based dip as a spearhead. The decision would have significant resource allocation consequences, since it was unlikely that funds for dip advertising and merchandising would be increased in 1987 beyond the $4.73 million budgeted for 1986.

Chip Dip Opportunity

One view expressed at the planning meeting was that Frito-Lay should capitalize on its foothold in the chip dip market and attempt to expand the market and build market share. Several arguments were made for this strategy. First, research indicated that only 20 percent of chips were currently eaten with dips; furthermore, only 45 percent of all U.S. households used dips in 1985, whereas 97 percent used salty snacks. "This indicated a major opportunity to build penetration through more aggressive advertising," according to a Frito-Lay executive. Second, research indicated that in 1985 the average number of times shelf-stable dips were purchased by households was four. It was felt that this frequency could be increased through frequency-building promotions such as on-pack coupon offers to encourage repeat sales. In 1985, the purchase frequency of all Frito-Lay's® Dips was 3.6 times per year. A third argument in favor of focusing attention on the chip dip market was the increased competitive activity: 40 new Mexican-style cheese dips had been introduced since 1983. Although many were regional products, each vied for shelf space in or near the salty snack section of supermarkets. At the same time, it was believed that Kraft would be introducing additional products that would compete in the chip dip market. A fourth argument was that historically Frito-Lay had not promoted dips aggressively. It was believed that the typical ratio of advertising and merchandising spending to sales (A/S ratio) for prepared dips was 10 percent.[1] Refrigerated salad dressings had an A/S ratio of 3 percent, and salad dressing dry mixes had an A/S ratio of 13.6 percent. In 1985, Frito-Lay's A/S ratio for its dip product line was 2.7 percent. Therefore, the 1986 advertising and merchandising budget had been more than double 1985 expenditures. (A breakdown of these expenses is shown in Exhibit 8.) A fifth argument was that Frito-Lay could spin off other products from its sour cream–based dip.

EXHIBIT 8

Planned Frito-Lay's® Dips Advertising and Merchandising Expenditures by Product Line, 1986

Product Line	*Consumer Advertising*	*Consumer Promotion*	*Trade Promotion*	*Total*
Mexican and cheese dips[a]	$1,170,000	$2,740,320	$ 56,790	$3,967,110
Sour cream dip	0	648,900	112,500	761,400
Total	$1,170,000	$3,389,220	$169,290	$4,728,510

[a] Total advertising and merchandising expenditures for Mexican and cheese dips were roughly proportional to 1985 sales of the two product lines.

[1] The A/S ratio is calculated by dividing total expenditures for consumer advertising and promotion and trade promotion by total sales for a given year.

Other executives argued that the opportunity in the chip dip category was less promising. They based their argument on three points. First, competitive activity was such that Frito-Lay could only hope to hold, not improve, its position in the chip dip category. The effort and expense necessary to increase penetration and/or increase purchase frequency in the congested chip dip category could be better spent on attacking vegetable dips, where the competition (such as Marie's) was less formidable and more fragmented. Second, Frito-Lay's recent sales growth in dips was due to new products (for example, cheese-based dips), and it was not clear that further product line extensions could produce continued growth. There was also significant potential for cannibalization of existing cheese dips if the line was expanded further. Third, the new sour cream dip represented a break with Mexican-style dips and cheese dips and was probably more suitable for vegetable dipping. To promote and distribute this new dip solely as a chip dip rather than as a vegetable dip could mean a missed opportunity.

Vegetable Dip Opportunity

Executives who voiced concern about focusing on the chip dip category also raised several points in favor of the vegetable dip opportunity. First, they noted that 33 percent of dip sales were linked to vegetables. Moreover, industry research indicated that only one-fourth of the dollar volume associated with vegetable dipping was accounted for by refrigerated salad dressings, such as Marie's. The remainder was accounted for by dip mixes and refrigerated dips, and no major competitors had a strong competitive position in the market. Second, research indicated that sour cream–based dips were more popular than cheese dips for vegetable dipping. Third, trend data indicated that consumers were becoming concerned about the nutritional value and salt content of prepared foods.[2] It was felt that this trend could affect preferences for vegetables and salty snacks and, as a result, dips. Fourth, the Frito-Lay's® Dips line now had a sour cream–based dip that had not yet been promoted and merchandised for vegetable dipping. Fifth, no major competitor had introduced a shelf-stable dip for vegetables. Frito-Lay had pioneered the shelf-stable business for chip dips, and some executives felt that a similar opportunity existed for vegetable dips. Finally, a cost analysis indicated that the gross margins would be largely unaffected. The gross margin on Frito-Lay's sour cream dip was 45 percent.

Other executives expressed the view that pursuing the vegetable dip segment would not be easy, however. These executives cited research indicating that supermarket executives preferred that dips suitable for vegetable dipping be handled by their produce warehouse. This meant that Frito-Lay's front-door delivery system would not be favored. Distribution through the produce warehouse would also involve dealing with supermarket produce buyers and managers. Frito-Lay had never dealt with these individuals in the past, and some company executives believed that a totally new sales approach would be necessary. Even though a complete cost analysis had not been conducted, it was estimated that selling expenses could increase to 25 percent of sales. Current sales expense was 22.7 percent. Freight expense would not be affected. As of 1986, the sour cream dip was not allocated any general and administrative overhead. Furthermore, Frito-Lay driver/salespeople were unfamiliar with merchandising practices in the produce section of supermarkets. This same research indicated that any new vegetable dip should be shelved next to refrigerated salad dressing or near produce.

---

[2] Bob Messenger, "Consumers See the Light . . . and the Lean, with a Touch of Pizzazz," *Prepared Foods* (November 1985): 46–49.

A second concern was that Frito-Lay's® Dips would lose some economies in advertising and merchandizing. Frito-Lay's® Dips had been promoted jointly with the company's chips in the past and thus traded on the "halo effect" of Frito-Lay salty snacks. Mirabito acknowledged that vegetable dips would have to "go it alone" because Frito-Lay's halo effect might not translate to vegetable dips.

A third concern expressed at the meeting was that any foray into vegetable dips would require more than a single item. In addition to the French onion flavor, other flavors (such as ranch style) would be necessary. Such line extensions would require added research and development expenses and promotional support, as had been the case with the successful introduction of cheese dips.

The planning meeting adjourned without resolution of the issue. Ben Ball asked Ann Mirabito to give the "chip dip versus vegetable dip" question further consideration. She was to prepare a recommendation for another meeting to be scheduled within 30 days.

CASE

South Delaware Coors, Inc.

Larry Brownlow was just beginning to realize the problem was more complex than he had thought. The problem, of course, was giving direction to Manson and Associates regarding what research should be completed by February 20, 1990, to determine market potential of a Coors beer distributorship for a two-county area in southern Delaware. With data from this research, Larry would be able to estimate the feasibility of such an operation before the March 5 application deadline. Larry knew his decision on whether to apply for the distributorship was the most important career choice he had ever faced.

■ LARRY BROWNLOW

Larry was just completing his MBA and, from his standpoint, the Coors announcement of expansion into Delaware could hardly have been better timed. He had long ago decided the best opportunities and rewards were in smaller, self-owned businesses and not in the jungles of corporate giants. Because of a family tragedy some three years earlier, Larry found himself in a position to consider small business opportunities such as the Coors distributorship. Approximately $500,000 was held in trust for Larry, to be dispersed when he reached age 30. Until then, Larry and his family were living on an annual trust income of about $40,000. It was on the basis of this income that Larry had decided to leave his sales engineering job and return to graduate school for his MBA

The decision to complete a graduate program and operate his own business had been easy to make. Although he could have retired and lived off investment income, Larry knew such a life would not be to his liking. Working with people and the challenge of making it on his own, Larry thought, were far preferable to enduring an early retirement.

Larry would be 30 in July, about the time money would actually be needed to start the business. In the meantime, he had access to about $15,000 for feasibility research. Although there certainly were other places to spend the money, Larry and his wife agreed the opportunity to acquire the distributorship could not be overlooked.

■ COORS, INC.

Coors' history dated back to 1873, when Adolph Coors built a small brewery in Golden, Colorado. Since then, the brewery had prospered and become the fourth-largest seller of beer in the country. Coors' operating philosophy could be summed

---

This case was prepared by Professor James E. Nelson and doctoral student Eric J. Karson, of the University of Colorado, as a basis for class discussion and is not designed to illustrate effective or ineffective handling of an administrative situation. Certain data have been disguised.

up as "hard work, saving money, devotion to the quality of the product, caring about the environment, and giving people something to believe in." Company operation is consistent with this philosophy. Headquarters and most production facilities are still located in Golden, Colorado, with a new Shenandoah, Virginia, facility aiding in nationwide distribution. Coors is still family operated and controlled. The company had issued its first public stock, $127 million worth of nonvoting shares, in 1975. The issue was enthusiastically received by the financial community despite its being offered during a recession.

Coors' unwillingness to compromise on the high quality of its product is well known both to its suppliers and to its consuming public. Coors beer requires constant refrigeration to maintain this quality, and wholesalers' facilities are closely controlled to ensure that proper temperatures are maintained. Wholesalers are also required to install and use aluminum can recycling equipment. Coors was one of the first breweries in the industry to recycle its cans.

Larry was aware of Coors' popularity with many consumers in adjacent states. However, Coors' corporate management was seen by some consumers to hold anti-union beliefs (because of a labor disagreement at the brewery some ten years ago and the brewery's current use of a nonunion labor force). Some other consumers perceived the brewery to be somewhat insensitive to minority issues, primarily in employment and distribution. These attitudes—plus many other aspects of consumer behavior—meant that Coors' sales in Delaware would depend greatly on the efforts of the two wholesalers planned for the state.

■ MANSON RESEARCH PROPOSAL

Because of the press of his studies, Larry had contacted Manson and Associates in January for their assistance. The firm was a Wilmington-based general research supplier that had conducted other feasibility studies in the South Atlantic region. Manson was well known for the quality of its work, particularly with respect to computer modeling. The firm had developed special expertise in modeling such things as population and employment levels for cities, counties, and other units of area for periods of up to 10 years into the future.

Larry had met John Rome, senior research analyst for Manson, in January and discussed the Coors opportunity and appropriate research extensively. Rome promised a formal research proposal (Exhibit 1) for the project, which Larry now held in his hand. It certainly was extensive, Larry thought, and reflected the professionalism he expected. Now came the hard part—choosing the more relevant research from the proposal—because he certainly couldn't afford to pay for it all. Rome had suggested a meeting for Friday, which gave Larry only three more days to decide.

Larry was at first overwhelmed. All the research would certainly be useful. He was sure he needed estimates of sales and costs in a form allowing managerial analysis, but what data in what form? Knowledge of competing operations' experience, retailer support, and consumer acceptance also seemed important for feasibility analysis. For example, what if consumers were excited about Coors and retailers indifferent, or the other way around? Finally, several of the studies would provide information that could be useful in later months of operation, in the areas of promotion and pricing, for example. The problem now appeared more difficult than before!

It would have been nice, Larry thought, to have had some time to perform part of the suggested research himself. However, there just was too much in the way of class assignments and other matters to allow him that luxury. Besides, using Manson and Associates would give him research results from an unbiased source. There would be plenty for him to do once he received the results anyway.

EXHIBIT 1

Research Proposal by Manson and Associates

Mr. Larry Brownlow
1198 West Lamar
Chester, PA 19345

January 16, 1990

Dear Larry:

It was a pleasure meeting you last week and discussing your business and research interests in Coors wholesaling. After further thought and discussion with my colleagues, the Coors opportunity appears even more attractive than when we met.

Appearances can be deceiving, as you know, and I fully agree some formal research is needed before you make application. Research that we recommend would proceed in two distinct stages and is described below.

Stage One Research, Based on Secondary Data and Manson Computer Models:

Study A: National and Delaware Per-Capita Beer Consumption for 1988–1992.
Description: Per-capita annual consumption of beer for the total population and for population age 21 and over in gallons is provided.
Source: Various publications, Manson computer model
Cost: $1,000

Study B: Population Estimates for 1986–1996 for Two Delaware Counties in Market Area.
Description: Annual estimates of total population and population age 21 and over are provided for the period 1986–1996.
Source: U.S. Bureau of Census, *Sales Management Annual Survey of Buying Power,* Manson computer model
Cost: $1,500

Study C: Estimates of Coors' Market Share for 1990–1995.
Description: Coors' market share for the two-county market area based on total gallons consumed is estimated for each year in the period 1990–1995. These data will be projected from Coors' nationwide experience.
Source: Various publications, Manson computer model
Cost: $2,000

Study D: Estimates of Number of Liquor and Beer Licenses for the Market area, 1990–1995.
Description: Projections of the number of on-premise sale operations and off-premise sale operations are provided.
Source: Delaware Department of Revenue, Manson computer model
Cost: $1,000

Study E: Beer Taxes Paid by Delaware Wholesalers for 1988 and 1989 in the Market Area.
Description: Beer taxes paid by each of the six presently operating competing beer wholesalers are provided. These figures can be converted to gallons sold by applying the state gallonage tax rate ($.06 per gallon).
Source: Delaware Department of Revenue
Cost: $200

Study F: Financial Statement Summary of Wine, Liquor, and Beer Wholesalers for Fiscal Year 1988.
Description: Composite balance sheets, income statements, and relevant measures of performance for 510 similar wholesaling operations in the United States are provided.
Source: Robert Morris Associates Annual Statement Studies, 1989 ed.
Cost: $49.50

Stage Two Research, Based on Primary Data:

Study G: Consumer Study.
Description: Study G involves focus-group interviews and a mail questionnaire to determine consumers' past experience, acceptance, and intention to buy

(continued on next page)

EXHIBIT 1 *(continued)*

Coors beer.[a] Three focus-group interviews would be conducted in the two counties in the market area. From these data, a questionnaire would be developed and sent to 300 adult residents in the market area, utilizing direct questions and a semantic differential scale to measure attitudes toward Coors beer, competing beers, and an ideal beer.
Source: Manson and Associates
Cost: $6,000

Study H: Retailer Study.
Description: Group interviews would be conducted with six potential retailers of Coors beer in one county in the market area to determine their past beer sales and experience and their intention to stock and sell Coors. From these data, a personal-interview questionnaire would be developed and executed at all appropriate retailers in the market area to determine similar data.
Source: Manson and Associates
Cost: $4,800

Study I: Survey of Retail and Wholesale Beer Prices.
Description: In-store interviews would be conducted with a sample of 50 retailers in the market area to estimate retail and wholesale prices for Budweiser, Miller Lite, Miller, Busch, Bud Light, Old Milwaukee, and Michelob.
Source: Manson and Associates
Cost: $2,000

Examples of the final report tables are attached [Exhibit 2, pages 123–127]. This should give you a better idea of the data you will receive.

As you can see, the research is extensive and, I might add, not cheap. However, the research as outlined will supply you with sufficient information to make an estimate of the feasibility of a Coors distributorship, the investment for which is substantial.

I have scheduled 9:00 A.M. next Friday as a time to meet with you to discuss the proposal in more detail. Time is short, but we firmly feel the study can be completed by February 20, 1990. If you need more information in the meantime, please feel free to call.

Sincerely,

John Rome
Senior Research Analyst

---

[a] A focus-group interview consists of a moderator's questioning and listening to a group of 8 to 12 consumers.

EXHIBIT 2

Examples of Final Research Report Tables

Table A
National and Delaware Residents' Annual Beer Consumption per Capita, 1988–1992 (Gallons)

	U.S. Consumption		*Delaware Consumption*	
Year	*Based on Entire Population*	*Based on Population Age 21 and Over*	*Based on Entire Population*	*Based on Population Age 21 and Over*
1988				
1989				
1990				
1991				
1992				

Source: Study A.

Table B
Population Estimates for 1986–1996 for Two Delaware Counties in Market Area

	Entire Population					
County	*1986*	*1988*	*1990*	*1992*	*1994*	*1996*
Kent						
Sussex						

	Population Age 21 and Over					
County	*1986*	*1988*	*1990*	*1992*	*1994*	*1996*
Kent						
Sussex						

Source: Study B.

Table C
Estimates of Coors' Market Share for 1990–1995

Year	***Market Share (%)***
1990	
1991	
1992	
1993	
1994	
1995	

Source: Study C.

(continued on next page)

EXHIBIT 2 *(continued)*

Table D
Estimates of Number of Liquor and Beer Licenses for the Market Area, 1990–1995

Type of License	*1990*	*1991*	*1992*	*1993*	*1994*	*1995*
All beverages						
Retail beer and wine						
Off-premise beer only						
Veterans beer and liquor						
Fraternal						
Resort beer and liquor						

Source: Study D.

Table E
Beer Taxes Paid by Beer Wholesalers in the Market Area, 1988 and 1989

Wholesaler	*1988 Tax Paid ($)*	*1989 Tax Paid ($)*
A		
B		
C		
D		
E		
F		

Source: Study E

Note: Delaware beer tax is $0.06 gallon.

Table F
Financial Statement Summary for 510 Wholesalers of Wine, Liquor, and Beer in Fiscal Year 1988

Assets	*Percentage*
Cash and equivalents	
Accounts and notes receivable, net	
Inventory	
All other current	
Total current	
Fixed assets, net	
Intangibles, net	
All other noncurrent	
Total	100.0

EXHIBIT 2 *(continued)*

Table F ***(continued)***

Liabilities	***Percentage***
Notes payable, short term	
Current maturity long-term debt	
Accounts and notes payable, trade	
Accrued expenses	
All other current	
Total current	
Long-term debt	
All other noncurrent	
Net worth	
Total liabilities and net worth	100.0
Income Data	
Net sales	100.0
Cost of sales	
Gross profit	
Operating expenses	
Operating profit	
All other expenses, net	
Profit before taxes	
Ratios	
Quick	
Current	
Debt/worth	
Sales/receivables	
Cost of sales/inventory	
Percentage profit before taxes, based on total assets	

Interpretation of Statement Studies Figures:
RMA recommends that Statement Studies data be regarded only as general guidelines and not as absolute industry norms. There are several reasons why the data may not be fully representative of a given industry:

1. The financial statements used in the Statement Studies are not selected by any random or statistically reliable method. RMA member banks voluntarily submit the raw data they have available each year, with these being the only constraints: (a) The fiscal year-ends of the companies reported may not be from April 1 through June 29, and (b) their total assets must be less than $100 million.
2. Many companies have varied product lines; however, the Statement Studies categorize them by their primary product Standard Industrial Classification (SIC) number only.
3. Some of the industry samples are rather small in relation to the total number of firms in a given industry. A relatively small sample can increase the chances that some of our composites do not fully represent an industry.
4. There is the chance that an extreme statement can be present in a sample, causing a disproportionate influence on the industry composite. This is particularly true in a relatively small sample.
5. Companies within the same industry may differ in their method of operations, which in turn can directly influence their financial statements. Since they are included in our sample, too, these statements can significantly affect our composite calculations.
6. Other considerations that can result in variations among different companies engaged in the same general line of business are different labor markets, geographical location, different accounting methods, quality of products handled, sources and methods of financing, and terms of sale.

For these reasons, RMA does not recommend that Statement Studies figures be considered as absolute norms for a given industry. Rather, the figures should be used only as general guidelines and in addition to the other methods of financial analysis. RMA makes no claim as to the representativeness of the figures printed in this book.

Source: Study F (Robert Morris Associates, © 1989).

EXHIBIT 2 *(continued)*

Table G
Consumer Questionnaire Results

	Percentage		*Percentage*
Consumed Coors in the past:		Usually buy beer at:	
Attitudes toward Coors:	%	Liquor stores	
Strongly like		Taverns and bars	
Like		Supermarkets	
Indifferent/no opinion		Corner grocery	
Dislike			
Strongly dislike			
Total	100.0	Total	100.0
Weekly beer consumption:		Features considered important when buying beer:	
Less than 1 can		Taste	
1-2 cans		Brand name	
3-4 cans		Price	
5-6 cans		Store location	
7-8 cans		Advertising	
9 cans and over		Carbonation	
Total	100.0	Other	
Intention to buy Coors:		Total	100.0
Certainly will			
Maybe will			
Not sure			
Maybe will not			
Certainly will not			
Total	100.0		

***Semantic Differential Scale, Consumers*[a]**

	Extremely	*Very*	*Somewhat*	*Somewhat*	*Very*	*Extremely*	
Masculine	—	—	—	—	—	—	Feminine
Healthful	—	—	—	—	—	—	Unhealthful
Cheap	—	—	—	—	—	—	Expensive
Strong	—	—	—	—	—	—	Weak
Old-fashioned	—	—	—	—	—	—	New
Upper-class	—	—	—	—	—	—	Lower-class
Good taste	—	—	—	—	—	—	Bad taste

[a] *Profiles would be provided for Coors, three competing beers, and an ideal beer.*

Source: Study G.

EXHIBIT 2 (*continued*)

Table H
Retailer Questionnaire Results

	Percentage		*Percentage*
Brands of beer carried:		Beer sales:	
Budweiser		Budweiser	
Miller Lite		Miller Lite	
Miller		Miller	
Busch		Busch	
Bud Light		Bud Light	
Old Milwaukee		Old Milwaukee	
Michelob		Michelob	
		Others	
Intention to sell Coors:			
Certainly will		Total	100.0
Maybe will			
Not sure			
Maybe will not			
Certainly will not			
Total	100.0		

Semantic Differential Scale, Retailers[a]

	Extremely	*Very*	*Somewhat*	*Somewhat*	*Very*	*Extremely*	
Masculine	—	—	—	—	—	—	Feminine
Healthful	—	—	—	—	—	—	Unhealthful
Cheap	—	—	—	—	—	—	Expensive
Strong	—	—	—	—	—	—	Weak
Old-fashioned	—	—	—	—	—	—	New
Upper-class	—	—	—	—	—	—	Lower-class
Good taste	—	—	—	—	—	—	Bad taste

[a] *Profiles would be provided for Coors, three competing beers, and an ideal bear.*

Source: Study H.

Table I
Retail and Wholesale Prices for Selected Beers in the Market Area

Beer	***Wholesale Six-Pack Price***[a] ***(dollars)***	***Retail Six-Pack Price***[b] ***(dollars)***
Budweiser		
Miller Lite		
Miller		
Busch		
Bud Light		
Old Milwaukee		
Michelob		

[a] *Price at which the wholesaler sold to retailers.*
[b] *Price at which the retailer sold to consumers.*

Source: Study I.

■ INVESTMENT AND OPERATING DATA

Larry was not completely in the dark regarding investment and operating data for the distributorship. In the past two weeks he had visited two beer wholesalers in his home town of Chester, Pennsylvania, who handled Anheuser-Busch and Miller beer, to get a feel for their operation and marketing experience. It would have been nice to interview a Coors wholesaler, but Coors management had instructed all of their distributors to provide no information to prospective applicants.

Although no specific financial data had been discussed, general information had been provided in a cordial fashion because of the noncompetitive nature of Larry's plans. Based on his conversations, Larry had made the following estimates:

Inventory		$240,000
Equipment:		
Delivery trucks	$150,000	
Forklift	20,000	
Recycling and miscellaneous equipment	20,000	
Office equipment	10,000	
Total equipment		200,000
Warehouse		320,000
Land		40,000
Total investment		$800,000

A local banker had reviewed Larry's financial capabilities and saw no problem in extending a line of credit on the order of $400,000. Other family sources also might loan as much as $400,000 to the business.

To get a rough estimate of fixed expenses, Larry decided to plan on having four route salespeople, a secretary, and a warehouse manager. Salaries for these people and himself would run about $160,000 annually, plus some form of incentive compensation he had yet to determine. Other fixed or semifixed expenses were estimated as follows:

Equipment depreciation	$35,000
Warehouse depreciation	15,000
Utilities and telephone	12,000
Insurance	10,000
Personal property taxes	10,000
Maintenance and janitorial services	5,600
Miscellaneous	2,400
	$90,000

According to the two wholesalers, beer in bottles and cans outsold keg beer by a three-to-one margin. Keg beer prices at the wholesale level were about 45 percent of prices for beer in bottles and cans.

■ MEETING

The entire matter deserved much thought. Maybe it was a golden opportunity, maybe not. The only thing certain was that research was needed, Manson and Associates was ready, and Larry needed time to think. Today is Tuesday, Larry thought—only three days until he and John Rome would get together for direction.

CHAPTER 5

Product and Service Strategy and Brand Management

The fundamental decision in formulating a marketing mix concerns the offering of an organization. Without something to satisfy target market wants and needs, there would be nothing to price, distribute, or communicate. In essence, the ultimate profitability of an organization depends on its product or service offering(s). Accordingly, issues in the development of a product and service strategy are of special interest to all levels of management in an organization.

The three basic kinds of offering-related decisions facing the marketing manager concern (1) modifying the offering mix, (2) positioning offerings, and (3) branding offerings. Aspects of each decision are described in this chapter.

In certain ways, offering decisions are extensions of product-market matching strategies described in Chapter 1. Like other marketing-mix decisions, offering decisions must be based on consideration of organization and marketing objectives, organization resources and capabilities, customer needs and wants, and competitive forces in the marketplace.

■ THE OFFERING PORTFOLIO

The Offering Concept

Before proceeding to a discussion of offering-related decisions, we should define the term *offering*. In an abstract sense, an *offering* consists of the benefits or satisfaction provided to target markets by an organization. More concretely, an offering consists of a tangible product or service (a physical entity) plus related services (such as delivery and setup), warranties or guarantees, packaging, and the like.

Use of the term *offering* rather than *product* or *service* has numerous benefits for strategic marketing planning. By focusing on benefits and satisfaction offered, it establishes a conceptual framework. This framework is potentially useful in analyzing competing offerings, identifying the unmet needs and wants of target markets, and developing or designing new products or services. It forces a marketer to go beyond the single tangible entity being marketed and to consider the entire offering, or extended product or service.

In a broader view, an organization's offerings are an extension of its business definition. Offerings illustrate not only the buyer needs served, but also the types of customer groups sought and the means (technology) for satisfying their needs.

The Offering Mix

Seldom do organizations market a solitary offering; rather, they tend to market many product or service offerings. The typical supermarket contains over 30,000 different products; General Electric offers over a quarter million. Banks provide hundreds of services to customers, including computer billing, automatic payroll deposits, checking accounts, and loans of numerous kinds. Similarly, hospitals maintain a complete "inventory" of services ranging from pathology to obstetrics to food services. The totality of an organization's offerings is known as its product or service *offering mix* or *portfolio*. This mix usually consists of distinct offering lines—groups of offerings similar in terms of usage, buyers marketed to, or technical characteristics. Each offering line is composed of individual offers or items.

Offering decisions concern primarily the width, depth, and consistency of the offering portfolio. Marketing managers must continually assess the number of offering lines (the width decision) and the number of individual items in each line (the depth decision). Although these decisions depend, in part, on the existing competitive or industry situation, as well as organizational resources, they are perhaps most often determined by overall marketing strategy. The options are many. At one extreme, an organization can concentrate on one offering; at the other, it can offer complete lines to its customers. In between, it can specialize in high-profit and/or high-volume offerings. Furthermore, managers must consider the extent to which offerings satisfy similar needs, appeal to similar buyer groups, or utilize similar technologies (the consistency decision).

Increasingly, organizations have turned to "bundling" as a means to enhance their offering mix. *Bundling* involves the marketing of two or more product or service items in a single "package." For example, IBM sells computer hardware, software, and maintenance contracts together. Bundling is based on the idea that consumers value the package more than the individual items. This is due to benefits received from not having to make separate purchases and enhanced satisfaction from one item given the presence of another. Moreover, bundling often provides a lower total cost to buyers and lower marketing costs to sellers. For instance, SBC Communications, Inc. offers a telephone service "bundle" that includes Internet, entertainment, and local telephone service with numerous add-on features such as caller ID and voice mail for one price of $137.00 per month. Priced separately, items in the bundle cost a buyer up to $185.00 per month.[1]

■ MODIFYING THE OFFERING MIX

The first offering-related decision confronting the manager is whether to modify the offering mix. Rarely, if ever, will an organization's offering mix stand the test of changing competitive actions and buyer preferences, or satisfy an organization's desire for growth. Accordingly, the marketing manager must continually monitor target markets and offerings to determine when new offerings should be introduced and existing offerings modified or eliminated.

Additions to the Offering Mix

Additions to the offering mix may take the form of a single offering or of entire lines of offerings. An example of adding a complete line of offerings is General Mills' introduction, several years ago, of salty snack items called Whistles, Bugles, and Daisies.

Whatever the reason for considering new offerings, three questions should direct the evaluation of this action:

- How consistent is the new offering with existing offerings?
- Does the organization have the resources to adequately introduce and sustain the offering?
- Is there a viable market niche for the offering?

First, in evaluating the consistency of the new offering with existing offerings, offering interrelationships—whether substitute, complementary, or whatever—must be carefully taken into account. This is necessary to avoid situations in which sales of the new offering may excessively cannibalize those of other offerings. Eastman Kodak did not originally introduce 35mm cameras and camcorders because of the potential for cannibalizing its core products—cameras. Today, a similar situation exists with electronic imaging cameras, which could cannibalize sales of existing cameras.[2] Determining a new offering's consistency also involves considering the degree to which the new offering fits the organization's existing selling and distribution strategies. For example, will the new offering require a different type of sales effort, such as new sales personnel or selling methods? The Metropolitan Life Insurance Company faced such a situation when it added automobile insurance to its line of life and health insurance, since the sales task for auto insurance differs from that for life insurance. Or will the new offering require a different marketing channel to reach the target market sought? Both the cannibalization question and the question of fit with sales and distribution strategies raise a fundamental third question relating to the buyers sought for the new offering. Will the new offering satisfy the target markets currently being served by the existing offering mix? If it will, then the sales and distribution issue may be settled, but the cannibalization question remains. If it will not, then the situation is just the opposite.

The second issue arising from the addition of new offerings relates to the adequacy of an organization's resources. In particular, the financial strength of the organization must be objectively appraised. New offerings often require large initial cash outlays for research, development, and introductory marketing programs. Gillette, for example, spent $750 million for research and development and another $300 million in advertising and marketing support to launch its Mach 3 razor.[3] Other costs of sustaining the new offering before it returns a profit to the organization must also be measured. These costs will be determined, in part, by the speed and magnitude of competitive response to new offerings in the market and by market growth itself. The experience of Royal Crown Company, the maker of RC Cola, is a case in point. The company pioneered the first can in 1954, the first diet cola in 1962, and the first caffeine-free cola in 1980. All three offerings achieved a respectable market presence only to lose it when larger competitors such as Coca-Cola and Pepsi-Cola introduced competitive products.[4]

Finally, one must determine whether a market niche exists for the new offering. Important questions here are whether the new offering has a relative advantage over existing competitive offerings and whether a distinct buyer group exists for which no offering is satisfactory. Careful market analysis is necessary to answer these questions.

New-Offering Development Process

Marketing managers are often faced with new-offering decisions. In dealing with the often-chaotic process of developing and marketing new offerings, most managers attempt to follow some sort of structured procedure.[5] This procedure typically includes four multifaceted steps: (1) idea generation/idea screening, (2) business analysis, (3) market testing, and (4) commercialization.

Briefly, the process is as follows. New-offering ideas are obtained from many sources—employees, buyers, and competitors—through formal (marketing research) and informal means. These ideas are screened, both in terms of organizational definition and capability and from the viewpoint of prospective buyers. Ideas deemed incompatible with organizational definition and capability are quickly eliminated. The match between prospective buyers and offering characteristics is assessed through questions such as the following. First, does the offering have a *relative advantage* over existing offerings? Second, is the offering *compatible* with buyers' use or consumption behavior? Third, is the offering *simple* enough for buyers to understand and use? Fourth, can the offering be *tested* on a limited basis prior to actual purchase? Fifth, are there *immediate benefits* from the offering, once it is used or consumed? If the answers to these questions are yes and the offering satisfies a *felt need*, then the new-offering idea passes on to the next stage. At that point, the idea is subjected to a business analysis to assess its financial viability in terms of estimated sales, costs, and profitability. Those ideas that pass the business analysis are then developed into prototypes, and various testing procedures are implemented. Marketing-related tests may include product concept or buyer preference tests in a laboratory situation, or even field market tests. Offering ideas that pass through these stages are commercially introduced into the marketplace in the hope that they will become profitable to the organization. Research on the new-offering development process indicates that upwards of 3,000 raw ideas are needed to produce a single commercially successful, innovative new product. This research also emphasizes that two major factors contribute to the success of new offerings: (1) a fit with market needs and (2) a fit with the internal strengths of the organizations.[6]

Although the stages just outlined are relatively straightforward from a managerial perspective, two require further elaboration: the business analysis and testing stages. Sales analysis and profit analysis are two fundamental aspects of the business analysis stage. Forecasting sales volume for a new offering is an enormously difficult task; nevertheless, preliminary forecasts must be made before further investigation of the offering is warranted. For the most part, profitability analyses are related to investment requirements, break-even procedures, and payback periods. Break-even procedures can be used to determine estimates of the number of units that must be sold to cover fixed and variable costs. An extension of this procedure—and one that is frequently used in evaluating new offerings—is to compute the payback period of the new offering. *Payback period* refers to the number of years required for an organization to recapture its initial offering investment. The shorter the payback period, the sooner an offering will prove profitable. Usually the payback period is computed by dividing the fixed costs of the offering by the estimated incoming cash flows from it. Though widely used, the method is limited in that it does not distinguish among offering investments according to their absolute sizes. A final method often used is to calculate the common return on investment (ROI). ROI equals the ratio of average annual net earnings (return) divided by average annual investment, discounted to the present time. Like the payback method, the ROI method does not always distinguish among offering alternatives according to their riskiness. Risk must still be subjectively assessed.

Test marketing is a major consideration in the development and testing stage. A test market is a scaled-down implementation of one or more alternative marketing strategies for introducing the new offering. Test markets provide several benefits to managers. First, they generate benchmark data for assessing sales volume when the product is introduced over a wider area. Second, if alternative marketing strategies are tested, the relative impacts of the two programs can be examined under actual market conditions. In a similar vein, test markets allow the manager to assess the incidence of offering trial by potential buyers, repeat-purchasing behavior, and quantities purchased. A manager should remember, however, that test markets of new offerings inform competitors of the organization's activities and thus may increase the magnitude and speed of competitive response. This happened to the Clorox Company. Its Wave laundry detergent with bleach was test-marketed for five years, only to be dropped after competitors introduced their own detergents with bleach supported by extensive marketing resources.[7]

Life-Cycle Concept

An important managerial tool related to the development and management of offerings is the concept of the life cycle. A *life cycle* plots sales of an offering (such as a brand of coffee) or a product class (such as all coffee brands) over a period of time. Life cycles are typically divided into four stages: (1) introduction, (2) growth, (3) maturity-saturation, and (4) decline. Exhibit 5.1 shows the general form of a product life cycle and the corresponding stages.

The sales curve can be viewed as being the result of offering trial and repeat-purchasing behavior. In other words,

$$\begin{aligned}\text{Sales volume} &= (\text{number of triers} \times \text{average purchase amount} \times \text{price}) \\ &\quad + (\text{number of repeaters} \times \text{average purchase amount} \times \text{price})\end{aligned}$$

Early in the life cycle, management efforts focus on stimulating trial of the offering by advertising, giving out free samples, and obtaining adequate distribution. The vast majority of sales volume is due to trial purchases. As the offering moves through its life cycle, an increasing share of volume is attributable to repeat purchases, and management efforts focus on retaining existing buyers of the offering through offering modifications, enhanced brand image, and competitive pricing.

Anticipating and recognizing movement into advanced stages of the life cycle are crucial to managing the various stages. Movement into the maturity-saturation stage is often indicated by (1) an increase in the proportion of buyers who are repeat purchasers (that is, few new buyers or triers exist), (2) an increase in the standardization of production operations and product-service offerings, and (3) an in-

EXHIBIT 5.1

General Form of a Product Life Cycle

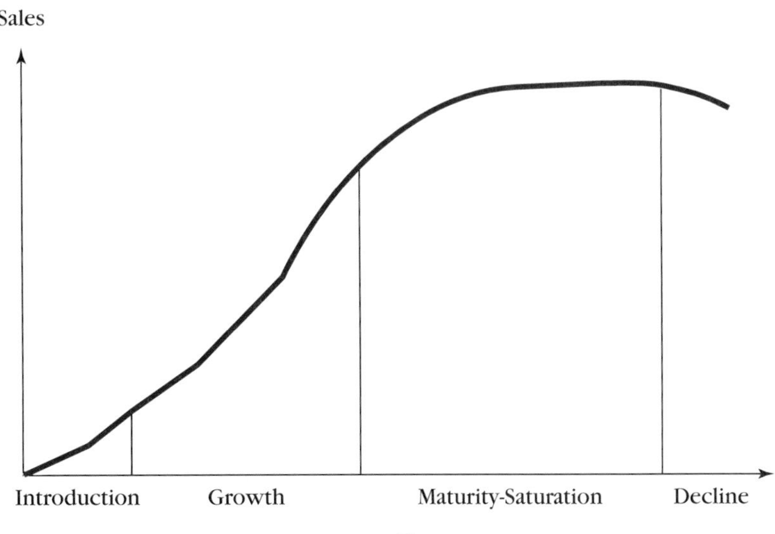

crease in the incidence of aggressive pricing activities of competitors. As the offering enters into and moves through this stage, management efforts typically focus on finding new buyers for the offering, significantly improving the offering, and/or increasing the frequency of usage among current buyers. Ultimately, the decline stage must be addressed. The decision criteria at this stage are outlined in the following discussion on modifying, harvesting, and eliminating offerings.

Services often follow a life cycle similar to the product life cycle described above. As a service firm approaches maturity, it typically modifies its operations to attract new buyers. Examples include McDonald's with its expanded menu and barbershops that become hair-stylist operations featuring hair-cutting services for men and women. Often service firms expand their geographical scope by reproducing facilities through franchising and licensing agreements to become multisite operators.

Modifying, Harvesting, and Eliminating Offerings

Modifying offerings is a common practice. Firms must always be on the lookout for new ways to improve the value their offerings provide consumers in terms of quality, functions, features, and/or price.

Modification decisions typically focus on trading up or trading down the offering. *Trading up* involves a conscious decision to improve an offering—by adding new features and higher-quality materials or augmenting the offering with attendant services—and raising the price. Examples of augmenting products with services are found in the computer industry. Manufacturers of computers enhanced the image and suitability of their products through programming services, information-system assistance, and user training. *Trading down* is the process of reducing the number of features or quality of an offering and lowering the price.

The dichotomy between trading up and trading down has been blurred in recent years as a result of competitive and cost pressures. In particular, many organizations have modified their offerings downward while maintaining or increasing the price. For example, many distillers have reduced the alcohol content of their beverages without changing prices. Some airlines have added more seats, thus reducing leg room, and eliminated certain extras without lowering fares. Consumer-packaged-goods firms have reduced the content of packages without reducing prices—a practice called *downsizing.*

The elimination of offerings as a specific decision is given less attention than new-offering or modification decisions. However, the elimination decision has grown in importance in recent years because of the realization that some offerings may be an unnecessary burden in light of potential opportunities. As an alternative to total elimination, management might consider harvesting the offering when it enters the late-maturity or decline stage of the life cycle. *Harvesting* is the strategic management decision to reduce the investment in a business entity in the hope of cutting costs and/or improving cash flow. In other words, the decision is not to abandon the offering outright but, rather, to minimize human and financial resources allocated to it. Harvesting should be considered when (1) the market for the offering is stable, (2) the offering is not producing good profits, (3) the offering has a small or respectable market share that is becoming increasingly difficult or costly to defend from competitive inroads, and (4) the offering provides benefits to the organization in terms of image or "full-line" capabilities, despite poor future potential.

Outright abandonment, or elimination, means that the offering is dropped from the mix of organizational offerings. Generally speaking, if the answer to each of the following questions is "very little" or "none," then an offering is a candidate for elimination.

1. What is the future sales potential of the offering?
2. How much is the offering contributing to the overall profitability of the offering mix?

3. How much is the offering contributing to the sale of other offerings in the mix?
4. How much could be gained by modifying the offering?
5. What would be the effect on channel members and buyers?

■ POSITIONING OFFERINGS

A second major offering-related decision confronting the manager concerns the positioning of offerings. *Positioning* is the act of designing an organization's offering and image so that it occupies a distinct and valued place in the target customer's mind relative to competitive offerings. There are a variety of positioning strategies available, including positioning by (1) attribute or benefit, (2) use or application, (3) product or service user, (4) product or service class, (5) competitors, and (6) price and quality.[8]

Positioning Strategies

Positioning an offering by attributes or benefits is the strategy most frequently used. Positioning an offering by attributes requires determining which attributes are important to target markets, which attributes are being emphasized by competitors, and how the offering can be fitted into this offering-target market environment. This kind of positioning may be accomplished by designing an offering that contains appropriate attributes or by stressing the appropriate attributes if they already exist in the offering. This latter tactic has been employed by a number of cereal manufacturers, who have emphasized the "naturalness" of their products in response to the growing interest in nutrition among a sizable number of cereal buyers.

In practice, operationalizing the positioning concept requires the development of a matrix relating attributes of the offering to market segments. Using toothpaste as an example, Exhibit 5.2 on page 136 shows how particular attributes may vary in importance for different market segments.[9] Several benefits accrue from viewing the market for toothpaste in this manner. First, the marketing manager can spot potential opportunities for new offerings and determine if a market niche exists. Second, looking at offering attributes and their importance to market segments permits subjective estimation of the extent to which a new offering might cannibalize existing offerings. If two offerings emphasize the same attributes, then they can be expected to compete with each other for the same market segment. Alternatively, if the offerings have different mixes of attributes, they probably will appeal to different segments. For this reason, Procter & Gamble's introduction of Crest tartar-control-formula toothpaste for adults did not have a major adverse effect on its sales of the existing Crest toothpaste for children. Third, the competitive response to a new offering can be judged more effectively using this framework. By determining which brands serve specific markets, one can evaluate offerings in terms of financial strength and market acceptance.

Organizations can also position their offerings by use or application. Arm & Hammer used this approach to position its baking powder as an odor-destroying agent in refrigerators and a water softener in swimming pools. Public television was originally positioned as a source of educational and cultural programming.

Positioning by user is a third strategy. This strategy typically associates a product or service with a user group. Federal Express positions its delivery service for the busy executive. Certain deodorant brands position themselves for females (Jean Naté by Charles of the Ritz), whereas others focus on males (Brut by Fabergé).

EXHIBIT 5.2

Attributes and Marketing Segment Positioning

	Market Segments			
Toothpaste Attributes	*Children*	*Teens, Young Adults*	*Family*	*Adults*
Flavor	*			
Color	*			
Whiteness of teeth		*		
Fresh breath		*		
Decay prevention			*	
Price			*	
Plaque prevention				*
Stain prevention				*
Principal brands for each segment	Aim, Stripe	Ultra Brite, McCleans	Colgate, Crest	Topol, Pearl Drops

Note: An asterisk (*) indicates principal benefits sought by each market segment.

Products and services can be positioned by product or service class as well. For example, margarine brands position themselves against butter. Savings associations position themselves as "banks."

An organization can position itself or its offerings directly against competitors. Avis positions itself against Hertz in the rental car business. Sabroso, a coffee liqueur, positions itself against Kahlua. For many years, the National Pork Producers Council positioned their product as being like poultry: "Pork: The Other White Meat." Often a political candidate will position himself or herself against the opponent.

Finally, positioning along a price-quality continuum is also possible. Hewlett-Packard consciously prices its line of office personal computers below Compaq and IBM in an attempt to convey a "value" position among corporate buyers. Ford Motor Company, on the other hand, has pursued a quality positioning stance evidenced by its "Quality Is Job One" advertising program.

The challenge facing a manager is deciding which positioning strategy is most appropriate in a given situation. The choice of a strategy is made easier when the following three questions are considered. First, who are the likely competitors, what positions have they staked out in the marketplace, and how strong are they? Second, what are the preferences of the target consumers sought and how do these consumers perceive the offerings of competitors? Finally, what position, if any, do we already have in the target consumer's mind? Once answered, attention can then be focused on a series of implementation questions:

1. What position do we want to own?
2. What competitors must be outperformed if we are to establish the position?
3. Do we have the marketing resources to occupy and hold the position?

The success of a positioning strategy depends on a number of factors. First, the position selected must be clearly communicated to targeted customers. Second, as the development of a position is a lengthy and often expensive process, frequent positioning changes should be avoided. Finally, and perhaps most important, the position taken in the marketplace should be sustainable and profitable.

Repositioning

Repositioning is necessary when the initial positioning of a product, service, or organization is no longer competitively sustainable or profitable or when better positioning opportunities arise. However, given the time and cost to establish a new position, repositioning is not advisable without careful study.

Examples of successful repositionings include the efforts of Johnson & Johnson's Baby Shampoo and Carnival Cruise Lines. Johnson & Johnson repositioned its shampoo from one used for babies to a shampoo for adults who wash their hair frequently and therefore needed a mild shampoo. This repositioning led to almost a five-fold increase in market share for the shampoo. Carnival Cruise Lines repositioned itself from a vacation alternative for older people to a "Fun Ship" for younger adults and families. After expanding its service offering to include Las Vegas–style shows, Camp Carnival, and Nautica Spa programs, Carnival became the largest and most successful company in the cruise industry.[10]

■ BRANDING OFFERINGS AND BRAND EQUITY

Branding offerings is a third responsibility of marketing managers. A brand name is any word, "device" (design, sound, shape, or color), or combination of these that are used to identify an offering and set it apart from competing offerings. The major managerial implication of branding offerings is that consumer goodwill, derived from buyer satisfaction and favorable associations with a brand, can lead to *brand equity*—the added value a brand name bestows on a product or service beyond the functional benefits provided.[11] This value has two distinct marketing advantages for the brand owner. First, brand equity provides a competitive advantage, such as the Sunkist label that signifies quality citrus fruit and the Gatorade name that defines sports drinks. A second advantage is that consumers are often willing to pay a higher price for a product or service with brand equity. Brand equity, in this instance, is represented by the premium a consumer will pay for one brand over another when the functional benefits provided are identical. Duracell batteries, Coca-Cola, Kleenex facial tissues, Louis Vuitton luggage, Lexus cars, Bose audio systems, and Microsoft software all enjoy a price premium arising from brand equity.

Brand equity also provides a financial advantage for the brand owner.[12] Successful, established brand names, such as Gillette, Nike, IBM, and Campbell's, have an economic value in the sense that they represent intangible assets. These assets enable their owner to enjoy a competitive advantage, to create earnings and cash flows in excess of the return on its tangible (plant and equipment) assets, and to achieve a high rate of return relative to competitors. The recognition that brands are assets and have an economic value is apparent in the strategic marketing decision to buy and sell brands. For example, Procter & Gamble bought the Hawaiian Punch brand from Del Monte in 1990 for $150 million and sold it to Cadbury Schweppes in 1999 for $203 million. This example illustrates that brands, unlike tangible assets that depreciate with time and use, appreciate in value when effectively managed. However, brands can lose value as well when they are not managed properly. The purchase and sale of Snapple brand noncarbonated fruit-flavored drinks and iced tea by Quaker Oats is a case in point. Quaker bought Snapple for $1.7 billion in 1994, only to sell it to Triarc Companies in 1997 for $300 million. The challenge of brand valuation is illustrated in the case study, Frito-Lay Company: Cracker Jack, at the end of this chapter.

Branding Decisions

Two branding decisions commonly confront marketing managers. The first relates to the strategy used to assign brands to multiple offerings or multiple lines of offerings. A manufacturer must decide whether to assign one brand name to *all* of the organization's offerings (such as General Electric), to assign one brand name to *each line* of offerings (Sears' appliances are Kenmore, and Sears' tools are Craftsman), or to assign individual names to *each offering* (Tide, Cheer, and Oxydol are all laundry detergents sold by Procter & Gamble). The branding strategy selected will depend on the consistency of the offering mix. If the offerings are related in terms of needs satisfied, then a common (family) brand strategy is often favored. A common brand name for offerings is also likely to be selected if the organization wishes to establish dominance in a class of product or service offerings, as in the case of Campbell soups. The decision to use a single brand name has certain advantages and disadvantages. Among the advantages is the fact that it is usually easier to introduce new offerings when the brand name is familiar to buyers—an outgrowth of brand equity. However, a single brand name strategy can have a negative effect on existing offerings if a new offering is a failure.

Some companies employ *sub-branding,* which combines a family brand with a new brand, when introducing new product or service offerings. The intent is to build on the favorable associations consumers have toward the family brand while differentiating the new offering. For example, ThinkPad is a sub-brand to the IBM name. Quaker Oats has recently used sub-branding for Gatorade with the introduction of Gatorade Frost and Gatorade Fierce, with unique flavors developed for each.

The second branding decision relates to supplying an intermediary with its own brand name. From the intermediary's perspective, the decision is whether or not to carry its own brands. Distributors favor carrying their own brands for a number of reasons.[13] By carrying a private brand, a distributor avoids price competition to some extent, since no other distributor carries an identical brand that consumers can use for comparison purposes. Also, any buyer goodwill attributed to an offering accrues to the distributor, and buyer loyalty to the offering is tied to the distributor, not the producer. If a distributor desires a private brand, it must locate a producer willing to manufacture the brand. A marketing manager is then placed in the position of having to decide whether to be the producer. A potential producer of private brands, or distributor brands, should consider a number of factors when making this decision.[14] If a producer has excess manufacturing capacity and the variable costs of producing a distributor's brand do not exceed the sale price, the possibility exists for making a contribution to overhead and utilizing production facilities. Even though a distributor's brand will often compete directly with a producer's brand, the combined sales of the brands and the profit contribution to the producer may be greater than if a competitor obtained the rights to produce the distributor brand. For these reasons and others, firms such as H. J. Heinz, Ralston Purina, and Dial produce private brands of pet foods, cereals, and bar soap for their distributors. However, a danger in producing private brands is the possibility of becoming too reliant on private-brand revenue, only to have it curtailed when a distributor switches suppliers or builds its own production plant. Overreliance on distributor brands will also affect trade relationships between a producer and distributor. As a generalization, the influence of a producer, in terms of price and channel leadership, is inversely related to the proportion of its output or revenue obtained from a distributor's brand.

Brand Growth Strategies

An organization has four strategic options for growing its brands (see Exhibit 5.3).[15] The options are dictated by whether a marketing manager wishes to extend existing

EXHIBIT 5.3

Brand Growth Strategies

		Product/Service Class Served by the Organization	
		New Product Class	*Existing Product Class*
Brand Name	*New Brand*	New Brand Strategy	Fighting/Flanker Brand Strategy
	Existing Brand	Brand Extension Strategy	Line Extension Strategy

brands or develop new brands and whether the manager chooses to deploy these brands in product classes presently served or not served by the organization.

The most frequently employed brand growth strategy is a *line extension strategy*. Line extensions occur when an organization introduces additional offerings with the same brand in a product class that it currently serves. New flavors, forms, colors, different ingredients or features, and package sizes are examples of line extensions. As an example, Campbell Soup Company offers regular Campbell soup, home-cooking style, chunky, and "healthy request" varieties, more than 100 soup flavors, and several different package sizes in the prepared soup product class. Line extensions respond to customers' desire for variety. They are also used to eliminate gaps in a product line that might be filled by competitive offerings or to neutralize competitive inroads. This strategy can also lower advertising and promotion costs because the same brand is used on all items, thus raising the level of brand awareness. Line extensions do involve risk. There is a likelihood of product cannibalism occurring rather than incremental volume gains as buyers substitute one item for another in the extended product line. Also, proliferation of offerings within a product line can create production and distribution problems and added costs without incremental sales. For example, just under 8 percent of personal-care and household products sold in the United States account for 84.5 percent of total sales. Such statistics led companies that market these products to prune their product lines in the late 1990s.[16]

Strong brand equity makes possible a *brand extension strategy*, the practice of using a current brand name to enter a completely different product class. This strategy can reduce the risk associated with introducing an offering in a new market by providing consumers the familiarity of and knowledge about an established brand. For instance, the equity in the Tylenol name as a trusted pain reliever allowed Johnson & Johnson to successfully extend this name to Tylenol Cold & Flu and Tylenol PM, a sleep aid. Fisher-Price, an established name in children's toys, was able to extend its name to children's shampoo and conditioners and baby bath and lotion products. Transferring an existing brand name to a new product class requires great care. For example, research indicates that the perceptual fit of the brand with and the transfer of the core product benefit to the new product class must exist for a brand extension to be successful. This happened with Tylenol and Fisher-Price, and both ventures produced sizable sales volume gains for the brands. However, it did not with Levi business attire and Dunkin Donuts cereal. Both efforts failed. Even successful brand extensions involve a risk. Too many uses for one brand name can dilute the meaning of a brand for consumers. Some marketing analysts claim this has happened to the Arm & Hammer brand given its extension to toothpaste, laundry detergent, cat litter, air freshener, carpet deodorizer, antiperspirant, and chewing gum.[17]

A variation on brand extensions is the practice of *co-branding*, the pairing of two brand names of two manufacturers on a single product. For example, Hershey Foods has teamed with General Mills to offer a co-branded breakfast cereal called Reese's Peanut Butter Puffs and with Nabisco to provide Chips Ahoy cookies using Hershey's chocolate morsels. Citibank co-brands MasterCard and Visa with American Airlines and Ford. Co-branding benefits firms by allowing them to enter new product classes and capitalize on an already established brand name in those product classes.

In situations in which an organization concludes that its existing brand name(s) cannot be extended to a new product class, a new brand strategy is appropriate. A *new brand strategy* involves the development of a new brand and often a new offering for a product class that has not been previously served by the organization. Examples of successful new brand strategies include the introduction of Prego spaghetti sauce by Campbell Soup, and Aleve, a nonprescription pain reliever, by Roche Holding, Ltd. In both examples, existing company brand names were not deemed extendable to the new product classes for which they were targeted.

A new brand strategy may be the most challenging to successfully implement and the most costly. The cost to introduce a new brand in some consumer markets ranges from $50 million to $100 million. In many ways, this strategy is akin to diversification, with all the attendant challenges associated with this product-market strategy. The marketing of Eagle brand snacks by Anheuser-Busch described in Chapter 1 is an example of a new brand strategy failure. Launching a new brand (Eagle) in a product class new to the company (salty snacks) meant competing with Frito-Lay, the market leader, and its well-entrenched brands. Without a cost/price or quality advantage, focused distribution, effective advertising, promotion, or sales effort, the Eagle brand never achieved more than a modest market share and operated at a loss for 17 years before its demise in 1996.[18]

Sometimes new brands are created for a product class already served by the organization when a line extension strategy is deemed inappropriate. These brands expand the product line to tap specific consumer segments not attracted to an organization's existing products/brands or represent defensive moves to counteract competition. As the name suggests, a *flanker brand strategy* involves adding new brands on the high or low end of a product line based on a price–quality continuum. The Marriott Hotel group has done this to attract different traveler segments. In addition to its medium-priced Marriott hotels, it has added Marriott Marquis hotels to attract the upper end of the traveler market. It has added Courtyard hotels for the economy-minded traveler and the Fairfield Inn for those with a very low travel budget. Each brand offers a different amenities assortment and a corresponding room rate. A *fighting brand strategy* involves adding a new brand whose sole purpose is to confront competitive brands in a product class being served by an organization. A fighting brand is typically introduced when (1) an organization has a high relative share of the sales in a product class, (2) its dominant brand(s) is susceptible to having this high share sliced away by aggressive pricing or promotion by competitors, or (3) the organization wishes to preserve its profit margins on its existing brand(s). Frito-Lay successfully used its Santitas brand tortilla chip as a fighting brand to confront lower-price and lower-quality regional tortilla chip brands. This was done without changing the premium price and quality of its flagship Doritos and Tostitos brand tortilla chips. Similarly, Kodak introduced its Funtime brand of film priced 20 percent below its dominant Kodak brand to compete against lower-priced film sold by Fuji and Konica.

Like line extensions, fighting and flanker brand strategies incur the risk of cannibalizing the other brand(s) in a product line. This is particularly likely with lower-priced brands. However, advocates of these brand strategies argue that it is better to engage in *preemptive cannibalism*—the conscious practice of stealing sales from an organization's existing products or brands to keep customers from switching to competitors' offerings—than lose sales volume.[19]

NOTES

1. "SBC to Launch Phone-Service 'Bundles' in Two Markets to Compete with AT&T," *Wall Street Journal* (August 24, 1999): B8.
2. "Film vs. Digital: Can Kodak Build a Bridge?" *Business Week* (August 2, 1999): 66-69.
3. Glenn Rifkin, "Mach 3: Anatomy of Gillette's Latest Global Launch," *Strategy & Business* (2nd quarter 1999): 34-41.
4. "Royal Crown Co. to Launch a 'Premium' Cola," *Wall Street Journal* (June 13, 1995): B10.
5. For an extended treatment of the new product development process, see C. Merle Crawford, *New Products Management*, 5th ed. (Chicago: Richard D. Irwin, 1997).
6. "A Survey of Innovation in Industry," *The Economist* (February 20, 1999): special supplement; and Greg A. Stevens and James Burley, "3,000 Raw Ideas = 1 Commercial Success!" *Research-Technology Management* (May-June 1997): 16-27.
7. B. Johnson, "Wash-day Washout," *Advertising Age* (June 3, 1991): 24.
8. Portions of the following discussion are based on Rajeev Batra, John G. Myers, and David A. Aaker, *Advertising Management,* 5th ed. (Upper Saddle River, NJ: Prentice Hall, 1996): 190-201.
9. This example is adapted from Russell Haley, "Benefit Segmentation: A Decision-Oriented Research Tool," in Ben Enis and Keith Cox (eds.), *Marketing Classics*, 7th ed. (Boston: Allyn and Bacon, 1991): 208-15.
10. "Few Icebergs on the Horizon," *Business Week* (June 14, 1999): 80-81.
11. For an extended discussion on brand equity, see Kevin Lane Keller, *Strategic Brand Management: Building, Measuring, and Managing Brand Equity* (Upper Saddle River, NJ: Prentice Hall, 1998).
12. This discussion is based on Roger A. Kerin and Raj Sethuraman, "Exploring the Brand Value-Shareholder Value Nexus for Consumer Goods Companies," *Journal of the Academy of Marketing Science* (Winter 1998): 260-73; "P & G Sells to Cadbury Hawaiian Punch Label in $203 Million Accord," *Wall Street Journal* (April 16, 1999): B2; and "Will Triarc Make Snapple Crackle?" *Business Week* (April 28, 1997): 64.
13. Stephanie Thompson, "The New Private Enterprise," *BRANDWEEK* (May 3, 1999): 36-48.
14. An argument for private branding by manufacturers is found in David Dunne and Chakravarthi Narasimhan, "The New Appeal of Private Labels," *Harvard Business Review* (May-June 1999): 41-52.
15. For different views on brand growth strategies, see David C. Court, Mark G. Leitter, and Mark A. Loch, "Brand Leverage," *The McKinsey Quarterly* (number 2, 1999): 100-110; John A. Quelch and David Kenny, "Extend Profits, Not Product Lines," *Harvard Business Review* (September-October 1994): 153-60; "Attack of the Fighting Brands," *Business Week* (May 2, 1994): 125.
16. "Make It Simple," *Business Week* (September 9, 1996): 96-105.
17. "When Brand Extension Becomes Brand Abuse," *BRANDWEEK* (October 26, 1998): 20-22.
18. "How Eagle Became Extinct," *Business Week* (March 4, 1996): 68-69.
19. For an extended discussion on product cannibalism and preemptive cannibalism, see Roger A. Kerin and Dwight Riskey, "Product Cannibalism," in Sidney Levy, ed., *Marketing Manager's Handbook* (Chicago: Dartnell Company, 1994): 880-95.

CASE

Zoëcon Corporation

Insect Growth Regulators

In January 1986, Zoëcon Corporation executives met to assess future growth and profit opportunities for its Strike® brand insect growth regulator (IGR) called Strike ROACH ENDER®. The meeting was prompted by a recent change in top management and corporate objectives, which now emphasized a focus on high financial-return businesses and products.

The first item on the agenda was the marketing program for Strike ROACH ENDER. This product had been in a consumer test market for six months in four cities: Charleston, South Carolina; Beaumont, Texas; Charlotte, North Carolina; and New Orleans, Louisiana. The results of the test market and future directions for the product were to be discussed. Ideas had already surfaced in informal meetings, however. Some executives believed Zoëcon (pronounced Zoy-con) should expand distribution of Strike ROACH ENDER to 19 cities in April 1986, with the intent of distributing the product nationally in April 1987. Other executives felt that Zoëcon should concentrate its effort on opportunities in the professional pest control market. Still other executives held the view that Zoëcon should reconsider any plans to market the product itself. Rather, these executives said Zoëcon should sell its IGR compound to firms actively engaged in reaching the consumer insecticide market. These firms included d-Con Company, S. C. Johnson and Son (Raid), and Boyle-Midway Division of American Home Products (Black Flag).

Further discussions indicated that some alternatives were mutually exclusive and others were not. For example, Zoëcon could sell to the consumer market under the Strike name or through other firms and also distribute its IGR to professional pest control operators. However, if Zoëcon was able to sell its IGR compound to, say, d-Con, then selling Strike ROACH ENDER would be infeasible. According to one Zoëcon executive, "The decision is basically how can we best allocate our technical, financial, and marketing resources for our IGR compounds."

■ ZOËCON CORPORATION

Zoëcon Corporation was founded in 1968 in Palo Alto, California, by Dr. Carl Djerassi to research endocrinological methods of insect population control. Djerassi was a pioneer in the development of chemical methods for human birth control, which subsequently led to the introduction of the birth control pill. The name Zoëcon is a combination of the Greek words *zoe* for life and *con* for control.

Zoëcon Corporation was acquired in 1983 by Sandoz, Ltd., a Swiss-based producer of pharmaceuticals, agrichemicals, and colors and dyes. Zoëcon's mission was to be the marketing arm of Sandoz, Ltd., in the animal health and insect control areas.

This case was prepared by Dr. Larry Smith, graduate student, under the supervision of Professor Roger A. Kerin, of the Edwin L. Cox School of Business, Southern Methodist University, as a basis for classroom discussion and is not designed to illustrate effective or ineffective handling of an administrative situation. Certain names and data have been disguised. The cooperation of Zoëcon Corporation in the preparation of this case is gratefully acknowledged.

EXHIBIT 1

Selected Zoëcon Products and Applications

Brand/Product	*Target Insects and Rodents*
Consumer	
Strike ROACH ENDER®	Cockroaches, fleas, ticks, mosquitoes, spiders, crickets
Strike FLEA ENDER®	
VAPORETTE® flea collars	
Methoprene	
Roach traps	
Insect strips	
Animal Health	
VET-KEM®—flea collars, dips, flea aerosols and foggers, flea powders, flea shampoos	Fleas, ticks, sarcoptic mange
ZODIAC®—flea collars, dips, flea aerosols and foggers, flea powders, flea and regular shampoos	
STARBAR®—flybait; cattle dusts, sprays, and dips; swine dusts, sprays, and dips; insect strips; rodenticides; pet products; Altosid® feed-through	Houseflies, cattle hornflies, grubs, lice, mosquitoes, rats and mice, fleas, ticks, and sarcoptic mange
Pest Control	
SAFROTIN®	Cockroaches, fleas, houseflies, pharaoh ants, stored-product pests, tobacco moths, cigarette beetles, mosquitoes, and blackflies
PRECOR®	
GENCOR®	
FLYTEK®	
PHARORID®	
DIANEX®	
KABAT®	
ALTOSID®	
TEKNAR®	

Source: Company records. STRIKE, ROACH ENDER, FLEA ENDER, VAPORETTE, VET-KEM, ZODIAC, STARBAR, SAFROTIN, PRECOR, GENCOR, FLYTEK, PHARORID, DIANEX, KABAT, ALTOSID, and TEKNAR are trademarks of Sandoz, Ltd.

Zoëcon sells (1) animal health products to small-animal veterinarians and clinics, (2) pest control chemicals for farm animals, (3) insecticides for household pets and pest control to supermarkets, pet stores, veterinarians, and pest control companies, and (4) products and chemical compounds to firms engaged in marketing pest control products to the consumer market. For example, Zoëcon produces the chemicals for the Black Flag Roach Motel sold by Boyle-Midway. The company recorded $100 million in sales from these products and a 25 percent pretax profit on sales. A partial list of company products and applications is shown in Exhibit 1.

■ INSECT CONTROL

The use of chemical toxins to control insect pests is commonplace. Although these toxins are potentially harmful to people as well as insects, recent advances in chemistry have reduced the threat to people. Surviving insects, however, may produce successive generations that are resistant to toxins.

Public concern over the toxic effect of agricultural and household insecticides has remained widespread despite the advances in chemistry. In particular, consumers have evidenced increasing concern that safer household insecticides be used where children and pets might come in contact with the residual chemicals. The demand for safer compounds caused a change in the focus of research and development from new insect adulticides, which kill adult insects, to chemical compounds that disrupt insect reproduction.

Insect Life Cycles

Insects reproduce by laying eggs. The life patterns after hatching from the egg vary among different insect species. The flea has a complete metamorphic cycle, passing in sequence through the egg, larval, and pupal stages to the adult stage in 23 days. Cockroach metamorphosis is incomplete. Wingless nymphs hatch from eggs and grow by shedding their exoskeletons, molting six times through six nymphal stages, called instars. Molting of the sixth instar produces winged, sexually mature adult roaches in 74 days.

Metamorphosis is controlled by the insect's endocrine system. In fleas, hormones regulate development and transition from larval to pupal to adult stages. Analogously, in roaches, molting is initiated when the brain produces a neurohormone that activates prothoracic gland production of a molting hormone. Additionally, a juvenile hormone is produced by the brain in decreasing amounts, until at the sixth and final molt no juvenile hormone is produced. This molting produces sexually mature adult cockroaches up to two inches long.

The life cycle of the cockroach is shown in Exhibit 2. It begins with formation of about 40 eggs in a capsule called an ootheca. The adult female produces one

EXHIBIT 2

Normal Life Cycle of the Cockroach

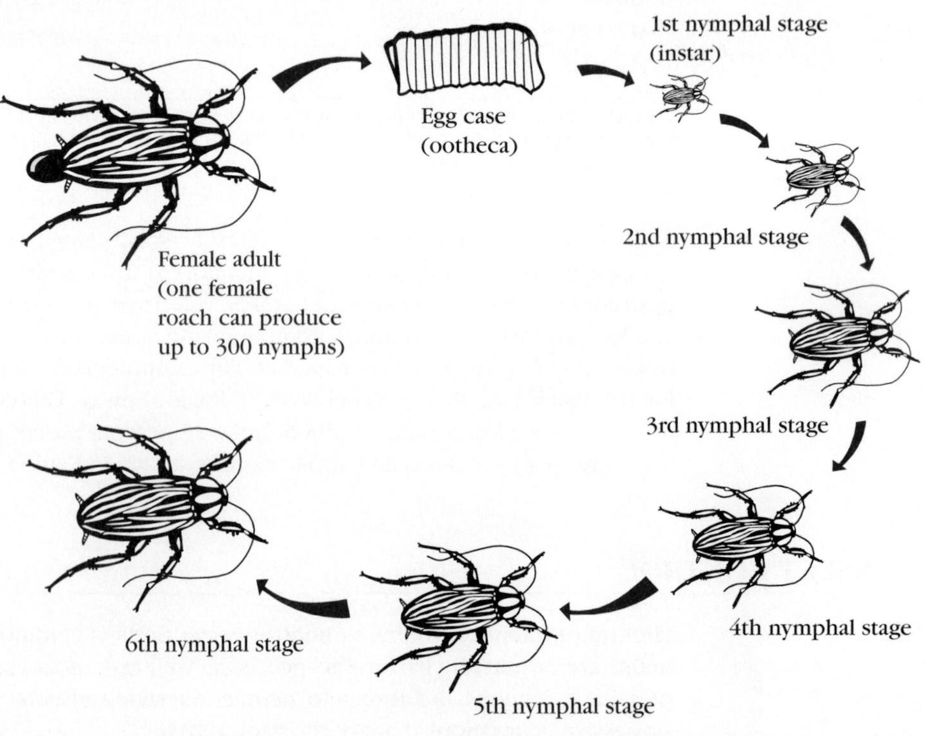

ootheca every 23 days over an average life span of 150 days, for a total of about 260 roaches. Research on cockroaches indicates that a roach population will increase geometrically if ample food, water, and shelter are available. Research also indicates that roaches are omnivorous and have a particular liking for beer.

Insect Growth Regulators

Insect growth regulators are effective against insects that are problems as adults, such as cockroaches. Roaches have been shown to carry bacteria, viruses, fungi, and protozoa, which cause diseases such as food poisoning, diarrhea, dysentery, hepatitis B, polio, and encephalitis. They are also capable of carrying organisms causing cholera, plague, typhus, leprosy, and tuberculosis. Furthermore, in susceptible individuals, cockroach contaminations may produce allergic reactions similar to hay fever, asthma, food allergies, and dermatitis.

Insect growth regulators are synthetic analogs of the natural insect juvenile hormones produced in the normal sequence of metamorphosis. The concentration of juvenile hormone produced decreases with each molting, to permit emergence of an adult insect after the pupal stage (for fleas) or after the last nymph stage (for roaches). If the larva or nymph is exposed to an IGR during the stage prior to molting, however, subsequent development into an adult is prevented or altered. Fleas exposed to an IGR during the larval stage pupate but fail to emerge to continue the reproductive cycle. Similarly, cockroaches exposed to an IGR in the sixth instar molt will become deformed, sexually immature adults incapable of reproducing.

As chemicals, IGRs are much less toxic than compounds typically used in household insecticides. Because they are synthetic chemical analogs of juvenile hormones specific to insects, they are not physiologically active in human or animal endocrine systems.

IGRs are extremely effective in eliminating insect populations. Only a few tenths of a milligram per square foot is required for effective control of insect reproduction. When an IGR is combined with an adulticide, many insects are killed and those that survive are prohibited from reproducing. In time, an insect infestation is controlled and, ideally, eliminated.

A unique feature of IGRs is that the immediate effects of an application are not observable. That is, since an IGR affects the reproductive cycle of an insect, it does not kill insects that come in contact with the compound. Controlled tests of a cockroach IGR indicate that a significant reduction in roach population occurs after 120 days and continues with applications spaced at 120-day intervals. When the IGR is combined with an adulticide, adult roaches and nymphs are killed upon contact with the adulticide. Short-term residual effects of the adulticide can repel roaches from treated areas, however. Therefore, the adulticide can hamper the effect of an IGR, since insects avoid treated areas.

PREMISE INSECTICIDE MARKET

The premise insecticide market is divided into two segments: the consumer market and the professional pest control market. The distinction is based on distribution systems and product forms. Insecticides for the consumer market are packaged in easy-to-use, do-it-yourself containers sold mostly through supermarkets. The professional pest control market consists of sales of insecticides, often in diluted form, to professional applicators. Orkin and Terminix are examples of professional applicators.

Consumer Market

Estimated annual sales for all consumer-disbursed insecticides in 1985 were $400 million at manufacturers' prices. Sales were forecasted to grow at an average rate of 10 percent per year through 1990. S. C. Johnson and Son, Inc. captured 45 percent of this market with its Raid brand. The Boyle-Midway Division of American Home Products accounted for 12 percent of the market with Black Flag, and d-Con Company captured 10 percent. No other company had a market share greater than 8 percent.

Supermarkets accounted for 70 percent of insecticide sales, followed by drugstores (9 percent) and a host of other retailers such as home improvement centers and house and garden outlets (21 percent). Aerosol sprays, including foggers, were the preferred method for applying insecticides and accounted for 74 percent of retail sales. Liquid sprays followed with 14 percent. Solids, strips, pastes, traps, and baits generated 12 percent of retail sales. Differences in packaging were based on consumers' preferences for quick-kill, residual control, or a margin of safety. Quick-kill dominated the consumer mindset, hence the popularity of aerosols and liquids that allowed for a "chase and squirt" routine when a roach was seen.

The consumer market was further subdivided into insect-specific insecticides. Ant and roach killers captured 40 percent of the market, flying insect killers 20 percent, flea killers 11 percent, and other insect-specific products 29 percent.

As expected, household insecticide sales were seasonal and varied by geography. The six-month period from May through October was the prime sales time for insecticides; 75 percent of annual sales were made during this period. The southern tier of 14 states (from the East Coast to the West Coast) accounted for 50 percent of annual sales.

Insecticides sold to the consumer market are heavily promoted. In 1983, the most recent year for which advertising expenditures were available, manufacturers spent $28.6 million for magazine, newspaper, television, radio, and outdoor advertising. For example, it was estimated that S. C. Johnson and Son spent $1.4 million to advertise Raid Ant & Roach Killer, Roach and Flea Killer, and Roach Traps. Boyle-Midway spent almost $3 million to advertise its Black Flag Roach & Ant Killer and Roach Motel. Past history of product introductions indicated that a minimum $10 million promotion investment was required to successfully launch a new product when consumers were familiar with the brand name.

Professional Pest Control Market

The professional pest control market produced revenues of $2.5 billion in 1985. Revenues were forecasted to be $3.7 billion in 1990, representing an annual average growth rate of 8 percent. About 6 percent of the revenues produced by pest control operators (PCOs) were accounted for by chemical compound cost.

The majority (52 percent) of professional pest control revenues resulted from general insect control (for example, of cockroaches, fleas, or ants). Termite control accounted for 21 percent of professional pest control revenues. The remaining 27 percent were from specialty pest control applications, especially rodent control.

This market was dominated by many small PCOs. There were an estimated 14,000 PCOs, of which only two (Orkin and Terminix) had annual sales greater than $100 million. About 28 PCOs had annual sales greater than $3 million, whereas over 6,000 had revenues under $50,000 annually.

Insecticides were sold to PCOs through distributors. These distributors purchased insecticides in bulk quantities (cases and pallets) from producers and then sold them to PCOs in smaller quantities. These distributors typically received an average gross margin of 27 percent on the selling price to PCOs. Although percentages varied, industry sources estimated that the producer's average gross profit on chemicals sold to the professional pest control market was 51 percent. By comparison, the average gross profit on insecticides sold to the consumer market was 55 percent.

Producer marketing expenses associated with selling to the professional pest control market were small in comparison to the costs of selling to the consumer market. As a general rule, about 27 percent of sales were spent for marketing to PCOs. Most of these expenses were for trade advertising and sales efforts.

ZOËCON PRODUCT DEVELOPMENT AND MARKETING

From its beginning, Zoëcon made a large commitment to ongoing research on IGRs. By the mid-1970s, Zoëcon research scientists, who comprised more than 25 percent of the company's employees, had synthesized more than 1,250 IGRs, and 175 patents had been issued for these inventions.

Development and Marketing of Flea Compound

The first commercialized IGR, methoprene, was introduced in 1974 for mosquito control. This IGR was made available in a variety of product forms over the years for multiple control uses. In 1980, Zoëcon obtained EPA approval for the use of methoprene under the trade name PRECOR® as a flea control compound. Given the company's already established trade relations with PCOs, veterinary clinics, and pet stores, Zoëcon began selling its flea control compound to these outlets. By 1985, Zoëcon executives estimated that the company had captured 80 percent of all flea product sales made through these outlets. Some company executives attributed the success of PRECOR to the fact that PCOs, veterinarians, and pet store sales personnel could explain the unique benefits and application of methoprene.

The early success of PRECOR led Zoëcon to look for opportunities outside of PCOs, animal clinics, and pet stores. Market analysis revealed that supermarkets accounted for a rapidly growing percentage of flea product sales volume. Since Zoëcon had no significant experience dealing with supermarkets, it approached the makers of d-Con, Black Flag, and Raid products about including PRECOR in their products. Only d-Con expressed interest. In 1981, d-Con introduced Flea Stop, a fogger for fleas containing only PRECOR—no adulticide was included among the ingredients. Flea Stop sold well in supermarkets, given the sales and marketing support provided by d-Con.

PRECOR's success prompted Zoëcon to again approach the makers of Black Flag and Raid in 1982. No agreement could be reached, however. This setback resulted in the decision by Zoëcon to develop its own brand for sales through supermarkets. In early 1983, Zoëcon introduced Strike FLEA ENDER®, which includes PRECOR and an adulticide, in 19 cities that accounted for the majority of flea product sales. By late 1983, Strike FLEA ENDER had captured 11 percent of flea product sales in those cities. This success led to an agreement with S. C. Johnson and Son, in December 1983, to include PRECOR in its Raid Flea Killer Plus. This agreement allowed Zoëcon to continue marketing PRECOR under the STRIKE brand name. Strike FLEA ENDER had an 18 percent market share in 1985; however, the product had not yet achieved its profit objective.

Development and Marketing of Roach Compound

Continuing research efforts resulted in the development of hydroprene, an IGR that was particularly useful for preventing normal cockroach maturation. This discovery was viewed as a major breakthrough in the creation of synthetic chemical analogs of naturally occurring insect juvenile hormones. In early 1984, Zoëcon obtained Envi-

EXHIBIT 3

Strike ROACH ENDER Print Advertisement

ronmental Protection Agency (EPA) registrations for hydroprene. By late 1984, the company was marketing hydroprene under the GENCOR® trade name only to PCOs, since pet stores and veterinary clinics had little or no use for this compound.

In late 1984, Zoëcon executives responsible for Strike FLEA ENDER proposed that a hydroprene-based product with the name Strike ROACH ENDER® be introduced to supermarkets. This proposal requested that Strike ROACH ENDER, which would contain hydroprene and an adulticide, be introduced in the same 19 cities where Strike FLEA ENDER was being sold. Top management believed that an opportunity existed but that Strike ROACH ENDER should be test-marketed before an investment in all 19 markets was made. Accordingly, a test market plan was drafted in early 1985.

Test-Marketing Strike Roach Ender

Two objectives were set for the test market: to determine consumer acceptance of the product and to qualify the trade and consumer marketing program. The four cities chosen for the test were Charlotte, North Carolina; Charleston, South Carolina; Beaumont, Texas; and New Orleans, Louisiana. These cities were considered representative of the 19-city market where 80 percent of roach insecticides were sold. The cities contained 1.17 million households, or 5.3 percent of the 22 million households in that market area. The test market ran from May through October 1985. Product shipments to supermarkets in the four cities began in April.

Segmentation and Positioning Research on roach insecticide users indicated that three segments existed, based on the primary benefit sought. The primary target market for Strike ROACH ENDER was the "end problem permanently" segment. A secondary market was the "product that lasts" segment. The "convenience/low cost" segment was not considered a primary or secondary target.

Strike ROACH ENDER was positioned as a scientific breakthrough with unique qualities desired by the targeted segments. A print advertisement for the product is shown in Exhibit 3.

Product Packaging and Price Strike ROACH ENDER was packaged in a 10-ounce aerosol spray and a 6-ounce fogger. The retail price for the aerosol was $4.49 and for the fogger was $3.99. These prices were 50 to 75 percent higher than those of existing roach insecticides. The premium price was justified on the basis of the product's unique compound and long-lasting effect. The higher price also provided supermarkets with a higher margin than they received from competitive products. Price and cost data are shown in Exhibit 4.

Consumer and Trade Promotion Television and newspaper advertising was used to build consumer awareness, and cents-off coupons were employed to stimulate product trial. The consumer promotion and media strategy focused on 25- to 54-year-old women living in households of three or more. A "blitz" strategy was used, with the heaviest promotion scheduled for the first three months of the test. A public relations effort was also launched, featuring press kit mailings to newspapers, guest ap-

EXHIBIT 4

Strike ROACH ENDER Package Economics

	10-oz. Aerosol	*6-oz Fogger*
Price to trade[a]	$3.14	$2.79
Cost of goods sold[b]	1.41	1.26
Zoëcon's gross profit	$1.73	$1.53

[a] Price to trade is the price at which Zoëcon sells directly to the retailer.

[b] Cost of goods sold includes the cost of the can, solvent, propellant, active ingredients, and freight. Note that the cost of goods sold represents virtually all of the variable costs associated with the product forms.

EXHIBIT 5

Strike ROACH ENDER Trade Promotion

pearances on local radio and television talk shows, and an 800-number consumer hotline to answer consumers' questions.

The trade promotion included discounts for first-time supermarket buyers, a calendar to assist buyers in coordinating store promotion with consumer advertising, freestanding in-store displays, and sales aids. Exhibit 5 shows a Strike ROACH ENDER trade promotion.

Test-Market Expenditures and Results The cost of the test market was $1,478,000. An itemized summary is shown in Exhibit 6.

Results of the test market were tracked by an independent marketing research firm. At the end of the test in November 1985, 57 percent of the households in the test cities were aware of the product, 6 percent of the households in the test cities had tried the product, and 30 percent of those households that had tried the prod-

EXHIBIT 6

Summary of Marketing Expenses for the Strike ROACH ENDER Test Market

Activity	*Expense*
Promotion and advertising[a]	$1,016,000
Setup/auditing[b]	377,000
Marketing research[c]	65,000
Miscellaneous[d]	20,000
	$1,478,000

[a] Includes consumer advertising and promotion to supermarket buyers.

[b] Includes point-of-purchase materials, monitoring of shelf placement, sales aids, and free goods.

[c] Includes consumer tracking studies (for example, product awareness and purchase behavior).

[d] Includes public relations campaign.

uct had repurchased during the test period. The average number of units purchased by all trier households was 1.3 units. Households that repurchased bought an average of 3.5 units in addition to their initial purchase. Sixty-six percent of Strike ROACH ENDER sales were of the aerosol spray; 34 percent were of foggers. This breakdown was identical for first purchases and subsequent purchases. Product shipments data indicated that 11,700 cases (at 12 units per case) of 10-ounce aerosol units and 6,300 cases (at 12 units per case) of 6-ounce fogger units were shipped to supermarket warehouses in the four cities during the test period.

■ JANUARY MEETING

When Zoëcon executives met in January 1986, the first item on the agenda was to review the test-market results and prepare marketing plans for 1986. Different points of view had already been expressed in informal discussions among Zoëcon executives. One position advanced was that Strike ROACH ENDER distribution should be expanded to the 19 cities where Strike FLEA ENDER was being sold. Marketing research indicated that these 19 cities accounted for 80 percent of roach insecticide volume. These executives reasoned that the up-front investment in marketing research, public relations, and set-up/auditing costs would not have to be repeated in the expanded distribution. Rather, the primary direct costs associated with the rollout to all 19 cities would be for promotion and advertising.

A second view was that Zoëcon should direct its resources to PCOs. These executives noted that GENCOR® (hydroprene) had been well received by PCOs in late 1984 and many PCOs were promoting its benefits to their customers. These executives felt that an ongoing investment of $500,000 per year above the 27 percent of sales typically budgeted for trade advertising and sales efforts would accelerate its use.

A third opinion was that Zoëcon should pursue opportunities for selling hydroprene to the makers of d-Con, Black Flag, and Raid for use in their products. This strategy had worked in the past for PRECOR (methoprene). A product cost analysis performed on Strike ROACH ENDER indicated that the cost of goods sold for the 10-ounce aerosol package without hydroprene would be $0.80. For the 6-ounce fogger package without hydroprene, the cost of goods sold would also be $0.80. Furthermore, Zoëcon could realize a 50 percent gross margin on hydroprene sold to another insecticide marketer with no investment in marketing or sales. These costs would be absorbed by the marketer of the product—d-Con, Black Flag, or Raid. Executives favoring this option believed the test-market experience could be used to interest insecticide marketers in the product. Specific aspects of the proposal, including the price for hydroprene, would have to be developed if this option was adopted. Executives favoring the continued marketing of Strike ROACH ENDER cautioned that this action could spell the end for Zoëcon's presence in the consumer market.

Zoëcon executives present at the January 1986 meeting were acutely aware of the importance of the decision they faced. Moreover, the peak season for roach insecticides was approaching, and a decision needed to be made quickly.

CASE

Ms-Tique Corporation

On Friday, January 7, 2000, Phoebe Masters, the newly appointed Product Manager for hand and body lotions at Ms-Tique Corporation, was faced with her first decision one day after her promotion. She had to decide whether to introduce a new package design for the company's Soft and Silky Shaving Gel. The major questions were whether a $5^1/_2$-ounce or a 10-ounce aerosol container should be introduced and whether she should approve additional funds for a market test. Timing was critical because the incidence of women's shaving would increase during the spring months and reach its peak during the summer months.

THE COMPANY AND THE PRODUCT

Soft and Silky Shaving Gel is marketed by Ms-Tique Corporation, a manufacturer of women's personal-care products with sales of $225 million in 1999. The company's line of products includes facial creams, hand and body lotions, and a full line of women's toiletries. Products are sold by drug and food-and-drug stores through rack jobbers. Rack jobbers are actually wholesalers that set up retail displays and keep them stocked with merchandise. They receive a margin of 20 percent off the sales price to retailers.

Soft and Silky Shaving Gel was introduced in the spring of 1986. The product was viewed as a logical extension of the company's line of hand and body lotions and required few changes in packaging and manufacturing. The unique dimension of the introduction was that Soft and Silky Shaving Gel was positioned as a high-quality women's shaving gel. The positioning strategy was successful in differentiating Soft and Silky Shaving Gel from existing men's and women's shaving creams and gels at the time. Moreover, rack jobbers were able to obtain product placement in the women's personal-care section of drug and food-and-drug stores, thus emphasizing the product's positioning statement. Furthermore, placement apart from men's shaving products minimized direct price comparisons with men's shaving creams, since Soft and Silky Shaving Gel was premium-priced—with a suggested retail price of $3.95 per $5^1/_2$-ounce tube. Retailers received a 40 percent margin on the suggested retail selling price.

Soft and Silky Shaving Gel has been sold in a tube since its introduction. This packaging was adopted because the company did not have the technology to produce aerosol containers in 1986. Furthermore, the company's manufacturing policy was and continues to be to utilize existing production capacity whenever possible. As of early 2000, all products sold by Ms-Tique Corporation were packaged in tubes, bottles, or jars.

This case was prepared by Professor Roger A. Kerin, of the Edwin L. Cox School of Business, Southern Methodist University, as a basis for class discussion and is not designed to illustrate effective or ineffective handling of an administrative situation. Certain data and names have been disguised.

EXHIBIT 1

Soft and Silky Shaving Gel Income Statement for the Year Ending December 31, 1999

Sales		$3,724,000
Cost of goods sold (incl. freight)[a]		784,000
Gross profit		$2,940,000
Assignable costs:		
Advertising and promotion costs	$1,154,540	
Overhead and administrative costs	421,560	$1,576,100
Brand contribution		$1,363,900

[a] For analysis purposes, treat the cost of goods sold and freight cost as the only variable cost.

Soft and Silky Shaving Gel had been profitable from the time of its introduction. Although the market for women's shaving cream and gels was small, compared to men's shaving cream and gels, Soft and Silky's unique positioning had created a "customer franchise," in the words of Heather Courtwright, the Soft and Silky brand assistant. "We have a unique product for the feminine woman who considers herself special." Soft and Silky Shaving Gel sales were $3,724,000 in 1999 with a 1,960,000 unit volume (see Exhibit 1).

WOMEN'S SHAVING

Research on women's shaving commissioned by Masters' predecessors over the past decade had produced a number of findings useful in preparing annual marketing plans for Soft and Silky Shaving Gel. The major findings and selected marketing actions prompted by these findings are described below.

Methods of Hair Removal and Shaving Frequency

Women use a variety of methods for hair removal. The most popular method is simply shaving with razors and soap and water. Shaving with razors and shaving cream and gels is the next most used method, followed by shaving with electric razors. Women typically have their own razors and purchase their own supplies of blades. Approximately 45 million women shave with a razor; 15 million women use electric shavers.

Over 80 percent of women shave at least once per week, and women who work outside the home shave more frequently than those who do not. On average, women shave eleven times per month and shave nine times more skin than men per shaving occasion (men shave 24 times per month on average). Shaving frequency varies by season, with the summer months producing the greatest shaving activity (see Exhibit 2). Accordingly, in-store promotions and multipack deals were scheduled during the summer.

Attitudes Toward Shaving

Women view shaving as a necessary evil. When queried about their ideal shaving cream or gel, women typically respond that they want a product that contains a moisturizer, reduces irritation, and makes shaving easier. It appears that four out of five women use a moisturizer after shaving.

EXHIBIT 2

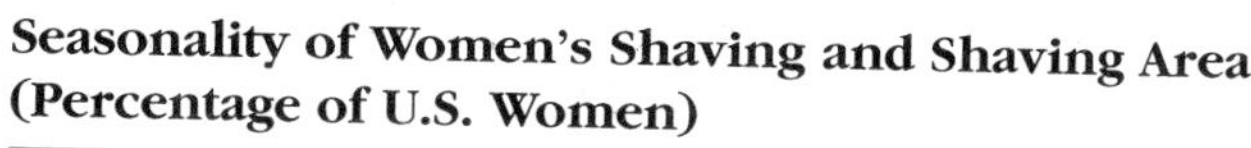

Seasonality of Women's Shaving and Shaving Area (Percentage of U.S. Women)

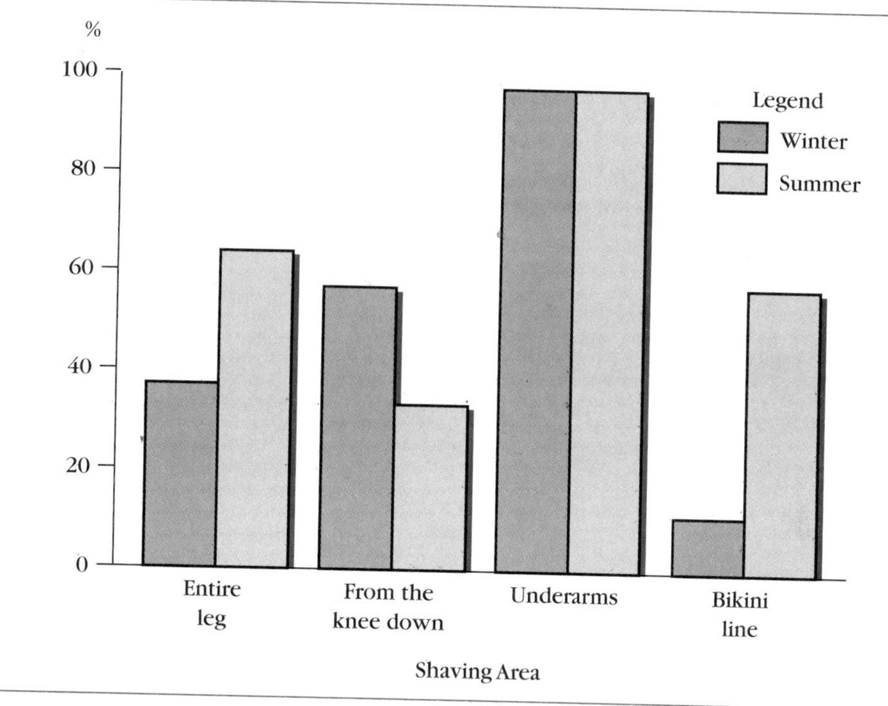

These specific findings resulted in a change in the Soft and Silky Shaving Gel ingredient formulation in 1990. Prior to 1990, the product contained only aloe. In 1990, three additional moisturizers were added to the product, including vitamin E. These ingredients were emphasized on the package and in-store promotions and media advertising.

Market Size and Competitive Products

Industry sources estimate the U.S. dollar value of women's "wet shaving" products to be over $300 million in 1999, at manufacturer's prices. Sales growth has been in the range of 3 to 5 percent per year since 1994. Razors account for the bulk of sales growth and annual sales.

Historically, women who used shaving cream or gels had few "women's-only" products to choose from. However, since 1994, a vibrant women's shaving cream and gel category has emerged due to new-product activity, increased advertising and promotion, and improved shaving technology. Some industry analysts pointed toward the introduction of Gillette's Sensor Razor for Women as one important growth stimulant. Other analysts cited improvements in the quality of shaving creams and gels for women and increased advertising. Until late 1993, only two competitive products were normally available in the drug and food-and-drug stores served by Ms-Tique Corporation rack jobbers. These products were S. C. Johnson's Skintimate (formerly called Soft Sense) and Soft Shave, a lotion sold by White Laboratories. By late 1999, seven major competing brands existed in the women's shaving cream or gel category even though all were not stocked by stores that carried Soft and Silky Shaving Gel. Exhibit 3 (page 156) shows representative brands, sizes, forms (cream, gel, lotion), and typical retail prices. Ms-Tique Corporation advertising and promotion for Soft and

EXHIBIT 3

Representative Women's Shaving Products

Brand (Manufacturer)	*Size*[a]	*Form*	*Price/Price per Oz.*
Skintimate (S. C. Johnson)	7 oz.	Gel	$2.48/$.35
Skintimate (S. C. Johnson)	10 oz.	Cream	$2.48/$.25
Satin Care (Gillette)	6 oz.	Gel	$1.97/$.33
Hers (Medtech Labs)	10 oz.	Cream	$1.78/$.18
Soft Shave (White Labs)	8 oz.	Lotion	$1.82/$.23
Barbasol Pure Silk (Pfizer)	7 oz.	Cream	$1.99/$.28
Aveeno (Ryoelle Labs-Div. of S. C. Johnson)	7 oz.	Gel	$3.69/$.53
Inverness Ultra-Lubricating Shaving Gel (Inverness Corp.)	6 oz.	Gel	$2.15/$.36
Soft and Silky Shaving Gel (Ms-Tique Corp.)	5.5 oz.	Gel	$3.95/$.72

[a] Several manufacturers also sold smaller 2, 2½, and 2¾ ounce sizes designed for travel purposes.

Silky Shaving Gel had responded to the increase in competition. Expenditures had increased each year since 1994, reaching 31 percent of sales in 1999.

By 1999, the dominant packaging for women's shaving cream or gels had become the aerosol container. Only a few shaving gels and brands were sold in tubes or plastic bottles, including Soft and Silky Shaving Gel, Soft Shave lotion, and Inverness Ultra-Lubricating Shaving Gel.

NEW PACKAGE DESIGN

The idea for a new package design was provided by Masters' brand assistant, Heather Courtwright. She originally proposed the new package to Masters' predecessor in July 1999. Her recommendation was based on four developments. First, unit sales volume for Soft and Silky Shaving Gel had declined and then plateaued in recent years (see Exhibit 4). Second, the growth of Soft and Silky Shaving Gel had strained manufacturing capacity. In the past, production of Soft and Silky Shaving Gel had been easily integrated into the firm's production schedules. However, growth in the entire line of hand and body lotions, coupled with Soft and Silky Shaving Gel sales, had overburdened production capacity and scheduling. Moreover, inspection of shipping records indicated that the product's fill rate (that is, Ms-Tique Corporation's ability to supply quantities requested by retailers) had dropped, leading to out-of-stock situations and lost sales. Third, the company had no manufacturing capacity expansion plans for the next three years. And finally, the aerosol packaging had become the dominant design for women's shaving creams and gels by 1999.

Courtwright's observations prompted a preliminary study of outsourcing opportunities for a new package design. Her study included visits to several firms specializing in "contract filling" and requests for production proposals. A contract filler purchases cans, propellants, caps, and valves from a variety of sources and then assembles these components, including the product fill (that is, shaving gel), into the final container. The production method is called pressure filling. In this method, the cap and valve are inserted in the can and then sealed. At the same time, a vacuum is created in the container. The product fill and propellant are then injected under high pressure through the valve into the can.

EXHIBIT 4

Soft and Silky Shaving Gel Unit Sales Volume, 1986–1999

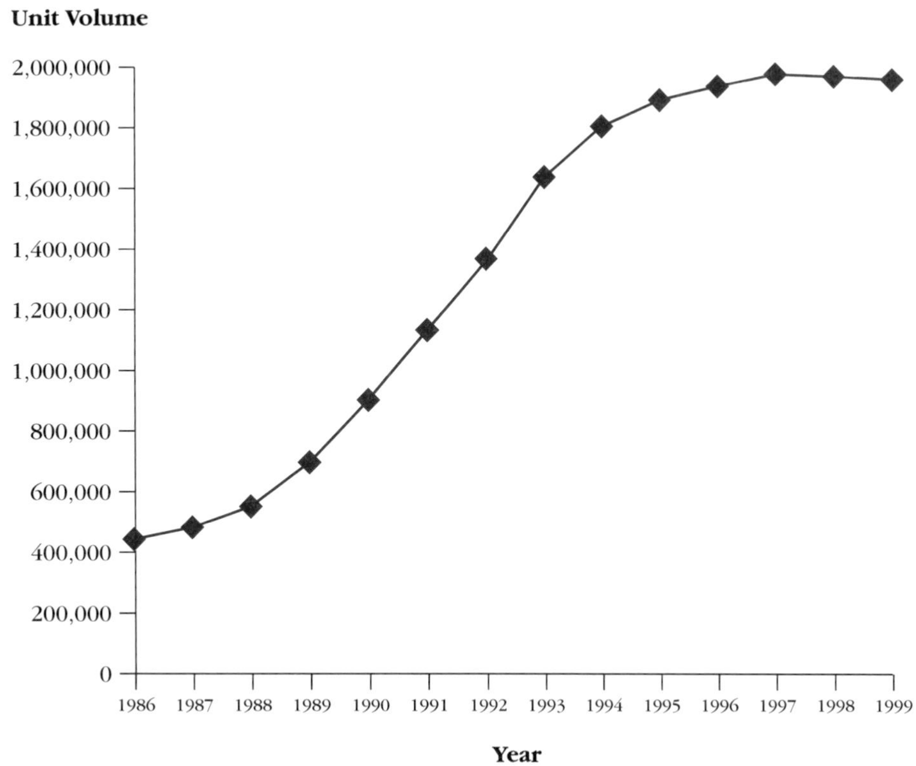

Her review of supplier proposals led her to choose one that was capable of meeting production requirements and providing certain "value-added" features. For example, the chosen supplier could deliver a propellant with no chlorofluorocarbons (CFCs), which are harmful to the earth's ozone layer. Also, the container's bottom would be rust-proof and leave no rust ring when wet. This feature was desired because most women shave in the bathtub or shower and tend to leave a wet can on the tub's porcelain, which can leave a rust stain. In addition, the supplier could produce and ship product directly from its manufacturing facility at a lower per unit cost than the tube container and was prepared to maintain an adequate safety stock of inventory. The only drawback in the supplier's proposal was that only 5½- and 10-ounce containers could be produced without making significant and expensive changes in its equipment. The typical sizes for women's shaving creams and gels were 7-ounce and 10-ounce containers.

The estimated total cost of producing and delivering to retailers a 10-ounce aerosol can of shaving gel was $0.29. A minimum order of 100,000 10-ounce cans would be required. Courtwright believed the suggested retail price would be set at $4.25 per 10-ounce can, reflecting Soft and Silky's premium-price strategy. The estimated total cost of producing and delivering to retailers a 5½-ounce aerosol can of shaving gel was $0.24, and the suggested retail price would be $3.50. A 100,000-unit minimum order would be required. Courtwright recognized that the price per ounce for the aerosol containers was lower than the price per ounce for the tube package. She said the lower price reflected competitive realities in the category:

"The dominant players (S. C. Johnson and Gillette) are very price competitive. We can retain our relative premium image even at the lower prices. I fully expect some cannibalization of the tube will take place just as I am confident the incremental volume will more than offset it." A one-time set-up charge for the Soft and Silky Shaving Gel production line and package graphics was $10,000, due and payable by Ms-Tique Corporation upon the signing of the supply agreement. This charge would be the same whether one or both sizes were produced.

PRELIMINARY TESTS

In November 1999, Courtwright received authorization from Masters' predecessor to spend $35,000 to assess consumer response to the proposed container. Her proposal was approved on the basis of the cost data provided and the recognition that use of a contract filler would require no incremental investment in company manufacturing capacity.

Courtwright commissioned a large marketing research firm to conduct four focus-group studies. Two focus groups would involve current users of Soft and Silky Shaving Gel, and two focus groups would involve users of shaving creams and gels other than Soft and Silky Shaving Gel and soap and water users. The principal information sought from these focus group studies was as follows:

1. Are present customers and noncustomers receptive to the new package?
2. At what rate would present customers convert to the aerosol can, and would noncustomers switch over to Soft and Silky Shaving Gel?
3. Where, in drug and food-and-drug stores, would customers and noncustomers expect to find the aerosol can?
4. Is the suggested retail price acceptable?

In addition, the marketing research firm was asked to examine analogous situations of package changes and report its findings.

In late December 1999, the marketing research firm presented its findings to Courtwright, two days after Masters' predecessor resigned to take a position with another company. There were five principal findings from the focus groups:

1. Customers and noncustomers were unanimously in favor of the aerosol can. The 10-ounce can was the favorite, since it would require fewer purchases.
2. Twenty percent of Soft and Silky Shaving Gel customers said they would convert to the 10-ounce can; 25 percent said they would convert to the $5^1/_2$-ounce can.
3. One-fourth of the noncustomers said they would switch over to the aerosol can irrespective of can size. These consumers' preference for the aerosol over the tube package was their principal reason (in addition to price) for not buying Soft and Silky Shaving Gel previously.
4. Customers expected to find the aerosol can next to the tube container. Noncustomers expected to find the aerosol container stocked with women's toiletries.
5. The pricing was acceptable and actually favored by current customers. Noncustomers thought the suggested retail price was somewhat high, but liked the value-added features and would try the product.

In addition to these findings, the marketing research firm presented ten case histories in which marketers of men's shaving cream had introduced a new package. (There was no distinction made with respect to size of package, whether the pack-

EXHIBIT 5

Soft and Silky Shaving Gel Sales Forecasts by Size and Type of Container

Forecast A: Low estimate for 5½-ounce aerosol package addition		
5½-ounce tube package volume		8,600,000 ounces
5½-ounce aerosol package volume:		
Cannibalized volume	2,145,174	
Net new volume	300,000	2,445,174
		11,044,174 ounces
Forecast B: High estimate for 5½-ounce aerosol package addition		
5½-ounce tube package volume		8,400,000 ounces
5½-ounce aerosol package volume:		
Cannibalized volume	2,345,174	
Net new volume	500,000	2,845,174
		11,245,174 ounces
Forecast C: Low estimate for 10-ounce aerosol package addition		
5½-ounce tube package volume		9,000,000 ounces
10-ounce aerosol package volume:		
Cannibalized volume	1,745,174	
Net new volume	800,000	2,545,174
		11,545,174 ounces
Forecast D: High estimate for 10-ounce aerosol package addition		
5½-ounce tube package volume		9,600,000 ounces
10-ounce aerosol package volume:		
Cannibalized volume	1,145,174	
Net new volume	1,500,000	2,645,174
		12,245,174 ounces

age change was from aerosol to nonaerosol, or vice versa, or previous sales performance.) Two statistics were highlighted: first-year sales with the combined packages and the cannibalization rate for the existing package. According to the report,

> It is difficult to draw one-to-one comparisons between the experience of other shaving creams and gels and that of Soft and Silky Shaving Gel, given its unique market position. We have tried to do so after examining ten product-design changes. Our estimates [Exhibit 5] are broken down into a "high" and a "low" forecast for each package size. Seven out of the ten products studied experienced the "high" situation presented; three experienced the "low" situation. We see the 10-ounce package as producing the largest increase in ounces sold. Even with the cannibalism effect operating, we believe that an additional package will produce higher sales, in ounces, than the Soft and Silky Shaving Gel forecasted volume of 10,745,174 ounces (1,953,668 5½-ounce tubes) for 2000. Only a market test can indicate what will actually occur.

■ THE PACKAGING AND TEST MARKET DECISION

Courtwright presented the research firm's findings to Phoebe Masters on January 7, 2000, one day after Masters became Product Manager for hand and body lotions. Masters listened attentively as Courtwright summarized the research findings and recommended that a market test be conducted to determine the best package size.

Courtwright's test-market recommendation included a proposal to introduce the new package design in a limited cross-section of drug and food-and-drug stores, including heavy-volume and low-volume stores, that presently carried Soft and Silky Shaving Gel. Test stores would be isolated geographically from nontest stores. The new package would be placed among women's toiletries, and the test would run for three months, beginning April 1, 2000. The April 1 start date was necessary to assure that adequate supply of the new package was available. One-half of the stores would carry the 5½-ounce container, and the other half would carry the 10-ounce container. The test would include a full complement of promotional aids, including newspaper ads and point-of-purchase displays, and would approximate a full-scale introduction.

Courtwright's estimated cost for the test market was $30,000, which included the cost of gathering marketing research data on the cannibalization rate and incremental sales growth. In addition, the $10,000 supplier set-up charge would have to be paid. However, Courtwright negotiated a 20,000 unit minimum order for each package size for the test market. No other incremental costs would be charged against the products. Sales and marketing efforts for the existing tube package would remain unchanged during the course of the test.

Late in the evening of Friday, January 7, 2000, Masters found herself considering whether the 5½-ounce or the 10-ounce container should be introduced. She believed it unwise to introduce both sizes, given the uncertainty of market acceptance, and packaging practices of most competitors. She also wondered whether Courtwright's test-market proposal should be adopted. Masters was confident that, given the product's sales history, the existing Soft and Silky Shaving Gel package would produce sales of 1,953,668 units (a .32 percent decrease from 1999) in 2000 if no new package was introduced. She was also confident that a new package would simultaneously cannibalize the existing package and generate incremental unit volume. Therefore, she knew that her decision on the package sizes and test market would have to focus on what was best for the Soft and Silky Shaving Gel product line, assuming an aerosol container would be marketed alongside the original tube container.

Masters also sensed that the new package had become a pet project for Courtwright. Courtwright had championed the idea for six months in addition to working on a variety of other assignments. Furthermore, she had heard that Courtwright felt that she, not Masters, should have been promoted to Product Manager for hand and body lotions given her association with the line for five years. Given the situation, Masters believed that her handling of this decision would affect her working relationship with Courtwright.

CASE

Manor Memorial Hospital

Downtown Health Clinic

In mid-April 2000, Sherri Worth, Assistant Administrator at Manor Memorial Hospital (MMH) in charge of MMH's Downtown Health Clinic (DHC), uncovered an unsettling parcel of news. During a call on the employee benefits director at a downtown department store, she was told that a firm was conducting a study to determine whether sufficient demand existed to establish a clinic five blocks north of MMH's Downtown Health Clinic. The description of the clinic's services sounded similar to those offered by the DHC, and the planned opening date was May 2001.

As Worth walked back to her office, she could not help but think about the possible competition. Upon arriving at her office, Worth called Dr. Roger Mahon, MMH's administrator, to tell him what she had learned. He asked her to contact other employee benefits directors and query patients to see whether they had been surveyed. He expressed concern for two reasons. First, a competitive clinic would attract existing and potential patients of the Downtown Health Clinic. Second, a clinic that provided similar services could hamper the DHC's progress toward achieving its service and profitability objectives. Mahon requested that Worth summarize the DHC's performance to date so that he could speak to members of the board of trustees' executive committee on what action, if any, the DHC should take to compete for patients.

■ THE HOSPITAL INDUSTRY AND AMBULATORY HEALTH CARE SERVICES

Health care, and specifically the hospital industry, has undergone a dramatic transformation in the past four decades. Until the 1960s, hospitals were largely charitable institutions that prided themselves on their not-for-profit orientation. Hospitals functioned primarily as workshops for physicians and were guided by civic-minded boards of trustees.

Federal legislation introduced in the 1960s created boom times for the hospital industry. The Hill-Burton Act provided billions of dollars for hospital construction, to be repaid by fulfilling quotas for charity care. Additional funds were poured into expansion and construction of medical schools. Medicare and Medicaid subsidized health care for the indigent, disabled, and elderly. These programs reimbursed hospitals for their incurred costs plus an additional return on investment. This period also saw dramatic increases in commercial insurance coverage, offered as employee fringe benefits and purchased in additional quantities by a more affluent public. Accordingly, health care became accessible to an overwhelming majority of U.S. citizens, regardless of where they lived or their ability to pay. Federal intervention had changed the concept of health care services from privilege to entitlement.

This case was prepared by Professor Roger A. Kerin, of the Edwin L. Cox School of Business, Southern Methodist University, as a basis for class discussion and is not designed to illustrate effective or ineffective handling of an administrative situation. Certain names and data have been disguised.

By the 1980s, however, skyrocketing health care costs had forced the federal government to reassess its role in health care. Stringent controls were placed on hospital construction and expansion, and utilization and physician-review programs were implemented to ensure against too-lengthy inpatient stays. By the end of the decade, hospitals were initiating voluntary cost-cutting programs to stave off additional government intervention. Despite all efforts, however, health care expenditures continued to outpace the Consumer Price Index into the 1990s.

The late 1980s and early 1990s ushered in a very different health care environment, and hospitals particularly were hard hit by the changes. On the one hand, the federal government sought to reduce health care costs through cutbacks in subsidy programs and cost-control regulations. On the other hand, innovations in health care delivery severely reduced the number of patients serviced by hospitals.

One innovation was preventive health care programs. These fall into two categories: health maintenance organizations (HMOs) and preferred provider organizations (PPOs). An HMO encourages preventive health care by providing medical services as needed for a fixed monthly fee. HMOs typically enter into contractual relationships with designated physicians and hospitals and have been successful in reducing hospital inpatient days and health care expenditures. PPOs establish contractual arrangements between health care providers (physicians and/or hospitals) and large employer groups. Unlike HMOs, PPOs generally offer incentives for using preferred providers rather than restricting individuals to specific hospitals or physicians. PPOs have the same effect on inpatient days and health care expenditures that HMOs have, and Mahon planned to expand the PPO for Manor Memorial Hospital using the Downtown Health Clinic as a link to large employers in the downtown area.

A second innovation has been ambulatory health care services and facilities. Ambulatory health care services consist of treatments and practices that consumers use on an episodic or emergency basis. Examples include physical examinations, treatment of minor emergencies (such as cuts, bruises, and minor surgery), and treatment of common illnesses (such as colds and flu).

Ambulatory health care facilities are split into two categories: (1) minor emergency centers, known by acronyms such as FEC (Free-Standing Emergency Clinic) and MEC (Medical Emergency Clinic) and (2) clinics that focus on primary or episodic care.[1] Although regulation is nominal, if a clinic positions itself as an emergency care center, expressing this focus in its name, it generally is required (or pressured by area physicians) to be staffed 24 hours a day by a licensed physician and to have certain basic life support equipment.

Three factors account for the growth of ambulatory health care services. First, advances in medical technology, miniaturization, and portable medical equipment have made more diagnostic and surgical procedures possible outside the traditional hospital setting. Second, consumers have adopted a more proactive stance on where they will receive their health and medical care. Consumers often choose the hospital at which they wish to be treated, and the incidence of "doctor shopping" is common. Third, the mystique of medical and health care has been altered with the growth of paramedical professionals and standardized treatment practices.

Most of the early centers emphasized quick, convenient, minor emergency care. Many new centers have positioned themselves as convenient, personalized alternatives to primary care physicians' practices. These operations typically employ aggressive, sophisticated marketing techniques, including branding, consistent logos and at-

[1] *Primary care* is the point of entry into the health care system. It consists of a continuous relationship with a personal physician who takes care of a broad range of medical needs. Primary care physicians include general practitioners, internal medicine and family practice specialists, gynecologists, and pediatricians.

mospherics, promotional incentives, and mass-media advertising (giving rise to vernacular designations such as "Doc-in-the-Box" and "McMedical"). Although ambulatory care facilities vary considerably among communities and owners, the following characteristics appear to be universal: (1) branding, (2) extended hours, (3) lower fees than emergency rooms, (4) no appointments necessary, (5) minor emergencies treated, (6) easy access and parking, (7) short waiting times, and (8) credit cards accepted.

■ MANOR MEMORIAL HOSPITAL

Manor Memorial Hospital is a 600-bed, independent, not-for-profit, general hospital located on the southern periphery of a major western city. It is one of six general hospitals in the city and twenty in the county. It is financially stronger than most of the metropolitan-based hospitals in the United States. It is debt-free and has the highest overall occupancy rate among the city's six general hospitals. Nevertheless, the hospital's administration and board of trustees have serious concerns about its patient mix, which reflects unfavorable demographic shifts. Most of the population growth in recent years occurred in the suburban areas to the north, east, and west. These suburban areas attracted young, upwardly mobile families from the city. They also attracted thousands of families from other states—families drawn to the area's dynamic, robust business climate.

As hospitals sprang up to serve the high-growth suburban areas, MMH found itself becoming increasingly dependent on inner-city residents, who have a higher median age and higher incidence of Medicare coverage. Without a stronger stable inflow of short-stay, privately insured patients, the financial health of the hospital would be jeopardized. Accordingly, in the summer of 1998, the board of trustees authorized a study to determine whether to open an ambulatory facility in the downtown area about ten blocks north of the hospital.

■ DOWNTOWN HEALTH CLINIC

The charter for the Downtown Health Clinic contained four objectives:

1. To expand the hospital's referral base
2. To increase referrals of privately insured patients
3. To establish a liaison with the business community by addressing employers' specific health needs
4. To become self-supporting three years after opening

The specific services to be offered by the DHC would include (1) preventive health care (for example, physical examinations and immunizations), (2) minor-emergency care, (3) referral for acute and chronic health care problems, (4) specialized employer services (for example, preemployment examinations and treatment of worker's compensation injuries), (5) primary health care services (for example, treatment of common illnesses), and (6) basic x-ray and laboratory tests. The DHC would be open 260 days a year (Monday–Friday) from 8:00 A.M. to 5:00 P.M.

The location for the DHC would be in the Greater West Office and Shopping Complex, situated on the corner of Main and West Streets (see Exhibit 1 on page 164). This location was chosen because a member of the board of trustees owned

EXHIBIT 1

Present and Planned Locations of Downtown Health Clinics and Service Areas

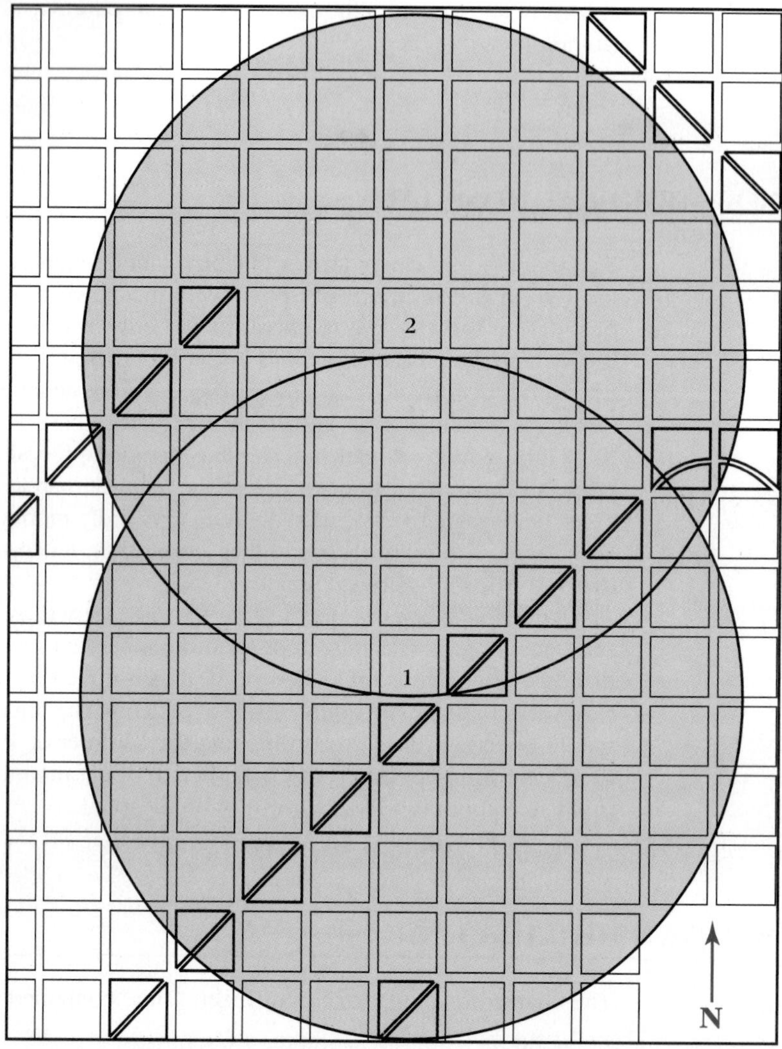

Key:

1. Original DHC and five-block service radius.
2. Planned location of competitor and five-block service radius.

the Greater West Complex and was willing to share construction, design, and equipment expenses with the hospital.

During the fall of 1998, construction plans for erecting the DHC were well under way, and the expense budget was developed (see Exhibit 2). During the winter months, MMH commissioned a study to determine the service radius of the DHC, estimate the number of potential users of the DHC, assess responsiveness to the services to be offered by the DHC, and review the operations of suburban ambulatory care clinics. The results indicated that the service area would have a five-block radius, since this was the longest distance office workers would walk. Discussions with city planners indicated the service area contained 11,663 office workers during the

EXHIBIT 2

Downtown Health Clinic: Preliminary 12-Month Expense Budget

Item	*Expenditure*
Physician coverage: 260 days times 8 hr/day at $66/hr	$137,280
Professional fees	43,720
Lease	76,500
Supplies	46,894
Utilities	6,630
Personnel, including fringe benefits (director, nurse, laboratory assistant, x-ray technician, receptionist)	168,376
Amortization	30,648
Annual expenditure	$510,048

Note: Expenditures were based on the assumption that the DHC would have 4 visits per hour, or 32 visits per day, when operating at full capacity.

9:00–5:00 Monday–Friday work week. The population in the area was expected to grow 6 percent per year, given new building and renovation activity. Personal interviews with 400 office workers, selected randomly, indicated that 50 percent would use or try the DHC if necessary and that 40 percent of these prospective users would visit the DHC at least once per year (see Exhibit 3 on page 166 for additional findings). Finally, the study of suburban ambulatory care facilities revealed the data shown in Exhibit 4 on page 167. Given their locations in suburban areas, these facilities were not considered direct competition, but their existence indicated that "the city's populace was attuned to ambulatory health care facilities," remarked Worth.

These results were viewed favorably by the board of trustees and "confirmed our belief that an ambulatory facility was needed downtown," noted Worth. The DHC was formally opened May 1, 1999. Except for the publicity surrounding the opening, however, no advertising or other types of promotion were planned. "Several members of the hospital staff shied away from advertising or solicitation, since it hinted at crass commercialism," said Worth.

Performance: May 1998–March 2000

A financial summary of DHC performance through March 1990 is shown in Exhibit 5 on page 168. According to Mahon:

> We are pleased with the performance to date and hope the DHC will be self-supporting by April 2001. We are getting favorable word of mouth from satisfied patients that will generate both new and repeat patients. We expect 410 patient visits in April [2000]. In addition, we have taken steps to improve our financial standing. For example, our bad debts have been costing us 4 percent of gross revenue. With a better credit and collection procedure established just last month, we will reduce this figure to 2 percent. We plan to initiate an 8 percent across-the-board increase in charges on May 1 and will experience only a 5 percent increase in personnel and professional services expenses next year.

Records kept by MMH revealed that the DHC was realizing its objectives. For example, the referral objective was being met, since the DHC had made 105 referrals to MMH and produced slightly over $378,000 in revenue and an estimated $30,000 in net profit. Almost all of these patients were privately insured. The service mix, though dominated by treatment of common illnesses and examinations, did indicate

EXHIBIT 3

Profile of DHC Service Area, Based on City and Survey Data

1999 Population Estimate (Source: City Planning Department)	
Total office worker population in five-block radius	11,663
Expected annual growth, 1998–2003	6.0% yr
Sex breakdown in five-block radius:	
Male	40%
Female	60%
Results from Personal Interviews (January 1998)	
Would use/try DHC if necessary for personal illness/exams	50%
Expected frequency of DHC use for personal illness/exams among those saying would use/try if necessary:[a]	
Once every other year	60%
Once per year	25%
Twice per year	10%
Three or more times per year	5%

Selected Cross-Tabulations

	Sex		
	Male	***Female***	***Total***
Would you use or try DHC if necessary?			
Yes	88[b]	168	256
No	72	72	144
Total	160	240	400

	Have Regular Physician (Excluding Gynecologist)		
	Yes	***No***	***Total***
Would you use or try DHC if necessary?			
Yes	58	198	256
No	130	14	144
Total	188	212	400

[a] No difference between males and females on frequency of use.

[b] Of the 160 males interviewed, 88 (55 percent) said they would use the DHC; 88 of the 256 interviewees (34 percent) who said they would use the DHC were male.

that the DHC was being used for a variety of purposes. A breakdown of the reasons for patient visits for the first 11 months of operations is as follows:

Personal illness exams	53%
Worker's compensation exam/treatment	25
Employment/insurance physical exams	19
Emergency	3
Total	100%

Patient records indicated that 97 percent of all visits were by first-time users of the DHC and 113 visits were by repeat patients. Approximately 5 percent of the visits in each month from October 1999 through March 2000 were repeat visits. "We

EXHIBIT 4

Suburban Ambulatory Care Clinics: Operations Profile

Operations	*EmerCenter #1*	*EmerCenter #2*	*Adams Industrial Clinic*	*Health First*	*Medcenter*
Opening	March 1990	November 1992	June 1992	May 1991	June 1997
Patients/year	9,030	6,000	8,400	5,700	8,661
Hours of operation	10:00 A.M.–10:00 P.M. Monday–Friday	10:00 A.M.–10:00 P.M. Monday–Sunday	8:00 A.M.–5:00 P.M. Monday–Friday	5:00 P.M.–11:00 P.M. Monday–Friday; 10:00 A.M.–10:00 P.M. Saturday–Sunday	8:00 A.M.–8:00 P.M. Monday–Sunday
Physicians/8-hr shift	2	2	2	2	2
Estimated patient visits/hour	3.8/hr	3.4/hr	5.0/hr	3.0/hr	3.0/hr
Estimated average charge per visit	$60.00	$62.00	$76.00	$62.00	$64.00
Services provided:					
Preventive health care			✔	✔	✔
Minor emergencies	✔	✔	✔	✔	✔
Employer services			✔		
X-ray/lab tests	✔	✔	✔	✔	✔
Miscellaneous	✔	✔	✔	✔	✔
Use direct-mail advertising	✔	✔		✔	✔

EXHIBIT 5

Downtown Health Clinic Financial Summary

	1999								2000			
	May	*June*	*July*	*Aug.*	*Sept.*	*Oct.*	*Nov.*	*Dec.*	*Jan.*	*Feb.*	*Mar.*	*Total Year to Date*
Gross revenue	$ 8,150	$ 16,774	$ 17,688	$19,394	$ 22,412	$ 22,812	$ 23,344	$ 23,516	$ 25,692	$ 27,758	$ 29,430	$ 236,970
Variable expenses:												
Bad debt	326	710	708	776	896	912	934	940	1,026	1,110	1,176	9,514
Medical/surgical supplies	13,182	1,596	1,870	1,286	2,126	2,426	3,322	1,224	1,052	3,106	2,156	34,300
Drugs	318	108	130	104	610	186	0	112	372	506	152	2,598
Office supplies	1,294	444	1,192	1,436	630	(380)	48	562	934	0	128	6,288
Total variable expense	$ 15,120	$ 2,858	$ 3,900	$ 3,602	$ 4,262	$ 3,144	$ 4,304	$ 2,838	$ 4,284	$ 4,776	$ 3,612	$ 52,700
Contribution	$ (6,970)	$ 13,916	$ 13,788	$15,792	$ 18,150	$ 19,668	$ 19,040	$ 20,678	$ 21,408	$ 22,982	$ 25,818	$ 184,270
Fixed expenses:												
Personnel	15,632	14,918	13,340	11,800	13,632	22,980	14,640	12,498	13,410	17,990	15,288	166,128
Professional services[a]	20,018	13,890	15,564	14,316	14,770	13,600	14,400	14,900	14,484	14,156	14,374	164,372
Facility[b]	6,444	5,074	5,780	5,810	5,244	5,310	5,240	5,226	5,672	5,244	5,438	60,482
Miscellaneous	1,410	214	266	280	476	90	222	152	212	246	114	3,682
Amortization	2,554	2,554	2,554	2,554	2,554	2,554	2,554	2,554	2,554	2,544	2,544	28,094
Total fixed expense	$ 46,058	$ 36,650	$ 37,504	$34,760	$ 36,676	$ 44,434	$ 37,056	$ 35,330	$ 36,332	$ 40,190	$ 37,768	$ 422,758
Net gain (loss)	$(53,028)	$(22,734)	$(23,716)	$ (18,968)	$(18,526)	$(24,866)	$(18,016)	$(14,652)	$(14,924)	$(17,208)	$(11,950)	$(238,488)
Number of patient visits	109	231	275	277	322	320	321	366	383	463	423	3,490
Number of working days	22	21	21	22	20	23	22	20	22	21	23	237

[a] Includes professional fees paid (see Exhibit 2).

[b] Includes lease payments, utilities, and maintenance.

are pleased that we are already getting repeat business because it shows we are doing our job," Worth commented. The average revenue per patient visit during the first 11 months was $67.90.[2] A breakdown of the average charge by type of visit follows. The average charge was to increase 8 percent on May 1, 2000.

Personal illness/exam	$50 per visit
Worker's compensation exam/treatment	$78 per visit
Employment/insurance physical examination	$94 per visit
Emergency	$134 per visit

In an effort to monitor the performance of the DHC, patients were asked to provide selected health care information as well as demographic information. This information was summarized monthly, and Exhibit 6 on page 170 shows the profile of patients visiting the DHC for the first 11 months of operation. In addition to this information, patients were asked for suggestions on how the DHC could serve the downtown area. Suggestions typically fell into three categories: service hours, services offered, and waiting time. Thirty percent of the patients suggested expanded service hours, with an opening time of 7:00 A.M. and a closing time of 7:00 P.M. One-half of the female patients requested that gynecological services be added.[3] A majority of the patients expressed concern about the waiting time, particularly during the lunch hours (11:00 A.M.–2:00 P.M.). A check of DHC records indicated that 70 percent of patient visits occurred during the 11:00 A.M.–2:00 P.M. period and that one-half of the visits were for personal illnesses.

Worth believed all three suggestions had merit, and she had already explored ways to expand the DHC's hours and reduce waiting time. For example, the reason for her call on the employee benefits director at a local department store was to schedule employee physical examinations in the morning or late afternoon hours to minimize crowding during the lunch hour. Nevertheless, she believed a second licensed physician might be necessary, with one physician working the hours from 7:00 A.M. to 3:00 P.M. and the other working between 11:00 A.M. and 7:00 P.M. The overlap during the lunch period would alleviate waiting times, she thought. Expanding from 9- to 12-hour days would entail a 33 percent increase in personnel costs, however, as well as the cost of another physician.[4]

Worth believed that scheduling was more of a problem than she or the MMH staff had expected. "You just can't schedule the walk-ins," she said, "and pardon me for saying it, but the people coming in with personal care needs have really caused the congestion." She added that the problem would get worse because the mix of patient needs was moving toward personal illnesses and examinations. "If the trend continues, we should have 20 percent more personal illness visits next year than last year."

Worth believed that gynecological services would be a plus, since 70 percent of the visits were made by women and almost all were under 35 years of age. She said:

> Women should see a gynecologist regularly at least once a year and often twice a year. We could add an additional 2,000 visits per year by having a hospital gynecologist work at the DHC two eight-hour days a week by appointment. An average charge per visit would be about $104 including lab work, and the physician cost would be $70 per hour.

---

[2] The average charge per patient visit excluded the charge for basic x-ray and laboratory tests.

[3] *Gynecology* is that branch of medicine dealing with the female reproductive tract.

[4] Expanded hours would be staffed by part-time personnel, who would receive the same wages as full-time personnel.

EXHIBIT 6

Profile of Downtown Health Clinic Patients: Personal Illness/Exam Visits Only

Occupation	
Clerical	48%
Professional/technical/managerial	23
Operator	19
Other	10
	100%
Sex	
Male	30%
Female	70
	100%
Referral Source	
Friend/colleague	35%
Employer	60
Other	5
	100%
Patient Origin	
Distance:	
One block	25%
Two blocks	28
Three blocks	22
Four blocks	15
Five blocks	8
More than five blocks	2
	100%
Direction:	
North of DHC	10%
South of DHC	25
Northeast of DHC	5
Southwest of DHC	15
East of DHC	20
West of DHC	10
Southeast of DHC	10
Northwest of DHC	5
	100%
Have Regular Physician	
Yes	18%
No	82
	100%

Worth had also given some thought to how the DHC could improve its relations with the business community. Currently, business-initiated visits (worker's compensation examinations and treatments and employment/insurance physical examinations) accounted for 44 percent of the visits to the DHC. Construction in the downtown area had stimulated worker's compensation activity, and growth in employment in the five-block service radius had contributed to employment physicals. Worth believed worker's compensation visits would stabilize at about 81 per month and then decline with slowed building activity. Employment physicals accounted for 50 visits per month and were expected to remain at this level with the current operating hours. Insurance physicals were not expected to increase beyond current levels, nor were emergency visits.

Commenting on her calls on businesses, Worth remarked:

> I have actively called on businesses under the guise of community relations because the MMH staff has not sanctioned solicitation. My guess, after talking with businesspeople, is that we could get virtually every new employment physical if we didn't interfere with employment hours and scheduled them before 8:00 A.M. or after 5:00 P.M. Given net new employment in the area and new employees due to turnover, I'd guess we could schedule an additional 65 employment physicals every month—that is, a total of 115 a month.

Worth added that she had also received approval to run an "informational advertisement" in the downtown weekly newspaper each week next year provided that the advertisement did not feature prices or appear to be commercial in its presentation. The weekly advertisement would cost $10,400 per year.

The Possibility of Competition

Worth's calls on local businesses and patient interviews indicated that someone was conducting a survey. She believed that Medcenter, a privately owned suburban ambulatory facility, was the sponsor. Medcenter appeared to be successful in its suburban location (see Exhibit 4) and had a reputation for being an aggressive, marketing-oriented operation. Even though Medcenter did not provide employer services at its suburban location, Worth thought the fact that an employee benefits director had been interviewed suggested that such services might be offered.

The proposed location for the new clinic was five blocks directly north of the DHC. Based on the research for the DHC, Worth estimated that the number of office workers within a five-block radius of the competitive clinic would be 11,652 in 2001 and 13,590 in 2002, and would grow at an annual rate of 7 percent through 2005 because of new construction and building renovation. Worth believed the competitor's service area had the same socioeconomic profile and the same usage and employment characteristics as the DHC's service area.

The overlap in service areas was due to the layout of the downtown area and the availability of high-quality street-level space. According to Worth, "It is possible that a third of our current personal illness/exam patients from the northern portion of our service area will switch to the new clinic and about 40 percent of potential personal illness/exam patients in this area will go to the new location." Worth went on to say that the overlap in service areas would cover 3,424 office workers in 2000.

The effect of the competing clinic on the volume of emergency, worker's compensation, and employment/insurance exam work was more difficult to assess. Worth felt that worker's compensation visits would not be materially affected because most construction was being undertaken in areas south, east, and west of the DHC. Emergency visits were so random that it was not possible to assess what effect the competing clinic would have. The projected volume of employment and insurance physicals could change with the addition of a competing clinic, however. Worth guessed, "At worst, we would see no increase in these types of visits over last year since we have not gotten many visits from this area."

A week after she first heard about the possibility of competition, Worth and Mahon met to review the information on the DHC. Just before Worth finished giving her overview, Mahon's administrative assistant interrupted to tell him he had to leave to catch a plane for a three-day hospital administration conference. As he left the room, Mahon asked Worth to draft a concise analysis of the DHC's position. He also asked her to specify and evaluate the alternatives for the DHC assuming Medcenter either did or did not open a facility. "Remember," Mahon said, "we have a lot riding on the DHC. Making it work involves not only dollars and cents, but our image in the community as well."

CASE

Procter & Gamble, Inc.

Scope

As Gwen Hearst looked at the year-end report, she was pleased to see that Scope held a 32 percent share of the Canadian mouthwash market for 1990. She had been concerned about the inroads that Plax, a prebrushing rinse, had made in the market. Since its introduction in 1988, Plax had gained a 10 percent share of the product category and posed a threat to Scope. As Brand Manager, Hearst planned, developed, and directed the total marketing effort for Scope, Procter & Gamble's (P&G) brand in the mouthwash market. She was responsible for maximizing the market share, volume, and profitability of the brand.

Until the entry of Plax, brands in the mouthwash market were positioned around two major benefits: fresh breath and killing germs. Plax was positioned around a new benefit—as a "plaque fighter"—and indications were that other brands, such as Listerine, were going to promote this benefit. The challenge for Hearst was to develop a strategy that would ensure the continued profitability of Scope in the face of these competitive threats. Her specific task was to prepare a marketing plan for P&G's mouthwash business for the next three years. It was early February 1991, and she would be presenting the plan to senior management in March.

■ COMPANY BACKGROUND

Based on a philosophy of providing products of superior quality and value that best fill the needs of consumers, Procter & Gamble is one of the most successful consumer goods companies in the world. The company markets its brands in more than 140 countries and had net earnings of $1.6 billion in 1990. The Canadian subsidiary contributed $1.4 billion in sales and $100 million in net earnings in 1990. It was recognized as a leader in the Canadian packaged-goods industry, and its consumer brands led in most of the categories in which the company competed.

Between 1987 and 1990, worldwide sales of P&G had increased by $8 billion and net earnings by $1.3 billion. P&G executives attributed the company's success to a variety of factors, including the ability to develop truly innovative products to meet consumers' needs. Exhibit 1 on page 174 contains the statement of purpose and strategy of the Canadian subsidiary.

P&G Canada has five operating divisions, organized by product category. The divisions, and some of the major brands, are:

1. *Paper products*: Royale, Pampers, Luvs, Attends, Always
2. *Food and beverage*: Duncan Hines, Crisco, Pringles, Sunny Delight

---

This case was prepared by Professors Gordon H. G. McDougall and Franklin Ramsoomair, of the Wilfrid Laurier University, as a basis for class discussion and is not designed to illustrate effective or ineffective handling of an administrative situation. Used with permission.

EXHIBIT 1

A Statement of Purpose and Strategy: Procter & Gamble, Canada

We will provide products of superior quality and value that best fill the needs of consumers.

We will achieve that purpose through an organization and a working environment which attracts the finest people, fully develops and challenges our individual talents; encourages our free and spirited collaboration to drive the business ahead; and maintains the Company's historic principles of integrity, and doing the right thing.

We will build a profitable business in Canada. We will apply P&G worldwide learning and resources to maximize our success rate. We will concentrate our resources on the most profitable categories and on unique, important Canadian market opportunities. We will also contribute to the development of outstanding people and innovative business ideas for worldwide company use.

We will reach our business goals and achieve optimum cost efficiencies through continuing innovation, strategic planning, and the continuous pursuit of excellence in everything we do.

We will continuously stay ahead of competition while aggressively defending our established profitable businesses against major competitive challenges despite short-term profit consequences.

Through the successful pursuit of our commitment, we expect our brands to achieve leadership share and profit positions and that, as a result, our business, our people, our shareholders, and the communities in which we live and work, will prosper.

Source: Company records.

3. *Beauty care*: Head & Shoulders, Pantene, Pert, Vidal Sassoon, Clearasil, Clarion, Cover Girl, Max Factor, Oil of Olay, Noxzema, Secret
4. *Health care*: Crest, Scope, Vicks, Pepto-Bismol, Metamucil
5. *Laundry and cleaning*: Tide, Cheer, Bounce, Bold, Oxydol, Joy, Cascade, Comet, Mr. Clean

Each division had its own Brand Management, Sales, Finance, Product Development and Operations line management groups and was evaluated as a profit center. Typically, within each division a Brand Manager was assigned to each brand (for example, Scope). Hearst was in the Health Care division and reported to the Associate Advertising Manager for oral care, who, in turn, reported to the General Manager of the division. After completing her business degree (B.B.A.) at a well-known Ontario business school in 1986, Hearst had joined P&G as a Brand Assistant. In 1987 she became the Assistant Brand Manager for Scope, and in 1988 she was promoted to Brand Manager. Hearst's rapid advancement at P&G reflected the confidence that her managers had in her abilities.

■ THE CANADIAN MOUTHWASH MARKET

Until 1987, on a unit basis the mouthwash market had grown at an average of 3 percent per year for the previous 12 years. In 1987, it experienced a 26 percent increase with the introduction of new flavors such as peppermint. Since then, the growth rate had declined to a level of 5 percent in 1990 (Exhibit 2).

The mouthwash market was initially developed by Warner-Lambert with its pioneer brand Listerine. Positioned as a therapeutic germ-killing mouthwash that eliminated bad breath, it dominated the market until the entry of Scope in 1967. Scope, a green, mint-tasting mouthwash, was positioned as a great-tasting, mouth-refreshing brand that provided bad-breath protection. It was the first brand that offered both effective protection against bad breath and a better taste than other mouthwashes. Its advertising focused, in part, on a perceived weakness of Listerine—a medicine

EXHIBIT 2

Canadian Mouthwash Market

	1986	*1987*	*1988*	*1989*	*1990*
Total retail sales (millions)	\$43.4	\$54.6	\$60.2	\$65.4	\$68.6
Total factory sales (millions)	\$34.8	\$43.5	\$48.1	\$52.2	\$54.4
Total unit sales (thousands)[a]	863	1,088	1,197	1,294	1,358
(% change)	3	26	10	8	5
(% change—"breath only")[b]	3	26	0	3	5
Penetration (%)[c]	65	70	75	73	75
Usage (number of times per week)[d]	2.0	2.2	2.3	2.4	3.0

[a] One unit or statistical case equals 10 liters or 352 fluid ounces of mouthwash.

[b] Excludes Plax and other prebrushing rinses.

[c] Percentage of households having at least one brand in home.

[d] For each adult household member.

Source: Company records.

breath (for example, "Scope fights bad breath. Don't let the good taste fool you")—and in 1976, Scope became the market leader in Canada.

In 1977, Warner-Lambert launched Listermint mouthwash as a direct competitor to Scope. Like Scope, it was a green, mint-tasting mouthwash and positioned as a "good tasting mouthwash that fights bad breath." Within a year it had achieved a 12 percent market share, primarily at the expense of Listerine and smaller brands in the market.

In the 1970s, Merrell Dow, a large pharmaceutical firm, launched Cepacol, which was positioned very close to Listerine. It achieved and held approximately 14 percent of the market in the early 1980s.

During the 1980s, the major competitive changes in the Canadian mouthwash market were:

- Listerine, which had been marketed primarily on a "bad breath" strategy, began shifting its position and in 1988 introduced the claim "Fights plaque and helps prevent inflamed gums caused by plaque." In the United States, Listerine gained the American Dental Association seal for plaque but, as yet, did not have the seal in Canada.
- Listermint added fluoride during the early 1980s and added the Canadian Dental Association seal for preventing cavities in 1983. More recently, Listermint had downplayed fluoride and removed the seal.
- In early 1987, flavors were introduced by a number of brands including Scope, Listermint, and various store brands. This greatly expanded the market in 1987 but did not significantly change the market shares held by the major brands.
- Colgate Fluoride Rinse was launched in 1988. With the seal from the Canadian Dental Association for cavities, it claimed that "Colgate's new fluoride rinse fights cavities. And, it has a mild taste that encourages children to rinse longer and more often." Colgate's share peaked at 2 percent and then declined. There were rumors that Colgate was planning to discontinue the brand.
- In 1988, Merrell Dow entered a licensing agreement with Strategic Brands to market Cepacol in Canada. Strategic Brands, a Canadian firm that markets a

variety of consumer household products, had focused its efforts on gaining greater distribution for Cepacol and promoting it on the basis of price.

- In 1988, Plax was launched on a new and different platform. Its launch and immediate success caught many in the industry by surprise.

THE INTRODUCTION OF PLAX

Plax was launched in Canada in late 1988 on a platform quite different from the traditional mouthwashes. First, instead of the usual use occasion of "after brushing," it called itself a "prebrushing" rinse. The user rinses before brushing, and Plax's detergents are supposed to help loosen plaque to make brushing especially effective. Second, the product benefits were not breath-focused. Instead, it claimed that "Rinsing with Plax, then brushing normally, removes up to three times more plaque than just brushing alone."

Pfizer Inc., a pharmaceutical firm, launched Plax in Canada with a promotion campaign that was estimated to be close to $4 million. The campaign, which covered the last three months of 1988 and all of 1989, consisted of advertising estimated at $3 million and extensive sales promotions including (1) trial-size display in three drugstore chains ($60,000), (2) co-op mail couponing to 2.5 million households ($160,000), (3) an instantly redeemable coupon offer ($110,000), (4) a professional mailer to drug and supermarket chains ($30,000), and (5) a number of price reductions ($640,000). Plax continued to support the brand with advertising expenditures of approximately $1.2 million in 1990. In 1990, Plax held a 10 percent share of the total market.

When Plax was launched in the United States, it claimed that using Plax "removed up to 300% more plaque than just brushing." This claim was challenged by mouthwash competitors and led to an investigation by the Better Business Bureau. The investigation found that the study on which Plax based its claim had panelists limit their toothbrushing to just 15 seconds—and didn't let them use toothpaste. A further study, where people were allowed to brush in their "usual manner" and with toothpaste, showed no overall difference in the level of plaque buildup between those using Plax and a control group that did not use Plax. Plax then revised its claim to "three times more plaque than just brushing alone." Information on plaque is contained in the Appendix.

THE CURRENT SITUATION

In preparing for the strategic plan, Gwen Hearst reviewed the available information for the mouthwash market and Scope. As shown in Exhibit 2, in 1990, 75 percent of Canadian households used one or more mouthwash brands, and, on average, usage was three times per week for each adult household member. Company market research revealed that users could be segmented on frequency of use; "heavy" users (once per day or more) comprised 40 percent of all users, "medium" users (two to six times a week) comprised 45 percent, and "light" users (less than once a week) comprised 15 percent. No information was available on the usage habits of prebrushing rinse users. Nonusers currently don't buy mouthwash because they either (1) don't believe they get bad breath, (2) believe that brushing their teeth is adequate, and/or (3) find alternatives like gums and mints more convenient. The most important reasons why consumers use mouthwash are:

Most Important Reason for Using a Mouthwash	%
It is part of my basic oral hygiene	40*
It gets rid of bad breath	40
It kills germs	30
It makes me feel more confident	20
To avoid offending others	25

* Multiple reasons allowed.

During 1990, a survey was conducted of mouthwash users' images of the major brands in the market. Respondents were asked to rate the brands on a number of attributes, and the results show that Plax had achieved a strong image on the "removes plaque/healthier teeth and gums" attributes (Exhibit 3).

Market share data revealed there was a substantial difference in the share held by Scope in food stores, 42 percent (for example, supermarkets) versus drugstores, 27 percent (Exhibit 4 on page 178). Approximately 65 percent of all mouthwash sales went through drugstores, while 35 percent went through food stores. Recently, wholesale clubs, such as Price Club and Costco, were accounting for a greater share of mouthwash sales.[1] Typically, these clubs carried Cepacol, Scope, Listerine, and Plax.

EXHIBIT 3

Consumer Perceptions of Brand Images

	All Users[a]					
Attributes	*Cepacol*	*Colgate*	*Listerine*	*Listermint*	*Plax*	*Scope*
Reduces bad breath	. . .	. . .	. . .	. . .	—	. . .
Kills germs	+	. . .	+	. . .	. . .	—
Removes plaque	. . .	. . .	. . .	. . .	+	—
Healthier teeth and gums	. . .	. . .	. . .	. . .	+	—
Good for preventing colds	. . .	. . .	+	. . .	. . .	. . .
Recommended by doctors/dentists	. . .	—	. . .	. . .	+	. . .
Cleans your mouth well	. . .	. . .	. . .	. . .	. . .	. . .

	Brand Users[b]					
Attributes	*Cepacol*	*Colgate*	*Listerine*	*Listermint*	*Plax*	*Scope*
Reduces bad breath	+	—	+	+	—	+
Kills germs	+	. . .	+	—	—	. . .
Removes plaque	—	+	+	—	+	—
Healthier teeth and gums	. . .	+	+	—	+	—
Good for preventing colds	+	—	+	—	—	—
Recommended by doctors/dentists	+	+	+	—	+	—

[a] Includes anyone who uses mouthwash. Respondents asked to rate all brands (even those they haven't used) on the attributes. A "+" means this brand scores *higher than average*. A ". . ." means this brand scored *about average*. A "—" means this brand scored *below average*. For example, Cepacol is perceived by those who use mouthwash as a brand that is good/better than most at "preventing germs."

[b] Includes only the users of that brand. For example, Cepacol is perceived by those whose "usual brand" is Cepacol as a brand that is good/better than most at "reducing bad breath."

Source: Company records.

[1] Wholesale clubs were included in food store sales.

EXHIBIT 4

Canadian Mouthwash Market Shares

	Units			*1990 Average*	
	1988	*1989*	*1990*	*Food*	*Drug*
Scope	33.0%	33.0%	32.3%	42.0%	27.0%
Listerine	15.2	16.1	16.6	12.0	19.0
Listermint	15.2	9.8	10.6	8.0	12.0
Cepacol	13.6	10.6	10.3	9.0	11.0
Colgate oral rinse	1.4	1.2	0.5	0.4	0.5
Plax	1.0	10.0	10.0	8.0	11.0
Store brands	16.0	15.4	16.0	18.0	15.0
Miscellaneous other	4.6	3.9	3.7	2.6	4.5
Total	100.0%	100.0%	100.0%	100.0%	100.0%
Retail sales (000,000)	$60.2	$65.4	$68.6	$24.0	$44.6

Source: Company records.

Competitive data were also collected for advertising expenditures and retail prices. As shown in Exhibit 5, total media spending of all brands in 1990 was $5 million, with Scope, Listerine, and Plax accounting for 90 percent of all advertising. Retail prices were calculated based on a 750-ml bottle, both Listerine and Plax were priced at a higher level in food stores, and Plax was priced at a premium in drugstores.

Information on the U.S. market for 1989 was also available (Exhibit 6 on page 180). In contrast to Canada, Listerine held the dominant share in the U.S. market. Since early 1989, Listerine had been advertised heavily in the United States as "the only nonprescription mouthwash accepted by the American Dental Association for its significant help in preventing and reducing plaque and gingivitis." In clinical tests in the United States, Listerine significantly reduced plaque scores by roughly 20 to 35 percent, with a similar reduction in gingivitis. In Canada, the 1990 advertising campaign included the claim that Listerine has been clinically proven to "help prevent inflamed and irritated gums caused by plaque build-up." Listerine's formula relied on four essential oils—menthol, eucalyptol, thymol, and methyl salicylate—all derivatives of phenol, a powerful antiseptic.

Listerine had not received the consumer product seal given by the Canadian Dental Association (CDA) because the association was not convinced a mouthrinse could be of therapeutic value. The CDA was currently reviewing American tests for several products sold in Canada. In fact, any proposed changes to the formulation of mouthwashes or advertising claims could require approval from various regulatory agencies.

THE REGULATORY ENVIRONMENT

1. **Health Protection Branch:** This government body classifies products into "drug status" or "cosmetic status" based on both the product's action on bodily functions and its advertising claims. Drug products are those that affect a bodily function (for example, prevent cavities or prevent plaque buildup). For "drug status" products, all product formulations, packaging, copy, and ad-

EXHIBIT 5

Competitive Market Data, 1990

Advertising Expenditures (000)

Scope	$1,700
Listerine	1,600
Plax	1,200
Listermint	330
Cepacol	170

Media Plans

	Number of Weeks on Air	*GRPs*[a]
Scope	35	325
Listerine	25	450
Plax	20	325

Retail Price Indices

	Food Stores	*Drugstores*
Scope	98	84
Listerine	129	97
Listermint	103	84
Colgate	123	119
Plax	170	141
Store brand	58	58
Cepacol	84	81
Total Market[b]	100	100

[a] GRP (Gross Rating Points) is a measurement of advertising impact derived by multiplying the number of persons exposed to an advertisement by the average number of exposures per person. The GRPs reported are monthly.

[b] An average weighted index of the retail prices of all mouthwash brands is calculated and indexed at 100 for both food stores and drugstores. Scope is priced slightly below this index in food stores and about 16 percent below in drugstores.

Source: Company records.

vertising must be pre-cleared by the Health Protection Branch (HPB), with guidelines that are very stringent. Mouthwashes like Scope that claim to only prevent bad breath are considered as "cosmetic status." However, if any claims regarding inhibition of plaque formation are made the product reverts to "drug status," and all advertising is scrutinized.

2. **The Canadian Dental Association:** Will, upon request of the manufacturer, place its seal of recognition on products that have demonstrated efficacy against cavities or against plaque/gingivitis. However, those products with the seal of recognition must submit their packaging and advertising to the CDA for approval. The CDA and the American Dental Association (ADA) are two separate bodies and are independent of each other and don't always agree on issues. The CDA, for example, would not provide a "plaque/gingivitis" seal unless clinical studies demonstrating actual gum health improvements were done.

3. **Saccharin/Cyclamate sweeteners:** All mouthwashes contain an artificial sweetener. In Canada, cyclamate is used as the sweetener, as saccharin is con-

EXHIBIT 6

Canada–U.S. Market Share Comparison, 1989 (% units)

Brands	*Canada*	*United States*
Scope	33.0	21.6
Listerine	16.1	28.7
Listermint	9.8	4.5
Cepacol	10.6	3.6
Plax	10.0	9.6

Source: Company records.

sidered a banned substance. In contrast, the United States uses saccharin because cyclamate is prohibited. Thus, despite the fact that many of the same brands compete in both Canada and the United States, the formula in each country is different.

THE THREE-YEAR PLAN

In preparing the three-year plan for Scope, a team had been formed within P&G to examine various options. The team included individuals from Product Development (PDD), Manufacturing, Sales, Market Research, Finance, Advertising, and Operations. Over the past year, the team had completed a variety of activities relating to Scope.

The key issue, in Hearst's mind, was how P&G should capitalize on the emerging market segment within the rinse category that focused more on "health-related benefits" than the traditional breath strategy of Scope. Specifically with the launch of Plax, the mouthwash market had segmented itself along the "breath-only" brands (like Scope) and those promising other benefits. Plax, in positioning itself as a prebrushing rinse, was not seen as, nor did it taste like, a "breath refreshment" mouthwash like Scope.

Gwen Hearst believed that a line extension positioned against Plax, a recent entry into the market, made the most sense. If the mouthwash market became more segmented, and if these other brands grew, her fear was that P&G would be left with a large share of a segment that focused only on "breath" and hence might decline. However, she also knew that there were questions regarding both the strategic and financial implications of such a proposal. In recent meetings, other ideas had been proposed, including "doing nothing" and looking at claims other than "breath" that might be used by Scope instead of adding a new product. Several team members questioned whether there was any real threat, as Plax was positioned very differently from Scope. As she considered the alternatives, Hearst reviewed the activities of the team and the issues that had been raised by various team members.

Product Development

In product tests on Scope, PDD had demonstrated that Scope reduced plaque better than brushing alone because of antibacterial ingredients contained in Scope. However, as yet P&G did not have a clinical database to convince the HPB to allow Scope to extend these claims into the prevention of inflamed gums (as Listerine does).

PDD had recently developed a new prebrushing rinse product that performed as well as Plax but did not work any better than Plax against plaque reduction. In fact, in its testing of Plax itself, PDD was actually unable to replicate the plaque reduction claim made by Pfizer that "rinsing with Plax, then brushing normally removes up to three times more plaque than brushing alone." The key benefit of P&G's prebrushing rinse was that it did taste better than Plax. Other than that, it had similar aesthetic qualities to Plax—qualities that made its "in-mouth" experience quite different from that of Scope.

The Product Development people in particular were concerned about Hearst's idea of launching a line extension because it was a product that was only equal in efficacy to Plax and to placebo rinses for plaque reduction. Traditionally, P&G had only launched products that focused on unmet consumer needs—typically superior performing products. However, Gwen had pointed out, because the new product offered similar efficacy at a better taste, this was similar to the situation when Scope was originally launched. Some PDD members were also concerned that if they couldn't replicate Plax's clinical results with P&G's stringent test methodology, and if the product possibly didn't provide any greater benefit than rinsing with any liquid, then P&G's image and credibility with dental professionals might be impacted. There was debate on this issue, as others felt that as long as the product did encourage better oral hygiene, it did provide a benefit. As further support they noted that many professionals did recommend Plax. Overall, PDD's preference was to not launch a new product but, instead, to add plaque-reduction claims to Scope. The basic argument was that it was better to protect the business that P&G was already in than to launch a completely new entity. If a line extension was pursued, a product test costing $20,000 would be required.

Sales

The sales people had seen the inroads Plax had been making in the marketplace and believed that Scope should respond quickly. They had one key concern. As stock-keeping units (SKUs) had begun to proliferate in many categories, the retail industry had become much more stringent regarding what it would accept. Now, to be listed on store shelves, a brand must be seen as different enough (or unique) from the competition to build incremental purchases—otherwise retailers argued that category sales volume would simply be spread over more units. When this happened, a retail outlet's profitability was reduced because inventory costs were higher, but no additional sales revenue was generated. When a new brand was viewed as not generating more sales, retailers might still list the brand by replacing units within the existing line (for example, drop shelf facings of Scope), or the manufacturer could pay approximately $50,000 per stock-keeping unit in listing fees to add the new brand.

Market Research

Market Research (MR) had worked extensively with Hearst to test the options with consumers. Its work to date had shown:

1. A plaque reassurance on current Scope (that is, "Now Scope fights plaque") did not seem to increase competitive users' desire to purchase Scope. This meant that it was unlikely to generate additional volume, but it could prevent current users from switching.

   MR also cautioned that adding "reassurances" to a product often takes time before the consumer accepts the idea and then acts on it. The issue in Hearst's mind was whether the reassurance would ever be enough. At best it might stabilize the business, she thought, but would it grow behind such a claim?

2. A "Better-Tasting Prebrushing Dental Rinse" product did research well among Plax users, but did not increase purchase intent among people not currently using a dental rinse. MR's estimate was that a brand launched on this posi-

> tioning would likely result in approximately a 6.5 percent share of the total mouthwash and "rinse" market on an ongoing basis. Historically, it has taken approximately two years to get to the ongoing level. However, there was no way for them to accurately assess potential Scope cannibalization. "Use your judgment," they had said. However, they cautioned that although it was a product for a different usage occasion, it was unlikely to be 100 percent incremental business. Hearst's best rough guess was that this product might cannibalize somewhere between 2 and 9 percent of Scope's sales. An unresolved issue was the product's name—if it were launched, should it be under the Scope name or not? One fear was that if the Scope name was used it would either "turn off" loyal users who saw Scope as a breath refreshment product or confuse them.

MR had questioned Hearst as to whether she had really looked at all angles to meet her objective. Because much of this work had been done quickly, they wondered whether there weren't some other benefits Scope could talk about that would interest consumers and hence achieve the same objective. They suggested that Hearst look at other alternatives beyond just "a plaque reassurance on Scope" or a "line extension positioned as a 'Better-Tasting Prebrushing Rinse.'"

EXHIBIT 7

Scope Historical Financials

Year	*1988*		*1989*		*1990*	
Total market size (Units) (000)	1,197		1,294		1,358	
Scope market share	33.0%		33.0%		32.4%	
Scope volume (Units) (000)	395		427		440	
	$(000)	**$/Unit**	**$(000)**	**$/Unit**	**$(000)**	**$/Unit**
Sales	16,767	42.45	17,847	41.80	18,150	41.25
COGS	10,738	27.18	11,316	26.50	11,409	25.93
Gross margin	6,029	15.27	7,299	15.30	6,741	15.32

Scope Marketing Plan Inputs
Scope "Going" Marketing Spending

Year	*1990*	*1989*	*1988*
Advertising (000)	$1,700	—	—
Promotion (000)	1,460	—	—
Total (000)	$3,160	$3,733	$2,697

Marketing Input Costs

Advertising:		(See previous table)
Promotion:	Samples	(Including Distribution): $0.45/piece
	Mailed couponing	$10.00 per 1,000 for printing distribution
		$0.17 handling per redeemed coupon (beyond face value) redemption rates: 10% to 15%
	In-store promotion	$200/store (fixed)
		$0.17 handling per redeemed coupon (beyond face value) redemption rates: 85%+

Source: Company records.

EXHIBIT 8

Scope 1990 Financials

	$(000)	$/Unit
Net sales[a]	18,150	41.25
Ingredients	3,590	8.16
Packaging	2,244	5.10
Manufacturing[b]	3,080	7.00
Delivery	1,373	3.12
Miscellaneous[c]	1,122	2.55
Cost of goods sold	11,409	25.93
Gross margin	6,741	15.32

[a] Net sales = P&G revenues.

[b] Manufacturing: 50 percent of manufacturing cost is fixed of which $200,000 is depreciation; 20 percent of manufacturing cost is labor.

[c] Miscellaneous: 75 percent of miscellaneous cost is fixed. General office overhead is $1,366,000. Taxes are 40 percent. Currently the plant operates on a five-day one-shift operation. P&G's weighted average cost of capital is 12 percent. Total units sold in 1990 were 440,000.

Source: Company records.

Finance

The point of view from Finance was mixed. On the one hand, Plax commanded a higher dollar price/liter and so it made sense that a new rinse might be a profitable option. On the other hand, they were concerned about the capital costs and the marketing costs that might be involved to launch a line extension. One option would be to source the product from a U.S. plant where the necessary equipment already existed. If the product was obtained from the U.S., delivery costs would increase by $1 per unit. Scope's current marketing and financial picture is shown in Exhibits 7 and 8 and an estimate of Plax's financial picture is provided in Exhibit 9.

EXHIBIT 9

Plax Financial Estimates ($/Unit)

Net Sales	*65.09*
COGS	
Ingredients	6.50
Packaging	8.30
Manufacturing	6.50
Delivery	3.00
Miscellaneous	1.06
Total	25.36

Notes: General overhead costs estimated at $5.88/unit.

Source: P&G estimates.

Purchasing

The Purchasing Manager had reviewed the formula for the line extension and had estimated that the ingredients cost would increase by $2.55 per unit due to the addition of new ingredients. But, because one of the ingredients was very new, Finance felt that the actual ingredient change might vary by ± 50%. Packaging costs would be $0.30 per unit higher owing to the fact that the setup charges would be spread over a smaller base.

Advertising Agency

The Advertising Agency felt that making any new claims for Scope was a huge strategic shift for the brand. They favored a line extension. Scope's strategy had always been "breath refreshment and good tasting" focused, and they saw the plaque claims as very different, with potentially significant strategic implications. The one time they had focused advertising only on taste and didn't reinforce breath efficacy, share fell. They were concerned that the current Scope consumer could be confused if plaque or any "nonbreath" claims were added and that Scope could actually lose market share if this occurred. They also pointed out that trying to communicate two different ideas in one commercial was very difficult. They believed the line extension was a completely different product from Scope with a different benefit and use occasion. In their minds, a line extension would need to be supported on a going basis separately from Scope.

■ WHAT TO RECOMMEND?

Hearst knew the business team had thought long and hard about the issue. She knew that management was depending on the Scope business team to come up with the right long-term plan for P&G—even if that meant not introducing the new product. However, she felt there was too much risk associated with P&G's long-term position in oral rinses if nothing was done. There was no easy answer—and compounding the exigencies of the situation was the fact that the business team had differing points of view. She was faced with the dilemma of providing recommendations about Scope, but also needed to ensure that there was alignment and commitment from the business team, or Senior Management would be unlikely to agree to the proposal.

■ APPENDIX

Plaque

Plaque is a soft, sticky film that coats teeth within hours of brushing and may eventually harden into tartar. To curb gum disease—which over 90 percent of Canadians suffer at some time—plaque must be curbed. Research has shown that, without brushing, within 24 hours a film (plaque) starts to spread over teeth and gums and, over days, becomes a sticky, gelatinous mat, which the plaque bacteria spin from sugars and starches. As the plaque grows it becomes home to yet more bacteria—dozens of strains. A mature plaque is about 75 percent bacteria; the remainder consists of organic solids from saliva, water, and other cells shed from soft oral tissues.

As plaque bacteria digest food, they also manufacture irritating malodorous byproducts, all of which can harm a tooth's supporting tissues as they seep into the crevice below the gum line. Within 10 to 21 days, depending on the person, signs of gingivitis—the mildest gum disease—first appear; gums deepen in color, swell, and lose their normally tight, arching contour around teeth. Such gingivitis is entirely reversible. It can disappear within a week after regular brushing and flossing are resumed. But when plaque isn't kept under control, gingivitis can be the first step down toward periodontitis, the more advanced gum disease in which bone and other structures that support the teeth become damaged. Teeth can loosen and fall out—or require extraction.

The traditional and still best approach to plaque control is careful and thorough brushing and flossing to scrub teeth clean of plaque. Indeed, the antiplaque claims that toothpastes carry are usually based on the product's ability to clean teeth mechanically, with brushing. Toothpastes contain abrasives, detergent, and foaming agents, all of which help the brush do its work.

CASE

Frito-Lay Company

Cracker Jack

In mid-July 1997, Lynne Peissig, Vice President and General Manager for New Ventures at the Frito-Lay Company, a division of PepsiCo, Inc., assembled the business team responsible for studying the possible acquisition of Cracker Jack from Borden Foods Corporation. Cracker Jack had been owned by Borden since 1964 and was one of the oldest and best-known trademarks in the United States. Borden's intention to sell the Cracker Jack brand and related assets had become public in June 1997. Peissig and the New Ventures Division initiated a study of the Cracker Jack business potential within days of the announcement.

The purpose of the all-day meeting was to (1) consolidate the findings of the business team, (2) outline a plan for how Cracker Jack might be marketed as a Frito-Lay brand, and (3) estimate the "fair market value" of the Cracker Jack business. The valuation would assist senior PepsiCo executives in determining an acquisition price should they decide to submit a bid on the Cracker Jack brand and related assets.

The effort of the business team benefited from the involvement of Frito-Lay brand marketing, sales, distribution, manufacturing, finance, legal, and research and development personnel and PepsiCo merger and acquisition staff working with the New Ventures Division. Peissig was scheduled to deliver a formal presentation and recommendation to senior PepsiCo executives within two weeks. She knew that the marketing issues identified, the plan outline, and the financial valuation by the business team would carry considerable weight in her recommendation to pursue or pass on the business opportunity made possible by the acquisition of the Cracker Jack brand and related assets.

FRITO-LAY COMPANY

Frito-Lay Company is a division of PepsiCo, Inc. Frito-Lay recorded an operating profit of $1.63 billion on net sales of $9.68 billion in 1996, which represented 31 percent of PepsiCo's net sales and 60 percent of PepsiCo's operating profit. The sales and operating profit compounded annual growth rate for Frito-Lay was 13 percent for the five-year period, 1991 to 1996. Frito-Lay Company is composed of Frito-Lay North America and Frito-Lay International. Frito-Lay North America, consisting of operations in the United States and Canada, recorded 68 percent of company sales and 79 percent of company operating profit in 1996.

The cooperation of the Frito-Lay Company in the preparation of this case is gratefully acknowledged. BAKED LAY'S, BAKED TOSTITOS, CHEE-TOS, DORITOS, FRITOS, FUNYUNS, LAY'S, ROLD GOLD, RUFFLES, SANTITAS, SUN CHIPS, TOSTITOS, SMARTFOODS, and GRANDMA'S are trademarks used by the Frito-Lay Company. After the acquisition, CRACKER JACK, SAILOR JACK, and BINGO would be trademarks used by the Frito-Lay Company. This case was prepared by Professor Roger A. Kerin, of the Edwin L. Cox School of Business, Southern Methodist University, with the assistance of Daniel Goe and Rebecca Kaufman, graduate students, as a basis for class discussion and is not designed to illustrate effective or ineffective handling of an administrative situation. Certain company information, including names of Frito-Lay executives, are disguised and not useful for research purposes.

Company Background

Frito-Lay is a worldwide leader in the manufacturing and marketing of snacks. Well-known company brands include Lay's and Ruffles potato chips, Fritos corn chips, Doritos, Tostitos, and Santitas tortilla chips, Chee·tos cheese-flavored snacks, and Rold Gold pretzels. Other well-known Frito-Lay brands include Sun Chips multigrain snacks and Funyuns onion-flavored snacks. In addition, the company markets a line of dips, salsas, nuts, peanut butter and cheese-filled sandwich crackers, processed beef sticks, Smartfood brand ready-to-eat popcorn, and Grandma's brand cookies.

The company is the leading manufacturer of snack chips in the United States, capturing 54 percent of the retail sales in this category in 1996. Nine of Frito-Lay's snack chips are among the top 10 best-selling snack brands in U.S. supermarkets (see Exhibit 1). Doritos tortilla chips and Lays and Ruffles potato chips each have the distinction of being the only snack chips with over $1 billion in retail sales in the world.

A major source of volume growth for Frito-Lay in the 1990s was due to the introduction of "better-for-you" low-fat and no-fat snacks. These snacks, including Baked Lay's potato crisps, Baked Tostitos tortilla chips, and Rold Gold pretzels, accounted for 47 percent of Frito-Lay's total pound volume growth in 1995 and 1996, and 40 percent of pound volume growth in 1994. Better-for-you products represented 15 percent of Frito-Lay's total snack volume in 1996, up from 5 percent in 1993.

Frito-Lay's U.S. snack food business spans every aspect of snack food production and distribution, from agriculture to stocking retailer shelves. During 1996 in the United States alone, Frito-Lay used 2.7 billion pounds of potatoes, one billion pounds of corn, and over 15 million pounds of cheese to produce its products. The company has 45 manufacturing plants in 26 states, including the world's largest snack food

EXHIBIT 1

Top-Selling Snack Chip Items in U.S. Supermarkets (Retail Sales in $ millions)

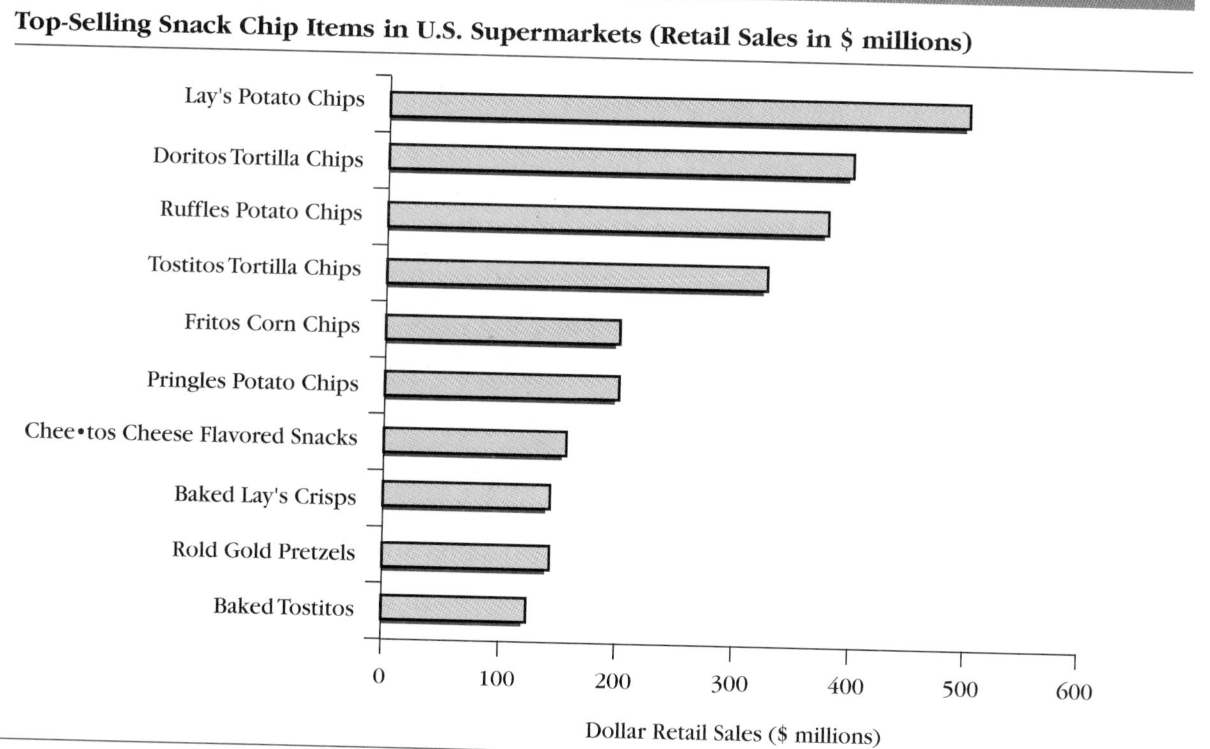

Source: 1996 PepsiCo, Inc., annual report.

plant in Frankfort, Indiana, and operates more than 1,800 warehouses and distribution facilities. Frito-Lay employs 17,500 sales people—the largest store-door-delivery sales force in the world—who make 750,000 sales and delivery calls on approximately 350,000 retail store customers each week. Frito-Lay's products receive constant attention from the company's sales force, which ensures constant replenishment of fresh product and proper facings of products on store shelves. Supermarkets and grocery stores accounted for more than 50 percent of Frito-Lay's total U.S. retail sales in 1996, followed by convenience stores (15 percent), mass merchandise/warehouse/club stores (11 percent), vending and food service operators (8 percent), and other retailers and institutions (10 percent).

Frito-Lay consistently ranks among the leading national advertisers in the United States, both in terms of dollars spent and creative execution. The company also uses trade and consumer promotions and sponsors special events, such as the Tostitos Fiesta Bowl postseason collegiate football game.

New Ventures Division

The New Ventures Division at Frito-Lay originated in December 1996 with a well-defined mission:

> To drive significant Frito-Lay growth by seeking and creating new business platforms and products which combine the best of Frito-Lay advantages with high-impact consumer food solutions.

According to Casey Joseph, Frito-Lay's Senior Vice President-Worldwide Marketing, the primary purpose of the New Ventures Division was to create meaningful growth outside of Frito-Lay's already successful existing snack businesses, and secondarily augment ongoing internal product development activities.

During the winter of 1997, the New Ventures mission manifested itself as a deliberate approach for identifying and developing sales and profit growth opportunities for Frito-Lay. After considerable discussion, three broad opportunity avenues emerged as possible routes for achieving meaningful future growth. One growth avenue consisted of opportunities for building Frito-Lay's existing snack business by expanding into new eating occasions for current or new products. Ongoing internal research and development efforts to identify "better-for-you" products for morning and all-day consumption fell into this category. A second growth avenue was the opportunity to successfully enter new product categories by capitalizing on Frito-Lay's store-door-delivery sales force strengths, broad distribution coverage, and brand marketing skills. This opportunity could be realized through internal research and development or through targeted distribution alliances and acquisitions. Possible new product categories for Frito-Lay included confectionaries (e.g., candies) and baked sweet pastries, single-serve cakes, or snack bars. A third growth avenue was labeled "opportunistic acquisitions" made possible by related food companies offering products or entire businesses for sale as a result of corporate restructuring. These acquisitions would be screened by the New Ventures Division on the basis of their strategic and operating fit with Frito-Lay's sales, distribution, manufacturing, and brand marketing capabilities and meaningful sales and profit growth potential.

The announcement by Borden of its intention to divest the Cracker Jack brand and related assets represented a potential fit with all three growth avenues. According to Lynne Peissig:

> Early in our discussions, the New Ventures Division came to believe that sweet snacks represented a potential incremental growth opportunity for Frito-Lay. Cracker Jack appeared to be a logical "step out" versus a "leap" into sweet snacks from a strategic perspective. It could provide the foundation for a sweet snack platform to build a successful business on and complement Frito-Lay's salty snack busi-

ness. Cracker Jack, with its strong brand equities, was certainly worth the time and effort to explore as an acquisition.

THE READY-TO-EAT CARAMEL POPCORN PRODUCT CATEGORY

The ready-to-eat (RTE) caramel popcorn product category recorded U.S. retail sales of $192 million in 1996 and $205 million in 1995. Manufacturer sales of RTE caramel popcorn were $167.3 million in 1996, down 6.2 percent from 1995. The decline in 1996 category dollar sales followed a steady annual sales increase since 1993. Pound volume in the RTE caramel popcorn category declined from 59.3 million pounds in 1995 to 57 million pounds in 1996, following a steady annual volume growth since 1993. Category sales and volume growth in the 1990s was due primarily to the introduction of new flavors (i.e., butter toffee) and low-fat and no-fat varieties of established brands.

Competitors

Several different types of competitors serve the RTE caramel popcorn category: (1) national brand firms, (2) seasonal/specialty firms, (3) regional firms, and (4) private label firms. National brand firms, which distribute products throughout the United States, include Borden Foods (Cracker Jack brand), International Home Foods, Inc. (Crunch 'n Munch brand), Lincoln Foods (Fiddle Faddle brand), and SIM-GT Licensing Corporation, which markets the Richard Simmons brand. A second category of competitors consists of seasonal/specialty firms that produce and market their caramel popcorn on a seasonal basis (often around December and the Christmas holiday season) or as a specialty item frequently sold in collectible tins. Seasonal/specialty firms include Houstons Foods and Harry and David. A large number of small, regional firms produce and distribute RTE caramel popcorn in only certain parts of the United States. Private brands are produced by regional or local manufacturers on a contractual basis for major U.S. supermarket chains. Estimated 1996 sales and pound volume market shares for individual national brands, seasonal/specialty/regional brands, and private labels are shown in Exhibit 2 on page 190.

International Home Foods, Inc. (Crunch 'n Munch) and Borden Foods (Cracker Jack) are the RTE caramel popcorn category dollar and volume market share leaders in the United States. Prior to 1996, International Home Foods was the consumer foods unit of American Home Products Corporation (AHP). AHP is a multinational human and animal health care and agricultural products company with net sales exceeding $14 billion in 1996. In November 1996, AHP sold a majority interest (80%) in the food unit for approximately $1.2 billion to a limited partnership, of which the investment firm of Hicks, Muse, Tate & Furst is the general partner. International Home Foods produces and markets name-brand preserved foods. Its nationally known products include Chef Boyardee pastas (which represents nearly 30% of sales), Bumble Bee tuna, Polaner fruit spread, and PAM cooking spray. The company also sells southwestern cuisine foods (Ro*Tel canned tomatoes, Dennison's canned chili, and Ranch Style beans) and snack foods (Crunch 'n Munch caramel popcorn and Jiffy Pop popcorn). International Home Foods recorded net sales of $942.8 million in 1996.

Borden, Inc. is owned by the investment firm of Kohlberg Kravis Roberts & Co., which purchased the company for $1.9 billion in 1994. Although widely known for its dairy products, Borden divested its dairy business in 1997. Today, the company makes pasta, soup mixes, and bouillon (Borden Foods), snack foods (Wise Foods and Cracker Jack), consumer adhesives (Elmer's products), and industrial adhesives, coat-

EXHIBIT 2

Caramel Corn Category Dollar and Volume Share at Retail: 1996

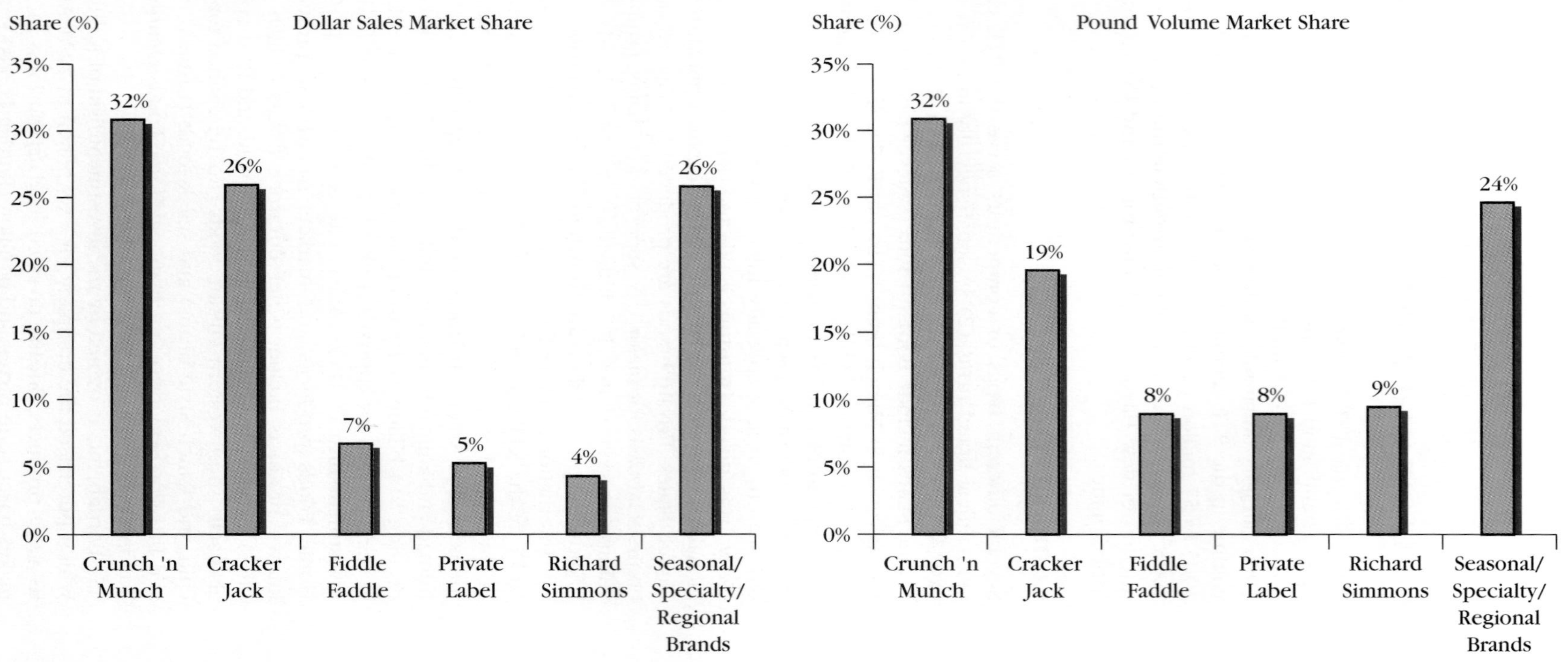

Share (%)

Dollar Sales Market Share

35%
30%
25%
20%
15%
10%
5%
0%

32%
26%
7%
5%
4%
26%

Crunch 'n Munch
Cracker Jack
Fiddle Faddle
Private Label
Richard Simmons
Seasonal/ Specialty/ Regional Brands

Share (%)

Pound Volume Market Share

35%
30%
25%
20%
15%
10%
5%
0%

32%
19%
8%
8%
9%
24%

Crunch 'n Munch
Cracker Jack
Fiddle Faddle
Private Label
Richard Simmons
Seasonal/ Specialty/ Regional Brands

Source: Company records.

ings, and resins (Borden Chemical). Borden, Inc. recorded net sales of about $5.8 billion in 1996.

The decision by Borden to divest itself of Cracker Jack and related assets was prompted by a strategic assessment of the company's focus and resources. The company chose to focus on its pasta business and expand into grain-based meals that would require a significant resource investment. As a consequence of this assessment and growth plan, Borden Foods announced that Cracker Jack, along with Borden Brands North America and Borden Brands International, would be sold in 1997.

Marketing Practice

RTE caramel popcorn is generally viewed among snack food industry analysts as an "undermarketed" category, when compared with microwave popcorn and most other snack categories. Most brands in the category offer both caramel and butter toffee flavors and feature both regular and low-fat/fat-free varieties in different package sizes. An exception is the Richard Simmons brand, which is sold only as a fat-free product.

Only Crunch 'n Munch and Cracker Jack have been recently advertised in consumer media. Crunch 'n Munch leads the category in advertising expenditures, outspending Cracker Jack by a wide margin since 1993 (see Exhibit 3, page 192). The last time Cracker Jack spent significant funds for consumer advertising occurred in 1992, when $2.1 million was spent to launch the brand's butter toffee flavor. Consumer and trade promotions are often used by national and regional brands. Consumer promotions include in-store and newspaper couponing and product sampling; trade promotions include sales aids and off-invoice allowances for retailers.

Supermarkets and grocery stores and mass merchandise/warehouse/club stores are the principal retail outlets for RTE caramel popcorn. Supermarkets and grocery stores account for an estimated 44.7 percent of category dollar sales. About 42 percent of sales occur in mass merchandise/warehouse/club stores (Target, Kmart, Wal-Mart). Drugstores account for 13 percent of sales. Remaining sales arise from a variety of other retail and food service outlets. In 1996, Crunch 'n Munch had an estimated 31 percent volume share in supermarkets and grocery stores, an 18 percent share in mass merchandise/warehouse/club stores, and a 13 percent share in drugstores. Cracker Jack's market share in these channels was 23 percent, 8 percent, and 11 percent, respectively, according to industry sources.

Retail outlets for RTE caramel popcorn are typically serviced via warehouse delivery systems. With a warehouse system, product is delivered from a manufacturer's plant or distribution center to a retailer's warehouse. The retailer assumes responsibility for distributing the product to its stores and stocking shelves.

Cracker Jack is the premium-priced brand in the RTE caramel popcorn category. Its total brand average price premium relative to Crunch 'n Munch has averaged about 28 percent over the past three years. Private (store) labels are typically the lowest-priced brands. Regional brands are often priced between national brands and private labels. In some areas, regional "gourmet" brands and seasonal/specialty brands are priced at or near national brands.

Caramel Popcorn Consumer

Industry research shows that RTE caramel popcorn is a snack primarily eaten at home in the afternoon and evening as a treat or reward. Four of five users eat RTE caramel popcorn at home, and 80 percent of eating occasions are in the afternoon or evening hours. Only about 12 percent of U.S. households consume RTE caramel popcorn. Average consumption frequency is also low relative to other snack categories at less than two purchases per year. Whereas two percent of U.S. households consume RTE caramel popcorn at least once in a typical two-week period, 70 per-

EXHIBIT 3

Competitive Spending for Consumer Media Advertising: 1993–1997

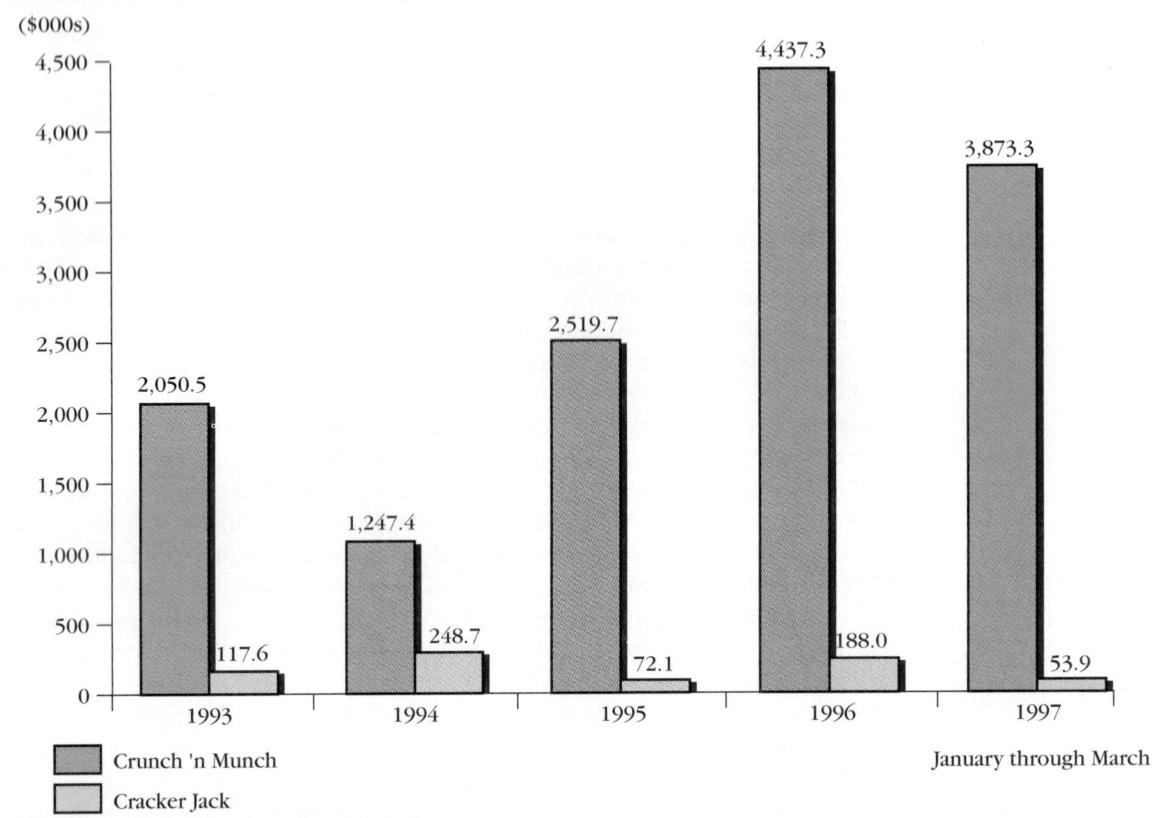

cent consume a salty snack (e.g., potato chips) and 31 percent consume candy (excluding gum and mints).

Industry research also shows that U.S. households with a female household head between the ages of 25 and 44, with children ages 4 to 17, is the heavy user of RTE caramel popcorn and Cracker Jack. This research further documents that:

1. Adult females consume 44 percent of caramel popcorn sold, adult males consume 29 percent, and children under age 18 consume 27 percent.
2. Fifty-four percent of heavy caramel popcorn users and 60 percent of heavy Cracker Jack purchasers reside in households with more than two members.
3. Fifty percent of heavy Cracker Jack purchasers and 42 percent of heavy caramel popcorn users are in households with children under age 18.

■ CRACKER JACK BRAND

Cracker Jack is one of the most recognized consumer food brands in the United States. The brand name enjoys a 97 percent awareness among persons between the ages of 15 and 60. Cracker Jack has a 95 percent brand name awareness among heavy users of caramel popcorn.

Brand Heritage

Cracker Jack is the original caramel popcorn. Invented by F. W. Ruekheim, the confection of popcorn, peanuts, and molasses was first made and sold in 1893 at the World's Fair Columbian Exhibition in Chicago, Illinois. The Cracker Jack name was coined in 1896 when a visiting salesman tasted the product and exclaimed, "That's a cracker jack!"—a nineteenth-century slang phrase meaning, "That's great." In 1899, Cracker Jack was packaged in moisture-proof boxes making possible broadened distribution of the product.

Three developments in the early 1900s had lasting effects on the image of Cracker Jack. In 1908, the brand was immortalized in the song, "Take Me Out to the Ball Game," with its lyric "Buy me some peanuts and Cracker Jack." In 1912, F. W. Ruekheim introduced the prize-in-every-box novelty, featuring magnifying glasses, little books, beads, metal trains and whistles, and baseball cards, among other items. More than 17 billion Cracker Jack toys have been distributed since 1912. A patriotic flair was added to the Cracker Jack box during World War I (1914–1918) with the inclusion of red, white, and blue stripes. A saluting Sailor Jack and his dog, Bingo, were also added to the box and soon became the national Cracker Jack logo. Sailor Jack and Bingo have appeared on Cracker Jack packages with only slight variations since 1918.

Cracker Jack Product Line and Positioning

For 100 years, the Cracker Jack product line consisted only of caramel-coated popcorn and peanuts, using the original recipe developed by F. W. Ruekheim. In 1992, a Butter Toffee flavor was introduced, followed by Nutty Deluxe in 1994, and Cracker Jack Fat Free (in Original and Butter Toffee flavors) in 1995. Approximately 23 percent of Cracker Jack dollar and pound volume sales growth between 1993 and 1995 could be attributed to these product introductions. The breakdown of Cracker Jack 1996 net dollar sales by formulation is shown below:

Product Formulation	***Net Dollar Sales (%)***
Original/Butter Toffee	63.0%
Original/Butter Toffee Fat Free	26.0
Nutty Deluxe	6.7
Other*	4.3
Total	100.0%

* The other category consists primarily of inventory with limited shelf-life sold to a number of prequalified off-price retailers.

Cracker Jack is sold in a variety of packages. The product is packaged in 1.05-ounce and 1.25-ounce single-serve boxes and bags (introduced in December 1996) and 7-ounce and 8-ounce family-size bags and bags-in-boxes (introduced in 1992). The combinations of flavors, package sizes, and package forms (boxes, bags, and bags-in-boxes) resulted in a product line with 32 separate items or stock-keeping units (SKUs) in 1996. Family-size bags-in-boxes accounted for 75 percent of net dollar sales; single-serve boxes accounted for 25 percent of net dollar sales in 1996. Single-serve and family-size bags represented an insignificant percentage of net dollar sales in 1996. Representative items in the Cracker Jack product line are shown in Exhibit 4 (page 194).

Cracker Jack positioning over the past 30 years focused on its brand heritage as a traditional fun treat. This positioning manifested itself in the primary message for Cracker Jack advertising as illustrated below:

1. "What do you want when you've gotta have something . . . candy coated popcorn, peanuts and a prize" (1960s)

EXHIBIT 4

Cracker Jack Product Line

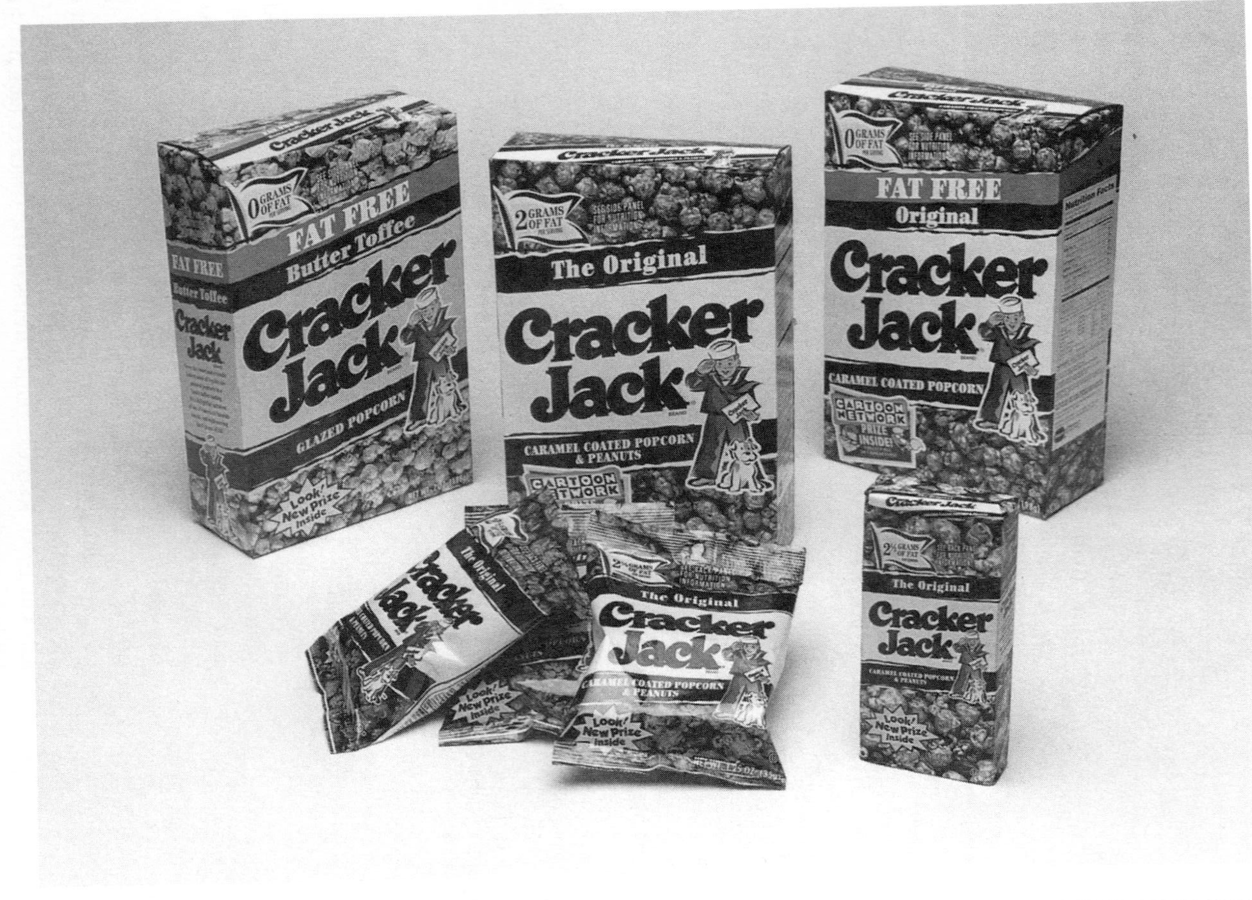

2. "When you're really good they call you Cracker Jack," featuring contemporary children excelling in athletics (1970s and early 1980s)
3. "Delicious then, delicious now," featuring a dual child/adult appeal reminding mothers how much they enjoyed Cracker Jack when growing up (mid-1980s)
4. "Only one snack says Cracker Jack," featuring its unique brand heritage (early 1990s). In 1992, the Butter Toffee flavor was introduced and positioned as a unique, all-family, all-occasion snack that provided a delicious-tasting, fun experience.

Cracker Jack's positioning was broadened in mid-1997 to emphasize the "better-for-you" qualities of Cracker Jack Fat Free in both Original and Butter Toffee flavors: "Cracker Jack, the sweet and crunchy fun snack you remember, has surprisingly less fat than you thought." The new positioning was being applied to all forms of brand communication, including packaging, consumer promotion, public relations, and consumer advertising.

Advertising and Promotion

Annual advertising and promotion spending for the Cracker Jack brand, as a percentage of sales, has ranged between 28 and 40 percent since 1993. Trade promotion, including incentives given retailers to reduce their cost or gain merchandising performance (off-invoice allowances, slotting fees, and market-development funds), represented the principal expense since 1993. Consumer promotion, including in-store and Sunday newspaper coupon insertions and redemption cost, and "other" promotions such as sales aids and samples accounted for the second largest expense item. Consumer advertising represented the smallest expense category. Cracker Jack has not been advertised nationally since 1993. However, as recently as 1980, Cracker Jack was the most advertised sweet snack in the United States, with a $6 million spending level.

The Cracker Jack toy surprise is another element of the advertising and promotion program. The choice of prizes is based on research among mothers and children to determine appeal. All toys must also pass rigorous safety testing to be considered as Cracker Jack prizes. In addition to long-time favorites, such as miniature baseball cards, Cracker Jack has licensed high-profile children's properties (e.g., Animaniacs, Looney Tunes, Wishbone, Scooby Doo) since 1995 to add value to the toy surprise. This effort has focused on promoting impulse purchases, particularly for Cracker Jack's highest gross margin items—the 1.05-ounce and 1.25-ounce single-serve box and bag.

Sales and Distribution

Cracker Jack sales volume is concentrated in the United States, where 98.9 percent of sales occur. Sales in Canada and a small export business represent the remaining 1.1 percent of volume. In 1996, 52 percent of Cracker Jack sales arose from supermarkets and grocery stores, 31 percent from mass merchandisers, 7 percent from drugstores, 4 percent from warehouse and club stores, and 6 percent from other outlets.

Cracker Jack is sold through a shared Borden sales force that also sells cheese and other Borden grocery brands such as Eagle Brand, Cremora, and ReaLemon. The retail grocery sales force includes 47 people who sell product to supermarkets and grocery stores through 65 independent food brokers. An independent broker organization of 20 people sells product directly to mass merchandise, military, drugstore, and club store customers.

Cracker Jack is shipped from 13 company distribution centers to retail store distribution centers or warehouses and subsequently delivered to retail outlets for stocking on store shelves by retail store personnel. Accordingly, Cracker Jack is typically placed in what is called the "warehouse-delivered snack aisles" of supermarkets and grocery stores versus the "direct-store delivery aisles," which are stocked and merchandised by a manufacturer's sales force and not retail store personnel.

Pricing

Borden Foods has employed a premium pricing strategy for Cracker Jack relative to competing national brands (e.g., Crunch 'n Munch). Cracker Jack prices have risen by an average of 5 to 6 percent per year since 1993. As a consequence, Cracker Jack's average retail price premium relative to Crunch 'n Munch was about 28 percent on a per-ounce basis since 1993. The price premium was expanded in January 1997, when the price for Cracker Jack was increased by 6 percent. However, this price premium margin quickly eroded when the 10- and 5-ounce Crunch 'n Munch packages were downsized to 8- and 4-ounce packages, respectively, without a change in price. The effect of this move was to reduce the Cracker Jack price premium for the 7-ounce and 8-ounce family-size packages to 14 percent.

Manufacturing

Borden Foods manufactures Cracker Jack at its Northbrook, Illinois, facility along with selected Borden Foods soup products. Cracker Jack equipment occupies about 32 percent of the facility's manufacturing space. This space houses 15 production lines, 11 box lines, and 4 bag lines. The production lines operate at approximately 33 percent capacity, and the box and bag lines operate at 85 percent capacity based on a five-day week and two eight-hour shifts per day. Approximately 450,000 to 500,000 packages are produced per day, warehoused at the site, and subsequently shipped to company distribution centers.

A unique feature of the production and packaging process is the Cracker Jack prize insertion activity. Prizes are collated on custom-made equipment designed by the company, and electric eyes are placed within the production lines to ensure that these prizes are inserted in boxes. In 1994, about 85 percent of the company's total capital expenditures was spent to automate the family-size bag-in-box packaging line and change the filling operation from a volumetric cup filler to a more accurate scale system.

Cracker Jack Strategy and Financial Performance: 1993–1996

Exhibit 5 contains Cracker Jack Direct Product Contribution Income Statements for the period 1993 to 1996.[1] Cracker Jack recorded a negative Direct Product Contribution in each of the three previous years (1994 to 1996). Borden's current management attributed this performance to a variety of sources. Beginning in 1992, prior management pursued a volume-based strategy that focused on introducing family-size packages (7- and 8-ounce bags and bags-in-boxes) while reducing emphasis on the smaller box packages (e.g., 1.25-ounce box). This strategy achieved its intended effect. Cracker Jack pound volume in supermarkets and grocery stores, mass mer-

[1] Direct Product Contribution Income Statements exclude certain direct and indirect expenses which customarily are allocated to products in accordance with Borden Foods' internal policies. These allocated expense categories, which change from time to time, represent the costs associated with the functional infrastructure of Borden Foods and include certain fixed sales and administrative expenses. In addition, costs related to certain systems, legal expenses, finance/accounting, and human resource/benefit services provided by Borden Foods Corporate headquarters have also been excluded in determining Direct Product Contribution. All financial information contained in these exhibits has been disguised and is not useful for external research purposes.

EXHIBIT 5

Cracker Jack Direct Product Contribution Income Statement: 1993–1996 ($ in Millions)

	1993	*1994*	*1995*	*1996*
Net trade sales	**$51.4**	**$ 51.7**	**$53.2**	**$48.4**
Cost of goods sold	26.0	33.8	32.2	27.1
Gross margin	**$25.4**	**$ 17.9**	**$21.0**	**$21.3**
Distribution expense	$ 4.6	$ 6.1	$ 5.5	$ 4.4
Trade promotion	11.4	16.0	15.6	8.6
Advertising, consumer, & other promotion	5.9	4.8	5.2	5.0
Variable sales	1.1	1.4	1.3	1.2
A & P management	0.3	0.4	0.8	0.8
Market research	0.3	1.0	2.3	2.5
Technical research	0.1	0.2	0.4	0.6
Direct product contribution[a]	**$ 1.7**	**($ 12.0)**	**($ 10.1)**	**($ 1.8)**
Other financial information:				
Depreciation expense	$ 1.5	$ 1.6	$ 1.4	$ 1.4
Capital expenditures	$ 1.4	$ 5.3	$ 0.8	$ 0.3
Working capital[b]	$16.4	$ 12.8	$ 6.3	$ 2.3

[a] Excludes effects of allocated selling costs, overhead, and other income and expense.

[b] Current assets (other than cash) minus current liabilities.

Explanatory Notes for Revenue and Expense Items:

Revenue recognition. Net trade sales are generally recognized when products are shipped. Liabilities are established for estimated returns, allowances, and consumer and trade discounts when revenues are recognized.

Cost of goods sold. Includes all variable costs associated with producing the product, including raw materials, packaging supplies, direct and indirect labor, and plant fixed overhead expenses including a BFC allocation for quality assurance and engineering.

Distribution expense. Expenses associated with moving finished good from distribution centers to customers and all handling and storage charges of moving goods into, within, and out of third-party warehouses.

Variable sales. Commission or other payments to brokers associated with volume.

A & P management. Costs associated with business unit marketing personnel.

Market research. Syndicated consumer information, taste tests, package tests, focus groups, and other market research.

Advertising costs. Production costs of future media advertising are expensed on the first airdate or print-release date of the advertising. All other advertising is expensed as incurred.

Trade promotion. All incentives to the trade related to tactics to reduce price or gain merchandising performance. Included are off-invoice allowances, slotting, and market development funds.

Consumer promotion. Promotion expenses targeted at consumers including coupon insertion and redemption and consumer refunds/premiums in return for certain purchase level requirements.

Other promotion. Includes sales aids, samples, packaging development, and racks.

Technical research. Costs associated with product or process research and development.

Note: All financial information in this exhibit has been disguised and is not useful for external research purposes.

chandisers, warehouse clubs, and drugstores combined increased to 12.4 million pounds in 1993, 13.5 million pounds in 1994, and 16.3 million pounds in 1995. However, the Cracker Jack gross margin percentage suffered due to a smaller margin contribution on large packages, which cannibalized higher margin small packages. In addition, rising material prices in 1994 and 1995 reduced margins since the added costs were not passed on with comparable price increases. Also, the introduction of Nutty Deluxe and Fat Free varieties in 1994 and 1995 was supported by a heavy financial investment in trade promotions. Even though these varieties accounted for almost one-fourth of Cracker Jack dollar and volume sales growth between 1993 and 1995, this growth was not large enough to offset the incremental trade promotion costs.

Direct Product Contribution improved in 1996 due to a number of changes made by current Borden management. For example, trade promotion spending was reduced. The number of Cracker Jack SKUs was reduced from 47 in 1995 to 32 in 1996, which reduced inventory levels and improved the sales mix gross margin. However, Cracker Jack dollar sales declined by 9 percent and unit volume fell to 11.2 million pounds in 1996.

Exhibit 6 shows the Cracker Jack balance sheet for the year ended December 31, 1996. In addition to the physical assets shown, other Cracker Jack assets include the trademarks Cracker Jack, the Sailor Jack and Bingo representation, Nutty Deluxe, and "When you're really good they call you Cracker Jack," and certain patents related to the manufacturing of Cracker Jack.

Cracker Jack Strategy and Financial Projections: 1997–2001

The financial performance of Cracker Jack through 1995 prompted a change in strategy in 1996. The new Cracker Jack strategy arose from a general strategic review of the entire Borden Foods Corporation begun in 1995. The strategy, adopted in 1996, had three objectives: (1) revitalize the base business, (2) improve operating efficiencies, and (3) extend the Cracker Jack trademark. These objectives would be realized by (1) expanded distribution within retail snack and food service marketing channels, (2) developing new packaging and flavors, (3) impactful product positioning,

EXHIBIT 6

Cracker Jack Balance Sheet: December 31, 1996 ($ in Millions)

Assets	
Cash and marketable securities	—
Net trade receivables*	$ 2.0
Inventories	4.2
Other current assets	0.2
Other long-term assets and intangibles	12.2
Net property, plant, and equipment	15.4
Total assets	**$34.0**
Liabilities and equity	
Trade and drafts payable*	$ 3.1
Other current liabilities	1.1
General insurance	2.2
Pension liability	0.3
Nonpension postemployment benefits	2.5
Total liabilities	**$ 9.2**
Owner's investment	**$24.8**

* Net trade receivables, trade and drafts payable, and certain other current liabilities are not being sold and are presented for informational purposes only.

Note: All financial information in this exhibit has been disguised and is not useful for external research purposes.

(4) enhanced gross margins via sustained price leadership, and (5) additional resources being allotted to consumer advertising.

Initial efforts in 1996 were designed to arrest the losses incurred in 1994 and 1995. The elimination of unprofitable trade promotions, the pruning of Cracker Jack SKUs from 47 to 32, and a higher gross margin resulted in a sizable improvement in the 1996 Direct Product Contribution. In late 1996 and early 1997, other actions were taken consistent with the new Cracker Jack strategy:

1. In December 1996, a single-serve (1.05- and 1.25-ounce) bag was introduced, primarily for distribution through vending machines and to Sam's Warehouse Clubs.
2. A 6 percent price increase was implemented in January 1997.
3. A new positioning that emphasized the low-fat content of Cracker Jack was initiated in mid-1997. This positioning—"Cracker Jack, the sweet and crunchy fun snack you remember, has surprisingly less fat than you thought"—highlighted the low-fat content of Original Cracker Jack (2.5 grams of fat per 1.25-ounce serving) and Cracker Jack Fat Free (0 grams of fat per serving).

Cracker Jack management believed that broadened distribution was the most important element of the new strategy. In December 1996, efforts were made to develop the vending machine business with the new single-serve bag using specialty distributors. Vending sales were projected to be almost $2 million in 1997. However, Cracker Jack management was of the view that the brand needed a totally new sales and delivery infrastructure to grow sales and product profitability. Specifically, the shared Borden sales force and broker/distributor network currently in use should be replaced by a direct-store-delivery (DSD) sales force. It was believed that a DSD sales force could provide product placement in grocery DSD snack aisles, which is the highest-velocity snack aisle in supermarkets. Limited, controlled store tests commissioned by Cracker Jack management indicated that placement in DSD snack aisles could initially boost dollar retail sales by as much as 38 percent. However, a DSD sales force is more resource intensive than Borden's present sales and distribution network. Borden Foods management was neither prepared to make the investments required nor equipped to handle a DSD sales force for Cracker Jack given the resource demands of other business opportunities.

Exhibit 7 on page 200 details projected Direct Product Contribution Income Statements prepared by Cracker Jack management for the period 1997 to 2001. The projections reflect the new strategy initiatives adopted by Borden's management and the integration of Cracker Jack into a national manufacturing, distribution, and sales infrastructure of a potential acquirer with an existing snack-related business.

The projection assumes significant revenue increases resulting from distribution expansion, primarily into grocery DSD, vending, and food service sales. It is also assumed that the acquirer would be willing and able to (1) fund trade promotions and consumer advertising to bolster sales of existing products and extend the product line and (2) raise prices. The projections also include capital expenditures, notably in 1999, that will be required to support the volume projections.

The Direct Product Contribution Income Statement projected for 1997 reflects Cracker Jack management's estimate of year-end results without a DSD sales force. Projected 1998 revenues demonstrate the estimated impact of a fully operational DSD sales force. These estimates focus exclusively on domestic opportunities for Cracker Jack and do not include potential export sales growth.

EXHIBIT 7

Cracker Jack Projected Direct Product Contribution Income Statements: 1997–2001 ($ in Millions)

	1997	*1998*	*1999*	*2000*	*2001*
Net trade sales	**$50.5**	**$78.5**	**$191.4**	**$209.1**	**$258.9**
Cost of goods sold	27.3	37.4	97.5	108.3	127.8
Gross margin	**$23.2**	**$41.1**	**$ 93.9**	**$100.8**	**$131.1**
Distribution expense	$ 4.4	$ 4.6	$ 9.7	$ 11.0	$ 13.0
Trade promotion	6.2	10.2	23.8	22.3	23.9
Advertising, consumer, & other promotion	5.3	11.3	19.9	20.1	24.8
Variable sales	1.4	2.4	3.6	3.9	4.6
A & P management	0.9	0.4	0.4	0.4	0.6
Market research	1.0	1.6	2.6	3.0	3.4
Technical research	0.7	0.8	1.8	2.1	2.6
Direct product contribution[a]	**$ 3.3**	**$ 9.8**	**$ 32.1**	**$ 38.0**	**$ 58.2**
Other financial information:					
Depreciation expense	$ 1.4	$ 1.9	$ 3.7	$ 4.2	$ 4.7
Capital expenditures	$ 0.4	$ 4.0	$ 19.3	$ 4.3	$ 6.4
Working capital[b]	$ 3.0	$ 5.0	$ 13.2	$ 14.4	$ 18.0

[a] Excludes effects of allocated selling costs, overhead, and other income and expense.

[b] Current assets (other than cash) minus current liabilities.

Note: All financial information in this exhibit has been disguised and is not useful for external research purposes.

PROJECT BINGO

The New Ventures team met in June 1997 to decide whether or not to explore the Cracker Jack acquisition. Following a review of financial and operating data supplied by Borden in its Offering Memorandum, the decision was made to examine Cracker Jack as an acquisition. The effort was code-named "Project Bingo."

Project Bingo consisted of commissioned studies, internal company reviews, and cross-functional team analyses and evaluations orchestrated by Lynne Peissig. The target completion date was July 15, 1997, with a presentation and recommendation to Frito-Lay senior management scheduled for August 1, 1997. A nonbinding open bid for Cracker Jack and its related assets from prospective buyers was due August 6, 1997. The top bidders would be invited to Northbrook, Illinois, for a plant visit and a Borden management presentation. A binding letter of intent and bid would be submitted by interested parties toward the end of September 1997. Peissig believed that bids for Cracker Jack would be submitted by a number of investment firms and consumer foods companies, including General Mills, Nabisco, and Procter & Gamble.

The data-gathering effort was substantially complete by mid-July 1997. Preliminary analyses had been conducted in four areas: (1) brand management, (2) sales and distribution, (3) manufacturing and product assurance, and (4) finance and administration.

Brand Management

The consensus opinion among the New Ventures team was that brand management considerations would drive Project Bingo. Two studies were commissioned, including (1) a brand awareness, image, equity, and usage study; and (2) a simulated test market.

Brand Awareness, Image, Equity, and Usage Study An independent research firm that specialized in ongoing brand-tracking studies for consumer goods companies submitted its report to Project Bingo's brand marketing team in late June 1997. The principal findings are summarized below:

1. The Cracker Jack name registers virtually universal awareness. However, Cracker Jack Fat Free, Butter Toffee, and Nutty Deluxe exhibit consumer awareness levels below 50 percent.
2. The Cracker Jack name evokes distinct imagery and icons in consumers' minds. These include the product form itself (caramel, popcorn, peanuts), the prize/toy in the box, the boy/sailor and dog on the box, and taste/flavor. Overall, Cracker Jack was perceived to be:
   - Traditional and old-fashioned in a way that evokes fond memories of growing up (but not very contemporary, and less contemporary than Crunch 'n Munch).
   - Popular with kids more than teens, adults, or the family.
   - More of a personal snack than a snack for sharing.
   - A good treat, but not necessarily extendible across eating occasions.
   - Fairly unique, particularly compared to other RTE caramel popcorn.
   - Not at all "better for you" compared to many other snacks.
   - Not as available for purchase, nor as easy to find in the stores as other RTE caramel popcorn.
   - Lacking a good variety of flavors/types.
3. Cracker Jack has a respectable brand equity due largely to its heritage and generally favorable image foundation. It is a recognized brand with a positive reputation that appears to have lost momentum (popularity) in recent years.
4. Only 7.1 percent of U.S. households consume Cracker Jack. These households consume less than one pound of Cracker Jack annually. Exhibit 8 (page 202) shows the major reasons why consumers do not buy Cracker Jack more often.

The study results were viewed favorably by the brand marketing team. According to one team member, "Cracker Jack is a trademark living off residual heritage with untapped opportunity."

Simulated Test Market Preliminary results from the simulated test market (STM) also proved "encouraging," according to a brand marketing team member. Unlike the brand awareness, image, equity, and usage study, the STM was commissioned to obtain an initial assessment of Cracker Jack's commercial potential.

The STM, conducted by another marketing research firm, consisted of four steps. First, consumers between the ages of 12 and 64, who had purchased a sweet or salty snack during the past three months, were recruited at shopping malls in 16 U.S. cities and escorted to a nearby research facility. These consumers were then exposed to an advertisement for Cracker Jack (see Exhibit 9, page 203). Following this exposure, consumers proceeded to a mock store setup where Cracker Jack was available for sale along with competing RTE caramel popcorn brands. Consumers were given money and could purchase whatever brands they wished, keeping any money left over. Finally, consumers who bought Cracker Jack were given two complimentary packages of Cracker Jack to take home. These consumers were called after a 2- to 3-week time period, asked a series of questions about the product, and offered a chance to repeat purchase the brand.

EXHIBIT 8

Most Important Reasons for Not Buying Cracker Jack More Often

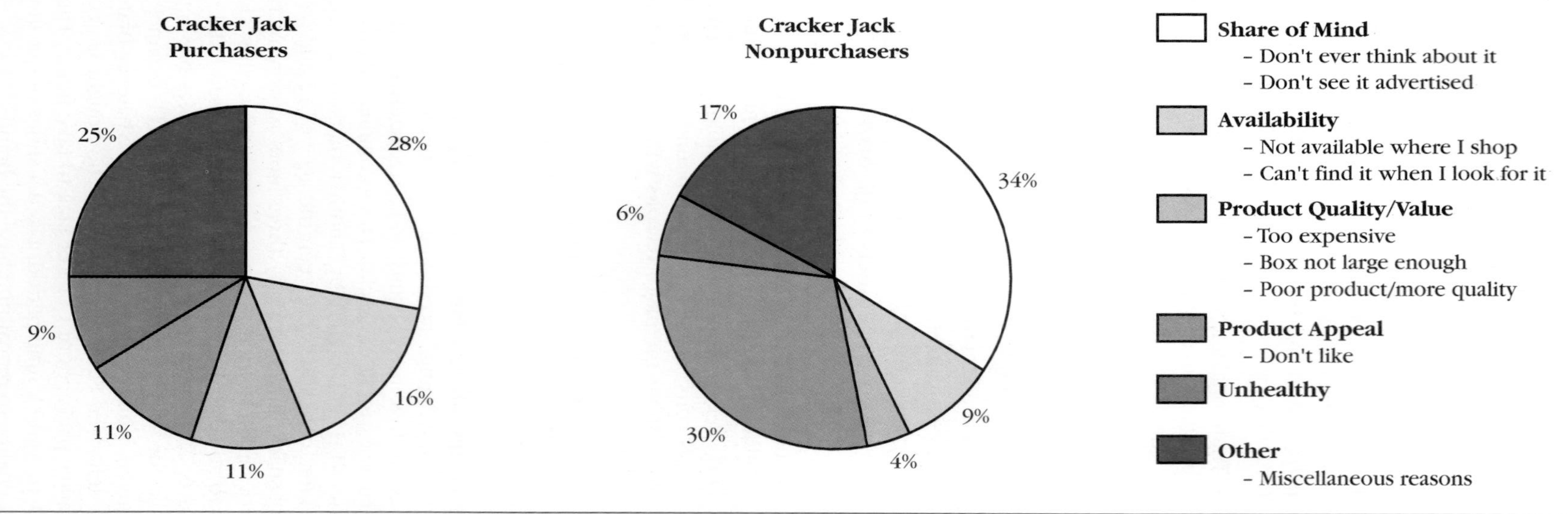

Source: Company records.

EXHIBIT 9

Cracker Jack Simulated Test Market Advertisement

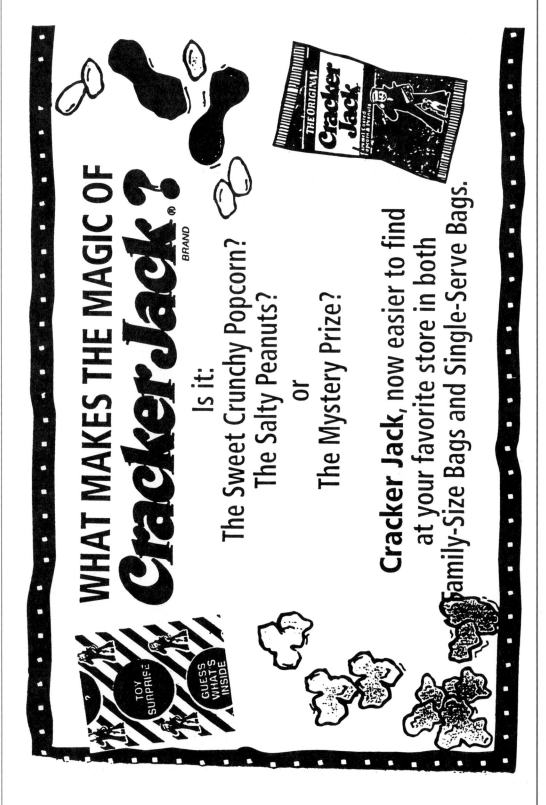

TOY SURPRISE

GUESS WHAT'S INSIDE

WHAT MAKES THE MAGIC OF

Cracker Jack® BRAND ?

Is it:

The Sweet Crunchy Popcorn?

The Salty Peanuts?

or

The Mystery Prize?

Cracker Jack, now easier to find at your favorite store in both Family-Size Bags and Single-Serve Bags.

THE ORIGINAL Cracker Jack

Diagnostic information was also gathered as part of the Cracker Jack STM. Consumer attitudes toward the brand (likes and dislikes) and usage intentions were obtained. These data were incorporated into computer simulation models that also included elements of the brand's intended marketing plan. The STM output included estimates of household brand trial and repeat rates, purchase amounts and frequency, product cannibalism, and first-year sales volume estimates.[2]

Fifteen different marketing plan options were tested in the Cracker Jack STM. Planned distribution coverage was set at levels comparable for Frito-Lay potato, corn, and tortilla chips. Two different store locations were tested: placement in the salty snack aisle versus the alternative snack aisle of stores. The present retail price of $1.69 for an 8-ounce box was tested, but the package type was varied to compare the 8-ounce box with a 7-ounce flex bag. Also, a $1.99 retail price was tested with an 8-ounce flex bag. Finally, three advertising and promotion expenditure levels ($15 million, $22 million, and $32 million) were simulated.

Diagnostic information gathered during the STM indicated that consumers had more "likes" than "dislikes" about Cracker Jack. Consumers gave favorable ratings to Cracker Jack's taste/flavor and texture/consistency. However, most consumers said there were not enough peanuts. Cracker Jack scored highly as an afternoon, early evening, and late evening snack, but low as a morning treat. Almost one-half (46%) of consumers said that the nuts, popcorn, and snack mix aisle was the preferred store location for buying Cracker Jack. The next most preferred store aisle was with salty snacks (24%), followed by the candy and cookie aisles and the checkout counter.

Exhibit 10 shows preliminary first-year pound and net sales dollar volume estimates for each of the marketing plan options. First-year net sales estimates ranged from $46.6 million to $124.4 million at manufacturer prices. Estimates of product cannibalism indicated that 22 percent of Cracker Jack pound volume would come from other Frito-Lay snack chip brands when the advertising and promotion expenditure was $32 million.[3] (*Case writer note:* Footnote 3 contains important information for case analysis purposes.) This percentage was 7 percent at the $15 million expenditure level. No estimates were made for the $22 million expenditure level. The incidence of product cannibalism did not vary by store location (salty snack versus alternative snack aisle). According to a New Ventures team member, "These preliminary results indicate that Cracker Jack has considerable upside potential given broadened availability through our extensive sales and distribution network and advertising and promotion support."

Cracker Jack Extensions In subsequent meetings with the brand marketing team, discussions focused on Cracker Jack extension possibilities beyond the first year. Brand marketing personnel believed that attention in the first year should focus on establishing the Cracker Jack base business given a new sales and distribution infrastructure. However, brand and flavor extensions should be pursued in the second and third year of Cracker Jack marketing as a Frito-Lay brand.

Several brand marketing team members advocated a brand extension in the second year. Specifically, they proposed that a Cracker Jack snack bar be introduced. Cereal marketers had experienced considerable success with these bars following the trend toward "grab-and-go" eating. For example, Kellogg's Rice Krispies Treats snack bar recorded over $100 million in supermarket retail sales over the past two years. Quaker

---

[2] For an extended description of STMs, see K. Clancy, R. Shulman, and M. Wolf, *Simulated Test Marketing: Technology for Launching Successful New Products* (New York: Lexington Books, 1994).

[3] Frito-Lay does not divulge profitability data on individual products and product lines. However, for case analysis and class discussion purposes, Frito-Lay snack chip brands can be assumed to have a gross profit of $1.05 per pound.

EXHIBIT 10

Cracker Jack Simulated Test Market First-Year Volume Projections

Marketing Plan Elements	*Preliminary Marketing Plan Options*														
Distribution/Product Placement	***Salty Snack Aisle***									***Alternative Snacks Aisle***					
Package form and retail (consumer) price	*8-oz. Bag-in-Box @ $1.69*			*7-oz. Flex Bag @ $1.69*			*8-oz. Flex Bag @ $1.99*			*8-oz Bag-in-Box @ $1.69*			*7-oz. Flex Bag @ $1.69*		
Advertising and promotion ($ million)[a]	*$15*	*$22*	*$32*	*$15*	*$22*	*$32*	*$15*	*$22*	*$32*	*$15*	*$22*	*$32*	*$15*	*$22*	*$32*
First-Year Volume Projections[b]															
Pound volume (millions)	24.3	34.0	40.7	22.6	31.6	37.8	26.0	36.4	43.8	20.5	32.2	38.9	19.0	29.9	36.2
Dollar sales volume (millions) @ manufacturer price to retailer (mfr. net sales)	$59.6	$83.4	$99.0	$55.1	$77.1	$92.5	$73.9	$103.7	$124.4	$50.4	$79.1	$95.7	$46.6	$72.6	$88.6

[a] Advertising and Promotion Breakdown:

	At $15 million	At $22 million	At $32 million
Consumer Advertising	$0	$10	$15
Consumer Promotion	8	5	10
Trade Promotion	7	7	7

[b] Volume forecasts are subject to a ± 15% accuracy range.

Note: All financial information in this exhibit has been disguised and is not useful for external research purposes.

Oats recently extended its oatmeal cereal with the launch of Fruit & Oatmeal Cereal bars supported by $20 million in trade promotion and consumer advertising. Brand marketing team members speculated that a Cracker Jack snack bar could generate $50 to $100 million in incremental manufacturer net sales in the second year if supported by a $10 million trade and consumer advertising and promotion program. It was believed that incremental snack bar sales would be somewhat dependent on first-year sales; that is, higher first-year sales would result in higher incremental snack bar sales.

A flavor extension, added to the current caramel and butter toffee flavors, might be introduced in the third year, according to brand marketing team members. A specific flavor had not been proposed, but likely candidates were chocolate and peanut butter. The snack bar and flavor extension might produce an incremental dollar sales boost of 5 to 10 percent over the second-year sales volume if supported by a $5 to $10 million trade and consumer advertising and promotion program.

Sales and Distribution

Frito-Lay sales and distribution personnel were consulted soon after the Cracker Jack acquisition opportunity became public. Their initial reaction was positive, noting that Cracker Jack would fit the existing Frito-Lay sales and distribution infrastructure.

Sales and distribution personnel raised two issues related to the acquisition. First, the number of Cracker Jack SKUs (32) seemed large. The typical Frito-Lay brand had five to ten SKUs and the number of Cracker Jack SKUs could present a challenge in getting retailer shelf and display space. Second, the estimated cost of a direct-store-delivery (DSD) like that employed by Frito-Lay appeared to be understated. According to industry analysts, the selling and distribution cost of a DSD sales force selling comparable products, was understated by a factor of one-half when stated as a percent of net sales.

Manufacturing and Product Assurance

Frito-Lay manufacturing and product assurance personnel were also favorably disposed toward the Cracker Jack acquisition. Like sales and distribution personnel, they expressed concerns about the number of Cracker Jack SKUs and the added complexity caused by this large number from a production perspective.

Without actually inspecting the Cracker Jack plant, manufacturing and product assurance personnel could not assess the condition of the facility and Cracker Jack production, box, and bag lines. However, they believed that it was highly unlikely that Frito-Lay would buy the Northbrook, Illinois, facility. The production, box, and bag lines might be purchased depending on their condition and relocated to an existing Frito-Lay manufacturing plant along with peanut and prize-insertion equipment. The ongoing capital expenditures projected by Borden management seemed appropriate if this were done.

Manufacturing personnel also said it was unlikely that Frito-Lay would need to make the substantial new plant and equipment capital expenditures indicated in Borden management's projection for 1999 (see Exhibit 7). Rather, Frito-Lay had a long-standing and successful relationship with an independent supplier that produced caramel popcorn, among other savory and salty snack products, and also had the manufacturing capacity to produce the equivalent of $100 million in sales. Space was available at existing Frito-Lay manufacturing facilities to install additional production, box, and bag lines if Cracker Jack sales exceeded $100 million. These lines could be added incrementally for a minimal capital investment. Each $10 million capital investment for production and lines was estimated to provide capacity to manufacture the equivalent of $50 million in sales. The equipment itself would be most likely depreciated over 15 years using the straight-line method.

A senior Frito-Lay manufacturing executive also believed that the Cracker Jack cost of goods sold could be 10 percent less than Borden management's projections. This cost reduction could be realized by simplifying the Cracker Jack product line and building the flex bag volume relative to Cracker Jack sold in boxes and bags-in-boxes.

Finance and Administration

Lynne Peissig engaged Frito-Lay planning personnel and PepsiCo merger and acquisition specialists to begin a valuation analysis of the Cracker Jack business in June 1997. By mid-July, a variety of data had been gathered pertaining to recent acquisitions in the consumer foods industry. According to Diane Tousley, the New Ventures division finance director, the transaction prices for these types of acquisitions represented one to three times net revenues and 10 to 12 times after-tax earnings of the acquired companies. The higher multiples were associated with businesses that had strong brand names or trademarks, established distribution channels and trade relations, and a positive earnings history.

Tousley acknowledged that these data needed to be supplemented with a more rigorous financial appraisal, including a discounted cash flow valuation for Cracker Jack (see Appendix: Note on Valuing a Business at the end of this case). She noted that Frito-Lay commonly applied a risk-adjusted discount rate to calculate the present value of after-tax future cash flows when performing a discounted cash flow analysis for new investments. (*Note*: According to the PepsiCo, Inc. annual report, 1997, p. 29, the effective 1997 PepsiCo, Inc. corporate income tax rate for continuing operations was 35.4 percent.) Depending on the level of the risk, the discount rate ranged from 12 to 18 percent with an average risk-adjusted discount rate of 15 percent. New Ventures team members agreed that an investment in Cracker Jack represented an "average risk" for Frito-Lay.

Revenue forecasts associated with marketing Cracker Jack as a Frito-Lay brand had not been finalized as of July 15, 1997. However, Peissig believed that the preliminary first-year sales projections provided by the STM and incremental dollar sales estimates resulting from brand and flavor extensions in the second and third year offered a starting point for making revenue forecasts. She also thought Cracker Jack dollar sales growth would likely stabilize at a rate of two or three percent in the fourth and fifth year following modest price and pound volume increases. Peissig added: "I suspect that considerable discussion will focus on Cracker Jack revenue projections when the business team is assembled."

Peissig also expected an animated discussion related to the Cracker Jack trade promotion and consumer advertising budget. She believed three years of focused brand development efforts supported by promotion and advertising spending would be necessary to rebuild and grow the business. After that, the Cracker Jack business might be sustained with an annual promotion and advertising budget representing about 4 to 8 percent of manufacturer net sales. Other costs would also be incurred by Cracker Jack. For example, Tousley estimated that initial and ongoing general and administrative costs associated with the marketing of Cracker Jack as a Frito-Lay brand would range from 4 to 7 percent of manufacturer net sales. These costs included product and process research and development, marketing research, and brand management and administrative salaries and fringe benefits.

Finally, Peissig believed that her presentation to senior PepsiCo executives should include consideration of the Cracker Jack acquisition relative to the internal development and commercialization of a new consumer food brand. According to industry sources, the financial investment to internally develop and launch a new brand (trademark) in a consumer food category was $75 to $100 million, including the cost of product research and development, test marketing, and a national introduction. The time interval from concept development to full-scale commercialization ranged from two to three years. The likelihood of a new product success was roughly one in ten.

APPENDIX: NOTE ON VALUING A BUSINESS

Estimating a company's fair market value is a necessary first step in determining the purchase price for an acquisition. Fair market value is the cash, or cash-equivalent, price at which an asset would trade between a willing buyer and seller, with each in command of all information necessary to value the asset and neither under any pressure to trade.

Valuation experts have developed a variety of valuation techniques to assist in establishing a company's fair market value, although this value often may not represent the final transaction price. In practice, a transaction price involves consideration of a variety of factors that may vary depending on the characteristics of the company to be acquired and the objectives of the buyer and seller. For example, obtaining valuable trade names, taking control of another entity, or acquiring an increased market share for a particular product may affect the final purchase price. Still, determination of a transaction or purchase price or a reasonable price range generally involves quantitative techniques. This appendix briefly describes the discounted cash flow (DCF) technique that is used by investment bankers, research analysts, and valuation experts to estimate a company's fair market value. It is assumed that the reader is familiar with the vocabulary and mechanics of present value and discounted cash flow analysis.[4]

The Discounted Cash Flow Technique

The DCF valuation approach is the most frequently used fair market valuation technique. It provides a "going concern" value, which is the value indicated by the future commercial possibilities of a business. Using this technique, fair market value is calculated by the summation of the present value of projected cash flows for a determined period plus the present value of the residual or terminal value at the end of the projection period for a business. Typically, a 5- to 10-year projection period of after-tax operating cash flows, with various terminal or residual value estimates, will be discounted back to the present by the risk-adjusted, weighted-average cost of capital for the acquiring company. The cash flows are derived from the projected income statements and working and fixed capital expenditure plans. This calculation produces a result that represents the fair market value to both debt and equity holders. To arrive at the (owner's) equity value, the outstanding debt at the time of the acquisition is subtracted from the total capital value.

Four key areas must be assessed for accuracy and appropriateness when using the DCF technique. These include the (1) assumptions underlying the projection of cash flows, (2) length of the projection period, (3) residual or terminal value at the end of the projection period, and (4) appropriate discount rate.

Financial Projection Assumptions and Projection Period Five factors form the basis for basic financial projections: (1) historical sales growth; (2) business plans of the

[4] For background reading on the time value of money, present value analysis, and discounted cash flow, see the most recent edition of S. Ross, R. Westerfield, and B. Jordan, *Fundamentals of Corporate Finance* (Burr Ridge, IL: Irwin McGraw-Hill) or R. Higgins, *Analysis for Financial Management* (Burr Ridge, IL: Irwin McGraw-Hill).

company to be acquired; (3) prevailing relevant business conditions including growth expectations and trends in light of competitive positioning, general market growth, and price pressure; (4) anticipated needs for working capital and fixed asset expenditures; and (5) historical and expected levels and trends of operating profitability. Each factor affects the estimation of projected cash flows for the business to be acquired.

Determining the length of the projection period is a matter of judgment. As a general rule, it is expected that at the end of the projection period, the operations of a business should be at a normal and sustainable operating level in order to more easily estimate a terminal or residual value (discussed next). Unusual circumstances, such as an excessive sales growth factor, an increase or decrease in operating profit margins, or an improvement in the accounts receivable or inventory levels, should no longer exist by the end of the projection period. For companies projecting normal sales growth rates and profitability margins, a 5- to 10-year projection period is usually employed.

Estimating the Terminal or Residual Value The value of a business at the end of the projection period is often the least analyzed element of a valuation. However, it can represent a significant portion of the company's entire fair market value. The proper method for estimating the terminal or residual value depends on the financial projection factors described earlier and the length of the projection period in addition to the specifics of the business. A trade-off exists between the degree of reliability inherent within the two factors (DCFs during the projection period and the terminal value) used to calculate an ultimate fair market value. A shorter projection period places greater importance on the ability to develop a meaningful terminal or residual value estimate. A longer projection period places less reliance on the estimated terminal value but makes the annual cash flow assumptions more important.

The two most frequently used approaches for estimating a terminal value are the income capitalization and the multiple techniques. Both techniques estimate the future value of the business at the end of the projection period. This future value is then discounted back to determine the present value.

The income capitalization technique method adjusts either after-tax earnings or cash flow from the final year of the projection period by the discount rate. This technique assumes that after-tax earnings will either be constant or increasing at a constant rate from the last year of the projection period and that the proper risk-adjusted weighted-average cost of capital is the discount rate. The multiple approach applies some multiplier to either after-tax earnings or cash flow from the last year of the projection period. The resulting terminal value is then discounted to its present value using the discount rate from the final year of the projection period. The multiples are developed from publicly traded comparable companies or recent merger and acquisition transactions. A point to remember about the income capitalization and multiple approaches is that the calculated terminal value is dependent on the assumptions underlying the projection period. For example, aggressive sales growth rates will overstate after-tax earnings or cash flow for the last year of the projection period, which will in turn overstate the terminal value. Similarly, multiples may be distorted because of extrinsic influences on recent merger and acquisitions transactions and the fact that two companies are rarely alike.

Discount Rate The proper discount rate is one of the most significant elements in a DCF. Because the present value changes inversely with changes in the discount rate, it is critical to the valuation to properly assess the inherent risk and thus the required yield of the business to be acquired.

The Capital Asset Pricing Model (CAPM) is generally accepted by the financial community as a means for estimating an investor's yield requirement and hence a company's cost of equity capital. Essentially, the CAPM states that the required cost of equity is equal to the cost of risk-free debt plus some additional risk premium relating to the company. A detailed discussion of CAPM can be found in most finance textbooks. The required rates of return on equity and debt are then weighted in order to arrive at the weighted-average cost of capital. The weighted-average cost of capital for *Fortune* 500 consumer goods companies averages around 10 to 12 percent.

Discounted Cash Flow Technique Illustration

Exhibit A-1 provides a simple illustration of the DCF computation for valuing a business. The upper portion of the illustration contains a five-year *pro forma* income statement, including projected business revenues, cost of goods sold, operating expenses, and earnings (net income) before interest and taxes. Also indicated is the provision for corporate income tax and after-tax earnings.

Cash Flow Calculation The bottom portion of Exhibit A-1 details the cash flow calculation. The projected cash flows are obtained by adjusting the *pro forma* income statement for noncash items and changes in balance sheet items affecting cash.[5] This is shown by first adding depreciation expense (a noncash cost) for each year to after-tax earnings. After-tax earnings plus depreciation represents the annual cash flow from operations for a business.

The cash flow from operations then needs to be adjusted to reflect cash outflows. This is done by subtracting the estimated year-to-year *increase* in working capital (current assets minus current liabilities) and planned capital expenditures for each year from the estimated cash flow from operations. Increases to working capital in this illustration suggest that current assets, such as inventories and accounts receivables, net of current liabilities (e.g., accounts payable), increase each year at a constant amount of $100,000 given the constant (10%) annual revenue growth rate over the projection period shown in Exhibit A-1. The dollar amount for capital expenditures reflect annual cash investments in plant and equipment. In summary, after-tax earnings plus noncash expenses (e.g., depreciation) minus projected increases to working capital and annual capital expenditures result in a projected total annual cash flow for a business.

Present Value of Projected Cash Flows and Residual or Terminal Value As described earlier, the fair market value of a business is calculated by the summation of the present value of projected cash flows for a determined period plus the present value of the residual or terminal value at the end of the projection period. Exhibit A-1 shows the present value calculation using a 15 percent discount rate (other discount rates are shown in Exhibit A-2 on page 212). The discount rate reflects the acquiring company's weighted-average cost of capital, plus any amount to be added for special risks entailed in the acquisition; hence, the frequently used term *risk-adjusted discount rate*. The summed, or cumulative, present value of projected cash flows over the 5-year projection period is $9,592,000, shown in Exhibit A-1.

As mentioned earlier, the residual or terminal value at the end of a projection period often represents a significant portion of the fair market value of a business. This is apparent in Exhibit A-1, which illustrates the multiple approach for estimating the residual or terminal value. In this illustration, an after-tax earnings (cash flow) multiple (12) is used, which is then discounted to its present value using the discount rate from the final year of the projection period. This results in a residual value of $22,704,000. The sum of the cumulative present value of projected cash flows ($9,592,000) and the present value of the residual or terminal value is the estimated fair market value shown as $32,296,000 in Exhibit A-1.

[5] For simplicity, deferred taxes and amortization of goodwill are omitted from this example.

EXHIBIT A-1

Business Valuation Discounted Cash Flow Illustration ($000s)

	Year 1	*Year 2*	*Year 3*	*Year 4*	*Year 5*	*Residual Value*	*Fair Market Value*
Revenues (10% growth)	$10,000	$11,000	$12,100	$13,310	$14,641		
Cost of goods sold (40% of revenues)	4,000	4,400	4,840	5,324	5,856		
Gross profit (60% of revenues)	6,000	6,600	7,260	7,986	8,785		
Operating expenses (20% of revenues)	2,000	2,200	2,420	2,662	2,928		
Earnings before interest and taxes (EBIT) (40% of revenues)	4,000	4,400	4,840	5,324	5,856		
Income tax provision on EBIT (40% of EBIT)	1,600	1,760	1,936	2,130	2,343		
After-tax earnings before interest and taxes on interest (24% of revenues)	$2,400	$2,640	$2,904	$3,194	$3,514		
Add noncash items, including depreciation expense	700	850	1,050	1,300	1,600		
Funds provided	$ 3,100	$ 3,490	$ 3,954	$ 4,494	$ 5,114		
Subtract:							
Increases to working capital	(100)	(100)	(100)	(100)	(100)		
Capital expenditures	(500)	(750)	(1,000)	(1,250)	(1,500)		
Total cash flows exclusive of interest (net of tax)	$2,500	$2,640	$2,854	$3,144	$3,514	$45,682[a]	
Present value factor at 15%	0.87	0.756	0.658	0.572	0.497	0.497	
Present value	$ 2,174	$ 1,996	$ 1,877	$ 1,798	$ 1,747	$22,704	
Total present value of cash flows							$ 9,592
Present value of residual							22,704
Fair market capital value for the firm							$32,296

[a] Residual value using an after-tax earnings (cash flow) multiple. After-tax earnings (cash flow) from Year 5 times the multiple selected of twelve ($3,514 × 12).

Alternatively, the income capitalization approach can be used. This approach adjusts either after-tax earnings or cash flow from the final year of the projection period by the discount rate. It can be assumed that after-tax earnings or cash flow will be either constant or increasing at a constant rate from the last year of the projection period.

The income capitalization approach for estimating a residual or terminal value can be applied given information contained in Exhibit A-1. Assuming that after-tax earnings (or cash flow) in Year 5 remain constant at $3,514,000 and a 15 percent discount rate applies, then the present worth of the residual value is $11,643,053 ([$3,514,000/.15] × 0.497). When added to the present value of projected cash flows, the estimated fair market value is $21,235,053 ($9,592,000 + $11,643,053). Alternatively, if a 10 percent annual growth in after-tax earnings (or cash flow) is ex-

EXHIBIT A-2

Present Value of $1.00 Discounted at Discount Rate K, for N Years

				Discount Rate (K)			
Period (N)	*12%*	*13%*	*14%*	*15%*	*16%*	*17%*	*18%*
1	0.893	0.885	0.877	0.870	0.862	0.855	0.847
2	0.797	0.783	0.769	0.756	0.743	0.731	0.718
3	0.712	0.693	0.675	0.658	0.641	0.624	0.609
4	0.636	0.613	0.592	0.572	0.552	0.534	0.515
5	0.567	0.543	0.519	0.497	0.476	0.456	0.437

pected in the future as was apparent in Exhibit A-1 projections, then the present value of a perpetually growing after-tax earnings (cash flow) stream can be estimated. This is done using the formula, E/K-g, where E represents after-tax earnings (cash flow) in the last year of the projection period, K is the discount rate, and g is the growth rate in perpetuity. Applying this formula, the estimated residual value is $70,280,000 ($3,514,000/[.15 – .10]). The present value of this amount is $34,929,160 (0.497 × $70,280,000). By adding the present value of the terminal value to the present value of projected cash flows, the estimated fair market value is $44,521,160.

Summary

The estimation of fair market value requires both a qualitative and quantitative appraisal of the future commercial possibilities of a business as a going concern. As demonstrated in this note, the determination of fair market value is by no means a simple matter and will often yield different dollar figures given different assumptions. The DCF valuation approach featured in this note, while conceptually correct, often requires a heavy dose of judgment in its application. Fair market value of a business lies in the eyes of the beholder, whether he or she is the buyer or the seller.

CASE

Swisher Mower and Machine Company

Evaluating a Private Brand Opportunity

In early 1996, Wayne Swisher, President and Chief Executive Officer (CEO) of Swisher Mower and Machine Company (SMC), received a certified letter from a major national retail merchandise chain inquiring about a private branding arrangement for SMC's line of riding mowers. Wayne Swisher had only recently assumed his position as President and CEO from Max Swisher, his father and company founder. Wayne Swisher was previously Vice President of Sales, a position he held for six years following completion of the MBA Program at Southern Methodist University in Dallas, Texas. Prior to graduate school, he had worked in a sales and marketing position for three years at a large *Fortune* 500 corporation.

The private branding proposal represented the first major decision he faced as President and CEO. He thought the inquiry presented an opportunity worth consideration, since unit volume sales of the SMC riding mower had plateaued in recent years. However, details concerning the proposal would have to be studied more closely.

■ COMPANY BACKGROUND

The origins of Swisher Mower and Machine Company can be traced to the mechanical aptitude of its founder, Max Swisher. He received his first patent for a gearbox drive assembly when he was 18 years old. Shortly thereafter, he developed a self-propelled push mower utilizing this drive assembly. He began selling these mowers to neighbors after converting his parents' garage into a small manufacturing operation and formed Swisher Mower and Machine Company in 1945. In the early 1950s, Swisher decided to integrate his drive mechanism into a riding mower and, after service in the Korean War, began selling these mowers under the Ride King name in 1956.

In 1966, unit volume for SMC riding mowers peaked at 10,000 units with sales of $2 million. In the early 1970s, sales volume began a downward trend as a result of poor economic conditions in the geographic markets served by SMC. From 1975 to

The cooperation of Swisher Mower and Machine Company in the preparation of this case is gratefully acknowledged. This case was prepared by Professor Roger A. Kerin, of the Edwin L. Cox School of Business, Southern Methodist University, and Wayne Swisher, Swisher Mower and Machine Company, as a basis for class discussion and is not designed to illustrate effective or ineffective handling of an administrative situation. Company financial and operating data are disguised and not useful for research purposes.

EXHIBIT 1

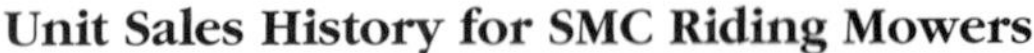

Unit Sales History for SMC Riding Mowers

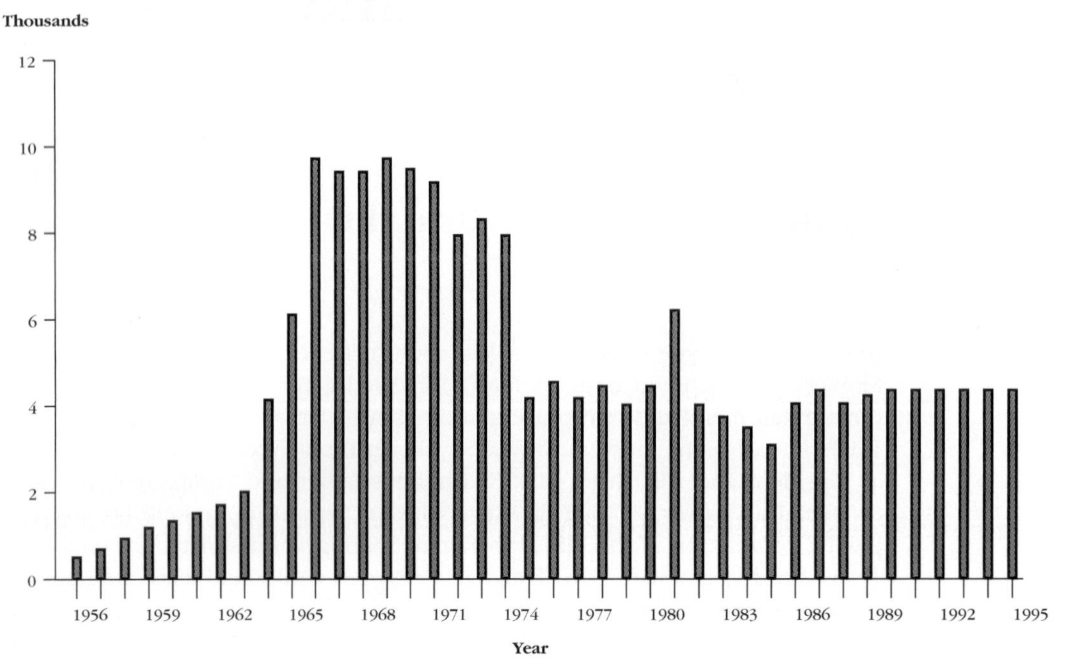

1989, unit volume remained relatively constant. Sales improved in the 1990s, with an average unit volume of 4,250 riding mowers. In 1995, the company sold 4,200 riding mowers and recorded total company sales of $4.3 million. Exhibit 1 shows SMC's riding mower unit sales history since 1956.

The company manufactures mowers at its plant in Warrensburg, Missouri, but utilizes outside suppliers for some machine tool work and subassembly. Its facilities have an annual production capacity of 10,000 riding mower units on a single 40-hour-per-week shift. The company's production facility and office space are rented from a related firm.

Max Swisher has always insisted that his company be customer-oriented in recognizing and providing for both dealer and end-user needs. Maintaining a "small company" image had also been an important aspect of Max Swisher's business philosophy, which in turn has resulted in personal relationships with dealers and customers alike. A special loyalty has been demonstrated to the original SMC dealers and distributors that helped build the sales foundation of the company. SMC continues to guarantee protection of these and other dealers' trade territories whenever possible.

Product Line

SMC produced three types of lawn mower units in early 1996. Its flagship product, the Ride King, is a three-wheel riding mower that has a zero turning radius. Developed by Max Swisher in the 1950s, this design is distinct from competitors' in that the single steerable front wheel is also the drive unit. This feature allows the mower to be put in reverse without changing gears and by simply turning the steering wheel 180 degrees. The company is credited with producing the first zero-turning-radius riding mower.

The manufacturer's list price for the standard Ride King is $650. Manufacturer gross profit margin on this unit is approximately 15 percent. The cost of goods sold for this product is approximately $100 for labor and $453 for parts.

SMC has a reputation for producing high-quality riding mowers that have a simple design allowing for ease of customer use and maintenance. These features and benefits are prominently displayed in the product literature for Ride King (see Exhibit 2, page 216). The reliability and ruggedness of the riding mower are demonstrated by the product's longevity. SMC mowers often run for more than 25 years before having to be replaced. The company provides a one-year warranty on all parts and labor. Riding mowers accounted for 63.6 percent of SMC's total sales and 57.8 percent of total gross profit in 1995.

Most current mowers' parts are interchangeable with the parts of older models that date back to 1956. Even though the patent for the zero-turning-radius drive unit has expired, no competitors have copied this exact design.

SMC also produced a "trailmower" called T-44. This unit consists of a trailer-type mower that has a cutting width of 44 inches. When hitched to any riding lawn mower, this unit effectively increases the cutting width by 44 inches. The "trailmower" can also be pulled behind all-terrain vehicles. The T-44 accounted for 8.2 percent of SMC's total sales and 13.2 percent of total gross profit in 1995. Exhibit 3 on page 217 shows the product literature for the T-44.

SMC deemphasized the sale of its self-propelled push mower in the early 1960s due to lagging sales and increased demand for the riding mower. When it phased out these units, the company began offering push lawn mower "kits." There are three different push mower kits available, and each consists of all the component parts necessary to assemble push mowers. Kits do not provide a material contribution to the company's gross profit. Kits accounted for 8.2 percent of SMC's total sales in 1995.

The replacement parts business for mowers accounts for the remainder (20 percent) of SMC sales. Since little standardization exists among mower parts in the industry, SMC must provide customers with replacement parts for its mowers. Replacement parts accounted for 29 percent of the company's total gross profit.

Plans were under way to broaden the SMC product line in 1996 with the introduction of a high-wheel string trimmer product. The "Trim-Max" is a high-wheel, walk-behind product that combines a trimmer, mower, and edger in one unit. Exhibit 4 on page 218 shows the product literature for the "Trim-Max."

Distribution and Promotion

SMC distributes its lawn mowers through farm supply stores, lawn and garden stores, home centers, and hardware stores located primarily in nonmetropolitan areas. About 75 percent of company sales are made in nonmetropolitan areas.

SMC sells the Ride King mower through wholesale distributors that supply independent dealers and directly to dealers. Wholesalers that represent SMC are located throughout the country, but they mainly supply farm dealers situated in the south central and southeastern United States. Wholesalers account for 30 percent of riding mower sales; direct-to-dealer sales account for 25 percent of sales.

Private-label riding mower sales account for 40 percent of SMC sales. Its private-label Big Mow mowers are produced for two buying networks: Midstates (Minneapolis, Minnesota) and Wheat Belt (Kansas City, Missouri). These two organizations represent independent farm supply stores and home centers in the upper and central midwestern United States and provide a central purchasing service. Even though these buying groups operate in roughly the same territory, their stores are not generally located in the same towns. Exhibit 5 on page 219 shows the geographic scope of SMC's distribution in the United States by brand name.

In recent years the company has developed distributor arrangements in parts of Europe and in the South Pacific. These arrangements produce 5 percent of total company sales.

EXHIBIT 2

Ride King Product Literature

SWISHER ZERO TURNING RADIUS MOWER

For a quick, clear cut around trees, shrubs, and lawn ornaments.

Swisher, the originator of the ZERO TURNING RADIUS MOWER, has continually refined the mower with updated operating features since its exclusive patent. Swisher's riding mowers are guided by a single, steerable front wheel, pivoting 360 degrees for sharp turns or reversing without stopping or changing gears. Its 32" cutting deck is powered by an 8HP Briggs & Stratton engine. Swisher's ZERO TURNING RADIUS MOWER is another innovation in a long line of Swisher lawn and garden equipment – developed over the past 50 plus years.

EXHIBIT 3

T-40 Product Literature

SWISHER T-44 TRAILMOWER

For quick, versatile mowing.

1. The ultimate way to save time on large areas, Swisher's T-44 TRAILMOWER quickly attaches to almost any lawn tractor or ATV for a faster, wider cut. The T-44 can be offset left or right; it features non-incremented, easy changing adjustment handles for variable ground clearance heights. For convenience, the optional remote ignition is located near the operators' position and features an optional 12 volt electric starter. Swisher's T-44 TRAILMOWER is another innovative product in a long line of Swisher lawn and garden equipment – developed over the past 50 plus years.

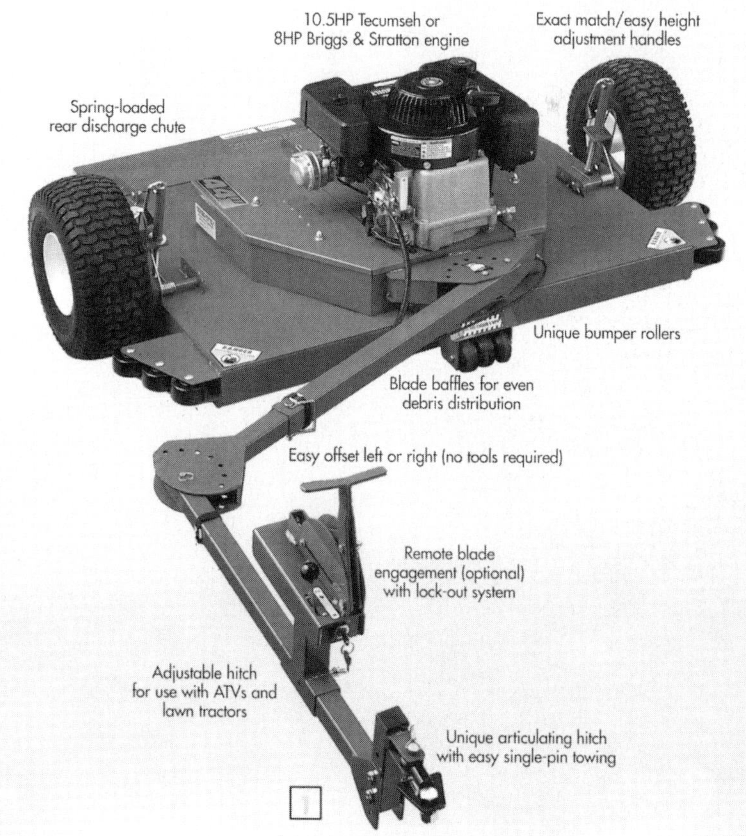

T-44 TRAILMOWER T-44 TRAILMOWER T-44 TRAILMOWER T-44 TRAILMOWER

EXHIBIT 4

Trim-Max Product Literature

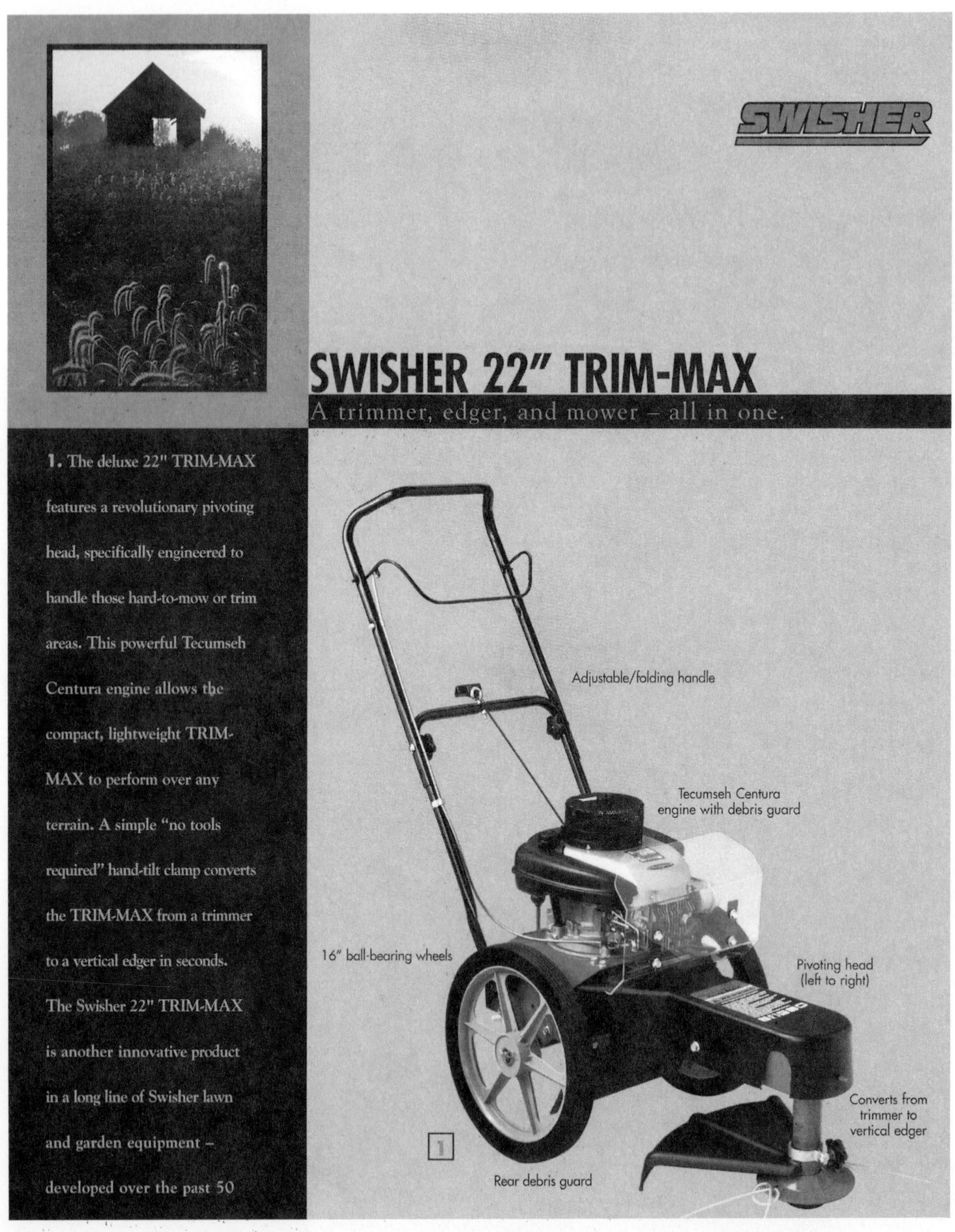

SWISHER
SWISHER 22" TRIM-MAX
A trimmer, edger, and mower – all in one.
1. The deluxe 22" TRIM-MAX features a revolutionary pivoting head, specifically engineered to handle those hard-to-mow or trim areas. This powerful Tecumseh Centura engine allows the compact, lightweight TRIM-MAX to perform over any terrain. A simple "no tools required" hand-tilt clamp converts the TRIM-MAX from a trimmer to a vertical edger in seconds. The Swisher 22" TRIM-MAX is another innovative product in a long line of Swisher lawn and garden equipment – developed over the past 50
Adjustable/folding handle
Tecumseh Centura engine with debris guard
16" ball-bearing wheels
Pivoting head (left to right)
Converts from trimmer to vertical edger
Rear debris guard
1

EXHIBIT 5

Geographic Scope of SMC Distribution

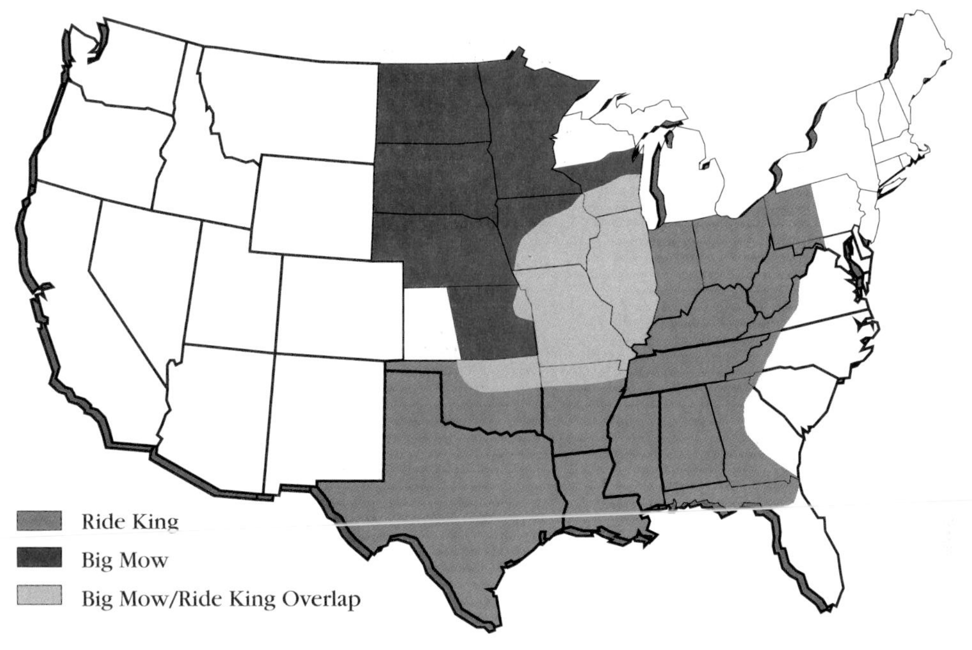

Prior to 1985, SMC advertising focused on trade-oriented promotion to wholesalers and dealers. Since 1985, SMC has used consumer advertising to promote Ride King through a co-op advertising program with its dealers utilizing radio, television, and newspapers. Ride King has been featured in publications such as *National Gardening, Country Journal,* and *Popular Mechanics,* among others.

Financial Position

SMC has remained a profitable company since its founding. The company has consistently generated a net profit return on sales of 10 percent or more annually. Moreover, SMC has been able to produce cash flow at levels large enough to minimize the need for any major short-term or long-term financing. During 1995, Ride King riding mower accounts receivable and inventory had turns of 8.1 and 5.8, respectively. Exhibit 6 (page 220) shows SMC financial statements for 1995.

■ RIDING LAWN MOWER INDUSTRY IN 1995

Riding lawn mowers are classified as lawn and garden equipment. This category is composed of numerous products, including walk-behind rotary mowers, riding mowers and tractors, garden tillers, snow throwers, and other outdoor power equipment designed primarily for the consumer market.

Industry sources estimated that the lawn and garden equipment industry produced sales of $5.5 billion in 1995, at manufacturers' prices. Of this amount, 74 percent was for finished goods and 25 percent was for engines. Components, including parts, accounted for the remainder of industry sales.

EXHIBIT 6

Swisher Mower and Machine Company Financial Statements: 1995[a]

Income Statement
(Year ended September 30, 1995)

Sales		$4,292,000
Cost of goods sold		3,587,150
Gross profit		$704,850
Sales and administrative expenses	$264,700	
Depreciation	2,300	
Total expenses		267,000
Income from continuing operations		$437,850
Other income (expenses)		(7,650)
Net income[b]		$430,200

Balance Sheet
(September 30, 1995)

Assets	
Current assets	$1,133,000
Net property and equipment	53,000
Total assets	$1,186,000
Liabilities and owner's equity	
Current liabilities	212,800
Owner's equity	973,200
Total liabilities and owner's equity	$1,186,000

[a] All figures disguised and not useful for research purposes.
[b] SMC is an "S" Corporation and therefore pays no corporate federal or state income taxes.

Sales Trends

Industry statistics show that riding mower unit volume is cyclical. Unit sales had grown in the early 1970s, but dropped dramatically in 1975 following a decline in the U.S. economy. By 1979, unit shipments had gradually risen, but with slowed economic conditions in the early 1980s, unit volume again declined. This same pattern was repeated during the 1983 to 1992 period. In 1993 and 1994, the industry posted record unit sales. Projections for 1995 and 1996 point toward further increases in unit volume. Exhibit 7 shows industry riding mower and lawn tractor unit sales for the period 1974 to 1994.

The riding lawn mower industry is highly seasonal. About one-third of riding lawn mower retail sales occur in March, April, and May. Over half of manufacturer shipments of these products occur in the four-month period from January to April.

Product Configuration

Riding lawn mowers are usually designed in two basic configurations: (1) front-engine lawn tractors and (2) rear-engine riding mowers. However, there are some mid-engine riding mowers on the market, such as those produced by SMC. Lawn tractors with larger engines (20 horsepower or more) are classified as garden tractors.

Riding lawn mowers are targeted at consumers who have large mowing areas, usually an acre or more. Front-engine lawn tractors are the most popular design fol-

EXHIBIT 7

Unit Sales of Riding Lawn Mowers and Lawn Tractors: 1974–1994

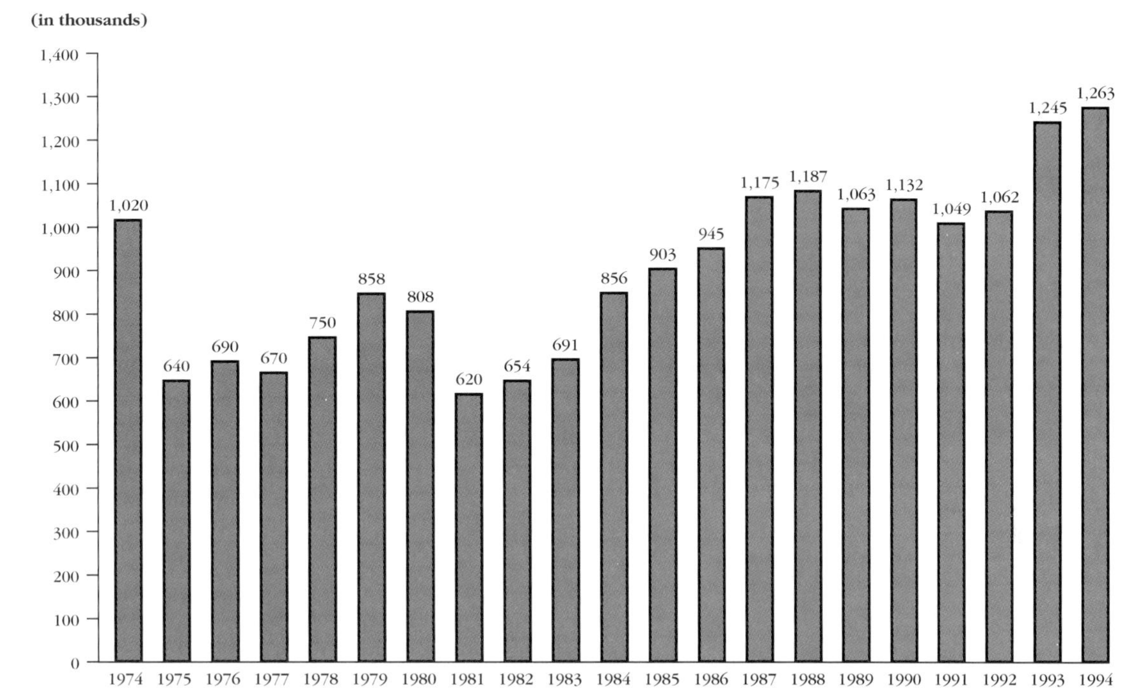

lowed by rear-engine and mid-engine models. According to industry surveys, the front-engine configuration (lawn and garden tractors) is perceived to be more powerful than the rear-engine configuration and capable of handling bigger jobs. Because the physical dimensions of the front-engine configuration tend to be larger than the rear-engine configuration, consumers tend to perceive lawn tractors and garden tractors as stronger and more durable.

Competition and Retail Distribution

Ten manufacturers comprised the major competitors in the riding lawn mower market in 1995: American Yard Products, Ariens, Honda, John Deere, Kubota, MTD, Inc., Murray of Ohio, Snapper, Toro, and Garden Way/Troy-Bilt.

Ariens, Honda, John Deere, Kubota, American Yard Products, Murray, MTD, Snapper, Toro, and Garden Way/Troy-Bilt sell their products through lawn and garden stores and specialty retailers. MTD, Murray, and American Yard Products also sell to national mass-merchandise stores. All of these companies manufacture riding mowers under a nationally branded name and engage in private-label production. Several companies produce a combination of nationally branded riding mowers and private labels for mass merchandisers (e.g., Sears, Wal-Mart, Kmart), home centers (e.g., Lowe's, Home Depot), and hardware chains (e.g., True Value Hardware).

Private-label riding mowers have captured a growing percentage of unit sales in the industry. It is estimated that private-label mowers currently account for 65 to 75 percent of total industry sales.

Each of the major competitors produces several riding mowers at different price points. Although retail prices vary by type of retail outlet, representative retail prices for national and private-label riding mowers typically range from $800 to $5,000.

Outdoor power equipment (OPE), including riding mowers, is distributed through a variety of retail outlets. National retail merchandise chains such as Wal-Mart, Home Depot, and Sears account for the largest percentage of sales. These chains, plus outdoor power equipment/farm equipment and supply stores, lawn and garden stores, discount department stores, home centers, and hardware stores, account for 90 percent of total industry sales (see Exhibit 8).

THE PRIVATE-BRAND PROPOSAL

The inquiry received by SMC concerning a private-brand arrangement requested a sample order of 700 standard riding mower units to be delivered in January 1997. The national retail merchandise chain expected to make an annual order of approximately 8,200 units. The proposed arrangement had features that made it quite different from SMC's typical manner of doing business with its other private-label organizations. The chain wanted to purchase the mowers at a price 5 percent lower than SMC's manufacturer's list price for its standard model. They also wished to be a house account without manufacturers' representatives or company sales representatives calling on them. They did not want any seasonal or promotional discounts but only a single guaranteed low price. Reorders would be at the same price. The mowers would be shipped free on board (FOB) factory (that is, the chain would pay for all freight charges).

The chain wanted to carry inventories in its regional warehouses, but did not want title to transfer to itself until the mowers were shipped to a specific company store. From that point, payment would be made in 45 days. However, the chain agreed to take title to mowers that had been in one of its warehouses for two months. A 45-day payment period would follow the title transfer.

There would be small changes in the appearance of the mower to help differentiate it from SMC's Ride King. The chain requested a different seat and a particular color and type of paint and specified that all parts be American-made or that the mower at least display an "American name" as its producer. The chain would supply all decals displaying its brand name.

The chain did not propose any mechanical specifications for the mower. The letter expressed satisfaction with the design and performance of the machine and noted that only minor cosmetic changes were necessary. SMC's standard warranty

EXHIBIT 8

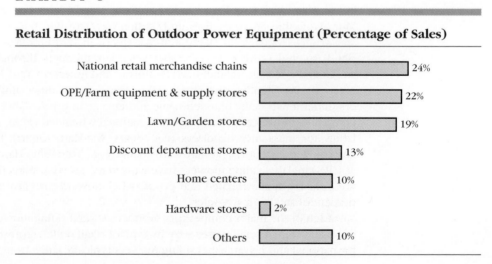

Retail Distribution of Outdoor Power Equipment (Percentage of Sales)

Outlet	Percentage of Sales
National retail merchandise chains	24%
OPE/Farm equipment & supply stores	22%
Lawn/Garden stores	19%
Discount department stores	13%
Home centers	10%
Hardware stores	2%
Others	10%

would be required for all mower parts. The chain expected SMC to reimburse it for any labor costs resulting from warranty work at $22.00 per hour. Replacement parts would be purchased at present price points and shipped FOB factory.

A two-year contract was offered, which could be automatically extended on a year-to-year basis. Either party could terminate the contract with a six-month notice. A new price would be negotiated at the end of the original two-year period. The contract would be negotiated annually thereafter. The chain also required SMC to assume liability for personal injury that might result from the use and maintenance of the mowers. The chain would supply all advertising related to the product and would not allow SMC to mention its relationship with the chain in any of its advertising or promotion.

EVALUATING THE PROPOSAL

The private-brand proposal required careful consideration, according to Wayne Swisher. The opportunity to expand production, given excess capacity, coupled with the added benefit of broadened distribution in metropolitan areas, seemed inviting. Moreover, increased sales of parts were likely, and the potential for selling the "trail-mower" was possible. At the same time, other factors would have to be considered. For example, SMC was self-insured and had not experienced any significant product-liability claims with some 175,000 units having been sold or used since 1956. However, if the private-brand proposal was pursued, greater exposure to liability claims was possible.

Furthermore, although increased production could be handled by paying overtime to SMC production workers, the cost of overtime, reflected in the direct labor cost, would represent an additional 4 percent of the current manufacturer's sales price for riding mowers. Additional direct material costs could represent another 1 percent of the current manufacturer's price. Additional overhead costs were estimated to be another 1 percent; other related costs, including additional inventory insurance, pilferage and breakage, additional wear and maintenance on machines, and a county property tax based on inventory, would account for an additional 1.5 percent.

A production agreement would create some one-time added costs for SMC. These costs would include arranging sources for specific materials that differed from those used in standard production and a rearrangement of production facilities to accommodate the new output levels. These one-time costs would be in the range of $10,000 to $12,000.

The added financing costs were of particular importance. Normally, SMC obtained short-term funds from local banks at 2.5 percentage points above the prime rate (currently 7 percent). These funds were used to finance accounts receivable and riding mower inventories, both of which would increase with the new arrangement. For example, the additional average inventory carried with this proposal would be 2,100 units.

Sales of SMC mowers by the national merchandiser could cannibalize some existing sales. Although the chain's outlets were located in metropolitan areas, there would be some overlap in trade areas with SMC's current dealers. Swisher felt that, as a result, SMC could initially lose approximately 300 units a year of Ride King sales volume. In addition, dealers directly affected would not welcome the added competition. Wayne Swisher believed that a small percentage of independent dealers would be likely to drop the SMC line.

Some aspects of the proposal might be negotiable, such as the title transfer and payment dates. From his experience, he knew that the unit price in the proposal was probably fixed and that the cosmetic changes were not negotiable. He knew that his bargaining position was limited because the chain would be approaching other manufacturers with the same opportunity. However, he also knew that SMC offered a highly differentiated and proven riding mower. This would be an advantage, because many other manufacturers' mowers were indistinguishable.

Wayne Swisher had been concerned for several years about SMC's future prospects. The private-brand arrangement might offer numerous benefits to SMC, but he wondered if other actions might be even more attractive. For example, a more aggressive advertising and sales effort to recruit new dealers and assist current dealers was being considered. Also, the new Trim-Max product was soon to be introduced under the Swisher name and an expanded line of "trailmowers" was a possibility. Still, he thought, the proposal is a "bird in the hand" while the other initiatives still had to prove themselves.

CHAPTER 6

Integrated Marketing Communication Strategy and Management

Marketing communication is the process by which information about an organization and its offerings is disseminated to selected markets. Given the role communication plays in facilitating mutually beneficial exchange relationships between an organization and prospective buyers, its importance cannot be overstated. The goal of communication is not just to induce initial purchases; it is also to achieve postpurchase satisfaction, thus increasing the probability of repeat sales. Even if prospective buyers possessed a pressing need and an organization possessed an offering that precisely met that need, no exchange would occur without communication. Communication is necessary to inform buyers of the following:

- The availability of an offering
- The unique benefits of the offering
- The where and how of obtaining and using the offering

Exactly how potential buyers are to be informed—the actual message communicated—is one of the most subjective communication decisions. Although message development can be somewhat aided by research, there are no guaranteed message strategies available for all offerings, markets, or organizations. Each individual situation must determine whether the message is to be hard-sell, humorous, or informational. Whatever message format is chosen, the message communicated should be desirable to those to whom it is directed, exclusive or unique to the offering being described, and believable in terms of the benefit claims made for the offering.

It is the task of the marketing manager to manage the communication process most effectively. Marketing managers have at their disposal specific communication activities, often called *elements, functions, tools*, or *tasks*. These include advertising, personal selling, and sales promotion. Collectively, the activities are termed the *marketing communication mix*.[1] Elements of the communication mix range from very flexible (for example, personal selling) to very inflexible (for example, mass advertising), and each has a unique set of characteristics and capabilities. To a certain extent, however, they are interchangeable and substitutable. It is the responsibility of the marketing manager to find the most effective communication mix at the least possible cost.

Marketing managers should not limit their thinking to which communication activity to use when designing communication strategies. Rare is the organization that employs only one form of communication. Rather, managers should broaden their perspective to think of *integrated marketing communications*—the practice of blending different elements of the communication mix in mutually reinforcing ways. In this context, attention is directed to which activity should be emphasized, how intensely it should be applied, and how communication activities can be most effectively combined and coordinated. For instance, advertising activities might be employed to develop offering awareness and comprehension; sales promotion might be used to increase purchase intention; and personal selling might be utilized to obtain final conviction and purchase.

Increasingly, marketers are looking to the Internet as a potential platform for integrated marketing communications. This technology has the capability to take consumers and industrial users through the entire purchase process, from creating awareness to providing information in an interactive manner, to placing an order, to customer service after the sale.[2] The role of the Internet in interactive marketing and electronic commerce is discussed in greater depth in Chapter 9.

■ INTEGRATED MARKETING COMMUNICATION STRATEGY FRAMEWORK

From a managerial perspective, the formulation of an integrated marketing communication strategy requires six major decisions. Once the offering and target markets have been defined, the manager must consider the following decisions:

1. What are the information requirements of target markets as they proceed through the purchase process?
2. What objectives must the communication strategy achieve?
3. How might the mix of communication activities be combined to convey information to target markets?
4. How much should be budgeted for communicating with target markets, and in what manner should resources be allocated among various communication activities?
5. How should the communication be timed and scheduled?
6. How should the communication process be evaluated as to its effectiveness, and how should it be controlled?

Theoretically, these questions are distinct and thus can be approached in a sequential manner. In practice, however, they are likely to be approached simultaneously, because they are closely interrelated.

■ INFORMATION REQUIREMENTS IN PURCHASE DECISIONS

The first step in designing an integrated marketing communication strategy is to determine how buyers purchase a particular offering and to define the role of information in the purchase process. This often requires use of a purchase-process (or adoption-process) model. Usually, such a model treats buyers as though they were moved through a series of sequential stages in their purchase processes, such as

Unawareness → Knowledge → Preference → Purchase

At any point in time, different buyers are in different stages of the model, and each stage requires a different communication strategy.

Most models allow the marketing manager to distinguish between solitary and joint decision making. In any purchase decision, the person or persons involved can play several possible roles—purchaser, influencer, decision maker, and/or consumer. In certain purchase situations, one individual may play more than one role. In other purchase situations, such as a joint purchase decision, the roles may be played by different individuals. Whereas a mother may be the family member who purchases breakfast cereal, her children may influence the brand purchase, and the father may consume the product. A similar situation could exist in an industrial setting. A purchasing agent may be the buyer, an engineer the influencer and decision maker, and a technician the user. Understanding who is playing the roles is a prerequisite for successfully determining what the communication message should be, as well as to whom it should be directed and how it should be communicated.

Similarly, the process used by buyers to purchase an offering influences the role of information, and hence the most effective communication strategy. For example, in industrial settings purchasing procedures are often prescribed. Therefore, understanding when, where, how, and what information is employed in the purchase decision will enable an organization to direct the proper communication to the proper individual at the proper time. These remarks also apply to communication directed toward consumers. Consider the case of consumers making a decision to buy a house. To communicate effectively, an organization must know *what* information these consumers think is necessary (price, location, size), *where* they will seek it (newspapers, the Internet, brokers, friends), *when* they will seek it (how far in advance, on what days), and *how* they will apply the information once obtained.

Finally, the way in which buyers perceive an organization and its offering is closely related to their information needs. The perceived importance of the offering and the perceived risk in making an incorrect purchase decision influence the extent to which buyers receive information, as well as their choice of information source(s). The more important or risky an offering is perceived to be (because of large dollar outlays, ego involvement, or health and safety reasons), the more likely it is that buyers will seek information from sources other than the organization providing the offering.

REASONABLE COMMUNICATION OBJECTIVES

The objectives set for communication programs will depend on the overall offering-market strategies of the organization and the stage of the product's life cycle. Communication objectives will differ according to whether the strategy being employed is market penetration, market development, or product development. For instance, a market penetration strategy will suggest communication objectives that emphasize more frequent offering usage or that build preference for or loyalty to the offering. On the other hand, a market development strategy will encourage communication that will stimulate awareness and trial of the offering.

Life-cycle stage plays a role in determining whether communication objectives should stimulate primary demand or selective demand. Early in the life cycle, communication efforts focus on stimulating *primary demand*—demand for the product or service class, such as dairy products, personal computers, or financial planning. Typically, the message conveyed focuses on introducing the benefits of a product or service or overcoming objections to the product or service. Later in the life cycle, when substitute products or services exist, communication efforts focus on stimulating *selective demand*—demand for a particular brand, product, or service such as Borden milk, Apple personal computers, or Merrill Lynch financial planning. Typically, the message conveyed extols the benefits of a particular competitive offering and seeks to differentiate that offering from others.

Objectives must also be delineated for individual communication tools. Both general and specific communication objectives need to relate directly to the tasks that the tools are to accomplish. Communication objectives and the tasks must be reasonable—*consistent* both among themselves and with other marketing elements, *quantifiable* for measurement and control purposes, and *attainable* with an appropriate amount of effort and expenditure and within a specific time frame.

■ INTEGRATED MARKETING COMMUNICATION MIX

Development of an integrated marketing communication mix requires the assignment of relative weights to particular communication activities, based on communication objectives. Although no established guidelines exist for designing an optimal communication mix, several factors that influence the mix need to be considered. These factors are:

- The information requirements of potential buyers
- The nature of the offering
- The nature of the target markets
- The capacity of the organization

Information Requirements of Buyers

As a starting point in crafting an integrated communication mix, an analysis of the relative value of the communication tools used at various stages in the purchase-decision process ought to be undertaken. Consider the purchase-decision process for a new automobile. Through advertising and an increasing number of Web sites, manufacturers seek to stimulate awareness of the new models and to indicate where they can be purchased. Sales personnel provide information on specific options available, financing, and delivery. Sales promotion, brochures, and catalogs provide descriptions of performance characteristics and other salient features. Which communication tool has the greatest impact on prospective buyers? The answer to this question, while admittedly difficult to arrive at, will lead to a weighing of the importance of the communication tools. The manager will achieve an effective communication mix only by understanding the information requirements of potential buyers and by meeting those requirements with the appropriate communication-mix elements.

Nature of the Offering

A major consideration in developing the communication mix is the organization's offering. A highly technical offering, one with benefits not readily apparent (such as performance or quality), or one that is relatively expensive is likely to require personal selling. On the one hand, advertising is a potent communication tool when the offering is not complex, is frequently purchased, is relatively inexpensive, or has benefits that readily differentiate it from competing offerings. Sales promotion lends itself to nearly every offering type because of the wide variety of forms it can assume. Its main use, however, is to induce immediate action on frequently purchased products.

Target-Market Characteristics

The nature of the target market is another consideration. A target market consisting of a small number of potential buyers, existing in close proximity to one another and each purchasing in large quantities, might suggest a personal selling strategy. In contrast, a mass market that is geographically scattered generally calls for an emphasis on advertising. However, firms are finding that direct marketing also can be used to reach a geographically dispersed target market. This realization has led many firms to substitute mail and telephone solicitations for mass media (radio, print, and television) advertising and use the Internet as a communication medium to complement advertising.

Organizational Capacity

A fourth consideration is the ability or willingness of the organization to undertake certain communication activities. The organization is continually faced with *make-or-buy decisions.* If an organization decides to employ a particular communication activity, should it perform the activity internally (that is, make it) or contract it out (in other words, buy it)?

One such make-or-buy decision is the choice between a company sales force and independent sales representatives.[3] The decision has both economic and behavioral dimensions. The economic dimension relates to the issue of fixed versus variable costs. The cost of independent representatives is variable; they are paid on sales commission only. A company sales force, on the other hand, typically includes a variable-cost component *and* a fixed-cost component. If independent representatives fail to sell, no costs are incurred; however, if a company sales force fails to sell, the fixed costs still have to be paid. These concepts are useful in determining whether independent representatives or company representatives are more cost-effective at different sales levels.

Suppose independent representatives received a 5 percent commission on sales and company sales personnel received a 3 percent commission in addition to incurring a salary and administration cost of $500,000. At what sales level would company representatives become more or less costly than independent representatives? This question can be resolved by setting the cost equations for both types of representatives equal to each other and solving for the sales level amount, as follows:

$$\frac{\text{Cost of company reps}}{0.03(x) + \$500{,}000} = \frac{\text{Cost of independent reps}}{0.05(x)}$$

where x = sales volume. Solving for x, we get $25 million as the sales volume at which the costs of company and independent representatives are equal.

The calculation indicates that if the sales volume were below $25 million, the independent representative would be cheaper; above that amount, the company sales force would be cheaper. Of course, a fundamental issue is the likelihood of achieving a $25 million sales level.

Behavioral dimensions of this decision focus on issues of control, flexibility, effort, and availability of independent and company sales representatives. There is considerable difference of opinion as to the relative advantages and disadvantages of company and independent representatives with respect to each factor. Proponents of a company sales force argue that this strategy offers greater control, since the company selects, trains, and supervises sales personnel. The sales effort is enhanced because sales personnel are representing only one company's product line. Flexibility exists because the firm can change sales-call patterns and customers and can transfer personnel. Finally, availability of sales personnel is superior, because an independent representative might not exist in a geographical area, whereas a company representative can be relocated. Proponents of independent sales representatives argue that selection, training, and supervision of sales personnel can be done equally well by sales agencies and at no cost to the firm. Flexibility is improved, since fixed investment in a sales force is minimal. Effort is increased, since independent representatives live on their commissions. Finally, availability is no problem, because the entrepreneurial spirit of these individuals will take them wherever effective demand exists. These economic and behavioral dimensions were carefully considered when Coca-Cola's Food Division decided to eliminate 110 sales positions and sell through independent agents (food brokers).[4]

Another make-or-buy decision relates to advertising. Often, it is advantageous to have intermediaries (such as wholesalers, retailers, and dealers) assume advertising costs and placement responsibilities. Cooperative advertising, in which a manufacturer shares the costs of advertising or sales promotion, is an example of this type of strategy.

Push versus Pull Communication Strategies

Two approaches that incorporate the topics just discussed are termed push and pull communication strategies. A *push communication strategy* is one in which the offering is pushed through a distribution channel in a sequential fashion, with each channel level representing a distinct target market. A push strategy concentrates on channel intermediaries, building relationships that can have long-term benefits. With such a strategy, advertisements are likely to appear in trade journals and magazines, and sales aids and contests are likely to be used as incentives to gain shelf space and distribution. A principal emphasis, however, is on personal selling to wholesalers and retailers. This strategy is typically used when (1) an organization has easily identifiable buyers, (2) the offering is complex, (3) buyers view the purchase as being risky, (4) a product or service is early in its life cycle, and/or (5) the organization has limited funds for direct-to-consumer advertising.

A *pull communication strategy* seeks to create initial interest among potential buyers, who in turn demand the product from intermediaries, ultimately pulling the offering through a channel. A pull strategy normally employs heavy end-user (consumer) advertising, free samples, and coupons to stimulate end-user awareness and interest. Consumers might be encouraged to ask their favorite retailer for the offering to pressure retailers into carrying the product. Pennzoil Motor Oil's "Ask for Pennzoil," Claritin's "Talk to your doctor . . .," and General Motors' "Ask for Genuine GM parts" advertising campaigns are prime examples of a pull communication strategy in practice.

The conditions favoring a pull strategy are virtually opposite to those favoring a push strategy. A central issue in choosing a push strategy is the ability and willingness of wholesalers and retailers to implement selling and sales promotion programs advocated by manufacturers. An important consideration in using a pull strategy is whether an *advertising opportunity* exists for a product or service. Such an opportunity exists when (1) there is a favorable primary demand for a product or service category, (2) the product or service to be advertised can be significantly differentiated from its competitors, (3) the product or service has hidden qualities or benefits that can be portrayed effectively through advertising, and (4) there are strong emotional buying motives involved, such as buyers' concern for health, beauty, or safety. The value of an advertising opportunity decreases if one or more of these conditions is not met. Nonprescription drugs and cosmetics often satisfy most of these conditions and are frequently advertised. Commodities such as unprocessed foods (for example, corn, oats, and wheat) are rarely advertised; however, when they are processed and dietary supplements and flavors are added to produce cereals, they are advertised effectively.

Nevertheless, push and pull communication strategies are often used together.[5] Investment in end-user advertising stimulates consumer demand and hence product or service sales volume. Investment in efforts to gain display space for products, promote specific services, and educate retail salespeople builds channel relationships that have long-term benefits.

COMMUNICATION BUDGETING

As one might expect, the question of how much to spend on communication is difficult to answer. Many factors, including those previously mentioned, must be considered in communication budget determination.[6] In general, the greater the geographic dispersion of a target market, the greater the communication expenditure required; the earlier an offering is in its life cycle, the greater the necessary expenditure; and so forth.

The primary rule in determining a communication budget is to *make the budget commensurate with the tasks required of the communication activities.* The more important communication is in a marketing strategy, the larger the amount of funds that should be allocated to it. Conceptually, budget determination is straightforward—set the budget so that the marginal costs of communication equal the marginal revenues resulting from it. This, however, requires an assessment of the effectiveness of communication.

Because it is difficult to evaluate communication effectiveness, attempts to establish a relationship between budget size and communication effectiveness have generally proven unproductive. For this reason, there is no widely agreed-on criterion for establishing the size of a communication budget. Instead, numerous guidelines have been suggested. These guidelines can be roughly grouped as *formula based* or *qualitatively based.*

The most widely used formula-based approach is the *percentage-of-sales approach*. Most frequently, past sales are employed, but anticipated sales are also occasionally used. Hence, when sales increase, communication activity increases. Although it creates certain conceptual problems (for example, which should come first—sales or communication?), this approach is commonly used as a starting point because of its simplicity. A second formula-based method is to allocate for communication a fixed dollar amount per offering unit, and then to calculate the communication budget by multiplying this per-unit allocation by the number of units expected to be sold. This method is most often used by durable-goods manufacturers such as appliance and automobile companies.

In practice, the formula-based approaches tend to be rather inflexible and not marketing oriented, so they are often supplemented by qualitatively based approaches. Management may use the *competitive-parity approach*, whereby an organization attempts to maintain a balance between its communication expenditures and those of its competitors. Another approach is to use *all available funds* for communication. This strategy might be employed in introducing a new offering for which maximum exposure is desired; it is also sometimes used by nonprofit organizations.

A final approach is termed the *objective-task* approach. Here an organization budgets communication as a function of the objectives set for a communication program and the costs of the tasks to be performed to accomplish the objectives. The approach involves three steps: (1) define the communication objectives, (2) identify the tasks needed to attain the objectives, and (3) estimate the costs associated with the performance of these tasks.

Although all of these approaches are useful, each has decided limitations. More often than not, managers use these approaches in conjunction with one another.

Communication Budget Allocation

Once a communication budget has been settled on, it must be allocated across the communication activities. This can be accomplished by using guidelines similar to those discussed previously for general communication budget determinations. Advertising and personal selling will be used to illustrate necessary budgetary allocation decisions. As a general rule, marketers of consumer products and services spend more for advertising as a percentage of their communication budget; marketers of industrial products and services spend more for personal selling as a percentage of their communication budget.[7]

Advertising Budget Allocation Decisions about advertising budget allocation revolve around media selection and scheduling considerations. Basically, there are five mass media—television, radio, magazine, newspaper, and outdoor (billboard)—that an organization can use in transmitting its advertising messages to target markets. Each of these media, or *channels*, consists of *vehicles*—specific entities in which advertisements can appear. In magazines, the vehicles include *Newsweek* and *Mechanics Illustrated. Newsweek* can be thought of as a mass-appeal vehicle, whereas *Mechanics Illustrated* might be considered a selective-appeal vehicle. Moreover, media can be *vertical* (reaching more than one level of a distribution channel) or *horizontal* (reaching only one level of a channel).

Media selection is based on numerous factors, the most important of which are cost, reach, frequency, and audience characteristics. Cost frequently acts as a constraint—for example, a one-minute national television commercial (spot) during the Super Bowl costs over $3 million, not including associated production costs. *Cost* is usually expressed as cost per thousand (CPM) readers, viewers, and so on, to facilitate cross-vehicle comparisons. *Reach* refers to the number of buyers potentially exposed to an advertisement in a particular vehicle. *Frequency* refers to the number of times buyers are exposed to an advertisement in a given time period; total exposure equals reach multiplied by frequency. The more closely the characteristics of the target market match those of a vehicle's audience, the more appropriate the vehicle.

Other considerations include the purpose of the advertisement (image building, price, and so on), product needs, and the editorial climate of the vehicle. Whereas price advertisements (those emphasizing an immediate purchase) are more likely to be found in newspapers than in magazines, the opposite is true for advertisements of products requiring color illustration and detailed explanation. Finally, audience characteristics determine which advertisements are acceptable, as well as which are appropriate. For example, 89 percent of wives either influence or make outright purchases of men's clothing. Knowing this, Haggar Clothing, a menswear marketer, advertises in women's magazines such as *Vanity Fair, Mademoiselle,* and *Redbook.*[8]

The timing, or scheduling, of advertisements is critical to their success. Purchases of many offerings (such as skis, snowblowers, and swimsuits) are seasonal or are limited to certain geographic areas. Thus, the advertising budgeting must take into account purchasing patterns. For example, advertising snowblowers in Ohio during the month of July is probably not a worthwhile endeavor.

There are numerous timing strategies that a marketing manager can employ when undertaking an advertising campaign. One alternative is to concentrate advertising dollars in a relatively short time period—a *blitz strategy*. This strategy is often used when new products or services are introduced. For example, movie studios spend 75 percent of a new film's advertising budget in the four to five days preceding the film's opening weekend.[9] Another alternative is to spend advertising dollars over the long term to maintain continuity. A *pulse strategy* might be employed, whereby an organization periodically concentrates its advertising but also attempts to maintain some semblance of continuity.

Sales-Force Budget Allocation The sales-force budgeting problem is two-faceted: How many salespeople are needed, and how should they be allocated? A commonly used formula is

$$NS = \frac{NC \times FC \times LC}{TA}$$

where

NS = number of sales people

NC = number of customers (actual or potential)

FC = necessary frequency of customer calls

LC = length of average customer call, including travel time

TA = average available selling time per salesperson (less time spent on administrative duties)

In most instances, the time period is one business year. Although this formula can be used for nearly all types of salespeople, from retail clerks to highly creative salespeople, it is more likely used with the latter.

Assume that the number of potential customers is 2,500 and four calls should be made per customer per year. If the length of the average call and travel time is two hours and there are 1,340 working hours per year available for selling (50 weeks × 40 hours × 67 percent available selling time per week), then

$$NS = \frac{2{,}500 \times 4 \times 2}{1{,}340} = 15 \text{ salespeople needed}$$

The formula is flexible. It is possible to create several different strategies simply by varying (1) how the various elements in this formula are defined and (2) the elements themselves, such as the frequency of calls with actual customers and potential customers.

A related decision concerns the allocation of salespeople. Every salesperson must have a territory, whether defined as square feet of selling space, a geographical area, or a delivery route. In determining how large the sales territory should be, decision makers should attempt to equate selling opportunities with the workload associated with each sales territory.

The question of how the sales force should be organized is perhaps more difficult to answer, as it directly relates to organization and marketing objectives, offering characteristics, competitor and industry practices, and the like. The alternatives include having salespeople specialize in certain offerings or in customer types or in a combination of offerings and customer types. For instance, Procter & Gamble and Black & Decker organize their sales forces by customer size with large customers (Wal-Mart and Home Depot) having "customer specialists" who focus on delivering superior customer service. Firestone Tire and Rubber has a sales force that calls on its own dealers and another that calls on independent dealers, such as gasoline stations. Lone Star Steel has a sales force that sells drilling pipe to oil companies and another that sells specialty steel products to manufacturers.

■ EVALUATION AND CONTROL OF THE COMMUNICATION PROCESS

As part of every communication strategy, there must be mechanisms for evaluation and control. Without them, a marketing manager would be hard-pressed to manage the communication process effectively. There would be no way to determine whether a strategy had achieved its objectives, nor would there be a way to make changes in a strategy in response to competitive activities or environmental occurrences, whether fortuitous or not.

Implicit in both mechanisms is the concept of *continuousness*. The marketing manager must continuously monitor the execution of any communication plan or strategy to ensure that the communication objectives are being attained.

Ideally, evaluation and control should incorporate some measure of sales or profits. Although this is possible for certain communication tools (the sales effectiveness of a direct-mail program can be judged in a relatively straightforward way), for others, it is not. It is nearly impossible to isolate the contribution of institutional advertising to any individual sales transaction.

Budgeting is the ultimate form of control because slashing or adding to the budget of a communication activity effectively eliminates or accentuates the activity itself. The budgeting element is illustrated by the decision to add an additional sales representative with a yearly salary and fringe benefits of $75,000 or to allocate the same amount to a direct-mail sales promotion program, when the product mix contribution margin is 25 percent. A simple break-even calculation ($75,000 ÷ 0.25) reveals that $300,000 in additional sales must be generated to cover the incremental cost. The issue is therefore whether the new sales representative or the sales promotion is more likely to achieve this break-even sales volume. Incremental analysis of this type is increasingly being viewed as the appropriate approach for evaluating and controlling expenditures for sales promotion, advertising, and personal selling.[10]

NOTES

1. Publicity is a fourth element often included in the communication mix, but it is not considered here for two reasons. First, publicity is often uncontrollable except through the broader public relations function of an organization; hence, it is not typically the responsibility of the marketing manager. Second, even if publicity is the responsibility of the marketing manager, it is often managed as a mixture of advertising and personal selling, and thus does not require separate treatment.
2. Judy Strauss and Raymond Frost, *Marketing on the Internet: Principles of Online Marketing* (Upper Saddle River, NJ: Prentice Hall, 1999).
3. Independent representatives are individuals or firms paid commissions for selling a manufacturer's product. These individuals or companies represent several noncompeting products that are sold to one or several categories of customers. They do not carry product inventories or take legal title to goods. Their functions vary from selling only a firm's products to broader activities including applications engineering, in-store merchandising support (point-of-purchase displays, stocking), and product maintenance. Independent representatives go by a variety of names, including broker, manufacturer's representative, and sales agent.
4. "Coca-Cola Foods' Teasley Focuses Marketing on Minute Maid Juices," *Wall Street Journal* (June 23, 1988): 32.
5. Portions of this discussion are based on Robert C. Blattberg and Scott A. Neslin, *Sales Promotion: Concepts, Methods, and Strategies* (Upper Saddle River, NJ: Prentice Hall, 1990): 466–71.
6. George E. Belch and Michael A. Belch, *Introduction to Advertising & Promotion: An Integrated Marketing Communications Perspective*, 5th ed. (Chicago: Irwin/McGraw-Hill, 2001).
7. "Business-to-Business Captures 37.4% of All Marketing Spending," *Advertising Age* (June 3, 1997): 46.
8. "Wearing the Pants," *BRANDWEEK* (October 20, 1998): 20–22.
9. "The Won and Lost Weekend," *The Economist* (November 29, 1997): 87–88.
10. Magid Abraham and Leonard Lodish, "Getting the Most Out of Advertising and Promotion," *Harvard Business Review* (May-June 1990): 50–58.

CASE

Throckmorten Furniture, Inc. (A)

Late in the evening of January 10, 2000, Charlton Bates, President of Throckmorten Furniture, Inc., called Dr. Thomas Berry, a marketing professor at a private university in the Northeast and a consultant to the company. The conversation went as follows:

BATES: Hello, Tom. This is Chuck Bates. I'm sorry to call you this late, but I wanted to get your thoughts on the tentative 2000 advertising program proposed by Mike Hervey of Hervey and Bernham, our ad agency.

BERRY: No problem, Chuck. What did they propose?

BATES: The crux of their proposal is that we should increase our advertising expenditures by $200,000. They suggested that we put the entire amount into our consumer advertising program for ads in several shelter magazines.[1] Hervey noted that the National Home Furnishings Foundation has recommended that furniture manufacturers spend 1 percent of their sales exclusively on consumer advertising.

BERRY: That increase appears to be slightly out of line with your policy of budgeting 5 percent of expected sales for total promotion expenditures, doesn't it? Hasn't John Bott [Vice President of Sales] emphasized the need for more sales representatives?

BATES: Yes, John has requested additional funds. You're right about the 5 percent figure too, and I'm not sure if our sales forecast isn't too optimistic. Your research has shown that our sales historically follow industry sales almost perfectly, and trade economists are predicting about a 4.2 percent increase for 2000. Yet, I'm not too sure.

BERRY: Well, Chuck, you can't expect forecasts to be always on the button. The money is one thing, but what else can you tell me about Hervey's rationale for putting more dollars into consumer advertising?

BATES: He contends that we can increase our exposure and tell our quality and styling story to the buying public—increase brand awareness, enhance our image, that sort of thing. He also cited industry research data that showed that as baby boomers [consumers born between 1946 and 1964] age they are becoming more home oriented and are replacing older, cheaper furniture with more expensive, longer-lasting pieces. Baby boomers will make up 44 percent of all U.S. households in 2000. All I know is that my contribution margin will fall to 25 percent next year because of increased labor and material cost.

BERRY: I appreciate your concern. Give me a few days to think about the proposal. I'll get back to you soon.

---

[1] Shelter magazines feature home improvement ideas, new ideas in home decorating, and so on. *Better Homes and Gardens* is an example of a shelter magazine.

After hanging up, Berry began to think about Bates' summary of the proposal, Throckmorten's present position, and the furniture industry in general. He knew that Bates expected a well-thought-out recommendation on such issues and a step-by-step description of the logic used to arrive at that recommendation.

THE COMPANY

Throckmorten Furniture is a manufacturer of medium- to high-priced wood bedroom, living room, and dining room furniture. The company was formed at the turn of the century by Charlton Bates' grandfather. Bates assumed the presidency of the company upon his father's retirement. Year-end net sales in 1999 were $75 million with a before-tax profit of $3.7 million.

Throckmorten sells its furniture through 1,000 high-quality department stores and independent furniture specialty stores nationwide, but all stores do not carry the company's entire line. The company is very selective in choosing retail outlets. According to Bates, "Our distribution policy, hence our retailers, should mirror the high quality of our products." As a matter of policy, Throckmorten does not sell to furniture chain stores or discount outlets.

The company employs ten full-time salespeople and two regional sales managers. Sales personnel receive a base salary and a small commission on sales. A company sales force is atypical in the furniture industry; most furniture manufacturers use sales agents or representatives who carry a wide assortment of noncompeting furniture lines and receive a commission on sales. "Having our own sales group is a policy my father established years ago," noted Bates, "and we've been quite successful in having people who are committed to our company. Our people don't just take furniture orders. They are expected to motivate retail salespeople to sell our line, assist in setting up displays in stores, and give advice on a variety of matters to our retailers and their salespeople." He added, "It seems that my father was ahead of his time. I was just reading in the *Standard & Poor's Industry Surveys* for household furniture that the competition for retail floor space will require even more support, including store personnel sales training, innovative merchandising, inventory management, and advertising."

In early 1999, Throckmorten allocated $3,675,000 for total promotional expenditures for the 1999 operating year, excluding the salary of the Vice President of Sales. Promotion expenditures were categorized into four groups: (1) sales expense and administration, (2) cooperative advertising programs with retailers, (3) trade promotion, and (4) consumer advertising. Sales costs included salaries for sales personnel and sales managers, selling-expense reimbursements, fringe benefits, and clerical/office assistance, but did not include salespersons' commissions. Commissions were deducted from sales in the calculation of gross profit. The cooperative advertising budget is usually spent on newspaper advertising in a retailer's city. Cooperative advertising allowances are matched by funds provided by retailers on a dollar-for-dollar basis. Trade promotion is directed toward retailers and takes the form of catalogs, trade magazine advertisements, booklets for consumers, and point-of-purchase materials, such as displays, for use in retail stores. Also included in this category is the expense of participating in trade shows. Throckmorten is represented at two shows per year. Consumer advertising is directed at potential consumers through shelter magazines. The typical format used in consumer advertising is to highlight new furniture and different bedroom, living room, and dining room arrangements. The dollar allocation for each of these programs in 1999 is shown in Exhibit 1.

EXHIBIT 1

Allocation of Throckmorten's Promotion Dollars, 1999

Sales expense and administration	$ 995,500
Cooperative advertising allowance	1,650,000
Trade advertising	467,000
Consumer advertising	562,500
	$3,675,000

Source: Company records.

THE HOUSEHOLD FURNITURE INDUSTRY

The household furniture industry is divided into three general categories: wood, upholstered, and other (ready-to-assemble furniture and casual furniture). Total furniture industry sales in 1999 were estimated to be $24.5 billion at manufacturers' prices.

Household wood furniture sales represent 48 percent of total household furniture sales, followed by upholstered furniture (40 percent) and other forms (12 percent), according to the American Furniture Manufacturers Association (AFMA). The principal types of wood furniture are dressers, tables, and dining room suites. Bedroom and dining room furniture account for the majority of wood furniture sales.

In recent years, wood furniture manufacturers have increased their emphasis on quality by monitoring the entire production process from the raw materials used to construction, finishes, and packaging. In addition to improving quality controls, companies also stress price points and basic styling features, and are trying to improve shipping schedules. Wood furniture manufacturers' sales rose only 2.1 percent in 1999, but are expected to rise by 4.2 percent in 2000, according to the AFMA.

More than 1,000 furniture manufacturers operate in the United States. Three manufacturers have annual sales of more than $1 billion and represent about 20 percent of industry sales. These are Furniture Brands International, Inc. (owner of the Broyhill, Lane, and Thomasville brands), Lifestyle Furnishings International, Inc. (Drexel Heritage, Henredon, and Lexington brands), and La-Z-Boy, Inc. Other well-known manufacturers include Ethan Allen, Bassett, Ladd, and Sherrill. The top 25 manufacturers account for 52 percent of U.S. furniture sales. Imports are not a factor in the U.S. household wood furniture industry.

Consumer Expenditures for Furniture

Consumer spending for wood furniture is highly cyclical and closely linked to the incidence of new housing starts, consumer confidence, and disposable personal income. Because wood furniture is expensive and often sold in sets, such as a dining room table and chairs, consumers consider these purchases deferrable.

Expenditures for furniture of all kinds have fluctuated as a percentage of consumer disposable personal income since 1979. It has been estimated that about 1 percent of a U.S. household's disposable income is spent for household furniture and home furnishings. The expected absolute growth in consumer disposable income has led industry economists to forecast a 5 percent increase in retail furniture sales over 1999 sales. Forecasted retail sales for 2000 are about $62.2 billion. Exhibit 2 on page 238 shows annual furniture sales at retail prices for the period 1989 to 1999.

EXHIBIT 2

Total Retail Furniture Sales in the United States, 1989–1999 (In Billions of Dollars at Retail Prices)

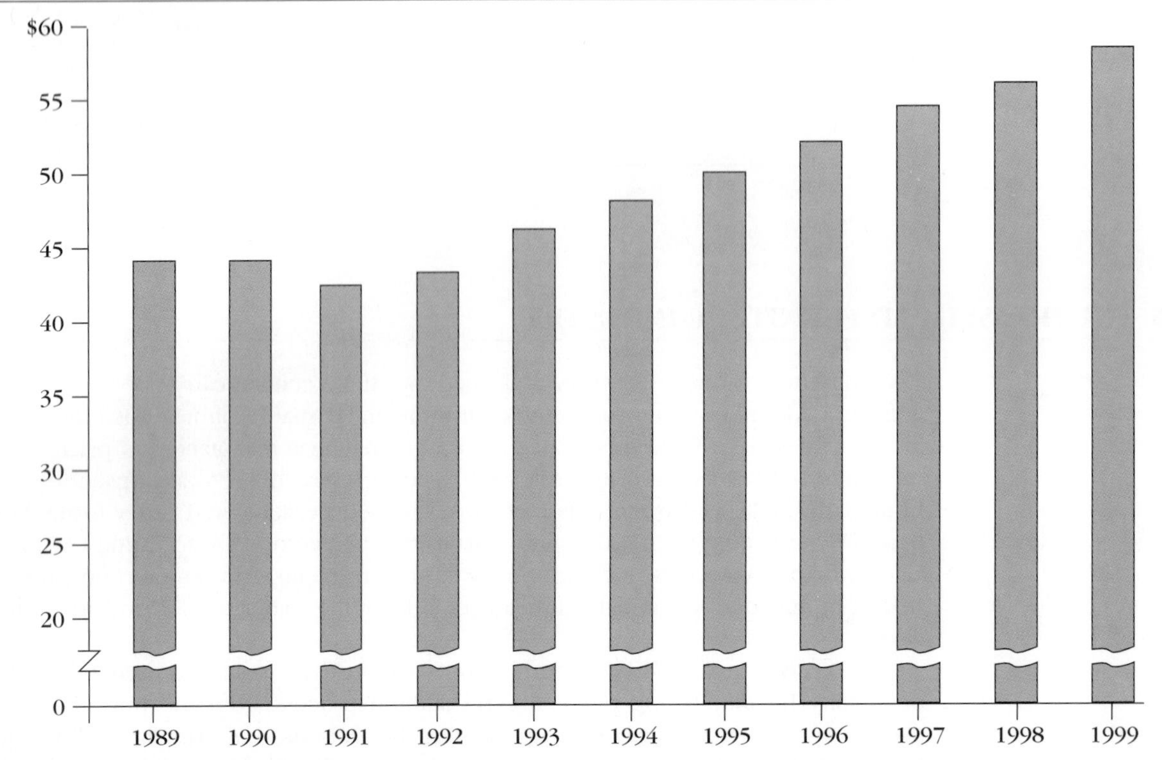

Source: U.S. Department of Commerce.

Furniture Buying Behavior

Even though industry research indicates many consumers consider the furniture shopping process to be enjoyable, consumers acknowledge that they lack the confidence to assess furniture construction, make judgments about quality, and accurately evaluate the price of furniture. Consumers also find it difficult to choose among the many styles available, fearing they will not like their choice several years later or that their selection will not be appropriate for their home and they will be unable to return it. According to a recent summary of furniture-buying behavior published in *Standard & Poor's Industry Surveys*:

> Consumers are quite finicky when it comes to buying furniture—a procedure fraught with concerns that are often not associated with buying other consumer durables, such as appliances and cars. With appliances and cars, consumers may have a more limited selection, they can do their own research, and they know what they are buying and what to expect. On the other hand, most consumers know little about evaluating the price or quality of furniture. It is also difficult for consumers to imagine how furniture will look in their homes, or whether they will still like their purchase in several years. Furthermore, there are questions about delivery—as in whether the item will arrive on time and in good condition and whether it can be returned for a full refund.
>
> The furniture industry's efforts to educate consumers over the past years have failed for the most part. These efforts have included in-depth market studies to learn what consumers look for when they buy furniture, improved distribution, and new programs for training sales personnel. Despite these efforts, consumers still find the

quality of furniture difficult to discern, and tend to base their furniture choice on price.

Results of a consumer panel sponsored by *Better Homes and Gardens* and composed of its subscribers provide the most comprehensive information available on furniture-buying behavior. Selected findings from the *Better Homes and Gardens* survey are reproduced in the appendix following this case. Other findings arising from this research are as follows:

- 94 percent of the subscribers enjoy buying furniture somewhat or very much.
- 84 percent of the subscribers believe "the higher the price, the higher the quality" when buying home furnishings.
- 72 percent of the subscribers browse or window-shop furniture stores even if they don't need furniture.
- 85 percent read furniture ads before they actually need furniture.
- 99 percent of the subscribers agree with the statement "When shopping for furniture and home furnishings, I like the salesperson to show me what alternatives are available, answer my questions, and let me alone so I can think about it and maybe browse around."
- 95 percent of the subscribers say they get redecorating ideas or guidance from magazines.
- 41 percent of the subscribers have requested a manufacturer's booklet.
- 63 percent of the subscribers say they need decorating advice to "put it all together."

Consumer research data have prompted both furniture retailers and manufacturers to stress the need for well-informed retail sales personnel to work with customers. For example, many manufacturers have established education centers where they train retail salespersons in the qualitative and construction details of the furniture they sell. Some manufacturers also distribute product literature to customers via retailers. Drexel Heritage, for instance, provides a series of books, entitled *Living with Drexel Heritage,* to its authorized retailers, who then give them to customers.

Distribution

Furniture is sold through over 100,000 specialty furniture and home furnishings stores, department stores, and mass-merchandise stores in the United States. Furniture and home furnishings are also sold by Internet companies. Industry trends indicate that the number of independently owned furniture stores has declined while furniture store chains have grown. The top 25 furniture retailers in the United States captured approximately 27 percent of total U.S. furniture retail sales. Heilig-Meyers Company is the largest furniture retailer, with sales that accounted for less than 5 percent of the retail furniture market. Other large retailers include Levitz, Pier 1 Imports, The Bombay Company, W. S. Badcock, Ethan Allen, This End Up, and Jennifer Convertibles. Well-known regional furniture retailers include Haverty's and Breuner's Home Furnishings.

A significant trend among furniture retailers is the movement toward the "gallery concept"—the practice of dedicating an amount of space and sometimes an entire free-standing retail outlet to one furniture manufacturer. There are currently 11,000 galleries, and it is estimated this number will reach 12,500 by 2002. Commenting on the gallery concept, Charlton Bates said:

> The gallery concept has great appeal for a furniture manufacturer, since product is displayed in a unique and comfortable setting without the lure of competitive brands. We have galleries in a small number of our furniture stores. The fact that we are not getting our full line in all of our retailers galls me because the opportunity to even discuss the gallery concept with many of our retailers doesn't exist.

EXHIBIT 3

Furniture Retailers that Upscale Shoppers (Household Income $100,000 and Up) Have Used for Ideas and Where They Buy

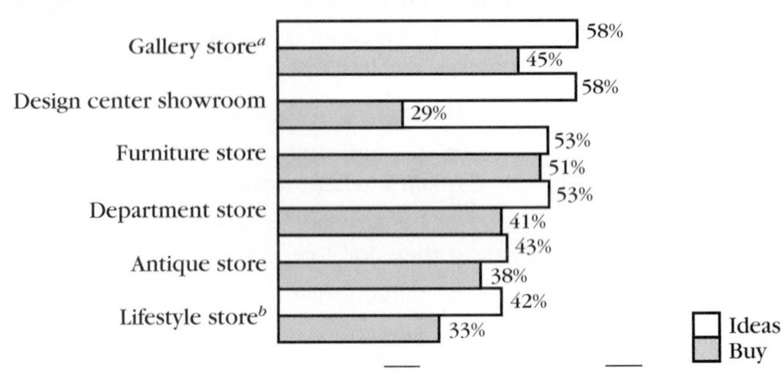

[a] *Furniture from single company*

[b] *Crate & Barrel, Pottery Barn, Ikea, etc.*

Bates added: "Galleries and upscale furniture and department stores attract and serve our target customer, the 36- to 54-year-old home owner with an annual household income over $100,000. That's where our customers get ideas and buy the quality furniture we sell" (see Exhibit 3).

The selling of furniture to retail outlets centers on manufacturers' expositions held at selected times and places around the country. The major expositions occur in High Point, North Carolina, in October and April. Regional expositions are also scheduled during the June–August period in locations such as Dallas, Los Angeles, New York, and Boston. At these *marts*, as they are called in the furniture industry, retail buyers view manufacturers' lines and often make buying commitments for their stores. However, Throckmorten's experience has shown that sales efforts in the retail store by company representatives account for as much as one-half of the company's sales in any given year.

Advertising Practices

Manufacturers of household furniture spend approximately 3.5 percent of annual net sales for advertising of all types (consumer, trade, and cooperative advertising).[2] This percentage has remained constant for many years. The typical vehicles used for consumer advertising are shelter magazines such as *Better Homes and Gardens, House Beautiful*, and *Southern Living*. Trade advertising directed primarily toward retailers includes brochures, point-of-purchase materials to be displayed on a retailer's sales floor, and technical booklets describing methods of construction and materials. Cooperative advertising, shared with retailers, usually appears in newspapers, but there are also some television and radio spots featuring the brands carried by retailers.

Since 1990, the Home Furnishings Council has promoted home furnishings in general through advertising and a nationally syndicated, interactive television show, *Haven*. This effort focuses on stimulating demand for furniture and home furnishings and increasing the percentage of consumer disposable income devoted to furniture purchases. Exhibit 4 shows one of the print advertisements sponsored by the Home Furnishings Council.

[2] "1999 Advertising-to-Sales Ratio for the 200 Largest Ad Spending Industries," *Advertising Age* (June 28, 1999): 58.

EXHIBIT 4

Home Furnishings Council Print Advertisement

Home Furnishings Tips From Kathie Lee Gifford.

Second In A Series:
"How Do I Start?!" My Answer: Don't Panic, Breathe Easy, And Read This.

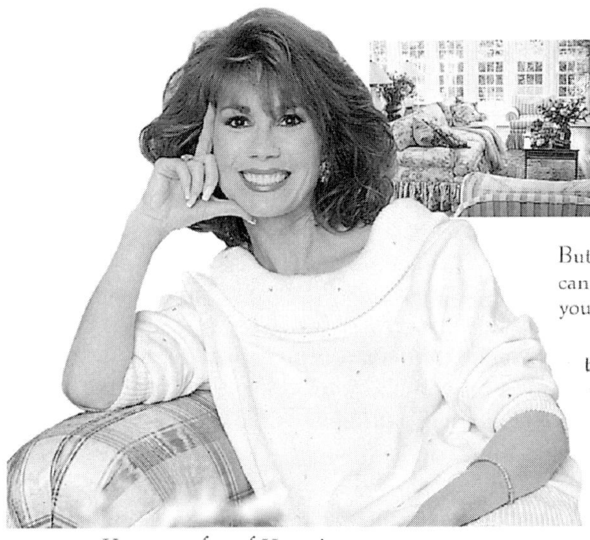

Nobody ever said that decorating a room, or a whole house, was a piece of cake. But it's definitely *not* hard, and can actually be fun—especially if you start off right.

You can do that by following the terrific "Getting Started" tips found in Haven. It's the incredibly easy to use, complete decorating guide that's *free* at home furnishings stores everywhere that display the "heart and home" sign of the Home Furnishings Council.

Here are a few of Haven's time-saving, money-saving, sanity-saving ideas on starting off right.

1. For Step One, you don't even have to step out of your home, just go through all the decorating magazines you've been saving to find the rooms, the home furnishings, the colors and styles you like. Then take a grand tour of your own home, to see what you like, and what you'd like to never see again. Put all your thoughts on paper.

2. Next comes my favorite part, visiting home furnishings stores and galleries.

3. Take advantage of all the help and advice that these stores' sales experts have to offer you. Tell them your budget (don't be timid about it!) so they can help you get the best value for your dollar. Show them the pictures you tore out of magazines, bring along your room dimensions, your likes and dislikes—the more they know, the more they can help.

4. And, most important, work with them to realistically plan your decorating in phases—no one expects you to buy *everything* you want at once.

See, making a beautiful home for the most wonderful family in the world *is* a whole lot easier than you thought.

For the store nearest you offering free copies of Haven, please call 1-800-521-HOME, ext. 345

Home Is Where The Heart Is.

Source: Courtesy of the Home Furnishings Council.

THE BUDGET MEETING

At the January 10 meeting attended by Hervey and Bernham executives and Throckmorten executives, Michael Hervey proposed that the expenditure for consumer advertising be increased by $200,000 for 2000. Cooperative advertising and trade advertising allowances would remain at 1999 levels. Hervey further recommended that shelter magazines account for the bulk of the incremental expenditure for consumer advertising.

John Bott, Throckmorten's Vice President of Sales, disagreed with the budget allocation and noted that sales expenses and administration costs were expected to rise by $50,000 in 2000. Moreover, Bott believed that an additional sales representative was needed to service Throckmorten's accounts, because 50 new accounts were being added. He estimated that the cost of the additional representative, including salary and expenses, would be at least $70,000 in 2000. "That's about $120,000 in additional sales expenses that have to be added into our promotional budget for 2000," Bott noted. He continued:

> We recorded sales of $75 million in 1999. If we assume a 4.2 percent increase in sales in 2000, that means our total budget will be about $3.9 million, if my figures are right—a $232,500 increase over our previous budget. And I need $120,000 of that. In other words, $112,500 is available for other kinds of promotion.

Hervey's reply to Bott noted that the company planned to introduce several new styles of living room and dining room furniture in 2000 and that these new items would require consumer advertising in shelter magazines to be launched successfully. He agreed with Bott that increased funding of the sales effort might be necessary and thought that Throckmorten might draw funds from cooperative advertising allowances and trade promotion.

Bates interrupted the dialogue between Bott and Hervey to mention that the $200,000 increase in promotion was about $32,000 less than the 5 percent percentage-of-sales policy limit. He pointed out, however, that higher material costs plus a recent wage increase were forecasted to squeeze Throckmorten's gross profit margin and threaten the company objective of achieving a 5 percent net profit margin before taxes. "Perhaps some juggling of the figures is necessary," he concluded. "Both of you have good points. Let me think about what's been said and then let's schedule a meeting for a week from today."

As Bates reviewed his notes from the meeting, he realized that the funds allocated to promotion were only part of the question. How the funds would be allocated within the budget was also crucial. A call to Tom Berry might be helpful in this regard, too.

APPENDIX: SELECTED FINDINGS FROM THE *BETTER HOMES AND GARDENS*® CONSUMER PANEL REPORT—HOME FURNISHINGS[3]

Question: If you were going to buy furniture in the near future, how important would the following factors be in selecting the store to buy furniture? (Respondents: 449)

Factor	*Very Important*	*Somewhat Important*	*Not Too Important*	*Not at All Important*	*No Answer*
Sells high-quality furnishings	62.6%	31.0%	3.8%	1.1%	1.5%
Has a wide range of different furniture styles	58.8	29.2	8.2	2.9	0.9

[3] Reprinted courtesy of the *Better Homes and Gardens*® Consumer Panel.

Factor	*Very Important*	*Somewhat Important*	*Not Too Important*	*Not at All Important*	*No Answer*
Gives you personal service	60.1	29.9	7.8	0.9	1.3
Is a highly dependable store	85.1	12.7	1.1	—	1.1
Offers decorating help from experienced home planners	26.5	35.9	25.4	10.9	1.3
Lets you "browse" all you want	77.1	17.8	3.3	0.7	1.1
Sells merchandise that's a good value for the money	82.0	15.6	0.9	0.2	1.3
Displays furniture in individual room settings	36.3	41.2	18.7	2.4	1.3
Has a relaxed, no-pressure atmosphere	80.0	17.1	1.6	—	1.3
Has well-informed salespeople	77.5	19.8	1.6	—	1.1
Has a very friendly atmosphere	68.2	28.1	2.4	—	1.3
Carries the style of furniture you like	88.0	10.0	0.9	—	1.1

Question: Please rate the following factors as to their importance to you when you purchase or shop for case-goods furniture, such as a dining room or living room suite, *1* being the most important factor, *2* being second most important, and so on, until all factors have been rated. (Respondents: 449)

Factor	*1*	*2*	*3*	*4*	*5*	*6*	*7*	*8*	*9*	*10*	*No Answer*
Construction of item	24.1%	16.0%	18.5%	13.1%	10.5%	6.9%	4.9%	1.6%	0.2%	1.1%	3.1%
Comfort	13.6	14.7	12.9	12.3	12.7	10.9	8.2	4.5	4.0	2.4	3.8
Styling and design	33.6	19.8	11.1	9.6	4.7	7.3	4.5	1.6	2.9	1.6	3.3
Durability of fabric	2.2	7.6	9.8	14.5	15.1	14.7	12.9	5.6	5.8	7.8	4.0
Type and quality of wood	10.9	17.8	16.3	15.8	14.7	5.8	5.3	3.1	4.9	2.0	3.4
Guarantee or warranty	1.6	3.8	1.6	5.3	8.7	10.0	13.8	25.2	14.5	11.1	4.4
Price	9.4	6.2	8.7	8.5	10.0	12.5	14.2	11.8	6.9	8.0	3.8
Reputation of manufacturer or brand name	6.2	3.6	4.7	5.6	6.2	6.2	12.7	17.1	22.7	11.6	3.4
Reputation of retailer	1.6	1.8	1.6	2.4	4.0	7.3	7.4	13.6	22.0	34.5	3.8
Finish, color of wood	4.7	7.6	10.2	8.0	8.9	13.4	10.7	10.0	10.2	12.7	3.6

Question: Below is a list of 15 criteria that may influence what furniture you buy. Please rate them from *1* as most important to *5* as least important. (Respondents: 449)

Criterion	*1*	*2*	*3*	*4*	*5*	*No Answer*
Guarantee or warranty	11.4%	11.1%	26.3%	16.9%	5.3%	29.0%
Brand name	9.1	6.5	14.3	25.6	11.6	32.9
Comfort	34.7	27.8	14.5	8.5	4.7	9.8

Criterion	*1*	*2*	*3*	*4*	*5*	*No Answer*
Decorator suggestion	4.0	2.4	2.7	8.2	44.8	37.9
Material used	14.9	24.1	14.9	13.4	6.2	26.5
Delivery time	0.7	0.5	1.3	2.9	55.2	39.4
Size	7.6	10.7	13.6	30.9	4.0	33.2
Styling and design	33.4	17.8	21.8	13.6	2.2	11.2
Construction	34.3	23.6	13.1	11.4	2.9	14.7
Fabric	4.0	25.6	24.9	14.0	4.5	27.0
Durability	37.0	19.4	13.6	6.9	4.9	18.2
Finish on wooden parts	5.8	14.7	16.7	10.7	16.7	35.4
Price	19.4	21.8	16.0	10.9	15.4	16.5
Manufacturer's reputation	4.2	9.1	15.4	22.9	14.3	34.1
Retailer's reputation	2.2	4.7	10.5	21.2	26.5	34.9

Question: Listed below are some statements others have made about shopping for furniture. Please indicate how much you agree or disagree with each one. (Respondents: 449)

Statement	*Agree Completely*	*Agree Somewhat*	*Neither Agree nor Disagree*	*Disagree Somewhat*	*Disagree Completely*	*No Answer*
I wish there were some way to be really sure of getting good quality in furniture	61.9%	24.7%	4.7%	4.2%	3.6%	0.9%
I really enjoy shopping for furniture	49.2	28.3	7.6	9.8	4.2	0.9
I would never buy any furniture without my husband's/wife's approval	47.0	23.0	10.9	9.8	7.1	2.2
I like all pieces in the master bedroom to be exactly the same style	35.9	30.7	12.7	11.1	7.6	2.0
Once I find something I like in furniture, I wish it would last forever so I'd never have to buy again	36.8	24.3	10.0	18.9	9.1	0.9
I wish I had more confidence in my ability to decorate my home attractively	23.1	32.3	12.5	11.6	18.7	1.8
I wish I knew more about furniture styles and what looks good	20.0	31.0	17.1	13.4	16.7	1.8
My husband/wife doesn't take much interest in the furniture we buy	6.5	18.0	12.3	17.8	41.4	4.0
I like to collect a number of different styles in the dining room	3.3	10.5	15.2	29.8	38.3	2.9
Shopping for furniture is very distressing to me	2.4	11.6	14.3	18.0	51.9	1.8

Question: Listed below are some factors that may influence your choice of furnishings. Please rate them with *1* being most important, *2* being second most important, and so on, until all factors have been rated. (Respondents: 449)

Factor	***1***	***2***	***3***	***4***	***5***	***No Answer***
Friends and/or neighbors	1.3%	16.9%	15.8%	22.1%	41.7%	2.2%
Family or spouse	62.8	9.4	14.3	9.8	2.0	1.7
Magazine advertising	16.3	30.3	29.6	17.6	4.2	2.0
Television advertising	1.1	6.7	14.7	32.5	42.3	2.7
Store displays	18.9	37.2	22.1	14.0	5.6	2.2

Question: When you go shopping for a *major piece* of furniture or smaller pieces of furniture, who, if anyone, do you usually go with? (Respondents: 449—multiple responses)

Person	***Major Pieces***	***Other Pieces***
Husband	82.4%	59.5%
Mother or mother-in-law	6.2	9.1
Friend	12.0	18.9
Decorator	4.2	1.6
Other relative	15.6	15.4
Other person	2.9	3.3
No one else	5.1	22.3
No answer	0.9	3.1

Question: When the time comes to purchase a *major* item of furniture or other smaller pieces of furniture, who, if anyone, helps you make the final decision about which piece to buy? (Respondents: 449—multiple responses)

Person	***Major Pieces***	***Other Pieces***
Husband	86.0%	63.5%
Mother or mother-in-law	2.4	4.5
Friend	3.6	8.0
Decorator	3.1	2.7
Other relative	10.0	12.9
Other person	1.6	1.8
No one else	7.1	24.3
No answer	0.9	2.2

CASE

Throckmorten Furniture, Inc. (B)

In April 2000, Throckmorten Furniture, Inc. merged with Lea-Meadows, Inc., a manufacturer of upholstered furniture for living and family rooms. The merger was not planned in a conventional sense. Charlton Bates's father-in-law died suddenly in early February 2000, leaving his daughter with controlling interest in Lea-Meadows. The merger proceeded smoothly, since the two firms were located on adjacent properties and the general consensus was that the two firms would maintain as much autonomy as was economically justified. Moreover, the upholstery line filled a gap in the Throckmorten product mix, even though it would retain its own identity and brand names.

The only real issue that continued to plague Bates was merging the selling effort. Throckmorten had its own sales force, but Lea-Meadows relied on sales agents to represent it. The question was straightforward, in his opinion: "Do we give the upholstery line of chairs and sofas to our sales force, or do we continue using the sales agents?" John Bott, Throckmorten's Vice President of Sales, said the line should be given to his sales group; Martin Moorman, National Sales Manager at Lea-Meadows, said the upholstery line should remain with sales agents.

■ LEA-MEADOWS, INC.

Lea-Meadows, Inc. is a small, privately owned manufacturer of upholstered furniture for use in living and family rooms. The firm is more than 75 years old. The company uses some of the finest fabrics and frame construction in the industry, according to trade sources. Net sales in 1999 were $5 million. Total industry sales of upholstered furniture manufacturers in 1999 were $9.8 billion. Forecasted 2000 industry sales for upholstered furniture were $10.4 billion. Company sales had increased 7 percent annually over the past five years, and company executives believed this growth rate would continue for the foreseeable future.

Lea-Meadows employed 15 sales agents to represent its products. These sales agents also represented several manufacturers of noncompeting furniture and home furnishings. Often, a sales agent found it necessary to deal with several buyers in a store in order to represent all the lines carried. On a typical sales call, a sales agent first visited buyers to discuss new lines, in addition to any promotions being offered by manufacturers. New orders were sought where and when it was appropriate. The sales agent then visited the selling floor to check displays, inspect furniture, and inform salespeople about furniture styles and construction. Lea-Meadows paid an agent commission of 5 percent of net company sales for these services. Moorman

This case was prepared by Professor Roger A. Kerin, of the Edwin L. Cox School of Business, Southern Methodist University, as a basis for class discussion and is not designed to illustrate appropriate or inappropriate handling of administrative situations. All names and data are disguised.

thought sales agents spent 10 to 15 percent of their in-store time on Lea-Meadows products.

The company did not attempt to influence the type of retailers that agents contacted, although it was implicit in the agency agreement that agents would not sell to discount houses. Sales records indicated that agents were calling on specialty furniture and department stores. An estimated 1,000 retail accounts were called on in 1998 and 1999. All agents had established relationships with their retail accounts and worked closely with them.

■ THROCKMORTEN FURNITURE, INC.

Throckmorten Furniture, Inc. is a manufacturer of medium- to high-priced wood bedroom, living room, and dining room furniture.[1] Net sales in 1999 were $75 million; before-tax profit was $3.7 million. Industry sales of wood furniture in 1999 were $11.8 billion at manufacturers' prices. Projected industry sales for 2000 were $12.3 billion.

The company employed 10 full-time sales representatives, who called on 1,000 retail accounts. These individuals performed the same function as sales agents but were paid a salary plus a small commission. In 1999, the average sales representative received an annual salary of $70,000 (plus expenses) and a commission of 0.5 percent on net company sales. Total sales administration costs were $130,000.

Throckmorten's salespeople were highly regarded in the industry. They were known particularly for their knowledge of wood furniture and willingness to work with buyers and retail sales personnel. Despite these advantages, Bates knew that all retail accounts did not carry the complete Throckmorten furniture line. He had therefore instructed Bott to "push the group a little harder." At present, sales representatives were making 10 sales calls per week, with the average sales call running three hours. Salespersons' remaining time was accounted for by administrative activities and travel. Bates recommended that the call frequency be increased to seven calls per account per year, which was consistent with what he thought was the industry norm.

■ MERGING THE SALES EFFORTS

Through separate meetings with Bott and Moorman, Bates was able to piece together a variety of data and perspectives on the question of merging the sales efforts. These meetings also made it clear that Bott and Moorman differed dramatically in their views.

John Bott had no doubts about assigning the line to the Throckmorten sales force. Among the reasons he gave for this view were the following. First, Throckmorten had developed one of the most well respected, professional sales forces in the industry. The representatives could easily learn the fabric jargon, and they already knew personally many of the buyers who were responsible for upholstered furniture. Second, selling the Lea-Meadows line would require only about 15 percent of present sales call time. Thus, he thought that the new line would not be a major burden. Third, more control over sales efforts was possible. Bott noted that Charlton Bates's father had created the sales group 30 years earlier because of the commitment it engendered and the service "only our own people are able and willing to

[1]Additional background information on the company and industry can be found in the case titled "Throckmorten Furniture, Inc. (A)."

give." Moreover, the company salespeople have the Throckmorten "look" and presentation style, which is instilled in every one of them. Fourth, Bott said that it wouldn't look right if both representatives and agents called on the same stores and buyers. He noted that Throckmorten and Lea-Meadows overlapped on all their accounts. He said, "We'd be paying a commission on sales to these accounts when we would have gotten them anyway. The difference in commission percentages would not be good for morale."

Martin Moorman advocated keeping sales agents for the Lea-Meadows line. His arguments were as follows. First, all sales agents had established contacts and were highly regarded by store buyers, and most had represented the line in a professional manner for many years. He, too, had a good working relationship with all 15 agents. Second, sales agents represented little, if any, cost beyond commissions. Moorman noted, "Agents get paid when we get paid." Third, sales agents were committed to the Lea-Meadows line: "The agents earn a part of their living representing us. They have to service retail accounts to get the repeat business." Fourth, sales agents were calling on buyers not contacted by the Throckmorten sales force. Moorman noted, "If we let Throckmorten people handle the line, we might lose these accounts, have to hire more sales personnel, or take away 25 percent of the present selling time given to Throckmorten product lines.

As Bates reflected on the meetings, he felt that a broader perspective was necessary beyond the views expressed by Bott and Moorman. One factor was profitability. Existing Throckmorten furniture lines typically had gross margins that were 5 percent higher than those for Lea-Meadows upholstered lines. Another factor was the "us and them" references apparent in the meetings with Bott and Moorman. Would merging the sales effort overcome this, or would it cause more problems? The idea of increasing the sales force to incorporate the Lea-Meadows line did not sit well with him. Adding new salespeople would require restructuring of sales territories, involve potential loss of commissions by existing salespeople, and be "a big headache." Finally, there was the subtle issue of Moorman's future. Moorman, who was 55 years old, had worked for Lea-Meadows for 25 years and was a family friend and godfather to Bates' youngest child. If the Lea-Meadows line was represented by the Throckmorten sales force, Moorman's position would be eliminated.

CASE

Cadbury Beverages, Inc.

Crush® Brand

In January 1990, marketing executives at Cadbury Beverages, Inc. began the challenging task of relaunching the Crush, Hires, and Sun-Drop soft drink brands. These brands had been acquired from Procter & Gamble in October 1989.

After considerable discussion, senior marketing executives at Cadbury Beverages, Inc. decided to focus initial attention on the Crush brand of fruit-flavored carbonated beverages. Three issues were prominent. First, immediate efforts were needed to rejuvenate the bottling network for the Crush soft drink brand. Second, according to one executive, "[we had] to sort through and figure out what the Crush brand equity is, how the brand was built . . . and develop a base positioning."[1] Third, a new advertising and promotion program for Crush had to be developed, including setting objectives, developing strategies, and preparing preliminary budgets.

Kim Feil was assigned responsibility for managing the relaunch of the Crush soft drink brand. She had joined Cadbury Beverages, Inc. on December 12, 1989, as a Senior Product Manager, after working in various product management positions at a large consumer goods company for five years. Recounting her first day on the job, Feil said, "I arrived early Wednesday morning to find 70 boxes of research reports, print ads, sales and trade promotions and videotapes stacked neatly from the floor to the ceiling." Undaunted, she began to sift through the mountains of material systematically, knowing that her assessment and recommendations would soon be sought.

■ CADBURY BEVERAGES, INC.

Cadbury Beverages, Inc. is the beverage division of Cadbury Schweppes PLC, a major global soft drink and confectionery marketer. In 1989, Cadbury Schweppes PLC had worldwide sales of $4.6 billion, which were produced by product sales in more than 110 countries. Cadbury Schweppes PLC headquarters are located in London, England; Cadbury Beverages, Inc., worldwide headquarters are in Stamford, Connecticut. Exhibit 1 on page 250 shows the product list sold worldwide by Cadbury Beverages, Inc. Exhibit 2 on page 251 details the product list for the United States.

History

Cadbury Schweppes PLC has the distinction of being the world's first soft drink maker. The company can trace its beginnings to 1783 in London, where Swiss na-

[1] Patricia Winters, "Fresh Start for Crush," *Advertising Age* (January 6, 1990): 47.

The cooperation of Cadbury Beverages, Inc. in the preparation of this case is gratefully acknowledged. This case was prepared by Professor Roger A. Kerin, of the Edwin L. Cox School of Business, Southern Methodist University, as a basis for class discussion and is not designed to illustrate effective or ineffective handling of an administrative situation. Certain information has been disguised and is not useful for research purposes. Crush is a registered trademark used by permission from Cadbury Beverages, Inc.

EXHIBIT 1

Worldwide Product List for Cadbury Beverages, Inc.

Carbonates	*Waters*	*Still Drinks/Juices*
Canada Dry	Schweppes	Oasis
Schweppes	Canada Dry	Atoll
Pure Spring	Pure Spring	Bali
Sunkist	Malvern	TriNaranjus
Crush		Vida
'C' Plus		Trina
Hires		Trina Colada
Sussex		Red Cheek
Old Colony		Allen's
Sun-Drop		Mitchell's
Gini		Mott's
		Clamato
		E. D. Smith
		Rose's
		Mr & Mrs "T"
		Holland House

tional Jacob Schweppe first sold his artificial mineral water. Schweppe returned to Switzerland in 1789, but the company continued its British operations, introducing a lemonade in 1835 and tonic water and ginger ale in the 1870s. Beginning in the 1880s, Schweppes expanded worldwide, particularly in countries that would later form the British Commonwealth. In the 1960s, the company diversified into food products.

In 1969, Schweppes merged with Cadbury. Cadbury was a major British candy maker that traced its origins to John Cadbury, who began his business making cocoa in Birmingham, England, in the 1830s. By the middle of this century, Cadbury had achieved market presence throughout the British Commonwealth, as well as other countries.

In 1989, Cadbury Schweppes PLC was one of the world's largest multinational firms and was ranked 457th in *Business Week*'s Global 1000. Beverages accounted for 60 percent of company worldwide sales and 53 percent of operating income in 1989. Confectionery items accounted for 40 percent of worldwide sales and produced 47 percent of operating income.

Soft Drinks

Cadbury Schweppes PLC is the world's third largest soft drink marketer behind Coca-Cola and PepsiCo. The company has achieved this status through consistent marketing investment in the Schweppes brand name and extensions to different beverage products such as tonic, ginger ale, club soda, and seltzer in various flavors. In addition, the company has acquired numerous other brands throughout the world, each with an established customer franchise. For example, Cadbury Schweppes PLC acquired the Canada Dry soft drink brands and certain rights to Sunkist soft drinks in 1986. In 1989, the company acquired certain soft drink brands and associated assets (for TriNaranjus, Vida, Trina, and Trina Colada) in Spain and Portugal and purchased the Gini brand, which is the leading bitter lemon brand in

EXHIBIT 2

U.S. Product List for Cadbury Beverages, Inc.

Schweppes	*Canada Dry*	*Sunkist*	*Crush, Hires, Sun-Drop*	*Mott's, Red Cheek, Holland House, Mr & Mrs "T," Rose's*
Tonic Water	Tonic Water	Sunkist Pineapple Soda	Crush Orange	Mott's 100% Pure Apple Juices
Diet Tonic Water	Sugar-Free Tonic Water	Sunkist Grape Soda	Crush Diet Orange	Mott's 100% Pure Juice Blends
Club Soda	Club Soda	Sunkist Fruit Punch	Hires Root Beer	Mott's Juice Drinks
Seltzer Water	Seltzer Waters	Sunkist Strawberry Soda	Hires Diet Root Beer	Mott's Apple Sauce
Sparkling Waters	Sparkling Mineral Waters	Sunkist Orange Soda	Hires Cream Soda	Mott's Apple Sauce Fruit Snacks
Grapefruit Soda	Barrelhead Root Beer	Sunkist Diet Orange Soda	Hires Diet Cream Soda	Mott's Prune Juice
Collins Mix	Barrelhead Sugar-Free Root Beer	Sunkist Sparkling Lemonade	Crush Strawberry	Clamato
Grape Soda	Wink	Sunkist Diet Sparkling Lemonade	Crush Grape	Beefamato
Ginger Ale	Ginger Ale		Crush Cherry	Grandma's Molasses
Diet Ginger Ale	Diet Ginger Ale		Crush Pineapple	Rose's Lime Juice
Raspberry Ginger Ale	Cherry Ginger Ale		Crush Cream Soda	Rose's Grenadine
Diet Raspberry Ginger Ale	Diet Cherry Ginger Ale		Sun-Drop Cherry Citrus	Red Cheek Apple Juice
Bitter Lemon	Bitter Lemon		Sun-Drop Diet Citrus	Red Cheek Juice Blends
Lemon Sour	No-Cal Brand Soft Drinks			Mr & Mrs "T" Margarita Salt
Lemon Lime	Cott Brand Soft Drinks			Mr & Mrs "T" Bloody Mary Mix
	Lemon Ginger Ale			Mr & Mrs "T" Liquid Cocktail Mixers
	Diet Lemon Ginger Ale			Mr & Mrs "T" Rich & Spicy
				Holland House Cooking Wines
				Holland House Dry Mixers
				Holland House Wine Marinades
				Holland House Smooth & Spicy
				Holland House Coca Casa Cream of Coconut
				Holland House Liquid Mixers

France and Belgium. Also, in October 1989, the company acquired all the Crush brand worldwide trademarks from Procter & Gamble for $220 million.

Cadbury Schweppes PLC (Cadbury Beverages, Inc.) was the fourth largest soft drink marketer in the United States in 1989, with a carbonated soft drink market share of 3.4 percent. (The three leading U.S. soft drink companies, in order, were Coca-Cola, PepsiCo, and Dr. Pepper/7Up.) Nonetheless, the company's brands were often the market leader in their specific categories. For example, Canada Dry is the top-selling ginger ale in the United States, Schweppes is the leading tonic water, and Canada Dry seltzers top the club soda/seltzer category. The combined sales of Sunkist and Crush brand orange drinks lead the orange-flavored carbonated soft drink category.

According to industry analysts, the 1989 acquisition of Crush meant that Canada Dry would account for 39 percent of Cadbury Beverages soft drink sales in the United States. Sunkist, Crush, and Schweppes would account for 22 percent, 20 percent, and 17 percent of U.S. sales, respectively. The remaining 2 percent of U.S. sales would come from other soft drink brands.[2]

CARBONATED SOFT DRINK INDUSTRY

American consumers drink more soft drinks than tap water. In 1989, the average American consumed 46.7 gallons of carbonated soft drinks, or twice the 23 gallons consumed in 1969. Population growth compounded by rising per capita consumption produced an estimated $43 billion in retail sales in 1989.

Industry Structure

There are three major participants in the production and distribution of carbonated soft drinks in the United States. They are concentrate producers, bottlers, and retail outlets. For regular soft drinks, concentrate producers manufacture the basic flavors (for example, lemon-lime and cola) for sale to bottlers, which add a sweetener to carbonated water and package the beverage in bottles and cans. For diet soft drinks, concentrate producers include an artificial sweetener, such as aspartame, with their flavors.

There are over 40 concentrate producers in the United States. However, about 82 percent of industry sales are accounted for by three producers: Coca-Cola, PepsiCo, and Dr. Pepper/7Up.

Approximately 1,000 bottling plants in the United States convert flavor concentrate into carbonated soft drinks. Bottlers are either owned by concentrate producers or franchised to sell the brands of concentrate producers. For example, roughly one-half of Pepsi-Cola's sales are through company-owned bottlers; the remaining volume is sold through franchised bottlers. Franchised bottlers are typically granted a right to package and distribute a concentrate producer's branded line of soft drinks in a defined territory and not allowed to market a directly competitive major brand. However, franchised bottlers can represent noncompetitive brands and decline to bottle a concentrate producer's secondary lines. These arrangements mean that a franchised bottler of Pepsi-Cola cannot sell Royal Crown (RC) Cola but can bottle and market Orange Crush rather than PepsiCo's Mandarin Orange Slice.

Concentrate producer pricing to bottlers was similar across competitors within flavor categories. Exhibit 3 shows the approximate price and cost structure for orange concentrate producers and bottlers.

---

[2] Patricia Winters, "Cadbury Schweppes' Plan: Skirt Cola Giants," *Advertising Age* (August 13, 1990): 22–23.

EXHIBIT 3

Approximate Price and Cost Structure for Orange Concentrate Producers and Bottlers

	Concentrate Producers			
	Regular (Sugar)		*Diet (Aspartame)*	
	$/Case	*Percentage*	*$/Case*	*Percentage*
Net selling price	$0.76	100%	$0.92	100%
Cost of goods sold	0.11	14	0.12	13
Gross profit	$0.65	86%	$0.80	87%
Selling and delivery	0.02	3	0.02	2
Advertising and promotion	0.38	50	0.38	41
General and administrative expense	0.13	17	0.13	14
Pretax cash profit/case	$0.12	16%	$0.27	30%

	Bottlers			
	Regular (Sugar)		*Diet (Aspartame)*	
	$/Case	*Percentage*	*$/Case*	*Percentage*
Net selling price	$5.85	100%	$5.85	100%
Cost of goods sold	3.16	54	3.35	57
Gross profit	$2.69	46%	$2.50	43%
Selling and delivery	1.35	23	1.35	23
Advertising and promotion	0.40	7	0.40	7
General and administrative expense	0.05	1	0.05	1
Pretax cash profit/case	$0.89	15%	$0.71	12%

The principal retail channels for carbonated soft drinks are supermarkets, convenience stores, vending machines, fountain service, and thousands of small retail outlets. Soft drinks are typically sold in bottles and cans, except for fountain service. In fountain service, syrup is sold to a retail outlet (such as McDonald's), which mixes the syrup with carbonated water for immediate consumption by customers. Supermarkets account for about 40 percent of carbonated soft drink industry sales. Industry analysts consider supermarket sales the key to a successful soft drink marketing effort.

Soft Drink Marketing

Soft drink marketing is characterized by heavy investment in advertising, selling and promotion to and through bottlers to retail outlets, and consumer price discounting. Concentrate producers usually assume responsibility for developing national consumer advertising and promotion programs, product development and planning, and marketing research. Bottlers usually take the lead in developing trade promotions to retail outlets and local consumer promotions. Bottlers are also responsible for selling and servicing retail accounts, including the placement and maintenance of in-store displays and the restocking of supermarket and convenience store shelves with their brands.

Flavor and Brand Competition Colas account for slightly less than two-thirds of total carbonated soft drink sales. Other flavors, such as orange, lemon-lime, cherry, grape, and root beer account for the remaining sales. Estimates of market shares for flavors in 1989 were as follows:

Flavor	*Market Share*
Cola	65.7%
Lemon-lime	12.9
Orange	3.9
Root beer	3.6
Ginger ale	2.8
Grape	1.1
Others	10.0
	100.0%

Diet soft drinks represented 31 percent of industry sales in 1989. Industry trend data indicate that sales of diet drinks accounted for a large portion of the overall growth of carbonated soft drink sales in the 1980s.

There are more than 900 registered brand names for soft drinks in the United States. Most of these brands are sold only regionally. Exhibit 4 shows the top 10 soft drink brands in 1989. Six of these brands were colas, and all 10 brands were marketed by Coca-Cola, PepsiCo, or Dr. Pepper/7Up.

Soft Drink Purchase and Consumption Behavior Industry research suggests that the purchase of soft drinks in supermarkets is often unplanned. Accordingly, soft drink purchasers respond favorably to price (coupon) promotions, in-store (particularly end-of-aisle) displays, and other forms of point-of-sale promotions (such as shelf tags). The importance of display is evidenced in the view held by an industry analyst who estimated that a brand is "locked out of 60 percent of the [supermarket soft drink] volume if it can't get end-aisle displays."[3] The typical supermarket purchaser of soft drinks is a married woman with children under 18 years of age living at home.

Soft drink buying is somewhat seasonal, with consumption slightly higher during summer months than winter months. Consumption also varies by region of the country. Per capita consumption in the East South Central states of Kentucky, Ten-

EXHIBIT 4

Market Share of Top 10 Soft Drink Brands in the United States, 1989

Brand	*Market Share*
1. Coca-Cola Classic	19.8%
2. Pepsi-Cola	17.9
3. Diet Coke	8.9
4. Diet Pepsi	5.7
5. Dr. Pepper	4.5
6. Sprite	3.7
7. Mountain Dew	3.6
8. 7Up	3.2
9. Caffeine-free Diet Coke	2.5
10. Caffeine-free Diet Pepsi	1.6
Top 10 brands	71.4
Other brands	28.6
Total industry	100.0%

[3] Patricia Winters, "Crush Fails to Fit on P&G Shelf," *Advertising Age* (July 10, 1989): 1, 42–43.

nessee, Alabama, and Mississippi was highest in the United States in 1989, with 54.9 gallons compared with the national per capita average of 46.7 gallons. In the Mountain states of Montana, Idaho, Wyoming, Colorado, New Mexico, Arizona, Utah, and Nevada, per capita consumption was 37.1 gallons—the lowest in the nation.

Consumption of diet beverages was more pronounced among consumers over 25 years of age. Teenagers, and younger consumers generally, were heavier consumers of regular soft drinks.

■ ORANGE CATEGORY

Orange-flavored carbonated soft drinks recorded sales of 126 million cases in 1989, or 3.9 percent of total industry sales sold through supermarkets.[4] Prior to 1986, annual case volume had hovered in the range of 100 to 102 million cases. In the mid-1980s, PepsiCo introduced Mandarin Orange Slice, and Coca-Cola introduced Minute Maid Orange. Entry of these two brands, supported by widespread distribution and heavy advertising and promotion, revitalized the category and increased supermarket sales to 126 million cases. Annual supermarket case volume for the period 1984-1989 was as follows:

Year	*Annual Supermarket Case Volume of Orange-Flavored Soft Drinks*
1984	102,000,000
1985	100,000,000
1986	126,000,000
1987	131,000,000
1988	131,000,000
1989	126,000,000

Major Competitors

Four brands captured the majority of orange-flavored soft drink sales in 1989. Mandarin Orange Slice marketed by PepsiCo was the category leader with a market share of 20.8 percent. Sunkist, sold by Cadbury Beverages, Inc., and Coca-Cola's Minute Maid Orange had market shares of 14.4 percent and 14 percent, respectively. Orange Crush had a market share of 7.5 percent. Other brands accounted for the remaining 43.3 percent of sales of orange-flavored soft drinks. Exhibit 5 on page 256 shows the market shares for the major competitors for the period 1985-1989.

The major competitors sold both regular and diet varieties of orange-flavored drink. As shown in Exhibit 6 on page 256, slightly over 70 percent of sales in this category were regular soft drinks. Orange Crush sales mirrored this pattern. Sunkist, however, exceeded the category average, with 82 percent of its case volume sales being the regular form. For Mandarin Orange Slice and Minute Maid Orange, case volume was almost evenly split between regular and diet drinks.

Major competitors also differed in terms of market coverage in 1989. Sunkist was available in markets that represented 91 percent of total orange category sales. By comparison, Orange Crush was available in markets that represented only 62 per-

[4] *Case author's note*: The soft drink industry uses supermarket sales and market shares as a gauge to assess the competitive position of different brands and flavors, since supermarket volumes affect sales through other retail outlets and fountain service. As an approximation and for analysis purposes, *total case* volume for a brand or flavor can be estimated as 2.5 times supermarket case volume. Therefore, total sales of orange-flavored soft drinks are $2.5 \times 126{,}000{,}000 = 315$ million cases.

EXHIBIT 5

Orange Carbonated Soft Drink Brand Market Shares, 1985–1989 (Rounded)

Brand	*1985*	*1986*	*1987*	*1988*	*1989*
Sunkist	32%	20%	13%	13%	14%
Mandarin Orange Slice	NA	16	22	21	21
Minute Maid Orange	NA	8	14	13	14
Crush	22	18	14	11	8
Total top four brands	54	62	63	58	57
Others	46	38	37	42	43

cent of orange category sales. Mandarin Orange Slice and Minute Maid Orange were available in markets that represented 88 percent of orange category sales. Exhibit 7 shows the market coverage by the four major competitors for the period 1985-1989.

Competitor Positioning and Advertising

Each of the four major competitors attempted to stake out a unique position within the orange category. For example, Minute Maid Orange appeared to emphasize its orange flavor, while Sunkist focused on the teen lifestyle. Mandarin Orange Slice and Minute Maid Orange appeared to be targeted at young adults and households without children. These brands also appeared to be emphasizing the "better for you" idea. Crush and Sunkist targeted teens and households with children at home. Exhibit 8 summarizes the apparent brand positionings of the major competitors and selected performance data compiled by the Crush marketing research staff.

Slightly over $26 million was spent on advertising by the four major brands in 1989. Mandarin Orange Slice and Minute Maid Orange accounted for 84 percent of all advertising expenditures in the orange category. Although both brands were advertised on network and cable television and both used spot television commercials in local markets, their advertising differed in other respects. Minute Maid Orange used outdoor billboards and network radio for advertising, but Mandarin Orange Slice did not. In comparison, Mandarin Orange Slice was advertised in magazines and newspapers, but Minute Maid Orange was not.

Crush and Sunkist spent less on advertising and used fewer advertising vehicles than did Minute Maid Orange and Mandarin Orange Slice. Crush was promoted most frequently on spot television and in newspaper and outdoor signage. Sunkist used newspapers, spot television, outdoor billboards, and some syndicated television.

EXHIBIT 6

Case Volume in 1989 by Type of Drink: Regular versus Diet

Type	*Total Soft Drinks*	*Total Orange*	*Crush*	*Sunkist*	*Mandarin Orange Slice*	*Minute Maid Orange*
Regular	68.9%	73.2%	71.3%	82.1%	49.0%	53.1%
Diet	31.1	26.8	28.7	17.9	51.0	46.9
	100.0%	100.0%	100.0%	100.0%	100.0%	100.0%

EXHIBIT 7

Market Coverage of Orange Category by Major Competitors, 1985–1989

	Year				
Brand	*1985*	*1986*	*1987*	*1988*	*1989*
Crush	81%	81%	78%	78%	62%
Sunkist	95	83	79	86	91
Mandarin Orange Slice	10	68	87	88	88
Minute Maid Orange	10	60	87	88	88

Two advertising trends were evident in the orange category since 1986. First, total expenditures for measured print and broadcast media declined each year since 1986, when $52.2 million was spent for advertising. In that year, Mandarin Orange Slice and Minute Maid Orange were introduced nationally. Second, competitors increased the variety of media used for advertising. In 1986, spot television and outdoor billboards were used almost exclusively. By 1989, a broader spectrum of vehicles was used, including broadcast media (network, spot, syndicated, and cable television and network radio) and print media (outdoor, magazines, and newspapers). Exhibit 9 on page 258 shows advertising expenditures for the four major brands for the period 1985-1989.

Competitor Pricing and Promotion

Concentrate pricing among the four major competitors differed very little. Typically, no more than a one-cent difference existed. The price differential between regular (with sugar) and diet (with aspartame) concentrate was virtually the same across competitors. The similarity in pricing as well as in raw material costs resulted in similar gross profit margins across competitors in the orange category. However, as noted in Exhibit 3, the gross profit margin differs between regular and diet soft drink concentrate.

EXHIBIT 8

Competitive Positioning and Performance, 1989

	Sunkist	***Mandarin Orange Slice***	***Minute Maid Orange***	***Crush***
Positioning	"Teens on the Beach"; "Drink in the Sun"	"Who's Got the Juice?" Contemporary youth culture	"The orange, orange" orange flavor, taste of real orange	"Don't just quench it, CRUSH it"; bold user imagery with thirst-quenching benefit
Target	Teens, 12-24	Young adults, 18-24	Young adults, 18-34	Teens, 13-29
Household size of purchaser	3-4 (children at home)	1-2 (no children)	1-2 (no children)	3-5 (children at home)
Package sales mix	Two-liter 51% Cans 42% Other 9%	Two-liter 54% Cans 42% Other 4%	Two-liter 54% Cans 41% Other 5%	Two-liter 64% Cans 31% Other 5%
Loyalty (percentage of brand buyer's orange volume)	36%	55%	48%	46%

Source: Crush Marketing Research Staff Report. Based on trade publications and industry sources.

EXHIBIT 9

Concentrate Producers' Advertising Expenditures for Broadcast and Print Media for Major Orange Soft Drink Brands, 1985–1989 (In Thousands of Dollars)

Brand	*1985*	*1986*	*1987*	*1988*	*1989*
Mandarin Orange Slice (total)	$17,809.4	$32,079.9	$29,555.8	$15,001.3	$11,388.1
Regular	12,739.4	27,704.2	20,123.2	10,247.9	11,199.5
Diet	5,070.0	4,375.7	2,676.4	1,881.9	
Regular and Diet			6,756.2	2,872.5	188.6
Sunkist (total)	$ 7,176.2	$ 4,013.0	$ 910.7	$ 1,719.3	$ 2,301.9
Regular	4,816.5	1,340.6	887.2	309.4	281.5
Diet	2,316.0	1,269.5	1.3		
Regular and Diet	43.7	1,402.9	22.2	1,409.9	2,020.4
Crush (total)	$ 4,371.2	$ 7,154.9	$ 4,296.7	$ 6,841.1	$ 1,853.6
Regular	3,282.7	4,712.9	2,729.8	2,561.6	1,382.2
Diet	1,004.6	2,413.1	959.4	1.2	127.7
Regular and Diet	83.9	28.9	607.5	4,278.3	343.7
Minute Maid Orange (total)	$ 174.4	$ 7,952.3	$ 9,027.2	$12,811.3	$10,463.1
Regular	174.4	7,508.2	7,211.6	9,252.5	10,191.9
Diet			1,745.1	3,450.2	
Regular and Diet		444.1	70.5	108.6	271.2

Advertising and promotion programs were jointly implemented and financed by concentrate producers and bottlers. Concentrate producers and bottlers split advertising costs 50-50. For example, if $1 million were spent for television brand advertising, $500,000 would be paid by the brand's bottlers and $500,000 would be paid by the concentrate producer. Bottlers and concentrate producers split the cost of retail-oriented merchandise promotions and consumer promotions 50-50.

A variety of merchandising promotions are used in the soft drink industry. One kind of promotion, called a "dealer loader," is a premium given to retailers. A common form is a "display loader" such as ice chests, insulated can coolers, T-shirts, or sweatshirts, which are part of an in-store or point-of-purchase display. After the display is taken down, the premium is given to the retailer. End-of-aisle displays and other types of special free-standing displays are also provided, as are shelf banners. Concentrate producers will often allocate 10 cents (for shirts) to 20 cents (for displays) per case sold to bottlers who implement these merchandising promotions. Consumer promotions include sponsorship of local sports and entertainment events, plastic cups and napkins with the brand logo, and stylish baseball caps, T-shirts, or sunglasses featuring the brand name. Assorted other promotions are also used, including coupons, on-package promotions, and sweepstakes. Concentrate producers will offer anywhere from 5 cents (for cups, caps, or glasses) to 25 cents (for local event marketing including cups, caps, or glasses) per case sold to bottlers who use these promotions. Examples of trade and consumer promotions are shown in Exhibits 10 (page 259) and 11 (page 260).

Concentrate producers occasionally offer bottlers price promotions in the form of distribution incentives. These incentives are typically based on case sales and are frequently used to stimulate bottler sales and merchandising activity. These incentives are often in the range of 15 to 25 cents per case depending on the amount of effort desired or needed.

EXHIBIT 10

Example of Crush Trade Promotion

HAVE A CRUSH ON US!
DEALER LOADERS

Item

- A Crush Adventure Back Pack
- B Beach Bag/Blanket
- C Neon Cap
- D Sony® Walkman
- E Dirty Dunk®

EXHIBIT 11

Example of Crush Consumer Promotion

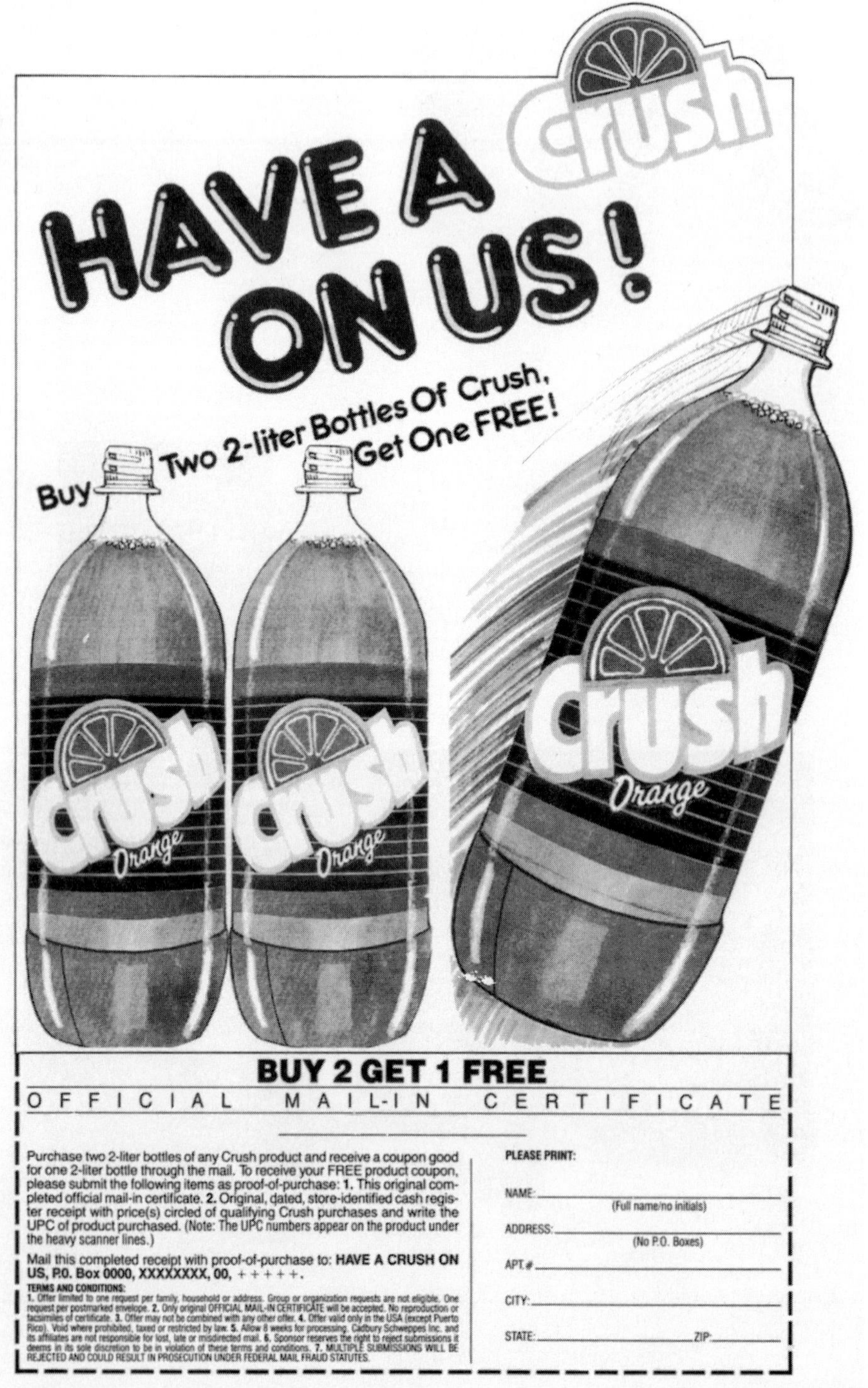

■ CRUSH MARKETING PROGRAM

In January 1990, several strategic marketing decisions were made concerning the Crush brand. Most notably, a decision was made to focus initial attention on the orange flavor. Even though the Crush line featured several flavors, orange (regular and diet) accounted for almost two-thirds of total Crush case volume. (Exhibit 12 shows the Crush product line.) Second, marketing executives at Cadbury Beverages, Inc. decided to focus immediate attention and effort on reestablishing the bottling network for the Crush line, particularly Orange Crush. Third, it was decided that careful consideration of Crush positioning was necessary to build on the existing customer franchise and provide opportunities for further development of the Crush brand and its assorted flavors. Finally, the executives agreed to the development of an advertising and promotion program, including the determination of objectives, strategies, and expenditures.

Bottler Network Development

Recognizing the traditional and central role that bottlers play in the soft drink industry, company marketing and sales executives immediately embarked on an aggressive effort to recruit bottlers for the Crush line. The Crush bottling network had gradually eroded in the 1980s due in part to Procter & Gamble's decision to test a distribution system for selling Crush through warehouses rather than through bottlers. This action, which centralized bottling in the hands of a limited number of bottlers that shipped product to warehouses for subsequent delivery to supermarkets and other retail outlets, had led many in the Crush bottler network to question their future role

EXHIBIT 12

Crush Product Line

EXHIBIT 13

Positioning of Crush, 1954–1989

Year	*Positioning*	*Target*	*Campaign*
1954	Natural flavor from Valencia oranges	All-family	"Naturally—it tastes better, Orange Crush"
1957-Late 1960s (est.)	Good for you; fresh juice from specially selected oranges	All-family	"Tastes so good . . . so good for you!"
1963-1964 (est.)	Introduced full line of flavors: grape, strawberry, grapefruit, root beer, cherry	All-family	No clear introduction effort: • "Thirsty? Crush that thirst with Orange Crush" • "Delicious, refreshing, satisfying—Grape Crush" • "Clean fruit taste—Grapefruit Crush" • "Mellow Crush Root Beer"
Early 1970s (est.)	Unique taste, the "change of pace" drink	All-family directed toward purchaser who is female 18-35, promotions targeted children/young adults	"Ask for Crush, the taste that's all its own."
1979-1980	Competitive taste superiority	Maintained early 1970s TV but focused on young males with sports	Added "There is no orange like Orange Crush . . ." to "Ask for Crush, the taste that's all its own."
1980	Competitive taste superiority in fruit flavors	Added new radio for 10-19 target	Same as above
1981	100% natural flavors, contemporary wholesome brand	13-39 Teens and young adults	"Orange lovers have a Crush on us"
1980-1985	Great, irresistible taste	13-39	"Orange lovers have a Crush on us"
1981-1982	Great taste	13-39	Test: "First Crush"
1983	More orangery taste	13-39	"Orange lovers"
1984	Sugar-free Crush, great taste of Nutrasweet	13-49	"Celebrate"
1986-1987	Taste with 10% real juice	Teens, 12-17	"Peel Me a Crush"
1987	The drink that breaks monotony	Teens, 12-17	Test: "Color Me Crush"
1987-1989	Bold user imagery with thirst-quenching benefit	Teens, 13-29	"Don't just quench it, Crush it"

with Crush. An outgrowth of this action was that Crush had the lowest market coverage of orange category sales potential among major competitors.

Recruitment efforts in early 1990 broadened the bottler network. By mid-1990, new bottling agreements had been arranged, and trade relations with 136 bottlers were established. The revitalized bottler network meant that Crush would be available in markets that represented 75 percent of total orange category sales in time for the Crush relaunch. The broadened bottler network would also require promotional support. According to Kim Feil, "We knew that reestablishing trade relations was an important first step. However, we also knew that new and existing bottlers would be gauging the kind and amount of advertising and promotional support we would provide when we relaunched Crush."

Positioning Issues

Numerous issues related to positioning were being addressed while the bottler recruitment effort was under way. First, since the company already marketed Sunkist, questions arose concerning the likely cannibalization of Sunkist sales if a clearly differentiated position for Orange Crush in the marketplace was not developed and successfully executed. A second issue concerned the relative emphasis on regular and diet Crush with respect to Mandarin Orange Slice and Minute Maid Orange. These two competitors had outpaced Crush and Sunkist in attracting the diet segment of orange drinkers. Third, viable positions had to be considered that did not run contrary to previous positionings and would build on the customer franchise currently held by Orange Crush. In this regard, a historical review of Crush positioning was conducted. The results of this effort are reproduced in Exhibit 13.

Company executives recognized that issues relating to positioning needed to be addressed in a timely manner. Without a clear positioning statement, the creative process underlying the advertising program could not be initiated.

Advertising and Promotion

Crush marketing executives were pleasantly surprised to learn that the Crush brand had high name awareness in the markets served by existing and new bottlers. According to the company's consumer awareness tracking research, of the four major brands, Crush had the highest orange-brand awareness in Seattle, San Francisco, New York, Miami, Los Angeles, Chicago, and Boston. Nevertheless, numerous issues had to be addressed concerning the Crush advertising and promotion program.

In particular, objectives for the advertising and promotion had to be established and communicated to the advertising agency that would represent Crush. Next, the relative emphasis on consumer advertising and on types of trade and consumer promotion had to be determined. Specifically, this meant setting the budget for advertising expenditures and the amounts to be spent on a per case basis for promotions. Ultimately, a *pro forma* statement of projected revenues and expenses would be necessary for presentation to senior management at Cadbury Beverages, Inc. Implicitly, this required a case volume forecast for Orange Crush that realistically portrayed market and competitive conditions and "the quality of my marketing program," said Feil.

CASE

Drypers Corporation

National Television Advertising Campaign

In late 1997, senior executives at Drypers Corporation were discussing the merits of spending upwards of $10 million on national television advertising in 1998 for its Drypers brand of disposable diapers. The matter was significant for two reasons. First, the company had not used television advertising in its 10-year history. Second, a $10 million expenditure represented a 33 percent increase in the company's combined advertising and promotion budget, which was budgeted at about $30 million in 1997.[1]

The reasoning behind the national television advertising campaign was explained as follows:

> In the United States, diapers are highly promoted since many retailers rely on their diaper products to attract customers to their stores. In addition, Procter & Gamble and Kimberly-Clark spend a significant amount on mass media advertising to create demand for their products. In contrast, Drypers has relied more heavily on promotional spending and cooperative merchandising arrangements with retailers. Promotional activity, such as couponing, is geared toward initiating consumer trial and has been especially effective at targeting spending when less than full distribution has yet to be achieved.[2]
>
> [Television] advertising will build consumer awareness for Drypers as a national brand that stands for quality and innovation. Awareness will boost demand, and increased demand will yield three important results. One, we will increase our penetration of grocery outlets. Two, increased grocery penetration will help mass merchants see us in a new light and help us break into this all-important retail channel. And three, we will move away from higher-cost, promotion-driven sales to brand-driven sales.[3]

The marketing rationale for television advertising was clear. However, discussions related to the national advertising campaign, including its short- and long-term sales and brand-building effect and profit impact, continued as part of the business planning process for 1998.

■ U.S. DISPOSABLE DIAPER AND TRAINING PANTS MARKET

The market for disposable diapers and training pants is often described as infants and children, primarily below age four, who use diapers and training pants, and their mothers, primarily between the ages of 18 and 49, who decide on the brand of diapers and

[1] Laurie Freeman, "Flanking Maneuver," *Marketing News* (October 27, 1997): 1, 16.
[2] Drypers Corporation, *U.S. Securities and Exchange Commission Form 10-K,* for the fiscal year ended December 31, 1997, at p. 9.
[3] Drypers Corporation, *1997 Annual Report,* p. 11.

This case was prepared by Professor Roger A. Kerin, of the Edwin L. Cox School of Business, Southern Methodist University, as a basis for class discussion and is not designed to illustrate effective or ineffective handling of an administrative situation. This case is based on published sources, including the Drypers Corporation annual reports, U.S. Securities and Exchange Commission Form 10-K and 10-Q reports, company news releases, published articles, and information provided by individuals knowledgeable about the industry. The information presented in the case does not necessarily depict the explicit situation faced by Drypers Corporation, but is introduced only for class discussion purposes. Where appropriate, quotes, statistics, and published information are footnoted for reference purposes.

EXHIBIT 1

Trends in the U.S. Disposable Diaper and Training Pants Market

	1994	*1995*	*1996*	*1997*
Infants (millions): birth to 30 months	10.0	9.8	9.7	9.7
Diapers sold (billions of units)	17.2	17.2	17.3	17.5
Diaper retail dollar sales (millions)	$3,880.0	$3,825.0	$3,855.0	$3,930.0
Children (millions): 18 months to 8 years	26.1	26.3	26.3	26.2
Training and youth pants sold (millions of units)	970.0	1,070.0	1,250.0	1,410.0
Training and youth pants retail dollar sales (millions)	$485.0	$510.0	$540.0	$595.0

training pants and usually make the purchase. A baby, on average, uses five diapers per day for 30 months, for a total of 5,475 diapers. At an average retail price in the range of 18 to 27 cents per diaper, each baby represents about $1,125.00 in retail sales.

The retail dollar value of unit volume of the U.S. disposable diaper market has recorded modest growth in recent years due to the trend in fewer infants under 30 months of age and diaper improvements in absorbency and leakage control. The retail dollar value of the U.S. disposable diaper market was estimated to be $3.93 billion in 1997. The retail dollar value of the training and youth pants market was estimated to be $595 million in 1997. Trends in U.S. retail sales, diaper and training pants unit volume, and population are shown in Exhibit 1.

Distribution Channels

Disposable diapers and training pants are distributed principally through grocery stores, drugstores, and mass merchants. Grocery stores accounted for approximately $2 billion in diaper and training pants retail sales in 1997. Grocery store distribution of diapers and training pants has been decreasing as a percentage of total retail sales since 1994. Grocery stores accounted for 51.2 percent of retail sales in 1997, compared with 60 percent in 1994.

Mass merchants and drugstores recorded diaper and training pants retail sales of about $1.9 billion in 1997. Mass merchants have increased their share of total diaper and training pants retail sales from 30 percent in 1994 to 39.4 percent in 1997. The drugstore share of diaper and training pants retail sales has declined from 10 percent in 1994 to 9.2 percent in 1997.

Competitors

Manufacturers of disposable diapers and training pants are typically grouped into three general categories: (1) premium-priced branded manufacturers, (2) value-priced branded manufacturers, and (3) private-label manufacturers. Procter & Gamble and Kimberly-Clark are the leading premium-priced branded manufacturers with their well-known Pampers and Huggies premium brands, respectively. They compete on the basis of product quality, product features and benefits, and price. Both manufacturers invest heavily in research and development. For example, Kimberly-Clark pioneered the first premium training pants for children and presently captures 77 percent of this market on a unit volume basis. Procter & Gamble and Kimberly-Clark also invest heavily in consumer advertising and marketing support for their brands. In 1997, Procter & Gamble spent an estimated $69.6 million in measured media advertising for its Pampers brand; Kimberly-Clark spent $75.6 million in measured media advertising for its Huggies brand. The following is a breakdown of their media expenditures:

		1997 Media Advertising ($ Millions)		
Manufacturer	***Brand***	***Television***	***Print***	***Total***
Kimberly-Clark	Huggies	$57.2	$18.5	$75.6
Procter & Gamble	Pampers	$52.8	$16.8	$69.6

Kimberly-Clark and Procter & Gamble brands commanded an estimated 78.9 percent of total U.S. retail dollar sales of disposable diapers and training pants in 1997. The combined share of these two companies has increased since 1994 (see Exhibit 2), due in part to their extensive distribution coverage in grocery, mass-merchant, and drugstore markets. For example, both companies sell their products in stores that account for over 90 percent of U.S. diaper and training pants sales. However, Kimberly-Clark and Procter & Gamble market shares differ by distribution channel. For example, Kimberly-Clark's 1997 market share in U.S. grocery stores is an estimated 40.6 percent whereas Procter & Gamble's market share is 34.1 percent. Kimberly-Clark has an estimated 41.8 percent share of the mass merchant and drugstore channel; Procter & Gamble's share is 39.4 percent.

Value-priced branded manufacturers, such as Drypers Corporation, typically market their products through grocery stores due to their general lack of national brand-name recognition and less extensive national production and distribution capabilities necessary to supply large mass-merchant and drugstore chains. Value-priced branded manufacturers' strategies vary widely, ranging from an emphasis on quality and "good value for the money" to simply low prices. Products vary from premium-quality to low-quality diapers. Few of these manufacturers engage in extensive research and development or invest in national advertising. Instead, they rely on in-store promotions and couponing, often using local or regional print advertising, and cooperative advertising and promotion programs with retailers.

Private-label manufacturers, such as Paragon Trade Brands, Inc. and Arquest, Inc. (the two largest U.S. private-label manufacturers), market their diapers and training pants under retailer-affiliated labels. These manufacturers typically emphasize lower

EXHIBIT 2

Combined Dollar Market Share for Disposable Diapers and Training Pants for Kimberly-Clark, Procter & Gamble, and Others: 1994–1997

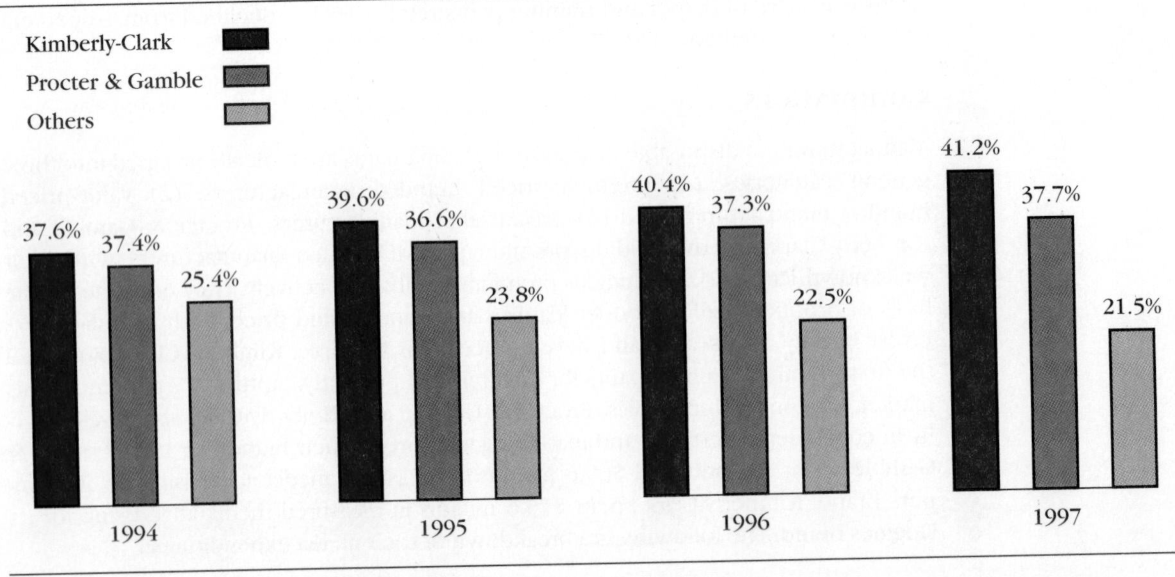

EXHIBIT 3

Dollar and Unit Market Share of Private-Label Diapers and Training Pants by Distribution Channel

	Private Label	
Distribution Channel	*Unit Share*	*Dollar Share*
Grocery stores	23.0%	15.9%
Drugstores	31.3	21.7
Mass merchandisers	21.5	15.3
U.S. market share for private-label diapers and training pants	23.2%	16.1%

price over quality and product features. Private-label manufacturers spend little on consumer advertising and marketing; however, retailers often promote their individual private-label brands. Private labels account for approximately 16 percent of 1997 retail dollar sales and 23 percent of unit sales for diapers and training pants. Private labels are the most prominent in the drugstore channel. The breakdown of private-label sales by channel is shown in Exhibit 3.

■ DRYPERS CORPORATION

Drypers Corporation (www.drypers.com) is a producer and marketer of premium-quality, value-priced disposable baby diapers and training pants sold under the Drypers brand name in the United States and under the Drypers name and other brand names internationally. The company also manufactures and sells lower-priced disposable diapers under other brand names (Comfees) in the United States and internationally, in addition to private-label diapers, training pants, and premoistened baby wipes. In 1997, branded products represent 88.9 percent of company net sales in the United States; sales of private-label and other products account for remaining sales. The company's Drypers premium-brand diapers and training pants account for 52.3 percent of total company net sales in 1997, down from 62.3 percent in 1996 and 61.3 percent in 1995. The company leases manufacturing, distribution, and administrative space in nine locations in the United States, Brazil, Puerto Rico, Argentina, and Mexico. Corporate headquarters are in Houston, Texas.

The company is the world's sixth largest producer of disposable baby diapers and the third largest marketer of brand-name disposable diapers in the United States. In 1997, the company's Drypers brand was the fourth largest selling diaper brand in the United States and the second largest selling training pants brand in U.S. grocery stores.

Company Sales and Profit History

Drypers Corporation has recorded double-digit sales growth since 1995. A tenfold increase in international sales accounted for much of the sales increase, as shown below:

	1995		*1996*		*1997*	
			(Dollars in Millions)			
Domestic[a]	$154.5	94.3%	$179.2	86.6%	$191.3	66.7%
International	9.4	5.7	27.8	13.4	95.7	33.3
Total net sales	$163.9	100.0%	$207.0	100.0%	$287.0	100.0%

[a]Domestic sales include the United States, Puerto Rico, and exports from these manufacturing operations.

The company's foreign-produced and exported products are sold in over 28 countries, but international marketing efforts have focused principally in Latin America. For example, in February 1997 the company acquired the Brazilian Puppet brand name and formed a joint venture to market this brand in Brazil. In addition, Drypers Corporation is the exclusive private-label supplier to Wal-Mart stores in Latin America and also supplies Drypers premium-branded products to Wal-Mart stores in Latin America.

The company has recorded a significant improvement in sales and profitability since 1995. In 1995, the company's financial performance was adversely affected by events outside its control.[4] Devaluation of the Mexican peso in December 1994, followed by economic uncertainty in Brazil, had a severe impact on sales and profitability. In addition, aggressive diaper promotional spending and pricing by Kimberly-Clark and Procter & Gamble in the United States and a rise in raw-material costs dampened the company's gross profit margin. These events occurred just as the company was converting its four regional U.S. brands (Drypers in the South, Baby's Choice in the West, Wee-Fits in the Midwest, and Cozies in the Northeast) into one common package design and brand name, Drypers. The lack of Drypers brand awareness in the markets previously served by regional brands materially affected sales.

Exhibit 4 shows abbreviated income statements for Drypers Corporation for the years ended December 31, 1995, 1996, and 1997. The company generated earnings before interest, taxes, depreciation, and amortization (EBITDA) of $28.8 million for 1997. This strong cash flow, along with sales growth, enabled the company to raise $115 million in capital through a bond offering. Proceeds from the issuance of bonds were used to refinance debt and finance additional production capacity in the United States and Latin America. The company's working capital stood at $48.7 million at the end of 1997.

EXHIBIT 4

Drypers Corporation Abbreviated Income Statements: 1995–1997 (Expressed as a Percentage of Net Sales)

	Year Ended December 31		
	1995	*1996*	*1997*
Net sales	100.0%	100.0%	100.0%
Cost of goods sold	69.6	60.9	61.2
Gross profit	30.4	39.1	38.8
Selling, general, and administrative expenses	32.8	34.0	31.3
Unusual expenses	1.9	—	—
Restructuring charge	2.6	—	—
Operating income (loss)	(6.9)	5.1	7.5
Interest expense, net	4.9	4.3	3.5
Other income	—	—	0.1
Income (loss) before income tax provision (benefit) and extraordinary item	(11.8)	0.8	4.1
Income tax provision (benefit)	(2.4)	0.2	0.8
Extraordinary item	—	—	(2.7)
Net income (loss)	(9.4)%	0.6%	0.6%

Source: Drypers Corporation, U.S. Securities and Exchange Commission, Form 10-K, 1997, at p. 17.

[4] Alexandra M. Biesada, "The Poop on Drypers," *Texas Monthly* (July 1996): 50ff.

Market Position

Drypers Corporation distributes its products principally through grocery stores in the United States. In 1997, the company estimated that its products were sold through 635 grocery retailers with an estimated 20,000 retail outlets. The sales of these retailers represented 66 percent of the total U.S. grocery store market for disposable diapers and training pants. In 1995, the company's distribution coverage in the grocery store channel represented 54 percent of the total U.S. grocery store market for these products. The company estimates that its brands captured 6.4 percent of the total dollar volume and 6.6 percent of the total unit volume for disposable diapers and training pants in the U.S. grocery store channel in 1997. However, in some grocery store markets, including Minneapolis, Minnesota, where Drypers are sold in grocery stores such as Super Valu and Cub Foods, the company estimates that its market share is as high as 20 percent, a figure comparable to Procter & Gamble's Pampers brand.

The company had less widespread distribution in mass-merchant and drugstore chain channels. As a consequence, Drypers' dollar market share in the total U.S. disposable diaper and training pants market is about 3.1 percent.[5] However, the company has recently obtained distribution through selected mass-merchant and drugstore chains, including Super Kmart stores of Kmart, Meijer, and Caldor. "We're trying to break into mass [merchants], to get on the shelf in Wal-Mart and Target," said Dave Olsen, Vice President of Marketing. "We're doing that by showing retailers that we really do have product differentiation in Drypers while maintaining our value position."[6] Terry Tognietti, co-CEO and President of Drypers North America, added, "What mass merchandisers want to see is that your product will move off the shelf on its own merit with little promotion, versus having them move it off the shelf for you."[7]

Marketing at Drypers Corporation

As the third largest marketer of brand-name disposable diapers in the United States, Drypers Corporation has found it necessary to compete against Kimberly-Clark and Procter & Gamble in novel ways. According to Terry Tognietti:

> We've always tried to compete with Kimberly-Clark and P&G in areas where they can't beat us by throwing money at us. When it comes to money, they beat us every time. So we need, and we try, to put ourselves in competitive situations where we are competing on ideas and quickness, not just who has the deeper pockets.[8]

Product Innovation and Pricing Drypers Corporation has demonstrated an ability to shift the ground rules in diaper marketing through product innovation. For example, in 1996 and 1997, the company was the first to introduce diapers that focused on skin care, in addition to diaper fit, absorbency, and leakage control. "We felt it was time for Drypers as a brand to begin to differentiate itself from the other brands," said Terry Tognietti. He added:

> We do not want to be just a high-quality, low-price, me-too diaper. We want consumers to buy Drypers because they're Drypers, and to do that, we've made significant strides in rolling out diapers that have different features—like the baking soda to address odor control, and the aloe vera as a skin-smoothing treatment.[9]

---

[5] Laurie Freeman, "Flanking Maneuver," *Marketing News* (October, 27, 1997): 16.
[6] *Ibid.*
[7] *Ibid.*
[8] *Ibid.*
[9] *Ibid.*

Drypers with Natural Baking Soda and Drypers with Aloe Vera, introduced in 1996 and 1997, respectively, were believed to be responsible for the increased penetration of the U.S. grocery store channel between 1995 and 1997. In addition, Drypers Corporation was presented the American Marketing Association's prestigious "Gold Edison" award in 1997 for the most innovative children's product on the basis of its Drypers with Aloe Vera product. The company also has provided value-added features to training pants, including a one-piece design and fit to make them look more like real underwear. These innovations, coupled with the addition of baking soda and aloe vera, have contributed to the company's market share in training pants. Drypers Corporation is second only to Kimberly-Clark in training pants sales, with a U.S. market share of 7.8 percent on a unit volume basis.

In 1997, Drypers Corporation entered into a licensing agreement to use the Sesame Street trademark and characters on the company's products, packaging, and advertising materials. This agreement was viewed as a validation of the company's product innovation efforts for children's products. "Children's Television Workshop is very careful who they license the Sesame Street characters to," according to Dave Olsen. "Sesame Street characters are seen as high end. That's the sizzle part."[10]

Drypers Corporation delivers on its value proposition with retail prices that are often 40 percent lower than premium-priced brands for comparable items. "Once consumers understand that our diapers are equal to the other national brands—and offered at a better price—we feel confident that we'll get our share of the diaper business," Terry Tognietti said.

Advertising, Promotion, and Sales Drypers Corporation has historically relied on print advertising in parent-oriented magazines and regularly places coupons in daily newspapers' food sections and Sunday newspaper free-standing inserts (FSIs). The company also does large volumes of direct mail, in-store promotions, and sampling in pediatricians' offices. For example, the company ships 8,000 to 10,000 diaper samples to pediatricians annually, along with several million coupons and/or diapers to day-care centers. Drypers Corporation's combined advertising and promotion budget was about $30 million in 1997. Of this amount, $3,219,000 was spent for advertising. Advertising expense in 1996 was $1,854,000.

The company does not have a dedicated sales force in the United States. Rather, the company uses in-house managers to coordinate brokerage companies that facilitate the distribution of products through grocery stores on a nonexclusive basis. This approach has expedited the company's entry into grocery store chains and independent grocers because of the favorable long-term relationships that many of these brokers have with these retailers. The use of brokers also minimized corporate overhead expense.

■ BUSINESS PLANNING FOR 1998

Senior executives at Drypers Corporation outlined an ambitious business plan for 1998. The company was registering its strongest year ever in 1997 in terms of sales and profitability, which was reflected in the upward trend in its common stock price (Exhibit 5). The time seemed right to continue existing efforts that had yielded favorable results and pursue new initiatives. The business plan focused on six key elements:

---

[10] *Ibid.*

EXHIBIT 5

Drypers Corporation High and Low Quarterly Common Stock Price: 1996–1997

	1996		1997	
	High	*Low*	*High*	*Low*
Quarter:				
First	$4.13	$2.75	$4.75	$3.63
Second	4.00	2.75	7.75	3.88
Third	4.25	2.63	7.94	6.13
Fourth	5.63	3.50	9.00	5.13

The Company's common stock, $.001 par value, was listed on the NASDAQ National Market under the symbol "DYPR" from March 11, 1994, through January 28, 1996. Effective January 29, 1996, the Company's stock began trading on the NASDAQ SmallCap Market. The table sets forth, for the periods indicated, the high and low sales prices of the common stock as reported by the NASDAQ National Market and the NASDAQ SmallCap Market.

Source: Drypers Corporation, U.S. Securities and Exchange Commission, Form 10-K, 1997, at p. 12.

1. Continue product innovation to differentiate the Drypers brand.
2. Offer "Everyday Value" branded products to consumers.
3. Continue to pursue international expansion opportunities.
4. Expand product lines to include additional consumer products.
5. Provide higher-margin products for retailers.
6. Increase brand awareness and retail penetration.

Each element is described below.

Continue product innovation to differentiate the Drypers brand. Drypers Corporation has built its business on meaningful product differentiation that creates value for its customers. The 1998 business plan continued this focus with the scheduled introduction of Drypers Supreme with Germ Guard Liner in September 1998. The product would position Drypers as the only diaper in the industry to include an antibacterial treatment.

Offer "Everyday Value" branded products to consumers. Drypers Corporation's value position emphasizes premium-quality, value-priced diapers and training pants that offer consumers the recognition and reliability of a national brand coupled with product quality and features comparable to premium-priced diapers at generally lower prices. The 1998 business plan reaffirmed this value position and ongoing efforts for continuous improvement.

Continue to pursue international expansion opportunities. The international disposable diaper market is estimated to be $12 billion in annual manufacturers' sales. Growth opportunities exist in regions of the world with low consumer penetration of disposable diapers, including Latin America, the Pacific Rim, and Eastern Europe. Drypers Corporation will continue to expand its operations in Argentina, Mexico, and Brazil and seek further expansion opportunities through acquisition, joint venture, or other arrangements in the Pacific Rim and Latin America.

Expand product lines to include additional consumer products. Drypers Corporation will seek to produce and market additional high-quality consumer products that occupy specialty niches in large and fragmented consumer product categories and can be sold primarily through grocery stores, drugstores, and mass merchants. In October 1997, Drypers Corporation acquired an option to purchase NewLund Laboratories, Inc., a start-up company with a breakthrough laundry detergent technology. The technology provides a detergent, fabric softener, and static-control product in a single-sheet form. The 1998 business plan included a scheduled roll-out of this product by year-end 1998.

Provide higher-margin products for retailers. Drypers Corporation will continue to sell its products to retailers at a generally lower price than leading premium-priced national brands, which allows retailers to offer a lower price to consumers while achieving substantially higher margins. The ability to maintain attractive profit margins for retailers and a favorable price–value relationship for consumers will continue as a result of the company's ongoing emphasis in four areas: (1) delivering innovative product features that differentiate its products, (2) producing high-quality products at substantially the same costs as leading national brand manufacturers, (3) significantly lower advertising, promotion, and research and development expenditures, and (4) maintaining a low corporate overhead structure.

Increase brand awareness and retail penetration. Drypers Corporation has been building its brand equity in a deliberate manner since 1992 with consolidation of the three largest U.S.-branded regional disposable diaper producers. By 1995, the different operations, technology, and the brands themselves had been converted to Drypers. Through distinctive product innovations in 1996 and 1997, the Drypers brand had differentiated itself in the marketplace. All of these efforts have been aimed at achieving a single, clear corporate objective: full U.S. distribution of Drypers diapers and training pants. The decision to invest in a national television media campaign in 1998 by senior Drypers Corporation executives was considered a logical step toward realizing this objective: "We strongly believe that this investment in a national television campaign to build brand awareness is key to achieving full product distribution and higher overall sales."[11]

The 1998 business plan included an expenditure budget for upwards of $10 million for a national television advertising campaign in the United States. The campaign would run during the first two quarters or six months of 1998, in combination with the company's existing promotional programs. In the second half of 1998, total advertising and promotion costs, as a percentage of sales, would be reduced to preadvertising levels. It was believed that building brand recognition through advertising should allow the company to gradually reduce its dependence on direct promotional spending and should increase the distribution of Drypers brand diapers and, in turn, increase sales in the second half of 1998.

Although it was clear why an investment in a national television advertising campaign should be made and what this investment should do, discussions continued as to what a national television advertising campaign would do. Discussions related to this initiative, including its short- and long-term sales and brand-building effect and profit impact, continued as the 1998 business plan took shape.

---

[11] Drypers Corporation, *1997 Annual Report,* p. 3.

CASE

Price Waterhouse

The 1980s witnessed widespread innovation in the public accounting industry in the United States. To better serve client needs, public accounting firms expanded their client services to include management consulting and industry-based specialties in addition to their traditional auditing and tax services, and they also broadened the international scope of their operations. Another innovation has been the addition of investment banking-related capabilities to further position public accounting firms as full-service financial counselors for their clients. Specifically, some public accounting firms have begun to assist their clients in assessing the merits of using and pursuing different forms of debt and/or equity financing and to conduct merger, acquisition, and divestiture analyses and negotiations. The latter function consists of bringing a potential seller and buyer together and helping them negotiate an agreement relating to the sale or purchase of securities or sometimes firms or divisions of companies.

The inclusion of investment banking-related services represents a significant change in the role public accounting firms have played. Historically, when it came to the buying and selling of companies, public accounting firms provided due diligence services, assisted their clients in assessing the accounting and tax implications of sale and purchase decisions, and provided postacquisition services including post-merger integration of accounting and management systems.[1] By offering direction and assistance in the strategy and negotiation phase that precedes the actual sale and purchase decision and on subsequent integration issues, public accounting firms have entered territory traditionally occupied by investment bankers.

Interest in providing investment banking-related services to its clients emerged at Price Waterhouse in the late 1980s. After considerable study, the firm decided in mid-1989 to offer these services and formed the Corporate Finance Group in early 1990. In early 1991, senior management was focusing attention on making these services achieve their potential and relating them to existing services offered by Price Waterhouse.

THE PUBLIC ACCOUNTING INDUSTRY

The public accounting industry in the United States can trace its roots to the early nineteenth century. At that time, British industrialists hired accountants who were given responsibility for overseeing their commercial interests in America. This responsibility for establishing checks and balances and assessing the accuracy of financial statements has remained an important function performed by the accounting profession.

[1] *Due diligence* refers to the practice of examining a company's records, financial statements, and other aspects of its operation prior to a sale or purchase decision.

The assistance of Price Waterhouse in the preparation of this case is gratefully acknowledged. This case was prepared by Angela Bullard and Lawrence Cervetti, graduate students, under the supervision of Professor Roger A. Kerin, of the Edwin L. Cox School of Business, Southern Methodist University, as a basis for class discussion and is not designed to illustrate effective or ineffective handling of an administrative situation. Selected information has been disguised and is not useful for research purposes.

Nature of Public Accounting

The purpose of accounting is to provide quantitative information, primarily financial in nature, that concerns economic entities and is intended to be useful in making economic decisions. Public accounting is an aspect of accounting that primarily focuses on the rendering of an opinion by an independent auditor as to whether an entity's financial statements are fairly presented. That is, the auditor attests that the accounting practices used in the preparation of financial statements are (or are not) in accordance with generally accepted accounting principles proposed by the Financial Accounting Standards Board.

The public accounting profession is composed of certified public accountants (CPAs), who have met certain educational requirements and have satisfied the statutory and administrative requirements to be registered or licensed as a public accountant. In addition, these individuals have successfully completed the Uniform CPA Examination administered by the American Institute of Certified Public Accountants. There are approximately 307,000 practicing certified public accountants in the United States.

Public Accounting Firms and Services

There are thousands of public accounting firms in the United States. Many of these firms are small professional corporations whose certified public accountants provide a variety of services (bookkeeping, tax preparation, and so forth) for small businesses and individuals. However, public accounting is typically associated with what is termed the "Big Six." The six largest public accounting firms in the United States are Arthur Andersen and Company, Ernst and Young, Deloitte and Touche, KPMG Peat Marwick, Coopers and Lybrand, and Price Waterhouse. These six firms combined produced U.S. revenues of approximately $10.9 billion and worldwide revenues in excess of $25 billion in 1990. Exhibit 1 profiles the Big Six accounting firms.

Public accounting firms, and particularly the Big Six, provide their clients with a wide range of services. Even though these firms still perform their traditional role of

EXHIBIT 1

Overview of the Big Six Accounting Firms: 1990

	Arthur Andersen and Co.	*Coopers and Lybrand*	*Deloitte and Touche*	*Ernst and Young*	*KPMG Peat Marwick*	*Price Waterhouse*
Revenues (billions)						
U.S. revenues	$2.28	$1.40	$1.92	$2.24	$1.83	$1.20
Worldwide revenues	$4.16	$4.10	$4.20	$5.01	$5.40	$2.90
U.S. professional staff (including partners)	19,992	10,898	18,800	16,911	15,000	9,560
Total number of partners	1,344	1,301	1,670	2,025	1,876	920
Number of U.S. offices	87	99	110	125	135	100
Percentages of revenue by function						
Auditing/advisory	35%	60%	57%	53%	53%	47%
Tax	23	20	23	25	27	29
Management consulting	42	20	20	22	20	24

Source: Based on company publications and *Public Accounting Report* (February 15, 1991). Information on Arthur Andersen and Company is both Arthur Andersen and Company public accounting and Arthur Andersen Consulting. Coopers and Lybrand revenue estimates are from *Public Accounting Report*, since the company does not disclose revenues.

attesting to the fairness of financial statements through the auditing function, they have expanded their services to include a variety of other activities, such as management consulting of various kinds, tax consulting and preparation, employee compensation and benefit studies, and various types of litigation support work. The expanded mix of services has broadened the appeal of public accounting firms by making many firms a "one-stop" source of business expertise. In 1990, almost one-half of the revenues generated by the Big Six firms arose from services other than auditing.

Several factors have fueled the addition of new services. First, the audit business, which had been the mainstay of public accounting firms and a continuing source of revenue and profit, has become an undifferentiated service in the eyes of many clients. This perception has resulted in the practice of competitive bidding, whereby the lowest bid for auditing services generally wins a proposal. Although still a valued service and profit center in 1990, auditing services were no longer generating the same profit margins as existed as recently as the mid-1980s. Second, the incidence of mergers and acquisitions in the 1980s shrank the client base for larger public accounting firms. Third, public accounting firms began to recognize that their clients needed assistance in a variety of areas and that many of these areas were allied with the skill and technical competence presently available within public accounting firms.

PRICE WATERHOUSE

Price Waterhouse was formed in 1860 in England by two chartered accountants, Samuel Lowell Price and Edwin Waterhouse. The firm opened its first office in the United States in 1890 under the name Jones, Caesar and Company. By 1990, Price Waterhouse operated 100 offices in the United States and had a total of 400 offices in 103 countries and territories worldwide. The U.S. firm reported fiscal 1990 net revenues of $1.2 billion.

Price Waterhouse is considered by many in the public accounting industry to be the most prestigious of the Big Six firms and lists more *Fortune* 500 firms among its clients than any other firm. In fiscal 1990, the U.S. firm was the auditor for 93 of the *Fortune* 500 companies. Current major clients include such well-known companies as IBM, Exxon, USX, DuPont, W. R. Grace, Borden, Walt Disney, Hewlett-Packard, Bristol-Myers, and Shell Oil. The firm also had a sizable client base among companies with annual sales under $150 million.

Client Services

The emphasis Price Waterhouse places on delivering exceptional client service is evident in the firm's "Client Bill of Rights," which encapsulates the client credo for all Price Waterhouse employees (see Exhibit 2 on pages 276–277). This credo applies to every service provided. Exhibit 3 on pages 277–278 lists and briefly describes the 16 prime service categories provided by Price Waterhouse.

Even though Price Waterhouse offers a wide variety of professional services, the firm in fiscal 1990 dedicated professional and financial resources to specific markets and services that offered the greatest potential for profitable growth. These included multinational corporations, the financial services industry, information technology consulting, specialized tax services, and services for rapidly growing and middle-market companies (those with annual revenues in the range from $10 million to $150 million). Special emphasis was placed on services for which business conditions created demand. These included services related to litigation consulting, reorganization and bankruptcy, and corporate finance.

EXHIBIT 2

Price Waterhouse's Client Bill of Rights

1. The Right to Professional Excellence
We will be technically proficient in all areas in which we provide advice. We will stay current on business and technical developments and seek counsel from appropriate firm professionals when in doubt about a course of action. We will keep abreast of all issues affecting our client so we can anticipate challenges and provide appropriate advice.

2. The Right to Be Served by Professionals Who Understand Our Business
We will learn all we can about our client's industry and business. We will get to know people within the client organization and outside it who have in-depth knowledge of the client's business, its culture, and its strategic objectives, and we will listen to our client to understand its needs. Being in the thick of our client's business—not on the sidelines—will allow us to identify and anticipate issues of concern to our client. While others may learn on the job, we will strive to know as much as possible about the client and its industry before we ever begin working with a client.

3. The Right to Proactive Advice and Creative Business Ideas
We will take the initiative in proposing actions to enhance our client's success, striving always to offer the innovative recommendations our client expects from its business advisers. We will demonstrate to our client that we expect to be and are qualified to be among those who are consulted about significant client events at the planning stage. We will be thought of as the "idea people." When asked for creative ways to help our client achieve its objectives, we will be the firm that says "Yes, can do. . . ."

4. The Right to Independent Viewpoints and Perspectives
We will advise our client about actions that are in its best long-term interests. Although we will keep client objectives clearly in mind as we aid in decision-making, we will not be sycophants. We will have the independence of spirit, the courage, and the confidence to discourage the client from pursuing a course of action that we believe to be ill-advised.

5. The Right to Effective Communication
We will keep our client contacts informed about the progress of our work and any issues that require their attention. Our written communication will be literate and clear, and our oral communication equally articulate. We will treat our client contacts as professional equals, extending to them and their staffs the same courtesy and respect we ourselves expect. In our communications with client executives and staff, we will demonstrate that we are well-rounded people they can relate to on levels other than the professional one; clients like to do business with people who are interesting and personable, just as we do.

6. The Right to a Wide Range of Professional Resources
We will tap the extensive resources of Price Waterhouse to provide our client with the most experienced and savvy business advice available. We will introduce our colleagues to our client contacts and, when relevant, involve them in client service planning and delivery. To promote well-coordinated services, we will ensure that all appropriate PW professionals are kept informed about services proposed and provided to a client.

7. The Right to Dependable Service
We will never miss a deadline or renege on a commitment. We will do it right the first time and complete the assignment better and faster than the client expects. We will avoid surprises about technical and reporting issues, fees, and staff turnover. When we are the best, we will let the client know; if we do not have the required depth in a particular area, we will have the confidence to direct the client elsewhere.

8. The Right to Service Anytime and Anyplace
We will always be available to our client, anytime and anyplace we are needed. That means spending more time in our client's office than in our own, being "on call" for our client at all times, and keeping in close touch with client contacts when we are not on the premises. And it means bringing the worldwide resources of the firm to bear on client issues, providing the services needed across town or across the globe.

EXHIBIT 2 *(continued)*

9. The Right to State-of-the-Art Technology

We will take advantage of the vast technological resources the firm has created to benefit PW professionals and clients. We will use internal tools to enhance the efficiency and cost-effectiveness of our services. And we will implement PW proprietary software and customize other products that will help our client attain better management information and more effective operations.

10. The Right to Value-Added Service

We will always be thinking about how our client can be more successful and of ways we can help it achieve its business goals. We will make our client's concerns our concerns and put its needs ahead of our own. We will challenge ourselves and our client, asking the tough questions, not being afraid to be wrong. We will be ever vigilant in identifying additional ways we can strengthen our client's competitive edge, ways in which we can offer even more than the client expects.

A central figure in rendering client service is the "engagement partner." This person is typically the senior professional who, along with a team of professionals, is assigned to a client to deliver the services desired. Engagement partners have other responsibilities beyond providing their technical knowledge. Increasingly, these individuals are responsible for identifying new clients and uncovering opportunities to match client needs with other Price Waterhouse services. For example, in fiscal 1990, Price Waterhouse was engaged to assist a long-term client, a commercial bank, in laying the groundwork for successful management of a troubled bank it had acquired in a neighboring state. The firm helped to establish management and control

EXHIBIT 3

Price Waterhouse Services

Audit and Business Advisory Services

Assist companies by enhancing management, strengthening financial controls, and improving competitiveness. In order to accomplish these goals, Price Waterhouse takes an approach based on an in-depth study of a business, its management philosophy and goals, and the environment in which it operates.

Middle-Market and Growing Companies (MMG)

Assist small and middle-market companies in all aspects of their operations. A group of specially trained business advisers provide services including tax assistance, compensation planning, audit procedures, and management training.

Employee Benefit Services

Assist companies in designing and implementing compensation and benefits programs that are both cost-effective and competitive, as well as fair. These programs include retirement plans, executive compensation programs, and employee benefit plans.

Government Services

Provide foreign, federal, state, and local governments and their respective quasi-governmental agencies with assistance in meeting their goals of reducing costs, increasing productivity, and improving services. Services include statistical and economic analyses, rate structures and strategies, and design and implementation of productivity improvement programs.

Industry Services

Monitor industry developments and participate in industry association activities in several industries in order to produce publications that explore business trends and conduct seminars and inform industry members of emerging issues.

EXHIBIT 3 *(continued)*

International Business Development Services
Assist U.S. companies with operations abroad and foreign companies with operations in the United States. Services include trade and customs consulting, tax planning, and marketing and strategic planning.

International Trade Services
Help improve the profitability and efficiency of an organization's international operations in areas that are directly related to trade at international levels. The focus lies in two areas, trade and investment development and trade information.

Inventory Services
Assist companies in managing inventory size, mix, pricing, cost, and value. Services include accounting and tax advisory and internal planning and implementation of systems.

Investment Management and Securities Operations Consulting
Work with organizations that sponsor, manage, and support securities and investment companies to provide assistance with systems development and implementation, operational efficiency evaluations, and business feasibility studies for new products and services. Also work closely with the accounting and tax services arms of PW to provide a comprehensive range of investment management services.

Management Consulting Services
Attempt to take advantage of new business technologies, implement innovative business strategies to improve operating efficiency, identify cost-effective solutions to business problems, and successfully implement changes that will solve these problems. PW operates the Technology Center to help identify and promote new technologies and develop strategies that can effectively take advantage of these technologies.

Corporate Finance Services
Assist middle-market clients in the sale of their business or the purchase of an additional business. Services include identification of buyers or acquisition candidates, financial analyses and projections, development of a negotiating strategy, private placement assistance, and acting as an agent in placing debt and/or equity securities with institutional investors.

Partnership Services
Offer experienced assistance in systems and tax accounting as well as determine the appropriateness of a Master Limited Partnership or syndication for a company and assist in developing and operating this type of partnership.

Personal Financial Services
Help executives with personal financial planning decisions and provide similar assistance to large populations of employee groups in order to help meet company objectives while offering employees financial peace of mind through financial and retirement planning, flexible benefits development, and benefits communication.

Litigation and Reorganization Consulting
Assist debtors, creditors, and other parties in Chapter 11 bankruptcy proceedings in order to successfully rehabilitate debtors and protect creditors' rights by evaluating debtor operations and developing solutions to their operating problems.

Tax Services
Attempt to minimize taxes and increase profitability by alerting clients to the tax consequences of their business decisions, informing them of legislative developments affecting their taxes, and advising them as to their best tax strategies.

Valuation Services
Determine the current value of assets, stock, and business interests for corporations and individuals for use in tax and business planning, mergers and acquisitions, financing, recapitalization, insurance, and litigation purposes.

systems, including employee training, for a multibillion-dollar portfolio of loans. In addition, the engagement partner recognized other opportunities, and Price Waterhouse was contracted to provide personal financial planning services to the senior executives of the acquired bank.

Corporate Finance Services

Price Waterhouse has provided numerous services related to the merger and acquisition (M&A) activities of its clients since the early 1900s. Early on, the firm typically became involved in the M&A process only after a client decided to purchase or sell its business or a division. According to a senior Price Waterhouse official, the M&A process can be distilled into three sequenced phases: (1) strategy, (2) execution, and (3) finalization and integration (see Exhibit 4). This official noted:

> We were often engaged to offer assistance in the execution and finalization and integration phase of the M&A process. We were rarely engaged to participate in the earlier strategy phase. Investment bankers were usually involved there, almost as a matter of tradition.

He added:

> The strategy phase is not only the starting point, but also lucrative in financial terms. In addition, it is a service that should have naturally occurred as a result of our auditing and management consulting business. Too often an engagement partner did not pursue this business, while investment bankers did.

The process of mergers and acquisitions is very complex and frequently conducted over a lengthy time period. It also often involves a great deal of personal and professional attention by the parties involved. "Deals aren't made easily," said a Price Waterhouse M&A specialist, "and companies require a significant amount of counseling not only in terms of technicalities, but in terms of strategic implications as well. A CEO wants to know and have confidence in the people giving the advice on whether to buy or sell and how best to do it."

Recognizing that the nature of corporate finance and the nuances of investment banking-related services require unique skills and abilities, particularly in the strategy phase of the M&A process, Price Waterhouse elected to recruit professionals

EXHIBIT 4

Anatomy of the Merger and Acquisition Process

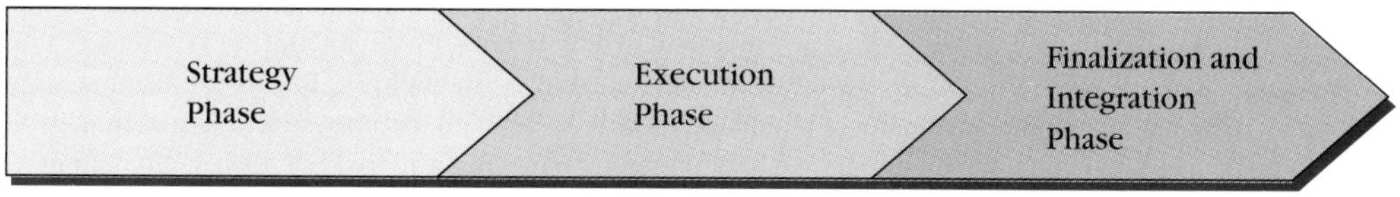

Strategy Phase	Execution Phase	Finalization and Integration Phase
• Identify objectives • Strategy development • Valuation analysis • Candidate identification • Financing strategy	• Descriptive memorandum • Strategy implementation • Alternatives evaluation • Negotiation assistance • Due diligence • Technical accounting and tax • Operations and systems evaluation	• Purchase price adjustments • Postcompletion integration: operational, organizational, systems, financial • Asset disposal planning

with such qualities and experience in early 1990 and to form the Corporate Finance Group, which also included accounting, tax, and consulting professionals who had experience with mergers and acquisitions. The decision to recruit corporate finance professionals, many of whom held MBA degrees with a corporate finance specialization and had extensive experience in the investment banking industry, was a departure from what other Big Six accounting firms had done. Other Big Six firms had tended to reassign accounting professionals to advance their corporate finance initiatives. According to some industry observers, these two different approaches regarding corporate finance initiatives resulted in an interesting situation in public accounting firms. One such observer commented:

> Both approaches have merit and will probably work, but the subtleties of how they will work present some fascinating professional and interpersonal dynamics. First, accounting and finance people are different in both their training and orientation. Surprisingly, few accountants have extensive formal training in finance, and few financial people are well-versed in accounting. This means that accountants in those firms that reassign them will have to learn the techniques and terminology of finance. On the other hand, firms that recruit corporate finance people will benefit quickly from the expertise and experience they bring. However, these corporate finance professionals may be looked at as outsiders and not be easily accepted into the public accounting culture. It is still the case in many public accounting firms that the non-CPA professionals often employed as management consultants are looked upon differently by their accountant colleagues.

■ INVESTMENT BANKING INDUSTRY

The movement by public accounting firms into the domain of investment banking-related services represented a significant departure from past practices. According to one industry observer,

> By moving "upstream" and becoming involved in decisions previously considered sacred territory by investment bankers, public accounting firms will have to develop or acquire new competencies. Advising on matters of capital structure, managing sensitive negotiations related to acquisitions, divestitures, and financing, assessing strategies for creating shareholder value, and a host of traditional activities upon which investment bankers have built reputations for many years will require new skills and possibly a new cultural orientation for accountants and public accounting firms. Investment banking is transaction-oriented, and investment bankers pride themselves on structuring deals. Many are effective salespeople, some view themselves as marriage brokers, and still others see their function as building relationships and becoming confidants of their clients. Some accountants will feel comfortable performing these roles and tasks, but many will not. For example, a partner with a long-term auditing client isn't likely to actively promote the notion that the client sell its business, since that would be running the risk of losing the client to the buyer's auditing firm.

Scope of Investment Banking

Simply put, an investment banker is an agent who joins buyers and sellers of money. Many investment bankers view themselves as facilitators of the flow of financial capital. Investment bankers are usually experts in financial markets and essentially provide their expertise to firms that wish to raise funds. For example, most of them have specific knowledge of potential buyers of financial securities. Since the role of investment bankers is primarily advisory in nature, building and sustaining relationships play a large part in their day-to-day activities.

Investment bankers perform several important services for their client firms. Specific services fall into three general categories:

1. *Assistance in raising capital.* Investment bankers are engaged to assist companies in raising capital to fund growth. These efforts divide into two categories: public security issues and private placements. *Public security issues* represent the most well-known investment banking function. Initial and secondary public offerings, as they are commonly known, consist of public offerings of debt or equity. Investment bankers may underwrite an issue and assume the risk of selling it in the open market. *Private placements* involve sales of new issues of debt (and occasionally equity) to a limited number of firms such as banks or insurance companies without a public offering. The issuing firm can be public or private.
2. *Merger and acquisition services.* When two firms want to merge their operations or when one firm acquires another, investment bankers are customarily asked to consult for the parties to the transaction. Their function often entails issuing opinions regarding the value of the acquired company or the fairness of the negotiated contract. Some larger investment banking firms often take a more active role and commit capital to help finance a merger or acquisition.
3. *General financial advisory services.* Investment bankers are paid for their knowledge of and access to capital markets. While they are predominantly involved directly in the capital-raising process, they may be engaged to assist in the valuation of a particular issue of securities or a company. Their advice is also sought in areas concerning the use of equity (for example, stock) and debt to fund company growth.

Investment Banking Firms

There are over 200 investment banking firms in the United States. However, industry observers typically recognize six firms as being industry leaders: Merrill Lynch, Pierce, Fenner and Smith; Lehman Brothers; Goldman Sachs; Morgan Stanley; First Boston; and Salomon Brothers. Other well-known firms are Dean Witter Reynolds; Alex Brown and Sons; Prudential Securities; and Smith Barney, Harris Upham and Company. Some firms are primarily regional. For example, Rauscher Pierce Refsnes, Inc. is prominent in the southwestern United States, William Blair in the upper Midwest, and Robinson Humphrey in the southeastern states. Even though investment banking firms provide a variety of services for their clients, they often differ in the extent to which they provide specific services. For example, in 1990, Alex Brown and Sons led the industry in initial public offerings; that is, securities issued for the first time to the public. Merrill Lynch and Goldman Sachs are industry leaders in the issuance of overall corporate debt and equity.[2] Morgan Stanley, First Boston, Lehman Brothers, and Goldman Sachs are typically viewed as leaders in the area of mergers and acquisitions. In addition, larger, national investment-banking firms tend to work with larger clients, while smaller or regional investment-banking firms work with smaller clients.

Credibility, reliability, and a history of past successes benefit established investment-banking firms. For these reasons and others, established firms typically experience a high incidence of repeat business from existing clients. Nevertheless, these firms are constantly seeking new clients through referrals and missionary efforts (for example, "cold calling"). Referrals often arise from existing clients and from other

[2] *Institutional Investor* (February 1991).

professionals (law firms and public accounting firms), financial institutions, and private investors.

Many larger banks in the United States are also involved in some investment banking-related activities. Although these banks are prohibited from issuing new securities by the Glass-Steagall Act of 1933, some of them have circumvented this prohibition by establishing foreign subsidiaries that operate in countries that allow banks to enter the securities field.[3] Moreover, there is evidence that the regulatory prohibitions on issuing new securities are being relaxed.

CORPORATE FINANCE INITIATIVE AT PRICE WATERHOUSE

The corporate finance initiative at Price Waterhouse prompted an extensive recruiting effort during much of 1990. By early 1991, about 35 corporate finance professionals were working out of six Price Waterhouse offices in the United States. These offices were located in New York, Chicago, Dallas, Los Angeles, San Francisco, and Atlanta.

Client Focus

The Corporate Finance Group was to focus primarily on what Price Waterhouse considered "middle-market" companies, or those companies with annual sales revenue between $10 million and $150 million. Companies in this category could already be clients of Price Waterhouse or not currently availing themselves of Price Waterhouse services. The decision to focus on "middle-market" companies was based on the view that larger, national investment banking firms typically directed their efforts toward larger companies, many of which were *Fortune* 1000 corporations. Furthermore, statistics on merger and acquisition activity indicated that approximately 45 percent of all such transactions were undertaken by "middle-market" companies.[4] However, Price Waterhouse officials acknowledged that by targeting such companies, they would be in direct competition with smaller, regional investment banking firms.

Service Focus

The Corporate Finance Group would provide a variety of services for new and prospective Price Waterhouse clients, including merger and acquisition advisory services, private placement advisory services, and general financial advisory services. According to a presentation made by one corporate finance professional, a sampling of services that could be provided included (1) exclusive sale assignments, (2) development and implementation of acquisition strategies, (3) structuring and financing of corporate recapitalizations, and (4) advice on financial restructuring options. Exhibit 5 details aspects of these four types of services. The mix of services provided by the Corporate Finance Group was intended to complement and expand the currently available expertise and services provided by Price Waterhouse.

Global Reach

The Corporate Finance Group would also benefit from the worldwide presence of Price Waterhouse in 103 countries and territories. This presence, involving thousands of clients, access to financing sources, and knowledge of foreign and domestic

---

[3] "Glass-Steagall Act Repeal: An Issue for 'Everybank,' " *American Banker* (July 6, 1990): 4.

[4] *Mergers & Acquisitions* (March-April, 1991): 40.

EXHIBIT 5

Representative Sampling of Service Opportunities for Corporate Finance Group

Opportunity	*Services Provided by CFG*
Exclusive sale assignment: Client wishes to sell all or a portion of its business.	1. Identify and evaluate financial alternatives, including • Selling off the entire business • Divestiture of operating unit(s) or significant assets 2. Assess likely range of value for business, operating unit, or assets 3. Identify interested buyers 4. Prepare descriptive memorandum 5. Evaluate proposals and negotiate with qualified buyers
Acquisition: Client believes the value of its business can be enhanced with a strategic acquisition.	1. Identify acquisition candidates 2. Perform a valuation analysis 3. Advise on bidding strategies 4. Approach target acquisition on behalf of client 5. Negotiate on behalf of client 6. Assist in financing if necessary
Recapitalization: Client wishes to realize a portion of the value of its business.	1. Identify and evaluate alternatives, including • Leveraged recapitalization • Leveraged employee stock ownership plan (ESOP) • Strategic alliance 2. Assess debt capacity 3. Identify appropriate financing sources 4. Prepare descriptive memorandum 5. Evaluate proposals and negotiate with lenders or investors
Financial restructuring: Client has a sound business but has inappropriate capitalization.	1. Identify and evaluate the strategic and financial alternatives to improve the client's financial strength and capital structure 2. Prepare descriptive memorandum for use in negotiations with lenders or investors

firms, affords information and technical resources that could strengthen the corporate finance initiative. A recent example involving an acquisition illustrates the benefits of Price Waterhouse's global reach:

> Learning that a major U.S. firm planned overseas acquisitions, a corporate finance specialist proposed to qualify an acquisition candidate in Western Europe. Given the mandate to act, the specialist drew on Price Waterhouse Europe's network to develop a list of targets with the right characteristics. Eventually, this search resulted in a successful offer for a company that happened to be audited by Price Waterhouse Europe.

Implementation

Field implementation of the corporate finance initiative at Price Waterhouse began in earnest in mid-1990 as the Corporate Finance Group began to take shape. According to a corporate finance specialist, "much of the first few months were devoted to making our presence and purpose known at Price Waterhouse." In this regard, corporate finance specialists often made presentations to the Price Waterhouse staff to introduce themselves and the services they could offer to present and prospective clients. Corporate finance specialists also spent time with auditing and management-consulting engagement partners to discuss opportunities for joint work on behalf of existing clients and opportunities for reaching new clients. During this period, corporate finance specialists occasionally accompanied an engagement partner on a visit to an existing client. Firms that were not Price Waterhouse clients were typically called on exclusively by corporate finance specialists. No advertising was employed. However, the Corporate Finance Group used brochures and formal presentation materials to communicate the nature and scope of its services. "These initial efforts were very useful in introducing our capabilities," said a corporate finance specialist. "However, interest in our services was dealt a blow in August [1990] by the invasion of Kuwait by Iraq and the subsequent threat of international turmoil. Companies were not disposed toward buying and selling businesses and pursuing private placements given the economic and political uncertainty during the fourth quarter of 1990."

Integration of the Corporate Finance Group

Even though potential demand for corporate finance services was negatively affected by the Persian Gulf conflict, efforts to build internal linkages within Price Waterhouse continued. A corporate finance specialist estimated that about 20 percent of the Price Waterhouse partners had embraced the Corporate Finance Group and its services by early 1991 and had actively communicated its capabilities to prospective clients. An engagement partner in the auditing area noted that this new service area was a "real plus" but added:

> Very often you have little time to describe the many services that Price Waterhouse provides. Most of a typical one-hour client meeting is spent listening to the client. If corporate finance service opportunities are not indicated by something the client says, they, like some other services, are put on a "second priority list" to be raised at a later time.

Another engagement partner, also in the auditing function, recounted an experience related to the Corporate Finance Group. He said:

> People in the CFG had been talking to my client about its business and had recommended that my client buy another company. However, our auditors had identified an underperforming division and recommended to the company president that it be sold. What started out as acquisition mindset ended up as a program for a divestiture.

A corporate finance specialist noted a missed opportunity for the Corporate Finance Group's private placement services:

> A few weeks ago our group read about a private placement by one of our blue chip clients after the placement happened. It seemed that the engagement partner was either not aware of the opportunity or did not bring it to our attention.

Some members of the Corporate Finance Group acknowledge that integration of their capabilities will take time, given the nature of their services. "What will be needed are a few large engagements," said a corporate finance specialist. "However," he added, "since acquisitions, divestitures, and private placements take months and sometimes a year or more to plan and execute, results are not immediately seen. And sometimes the effort does not produce tangible financial results if the deal fails."

Service Mix

One member of the Corporate Finance Group believed that the efforts of the group were "moderately successful" in that both external and internal relationships were being built and service proposals and engagements were being produced. No discernible pattern of service engagements had yet emerged, however.

Business conditions in early 1991 continued to indicate that corporate finance services were in demand and that these services offered significant potential for profitable growth. Given the nature of the services, exclusive sale assignments appeared to provide the greatest profit potential for Price Waterhouse, followed by private placements (including aspects of financial restructuring and recapitalization of companies). Private placements also had the potential for continuing repeat business. Acquisition assignments and engagements and general financial advisory services were next in order of profitability. However, as one engagement partner noted, "A client can buy and buy again, but it can only sell itself once."

CASE

Godiva Europe

In July 1991, Charles van der Veken, President of Godiva Europe, examined with satisfaction the financial results of Godiva Belgium for the last period, which showed an operating profit of 13 million Belgian francs. "We've come a long way," he thought to himself, remembering the financial situation he inherited just one year ago, which showed a loss of 10 million francs.[1] Over the course of the past year van der Veken had completely restructured the company. He started by firing the marketing and sales staff and then changed the retail distribution network by removing Godiva's representation from numerous stores. He then completely rethought the decoration and design of the remaining stores, and established precise rules of organization and functioning applicable to those stores. These changes made the Godiva-Belgium network of franchises comparable to those in the United States and Japan. For, while in all other countries Godiva stores conveyed an image of luxury and of high scale products, in Belgium, where the Godiva concept was originally conceived, this image was scarcely maintained. Fearing what he called the "boomerang effect," van der Veken had first focused on restructuring the Godiva retail network, an objective that was today on the road to realization. "It is time," thought van der Veken, "to communicate the desired image of Godiva more widely, now that we have a retail network capable of maintaining that image on the level of the Triad Countries."[2]

■ THE GODIVA EUROPE COMPANY

Godiva has its roots in Belgium, where the handcrafting of chocolates stems from a long tradition. Joseph Draps, founder of Godiva in the 1920s, took control of the family business upon the death of his father and created an assortment of prestigious chocolates for which he lacked a name. He finally chose the name "Godiva" because it had an international sound and a history, that of Lady Godiva:

> Lady Godiva is the heroine of an English legend. She was the wife of Leofric, Count of Chester in the 11th century, whom she married around 1050. Roger de Wendower (13th century) tells that Godiva implored Leofric to lower the taxes that were crushing Coventry. The Count would not consent unless his wife would walk through the town completely naked, which she did, covered only by her long hair. John Brompton (16th century) added that nobody saw her. According to a ballad from the 17th century, Godiva ordered all the inhabitants to remain at home. The only one to see her was an indiscreet Peeping Tom. Since 1678, every three years in Coventry, a Godiva Procession is held (Grand Larousse, Vol. 5, p. 522).

Godiva was purchased in 1974 by the multinational Campbell Soup Company. Godiva International is made up of three decision centers: Godiva Europe, Godiva

[1] In 1991, 34 Belgian francs (bf) = $1.00 U.S.

[2] The Triad Countries include the United States, Japan, and countries in Western Europe.

This case study was prepared by Professeur Jean-Jacques Lambin, of Louvain University, Louvain-la-Neuve, Belgium, with the cooperation of Jean-Francois Buslain and Sophie Lambin. Certain names and data have been disguised, and the case cannot be used as a source of information for market research. Used with permission.

EXHIBIT 1

Campbell Soup Organizational Structure

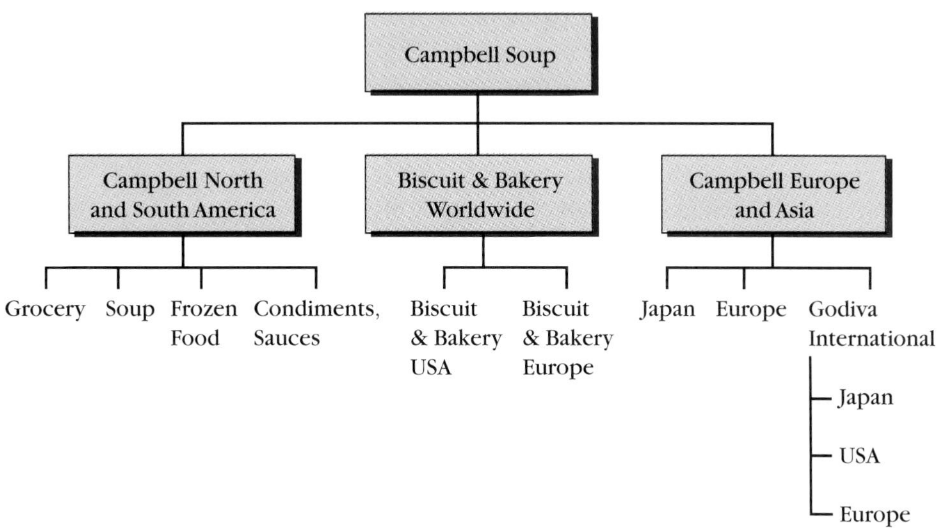

USA, and Godiva Japan, as shown in Exhibit 1. An essentially Belgian company in the beginning, Godiva has become an almost entirely triadic enterprise with a presence in the United States, Japan, and Western Europe.

Godiva Europe is headquartered in Brussels, Belgium. The company's factory, which has 3,000 tons of annual production capacity, is also situated in Brussels, from where products are exported to more than 20 countries throughout the world, including Japan. There is another production unit in the United States, which can provide about 90 percent of the needs of the U.S. market, with the remainder being imported from Belgium.

In 1990, Godiva Europe had annual sales of 926 million Belgian francs. The company is well placed to serve Belgium, its largest market. After Belgium, the principal European markets are France, Great Britain, Germany, Spain, and Portugal. Godiva USA and Godiva Japan distribute Godiva products to their respective markets and constitute the two other most important markets.

The largest part of European production volume (55 percent) is sold under the Godiva brand name, about 10 percent is sold through private labels arrangements, and another 10 percent is sold under the brand Corné Toison d'Or; 25 percent of Godiva Europe's production is sold directly to Godiva Japan and Godiva USA at a company transfer price. Thus, only 65 percent of the total sales are made in Europe under the brand name Godiva. A significant share of Godiva Europe's sales are made through more than 20 airport duty-free shops throughout the world. Those sales, free of a value-added tax (VAT), are made at the expense of local country sales, but they help to establish the international image of Godiva.[3]

Godiva Europe also owns the Corné Toison d'Or brand, which is distributed through 40 stores in Belgium, which are mostly located in the Brussels area. This brand has an image very similar to Godiva: a refined, handmade, luxury product. The acquisition of Corné Toison d'Or was made in 1989 to fully exploit the production

[3] A value-added tax is a government tax levied upon the value that is added to products as they progress from raw material to consumer goods.

capacity of the Brussels plant modernized two years earlier. The original objective was to differentiate the positioning of the brand Corné Toison d'Or from Godiva, but this objective was never pursued by management. A further complication stemmed from the fact that another Corné brand, Corné Port Royal, also exists in the Belgian market with a retail network of 18 stores.

Godiva USA has a factory in Pennsylvania that serves the U.S. market. Godiva Japan, which is solely concerned with marketing, distribution, and sales of Godiva chocolates, imports the product from Belgium. The Japanese market is very important for Godiva International because of the price level, 4,000 bf per kilogram compared to 2,000 bf in the United States, and 1,000 bf in Belgium.[4]

The reference market of Godiva International consists of the Triad Nations. As a branch of Campbell Soup Company, Godiva benefits from a privileged position. Godiva International is directly attached to the Campbell Soup Company Vice President Europe-Asia without an intermediary.

THE WORLD CHOCOLATE MARKET

Unlike coffee or tea, chocolate lends itself to multiple preparations. It can be eaten or drunk, munched or savored. The official journal of the European Community divides chocolate into four categories: bars of chocolate that are filled or not filled, chocolate candies or chocolates (called "pralines" in Belgium) such as Godiva's chocolates, and other chocolate preparations.

Chocolate consumption stabilized in the mid-1980s as a result of increasing raw material costs and an ensuing price rise of finished products. As depicted in Exhibit 2, the past three years have shown very good performances with worldwide consumption of confectionery chocolate (all categories included) of just over 3 million tons in 1989, or an increase of 30.7 percent compared with 1980 consumption. Overproportional consumption was observed in Japan (+54.2 percent), Italy (+102.1 percent), Australia (+45.1 percent), and the United States since 1980.

A distinction is made between industrial and chocolate pralines within the chocolate candies category. Industrial chocolates are sold in prewrapped boxes with or without brand names. The generic boxes are mostly sold through large retail chains at Christmas or Easter; brand boxes are luxurious, offer a high-quality assortment of chocolates, and emphasize the brand name on the package and through mass-media advertising. Typical of this subcategory is the brand Mon Chéri from Ferrero. The sales of generic boxes are stable in Europe, while sales of brand boxes are increasing. This suggests that consumers pay attention to brand names and to the quality image communicated by chocolate packaging and advertising.

EXHIBIT 2

Chocolate Confectionery World Consumption (In Thousands of Tons)

Year	*1980*	*1985*	*1986*	*1987*	*1988*	*1989*
Tons	2,359.6	2,778.1	2,780.2	2,862.0	2,990.8	3.083.6
Index	100	118	118	121	127	131

Source: IOCCC, December 1990, p. 45.

[4] 1 kilogram = 2.205 pounds.

Chocolate pralines, on the other hand, designate chocolate products that are handmade or decorated by hand. The distinctive characteristics of pralines are their delicate flavor and luxurious packaging. They are also highly perishable and fragile with regard to conservation and transport. Typically, Godiva chocolates belong to this last product category.

Chocolate Consumption per Country

The per capita consumption of chocolate varies among countries as shown in Exhibit 3. Chocolate consumption is higher in the northern part of Europe and lower in the Mediterranean region. In 1990, Switzerland had the highest per capita consumption, with 9.4 kilograms per person. The lowest per capita consumption rate is observed in Spain, with 1.2 kilograms per person.

Exhibit 3 also shows that the share of chocolate candies (namely, pralines) with respect to total chocolate confectionery consumption, is strongest in Belgium, with 44 percent against 41 percent in Great Britain, 37 percent in France, 35 percent in Italy, and 34 percent in Switzerland. Switzerland is the largest consumer of chocolate candies, followed closely by the United Kingdom and Belgium, while the other countries are found far behind these three leaders.

In examining the level of consumption reached in countries such as Switzerland, the United Kingdom, and Belgium, it is possible to get an idea of the enormous potential that the world chocolates market holds. In fact, countries like Spain, Italy, and Japan are susceptible to one day reaching such a level of consumption roughly comparable to Switzerland, the United Kingdom, and Belgium provided effective marketing programs are implemented. Available industry statistics do not allow more precise estimates of the share of "chocolate pralines" in the category of chocolate candies.

Evolution of Consumption

Growth rates of chocolate confectionery are also very different among countries as shown in Exhibit 4 on page 290. Countries experiencing the highest growth rates are Italy, Japan, the United Kingdom, and the United States. With the exception of the United Kingdom, these are the countries where the per capita consumption is the

EXHIBIT 3

Chocolate Confectionery Consumption per Country

	Per Capita Consumption in Kilograms in 1989		
Country	*Chocolate Candies*	*Chocolate Confectionery*	***Share of Chocolates in Confectionery Chocolate***
Belgium	2.65	6.09	43.5%
Denmark	1.17	5.61	20.9%
France	1.69	4.59	36.8%
Spain	0.14	1.21	11.6%
Italy	0.65	1.84	35.3%
Japan	0.44	1.59	27.8%
German Federal Republic	1.64	6.81	24.1%
Switzerland	3.17	9.41	33.9%
United Kingdom	2.96	7.15	41.4%
United States	1.14	4.77	23.9%

Source: IOCCC, Statistical Bulletin, Brussels, December 1990. Chocolate candies: candy bars, pralines, and other chocolate products. Solid and filled bars and chocolate products.

EXHIBIT 4

Evolution of Chocolate Confectionery Consumption: Average Yearly Growth Rates, 1980–1989

	Consumption (Kilograms per Person)		*Average Growth*	
Country	*1980*	*1989*	*1980 = 100*	*Average Growth Rate*
Belgium	6.04	6.09	100.8	1.76%
Denmark	4.80	5.61	116.9	1.79%
France	3.96	4.59	115.9	1.65%
Spain	nd	1.21	nd	—
Italy	0.92	1.84	200.0	8.00%
Japan	1.09	1.59	145.9	4.28%
German Federal Republic	6.56	6.81	103.8	0.42%
Switzerland	8.44	9.41	111.5	1.22%
United Kingdom	5.48	7.15	130.5	3.00%
United States	3.69	4.77	129.3	2.89%

nd = no data.

Source: IOCCC, December 1990, p. 49.

lowest. The largest consumer countries like Belgium, Germany, and Switzerland have probably reached a plateau in terms of per capita consumption.

Purchase Behavior of the Chocolate Consumer

Chocolate was imported to Europe by the Spanish at the time of the exploration of the New World. At that time, only the wealthy ate chocolate.

Today, chocolate is a mass-consumption product, accessible to everyone. Consumers are demanding and desire variety. In making chocolate a luxury product, chocolatiers have given chocolates a certain nobleness. The hand-worked character of production and refined decoration give chocolates their status. Chocolates are offered at holidays and other special occasions, and are eaten among friends in an atmosphere of warmth. They are not purchased like bars of chocolate; the behavior of the consumer of chocolate pralines is much more deliberate and involved. The higher prices of chocolate pralines with respect to the other categories of chocolate do not inhibit the consumer but limit more impulsive purchases.

The consumption of chocolate of all categories is associated with pleasure. A qualitative study of the Belgian market shows that this pleasure is associated with the ideas of refinement, taste pleasure, and gift: ". . . chocolate pralines are offered as a gift while chocolate bars are purchased for self-consumption. A praline would be mainly feminine, . . . women seem to appreciate them more and pralines are described by them as refined and fine." In addition, the strong and powerful taste, a particular form, the consistency of chocolate that melts in the mouth, and the feel of the chocolate to the touch are also factors to which the consumer is sensitive. Finally, the idea of health, of a pure product devoid of chemicals, is also in the consumer's mind.

■ GODIVA CHOCOLATES IN THE WORLD

The ancestry of chocolates can be traced to the chef of the Duke of Choiseul de Plessis-Praslin, an ambassador of Louis XIII of France, when he prepared almonds browned in caramelized sugar. However, chocolates as we know them today, a filling surrounded by chocolate, were born in Belgium. It was at the end of the nineteenth century that Jean Neuhaus, son of a confectioner from Neuchatel living in Brussels, created the first chocolates that he named "pralines."

The current concern of Godiva International is to convey a similar image of Godiva chocolates across the world: the image of a luxury chocolate that is typically Belgian. In what follows, the main characteristics of consumers in each country where Godiva is distributed will be briefly presented.

Belgium

Belgium is the birthplace of chocolates and where their consumption is strongest. While there are no significant differences in the consumption rate among the different Belgian regions, differences do exist among the four main socioprofessional categories, as shown in Exhibit 5.

In 60 percent of purchases, chocolates are offered as gifts, and consumers make a clear distinction between a purchase for self-consumption and for a gift. The customer prefers a package where he or she may select the assortment. However, the image of chocolate pralines has aged; chocolates have become a product more comparable to flowers than to a luxury product. The results of a brand image study conducted in the Brussels area (see Appendix A) shows that, while Godiva is strongly associated with the items "most expensive," "nicest packaging," and "most beautiful stores," it is not clearly perceived as very different from its main competitors, Neuhaus mainly, on items associated with superior quality or a significant quality differential. Neuhaus and Corné, two directly competing brands, are perceived in a very similar way, as shown in the perceptual map presented in Exhibit 6 on page 292.

In Belgium, Godiva holds a 10 percent market share and Léonidas 43 percent. Léonidas also has a large international coverage with more than 1,500 outlets throughout the world and a production capacity of 10,000 tons, or three times that of Godiva Europe. In 1991, the size of the total Belgian market for chocolate pralines was estimated to be 3.6 billion Belgian francs (VAT included) or about 8,800 tons. This estimate is based on the data presented in Exhibit 5.

France

French chocolate is darker, drier, and more bitter than Belgian chocolates. Belgian chocolates are, however, well known and appreciated due to Léonidas, which introduced chocolates in France and today holds the largest market share and sells through 250 boutiques. Belgian chocolates are represented as well by Jeff de Bruges, which belongs to Neuhaus. Godiva has a share in a small niche, which is also occupied by several French chocolatiers, none of whom have national market coverage. In France, chocolates are above all regarded as a gift that is offered on certain special occasions, and their purchase is very seasonal (60 percent of all purchases are made at Christmas), which poses problems of profitability during periods of lower sales. Estimates of market size are presented in Exhibit 7 on page 292.

EXHIBIT 5

The Demand for Pralines in Belgium: Average Expenditures per Household in 1988 (bf)

Regions	Belgium	Brussels	Wallonie	Flanders
	814	884	812	793
Households	Independent	White Collar	Blue Collar	Inactive
	1,239	800	567	755

Source: INS, *Enquête sur less budgets des ménages* (1988). The total population includes 3,876,549 households.

EXHIBIT 6

Brand Image Study: Chocolate Pralines in Belgium (Bubble Area = Awareness)

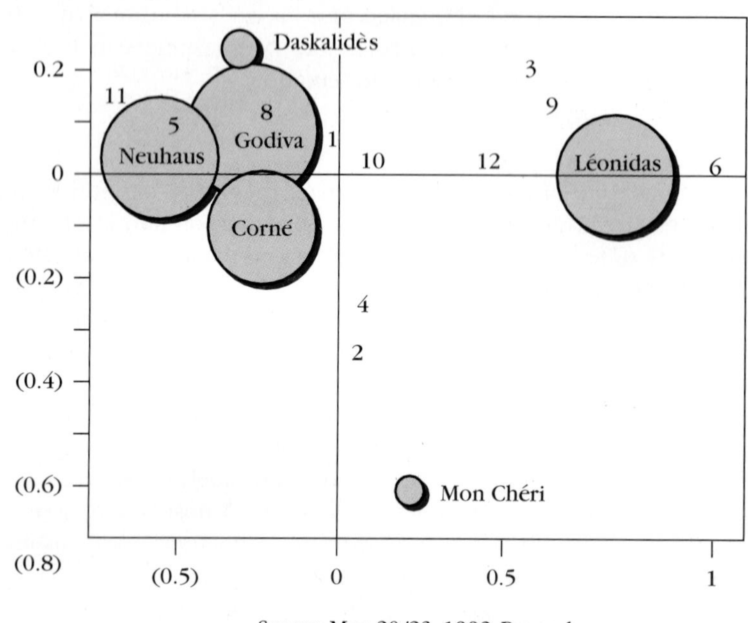

1. Queen of chocolate
2. Ideal for gift
3. For self-indulgence
4. Special occasions
5. Beautiful boutique
6. Attractive price
7. Nice packaging
8. Refined chocolate
9. Belgian chocolate
10. Taste I like best
11. Expensive chocolate
12. Worldly known brand

Survey May 20/23, 1992, Brussels
Sample Size = 128

United Kingdom

An assortment of confectionery products, in which different types of chocolate are mixed, is most appreciated in the United Kingdom. Godiva is currently being introduced to the British market and seeks to create the concept of high-quality and more refined Belgian chocolates. The change in mentality is progressing, but the British are viewed as rather conservative and the economic climate is not very favorable for a luxury product. Marks and Spencer, an upscale British retailer, is selling Belgian chocolates under the private brand name Saint Michael. The Belgian origin of the chocolates is clearly indicated in the packaging, however.

EXHIBIT 7

Estimated Consumption of Chocolates in France, 1988–1990 (In Tons)

Year	*1988*	*1989*	*1990*
Production	44,302	47,660	50,720
Imports (+)	9,677	10,478	11,546
Exports (–)	3,788	5,739	7,970
Total consumption	50,191	52,399	54,365
Per capita consumption	0.900 kg	0.935 kg	0.965 kg

Source: "Production des IAA," SCEES (Décembre 1991): 61 (bonbons de chocolat); Eurostat "Foreign Trade"—Categories; 1806.90.11 and 1806.90.19. The category "bonbons de chocolat" includes other products than chocolate pralines. Thus, total consumption is overestimated.

Spain and Portugal

In Spain and Portugal, chocolate pralines are a completely new concept. Godiva was the first to introduce chocolates a few years ago, and the reception was excellent. Godiva chocolates immediately acquired the image of a refined, luxury product. In Spain, Godiva is sold through the upscale department store Corte Inglese and by several franchises. Consumers' attitudes toward chocolate is very positive. Chocolates are principally offered as gifts and most often in luxurious boxes.

Germany

In Germany, a "chocolates culture" does not really exist. Germans appear to be satisfied with a classic chocolate bar and do not yet place much importance on the distinctive qualities of fine chocolates. Godiva pralines are distributed through five franchised dealers.

Other European Countries

In Holland, chocolate pralines are perceived as too expensive. In Italy and in the Nordic countries, chocolate praline consumption is still a very marginal phenomenon.

United States

Chocolates are very popular in the United States. Chocolates are given as presents on special occasions such as birthdays, Valentine's Day, and Christmas. Chocolates are typically offered in prewrapped packages, with an interior form to house them. The output of the Godiva facility in Pennsylvania almost suffices to cover the needs of present domestic consumption. A small proportion of the Brussels plant output is exported to the United States. The Belgian factory delivers only new products or some products that cannot be produced by the Pennsylvania plant, such as the Godiva golf balls and the chocolate cartridges. In addition to 95 company-owned stores, 800 outlets carry Godiva chocolates in the United States. These outlets are generally located in upscale department stores situated in suburban shopping malls, like Lord & Taylor, Neiman Marcus, Saks Fifth Avenue, Filenes, and I Magnin.

Japan

In Japan, the Godiva chocolate is perceived foremost as European (60 percent as Belgian and 40 percent as Swiss or French). Chocolates are a prestigious and luxury gift. A large problem of seasonality exists in Japan as 75 percent of purchases take place near Valentine's Day. A unique feature of this market is that Japanese women give Japanese men chocolates on Valentine's Day. The Japanese market is a very attractive market for Godiva International and is still expanding.

The Duty-Free Market

In addition to these countries, one must also include the duty-free market, which represents a very significant market segment in terms of output. The number of duty-free stores is still increasing, and sales are closely linked to the development of passenger traffic. Godiva holds a very strong position in this market where Léonidas is not present.

Generally speaking, the annual growth potential in Europe is very different and varies from country to country. In the United States, growth varies between 5 and 10 percent annually, while in Japan growth is very strong, varying between 20 and 25 percent annually.

GODIVA'S MARKETING STRATEGY

Godiva pralines are produced by four means of fabrication: those that are formed in a mold, those that are hollowed then filled, those where a solid filling is coated with chocolate, and finally those that are produced entirely by hand: handmade chocolates. Seventy percent of Godiva pralines are machine-made, and 30 percent are handmade. However, 60 percent of the 70 percent machine-made chocolates must be decorated by hand. Hand decoration is necessary to assure the quality level and the look of the praline.

Godiva strives to find an optimal compromise between automation and handwork, hoping both to ensure the profitability and to perpetuate the name of Godiva as a producer of handmade luxury chocolates. However, the difference in production costs between machine-made and handmade chocolates is considerable (handmade chocolates can cost up to seven times more than machine-made). Charles van der Veken often had second thoughts about the wisdom of maintaining this product policy. He thought:

> Isn't the investment in making hand-made chocolates disproportional to the expectations of our customers? Do they really perceive the added value of these handmade chocolates? Aren't these chocolates just a bit too sophisticated?

Whatever the case, the objective pursued by Godiva is to convert the European market to the quality level of the Godiva praline. The Belgian consumer is the reference point: "Shouldn't a product that has passed the test of the Belgian consumer, a fine connoisseur of chocolate and a demanding customer, be assured of success throughout the world?"

The Godiva facility in Belgium produces chocolates for the entire world, with the exception of the United States. Products exported from Belgian are identical for all countries, but sales by item are different. For example, in France the demand for drier and more bitter chocolates is stronger, while in the United Kingdom cream and white chocolates are more popular. The production capacity of the Belgian factory is not fully utilized, and there is a significant available capacity. Today, the U.S. factory still produces a slightly different and more limited assortment of chocolate pralines. These differences will progressively vanish, and the trend is toward similar production. The planning of production is particularly complex, however, because of the high seasonality of consumption combined with the emphasis on chocolate freshness.

Packaging Policy

Only packaging will distinguish one country from another in order to better meet national and local chocolate consumption habits. In the United States, the tradition is to purchase chocolates prewrapped, while in Europe and Japan the custom-made assortment dominates. What's more, in Japan, chocolates are purchased in very small quantities (given the price); thus, the beauty of the packaging becomes predominant, whereas in Europe and more precisely in Belgium, the value of the gift is more often related to the judicious assortment of chocolates that was chosen. As stated by a Godiva dealer, "Customers have very precise ideas on the type of assortment they want, even for gifts, and they don't like to buy prewrapped standard assortments."

Currently, the trend in packaging at Godiva is packaging by themes called "collections." With these "collections," Godiva leaves the food industry for the luxury products sector. These handmade creations constitute a research and development activity that ensures continuous innovation and provides renewed promotional displays in the Godiva boutiques. In these "collections," beautiful fabric boxes, handcrafted according to the principles of "haute couture," will illustrate through the calendar Valentine's Day, Spring, Easter, Mother's Day, Christmas, and so on. In Belgium, the price of such a box (1,000 bf) is exorbitant with respect to the price of the chocolates; thus, these boxes serve more often for in-store decoration than for sales.

For several years, Godiva has also tried to develop tea rooms attached to Godiva boutiques where customers can eat fine pastries or ice cream. The people who stop here see these rooms as havens of peace where they can rest between purchases while shopping and buy a few chocolates or even a box of chocolates.

Pricing Policy

Making a Godiva chocolate requires an enormous amount of manual labor and the gross margins are modest (35 to 40 percent on average). Top management of Campbell Soup requires a 15 percent rate of return on capital invested for Godiva, a normal rate of return for a luxury product.

From one country to another, the price differences are great, as shown in Exhibit 8. One of the main preoccupations of Godiva Europe is to standardize retail prices at the European level, in view of the unified European Union in 1993.

Previously, Godiva franchisees were held to a contract with the Godiva organization and had to be supplied within that country. From 1993 on, it will no longer be possible to keep French franchisees from getting their supplies directly from the Belgian factory, which sells its chocolates at a much lower price. This is why prices must be modified. This adaptation has been started in Belgium, with a 10 percent increase in prices effective August 1, 1991. The price of one kilo of Godiva chocolates is 1,080 bf, whereas the average market price for chocolates in Belgium is 450 bf per kilo.

This price policy, however, has not been easily accepted by the market, particularly in Belgium, where the price gap between the high and the low end of the market is already very large (see Exhibit 9 on page 296). Charles van der Veken observed that, in Belgium, a 10 percent price increase has generated a loss in volume of about 7 percent. He is also aware that this lost volume goes to Léonidas for the most part.

Distribution Policy

The ultimate goal that Godiva is pursuing in its distribution policy is to obtain across the world something akin to the Benetton model: boutiques with a uniform look. This "look" includes a logo with golden letters on a black background, a facade incorporating these same colors, interior fixtures in pink marble, glass counters, and so forth.

EXHIBIT 8

Price of One Kilo of Godiva Pralines (bf)

Country	*Price to Franchisees*	*Retail Price (VAT Included)*	*VAT (%)*
Belgium	640	1,080	6.0
France	763	1,920	18.6
Spain	640	2,145	6.0
United Kingdom	757	1,782	17.5
Italy	640	2,009	9.0
Holland	640	1,261	6.0
Germany	640	1,641	7.0
Portugal	640	2,408	16.0
United States	na	2,040	—
Japan	na	4,000	—

Source: Trade publications.

EXHIBIT 9

Retail Price Comparison Among Brands

Belgium		*France*		*United Kingdom*	
Brands (bf/kg)	*Price*	*Brands (ff/kg)*	*Price*	*Brands (£/lb)*	*Price*
Godiva	1,080	Godiva	320	Godiva	13.50
Neuhaus	980	Hédiard	640	Gérard Ronay	20.00
Corné PR	880	Fauchon	430	Valrhona	16.80
Corné TO	870	Maison ch.	390	Charbonel	14.00
Daskalidès	680	Le Notre	345	Neuhaus	12.00
Jeff de Bruges	595	Fontaine ch.	327	Léonidas	6.75
Léonidas	360	Léonidas	120	Thorton's	5.80

Source: Trade publications.

The current retail distribution problem lies in the great disparity between the Godiva boutiques in different countries, mainly in Europe and even more particularly in Belgium (Exhibit 10 shows the Godiva distribution network). Through the years the boutiques in Belgium have become less and less attractive. As a consequence, the Godiva brand image has aged. Abroad, however, Godiva benefits from an extremely prestigious image, and the boutiques merit their name. Nevertheless, Charles van der Veken fears the worst:

> If we don't react quickly, we could compromise the world brand image of Godiva. What would a Spanish tourist think in comparing the boutique of a local distributor in Brussels to the refined boutiques that he finds in Spain, although Belgium is the birthplace of chocolates?

EXHIBIT 10

The Godiva Distribution Network

Country	*Company-Owned Stores*	*Franchised Dealers*	*Department Stores and Others*	*Total Outlets*
Belgium	3	54	—	57
France	1	19	—	20
Spain	—	6	18	24
United Kingdom	2	—	15	17
Italy	—	2	—	2
Holland	—	2	—	2
Germany	—	4	1	5
Portugal	—	3	7	10
Total Europe	**6**	**90**	**41**	**137**
United States	95	—	800	895
Japan	—	22	67	89

Source: Trade publications and yellow pages.

Godiva's retail distribution action plan for Belgium covers a period of 18 months. A contract has been made with the franchisees in which Godiva imposes both exclusivity and design; all the boutiques must have completed renovation. Once the movement is well established in Belgium, Godiva hopes this will create a spillover effect to all of Europe, because the new boutiques will constitute a reference for the recruitment of new franchisees or for spontaneous requests for renovations.

This renovation movement has already begun and every two weeks a "new" boutique is inaugurated. The renovated boutiques have been transformed so that everything is in black and gold, and the entire interior decoration is redone according to the same single standard of luxury.

Generally, consumer reactions in Belgium seem favorable, although in certain respects consumers find the stores almost too beautiful. As for the franchisees, they feel as though they have a new business, and appear to be changing some of their former bad habits. If the effects remain favorable in the medium term, van der Veken said he will increase the margin provided to franchisees, which is still different from one country to the other (see Exhibit 8).

The Chairman of Godiva International, Mr. Partridge, has frequently questioned the wisdom of this costly exclusive distribution system because he believes chocolate is not really a destination purchase. In Europe, the adoption of a broader distribution system is difficult, however, because of the reluctance of consumers vis-à-vis prewrapped assortments of chocolates. Van der Veken is convinced, however, that the Godiva boutique is a key component of the Godiva image of a luxury good.

The Competitive Environment

The handmade luxury chocolate segment is occupied by many other brands. Exhibit 11 presents a ranking of the specialty brands for Belgium, France, and the United Kingdom, in descending order of market share. The strength of the Léonidas competitive position in Europe is clearly shown by this comparison. Léonidas was created in 1910. It did for chocolate pralines what Henry Ford did for the car: a mass-consumption product sold at a low price. Their recipe is simple: a price of 360 bf

EXHIBIT 11

Main European Competitors

Belgium		*France*		*United Kingdom*	
Brands	*Share*	*Brands*	*Share*	*Brands*	*Tons*
Léonidas	42.8%	Léonidas	62.0%	Thornton's	1,200
Godiva	10.3	Thornton's	18.0	Léonidas	300
Neuhaus	7.1	Jeff de Bruges	14.0	Godiva	40
Mondose	5.4	Godiva	3.0		
Corné TO	2.7	Le Notre	1.0		
Others	31.7	Others	2.0		

Source: Industry trade publications (market shares are calculated on sales revenues).

per kilogram, 8,600 square meters of industrial space, a production capacity of 10,000 tons. Léonidas is a very important competitor for Godiva. With total sales of over 2.6 billion Belgian francs, and a 32 percent operating profit margin, Léonidas has 1,500 stores worldwide, and is now expanding rapidly in the international market. The next major competitor is Neuhaus, which recently merged with Mondose and Corné Port Royal and which is also pursuing an international development strategy. The "others" include the many small confectionery-chocolatiers who nibble at the market share of the larger companies in offering fresh, original products made from pure cocoa.

However, given its broad market coverage, Charles van der Veken believes that Godiva has a significant competitive advantage due to its integration into Campbell Soup 13 years ago, which provided Godiva with an opportunity for global expansion much more quickly than its competitors. Thus, Godiva is present everywhere, and even if it often skirts a competitor in a particular market, it is rarely the same one across the world. Godiva can thus currently be considered the global leader in the luxury chocolate segment.

Only in Belgium is Godiva having difficulties making use of its competitive advantage. The volume growth has proven important everywhere, except in Belgium. According to Charles van der Veken, the market is already too saturated, and it is up to the best to make the difference.

Advertising Strategy

Today, Godiva does not need to make itself known on the international level: Its brand name is already globally recognized. Its current concern, in line with the policy that has been pursued for the past several months, is to create a common advertising message for the entire world. However, this will not be an easy task, as evidenced by a comparison of the situation in Belgium, the United States, and Japan. In the United States and Japan, the product is relatively new and has a strong image inasmuch as there is no direct competitor. In Belgium, the consumer has followed the evolution of Godiva chocolates and the progressive commoditization of the brand. It is therefore more difficult to impress Belgians with a product that is already well known. What's more, Belgians are in daily contact with other brands of chocolates, with which they can easily compare Godiva.

Thus, as van der Veken pointed out, Godiva finds itself faced with very different worlds. Until now, in the United States advertising was focused on prestige, luxury, and refinement, with a communication style similar to the one adopted by Cartier, Gucci, or Ferrari. These advertisements were presented in magazines well adapted to the desired positioning: gourmet, fashion, or business magazines that cater to higher-income echelons (see Exhibit 12).

In Belgium, however, this type of advertising tended only to reinforce the aged, grandmotherish image of Godiva chocolates. What's more, the gap between the "perceived image" (a food item interchangeable with others of the same type) and the "desired image" (an exceptional luxury product) was so large that spectacular results could not be expected.

A study performed by Godiva seems to show that nobody could remember these advertisements, nor the promises that were made. In Belgium, Godiva had also made use of event marketing: being represented at events at which the target population had a large chance of being present. Thus, two years ago, Godiva was the sponsor of a golf competition in Belgium that held its name (Godiva European Masters). Such actions are, however, extremely costly, and their effectiveness is difficult to measure. The total advertising budget of Godiva Europe is 31 million Belgian francs per year.

EXHIBIT 12

Typical Godiva Print Advertisement in the United States

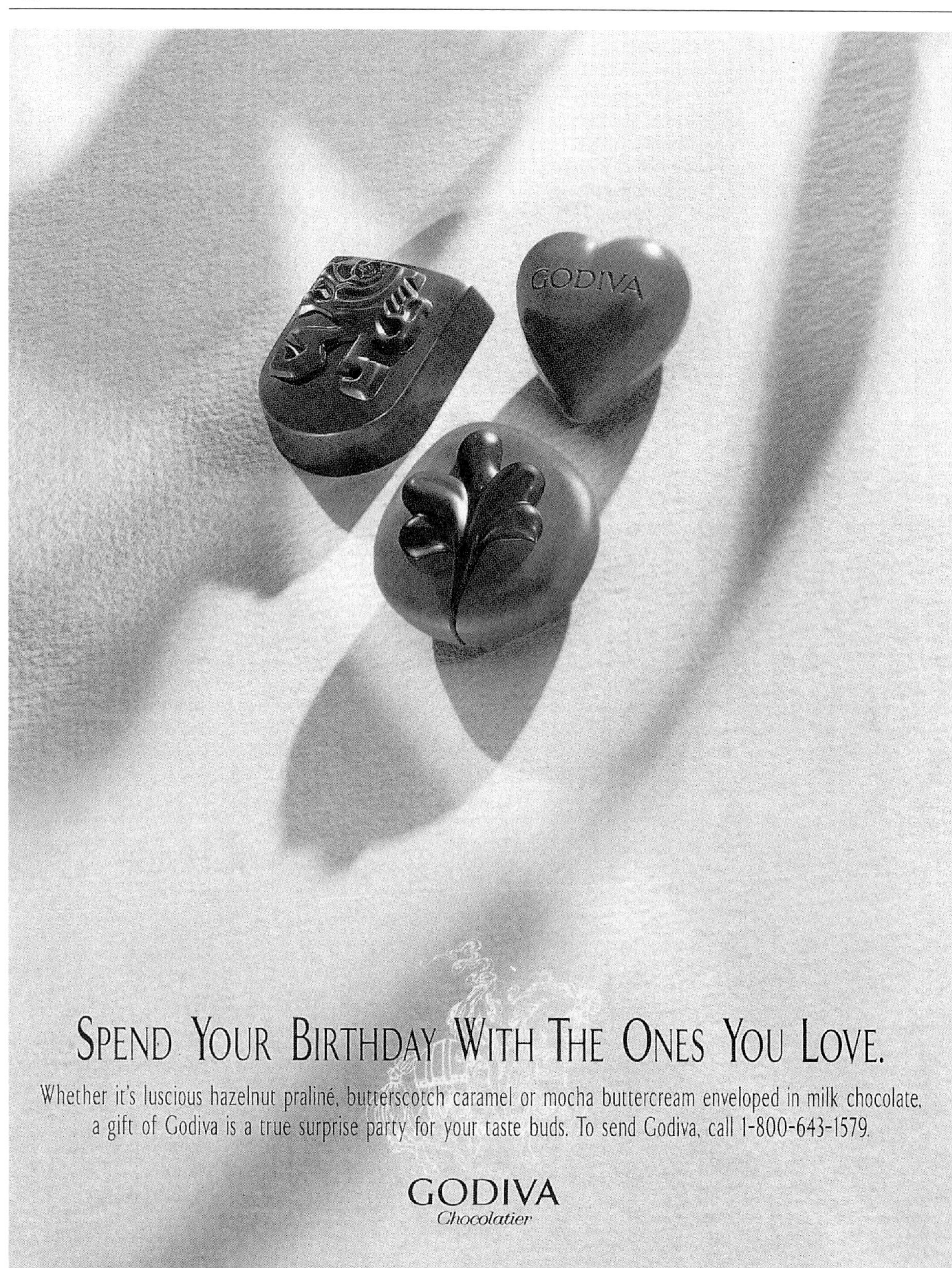

GODIVA
SPEND YOUR BIRTHDAY WITH THE ONES YOU LOVE.
Whether it's luscious hazelnut praliné, butterscotch caramel or mocha buttercream enveloped in milk chocolate, a gift of Godiva is a true surprise party for your taste buds. To send Godiva, call 1-800-643-1579.
GODIVA
Chocolatier

EXHIBIT 13

The Briefing from Godiva International

1. **Current Positioning**
   - To adults who want a quality product for special moments, Godiva is an accessible luxury branded by Godiva Chocolatier and distinguished by superior craftsmanship.
2. **Consumer Benefit**
   - Whether you give Godiva or consume it yourself, you will relish its uniquely sensual pleasures: taste and presentation.
3. **Promise**
   - Using the finest ingredients and Belgian recipes for a remarkable taste experience.
   - Godiva heritage of fine chocolate making.
   - Beautifully crafted packaging.
   - Handcrafted in fine European heritage/style.
   - Created by an expert chocolatier.
4. **Psychographic Characteristics**
   - Godiva purchasers are discerning and driven by quality expectations. While they are value-oriented, they will pay a higher price if a significant quality differential exists, since they aspire to have or share the best.
   - Godiva men and women are sensual individuals, enjoying the pleasures that things of exceptional look, feel, taste, sound, and smell can offer them.
5. **Competitive Frame**
   - Gift: flowers, perfume, wine, other fine chocolates, giftables of the same price range.
   - Self-consumption: any item meant to provide a range of self-indulgences at Godiva's basic price-points.
6. **Target Audience**
   - The Godiva target covers a range of demographic characteristics:
     - Broad age range (25–54 primarily)
     - Women and men
     - Across breadth of income levels, but with reasonable to high disposable incomes.
7. **Advertising Objectives**
   - To revitalize Godiva's worldwide premium position most specifically as it pertains to the superior quality of the chocolate product.
   - To motivate our current Godiva franchise to purchase on more frequent occasions (gifting and self-consumption).
   - To motivate current purchasers of competitive chocolates and nonchocolate giftables to convert to the Godiva franchise.
8. **Message**
   - Godiva chocolates are expertly crafted to provide an unparalleled sensory experience.
9. **Tone and Manner**
   - Luxurious—Energetic—Modern—Upscale—Emotionally involving.

■ THE ADVERTISING DECISION

Aware of this problem, Godiva Europe is in the process of evaluating its advertising strategy. The following situation had to be solved: creating a common advertising message targeted at the three main markets while taking into consideration the inevitable cultural differences among countries.

Godiva USA had just sent Charles van der Veken the briefing of an international advertising campaign, which is summarized in Exhibit 13. He said that adopting this advertising style on the European market worried him to a certain degree:

> The least one can say is that differences of mentality exist between our two continents. We certainly need to wake up our old-fashioned Godiva, but we should also be careful of overly radical changes.

Reflecting with his marketing staff, van der Veken tended to define the advertising objective in the following manner.

> The objective of Godiva USA is to increase the frequency of the purchase of chocolates for gifts as well as for self consumption, whereas Belgium wants to make its brand image more youthful. Thus, the United States should adjust its advertising slightly "downward," in making the product more accessible through convivial advertising and less "plastic beauty." Belgium should strive, jointly with other marketing efforts (redesign of boutiques, increased quality of service, creation of "collections"), to adjust its advertising slightly "upward," in affirming itself as a prestigious luxury product, only younger.

The upward adjustment for Belgium was a daring challenge. Charles van der Veken wondered if it would not be preferable to pass through a transitory period before beginning a global marketing campaign, which would take into consideration the historical and cultural context of Belgium.

Just then, Mrs. Bogaert, van der Veken's assistant, entered his office holding a fax from Godiva International:

> The campaign cannot be launched in time for Christmas; prepare as quickly as possible your advertising campaign for Belgium and contact your agencies. Meeting in five weeks in New York for the confirmation of our projects.

Charles van der Veken immediately called his Director of Marketing, informed her of the freshly arrived news, and asked her to submit for the Belgian market a campaign project based on the American model, targeted in a first step to the Belgian market, but which could be extended to the other European markets, if not to the entire world. Together they agreed on objectives in three main categories:

1. Qualitative objectives:
   - Rapidly reinforce the luxury image of Godiva
   - Make visibility a priority
2. Quantitative objectives:
   - Increase the frequency of purchase
3. Other objectives:
   - Concentrate all efforts on Belgium during several months (months of peak sales)
   - Synergy of all other methods of promotion and advertising

An additional 13 million bf advertising budget would be allocated to the campaign. After some thought, it seemed possible to Mr. van der Veken that a triad campaign would, on a long-term basis, be feasible in spite of cultural differences. He did not believe, however, that business generated in the other European countries would be high enough today to justify the same advertising budget as for Belgium. This became even more obvious when one considered that, in terms of media costs and for a same impact, 1 bf in Belgium is equivalent to 1.6 bf in France and 1.9 bf in the United Kingdom.

Charles van der Veken was also convinced that a European advertising campaign was useless without having first improved and reinforced Godiva European distribution.

APPENDIX: RESULTS OF THE BRAND IMAGE STUDY IN THE BRUSSELS MARKET AREA

Aided Brand Awareness (%)

Brand Name	*Not at All*	*Only by Name*	*By Experience*	*Total*
Corné	24.2%	28.9%	46.9%	100%
Corné Toison d'Or	31.3	25.8	43.0	100
Corné Port Royal	69.3	16.5	14.2	100
Daskalidès	54.3	26.0	19.7	100
Godiva	2.3	19.5	78.1	100
Léonidas	2.3	10.9	86.7	100
Mon Chéri	4.7	23.6	71.7	100
Neuhaus	13.3	25.0	61.7	100

Don't know any of brands Corné, Corné Toison d'Or, Corné Port Royal: 22.7%. Known "by name" or "by experience" at least one of the following brands: Corné, Corné Toison d'Or, Corné Port Royal: 77.3%

Brand Image Analysis

	Brand Associated Most with Each Attribute (%)									
Attribute	*Corné (1)*	*Corné Toison d'Or (2)*	*Corné Port Royal (3)*	*Corné Total (1+2+3)*	*Daskalidès*	*Godiva*	*Léonidas*	*Mon Chéri*	*Neuhaus*	*Total*
The queen of chocolates	7.1%	5.5%	0.8%	(13.4%)		37.8%	27.6%	1.6%	19.7%	100%
Ideal for gift	11.0	3.1		(14.1)		29.1	26.8	10.2	19.7	100
For self-indulgence	4.8	3.2	0.8	(8.8)	0.8%	26.4	48.0	1.6	14.4	100
For special occasions	6.5	8.9	0.8	(16.2)	0.8	26.8	28.5	8.1	19.5	100
The most beautiful boutique	6.0	9.4		(15.4)		40.2	12.0	0.9	31.6	100
The most attractive price	3.3	2.5		(5.8)	0.8	5.7	81.1	4.9	1.6	100
The nicest packaging	7.2	7.2	0.8	(15.2)	0.8	49.6	6.4	3.2	24.8	100
The most refined chocolate	8.8	7.2	1.6	(17.6)	0.8	35.2	18.4	0.8	27.2	100
Typically Belgian chocolate	6.5	2.4		(8.9)		30.1	48.1	2.4	10.6	100
Taste I like best	5.6	4.0	1.6	(11.2)		32.3	37.9	3.2	15.3	100
The most expensive chocolate	6.7	8.4		(15.1)	2.5	40.3	5.9	0.8	35.3	100
Worldly known brand	4.0	0.8		(4.8)	0.8	42.7	39.5	4.8	7.3	100

Brand Preferences by Situation

For Self-Consumption		*For Gift*	
Corné:	2.4%	Corné:	3.9%
Corné Toison d'Or:	4.1	Corné Toison d'Or:	3.9
Corné Port Royal:	0.8	Corné Port Royal:	0.8
Daskalidès:	—	Daskalidès:	0.8
Godiva:	24.4	Godiva:	29.1
Léonidas:	48.0	Léonidas:	27.6
Mon Chéri:	2.4	Mon Chéri:	5.5
Neuhaus:	12.2	Neuhaus:	25.2
Other:	5.7	Other:	3.2
	100%		100%

CHAPTER 7

Marketing Channel Strategy and Management

Marketing channels play an integral role in an organization's marketing strategy. A *marketing channel* consists of individuals and firms involved in the process of making a product or service available for consumption or use by consumers and industrial users. Channels not only link a producer of goods to the goods' buyers, but also provide the means through which an organization implements its marketing strategy. Marketing channels determine whether the target markets sought by an organization are reached. The effectiveness of a communications strategy is determined, in part, by the ability and willingness of channel intermediaries to perform sales, advertising, and promotion activities. An organization's price strategy is influenced by the markup and discount policies of intermediaries. Finally, product strategy is affected by intermediaries' branding policies, willingness to stock and customize offerings, and ability to augment offerings through installation or maintenance services, the extension of credit, and so forth.

To the extent that a marketing manager has alternative channels available for reaching chosen target markets, the task facing the manager is to select those channels that meet three objectives. First, of all channel options, the chosen channel should provide the best coverage of the target markets sought. This means that the channel will locate the right offerings in the right place, in the right quantity, at the right price, and at a time when buyers wish to purchase them. Second, the channel should satisfy the buying requirements of the target markets sought. Buying requirements refer to buyers' needs for information about the offering, convenience of purchase, and services such as delivery that are incidental to purchasing. Finally, the chosen channel should maximize potential revenues returned to the organization while minimizing the costs of achieving adequate market coverage and satisfying buyer requirements. Channel profitability is determined by the profit margins earned (revenues minus costs) for each channel member and for the channel as a whole.

Marketing channel strategy and management has assumed greater significance with the onset of electronic commerce. Growth in the sophistication and usage of Internet/Web-based technology has revolutionized the way products and services are made available for consumption or use by consumers and industrial users. The Internet has challenged marketers to innovatively employ this technology in channel strategy and management in a manner that creates customer value at a profit.[1] This topic is addressed in chapter 9.

THE CHANNEL-SELECTION DECISION

Making the channel-selection decision is not so much a single act as it is a process of making various component decisions. The process of channel selection involves specifying the type, location, density, and functions of intermediaries, if any, in a marketing channel. However, before addressing these decisions, the marketing manager must conduct a thorough market analysis in order to identify the target markets that will be served by a prospective marketing channel. The target markets sought and their buying requirements form the basis for all channel decisions. In other words, the marketing manager needs answers to fundamental questions such as these: Who are potential customers? Where do they buy? When do they buy? How do they buy? What do they buy? By working backward from the ultimate buyer or user of an offering, the manager can develop a framework for specific channel decisions and can identify alternative channel designs.[2]

Consider Gateway, Inc., the world's second largest direct seller of personal computers behind Dell Computer. The company studied small business buyers of personal computers and concluded that an alternative channel design, featuring stores, was necessary to reach and service this market. Why? Gateway's research indicated that a large segment of these buyers prefer browsing in a store. They like to see, touch, test, and custom configure a computer system to meet their needs with the help of highly trained representatives. Gateway Country stores combine a showroom and service center that offer special computers, training programs, a business version of the company's successful Your:) ware leasing program and services geared to particular categories of small businesses—real estate, law, and physicians' offices. However, Gateway Country stores do not stock computers. Customers who want to buy a computer must still order one from Gateway, which will custom-build the system to the customer's specifications and ship it to his or her office. In this way, Gateway retains the economic benefits of direct selling. The initial results have been impressive. Computer industry analysts estimate that 80 percent of Gateway's sales growth can be attributed to Gateway Country stores.[3]

The Design of Marketing Channels

Exhibit 7.1 illustrates traditional channel designs for consumer and industrial offerings. Also indicated is the number of levels in a marketing channel, which is determined by the number of intermediaries between the producer and the ultimate buyers or users. As the number of intermediaries between the producer and the ultimate buyer increases, the channel increases in length.

Direct versus Indirect Distribution The first decision facing a manager is whether the organization should (1) use intermediaries to reach target markets or (2) contact ultimate buyers directly using its own sales forces or distribution outlets, or the Internet through a marketing Web site or electronic storefront. If the manager elects to use intermediaries, then the type, location, density, and number of channel levels must be determined.

Organizations usually elect to contact ultimate buyers directly rather than through intermediaries when the following conditions exist. Direct distribution is usually employed when target markets are composed of buyers who are easily identifiable, when personal selling is a major component of the organization's communication program, when the organization has a wide variety of offerings for the target market, and when sufficient resources are available to satisfy target market requirements that would normally be handled by intermediaries (such as credit, technical assistance, delivery, and post-sale service). Direct distribution must be considered when intermediaries are not available for reaching target markets, or when interme-

EXHIBIT 7.1

Traditional Marketing Channel Designs

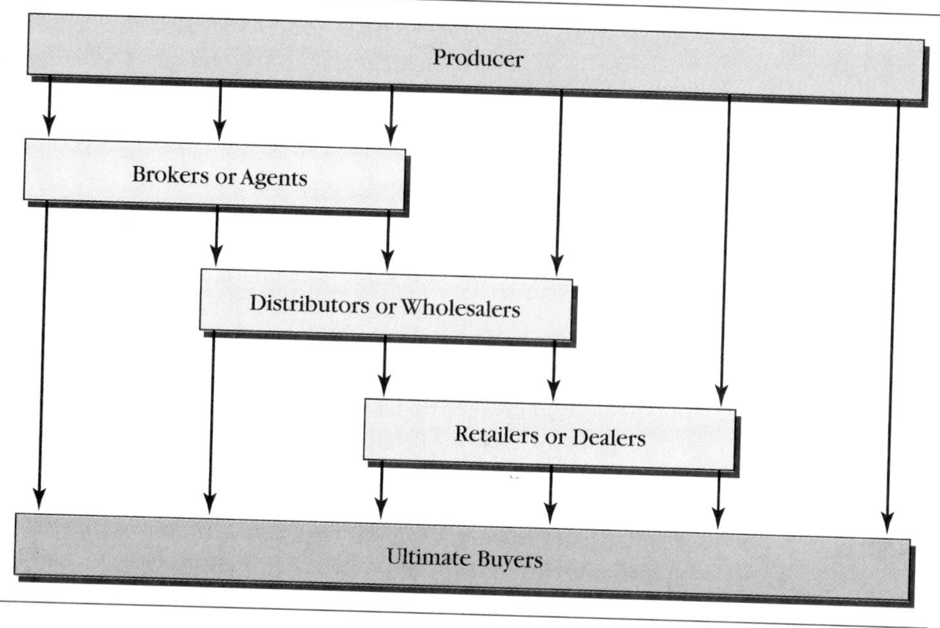

diaries do not possess the capacity to service the requirements of target markets. For example, Procter and Gamble sells its soap and laundry detergents direct, door to door in the Philippines because there are no other alternatives in many parts of the country. Also, when Ingersoll-Rand first introduced pneumatic tools, a direct channel was used because considerable buyer education and service was necessary. As buyers became more familiar with these products, the company switched to using industrial distributors. Certain characteristics of offerings also favor direct distribution. Typically, sophisticated technical offerings such as mainframe computers, unstandardized offerings such as custom-built machinery, and offerings of high unit value are distributed directly to buyers. Finally, the overall marketing strategy might favor direct distribution. An organization might seek a certain aura of exclusivity not generated by using intermediaries, or an organization might want to emphasize the appeal of "buying direct," presumably important to certain market segments. Direct distribution may also be appropriate if the organization seeks to differentiate its offering from others distributed through intermediaries. A part of the successful differentiation strategy used by Dell Computer Corporation is its emphasis on Internet purchases of personal computers.

Even though a variety of conditions favor direct distribution, an important caveat must be noted. The decision to market directly to ultimate buyers involves the absorption of all functions (contacting buyers, storage, delivery, and credit) typically performed by intermediaries. The marketing principle "You can eliminate intermediaries, but not their functions" is particularly relevant to the manager considering direct distribution. This point is occasionally overlooked by marketing managers when they elect to distribute directly. The costs of performing these functions can be prohibitive, depending on the organization's financial resources and the opportunity cost of diverting financial resources from other endeavors. Therefore, even though all signs favor direct distribution, the capacity of the organization to perform tasks normally assigned to intermediaries may eliminate this alternative from final consideration. A similar caveat must be noted with respect to intermediaries who consider acquiring functions typically performed by channel members above or below them in the channel (for example, a retailer who wishes to perform wholesaling functions). 7-Eleven convenience stores eliminated much of its warehousing of merchandise in favor of using independent wholesalers. The reasons cited for this decision were that independent wholesalers could perform these functions more efficiently and at a lower cost.[4]

Electronic Marketing Channels The phenomenal growth of the Internet and the World Wide Web adds a technological twist to the analysis of direct versus indirect distribution.[5] A popular view is that traditional intermediaries—retailers, wholesalers, brokers—are superfluous when producers and buyers everywhere can be linked directly to each other via electronic marketing channels. *Electronic marketing channels* employ some form of electronic communication, including the Internet to make products and services available for consumption or use by consumers and industrial users. The elimination of traditional intermediaries and direct distribution through electronic marketing channels is called *disintermediation.* Electronic marketing channels have the potential to revolutionize how products and services are marketed, and disintermediation is seen as the driving force behind this revolution.

Exhibit 7.2 shows the electronic marketing channels for books (Amazon.com), automobiles (Auto-By-Tel.com), reservations services (Travelocity.com), and personal computers (Dell.com).[6] A feature of these channels is that they often combine electronic ("cybermediaries") and traditional intermediaries. The inclusion of traditional intermediaries for product marketing (distributors for books and dealers for cars) is due to the logistics function they perform—namely, handling, storage, shipping, and so forth. This function remains with traditional intermediaries or with the producer, as evident with Dell Computer Corporation and its Dell.com direct channel. It is also noteworthy that two-thirds of the sales through Dell.com involve human sales representatives—a common practice with direct distribution as described earlier.[7]

EXHIBIT 7.2

Representative Electronic Marketing Channels

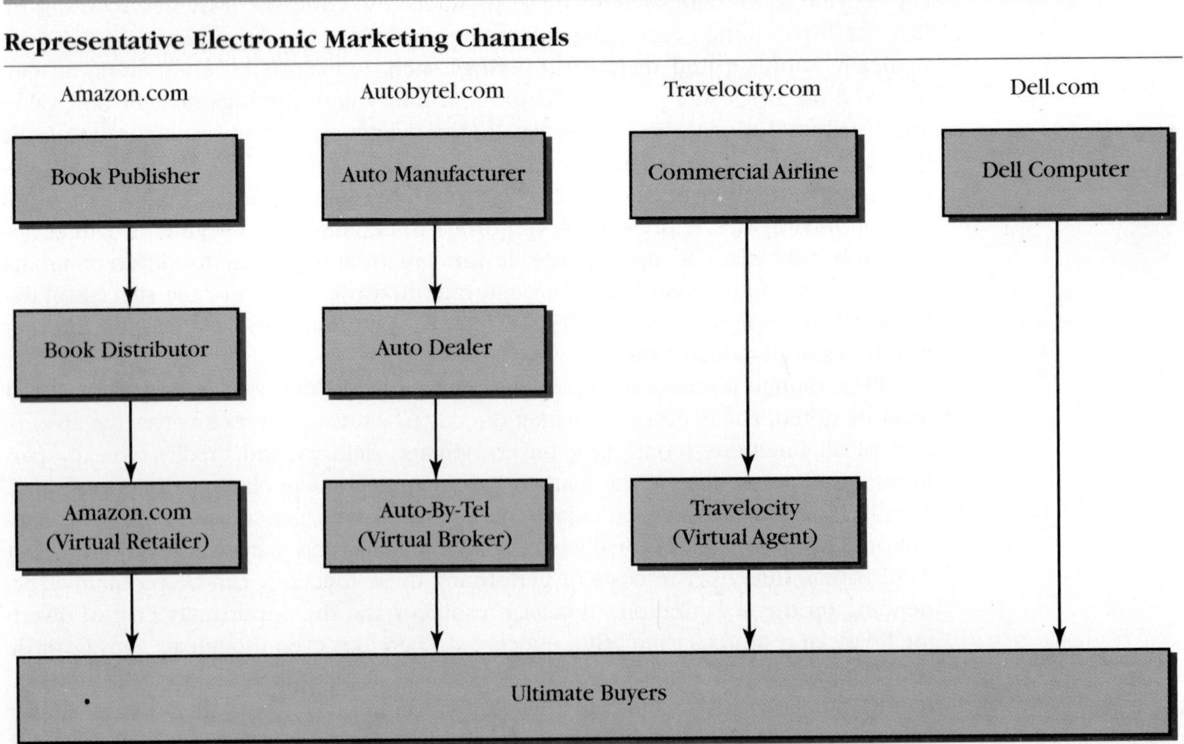

Many services can be distributed through electronic marketing channels, such as travel reservations marketed by Travelocity.com, financial securities by Schwab.com, and insurance by MetLife.com. Software also can be marketed this way. However, many other services such as health care and auto repair still involve traditional intermediaries.

Electronic marketing channels represent yet another, albeit important, channel design option available for marketers. Like all options, it too must be assessed on its revenue-producing capability relative to the costs of achieving market coverage and satisfying buyer requirements.

Channel Selection at the Retail Level

In the event that traditional intermediaries are chosen as the means for reaching target markets, the channel-selection decision then focuses on the type and location of intermediaries at each level of the marketing channel, beginning with the retail level.

Consider the case of a manufacturer of sporting goods. If retail outlets are chosen, the question becomes, What type of retail outlet? Should hardware stores, department stores, sporting goods stores, or some combination be selected to carry the line of sporting goods? Also, where should these retail outlets be located? Should they be in urban, suburban, or rural areas, and in what parts of the country?

Type and place decisions depend on the buying requirements of the target markets and the potential profitability of the outlets to the manufacturer. If retail outlets are to play a role in providing information about the offering to potential buyers, which of the retail outlets will most actively promote the line through point-of-purchase displays, store-sponsored advertising (including cooperative advertising), and/or knowledgeable sales personnel? Which of the stores will carry a reasonable inventory to attract buyers interested in selection and variety? Which outlets carry competing or complementary products? Which outlets are conveniently located for buyers? The profitability of a retail outlet relates to the potential volume in the trade area served by the outlet, the merchandising skill of store management, and the store's competitive environment.

Next, the density of intermediaries at the retail level of distribution must be determined. *Density* refers to the number of intermediaries carrying the organization's offering in a particular geographical area. Three degrees of density at the retail level are intensive distribution, exclusive distribution, and selective distribution.

1. *Intensive distribution* at the retail level means that a manager attempts to distribute the organization's offerings through as many retail outlets as possible. More specifically, a manager may seek to gain distribution through as many outlets of a specific type (such as drugstores) as possible. In its extreme form, intensive distribution refers to gaining distribution through almost all types of retail outlets, as soft drink and candy manufacturers do. For example, Coca-Cola's retail distribution objective is to place its products "within an arm's reach of desire."
2. *Exclusive distribution* is the opposite of intensive distribution in that typically *one* retail outlet in a geographic area or *one* retail chain carries the manufacturer's line. Usually, the geographic area constitutes the defined trade area of the retailer. Mark Cross wallets and Regal shoes are distributed under an exclusive distribution arrangement. Sometimes retailers sign exclusive distribution agreements with manufacturers. For instance, Radio Shack now sells only Compaq's Presario home computers and Thomson SA's RCA brand of audio and video products in its 7,000 stores.[8]

   Occasionally, the exclusive-distribution strategy involves a contractual arrangement between a retailer and a manufacturer or service provider that gives the retailer exclusive rights to sell a line of products or services in a defined area in return for performing specific marketing functions. A common form of an exclusive agreement is a franchise agreement. Franchise agreements now exist in more than 70 industry categories ranging from tax-preparation services (H & R Block) to donuts (Dunkin' Donuts). There are nearly 3,000 franchise retail chains in the U.S. with 600,000 units, which account for 41 percent of all retail sales.[9]

3. *Selective distribution* is between these two extremes. This strategy calls for a manufacturer to select a few retail outlets in a specific area to carry its offering. This approach is often used for marketing furniture, some brands of men's clothing, and quality women's apparel. Selective distribution weds some of the market coverage benefits of intensive distribution to the control over resale evident with the exclusive distribution strategy. For this reason, selective distribution has become increasingly popular in recent years among marketers.

The popularity of selective distribution has come about also because of a phenomenon called effective distribution. *Effective distribution* means that a limited number of outlets at the retail level account for a significant fraction of the market potential. An example of effective distribution is a situation in which a marketer of expensive men's wristwatches distributes through only 40 percent of available outlets, but these outlets account for 80 percent of the volume of the wristwatch market. Increasing the density of retail outlets to perhaps 50 percent would probably increase the percentage of potential volume to 85 percent; however, the attendant costs of this action might lead to only a marginal profit contribution at best.

The decision as to which of the three degrees of density to select rests on how buyers purchase the manufacturer's offering, the amount of control over resale desired by the manufacturer, the degree of exclusivity sought by intermediaries, and the contribution of intermediaries to the manufacturer's marketing effort. General Motors considered these factors when it announced plans to pare its franchised Oldsmobile dealerships by almost 20 percent by 2002.[10]

Intensive distribution is often chosen when the offering is purchased frequently and when buyers wish to expend minimum effort in its acquisition. Almost by definition, convenience goods such as confectionery products, personal care products, and gasoline fall into this category. Limited-distribution strategies (exclusive and selective) are chosen when the offering requires personal selling at the point of purchase. Major appliances and industrial goods are typically distributed exclusively or selectively.

The density of retail distribution varies inversely with the amount of control over resale desired by the manufacturer. As the density of retail outlets increases, the number of intermediary levels often increases, further removing the manufacturer from the ultimate consumer. A manufacturer's control over resale declines sharply in these cases. If control over resale is important, then a strategy of more limited distribution is used. Interests of intermediaries in improving their own competitive advantage also limit distribution. If the nature of the offering demands considerable investment by an intermediary in terms of service capabilities, specialized selling at the point of sale, or unique display methods, limited distribution in the retailer's trade area may be required.

Channel Selection at Other Levels of Distribution

After having determined the nature of retail distribution, the marketing manager must then specify the type, location, and density (if any) of intermediaries that will be used to reach retail outlets. These specific selection decisions closely parallel the retail network decisions made earlier.

If a second-level intermediary (wholesaler, broker, or industrial distributor) is decided on, the question becomes, What type of wholesaler? Should the manager select a specialty wholesaler, which carries a limited line of items within a product line; a general-merchandise wholesaler, which carries a wide assortment of products; a general-line wholesaler, which carries a complete assortment of items in a single retailing field; or a combination of wholesalers? Obviously, an important consideration is what types of wholesalers sell to the retail outlets desired. When Mr. Coffee decided to use supermarkets to sell its replacement coffee filters, it had to recruit food brokers to call on these retailers. Often, the decision is based on what is available. If the available wholesalers do not meet the requirements of the manufacturer in terms of satisfying retailers' requirements for delivery, inventory assortment and volume, credit, and so forth, then direct distribution to retailers becomes the only viable alternative. However, careful study of a wholesaler's role in distribution should precede any decision to bypass them, particularly in countries outside the United States. The Gillette Company's experience in Japan is a case in point.[11] Gillette attempted to sell its razors and blades through company salespeople in Japan as it does in the United States, thus eliminating wholesalers traditionally involved in marketing toiletries. Warner-Lambert Company sold its Schick razors and blades through the traditional Japanese channel involving wholesalers. The result? Gillette captured 10 percent of the Japanese razor and blade market and Schick captured 62 percent.

The location of wholesalers is determined by the location of retail outlets to the extent that geographical proximity affects logistical considerations such as transportation costs and fast delivery service. The density of wholesalers is influenced by the density of the retail network and wholesaler service capabilities. Generally, as the density of retail outlets increases, the density of wholesalers necessary to service them also increases. Retail bookseller Barnes & Noble, Inc. recently faced this issue. It attempted to acquire the Ingram Book Group, the largest U.S. book wholesaler with 11 strategically placed distribution locations. The addition of these wholesalers could have cut transportation costs to its more than 1,000 stores and reduced delivery time for its growing online customers reached through barnesandnoble.com, the Internet bookseller. The acquisition did not materialize, and Barnes & Noble found it necessary to expand its own wholesale distribution network.[12]

Similar kinds of decisions are required for each level of distribution in a particular marketing channel; their determination will depend on the extent of market coverage sought and the availability of intermediaries. Suffice it to say that the number of levels in a marketing channel generally varies directly with the breadth of the market sought.

■ DUAL DISTRIBUTION

The discussion thus far has focused on the selection of a single marketing channel. However, many organizations use multiple channels simultaneously, a practice called dual distribution. *Dual distribution* occurs when an organization distributes its offering through two or more different marketing channels that may or may not compete for similar buyers. For example, General Electric sells its appliances directly to house and apartment builders but uses retailers to reach consumers. Mattel distributes its toys through traditional retailers (Toys 'R' Us), cybermediaries (etoys.com), and direct through its Web site, mattel.com.

Dual distribution is adopted for a variety of reasons. If a manufacturer produces its own brand as well as a private store brand, the store brand might be distributed directly to that particular retailer, whereas the manufacturer's brand might be handled by wholesalers. Or a manufacturer may distribute directly to major large-volume retailers, whose service and volume requirements set them apart from other retailers, and may use wholesalers to reach smaller retailer outlets. Finally, geography itself may affect whether direct or indirect methods of distribution are used. The organization might use its own sales group in high-volume and geographically concentrated markets but use intermediaries elsewhere. In some instances, companies use multiple channels when a multibrand strategy is used (see Chapter 5). Hallmark sells its Hallmark brand greeting cards through its franchised Hallmark stores and select department stores, and its Ambassador brand of cards through discount and drugstore chains.

The viability of the dual-distribution approach is highly situational and will depend on the relative strengths of the manufacturer and retailers. If a manufacturer decides to distribute directly to ultimate buyers in a retailer's territory, the retailer may drop the manufacturer's line. The likelihood of this depends on the importance of the manufacturer's line to the retailer and the availability of competitive offerings. If a retailer accounts for a sufficiently large portion of the manufacturer's volume, elimination of the line could have a negative effect on the manufacturer's sales volume. This happened to Shaw Industries, the world's largest carpet and rug manufacturer. When Shaw Industries announced it would begin operating its own retail stores and commercial dealer network, Home Depot dropped Shaw Industries as a carpet and rug supplier and switched to Mohawk Industries' products.[13]

A major consideration in dual distribution is whether additional marketing channels will provide incremental sales revenue or simply cannibalize the sales revenue from existing channels. The reluctance of many companies to add electronic marketing channels is that incremental sales may not offset cannibalized sales.[14]

■ SATISFYING INTERMEDIARY REQUIREMENTS AND TRADE RELATIONS

The role of intermediaries in channel selection has been cited several times; however, a number of specific points require elaboration. The impression given so far may be that intermediaries are relatively docile elements in a marketing channel. Nothing could be further from the truth!

Even though reference has been made to "selecting" intermediaries, selection in actual practice is a two-way street. Intermediaries often choose those suppliers with whom they wish to deal. For instance, Goodyear Tire & Rubber Company was recently selected as the exclusive supplier to Penske Auto Center, Inc.[15] This action meant that competing brands such as Uniroyal, Michelin, and BF Goodrich from France's Groupe Michelin and Firestone from Japan's Bridgestone Corporation would no longer be sold through 860 Penske automobile service centers. Similarly, the largest soft-drink bottler in Venezuela dropped Pepsi-Cola and began bottling Coca-Cola in an overnight conversion. The result was that Pepsi-Cola lost its distribution in its sixth-largest market in the world.[16]

Intermediary Requirements

Experienced marketing managers know that they must be sensitive to possible requirements of intermediaries that must be met in order to establish profitable exchange relationships. Intermediaries are concerned with the adequacy of the manufacturer's offering in improving its product assortment for its own target markets. If the product line or individual offering is inadequate, then the intermediary must look elsewhere. Intermediaries also seek marketing support from manufacturers. For wholesalers, support often involves promotional assistance; for industrial distributors, it includes technical assistance. As noted previously, intermediaries concerned with competition usually seek a degree of exclusivity in handling the manufacturer's offering. The ability of the intermediary to provide adequate market coverage, given an exclusive agreement, will determine whether this interest can be satisfied by the manufacturer. Finally, intermediaries expect a profit margin on sales consistent with the functions they are expected to perform. In short, trade discounts, fill-rate standards (that is, the ability of the manufacturer to supply quantities requested by intermediaries), cooperative advertising and other promotional support, lead-time requirements (that is, the length of time from order placement to receipt), and product-service exclusivity agreements each contribute to the likelihood of long-term exchange relationships. A manager who fails to recognize these facts of life often finds that the functions necessary to satisfy buyer requirements, such as sales contacts, display, adequate inventory, service, and delivery, are not being performed.

Trade Relations

Trade relations also are an important consideration in marketing channel management and strategy. Marketing managers recognize that conflicts often arise in trade relations.[17] *Channel conflict* arises when one channel member (such as a manufacturer or an intermediary) believes another channel member is engaged in behavior that is preventing it from achieving its goals. Four sources of conflict are most common. First, conflict arises when a channel member bypasses another member and sells or buys direct. When Wal-Mart elected to purchase products direct from manufacturers rather than through manufacturers' agents, these agents picketed Wal-Mart stores and placed ads in the *Wall Street Journal* critical of the company. Second, there can be conflict over how profit margins are distributed among channel members. This happened when Compaq Computer Corporation and one of its retailers disagreed over how price discounts were applied in the sale of Compaq's products. Compaq stopped selling to the retailer for 13 months, and sales of both companies suffered. A third source of conflict arises when manufacturers believe wholesalers or retailers are not giving their products adequate attention. For example, H. J. Heinz Company became embroiled in a conflict with supermarkets in Great Britain because the supermarkets were promoting and displaying private brands at the expense of Heinz brands. The fourth source of conflict occurs when a manufacturer engages in dual distribution, and particularly when different retailers or dealers carry the same brands. For instance, the launch of Elizabeth Taylor's Black Pearls fragrance by Elizabeth Arden was put on hold when department store chains such as May and Dillard refused to stock the item once they learned that mass merchants Sears and JCPenney would also carry the brand. Elizabeth Arden subsequently introduced the brand only through department stores.

Conflict can have destructive effects on the workings of a marketing channel. To reduce the likelihood of conflict, one member of the channel sometimes seeks to coordinate, direct, and support other channel members. This channel member assumes the role of a *channel captain* because of its power to influence the behavior of other channel members.

This type of power can take four forms. First, economic power arises from the ability of a firm to reward or coerce other members, given its strong financial position or customer franchise. Microsoft Corporation and Wal-Mart have economic power. Expertness is a second source of power. For example, American Hospital Supply helps its customers—hospitals—manage order processing for hundreds of medical supplies. Identification with a particular channel member may also bestow power on a firm. For instance, retailers may compete to carry Ralph Lauren, or clothing manufacturers may compete to be carried by Neiman-Marcus or Nordstrom's. Finally, power can arise from the legitimate right of one channel member to dictate the behavior of other members. This would occur under contractual arrangements (such as franchising) that allow one channel member to legally direct how another behaves.

CHANNEL-MODIFICATION DECISIONS

An organization's marketing channels are subject to modification, but less so than product, price, and promotion. Shifts in the geographical concentration of buyers, the inability of existing intermediaries to meet the needs of buyers, and the costs of distribution represent common reasons for modifying existing marketing channels. Sanyo Electric, Inc., eliminated many of its distributors when managers observed that 20 distributors could cover the same market that 90 had in previous years.[18] Compaq Computer Corporation recently pared the number of distributors that carry its products from 39 to four, which accounted for about 50 percent of the company's North American personal computer distribution business. The action was taken to lower its distribution costs and speed deliveries to customers.[19] An organization might initiate a channel-modification program if the product-market strategy changed with the adoption of a market development or diversification strategy. Honda (Acura), Toyota (Lexus), and Nissan (Infiniti) created separate dealer networks to sell their new luxury models designed for upscale consumer markets. Whatever the reason for modifying an organization's marketing channels, at the base of the channel-modification decision should lie the marketing manager's intent to better achieve the three channel objectives cited earlier. The approach taken in making these decisions involves an assessment of both the benefits and the costs of making a change.

Qualitative Factors in Modification Decisions

The qualitative assessment of a modification decision rests on a series of questions. These questions imply that the modification decision involves a comparative analysis of the existing and new channels.

1. Will the change improve the effective coverage of the target markets sought? How?
2. Will the change improve the satisfaction of buyer needs? How?
3. Which marketing functions, if any, must be absorbed in order to make the change?
4. Does the organization have the resources to perform the new functions?
5. What effect will the change have on other channel participants?
6. What will be the effect of the change on the achievement of long-range organizational objectives?

Quantitative Assessment of Modification Decisions

A quantitative assessment of the modification decision considers the financial impact of the change in terms of revenues and expenses. Suppose an organization is considering replacing its wholesalers with its own distribution centers. Wholesalers receive $5 million annually from the margin on sales of the organization's offering. The organization's cost of servicing the wholesalers is $500,000 annually. Therefore, the cost of using wholesalers in this instance is the margin received by wholesalers plus the $500,000 devoted to servicing them, for a total of $5.5 million. Stated differently, the organization would save this amount if the wholesalers were eliminated.

If it eliminated the wholesalers, however, the organization would have to assume their functions, including the costs of sales to retail accounts formerly assumed by the wholesalers. Sales administration costs would be incurred also. In addition, since the wholesalers carry inventories to service retail accounts, the cost of carrying the inventory would have to be assumed, as well as the expenses of delivery and storage. Finally, since wholesalers extend credit to retailers, the cost of carrying the accounts receivable must be included.

Once the costs incurred by eliminating the wholesaler have been estimated, an evaluation of the modification decision from a financial perspective is possible. Such an evaluation is shown below with illustrative dollar values.

Cost of Wholesalers		***Cost of Distribution Centers***	
Margin to wholesalers	$5,000,000	Sales to retailers	$1,500,000
Service expense	500,000	Sales administration	250,000
Total cost	$5,500,000	Inventory cost	935,000
		Delivery and storage	1,877,000
		Accounts receivable	438,000
		Total cost	$5,000,000

Since using wholesalers costs $5.5 million and the cost of distribution centers would be $5 million, a cost perspective suggests selection of the latter option. However, the effect on revenues must be considered. This effect can be determined by first addressing the questions noted earlier and then translating market coverage, the satisfaction of buyer needs, and channel-participant response into dollar values.

NOTES

1. "Internet Anxiety," *Business Week* (June 28, 1999): 79–88.
2. Louis W. Stern, Adel El-Ansary, and Anne T. Coughlan, *Marketing Channels,* 5th ed. (Upper Saddle River, NJ: Prentice Hall, 1996): Chapter 5.
3. "Gateway to Use Its Stores to Lure Small Businesses," *Wall Street Journal* (April 8, 1999): B1, B4; "About Gateway," www.gateway.com. January 3, 2000.
4. "Southland Loses $39 Million after Charge for Closures," *Dallas Morning News* (February 20, 1993): C3.
5. Portions of this discussion are based on Bert Rosenbloom, *Marketing Channels,* 6th ed. (Fort Worth: The Dryden Press, 1999): Chapter 15.
6. "A Survey of Business and the Internet," *The Economist* (June 26, 1999): special section.
7. "Random Access: Dell's Sell," *Forbes ASAP* (February 22, 1999): 16.
8. "Inside Radio Shack's Surprising Turnaround," *Wall Street Journal* (June 8, 1999): B1, B16.
9. "Franchising the American Dream," *Time* (November 7, 1998): 178.
10. "Who Will Deal in Dealerships?" *The Economist* (February 14, 1998): 61–62.
11. "Gillette Tries to Nick Schick in Japan," *Wall Street Journal* (February 4, 1991): B3, B4.
12. "Barnes & Noble Likely to Build Centers for Distribution If Ingram Deal Fails," *Wall Street Journal* (June 2, 1999): B8.
13. "Carpet Firm's Dynamic Chief Must Weave Succession," *Wall Street Journal* (August 19, 1998): B4.
14. "The Bottom Line," *Wall Street Journal* (July 12, 1999): R12.
15. "Penske Auto Center Gives Goodyear Exclusive Tire Pact," *Wall Street Journal* (October 10, 1995): B9.
16. "Pepsi Seeing Red Over Coke's Venezuela Coup," *Dallas Morning News* (August 22, 1996): D1, D10.
17. For an overview on channel conflict, see Christine B. Bucklin, Pamela A. Thomas-Graham, and Elizabeth A. Webster, "Channel Conflict: When Is It Dangerous?" *The McKinsey Quarterly* (Number 3, 1997): 36–43.
18. "Sanyo Sales Strategy Illustrates Problem of Little Distributors," *Wall Street Journal* (September 10, 1985): 31.
19. "Compaq's Paring of PC Distributors Is Boon for 4 Firms," *Wall Street Journal* (May 11, 1999): B10.

CASE

Dell Computer Corporation

The Higher Education Market

Diane Jeni hung up the phone slowly. "This could be interesting," she thought to herself. Turning around, she took another look at the whiteboard in her office.

Goals for Planning Year 96/97	
Revenue	$150 MM
Units	69,000

Those were the financial goals she'd been given by Matthew Roberts, Vice President of Dell's Education, State & Local Government (ESL) Business Unit. It was early 1996, and Jeni was the marketing manager responsible for the higher education portion of ESL's business. She was concerned because for the past two quarters business had seemed soft. Reflecting on the current uncertainty in the higher education market, she wondered whether this uncertainty offered a window of opportunity for Dell. Although the number of students expected to enroll in higher education institutions was projected to increase steadily over the next few years, the competitive environment was in flux. Until recently the education market, kindergarten through higher education, had been dominated by Apple Computer. But now, at least according to articles just published in *Business Week* and the *Los Angeles Times*, Apple seemed to be leaderless and in financial disarray, and the phone call she had just received led her to believe that other competitors might also be scaling back their efforts to capture the higher education market.

Glancing at her watch, Jeni realized that she was late for a meeting with other members of the Higher Education Planning Team. She hurried off to join them.

THE COMPANY

Dell Computer Corporation designs, manufactures, markets, services, and supports a wide range of computer systems, including desktop personal computers, notebook computers, and network servers. It also markets peripheral computer hardware and software, as well as service and support programs. According to most industry observers, Dell Computer is the world's leading direct marketer of personal computer systems.

The story of Dell Computer Corporation is the story of Michael Dell and his strategic vision. As a college freshman in 1983, Michael Dell began selling personal computer disk drive kits and related parts to personal computer (PC) enthusiasts at local meetings of PC users. Within a few months, he was selling "gray market" IBM PCs out of his dormitory room. By April 1984, Dell had dropped out of college and

This case was prepared by Professor Robert A. Peterson, The University of Texas at Austin, as a basis for class discussion and is not designed to illustrate effective or ineffective handling of an administrative situation. Certain corporate information is disguised. Consequently, the case is not useful for research purposes.

EXHIBIT 1

Dell Computer Corporation's Net Sales, Fiscal Years 1991–1996[a] ($ in Thousands)

	1991	*1992*	*1993*	*1994*	*1995*	*1996*
Americas[b]	$397,000	$648,000	$1,459,000	$2,037,000	$2,40 0,000	$3,474,000
Other	149,000	241,000	554,000	836,000	1,075,000	1,822,000
Total	$546,000	$889,000	$2,013,000	$2,873,000	$3,475,000	$ 5,296,000

[a] Fiscal years generally run from February through January.

[b] Includes North and South America.

Source: Annual reports of the company.

was devoting all of his energies to his burgeoning business. Operating out of a small storefront, he began to assemble and market some of the first IBM clones under the brand name PC's Limited. By 1986, PC's Limited had grown to 400 employees and reached $69.5 million in annual revenues.

In 1988, at the age of 23, Dell took his company public. By the end of January 1990, annual sales had reached $388.6 million, and Michael Dell was named *Inc.* magazine's Entrepreneur of the Year. The following year *Fortune* listed Dell Computer Corporation as one of the 100 fastest growing companies in the United States. During the next few years the company continued to expand rapidly, both in the United States and internationally. By the end of 1995, Dell Computer employed approximately 8,400 people in more than 130 countries worldwide. (See Exhibits 1 and 2 (page 318) for pertinent sales and operating information.) At the beginning of 1996, Dell Computer was ranked 250th on the *Fortune* 500 list.

Oversimplifying a bit, Dell Computer is organized around three distinct customer groups: major accounts (large corporations, government agencies, and educational and medical institutions), individuals, and small and medium-sized businesses. The former are reached through Dell's Major Accounts Division, the latter two through the Dell Direct Division. As suggested by the sources of its revenues in the boxed insert, nearly two-thirds of Dell Computer's sales are derived from its major accounts. Among Dell Computer's major account customers are seven of the world's eight largest automobile manufacturers, seven of the nine largest airlines, and nine of the ten largest telecommunications companies. Dell itself is among the seven largest computer vendors in the world. Sales to consumers constitute less than 10 percent of Dell Computer's revenues.

Dell Computer Revenues ($ in Billions)

Customer Group	*FY 1995*	*FY 1996*
Major corporate, government, medical, and education accounts	$2.31	$3.36
Individuals, small and medium-sized businesses	1.16	1.93
Total	$3.47	$5.29

Source: 1996 Annual Report.

The Strategic Vision

According to analysts who follow the company, the success of Dell Computer Corporation can be traced to Michael Dell's strategic vision of a high-performance/low-price personal computer marketed directly to end users. Dell computers, although not designed to be the most powerful or the most technically advanced computers, were of higher-than-average quality and very reliable. Dell computers were also not designed to be the lowest cost PCs available. The key strategic concept of Michael

EXHIBIT 2

Dell Computer Corporation Operating Results, Fiscal Years 1991–1996*

	Percentage of Net Sales					
	1991	*1992*	*1993*	*1994*	*1995*	*1996*
Net sales	100.0%	100.0%	100.0%	100.0%	100.0%	100.0%
Cost of sales	66.7	68.3	77.7	84.9	78.8	79.8
Gross profit	33.3	31.7	22.3	15.1	21.2	20.2
Operating expenses						
Selling, general and administrative	21.0	20.5	13.3	14.7	12.2	11.3
Research, development, and engineering	4.1	3.7	2.1	1.7	1.9	1.8
Total operating expenses	25.1	24.2	15.4	16.4	14.1	13.1
Operating income (loss)	8.2	7.5	6.9	(1.3)	7.1	7.1
Other income (expense)	(3.2)	(1.8)	.2	—	(1.0)	.1
Income (loss) before taxes	5.0	5.7	7.1	(1.3)	6.1	7.2

* Fiscal years generally run from February through January.

Source: Annual reports of company.

Dell can be described as a combination of "relatively high performance" and "relatively low price" that provides exceptionally high value for buyers.

However, perhaps more important than the high-performance-to-price ratio was the manner in which Dell Computer marketed its products. Rather than marketing its computers through one of the currently existing (indirect) distribution channels—traditional dealers, mass merchandisers, value-added resellers (VARs), and so forth—or by means of a sales force, Dell Computer initially marketed its computers directly to end users by means of direct response advertising in selected computer magazines. Later, it added telemarketing activities, an indirect sales force, and field sales representatives. During the first few years of its existence, all products were distributed directly from the Dell factory to the end user by UPS or Airborne Express. This type of marketing provided a single source for complete computing solutions, as well as total accountability to customers. No intermediaries, wholesalers, or retailers were used in the initial distribution channel. The industry recognized Dell as the pioneer of a unique form of direct-relationship marketing.

Interestingly enough, Michael Dell's direct marketing approach did not spring full-grown from his imagination. By age 13, he had already created a successful mail-order stamp-trading business.

As Dell Computer grew rapidly through its manufacturer–direct marketing strategy, its strategic vision evolved to include three key elements: maintaining a direct relationship with the end users of its products, developing high-quality products that are custom-configured and sold at reasonable prices, and providing industry-leading service and support.

The first key element, maintaining direct relationships with end users of its products, has always been standard practice in all distribution channels used by Dell. For example, even when Dell attempted to market its products through mass merchandisers such as CompUSA, Sam's Club, and Best Buy (a practice stopped in 1994), it required all end-user buyers to register their computers with Dell at the time of purchase. This process enabled the company to enter the new buyer into its catalog/mail-out database and immediately begin a direct relationship with the buyer.

The second key element of Dell Computer's success is its commitment to developing high-quality products that are custom-configured and sold at reasonable prices. The company prides itself on providing the highest-quality components and testing standards in the industry, and through innovative market segmentation it offers a combination of competitively priced products and promotional bundles targeting specific market segments.

The third key element of Michael Dell's strategic vision that contributed to the success of Dell Computer Corporation is the unrelenting emphasis on the customer. Since customer satisfaction is dogma at Dell Computer, industry-leading warranty packages, installation, maintenance, repair services, and user support have always been first priority. Dell Computer was the first company in the industry to offer manufacturer-direct, toll-free, 24-hour technical support service and next-day, on-site service programs that have become standard in the industry.

Distinctive Competency

The distinctive competency of Dell Computer in its early years resided in its innovative direct selling model more than anything else. Indeed, in several interviews in the 1980s, Michael Dell stressed his belief that the company's distribution channel was *the* most efficient way to market personal computers. Even the company's advertising reflected Dell's belief. For example, in the mid-1980s, company print advertisements contained a picture of a computer store with a red X drawn through it and featured the line "and you don't have to go there to buy it."

The success of the Dell selling model opened the door to literally hundreds of small PC manufacturers who found that they only needed a telephone number and/or a post office box to enter the marketplace. Ultimately, Dell Computer's success prompted even its largest competitors to expand into the direct channel. In 1992 both IBM and Compaq began offering new PC lines through direct distribution channels. IBM created a direct sales operation in late 1992 called Ambra, and Compaq created Compaq Direct in attempts to "Dell-ize" their selling methods.

What currently keeps Dell Computer competitive in the PC market is its ability to efficiently deliver new value-added services. It is becoming more and more difficult to distinguish among personal computers on the basis of technology alone, and customers expect more value at lower prices. Therefore, Dell approaches the PC market (which has effectively become a commodity market because of the industry's adoption of open standards) with an array of custom-made products and services. These products and services clearly set the company apart from its competitors.

In addition to its direct selling model, Dell Computer Corporation possesses a second distinction that sets the company apart from its competitors. The computers it sells are "built to order" in that virtually all of its computers are assembled and shipped within three to five days of payment receipt. One implication of this built-to-order production and marketing strategy is that each buyer can have a computer that has been configured specifically to fit its exact needs (including a unique suite of preloaded software). It also means that the company has a minimal finished product inventory (and thus minimal inventory carrying costs) and can take advantage of the constantly decreasing component prices that have characterized the industry in recent years. Simultaneously, the company has minimized the risk of having too many obsolete components in inventory.

Michael Dell's strategic vision has been very successful in part because the company focuses on sophisticated buyers and users (such as those typically found in large corporations). These are not first-time buyers or users but individuals who are very knowledgeable about their computer needs and are comfortable in ordering a computer system from a catalog or over the telephone. They also tend to want higher performance systems than first-time buyers and to be less price sensitive.

Product Offering

Dell Computer's product offering consists of desktop computers, notebook computers, and network servers. With respect to desktop computers, Dell offers two product lines, the OptiPlex and the Dimension. The OptiPlex line was developed for major account customers that need advanced features, high performance, and the ability to network with other computers. OptiPlex computers use industry-standard architecture and components and support a wide range of industry-compatible operating and network systems; they are designed to be easily upgradable as new technology becomes available. At the present time, the OptiPlex line offers a three-year warranty and extensive service and support programs. In general, OptiPlex computers are slightly more expensive than Dimension computers. Major competitors are Compaq, IBM, and Hewlett-Packard.

The Dimension line of desktop computers was developed for smaller, independent users, such as small businesses and self-sufficient home users. Although designed for technologically sophisticated users, the Dimension line is intended to be a more aggressively priced computer line than the OptiPlex. As such, it competes head-to-head with Gateway. The Dimension line has a one-year warranty and is sold primarily through the Dell Direct Division.

The company also offers a notebook computer product line called the Dell Latitude line. This product line is designed for the high-end notebook customer looking for a desktop alternative or a powerful multimedia system. In addition, Dell Computer offers the PowerEdge line of network servers that can be configured for various uses. Finally, in addition to its computer products, Dell Computer offers a wide range of peripheral hardware and software products through its Dellware Catalog. This catalog, which is distributed quarterly to more than a million owners of Dell computers, offers more than 6,500 popular software and hardware add-ons.

Company Sales Organization

At the beginning of 1996, Dell Computer Corporation's worldwide operations were organized according to four geographical regions. Dell Americas focuses on the United States, Canada, and Latin America. Dell Europe focuses on Western European countries. All products sold in this region are assembled at Dell's plant in Limerick, Ireland. Dell Japan focuses only on that country; it was created to focus on what was thought to be (and has turned out to be) a major marketing opportunity. Dell Asia Pacific focuses on Pacific Rim countries (except for Japan) and countries such as Australia. In 1995 Dell opened an assembly plant in Penang, Malaysia, to service this region.

Over time, the company evolved from (1) relying solely on direct marketing to (2) utilizing direct-response ads and telemarketing to (3) employing field account teams. These teams consist of sales representatives, customer service specialists, and systems engineers that are charged with (1) developing comprehensive relationships with large businesses and institutions and (2) building repeat sales through focused customer management. In general, smaller businesses and individuals tend to purchase from Dell because of its low prices (but typically purchase only a small number of low-margin computers). Larger corporations, government agencies, and medical and educational institutions are much larger markets for large numbers of higher priced (and higher margin) computers.

The Education, State & Local Government Business Unit is one of five business units in Dell Americas. The others focus respectively on the federal government (FED), large corporations (LCA), medium-sized businesses (PAD), and individuals and small businesses (Dell Direct). ESL possesses the general sales structure set forth in Exhibit 3. Inside sales managers concentrate most of their attention on inbound tele-

EXHIBIT 3

ESL Sales Organization

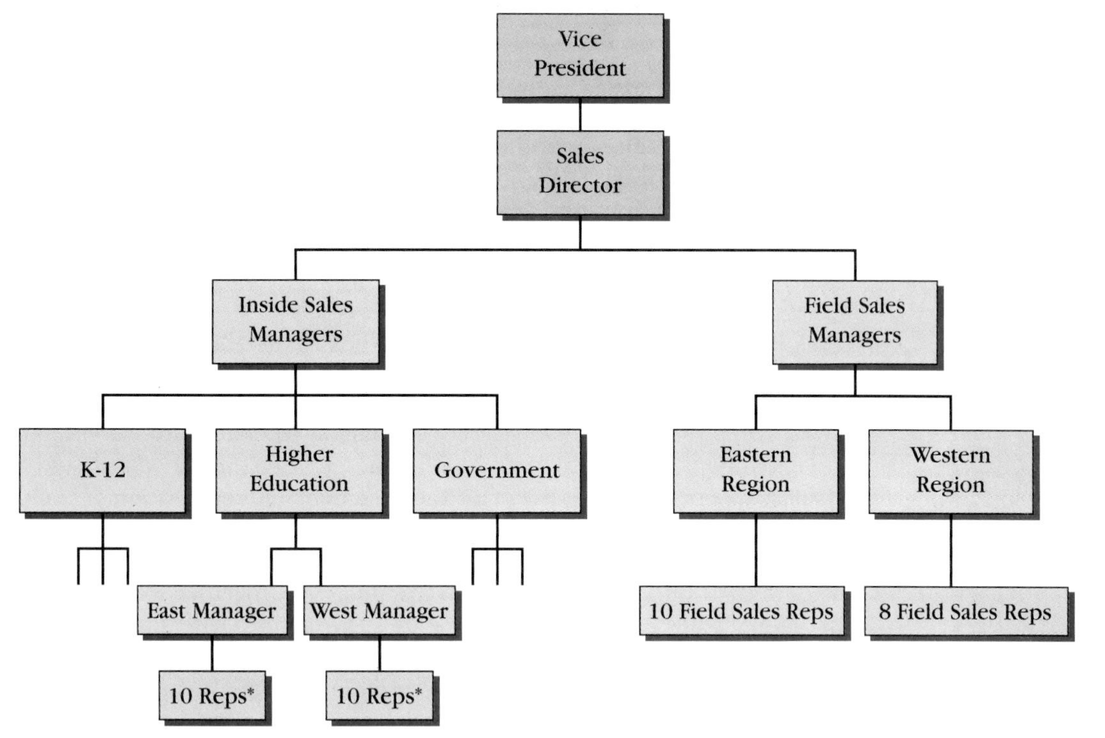

*Primarily inbound telephone sales.

Source: Company records.

phone ordering; typically, telephone sales representatives report to a sales manager. ESL field sales managers are tasked with originating and servicing major accounts on a face-to-face basis and in turn supervise field sales representatives. In addition, the unit has a marketing program manager dedicated to the higher education market, as well as several marketing-related support positions.

Regardless of how a sales lead is generated in the United States, the typical way to purchase a Dell Computer is to telephone the company. This is so even if the buyer is a major corporate customer making a large repeat purchase and a Dell sales team and Dell field engineers currently interact with the corporation's employees. Although provisions are being made for electronic data interchanges with major accounts and a World Wide Web site on the Internet is being expanded, the telephone remains the primary means of communicating.

When a telephone call is made to Dell (1-800-BUY-DELL), a computer voice answers and directs the caller to choose one of the following options:

- Dial the extension number, if known, to reach an individual.
- Dial "2" to make an institution, education, or large business purchase.
- Dial "3" to make a small business or personal purchase.
- Dial "4" to report problems with an order.
- Dial "5" if technical support is required.
- Stay on the line for an operator if none of these options is appropriate.

By answering a series of queries, the caller is channeled to the appropriate source for taking computer orders, responding to inquiries, or resolving problems. Dial-in options 2 and 3 correspond to Dell's two major business segments in the United States.

■ THE HIGHER EDUCATION MARKET

The higher education market in the United States consists of more than 3,600 institutions of higher learning. These institutions, though, are far from uniform and are widely scattered geographically. Less than half (about 1,500) are two-year junior colleges or community colleges. There are 92 large state-supported universities, as well as some six dozen elite private universities, that offer bachelor's degrees, master's degrees, and doctoral degrees. In addition, there are both public (500+) and private four-year colleges (1,500+). The educational missions of these various institutions differ considerably, as do enrollments; enrollments vary from 200 or so undergraduate students to more than 52,000 undergraduate and graduate students.

In academic year 1995–1996, nearly 14.4 million students enrolled in higher education institutions, and by the year 2000 about 15.5 million students should be enrolled. Slightly less than 40 percent of these students attended a junior college or community college. About 12 percent were graduate students; foreign students comprised 3 percent of all college students. Exhibit 4 shows the number of high school graduates in the United States from 1980 through 1995, together with the projected number of graduates each year through 2004. According to federal government estimates, approximately 62 percent of all high school graduates enroll in an institution of higher learning. Of those who were to enroll in a college or university in the fall of 1996, nearly half were expected to have their own computer.

Of the approximately 1.4 million full-time college and university administrators, faculty, and staff members in the United States, more than 800,000 are faculty mem-

EXHIBIT 4

High School Graduates (Millions)

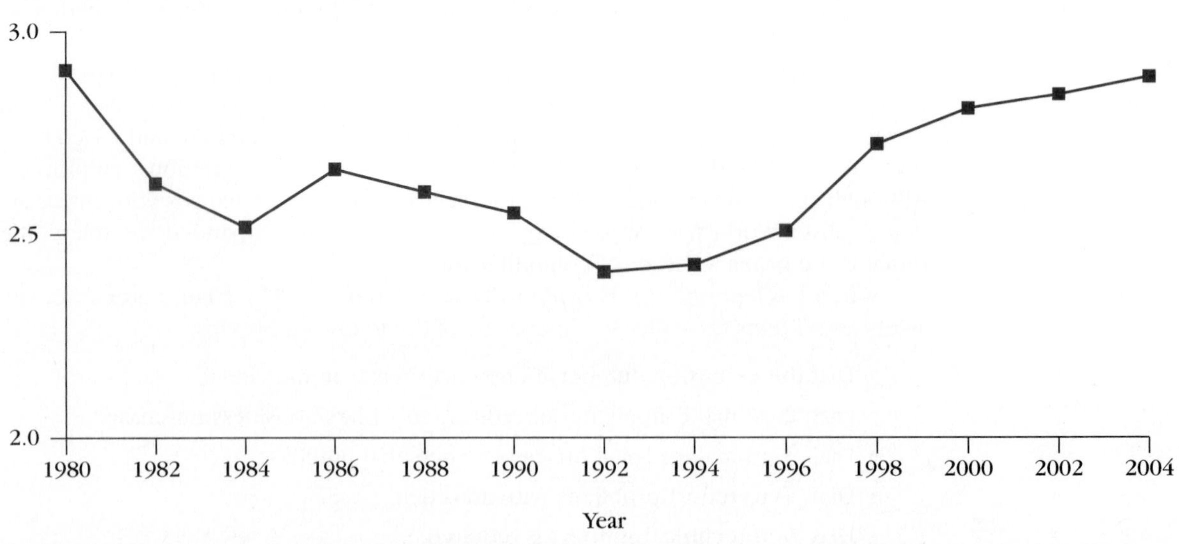

Source: Kenneth C. Green, "Campus Computing, 1995," Sixth National Survey of Desktop Computing in Higher Education, November 1995.

EXHIBIT 5

Ownership of Personal Computers

	1991		1993		1995	
Type of Institution	*Students*	*Faculty*	*Students*	*Faculty*	*Students*	*Faculty*
Public university	19%	42%	27%	50%	33%	62%
Private university	32%	54%	39%	63%	40%	68%
Public 4-year college	17%	43%	21%	45%	28%	54%
Private 4-year college	18%	43%	23%	50%	32%	58%
Community college	15%	31%	18%	39%	26%	46%

Source: Kenneth C. Green, "Campus Computing, 1995," Sixth National Survey of Desktop Computing in Higher Education, November 1995.

bers. Many of these faculty members use computers provided by their institutions. Even so, a sizable number have purchased their own computers. Exhibit 5 shows the percentage of college and university faculty members who have their own computers. For comparison, student ownership is also provided. Ownership within both groups has steadily increased since 1991.

The higher education market for computers, estimated to be $5 to $6 billion annually, is divided into two distinct segments. One segment consists of the higher education institutions themselves, primarily departments or specific organizational units. The second segment consists of faculty, staff, and students (FSS). This segment is estimated to account for 75 to 80 percent of the total market potential. The two segments differ with respect to their computing needs and purchasing behaviors. The department segment is essentially a type of major account that requires many computers, large-scale computing capacity, and networking capabilities. Purchases are frequently made through long-term contracts. The FSS segment is very "consumer-like" in that segment members tend to be relatively price conscious and to purchase low volumes of equipment (typically single units), often by personal check or credit card.

In 1995, the higher education market accounted for about 40 percent of ESL unit sales. One analyst in the ESL unit estimated that unit sales were split 80–20 between the department and FSS segments in 1995.

Microcenters

Eighty-one college or university microcomputer centers, or "microcenters," exist in the United States. These microcenters, which are usually owned by larger colleges or universities and are frequently part of a campus bookstore, coordinate the computer purchases of the respective colleges and universities and serve as computer resellers for their faculties, staffs, and students. For the FSS segment, microcenters effectively act as full-service (sales, service) retail stores. Only individuals associated with a college or university that has a microcenter are allowed to buy a computer and software from the center at a price that has traditionally been less than that available from retail stores. What differentiates microcenters from other higher education retailing operations selling computers is that microcenters carry an inventory of computers. Apple Computer, which has the largest share of the higher education market (estimated to be in the neighborhood of 56 percent), requires a microcenter to stock inventory before it will enter into a higher education contract.

Microcenters carry the computers of companies that have specific higher education programs (e.g., Apple and Dell). They cannot sell or advertise the computers to the general public. Generally, microcenters stock computers that provide the best quality and price values. Lower-quality computers are not stocked because of the higher warranty costs incurred over the lifetime of the computer.

Microcenters are essentially customer driven because they always try to find the best value for their customers. The type of computers they offer depends largely on customer demand. Microcenters want to meet the needs of their customers and as a policy will not recommend one computer over another. Their customers are primarily students because the institutions themselves do not necessarily purchase their computers through them.

Because students are microcenters' main customers, the choice of computer carried is largely dependent on price. Historically, Apple gave the highest discounts to higher education, relative to other channels, although in the past year other PC manufacturers have increased their discounts to become more competitive. Microcenters make money primarily through the sale of computers, not hardware peripherals or software.

Because of its focus on education, Apple Computer has traditionally supported campus microcenters by its generous pricing and promotional programs. In effect, Apple Computer has covered the overhead of the microcenters in return for being allowed to dominate shelf space and advertising programs. Most microcenters also offer one or two other brands of computers so that the institution and the FSS segment have a non-Macintosh choice.

In 1991, Dell Computer launched a microcenter-focused program to leverage its relationship with those colleges and universities having campus microcenters. This program represented a departure from Dell's direct selling approach and created a new retail distribution channel as part of Dell Computer's higher education strategy. At the end of 1995, Dell Computer offered its products through numerous university microcenters. Collectively, the combined enrollment of these universities was about 1.3 million students. Microcenter sales accounted for 35 to 40 percent of Dell's revenues in the higher education market in FY 1996. The rest of Dell Computer's higher education market revenues resulted from purchases made directly from educational institutions calling Dell's 1-800 number.

Although large higher education institutions tend to be characterized by decentralized computer buying (thus fragmenting the market), recent computer networking requirements have resulted in more centralized network support and maintenance functions. Smaller colleges, though, tend to be characterized by both centralized purchasing and centralized support. In general, there is little consistency across colleges and universities in terms of purchasing institutional computers.

Most Dell computers sold in the higher education market are bundled with software and peripheral products into a system. The average higher education system price for the OptiPlex line in 1995 was $2,381. This compares with an average higher education system price of $2,423 for the Dimension line and an average system price of $3,060 for the Latitude notebook line. In 1995, the average gross margin of an OptiPlex computer in the higher education market was 24 percent. The average gross margin of a Dimension computer was 15 percent in the higher education market, whereas that for a Latitude notebook was 21 percent. Exhibit 6 contains a typical Dell advertisement for the education market.

Because of Apple Computer's financial problems, considerable uncertainty existed in the higher education marketplace. Apple was expected to restructure its campus reseller program, probably by reducing its financial support of that channel. Simultaneously, rumors circulated that Compaq Computer, the largest manufacturer and marketer of personal computers, would also be entering the higher education market. The difficulty that the uncertainty presented for companies like Dell was compounded by stagnant or even declining higher education budgets, especially for infrastructure equipment such as computers.

EXHIBIT 6

Typical Dell Computer Corporation Advertisement for Education Market

IF NOT APPLE, WHO?

(Hint)

If Apple's not in your future plans, why not build your computer infrastructure around industry standard technology? Dell has every type of system schools could possibly need, a sales team dedicated to the education market and the unique ability to quickly customize our systems for teachers, students, administrators and harried technology coordinators.

☆ Guaranteed network compatibility on all industry standard, non-proprietary network operating systems

☆ Guaranteed next-business-day on-site service[‡] for desktops and servers

☆ Customization of computers, from the classroom to the District Superintendent's Office

☆ Ability to preload software available through Dell

☆ Variety of multimedia software for creating learning stations

☆ Computers drop shipped to each school in your district

☆ Educational software alliances with Computer Curriculum Corporation and Jostens Learning

☆ Administrative software alliance with McGraw-Hill School Systems

☆ Networking partnership with 3Com

☆ Platform partnerships with Intel® and Microsoft

3Com Network Ready

DESKTOP: DELL® OPTIPLEX® G 5133L
133MHz PENTIUM® PROCESSOR

- 16MB EDO RAM/1GB EIDE HDD
- 64-bit PCI Local Bus Video/1MB Video Memory (Upgradeable to 2MB)
- 14LS Monitor (13.2" v.i.s., .28NI)
- Low-Profile Chassis
- Factory Installed MS® Windows® 95 (30 Days Free Support)
- 3 Year Limited Warranty[†]

★ ***Add an 8X EIDE CD-ROM for just $149 more.***
★ ***Double your RAM to 32MB for just $199 more.***

$1574 Product Code #300237

NOTEBOOK: DELL LATITUDE® LM P100SD
100MHz PENTIUM PROCESSOR

- Large 11.3" Dual Scan SVGA Color Display (800 x 600 Resolution)
- 8MB RAM
- 810MB Upgradeable HDD (1.3GB Max)
- Upgradeable Modular 6X Speed CD-ROM
- Multi-Function Options Bay w/CD-ROM, Floppy or Optional 2nd Li-Ion Battery
- Smart Lithium Ion Battery
- PCI Bus Architecture w/256KB L2 Cache
- Integrated 16-bit Sound with Stereo Speakers and Line-out Jacks
- 128-bit High Performance Video Controller with Integrated Video RAM
- Infrared Port for Wireless Connectivity
- Playback Software for Full Motion Video Clips
- Touchpad Pointing Device with Palmrest
- Win95 Mobile Solution Pack Software Bundle
- 3 Year Limited Warranty

★ ***Upgrade to a 133MHz Pentium processor with a 12.1" Active Matrix Display for $800.***

$2599 Product Code #500769

NOTEBOOK: DELL LATITUDE LM P100SD
100MHz PENTIUM PROCESSOR

All of the above features plus:

- 16MB RAM (40MB Max RAM)
- 810MB Upgradeable Hard Drive (1.3GB Max)
- MS Office Pro V7.0, Win95
- Dual Compartment Carrying Case

★ ***Add a 28.8 XJACK® /Cabled Modem for Internet Access for only $259 more.***

$2999 Product Code #500770

DESKTOP: DELL OPTIPLEX GX 5166M
166MHz PENTIUM PROCESSOR

- 32MB EDO RAM/2GB EIDE HDD
- 256KB Pipeline Burst Cache (Upgradeable to 512KB)
- 64-bit PCI Local Bus Video/ 2MB Video Memory
- 15TX Monitor (13.7" v.i.s., .26NI)
- Mid-Size Chassis
- Full-Motion MPEG Video
- Integrated 3Com® EtherLink® III
- Integrated Sound Blaster Compatible Audio
- Factory Installed MS Office Pro for Windows 95
- Factory Installed MS Windows 95 (30 Days Free Support)
- 3 Year Limited Warranty

★ ***Add an 8X EIDE CD-ROM for $149 more.***

PICTURED SYSTEM

$2649 Product Code #300235

SERVER: DELL POWEREDGE® SP
133MHz PENTIUM PROCESSOR
(Expandable to Dual Processor)

- 32MB Parity RAM/512KB L2 Cache
- 2GB SCSI Hard Drive
- 15LS Monitor (13.7" v.i.s., .28NI)
- PCI SCSI Controller 2940
- 3Com PCI 10/100 Ethernet Adapter
- 6X SCSI CD-ROM Drive
- SafeSite™ Server Management System
- 1 Year DirectLine™ NOS support
- 3 Year BusinessCare℠ Service Program
- 3 Year Limited Warranty

★ ***Factory Installed MS Windows NT® Server 3.51***

$5498 Product Code #200125

DELL®
800-433-2958
http://www.dell.com
Mon-Fri 7am-9pm CT • Sat 10am-6pm CT
Sun 12pm-5pm In Canada,[‡] call 800-839-0148
Keycode #20010

Source: Company records.

Moreover, the PC market in general had recently been barraged by the aggressive pricing policies of mass merchandisers such as CompUSA and Best Buy. One consequence was that margins available to microcenters were under increasing pressure. To keep in touch with the microcenters that Dell used, Jeni, along with the higher education sales team, established an advisory council of microcenter managers from which it obtained periodic input. On the basis of a recent survey of its council, one ESL analyst concluded that Dell

- could do a better job providing and coordinating product information to microcenters;
- had potential pricing problems both across Dell divisions and between product lines; and
- needed improvement in its service and support activities for microcenter purchases.

Apparently, however, Dell was not the only company doing a less than satisfactory job with the microcenter business.

■ THE PHONE CALL

Jeni's phone call was from one of the more influential members of the College Reseller Association, a national group of microcenter managers that worked to promote the microcenter channel. Apparently concerned about ensuring the financial well-being and competitiveness of its members, the Association wanted to meet with each of the leading computer hardware manufacturers to discuss how it might be able to negotiate more aggressive prices or discounts for its members. The meetings were to be held over the next two weeks, and it was the Association's intention to select one vendor whose program it would endorse over the coming academic year. Although the Association was clear that its endorsement would by no means be a mandate to its members to buy from that vendor, it would certainly encourage all of its members to at least consider the endorsed vendor. This posed yet another challenge in Jeni's development of a higher education plan. Should Dell aggressively try to become the vendor of choice in this market or, given the uncertainty surrounding the future of the channel, should the company back off from this strategy?

■ THE HIGHER EDUCATION PLANNING TEAM

Dell Computer's Higher Education Planning Team was created early in 1996. Knowing that she would be asked to construct a plan to meet the financial objectives for higher education next year, Jeni pulled together a team of people within ESL to analyze the situation and provide input. This team included several sales managers, a financial analyst, a research analyst, and some of the account executives who worked with higher education customers on a daily basis. After collecting and summarizing information for nearly a month, Jeni condensed it into several reports. Some of the information is presented in Exhibits 7 through 9 (pages 327 and 328).

From the reports, Jeni and the planning team knew that enrollment in higher education institutions was likely to increase over the next decade because of the projected number of high school graduates. They noted that the average age of college and university students was likely to increase, as were the number and percentage of

EXHIBIT 7

Selected Responses to a Survey of the Readership of a Higher Education Publication (Part 1)

	Subgroup				
Response	*Senior Administrators*	*Department Directors/ Managers*	*Academic Officers*	*Faculty Members*	*Information Technology Administrators*
Use of PC					
Research	37%	44%	65%	78%	61%
Instruction	29%	44%	70%	90%	52%
Reports	93%	94%	94%	76%	94%
Communication	91%	93%	90%	86%	95%
Access records	58%	66%	65%	46%	69%
Internet	83%	85%	84%	79%	93%
Involved in purchasing or selecting institution's computers in past 12 months	70%	70%	74%	49%	90%
Mean number of computers purchased	59	26	37	30	160
Will be involved in purchasing or selecting institution's computers in next 12 months	71%	60%	70%	42%	86%

Source: Adapted from a 1996 *Chronicle of Higher Education* report titled "Information Technology and Higher Education."

EXHIBIT 8

Selected Responses to a Survey of the Readership of a Higher Education Publication (Part 2)

	Subgroup				
Response	*Senior Administrators*	*Department Directors/ Managers*	*Academic Officers*	*Faculty Members*	*Information Technology Administrators*
Desktop computer brands considered for institutional purchases					
Apple Macintosh	49%	47%	52%	51%	62%
IBM	57%	43%	47%	47%	43%
Compaq	23%	16%	20%	20%	33%
Dell	21%	18%	19%	19%	41%
Hewlett-Packard	21%	14%	17%	19%	33%
Digital	16%	9%	12%	10%	25%
Other	40%	32%	38%	31%	48%

Source: Adapted from a 1996 *Chronicle of Higher Education* report titled "Information Technology and Higher Education."

EXHIBIT 9

Selected Responses to a Survey of the Readership of a Higher Education Publication (Part 3)

	Subgroup				
Response	*Senior Administrators*	*Department Directors/ Managers*	*Academic Officers*	*Faculty Members*	*Information Technology Administrators*
Source of institutional computer purchases in past 12 months*					
Direct from manufacturer	4%	29%	35%	20%	52%
Campus computer center	18%	25%	21%	14%	22%
Computer-only reseller	23%	16%	17%	9%	47%
Bookstore	10%	9%	8%	4%	15%
None purchased	28%	33%	31%	58%	8%
Preferred source of institutional computer purchases					
Direct from manufacturer	50%	43%	50%	42%	43%
Campus computer center	16%	28%	21%	23%	18%
Computer-only reseller	22%	21%	18%	22%	26%
Bookstore	12%	8%	11%	13%	13%

* Percentages reflect the use of multiple sources.

Source: Adapted from a 1996 *Chronicle of Higher Education* report titled "Information Technology and Higher Education."

minority students. They further noted that both student and faculty ownership of computers continued to grow (even though Dell did not currently have programs specifically targeted to individuals).

From other sources the planning team knew that institutions of higher education were somewhat behind business and government in the use of personal computers, and that some faculty members were even less knowledgeable about computers than were their students (an estimated two-thirds of the freshmen projected to enter in the fall of 1996 would have received computer instruction in high school). Given the increased emphasis on the computer as a learning tool, and on the need to be computer literate in both educational and work environments, the team wondered whether the market for computers was likely to grow in higher education through the remainder of the decade. This question was again raised by one research finding that indicated that about 34 percent of colleges and universities currently recommended or required students to have their own computers (the range was from 11 percent for community colleges to 48 percent for private colleges and universities). Of those institutions recommending or requiring a computer, one in seven specified that a particular brand, configuration, or type of computer be owned.

The Meeting

The meeting Jeni called was a brainstorming session. Now that everyone on the team had a chance to review the data, it was time to throw some ideas out on the table for discussion. Jeni had asked Sylvia Drum, ESL's director of marketing, to facilitate the meeting. Drum began by thanking the team for all the background work that had been done thus far, and then said she would like to open the floor to get the team's initial impressions on what the options were for addressing the higher education market in the upcoming year. As the team members spoke, Drum documented their thoughts and comments on the whiteboard:

Do nothing—the uncertainty in the market will cause people to look for alternatives—we're already one of the top PC companies in the country, we'll get the business—invest in other segments where there seems to be great growth opportunity, such as K-12 or state government.
Go all out with the microcenters—a window of opportunity—we could own this channel with all the uncertainty in the market.
Develop a student purchase program—huge market—renewable every year—but what do we sell them (Dimension or Optiplex?)—what about notebooks?
Scale back on microcenters—their future is too risky—too many eggs in one basket—go after direct business from universities instead of relying on microcenters.

Interesting, thought Drum. They all seem to have very strong opinions as to the "correct answer." "OK," she said to the team, "it appears that all of you have been doing a lot of thinking about this. Now comes the hard part. We need to choose. And choosing is difficult because it means focusing on the one or two areas where we believe we can be successful next year and letting some of the other options and ideas sit on the shelf for a while. So let me give you a little more information, and then I'm going to turn the meeting back to Diane."

"First, assume that our total marcom [marketing/communications] budget for higher education is going to be $1 million next year. That needs to cover advertising, direct mail, trade shows, computer fairs, and any other marketing communications activities, including the Internet. Second, let's assume that four of the people in the field organization can be dedicated to higher education beginning October 1. Further assume that we will have the ability to hire eight additional sales reps for this business unit by the end of December. Finally, should you come up with a plan that can deliver substantial upside to the revenue target, don't be afraid to ask for additional resources—people or dollars—to attain it. Of course, you need to be reasonable.

"I know that Matthew Roberts is looking for a first-pass recommendation by the end of next week—so we don't have much time. I would like to see a preliminary recommendation by the beginning of next week, and the financials to support it." She then asked Jeni to take over, and left as the team began debating the various pros and cons of the options listed on the whiteboard.

CASE

Amway Japan Limited

In April 1997, overlooking the cherry trees in full bloom outside his office at Amway Japan Limited (AJL) in Tokyo, Bruce L. Stephens, President of AJL, pondered how to reverse the first performance decline the company has experienced since entering the Japanese direct selling market in 1979.

Established as the tenth overseas subsidiary of Amway Corporation of Ada, Michigan, AJL had grown to become the most successful company in the Amway group, accounting for 30 percent of its worldwide estimated retail sales of $6.8 billion in 1996. In FY 1996, AJL's net sales were up 19.2 percent to ¥212.2 billion ($1.9 billion); net income grew 21.8 percent to ¥28.1 billion ($257 million).[1] The number of its core distributorships expanded 11.6 percent to exceed the all-time record of one million.[2] Exhibit 1 summarizes AJL's recent performance.

AJL's first half results in FY 1997, however, showed net sales declining to ¥96.3 billion, down 11.6 percent from the first half of the previous year, and net income down 27.6 percent to ¥11.6 billion. AJL's revised year-end forecasts projected 1.3 percent annual sales growth which would bring net sales to ¥215 billion, and a 6.8 percent decline in net income to ¥26.2 billion.

Bruce L. Stephens, 1966 Harvard MBA, joined Amway Corporation in 1990 as General Manager of Amway GmbH in Germany and became President of AJL in 1991. He had previous experience in the Asia operation of U.S. firms including PepsiCo, RJR Tobacco, Seagram, and Tupperware. Having succeeded in doubling AJL's sales during the five years of his presidency, Stephens now needed to develop a strategy not only for rebuilding growth in the second half of FY 1997, but also for achieving AJL's long-term goal of sales of ¥300 billion by FY 2000.

■ DIRECT SELLING INDUSTRY

The direct selling industry was growing at 8 percent annually, with worldwide sales of $72 billion in 1995, and more than 20 million people in the world engaged in direct selling, on either a part-time or full-time basis. In 1996, Japan was the largest market, with sales of $30 billion and 2 million distributors, followed by the U.S. with $18 billion sales and 7 million distributors. Exhibit 2 on page 332 overviews the industry, with particular details on Japan and the U.S.

---

[1] Exchange rate was approximately ¥109/$1 in 1997.

[2] Amway used "distributorship" as an official counting unit for its distributor membership. Under this counting method, a single person, a married couple, and parent-child team were considered as one "distributorship." In practice, the terms "distributorship" and "distributor" were used interchangeably.

Doctoral Candidate Yoshinori Fujikawa of Harvard Business School and Dr. Patrick Reinmoeller of Japan Advanced Institute of Science and Technology prepared this case under the supervision of Professors David J. Arnold and John A. Quelch as the basis for class discussion rather than to illustrate either effective or ineffective handling of an administrative situation. Some figures and names were disguised for security and competitive reasons.

EXHIBIT 1

Selected Financial and Company Data, FY 1992–FY 1996[a]

	FY 1992	FY 1993	FY 1994	FY 1995	FY 1996	FY 1996[d]	FY 92–FY 96	
Income Statement Data (¥ Million Except for Per-Share Amounts)						($ Thousand)	% Sales	CAGR (%)
Net sales	¥123,253	¥130,028	¥157,556	¥177,991	¥212,196	$1,946,752	100.0%	14.5%
Cost of sales[b]	¥36,087	¥37,319	¥43,576	¥47,515	¥55,588	$509,982	26.2%	11.4%
Gross profit	¥87,166	¥92,709	¥113,980	¥130,476	¥156,608	$1,436,771	73.8%	15.8%
Operating expenses:								
Distributor incentives[c]	¥31,908	¥34,001	¥42,652	¥47,885	¥57,044	$523,339	26.9%	15.6%
Distribution expenses	¥7,653	¥7,773	¥8,324	¥8,853	¥9,839	$90,266	4.6%	6.5%
Selling and administrative expense	¥15,188	¥16,810	¥19,616	¥24,022	¥28,355	$260,138	13.4%	16.9%
Total operating expenses	¥54,749	¥58,584	¥70,592	¥80,760	¥95,238	$873,743	44.9%	14.8%
Operating income	¥32,417	¥34,125	¥43,388	¥49,716	¥61,370	$563,028	28.9%	17.3%
Other income	¥3,487	¥2,485	¥2,557	¥1,733	¥1,309	$12,009	0.6%	−21.7%
Income before income taxes	¥35,904	¥36,610	¥45,945	¥51,449	¥62,679	$575,037	29.5%	14.9%
Income taxes	¥19,373	¥20,759	¥25,341	¥28,387	¥34,598	$317,413	16.3%	15.6%
Net income	¥16,531	¥15,851	¥20,604	¥23,062	¥28,081	$257,624	13.2	14.2%
Net income per share	¥110.49	¥105.94	¥137.70	¥154.13	¥187.83	$1.72		14.2%
Cash dividends per share	¥50.00	¥60.00	¥140.00	¥190.00	¥125.00	$1.15		25.7%
Shares outstanding (thousands)	149,625	149,625	149,625	149,625	149,502	149,502		0.0%
Balance Sheet Data (¥ Million Except for Per-Share Amounts)						($ Thousand)		CAGR (%)
Inventory	¥10,300	¥9,900	¥11,000	¥11,400	¥12,500	$114,679		5.0%
Working capital	¥57,000	¥62,300	¥68,900	¥43,600	¥27,000	$247,706		−17.0%
Total assets	¥93,000	¥102,000	¥116,500	¥121,800	¥116,200	$1,066,055		5.7%
Total shareholder's equity	¥64,700	¥72,300	¥79,200	¥77,900	¥63,900	$586,239		-0.3%
ROA	18.4	16.3	18.9	19.4	23.6	23.6		6.4%
ROE	27.2	23.1	27.2	29.4	39.6	39.6		9.8%
Other Data								CAGR (%)
Number of employees	746	769	871	960	1,044			8.8%
Number of core distributors	752,000	816,000	896,000	980,000	1,093,000			9.8%
Number of direct distributors	4,600	4,800	5,900	7,100	8,500			16.6%
Core distributor renewal rate	67.6%	71.7%	72.8%	71.8%	73.0%			1.9%

[a] Fiscal year ended August 31. For example, FY 1996 was from September 1, 1995 to August 31, 1996.

[b] Approximately 65% of the AJL's cost of sales for FY 1992–FY 1996 represented purchase of products from Amway Corporation (Ada, Michigan) which AJL paid in yen. Prices of these products were determined with an implicit dollar/yen exchange rate which AJL calculated to be ¥91/$1.00 until FY 1996 and which has changed to ¥107/$1.00 from FY 1997.

[c] Distributor incentives, which were principally in the form of bonus payments to distributors based on performance, fluctuated with the sales volume.

[d] The U.S. dollar amounts were calculated at the approximate rate of exchange prevailing on August 31, 1996, of ¥109/$1.00.

Source: Amway Japan Limited annual reports 1994–1996.

EXHIBIT 2

World Direct Selling Industry, 1995

Country	*Sales ($ Million)*	*Distributors (000)*	*Country*	*Sales ($ Million)*	*Distributors (000)*
Japan	30,320	2,000	Netherlands	130	34
United States	16,550	6,300	Belgium	128	14
Germany	2,630	191	New Zealand	117	68
Mexico	2,000	900	Hong Kong	109	105
Brazil	1,950	850	Chile	108	80
Taiwan	1,770	2,000	Sweden	100	30
United Kingdom	1,474	450	Singapore	99	35
Korea	1,330	157	Poland	92	165
Italy	1,320	400	Portugal	83	34
France	1,100	250	Norway	80	8
Argentina	1,014	350	Finland	79	8
Australia	1,000	400	Turkey	75	110
Canada	844	600	Philippines	74	420
Spain	691	84	India	60	10
Malaysia	510	350	Hungary	59	116
Thailand	448	250	Uruguay	46	29
South Africa	300	100	Israel	45	8
Switzerland	196	6	Denmark	35	4
Austria	190	6	Slovenia	28	5
Indonesia	160	600	Czech Republic	22	19
Peru	160	100	Greece	22	24
			Ireland	22	6

Percent of Sales by Major Product Groups	*U.S.*	*Japan*
• Personal care products (cosmetics, skin care, etc.)	38.8%	41.0%
• Home/family care (cleaners, cookware, etc.)	34.4%	19.1%
• Services/miscellaneous/others (long distance calls, etc.)	10.3%	n.a.
• Wellness (vitamins, etc.)	9.2%	17.3%
• Leisure/educational (books, games, etc.)	7.3%	22.6%

Locus of Sales	*U.S.*	*Japan*
• In the home	59.0%	44.0%
• Over the phone	15.9%	n.a.
• In a workplace	14.8%	12.0%
• At a public event (fair, exhibition, shopping mall, etc.)	4.3%	6.0%
• Other locations	6.0%	38.0%

Sales Approach (Reported as % of Sales)	*U.S.*	*Japan*
• Individual/one-to-one selling	64.9%	n.a.
• Party plan/group sales	32.1%	n.a.
• Customer placing order directly with firm	1.6%	n.a.
• Others	1.4%	n.a.

Demographics of Salespeople	*U.S.*	*Japan*
• Female/Male	79%/21%	85%/15%
• Part-time/Full-time	89%/11%	90%/10%

Source: World Federation of Direct Selling Associations, U.S. Direct Selling Association, Japan Direct Selling Association.

Direct selling was a face-to-face method of selling to the consumer, not relying on fixed retail stores, product advertising, or direct mail. Salespeople called on consumers to show sample products and to obtain orders. The goods were then supplied by the company, either directly to the consumer or through the salespeople. Direct selling was considered as particularly suited to high quality household and personal products that benefited from detailed explanation or demonstration. Direct selling was usually distinguished from direct marketing, which comprised mail-order retailing, telemarketing, television direct response, and electronic shopping.

Direct selling companies employed several different approaches: door-to-door, person-to-person, and party plan. Traditional direct sales programs were often described as "door-to-door" business. The person contacting customers typically worked for the company as a sales representative. Closely supervised by the company, the individual was usually assigned a limited geographic territory and specific hours in which to sell the company's products. Normally, the salesperson only sought to sell to customers and would not recruit others to form a distributor network. Avon employed such a method, selling cosmetics through its army of "Avon Lady" representatives.

In contrast, the "person-to-person" method relied upon independent businesspeople acting as distributors for household or nutritional product companies such as Amway, Nu Skin, and Shaklee. The distributors purchased products wholesale from the manufacturer and sold them to end customers, who were typically their friends, families, and acquaintances. The method was also known as "network marketing" or "multilevel marketing," since the independent distributors often sponsored subdistributors, who in turn recruited others to expand their sales network. A distributor's compensation included margins on any direct sales to customers and a percentage of the sales of the entire sales group that (s)he sponsored.

In the "party plan" method, the salesperson, frequently called a counselor, consultant, or advisor, demonstrated products to a group of customers in the home of one customer. The hosting customer commonly received a commission, some free gifts, or extra price discounts. The sales associate usually followed up with customers to see if they needed more products, might be interested in hosting their own party, or even would like to represent the company. Some salespersons were employees of the company; others were independent. Tupperware (kitchenware) and Mary Kay (cosmetics) were known for this method.

AMWAY CORPORATION AND AMWAY JAPAN LIMITED

Amway, one of the largest direct selling companies in the world, operated in more than 70 countries and territories in 1996 with worldwide estimated retail sales of $6.8 billion, triple its sales in 1990. In 1996, Amway ranked fifth among the world's household products companies. Exhibit 3 (pages 334 and 335) summarizes Amway's global expansion and ranking. Amway group included Amway Corporation, headquartered in Ada, Michigan, and 44 international affiliates including the two publicly held companies, Tokyo-based Amway Japan Limited (AJL), which generated $1.9 billion, and Hong Kong-based Amway Asia Pacific Ltd., which recorded sales of $717 million in Australia, New Zealand, Malaysia, Thailand, Taiwan, Macao, Hong Kong, and China. Amway's largest markets included North America, Japan, Korea, and Italy. Approximately 70 percent of Amway's worldwide sales were generated outside North America and 50 percent from Asian markets.

Amway Corporation was founded in 1959 by Jay Van Andel and Richard M. DeVos, with the vision "to be the best business opportunity in the world." Starting with their first product, L.O.C. (Liquid Organic Cleaner) and the subsequently introduced laundry detergent, SA8, the co-founders offered a small circle of their friends the op-

EXHIBIT 3

Amway Worldwide Expansion and Sales Ranking, 1996

Amway's Worldwide Expansion

1962	Canada	1991	Korea
1971	Australia		Hungary
1973	United Kingdom		Brazil
1974	Hong Kong	1992	Portugal
1975	Germany		Indonesia
1976	Malaysia		Poland
1977	France	1993	Argentina
1978	Netherlands	1994	Czech Republic
1979	Japan		Turkey
1980	Switzerland		Slovakia
1982	Taiwan	1995	Slovenia
1983	Belgium		Uruguay
1985	Austria		El Salvador
	Panama		Honduras
	Italy		Chile
	New Zealand		China
1986	Spain	1996	Costa Rica
1987	Thailand		Greece
	Guatemala		Columbia
1990	Mexico		

Source: Amway Corporation, 1996 annual review.

Ranking	***Company***	***Headquarters***	***Sales ($ Billion)***
1	Unilever	United Kingdom	22.5
2	The Procter & Gamble Company	Cincinnati, OH	20.5
3	L'Oreal	France	9.4
4	Colgate-Palmolive Company	New York, NY	7.8
5	**Amway**	**Ada, MI**	**6.8**
6	Kao	Japan	6.4
7	Henkel KGaA	Germany	5.4
8	Shiseido	Japan	4.9
9	S.C. Johnson Wax	Racine, WI	3.8
10	The Este Lauder Companies	New York, NY	3.2
11	Joh. A. Benckiser GmbH	Germany	3.2
12	Reckitt & Coleman	United Kingdom	3.1
13	**Avon Products**	**New York, NY**	**2.9**
14	Wella AG	Germany	2.3
15	The Clorox Company	Oakland, CA	2.2
16	Sanofi	France	2.2
17	Revlon, Inc.	New York, NY	2.1
18	Lion	Japan	2.1
19	Beiersdorf AG	Germany	2.0

EXHIBIT 3 (continued)

Ranking	*Company*	*Headquarters*	*Sales ($ Billion)*
20	**Pola**	**Japan**	**1.9**
21	Kanebo	Japan	1.9
22	Sara Lee Corporation	Chicago, IL	1.8
23	Bristol-Myers Squibb Corporation	New York, NY	1.7
24	LVMH	France	1.7
25	Alberto-Culver Company	Melrose Park, IL	1.5
26	Ecolab, Inc.	St. Paul, MN	1.5
27	The Dial Corporation	Phoenix, AZ	1.4
28	The Gillette Company	Boston, MA	1.3
29	Johnson & Johnson	New Brunswick, NJ	1.2
30	**Mary Kay, Inc.**	**Dallas, TX**	**1.0**
31	**Nu Skin International**	**Provo, UT**	**1.0**
32	LG Household & Health Care	Korea	0.9
33	Pacific Corporation	Korea	0.9
34	The Limited	Columbus, OH	0.8
35	Natura Cosmetics	Brazil	0.8

Note: Bolded companies employed direct selling methods.
Source: *Household and Personal Products Industry (HAPPI)*, Internet home page, 1997.

portunity to become independent distributors using their direct sales approach, later known as the Amway Sales and Marketing Plan.

Growth was rapid, and the number of products grew to 150 by 1970. By 1997, distributors marketed 400 Amway brand products in the U.S., ranging from home care, housewares, personal care, to nutrition products. Research, development, and manufacture of products were mainly carried out in Ada, Michigan, with additional production facilities located in California, China, and South Korea. In the U.S. market, Amway also marketed 6,500 non-Amway brand name items through catalogues as well as a variety of services including voice messaging and long distance phone services. Amway's overseas affiliates mainly imported Amway products from the U.S., but in some cases also sold locally sourced products.

The core of the Amway direct selling method was the large network of independent distributors, which expanded to over 2.5 million worldwide in 1997. They were introduced into the Amway business by other distributors, and sold Amway products using the Amway Sales and Marketing Plan. Under the Plan, they earned income from the markup of products, a performance incentive based on a percentage of their sales volume, and other incentives based on the sales volume of those they sponsored.

Amway Corporation was privately held by the DeVos and Van Andel families. Major strategic issues were governed by the Policy Board, composed of the co-founders and their eight children. The Board was created in 1992 as an outgrowth of the founders' two-man Policy Committee. The day-to-day affairs of Amway's global operations were directed by Chairman Steve Van Andel and President Dick DeVos, the eldest sons of the two founders. The two second-generation leaders shared the Office of Chief Executive, leading a Global Senior Management Team in which Bruce L. Stephens of AJL participated.

Throughout its history, Amway had remained closely linked to its founders and their families. Every employee and distributor worldwide participated in a program to learn the company history and founding families business philosophy, known as "Founders' Vision, Mission, Fundamentals, and Values" (see Exhibit 4, page 336).

EXHIBIT 4

Founders' Vision, Mission, Fundamentals, and Values

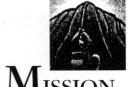

Founders' Fundamentals

Rich DeVos and Jay Van Andel built the Amway business on the following principles, which they and their families believe constitute a sound foundation for a meaningful life.

Freedom
Freedom is our natural state and most conducive environment in which to live, work, achieve, and grow. It allows for our belief in God and for the opportunity to build a meaningful, purposeful life. The Amway business recognizes, supports, and expands our freedom, which is both personal and economic. Thus, it is our responsibility to ensure, protect, and sustain our freedom.

Family
The family is our primary social structure, providing love and nurturing, heritage and legacy. The family provides us with a consistent set of values, and a framework for growth and the ability to thrive as individuals. The Amway business respects and supports the family, as evidenced by the Amway Policy Board and the prominence of "family" in Amway distributorships.

Vision

To be the best business opportunity in the world.

Hope
Hope gives us the power to transform our lives in positive ways. It is a force that allows us to envision dreams, establish goals, and achieve great things. By offering hope, we open windows of possibility for others, and it is why Amway speaks so meaningfully to the needs of people around the world.

Reward
Reward involves the shared action of giving and receiving. Reward helps us grow, either as the giver or the recipient, and there are many ways we are rewarded. At the most basic, it is to be acknowledged and loved as a person. To be rewarded also means to be recognized for one's commitments, valued for one's contributions, and compensated for one's efforts. Reward helps productivity flourish by providing both closure for one action and impetus for a new action. Reward is integral to the Amway business as we help each other grow as people and as entrepreneurs.

Values

These are the essential and enduring standards, not to be compromised, by which we operate the Amway business.

Partnership
Amway is built on the concept of partnership, beginning with the partnership between our founders. The partnership that exists among the founding families, distributors, and employees is our most prized possession. We always try to do what is in the long-term best interest of our partners, in a manner which increases trust and confidence. The success of Amway will reward all who have contributed to its success.

Integrity
Integrity is essential to our business success. We do what is right, not just whatever "works." Amway's success is measured not only in economic terms, but by the respect, trust, and credibility we earn.

Personal Worth
We acknowledge the uniqueness created in each individual. Every person is worthy of respect, and deserves fair treatment and the opportunity to succeed to the fullest extent of his or her potential.

Mission

Through the partnering of Distributors, Employees, and the Founding Families, and the support of quality products and service, we offer all people the opportunity to achieve their goals through the Amway Sales and Marketing Plan.

Achievement
We are builders and encouragers. We strive for excellence in all we do. Our focus is on continuous improvement, progress, and achievement of individual and group goals. We anticipate change, respond swiftly to it, take action to get the job done, and gain from our experiences. We encourage creativity and innovation.

Personal Responsibility
Each individual is responsible and accountable for achieving personal goals, as well as giving 100 percent effort in helping achieve corporate or team goals. By helping people help themselves, we further the potential for individual and shared success. We also have a responsibility to be good citizens in the communities where we live and work.

Free Enterprise
We are proud advocates of freedom and free enterprise. Human economic advancement is clearly proven to be best achieved in a free market economy.

Source: Company material.

Amway Japan Limited (AJL) was founded in 1977 and began operations in 1979 as the exclusive distribution vehicle in Japan for Amway Corporation. AJL was a publicly traded company on the Tokyo's Over-The-Counter Exchange since 1991, and became the tenth Japanese company to be listed on the New York Stock Exchange in 1994. The co-founders of Amway Corporation and the members of their families owned over 80 percent of AJL's shares. In 1996, AJL was the largest direct selling company in Japan and also the third largest foreign firm in Japan, after IBM Japan and Coca-Cola Company Japan (see Exhibit 5, page 338).

■ AMWAY BUSINESS

The Amway Business was based on a direct selling system in which distributors promoted and delivered a variety of Amway products to customers on a person-to-person basis. Amway products were exclusively distributed by AJL, not sold at regular retail stores, and there were no media advertisements for promoting particular products.

Amway Product

AJL started its operation with a small product line of household cleaners and detergents. In 1983, three hair care products and three nutritional supplements were added as the first products jointly developed by Amway Corporation and AJL. The cosmetics line, branded Artistry, followed in 1986. The "big ticket items" selling at over ¥150,000 (about $1,400), such as Amway Queen Cookware and Amway Water Treatment System, had functioned as major drivers for the recent sales expansion.

During the 1990s, the product line expanded rapidly. In 1997, AJL marketed some 140 items in the four product categories, including Personal Care (which accounted for 32.4 percent of FY 1996 sales), Housewares (29.5%), Nutrition (23.8%), and Home Care (10.2%). Exhibit 6 on page 339 illustrates the sales performance of each category from FY 1992 to FY 1996.

New products had played an important role in AJL's growth. New products, defined as products introduced during the preceding two years, accounted for a substantial share of AJL's total sales, ranging from 25 percent to 40 percent every year. Recent successful new products included Skin Care products in the line of the Artistry brand cosmetics, Amway Water Treatment System, and Triple X, an all inclusive dietary supplement. These products led their respective product categories in sales and collectively accounted for 47 percent of sales in 1996 (see Exhibit 6).

In 1997, approximately 65 percent of AJL's entire product line was imported from Amway Corporation, usually with the package design and product formula modified to suit Japanese consumer culture and lifestyles. In addition, AJL also developed some products solely for Japanese market, in cooperation with other suppliers. Examples of such joint product development included a kitchen knife set developed with Henckels of Germany, and the Amway Induction Range and a coffee maker developed with Sharp Corporation.

Amway Distributors

Amway distributors contracted with AJL on an annual basis. AJL's distributor contract renewal rate had stayed at about 70 percent in the 1990s, much higher than the industry average of a 50 percent level. In FY 1996, approximately 1.6 million people in Japan were Amway distributors, 1.1 million of whom renewed and remained as AJL's "core distributors" for FY 1997.

New distributors joined Amway by signing a contract provided by an existing Amway distributor. Through the contracting, distributors were connected to each

EXHIBIT 5

Ranking of Direct Selling Companies and Foreign Firms in Japan

Top 20 Direct Sales Companies in Japan by Sales, FY 1995 and FY 1996

Ranking	*Company*	*Main Business*	*FY 1996 Sales (¥ Million)*	*FY 1995 Sales (¥ Million)*	*Growth (%)*
1	**Amway Japan Limited**	**Household products**	**¥212,196**	**¥177,991**	**19.2%**
2	Duskin	Dust-control product, Rental	¥176,668	¥172,843	2.2%
3	Yakult	Beverage	¥159,569	¥160,252	−0.4%
4	Gakushu Kenkyusha	Books, Tutorial materials	¥113,328	¥117,372	−3.4%
5	Miki Corporation	Health food	¥100,662	¥102,540	−1.8%
6	Pola Corporation	Cosmetics	¥100,260	¥102,200	−1.9%
7	Brother Sales Ltd.	Sewing machines	¥96,638	¥94,917	1.8%
8	Taihei	Food	¥69,175	¥68,647	0.8%
9	Yamahisa	Household products	¥64,680	¥60,204	7.4%
10	Janome Sewing Machine	Sewing machines	¥60,339	¥62,667	−3.7%
11	Asahi Solar	Household products	¥55,500	¥41,446	33.9%
12	Charle	Underwear	¥50,335	¥50,299	0.1%
13	Shinko Sangyo	Household products	¥49,706	¥46,810	6.2%
14	Noevir	Cosmetics	¥45,446	¥43,059	5.5%
15	Nu Skin Japan	Cosmetics	¥41,505	¥23,000	80.5%
16	Chandeal	Underwear	¥40,000	¥32,000	25.0%
17	Maruhachi Mawata	Bedding products	¥38,249	¥35,074	9.1%
18	Nippon Menard Cosmetics	Cosmetics	¥36,000	¥37,000	−2.7%
19	Fuji Yakuhin	Medical drugs, Cosmetics	¥35,958	¥30,854	16.5%
20	Herbalife of Japan	Health food	¥34,000	¥8,200	314.6%

Source: Teikoku Data Bank.

Top 10 Foreign Companies in Japan, by Income, FY 1996

Ranking	*Overall Ranking**	*Company*	*FY 1996 Declared Income (¥ Million)*	*Annual Growth (%)*
1	24	IBM Japan	¥117,048	146.1%
2	52	Coca-Cola Company Japan	¥65,778	−0.9%
3	65	Amway Japan Limited	¥57,958	19.9%
4	123	Isuzu Motors	¥33,225	n.a.
5	144	Motorola Japan	¥28,972	50.6%
6	181	American Life Insurance Company	¥23,600	23.9%
7	182	Nestlé Japan	¥23,515	0.8%
8	187	McDonald's Japan	¥22,565	25.4%
9	188	Alcan Aluminum Limited	¥22,562	n.a.
10	190	Banyu Pharmaceutical	¥22,519	1.6%

* Ranking among all firms including Japanese companies.
Source: *Shukan Diamond*, July 1997.

EXHIBIT 6

Net Sales by Product Category and Best-Selling Products

a. Sales by Product Category, FY 1992–FY 1996

Category	Main Products	FY 1992	FY 1993	FY 1994	FY 1995	FY 1996	FY 1996 ($ Million)	Sales %	CAGR FY 92–96
		(¥ Million)							
Home Care	Laundry, kitchen and household detergents, metal cleaner, air freshners, car care, etc.	¥22,300	¥21,800	¥21,500	¥22,400	¥21,600	$198	(10.2%)	–0.8%
Housewares	Amway Queen Cookware, Amway Water Treatment System, etc.	¥25,400	¥26,600	¥46,500	¥50,600	¥62,700	$575	(29.5%)	25.3%
Nutrition	Nutritional supplements, coffee, pastas, etc.	¥32,300	¥33,700	¥37,000	¥42,400	¥50,400	$462	(23.8%)	11.8%
Personal Care	Cosmetics, toiletry products, fashion jewelry, fashion goods, etc.	¥38,000	¥41,900	¥46,000	¥55,500	¥68,600	$629	(32.3%)	15.9%
Others	Starter kit, sales slips, sales forms, etc.	¥5,300	¥6,000	¥6,600	¥7,100	¥8,900	$82	(4.2%)	13.8%
Total sales		¥123,300	¥130,000	¥157,600	¥178,000	¥212,200	$1,947	(100.0%)	14.5%

Source: Company materials.

b. Top Five Best Sellers, FY 1994–FY 1996

FY 1994 Product	Category	FY 1995 Product	Category	FY 1996 Product	Category
1 Water Treatment System	Houseware	1 Skin Care	Personal Care	1 Skin Care	Personal Care
2 Queen Cookware Set	Houseware	2 Water Treatment System	Houseware	2 Water Treatment System	Houseware
3 Acerola C	Nutrition	3 Queen Cookware Set	Houseware	3 Queen Cookware Set	Houseware
4 Dish Drops (1 Liter)	Home Care	4 Triple X	Nutrition	4 Triple X	Nutrition
5 Wheat Germ E	Nutrition	5 A.W.P.	Personal Care	5 Base Make Up	Personal Care
Top five sales (¥ million)	¥48,317	Top five sales (¥ million)	¥81,664	Top five sales (¥ million)	¥98,934
% Total sales	31%	% Total sales	46%	% Total sales	47%

Source: Company materials.

other in a vertical relationship between the sponsoring distributors, dubbed "up-lines," and the new distributors, called "down-lines." Distributors were rewarded for the sales generated by their down-lines in addition to their own sales. The only up-front investment required to become a distributor was the purchase of a starter kit at ¥8,400 (approximately $77), which included Amway business manuals. Each distributor remained an entrepreneurial salesperson who could decide how to participate in the Amway business, with the only requirement being observance of the Amway Code of Ethics and Rules of Conduct, shown in Exhibit 7.

Amway distributors could buy Amway products at a discount, typically 30 percent off the suggested retail price. Approximately 70 percent of 1.1 million core distributorships were categorized as "consumer-type distributors," who maintained their distributorship solely for this discount privilege. These distributors rarely participated in meetings or events, and contacted the up-line distributors or AJL, except for placing orders. Half the orders were placed through up-lines and half directly to AJL.

Distributors could also earn income from their sales of Amway products to end consumers and/or from the sales of their sponsored down-line distributors. In 1997, about 30 percent of the AJL's core distributorships were categorized as "business-

EXHIBIT 7

Amway Code of Ethics and Rules of Conduct

Amway Code of Ethics

The basic precept of the Amway Business is "Do unto others as I would have them do unto me."

(1) The distributors must understand that their behavior has considerable effects not only on their own business but also on other distributors, and must always act responsibly with well-rounded character and sincerity.

(2) The distributors must sincerely represent only the truth when introducing Amway products and the Amway business to prospects.

(3) The distributors must, among other things, take great care of customers. If complaints concerning the products arise from any customer, the distributors should promptly address such complaints in accordance with Amway's rules and with a modest attitude.

Amway Rules of Conduct

The Rules of Conduct stipulate the rules relating to the Amway business and to the conduct of distributors. The distributors must faithfully observe and act in accordance with the Rules of Conduct in order to develop the Amway business in a sound manner.

Detailed rules were described under the following headings:

Rule 1: Application for Distributorship
Rule 2: Term and Renewal of Distributorship
Rule 3: Sales of Amway Products
Rule 4: Sponsoring Activities and Sponsor's Responsibility
Rule 5: Recognition of Distributor Qualification
Rule 6: Meetings and Other Business Activities
Rule 7: Use of Amway's Tradename, Trademarks and Writings
Rule 8: Distributorship in Case of Marriage or Divorce
Rule 9: Inheritance and Testamentary Gift of Distributorship
Rule 10: Requalification of Distributorship (Rules of Inactivity)
Rule 11: Termination and Expiration of Distributorship
Rule 12: Penalty

Source: Company material.

type distributors," who conducted marketing and sponsoring activities. A business-type distributor's source of income consisted of the following: (1) the mark-up on products sold, about 30 percent of the suggested price; and (2) a performance incentive calculated on a sales volume, ranging from 3 percent to 25 percent of the sales.

Various nonpecuniary incentives and rewards were also provided for the business-type distributors, who were explicitly ranked according to their sales achievements. Amway offered 10 achievement levels worldwide, symbolized by different names and ornamental pins, such as Diamond Direct Distributors and Crown Ambassadors. Each time the distributors moved up in the ladder, their success was officially recognized within the distributor community: for example, their photos and sales records were shown in the monthly distributor magazine, AMAGRAM. Moving up in the hierarchy also created further opportunities to be publicly commended, ranging from an invitation to a party with founding families to an opportunity to speak at junior distributor conferences or to participate in international conventions, usually held in resorts at places such as Hawaii and Guam.

Distributors who achieved a level higher than Direct Distributors (DDs) grew to 8,500 in FY 1996 from 5,500 in FY 1994. The DD status was entitled to distributors who had achieved certain volume levels, which typically required a sales network of approximately 150 down-line distributors. Their motives varied across DDs. Some wanted supplemental part-time income; others wanted to gain financial independence from their previous jobs; and still others wanted the social recognition and personal contacts that an Amway business could offer. Although their skills and personal investments in operating the business varied from distributor to distributor, annual gross income of an average DD was estimated to be ¥5 million ($46,000). Some highly successful DDs earned as much as ¥25 million ($230,000) a year.

Business-type distributors regularly contacted AJL for placing orders and participating in various events. Up-line distributors usually combined several of their down-lines' orders into a single batch order. The regularly organized rallies, conventions and other events functioned as motivation vehicles. These events typically included successful distributors' speeches, new product explanation, and narration of the Amway mission and values. All the elements helped to create a highly emotional atmosphere, stimulating further endeavor.

Legal and Public Relations Issues

Amway's business, especially its Sales and Marketing Plan, was often described as "multi-level marketing" or "network marketing." Its multiplicative model of sales expansion based on distributors' sponsoring activities had drawn legal and social attention in several major markets including the U.S. and Japan. It had on occasion been confused with a "pyramid scheme," fraudulent money making.

During the 1970s, the U.S. Federal Trade Commission (FTC) investigated a number of sales plans, including Amway, as a result of consumer and distributor losses at the hands of a number of direct selling businesses, including some which imitated Amway. In 1979, the FTC ruled that Amway's plan was not a questionable practice. The major reasons why the FTC ruled in Amway's favor included: distributors earned income based on the actual sales of their network; distributors could not make money from recruiting per se; distributors were not forced to buy a high volume of inventory; and the company was willing to buy back the unsold products so that the distributor would not suffer any major losses.

In Japan, the "Door-to-Door Sales Law" regulated direct sales practices, mail order businesses, and chain sales transactions. The law was first enacted in 1976 and was revised in 1984, 1988, and 1996. In addition, there existed another law known as the "Law on the Prevention of Endless Chain Schemes," enacted in 1979, which prohibited pyramid schemes. During the 1970s, a number of companies employing "pyramid schemes" caused social problems when they abused their sales systems and Japanese consumers incurred large financial losses. Although AJL's business was legitimate under these Japanese laws, there remained some public confusion between Amway and pyramid schemes. Exhibit 8 summarizes various consumer and distributor survey results.

EXHIBIT 8

Consumer and Distributor Survey Results

a. Consumers' Image toward Amway, 1996

Response	*%*	*Comments*
• Favorable	33%	"Quality products"
• Neutral	35%	"Direct sales," "American company"
• Unfavorable	32%	"Pyramid sales," "Expensive products"

b. Consumers' Awareness and Purchase Experience of Amway by Age and Sex

Age and Sex	*Aided Awareness (%)*		*Ever Purchased (%)*	
	1995	*1996*	*1995*	*1996*
Total	57	68	25	28
Male	45	57	11	14
Female	70	79	41	43
Male				
20–29 years old	51	63	10	13
30–39	61	82	19	20
40–49	43	50	10	13
50 and older	22	53	7	9
Female				
20–29 years old	74	83	32	37
30–39	82	93	50	55
40–49	69	76	47	46
50 and older	55	66	34	36

c. Consumers' Awareness and Purchase Experience by Direct Selling Companies

Company	*Aided Awareness (%)*		*Ever Purchased (%)*	
	1995	*1996*	*1995*	*1996*
Amway	57	68	19	16
Avon	56	57	15	15
Charle	57	60	16	15
Japan Healthy Summit	n.a.	3	13	12
Miki Shoji	35	36	8	8
Nihon Forever Living	n.a.	1	6	6
Noevir	72	76	n.a.	3
Nu Skin	10	13	2	2
Pola	92	92	1	1
Shaklee	6	6	n.a.	0
Tupperware	51	51	n.a.	0
X-1	3	3	0	0

EXHIBIT 8 (continued)

d. Distributor Satisfaction Survey

Satisfied with Amway Products?	***Current User***		***Current Non-User***	
	1995	*1996*	*1995*	*1996*
• Satisfied with Quality	88%	87%	64%	61%
• Satisfied with Price	69%	62%	45%	41%
• Overall Satisfaction	74%	71%	42%	40%
Want to Buy Amway Products?	***Current User***			
	1995	*1996*		
• Want to buy	55%	56%		
• Don't know	23%	25%		
• Don't want to buy	22%	19%		

Source: Company material.

AJL'S ROLE IN AMWAY BUSINESS: HELP DISTRIBUTORS TO GROW THEIR BUSINESS

AJL provided distributors a wide variety of support to help them to grow their business. Major activities included customer services, distributor relationship, logistics, marketing, and public relations. Exhibit 9 on page 344 illustrates AJL's organization chart in 1997.

Customer Service and Customer Satisfaction (CS)

The CS Department, which belonged to the Distributor Relations Division, was primarily responsible for handling incoming calls and claims from Amway distributors and end users. A customer free dial service was initially centralized at Tokyo headquarters, but, by the mid-1990s, the task was decentralized into eight regional CS centers. In 1996, these CS centers received approximately 1.2 million incoming calls, about 90 percent from distributors and 10 percent from end customers. Many of the consumer-type distributors and end consumers regarded AJL as more competent and trustworthy than their up-line distributors. About 60 percent of the inquiries were product related and 40 percent business related.

About 130 operators in Tokyo and an additional 180 in regional centers responded to the calls, about 30 percent of whom were engaged in analysis of the call data. The data were grouped by the product categories or the demographics. Monthly purchase data were also added to the database. However, if the contracts were not renewed at the end of each year, all data would be cleared and no follow-up efforts were made. One CS manager explained, "it is very hard to follow up although mail questionnaires are sent to people who decided to leave Amway. Their sales data are erased after one month."

The current concern of the CS Department was how to reduce the number of claims and how to handle the calls more efficiently. Further distributor education could be one way of reducing the number of minor inquiries, which were usually covered in the catalogues and other printed materials. One CS manager explained, "the constant top ten questions could effectively be answered by distributors. However, a complicated question could only be handled in more individualized conversation."

EXHIBIT 9

AJL Organization Chart, April 1997

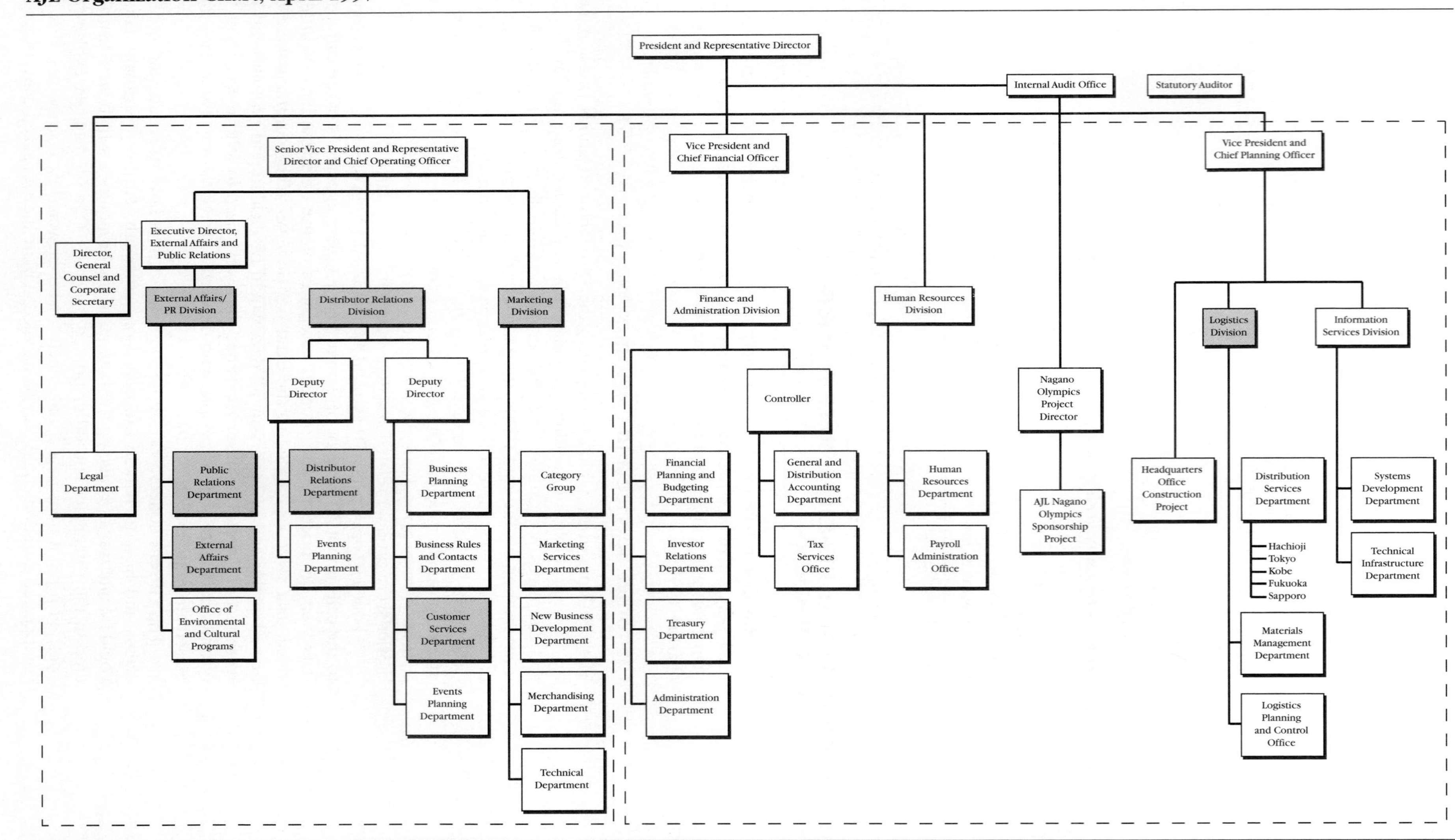

Note: Shaded boxes indicate the divisions and departments discussed in the case.
Source: Company material.

In order to address the increasing number of inquiries, an automatic system called VPS (voice-processing system) was developed. In 1996, about 400,000 of all incoming calls were answered by VPS. The system was capable of responding to simple questions and also taking orders. Other information technologies were also at the experimental stage of application. AJL established an Amway homepage in 1996 for providing distributors more information on product and distributor support activities. Another technology at a developmental stage was satellite broadcasting, through which visual information and data were broadcast to regional offices and distributor centers. For example, the 1996 National Convention in Tokyo was broadcast to all the regional offices. Interdepartmental communication was also expected to improve dramatically when groupware software such as Lotus Notes was introduced within a year to connect CS to other AJL divisions and departments. However, according to a CS manager, the CS database would remain accessible only by CS managers, not by other divisions or departments. The CS Department would maintain its primary role to analyze data and customize the results before CS managers reported specific issues to other divisions or departments.

Distributor Relations (DR)

The DR Department, which was also a part of Distributor Relations Division, served as an interface between AJL and business-type distributors who were above the Direct Distributor level (collectively called DDs). In 1996, there were 106 DR Staff and 30 DR Coordinators to provide information, counseling, and recognition to 8,500 DDs.

DR Staff members organized large-scale meetings for training DDs in the Amway business and its business ethics and philosophy. AJL devised various education programs for distributors at every stage of their advancement to the next ranking. In 1996, about one thousand such meetings were organized throughout Japan.

DR Coordinators organized smaller-scale individual meetings, serving as a consulting function for each distributor. Coordinators conducted business analysis on issues such as how much sponsoring should be done for the particular distributor group, how much sales should be generated for the specific time frame, and so forth. DR Coordinators also tried to provide specific action plans to improve an individual distributor's performance.

The DR Department was also responsible for organizing a number of events such as tours, rallies, and seminars, which totaled several thousand a year ranging from a national convention to small gatherings at the local level. These events served the purpose of providing recognition and motivation to the distributors. The distributors were commended publicly for their sales achievements.

Logistics

The Logistics Division was responsible for quick and accurate order processing, packing, and delivery of Amway products. In FY 1996, AJL handled a daily average of 19,000 orders (4.6 million for the year). Every order resulted on average in six cartons to be shipped. During the 1990s, total quality control programs had shortened the delivery lead time from 3–5 days to 1–2 days. In addition to routine picking and packing tasks, AJL's six nationwide Regional Distribution Centers (RDCs) performed the quality control function for the Amway products, including those imported from the United States. Japanese customers were well known for their sensitivity to even slight tears of the packaging.

Marketing

The Marketing Division planned and implemented AJL's marketing strategies, new product development, and merchandising. While the DR Division primarily served the upper-level business-type distributors (DDs and above), the Marketing Division focused on lower-level business-type distributors and consumer-type distributors. Its function was to provide distributors with useful information about new product introductions, product promotions, sales system improvement, and schedules for seminars and events through periodicals.

More strategic tasks included conducting segmentation analysis and formulating target marketing plans. Until the 1990s, AJL had not collected or utilized distributors' profiles and purchase data extensively. However, AJL had built a distributor database by the mid-1990s and rolled out "Targeted Marketing Initiatives" in 1996. Through segmenting the data, AJL tried to refine its understanding of distributors' buying habits and to provide them more customized information for their particular areas of interests.

The preliminary segmentation study was started in FY 1993 together with a leading consulting company. The immediate finding of the detailed data analysis was that distributors in different demographic groups tended to focus their sales efforts on very different product categories: some specialized in Nutrition category while others focused on selling beauty- and fashion-related products in the Personal Care category, and the like. The preliminary segmentation study distinguished the nine different distributor segments as shown in Exhibit 10.

A successful example of "Targeted Marketing Initiatives" included the launch of Club Artistry program in 1996. Distributors received gifts and other rewards such as resort hotel stays based on their purchase volumes of skin care products. After analyzing the segmentation data, AJL offered the Club invitation only to the younger female distributors who had been heavy purchasers of Artistry products. The launch of the Club was an immediate success. Within days, about 250,000 distributors joined the Club, prompting AJL to close membership temporarily.

Another example was the launch of Invictus, a line of high-quality skin care products for men. The launch program for Invictus was tailored to the preidentified younger male distributor segment. AJL tested a new communication medium in the launch process by redesigning the monthly magazine AMAGRAM. Several modified versions of the AMAGRAM were designed so as to target different distributor demographics such as single male, single female, and young families. According to a marketing manager, this new medium proved to generate more favorable feedback and sales productivity than other media such as direct mailing of product leaflets.

Public Relations and External Affairs

There were two departments in the PR&EA Division. The Public Relations Department aimed at improving Amway's image in the mass media and Japanese society, while the External Affairs Department was responsible for establishing good relations with government and other public organizations.

During the 1980s, several pyramid scheme companies collapsed, causing a series of consumer problems including substantial financial loss and suicides of the program members. The fraudulent nature of the pyramid schemes was explained by the mass media as an example of direct selling. AJL's rapid growth during the 1980s started to gain Japanese consumers' attention and suspicion. However, until PR was established as a formal department in 1987, AJL made little effort to publicize the company. Both the positive and negative reputation of Amway had been formed mainly through word-of-mouth.

While the growing network of distributors helped to diffuse some information about Amway, some tended to promote a partial image of Amway, emphasizing the quick and easy money-making aspect of the business. As a result of AJL's inaction during the period, Japanese consumers, and media in particular, developed skepticism about Amway. Some distributors' misconduct, such as coercive recruitment of down-line distributors, was occasionally covered by the press.

EXHIBIT 10

AJL's Distributor Segments, FY 1997 (Estimated)

Segment	*Description*	*% Sales*
DD and Above	• Business-type distributors with DD and above achievements	30.7%
Below DD and Consumer-Type Distributors	• Other lower-level business-type distributors and consumer-type distributors	69.3%
1. GMS (General Merchandising Store Type)	• Highest productivity • Balanced product categories • Mostly young family with children	15.0%
2. PC/NT (Personal Care + Nutrition)	• Second highest productivity • Close to business-type distributors • Relatively young	11.3%
3. HC/NT (Home Care + Nutrition)	• Family oriented • Potential in home/family products	2.8%
4. HC/PC (Home Care + Personal Care)	• Largest number of distributors • Young family • Potential for children's item	10.1%
5. HC (Home Care Specialists)	• High disposable income • Conservative life style • Need for reliable information	2.2%
6. PC (Personal Care Specialists)	• Youngest segment • High potential in personal use item • 94% female, 46% single	7.8%
7. NT (Nutrition Specialists)	• Belief in only Nutrition products • High potential in items for young male and aging population	2.9%
8. Others	• Gift related • Other unsegmented distributors	17.2%

Source: Company material.

In 1989, so widespread was skepticism that AJL undertook its first corporate advertising after 10 years of operation in Japan. However, some major newspapers and TV networks had not accepted AJL requests for advertising until the mid-1990s. Especially, Asahi Shimbun, the nation's leading newspaper with a readership of about five million, had refused Amway advertisements, influencing other media to maintain their closed door policies toward AJL. The Newspaper Advertising Review Council (NARC), for example, continued to give an "X" rating to AJL, meaning that acceptance of AJL advertising depended on the judgment of the leading companies in the industry.

The public listing of AJL on the Tokyo OTC Exchange and New York Stock Exchange boosted its corporate image, and its first advertising in Asahi Shimbun appeared in December 1996. The first campaign featured the message "Real Amway" with pictures of a baby, a kitchen, and fruit stressing the superior quality of Amway's traditional cleaning products such as L.O.C. cleaner and SA8 detergent (see Exhibit 11). The following texts appeared in the advertisements:

EXHIBIT 11

AJL's Corporate Advertisement Example

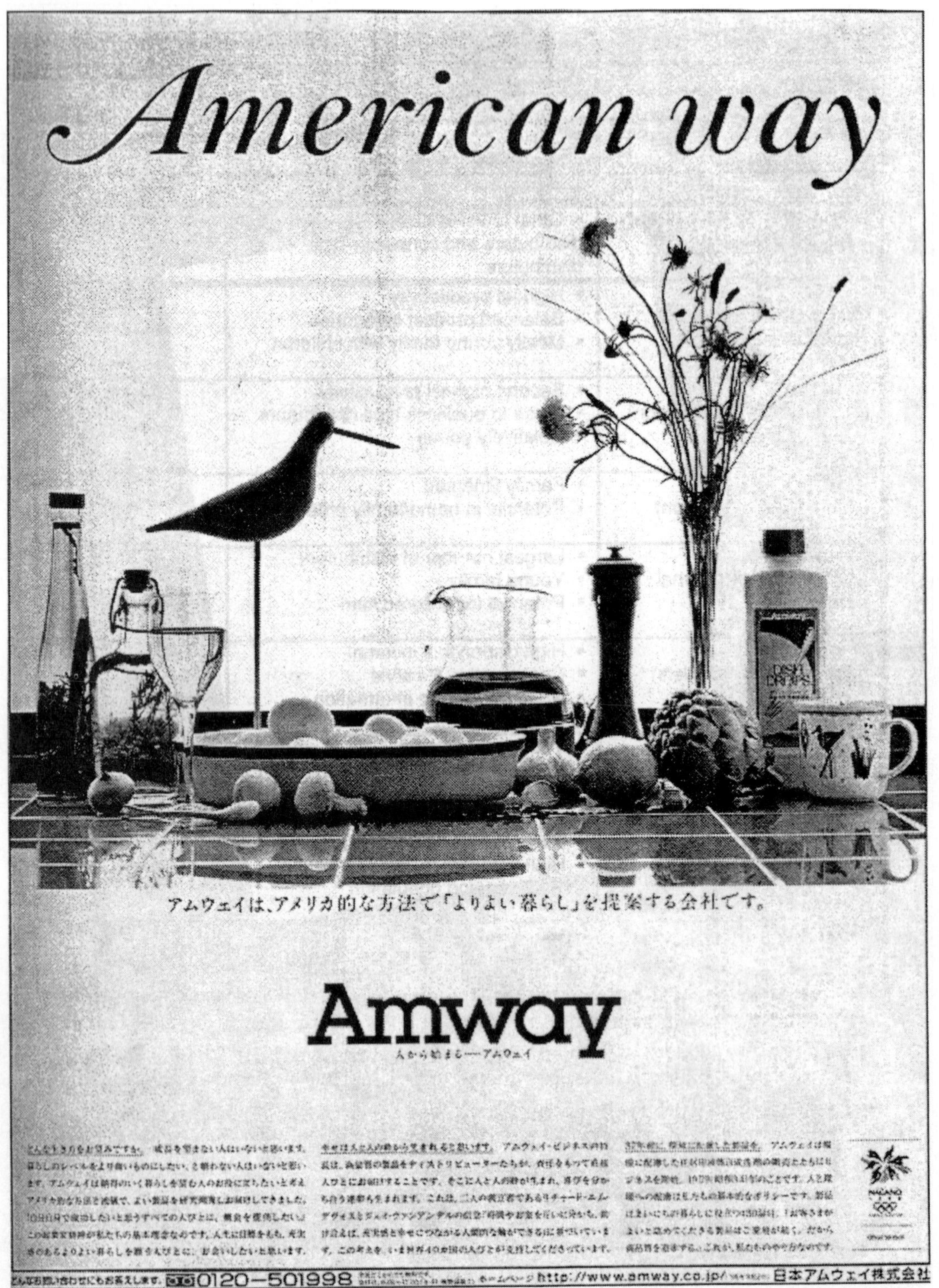

Source: Company material.

"Our business—direct selling—is communication between people."
"The way we do . . . it is to develop high quality products which are directly sold to the people by our distributors."
"Distributors who buy for themselves are the majority . . . there are also couples who enjoy running their business to realize their dreams."

AJL's appearance in Asahi Shimbun helped to convince other newspapers and magazines to change their stances. Amway frequently bought tie-up spaces in major business magazines and wrote comprehensive texts on the company and its business. The tie-up pages were similar in design to regular editorial articles but different in some aspects: Every page was headed or footed with a remark that the contents were provided by the company for promotional purposes. Press conferences and news releases were also used to diffuse corporate information, with particular emphasis on sound financial results. Presentations were often conducted for stock analysts of major security houses and financial media.

As a part of its PR strategy, AJL had also actively sponsored various events, including sports, environmental activities, and art performances. In the past, AJL sponsored the Japanese tours of major orchestras such as the American Symphony Orchestra and the New York Philharmonic. Contemporary American Art had been exhibited in several major Japanese museums. "Porgy and Bess" and Yo Yo Ma concerts were also sponsored by AJL. Amway had also made a decision to sponsor the 1998 Winter Olympic Games in Nagano. Environmental issues were also addressed through Amway Nature Center which frequently conducted fund-raising campaigns in the form of Amway distributors' purchase of the Center's goods (e.g., T-shirts and pencils) for use at Amway meetings and conferences.

■ CHALLENGES AND OPPORTUNITIES IN 1997

1997 Decline

AJL's disappointing first-half results in FY 1997 reflected downturns in all four product categories. Category-by-category analysis had revealed, however, that approximately 70 percent of the total sales decline was due to a fall in sales in the Housewares category. Housewares suffered far more than the other three, with sales down 25.9 percent to ¥24.9 billion, led by declines in sales of Amway Queen Cookware and the Amway Water Treatment System. Home Care category sales showed the second biggest decline, down 10.5 percent to ¥9.7 billion. This partly reflected AJL's strategic decision during the second quarter of FY 1996 to reduce the price of certain Home Care products for competitive reasons. Sales in Personal Care, the largest category, declined 5.2 percent to ¥33.3 billion, reflecting a decline in sales of Artistry cosmetics and skincare. Sales in the Nutrition category meanwhile dipped 1.8 percent, as a decline in sales of Triple X was almost offset by a rise in sales of new products such as herbal food supplements.

Challenge for the Future

Stephens was concerned with the following issues: (1) fluctuating distributor motivation; (2) growing dissatisfaction with Amway products; (3) increasing difficulty in controlling the distributor network; and (4) the changing market environment.

Fluctuating Distributor Motivation Historically, AJL had relied greatly on several top distributors. The top five distributors and their down-lines were believed to account for a substantial portion of AJL's total sales in 1996. In 1996, the company's top distributor, Kaoru Nakajima, pursued the Double Crown Ambassador DD, the highest recognition level of the Amway distributors which nobody had ever achieved worldwide. Working with his down-line distributors, Nakajima tried to achieve a particular sales goal within a certain time frame so that he and his entire down-line would be invited to his commendation ceremony at New York's Radio City Music Hall. After successfully accomplishing the goal and enjoying the trip to New York City, the group was said to slow down their sales effort in 1997.

The reduced level of distributor motivation was reflected in a decrease in the rate at which existing distributors were sponsoring new distributors. This in turn had a negative impact on sales, particularly of expensive durable items such as the Amway Queen Cookware and the Amway Water Treatment System, because these were the items that new distributors typically bought when they first joined Amway to get large savings.

Growing Dissatisfaction with Amway Products AJL had put an emphasis on introducing high-quality products. However, as Stephens explained, "(AJL) tended to believe in the high-quality image of our products. However, the price–value trade-off of our products is becoming a great concern among distributors and leaders as indicated in the distributor satisfaction survey." (See Exhibit 8 for distributor satisfaction survey result.)

Distributors' dissatisfaction with AJL's high prices was also prompted by an increasing awareness of the gap between AJL's and other foreign Amway affiliates' pricing, due to easy access to international pricing information through the Internet. Distributors also became sensitive with the relatively higher price of Amway products as competitors such as Nu Skin and Shaklee had introduced similar personal care or nutrition products at lower prices.

In addition, AJL had to cope with an increase of approximately 21 percent in product procurement prices from Amway Corporation effective September 1, 1996. The price adjustment was mainly a result of continuing depreciation of the yen against the dollar since 1995. While finance executives saw AJL in a very strong position to absorb the increased import prices, it had caused a deterioration in its operating margins (see Exhibit 1).

Increasing Difficulty in Controlling the Distributor Network With an ever-expanding distributor network, it had become more difficult to control some distributors' misconduct, such as coercive recruiting of or selling to their down-lines. It is one of the reasons for the increasing number of AJL-related inquiries to various consumer organizations, as a result of which, the image of AJL had remained unfavorable (see Exhibit 12).

Stephens asserted that AJL's extraordinary success in the Japanese market had made the company a target for some journalists, although he also acknowledged that:

> We cannot hope to solve the problem if we lay all the blame on hostile journalism. AJL must do whatever we can to prevent social problems arising from distributors by establishing healthy systems and continuing to provide extensive education programs.

However, as a senior executive of the DR Division stated, "distributors are not Amway employees after all. They joined Amway because they wanted to operate their business as entrepreneurs who are free from any formal control. I am not sure how much Amway should and can control the individual distributor's conduct. In addition, eliminating these activities was virtually impossible with the existing AJL's distributor support staffing. It has become more difficult to adequately communicate with and effectively deliver education programs to an increasing number of distributors."

EXHIBIT 12

Product Inquiries and Complaints

a. Inquiries from Distributors to AJL, FY 1990-FY 1996

FY	*Amway Business*	*Amway Product*	*Total*
1990	278,741	18,869	297,610
1991	328,614	29,874	358,488
1992	305,408	32,297	337,705
1993	354,510	41,006	395,516
1994	517,511	219,751	737,262
1995	630,337	240,971	871,308
1996	729,009	269,587	998,596

Note: FY 1990-FY 1993 figures include only Distributor Inquiry Center.
FY 1994-FY 1996 figures include both Distributor and Customer Inquiry Centers.
Source: Company materials.

b. Number of Inquiries and Complaints to Consumer Center, 1994-1996

	1993	*1994*	*1995*
Total	233,999	273,931	342,073
Multilevel marketing	5,341	6,658	9,738
Amway	1,013	1,419	1,520
AJL's % share in Multilevel marketing	19.0%	21.3%	15.6%
AJL's rank in Multilevel marketing	1st	1st	1st

Note: Figures were based on number of calls. No distinction was made between inquiries and complaints.
Source: Japan Consumer Information Center.

Recently, increasing Internet postings had exacerbated this problem. With major Web browser software, the keyword "amway" would bring Internet users to a mixed list of official Amway Web sites as well as the skeptics' home pages that attacked Amway. Respecting free speech rights, AJL did not take any explicit countermeasures to address such negative postings on the Internet.

Changing Market Environment Stephens also saw both threats and opportunities in ongoing change in the Japanese market environment. Exhibit 13 on page 352 shows some selected demographic and macroeconomic figures.

> Japan is experiencing a period of great political, economic, and social changes. Remarkable changes in people's values and judgment criteria are arising from a variety of aspects: low birth rates, aging of the population, changes in lifestyles, shifts in purchasing behavior, rising share of female labor force, changes in employment patterns, and growing interest in healthy lifestyles . . .
>
> The distribution sector saw a definite change in consumer behavior, and as a result, new styles of sales such as non-store sales and consumer participation-type direct selling have come to draw significant public interest. Door-to-door sales still account for only about 2 percent of total retail sales . . . but, are growing while the retail industry as a whole is not.
>
> Current trends of increasing corporate restructuring and diminishing life-time employment system . . . indicate continuing oversupply in the labor market. Many

EXHIBIT 13

Selected Demographics and Macroeconomic Data

Unemployment Rate, 1993-1996

	1993	*1994*	*1995*	*1996*
Male	2.4%	2.8%	3.1%	3.3%
Female	2.6%	3.0%	3.2%	3.3%

Source: Management and Coordination Agency.

Demographic Change in Japan, 1980-2000

	1980	*1990*	*2000*
% Elderly people (over 65)	9.1%	12.0%	17.0%
% Household with elderly	22.7%	26.4%	—
Birth rate (per 100 persons)	1.36	1.00	1.11
Number of children/female	1.75	1.54	1.60

Source: Japan Direct Selling Association.

Retail and Direct Selling Industry, 1994-1996

	1994	*1995*	*1996*	*CAGR*
Total retail industry (¥ billion)	144,823	144,677	145,920	0.4%
Direct selling industry (¥ billion)	3,130	3,230	3,340	3.3%
% Direct selling/total retail	2.2%	2.2%	2.3%	

Source: Japan Direct Selling Association.

> women want a business career but do not want, or cannot get, traditional salaried employment opportunities. Many older people will have a need, or want, for additional income after retirement from regular employment. There still exists a potential for new distributors to be served by AJL.
>
> Price slashing became common among the distribution industry as discount and convenience stores began to spread quickly. This trend became even more pronounced as a result of the increasing corporate overseas outsourcing and government deregulation.
>
> Price slashing has now taken root in Japanese society as a long-term trend. People's worship of high-priced, high-quality products seems now a thing of the past.

In 1997, AJL also had to cope with the effect of revisions to Japan's Door-to-Door Sales Law that took effect in November 1996. Varying interpretations of the revised law had created uncertainties among distributors about whether they were in full compliance. Lack of clarification of the new law's implications to Amway's business significantly inhibited its sales efforts. The incomplete understanding of the revision especially impacted negatively on sales of expensive durable products over ¥20,000, to which the new law was believed to be applied.

Strategic Options: Penetration or Productivity

While trying to address these issues, Stephens also emphasized the importance of leveraging the core strength AJL had long accumulated:

> As we face these challenges, we are going to keep our focus firmly fixed on preserving and strengthening the full power of our most important single asset, which is our partnership with our distributors. . . . A strong, positive relationship exists between AJL and distributors, based on the Amway Sales and Marketing Plan. Continued increases in the number of renewed distributors have succeeded in establishing the most extensive network of its kind in Japan. Furthermore, the renewal rate of distributors has been over 70 percent for the past years. This is a very high level relative to other direct selling companies not only in Japan, but also worldwide. Distributors' strong loyalty to AJL and our products further strengthens the distributor network. . . .

Although Stephens was confident that the ongoing "Targeted Marketing Initiatives" would contribute to further growth of the company, he pondered how to maximize the potential AJL possessed with its distributor network. Since AJL's direct day-to-day contacts with distributors ranged from order processing, delivery, inquiry calls, to field meetings, AJL held unlimited opportunities to cultivate value from each such direct interaction with distributors.

Stephens saw three levers for boosting AJL's sales in the future: (1) sponsoring, (2) retention, and (3) productivity.

First, "sponsoring" was to increase the number of distributors further. The growing number of distributors had been the engine of AJL's success to date. Given the potential of the direct selling in the ongoing change of the Japanese market, sticking to the proven strategy seemed still to be the way to go.

Second, AJL could generate sales further by improving "retention." Although AJL's distributor renewal rate of 70 percent was already much higher than the industry average of 50 percent, the figure also meant that a half million distributors out of 1.6 million left Amway in 1996. Focusing on this large group of nonrenewing people could provide an opportunity for sales improvement. Little effort had been made to follow up those leaving. As a senior DR executive put it: "you cannot bother somebody who was upset with something by asking questions about it."

Finally, AJL could also pursue future growth by increasing "productivity," that is, sales per distributor. As a marketing manager emphasized, the network of 1.1 million core distributors with a 70 percent renewal rate might have been "already huge enough." Concentrating on tapping sales productivity of the established distributor network could be the key to further growth.

Having analyzed the complex situation AJL faced in 1997, Stephens devised a little diagram to straighten up his strategic thinking. As shown in Exhibit 14 (page 354), it had two dimensions: one was labeled "penetration" strategy; the other was "productivity." Stephens saw three strategic options for AJL: (1) penetration growth, (2) productivity growth, and (3) both. Stephens needed to come up with a clear strategic direction based on thorough analysis of both pros and cons of each strategic choice.

■ STAYING THE COURSE

Stephens declared his determination to develop AJL's strategy for delivering growth both in the near-term and the longer-term as follows:

> First, . . . we are taking specific steps to cope with the special challenges we face in FY 1997 and to rebuild growth in the second half of the year.
>
> Second, we are simultaneously continuing to make the investments we need to make to further reinforce the core strengths of our business for the future. These core strengths are our direct selling system, which is the bedrock of our business. Our partnership with our more than one million core distributorships, which is our most

EXHIBIT 14

Strategic Options

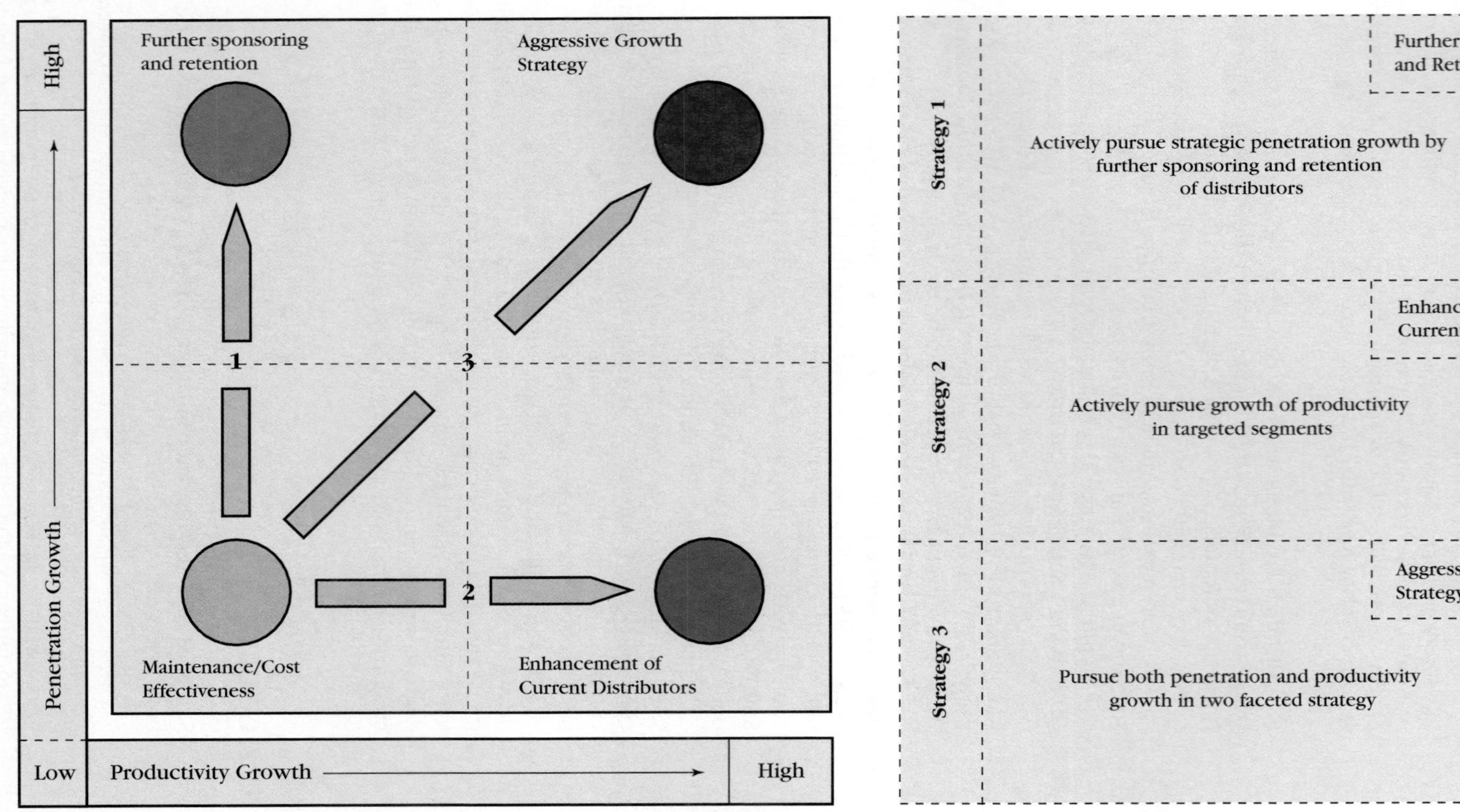
High
Penetration Growth
Low
Productivity Growth
High
Further sponsoring
and retention
Aggressive Growth
Strategy
1
3
2
Maintenance/Cost
Effectiveness
Enhancement of
Current Distributors
Strategy 1
Further Sponsoring
and Retention
Actively pursue strategic penetration growth by
further sponsoring and retention
of distributors
Strategy 2
Enhancement of
Current Distributors
Actively pursue growth of productivity
in targeted segments
Strategy 3
Aggressive Growth
Strategy
Pursue both penetration and productivity
growth in two faceted strategy

Source: Company material.

important single asset. And our broad and diverse product line-up targeted to the Japanese market and meaningfully differentiated from competing products.

And third, we are continuing aggressively to exploit all available means to leverage our core strengths to the maximum possible extent.

We are not taking any easy options for short-term gain. We are continuing to make the investments we need to make to secure our future.

We are staying the course.

CASE

Goodyear Tire and Rubber Company

In early 1992, Goodyear Tire and Rubber Company executives were reconsidering a proposal made by Sears, Roebuck and Company. Sears management had approached Goodyear about selling the company's popular Eagle brand tire in 1989. The proposal was declined. At the time, Goodyear's top management believed that such an action would undermine the tire sales of company-owned Goodyear Auto Service Centers and franchised Goodyear Tire Dealers, which were the principal retail sources for Goodyear brand tires. However, following a $38 million loss in 1990 and a change in Goodyear top management in 1991, the Sears proposal resurfaced for consideration.

Two factors contributed to the renewed interest in the Sears proposal.[1] First, between 1987 and 1991, Goodyear brand tires recorded a 3.2 percent decline in market share for passenger car replacement tires in the United States. This share decline represented a loss of about 4.9 million tire units. It was believed that the growth of warehouse membership club stores and discount tire retail claims coupled with multibranding among mass merchandisers contributed to the market share erosion (see Exhibit 1). Second, it was believed that nearly 2 million worn-out Goodyear brand tires were being replaced annually at some 850 Sears Auto Centers in the United States. According to a Goodyear executive, the failure to repurchase Goodyear brand tires happened by default "because the remarkable loyalty of Sears customers led them to buy the best tire available from those offered by Sears," which did not include Goodyear brand tires.

The Sears proposal raised several strategic considerations for Goodyear. First, as a matter of distribution policy, Goodyear had not sold the Goodyear tire brand through a mass merchandiser since the 1920s, when it sold tires through Sears. A decision to sell Goodyear brand passenger car tires again through Sears would represent a significant change in distribution policy and could create conflict with its franchised dealers. Second, if the Sears proposal was accepted, several product policy questions loomed. Specifically, should the arrangement with Sears include (1) only the Goodyear Eagle brand or (2) all of its Goodyear brands? Relatedly, should Goodyear allow Sears to carry one or more brands exclusively and have its own dealers carry certain brands on an exclusive basis? Goodyear presently has 12 brands of passenger and light-truck tires sold under the Goodyear name, ranging from lower-priced tire brands to a very expensive special high-speed tire for a Corvette that bears the Goodyear name.

---

[1] "Newsfocus," *Modern Tire Dealer* (March 1992), p. 13.

This case was prepared by Professor Roger A. Kerin, of the Edwin L. Cox School of Business, Southern Methodist University, as a basis for class discussion and is not designed to illustrate effective or ineffective handling of an administrative situation. The case is based on published sources. The author wishes to thank Professor Arthur A. Thompson, Jr., of the University of Alabama, for kindly granting permission to extract information from his industry note, "Competition in the World Tire Industry, 1992," for use in this case, the Goodyear Tire and Rubber Company for comments on a previous draft of the case and permission to reproduce its advertising copy, and Michelin Tire Corporation for permission to reproduce its advertising copy.

EXHIBIT 1

U.S. Market Share of Replacement Tire Sales by Type of Retail Outlet, 1982 and 1992

Type of Retail Outlet	*1982*	*1992**
Traditional multibrand independent dealers	44%	44%
Discount multibrand independent dealers	7	15
Chain stores, department stores	20	14
Tire company stores	10	9
Service stations	11	8
Warehouse clubs	—	6
Other	8	4
	100%	100%

* Estimate.

Source: Goodyear Tire and Rubber Company.

THE TIRE INDUSTRY

The tire industry is global in scope, and competitors originate, produce, and market their products worldwide.[2] World tire production in 1991 was approximately 850 million tires, of which 29 percent were produced in North America, 28 percent in Asia, and 23 percent in Western Europe. Ten tire manufacturers account for 75 percent of worldwide production. Groupe Michelin, with headquarters in France, is the world's largest producer and markets the Michelin, Uniroyal, and BF Goodrich brands. Goodyear is the second largest producer, with Goodyear, Kelly-Springfield, Lee, and Douglas being its most well-known brands. Bridgestone Corporation, a Japanese firm, is the third largest tire producer. Its major brands are Bridgestone and Firestone. These three firms account for almost 60 percent of all tires sold worldwide.

The Original Equipment Tire Market

The tire industry divides into two end-use markets: (1) the original equipment tire market and (2) the replacement tire market. Original equipment tires are sold by tire manufacturers directly to automobile and truck manufacturers. Original equipment tires represent 25 to 30 percent of tire unit production volume each year. Goodyear is the perennial market share leader for original equipment tires capturing 38 percent of this segment in 1991. Exhibit 2 on page 358 shows the original equipment tire market shares for major tire suppliers.

Demand for original equipment tires is derived; that is, tire volume is directly related to automobile and truck production. Overall original equipment tire demand is highly price inelastic given the derived demand situation. However, the price elasticity of demand for individual tire manufacturers (brands) was considered highly price elastic, since car and truck manufacturers could easily switch to a competitor's brands. Accordingly, price competition among tire manufacturers was fierce and motor vehicle manufacturers commonly relied upon two sources of tires. For example, General Motors split its tire purchases among Goodyear, Uniroyal/Goodrich, General Tire, Michelin, and Firestone brands in the early 1990s. Even though the original

[2] Portions of the tire industry overview are based on "Competition in the World Tire Industry, 1992," in Arthur A. Thompson, Jr., and A. J. Strickland III, *Strategic Management: Concepts & Cases*, 7th ed. (Homewood, IL, 1993), pp. 581–614.

EXHIBIT 2

Manufacturer Brand U.S. Market Share for Original Equipment Passenger Car Tires

Original Equipment (OE) Buyer	*Tire Manufacturer (Brand)*						
	Goodyear	*Firestone*	*Michelin*	*Uniroyal Goodrich*	*General Tire*	*Dunlop*	*Bridgestone*
General Motors	33.5%	1.5%	14.5%	32.5%	18.0%	0.0%	0.0%
Ford	26.0	39.0	23.5	0.0	11.5	0.0	0.0
Chrysler	83.0	0.0	0.0	0.0	17.0	0.0	0.0
Mazda	15.0	50.0	0.0	0.0	0.0	0.0	35.0
Honda of U.S.	30.0	0.0	47.0	0.0	0.0	16.0	7.0
Toyota	15.0	40.0	0.0	0.0	3.0	42.0	0.0
Diamond Star	100.0	0.0	0.0	0.0	0.0	0.0	0.0
Nissan	0.0	35.0	22.0	0.0	35.0	8.0	0.0
Nummi (GM-Toyota)	50.0	50.0	0.0	0.0	0.0	0.0	0.0
Volvo	0.0	0.0	100.0	0.0	0.0	0.0	0.0
Saturn	0.0	100.0	0.0	0.0	0.0	0.0	0.0
Isuzu	15.0	35.0	0.0	50.0	0.0	0.0	0.0
Subaru	0.0	0.0	100.0	0.0	0.0	0.0	0.0
Hyundai	35.0	0.0	65.0	0.0	0.0	0.0	0.0
Overall OE market share	38.0%	16.0%	16.0%	14.0%	11.5%	2.75%	1.25%

Source: *Modern Tire Dealer*, January 1991, p. 27.

equipment market was less profitable than the replacement tire market, tire manufacturers considered this market strategically important. Tire manufacturers benefited from volume-related scale economics in manufacturing for this market. Furthermore, it was believed that car and truck owners who were satisfied with their original equipment tires would buy the same brand when they replaced them.

The Replacement Tire Market

The replacement tire market accounts for 70 to 75 percent of tires sold annually. Passenger car tires account for 75 percent of annual sales. Primary demand in this market is affected by the average mileage driven per vehicle. Every 100-mile change in the average number of miles traveled per vehicle produces a 1 million unit change in the unit sales of the replacement market, assuming an average treadwear life of 25,000 to 30,000 miles per tire.[3] Worldwide unit shipments in this segment have been "flat" due in part to the longer treadlife of new tires. Exhibit 3 shows original equipment and replacement unit sales in the United States for the period 1987 to 1991.

Tire manufacturers produce a large variety of grades and lines of tires for the replacement tire market under both manufacturers' brand names and private labels. Branded replacement tires are made to the tiremaker's own specifications. Some private-label tires supplied to wholesale distributors and large chain retailers are made to the buyer's specifications rather than to the manufacturer's standards.

The major tire producers often used network TV campaigns to promote their brands, introduce new types of tires, and pull customers to their retail dealer outlets. Their network TV ad budgets commonly ran from $10 million to $30 million, and their budgets for cooperative ads with dealers were from $20 million to $100 mil-

[3] "Competition in the World Tire Industry, 1992," p. 587.

EXHIBIT 3

Unit Tire Sales in the United States, 1987–1991

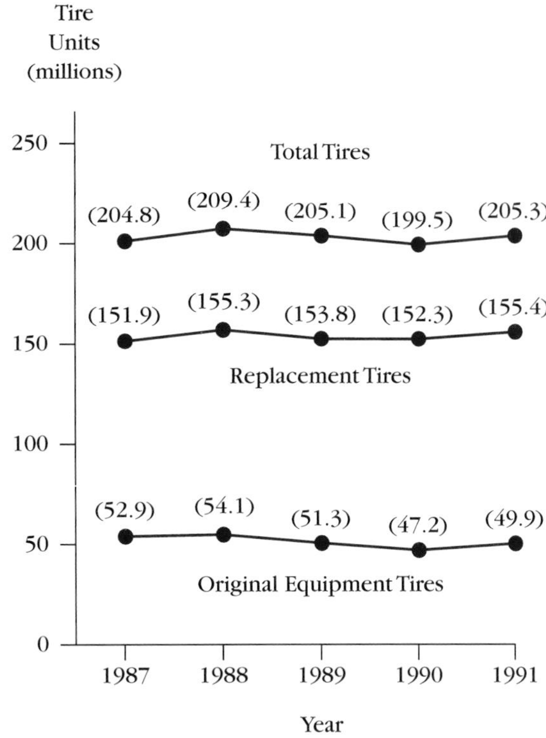

Source: *Modern Tire Dealer*, 1993 Facts/Directory.

lion. Print media were also used extensively. As an illustration, a Michelin print ad featuring the slogan "Michelin, Because So Much Is Riding on Your Tires" is shown in Exhibit 4 (page 360). Several tire companies also sponsored auto racing events to promote the performance capabilities of their tires.

Goodyear is the perennial market-share leader in the U.S. replacement tire market. The company holds a leadership position in the passenger car, light-truck, and highway truck product categories (see Exhibit 5 on page 361).

Retail Distribution Major brand-name tire manufacturers capitalized on their reputation and experience as producers of original equipment tires by building strong wholesale and retail dealer relationships and networks through which to sell their brand-name replacement tires to vehicle owners. The tire industry uses "retail points of sale" to gauge the retail coverage of tire manufacturers and their brands. Goodyear brand tires have the broadest retail coverage with almost 8,000 "retail points of sale," most of which are company-owned Goodyear Auto Service Centers or franchised Goodyear Tire Store dealers with multiple locations. Groupe Michelin is estimated to have almost 14,000 "points of sale" for its three major brands—Michelin, Goodrich, and Uniroyal. The number of "retail points of sale" for major tire brands is shown in Exhibit 6 on page 361.

Retail Marketing[4] Independent tire dealers usually carried the brands of several different major manufacturers and a discount-priced private-label brand so as to give re-

[4] This material is extracted from "Competition in the World Tire Industry, 1992," pp. 588–591.

EXHIBIT 4

Michelin Print Advertisement

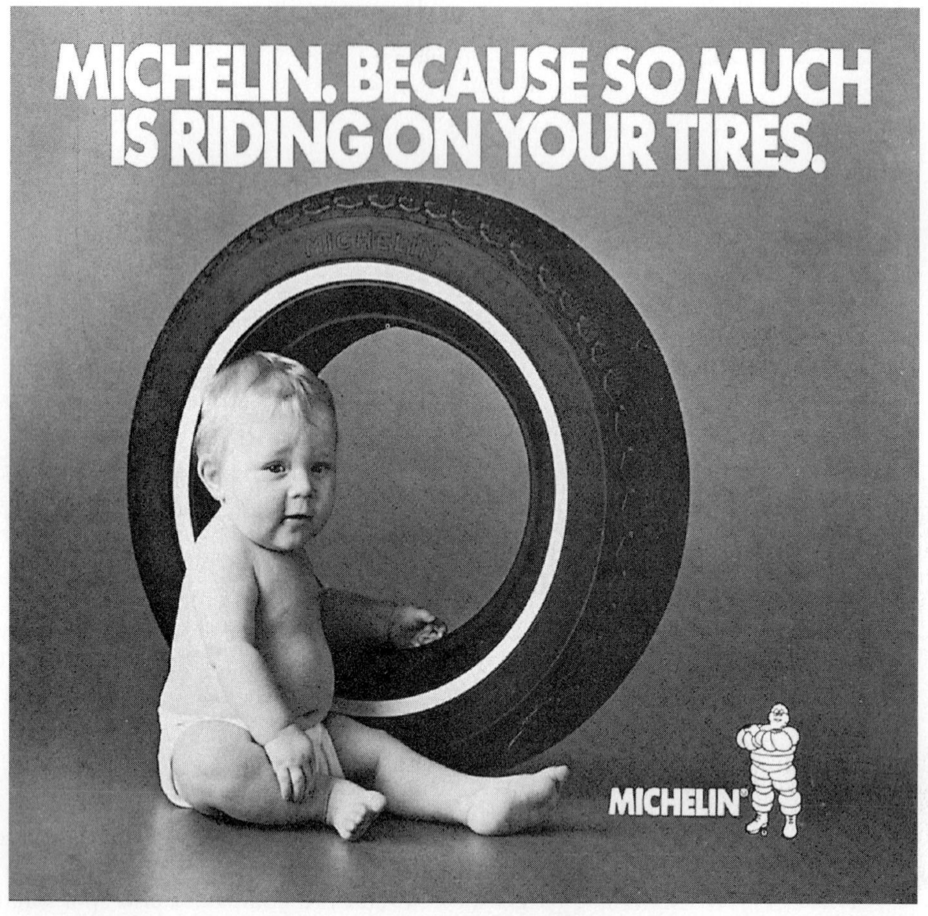

placement buyers a full assortment of qualities, brands, and price ranges to choose from. Service stations affiliated with Exxon, Chevron, and Amoco marketed Atlas brand tires produced by Firestone (Bridgestone). Other service stations, especially those that emphasized tire sales, stocked one or two manufacturers' brand tires and a private-label brand. Retail tire outlets that were owned or franchised by the manufacturers (that is, Goodyear Tire Stores and Firestone Auto Master Care Centers) carried only the manufacturer's name brands and perhaps a private-label or lesser-known, discount-priced line made by the manufacturer. Department stores and the major retail chains such as Montgomery Ward and Sears Roebuck and Company occasionally carried manufacturers' label tires but usually marketed only their own private-label brands.

Manufacturers found it advantageous to have a broad product line to appeal to most buyer segments to provide tires suitable for many different types of vehicles driven under a variety of road and weather conditions. When vehicle owners went to a tire dealer to shop for replacement tires, they had a variety of tread designs, tread widths, tread durabilities, performance characteristics, and price categories to

EXHIBIT 5

Estimated U.S. Market Shares of the Top Ten Brands in the Replacement Tire Market, 1991

Passenger Car Tires		*Light-Truck Tires*		*Highway Truck Tires*	
Brand	*Share*	*Brand*	*Share*	*Brand*	*Share*
Goodyear	15.0%	Goodyear	11.0%	Goodyear	23.0%
Michelin	8.5	BF Goodrich	10.0	Michelin	15.0
Firestone	7.5	Firestone	5.0	Bridgestone	11.0
Sears	5.5	Michelin	6.0	General Tire	7.0
General	4.5	Cooper/Falls	5.0	Firestone	6.0
BF Goodrich	3.5	Kelly-Springfield	5.0	Kelly-Springfield	6.0
Bridgestone	3.5	Armstrong	4.0	Dunlop	6.0
Cooper	3.5	General Tire	4.0	Yokohama	5.0
Kelly-Springfield	3.0	Bridgestone	3.0	Cooper	4.0
Multi-Mile	3.0	Dunlop	2.0	Toyo	3.0
Others	42.5%	Others	44.0	Others	14.0
	100.0%		100.0%		100.0%

Source: Modern Tire Dealer, January 1991, p. 27; *Market Data Book*, 1991; *Tire Business*, January 1992, p. 13.

choose from. Car and light-truck owners were often confused by the number of choices they had; few buyers were really knowledgeable about tires. Many buyers ended up choosing a tire on the basis of price, while others followed the recommendation of the local dealer whom they regularly patronized. The retail prices of replacement tires ranged from retreaded (or recapped) tires selling for under $20 to $35 each to top-of-the-line tires going for $125 to $175 each. Tire dealers ran fre-

EXHIBIT 6

Estimated Number of Retail Points of Sale for Major Tire Brands in the United States, 1991

Tire Brand (Parent Company)	*Number of Retail Points of Sale*
Armstrong (Pirelli)	978
Bridgestone (Bridgestone Corp.)	5,960
Cooper (Cooper Tire and Rubber)	1,518
Dunlop (Sumitomo)	2,046
Firestone (Bridgestone Corp.)	4,208
General (Continental A.G.)	2,107
Goodrich (Groupe Michelin)	4,215
Goodyear (Goodyear Tire and Rubber)	7,964
Kelly-Springfield (Goodyear Tire and Rubber)	2,421
Michelin (Groupe Michelin)	7,159
Pirelli (Pirelli Group)	2,133
Uniroyal (Groupe Michelin)	2,321

Source: Market Data Book, 1991; *Tire Business*, January 1992, p. 14.

quent price promotion ads in the local newspapers, making it easy for price-sensitive buyers to watch for sales and buy at off-list prices. In recent years, consumers had become more price conscious and less brand loyal (thus eroding the importance of securing replacement sales through original equipment sales to vehicle manufacturers). However, it was often difficult for car owners to comparison shop on the basis of tire quality and tread durability because of the proliferation of brands, lines, grades, and performance features. Manufacturers had resisted the development of standardized specifications for replacement tires, and there was a general lack of common terminology in describing tire grades and construction features.

In most communities, the retail tire market was intensely competitive. Retailers advertised extensively in newspapers, on outdoor billboards, and occasionally on local TV to establish and maintain their market shares. Price was the dominant competitive appeal. Many dealers featured and pushed their private-label "off-brand" tires because they could obtain higher margins on them than they could selling the name-brand tires of major manufacturers. Dealer-sponsored private-label tires accounted for 15 to 20 percent of total replacement tire sales in the United States in 1991. Surveys showed dealers were able to influence a car owner's choice of replacement tires, both as to brand and type of tire. Most replacement car tire buyers did not have strong tire brand preferences, making it fairly easy for tire salespeople to switch customers to tire brands and grades with the highest dealer margins. Normal dealer margins on replacement tires were in the 35 to 40 percent range, but many dealers shaved margins to win incremental sales.

Retailer Profitability Since the mid-1970s, tire retailers' profit margins had been under competitive pressure, partly because of stagnant growth in tire sales and partly because of declining retail prices since 1980. To bolster profitability, tire dealers had expanded into auto repair services (engine tune-ups, shock-absorber and muffler replacement, and brake repair), retreading, and automobile accessories. Some tire retailers were experimenting with becoming "total car care centers." Auto service work was very attractive because gross profit margins were bigger than the margins earned on replacement tire sales. A recent survey of independent tire dealers indicated that 38.2 percent of their sales and 45.8 percent of their earnings came from automobile service.[5]

■ GOODYEAR TIRE AND RUBBER COMPANY

Goodyear Tire and Rubber Company, headquartered in Akron, Ohio, was founded in 1898 by Frank and Charles Seiberling. The company began as a supplier of bicycle and carriage tires, but soon targeted the fledgling automotive industry. The introduction of the Quick Detachable tire and the Universal Rim (1903) helped make Goodyear the world's largest tire manufacturer by 1916, the same year the company introduced the pneumatic truck tire. Goodyear held the distinction as the world leader in tire production until November 1990, when Groupe Michelin acquired the Uniroyal Goodrich Tire Company (then the second largest U.S. tire manufacturer) for a purchase price of $1.5 billion.

Goodyear's principal business is the development, manufacture, distribution, and sale of tires throughout the world. Tires and tire tubes represented 83 percent of Goodyear's corporate sales of $10.9 billion in 1991. Corporate-wide earnings in 1991 were $96.6 million. In addition to Goodyear brand tires, the company owns the

[5] "Dealer Attitude Survey Concerning Automotive Service," *Modern Tire Dealer* (Spring 1992), p. 1.

Kelly-Springfield Tire Company, Lee Tire and Rubber Company, and Delta Tire. The company also manufactures private-label tires.

Goodyear controls 20 to 25 percent of the world's tire manufacturing capacity and about 37 percent of U.S. tire-making capacity. Sales outside of the United States accounted for about 42 percent of company revenues.

Market Presence

Approximately 60 percent of Goodyear worldwide sales were in the tire replacement market and 40 percent were to the original equipment market. The Goodyear brand is the market share leader in North America and in Latin America and number two throughout Asia outside of Japan (behind Bridgestone). The Goodyear brand is third in market share in Europe behind Michelin and Pirelli. Goodyear is second to Groupe Michelin (Michelin, Uniroyal-Goodrich) in terms of worldwide market share for auto, truck, and farm tires (see Exhibit 7). The company operates 44 tire products plants in 28 countries and seven rubber plantations.

Tire Product Line and Pricing

Goodyear produces tires for virtually every type of vehicle. It has the broadest line of tire products of any tire manufacturer. The broad market brand names sold under the Goodyear umbrella include the Arriva, Corsa, Eagle, Invicta, Tiempo, Decathlon, Regatta, S4S, T-Metric, Wrangler (light-truck tire), and Aquatred. The Aquatred brand was the most recent introduction and featured a new tread design that prevented hydroplaning (see Exhibit 8 on page 364). Sales of this brand were expected to reach 1 million units in 1992 based on initial sales figures.

The Goodyear name is one of the best known brand names in the world. Goodyear brand tires have been traditionally positioned and priced as premium quality brands. Nevertheless, the company has recently introduced mid-priced tire brands. These include the Decathlon and T-Metric brands with lower treadwear and traction performance characteristics than its other brands (see Exhibit 9 on page 365).

Kelly-Springfield Tire Company and Lee Tire and Rubber Company, two Goodyear subsidiaries, also sell some 16 tire brands and engage in private-label manufacturing. For example, Wal-Mart sells the Douglas brand made by the Kelly-Springfield unit.

Goodyear Advertising and Distribution

Goodyear is one of the leading national advertisers in the United States. The company also has maintained a high profile in auto racing to emphasize the high-

EXHIBIT 7

Worldwide Market Shares of Tire Makers, 1990

Tire Manufacturer (Brands)	*Market Share*
Michelin/Uniroyal-Goodrich	21.5%
Goodyear	20.0
Bridgestone/Firestone	17.0
Continental/General	7.5
Pirelli/Armstong	7.0
Sumitomo/Dunlop	7.0
Others	20.0
	100.0%

Source: Goodyear Tire and Rubber Company, 1991 annual report, p. 5.

EXHIBIT 8

Aquatred Print Adverisement

ONE GALLON PER SECOND.

POURING BUCKETS? GOODYEAR AQUATRED® PUMPS UP TO A GALLON OF WATER AWAY AS YOU DRIVE.

The award-winning* Aquatred, with its deep-groove AquaChannel,™ moves

up to one gallon of water away per second at highway speeds. This keeps more of the tire's tread area in contact with the road for superb wet traction. **ONLY FROM GOODYEAR.** For your nearest Goodyear retailer call 1-800-GOODYEAR.

TREADLIFE 60000 WARRANTY

Aquatred features a 60,000-mile treadlife limited warranty. Ask your retailer for details.

*Which awards? *Popular Science*, 1991 Best of What's New. *Popular Mechanics*, 1992 Design & Engineering Award. *Fortune*, a 1992 "Product of the Year." Industrial Designers Society of America, Gold Industrial Design Excellence IDEA Award. *Discover*, Discover Award for Technological Innovation.

THE BEST TIRES IN THE WORLD HAVE GOODYEAR WRITTEN ALL OVER THEM.

Experience Goodyear traction for your high-performance, passenger and multi-purpose vehicles.

EAGLE GS-C.® *Dual tread zone for high-performance traction.*

AQUATRED.® *Deep-groove design for outstanding wet traction.*

WRANGLER GS-A.® *"Triple Traction" tread for all-surface traction.*

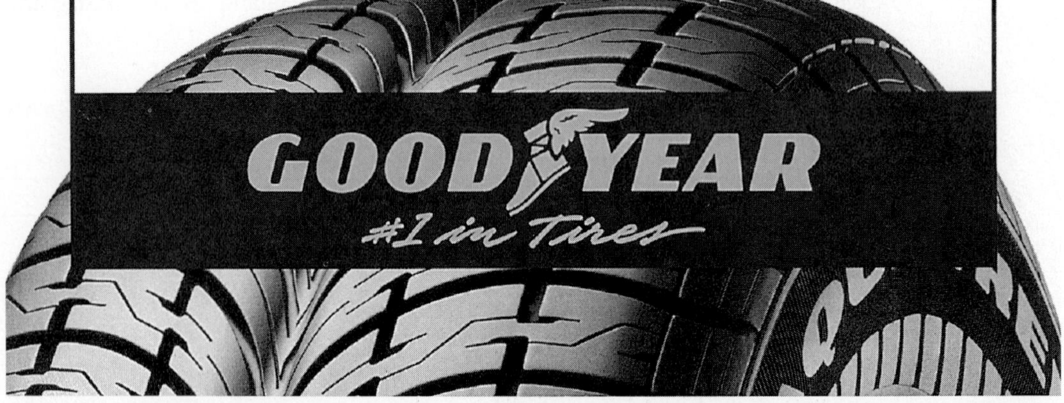

Source: Courtesy of the Goodyear Tire and Rubber Company.

EXHIBIT 9

Goodyear Brand Passenger-Car Tires (Including Minimum Assigned Grades for Treadwear, Traction, and Temperature)

	Treadwear[a]			
Brand	*Rim Diameter 13″*	*All Others*	***Traction***[b]	***Temperature***[c]
Aquatred	320	340	A	B
Arriva	260	310	A	B
Corsa GT	280	280	A	B
Decathlon	220	240	B	C
Eagle GA	280	300	A	B
Eagle GA (HNIZ)	280	300	A	A
Eagle GS-C	—	220	A	A
Eagle GS-D	—	180	A	A
Eagle GT (H)	—	200	A	A
Eagle GT II	—	320	A	B
Eagle GT + 4	—	240	A	B
Eagle GT + 4 (HNIZ)	—	240	A	A
Eagle ST IV	280	300	A	B
Eagle VL	—	220	A	A
Eagle VR	—	220	A	A
Eagle ZR	—	220	A	A
Invicta	—	280	A	B
Invicta GA	—	280	A	B
Invicta GA (HN)	—	280	A	A
Invicta GA (L)	—	300	A	B
Invicta GA (L) (HN)	—	220	A	A
Invicta GFE	280	300	A	B
Invicta GL	260	280	A	B
Invicta GL (H)	—	280	A	A
Invicta GLR	260	280	A	B
Invicta GS	320	340	A	B
Regatta	300	320	A	B
S4S	240	280	A	B
Tiempo	240	280	A	B
T-Metric	240	240	B	C

Note: The U.S. Department of Transportation (DOT) requires tire manufacturers to state the size, load and pressure, treadwear, traction, and temperature on their tires. This information is provided by manufacturers based on their own tests and not provided by the DOT. Treadwear, traction, and temperature are all useful quality indicators and appear on the tire sidewall.

[a] Treadwear. This is an index based on how quickly the tire tread wears under conditions specified by the U.S. Government, relative to a "standard tire." The index does not specify how long a tire tread will last on a car because driving conditions vary. However, a tire with a treadwear index of 200 should wear about twice as long as a tire with an index of 100 under similar conditions.

[b] Traction. This is a measure of a tire's ability to stop on wet pavement under specific conditions. Grades range from A (highest) to C (lowest).

[c] Temperature. This is a measure of a tire's resistance to heat buildup under simulated high-speed driving. Grades range from A (highest) to C (lowest).

Source: "How to 'Read' a Tire," *Consumer Reports* (February 1992): 78.

performance capabilities of its tires and the company's commitment to product innovation. The Goodyear name is prominently featured on the company's well-known blimps frequently seen at special events in communities throughout the United States. The company's advertising slogan, "The best tires in the world have Goodyear written all over them," communicates the Goodyear positioning as a high-quality, worldwide tire manufacturer and marketer.

Goodyear distributes its tire products through almost 8,000 retail points of sale in the United States and some 25,000 retail outlets worldwide. The company operates about 1,000 company-owned Goodyear Auto Service Centers and sells through 2,500 franchised Goodyear Tire Dealers in the United States, many of which are multisite operators. These retail outlets account for a major portion of Goodyear brand annual tire sales. In addition, the company sells its tires through some multibrand dealers. As of early 1992, the company did not typically sell Goodyear brand tires through discount multibrand dealers, mass-merchandise chain stores, or warehouse clubs.[6]

■ STRATEGIC CONSIDERATIONS IN BROADENING DISTRIBUTION

Interest in reconsidering Sears Auto Centers for selling Goodyear brand tires meant that Goodyear executives would have to revisit the company's long-standing distribution policy. Furthermore, a product policy question relating to which brands might be sold through Sears had to be considered. Decisions on these policy issues were further complicated by Goodyear Tire dealer franchisee reaction to broadened distribution and estimates of incremental sales possible through expanded distribution.

An immediate reaction was forthcoming from franchised Goodyear tire dealers who heard about the Sears proposal. According to comments appearing in the *Wall Street Journal*, one dealer said, "We went with them through thick and thin, and now they're going to drown us."[7] Other dealers indicated they would add private-label brands to their product line. One dealer said: "We [will] sell what we think will give the customer the best value, and that's not necessarily Goodyear." While it was clear that some franchise dealers were critical of broadened distribution of any kind, the pervasiveness of this view was unknown. Furthermore, it was not readily apparent how many dealers would actually carry competitive brands.

Tire industry analysts expected Sears to benefit from carrying Goodyear brand tires. According to market share estimates made by *Modern Tire Dealer*, an industry trade publication, Sears' share of the U.S. replacement passenger car tire market had declined from 6.5 percent in 1989 to 5.5 percent in 1991.[8] Goodyear brand tires would certainly enhance the company's product mix and draw tire buyers who were already Sears customers. The extent of the draw, however, would depend on how many or which Goodyear brands were sold through Sears Auto Centers.

Cannibalization of company-owned Goodyear Auto Service Center and franchised Goodyear Tire Dealers tire sales also meant that Goodyear executives had to consider the incremental replacement passenger car tire sales from broadened distri-

---

[6] Goodyear brand tires could sometimes be purchased at discount multibrand dealers because of "diverting." Diverting is the practice whereby a manufacturer's authorized distributors/dealers sell the manufacturer's products to unauthorized distributors/dealers who, in turn, distribute the manufacturer's products to customers. This practice is common for many consumer products. See W. Bishop, Jr., "Trade Buying Squeezes Marketers," *Marketing Communications* (May 1988): pp 52–53.

[7] "Independent Goodyear Dealers Rebel," *Wall Street Journal* (July 8, 1992): p B2.

[8] Statistics reported in *Modern Tire Dealer* (January 1991): 27; "Tire Makers Are Traveling Bumpy Road as Car Sales Fall, Foreign Firms Expand," *Wall Street Journal* (October 19, 1990): B1.

bution. In other words, even though distribution through Sears could increase sales of Goodyear brand tires from the manufacturer's perspective, the danger would be that company-owned and franchised Goodyear Tire Dealers might incur a loss in unit sales. This could be particularly evident in communities where Sears had a strong market presence.

CASE

Hendison Electronics Corporation

The corporate planning process for Hendison Electronics Corporation had just concluded, and Richard Hawly, Vice President of Marketing, was reviewing the corporate goals for 1997. Even though Hawly had participated in the deliberations and the drafting of the final document, he was impressed with the ambitious goals. For example, the corporate plan established a sales goal of $92.5 million for 1997, when sales volume for 1996 was estimated to be $67.5 million.

During the planning process, a number of fellow executives had voiced concern over whether the distribution approach used by Hendison was appropriate for the expanded sales goals. Hawly felt that their concerns had merit and should be given careful consideration. Though he had considerable latitude in devising the distribution strategy, the final choice would have to be consistent with the overall marketing program for the company in 1997. A recommendation and supporting documentation had to be prepared in a relatively short time to permit an integrated marketing program introduction in January 1997.

■ THE COMPANY

Hendison Electronics Corporation was formed in 1961 by Mark Hendison, who had a PhD in electrical engineering. The company introduced a stereo radio unit in 1964 and a line of television sets in 1966. By the early 1990s, the company had expanded its product line to include a full line of home entertainment equipment.

Hendison is an assembler rather than a manufacturer of home entertainment equipment. As an assembler, the company purchases components under contract from large (usually foreign) manufacturers. These components are then identified as Hendison Electronics Corporation products and placed in consoles or other packages for sale under the Hendison brand name.

Hendison distributes its products directly to 425 independent specialty home entertainment dealers and 50 exclusive dealers which are of standard industry size in terms of selling space. Combined, these 475 dealers service 150 markets in 11 western and Rocky Mountain states. The exclusive dealers, however, are the sole company representatives in 50 markets. According to Hawly, this disparity in market coverage occurred as a result of the company's early difficulty in gaining adequate distribution.[1]

[1] Exclusive dealerships had chosen to operate in this manner. This was not the policy of Hendison Electronics Corporation. However, Hendison did not pursue additional dealers in these markets for the purpose of carrying company products.

This case was prepared by Professor Roger A. Kerin, of the Edwin L. Cox School of Business, Southern Methodist University, as a basis for class discussion and is not designed to illustrate effective or ineffective handling of an administrative situation. Certain names and data have been disguised.

The independent dealers typically carry ten or more brands of home entertainment equipment products, whereas the exclusive dealerships carry only Hendison products and noncompetitive complementary products. Dealerships are located in market areas with populations of approximately 100,000 or fewer. In contrast, major competitors tend to be national in scope. Partially as a result of that—and partially because of economies of scale in advertising and distribution—these firms had been selling an increasing proportion of their products through mass merchandisers such as chain and discount stores. The overwhelming majority of these stores were located in retail trading areas with 1 million or more inhabitants.

The company employs ten sales representatives, each responsible for a territory that is generally delineated by state borders. These representatives deal primarily with the independent dealers and call on them twice a month on average.

THE HOME ENTERTAINMENT INDUSTRY

The home entertainment industry experienced double-digit dollar sales growth in the 1980s with the rise in consumer disposable income, changes in lifestyles, and product innovation. However, dollar sales volume growth slowed in the 1990s due in part to lower prices at both the equipment manufacturer and retail sales level. Sales growth, at manufacturer prices, was 4.5 percent between 1995 and 1996. Manufacturer dollar sales were $20.5 billion in 1996. Projected sales for 1997 were $21 billion, representing a 2.4 percent increase.

Thomason (GE and RCA brands), Zenith, Matsushita (Panasonic and Quasar brands), Sony, and North American Philips (Magnavox, Sylvania, and Philco brands) account for the bulk of dollar and unit sales in the home entertainment industry. Private brands, produced by several of these companies and many others, are also important in the industry.

The product mix in the home entertainment industry consists of five major categories: television, compact disc players, videocassette players, audio systems, and tape players and recorders. Television is the largest single category in terms of dollar sales volume. These product categories vary dramatically in terms of market saturation in the United States. For example, 99 percent of U.S. households have a television set, 75 percent have a videocassette player, and 48 percent have a tape player or recorder. By comparison, 20 percent of U.S. households have a compact disc player, but only 8 percent have a portable compact disc player. Exhibit 1 on page 370 shows home entertainment product unit and dollar sales for 1995 and 1996 and projected sales for 1997.

In 1993 the company commissioned a study on the socioeconomic characteristics and purchase behavior of buyers of home entertainment products. The study reported that these purchasers had household incomes above the median household income of the U.S. population as a whole. The research also revealed the following:

1. In-store demonstration, friend or relative recommendation, dealer or salesperson presentation, and advertising are dominant influences when buyers decide what brand of home entertainment products to purchase.
2. The median number of shopping trips made before purchasing home entertainment products was 2.4.
3. The most frequently shopped outlets for home entertainment products were radio/TV stores.

EXHIBIT 1

Home Entertainment Product Sales Overview and Forecast (Units in Thousands; $ Value in Millions)

	1995			1996			1997		
Product	*Unit Sales*	*Mfrs. $ Value*	*Average $ Price*	*Unit Sales*	*Mfrs. $ Value*	*Average $ Price*	*Unit Sales*	*Mfrs. $ Value*	*Average $ Price*
Total TV	26,499	8,889	335	27,925	9,409	337	28,920	9,708	336
Direct-view color	24,634	7,915	321	26,000	8,317	320	26,990	8,543	317
Color only	23,005	7,316	318	23,700	7,489	316	24,160	7,538	312
Stereo	9,767	4,288	439	10,665	4,533	425	11,476	4,854	423
Nonstereo	13,239	3,028	229	13,035	2,956	227	12,684	2,684	212
TV/VCR combos	1,629	599	368	2,300	828	360	2,830	1,005	355
Projection TV	465	841	1,808	535	962	1,798	585	1,038	1,775
Monochrome TV	550	40	72	530	37	70	480	33	69
LCD TV, color	300	60	200	310	61	196	320	62	195
LCD TV, mono	550	33	60	550	32	59	545	32	59
Total VCR	15,536	4,809	310	15,700	4,768	304	15,925	4,716	296
Decks	12,448	2,851	229	12,500	2,800	224	12,580	2,742	218
Stereo	3,248	997	307	3,560	1,050	295	4,200	1,218	290
Nonstereo	9,200	1,854	211	8,940	1,750	196	8,380	1,524	211
Videocassette player	449	61	135	400	52	130	360	46	127
Videodisc players	287	123	429	305	130	425	325	137	420
C-Band Sat. systems	338	395	1,170	369	406	1,100	330	330	1,000
Total audio systems	5,216	1,464	281	5,325	1,468	276	5,475	1,473	269
Rack systems	1,116	545	488	1,000	495	495	975	483	495
Compact systems	4,100	919	224	4,325	973	225	4,500	900	220
Separate components	-0-	1,635	-0-	-0-	1,750	-0-	-0-	1,790	-0-
Total CD players*	20,425	3,552	174	24,550	4,026	164	27,000	4,239	157
Portable CD players	11,276	1,289	114	14,620	1,579	108	16,540	1,720	104
Total Tape	32,343	909	29	30,940	803	26	30,285	787	26
Tape players**	15,717	397	25	15,640	375	24	15,295	367	24
Tape recorders**	16,626	501	30	15,300	428	28	14,990	420	28

* Includes portables and home decks; ** includes radio combinations.

Sources: U.S. Department of Commerce; Electronic Industries Association; Hendison Electronics Corporation estimates.

The vast majority of home entertainment products are distributed through five types of retail outlets: (1) home furnishings/furniture stores, (2) housewares/hardware stores, (3) auto supply stores, (4) department stores/mass merchandisers (such as Circuit City), and (5) radio/TV stores. The volume of home entertainment merchandise sold by these outlets is unknown because of the variety of merchandise offered. However, selected data on the radio/TV store group with a more homogeneous product mix are available (see Exhibit 2). These types of dealers represent all of Hendison's accounts and operate with a gross margin of 27.5 percent.

EXHIBIT 2

Number and Retail Sales of Radio/TV Stores in the Western and Rocky Mountain States

State	*Number*	*Sales ($ in Thousands)*
Arizona	289	$ 412,175
California	2,375	3,952,615
Colorado	331	450,298
Idaho	86	75,073
Montana	81	96,020
Nevada	88	138,493
New Mexico	113	106,872
Oregon	286	331,815
Utah	124	143,010
Washington	457	457,482
Wyoming	59	50,630
11-state total	4,289	$6,214,483

Source: Hendison Electronics Corporation estimate.

HENDISON ELECTRONICS CORPORATION PLANNING INITIATIVES FOR 1997

The following is an excerpted version of the company's planning initiatives.

General Corporate Objective

Our customer is the discriminating purchaser of home entertainment products who makes the purchase decision in a deliberate manner. To this customer we will provide, under the Hendison brand, quality home entertainment products in the higher-priced brackets that require specialty selling. These products will be retailed through reputable electronics specialists who provide good service.

Company Mission, Strategy, and Goals

The company's mission is to serve the discriminating purchaser of home entertainment products who approaches a purchase in a deliberate manner with heavy consideration of long-term benefits. We will emphasize home entertainment products with superior performance, style, reliability, and value that require representative display, professional selling, trained service, and brand acceptance—retailed through reputable electronics specialists to those consumers whom the company can most effectively service. This will be accomplished by:

1. A focused marketing effort to serve the customer who approaches the purchase of a home entertainment product as an investment.
2. Concentration on our areas of differential advantage: high-technology television, audio, and related home entertainment products with innovative features, superior reliability, and high performance levels—products that generally sell for more than $500 at retail.
3. Emphasis on products requiring display, demonstration, and product education, which must be delivered to and serviced in the home, to be sold through reputable merchants that specialize in home entertainment products and provide good service.

4. Concentration on distribution in existing markets, and general exclusion of large core cities with populations of 1 million or more.
5. Developing brand acceptance by obtaining in every market served a market position of at least $16.25 sales per capita, which our research indicates is possible.

Hendison's 1997 marketing strategy represented a significant departure from the company's previous marketing posture. For many years the company had assembled and marketed good-quality, medium- and promotionally priced home entertainment products. In the last few years, however, the company had begun to emphasize more expensive and more luxurious home entertainment equipment.

Although this was not stated in the overall marketing strategy, the company had also become more aggressive in its advertising. The advertising budget for 1997 included television advertising, which the company had previously eschewed in favor of local newspaper advertising on a cooperative basis with dealers. In 1997, television advertising would be allotted $7.5 million and would be directed at the 100 highest-potential markets, 50 markets served by exclusive dealers and 50 other current markets that had the next highest potential which had yet to be determined.

The overall direction of the marketing program had been reaffirmed in the recent corporate planning sessions. The sales target of $92.5 million was viewed as both ambitious and necessary. Hendison's senior managers were of the firm belief that the company had to attain a larger, critical mass of sales volume to preserve its buying position with component suppliers, particularly with respect to component prices and discounts.

Even though there was agreement on the marketing effort and the need to expand sales volume, different viewpoints were raised concerning the capacity of present dealers to deliver $92.5 million in sales. This matter had consumed much of Hawly's time recently.

THE DISTRIBUTION STRATEGY ISSUE

Hawly was well aware of the value that Hendison placed on its dealers and the importance of developing a close linkage between the company and the dealers. The company had long emphasized that dealers are an asset that must be consistently supported.

Hawly saw his charge as determining the characteristics, the number, and the locations of the dealers Hendison would need to meet its sales goal of $92.5 million in 1997. Initially this would involve identifying the types of dealers that would satisfy the needs of the kind of customer the company sought and that would work closely with the company in meeting corporate objectives.

A number of different viewpoints had been voiced by Hawly's fellow executives. One viewpoint favored increasing the number of dealers in the markets currently served by the company. The reasoning behind this position was that it would be difficult for existing dealers to attain the sales goal specified in the corporate plan. Executives expressing this view noted that even with a 2.4 percent increase in sales following the industry trend, it would be necessary to add at least another 100 dealers. They said these dealers would be likely to be independent (nonexclusive) dealers located in the 100 markets not served by exclusive dealerships. Hawly believed that adding another 100 dealers over the next year would not be easy and would require increasing the sales force that serviced nonexclusive dealers. Executives acknowledged that this plan had more merit in the long run of, say, three to four years. However, their idea had merit as a long-term distribution policy, they thought. The incremental direct cost of adding a sales representative was $80,000 per year.

A second viewpoint favored the development of an exclusive franchise program, since 27 nonexclusive dealers had posed such a possibility in the last year. Each of these dealers represented a different market and each of these markets was considered to have high potential and be a candidate for the new advertising program. These dealers were prepared to sell off competing lines. They would sell Hendison brand home entertainment products exclusively in their market for a specified franchise fee. In exchange for the dealer's contractual obligation to promote, merchandise, and service Hendison brand products in a specified manner consistent with corporate objectives, Hendison Electronics Corporation would drop present dealers in their markets and not add new dealers. Further, these dealers noted, the company's current contractual arrangements with its independent dealers allowed for cancellation by either party, without cause, with 90-days advance notification. Thus, the program could be implemented during the traditionally slow first quarter of the upcoming year. If adopted, company executives believed the franchise program in these 27 markets could be served by the television advertising program. The other 50 markets served by exclusive dealers would be unaffected, since this advertising program was already being applied. The remaining 73 markets would also be unaffected, except for increased advertising in 23 high-potential markets.

A third viewpoint called for a general reduction in the number of dealerships without granting any exclusive franchises. Executives supporting this approach cited a number of factors favoring it. First, analysis of dealers' sales indicated that 50 of Hendison's dealers (all exclusive dealers) produced 80 percent of company sales. Second, an improvement in sales-force effort and possibly increased sales might result if more time were given to fewer dealers. These executives acknowledged that committing Hendison to an exclusive franchise program would limit its flexibility in the future. Although a number had not been set, some consideration had been given to the idea of reducing the number of dealers in the 150 markets served by the company from 475 to 250. This would mean that the 50 exclusive dealers would be retained and 200 nonexclusive dealers would operate in the remaining 100 markets, of which the top 50 would benefit from the television advertising program.

A fourth viewpoint voiced by several executives was not to change either the distribution strategy or the dealers. Rather, they believed that the company should do a better job with the current distribution system. It was their opinion that additional sales personnel and the expanded television advertising budget should be sufficient. Moreover, they argued that because of slowed growth, this was not the time for major changes in distribution policy and practices.

CASE

Chesterton Carpet Mills, Inc.

In early July 1999, Suzanne Goldman was scheduled to meet with Robert Meadows, President of Chesterton Carpet Mills, Inc. Goldman expected the meeting would relate to the recent board of directors meeting. In her position as Special Assistant to the President, or "troubleshooter," as she called herself, Goldman had noticed that such meetings often led to a project of some type. Her expectations were met, as Meadows began to describe what had happened at the board meeting.

> The directors were generally pleased with the present state of the industry and our performance last year. Even though we lagged behind industry sales growth, we recorded a profitable sales growth of 3.6 percent. Our net profit margin of 4 percent is respectable and our cash flow is more than sufficient to fund our present initiatives. Board members were quite complimentary in their comments about senior management and the recommended bonuses and raises were approved. You deserve the credit for pulling together a really professional packet of materials for the meeting.
>
> The possibility of establishing our own distribution centers or wholesale operation was raised, given the recent developments in the industry and our competitive position. We looked at this issue ten years ago and concluded it wasn't strategically in our interest to do so. Besides we were too small and couldn't afford it. Would you examine such a program for me for fiscal 2000 and prepare a position paper for the October board meeting? Focus only on residential business, since we handle contract sales on a direct basis already, assume the same sales level as in fiscal 1999 to be conservative, and address both the strategic and economic aspects of a change in distribution practices. Remember that our policy is to finance programs from internal funds except for capital expansion. I know you'll do the same comprehensive job that you did on the advertising and sales program last year.

THE U.S. CARPET AND RUG INDUSTRY

U.S. consumers and businesses spend about $50 billion annually for floorcoverings. The largest category of floorcoverings is carpet and rugs, followed by resilient coverings (vinyl), hardwood, ceramic tile, and laminates.

This case was prepared by Professor Roger A. Kerin, of the Edwin L. Cox School of Business, Southern Methodist University, as a basis for class discussion and is not designed to illustrate effective or ineffective handling of an administrative situation. Certain names and data have been disguised.

Carpet and Rug Industry Sales and Trends

The U.S. carpet and rug industry recorded sales of $10.3 billion at manufacturer's prices in 1998.[1] Carpet and rug retail sales were estimated to be $15.8 billion. These figures represented about a 6.6 percent increase in sales from 1997.

Industry sales are divided between "contract," or commercial, sales for institutions and businesses and residential sales for household replacement carpets. The residential segment accounted for about 57 percent of sales; the contract segment accounted for 43 percent of sales in 1998. The percentages reflected a five percentage point decline in residential sales since 1995.

It is estimated that carpet and rugs commanded 70.8 percent of total U.S. floorcovering sales in 1998, down from 73.4 percent in 1995, and 82 percent in 1985. Resilient floorcoverings have shown a similar decline in market share while hardwood, ceramic tile, and laminate floorcoverings have grown (see Exhibit 1). In addition, U.S. carpet and rug manufacturers have experienced a decline in sales outside the United States. Since 1980, the export market for U.S.-made carpet and rugs has become highly competitive. As recently as 1970, U.S. companies supplied 51 percent of the world's carpet; by 1997, this percentage had declined to 45 percent.

Some industry analysts claim that the carpet and rug industry itself is partially to blame for the present situation. Lack of marketing, particularly in the residential carpet and rug replacement segment, is an often-cited problem area. Even though manufacturers continue to improve the quality of their products and develop new patterns, critics say the industry has not communicated these value-added dimensions to consumers and differentiated carpet and rugs from other floorcoverings. They note that the industry as a whole spends 2.1 percent of its sales on consumer advertising. For comparison, other manufacturers of consumer durable products such as household furniture and household appliances spend 4.2 percent and 2.5 percent of sales, respectively, for advertising. Instead, price had become the dominant marketing tool for much of the past decade and manufacturers focused attention on cost reduction and achieving economies of scale. A result of these efforts was an erratic upward trend in dollar sales over the past decade, but marginal profitability for the industry as a whole.

EXHIBIT 1

U.S. Floorcovering Market Shares

	Market Share				
Floorcovering Type	*1998*	*1997*	*1996*	*1995*	*1994*
Carpet and rug	70.8%	71.1%	72.9%	73.4%	73.6%
Resilient	11.6	12.5	13.5	14.5	14.5
Hardwood	7.6	7.5	6.9	6.4	6.1
Ceramic	7.0	6.7	5.0	4.6	5.0
Laminate	3.0	2.2	1.7	1.1	.8
	100.0%	100.0%	100.0%	100.0%	100.0%
Total sales ($ in millions)	$15,436	$14,422	$13,893	$13,344	$13,509

[1] This overview is based on interviews with individuals knowledgeable about the carpet and rug industry and information contained in *The Tufted Carpet Industry History and Current Statistics 1999* (Dalton, GA: The Carpet and Rug Institute, 1999); Kimberly Gavin, "Carpet: State of the Industry," *Floor Covering Weekly* (March 15, 1999): 1, 28; "The Focus Top 100," *Floor Focus* (May 1999): 19–25.

Competitors

The U.S. carpet and rug industry is undergoing a period of consolidation begun in the mid-1980s. Mergers, acquisitions, and bankruptcies among manufacturers brought about by declining demand for carpet and rugs, excess manufacturing capacity, and dwindling profit margins reduced the number of carpet and rug manufacturers from more than 300 in the mid-1980s to about 100 companies in 1998. This number includes 96 U.S.-based companies and 4 Canadian-based companies, most of which are privately held companies. Mergers and acquisitions since 1995 reflected a push to build further economies of scale in the production and distribution of carpet and rugs.

By 1998, it was estimated that 10 companies in the industry produced 91 percent of carpet and rug sales in the United States. The sales distribution in the residential segment was even more skewed. Three companies—Shaw Industries, Mohawk Industries, and Beaulieu of America—accounted for about 85 percent of U.S. residential carpet and rug sales.

The U.S. industry sales leader is Shaw Industries, with 1998 sales of $3.5 billion. The company also has the distinction of being the largest carpet and rug manufacturer in the world. Exhibit 2 lists the top 20 North American floorcovering manufacturers based on annual sales in 1997 and 1998.

EXHIBIT 2

Sales of the Top 20 North American Floorcovering Manufacturers in 1997 and 1998

	Sales ($ in Millions, United States only)	
Manufacturer	*1998*	*1997*
1. Shaw Industries	$3,542.2	$2,626.0
2. Mohawk Industries	2,639.2	2,327.3
3. Armstrong World Industries*	2,074.6	1,120.0
4. Beaulieu of America	1,500.0	1,100.0
5. Interface Flooring	780.0	710.0
6. Collins & Aikman Corp.	574.0	513.0
7. Mannington Mills*	475.0	435.0
8. Lear Corporation	465.0	410.0
9. Burlington Industries	490.0	445.0
10. The Dixie Group	415.0	340.0
11. Dal-Tile*	338.0	301.0
12. Milliken Carpets	290.0	260.0
13. Congoleum*	259.1	252.5
14. Domco*	236.4	252.9
15. Perstorp*	201.0	150.0
16. Tarkett*	162.0	183.0
17. Kraus Carpet	185.0	175.0
18. C&A Floorcoverings	170.0	158.0
19. Royalty Carpet Mills	163.0	108.0
20. Gulistan Carpet	155.0	145.0

* Manufacturer produces floorcoverings other than carpet and rugs.
Source: "The Focus Top 100," *Floor Focus* (May 1999): 19.

Wholesale and Retail Distribution

Wholesale and retail distribution in the U.S. carpet and rug industry has undergone three distinct changes since the mid-1980s.

Mid-1980s: Direct Distribution In the mid-1980s, the largest carpet and rug manufacturers began to bypass floorcovering wholesalers (distributors) and sell directly to retailers in greater numbers. In many instances, direct distribution involved establishing sales offices located in manufacturer-operated distribution centers. The intent was to capture the margins paid to floorcovering wholesalers and offset declining and often negative manufacturer profit margins at the time. Lacking the capital to invest in distribution centers, smaller manufacturers continued to rely on floorcovering wholesalers that were increasingly expanding their product line to include ceramic, hardwood, and resilient floorcoverings. Although no statistics were available, it was believed that the majority of carpet and rug sales for residential use were distributed through company distribution centers to retailers by 1990. However, the majority of carpet and rug manufacturers still used floorcovering wholesalers.

Distribution through floorcovering wholesalers remained popular with the majority of carpet and rug manufacturers because of the retail distribution of residential carpet and rugs. In the mid-1980s, independent (and often small) floorcovering specialty stores were responsible for 58 percent of residential carpet and rug sales volume. Department stores and furniture stores accounted for 21 percent and 19 percent, respectively, of residential sales volume. Mass merchandisers, chain stores, and discount stores were relatively minor retail outlets for carpet and rugs until the early 1990s.

Early 1990s: Wholesale and Retail Consolidation The early 1990s was marked by a second significant change in wholesale and retail distribution for residential carpet and rugs in the United States. Department stores, furniture outlets, and independent retail stores were being replaced by large mass-merchandise and discount stores (Kmart and Wal-Mart) and later by home centers such as Home Depot. The growing number of large retailers that were capturing an increasing share of residential carpet and rug sales spawned a new phenomenon in the retail floorcovering industry among specialty outlets: the buying group. A retail buying group is an organization of similar retailers which combine their purchases to obtain price (quantity) discounts from manufacturers. These pooled purchases allowed independent specialty floorcovering retailers to buy less inventory per order while still getting a lower price, which reduced their costs and pressure for markdowns caused by overordering. Lower carpet and rug cost plus an emphasis on service gave independent specialty floorcovering retailers a basis with which they could compete against their larger competitors. Logistical aspects of shipping and storing inventory varied from group to group. Some buying groups took physical custody of goods through a central warehouse which often replaced floorcovering wholesalers. Others simply requested manufacturers to deliver the goods directly to buying-group members from the manufacturer's mill or distribution center.

By 1995, three retail buying groups—CarpetMax, Carpet One, and Abby Carpets—registered $3 billion in floorcovering purchases. Another 10 smaller buying groups made another $1 billion in purchases. According to one industry observer, almost one-half of all U.S. residential carpet and rug sales volume was accounted for when buying group purchases were combined with those of large to medium-size carpet store chains (e.g., Carpet Exchange), mass merchandisers and discount stores, and home centers (e.g., Home Depot). Although estimates varied, about 40 percent of the roughly 23,000 retail outlets that carried carpet and rugs were members of buying groups, large mass-merchandise, discount, or home center chains. By 1998, CarpetMax, Carpet One, and Home Depot accounted for 45 percent of total U.S. floorcovering sales.

Increased consolidation of retail purchasing evident in buying groups, chain stores, and large mass-merchandise, discount, and home center stores had either a positive or negative effect on manufacturers. Even with price discounting, and assuming the retail buying organization operated a central warehouse, it was easier and less expensive for a manufacturer to supply one location with large orders than to supply several separate retailers with smaller orders. On the other hand, if a buying organization flexed its buying power and persuaded manufacturers to take lower-than-normal margins (prices) and ship to diverse locations, a manufacturer risked seeing a lower dollar volume and profit.

Direct distribution by manufacturers in the mid-1980s followed by consolidated purchasing and warehousing by retailers in the early 1990s put many floorcovering wholesalers in a precarious position in the residential segment of the carpet and rug industry. Wholesalers that typically served small and medium-sized independent floorcovering specialty stores were particularly vulnerable to the ascension of retail buying groups that operated their own warehouse facility. These wholesalers advocated their role in distribution to both manufacturers and retailers. They argued that working with a buying group was worthwhile to a manufacturer only if the functions performed by the buying group were not only better than those offered by floorcovering wholesaler, but significant enough to justify the price discounts demanded by a buying group. Similarly, they argued that retailers benefited from wholesaling functions above and beyond the warehousing function. Nevertheless, the absolute number of floorcovering wholesalers had declined in recent years and was expected to decline further. The share of wholesaler floorcovering sales was projected to decline from 26 percent in 1995 to less than 23 percent in 2000.

Mid-1990s: Forward Integration into Retailing In late 1995, the carpet and rug industry watched as yet another change in distribution practices unfolded. On December 12, 1995, Shaw Industries, the largest carpet and rug manufacturer and sales leader, announced plans to engage itself directly in the residential and contract segments of the floorcovering industry. It would do this by operating its own retail stores and commercial dealer network. In announcing this initiative, Robert E. Shaw, the President and CEO of Shaw Industries said:

> We have realized for some time that the manufacturer must become significantly involved in the retail environment to enhance the viability of our industry. Today, our industry offers products of exceptional quality and unsurpassed value, yet we continue to lose consumer dollars to other product groups. Moreover, because consumers have traditionally price-shopped our products, profits have stagnated for years, from fiber producer to manufacturer to retailer.
>
> Although our industry has matured considerably in recent years, the current structure cannot address many fundamental problems the industry is facing. A manufacturer–dealer affiliation was inevitable, since the only practical way to improve these adverse conditions is by consolidating the combined resources of the two.[2]

Shortly afterward, Shaw Industries announced that it had purchased a number of commercial carpet dealers and contractors and Carpetland USA, a retail chain of 55 stores.

In response to this initiative, Home Depot dropped Shaw Industries as a carpet and rug supplier and switched to Mohawk Industries. Carpet One and Abbey Carpets, two buying groups, asked their members not to do business with Shaw. Other carpet manufacturers courted floorcovering specialty stores with promises to sup-

[2] Quoted in "The North American Top 50 Carpet & Rug Manufacturers," *Carpet & Rug Industry* (April 1996): 12–13.

port them with product and not to enter the retail market as competitors. Shaw Industries countered these actions by creating its own retail buying group—the Shaw Alignment Incentive Program—which operated 275 retail stores in 26 states with annual sales of $575 million by mid-1998. Then, in June 1998, Shaw Industries announced it would sell off its retail stores to the Maxim Group, the owner of CarpetMax floorcovering stores, for about $93 million.[3]

THE COMPANY

Chesterton Carpet Mills, Inc., is a privately held manufacturer of a full line of medium- to high-priced carpet primarily for the residential segment. The company markets its products under the Masterton and Chesterton brand names. Contract sales to institutions and businesses are also made but account for only 28 percent of company sales and occur principally in the southeastern United States. The company had no export sales. Total company sales in Fiscal 1999 were $75 million, with a net profit before tax of $3 million. Exhibit 3 shows abbreviated company financial statements.

Chesterton Carpet Mills currently distributes its line through seven floorcovering wholesalers located throughout the United States. These wholesalers, in turn, supplied 4,000 retail accounts, including department stores, furniture stores, and floorcovering specialty stores. Inspection of distribution records revealed that 80 percent of residential segment sales were made through 50 percent of its retail accounts. This relationship exists within all market areas served by Chesterton Carpet Mills. Meadows believed these sales-per-account percentages indicated that at the re-

EXHIBIT 3

Chesterton Carpet Mills, Inc. Financial Statements (For the Fiscal Year Ending June 30, 1999)

Income Statement	
Net sales	$ 75,000,000
Less cost of goods sold	56,250,000
Gross margin	$ 18,750,000
Distribution expenses	$ 2,250,000
Selling and administrative expenses	11,250,000
Other expenses	2,250,000
Net income before tax	$ 3,000,000

Balance Sheet	
Current assets	$ 26,937,500
Fixed assets	24,000,000
Total assets	$ 50,937,500
Current liabilities	$ 10,312,500
Long-term debt and net worth	40,625,000
Total liabilities and net worth	$ 50,937,500

Source: Company records.

[3] "Shaw Industries to Sell Retail Arm to Maxim Group," *Wall Street Journal* (June 24, 1998): B11.

tail level the company was gaining adequate coverage, if not over coverage. The review of distribution records also indicated that it cost Chesterton Carpet Mills 6 percent of its residential segment sales to service the seven floorcovering wholesalers.

Advertising by Chesterton Carpet Mills appeared primarily in shelter magazines and newspapers. The emphasis in advertisements was on fiber type, colors, durability, and soil resistance. A cooperative advertising program with retailers had been expanded on the basis of Goldman's recommendation. According to Goldman, "The co-op program is being well received and has brought us into closer contact with retail accounts." The company employed two regional sales coordinators, who acted as a liaison with wholesalers, assisted in managing the cooperative advertising program, and made periodic visits to large retail accounts. In addition, they were responsible for handling contract sales for institutions and businesses.

Floorcovering wholesalers played a major role in Chesterton Carpet Mills' marketing strategy. Its seven wholesalers had long-term relationships with the company. Two had represented Chesterton Carpet Mills products for over 30 years, four had been with the company for 20 to 25 years, and one had been with the company for 10 years. Chesterton Carpet Mills' wholesalers maintained extensive sales organizations, with the average wholesaler employing 10 salespeople. On average, retail accounts received at least one sales call per month. Goldman's earlier evaluation of the sales program revealed that wholesaler sales representatives performed a variety of tasks, including checking inventory and carpet samples, arranging point-of-purchase displays, handling retailer questions and complaints, and taking orders. About 25 percent of an average salesperson's time was spent on nonselling activities (preparing call reports, acting as a liaison with manufacturers, traveling, and so forth). About 40 percent of each one-hour sales call was devoted to selling Chesterton Carpet Mills carpeting; 60 percent was devoted to selling noncompeting products. This finding disturbed company management, which felt that a full hour was necessary to represent the product line. In addition to making sales, wholesalers also stocked carpet inventory. Chesterton Carpet Mills' wholesalers typically carried sufficient stock to keep the number of their inventory turnovers at five per year. Chesterton Carpet Mills' executives felt that inventory levels sufficient for four turns per year were necessary to service retailers properly, however. Finally, wholesalers extended credit to retail accounts. In return for these services, wholesalers received a 20 percent margin on sales billed, at the price to retailers.

At a June 1999 meeting with its wholesalers, Chesterton Carpet Mills executives were informed that several wholesalers were feeling increased pressure to shave their profit margins to accommodate retailer pricing demands. It seemed that an increasing number of their retail accounts had joined regional retail buying groups and were seeking price breaks comparable to those made possible through their group purchases. Subsequent probing on this topic led Chesterton Carpet Mills executives to conclude that about 1,200 of the company's current retailers were members of buying groups; they represented about a third of the company's residential segment sales. The meeting concluded with Chesterton Carpet Mills executives agreeing to consider a reduction in its price to wholesalers that could be passed on to retailers. At the same time, wholesalers agreed to consider a modest reduction in their margins as well. The "Margin Sharing" proposal, so named by a wholesaler, would be given top billing at the next meeting in January 2000. In the meantime, price accommodations would be made where and when it was necessary to meet the competition.

■ DIRECT DISTRIBUTION EXPERIENCE OF COMPETITORS

Following her meeting with Meadows, Goldman sought out information on competitors' experience with direct distribution. Despite conflicting information from trade publications and knowledgeable industry observers, she was able to arrive at several important conclusions. First, competitors with their own warehousing or direct distribution operations located them in or near seven metropolitan areas: Atlanta, Chicago, Dallas-Fort Worth, Denver, Los Angeles, New York City, and Philadelphia. Chesterton Carpet Mills had wholesalers already operating in these metropolitan areas, except for Dallas-Fort Worth and Atlanta. The company serviced these two areas from wholesalers located in Houston, Texas, and Richmond, Virginia, respectively. Second, a minimum volume of approximately $5 million in wholesale sales was necessary to operate a warehouse operation economically. The average warehouse operation could be operated at an annual fixed cost (including rent, personnel, operations) of $700,000. Goldman was informed that suitable warehouse space was available in the metropolitan areas under consideration; therefore, the company would not have to embark on a building program. Third, salaries and expenses of highly qualified sales representatives would be about $70,000 each annually. One field sales manager would be needed to manage eight sales representatives. Salary and expenses would be approximately $80,000 per field sales manager per year. Sales administration costs (including fringe benefits) were typically 40 percent of the total sales force and management costs per year. Delivery and related transportation costs to retail accounts were estimated to be about 4 percent of sales, and inventory and accounts receivable carrying costs were 10 percent. Retail accounts receivable take about 90 days to collect, on average. Though these figures represented rough approximations, in Goldman's opinion and in the opinion of others with whom she conferred, they were the best estimates available.

In late September 1999, just as Goldman was about to draft her position paper for Robert Meadows, she received a disturbing telephone call from a long-time successful wholesaler of the company's products. The wholesaler told her that he and others were disappointed to hear of her inquiries about direct distribution possibilities given what transpired at the June meeting. Through innuendo, the wholesaler threatened a mass exodus from Chesterton Carpet Mills once the first company warehouse operation was opened. He implied that plans were already under way to establish a trade agreement with a competitor. This conversation would have significant impact on her recommendation if direct distribution was deemed feasible. In short, a rollout by market area looked less likely. A rapid transition would be necessary, which would require sizable cash outlays and an aggressive sales force recruiting program.

CHAPTER 8

Pricing Strategy and Management

Whether or not it is so recognized, pricing is one of the most crucial decision functions of a marketing manager. According to one marketing authority: "Pricing is an art, a game played for high stakes; for marketing strategists, it is the moment of truth. All of marketing comes to focus in the pricing decision."[1] To a large extent, pricing decisions determine the types of customers and competitors an organization will attract. Likewise, a single pricing error can effectively nullify all other marketing-mix activities. Despite its importance, price rarely serves as the focus of marketing strategy, in part because it is the easiest marketing-mix activity for the competition to imitate.

It can be easily demonstrated that price is a direct determinant of profits (or losses). This fact is apparent from the fundamental relationship

Profit = total revenue − total cost

Revenue is a direct result of unit price times quantity sold, and costs are indirectly influenced by quantity sold, which in turn is partially dependent on unit price. Hence, price simultaneously influences both revenues and costs.

Despite its importance, pricing remains one of the least understood marketing-mix activities. Both its effects on buying behavior and its determination continue to be the focus of intensive study.[2]

PRICING CONSIDERATIONS

Although the respective structures of demand and cost obviously cannot be neglected, other factors must be considered in determining pricing objectives and strategies. Most important, the pricing objectives have to be consistent with an organization's overall marketing objectives. Treating the maximization of profits as the sole pricing objective not only is a gross oversimplification, but may undermine the broader objectives of an organization. Other pricing objectives include enhancing product or brand image, providing customer value, obtaining an adequate return on investment or cash flow, and maintaining price stability in an industry or market.

EXHIBIT 8.1

Conceptual Orientation to Pricing

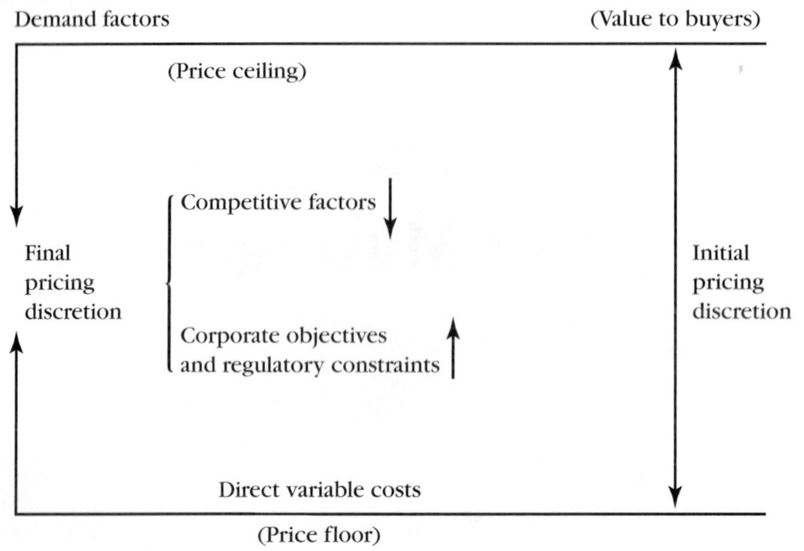

Source: Kent B. Monroe, *Pricing: Making Profitable Decisions*, 2nd ed. (New York: McGraw-Hill, 1990). Reproduced with permission of McGraw-Hill, Inc.

Exhibit 8.1 shows how numerous factors affect a marketing manager's pricing discretion. Demand for a product or service sets the price ceiling. Costs, particularly direct (variable) costs, determine the price floor. More broadly, consumer value perceptions and buyer price sensitivity will determine the maximum price(s) that can be charged. The Campbell Soup Company was recently reminded of this fact.[3] The company spent seven years and $55 million developing a line of Intelligent Quisine (IQ) food products. The 41 breakfasts, lunches, dinners, and snacks would be the first foods "scientifically proven to lower high levels of cholesterol, blood sugar, and blood pressure." After 15 months in test market, Campbell Soup yanked the entire IQ line. Consumers found the products too expensive and lacking in variety. On the other hand, the price(s) chosen must at least cover unit variable costs; otherwise, for each product sold or service provided, a loss will result. Some companies that sell products via the Internet have come to recognize that unit variable costs of a transaction (including order fulfillment and distribution expenses), often exceed the price of the products bought. The result? Skyrocketing dollar sales and huge financial losses.[4]

Although demand and cost structures set the upper and lower limit of prices, government regulations, the price of competitive offerings, and organizational objectives and policies narrow a manager's pricing discretion. Regulations prohibiting predatory pricing, the level of differentiation among competitive offerings, and the financial goals set by the organization are all factors that may affect the price range within broad demand and cost boundaries.

There are still other factors that must be considered in pricing a product or service. The life-cycle stage of the product or service is one factor—greater price discretion exists early in the life cycle than later. The effect of pricing decisions on profit margins of marketing channel members must be assessed. The prices of other products and services provided by the organization must be considered as well; that is, price differentials should exist among offerings such that buyers perceive distinct value differences.

Price as an Indicator of Value

In determining value, consumers often pair price with the perceived benefits derived from a product or service. Specifically, *value* can be defined as the ratio of perceived benefits to price:[5]

$$\text{Value} = \frac{\text{perceived benefits}}{\text{price}}$$

This relationship shows that for a given price, value increases as perceived benefits increase. Also, for a given price, value decreases as perceived benefits decrease. Seasoned marketers know that value is more than a low price. According to a Procter & Gamble executive, "Value is not just price, but is linked to the performance and meeting expectations of consumers."[6]

For some products, price alone influences consumers' perception of quality—and ultimately value. For example, in a *Better Homes and Gardens* survey of home furnishing buyers, 84 percent agreed with the statement "The higher the price, the higher the quality." For computer software, it has also been shown that consumers believe a low price implies poor quality.

Price also affects consumer perceptions of prestige so that as price increases, demand for the item may actually rise. Rolls-Royce automobiles, Cartier jewelry, Chanel perfumes, fine china, Swiss watches, and Lalique crystal may sell worse at lower prices than at higher ones. The recent success of Swiss watchmaker TAG Heuer is an example. The company raised the average price of its watches from $250 to $1,000, and its sales volume increased sevenfold.[7]

Consumer value assessments are often comparative. In such cases, determining value involves a judgment by a consumer as to the worth and desirability of a product or service relative to substitutes that satisfy the same need. A consumer's comparison of the costs and benefits of substitute items gives rise to a "reference value." Although Equal, a sugar substitute containing Nutrasweet, might be more expensive than sugar, some consumers value it more highly than sugar because it has no calories. Retailers have found that they should not price their store brands more than 20 to 25 percent below manufacturers' brands. When they do, consumers often view the lower price as signaling lower quality.[8]

Price Elasticity of Demand

An important concept used to characterize the nature of the price-quantity relationship is that of *price elasticity of demand*. The coefficient of price elasticity, *E*, is a measure of the relative responsiveness of the *quantity* of a product or service demanded to a change in the *price* of that product or service. In other words, the coefficient of price elasticity measures the ratio of the percentage change in the quantity purchased of a product or service to the underlying percentage change in the price of the product or service. This relationship can be expressed as follows:

$$E = \frac{\text{percentage change in quantity demanded}}{\text{percentage change in price}}$$

If the percentage change in quantity demanded is greater than the percentage change in price, demand is said to be *elastic*. In such cases, a small reduction in price will result in a large increase in the quantity purchased; thus, total revenue will rise. Conversely, if the percentage change in quantity demanded is less than the percentage change in price, demand is *inelastic*, and a price reduction will have less of an impact on revenues. Price elasticity of demand is an important factor, for example, in the setting of airline prices for business and leisure fares.[9] Business fares are less price elastic than leisure fares.

A number of factors influence the price elasticity of demand for a product or service. In general,

- The more *substitutes* a product or service has, the greater its price elasticity.
- The more *uses* a product or service has, the greater its price elasticity.
- The higher the *ratio* of the price of the product or service to the income of the buyer, the greater the price elasticity.

Product-Line Pricing

In practice, it is common to apply the concept of price elasticity simultaneously to more than one product or service. By computing the *cross-elasticity of demand* for product A and product B, it is possible to measure the responsiveness of the quantity demanded of product A to a price change in product B. A negative *cross-elasticity coefficient* indicates that the products are complementary; a positive coefficient indicates that they are substitutes. An understanding of the implications of cross-elasticity is especially important for successful implementation of product-line pricing, in which product demand is interrelated and the goal is to maximize revenue for the entire line and not just for individual products or services.

Consider a marketer of cameras and films (or of copying machines and paper, or of video game machines and video games). Should the marketer price cameras very low, perhaps close to or even below cost, in order to promote film sales? Film could then be marketed at relatively high prices. Or should an opposite strategy be employed—selling high-priced cameras but low-priced film? Examples of these alternative tie-in pricing strategies are readily available. For instance, Nintendo, a leader in video games, has traditionally priced its hardware at or near cost and made its profit on its software.[10] The important point is that in most organizations, products are not priced in isolation. In certain instances, individual products may be sold at a loss merely to entice buyers or to ensure that the organization can offer potential buyers complete product lines. In such situations, the price may bear little relationship to the actual cost of a product.

In addition, product-line pricing involves determining (1) the lowest-priced product price, (2) the highest-priced product and price, and (3) price differentials for all other products in the line. The lowest- and highest-priced items in the product line play important roles. The highest-priced item is typically positioned as the premium item in quality and features. The lowest-priced item is the traffic builder designed to capture the attention of the hesitant or first-time buyer. Price differentials between items in the line should make sense to customers and reflect differences in their perceived value of the products offered. Behavioral research also suggests that the price differentials should get larger as one moves up the product line to more expensive items.

Estimating the Profit Impact from Price Changes

In Chapter 2, the basic principles of break-even analysis and leverage were described. These same principles can be applied to assessing the effect of price changes on volume.[11]

The impact of price changes on profit can be determined by looking at cost, price, and volume data for individual products and services. Consider the data shown in the top half of Exhibit 8.2 for two products, alpha and beta. These products have identical prices ($10), unit volumes (1,000 units), and net profits ($2,000), but their cost structures differ. Product alpha has a unit variable cost of $7 and assignable fixed costs of $1,000. Product beta has a unit variable cost of $2 and assignable fixed costs of $6,000. The unit break-even volume for product alpha is 333.3 units ($1,000/$3). Product beta's unit break-even volume is 750 units ($6,000/$8).

The calculation for determining the unit volume necessary to break even on a price change is as follows (percentages expressed in whole numbers):

$$\text{Percentage change in unit volume to break-even on a price change} = \frac{-\,(\text{percentage price change})}{\left(\text{original contribution margin}\right) + \left(\text{percentage price change}\right)}$$

For example, if a product has a 20 percent contribution margin, a 5 percent price decrease will require a 33 percent increase in unit volume to break-even:

$$+33 = \frac{-(-5)}{[20] + [-5]}$$

Alternatively, a product with the same contribution margin can absorb a 20 percent decline in unit volume if its price increases 5 percent without incurring a loss in profit:

$$-20 = \frac{-(+5)}{[20] + [+5]}$$

The lower half of Exhibit 8.2 illustrates the potential profit impact of price changes for products alpha and beta. For product alpha to profit from a 10 percent price cut, its unit volume would have to increase by 50 percent. In contrast, unit sales of product beta, with its larger contribution, would only have to increase by slightly more than 14 percent for a profit to be realized.

The same type of analysis can be applied to price increases. For example, if product alpha's price were increased 10 percent, its unit volume could decrease by 25 percent before profits would decline. On the other hand, product beta, with its higher contribution, could absorb only an 11 percent volume decline with a 10 percent price increase. Other price change effects are shown in Exhibit 8.2 for illustrative purposes.

EXHIBIT 8.2

Estimating the Effect of Price Changes

	Product Alpha	***Product Beta***
Cost, Volume, and Profit Data		
Unit sales volume	1,000	1,000
Unit selling price	$10	$10
Unit variable cost	$7	$2
Unit contribution (margin)	$3 (30%)	$8 (80%)
Fixed costs	$1,000	$6,000
Net profit	$2,000	$2,000
Break-Even Sales Change		
For a 5% price reduction	+20.0%	+6.7%
For a 10% price reduction	+50.0%	+14.3%
For a 20% price reduction	+200.0%	+33.3%
For a 5% price increase	−14.3%	−5.9%
For a 10% price increase	−25.0%	−11.1%
For a 20% price increase	−40.0%	−20.0%

■ PRICING STRATEGIES

Because of the difficulty of estimating demand, most pricing strategies have a decided reliance on cost as a basic foundation. To a great extent, price strategies can be termed either full-cost or variable-cost strategies. *Full-cost price strategies* are those that consider both variable and fixed costs (sometimes termed *direct* and *indirect costs*). *Variable-cost price strategies* take into account only the direct variable costs associated with offering a product or service.

Full-Cost Pricing

Full-cost pricing strategies generally take one of three forms: markup pricing, break-even pricing, and rate-of-return pricing. *Markup pricing* is a strategy in which the selling price of a product or service is determined simply by adding a fixed amount to the (total) cost of the product. The fixed amount is usually expressed as a percentage of either the cost or the price of the product. If it costs \$4.60 to produce a product and the selling price is \$6.35, the markup on *cost* would be 38 percent, and the markup on *price* would be 28 percent.

Markup pricing is frequently used in routine pricing situations, such as with grocery or clothing items, but it is also sometimes employed in pricing unique products or services—for example, military equipment or construction projects. Markup pricing may well be the most common type of pricing strategy. Although it possesses decided drawbacks (especially if a single percentage is applied across products without regard to their elasticities or competition), its simplicity, flexibility, and controllability make it highly popular.

As noted in Chapter 2 when discussing the financial aspects of marketing management, break-even analysis is a useful tool for determining how many units of a product or service must be sold at a specific price for an organization to cover its total costs (fixed plus variable costs). Through judicious use of break-even analysis, it is also possible to calculate the break-even price for a product or service. Specifically, the break-even price of a product or service equals the per-unit fixed costs plus the per-unit variable costs.

Rate-of-return pricing is slightly more sophisticated than either markup or break-even pricing. Still, it contains the basic ingredients of both of these strategies and can be viewed as an extension of them. In a *rate-of-return pricing strategy*, price is set so as to obtain a prespecified rate of return on investment (capital) for the organization. Since rate of return on investment (ROI) equals profit (Pr) divided by investment (I),

$$\text{ROI} = \text{Pr}/I = \frac{\text{revenues} - \text{cost}}{\text{investment}} = \frac{P \cdot Q - C \cdot Q}{I}$$

where P and C are, respectively, unit selling price and unit cost, and Q represents the quantity sold.

By working backward from a predetermined rate of return, it is possible to derive a selling price that will obtain that return rate. If an organization desires an ROI of 15 percent on an investment of \$80,000, total costs per unit are estimated to be \$0.175, and a demand of 20,000 units is forecast, then the necessary price will be

$$\frac{(\text{ROI}) \times I + CQ}{Q} = P = \frac{(0.15)\ \$80{,}000 + \$0.175 \times 20{,}000}{20{,}000} = 0.775$$

or roughly \$0.78.

This pricing strategy, popularized by General Motors, is most commonly used by large firms and public utilities whose return rates are closely watched or are regulated by government agencies or commissions. Like other types of full-cost pricing strategies, rate-of-return pricing assumes a standard (linear) demand function and insensitivity of buyers to price. This assumption often holds true only for certain price ranges, however.

Variable-Cost Pricing

An alternative to full-cost pricing strategies is a variable-cost, or contribution pricing, strategy. This type of strategy is sometimes used when an organization is operating at less than full capacity and fixed costs constitute a great proportion of total unit costs. The basic idea underlying *variable-cost pricing* is that, in certain short-run pricing situations, the relevant costs to consider are the variable costs, not the total costs. Specifically, in this strategy, variable unit cost represents the minimum selling price at which the product or service can be marketed. Any price above this minimum represents a contribution to fixed costs and profits.

Variable-cost pricing is a form of demand-oriented pricing. As such, it can serve two different purposes: (1) stimulate demand and (2) shift demand. Since variable-cost prices are lower than full-cost prices, the assumption is that they will *stimulate demand* and increase revenues, and hence will lead to economies of scale, lower unit costs, and greater profits. This is why airlines offer different classes of fares, hotels offer special weekend rates, and movie theaters have discounts for senior citizens. Variable-cost pricing also makes sense because fixed costs must be met no matter whether a product or service is sold—the airline must maintain its flight schedule whether or not there are any passengers; the hotel or movie theater has to remain open even if it is only partially filled—and the incremental (variable) costs of serving one more customer are minimal.

Consider a bus line making a daily run from Duluth to Minneapolis, Minnesota. The price of a one-way ticket is $30.00, and on an average trip the bus is 60 percent full. If unit fixed and variable costs are, respectively, $7.50 and $2.00, should the bus line offer a half-price fare for children under five years of age? Ignoring price elasticity and the like for the moment, the answer is yes, the reduced fare should be offered. The reduced fare ($15.00) covers the variable costs ($2.00) and makes a contribution of $13.00 to fixed costs. Since the bus line will make the trip regardless of how many passengers there are, in the short run every reduced-fare ticket sold contributes $13.00 to fixed expenses. Such a pricing approach always assumes that no more profitable use may be made of the revenue-generating activity.

In addition to stimulating demand, variable-cost pricing can be used to *shift demand* from one time period to another. Movie theaters sometimes have lower matinee ticket prices to encourage customers to switch from evening to afternoon attendance. Likewise, certain utilities (such as telephone companies) have different price schedules to shift demand away from peak load times and smooth it out over extended time periods.

New-Offering Pricing Strategies

Full- and variable-cost pricing strategies are *technical strategies* that can be used when an organization initially sets its prices or when it changes them. When pricing a new product or service, however, a manager also has to consider other, more *conceptual* strategies.

When introducing a new product or service to the marketplace, an organization can employ one of three alternative pricing strategies. With a *skimming pricing strategy*, the price is set very high initially and is typically reduced over time. A skimming strategy may be appropriate for a new product or service if any of the following conditions hold:

1. Demand is likely to be price inelastic.
2. There are different price-market segments, thereby appealing first to buyers who have a higher range of acceptable prices.
3. The offering is unique enough to be protected from competition by patent, copyright, or trade secret.
4. Production or marketing costs are unknown.
5. A capacity constraint in producing the product or providing the service exists.
6. An organization wants to generate funds quickly to recover its investment or finance other developmental efforts.
7. There is a realistic perceived value in the product or service.

Many of these conditions were present in 1998 when Gillette decided to price its innovative Mach3 shaving system 35 percent higher than its hugely successful SensorExcel shaving system introduced four years earlier. Mach3 is projected to log $1.8 billion in annual worldwide sales using this strategy in some 100 countries.[12]

At the other extreme, an organization may use a *penetration pricing strategy*, whereby a product or service is introduced at a low price. This strategy may be appropriate if any of the following conditions exist:

1. Demand is likely to be price elastic in the target market segments at which the product or service is aimed.
2. The offering is not unique or protected by patents, copyrights, or trade secrets.
3. Competitors are expected to enter the market quickly.
4. There are no distinct and separate price-market segments.
5. There is a possibility of large savings in production and marketing costs if a large sales volume can be generated.
6. The organization's major objective is to obtain a large market share.

Sega Enterprises most likely considered several of these factors and consciously chose a penetration strategy when it introduced the Dreamcast video game machine in late 1999 at a price that was 33 percent less than the traditional debut price for new-generation video game machines.[13]

Between these two extremes is an *intermediate pricing strategy*. As might be expected, this type of strategy is the most prevalent in practice. The other two types of introductory pricing strategies are, so to speak, more flamboyant; given the vagaries of the marketplace, however, intermediate pricing is more likely to be used in the vast majority of initial pricing decisions.

Pricing and Competitive Interaction

No discussion of pricing strategy and management is complete without mention of competitive interaction.[14] Because price is the one element of the marketing mix that can be changed quickly and easily, competitive interaction is common. Competitive interaction in a pricing context refers to the sequential action and reaction of rival companies in setting and changing prices for their offering(s) and assessing likely outcomes, such as sales, unit volume, and profit for each company and an entire market. Competitive interaction is like playing chess. Those players who make moves one at a time, seeking to minimize immediate losses or to exploit immediate opportunities, invariably are beaten by those who can envision the game a few moves ahead.

Somewhat surprisingly, research and practice suggest that marketing managers infrequently look beyond an initial pricing decision to consider competitor countermoves, their own subsequent moves, and outcomes. Two remedies are often proposed to overcome this nearsightedness. First, managers are advised to focus less on short-term outcomes and attend more to longer-term consequences of actions. Competitive interactions are rarely confined to one period; that is, an action followed by a reaction. Also, the consequences of actions and reactions are not always immediately observable. Therefore, managers are advised to "look forward and reason backward" by envisioning patterns of future pricing moves, competitor countermoves, and likely outcomes. Second, managers are advised to step into the shoes of rival managers or companies and answer a number of questions:

1. What are competitors' goals and objectives? How are they different from our goals and objectives?
2. What assumptions has the competitor made about itself, our company and offerings, and the marketplace? Are these assumptions different from ours?
3. What strengths does the competitor believe it has and what are its weaknesses? What might the competitor believe our strengths and weaknesses to be?

Failure to answer these questions can lead to misjudgments about the price(s) set or changed by competitors and misguide subsequent pricing moves and countermoves among competitors. Misreading the situation can result in price wars.

Over the past decade, price wars have broken out in a variety of industries: from personal computers to disposable diapers, from soft drinks to airlines, and from grocery retailing to long-distance telephone services.[15] Price wars do not just happen. Managers expecting that a lower price will result in a larger market share, higher unit sales, and greater profit for their offering(s) often initiate them. This may indeed occur. However, if competitors match the lower price, other things being equal, the expected share, sales, and profit gain is lost. More importantly, the overall price level resulting from the lower price benefits none of the competitors.

Certain industry settings tend to be prone to price wars. Exhibit 8.3 shows that the risk of price wars is higher or lower when an industry exhibits certain characteristics. For example, if a product or service supplied by the industry is undifferentiated, price tends to be an important buying factor. This situation increases the likelihood of price competition and price wars. A stable or declining market growth rate coupled with low capacity utilization by companies tends to result in corporate unit volume growth objectives, often promoted through price cutting. Clearly visible competitor prices, highly price sensitive consumers, and declining costs in an industry also increase the risk of price wars.

EXHIBIT 8.3

Industry Characteristics and the Risk of Price Wars

	Risk Level	
Industry Characteristics	*Higher*	*Lower*
Product/Service type	Undifferentiated	Differentiated
Market growth rate	Stable/Decreasing	Increasing
Price visibility to competitors	High	Low
Consumer price sensitivity	High	Low
Overall industry cost trend	Declining	Stable
Industry capacity utilization	Low	High
Number of competitors	Many	Few

NOTES

1. E. Raymond Corey, *Industrial Marketing: Cases and Concepts,* 4th ed. (Upper Saddle River, NJ: Prentice Hall, 1991): 256.

2. For an extensive treatment of pricing, see Kent B. Monroe, *Pricing Making Profitable Decisions,* 2nd ed. (New York: McGraw-Hill, 1990); Thomas T. Nagle and Reed K. Holden, *The Strategy and Tactics of Pricing,* 2nd ed. (Upper Saddle River, NJ: Prentice Hall, 1995); or Robert J. Dolan and Hermann Simon, *Power Pricing* (New York: The Free Press, 1996).

3. Vannessa O'Connell, "How Campbell Saw a Breakthrough Menu Turn into Leftovers," *Wall Street Journal* (October 6, 1998): A1, A12.

4. Mary Beth Grover, "Lost in Cyberspace," *Forbes* (March 8, 1999): 124–28.

5. For a comprehensive review of the price-quality-value relationship, see Valarie A. Zeithaml, "Consumer Perceptions of Price, Quality, and Value," *Journal of Marketing* (July 1988): 2–22. Also see Rolf Leszinski and Michael V. Marn, "Setting Value, Not Price," *The McKinsey Quarterly* (Number 1, 1997): 98–115.

6. "Laundry Soap Marketers See the Value of 'Value'!" *Advertising Age* (September 21, 1992): 3, 56.

7. Jean-Noel Kapferer, "Managing Luxury Brands," *The Journal of Brand Management* (July 1997): 251–60; "Buying Time," *Fortune* (September 8, 1997): 192.

8. "Store-Brand Pricing Has to Be Just Right," *Wall Street Journal* (February 14, 1992): B1.

9. "Business Fares Increase Even as Leisure Travel Keeps Getting Cheaper," *Wall Street Journal* (November 3, 1997): A1, A6.

10. "Giants of Video-Game Industry Rallying for Rebound," *Wall Street Journal* (May 31, 1996): B3.

11. This discussion is based, in part, on George E. Cressman, Jr., "Snatching Defeat From the Jaws of Victory," *Marketing Management* (Summer 1997): 9–19.

12. Mark Morement, "How Gillette Brought Its Mach3 to Market," *Wall Street Journal* (April 15, 1998): B1, B8; "The Big Push: Gillette Lets Fly $100 Mil Campaign for Mach3," *Advertising Age* (April 5, 1999): 46.

13. "Sega Is Pricing Game Machine on the Low Side," *Wall Street Journal* (April 16, 1999): B7.

14. This discussion is based on Bruce Clark, "Managing Competitive Interactions," *Marketing Management* (Fall/Winter 1998): 9–20; Joe E. Urbany and David B. Montgomery, "Rational Strategic Reasoning: An Unnatural Act?" *Marketing Letters* (August 1998): 285–300.

15. This discussion is based on Michael R. Baye, *Managerial Economics and Business Strategy,* 2nd ed. (Chicago: Richard D. Irwin, 1997): Chapters 9 and 10; Robert A. Garda and Michael V. Marn, "Price Wars," *The McKinsey Quarterly* (Number 3, 1993): 87–100; and Akshay R. Rao, Mark E. Bergen, and Scott Davis, "How to Fight a Price War," *Harvard Business Review* (March–April 2000): 107–116.

CASE

Southwest Airlines

In late January 1995, Dave Ridley, Vice President-Marketing and Sales at Southwest Airlines, was preparing to join Joyce Rogge, Vice President-Advertising and Promotion, Keith Taylor, Vice President-Revenue Management, and Pete McGlade, Vice President-Schedule Planning, for their weekly "Tuesday meeting." The purpose of this regularly scheduled meeting was to exchange ideas, keep one another informed about external and internal developments pertaining to their areas of responsibility, and coordinate pricing and marketing activities. This informal gathering promoted communication among functional areas and fostered the team spirit that is an integral part of the Southwest corporate culture.

A recurrent "Tuesday meeting" topic during the past six months had been the changing competitive landscape for Southwest evident in the "Continental Lite" and "Shuttle By United" initiatives undertaken by Continental Airlines and United Airlines, respectively. Both initiatives represented targeted efforts by major carriers to match Southwest's price *and* service offering—a strategy that no major carrier had successfully implemented in the past. In early January 1995, Continental's effort was being scaled back due to operational difficulties and resulting financial losses.[1] However, United's initiative remained in effect. Launched on October 1, 1994, "Shuttle By United" was serving 14 routes in California and adjacent states by mid-January 1995, nine of which were in direct competition with Southwest. When "Shuttle By United" was announced, United's CEO predicted: "We're going to match them (Southwest) on price and exceed them on service."[2] In response to United's initiative, Southwest's Chairman Herb Kelleher said, the "United Shuttle is like an intercontinental ballistic missile targeted directly at Southwest."

Just as the meeting began, a staff member rushed in to tell the group that United had just made two changes in its "Shuttle By United" service and pricing. First, its service for the Oakland-Ontario, California market would be discontinued effective April 2, 1995. This market had been among the most hotly contested routes among the nine where United and Southwest competed head-to-head and Southwest had lost market share on this route since October 1994. Second, the one-way walk-up first class and coach fare on all 14 "Shuttle By United" routes had just been increased by $10.00. "Shuttle By United" had previously matched Southwest's fare on the nine competitive routes and, as of mid-January 1995, had been increasing the number of flights on these routes and the five routes where they did not compete.

Changes in United's pricing and service for its shuttle operation caught Southwest executives by surprise. The original agenda for the "Tuesday meeting" was im-

---

[1] Bridget O'Brian, "Continental's CALite Hits Some Turbulence in Battling Southwest," *Wall Street Journal* (January 10, 1995): A1, A5.

[2] Quoted in Jon Proctor, "Everyone Versus Southwest," *AIRWAYS Magazine* (November/December 1994): 6-13.

The cooperation of Southwest Airlines in the preparation of this case is gratefully acknowledged. This case was prepared by Professor Roger A. Kerin, of the Edwin L. Cox School of Business, Southern Methodist University, as a basis for class discussion and is not designed to illustrate effective or ineffective handling of an administrative situation. Certain information is disguised and not useful for research purposes.

mediately set aside. Attention focused on (1) what to make of these unexpected developments and (2) how Southwest might respond, if at all, to the new "Shuttle By United" initiatives.

■ THE U.S. PASSENGER AIRLINE INDUSTRY

The U.S. Department of Transportation classified U.S. passenger airlines into three categories on the basis of annual revenue.[3] A "major carrier" was an airline with more than $1 billion in annual revenue. A "national carrier" had annual revenues between $100 million and $1 billion, and a "regional and commuter airline" had annual revenues less than $100 million. Major carriers accounted for more than 95 percent of domestic passengers carried in 1994. Five carriers—American Airlines, Continental Airlines, Delta Airlines, Northwest Airlines, and United Airlines—accounted for over 80 percent of all major carrier domestic passenger traffic. Exhibit 1 shows major air carrier estimated market shares for 1994 in the United States.

Industry Background

The status of the U.S. passenger airline industry in early 1995 could be traced to 1978. Prior to 1978, and for 40 years, the U.S. airline industry was regulated by the federal government through the Civil Aeronautics Board (CAB). The CAB regulated airline fares, routes, and company mergers, and CAB approval was required before any changes in fares or route systems could be made. In this capacity, the CAB assured that individual airlines were awarded highly profitable and semi-exclusive routes necessary to subsidize less profitable routes which they were also assigned in the public interest. Price competition was suppressed, airline cost increases were routinely passed along to passengers, and the CAB allowed airlines to earn a reasonable rate of return on their investments. In 1978, the Airline Deregulation Act was passed. This Act allowed airlines to set their own fares and enter or exit routes without CAB approvals. Jurisdiction for mergers was first transferred to the U.S. Department of Transportation and subsequently assigned to the U.S. Justice Department in 1988. The CAB was dissolved in 1985.

EXHIBIT 1

Estimated Market Shares for Major U.S. Carriers in 1994 Based on Revenue Passenger Miles Flown

Carrier	*Market Share (%)*	*Carrier*	*Market Share (%)*
1. United Airlines	22.1	6. USAir	7.8
2. American Airlines	20.2	7. Trans World Airlines	5.1
3. Delta Airlines	17.6	8. Southwest Airlines	4.4
4. Northwest Airlines	11.8	9. America West Airlines	2.5
5. Continental Airlines	8.5		

Source: Southwest Airlines company records. Figures rounded.

[3] This section is based on information provided in *FAA Aviation Forecasts* (Washington, D.C.: U.S. Department of Transportation, March 1995); Standard & Poor's *Industry Surveys* (New York: Standard & Poor's, January 1995); *U.S. Industrial Outlook* 1995 (Washington, D.C.: U.S. Department of Commerce, January 1995); Timothy K. Smith, "Why Air Travel Doesn't Work," *Fortune* (April 3, 1995): 42–56; and Jon Proctor, "Everyone Versus Southwest," *AIRWAYS Magazine* (November/December 1994): 6–13.

Deregulation and a Decade of Transition Public policy makers and industry analysts expected that deregulation would proceed in an orderly manner with multiple existing major carriers serving previously semi-exclusive routes, bringing about healthy price competition. However, the carriers responded to deregulation with unexpected changes in their operations that would have long-term effects on the industry.

Two changes in particular were noteworthy. First, major carriers turned their attention to serving nonstop "long-haul" routes anchored by densely populated metropolitan areas or city-pairs which had been highly profitable in a regulated environment. This meant that longer routes such as New York to Los Angeles and Chicago to Dallas were favored over "short-haul" routes between smaller city pairs such as Baltimore and Newark, New Jersey. As major carriers pruned or reduced service on these short-haul routes, existing regional carriers and new airlines filled the void. In 1978, the United States had 36 domestic carriers; by 1985 the number had grown to 100. Second, major carriers almost uniformly abandoned point-to-point route systems and adopted the hub-and-spoke route system. Point-to-point systems involved nonstop flights between city-pairs and often "shuttle" flights back and forth between city-pairs. The hub-and-spoke system featured "feeder flights" from outlying cities to a central hub city, where passengers would either continue their trip on the same plane or transfer to another plane operated by the same carrier to continue to their final destination. The key to this route system was to schedule numerous feeder flights into the hub airport to coincide with the more profitable long hauls, with each spoke adding passengers to the larger aircraft flying these longer distances. Potential increased revenue and some cost economies from flying more passengers longer distances, however, were offset by increased costs resulting from reduced utilization of aircraft as they waited to collect passengers, the capital investment in hub facilities, and the need for a larger ground staff.

Competition to survive and succeed intensified in the airline industry immediately following deregulation. Newly formed airlines and regional carriers, which had been permitted to serve only regional markets in a regulated environment, expanded both the number and length of their routes. These carriers typically retained the point-to-point route system which was more economical to operate than hubs. Absent the higher costs associated with the hub-and-spoke system and lower debt than older major carriers had assumed during the regulation era, these carriers had an immediate cost advantage. This advantage resulted in lower fares on both short- and long-haul routes. Price competition quickly erupted as all airlines scrambled to fill their seats. Price competition lowered the average fares paid on the formerly profitable long-haul routes serviced by major carriers while their operating costs remained high. The profit squeeze caused major carriers to cut their schedules and further reduce the number of short-haul routes.

Within five years after deregulation, the major carriers found themselves in a price-cost predicament best described by a senior airline executive: "Either we don't match (fares) and we lose customers, or we match and then because our costs are so high, we lose buckets of money."[4] This situation continued through the remainder of the 1980s as a price war of attrition was waged, ultimately resulting in a flurry of acquisitions by major carriers. Noteworthy acquisitions included Ozark Airlines by Trans World Airlines (TWA), Western Airlines by Delta, and Republic Airlines by Northwest in 1986. In 1987, AMR (American Airlines' parent company), acquired Air California and USAir acquired Pacific Southwest Airlines.

[4] William M. Carley, "Rough Flying: Some Major Airlines Are Being Threatened by Low-Cost Carriers," *Wall Street Journal* (October 12, 1983): 23.

Financial Calamity in the Early 1990s Acquisition activity in the mid-1980s led industry analysts to believe the U.S. airline industry would soon evolve into an oligopoly with a few carriers capturing a disproportionate share of domestic traffic. By the late 1980s, eight airlines controlled 91 percent of U.S. traffic, but their financial condition was fragile due to a decade of marginal profitability.

Carrier bankruptcy and collapse marked the early 1990s due to a recession, a doubling of fuel prices during the Gulf War in 1991, and excess capacity in the industry. The U.S. airline industry recorded a cumulative deficit of $12 billion from 1990 through 1993. (See Exhibit 2, which plots U.S. air carrier operating revenues and expenses for fiscal years 1979 to 1994.) Between 1989 and 1992, Pan American Airlines (Pan Am), Continental Airlines, America West Airlines, Midway Airlines (a national carrier), Eastern Airlines, and TWA all filed for protection under Chapter 11 of the U.S. Bankruptcy Code. Eastern, Pan Am, and Midway ceased operations in 1991. Continental and TWA emerged from bankruptcy in 1993 as did America West in late 1994, and the industry as a whole recorded a modest operating profit in the 1994 fiscal year. Exhibit 3 shows 1994 financial and operating statistics for major U.S. carriers.

As existing airlines collapsed, new airlines were formed. The majority of new carriers, such as ValuJet, Reno Air, and Kiwi International Airlines, positioned themselves as "low-fare, low-frill" airlines. Benefiting from a cheap supply of aircraft grounded by major carriers from 1989 to 1993, the availability of furloughed airline personnel, and cost economies of point-to-point route systems, these new entrants had cost structures that were again significantly below most major carriers. For example, Kiwi was started by former Eastern and Pan Am personnel and was largely

EXHIBIT 2

U.S. Air Carrier Operating Revenues and Expenses, 1979–1994

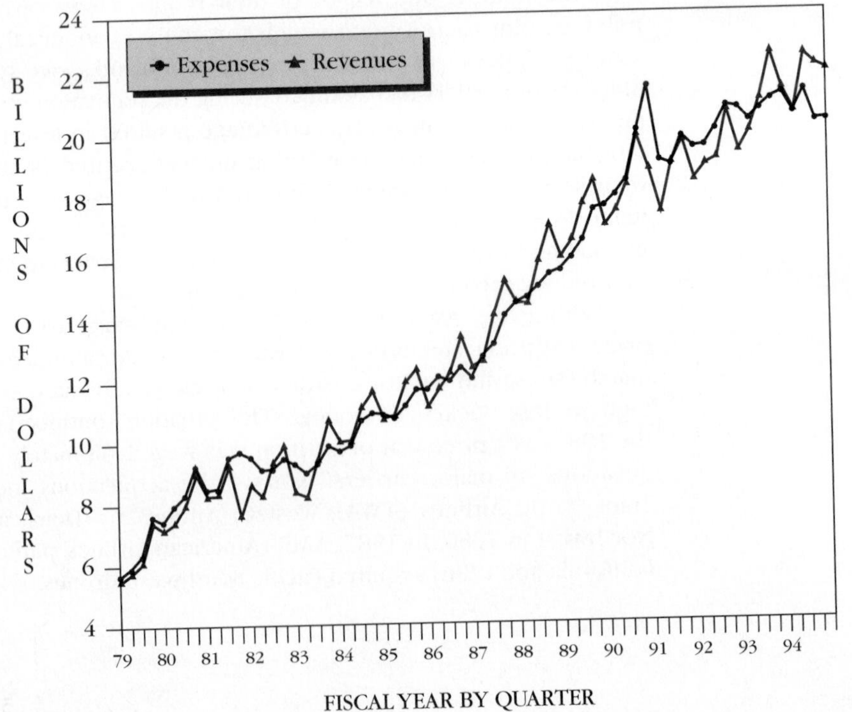

Source: U.S. Department of Transportation.

EXHIBIT 3

1994 Financial and Operating Statistics for Major Carriers in the United States

	American Airlines (AMR)	America West Airlines	Continental Airlines	Delta Airlines	Northwest Airlines	Southwest Airlines	Trans World Airlines	United Airlines (UAL)	USAir
Financial Data ($ millions)									
Operating revenue	$14,895	$1,409	$5,670	$12,062	$8,343	$2,592	$3,408	$13,950	$6,997
Passenger	13,616	1,320	5,036	11,197	7,028	2,498	2,876	12,295	6,358
Freight/other	1,279	89	634	865	1,315	94	532	1,655	6 39
Operating expenses[a]	$14,309	$1,319	$5,921	$12,151	$7,879	$2,275	$3,883	$13,801	$7,773
Operating income	$586	$90	$(251)	$(89)	$464	$317	$(475)	$149	$(776)
Other income (expense)	$(593)	$2	$(399)	$(325)	$52	$(17)	$39	$22	$91
Net income before tax	$(7)	$92	$(650)	$(414)	$516	$300	$(436)	$171	$(685)
Operating Statistics									
Available seat miles (millions)	157,047[e]	18,060	65,861[f]	130,198	85,016	32,124	39,191	152,193	61,540
Revenue passenger miles (millions)	101,382	12,233	31,588	86,296	57,872	21,611	24,906	108,299	37,941
Load factor (%)	64.6	67.7	63.1	66.3	68.1	67.3	63.5	71.2	61.3
Yield (¢)[b]	13.40	10.79	11.44	12.97	12.14	11.56	11.31	11.35	16.76
Cost per available seat mile (¢)[c]	9.11	7.30	7.86	9.33	9.26	7.08	9.91	9.06	12.63
Labor productivity[d]	1,739	1,695	1,668	1,915	1,968	2,019	1,502	2,125	1,451

[a] Operating expenses include interest expense.

[b] Passenger revenue per revenue passenger mile.

[c] Operating expenses including interest expense per available seat mile.

[d] Thousands of available seat miles per employee.

[e] Includes the American Eagle commuter airline and transportation business only.

[f] Continental Airlines operating statistics are for jet operations only.

Source: Company annual reports. Data and calculations (all rounded) are useful for case analysis, but not for research purposes. Revenue, expense, and operating statistics also include international operations.

funded by its employees (pilots paid $50,000 each to get jobs; other employees paid $5,000). These new "low-fare, low-frill" carriers reported combined revenues of about $1.4 billion in 1994 compared with $450 million in 1992. Although accounting for a small percentage of industry revenue, their pricing practices depressed fares on a growing number of routes also served by major carriers. In 1994, 92 percent of airline passengers bought their tickets at a discount, paying on average just 35 percent of the posted full fare.

Industry Economics and Carrier Performance

The financial performance of individual carriers and the U.S. airline industry as a whole could be attributed, in part, to the underlying economics of air travel. The majority of a carrier's costs (e.g., labor, fuel, facilities, planes) were fixed, regardless of the numbers of passengers served. The largest single cost to a carrier was people (salaries, wages, and benefits) followed by fuel. These two cost sources represented almost one-half of an airline's costs and were relatively fixed at a particular level of operating capacity. Fuel costs were uncontrollable and the industry had been periodically buffeted with skyrocketing fuel prices, most recently during the Gulf War in 1991. Fuel cost was expected to increase by 4.3 cents per gallon in late 1995 based on a tax imposed by the Revenue Reconciliation Act of 1993. Industry observers estimated that this tax would cost the U.S. airline industry an additional $500 million annually in fuel expense.

Labor cost, by comparison, was a controllable expense within limits, and more than 100,000 airline workers lost their jobs between 1989 and 1994. Recent efforts by major carriers to reduce labor cost included United Airlines, which completed an employee buyout of 55 percent of the company in exchange for $4.9 billion in labor concessions in the summer of 1994. In the spring of 1994, Delta Airlines announced a three-year plan to reduce operating expenses by $2 billion, which would involve 12,000 to 15,000 jobs being eliminated.

Carrier Operating Performance Whereas the majority of a carrier's costs were fixed at a particular capacity level regardless of the number of passengers carried, a carrier's passenger revenues were linked to the number of passengers carried and the fare paid for a seat at a particular passenger capacity level. A carrier's passenger capacity is measured by the available seat miles (ASMs) it can transport given its airplane fleet, flight scheduling, and route length. An ASM is defined as one seat flown one mile whether the seat is occupied by a passenger or is empty. Carrier productivity is typically tracked by dividing a carrier's total operating cost by available seat miles. Carrier utilization is measured by what is termed a load factor. Load factor is computed by dividing a carrier's revenue passenger miles (RPMs) by its available seat miles. An RPM is defined as one seat flown one mile with a passenger in it and is a measure of a carrier's traffic. Yield is the measure of a carrier's passenger revenue-producing ability and is expressed as an average dollar amount received for flying one passenger one mile. Yield is calculated by dividing passenger revenue by revenue passenger miles.

The following expression shows how yield, load factor, and cost combine to determine the profitability of passenger operations for individual carriers, routes, and the industry:

$$\text{Operating income} = (\text{yield} \times \text{load factor}) - \text{cost, or}$$

$$\frac{\text{Operating income}}{\text{ASM}} = \left(\frac{\text{passenger revenue}}{\text{RPM}} \times \frac{\text{RPM}}{\text{ASM}}\right) - \frac{\text{operating cost}}{\text{ASM}}$$

By setting operating income to zero and monitoring yield and cost, individual carriers frequently computed a break-even load factor for passenger operations which

EXHIBIT 4

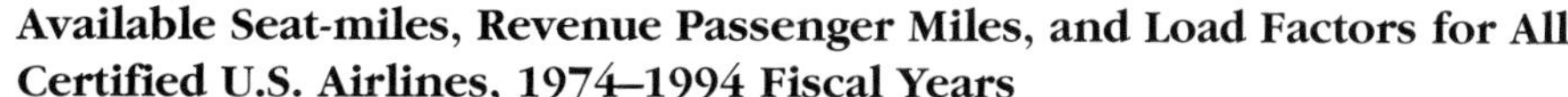

Available Seat-miles, Revenue Passenger Miles, and Load Factors for All Certified U.S. Airlines, 1974–1994 Fiscal Years

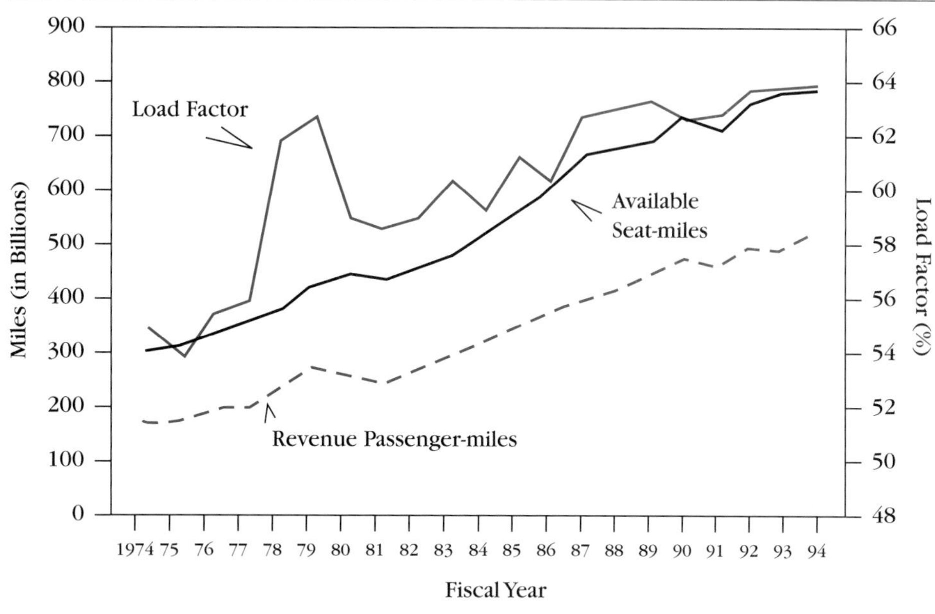

Source: U.S. Department of Transportation.

was continually compared with actual load factors. Actual load factors higher than the break-even load factor produced an operating income for passenger operations; actual load factors below a break-even load factor resulted in an operating loss.

Industry Trends Exhibit 4 charts available seat-miles, revenue passenger miles, and load factors for all FAA certified airlines for the 1974 fiscal year through the 1994 fiscal year. While revenue passenger miles and available seat miles for the industry have shown an upward trend, load factor fluctuated due to periodic imbalances between industry capacity and passenger demand. For example, domestic airline capacity (ASMs) increased by only 1.6 percent in fiscal year 1994 while revenue passenger miles increased 6.5 percent, producing a load factor of 64.3 percent. This figure represented the highest industry load factor ever achieved on domestic routes. Domestic passenger yields evidenced a long-term downward trend for 25 years in real (adjusted for inflation) dollars. In terms of real yield (discounting fares for inflation), fares in the years 1969 to 1971 produced an average yield of 21.4 cents in 1994 dollars. By 1994, the average industry yield was 12.73 cents.

Cost per available seat mile also exhibited a downward trend since 1978 despite periodic fluctuations in fuel prices. Nevertheless, labor cost reduction and productivity improvements coupled with the gradual addition of more fuel-efficient and lower cost maintenance planes by major carriers had not kept pace with the declining yields in the industry. Efforts by major carriers to reduce labor cost, described earlier, reflected the continuing attention to reducing the cost per available seat mile.

The Airline-Within-an-Airline Concept

Only Southwest Airlines, among the major carriers, appeared able to effectively navigate the economics of air travel and avoid the financial calamity that had befallen the airline industry in the early 1990s. Operating primarily short-haul, point-to-point routes, with minimal amenities, and able to make a fast turnaround of its aircraft between flights, Southwest had much lower operating costs than other major carriers. Lower operating costs were passed on to customers in the form of consistently low fares. From 1990 through 1994, Southwest more than doubled its operating revenues and almost quadrupled its operating income. Its operating practices and financial performance prompted a 1993 U.S. Department of Transportation study to conclude: "The dramatic growth of Southwest has become the principal driving force in changes occurring in the airline industry . . . As Southwest continues to expand, other airlines will be forced to develop low-cost service in short-haul markets."[5]

With Southwest's operating practices as a blueprint, several major carriers had already explored ways to implement a low-cost airline service in short-haul markets and produce a "clone" of Southwest. An outcome of this effort was the "airline-within-an-airline" concept. This concept involved operating a point-to-point, low-fare, short haul, route system alongside a major carrier's hub-and-spoke route system.

Continental Lite Continental was the first major carrier to implement this concept. Having just emerged from bankruptcy with lower operating costs and armed with a preponderance of consumer research showing that 75 percent of customers choose an airline on the basis of flight schedule and price, Continental unveiled what came to be known as "Continental Lite" on October 1, 1993. This service initially focused on Continental routes in the eastern and southeastern United States. By December 1994, Continental had converted about one-half of its 2,000 daily flights into low-fare, short-haul, point-to-point service, but was experiencing operating difficulties. In early January 1995, with operating difficulties resulting in a sizable financial loss, the "Continental Lite" initiative began folding back into Continental's hub-and-spoke system.

Shuttle By United United, the world's largest airline in 1994, inaugurated its "airline-within-an-airline" on October 1, 1994. Branded "Shuttle By United," this initiative followed the United employee buyout in the summer of 1994 when employee wage cuts and more flexible work rules made possible a lower cost shuttle operation alongside the United hub-and-spoke route system. "Shuttle By United" was designed to be a high-frequency, low-fare, minimal amenity, short-haul flight operation initially serving destinations in California and adjacent states. If successful, United executives noted that the initiative could be expanded to 20 percent of United's domestic operations, and particularly to areas where the airline had a significant presence. One such area was the midwest, where United operated a large hub-and-spoke system out of Chicago's O'Hare Airport.

Beginning with eight routes, six of which involved United's San Francisco hub, "Shuttle By United" expanded to 14 routes by January 1995. Eight of the 14 routes involved point-to-point routes separate and apart from United's San Francisco hub. Nine of the routes competed directly with Southwest. In early December 1994, United executives reported that the initiative was exceeding expectations and some routes were profitable. "The Shuttle is working well," said its president, A. B. "Sky" Magary.[6]

---

[5] U.S. Department of Transportation press release, May 11, 1993.

[6] Quoted in Michael J. McCarty, "New Shuttle Incites a War Between Old Rivals," *Wall Street Journal* (December 1, 1994): B1, B5.

■ SOUTHWEST AIRLINES

Southwest Airlines was the eighth largest airline in the United States in 1994 based on the number of revenue passenger miles flown. Southwest recorded net income of $179.3 million on total operating revenue of $2.6 billion in 1994, thus marking 22 consecutive years of profitable operations—a feat unmatched in the U.S. airline industry over the past two decades. According to Southwest's Chairman, President, CEO, and co-founder, Herb Kelleher, Southwest's success formula could be succinctly described as, "Better quality plus lesser price equals value, plus spiritual attitude of our employees equals unbeatable."

The Southwest Model

Southwest began scheduled service on June 18, 1971, as a short-haul, point-to-point, low-fare, high-frequency airline committed to exceptional customer service. Beginning with three Boeing 737 aircraft serving three Texas cities—Dallas, Houston, and San Antonio—Southwest presently operates 199 Boeing 737 aircraft and provides service to 44 cities primarily in the midwestern, southwestern, and western regions of the United States. Fifty-nine percent of Southwest's capacity, measured in available seat miles flown, was deployed in the western United States, 22 percent in the southwest (Texas, Oklahoma, Arkansas, and Louisiana), and 19 percent in the midwest. Exhibit 5 shows the Southwest route map in early 1995.

EXHIBIT 5

Southwest Airlines Route Map in Early 1995

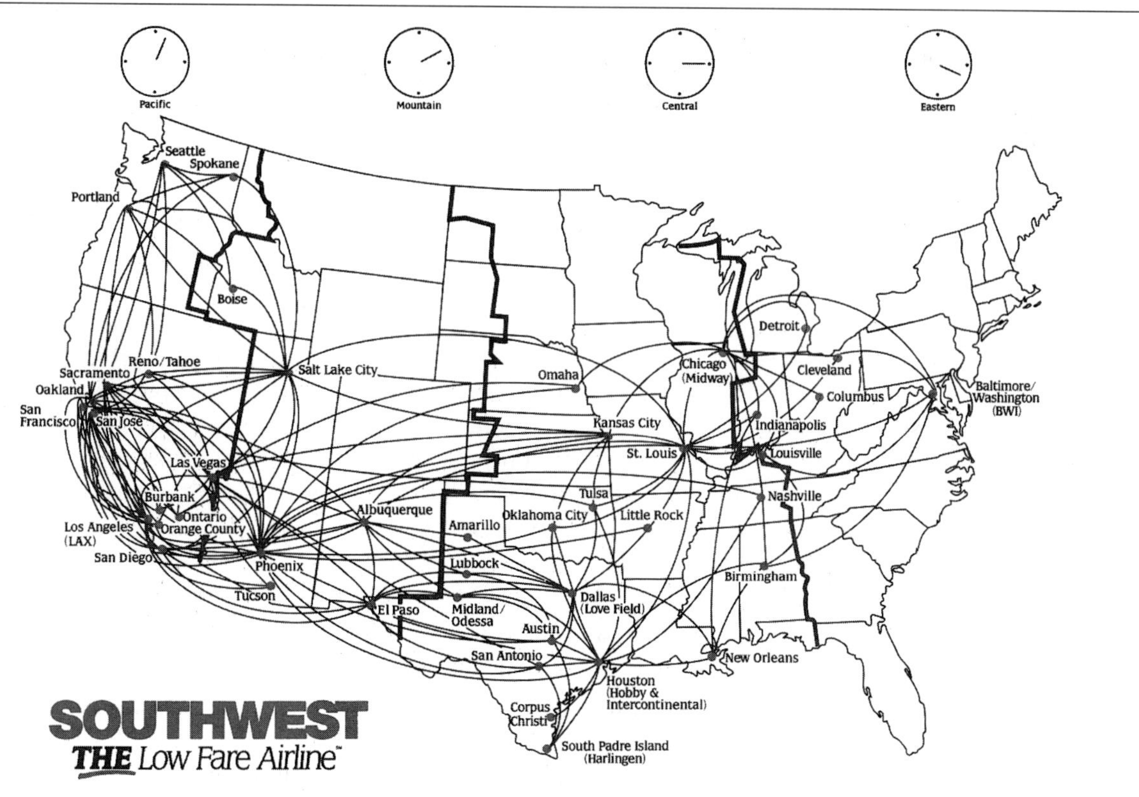

Source: Courtesy of Southwest Airlines.

Except for the acquisitions of Muse Air in 1985 and Morris Air in 1993, Southwest's management has steadfastly insisted on growing internally and refining and replicating what came to be known as the "Southwest Model" in the airline industry. This model was a mixture of a relentless attention to customer service and operations, creative marketing, and Southwest's commitment to its people. A healthy dose of fun was added for good measure.

Customer Service Southwest's attention to customer service was embodied in the attitudes of its people. According to Herb Kelleher:

> What we are looking for, first and foremost, is a sense of humor. Then we are looking for people who have to excel to satisfy themselves and who work well in a collegial environment. We don't care that much about education and expertise, because we can train people to do whatever they have to do. We hire attitudes.[7]

A sense of humor, compassion for passengers and fellow workers, a desire to work, and a positive outlook manifested themselves in customer service at Southwest. Pilots could be found assisting at a boarding gate; ticket agents could be seen handling baggage. So important was the attention to customer service that Southwest chronicled legendary achievements in an internal publication titled *The BOOK on Service: What Positively Outrageous Service Looks Like at Southwest Airlines*.

The Southwest focus on customer service also produced tangible results. In 1994, Southwest won the annual unofficial "triple crown" of the airline industry for the third consecutive year by ranking first among major carriers in the areas of on-time performance, baggage handling, and overall customer satisfaction (see Exhibit 6). No other airline had ever won the "triple crown" for even a single month.

Operations Southwest dedicated its efforts to delivering a short-haul, low-fare, point-to-point, high-frequency service to airline passengers. As a short-haul carrier with a point-to-point route system, it focused on local, not through or connecting, traffic that was common among carriers using a hub-and-spoke system. As a result, approxi-

EXHIBIT 6

U.S. Department of Transportation Rankings of Major Air Carriers for 1994 by On-time Performance, Baggage Handling, and Customer Satisfaction

On-Time Performance		*Baggage Handling*		*Customer Satisfaction*	
Southwest	1	Southwest	1	Southwest	1
Northwest	2	America West	2	Delta	2
Alaska	3	American	3	Alaska	3
United	4	Delta	4	Northwest	4
American	5	Alaska	5	American	5
America West	6	United	6	United	6
Delta	7	TWA	7	USAir	7
TWA	8	USAir	8	America West	8
USAir	9	Northwest	9	TWA	9
Continental	10	Continental	10	Continental	10

Source: U.S. Department of Transportation.

[7] Quoted in Kenneth Labich, "Is Herb Kelleher America's Best CEO?" *Fortune* (May 2, 1994): 28–35.

mately 80 percent of its passengers flew nonstop. In 1994, the average passenger trip length was 506 miles and the average flight time was slightly over one hour. From its inception, Southwest executives recognized that flight schedules and frequency were important considerations for the short-haul traveler. This meant that Southwest aircraft had to "turn" quickly to maximize time in the air and minimize time on the ground. Turn referred to the elapsed time from the moment a plane arrived at the gate to the moment when it was "pushed back," indicating the beginning of another flight.[8] More than half of Southwest's planes were turned in 15 minutes or less while the remainder were scheduled to turn in 20 minutes. The U.S. airline industry turn time averaged around 55 minutes. A result of this difference was that Southwest planes made about ten flights per day, which was more than twice the industry average.

Southwest's operations differed from major carriers in other important ways. First, Southwest generally avoided major airline hubs in large cities. Instead, airports in smaller cities or less congested airports in larger cities were served. Midway Airport in Chicago, Illinois, and Love Field in Dallas, Texas, were examples of less congested airports in larger cities from which Southwest operated. Less congestion meant Southwest flights experienced less aircraft taxi time and less airport circling while awaiting landing permission. The practice of using secondary rather than hub airports also meant that Southwest did not transfer passenger baggage to other major airlines. In fact, Southwest did not coordinate baggage transfers with other airlines even in the few hub airports it served, such as Los Angeles International Airport (LAX).

Second, Southwest stood apart from other major carriers in terms of booking reservations and providing seat assignments. Rather than making reservations through computerized reservations systems, passengers and travel agents alike had to call Southwest. As a result, fewer than one-half of Southwest's seats were booked by travel agents. (Most airlines rely on travel agents to write up to 90 percent of their tickets.) Savings on travel agent commissions to Southwest amounted to about $30 million per year. Also, contrary to other major airlines, Southwest did not offer seat assignments. As Herb Kelleher said, "We still reserve your seat. We just don't tell you whether it's 2C or 38B!" Instead, reusable, numbered boarding passes identified passengers and determined boarding priority. The first 30 passengers checked in at the gate board first, then a second group of 30 (31–60) boarded, and so forth.

Third, only beverages and snacks were served on Southwest flights. The principal snack was peanuts, and 64 million bags of peanuts were served in 1994. Cookies were offered on longer flights.

Finally, Southwest flew only Boeing 737 jets in an all-coach configuration since no fare classes (first class, economy, business, etc.) existed. This practice differed from other major carriers which flew a variety of jet aircraft made by Airbus Industries, Boeing, and McDonnell Douglas, and reduced aircraft maintenance costs. Southwest's fleet was among the youngest of the major airlines at 7.6 years and had 25 new Boeing 737 aircraft scheduled for delivery in 1995. In 1994, less than one percent of Southwest flights were canceled or delayed due to mechanical incidents and Southwest was consistently ranked among the world's safest air carriers.

The combined effect of Southwest's operations was apparent in its cost structure. In 1994, Southwest's 7.08-cent cost per available seat mile was the lowest among major U.S. carriers.

---

[8] Numerous activities occurred during a turn's elapsed time. Passengers got on and off the plane and baggage was loaded and unloaded. The cabin and lavatories were tidied and the plane was refueled, inspected, and provisioned with snacks and beverages.

Marketing Creative marketing was used to differentiate Southwest from other airlines since its beginning. As Herb Kelleher put it, "We defined a personality as well as a market niche. [We seek to] amuse, surprise and entertain."

Southwest's marketing orientation was intertwined with its customer and operations orientation. In this regard, service, convenience, and price represented three pillars of Southwest's marketing effort. As with customer service and operations, Southwest's unique twist on marketing set it apart from other airlines. In the domain of pricing, for example, Southwest had always viewed the automobile as its primary competitor, not other airlines. According to Colleen Barrett, Southwest's Executive Vice President with responsibility for Customers: "We've always seen our competition as the car. We've got to offer better, more convenient service at a price that makes it worthwhile to leave your car at home and fly with us instead." In 1994, Southwest's average passenger fare was $58.44. Marketing communications continually conveyed the benefits to customers of flying Southwest. Advertising campaigns over the past 24 years featured Southwest service in "The Love Airline" campaign, convenience in "The Company Plane" campaign, and most recently, low price in "*The* Low Fare Airline" campaign (see Exhibit 7).

Southwest offered a frequent flyer program called "The Company Club," but again with a difference. Consistent with its focus on flight frequency and short-hauls, passengers received a free ticket to any city Southwest served with eight round-trips completed within 12 months. For 50 round-trips in a 12-month period, Southwest provided a companion pass valid for one year. Having no mileage or other qualifying airlines to track, the costs of "The Company Club" were minimal compared with other frequent flyer programs and rewarded the truly frequent traveler.

Southwest also flew uniquely painted planes that signified places on its route structure. Planes were painted to look like Shamu the Killer Whale to highlight Southwest's relationship with both Sea World of California and Texas. Other planes were painted to look like the Texas state flag and called "The Lone Star Over Texas" while others, such as "Arizona One," featured the Arizona state flag (see Exhibit 8 on page 406).

People Commitment The bond between Southwest and its workers was generally regarded by the company as the most important element in the Southwest model. Herb Kelleher referred to this bond as "a patina of spirituality." He added:

> I feel that you have to be with your employees through all their difficulties, that you have to be interested in them personally. They may be disappointed in their country. Even their family might not be working out the way they wish it would. But I want them to know that Southwest will always be there for them.[9]

The close relationship among all Southwest employees contributed to Southwest's recent listing as one of the top ten best companies to work for in a recent study of U.S. firms. The study noted that the biggest plus at Southwest was that "it's a blast to work here"; the biggest minus was that "you may work your tail off."[10]

Southwest's commitment to its people was evident in a variety of forms. The company had little employee turnover compared with other major airlines and was the first U.S. airline to offer an employee profit-sharing plan. Through this plan, employees owned about 10 percent of Southwest stock. Eighty percent of promotions were internal and cross-training in different areas as well as team building were emphasized at Southwest's "People University."

---

[9] Quoted in Kenneth Labich, "Is Herb Kelleher America's Best CEO?" *Fortune* (May 2, 1994): 28–35.

[10] Robert Levering and Milton Mosckowitz, *The 100 Best Companies to Work for in America* (New York: Doubleday/Currency, 1993).

EXHIBIT 7

Representative Southwest Airlines Print Advertising Campaign

WHEN YOU WANT A LOW FARE, LOOK TO THE AIRLINE THAT OTHER AIRLINES LOOK TO.

Call your travel agent or **1-800-I-FLY-SWA**

Source: Courtesy of Southwest Airlines.

EXHIBIT 8

Southwest Airlines Aircraft

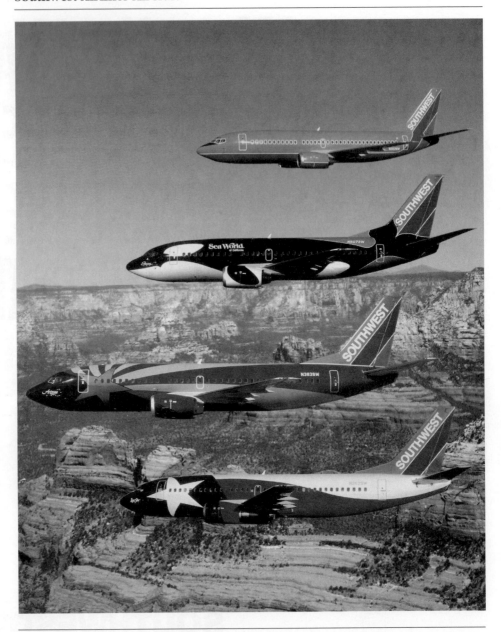

Source: Courtesy of Southwest Airlines.

Competitive and Financial Performance

Southwest's attention to customer service and efficient operations, creative marketing, and people commitment produced extraordinary competitive and financial results.

Competitive Performance According to the U.S. Department of Transportation, Southwest carried more passengers than any other airline in the top 100 city-pair

markets with the most passengers in the 48 contiguous United States.[11] These 100 markets represented about one-third of all domestic passengers. In its own top 100 city-pair markets, Southwest had an average 65 percent market share compared with about a 40 percent market share for other airlines in their own top 100 city-pair markets. Southwest consistently ranked first or second in market share in more than 90 percent of its top 50 city-pair markets. In Texas, where Southwest began operations in 1971, it ranked first in passenger boardings at ten of the 11 Texas airports served and had an intra-Texas market share of 70.8 percent in mid-1994. Southwest recorded a market share of 56.4 percent in the intra-California market in mid-1994, compared with a market share of less than three percent in 1989.

Financial Performance Southwest's average revenue and income growth rate and return on total assets and stockholders' equity were the highest of any U.S. air carrier during the 1990s. Exhibit 9 provides a five-year consolidated financial and operating summary for Southwest Airlines.

Even though Southwest achieved record revenue and income levels in 1994, net income in the fourth quarter 1994 (October 1–December 31, 1994) fell 47 percent compared to the fourth quarter 1993. The last time Southwest reported quarterly earnings that were less than the same quarter a year earlier was in the third quarter of 1991. Fourth quarter 1994 operating revenues were up only three percent compared to the same period in 1993. This result was considerably less than the double-digit gains in operating revenues recorded in each of the preceding three quarters compared to 1993. Southwest's fourth quarter financial report sent the company's stock price reeling to close at a 52-week low of $15.75 in December 1994 in New York Stock Exchange composite trading, down from a record $39.00 in February 1994.

Southwest's fourth quarter 1994 earnings performance reflected the cumulative effect of numerous factors. These included the conversion of recently acquired Morris Air Corporation to Southwest's operations, competitors' persistent use of fare sales which Southwest often matched, and the airline-within-an-airline initiatives launched by Continental and United. Commenting on the fourth quarter financial and operating performance, Herb Kelleher said:

> While these short-term results will be disappointing to our shareholders, the recent investments made to strengthen Southwest Airlines are vitally important to our long-term success. We are prepared emotionally, spiritually and financially to meet our increased competition head-on with even lower costs and even better customer service.[12]

SOUTHWEST VS. SHUTTLE BY UNITED

The maiden flight for "Shuttle By United" departed Oakland International Airport for Los Angeles International Airport at 6:25 A.M. on Saturday, October 1, 1994. Later that morning, United's executive vice president of operations, who flew in from United's world headquarters near Chicago to mark the occasion, spoke to the media. He said:

> What we're doing is getting back into the market and getting our passengers back. We used to own Oakland and LA, and then Herb (Kelleher) came in. What we have to do is protect what's ours.[13]

[11] U.S. Department of Transportation press release, May 11, 1993.

[12] Quoted in Terry Maxon, "Southwest Forecasts Dip in Earnings," *The Dallas Morning News* (December 8, 1994): D1, D3.

[13] Quoted in Catherine A. Chriss, "United Shuttle Takes Wing," *The Dallas Morning News* (October 3, 1994): 1D, 4D.

EXHIBIT 9

Southwest Airlines Five-year Financial and Operating Summary (Abridged)

Selected Consolidated Financial Data[a]					
(In Thousands Except Per-Share Amounts)	*1994*	*1993*	*1992*	*1991*	*1990*
Operating revenues:					
Passenger	$2,497,765	$2,216,342	$1,623,828	$1,267,897	$1,1 44,421
Freight	54,419	42,897	33,088	26,428	22,196
Charter and other	39,749	37,434	146,063	84,961	70,659
Total operating revenues	2,591,933	2,296,673	1,802,979	1,379,286	1,237,276
Operating expenses	2,275,224	2,004,700	1,609,175	1,306,675	1,150,015
Operating income	316,709	291,973	193,804	72,611	87,261
Other expenses (income), net	17,186	32,336	36,361	18,725	(6,827)[f]
Income before income taxes	299,523	259,637	157,443	53,886	80,434
Provision for income taxes[c]	120,192	105,353	60,058	20,738	29,829
Net income[c]	$179,331	$154,284[d]	$97,385[e]	$33,148	$50,605
Total assets	$2,823,071	$2,576,037	$2,368,856	$1,854,331	$1,480,813
Long-term debt	$583,071	$639,136	$735,754	$617,434	$327,553
Stockholders' equity	$1,238,706	$1,054,019	$879,536	$635,793	$607,294
Consolidated Financial Ratios[a]					
Return on average total assets	6.6%	6.2%[d]	4.6%[e]	2.0%	3.5%
Return on average stockholders' equity	15.6%	16.0%[d]	12.9%[e]	5.3%	8.4%
Debt as a percentage of invested capital	32.0%	37.7%	45.5%	49.3%	35.0%
Consolidated Operating Statistics[b]					
Revenue passengers carried	42,742,602[g]	36,955,221[g]	27,839,284	22,669,942	19,830,941
RPMs (thousands)	21,611,266	18,827,288	13,787,005	11,296,183	9,958,940
ASMs (thousands)	32,123,974	27,511,000	21,366,642	18,491,003	16,411,115
Load factor	67.3%	68.4%	64.5%	61.1%	60.7%
Average length of passenger haul	506	509	495	498	502
Trips flown	624,476	546,297	438,184	382,752	338,108
Average passenger fare	$58.44	$59.97	$58.33	$55.93	$57.71
Passenger revenue per RPM	11.56¢	11.77¢	11.78¢	11.22¢	11.49¢
Operating revenue per ASM	8.07¢	8.35¢	7.89¢	7.10¢	7.23¢
Operating expenses per ASM	7.08¢	7.25¢[h]	7.03¢	6.76¢	6.73¢
Number of employees at year-end	16,818	15,175	11,397	9,778	8,620
Size of fleet at year-end[i]	199	178	141	124	106

[a] The Selected Consolidated Financial Data and Consolidated Financial Ratios for 1992 through 1989 have been restated to include the financial results of Morris.

[b] Prior to 1993, Morris operated as a charter carrier; therefore, no Morris statistics are included for these years.

[c] Pro forma assuming Morris, an S Corporation prior to 1993, was taxed at statutory rates.

[d] Excludes cumulative effect of accounting changes of $15.3 million ($.10 per share).

[e] Excludes cumulative effect of accounting change of $12.5 million ($.09 per share).

[f] Includes $2.6 million gains on sales of aircraft and $3.1 million from the sale of certain financial assets.

[g] Includes certain estimates for Morris.

[h] Excludes merger expenses of $10.8 million.

[i] Includes leased aircraft.

Source: Southwest Airlines 1994 *Annual Report*.

At the time, Dave Ridley believed that the Oakland flight had "symbolic significance" for two reasons. First, until the late 1980s, United was the dominant carrier at the Oakland airport, but left in the early 1990s following head-to-head competition with Southwest. Second, Oakland had become the main base of Southwest's Northern California operation and was the fastest growing of California's ten major airports in terms of air traffic.

Shuttle By United[14]

Created by a team of United Airlines managers and workers over the course of a year and code-named "U2" internally, "Shuttle By United" was designed to replicate many operational features of Southwest: point-to-point service, low fares, frequent flights, and minimal amenities. Lowering operating cost was a high priority since United's cost for shorter domestic routes (under 750 miles) was 10.5 cents per available seat mile. United's targeted cost per seat mile was 7.5 cents for its shuttle operation.

Like Southwest, "Shuttle By United" featured Boeing 737 jets with a seating capacity of 137 passengers, focused on achieving 20-minute aircraft turns, and offered only beverage and snack (peanuts and pretzels) service. Management and ground crews alike had attended "enculturalization" and motivational classes that emphasized teamwork and customer service. Unlike Southwest, "Shuttle By United" provided first-class (12 seats) and coach seating. Rather than boarding passengers in groups of 30 like Southwest, a boarding process—known as WILMA for windows, middle, and aisle seat—was used for seat assignments. Passengers assigned window seats boarded first, followed by middle seat travelers, and then aisle customers. United's "Mileage Plus" frequent flyer program was available to passengers, with an option that matched Southwest's offer of one free ticket for each eight shuttle round trips.

"Shuttle By United" was inaugurated with eight routes. Six of these were converted United routes involving the airline's San Francisco hub. Only three of the original eight routes competed directly with Southwest: San Francisco–San Diego, Oakland–Los Angeles, and Los Angeles–Sacramento. On these three routes, the "Shuttle By United" one-way, walk-up coach fare, was identical to Southwest's $69.00 "California State Fare," which was Southwest's highest fare on all seats and flights within California.[15] One-way walk-up coach fares varied on the five noncompeting routes. Service from San Francisco to Burbank and to Ontario was priced at $104.00. Fares for the remaining San Francisco routes were $89.00 to Los Angeles, $99.00 to Las Vegas, and $139.00 to Seattle. The "Shuttle By United" first-class fare was typically $20.00 higher than its coach fare. "Shuttle By United" was advertised heavily using print and electronic media.

"Shuttle By United" soon expanded its route system to include six additional routes. All six routes competed directly with Southwest. Service out of Oakland included Oakland–Burbank, Oakland–Ontario, and Oakland–Seattle. Los Angeles to Phoenix and to Las Vegas and San Diego–Sacramento rounded out the new service. Except for the Oakland–Seattle route, all one-way walk-up coach fares were $69.00 for Southwest and "Shuttle By United." A one-way walk-up coach fare of $99.00 was charged on the Oakland–Seattle route by the two airlines. "Shuttle By United" also in-

[14] Portions of this discussion are based on Jesus Sanchez, "Shuttle Launch," *Los Angeles Times* (September 29, 1994): D1, D3; Randy Drummer, "The Not-So-Friendly Skies," *Daily Bulletin* (September 30, 1994): C1, C10; "United Brings Guns to Bear," *Airline Business* (November 1994): 10; Michael J. McCarthy, "New Shuttle Incites a War Between Old Rivals," *Wall Street Journal* (December 1, 1994): B1, B5.

[15] Walk-up fares refer to the fare available at any time, with no restrictions, no penalties, and no advance purchase requirements.

EXHIBIT 10

Cities Served by Shuttle By United

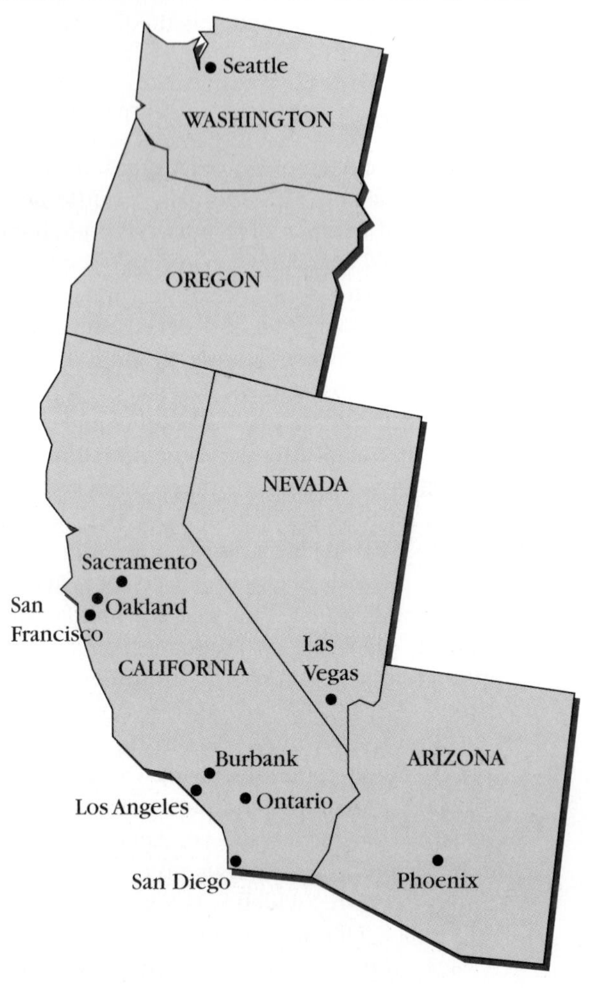

Note: The map is not drawn to scale.

creased its flight frequency in 12 of 14 city-pair markets, primarily out of its San Francisco hub. Cities served by "Shuttle By United" appear in the map shown in Exhibit 10.

In early December 1994, United reported that the cost per available seat mile of its shuttle operation had not yet achieved its targeted 7.5 cents. In an interview, "Sky" Magary said, "We're vaguely better than halfway there."[16]

Southwest Airlines

Southwest's planning for United's initiative began months before the "Shuttle By United" scheduled October 1 launch. In June 1994, a Southwest spokesperson said the airline would "vigorously fight to maintain our stronghold in California."

Prior to the launch of "Shuttle By United," Southwest committed additional aircraft to the California market to boost flight frequencies on competitive routes. By

[16] Michael J. McCarthy, "New Shuttle Incites a War Between Old Rivals," *Wall Street Journal* (December 1, 1994): B1, B5.

mid-January 1995, Southwest had deployed 16 percent of its total capacity (in terms of available seat miles flown) to the intra-California market. Thirteen percent of Southwest's total available seat-mile capacity overlapped with "Shuttle By United" by late January 1995.

Southwest also boosted its advertising and promotion budget for the intra-California market, with particular emphasis in city-pairs where "Shuttle By United" competed directly with Southwest. Southwest's "*The* Low Fare Airline" advertising campaign spearheaded this effort. Southwest's walk-up fare remained at $69.00 during the fourth quarter of 1994, unchanged from the fourth quarter of 1993. However, Southwest's 21-day advance fares and other discount fares were being heavily promoted. The effect of this pricing was that Southwest's average passenger fare in the markets also served by "Shuttle By United" (excluding Oakland–Seattle) was $44.00 during the fourth quarter of 1994 and into early January 1995, compared with $45.00 in the third quarter of 1994. The average 1994 fourth-quarter fare for the Oakland–Seattle route was $51.00, down from $60.00 in the third quarter of 1994. Dave Ridley estimated that the average passenger fare for "Shuttle By United" was five to ten percent higher than the average Southwest fare in the nine markets where it competed directly with Southwest, and about $20.00 higher than the average Southwest fare in the five markets served out of San Francisco where it did not compete directly with Southwest. The difference in average passenger fares between the airlines was due to first-class seating offered by "Shuttle By United" in competitive markets and generally higher fares in non-competitive markets.

■ THE TUESDAY MEETING

The original agenda for the "Tuesday meeting" in late January 1995 focused mostly on operational issues. For example, Southwest would begin scheduled service to Omaha, Nebraska, in March 1995, and advertising, sales, promotion, and scheduling matters still required attention. Southwest's "ticketless" travel system, or "electronic ticketing" was also on the agenda. This system, whereby travelers make reservations by telephone, give their credit card number and receive a confirmation number, but receive no ticket in the mail, was scheduled to go nationwide on January 31, 1995, after a successful regional test. Final details were to be discussed.

Dave Ridley also intended to apprise his colleagues of the competitive situation in California. A staff member had prepared a report showing fourth quarter load factors by route for Southwest and estimated load factors for "Shuttle By United." He wanted to share this information with the group (see Exhibit 11, page 412), along with other recent developments. For example, a few days earlier, "Shuttle By United" had reduced its one-way walk-up coach fare on the San Francisco–Burbank route to $69.00. This fare was identical to the one charged on the Oakland–Burbank route by both airlines. In addition, Southwest's consolidated yield and load factor for January 1995 were tracking lower than the consolidated yield and load factor for January 1994. If present traffic patterns continued, Southwest's consolidated load factor would be about five points lower in January 1995 as compared to January 1994.

Unexpected news that "Shuttle By United" intended to discontinue some service and raise fares altered the original meeting agenda and posed a number of questions for Southwest executives. For instance, did the fare increase signify a major modification in United's "We're going to match Southwest" strategy? If so, what were the implications for Southwest? How might Southwest react to these changes, if at all? Should Southwest follow with a $10.00 fare increase of its own or continue with its present price and service strategy? What might be the profit impact of United's action and Southwest's reaction, if any, for each airline? And how, if at all, was United's pricing action linked to the announced withdrawal from the Oakland–Ontario market?

EXHIBIT 11

Daily Scheduled City Pair Round Trips by Southwest Airlines and "Shuttle By United" and Quarterly Load Factor Estimates

		Southwest Airlines Daily Round-Trip Flights		*Shuttle By United Daily Round-Trip Flights*		*1994 4th-Quarter Load Factor*		*1994 3rd-Quarter Load Factor*		*1993 4th-Quarter Load Factor*	
Market (City Pair)	***Air Miles***	*October–December 1994*	*Mid-January 1995*	*October–December 1994*	*Mid-January 1995*	*United*	*Southwest*	*United*	*Southwest*	*United*	*Southwest*
San Francisco–Los Angeles	338	← No Service →		31	40	66%	—	77%	—	68%	—
San Francisco–Burbank	359	← No Service →		11	12	60%	—	70%	—	64%	—
San Francisco–Ontario	364	← No Service →		11	12	47%	—	63%	—	64%	—
San Francisco–Las Vegas	417	← No Service →		9	10	73%	—	85%	—	74%	—
San Francisco–Seattle	678	← No Service →		13	16	74%	—	89%	—	77%	—
San Francisco–San Diego	417	12	12	10	12	77%	61%	87%	68%	84%	70%
Oakland–Los Angeles	338	19	25	10	15	62%	59%	—	74%	—	63%
Oakland–Burbank	326	13	16	7	11	40%	63%	—	80%	—	7 0%
Oakland–Ontario	362	12	14	7	7	32%	57%	—	68%	—	65 %
Oakland–Seattle	671	4	7	4	5	52%	66%	—	77%	—	—
Los Angeles–Sacramento	374	5	6	5	6	81%	65%	73%	53%	67%	—
Los Angeles–Phoenix	366	25	23	9	10	48%	61%	—	60%	—	56%
Los Angeles–Las Vegas	241	13	19	10	12	61%	65%	—	73%	—	61%
San Diego–Sacramento	481	9	9	5	5	50%	68%	—	78%	—	67%

Source: Southwest Airlines company records. For analysis purposes, load factors can be applied to daily round-trip flights for both airlines on both legs of a round trip.

CASE

Burroughs Wellcome Company

Retrovir

"I think that Burroughs Wellcome is very interested in getting all their money back as soon as possible, because the sun won't shine forever."[1]

Cofounder of Project Inform,
an AIDS treatment information agency (1987)

"Once the drug is out on the marketplace, the company controls the pricing."[2]

Dr. George Stanley,
Food and Drug Administration (1987)

"To make AZT accessible to everyone who should be on it, Burroughs Wellcome has an obligation to give up a significant amount of money to allow people to get access."[3]

Executive Director,
National Gay and Lesbian Task Force (1989)

"There's no plan to make another price cut."[4]

Sir Alfred Sheppard,
Chairman of the Board, Wellcome PLC (1989)

In January 1990, Burroughs Wellcome executives were under continued pressure to reduce the price of Retrovir. Retrovir brand zidovudine is the trade name for a drug called azidothymidine (AZT), which had been found to be effective in the treatment of acquired immune deficiency syndrome (AIDS) and AIDS-related complex (ARC). AIDS is a disease caused by a virus that attacks the body's immune system and damages the system's ability to fight off other infections. Without a functioning immune system, a person becomes vulnerable to infection by bacteria, protozoa, fungi, viruses, and other malignant agents, which may cause life-threatening illnesses, such as pneumonia, meningitis, and cancer. AIDS is caused by HIV (human immunodeficiency virus), a human virus first discovered in 1983. AZT is classified as an antiviral drug that interferes with the replication of HIV. As such, AZT is a treatment, not a cure, for AIDS.

In 1987, Burroughs Wellcome obtained approval from the U.S. Food and Drug Administration to market Retrovir, the first and, as of 1990, the only drug authorized for the treatment of AIDS. Soon after Burroughs Wellcome made Retrovir available for prescription sales on March 19, 1987, the company became embroiled in controversy related to the price of the drug. Critics charged that Burroughs Wellcome, which sold the drug to wholesalers at a price of $188 for a hundred 100-milligram

[1] "The Unhealthy Profits of AZT," *The Nation* (October 17, 1987): 407.

[2] Ibid.

[3] "AZT Maker Expected to Reap Big Gain," *New York Times* (August 29, 1989): 8.

[4] "Wellcome Seeks Approval to Sell AZT to All Those Inflicted with AIDS Virus," *Wall Street Journal* (November 17, 1989): B4.

This case was prepared by Professor Roger A. Kerin, of the Edwin L. Cox School of Business, Southern Methodist University, with the assistance of Angela Bullard, graduate student, as a basis for class discussion and is not designed to illustrate effective or ineffective handling of an administrative situation. The case was prepared from published sources. Quotes, statistics, and published operating information are footnoted for reference purposes.

capsules, engaged in price gouging of a "highly vulnerable market." The company's President, T. E. Haigler, responded that the high price was due to the "uncertain market for the drug, the possible advent of new therapies, and profit margins customarily generated by significant new medicines."[5]

Nevertheless, the company reduced its price by 20 percent in December 1987, and again by 20 percent in September 1989. Prior to the 1989 price reduction, the Subcommittee on Health and the Environment of the U.S. House of Representatives had launched an investigation into possible "inappropriate" pricing of Retrovir. Soon after the announced price reduction in 1989, the chairman of the House subcommittee said that this was "a good first step. But I think the company can do better."[6] In November 1989, the Chairman of Wellcome PLC, the parent company of Burroughs Wellcome, was quoted as saying, "There's no plan to make another price cut."[7] However, pressure to again reduce the price continued.

■ ACQUIRED IMMUNE DEFICIENCY SYNDROME

Acquired immune deficiency syndrome can be traced to a blood sample taken and stored in the Central African nation of Zaire in 1959 (see Exhibit 1 for a chronology of important events). It was not until 1982, however, that the Centers for Disease Control and Prevention in Atlanta, Georgia, labeled the disease and warned that it

EXHIBIT 1

AIDS Chronology, 1959–1990

1959	Blood sample taken and stored in the Central African nation of Zaire. Retesting the sample in 1986, physicians discover it to be HIV-infected.
1978	Doctors determine that a child in New York died as a direct result of immune system breakdown.
1981	The Centers for Disease Control (CDC) reports breakdowns of the immune systems of several male homosexuals with the resulting occurrence of infectious diseases and cancers.
1982	CDC names the "mystery disease" acquired immune deficiency syndrome (AIDS) and warns that it may be spread by a virus in bodily fluids such as blood and semen.
1983	Scientists at the Pasteur Institute in Paris, France, isolate a suspected AIDS-causing virus.
1984	U.S. researchers identify an AIDS-causing virus as the same one isolated by the French scientists.
1985	A test is licensed to detect an AIDS-causing virus in blood.
1986	The AIDS-causing virus is named human immunodeficiency virus, or HIV.
1987	U.S. Food and Drug Administration permits sale of azidothymidine (AZT), which eases some of the symptoms of AIDS and AIDS-related complex (ARC).
1988–1990	AIDS fatalities continue to increase while the pharmaceutical industry searches for a cure.

[5] "The High-Cost AIDS Drug: Who Will Pay for It?" *Drug Topics* (April 6, 1987): 52.

[6] "How Much for a Reprieve from AIDS?" *Time* (October 2, 1989): 81.

[7] "Wellcome Seeks Approval to Sell AZT . . . ," *Wall Street Journal* (November 17, 1989): B4.

might be spread by a virus in bodily fluids such as blood and semen. In 1983 and 1984, French and American scientists isolated a suspected AIDS-causing virus that was subsequently named human immunodeficiency virus, or HIV, in 1988. HIV is a retrovirus that can become an extra link in the genetic code, or DNA, of a cell. HIV inhibits and eventually destroys the T-4 cell, which is a key part of a person's immune system that attacks foreign germs. Without T-4 cells, people succumb to all manner of infections. The identification of HIV was a major breakthrough, especially since, prior to 1984, it was not established in the scientific community that retroviruses like HIV caused human diseases.

Incidence and Cost of HIV and AIDS

Efforts to track and forecast the incidence and cost of HIV and AIDS began in earnest in 1986. Research focused on identifying high-risk individuals, determining the geographical concentration of the disease, and arriving at estimates of the number of people afflicted with HIV and AIDS.[8] This research found that almost 90 percent of AIDS victims were homosexual men or intravenous drug users. One-half of all reported AIDS cases were in the San Francisco, Miami, New York City, Los Angeles, and Houston metropolitan areas.

Tracking and forecasting the incidence of AIDS cases and HIV infections proved to be more difficult. The CDCP reported 5,992 AIDS cases in 1984 and 35,198 cases in 1989. Estimates of HIV infections in 1990 ranged between 800,000 and 1,300,000 Americans, depending on the estimation procedure employed. The incidence of AIDS cases in the period 1981-1989 is charted in Exhibit 2 on page 416. The fatality rate for persons inflicted with AIDS was about 91 percent in 1981 and 46 percent in 1989.

Treating AIDS patients has proved to be extremely expensive. According to a 1987 study by the Rand Corporation, an internationally recognized research organization, the lifetime medical costs of an AIDS patient in his thirties were estimated to be between $70,000 and $141,000. For comparison, the lifetime cost of treating a person in his thirties with digestive tract cancer was $47,000; leukemia, $29,000; and a heart attack, $67,000.

An estimated 40 percent of persons with AIDS have received care under the Medicaid Program, which is administered by the Health Care Financing Administration and funded jointly by the federal government (55 percent) and individual states (45 percent). Estimated annual costs for AIDS care and treatment funded by Medicaid ranged between $700 million and $750 million in 1988. Medicaid spending for AIDS was estimated to reach $2.4 billion in 1992. In addition, private insurers paid $250 million annually in AIDS-related medical payments.

Anti-HIV Drug Treatment

The identification of HIV in the mid-1980s prompted numerous pharmaceutical companies to search for antiviral drugs. Burroughs Wellcome led the research effort in part because of its prior development of drugs that combat viral diseases. In addition to AZT supplied by Burroughs Wellcome, other compounds were in various stages of

---

[8] Portions of this material are based on statistics reported in Brad Edmundson, "AIDS and Aging," *American Demographics* (March 1990): 28-34; Fred J. Hellinger, "Forecasting the Personal Medical Care Costs of AIDS from 1988 through 1991," *Public Health Reports* (May-June 1988): 309-319; William L. Roper and William Winkenwerder, "Making Fair Decisions about Financing Care for Persons with AIDS," *Public Health Reports* (May-June 1988): 305-308; Centers for Disease Control, "Human Immunodeficiency Virus Infection in the United States: A Review of Current Knowledge," *Morbidity and Mortality Weekly Report* (December 18, 1987): 2-3, 18-19; "Now That AIDS Is Treatable, Who'll Pay the Crushing Cost?" *Business Week* (September 11, 1989): 115-16; Centers for Disease Control, "HIV/AIDS Surveillance Report" (U.S. Department of Health and Human Services, Public Health Services: December 1990).

EXHIBIT 2

AIDS Cases, 1981–1989

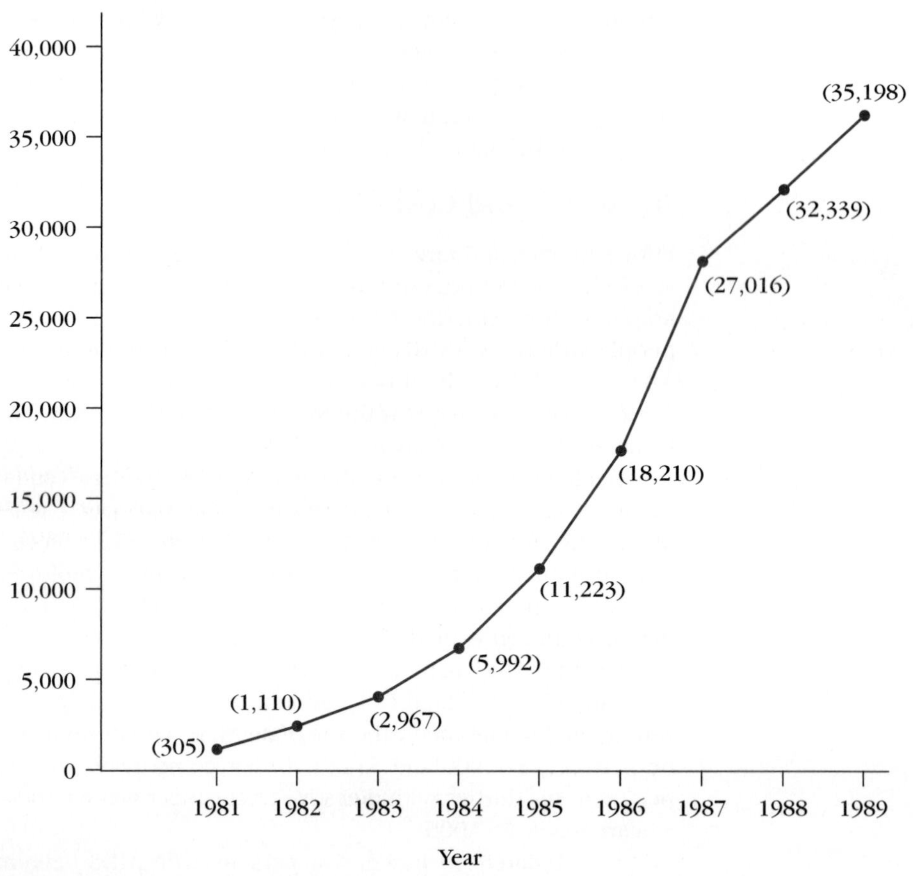

Source: Based on Centers for Disease Control and Prevention, "HIV/AIDS Surveillance Report" (U.S. Department of Health and Human Services, Public Health Services: December 1990).

development and commercialization.[9] One antiviral drug has been given limited approval by the FDA and is available to patients who have a negative reaction to AZT. This drug, produced by Bristol Myers and called DDI, is an antiviral drug that appears to inhibit reproduction of HIV and slow the damage it causes. DDI was initially studied for AIDS use by the National Cancer Institute. Like AZT, it interferes with the ability of HIV-infected cells to produce new viruses and slows the progression of HIV infection, but does not eradicate or eliminate the infection. The principal advantage of DDI over AZT is that it appears to be less toxic. DDC, developed by Hoffman-LaRoche, was in clinical trials in 1989. Other drugs produced by Glaxo and Triton Biosciences, Inc. were being tested as well. Industry analysts believed that one or more of these drugs would obtain FDA approval for prescription sales by 1991.

[9] Portions of this material are based on "A Quiet Drug Maker Takes a Big Swing at AIDS," *Business Week* (October 6, 1986): 32; "There's No Magic Bullet, but a Shotgun Approach May Work," *Business Week* (September 11, 1989): 118.

■ BURROUGHS WELLCOME COMPANY

Burroughs Wellcome is the American subsidiary of Wellcome PLC, an English public limited company with headquarters in London.[10] Wellcome PLC is a multinational firm with manufacturing operations in 18 countries and employs 20,000 people. Approximately 18 percent of the company's employees are engaged in research and development efforts. The company's primary business, which accounts for 89 percent of its fiscal 1989 revenue, is human health care products, both ethical (prescription) and over the counter (nonprescription). Two ethical products account for 34 percent of its human health care revenue: Zovirax and Retrovir. Zovirax, which is used in the treatment of herpes infection, is the company's single largest-selling product with annual sales of $492 million in 1989. Retrovir is its second largest-selling product with sales of $225 million in fiscal 1989. In addition, the company markets Actifed and Sudafed, cough and cold preparations, as over-the-counter products. These two products combined account for annual sales of $253 million. Wellcome PLC had an animal health care business that accounted for about 11 percent of company revenue. This business was divested in late 1989.

North America represents the largest market for the products sold by Wellcome PLC, with annual sales of $997 million. Sales in the United States are roughly equivalent to 42 percent of Wellcome PLC's worldwide sales. The United Kingdom is the company's second largest market and accounts for about 10 percent of worldwide sales.

EXHIBIT 3

Selected Financial and Operating Ratios of Wellcome PLC

	*Fiscal Year**		
	1989	*1988*	*1987*
Financial Ratios			
Gross profit margin (gross profit/sales)	70.6%	68.1%	67.5%
Return on sales (net income before tax/sales)	20.0	17.7	14.9
Return on assets (net income before tax/total assets)	20.0	18.0	15.0
Return on equity (net income before tax/common equity)	35.0	36.0	32.0
Operating Ratios			
R&D expenditures/sales	13.4	13.1	12.6
Selling, general, and administration costs/sales	36.9	36.5	39.2

* Fiscal year ends August 31.

Source: Wellcome PLC annual reports.

[10] Much of this material is described in Wellcome PLC's 1989 and 1990 annual reports; "Burroughs Wellcome Company," Burroughs Wellcome news release, December 13, 1990; Brian O'Reilly, "The Inside Story of the AIDS Drug," *Fortune* (November 5, 1990): 112–29. Financial figures and percentages represent approximations, since information is reported in U.S. dollars and the British pound sterling. These figures are not useful for research purposes.

EXHIBIT 4

Selected Financial and Operating Ratios for Pharmaceutical Firms in the United States, 1989

	Pharmaceutical Firm					
	Merck & Co.	*Pfizer, Inc.*	*Abbott Labs*	*Upjohn*	*Schering-Plough*	*Eli Lilly*
Financial Ratios*						
Gross profit margin	76.3%	63.6%	52.5%	69.8%	73.8%	69.9%
Return on sales	34.8	16.2	22.2	15.8	20.4	31.9
Return on assets	33.8	11.0	24.6	14.2	17.9	22.7
Return on equity	64.9	20.2	43.8	26.5	33.0	35.4
Operating Ratios						
R&D/sales	11.5	9.4	9.3	14.0	10.3	14.5
SG&A/sales	30.7	37.2	20.5	40.3	42.3	27.5

* See Exhibit 3 for definitions of ratios.

Source: Company annual reports.

Wellcome PLC recorded total revenues of $1.75 billion and net profit before tax of $262.1 million in fiscal 1987. Total revenues for fiscal 1989 (fiscal year ended August 31, 1989) were $2.1 billion with net profit before taxes of $475 million.[11] Selected financial and operating ratios for Wellcome PLC for the fiscal years 1987–1989 are shown in Exhibit 3 on page 417. Exhibit 4 presents comparative statistics for other major firms in the U.S. pharmaceutical industry. Percentage sales and the net income growth since fiscal 1985 for Wellcome PLC are shown below:

Fiscal Year	*Sales Growth*	*Net Income Growth*
1985–1986	0.2%	7.2%
1986–1987	12.6	47.3
1987–1988	10.4	35.1
1988–1989	12.6	42.9

■ DEVELOPMENT OF RETROVIR

Burroughs Wellcome's AIDS research program began in June 1984 with an extensive search for likely drug candidates. According to Philip Furman, head of virus research, "We looked at all our known antivirals on the off chance that one would work against retroviruses."[12]

[11] These figures are based on the average exchange rate of $1.55 = £1 in 1987, $1.68 = £1 in 1989 (Wellcome PLC 1990 *Annual Report*).

[12] This material is based on "The Development of Retrovir," Burroughs Wellcome news release, June 1990; L. Wastila and L. Lasagna, "The History of Zidovudine (AZT)," *Journal of Clinical Research and Pharmacoepidemiology*, Vol. 4 (1990): 25–29; "The Inside Story of the AIDS Drug," *Fortune* (November 5, 1990): 112–29; "AIDS Research Stirs Bitter Fight over Use of Experimental Drugs," *Wall Street Journal* (June 18, 1986): 26.

Laboratory Testing

Burroughs Wellcome scientists examined hundreds of compounds over a period of five months, but none proved acceptable. In November 1984, AZT was found to inhibit animal viruses in a laboratory setting. AZT had been synthesized in 1964 by a researcher at the Michigan Cancer Foundation. It was hoped then that the drug would be useful in the treatment of cancer, but when investigated, it was found to have no potential as an anticancer agent. In the early 1980s, Burroughs Wellcome scientists resynthesized AZT in their exploration of compounds with possible effectiveness against bacterial infection. This research provided information about the spectrum of the drug's antibacterial activity and its toxicity and metabolism in laboratory animals, but intensive development was not pursued. The drug was not examined again until late 1984 when it showed promise as an AIDS treatment. (Exhibit 5 on page 420 details significant events in the development of Retrovir.)

Following *in vitro* demonstration of its potential by Burroughs Wellcome's scientists, 50 coded compounds including AZT were sent to Duke University, the National Cancer Institute (NCI), and the FDA for independent testing to assess their *in vitro* activity against the human retrovirus.[13] Early in 1985 these tests showed that AZT was, in fact, active against HIV in the test tube. The company then began extensive preclinical toxicologic and pharmacologic testing in the spring of 1985. At the same time, work began on scaling up synthesis of the drug in preparation for clinical testing in patients with HIV. On June 14, 1985, Burroughs Wellcome submitted an application to the FDA to obtain Investigational New Drug (IND) status for the compound, which would allow its use in a limited number of severely ill AIDS and ARC patients. A week later, the FDA notified Burroughs Wellcome that the submitted data were sufficient to allow clinical studies in humans to be initiated.

Human Testing

Retrovir was administered to patients for the first time on July 3, 1985, at the Clinical Center of the National Institutes of Health (NIH) in Bethesda, Maryland. This initial (Phase I) study, conducted under a protocol developed by Burroughs Wellcome in collaboration with scientists at the NCI, Duke University, the University of Miami, and UCLA, involved 40 patients infected with HIV. The purpose of Phase I testing was to determine how Retrovir acted in the body, the appropriate dosage, and potential adverse reactions or side effects. Initial results were encouraging. Some of the patients showed evidence of improvement, including an increased sense of well-being, weight gain, and positive changes in various measures of the immune system function. Extended treatment, however, lowered production of red blood cells and certain white blood cells in some patients who had taken high doses.

By early 1986, sufficient data on Retrovir were available to proceed with more extensive human testing. The need now was to prove that the drug could provide useful therapy for AIDS and ARC patients. More volunteers and an objective basis for comparison were essential to the conduct of the Phase II trial. A double-blind, placebo-controlled trial, conducted and financed by Burroughs Wellcome, began on February 18, 1986. A total of 281 patients participated. Safeguards built into the study provided for data to be reviewed periodically by a board of impartial experts convened under the auspices of the National Institute of Allergy and Infectious Diseases (NIAID). If either the placebo or the drug-treated group did either so poorly or so well that it would be unethical to continue the trial, the study would be stopped.

About this time, both the medical community and the general public had heard of the Phase II trial. As publicity about the trial gained momentum, AIDS patient-

[13] *In vitro*, a Latin phrase meaning "in glass," is used medically to mean to isolate from a living organism and artificially maintain in a test tube.

EXHIBIT 5

Retrovir Milestones, 1984–1990

June 1984	Burroughs Wellcome begins an AIDS research program to search for chemical compounds that might be effective against HIV.
November 1984	Burroughs Wellcome scientists identify AZT as potentially useful against AIDS.
Spring 1985	*In vitro* activity of AZT against HIV is confirmed by laboratories at Duke University, FDA, and NCI. This confirmatory work, requested by Burroughs Wellcome, is done on coded samples whose chemical identity is not revealed to the outside laboratories.
Spring 1985	Burroughs Wellcome continues toxicologic and pharmacologic testing of AZT. Work begins on scaling up synthesis of the drug, as the compound has never been produced beyond the few grams used for research purposes.
June 1985	FDA permits Burroughs Wellcome to begin clinical trials of AZT in humans.
July 1985	AZT is designated an "orphan drug" for the treatment of AIDS (a designation made when the affected population is less than 200,000).
July 1985	Burroughs Wellcome begins a collaborative Phase I study with NCI and Duke University to assess AZT's safety and tolerance in humans.
December 1985	Enrollment in the Phase I study, eventually involving 40 patients and investigators from NCI, Duke University, University of Miami, and UCLA, continues. Patient responses are encouraging.
February 1986	Burroughs Wellcome initiates and is the sole sponsor of a Phase II study at 12 academic centers, eventually involving 281 patients.
September 1986	The Phase II study is halted when an interim analysis by an independent data safety and monitoring board shows a significantly lower mortality rate in patients receiving AZT compared to those randomized to receive a placebo.
October 1986	Burroughs Wellcome, National Institutes of Health, and FDA establish a Treatment IND (Investigational New Drug) program as a means of providing wider access to AZT prior to FDA clearance.
December 1986	Burroughs Wellcome completes submission of a New Drug Application to FDA.
March 1987	The FDA clears Retrovir brand zidovudine (AZT) as a treatment for advanced ARC and AIDS.
February 1988	Burroughs Wellcome is issued a U.S. patent for the use of Retrovir as a treatment for AIDS and ARC based on the innovative work done by company scientists.
August 1989	Controlled clinical trials indicate that certain HIV-infected early symptomatic and asymptomatic persons can benefit from Retrovir with fewer or less severe side effects.
October 1989	Burroughs Wellcome establishes a Pediatric Treatment IND program, providing wider access to Retrovir for medically eligible children prior to FDA clearance.
January 1990	The FDA clears modified dosage guidelines for therapy with Retrovir patients with severe HIV infection.

Source: Abridged from a Burroughs Wellcome news release, "Retrovir Milestones," dated December 13, 1990.

advocacy groups became impatient with what they perceived as an overly tedious and unnecessary process. They began accusing Burroughs Wellcome and the FDA of delaying the drug's availability. These critics argued that withholding potentially effective therapy from AIDS patients was inhumane and unethical, as was the use of a placebo. David Barry, Vice President and head of the research, medical, and development divisions, defended the trial process, asserting that, if placebo controls were removed, "it could destroy the most modern and rapid clinical research plans ever devised."[14]

In September 1986, the review board recommended that the administration of the placebo be terminated. Analysis of the data had shown a significantly lower mortality rate among those patients who had received Retrovir for an average period of six months. When the trial stopped, there had been 19 deaths among the 137 patients receiving the placebo and 1 death among those patients taking Retrovir. The group receiving Retrovir also had a decreased number of infections. In addition, the weight gain, improvements in the immune system, and ability to perform daily activities noted in the Phase I trial were confirmed. However, patients involved in the Phase II trial also experienced adverse reactions similar to those reported in the earlier trial. Since it was no longer appropriate to withhold drug treatment from placebo-treated patients, all patients who had formerly received the placebo were offered Retrovir treatment with the agreement of the FDA.

Expanded distribution of the drug meant that the company would have to obtain a larger supply of thymidine, a biological chemical first harvested from herring sperm and a key raw material in AZT. In 1986, the world's supply of thymidine was 25 pounds. Recognizing that this supply would be exhausted quickly, the head of technical development at Burroughs Wellcome began a worldwide search for a thymidine supplier, recognizing that it took months and 20 chemical reactions to produce this material. This search uncovered a small German subsidiary of Pfizer, Inc., a New York-based pharmaceutical firm, which had produced thymidine in the 1960s. This company was persuaded to produce thymidine by the ton.

In March 1987, the FDA released Retrovir for treatment for adult patients with symptomatic HIV infection, those patients for whom the drug had been shown to be beneficial in clinical trials. Although no hard figures were available, it was believed that about 50,000 individuals in the United States had symptomatic HIV infection. The recommended dosage for symptomatic HIV patients was 1,200 milligrams every day, administered in 12 100-milligram capsules.

Research and Development Costs

The direct research and development costs associated with Retrovir were estimated to be about $50 million, according to industry analysts.[15] This cost was considered low, since the typical cost of developing a new drug in the United States is $125 million. Indeed, Wellcome PLC had spent $726 million for research and development on dozens of drugs in the five years preceding approval of Retrovir without producing a major commercial success. However, when the costs of new plant and equipment to produce Retrovir were also considered, total research and development cost estimates ranged from $80 million to $100 million. Furthermore, the company provided the equivalent of $10 million of the drug free to 4,500 AIDS patients and supplied free of charge a metric ton of AZT to the National Institutes of Health's AIDS Clinical Trials Group.

[14] David Barry, testimony before the House Committee on Government Operations Subcommittee on Intergovernmental Relations and Human Resources, July 1, 1987.

[15] Cost estimates have been made by industry analysts and have not been confirmed or denied by Burroughs Wellcome.

Burroughs Wellcome's research and development effort did benefit from AZT being designated as an "orphan drug" in 1985 under provisions of the Orphan Drug Act of 1983. This act, which applies to drugs useful in treating 200,000 or fewer people in the United States, confers special consideration to suppliers of these drugs. For example, the orphan drug designation for Retrovir provided a seven-year marketing exclusivity after its commercial introduction, tax credits, and government subsidization of clinical trials.

■ MARKETING OF RETROVIR

Initial distribution of Retrovir was limited because of its short supply in March 1987. A special distribution system was set up to ensure availability of the drug to those patients who had been shown to benefit from its use. This system remained in place until September 1987, when supplies were adequate and broader distribution was possible.

The initial price set for Retrovir to drug wholesalers in March 1987 was $188 for a hundred 100-milligram capsules. This price represented an annual cost to AIDS patients ranging from $8,528 to $9,745 depending upon wholesaler and pharmacy margins, which combined ranged from 5 to 20 percent. An immediate controversy was created, with the public, media, and AIDS patient-advocacy groups seeking justification of the price for Retrovir, a decrease in its price, or federal subsidization. Critics pointed out that, for comparison, the annual cost of interferon, a cancer-fighting drug, was only $5,000. The cofounder of Project Inform, an AIDS treatment information agency, said, "I think that Burroughs Wellcome is very interested in getting all their money back as soon as possible, because the sun won't shine forever."[16] Congressional hearings resulted in the chairman of the House Subcommittee on Health and the Environment charging that Burroughs Wellcome's "expectation was that those people who want to buy the drug will come up with the money" and that the government would "step in" to subsidize those who could not.[17] Congress subsequently created a $30 million emergency fund for AIDS patients who were unable to afford the cost of AZT.[18]

Company officials acknowledged that the pricing decision was difficult to make. According to one official, "We didn't know the demand, how to produce it in large quantities, or what competing drugs would come out in the market. There was no way to find out." Another company official said, "I guess we assumed that the drug . . . would be paid in some manner by the patient himself out of his own pocket or by third-party payers. We really didn't get into a lot of calculation along those lines."[19]

On December 15, 1987, the capsule price of Retrovir was reduced by 20 percent. The company announced that the price reduction was made possible because of cost savings achieved in the production process and an improved supply of synthetically manufactured thymidine. The company continued its research on AZT throughout 1988 into 1989, including treatments for children with HIV infection. In August 1989, this research program indicated that Retrovir produced positive results in postponing the appearance of AIDS in HIV-infected people. This development expanded the potential users of the drug to between 600,000 and 1 million people. (However, industry sources believe that fewer than one-half of the people with HIV

[16] "The Unhealthy Profits of AZT," *The Nation* (October 17, 1987): 407.

[17] FDC Reports—the Pink Sheet 49 (11): 5, 1987.

[18] "Find the Cash or Die Sooner," *Time* (September 5, 1988): 27.

[19] "The Inside Story of the AIDS Drug," *Fortune* (November 5, 1990): 124–25.

have been tested and told of their condition and would thus be seeking treatment.) FDA approval for marketing to this larger population was expected by March 1990.

Recognizing the expanded potential patient population and anticipated production economies, the capsule price of Retrovir was again reduced by 20 percent in September 1989. In reference to this price reduction, Burroughs Wellcome's *1989 Annual Report* noted:

> In arriving at our decision to reduce the price, we carefully weighed a number of factors. These included our responsibility to patients and shareholders, the very real remaining uncertainties in the marketplace, and the vital need to fund our continuing research and development programmes.[20]

The new price to drug wholesalers was set at $120 for a hundred 100-milligram capsules. The retail price to users was about $150 for a hundred 100-milligram capsules. Industry analysts estimated that the direct cost of manufacturing and marketing Retrovir was 30 cents to 50 cents per capsule.[21]

EXHIBIT 6

Retrovir Sales Volume, Fiscal 1987–1989

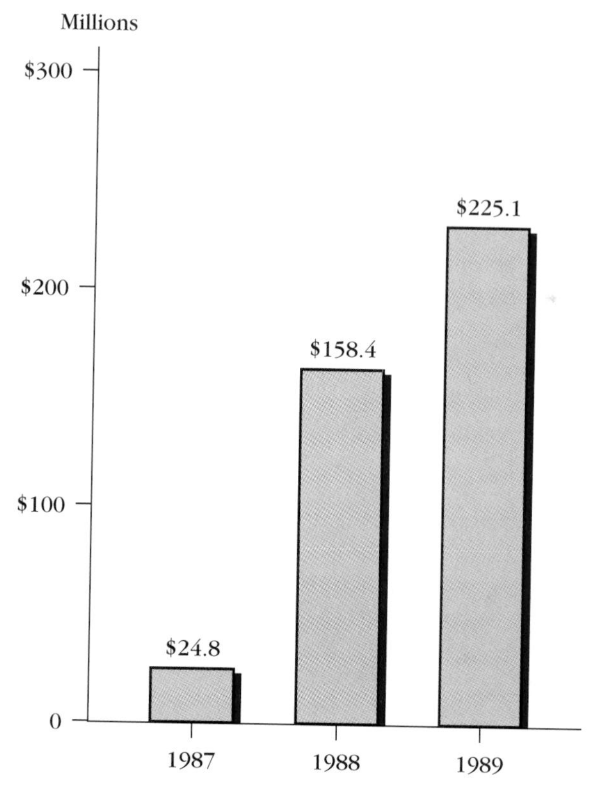

Note: U.S. dollar sales volume computed using average exchange rate £1 = $1.55 (1987), £1 = $1.76 (1988), £1 = $1.68 (1989).

Source: Wellcome PLC, 1990 *Annual Report.*

[20] Wellcome PLC 1989 *Annual Report*: 13.

[21] "How Much for a Reprieve from AIDS?" *Time* (October 2, 1989): 81.

Sales of Retrovir since its introduction are shown in Exhibit 6 on page 423. Unit volume for Retrovir in fiscal 1990 was forecasted to be 53 percent higher than fiscal 1989 unit volume.

Patient-advocacy groups continued to criticize the pricing of Retrovir. AIDS activists chanted such slogans as "Be the first on your block to sell your Burroughs Wellcome stock" while picketing stock exchanges in London, New York, and San Francisco. The executive director of the National Gay and Lesbian Task Force said, "To make AZT accessible to everyone who should be on it, Burroughs Wellcome has an obligation to give up a significant amount of money to allow people to get access."[22] Members of Senator Edward Kennedy's staff began researching possible ways to nationalize the drug by invoking a law that allows the U.S. government to revoke exclusive licenses in the interest of national security. In addition, there were published reports that the American Civil Liberties Union was considering a suit against Burroughs Wellcome. The suit would challenge the 17-year-use patent awarded Burroughs Wellcome for Retrovir, arguing that government scientists discovered AZT's efficacy against HIV.[23] The Subcommittee on Health and the Environment of the U.S. House of Representatives, which had already launched an investigation into possible "inappropriate" pricing of the drug, continued its hearings. However, Sir Alfred Sheppard, the company's Chairman, remained firm, saying "There's no plan to make another price cut." Later in 1990, he added, "If we wrapped the drug in a £10 note and gave it away, people would say it cost too much."[24]

In January 1990, the FDA approved modified dosage guidelines for Retrovir. These guidelines reduced the recommended adult dosage to 500 milligrams per day for some symptomatic AIDS patients from the original recommended dosage of 1,200 milligrams per day established in 1987. However, some clinicians warned that lower dosages should be prescribed cautiously. Also in January, congressional lobbyists began a campaign to curb "excessive profits earned by the drug industry as a whole." Industry observers were speculating that the price of Retrovir might have to be cut again sometime in 1990 because of continued pressure from the U.S. Congress, the media, and AIDS patient-advocacy groups.[25]

---

[22] "AZT Maker to Reap Big Gain," *New York Times* (August 19, 1989): 8.

[23] "A Stitch in Time," *The Economist* (August 18, 1990): 21–22.

[24] "The Inside Story of the AIDS Drug," *Fortune* (November 5, 1990): 124–25.

[25] "Profiting from Disease," *The Economist* (January 27, 1990): 17–18.

CASE

Afton Industries

In January 1999, the Director of Sales and the Director of Planning and Administration at Afton Industries met to prepare a joint recommendation to the president on the firm's line of asphalt shingles. Afton Industries had been a regional price leader over the years; that is, when the company announced its price on asphalt shingles, competitive shingle manufacturers followed.

In January 1998, Afton raised the average price per square of its asphalt shingles from $40.50 to $44.50.[1] Although the company was strong financially, the price increase was prompted in part by a decision by Afton's board of directors to embark on an extensive plant modernization and expansion program. The price increase was one of several changes directed by the board to improve the company's working capital position. Contrary to previous price increases, Afton's major competitors did not follow suit. The company experienced a five-percentage-point decline in market share during 1998.

THE RESIDENTIAL ASPHALT SHINGLE INDUSTRY

Asphalt shingles are the dominant residential roofing product in the United States, accounting for about 93 percent of roofing applications. About 80 percent of asphalt shingles are used to reroof and remodel existing homes, and 20 percent are used for new construction. Other roofing materials include wood, metal, clay tile, and slate, all of which are more expensive than asphalt shingles to produce and install (see Exhibit 1, page 426).

Anatomy of an Asphalt Shingle

Asphalt shingles are named for the sticky, tarry, water-repellent substance that holds them together. They are basically large, rectangular sheets about 1 × 3 feet, made of cellulose or fiberglass, and impregnated with asphalt, a petroleum byproduct.

Asphalt shingles are categorized as either organic based or fiberglass based. Organic-based asphalt shingles are manufactured with a base (also termed *mat* or *substrate*) made of various cellulose fibers, such as recycled waste paper and wood fibers. This organic base is then saturated with specially formulated asphalt coating, surfaced with weather resistant mineral granules, and colored with a hard ceramic glaze. Fiberglass-based asphalt shingles are manufactured with mat composed entirely of glass fibers of varying lengths and orientations. This fiberglass base is then surfaced with a specially formulated asphalt coating, followed by weather-resistant

[1] A *square* is a unit of measurement used in the roofing industry. One square contains approximately 80 shingles and covers 100 square feet. A rule of thumb in the industry holds that 25 squares are needed to roof a typical single-family dwelling.

This case was prepared by Professor Roger A. Kerin, of the Edwin L. Cox School of Business, Southern Methodist University, as a basis for class discussion and is not designed to illustrate effective or ineffective handling of an administrative situation. Certain names and data have been disguised.

EXHIBIT 1

Comparison of Roofing Material per 100 Square Feet of Coverage

Roofing Material	*Asphalt*	*Wood*	*Clay Tile*	*Slate*
Retail price of material*	\$20–\$140	\$95–\$170	\$140–\$850	\$320–\$1200
Installation cost	\$31–\$76	\$67–\$135	\$120–\$200	\$110–\$150
Weight in pounds	195–430	300–400	900±	900±
Typical life span in years	15–30	15–30	50	50–100+

* Not including underlayment.
Source: Company records.

mineral granules. In addition to adding color, mineral granules protect the asphalt from the sun's ultraviolet rays, and their weight increases the shingles' resistance to wind. In general, organic-based asphalt shingles fare better in cold weather regions. Fiberglass-based shingles fare better in hot weather regions. Asphalt shingled roofs are typically replaced about every 17 years.

Industry Size and Structure

About 135 million asphalt shingle squares were manufactured in the United States in 1998—nearly enough to cover 5.4 million homes. The industry has recorded consistent growth since 1991 with dollar sales reaching approximately \$6.5 billion in 1998, at manufacturers' prices. The seven-year expansion in the asphalt shingle industry has been the longest in more than a generation. Historically, the industry has been cyclical in nature, marked by three to four years of sales growth followed by a sales slowdown and decline.

There are about 35 asphalt roofing manufacturers in the United States. These manufacturers operate 110 production facilities. While about half of shingle manufacturers operate a single plant and compete regionally, larger manufacturers such as GAF Materials Corporation, Georgia-Pacific, and Owens Corning each operate more than 10 plants located throughout the continental United States. Some manufacturers specialize in fiberglass-based or organic-based asphalt shingles. For example, GAF and Owens Corning do not have organic-based shingle plants. No large, national shingle manufacturer had a plant in Afton's region.

Sales and marketing efforts for asphalt shingles focus on roofing material distributors. Distributors provide a warehousing function for shingle manufacturers and sell shingles to roofing contractors or applicators who install the shingles. Research conducted by the National Roofing Contractors Association indicates that the type of asphalt shingle to install and specific manufacturer to use depends on whether a project involves new construction or reroofing work. For new construction, architects or builders typically decide which type of shingle should be used. Roofing contractors usually decide which manufacturer to use. For reroofing, roofing contractors play an influential role in both shingle and manufacturer choice. In deciding between roofing materials, contractors report that shingle performance and level of manufacturer service were the dominant choice considerations, followed by shingle warranty and price. In general, homeowners have little knowledge about shingles and manufacturers and leave the brand choice, particularly for reroofing, to the roofing contractor, provided the price and manufacturer's warranty are acceptable.[2]

[2] "Shingles and Siding: A Roof Over Your Head," *Consumer Reports* (August 1997): 26–30.

■ AFTON INDUSTRIES

Afton Industries produces only organic-based asphalt shingles for the residential market in the upper-midwestern United States at a single manufacturing facility. The company also distributes a line of roofing accessory products under the Afton brand name. The company was formed in the early 1960s and is a privately held corporation. Company sales in 1998 were $32 million.

The company's line of asphalt shingles and service are highly regarded by roofing material distributors and among established, reputable roofing contractors in the region. All major distributors carry its products. Afton markets three separate lines of asphalt shingles. The premium line, priced at $55 per square, is a very heavy, laminated shingle with a prorated 40-year warranty. Laminated shingles create a three-dimensional visual effect that mimics wood or slate. This line also comes in a variety of colors. The moderately priced line, priced at $40 per square, is a less heavy shingle with a prorated 30-year warranty and fewer color options. The value line, with a $32-per-square price, is the lightest-weight shingle, has a prorated 20-year warranty, and comes in two colors—gray and brown. In 1997 and 1998, the premium line accounted for about 35 percent of Afton's shingle square volume. The moderately priced and value line represented 55 percent and 10 percent of volume, respectively.

Like other asphalt roofing manufacturers, Afton benefited from the seven-year economic expansion in the roofing industry. Asphalt shingle square volume had more than doubled in Afton's region since 1991. The company had increased its dollar sales and shingle market share during the period (see Exhibit 2). Afton's shingle

EXHIBIT 2

Regional Asphalt Shingle Volume and Afton Industries Volume: 1991–1998

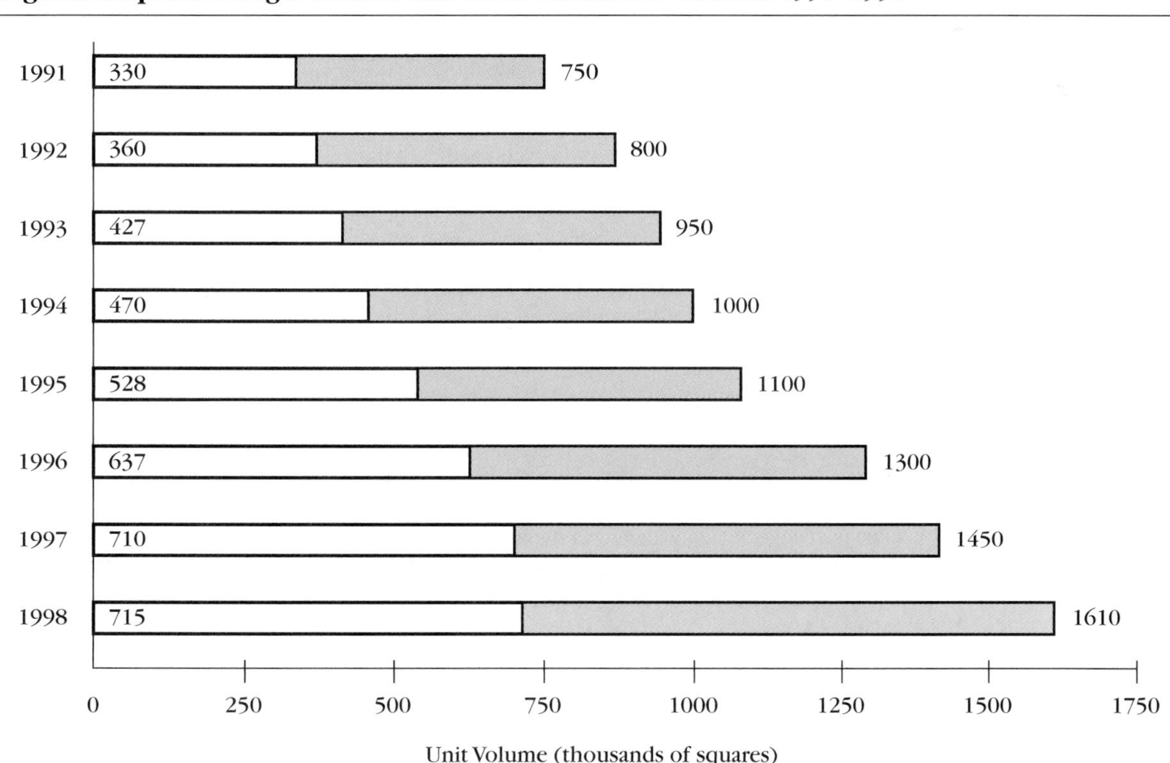

Source: Company records.

sales growth had strained production capacity and prompted an extensive plant modernization and expansion begun in 1997 and completed in 1998. Afton's senior management acknowledged that the plant's modernization and expansion should have been completed in 1997, when two of its major competitors expanded their shingle production capacity. These competitors, with added capacity, were probably seeking to increase their market share, Aftons' senior management thought. Afton's senior management speculated that this objective contributed to their unwillingness to raise shingle prices in 1998.

Afton increased its average price per square twice during the past seven years and major competitors in the region followed within a month or so of the announcement date. Each price increase averaged 10 percent. However, the recent price increase was not met. Even though Afton's unit volume continued to climb during the spring and summer construction months, Afton's director of sales observed a sales slowdown in September 1998. By calendar year-end 1998, Afton recorded a unit sales volume of 715 million squares. Afton's 1998 volume, although higher than 1997, represented an estimated market share of 44 percent—5 percentage points below the unit market share registered in 1997. Afton's President instructed the Director of Sales and the Director of Planning and Administration to prepare a recommendation on the company's pricing and competitive position soon after the end-of-year volume total was confirmed.

Regional Economic Projections for the Roofing Industry

During the course of their initial meeting, Bob Shearer, the Director of Sales, presented historical data on housing starts and the age of the existing housing stock (to estimate reroofing potential) in the region. Dan Egan, the Director of Planning and Administration, supplied published 1999 economic projections for the U.S. roofing industry as a whole and for Afton's region. The projections generally pointed toward a slowdown. According to one report:

> The construction industry is reaching the peak of the current economic cycle. Single-family dwelling unit construction is predicted to retreat seven percent as a result of slower income growth and sagging consumer confidence. Low mortgage rates, possibly reaching as low as six percent, will help limit the extent of the decline.[3]

In another report, based on a survey of roofing contractors nationwide and in Afton's region, was more optimistic in its economic outlook:

> Roofing contractors throughout the United States seem to agree that business conditions during 1999 are anyone's guess. Most tend to project a modest increase in reroofing and new construction over 1998 sales or no increase at all.[4]

Roofing contractors in Afton's region were optimistic that shingle volume would increase 2 percent overall, growing in the first six months of the calendar year, then declining in the second six months. Representative comments from large, established roofing contractors in the survey were as follows:

> [We] believe the roofing market will soften a bit during 1999. We don't have a backlog as big as last year's [1998]. In addition, homeowners won't commit to major capital expenditures, such as reroofing. They're adopting wait-and-see attitudes.

---

[3] "An Economic Outlook," *Professional Roofing Magazine* (January 1999): 6–7.

[4] "In Which Direction Is the Industry Headed?" *Professional Roofing Magazine* (December 1998): 15–20.

Another large contractor noted:

> I don't know what has happened. We had a flat fall [1998] season, and I know a number of well-known contractors, including myself, who are suffering. Contractor pricing concerns me. Prices seem to be lower than five years ago. Businesses have grown in terms of revenues, not bottom lines.

Shearer and Egan believed both the formal economic projections and roofing contractors' estimates had merit. Looking forward to 1999, they agreed that a favorable forecast meant about a 2 percent increase in square volume over 1998 volume in Afton's region. An unfavorable forecast meant a 5 percent decline in square volume compared to 1998 volume in Afton's region. Both executives were inclined to give greater weight to professional economists' estimates. Egan said, "I tend to think there is a 50 to 60 percent chance of two percent growth in 1999 and a 40 to 50 percent chance of a five percent decline." Shearer felt that Egan's views were reasonable and, like Egan, believed that the pricing recommendation should consider both the favorable and unfavorable forecast.

Planning Considerations

A week later, the executives met and discussed their options, knowing their recommendation was due the next day. After a lengthy discussion, they concluded two options existed. They could recommend maintaining Afton's average price per square at $44.50, or returning the average price to $40.50. The option of recommending a further price increase was dismissed on the grounds that the price differential between Afton Industries and its competitors would be too great. An average price below $40.50 was out of the question, as was reducing Afton's $44.50 average price by a few dollars. In Shearer's opinion, it was unlikely that competitors would increase or decrease their prices in 1999, regardless of whether Afton lowered its average price to $40.50 or maintained the $44.50 average price. "There is too much uncertainty in the marketplace right now," Shearer said.

During the discussion, Shearer commented that if Afton kept its average price at $44.50 per square and asphalt shingle sales grew by two percent, it was highly likely that Afton could realize a market share gain of one percentage point to 45 percent. He believed that the "fly-by-night" roofing contractors that populated the region during the boom times and fed on demand not satisfied by established roofing contractors would see less opportunity and do something else. He added, "Without licensing requirements to be a roofer in many areas of our region, all you have to do is hang out a shingle saying you're a roofing contractor." Shearer believed market demand would be even more important with a 5 percent decline in shingle volume in driving out fly-by-night roofing contractors who often priced low to get business. He noted, "We could very well achieve a 46 percent market share if market demand actually drops. We experienced an increase in market share during the previous downturn in the late 1980s."

Shearer believed that reducing Afton's average shingle price to $40.50 per square would return the region to the traditional price tiers and differentials among competitors. Also, it would remove the economic incentive for some roofing contractors to recommend a competitor's shingles to homeowners and builders. According to Afton sales representatives, many roofing contractors that purchased lower-priced shingles from competitors were marking up the product in such a manner that the installed price to homeowners and builders was equal to Afton's shingle price at its typical markup levels. The installed price parity was annoying to competitors because they had no price advantage at the point of sale or in the bidding for new construction. However, this pricing practice did improve roofing contractor profit margins slightly and did give competitors an edge over Afton for reroofing jobs when the roofer selected the shingle manufacturer. Shearer said that this practice was more prominent among "marginal roofers," as he called them, and would decrease with the departure of many fly-by-night roofing contractors following slowing or declining shingle demand. Shearer believed that reducing Afton's average shingle price to $40.50 could increase Afton's market share to 47 percent in a slowing market (2 percent growth). He added, "I think we can recapture our 49 percent market share if shingle demand actually declines by 5 percent." Egan thought Shearer's market share estimates were optimistic, but generally agreed with his assessment.

"We also have to consider our costs," injected Dan Egan. During the previous week, he had requested and obtained a production cost breakdown on the company's line of shingles at various levels of output from the company controller (Exhibit 3). The costs represented standard costs—predetermined costs under projected conditions—which were established to coincide with the recent plant modernization and expansion. "Pat (the company controller) assures me that these costs are reasonable and attainable given our engineering study," said Egan. He added, "I think our product costs are roughly the same as our competitors."

Tom Afton, the President of Afton Industries, knocked on the door just as Egan completed his sentence. "Any progress on the pricing recommendation?" Afton asked. "You bet," replied Shearer. "We'll have it ready for our meeting tomorrow." Egan looked at Shearer and said, "Let's order in some food for dinner."

EXHIBIT 3

Afton's Estimated Total Cost per Square at Various Production Volumes

	Production Volume in Squares			
Cost Item	*700,000*	*725,000*	*750,000*	*775,000*
Direct labor	$ 17.50	$ 15.75	$ 13.50	$ 11.20
Direct material	7.00	7.00	7.00	7.00
Scrappage	2.10	2.05	2.00	1.95
Product line expense				
Direct expense[a]	3.47	3.45	3.40	3.38
Indirect expense[b]	2.30	2.22	2.15	2.08
Selling, general and administrative expense[c]	3.75	3.58	3.43	3.29
Total cost per square	$ 36.12	$ 34.05	$ 31.48	$ 28.90

[a] Includes supplies, repairs, power, etc. (all variable costs).

[b] Includes depreciation, supervision, etc. (all fixed costs).

[c] All fixed cost but allocated on a per square basis for expository purposes.

Source: Company records.

CASE

Augustine Medical, Inc.

The Bair Hugger® Patient Warming System

In July 1987, Augustine Medical, Inc., was incorporated as a Minnesota corporation to develop and market products for hospital operating rooms and postoperative recovery rooms. The first two products the company planned to produce and sell were a patented patient warming system designed to treat postoperative hypothermia in the recovery room and a tracheal intubation guide for use in the operating room and in emergency medicine.

By early 1988, company executives were actively engaged in finalizing the marketing program for the patient warming system named Bair Hugger® Patient Warming System. The principal question yet to be resolved was how to price this system.

■ THE BAIR HUGGER® PATIENT WARMING SYSTEM

The Bair Hugger® Patient Warming System is a device designed to control the body temperature of postoperative patients. Specifically, the device is designed to treat the hypothermia (a condition defined as a body temperature of less than 36 degrees Centigrade or 96 degrees Fahrenheit) experienced by patients after operations.

Medical research indicates that 60 to 80 percent of all postoperative recovery room patients are clinically hypothermic. Several factors contribute to postoperative hypothermia. They are (1) a patient's exposure to cold operating room temperatures (which are maintained for the surgeons' comfort and for infection control), (2) heat loss due to evaporation of the fluids used to scrub patients, (3) evaporation from the exposed bowel, and (4) breathing of dry anesthetic gases.

The Bair Hugger® system consists of a heater/blower unit and a separate inflatable plastic/paper cover, or blanket. A photo of the system is shown in Exhibit 1 on page 432. The heater/blower unit is a large, square, boxlike structure that heats, filters, and blows air through a plastic cover. An electric cord wraps around the back of the unit for storage, and the unit is mounted on wheels for easy transport. The blower tubing attaches to the warming cover through a simple cardboard connector strap and can be retracted into the top of the unit for storage. Temperature is set by a dial with four settings on the top of the unit. A top lid opens to a storage bin that holds 12 warming covers for easy access. The disposable warming covers come packaged in 18-inch-long tubes. When unrolled, the plastic/paper cover is flat and covers an average-sized patient from shoulders to ankles. The blanket consists of a layer of thin plastic and a layer of plastic/paper material laminated into full-length

This case was prepared by Professor Roger A. Kerin, of the Edwin L. Cox School of Business, Southern Methodist University; Michael Gilbertson, of Augustine Medical, Inc.; and Professor William Rudelius, of University of Minnesota, as a basis for class discussion and is not designed to illustrate effective or ineffective handling of administrative situations. Certain names and data have been disguised. The assistance of graduate students Anne Christensen, Joanne Perty, and Laurel Wichman of the University of Minnesota is appreciated. The cooperation of Augustine Medical, Inc., in the preparation of the case is gratefully acknowledged.

EXHIBIT 1

Bair Hugger® Patient Warming System

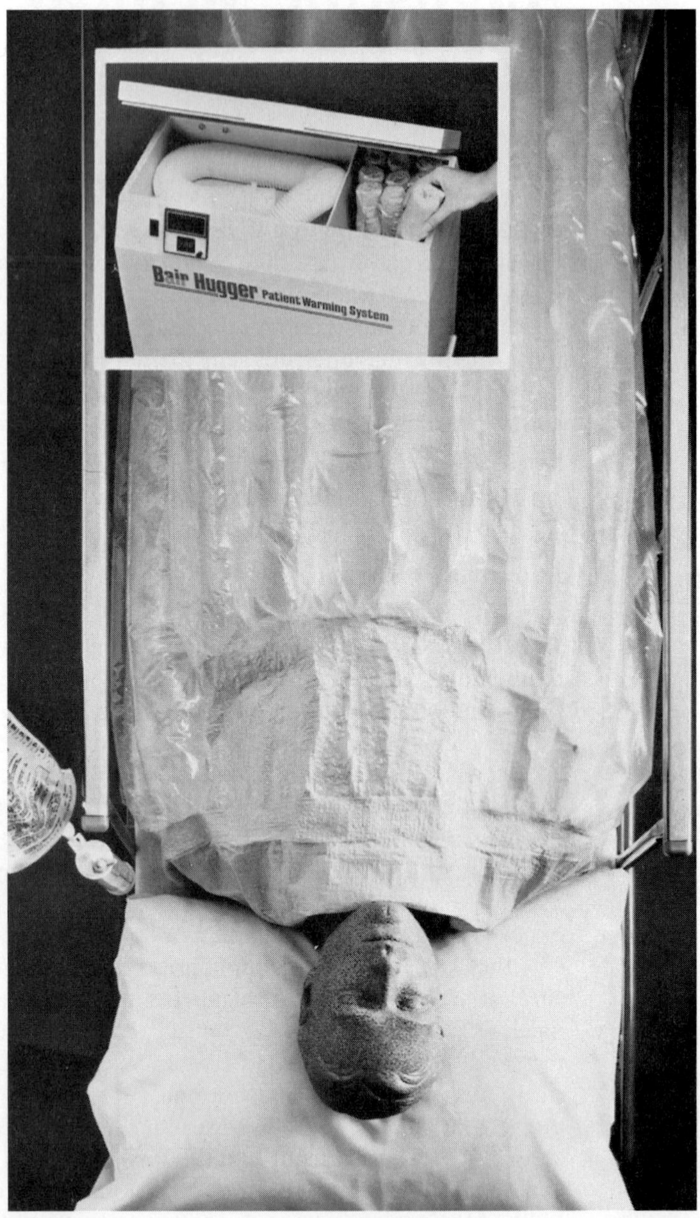

channels. Small holes punctuate the inner surface of the cover. When inflated through a connection at the feet of the patient, the tubular structure arcs over the patient's body, creating an individual patient environment. The warm air exits through the slits on the inner surface of the blanket, creating a gentle flow of warm air over the patient. The warming time per patient is about two hours.

The plastic cover was patented in 1986; there is no patent protection for the heater/blower unit.

■ COMPETING TECHNOLOGIES

Many competing technologies are available for the prevention and treatment of hypothermia. These technologies generally fall into one of two broad types of patient warming: surface warming or internal warming.

Surface-Warming Technologies

Warmed hospital blankets are the most commonly used treatment for hypothermia in recovery rooms and elsewhere. An application of warmed hospital blankets consists of placing six to eight warmed blankets in succession on top of a patient. Almost all patients receive at least one application; it is estimated that 50 percent of the postoperative patients require more than one application. The advantages of warmed hospital blankets are that they are simple, safe, and relatively inexpensive. The main disadvantage is that they cool quickly, provide only insulation, and require the patient's own body heat for regenerating warmth.

Water-circulating blankets are the second most popular postoperative hypothermic treatment. Water-circulating blankets can be placed under a patient, over a patient, or both. If a blanket is placed just under the patient, only 15 percent of the body's surface area is affected. However, hospitals typically place water-circulating blankets either just over the patient or over and under the patient, forming an insulated environment that encloses 85 to 90 percent of the body's surface area. The disadvantages of water-circulating blankets are that they are heavy and expensive and can cause burns on pressure points. Moreover, although a widely used and accepted method of warming, especially for more severe cases of hypothermia, water-circulating blankets are considered only slightly to moderately effective.

Electric blankets are generally unacceptable as a hypothermic treatment because of the risk of burns to the patient and of explosion in areas where oxygen is in use.

Air-circulating blankets and mattresses are not in common use in the United States, although variations on this technology have been used in the past. This technology relies on warmed air flowing over the body to transfer heat to the patient. The advantages of warmed-air technology are that it is safe, lightweight, and theoretically more effective than warmed hospital blankets or water-circulating blankets. Products using this technology are not widely found in the U.S. market, however.

Thermal drapes, also known as reflective blankets, have recently been introduced and are gaining acceptance as a preventive measure used in the operating room. They consist of head covers, blankets, and leggings placed on the uninvolved portions of the patient's body. Their use is recommended when 60 percent of a patient's body surface can be covered. The advantages of this technology are that it is simple, safe, and inexpensive and has been shown to reduce heat loss. The disadvantage is that it merely insulates the patient and does not transfer heat to someone who is already hypothermic.

Infrared heating lamps are popular for infant use. When placed a safe distance from the body and shone on the skin, they radiate warmth to the patient. The advantages of heat lamps are that they are effective and illuminate the patient for observation or therapy. A disadvantage is that since the skin needs to be exposed, modesty prevents widespread use among adults. (They are, however, used in adult skin-graft operations.) Nurses dislike radiant heat lamps and panels because they tend to heat the entire recovery room and are uncomfortable to work under.

Partial warm-water immersion has been used in the past, especially in cases where a patient was deliberately cooled to slow down metabolism. With this method, the patient is placed in a bath of warm water and watched carefully. The advantages of this technology are that it transfers heat very effectively and it is simple. The disadvantages are that the system is inconvenient to set up and requires close monitoring of the patient, which increases labor costs. In addition, water baths must be carefully watched for bacterial growth, and they are very expensive to purchase and use.

Increasing room temperature is the most obvious way to prevent and treat hypothermia, but it is seldom used. The advantages of this method are that it is simple and relatively inexpensive and has been proven effective at temperatures of over 70 degrees Fahrenheit. The disadvantage is that warm room temperatures are not acceptable to the nurses and surgeons who must work in the environment. Furthermore, warm temperatures increase the risk of infection.

Internal-Warming Technologies

Inspiring *heated and humidified air* is a fairly effective internal-warming technique currently being used with intubated patients (those having a breathing tube in the trachea). However, delivery of heated and humidified air by mask or tent to nonintubated patients is not acceptable in postoperative situations, because mask or tent delivery would interfere with observation and communication and, in the case of a tent, might increase the chance of infection. The fact that the patient must be intubated is a disadvantage, since the vast majority of postoperative patients are not intubated.

Warmed intravenous (I.V.) fluids are used in more severe hypothermic cases to directly transfer heat to the circulatory system. Warmed I.V. fluids are very effective because they introduce warmth directly into the circulatory system. The disadvantages of this technology are that it requires very close monitoring of the patient's core temperature and high physician involvement.

Drug therapy diminishes the sensation of cold and reduces shivering but does not actually increase body temperature. Although drug therapy is convenient and makes patients feel more comfortable, it does not warm them and in fact slows their recovery from anesthesia and surgery.

■ COMPETITIVE PRODUCTS

A variety of competitive products that use the above-mentioned technologies are available (see Exhibit 2). A review of competitors' sales materials and interviews with hospital personnel provided the following breakdown of competitive products.

Warmed Hospital Blankets

For treating adult hypothermia, hospitals use their own blankets, which they warm in large heating units. Many manufacturers produce heating units for hospital use. The cost of laundering six to eight two-pound hospital blankets averages $0.13 per pound. Laundering and heating costs are absorbed in hospital overhead.

Water-Circulating Blankets

Several manufacturers produce water-circulating mattresses and blankets, but Cincinnati Sub-Zero, Gaymar Industries, and Pharmaseal are the major suppliers. Prices of automatic control units that measure both blanket and patient temperatures range from $4,850 to $5,295. Manual control units are priced at about $3,000, although they appear to be discounted by as much as 40 percent in actual practice.

The average life of water-circulating control units is 15 years. Reusable blankets list at from $168 to $375, depending on quality. Disposable blankets list at from $20 to $26. Volume discounts for blankets can reduce the list price by almost 50 percent.

EXHIBIT 2

Representative Competitive Products and Prices

Product	*List Price*	*Company*	*Estimated Size of Company (Sales, Employees)*	*Comments*
Blanketrol 200	$2,995/manual unit; $4,895/automatic unit; $165–$305/reusable blanket; $20/disposable blanket	Cincinnati Sub-Zero	$10 million; 90 employees	Hypothermia equipment is a small part of its overall business.
MTA 4700	$4,735/unit; $139/reusable blanket; $24/disposable blanket	Gaymar Industries	$17 million; 150 employees	Hypothermia equipment seems to be a major part of its business.
Aquamatic	$4,479/unit	American Hamilton (division of American Hospital Supply)	$3.3 billion; 31,300 employees	Hypothermia equipment is a very minor part of American Hospital Supply's business.
Climator	$4,000/unit	Hosworth Air Engineering Ltd.	Not available	The company could begin distribution of hypothermia equipment in the United States in 1988.

Water-circulating blanket technology has changed little over the past 20 years except for the addition of solid state controls. There is little differentiation among the products of different firms.

Reflective Thermal Drapes

O.R. Concepts sells a product named the Thermadrape, which comes in both adult and pediatric sizes. Adult head covers list for $0.49 each; adult drapes list for $2.50 to $3.98, depending on size; leggings are priced at $1.50 each.

Air-Circulating Blankets and Mattresses

Two competitors are known to provide an air-circulating product like the Bair Hugger® Patient Warming System; however, neither is currently sold in the United States. The Sweetland Bed Warmer and Cast Dryer was in use 25 years ago but is no longer manufactured. This product consisted of a heater/blower unit that directed warm air through a hose placed under a patient's blanket. The Hosworth-Climator is an English-made product that provides a controlled-temperature microclimate by means of air flow from a mattress. The Climator comes in a variety of models for use in recovery rooms, intensive care units, burn units, general wards, and patients' homes. The model most suitable for postoperative recovery rooms is priced at $4,000. This product could be distributed in the United States sometime in 1988. A summary of representative competitor products and list prices is shown in Exhibit 2.

THE HOSPITAL MARKET

Approximately 21 million surgical operations are performed annually in the United States, or 84,000 operations per average eight-hour work day. Approximately 5,500 hospitals have operating rooms and postoperative recovery rooms.

Research commissioned by Augustine Medical, Inc., indicated that there are 31,365 postoperative recovery beds and 28,514 operating rooms in hospitals in the United States. An estimated breakdown of the number of postoperative hospital beds and the percentage of surgical operations is shown below:

Number of Postoperative Beds	*Number of Hospitals*	*Estimated Percentage of Surgical Operations*
0	1,608	0%
1-6	3,602	20
7-11	1,281	40
12-17	391	20
18-22	135	10
23-28	47	6
29-33	17	2
>33	17	2

Given the demand for postoperative recovery room beds, the research firm estimated that hospitals with fewer than seven beds would not be highly receptive to the Bair Hugger® Patient Warming System. The firm also projected that one system would be sold for every eight postoperative recovery room beds.

Interviews with physicians and nurses, followed by a demonstration of the system, yielded a variety of responses:

1. Respondents believed that the humanitarian ethic "to make the patient feel more comfortable" is important.
2. Respondents felt that the Bair Hugger® Patient Warming System would speed recovery for postop patients.
3. Respondents wanted to test the units under actual conditions in postoperative recovery rooms. They were reluctant to make any purchase commitments without testing. A typical comment was "No one today, in this market, ever buys a pig in a poke."
4. Respondents felt that the product was price-sensitive to alternative methods. Respondents were very receptive to the notion of using the heater/blower free of charge and only paying for the disposable blankets. Physicians wanted to confer with others who would be responsible for using the product to administer the warming treatment, however, such as the head nurse in postoperative recovery rooms and the chief anesthesiologist.
5. Respondents believed that the pressure to move patients through the operating room and out of postop is greater than in the past. Efficiency is the byword.
6. Capital expenditures in hospitals were subject to budget committee approval. Although the amounts varied, expenditures for equipment over $1,500 were typically subject to a formal review and decision process.

■ AUGUSTINE MEDICAL, INC.

Augustine Medical, Inc., was founded in 1987 by Dr. Scott Augustine, an anesthesiologist. His experience had convinced him that hospitals needed and desired a new approach to warming patients after surgery. His medical knowledge, coupled with a technical flair, prompted the development of the Bair Hugger® Patient Warming System.

The Bair Hugger® Patient Warming System has several advantages over water-circulating blankets. First, warm air makes patients feel warm and stop shivering. Second, the system cannot cause burns, and water leaks around electrical equipment are

EXHIBIT 3

Sales Literature for the Bair Hugger® Patient Warming System

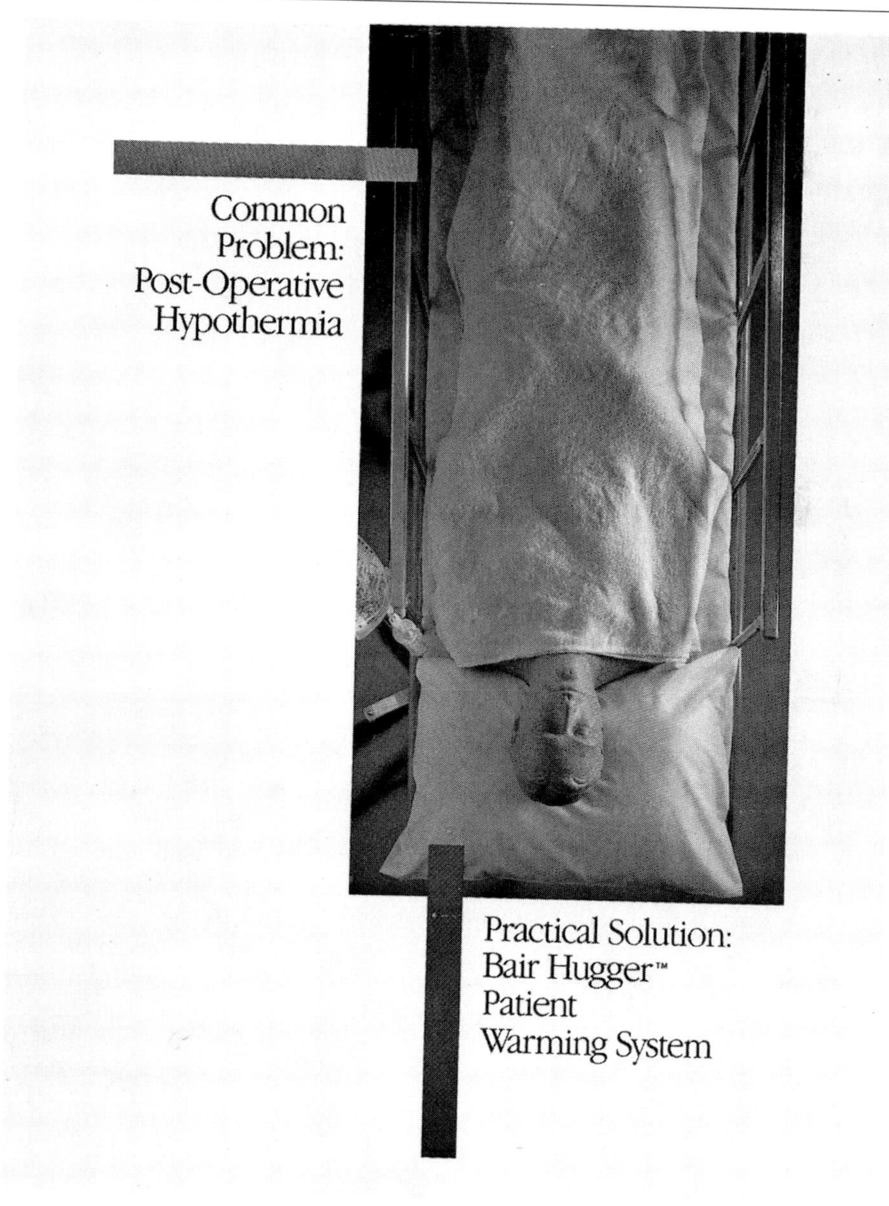
Common
Problem:
Post-Operative
Hypothermia
Practical Solution:
Bair Hugger™
Patient
Warming System

EXHIBIT 3 ***(continued)***

A Warm Welcome for Your Recovery Room Patients

Augustine Medical, Inc.'s new Bair Hugger™ Patient Warming System is the most practical and comforting solution for post-operative hypothermia available today.

Every year more than 10,000,000 hospital patients experience the severe discomfort and vital signs instability associated with post-operative hypothermia. Years later, patients can still vividly recall this discomfort. Augustine Medical's new Patient Warming System is a warm and reliable solution to post-operative hypothermia.

1. PATENTED SELF SUPPORTING DESIGN
   As the tubes fill with air, the Warming Cover naturally arches over the patient's body.
2. TISSUE PAPER UNDERLAYER
   The tissue paper underlayer of the Warming Cover is soft and comfortable against the patient's skin.
3. AIR SLITS
   Tiny slits in the underlayer allow warm air from the Heat Source to gently fill the space around the patient.
4. SHOULDER DRAPE
   The shoulder drape is designed to tuck under the chin and shoulders, trapping warm air under the cover and preventing air flow by the patient's face.
5. DISPOSABLE COVERS
   The disposable Covers prevent cross contamination and reduce laundry requirements.

A Practical Solution to Post-Operative Hypothermia

The Bair Hugger™ Patient Warming System consists of a Heat Source and a separate disposable Warming Cover that directs a gentle flow of warm air across the body and provides for safe and comfortable rewarming.

The Bair Hugger Heat Source uses a reliable, high efficiency blower, a sealed 400W heating element, and a microprocessor-based temperature control to create a continuous flow of warm air. There are no pumps, valves or compressors to maintain. Special features include built-in storage space for the air hose, power cord and a convenient supply of disposable Warming Covers. The Heat Source complies with all safety requirements for hospital equipment.

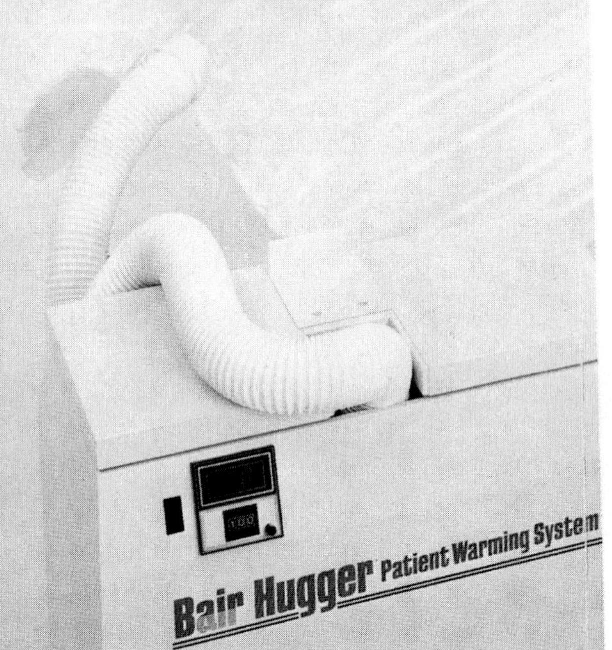

not a problem, as they are with water-circulating blankets. Third, the disposable blankets eliminate the potential for cross-contamination among patients. Finally, the system does not require that the patient be lifted or rolled. Augustine's personal experience indicated that all of these features would be welcome by nurses and patients alike. Features and benefits of the Bair Hugger® Patient Warming System are detailed in the company's sales literature, shown in Exhibit 3 on pages 437 through 440.

Investor interest in Augustine Medical and the medical technology it provided produced an initial capitalization of $500,000. These funds were to be used for further research and development, staff support, facilities, and marketing. It was believed that this initial investment would cover the fixed costs (including salaries, leased space, and promotional literature) of the company during its first year of operation. The company would subcontract the production of the heater/blower unit and would manufacture warming covers in-house using a proprietary machine. Only minor assembly would be performed by the company.

EXHIBIT 3 ***(continued)***

THE BAIR HUGGER™
PATIENT WARMING SYSTEM
IS SO EASY TO USE.

Remove a new Warming Cover from the storage compartment and unroll over the patient.

Connect the heater hose to the inlet of the Warming Cover and turn on the heater.

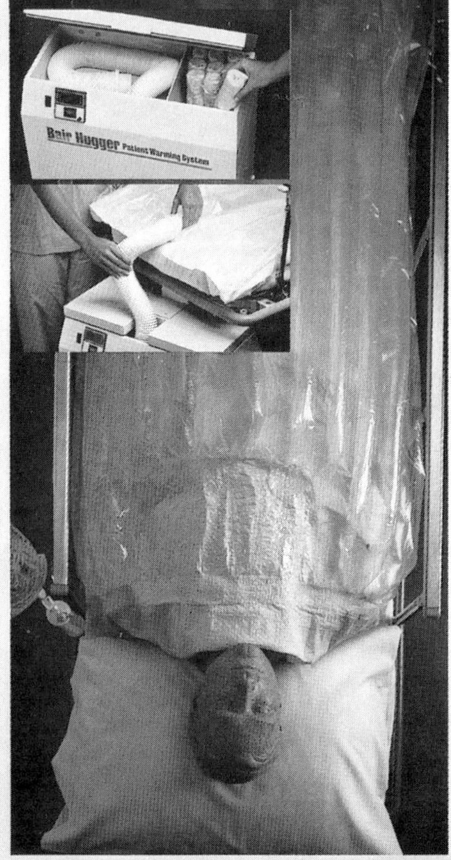

6. SIMPLE CONTROLS
A preprogrammed temperature range and a preset high temperature limit of 110°F make the Bair Hugger safe and simple to use.
7. INTERNAL WARMING COVER STORAGE
The storage compartment provides a convenient supply of Warming Covers ready for immediate use.
8. INTERNAL HOSE STORAGE
The hose retracts into its own compartment for ready access.
9. LIGHTWEIGHT, COMPACT DESIGN
The Heat Source is designed for convenience and portability. While in use, it tucks under the foot of the gurney. The unit's light weight and small size make it simple to move and store.
10. BUILT-IN POWER CORD STORAGE
The power cord storage holds up to 12 feet of cord, making the Heat Source portable and easy to store.
11. 5μ AIR FILTER
The air filter assures dust-free air circulation through the Bair Hugger Warming Cover. The filter is simple to change when necessary.

The Bair Hugger™ Warming Cover:

The Warming Cover consists of a layer of plastic and a layer of tissue paper laminate bonded together into long tubular channels. The self-supporting Warming Cover is designed to arch over the patient's body creating a warm, comfortable environment.

The Warming Cover is convenient to use because no straps, tapes or other fasteners are required to stabilize the cover and the patient does not have to be disturbed or moved.

When the Warming Cover is completely inflated, warm air from the Heat Source exits the tubular channels through slits in the Cover's soft underlayer, surrounding the patient with a gentle flow of warm air.

The Bair Hugger® Patient Warming System would be sold by and through medical products distributor organizations in various regions around the country. These distributor organizations would call on hospitals, demonstrate the system, and maintain an inventory of blankets. The margin paid to the distributors would be competitively set at 30 percent of the delivered (that is, less discounts) selling price on the heater/blower unit and 40 percent of the delivered (discounted if necessary) price on the blankets.

Preliminary estimates from subcontractors and a time-and-motion study on assembly indicated that the direct cost of the heater/blower unit would be $380. The cost of materials, manufacturing, and packaging of the plastic disposable blankets was estimated to be $0.85 per blanket.

EXHIBIT 3 ***(continued)***

A Warm and Practical Discovery: Bair Hugger™ Patient Warming System

Post-Operative Hypothermia–A Common Problem

As a practicing anesthesiologist, Dr. Scott D. Augustine observed that there was no practical treatment for the common problem of post-operative hypothermia. An extensive review of post-operative hypothermia revealed several important facts:

- Post-operative hypothermia (T<36°C or <96.7°F) occurs in 60-80% of all post-operative patients (1). This extremely common problem affects more than 10,000,000 surgical patients every year.
- Several factors contribute to post-operative hypothermia including the patient's exposure to cold operating room temperatures, heat loss due to evaporation of fluids used to scrub the patient, evaporation of moisture from exposed bowels, and the breathing of dry anesthetic gases.
- Unlike environmental hypothermia, post operative hypothermia is not usually life threatening. However, it can have serious side effects for older or unstable patients. Negative effects include a decrease in cardiovascular stability and an increase in oxygen consumption of up to 400% during unaided rewarming, as well as severe shivering and significant patient discomfort (2).
- Patients with unstable body temperatures require intensive nursing care, which means higher costs. Recovery room time may also be prolonged due to the instability caused by post-operative hypothermia.

Variety of Treatments–Only One Practical Solution

Many methods have been used to try to warm patients after surgery including warmed hospital blankets, water mattresses and heat lamps (3). Studies have shown, though, that these methods are ineffective.

The most common method of treating hypothermia–heated hospital blankets–does not actively heat the patient. The small amount of heat retained by a cotton blanket quickly dissipates, thereby requiring patients to rewarm themselves. Because multiple blankets are typically used, this method is both inconvenient and time-consuming for nursing staff and produces large amounts of laundry.

Another common method used to try to rewarm post-operative hypothermia patients is the use of a water circulating mattress. Water circulating equipment is heavy, complex, expensive and prone to leakage. While water mattresses have been used for many years, there is no clinical evidence that documents their effectiveness (4, 5). This lack of effectiveness can be explained by the minimal body surface area in contact with the mattress, (only 15%) and the lack of blood flow to this area. The weight of the patient creates a pressure which prevents normal cutaneous blood flow. The heat in the mattress cannot be transported away from the skin and the contact surface becomes an insulator effectively minimizing potential heat transfer to the patient.

New Approach Needed

As Dr. Augustine discussed the problem of post-operative hypothermia with doctors, nurses, and industry experts he became convinced that a new approach to warming patients was needed. A survey of anesthesiologists showed that most were dissatisfied with the current technology available for treating hypothermia. A new technology was definitely needed.

As a result of his research, Dr. Augustine developed the Bair Hugger™ Patient Warming System. Numerous studies and reports have shown that increased ambient room temperatures will prevent hypothermia (6-10). Indeed, before the advent of air conditioning, the average ambient temperature of the OR was higher and hyperthermia in the peri-operative period was not uncommon. Surgical patients will predictably lose or gain heat depending on the ambient temperature of the surrounding environment. The Bair Hugger™ System simulates a warm room by surrounding the patient in a gentle flow of warm air–A Focused Thermal Environment™.

The Bair Hugger™ Patient Warming System combines the convenience and effectiveness of warm air to safely rewarm hypothermic patients. The Warming System's minimal cost is rapidly recovered in saved nursing time, reduced linen expenses and lower overall recovery room costs. There is now a practical and cost-effective solution to post-operative hypothermia.

Two-week Free Trial

To arrange for a free two-week trial of the Bair Hugger™ Patient Warming System, fill out the enclosed reply card or call us collect at (612) 941-8866.

SPECIFICATIONS HEATER/BLOWER UNIT	
Size	26" high x 14" deep x 22" wide
Weight	65 lbs.
Power Requirements	110VAC
Temperature Range	Ambient to 110°F Max
Enclosure	Enameled steel
Displayed Variables	Temperature °F
Power Cable	12 Feet long
Display	.5 inch (1.2 cm) Character LCD
COVERS	
Size	54" x 36"
Weight	8 ounces
Material	Polyethylene and tissue paper laminate.

AUGUSTINE MEDICAL INC.

PRACTICAL SOLUTIONS TO COMMON PROBLEMS IN ACUTE CARE™

10393 West 70th St., Suite 100 Eden Prairie, Minnesota 55344

References: (1) Vaughan MS, Vaughan RW, Cork RC: Anesthesia and Analgesia 60:746-751, 1981. (2) Bay J, Nunn JG, Prys-Roberts C: British Journal of Anaesthesia 40: 398-406, 1968. (3) Kucha DH, Nichols GH, Christ NM, Bynum JW: Military Medicine 139:388-390, 1974. (4) Morris RH, Kumar A: Anesthesiology 36:408-411, 1972. (5) Goundsouzian NG, Morris RH, Ryan JF: Anesthesiology 39:351-353, 1973. (6) Morris, RH: Annals of Surgery 173:230-233, 1971. (7) Morris RH, Wilkey BR: Anesthesiology 32:102-107, 1970. (8) Clark RE, Orkin LR, Rovenstine EA: JAMA 154:311-319, 1954. (9) Bigler JA, McQuistow WO: JAMA 146:551, 1951. (10) Harrison GG, Bull AB, Schmidt HJ: British Journal of Anaesthesia 40:398-406, 1960.

The central issue at this time was the determination of the list price to hospitals for the heater/blower unit and the plastic blankets, given the widespread incidence of price discounting. Immediate attention to the price question was important for at least three reasons. First, it was felt that the price set for the Bair Hugger® Patient Warming System would influence the rate at which prospective buyers would purchase the system. Second, price and volume together would influence the cash flow position of the company. Third, the company would soon have to prepare price literature for its distributor organizations and for a scheduled medical trade show, where the system would be shown for the first time.

CASE

Seagram in Taiwan

Scotch and Cognac Pricing

In January 1998, Ian Swanson, vice president of finance at Seagram Greater China, was contemplating what actions to take in light of the proposed changes to the import duty rates applied on scotch and cognac in Taiwan. Given that the Taiwanese spirits market had become very competitive in recent years, careful management of these rate changes was critical for ensuring Seagram's future market share and profitability in Taiwan. This left Swanson with the challenging task of trying to determine what pricing levels to recommend based upon the new import duty regime.

■ SEAGRAM SPIRITS AND WINE GROUP

The Seagram Spirits and Wine Group is a division of Montreal-based Seagram Company Limited, and one of the leading producers and marketers of premium spirits and wines in the world. The group enjoyed strong market positions throughout most mature Western economies, and had made significant in-roads in the emerging markets of Asia Pacific, India, and eastern Europe. In 1997, the group had outpaced the spirits industry by increasing EBITDA (earnings before interest, taxes, depreciation, and amortization) by more than 8 percent over the previous year to US$813 million, even though revenues had decreased from US$5.199 billion to US$5.121 billion. The decline in the group's revenues was concentrated primarily in Asia and Europe, where weakened consumer spending and increased competition had eroded company sales volumes. Over the past several months, many Asian currency and equity markets experienced sharp devaluations, in turn exacerbating the previous decline in sales throughout the region. Although Taiwan's equity and currency markets were largely unaffected in comparison to other countries, consumer confidence had still taken a noticeable drop.

Seagram Greater China (Seagram GC) was a separate management group within the Spirits and Wine Group. The main office for Seagram GC was in Hong Kong, where a staff of marketing and finance professionals oversaw the company's sales, marketing, and distribution efforts in China, Hong Kong, and Taiwan. Previous reengineering efforts had led the company to adopt a decentralized organizational structure using "Shared Service Centers" to provide back-office support to Seagram GC's field operations in China, Hong Kong, and Taiwan. This structure was designed to

---

Tom Gleave prepared this case under the supervision of Professor Claude Lanfranconi solely to provide material for class discussion. The authors do not intend to illustrate either effective or ineffective handling of a managerial situation. The authors may have disguised certain names and other identifying information to protect confidentiality.

achieve greater cost efficiencies, as well as more effective marketing and brand development at the local level. For example, the Shared Service Centers provided specific accounting and financial reporting support to each of the three local offices, therefore negating the need to produce financial statements at the local level. The primary responsibilities for the local general managers included the execution of marketing plans that were developed in Hong Kong, as well as the development and management of key accounts. The Hong Kong office maintained responsibility for the procurement of Seagram products from the company's various manufacturing facilities located throughout the world. These products were, in turn, imported into Seagram GC's three local operations at a preset transfer price.

The focus of the group's marketing efforts was on its global scotch whisky and cognac brands, with a strong emphasis placed upon the sale of premium and super premium varieties within each of these product categories. Given the advent of Pan-Asian television coverage in recent years, Seagram GC had been able to develop effective advertising campaigns for the company's brands throughout Greater China. In particular, it was able to substantially increase awareness for both Chivas Regal and Martell Cordon Bleu, the company's flagship premium scotch and premium cognac, respectively. Chivas Regal was considered the company's single most important financial driver and was viewed as a cornerstone to Seagram's future success worldwide.

TAIWAN'S SCOTCH AND COGNAC MARKETS

Sales volume in the Taiwanese spirits market was approximately 1,522,000 nine-liter cases in 1996, and was forecasted to reach about 1,777,000 cases by 2000 (see Exhibit 1). Seagram believed that Taiwan's scotch consumers were very image conscious, with a core group of drinkers (comprising 20 percent of the company's customer base) accounting for 80 percent of the sales volume. (See Exhibit 2 for a breakdown of Seagram's brands.) Although brand consciousness was very high among Taiwan's scotch consumers, brand loyalty was not for a number of reasons, including price. This led many drinkers to switch brands on a regular basis. Within the overall market, premium scotch sales had grown rapidly between 1993 and 1996, after the Taiwanese government removed its previous ban on imported spirits; however, by 1997, sales growth had become less dramatic. Since entering the Taiwanese market in 1993, Seagram had captured dominant shares in both the premium and super-premium segments with its Chivas Regal and Royal Salute brands respectively. United Distillers/Hennessy (UD/Hennessy), Seagram's key competitor worldwide, had gained the largest share in the standard segment with Johnny Walker Red Label, whereas Seagram consciously neglected to participate in this category in Taiwan.

In stark contrast to the sales curve experienced in the premium scotch segment, sales volume in the premium cognac segment had started to decline by 1996 and showed little hope for recovery. This decrease was attributed to two main factors. First, consumers had become much more price conscious in their purchases of spirits and, therefore, sought lower cost alternatives to cognac. Second, a dramatic decrease in "on-premise" sales had taken place after the Taiwanese police forces began making concerted efforts to close many of the unlicensed nightclubs that had sprung up in recent years. In terms of market positioning, the Hennessy brand enjoyed dominant share in the standard cognac category, and was a close competitor in the premium category. According to Ian Swanson, this was "largely due to price leadership and heavy marketing spending in the standard category."

Since 1993, Taiwan's spirits importers had to contend with growing competitive pressures from a variety of other sources. For example, many traders and brokers en-

EXHIBIT 1

1996 Market Volume and Growth Rates

		1996 Volumes (%)		
Spirits Category	***# Cases*** [a]	***Seagram***	***UD/Hennessy***	***Other***
Super premium scotch	128,000	55	36	9
Premium scotch	333,000	60	24	16
Standard scotch	21,000	0	58	42
Other whisky (i.e., Japanese)	400,000	0	0	100
Premium cognac	118,000	41	37	22
Standard cognac	65,000	18	56	26

		Compounded Annual Growth Rates (%)		
Spirits Category	***Actual Total***	***1990–1996 Seagram***	***Forecast Total***	***1996–2000 Seagram***
Super premium scotch	67	69	–1	0
Premium scotch	22	26	3	–1
Standard scotch	8	0	75	124
Other whisky	77	12	–1	111[b]
Premium cognac	1	11	–1	–4
Standard cognac	–6	0	1	–2

[a] The basic sales volume unit in the spirits business was a box of 12,750 milliliter bottles.

[b] This large growth rate is based upon a very small sales base.

EXHIBIT 2

Current Landed Costs and Target Retail Pricing (NT$ per Bottle)

Product Category	***Landed Cost***	***Target Price***
Super Premium Scotch		
Seagram—Royal Salute (21 years)	832	2,170
UD/Hennessy—Johnny Walker Premier	832	2,300
Premium Scotch		
Seagram—Chivas Regal (12 years)	272	680
UD/Hennessy—Johnny Walker Black Label	272	650
Other Whisky		
Japanese	180	480
Cognac Premium		
Seagram—Martell XO	976	2,080
Seagram—Martell Cordon Bleu	784	1,960
UD/Hennessy—XO		2,200
Cognac Standard		
Seagram—Martell VSOP	464	1,100
UD/Hennessy—VSOP	464	1,100

gaged in "unauthorized commercial activity," which had impacted the market by purchasing discounted spirits (including Seagram products) on the open market, and then selling these items through conventional trading channels.[1] Being the market leader, Seagram suffered more than its competitors from this activity. Additionally, many domestic producers began to market numerous types of "look-alike" products. These products were generally inferior in quality when compared to their original counterparts, however, substantively cheaper pricing, coupled with near identical packaging, allowed the "look-alikes" to secure significant market share. The entry of "Japanese whisky" also had a major impact on the sales and marketing efforts of the importers, as brands such as Suntory became increasingly popular with price-conscious consumers. The popularity of Japanese whisky was due to a favorable duty regime coupled with heavy marketing expenditures by Suntory in recognition of the temporary opportunity these measures presented ahead of any duty reform.

The increased level of competitiveness of the Taiwanese market, coupled with the lack of product loyalty, caused some industry players (like UD/Hennessy) to invest more money in brand building in order to compete effectively. These players believed that focused and continued investment directed toward understanding consumer and market dynamics was crucial for future volume and profit growth. Seagram's took a different position, however, by decreasing advertising and promotion expenditures in Taiwan from US$12.5 million in 1996 to US$11.1 million in 1997. The rationale for this decision was that gains in market share were becoming disproportionately expensive in comparison to earlier gains. Moreover, it was crucial for the Greater China division to meet the preestablished profit targets it had set with Seagram's head office.

■ DISTRIBUTION CHANNELS

Upon entering the Taiwanese market, Seagram established relationships with five different distributors scattered throughout the island. By 1996, however, it had moved to an exclusive distributorship arrangement with Formosa Trading Limited because its previous relationships had become dysfunctional. This was because a lack of exclusive distribution rights among the original five distributors had encouraged all of the parties to undercut each other in order to achieve greater sales volume leading to retail price erosion. Additionally, the five distributors had started to engage in "unauthorized commercial activity" by trading in discounted spirits. These factors led Seagram to develop a compensation program for Formosa Trading that was designed to encourage higher sales volumes and provide timely and useful market information, while refraining from engaging in unauthorized commercial activity.

In becoming the exclusive distributor for Seagram's products in Taiwan, Formosa was charged with the responsibility for servicing four main types of accounts, namely liquor stores, convenience stores, hypermarkets, and on-premise licensees. Recent and forecasted sales for each channel were as follows:

Channel Type	*1996 (%)*	*2000 (%)*
Liquor stores	15	7
Convenience stores	10	10
Hypermarkets	30	35
On-premise licensees	45	48

[1] Many businesses in Asia experienced situations where they were faced with the prospect of trying to sell their products at prices that were more expensive than identical "unauthorized" products entering the market. This was because traders could source identical products (including spirits) more cheaply from other markets (such as Latin America), then sell the goods in markets where the base price was suitably high enough to make a profit.

Since their introduction in 1994, hypermarkets such as Makro, Carrefour, and Wal-Mart had made the most noticeable impact on the distribution of spirits in Taiwan, having grown to control over 30 percent of the island's sales. The general marketing strategy adopted by these retailers was to offer customers "everyday low prices" for the products carried. Therefore, merchandise was usually purchased in large quantities, and often directly from suppliers, so that the hypermarkets could benefit from volume discounts and cheaper prices. The impact of the success of this new retailing format was immediate and had affected the spirits industry in three significant ways. First, many on-premise establishments realized that they could buy spirits cheaper from the hypermarkets than from some of their distributors. This caused some of the smaller liquor distributors to go bankrupt. Second, the hypermarket format encouraged home consumption at a time when greater numbers of consumers were seeking increased affordability and convenience. Third, the buying power of the hypermarkets forced the industry to "match" unauthorized commercial activity prices that could be obtained on the open market.

■ TAIWAN'S DUTY REGIME

Prior to 1993, the Taiwanese market was officially closed to imported spirits. In early 1993, these restrictions were lifted, although the import duty rates that were simultaneously imposed were so prohibitive that many industry players refrained from entering the market. For example, a flat duty of NT$1,000 (in early January NT$33.5 = US$1.00) was levied on each liter of imported cognac, amounting to about 38 percent of the target retail price for Seagram's Martell Cordon Bleu and 68 percent for Martell VSOP. Similarly, a rate of NT$440 was charged for each liter of imported scotch, while other whiskies (including Japanese whiskies) were charged NT$198 per liter. These duty rates equated to about 48 percent of the target price for Chivas Regal and about 31 percent for Japanese whisky. (See also Exhibit 2.) Despite these barriers to entry, scotch and cognac became highly sought products, particularly by wealthy business executives. This allowed companies like Seagram and UD/Hennessy to capture significant share in specific product segments. However, by 1995, the Taiwanese spirits market began to change considerably due to the increasing acceptance of Japanese whisky, as well as the proliferation of "look-alike" brands. These developments, particularly the success of Japanese whisky, caused the scotch and cognac importers to seek greater equality from the Taiwanese government with respect to duty rates. Several years previously, the Imported Distillers Association had successfully argued a case before the European Union claiming that wide differences in duty rates levied throughout Europe was discriminatory. The success of this lobbying effort led the Imported Distillers Association to file a similar claim with the Taiwanese government, while raising the spectre of possible retaliation from the World Trade Organization if there was a failure to address the issue. This led the Taiwanese government to introduce proposed legislation that would see import duty rates be applied uniformly across all categories of spirits. The bill, which was expected to become law sometime in 1998, proposed that the following formula be applied to each liter of imported spirits:

1. Base rate: 12.5 percent of the landed cost[2]
2. Add: NT$170
3. Add: 5 percent value-added tax (based upon the cumulative total of items 1 and 2)

[2] Seagram's landed costs included the transfer price from Hong Kong, freight, handling, and insurance charges. Swanson stated that "insurance, freight and handling costs are essentially the same at about NT$30 per bottle among the key competitors."

It appeared to Ian Swanson that, based upon the proposed duty changes, Seagram GC had the potential to boost profits significantly in the Taiwanese market. Swanson commented:

> The current duty rate for a liter of imported standard cognac (VSOP) is NT$1,000. This would be reduced to NT$319 under the proposed duty regime. Therefore, the company essentially has two options. After the duties change, we could try to enhance our margins by recouping the duty savings, or we could reduce prices accordingly in order to generate sales volume.

■ PRICING TRADE-OFFS

In attempting to determine the best possible pricing regime for Seagram's range of scotch and cognac products in Taiwan, Swanson needed to balance several important factors. In examining the situation, he stated:

> This situation is very similar to a "prisoner's dilemma" in that we need to protect our downside risk, yet be prepared to exploit any upside potential. On the one hand, if the competition drops its prices when the duties change, we will need to move immediately or else risk a loss of market share, the cost of which can be tremendously expensive to reacquire. On the other hand, if we drop our prices, we risk destroying our highly valued brand equity in our premium and super premium categories. This leaves us with four possible scenarios: we hold prices while the competition cuts prices; we cut prices while the competition holds; we both hold; or we both cut. Clearly, there is no way to precisely predict what will happen, but educated guesses can be made based upon the strategies and competencies of our competitors and ourselves, as well as trends in the marketplace.
>
> In terms of Chivas Regal, we believe that by passing on 100 percent of the duty savings, we could gain up to 25 percent of the volume that is now being consumed by Japanese whisky drinkers, because the retail prices would be much closer together. Even if we pass on only 75 percent of the savings, volume should increase by 10 percent. If we don't pass on most of the duty savings, and the competition does, we risk losing all of our volume. Overall, we believe that there is a 90 percent probability that if either we or UD/Hennessy drops prices, so will the other.
>
> In the standard cognac category, passing on of 100 percent of the duty savings could potentially increase our volume by as much as 10 percent, presuming UD/Hennessy does not pass on the full amount. Given that they are the price-leader in this category, the more likely scenario would be for us to pass on 75 percent of the savings to the consumer and reinvest the remainder to build the brand. Since the duty drop will make standard scotch more price competitive with the premium scotch, there is a real opportunity for growing the entire VSOP category, however, volume growth would not be immediate. Another possibility would be for us to pass on 50 percent of the savings fully recognizing that volumes would likely decline by 50 percent or more. One thing is certain in this category, duty savings will be passed on—the question is "How much?"

■ DECISION

In trying to determine how to take advantage of Taiwan's proposed duty changes, Ian Swanson recognized that each of the options he faced would have different impacts in terms of overall sales volume and financial contribution. Therefore, given the data that were available to him, it was important that he first, clearly identify the main alternatives that would be available to Seagram in light of the proposed changes, then evaluate their net impact in Taiwan. Ultimately, however, Swanson needed to assess the impact of these pricing recommendations on Seagram's overall global operations.

CASE

Texas Instruments

Global Pricing in the Semiconductor Industry

Mr. John Szczsponik, Director of North American Distribution for Texas Instruments' Semiconductor Group, placed the phone back on its cradle after a long and grueling conversation with his key contact at Arrow, the largest distributor of Texas Instruments' semiconductors. With a market-leading 21.5 percent share of total U.S. electronic component distributor sales in 1994, Arrow was the most powerful distribution channel through which Texas Instruments' important semiconductor products flowed. It was also one of only two major American distributors active in the global distribution market.

Arrow's expanding international activities had made it increasingly interested in negotiating with its vendors a common global price for the semiconductors it sold around the world. In the past, semiconductors had been bought and sold at different price levels in different countries to reflect the various cost structures of the countries in which they were produced. Semiconductors made in European countries, for example, were usually more expensive than those made in Asia or North America, simply because it cost manufacturers more to operate in Europe than in the other two regions. Despite these differences, large distributors and some original equipment manufacturers were becoming insistent on buying their semiconductors at one worldwide price, and were pressuring vendors to negotiate global pricing terms. Szczsponik's telephone conversation with Arrow had been the third in the past month in which the distributor had pushed for price concessions based on international semiconductor rates:

> Yesterday they discovered that we're offering a lower price for a chip we make and sell in Singapore than for the same chip we manufacture here in Dallas for the North American market. They want us to give them the Singapore price on our American chips, even though they know our manufacturing costs are higher here than in the Far East. We can't give them that price without losing money!

In anticipation of increased pressure from Arrow and other large distributors, Szczsponik had organized a meeting with Mr. Kevin McGarity, Senior Vice President in the Semiconductor Group and Manager of Worldwide Marketing, to begin developing a cohesive pricing strategy. They were both to meet with Arrow executives in four days, on February 4, 1995, to discuss the establishment of common global pricing for the distributor.

Szczsponik knew that he needed to answer some basic questions before meeting with Arrow:

> Global pricing might make Arrow's job of planning and budgeting a lot easier, but our different cost structures in each region make it difficult for us to offer one price worldwide. How do we tell Arrow, our largest distributor, that we aren't prepared to

This case was developed by Profs. Per V. Jenster, CIMID, B. Jaworski, USC, and Michael Stanford as a basis for classroom discussion rather than to highlight effective or ineffective management of an administrative situation.

negotiate global pricing? Alternatively, how can we reorganize ourselves to make global pricing a realistic option? And what implications will a global pricing strategy have in relationship to other international customers?

With only two hours to go before his meeting with McGarity, Szczsponik wondered how they could respond to Arrow's request.

THE SEMICONDUCTOR INDUSTRY

Semiconductors were silicon chips which transmitted heat, light, and electrical charges and performed critical functions in virtually all electronic devices. They were a core technology in industrial robots, computers, office equipment, consumer electronics, the aerospace industry, telecommunications, the military, and the automobile industry. The majority of semiconductors consisted of integrated circuits made from monocrystalline silicon imprinted with complex electronic components and their interconnections (refer to Exhibit 1 for the key categories of semiconductors). The remainder of semiconductors were simpler discrete components that performed single functions.

EXHIBIT 1

Key Semiconductor Categories

Total Semiconductor 100% = $59.8b
Discrete Components (16.6%)
Optoelectronics (3.8%)
Diodes, Rectifiers, Transistors (12.8%)
Integrated Circuits (83.4%)
Analog (14.6%)
Amplifiers, etc (8.7%)
Special Consumer (5.9%)
Digital (68.8%)
Digital Bipolar (5.3%)
Logic (4.2%)
Memory (1.1%)
MOS (63.5%)
Logic (15.5%)
Microprocessors (23.2%)
Memory (24.8%)
Non-volatile memory (5.8%)
SRAM (4.8%)
Dram (14.2%)

Source: Analysts' reports.

The pervasiveness of semiconductors in electronics resulted in rapidly growing sales and intense competition in the semiconductor industry. Market share in the industry had been fiercely contested since the early 1980s, when the once-dominant U.S. semiconductor industry lost its leadership position to Japanese manufacturers. There followed a series of trade battles in which American manufacturers charged their Japanese competitors with dumping and accused foreign markets of excessive protectionism. By 1994, after investing heavily in the semiconductor industry and embarking on programs to increase manufacturing efficiency and decrease production costs, American companies once again captured a dominant share of the market (refer to Exhibit 2 for the top ten semiconductor manufacturers).

In 1994, total shipments of semiconductors reached $99.9 billion, with market share divided among North America (33%), Japan (30%), Europe (18%), and Asia/Pacific (18%). The industry was expected to reach sales of $130 billion in 1995, and $200 billion by the year 2000. To capture growing demand in the industry, many semiconductor manufacturers were investing heavily in increased manufacturing capacity, although most industry analysts expected expanding capacity to reach rather than surpass demand. Combined with record low inventories in the industry and reduced cycle times and lead times, a balancing of supply and demand was causing semiconductor prices to be uncharacteristically stable. The last three quarters of 1994 had brought fewer fluctuations and less volatility in the prices of semiconductors (refer to Exhibit 3 for a history of semiconductor price stability) despite their history of dramatic price variations.

Regardless of price stability, most semiconductor manufacturers were looking for competitive advantage in further cost reduction programs, in developing closer relationships with their customers, and in creating differentiated semiconductors which could be sold at a premium price. Integrated circuits were readily available from suppliers worldwide and were treated as commodity products by most buyers. Any steps manufacturers could take to reduce their production costs, build stronger relationships with customers, or create unique products could protect them from the price wars usually associated with commodity merchandise.

EXHIBIT 2

Top Ten Semiconductor Manufacturers ($ in thousands)

1980		*1985*		*1990*		*1992*	
Company	*Sales $*	*Company*	*Sales $*	*Company*	*Sales $*	*Company*	*Sales $*
1. Texas Instruments	1,453	NEC	1,800	NEC	4,700	Intel	5,091
		Motorola	1,667	Toshiba	4,150	NEC	4,700
2. Motorola	1,130	Texas Instruments	1,661	Motorola	3,433	Toshiba	4,550
3. Philips	845	Hitachi	1,560	Hitachi	3,400	Motorola	4,475
4. NEC	800	National	1,435	Intel	3,171	Hitachi	3,600
5. National	745	Toshiba	1,400	Texas Instruments	2,518	Texas Instruments	3,150
6. Intel	630	Philips	1,080	Fujitsu	2,300	Fujitsu	2,250
7. Hitachi	620	Intel	1,020	Mitsubishi	1,920	Mitsubishi	2,200
8. Fairchild	570	Fujitsu	800	Philips	1,883	Philips	2,041
9. Toshiba	533	Advanced Micro Devices	795	National	1,730	Matsushita	1,900
10. Siemens	525						

Source: Analysts' reports.

EXHIBIT 3

History of Semiconductor Stability

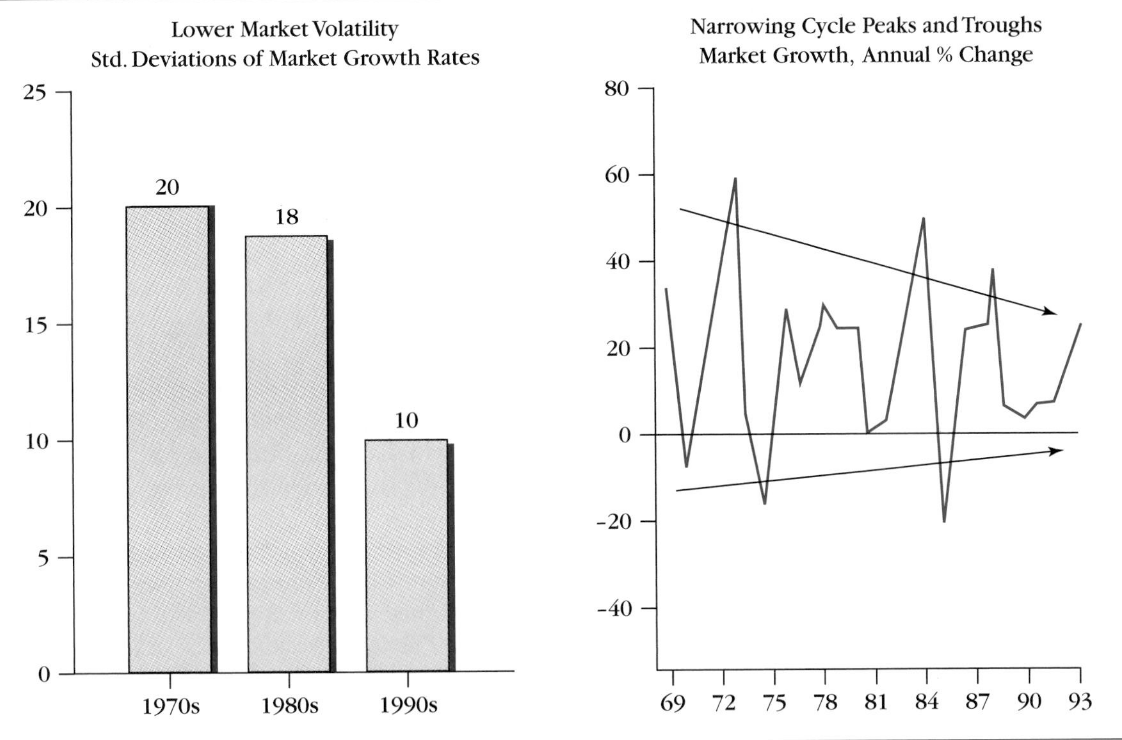

■ TEXAS INSTRUMENTS INCORPORATED

Established in 1951 as an electronics company serving the American defense industry, by 1995 Texas Instruments was a leading manufacturer of semiconductors, defense electronics, software, personal productivity products and materials, and controls. Its 1994 sales of $10.3 billion, a 21% increase from the previous year, was split among components ($6.8 billion), defense electronics ($1.7 billion), digital products ($1.66 billion), and metallurgical materials ($177 million). 1994's profits of over $1 billion came almost entirely from its components business. Components made a profit of $1.1 billion, while defense electronics made $172 million (refer to Exhibit 4 on page 452 for income statements).

1994's performance was record-breaking for Texas Instruments. It marked the first time the company exceeded sales of $10 billion and over $1 billion in profit, and followed a history of volatile financial results. Although Texas Instruments was often considered the pioneer of the American electronics industry—it was one of the first companies to manufacture transistors and developed the first semiconductor integrated circuit in 1958—it struggled to maintain its position in the electronics industry through the intense competition of the 1980s. After receiving market attention with its development of such innovative consumer products as the pocket calculator and the electronic wrist watch, Texas Instruments lost its business in both markets to cheap Asian imports. Meanwhile, it struggled to keep up with orders for its mainstay business in semiconductors through the 1970s, only to see demand for its pioneer semiconductors shrink during the recession of the early 1980s. Faced with heavy losses in many of its core areas, Texas Instruments reorganized its busi-

EXHIBIT 4

Income Statements

	Texas Instruments Key Financial Numbers				
	1994	*1993*	*1992*	*1991*	*1990*
Sales ($ millions)	10,200	8,523	7,049	6,628	6,395
Operating margin (%)	17.5	16.8	9.1	5.0	0.7
Net profit ($ millions)	715	459	254	169	0.7
Working capital ($ millions)	1,800	1,313	961	813	826
Long-term debt ($ millions)	800	694	909	896	715
Net worth ($ millions)	2,975	2,315	1,947	1,955	2,358

nesses to foster innovation and embarked on a program of cost-cutting. By 1985, the company had refocused its efforts on its strengths in semiconductors, relinquishing market dominance in favor of greater margins. While the company continued to grow its technological leadership, it also sought to build stronger relationships with its customers.

By 1995, Texas Instruments had developed a strong position in the electronics industry, despite its reputation as a technological leader rather than a skilled marketer of its products. The company continued to remain powerful in the semiconductor industry, in part because it was the only American company that continued to manufacture dynamic random access memory chips in the face of fierce Japanese competition in the 1980s. The company had manufacturing sites spread throughout North America, Asia, and Europe, and was pursuing its strategy of increasing manufacturing capacity and developing manufacturing excellence.

The Semiconductor Group

In 1958, Texas Instruments engineer Jack Kilby developed the first integrated circuit, a pivotal innovation in the electronics industry. Made of a single semiconductor material, the integrated circuit eliminated the need to solder circuit components together. Without wiring and soldering, components could be miniaturized and crowded together on a single chip. Only a few years after Kilby's invention, electronics manufacturers were demanding these integrated circuits, or chips, in smaller sizes and at lower costs, a move that led to unprecedented innovation in the electronics industry. Soon chips became a commodity, and chip manufacturers relied on high-volume, low-cost production of reliable chips for success. Only a few manufacturers had strong positions in the production of differentiated semiconductors.

Forty years after its discovery, Texas Instruments still remained dependent on its semiconductor sales, which fell primarily in integrated circuits. The Semiconductor Group, a part of the Components Division, had total sales of $2 billion in 1994, the third consecutive year in which Texas Instruments' semiconductor revenues grew faster than the industry. The company's return to financial success in the early 1990s was based on its strong performance in semiconductor sales and profits, both of which were at record levels in 1994. Management in the company expected semiconductor sales to continue to grow strongly and was planning heavy capital expenditures on new or expanded plants in the United States, Malaysia, and Italy to increase the company's capacity.

The Semiconductor Group divided its business into two segments: standard products and differentiated products. Standard semiconductors, which accounted for 90% of the Group's sales, included products which could be substituted by competitors. Standard semiconductors performed in the market much like other products for which substitutes were readily available. Texas Instruments, like its competitors, competed for market share in these commodity products based primarily on the price it offered to original equipment manufacturers and distributors. The remaining 10% of the company's semiconductor business came from differentiated products, of which Texas Instruments was the sole supplier. Because substitutes for these products were not available in the marketplace, differentiated products commanded higher margins than their standard counterparts and were receiving greater strategic emphasis on the part of Group management. While the company continued to hold a strong position in standard semiconductors, it was searching for a strategy that would allow it to achieve a higher return on development and manufacturing investments. Managers at Texas Instruments believed that higher returns were possible only by developing more successful differentiated semiconductors.

ELECTRONICS DISTRIBUTION MARKET

Texas Instruments sold its semiconductors through two channels: directly to original equipment manufacturers and through a network of electronics distributors. Szczsponik estimated that 70 percent of the Group's U.S. customers dealt directly with Texas Instruments. The remainder bought their semiconductors through one or more of the seven major semiconductor distributors that served the North American market (refer to Exhibit 5 for information on the top electronics distributors). Whether an original equipment manufacturer dealt directly with Texas Instruments or bought from a distributor depended on the manufacturer's size. The largest original equipment manufacturers were able to negotiate better prices from semiconduc-

EXHIBIT 5

Top Electronics Distributors

Company		*1994*	*1993*	*1992*	*1991*	*1990*
Arrow Electronics	Sales ($ billions)	3.973	2.536	1.622	1.044	.971
	Share (%)	21.5	17.4	14.8	11.0	10.2
Avnet	Sales ($ billions)	3.350	2.537	1.690	1.400	1.429
	Share (%)	18.1	17.4	15.4	14.8	15.0
Marshall Industries	Sales ($ billions)	.899	.747	.605	.563	.582
	Share (%)	4.8	5.1	5.5	6.0	6.1
Wyle Laboratories	Sales ($ billions)	.773	.606	.447	.360	.359
	Share (%)	4.2	4.2	4.1	3.8	3.8
Pioneer Standard	Sales ($ billions)	.747	.540	.405	.360	.343
	Share (%)	4.0	3.7	3.7	3.8	3.6
Anthem	Sales ($ billions)	.507	.663	.538	.420	.408
	Share (%)	2.7	4.6	4.9	4.4	4.3
Bell Industries	Sales ($ billions)	.395	.308	.282	.257	.239
	Share (%)	2.1	2.1	2.6	2.7	2.5

Source: Lehman Brothers, "Electronic Distribution Market," December 22, 1994.

tor manufacturers than were the distributors and therefore bought directly from the manufacturers. Because mid-sized and small original equipment manufacturers were fragmented, and thus more difficult to serve, these customers were served more efficiently through the distribution channel. Szczsponik explained:

> The semiconductor market can be divided into three tiers. Fifty percent of our sales in semiconductors go to the top tier of perhaps 100 large electronics manufacturers who deal with us directly. The next 46 percent of sales come from 1,400 medium-sized companies at the next level, half of whom deal directly with us and half of whom buy through distributors. The remaining 4% of sales are to 150,000 smaller companies at the bottom tier in the market, who deal only through distributors. Distributors have a clearly defined role in servicing mid-sized and small buyers.

Distributors were considered to be clearinghouses for the semiconductor industry. Each distributor dealt with products from all the major semiconductor manufacturers. For example, Arrow Electronics sold semiconductors manufactured by Motorola and Intel as well as those made by Texas Instruments. The distributors specialized in handling logistics, material flows, sales and servicing for electronics manufacturers who were either too small to negotiate directly with the major semiconductor manufacturers or lacked sufficient expertise in logistics management. In addition, the distributors sometimes knitted packages of different products together for the smaller original electronics manufacturers as an added service. Some also performed varying scales of assembly operation.

The electronics distribution network had originally consisted of a large group of smaller companies. By 1995, however, industry consolidation had left almost 40 percent of the distribution market in the hands of its two largest competitors, Arrow Electronics and Avnet. The seven largest distributors captured 58 percent of sales in the market (refer to Exhibit 6 for the sales and market shares of the top distributors). This trend toward consolidation had had a major impact on the nature of the relationships among semiconductor manufacturers and the distributors through which they sold their products. According to Szczsponik:

> Fifteen years ago, 30 distributors were active in the industry and it was clear that the semiconductor manufacturers controlled the distribution network. With the consolidation of the distribution network into only 7 or 8 powerful players, however, power is shifting. It's hard to say if we are more important to them or they are more important to us.

EXHIBIT 6

Total Sales and Market Share of Top Distributors

		1994	*1993*	*1992*	*1991*	*1990*
Industry Total	Sales ($ billions)	16.22	12.95	10.18	9.06	9.17
Top 25	Sales ($ billions)	13.41	10.69	8.11	7.10	7.20
	Share (%)	82.7	82.5	79.7	78.4	78.5
Top 7	Sales ($ billions)	10.75	8.42	6.36	5.05	5.00
	Share (%)	58.0	57.9	57.9	53.5	52.5
Top 2	Sales ($ billions)	7.32	5.07	3.31	2.44	2.40
	Share (%)	39.6	34.8	30.2	25.8	25.2

Source: Lehman Brothers, "Electronic Distribution Market," December 22, 1994.

Price Negotiations and Global Pricing Issues

Since the vast majority of semiconductors were considered commodity products, the buying decisions of distributors were based almost entirely on price. Distributors forecast the demand for the various semiconductor products they carried and negotiated with vendors for their prices. Since semiconductor prices were notoriously volatile, the price levels negotiated between manufacturers and distributors played a vital role in the distributors' profitability. The Semiconductor Group at Texas Instruments combined the practices of forward pricing and continuous price negotiations to set prices with its distributors.

Forward Pricing The cost of semiconductor manufacturing followed a generally predictable learning curve. When a manufacturer first began producing a new type of chip, it could expect only a small percentage of the chips it produced to function properly. As the manufacturer increased the volume of its production, it both decreased the costs of production and increased the percentage of functioning chips it could produce. This percentage, termed "yield" in the industry, and the standard learning curve of semiconductor manufacturing together had a large impact on the prices semiconductor manufacturers set for their products (refer to Exhibit 7 for the price curve of semiconductor products). This yield was important to TI; a 7 percent increase in overall yield was equivalent to the production of an entire Wafer Fab plant, an investment of $500 million.

According to Jim Huffhines, Manager of DSP Business Development in the Semiconductor Group, managers could predict with considerable accuracy the production cost decreases and yield improvements they would experience as their production volumes increased:

> We know the manufacturing costs for any given volume of production. We also know that these costs will decrease a certain percentage and our yields will increase a certain percentage each year. These predictions are the basis of the forward prices we set with both original equipment manufacturers and distributors.

Continuous Price Adjustments Production costs and yield rates were not the only contributing factors to price levels for standard semiconductors: market supply and

EXHIBIT 7

Forward Pricing Curve

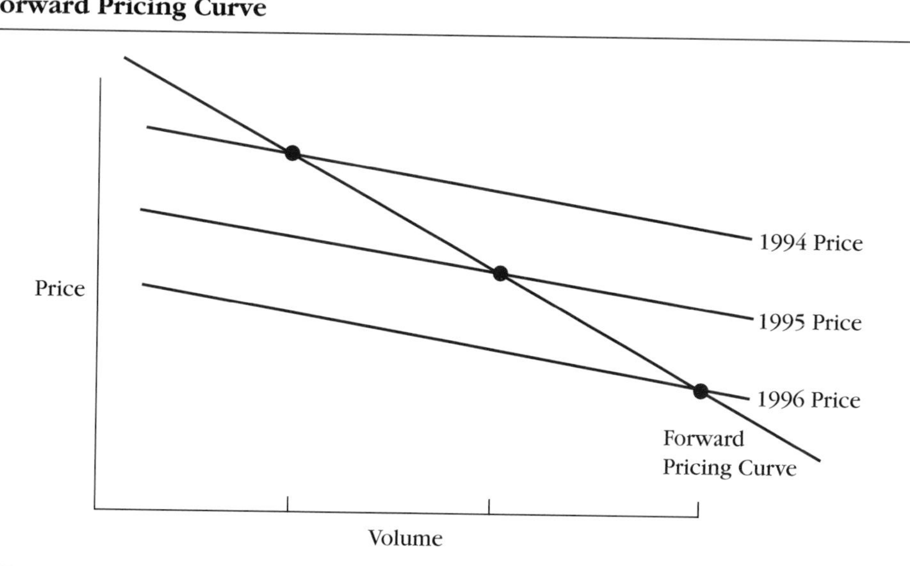

demand also played a powerful role in establishing prices. As a result of volatile prices caused by shifts in supply and demand, distributors often held inventories of semiconductors that did not accurately reflect current market rates. To protect distributors from price fluctuations, most semiconductor manufacturers offered to reimburse distributors for their overvalued inventories. Szczsponik explained:

> Semiconductor prices have fallen by 15% over the past 9 months. If Arrow bought semiconductors from me for $1.00, nine months ago, they are worth only 85¢ now. Arrow is carrying a 15% "phantom" inventory. If Arrow sells those semiconductors now, we give it price protection by agreeing to reimburse it the 15¢ it has lost per semiconductor over the past three quarters.

At the same time, distributors had at their disposal sophisticated systems for monitoring semiconductor prices from each of the major manufacturers, and were constantly in search of price adjustments from vendors when placing their orders. Szczsponik continued:

> Distributors have access to the prices of products from all the semiconductor manufacturers at any given time, and some anywhere in the world. The largest distributors have a staff of 20 to 30 people shopping around continuously for the best prices available for different types of semiconductors; add to this group a staff of accountants managing the price adjustment transactions. For example, they may call us to say that Motorola has quoted them a certain price for a semiconductor, and ask us if we can beat their price. In total, we get close to 150,000 of these calls requesting adjustments from distributors a year, and do over 10% of our sales through price adjustments. I have 10 people on my staff who negotiate price adjustments for distributors: 5 answer their calls, and 5 work with our product managers to make pricing decisions. These decisions are critical: if we make a mistake in our pricing, we lose market share in a day that can take us 3 months to recapture. At the same time, through our negotiations with distributors, we capture masses of data regarding the pricing levels of our competitors and the market performance of our different products. These data are critical to our ability to set prices.

As the distribution network consolidated into a small number of powerful companies, Szczsponik had begun to notice that his price negotiations were increasingly focused not only on beating the competition in North America, but on beating prices available around the world, including those of TI in other regions. With distributors becoming more active in the global market, they were more often exposed to semiconductor price levels from Europe and Asia. Industry analysts expected North American distributors to become more active in global markets as they pursued aggressive expansion campaigns in Europe and Asia. Although Texas Instruments' current contracts with its distributors prevented them from selling semiconductors outside of the region in which they were purchased, distributors were becoming insistent on access to freer global supplies and markets. While the concept may have appeared reasonable to the distributors, it was somewhat more complicated for Texas Instruments. Kevin McGarity elaborated:

> Because business is different everywhere in the world, our international distribution channels have evolved independently. They aren't subjected to the same costs, and don't operate under the same methods and calculation models. In the United States, for example, we offer a 30-day payment schedule for our customers. If they don't pay us within 30 days, we cut off their supply, no matter who they are. Italy operates under a 60-day schedule. Europeans include freight in their prices; we don't in North America. Finally, the cost of producing semiconductors varies by country. Europe tends to be more expensive than North America or Asia, simply because their infrastructure is more costly. So when one of our large distributors phones with the Singapore price for semiconductors manufactured in Düsseldorf, he is crossing boundaries that may be invisible to him but are very real to us.

Preparing for the Meeting with Arrow

With sales of almost $4 billion in 1994, Arrow Electronics was the largest semiconductor distributor in North America, of which TI products accounted for approximately 14 percent. Its aggressive growth had taken the company into global markets and had given it increased exposure to fluctuating price and exchange levels in different international markets. Seeking to minimize its costs, Arrow had begun to pressure semiconductor manufacturers to set standard global prices for each of their products. Motorola, one of Texas Instruments' largest competitors in the semiconductor industry, was rumored to be preparing for global pricing. Management at Texas Instruments, however, was unsure of the wisdom of moving toward global pricing. According to Szczsponik, the pros and cons to global pricing seem unevenly balanced:

> The large distributors want global pricing to reduce their costs and simplify their planning. But does it make sense for us? Right now our organization's calculation systems and costs in each country are too different for us to offer standard global prices. There are other things to consider as well. If we set global prices, we will no longer continue our price adjustment negotiations with the distributors. This may save us the cost of staffing our negotiations team, but it also takes away from us a powerful tool for gathering information on our customers' prices and our product performance. As soon as we stop negotiating price adjsutments, we lose our visibility in the market.

To prepare for his decision with McGarity and the forthcoming meeting with Arrow Electronics, Szczsponik knew TI had to make some fundamental decisions regarding global pricing. Who held the power in the relationships Texas Instruments had with its distributors? What was the source of the negotiating strength each party would bring to the meeting? Finally, what position should the Semiconductor Group take with its distributors regarding global pricing? And what organizational implications would such a decision imply?

CHAPTER 9

Interactive Marketing and Electronic Commerce

Many consumers and organizations populate two parallel and complementary market environments today. One is the familiar market*place* where buyers and sellers engage in exchange relationships in a physical environment inhabited by people and objects. The other is the new market*space,* an information- and communication-based electronic exchange environment occupied by computer and telecommunication technologies and digitized offerings.[1]

The marketspace has significant implications for marketing practice. Even though the fundamental purpose and perspectives of strategic marketing management still apply, the setting is very different with an emphasis on electronic commerce and interactive marketing. This chapter describes the marketing opportunities and strategic challenges facing companies in the new marketspace.

■ ELECTRONIC COMMERCE

Electronic commerce is made possible by a family of electronic networks, most prominently the Internet, on which the well-known World Wide Web operates.[2] *Electronic commerce* is "any activity that uses some form of electronic communication in the inventory, exchange, advertisement, distribution, and payment of goods and services.[3] Included in this definition is electronic data interchange (EDI), which involves the exchange of business data in digital form between a company and its suppliers, customers, and collaborators.

Marketing Opportunity in Marketspace

Electronic commerce offers a new way or means for satisfying buyer needs. As such, it represents a marketing opportunity as described in Chapter 4. There are six general categories of products and services that appear to be particularly suited for electronic commerce.[4] One category consists of items for which product information is an important part of the purchase decision, but prepurchase trial is not necessarily critical. Items such as computers and computer accessories, marketed by Dell (dell.com), consumer electronics sold by Sony (sony.com), and Internet equipment distributed by Cisco Systems fall into this category. So do books, which accounts for the sales growth of Amazon.com and Barnes & Noble (bn.com). A second category includes items for which audio or video demonstration is important. This category consists of compact discs (CDs) and videos sold by columbiahouse.com and tower-records.com. The third category contains items that can be delivered digitally, including computer software, travel reservations and confirmations, brokerage services, and electronic ticketing. Microsoft Corporation, travelocity.com, ticketmaster.com, and schwab.com (stockbrokers) successfully market these products and services.

Unique items, such as collectibles and specialty goods, foods, and gifts, represent a fourth category. Collectible auction houses (e.g., auctions-on-line.com), wine merchant Virtual Vineyards (wine.com), and flower and gift marketer 1-800-Flowers (1800flowers.com) market these products. A fifth category includes items that are routinely purchased and for which convenience is very important. Many consumer-packaged goods, including grocery products and vitamins and herbal supplements, fall into this category, which has benefited netgrocer.com and vitaminshoppe.com. Maintenance, repair, and operating (MRO) supplies purchased by businesses also fit this category. Boeing Company, for example, sells over $100 million in spare parts to 65 airlines around the world through Boeing On-Line.[5] A final category of items consists of highly standardized products and services for which information about price is important. Certain kinds of insurance (auto and homeowners), home improvement products, casual apparel, and toys make up this category. These six categories are expected to dominate electronic commerce dollar sales through 2003.[6]

Profit Opportunities in Marketspace

Despite the marketing opportunity made possible by electronic commerce, not all companies have realized its profit potential. As often as not, companies have found the pathway to profit in the new marketspace to be more illusionary than real.[7]

Electronic commerce can assume numerous forms. The six most prominent forms, termed *business models,* are described next.[8]

Sales Revenue Model The sales revenue model involves marketing products and services through the Internet. Companies that adopt this model seek to earn a margin on actual sales or a fee charged for rendering a service. This model describes CDNow and Cisco Systems, which earn a margin (price minus cost) on items sold, and Auto-By-Tel, which receives much of its revenue from fees paid by automobile dealers for assistance in referring customers to them.

The sales revenue model epitomizes the practice of selling real products and services for real money using Internet/Web-based technology. Few companies that market consumer products, however, actually make an operating profit using the sales revenue model exclusively. This is illustrated by Exhibit 9.1, which shows the economics of operating traditional versus electronic retail outlets for products such as books.[9] As indicated, electronic retailers typically sell their wares for less to consumers, but their total operating expenses, on a per-sale or order basis, are typically higher than traditional retailers. This lesson was learned by Egghead, Inc., a leading software retailing chain in the 1980s.[10] The company closed its 200-plus retail stores and became Egghead.com, an electronic retailer, in 1998. The result? Gross profit margins were halved, and sales, general and administrative (SG&A) expenses skyrocketed, resulting in a sizeable operating loss.

Advertising Support Model Companies often complement the sales revenue model with the advertising support model. This model emphasizes the selling of advertising on a company's Web site. Buy.com has adopted this model and claims to offer "the

EXHIBIT 9.1

Operating Economics of Traditional versus Electronic Retailers (Per Average Sale/Order of $100)

Revenue/Cost Item	*Traditional Retailer*		*Electronic Retailer*	
Average sale/order	$100.00		$100.00	
(Discount)	−8.00		−20.00	
Shipping & handling	—		11.00	
Consumer pays		$92.00		$91.00
Less:				
Cost of sales	67.41		57.60	
Shipping & handling	2.88		9.90	
Gross profit per sale/order		$21.71		$23.50
Less Operating Expenses:				
Rent	$ .96		$ 4.55	
Labor and store expenses	10.75		—	
Web site development	—		2.90	
Marketing	2.50		17.29	
Total operating expense	$ 14.21		$ 24.74	
Operating profit per sale/order		$ 7.50		−$1.24

lowest prices on Earth."[11] The company often lists prices at or below its cost with the expectation of building a large enough audience so that the company can overcome the profit shortfall by selling advertising to other companies on its Web site.

Other companies rely almost exclusively on the advertising support model to generate revenue. Encyclopaedia Brittannica posts the entire contents of its 32-volume printed book on the Internet for free. Its only revenue source is advertising.[12] Advertising is a major revenue source for search engines, such as Yahoo, Lycos, Excite, LookSmart, and All the Web. These search engines invest heavily in advertising, both on-line and off-line, through traditional mass media with the objective of attracting more viewers and increasing Web site visit time.

Cost Elimination Model A valuable feature of Internet/Web-based technologies is that they are capable of acquiring, storing, retrieving, and delivering data and information at an extremely low variable cost. In situations in which information delivery is central to a company's business or information technologies can be substituted for other, more expensive, means of data and information management, the adoption of Internet/Web-based technologies can be justified purely for cost reasons. Airlines and banks are two examples.[13] An Internet banking transaction costs one cent, compared with 27 cents at an automated teller machine (ATM) or 52 cents over the telephone. Processing an airline ticket on the Internet costs $1, versus $8 with a travel agent.

Cisco Systems, which sells equipment that powers the Internet, embraces the cost elimination model.[14] Its customers can select products from an electronic catalog, and the entire buying process of ordering, contract manufacturing, order fulfillment, and payment is made possible by a sophisticated application of Internet/Web-based technology. The company estimates that it saves $500 million annually by eliminating the cost of printed product manuals and catalogs, digitally distributing software, and using the Web to communicate with customers and suppliers.

Subscription Support Model This approach generates revenue from users in the form of monthly or annual subscriptions based on the value of the content or service provided. This model is analogous to a consumer's subscription to a newspaper or magazine. For example, Dow Jones & Company, Inc. provides the *Wall Street Journal Interactive* (wsj.com), which uses a subscription model. Large on-line services such as America Online, CompuServe, and MSN also rely on member subscriptions as a source of revenue.

Information Trading Model With this model, a company gathers information about consumer interests or purchase intentions and sells the information to a retailer or manufacturer for a fee. For example, Popular Demand, Inc. operates a Web site that pools consumers based on their interests in products and services. These customers are introduced anonymously to merchants that pay Popular Demand anywhere from $10 to $150 for each customer they can sell to via e-mail and the Web.[15]

Infomediary Model The sixth model represents an innovation made possible by Internet/Web-based technology. An *infomediary* sells information about a market and creates a platform on which buyer and sellers can do business in marketspace.[16] An infomediary is literally a virtual market and typically earns a commission or transaction fee for its service.

Infomediaries have gained popularity in highly fragmented markets composed of many small buyers and sellers who are geographically dispersed but share a common interest. There are three types of infomediaries. First, there are aggregators, which help buyers select products by providing up-to-the-minute price and product information and a single contact point for service. For example, Chemdex Corporation (chemdex.com) provides a virtual market for academic researchers and companies in the pharmaceutical and biotechnology business to sell and purchase supplies. Next, there are auctioneers, such as e-Bay. On-line auctioneers offer a reliable channel for sellers to dispose of items and buyers to acquire wanted items at an agreed-upon price. Exchanges represent the third type of infomediary. They act as neutral third parties in bid/ask offers and enforce market rules and settlement terms, much like a stock exchange. An example is National Transportation Exchange, Inc. (nte.net). It connects shippers with loads of merchandise they want to deliver cheaply and transportation firms that have space available.

Is there one best business model for electronic commerce? Probably not. According to one authority on electronic commerce:

> As with businesses that have come before it, there are countless "right" answers, endless combinations of business models, and infinite permutations of key themes and approaches. . . . Business models themselves do not offer solutions; rather how each business is run determines its success. So the success of e-commerce businesses will hinge largely on the art of management even as it is enabled by the science of technology.[17]

■ INTERACTIVE MARKETING

Companies that have achieved success in electronic commerce share a common bond, regardless of business model. Each has taken advantage of the unique characteristics of Internet/Web-based technology. Specifically, these companies have been able to develop and profitably execute a marketing strategy that delivers a customer value proposition rooted in the interactive capabilities of Internet/Web-based technology.[18]

The Customer Value Proposition in Marketspace

In the new marketspace, the provision of direct, on-demand information is possible from marketers *anywhere* to customers *anywhere*, at *anytime*. In addition, interactive two-way Internet/Web-based communication capabilities in marketspace allows a customer to tell a marketer exactly what his or her buying interests and requirements are, making possible the transformation of product or service into a specialized solution for an individual. These features of Internet/Web-based technologies, among others, have resulted in the identification of numerous sources of customer value creation in marketspace.

There are at least six basic sources of customer value creation in marketspace, any combination of which can provide a basis for a customer value proposition. These are convenience, cost, customer service, choice, customization, and coordination (see Exhibit 9.2).[19] The meaning of each is described next.

Convenience is a frequently chosen element of a value proposition, particularly as a point of difference with traditional retailers or industrial distributors. In particular, a buyer's cost of external search for products and services in the traditional marketplace, including time spent and often the hassle of physically shopping, is reduced in marketspace. However, for convenience to remain a source of customer value creation, Web sites must be easy to locate and navigate, and image downloads must be fast. A commonly held view among electronic commerce marketers is the "eight-second rule": Customers will abandon their efforts to enter a Web site if download time exceeds eight seconds.[20] Furthermore, the more clicks and pauses between clicks required to make a purchase or access information, the more likely it is a customer will exit a Web site.

Cost is a second commonly chosen element of a customer value proposition. Like convenience, cost is often used to attract customers from traditional retailers and industrial distributors. Research indicates that almost 90 percent of the 30 most

EXHIBIT 9.2

Sources of a Customer Value Proposition in Marketspace

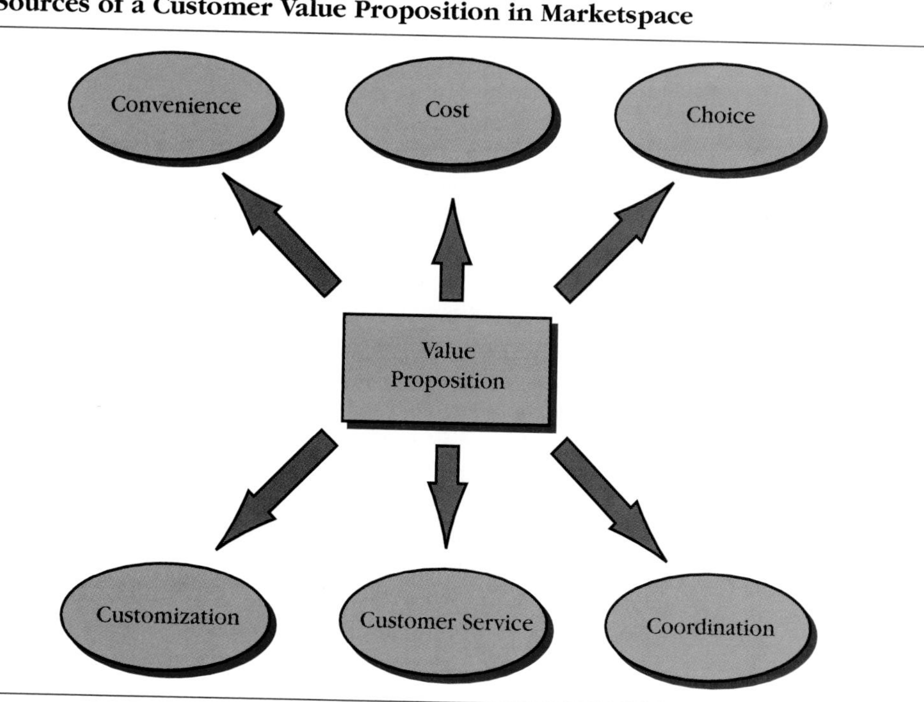

popular items bought on-line can be purchased at the same price or cheaper than in retail stores.[21] Lower prices, made possible by the capabilities of Internet/Web-based technology, have certainly stimulated on-line buying. However, cost alone is unlikely to provide a sufficient basis on which to build a value proposition.[22] Indeed, part of the cost/price advantage of companies that market via the Internet is the absence of a sales tax. The Internet Freedom Tax Act of 1998 specifically exempts electronic commerce from taxes through October 21, 2001. One way or another, this is likely to change. Furthermore, as the demand for customer service grows, it is reasonable to speculate that cost/price increases will follow.

Customer service has risen in importance an an element of a value proposition. Customers lured into marketspace with low prices and one-click ordering still expect the same level of customer service they receive in the traditional marketplace. They expect orders to be filled on time, complaints to be answered, and knowledgeable people to respond to their questions. Dell Computer Corporation is a success story in this regard. The company offers not only competitive prices, but also exceptional customer service. In fact, two-thirds of the sales through the Dell Direct Web site (dell.com) involve human sales representatives who work closely with buyers before, during, and after a sales transaction.[23]

Two additional sources of customer value creation—choice and customization—arise from interactive two-way Internet/Web-based communication capabilities that makes possible a highly personalized exchange environment for prospective buyers.[24] *Choice*, as an element of a value proposition, has two dimensions. First, choice can refer to the breadth and depth of a product-service assortment offered to consumers. For example, iqvc.com, a marketspace general merchant, touts that its Web site offers over 100,000 items. A second dimension is choice assistance. Here, interactive communication capabilities of Internet/Web-based technologies invites customers to engage in an electronic dialogue with marketers for the purpose of making informed choices. Garden Escapes, Inc. (garden.com) is a case in point. The company provides visitors with a computer-aided design for residential landscaping based on a customer's expressed preferences. Using state-of-the-art garden design techniques and working with plants and shrubs appropriate to specific geographic regions, customers can create and then see what their landscape will look like instantaneously. If it meets with their approval, items can be purchased, with delivery schedules in time for the best planting.

Customization is probably the most powerful basis for a customer value proposition. Customization is the ultimate form of product-service differentiation, with its focus on providing one-of-a-kind offerings that fit a customer's specific needs. For example, Mattel at barbie.com invites customers to design their own doll. They can specify the doll's skin tone, eye and hair color, hairdo, clothes, and accessories and give her a name. Customers can fill out a questionnaire, and a computer-generated personality profile for the custom-made Barbie is prepared. An added benefit of customization to companies is price differentiation. Because no two products are exactly alike, no two customers will necessarily pay the same price.

Coordination is quickly becoming an important dimension of a customer value proposition. Its importance has increased as a result of the growing parallel presence of companies in both the traditional marketplace and the new marketspace. Coordination typically refers to how well sales, customer service, promotion, and distribution activities reinforce each other in the different exchange environments to create value for customers. At Circuit City, for instance, customers can place an order on-line at circuitcity.com and pick up the item at their local store. The customer avoids shipping charges and the wait for delivery. Gateway Computer, described in Chapter 7, is another example. This direct marketer of personal computers and an early marketspace pioneer now operates showrooms where customers can see, touch, test, and custom configure a computer system with the help of highly trained company representatives. Coordination occurs in a variety of other ways, depending on how companies choose to operate their marketing Web site(s).

Marketing Web Sites

A customer value proposition manifests itself in a company marketing Web site and the technological and operational infrastructure that supports it. Marketing Web sites engage consumers in interactive communication or dialogue for the purpose of selling a company's product or service or moving the consumer closer to a purchase. They come in two general forms: (1) transactional sites and (2) promotional sites.

Transactional Web Sites Transactional Web sites are essentially electronic storefronts such as those operated by L. L. Bean and FAO Schwartz. They focus principally on converting an on-line browser into an on-line buyer. Successful transactional Web sites feature well-known, branded products and services. Gap clothes, for example, have sold well via its Web site (gap.com) because most consumers know the brand and the merchandise. The Gap generates more sales volume from its Web site than any of its stores save one.[25] A truly multifunctional transactional Web site is operated by Cisco Systems, a company that sells about 80 percent of the routers and networking gear for the Internet. Its site, Cisco Connection Online, blends technical support with every step in selling and servicing its products (all of which are custom-built to a customer's specifications), before and after a transaction. For example, Cisco's Configuration Agent software walks its business customers through the dozens of components that typically go into one of its products. Its Status Agent software lets customers track the progress of their orders on-line. In fact, the whole process of ordering, contract manufacturing, fulfillment, and payment is automated, and 55 percent of orders pass through Cisco's system without being touched by a human.[26]

Promotional Web Sites Promotional Web sites have a very different purpose than transactional sites. They promote a company's products and services, and provide information on how items can be used and where they can be purchased. These sites often engage the visitor in an interactive experience involving games, contests, and quizzes with electronic coupons and other gifts as prizes. Procter & Gamble maintains separate promotional Web sites for 24 of its leading brands, including Pringles potato chips, Vidal Sassoon hair products, Scope mouthwash, and Pampers diapers. Promotional sites can be effective in generating interest in and trial of a company's products and services.[27] General Motors reports that 80 percent of the people visiting a Saturn store first visited the brand's Web site (saturn.com). The Metropolitan Life Insurance Web site (metlife.com) is a proven vehicle for qualifying prospective buyers of its insurance and financial services. These sites also can be used for customer research and feedback. Cathay Pacific Airlines is a case in point. Its Web site (cathay-usa.com) is used to interview frequent fliers to determine their travel preferences and buying habits in addition to offering travel promotions.

Marketing Web Sites and Integrated Marketing Communications Marketing Web sites have the potential for creating a platform for integrated marketing communications, as described in Chapter 6. Most companies employ a mix of communication tools to achieve various objectives in the marketing communication process, judiciously combining personal selling and advertising. Marketing Web sites and the Internet/Web-based technology that supports them play a unique role in an integrated marketing communication mix, as described below:

> Personal selling is usually the largest single item in the industrial marketing communications mix. On the other hand, broadcast advertising is typically the dominant way used to reach consumers by marketers. Where do Web sites fit? The Web site is some-

thing of a mix between direct selling (it can engage the visitor in a dialogue) and advertising (it can be designed to generate awareness, explain/demonstrate the product, and provide information—without interactive involvement). It can play a cost-effective role in the communication mix, in the early stages of the process-need recognition, development of product specifications, and supplier search, but can also be useful as the buying process progresses toward evaluation and selection. Finally, the site is also cost-effective in providing feedback on product/service performance. Web sites might typically be viewed as complementary to the direct selling activity by industrial marketers, and as supplementary to advertising by consumer marketers.[28]

■ STRATEGIC MARKETING MANAGEMENT IN THE NEW MARKETSPACE

The existence of parallel market environments presents a variety of strategic challenges for companies. Companies that have historically prospered in the traditional marketplace are challenged to define the nature and scope of their presence in the new marketspace. At the same time, companies whose origins and fortunes are tied to the marketspace, such as Amazon.com, e-Toys.com, e-Bay.com, and others, are challenged to refine the nature and scope of their presence in the new marketspace, and increasingly, the traditional marketplace as these two market environments converge.[29]

Revisiting Business Definitions and Growth Opportunities

At a fundamental level, the new marketspace has caused companies that have successfully competed in the traditional marketplace to revisit their business definition. As described in Chapter 1, an organization defines its business in terms of the customers it wishes to serve, the particular needs of those customer groups it wishes to satisfy, and the means or technology by which the organization will satisfy those customer needs. The advent of electronic commerce has meant that these companies have had to grapple with how Internet/Web-based technology alters their approach to creating long-term and mutually beneficial exchange relationships with customers, including intermediaries that market their offerings and ultimate buyers who consume or use their products and services.[30] The transformation of Egghead to Egghead.com, described earlier, is an example of how one company has responded to the new marketspace.

The new marketspace represents an environmental growth opportunity that may not represent an organizational opportunity for every company. As recently as January 2000, only 15 percent of U.S. manufacturers used transactional Web sites to sell directly to consumers, and 57 percent of manufacturers state that they never plan to market their products on-line with transactional Web sites.[31]

As detailed in Chapter 1, organizational opportunities arise from the fit between an organization's distinctive competency and the success requirements in a market. In addition to delivering a meaningful customer value proposition, success in the new marketspace requires a sophisticated "back office" technological and operational infrastructure capable of processing orders, distributing products and services, managing large-scale customer databases, and handling customer payments and inquiries. Many mail-order and direct-marketing firms already had these competencies in place and the transition to electronic means for reaching customers proved to be easier than that faced by "brick-and-mortar" retailers such as Wal-Mart and manufacturers such as Levi Strauss & Company. Not surprisingly, Wal-Mart and Levi Strauss have "outsourced" the back-office chores for their transactional Web sites to Fingerhut Companies, Inc., a large catalog company.[32]

As large and small companies alike continue to explore the marketspace as a growth opportunity, they are advised to apply the same perspectives and tools (e.g., SWOT analysis) that can be employed to judge any opportunity. By objectively assessing this opportunity, the nature and scope of a company's presence in the new marketspace can be determined.

Managing Product-Market Convergence

Another strategic marketing challenge will be managing product-market convergence. Fewer and fewer products and services and their supporting marketing programs will be relegated to either the marketplace or the marketspace in the future. Instead, it will be commonplace for companies to maintain a presence in both market environments of some kind and measure. This is already apparent in retailing.[33] Fully 62 percent of on-line retail sales were made by "multichannel retailers"—those that combine selling through stores, the Internet, catalogs, and the telephone. Multichannel retailers are expected to capture 85 percent of on-line retail sales in 2004.

Coordination of Marketing Effort Manufacturers have chosen a variety of coordinated approaches for managing product-market convergence. Some employ promotional Web sites to support their traditional sales channel, including retail stores and build customer relationships. The Clinique division of Estée Lauder Companies is an example. It reports that 80 percent of current customers who visit its Web site (clinique.com) later purchase a Clinique product at a department store; 37 percent of non-Clinique buyers make a purchase after visiting the site.[34]

Another approach is that used by Ethan Allen, which uses retail stores, catalogs, and the Internet to sell its furniture. The company recognizes that product-market convergence is inevitable. It therefore compensates its stores for sales that occur via the Internet. Stores that help to make a sale that later occurs on-line through its transactional Web site or that provide delivery and service receive 25 percent of the sales price. If the furniture is shipped directly from the factory, the local store receives 10 percent of the sales price.[35]

Managing Trade Relations Another challenge arising from product-market convergence is the management of marketing channel trade relations. At issue is the conflict situation that may arise when a manufacturer elects to engage in dual distribution using a transactional Web site. For intermediaries, this form of dual distribution poses a dual threat: (1) cannibalization of their sales and (2) the possibility of disintermediation.

Cannibalism involves the diversion of sales from traditional intermediaries to a manufacturer's transactional Web site. The threat is very real.[36] Research firm Juniper Communications estimates that only 6 percent of sales via the Internet represented new or incremental business, while 94 percent simply represented diversions from traditional intermediaries. Still, cannibalism can be mitigated somewhat through effective market segmentation. Hewlett-Packard, for example, sells its products via the Internet to small businesses, but relies on its traditional intermediaries to sell to individual customers. However, market segmentation and a good faith effort to coordinate a dual distribution strategy can still lead to channel conflict. This happened to Compaq Computer Corporation.[37] The company created a unique product line for Internet buyers, available directly from Compaq, and targeted small and medium-sized businesses, which did not overlap with its dealers' sales focus. It even created a way for dealers to profit from Internet referrals. The result? Compaq dealers, feeling left out by the direct-sales Internet strategy and competing product line, shunned all Compaq personal computers. Compaq sales and profits dropped sharply as a result.

The reaction of Compaq dealers was also driven by the threat of disintermediation—the practice whereby an intermediary member is dropped from a marketing channel. Disintermediation is considered a serious threat by channel intermediaries (e.g., wholesalers, retailers, distributors, dealers, agents, and brokers). Its effect has already been seen.[38] Examples include on-line financial sites substituting for stock brokers, travel sites supplanting travel agents, and on-line insurance replacing insurance agents. Wholesalers and distributors of MRO supplies and electrical products and components in business-to-business marketing settings have been also bypassed through direct sales from manufacturers of these products to industrial buyers.

Disintermediation is considered much more serious than cannibalization by intermediaries. Whereas cannibalism affects only a portion of an intermediary's sales, disintermediation affects their survival. The threat of disintermediation has caused many intermediaries to seek out new ways to create a value proposition for their customers and suppliers. For example, Marshall Industries, a distributor of electrical components, now conducts all of its business on the Internet. It provides some 40,000 customers with a range of Internet/Web-based services from technical data sheets to interactive training sessions and product seminars and offers an electronic design center where engineers experiment with different design possibilities. Such actions create value for Marshall Industries' customers and suppliers and improve overall trade relations within the marketing channel.

Mastering the Economics of the New Marketspace

Companies will need to master the economics of the new marketspace to realize its profit potential. As emphasized in Chapters 2 and 8, profit = total revenue − total cost. This fundamental relationship exists in the new marketspace just as it does in the traditional marketplace. Similarly, as Internet/Web-based companies increase their presence in the traditional marketplace, knowledge of basic cost–volume–profit relationships is necessary. For example, the move by Gateway to operate showrooms and the recent opening of distribution warehouses by Amazon.com introduce new operating costs and cost behavior for consideration.

Understanding Cost Structure and Revenue Sources Mastering the economics of the new marketspace also requires that attention be given to cost structure and revenue sources. Exhibit 9.1 illustrated the operating economics of traditional versus electronic retailers of products such as books. This illustration highlights two important aspects of cost structure in marketspace. First, gross profit (margin) per sale is often lower. Second, operating costs, most of which are fixed, are higher. What is not shown is that revenues in marketspace often come from sources other than product (service) sales. For example, electronic retailers receive revenue from the sale of advertising on their Web site, sales of consumer information/databases, and shipping and handling markups on merchandise sold. These three sources account for about 12 percent of an electronic retailer's revenues. Traditional retailers generate less than one percent of revenues using these methods.[39]

Considering Relevant, Sunk, and Opportunity Costs in Marketing Decisions The new marketspace has given greater prominence to the concepts of relevant, sunk, and opportunity costs in strategic marketing management. A decision whether to market a company's offerings in marketspace incorporates an explicit or implicit consideration of each. Many executives view the foregone benefits of not marketing their offerings via the Internet as an opportunity cost incurred by their company. This cost is relevant in the sense that potential sales volume and associated profit margins are foregone. Real sales and profit are also lost, resulting from customers switching to the Internet to make purchases, and represent a relevant cost.

Sunk costs often incorrectly play a role in the decision whether a company chooses to market its offerings in the new marketspace. This is apparent in the fact that some companies consider their prior investments in the marketplace as relevant costs when making an entry decision. Although actual outlays, these earlier expenditures are sunk and should not weigh in the decision whether to market products and services via the Internet. A company's decision to not market its offerings in the marketspace for fear of cannibalizing sales and profits of an existing business is yet another manifestation of the sunk cost fallacy described in Chapter 2.

For companies to reap the benefits of information technology, the economics of electronic commerce and interactive marketing will need to be harnessed. It is very simple to establish a presence in the new marketspace, but quite difficult to create and deliver a profitable value proposition rooted in the interactive capabilities of Internet/Web-based technology.

NOTES

1. For early but still relevant descriptions of how the marketspace will influence marketing practice, see Jeffrey F. Rayport and John J. Sviokla, "Managing in the Marketspace," *Harvard Business Review* (November-December 1994): 141-53; and Robert A. Peterson, Sridar Balasubramanian, and Bart J. Bronnenberg, "Exploring the Implications of the Internet for Consumer Marketing," *Journal of the Academy of Marketing Science* (Fall 1997): 329-46.

2. The family of electronic networks that presently make possible electronic commerce include the Internet, Intranet, and Extranet. The Internet is an integrated global network of computers that gives users access to information and documents. The Internet is a network upon which the World Wide Web runs. An Intranet is an Internet/Web-based network used within the boundaries of an organization. It serves primarily as a business support function network and facilitates the internal, electronic exchange of corporate data and files. An Extranet is an Internet/Web-based network that permits private business-to-business communication between a company and its suppliers, distributors, and other partners, such as advertising agencies.

3. International Trade Administration definition reported in A. J. Campbell, "Ten Reasons Why Your Company Should Use Electronic Commerce," *Business America* (May 1998): 12.

4. "A Hard Sell Online? Think Again," *Business Week* (July 12, 1999): 142-43; Paul Foley and David Sutton, "Boom Time for Electronic Commerce—Rhetoric or Reality?" *Business Horizons* (September-October 1998): 21-30; "Future Shop," *Forbes ASAP* (April 6, 1998): 37-55; and "When the Bubble Bursts," *The Economist* (January 30, 1999): 23-25.

5. "Log On, Link Up, Save Big," *Business Week* (June 22, 1998): 132-38.

6. "Keeping Track of E-Commerce," *New York Times* (September 22, 1999): 58.

7. "A Cold Bath for dot.com Fever," *U.S. News & World Report* (September 13, 1999): 36-38.

8. Portions of this discussion are based in Jeffrey F. Rayport, "The Truth About Internet Business Models," *Strategy & Business* (Third Quarter, 1999): 5-7; and John Deighton, "Note on Marketing and the World Wide Web," Harvard Business School Note #9-597-037, Revised January 20, 1999.

9. This example is based on Mary Beth Grover, "Lost in Cyberspace," *Forbes* (March 8, 1999): 124-28.

10. "Grade-A Challenges," *Forbes* (March 8, 1999): 128.

11. J. William Gurley, "Buy.com May Fail, But If It Succeeds, Retailing May Never Be the Same," *Fortune* (January 11, 1999): 150-52.

12. "Mindful of the Times," *Dallas Morning News* (October 19, 1999): A1, A9.

13. "The Net Imperative," *The Economist* (June 26, 1999), special section: Business and the Internet.

14. "Cisco@speed," *The Economist* (June 26, 1999), special section: Business and the Internet.

15. Gregory Dalton, "Online Data's Fineline," *Information Week Online* (March 29, 1999).

16. "The Rise of the Infomediary," *The Economist* (June 26, 1999), special section: Business and the Internet.

17. Jeffrey F. Rayport, "The Truth About Internet Business Models," p. 7.

18. "Successful Online Businesses Tapping Advantages of Medium, Panel Says," *Dallas Morning News* (September 24, 1999): 3D; and Shikhar Ghosh, "Making Sense of the Internet," *Harvard Business Review* (March–April 1998): 126–35.

19. This value proposition framework is adapted from Eric N. Berkowitz, Roger A. Kerin, Steven W. Hartley, and William Rudelius, *Marketing*, 6th ed. (Burr Ridge, IL: Irwin/McGraw-Hill, 2000): 211-13.

20. Jonathan Mandell, "Speed It Up, Webmaster, We're Losing Billions Every Second," *New York Times* (September 22, 1999): D58.

21. "The Cybershopper's Best Friend," *Business Week* (May 4, 1998): 84.

22. Timothy Hanrahan, "Price Isn't Everything," *Wall Street Journal* (July 12, 1999): R20.

23. "Random Access: Dell's Sell," *Forbes ASAP* (February 22, 1999): 16.

24. Ward Hanson, *Principles of Internet Marketing* (Cincinnati, OH: South-Western College Publishing, 2000): Chapter 7.

25. " 'Clicks and Mortar' at gap.com," *Business Week* (October 18, 1999): 150–52.

26. "Cisco@speed," *The Economist* reference cited.

27. These examples are found in "Met Life Backs Local Agents with Sidewalk Sponsorship," *Marketing News* (January 18, 1999): 38; and "Branding on the Net," *Business Week* (November 9, 1998): 78–86.

28. Richard T. Watson, Pierre Berthon, Leyland F. Pitt, and George M. Zinkham, *Electronic Commerce: The Strategic Perspective* (Ft. Worth, TX: The Dryden Press, 2000): 79.

29. "The Real Revolution," *The Economist* (June 26, 1999), special section: Business and the Internet.

30. For an informative roundtable discussion on this topic, see "Retailing: Confronting the Challenges that Face Bricks-and-Mortar Stores," *Harvard Business Review* (July–August 1999): 159–68.

31. Ernst & Young LLP, "The Second Annual Ernst and Young Internet Shopping Study: The Digital Channel Continues to Gather Steam" (1999): 26.

32. "Finding E-Commerce Riches in the Back Office," *Business Week* (July 26, 1999): 84.

33. "The Real Internet Revolution," *The Economist* (August 21, 1999): 53–54.

34. "A Shameless Bribe," *Online Media Strategies for Advertising: A Supplement to Advertising Age* (Spring 1998): 60A.

35. Peter Pike, "Click-and-Mortar Companies/Home Depot Plays Godfather," Pikenet Dispatch, www.pikenet.com, August 8, 1999.

36. Jerry Useem, "Internet Defense Strategy: Cannibalize Yourself," *Fortune* (September 6, 1999): 121-34.

37. Gary McWilliams, "Dealer Loses?" *Wall Street Journal* (July 12, 1999): R20.

38. Ward Hanson, *Principles of Internet Marketing*, 379–80; "Industry Norms Will Be Transformed," *Electronic News Online* (August 29, 1999).

39. The Boston Consulting Group and Shop.org, "Online Retailing to Reach $36 Billion in 1999," www.bcg.com, August 20, 1999.

CASE

Peapod

Moving to the Internet

Ravi Chiruvolu, Peapod's Director of Business Development, leaned back in his office chair and looked out the window at the Old Orchard business park. It was a gray, rainy day, and the surroundings were marred by ongoing renovations. The scene began to remind him all too well of the current situation he faced at Peapod. "All of Peapod is renovating," he mused, "and hopefully before too long we should have a rock-solid foundation in place to grow from."

In many respects, Peapod was in an enviable position. Within a few short years, Peapod had established itself as the undisputed leader in a new industry that it had virtually created on its own. The past two years had been filled with rapid growth, and the outlook for the following year was even better. Andrew B. Parkinson, a co-founder of Peapod, and its Chairman, President, and Chief Executive Officer, commented in the company's recent quarterly report:

> Peapod continued in 1997 to solidify its leadership role in online grocery shopping and Internet commerce generally. Recent independent data regarding Internet shopping, and demand for online grocery solutions in particular, confirm Peapod's leadership position and suggest exciting growth opportunities for the industry. Our priorities for 1998 will allow us to complete and execute a refined business model, lead this industry growth and enhance the long-term value of our franchise.

Parkinson's comments specifically did *not* mention that while Peapod was the most successful of the fledgling on-line grocery stores, its stock price had tanked over the last few months. Ironically, this had created an entry barrier for some of Peapod's potential competitors. Companies such as OnCart were having a tougher time raising capital simply because Peapod was doing so poorly in the stock market. Nevertheless, the closest rival, NetGrocer.com, had just launched a national service for nonperishable goods in partnership with Federal Express. Peapod's service was currently available only locally in seven large metropolitan markets. Wall Street analysts were already none too pleased with Peapod's negative cash flow, and it was not clear how they would react if Peapod were to lose its first mover advantage in the larger national market. Being the first mover had brought them many benefits in the past, such as brand recognition and free media coverage. Now, however, their dominance was being challenged by a new series of players.

Peapod also knew the pitfalls of being the first mover. From the start, it had tried to ensure some strategic flexibility so as to take advantage of new opportunities by continually evolving its technology, distribution model, and services. Many developments were under way in each of these areas that would help Peapod maintain its

---

Kellogg students Dave Aufhauser, Dan Glennon, Marianne Jensen, Andrea Moretti-Adimari, Martin Sansing, and Leif Welch prepared this case under the supervision of Professor Mohanbir Sawhney as the basis for class discussion rather than to illustrate either effective or ineffective handling of an administrative situation.

leadership position. However, the upcoming transformation from dial-up access to access via the Internet presented some of the largest challenges and opportunities the company had faced thus far.

Within a few months Peapod would release version 5, the latest revision of its proprietary user interface software. Version 5 represented a significant technological shift for Peapod since it would require users to access Peapod strictly over the Internet.[1] Prior to the version 5 software, most users[2] placed their order by dialing Peapod directly, using a modem and phone line. By transferring all access to the Internet, Peapod would be able to reduce the costs associated with its (800) access lines. The cost savings of $0.06 per minute were significant to Peapod. However, it meant that most customers would experience slower access to Peapod's site. In addition, Peapod was only a few months away from introducing a reduced-capability hypertext markup language (HTML) version of its software. This simplified trial version would allow new customers to place orders directly on Peapod's Web site without downloading the full proprietary application.

Many people within Peapod, including Ravi, felt that the new software and access strategy would help simplify the customer interface and provide access to additional consumers within the existing metropolitan markets. Although the Web site could be accessed nationwide, the software would ask consumers for their zip code to determine if they were in an area serviced by Peapod. This created a dilemma of what the site could offer to consumers who were in nonserviced areas. Simply offering them nothing and turning them away would almost certainly create a negative first impression of Peapod that would be difficult to overcome later. The decision to offer them something was easy, but the decision of what to offer them was very difficult to answer.

Ravi knew that Peapod could no longer afford to postpone entry into the much larger national marketspace offered by the Web. However, this decision only led to more complex questions. What services or content should be offered nationally? How would fulfillment be handled? How would Peapod's existing business model transform into one that also supported a national presence on the Web? And, perhaps most importantly, how could this concept be sold internally to Peapod's own management? It was Ravi's job to help answer these questions. Given the dynamic nature of the industry, decisiveness was paramount to survival.

■ HISTORY OF PEAPOD

Founded in 1989, Peapod was the largest and most successful company that provided on-line grocery shopping via a virtual supermarket. Billed as "Smart Shopping for Busy People," Peapod's service was designed to provide consumers with a convenient and timesaving alternative to shopping in brick-and-mortar stores. By partnering with local grocery retail chains and implementing sophisticated product and customer management software, Peapod was able to offer a valuable service to consumers. Additionally, grocery retailers and consumer goods companies were able to derive significant benefit from a relationship with Peapod.

[1] Prior to the version 5 software, Peapod's Web site provided only general company information and the ability to download the proprietary shopping application (version 4). Version 4 was also direct-mailed to consumers.

[2] Peapod's version 4 software allowed users to select between the Internet and a dial-up connection. Peapod data indicates that 95 percent of Peapod's users placed their orders over a direct dial-up connection. The remaining 5 percent placed their orders over the Internet.

Consumer Services

The Peapod experience began when a consumer loaded the proprietary Peapod shopping application onto his or her personal computer (PC) in the home or office. When ready to order, the consumer simply selected the items from the virtual isles and shelves of the store on their screen. Once the user had finished building his or her shopping list, the order was placed with Peapod, using a modem and dial-up connection. When ordering, the user specified the delivery time and paid with a credit card. The order was then routed to the Peapod affiliated grocery store nearest the user's home. The customer's order was handpicked from the store shelves by Peapod's staff and delivered to the user's home.

The Peapod approach offered consumers many advantages over traditional grocery shopping. It allowed shoppers to avoid the long checkout lines, crowded parking lots, traffic, and other hassles typically associated with a trip to the local supermarket. Instead, using their PCs, users could order groceries 24 hours a day, seven days a week and schedule delivery within a 90-minute window of their choice. Additionally, users had a choice of shopping methods, which included browsing the aisles, conducting word or category searches, or using personalized standard shopping lists of frequently purchased items. As the user shopped, the software automatically kept a running on-line total of the bill. If desired, the user could investigate detailed nutritional information on the grocery items. Features allowed consumers to sort items on variables such as price, sale information, or nutritional data (e.g., fat content, calories, cholesterol, and sodium). Peapod also offered both electronic and telephone customer support.

Technology was central to Peapod's business model. In additon to the vast selection of products available (roughly 30,000 stock-keeping units [SKUs]), Peapod's systems were linked directly to the information systems of its retail partners, allowing consumers to take advantage of up-to-date pricing and promotional information. Peapod's database created sophisticated user profiles from the customer information collected. This included customers' on-line shopping behavior, purchase histories, as well as on-line attitudinal surveys and demographic data. Based on these profiles, Peapod's proprietary targeting engine delivered customized one-to-one advertising and promotions. These proprietary technologies enabled Peapod to derive revenue from consumers, grocery retailers, and consumer goods companies.

As of March 1998, Peapod was located in seven metropolitan markets: Chicago, San Francisco/San Jose, Columbus, Boston, Houston, Atlanta, and Dallas. In addition, Peapod's expansion plans called for entry into several more metropolitan markets within the year. As of January 1998, Peapod had over 75,000 members, and its membership growth mimicked the overall growth trends for e-commerce, although the demographic mix was different. While studies suggested that 60 to 70 percent of Internet users in 1996–1997 were male, Peapod's customers were predominantly upper-middle-class women.

Although Peapod continuously worked to refine the local pricing structure in each market, in Chicago, the largest market, the service was priced as follows: a $4.95 one-time fee to join; a flat-rate $4.95 charge for each order; and an additional per-order charge of 5 percent of the total grocery bill.

Grocery Retailer Alliances

In addition to individual consumer sales, the relationships Peapod had with retail partners in each metropolitan market were a significant source of revenue. Under its retail agreements, Peapod's retail partners generally paid various fixed and transaction-based fees and provided annual marketing support, which was used to advertise and promote the Peapod service.

From its inception, Peapod's ability to provide on-line shopping and delivery services to its users had depended on its affiliations with local grocery retail partners. In each metropolitan market, Peapod partnered with a single major grocery chain, which provided product sourcing, assistance with fulfillment, and marketing arrangements. In each partnership, Peapod provided its on-line shopping system, including the user application and the system hosting and network management services necessary to operate the service. Partner systems were linked to Peapod's proprietary merchandising software, which allowed retailers to electronically transmit product and pricing changes to Peapod on a real-time basis.

Additionally, Peapod provided retailers with the management expertise to run an on-line service. Peapod's approach was to provide an on-line shopping channel solution to the retailer that was significantly more attractive to the retailer than developing this capability in-house.

Interactive Marketing Services

Peapod continuously collected and archived information regarding consumer buying behavior and preferences in its extensive database. This uniquely positioned Peapod as an innovator in interactive marketing services. By partnering with consumer goods companies, Peapod was able to offer advertising, promotion, and market research services. Peapod first offered these services in 1995, and has since provided interactive marketing services to companies such as Anheuser-Busch, Inc., Bristol-Myers Squibb Company, Frito-Lay, Inc., The Gillette Company (USA), Inc., Helene Curtis, Inc., Kellogg Company, Kraft Foods, Inc., Nestle U.S.A., Inc., Novus Services, Inc. (Discover Card), Ore-Ida Foods, Inc., Ralston Purina Company, The J. M. Smucker Company, and Tropicana Products, Inc.

The consumer goods companies valued the appealing demographic profile of Peapod's membership base and the unique capabilities and content of its database. Using its proprietary targeting engine on the database content, Peapod was able to deliver highly targeted, one-to-one advertising and promotion, such as electronic coupons, as well as conducting cost-effective, high-quality marketing research. The level of sophistication of Peapod's systems had been developed to record every mouse click, page view, redemption and ultimate sale on a per-user basis. Consumer goods companies, in particular, found these capabilities useful when faced with the daunting task of evaluating a marketing program. Marketing programs that would ultimately be executed in traditional media could be analyzed for response rates before making large commitments (see Exhibit 1 for descriptions of interactive marketing services offered by Peapod).

Financial Performance

Entry into new markets, expansion of existing markets, and the general growth of e-commerce, had contributed to impressive growth for Peapod's core consumer services business. Additionally, revenues from Peapod's interactive marketing services had also roughly doubled over the previous year. Exhibit 2 on page 476 presents detailed growth statistics for Peapod's recent calendar year. Peapod's business was growing by all measures except profit. In fact, Peapod was losing money and had never made a profit in its history. Fortunately, the losses were growing more slowly than the revenues, and could be attributed to the rapid expansion into new markets. As with many new and unproven e-commerce companies, the market expressed its uncertainty with its pocketbook; Peapod's stock price had steadily declined since its initial purchase offer (IPO) in June 1997 (see Exhibit 3 on page 476).

Peapod's management felt very positive about the future and had, in addition to the version 5 software, several new projects in the pipeline that it felt would push

EXHIBIT 1

Revenue Streams That Were Currently Being Tested by Peapod

Banner Advertising: The standard Peapod advertising unit is a banner or half-banner ad that runs in the product's home screen and other high-traffic areas. Because the banner ad includes a direct link to the brand's on-line shelf location or information module, a member can quickly purchase the advertiser's product.

Enhanced Content Advertising: Peapod's flexible format allows additional content in the form of an information module to be added to more fully explain, in an exciting interactive format, the many uses of an advertiser's products. For example, a major national consumer goods manufacturer sponsors an interactive recipe planning module that promotes usage of the sponsor's brand ingredients and allows automatic addition of these ingredients to the member's "virtual" shopping basket. A Peapod member can review a menu of time-saving topics, select and view a list of recipes, examine individual recipes containing the sponsor's products and then quickly purchase those products as part of the member's grocery order. Through this program, the sponsor is able to provide helpful information to consumers at the time purchase decisions are being made. In addition, the sponsor can test which recipes are viewed by members and which ones result in incremental sales.

Electronic Couponing: Peapod's database and membership profile enable it to deliver highly targeted, one-to-one promotion programs such as electronic coupons. These programs can be offered to all users or targeted to specific members, such as consumers of competing products. Furthermore, the electronic coupons eliminate much of the printing, distribution, and expense normally associated with paper coupons.

Stimulus–Response Testing: Through Peapod's stimulus–response testing, a consumer goods company can accurately target communication and promotion programs, such as those described above, in innovative ways, thereby generating research data that would be difficult to otherwise obtain. Stimuli (i.e., incentives) can be delivered on-line with subsequent purchase behavior among test and control households tracked to calculate a return on investment for the sponsor's program. Through such a program, a consumer goods company can discover, among other things, how much incentive is needed to draw customers away from the competition and which tactics can maintain or increase purchases of the brand by current customers. Consumer goods companies can use this methodology to test alternative coupon events and tie-in promotions (e.g., offering a free jar of jelly with the purchase of several loaves of bread) as well as point-of-sale, direct mail and FSI promotion programs, and new product concepts. For example, sponsors have tested the impact of delivering an everyday-low-price message exclusively to consumers planning on buying competitive brands. In another example, a sponsor experimented with innovative media placements. This sponsor created a virtual display including an electronic coupon program for a personal care product in the high-traffic Peapod produce aisle, a placement that would have been difficult to implement in a traditional retail environment. This placement led to a substantial increase in use of this product by Peapod members.

Information Research Services: The Company has a relationship with The M/A/R/C Group, a national marketing research organization, to develop and market custom and syndicated research applications to bring the value-added research benefits of Peapod to consumer goods companies. Customers for such research products include ConAgra, Inc., Johnson & Johnson, and Procter & Gamble Co. A custom on-line survey tool has recently been developed that the Company believes will allow qualitative, attitudinal insights from highly targeted consumer groups to be gathered quickly and efficiently, and linked to data on shopping behavior.

The Company is also developing, in conjunction with The M/A/R/C Group, syndicated research tools by utilizing Peapod's membership pool. The first such report is entitled "On-line vs. In-Line" and identifies the characteristics and motives of on-line shoppers. Peapod believes that the nature of its database, which maintains extensive and detailed data tied to individual purchasers, enables it to provide improved research and data products without the cost of scanning and demographic research. Additionally, Peapod's membership base allows the Company to create and maintain highly targeted research panels at a cost the Company believes to be substantially lower than the consumer panels of current research firms.

To date, substantially all of Peapod's interactive marketing sales have been made through sponsorship agreements under which the Company provides a variety of bundled interactive marketing products and services. In 1997, the Company began offering individual interactive marketing services such as banner ads and electronic coupon programs on a shorter-term basis, in a manner more similar to typical advertising and promotion programs.

Source: Peapod prospectus dated May 12, 1997.

EXHIBIT 2

Growth Statistics for Peapod

	1996	*1997*	*Growth (Drop)*
Revenue	$29.2M	$59.6M	104%
Grocery sales	$22.0M	$43.5M	98%
Member and retailers services revenues	$6.1M	$13.9M	128%
Interactive marketing services revenues	$1.1M	$2.2M	108%
Grocery operations expense	$8.1M	$17.5M	115%
Households in service areas	3.25M	6.5M	100%
Members	33,300	71,500	115%
Total orders	201,000	396,600	97%
Profit (loss)	($9.6M)	($13.0M)	(35%)

Peapod toward profitability at a faster rate. Commenting on the past year's financial performance and the future prospects of Peapod, CEO Andrew B. Parkinson stated:

> 1997 was an exciting year for Peapod. Our dramatic growth in membership, orders and revenues showed a consistently increasing consumer demand for our service. We also made positive progress in streamlining our operations, and gained economies of scale in many overhead categories. We are further encouraged by the early consumer receptivity to our next generation of online shopping software, version 5.0, which went into beta testing during the fourth quarter. This product will provide our members with Internet access to Peapod, improved performance and ease-of-use, and new Internet content and multimedia capabilities.

EXHIBIT 3

Peapod's Stock Price Since IPO (June 1997)

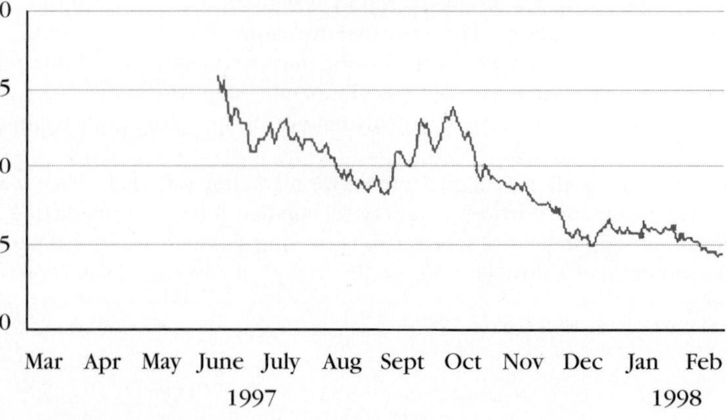

Source: http://www.quicken.com.

> We expect another productive year in 1998. On the basis of several research initiatives we conducted during 1997, we believe that we can accelerate our long-term revenue growth and build a more loyal membership franchise by more aggressively centralizing our fulfillment operations into warehouses. This should improve our service quality, cost structure and scalability, and allow us to reduce consumer fees. We believe the impact of reduced fees on membership and order levels can be meaningful over time.
>
> Specifically, in 1998, Peapod will focus on centralizing operations in select major cities and completing technology solutions, such as version 5.0 and our new hand-held scanner picking system, which will improve service quality and reduce costs. We will also continue to grow membership and orders, particularly in markets in which we operate a service model with centralized fulfillment and lower consumer fees. Because we will be implementing this model during 1998, much of our membership and order growth will likely occur in the second half of the year. We expect Interactive Marketing Services revenues to continue to grow in 1998, and to scale more aggressively in future periods as membership grows.

Strategic Issues in the Current Business

Management knew that these concerns were critical to Peapod's survival. Existing local operations were far from flawless, and customer service needed to be improved. For a company that claimed to offer consumers greater convenience, Peapod had problems that reached into the very core of its value proposition. A main concern was the churn rate, or the degree to which existing customers left the service to be replaced by new members. Two causes were determined to contribute to the high membership turnover:

- First, supermarkets regularly experienced stock-outs averaging up to 10 percent of their SKUs. A shopper in the physical store could automatically adjust to this condition by making an appropriate substitution on the spot from the available choices. However, the company's pickers were forced to use a best guess as to what the correct substitute would be. Unfortunately, more often than not, the shopper would be annoyed at not receiving what had been ordered. This problem was accentuated by price-promoted items, which attracted a higher proportion of on-line orders than nonsale items. A higher number of orders for particular items resulted in a greater chance of a stock-out, which ultimately translated into a higher number of dissatisfied on-line shoppers.
- Second, Peapod's pickers were subject to human error. Pickers occasionally made mistakes when picking items in the grocery store. According to Peapod statistics, a staggering 2 percent of items were incorrectly picked. Given an average order size of about 100 items, this means that most orders were delivered with about two wrong items.

Management felt that operations and logistics were key areas for improvement. By streamlining these areas, Peapod felt that it could improve financial performance and customer service. Based on this belief, Peapod began building warehouses to consolidate the fulfillment side of its business. Nevertheless, every area of the local business needed attention, as summarized by Exhibit 4 on page 478.

Given the interlinkages between the different parts of the business, the decision as to what to offer on the Website had implications for the entire business. Ravi had been following how other companies were using the Web, and he realized that a myriad of possibilities existed for Peapod. A matrix summarizing how different companies use the Internet is presented in Exhibit 5 on page 478.

EXHIBIT 4

Strategic Issues for Peapod's Current Business

Activity	*Issues*
Purchasing	• Should this be done by the company or in partnership with the retailer? • How many SKUs should be offered?
Warehousing	• How much should the company invest in state of the art warehousing? • Should Peapod or a third party manage this?
Delivery	• Should Peapod invest in company trucks rather than relying on the "pickers" using their own cars? • Should there be different delivery prices for different times of day?
Customer service	• How could Peapod improve its customer service to improve on its current low retention rate?
Demand building	• Was home mailing of the software (like AOL) the best way to do this?
Customer interface	• What should Peapod's Web site look like?

MARKET ANALYSIS AND OUTLOOK

Trends in Internet Use

In 1997, Morgan Stanley estimated that there were about 35 million Internet users, and that this number would grow at a compounded annual growth rate of approximately 60 percent over the next three years, so that about 150 million people would use the Internet in the United States by the year 2000.[3]

Jupiter Communications projected that by the year 2002, about 57 million U.S. households would be on-line. Adoption would be encouraged by an expanding range of household access devices, appealing content, and increased bandwidth. Non-PC access devices, such as phone and television, were expected to grow rapidly, and were projected to account for just under one-third of the access channel market

EXHIBIT 5

Matrix of Categorized Corporate Web Sites for Design of Peapod National Site

	Conversation	Collaboration	Commerce/Care
Creating New Businesses	Parentsoup Wired C/Net	? ↑	E*trade Amazon.com Garden.com
Extending Relationships	IBM ESPN Pathfinder	TI (DSPs) Fiat (Italy)	Barnes & Noble E&Y DLJDirect
Deepening Existing Relationships	Lexus Clinique Ragu	TI (Calculators) Intel	Dell Cisco Fidelity

Source: Mohan Sawhney, lecture notes for technology marketing course.

[3] Morgan Stanley Internet Retail Report, May 1997.

for on-line households by 2002. Although PCs would remain the largest access channel, more affordable technologies would speed up the evolution of the on-line industry into a mass medium.

Food Retailing on the Internet

In 1996, on-line grocery sales reached $27.5 million, representing only 4 percent of total on-line consumer spending. At this early stage in the market's development, estimates of the size of the Internet food retailing market were highly speculative and varied considerably. For example, Morgan Stanley projected that total Internet retailing would grow from $600 million in 1996 to $21 to $57 billion by the year 2000. Morgan Stanley believed that the biggest retail opportunities on the Internet would be in products that were currently sold via mail order, and that bulky, low-value items, such as groceries, would represent only a small component of this. Nevertheless, even if groceries only accounted for 1 percent of the e-commerce market, this would still be a $200 million to $600 million market by the year 2000.

Forrester, by contrast, projected total on-line consumer shopping in the year 2000 at a much lower $6.5 billion, but with a higher share for food and drink of 5 percent, giving a potential food grocery market of $330 million. Jupiter was the most optimistic, predicting on-line grocery spending to increase to $6.6 billion by 2002. This would represent 17 percent of its forecast for total on-line consumer spending, but only about 1 percent of the overall U.S. grocery market of almost $500 billion. Jupiter believed that the sale of dry goods would drive the majority of on-line grocery sales in the future. Dry goods represented approximately 40 percent of household grocery budgets.

Although these projections varied widely, it was clear that there would be strong growth in the on-line grocery market, as a result of frequent and relatively high dollar purchases. The average on-line grocery order was currently $100 to $125, which was three times the average of traditional grocery stores. With household food budgets fairly static, the key to growth and survival in the on-line grocery business was customer acquisition rather than increased spending per customer.

The On-line Grocery Shopper

Current Customer Profile According to CommerceNet/Nielsen Media research, Food and Drink was among the top three categories of merchandise for on-line purchases among women in the 25 to 34 age group.[4] This was in line with the fact that 75 percent of Peapod's current customer base were females. Currently, on-line grocery shopping appealed mainly to high-income households with time-compressed lifestyles, willing to pay the additional cost in subscription and delivery fees. Unfortunately, women were currently less active in e-commerce than men. Research data tracked by PC meter showed that the majority of Internet shoppers were males in the 25 to 49 age group. Only 8 percent of female Web users surveyed had made an on-line purchase, compared with 18 percent of male Web users. Males were also more likely to search for product information on the Web prior to making a purchase.

Some predicted that a key segment for on-line grocery shopping in the future would be seniors, as current users aged and the technology became available to the mass market. In fact, research by Media Metrix indicated that older baby boomers and retirees (45+ age group) spent nearly one-third more time using their home PCs than the generation-X age group (18 to 34). People aged 55+ spent nearly two-thirds more time using the home PC than the 18- to 24-year-olds, and three times more than teens (12 to 17 years old).

[4] *Ibid.*

Trends in Consumer Behavior In a 1996 study, the International Foodservices Distributor Association (IFDA) identified some key trends in the food industry:

- A shift toward purchasing food prepared outside the home, either through dining out or through pre-prepared meal delivery, due primarily to baby boomers who were now "empty nesters."
- People felt increasingly time-starved as they worked long hours. In addition, a majority of people perceived grocery shopping a chore (as many as 80 percent, according to a study commissioned by NetGrocer). This led to a demand for more convenient and time-saving methods of performing routine chores such as grocery shopping.
- Disposable incomes were increasing, as a result of more dual-income households. This led to a demand for higher-quality food.
- As consumers became more concerned with improving their lifestyle and health, they were also becoming more selective in the food they ate. This led to a demand for more information about food ingredients to help consumers make choices about food.

Consumers wanted to select their food more carefully, yet they would rather reduce the amount of time they spent grocery shopping. The higher disposable incomes suggested that some segments of consumers would be willing to pay a premium for services that would help them achieve the two, sometimes conflicting, goals of:

- Gathering information to help select products that would best satisfy the consumer's needs;
- Saving time and avoiding hassle when purchasing the products.

Consumers were increasingly using the Internet to gather information on purchases that were subsequently made off-line. A CommerceNet survey indicated that approximately 73 percent of users spent some of their on-line time searching for information about specific products or services. Of this group, 53 percent went on to make a purchase either on- or off-line, and only 15 percent made a purchase on-line. As e-commerce became more widely accepted, more people would choose to make on-line transactions. This suggested that transaction-based sites should initially focus on attracting eyeballs through content, in anticipation of the arrival of mass-market e-commerce.

Competition

In 1997, Peapod was competing with a number of providers of grocery products and services, including traditional grocery retailers and convenience stores, other interactive or Internet-based grocery providers, and providers that fulfilled orders obtained via telephone or facsimile. These grocery retailers were competing for the same customer base located in the seven metropolitan areas in which Peapod conducted its business. In general, the grocery retail market was extremely competitive, with net margins averaging less than 2 percent.

Because of the large capital investments required to develop and operate on-line grocery shopping and delivery systems, large, well-capitalized retailers or technology companies posed the most significant long-term competitive threat. By 1998, many traditional supermarkets were viewing the Internet as a distribution outlet that could be integrated into their existing business model, in order to both enhance and defend it. In fact, according to a 1997 survey taken by *Supermarket News*, 14.5 percent of retail grocery outlets expected to see on-line services used for shopping and targeted marketing initiatives by the year 2000. Many of these retailers were emerging with warehouse-based distribution models in an attempt to lead the development of the new channel. Although Peapod hoped to partner with many of these grocery retailers, some retailers would choose to develop their own systems, or align with other parties.

In some instances, new entrants with purely technical capabilities were partnering with local grocers to deliver food to consumers' homes. All electronic grocers were competing on several factors, including the ease of use, functionality and reliability of the shopping and ordering system, product selection, price, customer service, and general brand awareness. Key players in the electronic grocer arena included:

NetGrocer: Twenty-five percent owned by CUC International, NetGrocer was one of the first companies to serve a national market. The start-up focused solely on nonperishable dry goods, which were easy to ship nationally and accounted for upward of forty percent of most households' supermarket budgets. It targeted middle-income families with low-cost, lesser-known labels with limited selection. Using a centralized warehouse and a delivery agreement with FedEx, NetGrocer's value proposition was to match or undercut store pricing by cutting retail out of the distribution chain. The company's customer base was 10,000 at the end of 1997 and was expected to reach 100,000 by the end of 1998. Exhibit 6 shows the profitability of the Net.Grocer business model for different types of orders.

OnCart: Formerly Shoppers Express, OnCart operated grocery businesses both nationally and locally in Atlanta, Phoenix, Los Angeles, Dallas, Columbus, and Seattle. The national service, in partnership with UPS, offered nonperishable goods anywhere in the United States with free delivery for orders over $50. Residents of the local areas served could also get perishables delivered using OnCart's own trucks. OnCart partnered locally with regional grocery chains Krogers and Pavilions. It was planning to serve 4 to 6 new cities in 1998. In addition, the firm announced plans to begin offering content including customized meal planning, diet and nutrition advice, and a recipe database. In March 1998, there were rumors that OnCart was in financial difficulty and about to exit the on-line grocery business.

Wal-Mart Online: This distribution outlet opened in June 1997, offering a range of food by mail, including frozen dishes and some produce. With strong buying power and scale, Wal-Mart Online was expected to evolve into a fierce national competitor.

EXHIBIT 6

Profitability of Product Orders for NetGrocer (February 1998)

Estimated Variable Contribution to NetGrocer of Representative Transactions

Size of order	$15.00	$30.00	$60.00	$120.00
Shipping charge[a]	$2.99	$2.99	$5.99	$5.99
Total revenues	$17.99	$32.99	$65.99	$125.99
COGs (@ 70% of sales)	$10.50	$21.00	$42.00	$84.00
Shipping and Material (@ $8/box)[b]	$8.00	$8.00	$16.00	$32.00
Picking and Packing (@ 10% of sales)	$1.50	$3.00	$6.00	$12.00
Warehouse Management (@ 8% of sales)[c]	$1.20	$2.40	$4.80	$9.60
Total Variable Cost on Transactions	$21.20	$34.40	$68.80	$137.60
Variable Contribution on Transaction	–$3.21	–$4.40	–$8.80	–$17.60

[a] Flat fee of $2.99 for purchases totaling <$50 and $5.99 for purchases >$50.

[b] Assumes that a box holds up to $30 of grocery.

[c] Lumpy-fixed cost assumed to be variable.

Source: Peapod management estimates.

Finally, there was also the threat from services that delivered pre-prepared food to the home. Cybermeal.com, for example, leveraged a network of restaurants with delivery services. This aggregation simplified selection and ordering. Currently, delivery was carried out by the restaurants, but as this service took off, it would be feasible to move to a centralized delivery fleet, and perhaps even a centralized kitchen that prepared meals to order at lower cost than a restaurant.

MOVING TOWARD AN INTERNET BUSINESS MODEL

By moving its platform from proprietary software to the Internet, Peapod now faced a completely new set of business dynamics, as the Internet offered Peapod the opportunity to deliver a very different value proposition to its customers. In order to deliver a new value proposition, Peapod would have to adjust its current business model, perhaps by partnering with different firms (or with the same firms differently).

Edmund's and Amazon.com represented two examples of Internet-based companies that, in very different ways, had successfully used their business designs to offer customers a strong value proposition.

> **Amazon.com:** Amazon.com adopted a "transaction-centric" model that relied on bringing customers into a virtual bookstore via an electronic interface, rather than to a physical store. Amazon.com did not have to invest in capital to buy real estate or construct buildings. Instead, it invested primarily in programming tools to manage customer interfaces, Web site content, and to pay for on-line advertising. Amazon.com's cost structure was therefore lower than those of firms that operated under the traditional bookstore model. Customers used a search engine to find books from a collection of over 2.5 million books, far larger than that offered by any bricks-and-mortar retailer. The books could then be easily ordered on-line, and were delivered to the customer's home. Amazon.com held little inventory. It simply took orders, purchased the books from wholesalers or publishers, and repackaged and sent them to the customers. The process meant close partnerships with distributors, particularly the largest book wholesaler, Ingram Book Group, which represented about 60 percent of Amazon.com's sales. Amazon.com also added Web content such as author interviews, excerpts from book reviews by critics and readers, and book recommendations based on user purchases. Thus, Amazon.com partnered with published book reviewers, book authors, and customers themselves to augment its value to customers.
>
> **Edmund's:** Edmund's had adopted the "metamediary" model in the automotive arena, by seamlessly integrating a set of product markets that were cognitively related, but disconnected in the physical marketplace. Edmund's extracted value by being strategically located between the buyer and seller communities. Edmund's printed publications offered extensive pricing information on new and used vehicles as well as proprietary product reviews, including the extensive new vehicle tests. This information was offered for free on its Web page, and was supplemented on-line with user-generated content in Edmund's "town hall" discussion forums and via relationships with other network partners in the value Web. Visitors to the site had access to auto listings through Auto-By-Tel, and could purchase auto insurance, warranties, financing and repair manuals from other partners (Edmund's collected referral fees from its partners). Each partnership was exclusive, carrying Edmund's implicit seal of approval that the partner was "best in its kind." Thus, Edmund's represented a convenient and reliable one-stop shop for customer's automotive-related needs.

Could Peapod draw some inferences from these successful electronic commerce businesses? What was Peapod's new marketspace, that is, who were its customers and what did they want? What business design would be most appropriate to deliver this value, and who were the players?

EXHIBIT 7

Segmentation Dimensions of Potential Peapod Users

Demographics *(Who They Are)*	***Grocery Shopping Focus*** *(What They Want)*	***Internet Involvement*** *(Are They Tech-Savvy?)*
Gender	Convenience	Not on Internet
Income	Cost	Leisure-surfing
Age	Health	Information seeking
	Variety	Newsgroup members
	Pre-prepared	Transaction executers

Understanding the Customers

Traditional marketing approaches segment the market by focusing on consumer demographics. However, the demographic information that Peapod had access to from existing reports was not sufficient to perform a segmentation analysis. Commissioning a market research firm to do a more detailed study was not a viable option either, given Peapod's limited resources. Therefore, the project was given to a group of students from the Kellogg Graduate School of Management. The students immediately identified the dimensions that would traditionally be used to segment potential Peapod users (see Exhibit 7).

Since little meaningful demographic data was available, they chose a "response-based" segmentation, which was conceptually the inverse of the standard socio-demographic approach. Since consumers would only access Peapod's new site through the Web, the students developed a characterization of Internet/Web users. This, they felt, was the most appropriate response-based approach to segmenting the potential users. The mindsets of Web users as defined for Peapod are shown in Exhibit 8.

The segments shown in Exhibit 8 were not exclusive, meaning that a person could be in different segments at the same time, or move between segments as familiarity and comfort with the Internet grew. Most consumers started in the bottom left corner as leisure surfers. Then, over time, they progressed to become more active, either by using the Internet for entertainment or as an efficiency tool. The smallest segment thus far consisted of those who were willing to make a transaction over the Internet, the Spenders. E-commerce sites choosing to offer only a pure transaction engine would limit themselves to the smallest user segment based on this segmentation.

In addition to consumers' Web attitudes, the future occasions of use for Peapod's service were examined. The scenarios developed are described in Exhibit 9 on page 484. This analysis provided an added dimension that would help Peapod frame how consumers would use the Peapod site.

EXHIBIT 8

Internet/Web Attitudes of Potential Peapod Users

	Entertainment Tool	***Efficiency Tool***
Active	Participate in news groups **"The chatters"**	Willing to make transaction **"The spenders"**
Passive	**"The surfers"**	Info search only—no transaction **"The searchers"**

EXHIBIT 9

Hypothetical Occasions of Use for Peapod

	Scenario/Concerns
Cost-conscious/Searcher	• Young families with children seek coupons • Struggling twenty-something couple logged on to find cheap cans of soup
Variety-seeking/Chatter	• Student wants ethnic meal to woo a first date • Middle-aged woman throwing party needs advice to impress neighbors
Convenience-seeking	• Single dad with kids wants regular grocery needs fulfilled so he can spend more time with kids and worry less • Busy mom logs in, clicks update grocery list, adds two items, and food is there two hours later
Health-seeking	• Health-conscious newlyweds seek foods high in phytochemicals and low in pesticide residues to maximize future reproductive capabilities • Image-conscious yuppie seeks a meal plan to keep her fat intake under 20.523 grams per day

The next step was to choose which segments to target and ultimately how Peapod should position itself in the increasingly competitive on-line food marketspace. Peapod's marketing group reasoned that while Internet giants such as AOL should worry about attracting non-Internet users, Peapod should initially focus on current Internet users. In essence, it was not Peapod's job to build Internet usage, but rather to make current Internet users Peapod users. At the same time, some key features of digital industries made on-line targeting and positioning on the Internet different from conventional industries, namely:

- There were increasing economies of scale because a network's value increased with its size.
- It was much cheaper to personalize the service and the marketing message on the Web.
- The consumer received information from active choices (clicking on links) rather than from passive exposure.

These features made it easier to target multiple segments, thereby dampening the trade-offs that existed in conventional industries. Nevertheless, it was still true that the complexity of Peapod's business design would increase significantly as the number of targeted customer segments grew.

Peapod's Business Network

Many types of partners could potentially play a role in Peapod's value web.

- Retailers
- Distributors
- Consumer packaged goods companies (CPGs)
- Advertisers
- Content providers
- Technology providers

Peapod had already established relationships with firms in the first four categories. However, the makeup of the firms in the business value web would change with the choices Peapod made for its business design and value proposition. A description of each firm category and the potential value transferred between a firm and Peapod follows.

Retailers and Distributors Peapod had many existing relationships with local market retail and distribution partners. For example, Peapod partnered with Jewel/Osco in Chicago. This partnership allowed Peapod to tap the retailers' existing customer bases and offer an alternative channel for the same products at the same price. This price parity was very important to the retailers. In the value exchange, Peapod gained a sourcing partner and the local retailer gained another distribution channel. However, one possibility going forward was to bypass the local retailer entirely by sourcing directly from the manufacturer—migrating to a national service might in fact force this direction, since the local retailers did not have national capability. All benefits (e.g., national coverage) and disadvantages (e.g., hurting relationships with local retailers) needed to be fully evaluated.

A national Peapod model also raised issues on distribution and warehousing. For example, should Peapod build a national distribution capability, or establish new partnerships with UPS or FedEx? Should Peapod build its own warehouses or outsource?

Consumer Packaged Goods Companies Consumer packaged goods companies included conglomerates such as Kraft, Procter & Gamble, General Mills, and Colgate. These companies spent billions of dollars every year on advertising—print, electronic media, sponsorship, and outdoor billboards. A relatively small but increasing share of this budget was spent on Internet advertising.

Partnerships offered CPGs access to valuable demographic information, tracked by Peapod's Internet Marketing Services division, to be used for more effective targeted marketing and advertising. Additionally, Peapod could serve as an additional distribution channel for the CPG. The CPG, in turn, could offer Peapod targeted promotions such as electronic coupons, to boost sales. In addition, by bypassing local retailers and selling directly to Peapod, the CPG could split the retailers' margins with Peapod.

Advertisers Advertising was important to Peapod in two ways. First, it was a means to build the Peapod brand. Second, it was a potential source of revenue.

Advertising on the Web was constantly evolving. Its effectiveness was unproven to date, though one could argue that conventional measurements of effectiveness—cost per thousand (CPM), the same measure used for TV, radio, and print advertising—were not appropriate for Web advertising. In any case, Web advertising was evolving into closer alliances, sometimes called sponsorships. The typical banner ad cost $20 to $80 CPM and ranged in contract from a week to several months. A sponsorship usually involved a fixed fee, shared advertising revenues, and a longer-term working relationship. There was often a fine, blurry line between sponsorship deals and distribution partnerships such as that between Amazon and Yahoo, which consisted of a multimillion dollar, two- to three-year contract.

If, for example, Peapod wanted to be the exclusive food information source within Yahoo, there were a number of ways it could approach this idea. First, it could simply purchase advertising in the form of banner ads on the Yahoo site. Second, it could become a Yahoo "sponsor" and work closely with the company to better steer eyes to the Peapod site. Third, it could be a feature on the Yahoo marketplace. Finally, it could partner with Yahoo to become a part of Yahoo content—the latter was the most costly but most effective way to build brand, traffic, and transactions on the Web.

Advertising by other firms on www.peapod.com offered Peapod an alternative revenue source. This would complement Peapod's potential effort to build a more content-based business. For example, assuming the Peapod site achieves sufficient traffic, a niche food provider such as Omaha Steaks might be prepared to offer referral fees or to pay a premium for advertising on the Peapod site, where browsers have food on their mind, versus higher traffic generic sites such as Yahoo. However, the Web medium for advertising was still unproven. A second concern was that building an advertising business deviated significantly from Peapod's retailing core competencies. Peapod did not have advertisement selling and servicing capabilities, nor significant resources to build them.

Content Providers Content providers offered value to Peapod by delivering relevant, targeted content to customers. Peapod could potentially build its own brand through association with well-branded sites. In return, content providers would receive distribution of the content and access to eyeballs. They also would receive targeted information on customers, which could be used for future value offerings. This relationship could be reversed, with Peapod placing itself on other content sites, as well as content providers being on Peapod's site (see Exhibit 10 for a sample of food- and nutrition-related sites).

There existed hundreds of food-related sites on the Web, most of which fell into one of several broad categories: Cooking-enthusiast sites offered features for hobby-cooks or food lovers such as searchable recipe archives, chat rooms, message boards, indexed links to other sites and advice and other cooking information. One example was Cookbooks OnLine, which had a recipe archive with over one million recipes.

Some of these sites were connected to brand name sites, such as the Epicurious site, which was the Web home of *Bon Appetit* and *Gourmet* magazines. Other sites catered to particular interest groups with certain targeted interests such as vegetarianism or ethnic cuisine, or they focused on particular foods, such as chili or cheese. For the most part, this category was extremely fragmented and none appeared to be especially well positioned for mind-share consolidation.

Health-related sites focused more on the nutritional or diet aspects of food. There were many sites that targeted dieters and provided information such as calorie content, food ingredients, diet strategies, and, of course, recipe archives. Health-related sites often catered to people with specific health concerns such as diabetes sufferers. There was concern about the quality of the information provided, so a relationship with an established source such as Jenny Craig or the Mayo Clinic could bring credibility to a site.

One content site Peapod had singled out as a potential partner because of its demographic makeup was iVillage. iVillage, which called itself the "Woman's Network," catered to women with content related to topics including beauty care, health and fitness, relationships and parenting, financial and career, and food and nutrition. Content included features, expert advice, news, and more, similar to that offered by many popular women's print magazines. Food-related content included a searchable recipe archive, which generated shopping lists for recipes, cooking basics and features, and expert advice on cooking and nutrition, as well as chats and message boards. iVillage had an existing relationship with OnCart, but this relationship was in doubt because of OnCart's continuing financial problems.

Manufacturers or retailers of food often set up product-specific sites. These were not content sites, but rather focused marketing vehicles to communicate and strengthen brand equity. Most of the major packaged goods companies had set up sites for their companies or specific brands. These sites were replete with product or cooking information, recipes, and frequently promotions.

Technology Issues and Partnering

Plotting Peapod's strategic course was further complicated by the choices related to technology. The strategic use of technology was what gave Peapod its competitive advantage. Peapod had achieved not only competency, but also expertise with the

EXHIBIT 10

Sample of Food and Nutrition-Related Web Sites

Cooking- and Food-Related Sites

Epicurious
http://www.food.epicurious.com
Home of Conde Nast's *Gourmet* and *Bon Appetit* magazines. Searchable recipe index, restaurant guides, wine suggestions, articles from magazine affiliates.

Cookbooks Online
http://www.cookbooks.com/reg.htm
A searchable recipe archive with over one million recipes that recently began charging a subscription fee.

Culinaria Online!
http://www.culinaria.com/
Recipe archive with a linked glossary of terms and cooking tutorials.

Meals Online
http://www.meals.com/
Personalized meal planning from a variety of recipes and foods. Can be placed on a weekly calendar; can generate a grocery list. Also has chat rooms and chef advice.

SOAR (Searchable Online Archive of Recipes)
http://soar.Berkeley.edu/recipes/
Large searchable recipe archive with categorized index.

Top Food Chain
http://nexus.trident.org/sl/cooking/
An extensive index of links to food-related Web sites.

Global Gastronomer
http://www.cs.yale.edu/homes/hupfer/global/gastronomer.html
An index of links to food-related Web sites organized by country. Includes related cultural links.

Diet- and Nutrition-Related Sites

The American Dietetic Association
http://www.eatright.org
Includes a quiz of your nutrition knowledge, healthful recipes, and answers to food and nutrition questions. Offers links to other reliable sites and referrals to registered dietitians around the country.

The Consumer Information Center
http://www.pueblo.gsa.gov
Puts food, nutrition, and other health information at your fingertips. Makes available copies of printed publications, some of which are free.

The International Food Information Council Foundation
http://www.ificinfo.health.org
Provides scientifically sound material concerning food safety and nutrition.

Calorie Control Council
http://www.caloriecontrol.org
Contains tips on cutting fat, deciphering food labels, maintaining a healthy weight, recipes, and trends. Has a calculator to figure out the calories and fat content in various foods and beverages.

Weigh2Go-Online
http://www.ibdn.com/weigh2go/nfolinks.htm
Health, nutrition, and fitness news.

development of databases and sophisticated software to access the database information. However, it was uncertain how well the company's skill would transfer to the new demands of a national Web presence. Expansion into a national Web-based presence meant that Peapod would have to develop additional content, databases, and applications to supplement the product information and the transaction engine that were the current components that consumers dealt with.

A chief concern was Peapod's ability to develop content and applications for the new Web site. Any new content and applications would have to be continuously updated and refined to remain compelling to users and to stay one step ahead of the competition. Several new types of content and related application ideas were being considered, most of which would require development efforts above and beyond those already being done for Peapod's existing business-to-consumer and business-to-business applications.

To help identify the development issues surrounding the content ideas, Ravi consulted co-founder and Executive Vice President–Chief Technology Officer Thomas Parkinson. Thomas emphasized to Ravi that the added burden of developing new applications would increase the pressure on the company at a critical time. Both agreed that they could outsource the development work. However, the desire to reach profitability and please Wall Street made them shudder at the thought of dramatically increasing development costs. They also wondered if outsourcing critical technology would come back to haunt the company in the future. Further, they discussed the possibility of partnering with companies that already had compelling content or database/software development expertise.

Although partnering had the advantage of low cost to Peapod and seemed at first a good idea, it added another layer of complexity to the whole notion of national Web presence. If Peapod entered into partnerships with other technology and content companies, it meant that choices would have to be made about which capabilities to retain in-house and which capabilities to outsource. Thomas explained to Ravi that the key development efforts would include:

- Database development
- Applications to access database information
  - Business-to-consumer
  - Business-to-business
- Content development
- Content application development

The proliferation of the Web had resulted in hundreds of companies popping up over the past few years that offered capabilities in the development of Web pages and interactive applications. Given this trend, Peapod could outsource or gain through partnership all of its technology needs if necessary. Ravi considered that partnership was a two-way street—development costs could be reduced, but only at the expense of something given in return.

Peapod's Business Design

Ravi pulled out a chart from his drawer where he had been keeping a record of the deals done by AOL in the last six months. With every month that went by, gaining a share of eyeballs on the Internet was getting dramatically more expensive, particularly for the most-trafficked sites (see Exhibits 11 and 12 [page 490]). Along with this chart, he had created a list of strategic issues he knew had to be addressed as soon as possible. From this list he had to come up with some recommendations for the management team. Ravi's list of strategic issues was as follows:

Key Strategic Issues Faced by Peapod

1. Core promise of the Peapod brand
2. Web real estate or how to attract eyeballs to the site
3. Web site design—what the site should offer
4. Peapod's service offering
5. What product categories it should offer
6. Structure of the fulfillment side of the business

EXHIBIT 11

Most Popular Web Sites Ranked by Unique Visitor Traffic

Rank	*Property*	*Unique Visitor Traffic, Age 12+ (in thousands)*[d]
1	Yahoo/Four11[a]	31,923
2	Netscape[a]	24,460
3	Excite/Webcrawler[a]	19,830
4	Microsoft[a]	17,954
5	AOL.com[a,c]	14,337
6	Infoseek	13,750
7	Geocities	12,576
8	Lycos[a]	10,322
9	Walt Disney/ABC/ESPN[a]	9,053
10	MSN[a]	8,774
11	CNET[a]	8,402
12	AltaVista	7,790
13	ZDNet	6,951
14	Hotmail	6,713
15	Who Where/Angelfire[a]	5,657
16	CNN[a]	5,565
17	Mapquest[a,b]	4,866
18	Tripod	4,694
19	Wired[a]	4,404
20	Amazon[b]	4,323
21	Pathfinder[b]	4,116
22	Blue Mountain Arts[a,b]	3,979
23	MSNBC[b]	3,943
24	RealNetworks[a]	3,866
25	Looksmart[b]	3,842

[a] Site data based on aggregation of multiple domain names. A complete list of domain names/URLs for each site can be found at http://www.relevantknowledge.com/Press/sdindex.html.

[b] Web Property did not appear in January 1998 Top 25 Web Properties listing.

[c] At this time, Relevant Knowledge tracks AOL Interactive Services members' Web use through only a Netscape or MSIE browser, and not AOL's proprietary browser. Therefore, current data on AOL.COM only partially represents the Web behavior of AOL members. For a complete description of methodology, see http://www.relevantknowledge.com/Products/methodology.html.

[d] All numbers are estimates and are subject to the limitations inherent to survey methodology, such as sample variability, data collection flaws and nonrespondent bias. The effect of this cannot be determined to any precise mathematical degree. Projections have a statistical reliability of ± 277(000).

Source: Relevant Knowledge (2/2/98–3/1/98); ranked by number of Unique Visitors in the United States, age 12+.

EXHIBIT 12

Value of Web Real Estate ($ in thousands)

MNA	*Strategic Partner*	*Upfront Payment*	*Future Payments*	*Total*	*Term (years)*	*Date*	*Notes*
AOL	Intuit	$16,000	$14,000	$30,000	3	1997	
Excite	Netscape		8,250	8,250	1	1997	2.5 applied for advertising
Excite	Netscape	4,000		4,000	1	Jun-97	International
Excite	Preview Travel		15,000	15,000	2		
Infoseek	Bell Atlantic			6,000	1		
Infoseek	Netscape			12,500	2		
Yahoo	Netscape			30,000	2	1997	
Lycos	Electronic News		10,500	10,500	3		

Note: Numbers in $Thousand

Average Deal with Media Network Aggregators

Average deal ($thousand)	$14,531
Average term (years)	1.875
Average per year	$ *7,750*

In 1996, there were very few documented partnership deals. In 1997, deals averaged $7.7 million per year. In 1998, deals are expected to increase more as MNA sites gain eyeballs and eyeballs become more valuable.

The Peapod Brand

Until now, Peapod had been a transaction service using proprietary on-line software. Now, with the launch of an expanded and enhanced Peapod Web site, the company was standing at the threshold of numerous possibilities for developing its service. Since there was still no clear dominant player, Peapod had the opportunity to capture a dominant share of the national market for on-line transactional grocery business. No one could be certain how this emerging market would evolve, but Peapod has the opportunity to establish itself as an industry leader. A central question was what should the Peapod brand represent? The answer to this question would drive how Peapod would position itself. Possibilities included convenience, large selection, on-line groceries, low cost, high quality, fastest way to shop, etc.

Should Peapod remain a pure transactional site or should it introduce content and services to expand the service offering? Expanding the service offering would increase the stakes in terms of risks and potential rewards, while at the same time failing to adapt to market opportunities could rapidly cause it to become a "has been."

Attracting Eyeballs

The Internet was becoming increasingly congested with a vast number of sites on every possible topic. Although Peapod had benefited from a first mover advantage in the past, it was unlikely to benefit from the same "novelty factor" that had attracted attention to other first-in-kind sites such as Amazon.com. The Peapod site had to draw consumers in and keep them coming back. Clearly, two concepts were tantamount—location and positioning. Simply put, the old adage "location, location, location" perfectly described the three most important factors in driving traffic at the site. Hot locations on the Web were going for millions of dollars but Peapod was strapped for resources. Buying a location on a major site such as AOL or Yahoo could cost millions but so could developing and promoting Peapod's own stand-alone site. After a site was established, positioning was the key to customers returning to the site once they had checked it out. Peapod had to offer a compelling value proposition to ensure sustainable traffic and ultimately revenue. The central question was how should Peapod attract eyeballs to its new site without putting too much pressure on its cash flow?

Web Site Design

What should the Web site offer consumers? Should it be as simple as possible and offer only virtual "aisles" of food and transaction capability? Or should the site be more complex and offer content that the users may find helpful? Nutritional information was one form of content that had already been offered. There were many other possibilities for content or even applications that the site could provide (Exhibit 13 presents some of the ideas considered for the Peapod site). However, if consumers val-

EXHIBIT 13

Examples of Content and Applications for Peapod's National Web Site

Service	*Key Elements*	*Fit with Target*
Transaction engine	Needs refining at both the local and national levels. However, this represents Peapod's current core competency and competitive advantage.	For the Spenders who are looking for convenience in grocery shopping.
Coupons offer	An opportunity to download product coupons that can then be used at the local retail stores. This should parallel the structure of the transaction engine.	For the Searchers who are cost-conscious.
Ingredients database	Another element of the transaction engine is an ingredients database that gives more information on the food (similar to NetGrocer).	For the health-conscious Searchers.
Recipes database	This needs to be one of the largest databases available. However, the key differentiator to other such sites is the direct link to both the transaction engine and the product coupons.	This will appeal to all types of Variety-seekers and Searchers.
Chat rooms/message boards	An opportunity for users to share advice or recipes.	This will hopefully help to lock-in the Chatters.
Personal meal planner	A personalized meal planner that is linked to the other services and could emphasize certain diets.	This would generate great lock-in for Searchers and Spenders, especially those concerned with health or diet.
Idea generator	An additional feature that could be introduced, ideally leveraging off of both the recipe database and the diet planner, is a suggestion generator.	Such a service would be useful to all those who see decision making as a chore. There is an opportunity to introduce an element of fun in this feature, which would also help attract the Surfers.
Deliver meals	Similar to or in partnership with Cybermeals. Provides a link to restaurants with a delivery service in each area.	For those times when the consumer wants to treat himself/herself, or alternatively does not have the time to cook.

ued the Peapod shopping experience for the time it saved them would they want to wade through a variety of content areas on the site? Perhaps if the content were integrated into the value offered and solved a problem for consumers it could work. But, if a more complex site, rich in content, were designed how would it be maintained? Peapod did not have expertise in developing this kind of content, and it would be expensive to continuously update.

Service Offering

Probably the biggest question was what should Peapod try to sell through the site and to whom? What categories of physical products should Peapod offer to sell? This decision was heavily tied to the distribution options. For example, a consumer who lived in a remote area would find it very convenient to use the national courier service for large purchases of bulky products (e.g., soda), which are the most inconvenient to shop for in person. However, such a transaction would generate a loss for Peapod under all the delivery fee structures currently being used on the market. Therefore, should only certain types of items be offered nationally? Should all items be offered in local metropolitan markets where Peapod already had alliances with grocery chains? Although this type of segregation was relatively easy on the Web by using zip codes, would some consumers be turned off by an incomplete service in remote areas?

Product Offering

In some cases, there was simply no choice; it didn't make practical sense to overnight ship a box of ice cream bars. However, given that it was more expensive to ship certain types of products, was it wise to completely eliminate some types of products? For instance, 50-pound bags of dog food were a pain to deliver regardless of where they were going. Therefore, it may be possible to generate higher returns by concentrating only on those product areas that offered a high margin to density ratio. As an example, spices were small, lightweight (easy to ship), and could offer good margins. Similar issues existed along other dimensions. Produce was a type of product that consumers often liked to examine for themselves prior to purchase. Virtual shopping would not allow the inspection of individual pieces of fruit. Therefore, to reduce returns or customer dissatisfaction it might be wise to avoid at least some types of produce. While these issues could be quantified (see Exhibits 14 and 15) and certain types of products eliminated, where should the line be drawn? Would consumers be disinterested if they could not buy everything they needed in one place?

Fulfillment

How would the new service offering have to be supported by the fulfillment side of the business? Did it make sense to continue with the local alliances with grocery chains? Did in-store pickers continue to make sense if volume grew beyond some point? For national orders it probably made more sense to build and ship orders from a warehouse type of fulfillment center. However, should Peapod vertically integrate to accomplish this or should this activity be outsourced? Further, should there be one national warehouse or regional warehouses? And again, if fulfillment were done in this fashion, how would the existing alliances with grocery chains be handled?

Another idea was to partner with many smaller grocery stores in local markets. Something like the Amazon affiliates program could be implemented where local stores across the country could handle local fulfillment for Peapod. Finally, Peapod could try to leverage its relationships with CPG companies or specialty food compa-

EXHIBIT 14

Volume and Value Density of Grocery Items

Value to Volume Ratio ($/cc)

Value to Weight Ratio ($/lb)	Low (Value to Volume)	High (Value to Volume)
High	**Fluffy stuff** Diapers Soda Paper plates	**Catalog stars** Cosmetics Preserved meats Wine
Low	**Bulky dogs** Paper towels Kitty litter Cleaning supplies	**Heavy nuggets** Canned goods Fruit Candy

EXHIBIT 15

Graph of Grocery Item Types with Respect to Consumer's Sensory Needs for Purchase Consideration

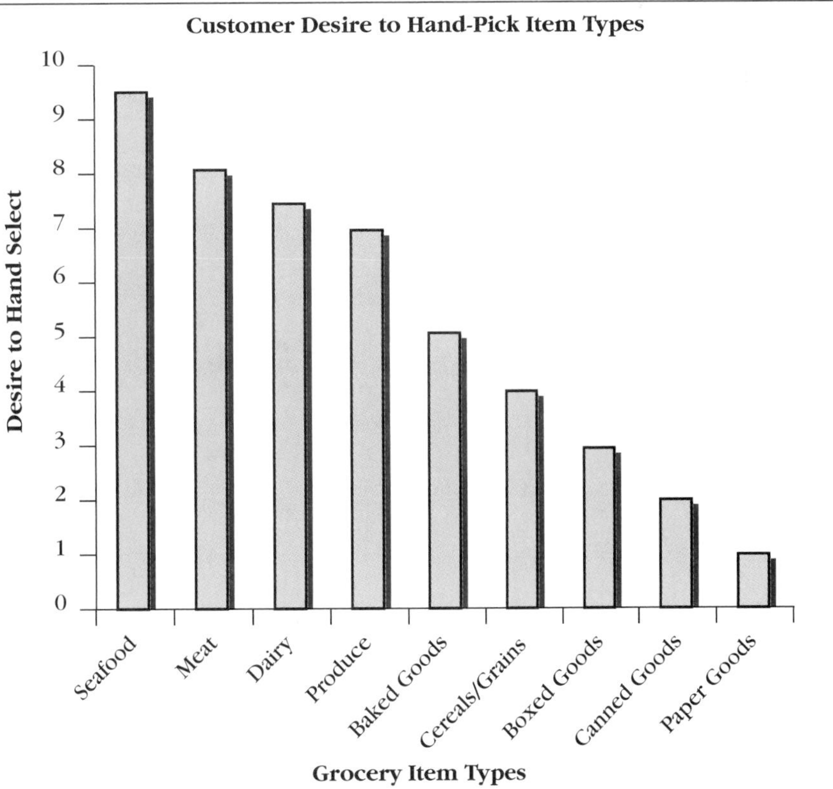

(Casewriter estimates)

nies and follow the Edmund's model of revenues from referrals. If Peapod's partners were willing to ship their product directly to the customer, Peapod could become a virtual store without having to invest in an expensive national distribution network. Although most CPG companies currently did not have the capability to ship small batches to individual customers, some large companies, such as Pepsi and P&G, were experimenting with this concept. This would avoid a direct "me too" strategy of Net-Grocer, and more importantly, allow for "monthly deliveries" of durable products such as soda, which were heavy to carry and thus had significant e-commerce convenience potential for consumers.

CASE

Amazon.com

Winning the On-Line Book Wars

In January 1998, Jeffery Bezos, the Chief Executive Officer of Amazon.com, was reflecting on the eventful year that had just concluded and the challenges that lay ahead. While Amazon.com had achieved success beyond anyone's expectations in 1997, the year ahead promised to be a battle of attrition against competition. Bezos realized that Amazon.com was faced with new challenges in achieving profitability and expanding its on-line bookselling franchise.

In less than three years that Amazon.com had been in business, Jeff Bezos and his rapidly expanding on-line book company had become a sensation among book lovers, and for many analysts and journalists, a barometer for the success of Internet commerce. Instead of just offering an on-line book catalog, Amazon.com had used technology to transform the behavior of book lovers and book buyers. After two years of absolute supremacy and an extended honeymoon with the trade press, competition was heating up and margins had come under pressure. While Amazon.com had held its own against the competition and revenues had increased dramatically to $147.8 million in 1997, a 938 percent increase over 1996, the company's losses continued to widen. Following a successful initial purchase offering (IPO) in the second quarter, Wall Street was beginning to question when Amazon.com would make money.

Despite these pressures, Bezos was adamant that Amazon.com would never push for profitability at the expense of compromising its core values. According to Bezos:

> I think the main reason that Amazon.com has been successful so far is that we have focused on the customer value proposition. We have gotten a lot of repeat business. We have gotten more than a million unique customers. And it's very, very simple, really. We have focused on three things. One is having a larger selection than anyone else. The second is having lower prices or competitive prices. And the third is making the store as easy as possible to use and very convenient. So you save time when you are buying. Also the books get shipped to your home or office. That also saves you time. People are busy in the late 20th century.

In a recent interview, Bezos commented on the profitability issue:

> In the short run, our strategy is not to make money. In this critical formative period, it's more important to spend significant money branding the site. We'll be in the harvest mode in the future. Brand comes first, profits later.

Despite these public statements, Bezos realized that Wall Street's patience was limited, and that there would be severe pressures from investors for Amazon.com to

---

Kellogg student David Contreras prepared this case under the supervision of Professor Mohanbir Sawhney as the basis for class discussion rather than to illustrate either effective or ineffective handling of an administrative situation.

improve its margins and to achieve profitability. Bezos was faced with two key strategic questions: What actions should Amazon.com take to improve its structural margin advantage over its competitors, and to overcome the disadvantages of its current business design? And what growth initiatives should it pursue to expand its franchise and grow its business? Bezos knew that these strategic decisions would determine if Amazon.com could manage its explosive growth and mature into a viable retailing giant. He was also painfully aware that the business and investment community was watching every move, and the margin for error was very small. In the extremely volatile world of technology stocks, a small misstep could brutally punish Amazon.com's stock.

■ HISTORY OF AMAZON.COM

An Idea Whose Time Had Come

In 1994, the potential growth of the Internet offered tremendous opportunities to young entrepreneurs. Jeffery Bezos, a computer science and electrical engineering Princeton graduate, was the youngest senior vice president at D. E. Shaw, a Wall Street-based investment bank. That year, he realized that Internet usage was increasing at the rate of 2,300 percent a year. He became convinced that anything growing that fast was going to become ubiquitous very quickly, and that this was his wake-up call.

After researching about 20 potential product categories, Bezos identified two categories that could be sold successfully on the Internet: music and books. He chose books based on the fact that there are too many titles for a single store to stock, and that the two major incumbents in the market, Barnes & Noble and Borders, jointly accounted for less than 25 percent of total sales. In contrast, the music business was dominated by six major record companies. These companies could lock out a new business threatening the traditional record-store format. Bezos and his wife Mackenzie (and dog) decided to move from Manhattan to Seattle to start his new venture. He chose Seattle for several reasons. Washington is a small state with a small population. The small local market was an advantage for a mail-order business, because sales taxes are charged to customers living in any state where mail-order businesses have a presence. The second reason was Seattle's abundant supply of skilled programmers associated with Microsoft. In fact, several Microsoft executives would later move to Amazon.com. The third reason was the incredible inefficiencies in the existing book distribution process, which resulted in between 40 percent and 50 percent of all published books being shipped back unsold to the publisher. The final reason was the proximity of Seattle to Roseburg, Oregon, where Ingram, the largest book wholesaler, had one of its largest warehouses.

Bezos quickly wrote a business plan, raised several million dollars from private investors, and launched Amazon.com in July 1995 on the Internet. Initially, Bezos was concerned that sales would be so slow that he would not be able to meet the 10-book minimum that his first distributors required. He found in a big distributor's catalog a book entry he suspected was not available—an obscure publication about lichen (a thallophytic plant). His plan was simple: if Amazon.com needed three books, it would pad the order with seven copies of the lichen book. Although creative, this turned out not to be necessary, because sales took off rapidly. With its vast selection of 2.5 million titles, Amazon provided a compelling value proposition to book buyers—the ability to buy almost any book in print in the English language, any time, from the comfort of their home or office, and at a substantial discount.

In May 1997, Amazon.com went public. The shares in the IPO, which were priced at $18, jumped 31 percent the first day of trading, and had more than tripled to $60 by the end of the year. Sales at Amazon.com increased rapidly every quarter. Net sales for the fourth quarter of 1997 soared to $66.0 million, a 74 percent increase over net sales of $37.9 million for the third quarter, and a 680 percent increase over net sales of $8.5 million for the fourth quarter of 1996. Net sales for fiscal 1997 were $147.8 million, a 938 percent increase over net sales of $15.7 million for fiscal 1996. However, losses continued to grow. The company reported a net loss of $27.6 million in 1997, compared with a net loss of $5.8 million in 1996. Exhibits 1 and 2 (page 498) show the financial statements for Amazon.com during its young existence.

By the end of the year, Amazon.com's cumulative customer accounts had grown to 1,510,000, an increase of 61 percent from 940,000 customer accounts at the end of September 1997; and 739 percent from 180,000 customer accounts at December 31, 1996. Repeat business represented more than 58 percent of orders placed during the quarter ended December 31, 1997. International sales were surprisingly large, at over a quarter of overall sales in 1997, indicating strong international growth potential.

EXHIBIT 1

Amazon.com Balance Sheet ($ in Thousands)

	1997	*1996*	*1995*
Total assets	**$149,006**	**$8,271**	**$1,084**
Current assets	$137,335	$7,140	$1,027
Cash and cash equivalents	109,810	6,248	996
Short-term investments	15,256	—	—
Inventories	8,971	571	17
Prepaid expenses and other current assets	3,298	321	14
Long-term assets	11,671	1,131	57
Equipment, net	9,265	985	57
Deposits	166	146	—
Deferred charges	2,240	—	—
Liabilities and shareholder equity			
Current liabilities	$43,818	$4,870	$107
Accounts payable	32,697	2,852	99
Accrued advertising	3,454	598	—
Accrued product development	—	500	—
Other accrued liabilities	7,667	920	8
Long-term debt	76,521	—	—
Long-term lease obligations	181	—	—
Total liabilities	$120,520	$4,870	$107
Shareholders' equity	28,486	3,401	977
Preferred and common stock	239	165	—
Additional paid-in capital	63,792	9,873	na
Deferred compensation	(1,930)	(612)	na
Accumulated deficit	(33,165)	(6,025)	na
Total liabilities and shareholders' equity	**$149,006**	**$8,271**	**$1,084**

Source: Company filings.

EXHIBIT 2

Amazon.com Income Statement ($ in Thousands Except for Per-Share Data)

	4Q 1997 (Quarter ending 12/31)	*4Q 1996 (Quarter ending 12/31)*	*FY 1997 (FY ending 12/31)*	*FY 1996 (FY ending 12/31)*
Net sales	$66,011	$8,468	$147,758	$15,746
Cost of sales	53,119	6,577	118,945	12,287
Gross profit	12,892	1,891	28,813	3,459
Gross margin	19.5%	22.3%	19.5%	21.9%
Operating expenses				
Marketing and sales	16,306	2,938	38,964	6,090
Product development	4,520	901	12,485	2,313
General and administrative	1,920	447	6,573	1,035
Total operating expenses	22,746	4,286	58,022	9,438
Loss from operations	$(9,854)	$(2,395)	$(29,209)	$(5,979)
Interest income	517	96	1,619	202
Net loss	$(9,337)	$(2,299)	$(27,590)	$(5,777)
Net loss per share	$(0.39)	$(0.10)	$(1.17)	$(0.25)
Shares outstanding	23,885	22,969	23,602	22,655

Source: Company filings.

Perhaps most significant, by the end of 1997, Amazon.com's best-seller lists had started to look more like the traditional bookstores' best-seller lists, indicating that Amazon.com's customers in particular, and on-line shoppers in general, were becoming more representative of the general population. Amazon.com's best-seller titles for 1997 are listed in Exhibit 3. Looking at this list, Amazon.com Senior Vice President David Risher noted, "Our top-selling title in 1996 was David S. Siegel's 'Creating Killer Web Sites.' In 1997, our number-one best-seller was Jon Krakauer's 'Into Thin Air,' an anguishing personal account of an ill-fated Mount Everest expedition. I can think of no better illustration of the changes in Internet shopping over the past year."

EXHIBIT 3

Amazon.com Best Seller Titles for 1997

Rank	*Book Title*	*Author*
1.	*Into Thin Air: A Personal Account of the Mount Everest Disaster*	Jon Krakauer
2.	*Cold Mountain*	Charles Frazier
3.	*The Perfect Storm: A True Story of Men Against the Sea*	Sebastian Junger
4.	*Angela's Ashes: A Memoir*	Frank McCourt
5.	*Creating Killer Web Sites: The Art of Third-Generation Site Design*	David S. Siegel
6.	*Songs in Ordinary Time*	Mary McGarry Morris
7.	*Visual Explanations: Images and Quantities, Evidence and Narrative*	Edward R. Tufte
8.	*The Visual Display of Quantitative Information*	Edward R. Tufte
9.	*Stones from the River*	Ursula Hegi
10.	*The God of Small Things*	Arundhati Roy

■ THE U.S. BOOK INDUSTRY

The U.S. book market was estimated at $17 billion in 1996, with 1.7 billion units sold. The market was expected to grow at a cumulative aggregate growth rate of 5 percent for the next five years, becoming a $21 billion business by 2000. Worldwide, the book market was estimated to be worth $82 billion, growing to $90 billion by 2000. The mail-order book business in the United States was valued at $588 million, for 92 million units in 1996, representing only 4 percent of total consumer book sales by revenue and 6 percent by units sold. The share of mail-order books had been declining steadily over the years, due to innovations in book retailing, which made bookstores look more attractive relative to mail-order catalogs. The book market was highly fragmented at the publisher level, with 50,000 publishers and several thousand independent booksellers. However, the industry was consolidating rapidly at the retail as well as the publisher level.

The Early Days

Before the din and noise of the 1990s, the retail book industry was pastoral and quiet, a place where competition was a part of the business, but not cut-throat. Independent sellers were the primary retailers of books. They selected various titles that they felt would be interesting to their clientele, and negotiated purchases with wholesalers and publishers. These stores carved out their specific market within the community, much like the mom-and-pop department stores before discount giants like Wal-Mart arrived. Independent booksellers were characterized by their devotion to literature, their ties to the community, and their knowledge of individual customer tastes.

During the late 1970s through the 1980s, the industry saw the "mallization" of America. Gradually, the industry saw the growth of the "chain" bookstores, which often mirrored the construction of new malls. The fundamental changes represented by these chain stores became apparent as they began to wield more and more power with publishers. In addition, books became more of a commodity as retailers of all types began to sell them (groceries, discount stores, drugstores, etc.).

Book Superstores

The 1990s have been called the "decade of the superstore." Much like their music and electronic counterparts, these behemoths were able to offer prices substantially lower than traditional independent bookstores, because of their economies of scale. They bought massive quantities of books directly from publishers at substantially better terms than independent retailers, who bought from book wholesalers and distributors. In addition, because of the sheer size of these stores, the superstores offered more shelf space and a wider selection of book titles.

To further entice customers, book superstores offered in-house restaurants/coffee shops, author visitations, and comfortable chairs to relax and read in. Consumers responded by visiting these stores in droves. As more and more of these stores were constructed, independents had been squeezed out, finding themselves unable to compete. By 1997, in the $18 billion dollar retail book industry, just over half of American readers bought their books in chain stores or super stores. Out of some 30,000 American bookstores, chain outlets accounted for 13,500 outlets in 1996, and this number was growing steadily at the expense of independent retailers.

Barnes & Noble With over 1,000 stores and retail sales of over $2.4 billion dollars in 1996, Barnes & Noble was the leading retailer in the bookstore business. Leonard Riggio, Barnes & Noble's chief operating officer, began his book-selling career while attending New York University in the early 1960s. Working as a clerk in the university bookstore, he became convinced that he could do a better job serving the students, and decided to open a competing store of his own. With a small investment, Riggio established the Student Book Exchange in Manhattan's Greenwich Village in 1965. In a few short years, SBX became one of New York's most successful independent bookstores, known for its staff, selection, and service.

In 1971, Riggio's thriving business, which by then included six other college bookstores, acquired the flagship Barnes & Noble Bookstore on Fifth Avenue and 18th Street in Manhattan. This venerable bookstore had fallen into decline after years of neglect. Riggio and his staff revived the institution and soon transformed it into "The World's Largest Bookstore" by expanding its selection to over 150,000 titles, including complete departments in medical, engineering, and technical books, as well as the most complete general trade book selection of any bookstore in America.

In the years that followed, the newly energized Barnes & Noble introduced many revolutionary concepts to the book industry, becoming the first bookseller to discount books, to advertise on television, and the first bookseller to widely implement book selling and merchandise techniques that made bookstores more accessible and friendly. Innovations included public seating, restrooms, huge children's departments, community event programs, specialty book boutiques, and the juxtaposition of library-like selection with contemporary promotional displays.

Throughout the 1980s, Barnes & Noble simultaneously expanded its franchise and refined its book selling approach. Under the leadership of Steve Riggio, Barnes & Noble launched a bargain book catalog, which had grown to over 500,000 regular customers. Steve also established Barnes & Noble Books, a publishing division, which specialized in reclaiming out-of-print books and reissuing them in quality, affordable editions. In 1987, the company purchased B. Dalton Bookseller, a leading national bookseller with stores primarily in regional shopping malls, from the Dayton Hudson Corporation.

In the late 1980s, Leonard & Steve pioneered the concept of book superstores. These mammoth bookstores combined a vast and deep selection of titles with experienced book selling staff with a warm, comfortable, spacious atmosphere. They featured cafes, huge selections of magazines, community event centers, and spacious and well-stocked children's boutiques. In January 1998, Barnes & Noble operated 431 book superstores in 47 states and the District of Columbia under the "Barnes & Noble Booksellers," "Bookstop," and "Bookstar" trade names. It also operated 577 mall-based bookstores in 46 states and the District of Columbia under the "B. Dalton Bookseller," "Doubleday Book Shops," and "Scribner's Bookstore" trade names. Barnes & Noble was also the world's largest supplier of books through direct-mail catalogs, and published books under its own name for exclusive sale through its retail bookstores and mail-order catalogs. Exhibit 4 shows the balance sheet for Barnes & Noble, and Exhibit 5 on page 502 shows the store revenue pattern for Barnes & Noble's superstores and mall-based bookstores.

Barnes & Noble's key assets included a state-of-the-art 350,000-square-foot distribution center in New Jersey that stocked 400,000 titles, a well-established infrastructure for order processing and fulfillment through its mail-order business, its strong relationships with 20,000 publishers, and its deep relationships with authors. These assets, coupled with Barnes & Noble's immense scale, allowed it to achieve a very favorable cost position, and positioned it well to enter into the on-line bookselling business.

Borders, Inc. Borders began in 1971, when Tom and Louis Borders opened what they considered to be a "serious" bookshop in the heart of Ann Arbor, an academic community in southeastern Michigan. As it grew, the first Borders store became known as a place where customers could find a friendly, well-informed staff to find

EXHIBIT 4

Barnes & Noble Financial Data ($ in Millions Except Earnings per Share)

	1995	*1996*	*1997E*	*1998E*
Superstores	$1,350.00	$1,861.10	$2,290.90	$2,630.30
Increase	41.7%	37.9%	23.1%	14.8%
Superstore comp.	6.9%	5.2%	7.7%	6.0%
Mall bookstores	$603.00	$565.10	$505.80	$470.70
Increase	−6.8%	−6.3%	−10.5%	−7.0%
Mall store comp.	−4.1%	−1.0%	−2.0%	−1.0%
Other revenues	$23.90	$22.00	$22.60	$24.80
Total revenues	$1,976.90	$2,448.20	$2,819.40	$3,125.80
COGS, buying & occupancy	1,269.00	1,566.70	1,795.70	1,982.90
Gross profit	707.9	881.5	1,023.70	1,142.90
Selling and administrative	376.8	456.2	523.1	573.2
Rental expenses	182.5	225.5	257.7	285.8
Preopening expenses	3	2	4	6
EBITDA	136.5	179.6	228.8	269.8
Depreciation and amortization	47.9	59.8	74.5	85.7
Interest expense/(income), net	28.1	38.3	45.1	46.9
Pretax income	60.5	81.5	109.2	137.2
Income taxes/(credit)	26.1	30.2	43.7	54.9
Net income (before extra items)	34.3	51.3	65.5	82.3
Extraordinary items	87.3	0	0	0
Net income	($53.00)	$51.30	$65.50	$82.30
EPS	($1.70)	$1.48	$1.85	$2.30
Average shares outstanding (MM)	31.2	34.6	35.5	35.8
As % of sales				
Gross margin	35.8%	36.0%	36.3%	36.6%
Selling and administrative	19.1%	18.6%	18.6%	18.3%
Rental expenses	9.2%	9.2%	9.1%	9.1%
Preopening expenses	0.6%	0.7%	0.5%	0.5%
EBITDA	6.9%	7.3%	8.1%	8.6%
Depreciation and amortization	2.4%	2.4%	2.6%	2.7%
Interest expense/(income), net	1.4%	1.6%	1.6%	1.5%
Pretax income	3.1%	3.3%	3.9%	4.4%
Tax rate	43.2%	37.0%	40.0%	40.0%
Net income (before extras)	1.7%	2.1%	2.3%	2.6%

Source: Company reports, Morgan Stanley Research.

exactly what they were looking for, or browse solo for hours through shelves stocked with a vast selection, including everything from African poetry to Zoroastrian theology.

This venture was so successful that the Borders brothers decided to open more stores. Their strategy was to target suburban markets, where demand for this type of bookstore was untested. The concept worked. Borders was a hit everywhere it opened. In the early 1990s, Borders began selling music in addition to books. As the company expanded, the Borders brothers decided to go national, and became a pub-

EXHIBIT 5

Barnes & Noble Store Revenue Buildup Model ($ in thousands)

	1995	*1996*	*1997E*	*1998E*
Quarterly Superstore Roll-up Model				
Beginning stores	268	358	431	491
Stores added	20	25		
Stores closed	–7	–18	–9	–10
Ending stores	358	431	491	551
Average quarterly stores	301	393	463	520
Superstore revenues	$1,350.00	$1,885.90	$2,279.90	$2,630.30
Sales per avg. store	$ 4.49	$ 4.80	$ 4.93	$ 5.06
Change	9.20%	6.80%	2.70%	2.70%
Quarterly Mall Store Roll-up Model				
Beginning stores	698	639	577	514
Stores added	1	37		
Stores closed	–69	–70	–70	–40
Ending stores	639	577	514	483
Average quarterly stores	676	615	551	502
Mall store revenues	$ 603.00	$ 558.70	$ 507.70	$ 470.70
Sales per avg. store	$ 0.89	$ 0.91	$ 0.92	$ 0.94
Change	–0.70%	1.80%	1.40%	1.90%
Change in mall revenue	–6.80%	–7.40%	–9.10%	–7.30%
Revenues by segment				
Superstores	$ 1,350	$ 1,861.1	$ 2,290.9	$ 2,630.3
Mall store	603	565.1	505.8	470.7
Other	23.9	22.5	22.6	24.8
Total	$1,976.90	$2,448.20	$2,819.40	$3,125.80
Percentage of Total				
Superstores	68.30%	76.00%	81.30%	84.10%
Mall stores	30.50%	23.10%	17.90%	15.10%
Other	1.20%	0.90%	0.70%	0.70%
Total	100.00%	100.00%	100.00%	100.00%

Source: Morgan Stanley Research.

licly held company. At the same time, large book chains started emulating the Borders concept.

In 1992, Borders was acquired by Kmart Corporation. This affiliation lasted three years. In April 1995, Borders bought its stock back from Kmart and raised new capital through an initial public offering. The company is now an independent, publicly owned corporation. Its shares traded on the New York Stock Exchange under the symbol BGP.

By the end of 1996, Borders was the second largest operator of book superstores and the largest operator of mall-based bookstores in the United States. The Company operated 142 large format books and music superstores and 16 book superstores under the Borders name, 936 mall-based and other bookstores under the Waldenbooks name, and three music superstores under the Planet Music name. The company had sales of approximately $2.0 billion in 1996 and $1.8 billion in 1995. In 1996, the Company opened 41 new Borders books and music superstores. Borders superstores achieved average sales per square foot of $259 and average sales per superstore of $7.2 million in 1996.

Borders did have a Web site on the Internet, but it was only a "placeholder" for informational purposes. The company had not entered the on-line retail sales, but had announced its intentions to do so. It was generally recognized that the company had enough brand awareness and working capital to make an impact when it did enter the on-line bookselling business. However, the date for the launch of its Web site was delayed several times, and as of January 1998, the company had still not launched its commerce site.

Book Wholesaling and Distribution

The book development process begins with an author negotiating a publishing contract with a publisher like Simon and Schuster, Doubleday, or HarperCollins. If the publisher is convinced that the book project is commercially viable, the publisher buys the rights from the author, generally with the payment of an advance against royalties, and begins the process of publishing and promoting the book. The publisher is responsible for the production, promotion, and distribution of the book. Promotional media, book reviews by famous critics, and organized special events, such as author book signing sessions, are all vehicles used by publishers to create awareness and demand. Retailers place advance orders for a fraction of books that are supported with substantial promotional dollars. Other titles, called the backlist, are purchased by retailers based on the historical sales and/or anticipated demand of the individual title.

Independent bookstores could keep only about 25,000 books in inventory, and did not have the physical space or the capital to invest in large quantities of an individual title. This made it impractical for publishers to sell book titles in small lots to the 15,000 independent bookstores in the United States. Publishers therefore sold a majority of books to book wholesalers and distributors. Wholesalers were simply order takers, while distributors also had sales forces that sold to retailer accounts. Wholesalers and distributors acted as a buffer in the distribution channel, buying books in bulk from the publisher and selling them in smaller lots to retailers at a markup.

Publishers The U.S. book publishing industry was highly fragmented. The top 20 publishing companies represented 60 percent of all retail sales, with the top three being Warner Books–Time Warner (sales of $3.7 billion in 1995), Simon & Schuster–Viacom Corporation (sales of $2.2 billion in 1995), and Pearson–Financial Times (sales of $1.75 billion in 1995). Publishers typically guaranteed 100 percent refunds to distributors on unsold books. Book demand was notoriously hard to predict, so first print runs ranged from as low as 10,000 copies for new authors to 500,000 copies for well-known authors. This uncertainty had a huge impact on the profitability of publishers, arising from the cost of returns. Between 40 and 50 percent of all books printed were returned unsold by retailers. The returns represented not only a loss of revenue, but high transportation costs. Publishers made money on less than 10 percent of their titles, with the rest of the titles barely breaking even or losing money. The publisher's economics for a typical hardcover book are shown in Exhibit 6 on page 504.

Wholesalers The task of wholesalers is to distribute books to independent booksellers and retail chains, based on orders placed by them. Publishers supply books to wholesalers at approximately 50 percent of their retail price, who in turn get a gross margin of between 6 and 8 percent of the retail price. Unlike the fragmented publisher market, the book industry was highly concentrated at the wholesaler level. The market leader, Ingram Book Company, held over a 50 percent market share in 1997. The

EXHIBIT 6

Economics of a Typical Hardcover Book for Publishers

	($)	*Percentage of list price*
Book list price	$20	100%
Wholesaler margin	$ 9.70	48.5%
Manufacturing cost (printing, binding, jacket design, composition, typesetting, paper, ink)	$ 2.00	10%
Publisher overhead (marketing, fulfillment)	$ 3.00	15%
Returns and allowances	$ 3.00	15%
Authors' royalties	$ 2.00	10%
Publisher's operating profits	$ 0.30	1.5%

other large players were Baker & Taylor and Book Wholesalers. Due to their slim operating margins, information technology was critical to the success of wholesalers. For instance, Ingram was able to use electronic ordering and fast delivery to achieve a lower cost position and superior margins. The wafer-thin wholesaler margins were being squeezed further due to the rising popularity of superstores. Companies such as Barnes & Noble and Borders ordered initial supplies of major titles directly from publishers, cutting out wholesalers in the process. Wholesalers represented around 30 percent of publisher sales, and their average net profit was between 1 and 1.5 percent of gross sales. The structure of consumer book distribution channels is illustrated in Exhibit 7.

EXHIBIT 7

Consumer Book Distribution Channels

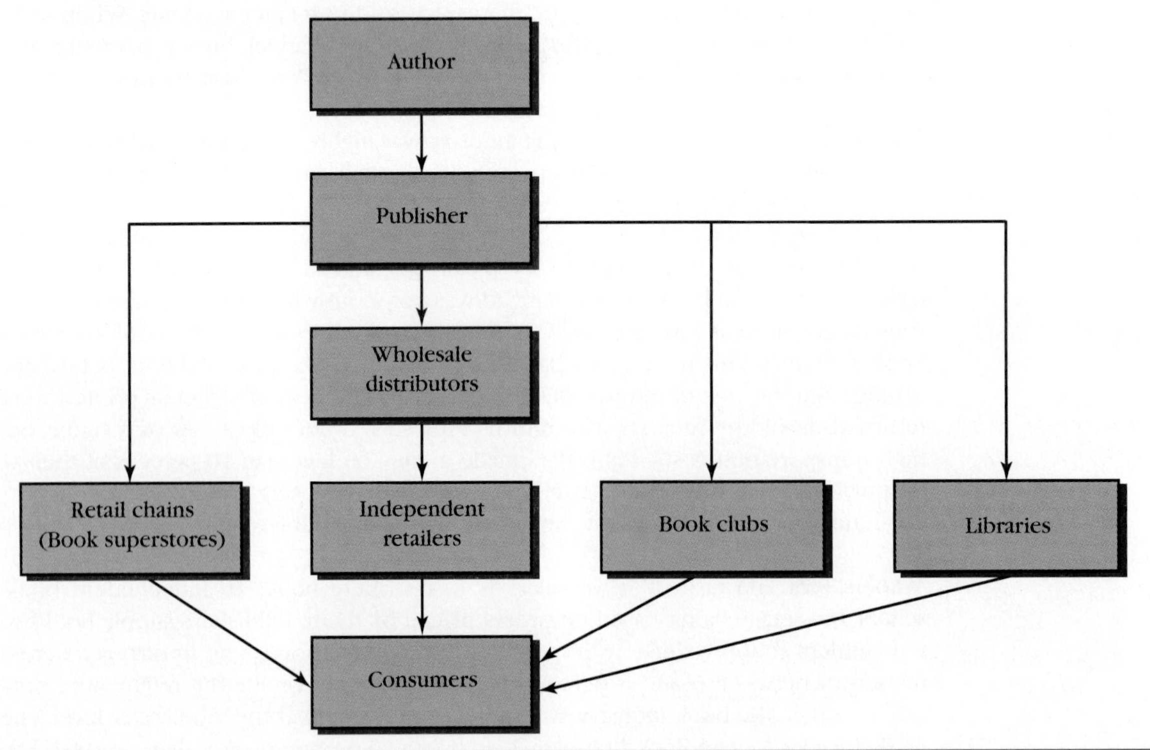

THE ON-LINE BOOKSELLING BUSINESS

On-line bookselling is one of the most developed retail concepts on the Internet. As a product category, books are particularly well suited to on-line sales. Books are popular, standardized, nonperishable, easy to ship, inexpensive, and can be effectively demonstrated and sampled on-line. On the Internet, books can be easily ordered and quickly delivered anywhere in the world. Additionally, on-line booksellers had unlimited "shelf space," so that customers can search and choose their favorite books from huge selections.

The on-line bookselling business operated with the same basic supply chain as traditional booksellers. The key difference was that on-line sellers like Amazon owned little real estate and carried very little inventory. They acted like retail brokers, taking orders from on-line clients and placing orders with wholesalers, who shipped the books to the retailer the next day, where they were repackaged and shipped to customers. Total turnaround time was usually three days or less.

Competition in the on-line bookselling business heated up in 1997, after Amazon.com's successful entry. On May 13, Barnes & Noble debuted its Web site with 30 percent discount on all hardcovers and 20 percent discount on all paperbacks. Amazon.com responded with 40 percent discounts on the Amazon 500, its best-sellers and other hot titles. Additionally, Amazon.com offered 10 percent discount on all of the other books. By mid-May, CUC's Book Stacks announced 40 percent discounts on New York Times best-sellers, in addition to its discounts of 15 to 30 percent on most of its 465,000 titles. Book Stacks offered members of its Frequent Buyers Club ($29.95 per year) discounts of 30 percent on 350,000 titles. It also offered Bookmarks, a sort of frequent buyer program for its customers. In addition to these large competitors, a large number of smaller book-related sites had begun to spring up all over the Web. Exhibit 8 lists the most popular retail book-related sites as of June 1997. Exhibit 9 (page 506) shows the strategic positioning of the main players in the book industry, in terms of their emphasis on the marketplace versus the marketspace, and the scope of their offerings.

EXHIBIT 8

Popular On-Line Bookselling Sites

A Sentimental Journey	Blackwell Science	Clarke & Stone	Mind's Eye Fiction
Adventurous Traveler Bookstore	Blue Moon Bookshop	Classic Gift Shoppe	Moon Travel
Albatross Specialty Booksellers	Book Look	Computer Manuals	New Badger Books
Albion Books	Book Stacks	Cook Inlet Book Company	Paper Ships Books & Crystals
Amazon.com	Books Now	The Cookbook Store	Planetary Publications
Annie's Book Stop of Kennewick	Book Serve	C. W. Hay Bookseller	Plum Choices
Antiquarian Booksellers	Book Site	Eastgate on the Web	Sasuga Japanese Bookstore
Armenian Reference Books	Book World!	Future Fantasy Bookstore	Thaddeus Books
Astrology Et Al Bookstore	Bookstore at Houghton Mifflin	Internet Book Shop	TOR Science Fiction & Fantasy
AudioBook Source	Breakwater Books	JoyMe by Mail	Traders Press Inc.
Audiobooks by Jincim	Cascadilla Press	LMG Enterprises	Waite Group Press
Bear Mountain	Charlesbank Bookshop	Macmillan Digital	

Source: The All Internet Shopping Directory.

EXHIBIT 9

Strategic Positioning Map for Players in the U.S. Bookselling Business

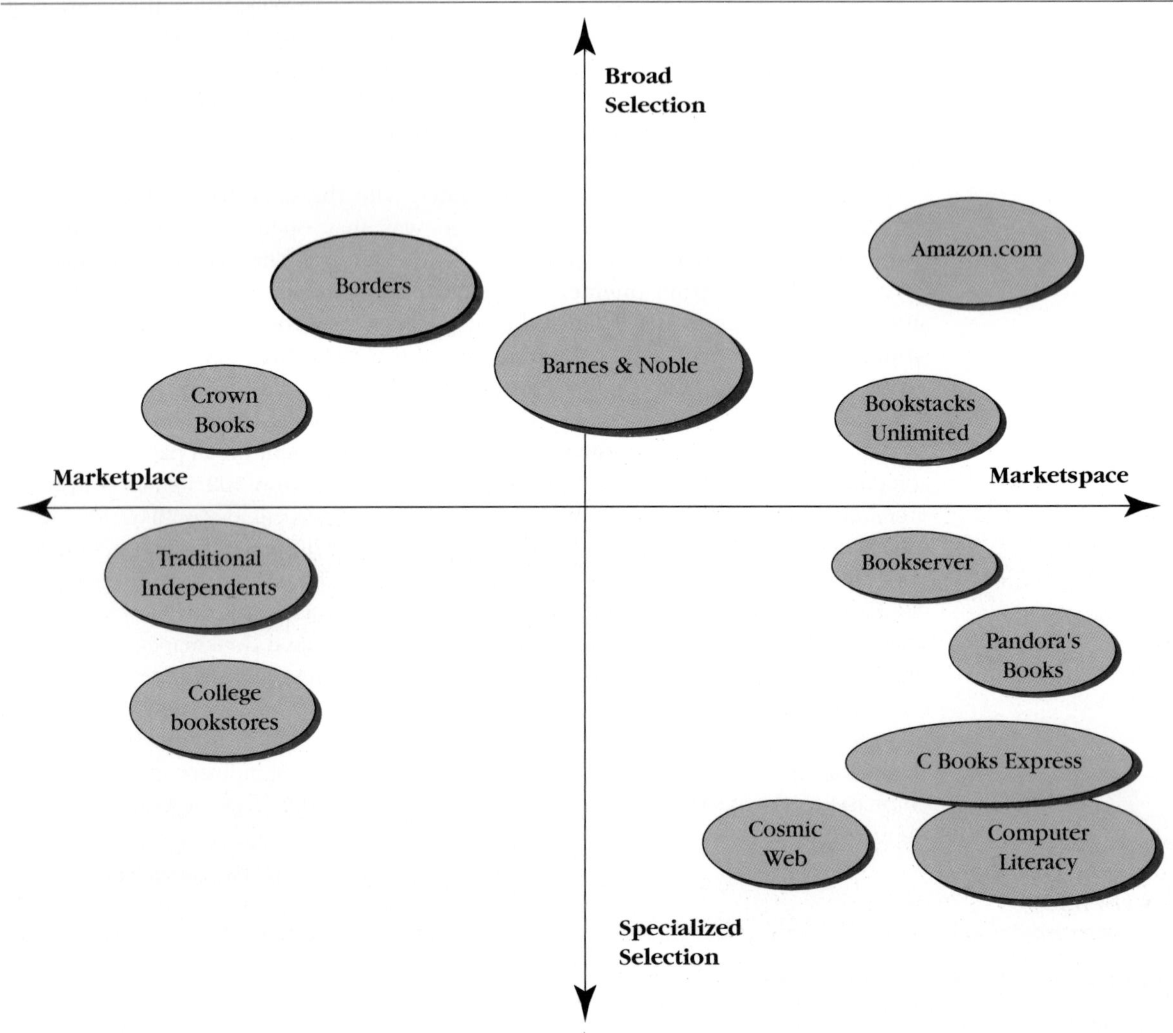

Amazon.com's Strategy and Business Design

While Amazon.com was the clear leader in Internet bookselling, it was not the first book seller on the Internet. However, Amazon was the first to sell books exclusively on the Internet with an organization and business processes designed expressly to support on-line sales and to transform the book-buying experience. From the beginning, Jeff Bezos carefully designed his business to take advantage of the Internet by offering a vast array of titles, a friendly shopping experience, a tightly managed supply chain, a responsive customer support organization, and strong investments in brand and traffic building. These moves were aimed at quickly developing relationships based on trust and positive feedback with a large number of customers. To emphasize the fact that the company offered over 10 times the selection of the largest traditional bookstore (2.5 million titles, including more than 1 million out-of-print books that are not readily available), he named the company after Earth's largest river, and chose the tagline "Earth's largest bookstore." Amazon.com's success could be attributed to several factors.

First Mover Advantage Heralded by many as the first real successful Web marketer, Amazon.com benefited from being the first in the industry. In the early days of the Internet, the on-line community was a tightly knit group, and word of a real Web-based seller spread quickly among the early adopters. Consequently, a loyal following appeared to support Amazon's early efforts, which many hoped would be an indicator of the potential success of electronic commerce in general. The business community at large was also hungry for a success story and was quick to pick up on Jeff Bezos's vision. Stories about the early success of Amazon.com created a virtuous circle. As in many other categories of electronic commerce, mind share led to traffic, which led to market share. Market share in turn led to publicity and a further increase in mind share.

Low Overhead Costs Amazon.com's on-line business design resulted in significantly lower overheads relative to brick-and-mortar-based retailers. Amazon.com shipped a book only when an order was received by a customer, instead of maintaining a large inventory of books, and waiting for them to sell or to be returned to the publisher. It kept a small inventory of popular books in its warehouses (less than 1,000 titles), with the rest being shipped directly from wholesalers. This direct shipping model allowed Amazon.com to borrow strength from the highly efficient logistics systems of large book wholesalers like Ingram. The low inventory levels also meant that Amazon.com could turn over its inventory 40 to 60 times a year, versus only 2 to 3 times a year for a traditional book superstore. Moreover, the fact that customers physically never entered the store meant that the inventory was stored in a warehouse that was far cheaper to operate than traditional bookstores, which relied on their prime location to attract customers. However, these cost advantages were somewhat offset by the lower profitability that resulted from paying the wholesalers for logistical services. Exhibit 10 compares the overhead structure for land-based bookstores with an on-line bookstore like Amazon.com.

Cross-Marketing—The Amazon Associates Program In July 1996, Amazon.com initiated an innovative cross-marketing program called the Amazon Associates Program. This program encouraged other Web sites to link book titles directly to Amazon.com. In return, the sites received a commission of between 5 and 15 percent for books sold due to traffic originating from their sites. This cross-marketing program provided Amazon.com with incremental sales and distribution reach into specialized audiences that the associates attracted to their sites. By the end of 1997, Amazon.com had signed up over 28,000 associates. In addition, Amazon.com struck several larger co-branding deals, such as the deal with Netscape where Amazon.com became the exclusive bookseller for popular books related to Netscape's products.

EXHIBIT 10

Comparison of Operating Models of Land-Based Versus On-Line Bookstore

	Traditional Book Superstore	*On-Line Bookstore (Amazon.com)*
Titles per store	175,000	2,500,000
Occupancy cost (% of revenues)	12%	<4%
Revenue per operating employee	$100,000	$300,000
Inventory turns	2-3X	40-60X
Sales per square foot	$250	$2,000
Rent per square foot	$20	$8

Source: Morgan Stanley Research.

Customer Service From its inception, Bezos strongly emphasized customer service at Amazon.com. He realized that the price advantage and variety advantage offered by Amazon.com would eventually be eroded by on-line competitors, and customer service would become Amazon.com's key competitive advantage. Every order placed was immediately acknowledged, and customers were informed the moment the order was shipped. Amazon.com instituted a no-questions-asked, money-back warranty and promptly credited customers for returned books. Every piece of electronic mail sent to Amazon.com's customer service department received a personalized reply. Dan Camacho, a publisher affairs executive at Amazon.com commented, "Our customer service representatives are much more than telemarketers. They are book lovers, and are very knowledgeable about books. In fact, customers who call in and speak to our representatives are amazed at their ability to talk about books, and to recommend books that they personally have read and liked."

■ THE ON-LINE BOOK-BUYING EXPERIENCE

From a customer perspective, Amazon.com's on-line business design resulted in a buying experience that was qualitatively very different from the traditional buying experience in a physical bookstore. The differences in the buying experience demonstrate that on-line bookselling is a very different business than conventional bookselling.

Convenience

On-line bookstores were available 24 hours a day, seven days a week, 365 days of the year.[1] Further, customers could visit on-line bookstores directly from the home or the office, and from anywhere in the world where Internet access was available. Traditional bookstores were limited to specific business hours.

Browsing Experience

Amazon.com tried to create a rich, entertaining Web site that encouraged clients to return to the site on a regular basis. The site offered professional book reviews, author interviews, reader comments, and personalized book recommendations. These features were designed to enhance reader involvement. While many readers found the on-line browsing experience vastly superior, others disagreed, noting that the ambience of a Barnes & Noble, with its comfortable overstuffed chairs and Starbucks coffee, could never be replicated on-line. Unlike grocery shopping, which consumers viewed as an unpleasant chore, people enjoyed visiting bookstores and browsing serendipitously for books that might "catch their eye."

Searching

The search capability was a strong differentiator for on-line bookstores. In physical bookstores, books were grouped physically by subjects, and customers had to walk the aisles to look for a book. Further, customers were limited to the number of books in each section selected for display. In an on-line store, customers could search through millions of books by title, topic, or author in a matter of seconds. In addition, on-line bookstores could record customer purchase histories and book

[1] In practice, however, system outages could seriously jeopardize this proposition. For instance, on January 7, 1998, Amazon.com's site went down for almost a day, resulting in lost sales of $600,000, and a drop of almost 10 percent in Amazon.com's stock price.

preferences and use these data to create personalized recommendations that could be dispatched via e-mail or displayed when customers visited the site.

Editorial Content

Amazon.com offered a lot of information and content to assist customers in making better book purchase decisions. Customers could not only get the publisher's comments offered by traditional books, they could also see professional book reviews and rankings from Amazon.com editors, excerpts, and titles from the *New York Times Book Review*, *The New Yorker*, *Entertainment Weekly*, National Public Radio, and *The Oprah Winfrey Show*, among others. Amazon.com also offered reader services that kept customers informed about new books. One service, called "Eyes," tracked every newly released book in the customer's designated subjects of interest, and generated e-mail messages whenever it found a new book that the customer might be interested in. Another service, called "Editors," was run by departmental editors, who informed readers of interesting new releases in specific subject areas. The editorial content was designed to create customer loyalty and to attract customers for reasons other than selection and price.

Delivery

In traditional bookstores, books chosen are typically on display unless customers place orders at the store. Out-of-stock books could take weeks to be delivered. On-line bookstores typically shipped books within 2 to 3 business days. However, they also took much longer to find and deliver out-of-print or hard-to-find books. Dan Camacho noted that Amazon.com had established an excellent network of relationships with sources of out-of-print books, and saw this as a competitive advantage for Amazon.com. On the other extreme, books that could be shipped straight from the warehouse by on-line booksellers could arrive faster than three days. Quicker shipping time was an advantage for on-line booksellers who had well-stocked and strategically located book warehouses.

Payment

In traditional bookstores, most customers bought a limited number of books that they could carry, and they could pay for the books in cash, checks, or with credit cards. On-line book buying had no limits on the number of books customers could buy, but payment methods were restricted to credit cards. Although security concerns about credit card payments were on the decline, some customers still felt uncomfortable about using credit cards on-line.

Marketing Communications

Physical bookstores spent significant amounts of money to publicize new books. While it might seem that on-line bookstores would have very low advertising expenses, marketing expenses for on-line bookstores were actually higher for on-line bookstores than for traditional bookstores. This was especially the case in the early stages when customer "eyeballs" were up for grabs, and building traffic was of paramount importance. One of the early opinions of the attractiveness of Web-based selling was that, because all sites were on the Internet, location no longer mattered. The problem with this logic is that location indeed did matter, and customers could not find an on-line bookseller just because it existed on the Internet! On-line booksellers had to find ways to attract traffic by advertising the existence of the site or by linking to other sites with relevant content. On June 8, 1997, Amazon.com announced agreements to advertise on the pages of three of the largest Web traffic sites: America Online, Yahoo!, and Excite. Amazon.com spent $6.1 million on marketing and sales efforts in 1996, and $38.9 million in 1997. Its biggest competitor, Barnes & Noble, also signed a $20 million deal with America Online for the privilege of being the exclusive bookseller on AOL, and getting access to 11 million AOL customers.

■ THE UNSEEN BATTLE—DISTRIBUTION AND SUPPLY CHAIN MANAGEMENT

Despite the publicity surrounding the competition among on-line booksellers to create world-class Web sites, experts opined that the on-line book war would eventually be won in the warehouse. According to Bezos, "the logistics of distribution are the iceberg below the waterline of on-line bookselling." If Amazon.com promised quick delivery, particularly to the digital-age technophiles that comprised its core customers, its fulfillment system had to deliver on the promise. At Amazon, everything from the Seattle, Washington location, to the culture in the distribution centers was designed for efficiency, accuracy, and speed. As margins were squeezed by competition, operating efficiencies and the lack of store overhead would determine if Amazon could ever make money in on-line bookselling.

Amazon's distribution system was based more on redistribution than warehousing, along the lines of Wal-Mart's famous cross-docking model. In fact, according to Dan Camacho, very few books were warehoused at Amazon.com's Seattle complex. The warehouse carried less than a thousand of the most popular titles. Rather, orders were placed on-line with wholesalers such as Ingram as they were received. The distributor shipped the books overnight to Seattle, where Amazon employees repackaged and shipped the orders to customers the next day.

Amazon.com worked with a dozen wholesalers, but obtained almost 60 percent of all books it sold through Ingram Book Group, a Nashville-based wholesaler. Ingram was the most influential force in Internet bookselling. Because of the fierce competition in the market, there was tremendous pressure for cheaper ways to get books into customers' hands. Ingram was a paragon of operational efficiency. It stocked nearly 500,000 titles in seven strategically located warehouses around the country. It shipped virtually all orders the day they were received. About 85 percent of shipments arrived at retailers' loading docks within 24 hours, and 95 percent within 48 hours. However, Ingram's efficiency came at the expense of its wholesale markup, which amounted to a couple of percentage points above the price of a book purchased directly from a publisher. On-line vendors also incurred considerable costs in repackaging and shipping books to their customers. These expenses weighed heavily in a low-margin business, negating the one major cost advantage intrinsic to the virtual bookshop: minimal investment in bricks and mortar.

To reduce its dependence on Ingram and to improve its structural margins, Amazon.com planned to move aggressively into self-distribution. In September 1997, it announced the expansion of its Seattle warehouse by 70 percent, and the leasing of a new warehouse in New Castle, Delaware. These moves would enable Amazon.com to stock 200,000 to 300,000 titles, and to buy the bulk of its books directly from publishers. To help implement its new distribution system, Amazon hired Richard Dalzell, a logistics expert, from Wal-Mart stores. The self-distribution strategy mirrored Barnes & Noble's strategy of gradually scaling back its purchases from wholesalers and increasingly buying directly from publishers.

Ingram in turn moved to defend its franchise and to make on-line booksellers even more dependent on Ingram. It announced that in 1998, it would introduce a new "drop-shipping" service to reduce on-line booksellers' operating costs. Ingram would offer its customers the option of shipping orders directly to consumers. Drop-shipping would cost more than the current wholesale shipping service, but would still be cheaper than repackaging and reshipping. Drop-shipping would also reduce delivery to consumers by a day or two at a minimum. However, these efficiencies would come at the cost of increased complexity in sorting, and the possibility of customer service being compromised if the wholesaler/distributor made mistakes in order fulfillment.

Traditional booksellers like Barnes & Noble entering the on-line bookselling business had an advantage over on-line booksellers in distribution, because they already possessed warehouses. This allowed them to ship books quicker, and to gain a few percentage points in margins by cutting out the wholesalers. However, the distribution systems used by traditional booksellers were designed to stock retail store shelves, and not to ship directly to customers. The retailer-oriented distribution systems created more overhead, fewer inventory turns, slower response time, and poorer service than highly focused and efficient wholesalers like Ingram. To adapt these systems, existing bookstore chains would have to reengineer the existing processes or start from scratch, both costly investments.

■ COMPETITIVE RESPONSE TO AMAZON.COM

Barnes & Noble (www.barnesandnoble.com)

Barnes & Noble (B&N) launched its Internet site (www.barnesandnoble.com) on May 13 to keep industry pioneer Amazon.com from dominating the Web and to preempt rival Borders Group Inc.'s entry. As the leading bookseller, B&N perceived the Internet as a critical new channel that allowed the company to leverage existing assets and strengths. These included a large important distribution center, sophisticated inventory tracking and replenishment systems, excellent economies of scale, national advertising campaign and brand name, and excellent relationships with 20,000 publishers and authors.

Revenues for barnesandnoble.com had doubled in each of the first three quarters that it had been in business, from $2.1 million in the first full quarter to $4 million in the second quarter, and an expected $8 million in the third quarter ending January 31, 1998. The company projected $100 million in sales for 1998, but analysts were skeptical, noting that barnesandnoble.com's sales were running short of projections. Moreover, with marketing costs in 1997 estimated at $30 million to $40 million, barnesandnoble.com would lose money even at a sales level of $100 million. The company reported over 250,000 individual accounts, and more than 40 percent of its business came from repeat buyers. This was far behind the 1.5 million accounts and 58 percent repeat business that Amazon.com boasted by the end of 1997.

However, analysts at Morgan Stanley concluded that, thanks to scale and asset sharing, the on-line division of B&N would potentially be more profitable than Amazon.com. It had the same structural low operating expenses as Amazon.com, but, unlike Amazon.com, it could share marketing and overhead expenses with its larger physical entity. This resulted in a significant structural margin advantage for B&N relative to Amazon.com in the on-line bookselling business. Exhibit 11 on page 512 provides a comparison of operating models for Amazon.com and B&N. The analysis assumes three scenarios for Amazon.com. The analysis shows that based on the best-case scenario, Amazon.com will begin to hit scale when it reaches a $200 million to $300 revenue run-rate sometime in 1998–99 and can potentially become profitable in 1999 after burning $25 to $50 million in cash. Amazon.com benefited from not having large operating expenses and large inventory typical of a retail channel such as B&N, but Amazon.com's gross margins were expected to be lower due to the dependence on wholesalers for inventory. While self-distribution would improve margins, these savings would be partially offset by the fixed costs and overheads that Amazon.com would incur in operating large book warehouses.

Features Barnes & Noble assumed a slightly different approach to its book site. Whereas Amazon.com focused on one-on-one interaction, B&N attempted to build an

EXHIBIT 11

Comparison of Operating Models of Amazon.com and Barnes & Noble at Scale Operations, Under Different Gross Margin Scenarios

	Amazon.com projections at scale operations ($200–$300 million revenue run rate)				
	Low Gross Margin Scenario	*OK Gross Margin Scenario*	*High Gross Margin Scenario*	***Amazon.com 1997 Results (Actuals)***	***B&N 1997 Results (Estimated)***
Revenue ($m)	100%	100%	100%	$147.8	$2,819
Gross margin	16%	20%	23–27%	19.5%	36%
SG&A/R&D	13%	16%	16–21%	39.3%	19%
Rent/Store expense	0%	0%	0%	0%	9%
Total operating expenses	13%	16%	16–21%	39.3%	
Pretax margin	3%	4%	5–10%	NM	4%
Inventory ($m)				$8.97	$835
Inventory turns				42	2.1
Employees				600	26,000
Revenue/Employee				$246,000	$92,000

NM, not meaningful.

Source: Morgan Stanley Research.

on-line community reflective of the casual reading-room atmosphere its real stores are known for. Connecting readers via literary forums, events, and live on-line interviews, the B&N site tried to create a distinct personality. It copied the design, navigation, and search functions of Amazon.com, even at level of the fonts used. Similar to Amazon.com, each subject area contained articles from B&N editors, interviews, and a top 10 list. B&N also provided personalization features, although these features were less developed and less well-thought-out than those of Amazon.com.

Pricing B&N priced its books aggressively, and entered the market with deeper discounts than other on-line or retail stores. Customers received across-the-board discounts of 30 percent on hardcovers and 20 percent on paperbacks. Typical discounts at B&N stores were 20 percent for hardcovers and 10 percent for paperbacks. In contrast, Amazon.com offered 40 percent off the "Amazon Top 500," and a 10 percent discount on other books. This meant that it was cheaper to buy the top 500 books at Amazon.com and to buy all others on barnesandnoble.com. B&N claimed that most on-line sales would come from outside the Amazon 500, based on the fact that in 1997, best sellers had accounted for less than 3 percent of B&N's sales on AOL.

Alliances B&N followed Amazon.com's lead in establishing a network of strategic alliances and partnerships to gain mind share and market share in on-line bookselling. On the technological side, B&N developed partnerships with Microsoft, Hewlett-Packard, Reach Networks, Business Data Services, and Interactive Bureau. Particularly important was its alliance with the Firefly Network, which allowed it to launch the Personalized Book Recommendations area using Firefly's collaborative filtering software. On the marketing side, B&N signed a $10 million deal to become the exclusive book retailing site on America Online. It offered more than 1 million titles to AOL's 11 million subscribers at a 30 percent discount on hardcover and a 20 percent discount for paperbacks. B&N also entered into exclusive agreements with on-line publishers and site networks, including the New York Times Online, CondeNet, Time Inc., New Media, ESPN SportsZone, CNN Interactive, Knight-Ridder New Media, ZDNet, and Wired Digital. It also became the exclusive book merchant on search and navigation engines like Lycos, Web-Crawler, and InfoSpace. Unlike Amazon.com, B&N did not focus on marketing its own site, relying instead on its brand name and distribution partnerships out of the gate.

Information Technology Infrastructure A combination of Unix and Windows NT technologies helped B&N to deliver some new capabilities via the Internet by leveraging the technology and expertise it used in many of its superstores. Most of the database information for the site already existed on B&N's Unix servers used by its bookstores. Additionally, B&N had begun to port to its Web site features such as author and book title searches that were developed for in-store use, and services such as order processing, that were developed for a merchandising data warehouse. To handle some of the hardware scalability, reliability, and fault-tolerance requirements for a 24-hour site, the company used a "modular distributed approach" in developing its information technology (IT) infrastructure. Instead of relying on a few large servers to power its entire site, B&N built a "Web farm" consisting of several Unix and Windows NT servers. By distributing applications across several servers and then duplicating them in geographically dispersed mirror locations, B&N hoped to minimize the risk associated with unexpected hardware downtime. The distributed architecture also gave B&N flexibility to grow the system as its needs expanded.

CUC International's Book Stacks (www.books.com)

Book Stacks Unlimited (www.books.com) was the on-line book venture of CUC International; the membership-based consumer services giant that had 66.3 million consumer accounts worldwide. An early entrant into the on-line bookselling business (October 1994), Books.com made a splash by knocking 40 percent off the suggested retail price for all *New York Times* best sellers. In addition, it discounted the majority of the titles in its on-line database by 15 percent. It also started a frequent buyer club in which members paid an annual fee of $29.95 to receive 30 percent off about 350,000 titles.

Books.com used a different business model than its competitors. It relied on CUC's membership model, where its revenues would primarily come from subscription fees, and not from transaction revenues. Its success would depend on how quickly the company could attract new members to the services, and how much the company could get customers to pay for subscribing to the service. Like its competitors, Book Stacks offered impressive search and index capabilities, as well as enhanced features such as chats and profiling. Book Stacks used agent technology to help readers determine whether certain titles fell within their areas of interest. The program, called Affinity, allowed customers to see what other titles had been bought by people who bought the book being evaluated. The service had been developed using five years of customer purchase information, was completely anonymous, and required no effort on the part of the consumer. Similar features were also offered by Amazon.com on its site, using the Group Lens collective filtering technology from Net Perceptions.

Niche Players

With the success of Amazon.com, many independent booksellers had created their own Web sites. To counter Amazon.com's size and variety advantage, these players emphasized their knowledge of specific subjects, and their friendly customer service. Many niche players focused their sales in one specific field, such as cooking, computer books, or self-improvement. While the number of niche players was too numerous to count, the niche business was growing, and many of these sites had become successful. Together, they posed a very real threat to the general-purpose "category killer" on-line bookstores like Amazon.com and Barnes & Noble.

The following were some notable niche players.

1stbooks.com Entrepreneurs David Hilliard and Tim Jacobs founded 1stbooks.com to provide authors with a new and inexpensive means of publishing and selling their works. 1stbooks was more than just a virtual store or another sales channel for the mega-publishers and mega-retailers. It was a vehicle for authors to inexpensively test the market and self-publish their works, without incurring the production expenses of regular publishers. Ownership of the book or work product and control of its publication were important to authors, in some cases even to their heirs. 1stbooks addressed this issue by structuring its site as a "pay for service" library, so that authors could "publish" their work and still retain full ownership and rights. For less than $500, they digitized the author's book and published it on the Web, along with a "digital book jacket." This "virtual cover" offered prospective readers much the same information as a traditional book jacket: a cover design or illustration, a summary of the book, and a biographical sketch of the author. "A typical book in the library can be purchased and downloaded for $5.95 to $9.95, less than the cost of most paperbacks. A few technical books are offered for as much as $25.00," noted Hilliard.

Buyers could download books electronically, and were offered a choice of formats. The site also offered authors full-service accounting and record keeping, as well as a detailed marketing, customer tracking, and prospect-to-sale ratio information. Authors received a royalty of 40 percent of the selling price, less any credit card fees, on each "book" sold. Commenting on his business model, Hilliard said, "The beauty of this concept is that it is a pure market-driven approach. The author is not at the mercy of the editor or the agent to determine whether there is an audience for the work."

Bargain Book Warehouse This niche player specialized in low shipping prices. It offered a flat shipping rate of $4.25 per order. The quality of the site's design, navigation, and load times were excellent, although the selection was somewhat limited. For customers who placed large orders, the BBW pricing approach would result in significant savings over the major on-line booksellers.

Used-Book Browsing Canadian company Advanced Book Exchange provided a single search engine for hundreds of used and antiquarian bookstores. Readers who were interested in obscure or out-of-print works were generally at the mercy of a few local shops in the physical world. ABS specialized in these hard-to-locate books. For instance, ABE was able to find three copies of an old autobiography published in 1950. Having found the store that carried the book, customers could contact the store directly, or place an electronic order using a credit card. The main obstacle with this business model was that most of these tiny offbeat stores were not sophisticated enough to accept credit cards.

In addition to these niche players, several publishers had investigated the possibility of selling their books directly to customers via the Internet. Companies like Simon and Schuster and Warner Books were large enough to make the investments needed to create traffic on their sites. However, there were questions about the level of brand equity that publishers possessed. Consumers generally bought books because of the author or the title, not because they had been published by a particular publisher.

■ STRATEGIC CHALLENGES

Operational Challenges

In the near term, Amazon.com's biggest challenge was to tweak its business design to improve its structural margin advantages and to achieve profitability. Amazon.com's financial success would depend upon two key metrics—its revenue growth, and its gross margin. While revenue growth had been explosive, and was expected to continue to be healthy through 1998, gross margins were a matter of serious concern. Amazon's gross margins were less than 20 percent, far below Barnes & Noble's gross margins of 36 percent. While its growing scale and self-distribution plans would improve gross margins, fierce price competition threatened to eat further into margins. Barriers to entry into the on-line bookselling business were low, and Amazon.com had watched several competitors enter the business by copying its successful processes and services, and undercutting it on price. Further, major competitors could leverage existing assets such as their physical store infrastructure (Barnes & Noble), or their existing membership base (CUC). Amazon.com could not rely on cross-subsidization or asset leveraging, and had to build everything from scratch.

Bezos wondered how to balance Amazon.com's aggressive pricing against the need to preserve margins, and how to balance marketing investments against the need to become profitable. He also wondered how to balance the need to keep lower inventories in Amazon.com's warehouses against the need to provide books quickly to customers. Already, Barnes & Noble was aggressively promoting the fact that it could ship books quicker to their customers, because it shipped over 50 percent of its books directly from its warehouses. Finally, Bezos was unclear about the extent to which Amazon.com should use the drop-shipping service offered by Ingram Books. While drop-shipping would reduce costs and improve speed of delivery, Amazon.com would run the risk of compromising service quality, and would become more dependent on Ingram. Some experts suggested that Amazon.com should focus on what it did best (customer relationship management and software), and leave the logistics and shipping to experts like Ingram, whose core competencies lay in shipping and warehousing.

Bezos's operational challenges were neatly summarized by an industry analyst, who observed, "Book selling and retail are two low-margin businesses. Even successful giants like Barnes & Noble are barely profitable, achieving net margins of 2 percent or less. Investors have to realize that Amazon.com is not an Internet company. It is a *retailer.* The retail business is one tough price-competitive business in the real world, and indications are that Internet retailing will be no different. In a world where customers are one mouse-click away from leaving, loyalty is tenuous at best. While Amazon.com will sell a lot of books, it has yet to show that it can ever make money."

Growing the Franchise

International Expansion In 1997, book superstores and on-line bookselling was primarily a U.S. phenomenon. In other parts of the world, such as Europe, Asia, or Latin America, book retailing was still in its infancy by comparison. Experts believed that this situation would soon change radically. Of the 3 million book titles in print worldwide, only 1.1 million were in English. This fact, coupled with the strong international sales that Amazon.com had seen in its early years, convinced Bezos that international expansion was an attractive way to grow Amazon.com's franchise.

The key to a successful international expansion would lie in overcoming language and cultural barriers, and in building a logistics and warehousing infrastructure that would be far more complex, difficult to set up, and inefficient than the well-oiled U.S. setup. Other factors that would inhibit development of on-line book sales in other countries included the slower acceptance of the Internet, the lack of trust in on-line transactions, and the ready availability of acceptable local bookstores. For these reasons, on-line bookstores had not been profitable outside the U.S. In Germany, for instance, ABC Bookworld, in Regensburg, Germany, had been on the Internet for well over two years, and expected to generate some 5.8 million dollars in sales in 1997. These numbers were insignificant compared to the United States.

In 1997, a Hong Kong-based company launched the first Chinese bookstore on the Internet. The site, Chinese Books CyberStore (www.chinesebooks.net), boasted a collection of 100,000 titles from China, Hong Kong, and Taiwan. Unlike Amazon.com, which competed directly with traditional bookstores, Chinese Books CyberStore enlisted the support of 17 publishing houses from Hong Kong, China, and Taiwan, including two that were shareholders. The cyberstore did not target readers who had easy access to traditional Chinese bookstores, according to Francis Lee, managing director of the store. Instead, the store aimed to serve overseas Chinese who found it difficult to buy Chinese-language books. Because it targeted Chinese-speaking readers, the site was primarily in Chinese. Readers could search a book by its title, author, publisher, year of publication, category, and even the International Standard Book Number, or ISBN. Once a book was selected and put into the shopping basket, the reader could see how many days it would take for delivery. For books that were out of stock or required special orders, the store would e-mail customers individually with delivery time details. Shipping time varied from three days to six weeks, depending on the type of delivery and the destination. The company charged $8.24 a book for delivery to Asia via courier.

Brand Extension into On-Line Music Sales At first glance, the $40 billion music industry seemed to be perfectly suited for the Web, for many of the same reasons as books: large selections, flexible searching, audio samples, and convenient buying. However, the total number of CD sales on-line represented less than 1 percent of sales overall. While many small on-line music sellers were cropping up all over the Internet in an attempt to tap into the money-making opportunity on the Internet, their attempts had been largely unsuccessful to date. Even CDNow (www.cdnow.com), the leading on-line music seller, only managed sales of $9.5 million for the nine-month period ending September 30, 1997, and reported losses of $4.1 million for this period. Analysts were skeptical about the ability of on-line brands to withstand competition from brick-and-mortar competitors that came to the Web merely to augment—not cannibalize—the sales of their physical stores. They believed that the on-line music sellers would find it difficult to create an independent business, and that the Internet instead would complement the major record labels' marketing efforts in the music business.

On-line music sellers faced technological challenges that did not affect the on-line bookselling business. While audio streaming technology was advancing rapidly, and companies like RealNetworks had released popular plug-ins that allowed consumers to hear CD-quality sound on their computers, listening to music on-line was still a tricky business. First, consumers needed to have speakers and sound cards on their computers. Second, consumers needed to download a plug-in before they could listen to music. Third, the sound quality was still poor for slower connections. The on-line bookselling business, in contrast, was not afflicted by any of these "chicken-and-egg" problems.

The poor performance of on-line music sellers was also attributable to their failure in brand-building. Major industry players tried to be everything to everyone, and no on-line music seller had succeeded in building a brand based on customer service. There was little perceived differentiation among retail sites, company sites, and fan sites. As a result, audiences were fragmented, and there were too many sites vying for the attention of consumers. This had resulted in customer confusion. The lack of a solid on-line music destination meant that consumers found it easier, faster, and more pleasant to buy music from a physical store.

Another challenge to on-line music sales was the unfamiliar on-line buying experience. Consumers were not used to the approach of reading content, hearing samples, and buying all in the same place and at the same time. People were used to walking into a music store and talking to someone. Experts believed that the on-line buying experience was far more "search-and-retrieval-oriented" and directed. In a physical store, people liked to browse, look, and listen before making any purchases.

Bezos wondered about the extent to which the problems of the on-line music business were intrinsic to the category, and to what extent they could be attributed to poor execution by the existing players. Clearly, Amazon.com could generate far more traffic than any of the existing players, but he was wary of entering into music sales until Amazon.com could be sure that it could provide a superior customer experience. Another issue that Amazon.com would have to contend with was the superior bargaining power of the half-dozen or so major record labels, who controlled most of the supply of music.

Backward Integration into Self-Publishing Amazon.com had succeeded in creating a large audience and loyal relationships with over a million consumers. These relationships ensured that millions of people visited the site, and trusted Amazon.com. This suggested the possibility that Amazon.com could become a publisher in its own right, along the lines of Barnes & Noble's successful self-publishing operation. Publishers played three key roles in marketing a book—production, promotion, and distribution. If Amazon.com could create an in-house production operation, it could easily handle its own promotion and distribution. In fact, Amazon.com would be far more effective and efficient at promoting the books that it published, because it would not need to spend money on advertising and promoting the books in physical bookstores. Self-publishing would also allow Amazon.com to create titles that would be available exclusively on its on-line store. This would promote differentiation and "lock-in" of the audience to Amazon's site.

Amazon.com's direct sales model offered an even more radical possibility—creating books based on audience input, by connecting authors directly with their audiences. Amazon currently provided every author with space on its Web site for providing more information about the book, samples and excerpts from the book, and author interviews with Amazon's editors. Bezos noted that Amazon.com had observed a strong correlation between the amount of information an author provided about a book, and the sales of the book. Extending this logic, Amazon.com could use this author–audience connection to test ideas for new books, and even to co-develop books with customer inputs on early drafts.

The self-publishing option had some important drawbacks, however. Publishing was a low-margin and high-risk business, and Bezos was not convinced that the economics of the publishing business were compelling enough to further Amazon.com's key objective of improving its operating margins. Another problem with backward integration would be the risk of upsetting publishers, who would see Amazon.com as a direct threat to their bread-and-butter business. Amazon.com had worked hard to build relationships with its publishers, and any strategic move that threatened these relationships would need to be evaluated very carefully. Finally, book production required a set of skills that were foreign to Amazon.com. While it would be possible to either acquire production skills or to outsource book production, Bezos was concerned that this would dilute Amazon.com's sharply focused business mission and strategy, at a time when competitors were nipping at its heels.

■ CONCLUSION

As he gathered his thoughts, Bezos was struck by the complexity of the decisions that he needed to make, and the magnitude of the impact these decisions would have on Amazon.com's future in 1998 and beyond. He recalled an old proverb, "The higher they rise, the harder they fall," and realized that the glowing praise that Amazon.com had received could swiftly turn into intense criticism if Amazon.com did not deliver on the sky-high expectations of the investment and business community. For Bezos and the 600 employees of Amazon.com, 1998 promised to be one hell of a ride.

CASE

Arrow Electronics, Inc.

In the spring of 1997, Jan Salsgiver, president of the Arrow/Schweber (A/S) group, a subsidiary of Arrow Electronics, reviewed the Express Parts Internet Distribution Service proposal with her colleagues Skip Streber, senior vice president for sales at A/S, and Steve Kaufman, chief executive officer of Arrow (see Exhibit 1, page 520). Express had developed an Internet-based trading system that would allow distributors to post inventories and prices on a bulletin board that customers could access to compare prices and place orders. By including distributors like A/S, Express planned to use the Internet to offer customers large and small an opportunity to shop for prices.

Express offered A/S an opportunity to sell to new customers and gain quick sales. Yet, it also could potentially affect Arrow's relationship with its current customers. It was quite possible that A/S's current customers would switch to buying part of their needs from Express rather than from A/S. In the process, Arrow's customers would be able to cherry pick products from different channels at the best possible prices. In addition, Express could also affect Arrow's relationship with its suppliers. It was possible that if A/S's suppliers saw Express as a legitimate option, they could decide to go directly to Express and disintermediate[1] Arrow from their distribution channel.

"As a distributor, amongst others, we need to know three things: how we create value for our customers for the prices we charge, how this value is different from what our suppliers can provide to our customers, and whether firms like Express can offer the same value or more for lower prices," commented Salsgiver. She continued, "We have a successful business model that is based on a portfolio of products and services that we offer our customers. Our customers come back to us because they get the most value from us for the prices they pay. If Express is going to change this equation, then we need to adapt our business model to accommodate the changes."

Salsgiver realized that she needed answers to several questions before she could decide on the Express proposal: How many of A/S's customers were likely to switch some of their purchases to Express? How would this affect A/S's sales and profitability? How would A/S's suppliers react to Express? And overall, was Express a threat or an opportunity to A/S?

Professor Das Narayandas prepared this case with the assistance of Research Associate Sara Frug as the basis for class discussion rather than to illustrate either effective or ineffective handling of an administrative situation. This case is based in part on a case developed by Stephen P. Kaufman, CEO of Arrow Electronics, for in-house executive training. Some proprietary data have been disguised.

[1] Disintermediation refers to the removal of a channel member (or intermediary) from a distribution channel.

EXHIBIT 1

Organization Chart

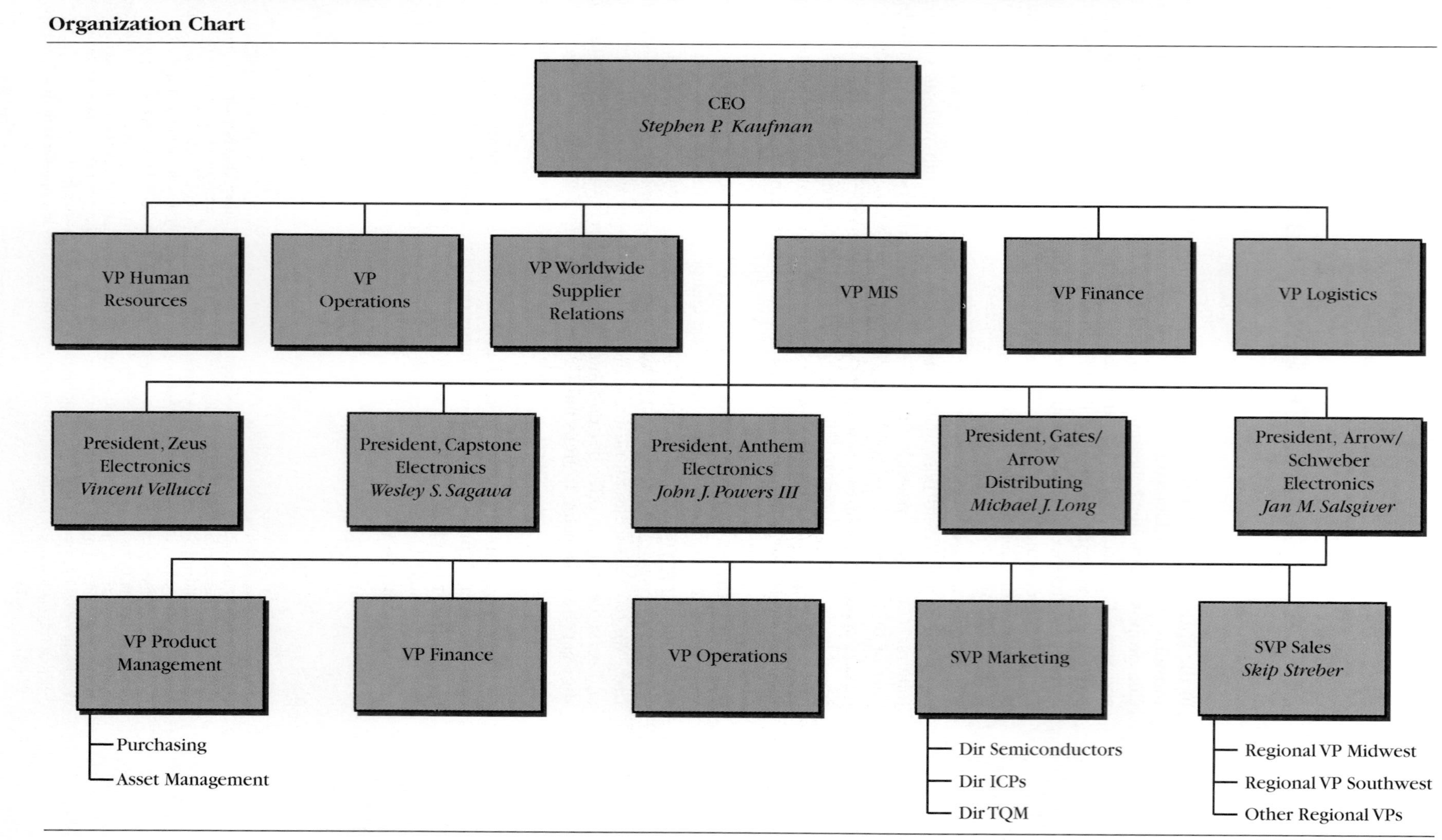
CEO
Stephen P. Kaufman
VP Human Resources
VP Operations
VP Worldwide Supplier Relations
VP MIS
VP Finance
VP Logistics
President, Zeus Electronics
Vincent Vellucci
President, Capstone Electronics
Wesley S. Sagawa
President, Anthem Electronics
John J. Powers III
President, Gates/Arrow Distributing
Michael J. Long
President, Arrow/Schweber Electronics
Jan M. Salsgiver
VP Product Management
Purchasing
Asset Management
VP Finance
VP Operations
SVP Marketing
Dir Semiconductors
Dir ICPs
Dir TQM
SVP Sales
Skip Streber
Regional VP Midwest
Regional VP Southwest
Other Regional VPs

Source: Company records.

■ THE ELECTRONICS INDUSTRY

In the six decades between Arrow's beginnings and the latter 1990s, the electronics industry evolved rapidly, incorporating numerous technological advances as they were developed. The advent of the transistor in 1947 signaled the beginning of a transition toward computers as a central product focus, with developments such as the integrated circuit in the late 1950s and the microprocessor in the early 1970s driving the change. Practical applications followed increasingly quickly upon the heels of technological advances, leading to a climate of planned obsolescence.

It was common for semiconductor and electronic component manufacturers like Intel and Motorola (hereafter referred to as suppliers) to deal directly with large original equipment manufacturers (OEMs). Suppliers franchised small numbers of distributors to manage sales to customers that they could not serve directly, whether because of diminutive size or voluminous service requirements. Between 65 percent and 75 percent of suppliers' sales were made directly by suppliers to their largest 200 customers. The remaining 25 percent to 35 percent of sales went through the distribution channels.

During the 1980s and early 1990s, as chip technologies developed and inventory became more rapidly obsolete, inaccuracies in demand estimation were increasingly exaggerated. Compounding this problem were a series of economic downturns during these years. Although by the mid-1990s the U.S. economy had improved, the industry was still characterized by volatility. Between August 1994 and February 1996, supplier shortages made it nearly impossible to live up to delivery commitments. Kaufman remembered: "Lead time stretched to 30–48 weeks—nearly every commodity was in short supply. However, this problem did not last very long. In February 1996, the situation reversed and the bottom dropped out of the memory market, producing vast oversupplies. Declines in dollar volume of sales across the board resulted from and in turn exacerbated excess inventory." Distributors suffered the effects of what one trade magazine called "a year best forgotten" in the semiconductor industry, during which Intel was the only top-five semiconductor manufacturer to increase sales, reflecting the precipitous drop in memory prices.

■ ARROW ELECTRONICS

Arrow Electronics was a broad-line distributor of electronics parts, including semiconductors and passive components. Founded in 1935 to sell radio equipment, the company had undergone a number of major changes in its history. In 1968, three Harvard Business School graduates teamed up and acquired a controlling interest in the company, which they grew to a number two position by 1980, largely through acquisitions. The latest management era had begun in the aftermath of a hotel fire in December 1980 that claimed the lives of five of the company's top six officers and eight other Arrow executives. During a shaky regrouping period coinciding with an overall economic recession, Stephen Kaufman became president in 1982 and the chief executive officer in 1986. Under Kaufman's leadership, however, Arrow had reached the number one position among electronics distributors by 1992.

Also by 1997, consolidation throughout the distribution world had allowed a small number of large companies to capture the top tier of the market. Arrow's closest competitor was Avnet Inc., which trailed it by over 20 percent in sales in 1996, though it had grown by 14 percent as opposed to Arrow's 10 percent during that year. The largest of the next group of competitors was only one quarter the size of Arrow in total sales volume, earning less than Arrow's largest operating group. This competition included foreign entrants Rabb Karcher and Future Electronics as well as long-time rivals Pioneer-Standard, Wyle, and Marshall Industries. In 1996, Arrow had performed solidly in a less than solid market, reaching over $6.5 billion in sales. (See Exhibit 2 for financial information.) In the comparatively more stable first half of 1997, Arrow saw an increase in sales compared to the first two quarters of 1996, but a decrease in net income.

Headquartered in Melville, New York, Arrow's North American operations were managed by a corporate marketing and purchasing group, finance and accounting, credit, human resources, management information systems, operations, and senior management (see Exhibit 1). Sales and marketing functions were divided among five distinct operating groups, each of which had its own P&L responsibility and maintained its own asset management and materials management. These operating groups were distinguished according to product and strategy concerns. Three groups, Arrow/Schweber, Anthem Electronics, and Zeus Electronics sold semiconductors, differing in customer base. Zeus sold to military and aerospace customers, while Anthem and A/S sold to industrial customers. Using product-driven strategies, on the other hand, Gates/Arrow Distributing sold mostly computer systems, peripherals, and software, while Capstone Electronics sold passive components.

■ ARROW/SCHWEBER

Arrow/Schweber was the largest of Arrow's working groups, with sales of $2.07 billion in 1996. A/S president Jan Salsgiver had assumed the helm in 1995 and worked

EXHIBIT 2

Consolidated Statement of Income ($ in Thousands Except Per-Share Data)

For the Year	*1996*	*1995*	*1994*
Sales	$6,534,577	$5,919,420	$4,649,234
Costs and expenses			
Cost of products sold	5,492,556	4,888,746	3,832,169
Selling, general and administrative expenses	604,412	574,166	487,982
Depreciation and amortization	36,982	33,299	27,759
Integration charges			45,350
	6,133,950	5,496,211	4,393,260
Operating income	400,627	423,209	255,974
Equity in earnings (loss) of affiliated company	(97)	2,493	
Interest expense, net	37,959	46,361	36,168
Earnings before income taxes and minority interest	362,571	379,341	219,806
Provision for income taxes	144,667	153,139	91,206
Earnings before minority interest	217,904	226,202	128,600
Minority interest	15,195	23,658	16,711
Net income	$ 202,709	$ 202,544	$ 111,889
Per common share			
Primary	$ 3.95	$ 4.21	$ 2.40
Fully diluted	3.95	4.03	2.31
Average number of common shares and common share equivalents outstanding			
Primary	51,380	48,081	46,634
Fully diluted	51,380	51,123	50,407

Source: Company records.

at headquarters with the sales and marketing VPs as well as VPs in charge of demand creation, value added services, and account development. As president of A/S, Salsgiver had been leading the operating group toward higher levels of technological expertise through technical certification for its field sales representatives and dedicated investments to enhance product management.

A/S's local operations were serviced through a branch structure. Each branch was headed by a General Manager and included Field Sales Representatives, Inside Sales Representatives, Product Managers, and Field Application Engineers. In addition, branches maintained administrative personnel, plus one or two other managers depending upon branch size. Six Regional VPs oversaw A/S's 39 branch managers.

Products and Suppliers

The Arrow/Schweber line card, that is, the set of products for which A/S was a franchised distributor, consisted of two categories of chips: standardized and proprietary. Standardized products were interchangeable chips produced by multiple suppliers. Proprietary products, on the other hand, were manufactured by only a single supplier. Only a franchised distributor could sell a supplier's standardized or proprietary products.

In an industry in which the top 10 suppliers provided 80 percent of the products on distributors' line cards, the A/S supplier list was long, including 56 suppliers in the spring of 1997 and increasing continually.

One of A/S's largest suppliers was Altera, a manufacturer of proprietary programmable logic devices (PLDs) that required a lot of value-added programming before a customer could use the product. As was typical in the industry, this manufacturer did virtually no programming itself. Roughly 20 percent of Altera's products were purchased directly by customers who had in-house programming skills. Altera sold the remaining 80 percent of their products through two franchised distributors. Each of these distributors had built capabilities to provide all the value-added programming required by each customer.

Intel, a semiconductor manufacturer, was another large supplier for A/S. Like Altera, Intel supplied mostly proprietary products, though its most popular line, the x86 chip, did not demand the sort of value-added support and programming or engineering that A/S provided for Altera's PLDs.

Texas Instruments and Motorola, the other two of A/S's "big four," balanced the line card by selling a 75/25 mix of standardized and proprietary products.

Customers

Mid- and small-sized original equipment manufacturers (OEMs) were A/S's traditional customer base and accounted for 56 percent of A/S's sales in 1996. Unlike large OEMs that purchased directly from suppliers, these OEMs often purchased through distributors because they were simply too small for the supplier to serve directly. However, suppliers still wanted to serve these customers, so they appointed franchised distributors to consolidate demand from the smaller OEMs. Suppliers allowed limited return privileges and price protection to these franchised distributors.

Franchised distributors offered customers the opportunity to order in small quantities and with short lead times,[2] a facility that suppliers were not willing to provide. Another important function provided by the distributor was credit. Suppliers had chosen not to build the structure to support credit management for all their

[2] In a business where the margins on a personal computer were typically less than a couple of hundred dollars, OEMs could have their margins wiped out completely when the supplier dropped the price of microprocessors by more than a hundred dollars, a phenomenon that usually happened two to three times a year. Customers therefore maintained minimal inventories and preferred to order products at the last minute and in small quantities.

customers. It fell upon the distributors to offer this benefit. In addition to the massive inventories distributors carried, they created value-added services for customers who needed more than just specific parts shipped against scheduled orders. Examples included the ability to receive all products necessary for a specific manufacturing run in a single shipment, as well as releasing products to shipment, based only on a forecast, not previously entered firm purchase orders. Kaufman explained, "This is very important to customers that have adopted just-in-time procurement systems. These customers want to be very sure that they have everything they need at the right time and in the right quantities. If not, they run the risk of having to stop their production lines."

Distributors' up-to-the-minute knowledge of available products could also be extremely valuable to OEMs in designing their equipment for manufacture.

Even when an OEM was large enough to purchase direct, a distributor could be attractive for particular value-added services. Salsgiver explained: "When a customer gets large enough, they want to buy only direct from the supplier, who can provide them with the technical support and low prices they want. As time passes, however, these customers begin to reach a stage where they want to hand off materials management as well. Most suppliers are not capable of providing this service, and, more important, are not interested in getting into this business. They don't want to take on any activity that does not have the high margins that electronic parts and components usually provide.[3] At this time they can become good distributor customers."

A second and growing new market were the contract manufacturers (CMs), who were in the business of building circuit boards or industrial computer systems for OEMs. OEMs would outsource the production of a prototype or even a whole product run to the CM, who would procure the components and assemble the piece. Between 1992 and 1996, the CM business had grown at 30 percent per year. During the same period, the percentage of A/S business going through the CM channel grew as well, reaching 20 percent of A/S's total sales by 1996. Said one A/S field sales representative: "Five years ago, the only CMs were small mom-and-pop operations used for overflow or testing demand. A few of them have grown to be multibillion dollar enterprises. However, there still are a large number of mid- and small-sized CMs. CMs tend to be very price sensitive. They selectively use our value-added services such as programming and supply-chain management, in addition to our quick delivery service. But they don't need our engineering services at all."

A/S served two other major customer segments. Amounting to 11 percent of A/S business were customers who purchased Intel x86 chips exclusively to manufacture PC clones. These customers could be differentiated from the traditional OEM customers insofar as they purchased in a purely commoditized fashion. The major value A/S could offer to these customers was credit that was unavailable through suppliers or other financial institutions.

The last segment was made up of customers who purchased industrial computer products. These customers were involved in various industries and tended to buy entire systems or at least assemblies from A/S. Streber explained: "These are computer product subassemblies that are used as a component inside industrial equipment such as elevators or medical equipment. For example, the heart of a blood gas analyzer is an Intel-based PC that we supply to the manufacturer of this equipment. These customers tend to order in smaller quantities and need highly customized solutions."

[3] For example, Intel's gross margins were over 55 percent in 1997, and were expected to stay above 50 percent in 1998 and 1999.

"OUR SUPPLIERS ARE OUR CUSTOMERS"

To a far greater extent than in most other industries, electronic component manufacturers made distributors responsible for demand creation. This tendency, Salsgiver explained, resulted from the nature of the electronics business:

> Suppliers have two fundamental needs from us. They need us to win business in their commodity products to help them grow and gain both profit and market share. They also need us to represent their new technologies and products to our customers. It's obviously critical for both of our future success to help customers design our suppliers' new proprietary devices into their products. Suppliers tend to price commodity products based on the competitive nature of the market. Our gross margins on standardized products run above the company average, in the range of 20 to 25 percent. However, suppliers are careful to try to ensure that our margins on the proprietary products run equal to or greater than commodity products, in an effort to reward us for our design work with our customers. This doesn't always work out.
>
> First, they franchise select distributors to sell their products and provide financial incentives such as price protection and limited return privileges to only these franchised distributors. More pointedly, suppliers refuse to honor warranties of products purchased through channels other than the ones they have designated.
>
> Second, many suppliers ship their proprietary products to us at list price or marginally below it. For example, one of our suppliers sets our book cost at a constant 5 percent below their list price. When we get a request for a price quote from a customer, we call the supplier back and give them the details of the customer and the opportunity. The supplier then decides how much of an additional discount they will provide us on this request. In this manner, they know exactly what we are doing, and they are also able to control prices. The level of discount provided varies depending on whether it is our *design win* or a *jump ball.*

Design Win

A/S, like other electronics distributors, generated demand by helping customers engineer their end products and making A/S-suppliers' chips integral to these designs. Suppliers kept track of which distributors did design work by assigning a number to the distributor/customer partnership. Explained Streber:

> When we start working on an opportunity and invest resources in a customer's project, we will call our supplier and give them all the details. The supplier then assigns a design number that recognizes the work we have done. This is called 'design registration.' Next, when the order materializes, and the customer shops across distributors for price, the supplier offers a much higher discount to the distributor credited with the design registration as compared to any other distributor. Unless another distributor is willing to take a hit, they will not be able to serve this customer since only the distributor with the design registration will be able to earn an acceptable margin at the suggested resale price.

Jump Ball

In some cases, the customer purchased according to manufacturer reputation or price, with no distributor doing any design work. These instances were called "jump balls" in the business. The supplier offered every distributor the same margin, which was significantly lower than the margin given with a design win. Jump balls could also occur when a customer switched from direct purchasing to distribution. Salsgiver explained:

> In these cases, the supplier has already created the demand for the product by doing the design work themselves, so they see the distributor's value only in credit and fulfillment, and they compensate minimally for these services.

Managing the Relationship with Suppliers

"Our suppliers are able to control our destiny in many ways," commented Kaufman. He continued:

> In the case of jump balls, our suppliers inform the customer about the various distributors they can buy from. Suppliers usually don't exclude a distributor from the list. But they do control the order of names in a list. This is an important factor. Being the first name on that list increases the chance of getting the sale. It is the supplier's way of rewarding one distributor over another.
>
> Another way suppliers manage demand flow is in the order in which they inform the distributors about an opportunity. Getting to know about an opportunity even a few minutes or hours before anyone else can give our sales reps all the time they need to secure the sale.
>
> Finally, suppliers can manage the flow of orders by managing the time they take in responding to a distributor's request for prices. The norm is that the supplier needs to get back within 24 hours of a request. If you have a good relationship, or if the supplier wants to reward you, you might get a response a lot faster. If you are not in the good graces of the supplier, you could be the victim of an overloaded sales rep who was so busy that it took all of 24 hours for them to process your request.

Kaufman continued:

> This does not mean that the distributor has no power. Usually, for the standardized products we will carry several lines. We can also favor one supplier over the other by recommending a particular supplier's product. If suppliers use jump balls to keep distributors in check, distributors are able to use design wins and competitive standardized products to counter-balance supplier power.
>
> In my mind, our relationships with our suppliers are as important as our relationships with any of our customers. Our suppliers are our customers.

Salsgiver further explained the relationship with suppliers:

> Suppliers want A/S and other distributors to get technology into the hands of the right customers. In this business, demand points are not always known. An operation in someone's garage this year could be the multi-billion dollar giant five years from now. Our suppliers want us to identify these growth opportunities and lock them in before anyone else does. Our job at A/S is to know our customers well enough to create demand for our suppliers' products. We maintain a separate account development group, calling on small companies and opportunities of the future. This is our ace of spades when it comes to managing our relationship with our suppliers.

■ ARROW'S SELLING EFFORT

Book and Ship (BAS)

A/S maintained 300 branch-based sales and marketing representatives (SMRs), who handled the daily phone calls from customers checking delivery, availability, and current price levels. One way a customer might order would be simply to request a quote directly from the SMR, in which case the representative would try to secure the business and arrange to ship the product. This was called a book and ship transaction. SMRs exercised pricing authority for daily orders. They obtained discount levels from the supplier and quoted prices to their assigned customers based on their knowledge of the customer's buying patterns, trends in that local market, and the current cost levels and availability of inventory on hand.

Each SMR used a computer terminal linked to a comprehensive real-time, on-line computer system (similar to an airline reservation system), which tracked the costs, prices, and movements of the 300,000 different part numbers in inventory, as well as the detailed ordering (A/S handled over 10,000 transactions a day) patterns and sales history for each of the company's 50,000 customers.

Value Added (VA)

Alternatively, an order could arise through field engineering facilitated by a field sales representative (FSR)—the typical design win situation. In this case, the customer's purchasing agent would speak to the SMR only to solidify details of the transaction. These transactions represented the culmination of tremendous effort and expenditure of resources. Field sales representatives, of which there were approximately 400, traveled to their customers (usually 10 to 20 customers per FSR), spending time with customers' design engineers to understand their current projects and to explain and promote the new products being introduced by Arrow's suppliers. They also spent time with customer purchasing personnel to build relationships, negotiate major contracts, and resolve any problems that might be arising in the flow of orders and deliveries.

FSRs worked hand in glove with field application engineers (FAEs), who served as technical support for the sales force when customers wanted detailed design assistance or problem solving on specific product design issues. They were in heavy demand from suppliers, who wanted Arrow to help smaller customers design-in their proprietary parts. FAEs were salaried and generally expensive to maintain.

Product managers (PMs) were manufacturers' advocates, ensuring that the FSRs and SMRs were up-to-date on the suppliers' latest products and marketing programs, and that the sales force was meeting its supplier-by-supplier sales budgets. The PMs also worked closely with the suppliers' local personnel to follow up on leads and referrals that came to A/S from the suppliers, as well as working with Arrow's corporate marketing department to make sure low-volume or ususual products were being ordered on a timely basis.

Streber pointed out that much of the involvement with the customer revolved around the changing understanding of value added:

> The meaning of value added has continuously changed in our business. In 1977, value added meant nothing more than providing an inventory buffer for the customer. In 1987, it meant altering components to meet customer needs, either by programming, packaging, or kitting[4] parts. In 1997, for our most important customers, it means building virtual organizations with us, through in-plant stores and the like. Today the true value-added is in order cycle management. In 1977, about 2 percent of our sales had a value-added component. By 2000, this number can reach as high as 80 percent (see Exhibits 3 and 4, pages 528–530).

Phantom Inventory

One of the results of the system of debits-to-cost used by suppliers was what Salsgiver called "phantom inventory." (See Exhibit 5 on page 531 for the overall Arrow inventory figures.)

"As strange as it sounds, the way our business works, we buy products all day long at a dollar per part, sell it at sixty cents, and make a decent profit." Salsgiver explained that because of the way the suppliers managed pricing, distributors ended up with inventory on the books at high costs, when in fact what they ended up paying was a

---

[4] "Kitting" meant gathering all the parts needed for a job into a single package, or kit. The customer would submit a bill of materials, and A/S would provide the complete set. Streber explained that this procedure worked well during the late 1980s, when customers were building to forecast, or in a "push manufacturing" environment, but had fallen off in popularity during the current "pull" (build-to-order) climate.

EXHIBIT 3

Value Added from Arrow/Schweber

Transacton Cost Reduction

Total Cost of Ownership Analysis

In today's competitive environment, the need to identify all the costs in a company's supply chain process is becoming increasingly important. Companies that understand their "total cost of ownership" find they are better prepared to make complex "make versus buy" and supplier selection decisions. Using Activity Based Costing (ABC) methodologies, Arrow/Schweber's Total Cost of Ownership financial model helps companies identify the total cost associated with a particular activity or process.

Automated Replenishment

Arrow CARES® is our PC Windows ®-based automated inventory replenishment system. A user-friendly materials management solution that can be easily and economically installed, CARES automates the purchasing and receiving process while dramatically reducing inventory and associated carrying costs. Designed to support high volume repetitive purchase items, CARES operates in a multiple bin, kanban environment using "pull" processes to replenish materials. Operating from the customer's stockroom or at point-of-use, CARES uses bar code technology to scan empty kanban bins. CARES then sends a replenishment signal to designated suppliers via EDI or fax transmission. While material is pulled from a second kanban, a replenishment bin is being shipped to support ongoing production requirements. Flexible, efficient, and user friendly, Arrow CARES provides an automated inventory management solution for our customers' entire supply base.

Electronic Data Interchange

As an integral part of all of Arrow/Schweber's value-added services, EDI allows us to move information faster and more accurately, driving cost out of the supply chain. EDI provides increased productivity and, as a result, makes our customers more competitive while reducing overhead, lowering inventory, and shortening cycle times. Whether sharing forecast information, placing purchase orders, or looking for advanced shipping notification, Arrow/Schweber supports the ANSI X.12 transactions our customers require.

In-Plant Terminals

By providing direct access to Arrow/Schweber's on-line, real-time computer system, our Customer Staffed Terminal enables our customers to check inventory availability, place purchase orders, cross parts, or view component specifications. A simple and easy way to access information makes Arrow/Schweber's customer staffed terminal a valuable tool for engineering and purchasing. For added value, our Arrow/Schweber Staffed Terminal provides on-site materials management for customers that handle high levels of order processing. On-site support for planning, purchasing, and engineering departments provides increased productivity and reduces acquisition costs.

Planning the Material Pipeline

In-Plant Stores

An Arrow/Schweber In-Plant Store provides on-site staffing to help manage material requirements. We maintain and manage a warehouse, stocked with the components our customers require, on-site at the customer's manufacturing facility. The In-Plant Store personnel are responsible for planning, purchasing, receiving, stocking, and fulfilling production and engineering requirements. Customers only take ownership of material once it has been delivered to them providing a significant reduction in inventory carrying costs.

Turnkey Service

Arrow/Schweber's Turnkey service provides complete management of a customer's printed circuit board assembly requirements. We combine our expertise in materials management with those of our certified turnkey partners to provide a flexible manufacturing strategy customized to meet our customer's unique requirements.

Our Turnkey service provides dedicated program management to support and facilitate our customers' production requirements, from prototype to production, decreasing a product's time-to-volume and time-to-market.

Improving Logistical Efficiency

Production Kitting

Arrow/Schweber's kitting service provides our customers prepackaged kits for delivery to a production facility designated by the customer. Our ISO 9002 Kitting division resides in Sparks, Nevada in one of our Primary Distribution Centers (PDC) providing customers with access to our extensive line card and inventory. Our dedicated Kitting project management oversees programs from quoting through delivery—managing ECO, pricing, and forecast changes. By supplying kits in a Just-In-Time (JIT) delivery process, we help reduce inventory related expenses such as stockouts, component obsolescence, and inventory carrying costs.

Device Programming

As the leading distributor of programmable products in North America, we do more than provide our customers with the industry's broadest line card. We are also uniquely positioned to provide solutions for every PLD application by offering a comprehensive resource of silicon and design support.

We serve our customers from four primary ISO 9002 certified programming centers. Each center is linked to a single network to provide an optimal means of matching demand to capacity, providing faster turnaround for our customers. Programming with Arrow/Schweber eliminates the need for costly capital equipment expenditures and reduces product obsolescence due to last minute firmware changes.

Complete Supply Chain Management

Business Needs Analysis

Arrow/Schweber's Business Needs Analysis provides an analysis of a customer's existing materials planning, acquisition, handling, and inventorying processes. After gaining a thorough understanding of a company's existing capabilities and desired goals, Arrow/Schweber is better able to make practical recommendations that provide sustainable results to our customer's bottom line.

Custom Computer Products (CCP)

Offering the most comprehensive computer customization capabilities in the industry, our ISO 9002-certified Custom Computer Products (CCP) Division is the premier nationwide source for complete system and subsystem integration, assembly, and testing. A valuable resource for design and development assistance, CCP is staffed by an in-house support team of engineers and technical personnel who offer total project management services, from concept to completion.

CCP offers this total project management from a facility certified by Intel for hardware and software design and product integration. Applications provided through CCP include disk drive formatting and custom drive configurations; software configuration and customization; custom packaging, painting, and labeling; run-in and diagnostic testing; complete functional, diagnostic, environmental, and confidence testing; extended warranty; local installation and on-site training; and nationwide field service programs. Using Arrow/Schweber's CCP service lowers production costs, reduces time to market, and enhances our customer's cash flow.

Source: Company records.

much lower figure. Nevertheless, this system made it look as though inventory never turned, making day-to-day management, not to mention projections, more difficult.

In addition to getting discounts for design wins on proprietary products, Arrow was sometimes able to negotiate with the supplier on an order-by-order basis for a special discount. A supplier that was anxious to fill its production lines for standardized products could "buy an order." This led to higher margins for Arrow on that order.

■ RELATIONSHIP WITH CUSTOMERS

Some customers chose to work with A/S on a transaction-by-transaction basis. These customers would place a request-for-quote (RFQ) for one or a few products with several distributors. The distributors would obtain current pricing information from their suppliers and offer a price to the customer. These customers could require several rounds of negotiations to obtain the best price.

EXHIBIT 4

Percent of Arrow Sales with Value-Added Content

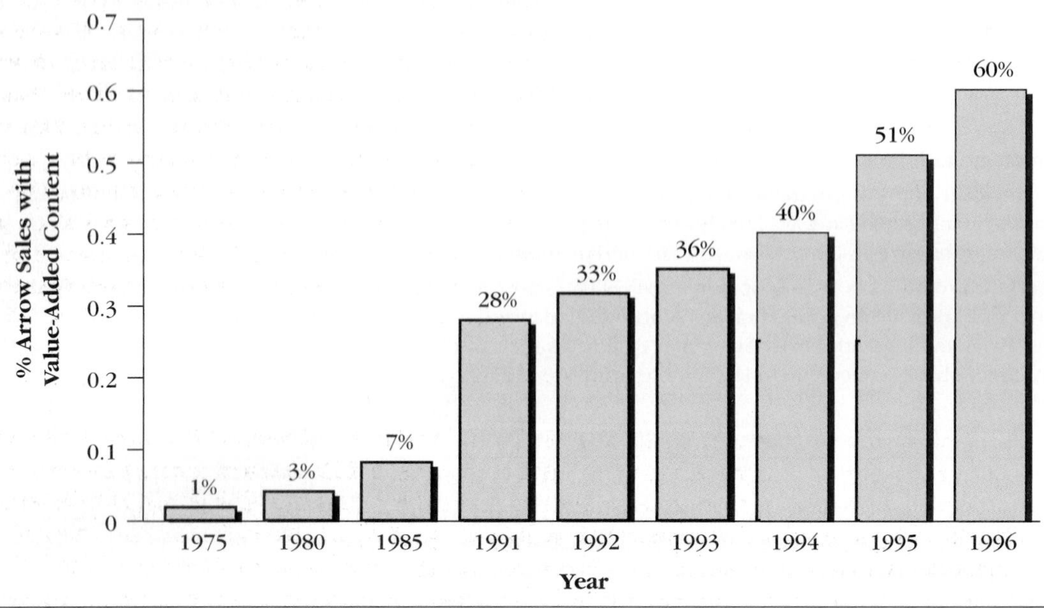

Source: Company records.

SMRs expressed some ambivalence about transactional customers. Explained one SMR: "I spend a good portion of my day speaking to these sorts of customers. They always know the current prices and will list gray market distributors' prices when I give my quote."

Added an FSR who called exclusively on CMs:

> We are currently able to provide credit and short delivery lead times on small orders to contract manufacturers, which they cannot receive either from the suppliers or from the non-franchised distributors otherwise known as brokers. This means that when an OEM asks a CM to build a board, the CM has an incentive to purchase through us. But CMs can design in our manufacturers' products just as easily as we can. If our suppliers decide to reward CM demand creation the way they reward such distributor activities, then it's going to be really tough to compete.

Kaufman commented:

> Roughly 25 percent of our sales today come from transactional customers. Typically, a majority of these sales are of the book and ship (BAS) type. We cannot afford to ignore this group for several reasons. In addition to accounting for a significant portion of our current sales, this customer segment is also a major source of relationship customers in the long run. Most of our relationship customers today started out as transactional customers. Customers want to check us out and monitor our performance over several orders before they are willing to get into any sort of agreement that goes beyond the transaction level. We are generally able to convert at least half of our transactional customers into relational customers over the long haul.

Other customers attempted to establish long-term relationships with a small number of distributors. Salsgiver explained:

> Most of our relationship customers do more than half of their business with their top distributor. These customers want the convenience of submitting an entire bill of items for a quote, finding it more valuable to have a steady partner than the rock

EXHIBIT 5

Consolidated Balance Sheet ($ in Thousands)

	December 31	
	1996	*1995*
Assets		
Current assets		
Cash and short-term investments	$ 136,400	$ 93,947
Accounts receivable, less allowance for doubtful accounts ($39,753 in 1996 and $38,670 in 1995)	902,878	940,049
Inventories	1,044,841	1,039,111
Prepaid expenses and other assets	36,004	31,610
Total current assets	2,120,123	2,104,717
Property, plant, and equipment at cost		
Land	8,712	14,527
Buildings and improvements	77,527	63,857
Machinery and equipment	127,633	112,883
	213,602	191,267
Less accumulated depreciation and amortization	98,377	73,932
	115,225	117,335
Investment in affiliated company	34,200	36,031
Cost in excess of net assets of companies acquired, less accumulated amortization ($57,802 in 1996 and $48,085 in 1995)	388,787	379,171
Other assets	52,016	63,762
	$2,710,351	**$2,701,016**
Liabilities and Shareholders' Equity		
Current liabilities		
Accounts payable	$ 594,474	$ 561,834
Accrued expenses	180,129	207,738
Short-term borrowings, including current maturities of long-term debt	71,504	117,085
Total current liabilities	846,107	886,657
Long-term debt	334,562	451,706
Other liabilities	68,488	68,992
Minority interest	92,712	97,780
Shareholders' equity		
Common stock, par value $1		
Authorized—120,000,000 and 80,000,000 shares in 1996 and 1995 Issued—51,196,385 and 50,647,826 shares in 1996 and 1995	51,196	50,648
Capital in excess of par value	549,913	530,324
Retained earnings	805,342	602,633
Foreign currency translation adjustment	8,753	18,398
	1,415,204	1,202,003
Less: Treasury stock (1,069,699 and 22,297 shares in 1996 and 1995), at cost	49,065	24
Unamortized employee stock awards	7,657	6,098
Total shareholders' equity	1,358,482	1,195,881
	$2,710,351	**$2,701,016**

Source: Company records.

bottom price over the long haul. That doesn't mean that they don't care about prices. It is very common for them to maintain a relationship with one or two other distributors in order to ensure continuous availability of products and to keep their primary distributor in check.

Most of our relationship customers buy a basket of products from us that includes BAS and VA products. Given the competitive nature of this business, we have found that it is difficult to get close to a customer through the "book and ship" business. Our approach is to use the value-added products as the first step to building a relationship. We provide customers with the best-in-class support in this category. Once the customer gets a chance to interact with us, they are able to see the true benefit of doing business with us rather than any other distributor.

Now comes a peculiar trait in our business. You would expect that the customer pays us high prices for the value-added services we provide. Well, that doesn't happen. The customer knows that there are several distributors that can provide these value-added services. They then use the threat of switching to other distributors to make sure that we don't charge too much of a premium for our services. While we try to demonstrate tangible financial benefits to justify our prices, there are times when we practically give away the value that we create for them and recover our profits in other areas. Our gross margins on value-added products run below the company average, in the range of 10 percent to 15 percent. We cross-sell our other products to these customers by offering them significant breaks on the value-added products in return for their commitment to buy the book and ship products exclusively from us. In a way, in these relationships the commodity products subsidize the specialty products.

Finding the right customers with which to develop a long-term relationship was very important. It was not uncommon for some customers simply not to appreciate the work done by A/S or even honor their own commitments. Martha Moranis, an SMR, related:

We had been pursuing a prospect for some time when a request came in from them for a highly allocated proprietary chip manufactured by one of our major suppliers. We saw this as a great opportunity to break into the account and establish a long-term relationship, and we agreed to obtain this product for them at a favorable price. In return, they promised to purchase one of their major needs exclusively from us at a price that allowed us a good margin. We jumped through flaming hoops to deliver on our side of the bargain, but once they had received their shipment, they seemed to change their mind about the agreement. When it came time for them to place their standing order, they tried to lower the price we had agreed upon and finally placed the order with another distributor. We could not do anything with the supplier because they saw it as a jump ball. In hindsight, we would have been better off not serving this customer at all.

The same set of actions on our part will get a very different response from some of our good customers. We have found that the best way to strengthen a relationship that is already strong is by helping our customers in their times of need. Our good customers will always remember what we did for them and usually reward us at a later date.

Long-term relationships had their own perils. One FSR related:

I once called on a customer who had a gatekeeper for a purchasing manager. This buyer had been there for fifteen years and had fallen into a routine of placing the same orders with the same distributors all the time. For some reason, he did not want to deal with us. We rotated this account through some of our best reps with no success. This buyer was "anti-Arrow" and we had no clue why. We tried to go around the buyer and work with engineering. This made things worse for us. We were told by the buyer that we could not design in any product that they currently purchased through our competition. This made it really tough to maneuver. Our chance arrived when a new buyer came in. This buyer was willing to work with us, and we ended winning significant amounts of business from this customer.

> This process can work in reverse as well. We can establish a solid relationship with a customer that is utterly obliterated when a new buyer with a different set of connections replaces the person with whom we used to work.

"There is another angle to building a relationship with a customer," added Kaufman. He continued:

> I think we need to go further to make the relationship virtually unbreakable. We need to get the customer to invest along with us in systems and processes that enable us to provide value-added services.
>
> It is easier for us when we are dealing with value-added products like PLDs where the customer has to have invested in product-related systems and processes that are customized to match our programming skills. But even with commodity products, where there is little that can be done at the product end, a customer that invests in supply-chain management initiatives along with us is very unlikely to terminate their relationship with us.
>
> The trend toward greater demand for value-added services is our best bet to counterbalance the high price sensitivities of our customers and the relational "cheating" that takes place in our business.

■ A/S AND THE INTERNET

During the early to mid-1990s, many electronics distributors had set up home pages on the Internet through which to present their companies, give line card information, and even sell products. In the move to the Internet, the prominence of independent, nonfranchised distributors on the landscape was unmistakable. These companies were seen by many franchised distributors as well as customers as being less than legitimate. They purchased their products from others' overstock, and because they lacked authorized reseller agreements, they could not use the manufacturers' warranties.

Although Arrow had established a closed system to allow its customers to obtain fixed price and availability information from a terminal in the customer plant, Arrow had been reluctant to establish a presence in the public domain. Preferring instead to watch and wait while others tested the waters, eventually Arrow had put up home pages for the company as a whole and its operating groups. Nevertheless, purchasing capability was not a feature of Arrow's new Web sites. Instead, they functioned as information centers with material about the various suppliers, searchable lists of parts, and news. Potential customers were directed from the Web page to the national 1-800 number for the group in question.

■ EXPRESS PARTS, INC.

Express Parts, Inc., was a new independent distributor. The company had developed an Internet-based trading system that revolved around a multidistributor bulletin board. Express said that its search engine could quickly cross-reference equivalent parts from multiple manufacturers based either on any manufacturer's part number or a technical description, and it estimated that over 50,000 OEMs across the United States would have access to the service. By gaining access to such a large market, Express proposed, A/S could increase its sales at less than half the cost of its existing branch network. The program worked as follows:

1. A/S would transmit its full list of available inventory and prices to Express each night. This list would be combined with similar lists from a limited number of other distributors.

2. Express would allow customers to sign onto its service via the Internet and search by part number or description. Upon making a selection, the customer would see a screen showing all products matching the search criteria, along with the quantity available for shipment and the price at which each distributor was prepared to sell. The customer would not actually know the distributor's name, since on the Internet screen used by the customer, each distributor would be identified only by an arbitrary letter. (See Exhibit 6.)
3. The customer could select any supplier/distributor combination, enter the quantity desired, and click the mouse to place the order. The order would instantly be transmitted to Express. Express would review the order, perform a credit check, accept and acknowledge it to the customer, and then send it electronically to the appropriate distributor.
4. After receiving the order, the distributor would pick the parts and "drop ship" the order on behalf of Express directly to the customer.[5] The distributor would then notify Express electronically that the shipment had been made, and Express would bill the customer.
5. A/S would be paid by Express 30 days later with no credit risk, minus Express's fee of 6 percent.

DECISIONS

Express's proposal had stirred significant debate among the A/S management team, which had now been discussing it for nearly a month. Express had told Salsgiver that they needed a decision within the week. This was, they said, because they were only going to ask a limited number of distributors to join, in order to avoid having too many duplicate and competitive lines.

Kaufman had asked Salsgiver to evaluate the impact that Express would have on A/S's business under different scenarios. "We need to have some idea of what this is going to do to our business," he had told Salsgiver. Salsgiver had commissioned a detailed study to look at this issue under different settings. Two outcomes were considered in this study. In the optimistic scenario, all transactional customers were assumed to switch purchases of their products from A/S to Express. In the pessimistic scenario, all transactional customers and roughly 40 percent of relationship customers were assumed to switch their purchases from A/S to Express in the future. These percentages were arrived at through a detailed bottom-up account product analysis. Exhibit 7 on page 536 provides the results of this study, which had stirred a lot of debate and little agreement. Salsgiver realized that this analysis only provided some direction but not all the answers she needed to make her decisions.

Salsgiver now considered the words of her colleagues as she composed her thoughts.

Kaufman: It is very important that we keep in mind our corporate objectives. With expenses at 11 percent, we cannot afford our overall gross margins for A/S to fall below 15 percent. We certainly don't want to accelerate the downward trend in margins that we've been seeing any more than is necessary.

[5] "Drop ship" was a process by which one company, in this case Arrow, would ship a product to a customer as an agent for a middleman, in this case Express, making it look as though the product came from the middleman. Legally, Arrow had "sold" the product to Express, who instantly resold it to the customer. Express was thus the legal party responsible for the transaction, did the billing and collecting, and was responsible for paying Arrow.

EXHIBIT 6

Express Parts Sample

Part Number Requested: SN74LS244N ***Part Description: LS Octal Buffer/Line Driver***

		Distributor											
		A		*B*		*C*		*D*		*E*		*F*	
Manufacturer	*Part Number*	*Qty*	*$*	*Qty*	*$*	*Qty*	*$*	*Qty*	*$*	*Qty*	*$*	*Qty*	*$*
Texas Instruments	SN74LS244N	62,507	.31	83,200	.28	5,000	.72	30,250	.67	89,660	.45	45,000	.62
Motorola	SN74LS244N	30,245	.42	77,700	.49	89,500	.25	82,300	.58	94,200	.26	145,000	.22
Natl Semiconductor	DM74LS244N	59,000	.30	12,400	.67	64,500	.53	73,000	.50	100,000	.23	2,200	.70
SGS Thomson	T74LS244B1	29,800	.55	28,000	.54	73,250	.59	62,900	.66	78,780	.39	40,245	.49
Philips	N74LS244N	76,400	.24	25,975	.62	25,000	.48	10,000	.70	47,120	.58	50,800	.55

Click on the price you want

Quantity ____

Quote ____

Order ____

Customer:

Name: ______________________

Address: ______________________

____

E-mail Address: ______________________

Source: Company records.

EXHIBIT 7

Market Segment Mix[a]

Market Segment	*Market Segment (% and $ of Total Business)*		*Value Added Business*[b]		*Standard Product Book & Ship Business*		*Optimistic Cannibalization of BAS Business*		*Pessimistic Cannibalization of BAS Business*	
	%	*$*	*%*	*$*	*%*	*$*	*%*	*$*	*%*	*$*
Core										
CM	20	460	57	262	43	198	30	59	70	139
OEM	56	1,300	72	936	28	364	25	91	60	218
X86	11	250	2	5	98	245	50	122	80	196
ICP[c]	13	300	80	240	20	60	35	21	80	48

[a] Calculations assume that value-added business is immune to Internet cannibalization.

[b] Includes scheduled orders and forecast sharing.

[c] Industrial Computer Products.

Source: Company records.

Ultimately, I think the Internet will never be anything more than an invitation to bargain. In the worst case scenario, all our current customers will get the lowest price from the Express system and use it as a starting point to bargain with us. I have yet to meet an industrial buyer who does not believe that he can do better by bargaining, especially on a price open to the public. With Express as a competitor, I think we will have to learn how to sell against "going out of business" prices on a regular basis. We have to have a much stronger value-in-use sales story than ever before.

Streber: I think Express gives us access to sales that would never have come our way in the past. I agree that any time the only value A/S brings to the table is in price and delivery, we are vulnerable to the Internet for competition. My feeling is that we will lose little or none of our business with relationship customers and about half of our business with transactional customers. But, if we do it right, this loss will be more or less compensated for by the additional business we get from Express. Express does not look like an attractive competitor, but it might give us one advantage. I would use it to sell to those customers that we cannot sell to using our current business model.

Currently, our SMRs spend a tremendous amount of time and energy trying to build new customers. When many of these customers call, we spend a lot of time trying to figure out whether we can build a relationship with them. We have found that most of the time, these customers are not interested in going beyond the transaction—all they want is to shop around for the lowest price. We could ask these customers to go to Express or possibly our own Internet site. For these price-sensitive, low-loyalty customers, the opportunity to offer standardized pricing over the Internet can minimize our efforts and even make it worthwhile for us since we might be able to significantly cut our costs to serve them. Finally, as long as we are the lowest, we will always get the sale.

By maintaining strong relationships with our suppliers, we will still be able to sell at competitive prices for design wins. As long as our suppliers believe that we create demand for them, they will give us the most favorable pricing. Express only responds to demand. I think if we quote anonymously on their system, given our ability to get the lowest prices, we might be able to hang on to a bit more of the business than our models indicate.

Salsgiver, however, was pessimistic:

> We all agree that Express will get the customer who is less likely to think long-term and is more likely to want to return to the old price-and-availability business. With Express, we are quite vulnerable in highly commoditized products like memory, for which it's very visible to any customer what a good price will be.
>
> I also think we are erring in making the absolute association between commodity products and transactional behavior on the one hand, and value-added products and relational behavior on the other. Although these generally line up, it does not always happen. This goes back to the point that Steve made. Even our relationship customers are going to use this as a tool to get lower prices from us. In the future, I think they will not appreciate what we do for them as much as they have in the past. The one thing that is in our favor over the long haul is the flux in the business. When product is scarce, a market may be good, but a friend is better. Our customers will be better off maintaining their relationship with us. We need to remind our customers of this.
>
> I also wonder how the Express proposal affects our suppliers. Suppliers franchise us because be add value for them. Arrow pays the bills for them—we stock products and schedule orders with enough size and scale. Currently, 70 percent of our commodity product sales to transactional customers are of products manufactured by our "big four" and other larger suppliers. To these suppliers, the Internet can mean lost control. For example, they can lose control over the point of sale information we currently can give them. In addition, they see a chance that prices for commodity products will fall down faster than they would like. Remember, it is the commodity product margin that is a major source of revenues for them. They use the money they make here to support the value-add and new proprietary products.

Salsgiver wondered, "How should we leverage all this information to our advantage?"

CASE

Vector Marketing Corporation

"CUTCO, The World's Finest Cutlery"

Michael J. Lancellot, chief executive officer of Vector Sales North America ("Vector"), glanced at his watch as he left the first staff meeting of the twenty-first century and mentally calculated whether he had time to call Erick Laine before his next appointment. "Growth," he murmured to no one in particular as he walked into his office, "that's the fundamental challenge facing Vector in the foreseeable future. How can we double our revenues in the next five years?"

The corporate long-range planning team was scheduled to meet in the next six weeks, and Lancellot was pressing to have a five-year marketing strategy ready to discuss at the meeting. He opened the "issues file" that Jim Stitt, president of ALCAS Corporation ("ALCAS"), Vector's parent company, had compiled over the holidays and thought back to the conversation that the two of them had earlier in the day. Stitt had talked about three major issues that needed to be addressed before the marketing strategy could be finalized: how much emphasis to place on international versus domestic marketing programs, whether to pursue the Internet as a marketing channel (and, if so, how), and what new products, if any, to add to the company's portfolio beyond the three garden tools scheduled for a June introduction. Of the three issues, if and how to pursue the Internet was deemed to be the most critical issue by both executives, as well as the one that needed immediate attention. Lancellot picked up his telephone to call Erick Laine.

Erick J. Laine, chairman and chief executive officer of ALCAS Corporation, put down his telephone, rose from his desk, and turned to look out his office window. The office overlooked the employees' parking lot, and he noticed a soft snow beginning to dust the vehicles. A smile spread across Laine's face as he recalled the year that had just ended. ALCAS had again experienced record sales. Company sales had increased 5 percent over 1998, to $130 million, employee profit-share bonuses were at peak levels for the fourth year in a row, and the company's 50th anniversary celebration the past summer had been a singular success.

Laine reflected with satisfaction on his recent telephone conversation with Michael Lancellot. Lancellot was correct, he thought. Sales growth was the fundamental issue facing the company. But how?

It was the beginning of the millennium, and Laine was contemplating the future of ALCAS. What would the future bring, both for his company and the country? He recalled reading a newspaper article that said U.S. households grew at an average annual rate of 1.5 percent in the 1980s and .8 percent during the 1990s and were expected to grow at an average annual rate of 1.1 percent until 2010. What would the size of the market be for the company in the next five, 10, or even 20 years? What would the com-

---

This case was prepared by Professor Robert A. Peterson, The University of Texas at Austin, as a basis for class discussion and is not designed to illustrate effective or ineffective handling of an administrative situation. Certain corporate information is disguised. Consequently, the case is not useful for research purposes.

position of the population be in the future and, more importantly, what would the company's market look like? What would the economy be like in the next few years? During the 1990s, consumer prices had been relatively stable, rising at an average annual rate of 3.0 percent per year (as compared with an average annual increase of 4.7 percent in the 1980s). Would this trend continue? These were certainly headache-causing questions, but Laine believed the answers held a wonderful future for the company.

Laine returned to his desk and picked up the telephone to call his wife Marianne. Perhaps, with the new snow, they could go cross-country skiing at their Cuba Lake home next Saturday.

■ ALCAS CORPORATION

Although ALCAS Corporation celebrated its 50th anniversary in 1999, its roots go back another half century. In 1902, ALCOA, the Aluminum Company of America, created the WearEver subsidiary to market aluminum cookware using in-home (non-store) demonstrations. In 1948, ALCOA and W. R. Case & Sons, then the country's leading cutlery manufacturer, formed a joint venture to manufacture high-quality kitchen cutlery that would be marketed through ALCOA's WearEver subsidiary. The joint venture was incorporated as Alcas Cutlery Corporation (Al for ALCOA and cas for Case), and a manufacturing facility was established in Olean, a small city on the western edge of New York. In 1949 the first CUTCO cutlery was produced (CUTCO was named for a company once owned by ALCOA, Cooking UTensil COmpany).

Case sold its 49 percent interest in Alcas Cutlery Corporation to ALCOA in 1972. Ten years later, in September 1982, ALCOA sold Alcas Cutlery Corporation through a leveraged buyout to a management team led by Erick Laine, then the president of Alcas Cutlery Corporation. Since 1982, Alcas Cutlery Corporation has been a privately held company. Company revenues at the time of the buyout were slightly less than $5 million.

In 1990, Alcas Cutlery Corporation changed its name to ALCAS Corporation. After a series of reorganizations and acquisitions, ALCAS morphed into a "family" consisting of five interrelated companies. As shown in Exhibit 1, ALCAS is the parent holding company of CUTCO Cutlery Corporation, Vector Marketing North America, CUTCO International, and KA-BAR Knives, all of which are subsidiaries administratively headquartered in Olean, and all of which are profit centers. CUTCO Cutlery Corporation manufactures the cutlery that Vector Marketing North America markets in the United States (through Vector Marketing Corporation) and Canada (through

EXHIBIT 1

ALCAS Corporate Structure

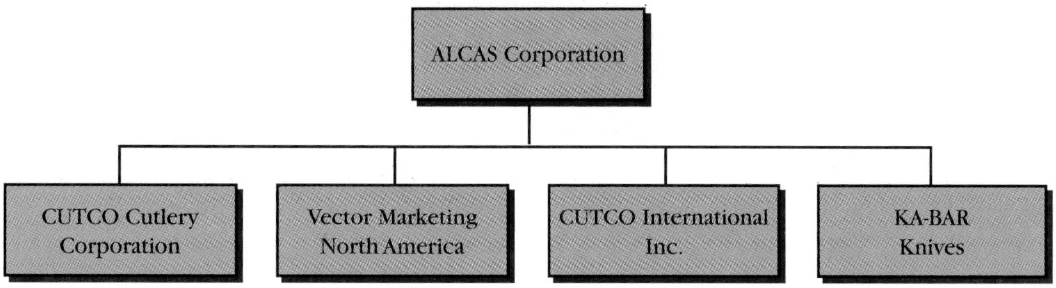

ALCAS Corporation
- CUTCO Cutlery Corporation
- Vector Marketing North America
- CUTCO International Inc.
- KA-BAR Knives

Source: Company records.

Vector Marketing Canada, Ltd.) and that CUTCO International markets in Australia, Costa Rica, Germany, Korea, and Puerto Rico.

KA-BAR Knives, a marketer of sport and utility knives established in 1898 under the name of Union Razor Company, was acquired by ALCAS in 1996 and is operated as a separate entity. KA-BAR knives are marketed domestically through independent sales representatives and internationally by in-house staff to direct marketers, wholesalers, and retailers. Cutco Cutlery Corporation manufactures 33 of the 63 KA-BAR knife products. The other 30 knife products are manufactured by a U.S. supplier and two suppliers located in Asia. Although KA-BAR knives range widely in price, the best-selling ones are priced between $30 and $50.

By the end of 1999, ALCAS (through CUTCO Cutlery Corporation) was the largest manufacturer of high-quality kitchen cutlery and accessories in North America. The corporate vision was to "become the largest, most respected and widely recognized cutlery company in the world." ALCAS had nearly 750 employees at its Olean headquarters. (See Exhibit 2 for a picture of the Olean headquarters.) Over time, it had eliminated nearly all outsourcing of product components to ensure that

EXHIBIT 2

ALCAS Headquarters

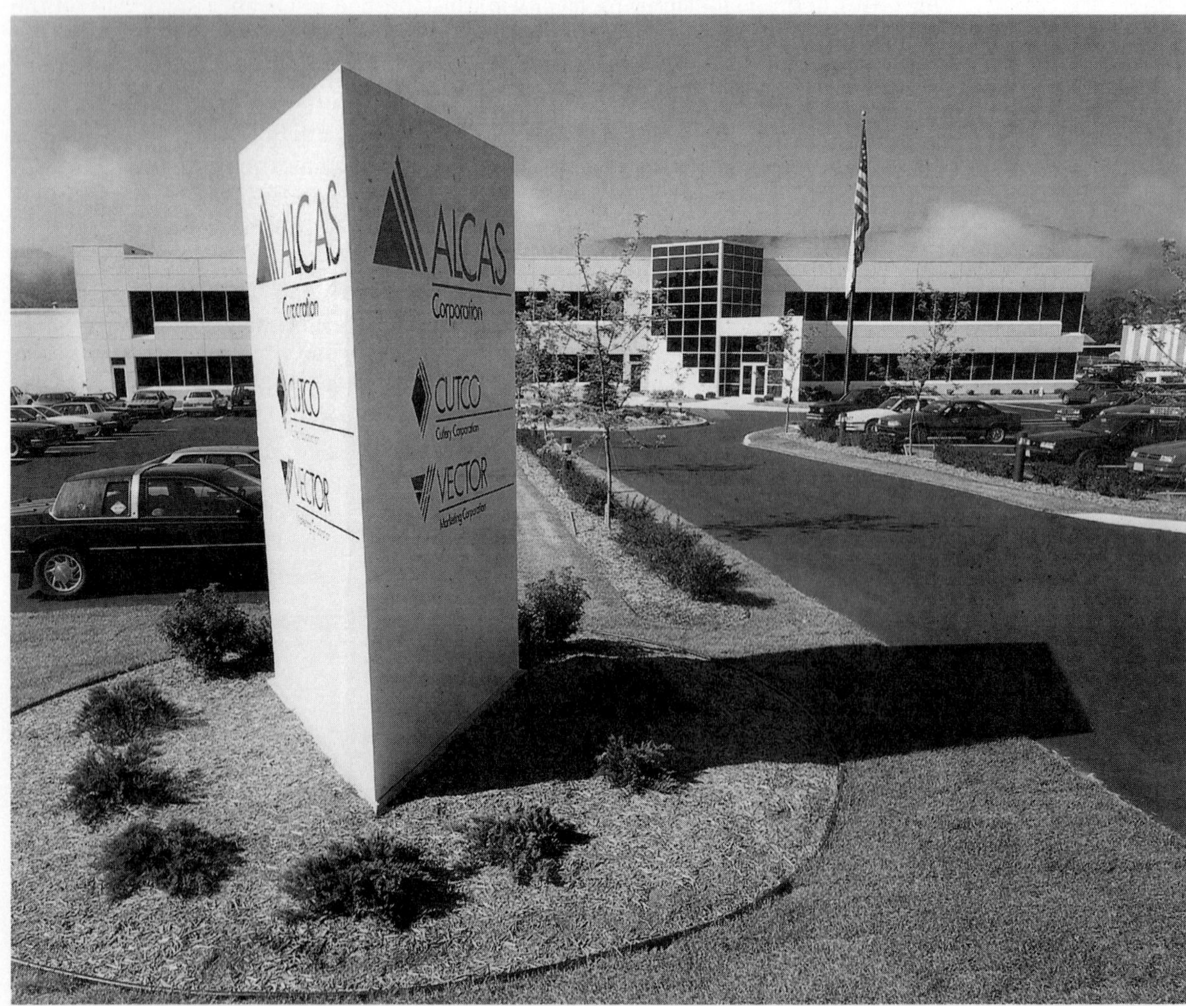

Source: Company records.

EXHIBIT 3

ALCAS Consolidated Sales, 1995–1999 ($ in Thousands)

	1995	*1996*	*1997*	*1998*	*1999*
Vector (direct sales)	$67,761	$ 83,786	$ 94,075	$102,102	$106,733
Vector (catalog)	5,773	7,521	8,167	9,386	10,662
CUTCO International	4,473	9,007	9,394	9,968	9,132
Misc. sales	2,106	1,575	1,869	2,290	3,554
Total	$80,113	$101,889	$113,505	$123,746	$130,081

Source: Company records.

only the highest quality materials and craftsmanship would be used in manufacturing CUTCO cutlery products. Exhibit 3 presents the revenues obtained by the various ALCAS entities over the period 1995-1999.

CUTCO Product Line

The first CUTCO cutlery was shipped by automobile from Olean to New Kensington, Pennsylvania, on April 29, 1949. The order consisted of six knives, two forks, a spatula, and two storage trays. The original product line consisted of nine basic pieces, including a table knife and fork, a carving knife and fork, a butcher knife, and a spatula. From the first product made, CUTCO cutlery was designed to be the finest cutlery in the world.

Presently, the CUTCO product line consists of 10 basic pieces that can be purchased individually or assembled in various sets ranging from a two-item gift pack to the Homemaker Set Plus Eight, which consists of the 10 basic pieces and eight table knives displayed in a wooden block. (Exhibit 4 on page 542 shows the Homemaker Set Plus Eight.) Retail prices in 1999 ranged from $21 for a vegetable peeler to $760 for the Homemaker Set Plus Eight. ALCAS also offers a complementary line of accessory kitchen products, including a potato masher, pizza cutter, professional spatula, cleaver, and various types of shears, as well as pocket and hunting knives and garden pruner. In 1999, the company added a five-piece set of flatware (teaspoon, dinner fork, table knife, soup spoon, and salad fork). Although the total CUTCO product line consists of approximately 250 SKUs (stock-keeping units), nearly double the number of a decade ago, 20 cutlery items account for 60 percent of sales. During the last half of the decade, prices of CUTCO products have been increased by an average of 5 percent every other year (e.g., 1995, 1997), primarily to offset rising labor and material costs.

In addition to being known for its outstanding quality, CUTCO cutlery is instantly recognizable because of its exclusive and unique wedge-lock handle and Double-D® knife blade grind. (Every CUTCO product has a full lifetime ["forever"] guarantee that includes free factory sharpening. If any product is found to be defective, it will be replaced at no cost to the customer.) First introduced in 1952, and improved considerably in 1972, the (universal) wedge-lock handle is ergonomically designed and scientifically contoured, creating a firm yet comfortable and safe grip by wedging the fingers apart across the handle while locking the thumb and fingers in place. Handles, which come in two colors, classic brown and pearl white, are made from a thermo-resin material that will not chip, crack, fade, or absorb moisture.

The Double-D® grind was added to certain knife blades in 1960. The grind consists of three razor-sharp edges angled and recessed in such a fashion that a blade can cut forward, backward, and straight down without the cutting edges becoming worn through contact with plates, cutting boards, or countertops. Unlike the typical

EXHIBIT 4

Homemaker Set Plus Eight

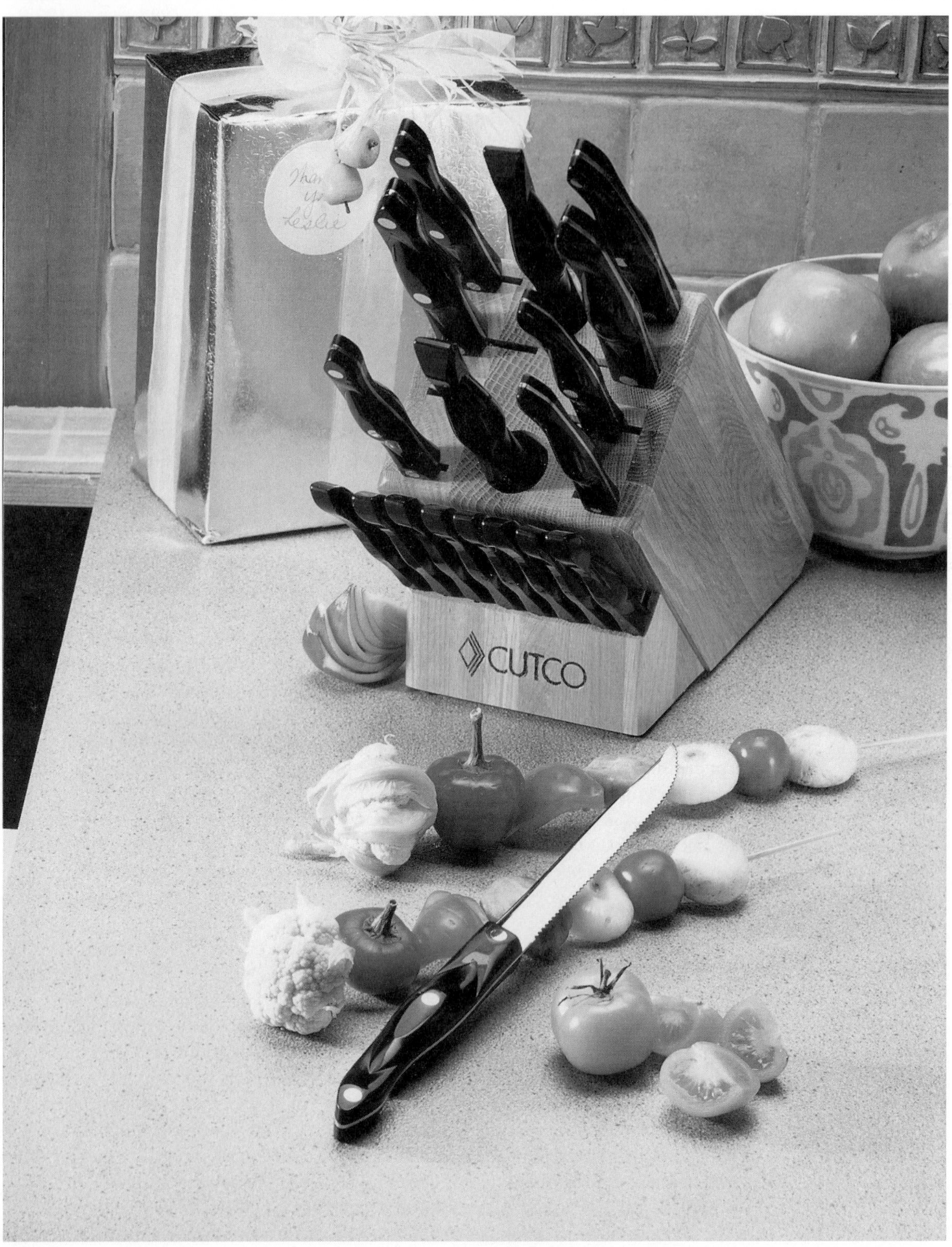

Source: Company records.

serrated knife blade, the Double-D® knife blade does not rip or tear what is being cut and can be resharpened (at the factory).

Marketing CUTCO Cutlery

CUTCO cutlery was marketed from 1949 through 1970 by a segment of the Wear-Ever sales force. In 1970, the CUTCO sales force was merged with the WearEver cookware sales force, and the two product lines were marketed together for the next decade. In 1981, WearEver decided to convert its sales force to a network of approximately 100 small, independent distributorships that would market the CUTCO product line. On January 1, 1982, Alcas Cutlery Corporation assumed the responsibility for all CUTCO marketing activities.

During the next three years, several multistate independent distributorships evolved through mergers and buyouts. In 1985, Alcas Cutlery Corporation took steps to re-create a nationwide in-house CUTCO sales and marketing infrastructure. It did so by acquiring the largest independent distributorship, Vector Marketing Corporation, which operated in the eastern United States. Vector Marketing Corporation became a wholly owned subsidiary. Shortly thereafter, Alcas acquired a second independent distributorship, CWE Industries, which operated in the western part of the country. The acquisition of BrekMar Corporation, which operated in the Midwest, and two southern-based distributorships followed, all of which were merged into Vector Marketing Corporation.

During the 50th anniversary celebration, Erick Laine reflected on the time when Vector Marketing Corporation became a subsidiary:

> The addition of Vector Marketing was the most significant organizational move we made since we purchased Alcas from ALCOA in 1982. Acquiring an in-house CUTCO marketing capability gave us complete control over our major market. Now, for the first time, CUTCO marketing decisions such as new office locations, expansion plans, rate of growth, and distribution methods were under the control of the company.

International expansion began in 1990, when Vector Marketing Canada, Ltd., was established. By the end of 1999, Canadian sales accounted for about 6 percent of ALCAS corporate revenues. CUTCO Korea had begun as a subsidiary of ALCAS Corporation in 1992. For cultural reasons, the standard VECTOR marketing approach was not very successful in Korea, but a change in the recruiting approach produced sales of nearly $8 million in Korea in 1996. Weakened Asian economic conditions in 1997 and 1998 caused sales to decline to $2 million in 1998, but in 1999 they rebounded to $5 million.

CUTCO International was created in 1994 to manage non-North American marketing efforts, and Korea was placed under its control that year. Australian and German sales organizations were established in 1996 under the direction of CUTCO International. The German operation was converted to an independently owned distributorship in 1999 because of accumulating losses. The Australian operation produced sales of about $2.5 million in 1999. A Puerto Rico office was also established in 1996 under the direction of Vector, but in 1999 responsibility for it was transferred to CUTCO International. Sales offices opened in Costa Rica in mid-1997; by 1999, sales were about $1 million. A year-end accounting review indicated that the CUTCO International operating margin was about 2.5 percent.[1]

One of the distinguishing features of CUTCO cutlery is that it has always been marketed through direct selling. This feature, which can be viewed as both a distinctive competency and a potential weakness, sets ALCAS apart from its major competi-

[1] All operating margins are disguised, although the relationships among them are representative.

tors, J. A. Henckels Zwillingswerk Inc. ("Henckels"), Chicago Cutlery, and Wusthof-Trident. These competitors have traditionally used department stores and mass merchandisers to market their products. Of the major competitors, Henckels, a German company, is the largest, with U.S. retail sales recently exceeding those of Vector. Although the "street" price of Henckels cutlery is typically 25 percent less than its list price, Vector prices and Henckels prices are very similar for comparable items.

■ VECTOR MARKETING CORPORATION

Vector Marketing Corporation sales efforts are organized by geographic location. At the end of 1999, the United States consisted of four geographic sales regions (central, northeast, southern, and western), each headed by a vice president and a sales director. Within each region are eight or nine divisions, and within these divisions are a total of approximately 200 district or permanent offices and another 200 branch ("summer") offices that operate for about 17 weeks every summer. A district office typically has a population base of at least 200,000 people.

The people actually selling CUTCO cutlery are independent contractors who effectively operate their own business. As such, these sales representatives are paid a commission on the products they sell. Although they are eligible for demonstration-based compensation, sales representatives usually move to a full commission compensation system that can exceed demonstration-based compensation. None of the sales representatives receive a salary from the company.

For the most part, sales representatives are college students who sell CUTCO cutlery during their school vacations. Fifty-five percent of the sales representatives are males. Each summer, thousands of college students are recruited to sell CUTCO products through a variety of methods that includes newspaper advertisements, direct mailings, the Internet, and on-campus recruiting. The most successful sales representatives earn more than $10,000 for a summer of selling; the average commission of the top 500 sales representatives in a typical summer is in excess of $5,500. The average commission for sales representatives working for an entire summer is $2,200. As a consequence of the "summer selling season," a majority of Vector's sales occurs between May and August each year. Vector is effectively an organization structured to facilitate the recruiting, training, and motivating of college students to sell CUTCO products.

Sales are made through in-home presentations that involve illustrations of the superiority of CUTCO cutlery through actual applications as well as rope-cutting demonstrations and the like. These presentations are prearranged through referrals and appointments; they are thought to be a key to company success. As Marty Domitrovich, vice president of the Central Region, frequently says:

> Selling yourself is paramount in any sales situation. I firmly believe that people buy from individuals they like, and there is no better way to make a solid impression than face to face. There is no substitute for the personal touch that comes from sitting across from someone in his or her home and allowing them to actually try your product. Personal, professional demonstrations sell CUTCO cutlery. Period.

Often, the first sale is made to a sales representative's parents, relatives, or neighbors. Interestingly enough, about one out of six sales is made each year to previous purchasers of CUTCO cutlery. Because CUTCO products tend to "sell themselves" after people have seen a live demonstration, there is relatively little need for a "hard sell" on the part of the sales representatives. Training emphasizes appointment setting, demonstrations, closing the sale, and referrals. There is no "cold calling" or door-to-door selling.

Sales representatives typically meet with their Vector managers on Monday evenings to discuss the prior week's activities and plan the current week's activities.

During these meetings, the sales representatives turn in their sales orders and the money collected. The sales managers express mail the orders and money to Olean, where orders are filled.

In 1999, Vector filled approximately 509,000 separate orders in the United States alone, with each order effectively representing one direct sales customer. Products are shipped directly to customers within three weeks during the summer selling season and within two weeks at other times. Both UPS and the U.S. Postal Service are used to deliver products. The operating margin of Vector in 1999 on direct sales was approximately 10.5 percent.[2]

To increase corporate revenues and motivate sales representatives, Vector employs a variety of promotional activities, events, and competitions. Not only are the sales representatives rewarded directly for the sales they make, they are also eligible to receive trophies, bonuses, trips, and even scholarships for achieving certain sales levels. Particularly successful sales representatives have an additional opportunity to establish and manage one of the branch offices. Managing a branch office requires a dedicated and active program of training throughout the school year.

The particular direct selling model that Vector uses differs from the direct selling models used by virtually all other direct selling firms. Only one other direct selling company uses college students as its primary sales force. The Southwestern Company in Nashville, Tennessee, uses college students to sell a variety of books and related educational material during summer vacations. However, the selling models of the two companies are very different. Vector trains sales representatives in small groups at each of its district or branch offices, whereas The Southwestern Company conducts centralized training programs in Nashville in which hundreds of sales representatives are trained simultaneously. Moreover, whereas Vector sales representatives use a referral system for sales leads, The Southwestern Company sales representatives focus on door-to-door sales presentations. Finally, whereas Vector sales representatives typically sell in their home cities, The Southwestern Company's sales representatives typically are assigned to a city away from their home.

Vector Catalog Sales

Because 90 percent of the sales representatives sell for only one summer, the customers that they create sometimes lose contact with CUTCO products and Vector. To maintain a continuing relationship with and service these customers, Vector mailed a flyer containing a few product specials to a sample of customers in 1985. This flyer was expanded to a 24-page catalog in 1988. Presently, as many as four 32-page catalogs are mailed to 2.8 million CUTCO customers in the fall and then to about 400,000 previous catalog buyers in the spring. Mailings are carefully timed (September to December and March to May) to prevent conflicts with the summer selling season. In 1999, catalog mailings generated about 97,000 orders, with a corresponding operating margin of 15 percent.[3] If the customer of a current Vector sales representative makes a catalog purchase, the representative and the representative's manager receive a commission (although the commissions are less than if the representative initiated the sale). If the sales representative is no longer actively selling for Vector, only the representative's manager receives a commision.

The Vector Customer

At the 50th anniversary celebration, Vector management estimated that about 9 million customers have purchased CUTCO cutlery at one time or another. Since 1989,

[2] All operating margins are disguised, although the relationships among them are representative.

[3] All operating margins are disguised, although the relationships among them are representative.

when Vector began systematically capturing and recording customers' names and addresses, more than 4.4 million customers have been added to the company's database. The "typical" Vector customer is a married homeowner with one or more older children. The typical customer is relatively affluent and holds a managerial or professional employment position. The annual income of a typical customer is more than $50,000; in certain geographic areas, the typical customer's annual income is in excess of $100,000. Most Vector customers have at least a bachelor's degree. Sixty percent are between 40 and 59 years of age. There is no discernible difference between Vector's direct sales customers and customers who purchase from its catalogs. The typical customer enjoys reading, traveling, cooking, and gardening.

■ A NOTE ON DIRECT SELLING

Direct selling is face-to-face selling away from a fixed business location. Thus, it is a form of nonstore retailing. The direct-selling industry consists of numerous well-known firms such as Amway, Avon, Mary Kay Cosmetics, and Tupperware. At the same time, however, the industry itself is relatively unknown, principally because it is "invisible." By definition, there are no physical stores, and because direct selling is essentially a push marketing strategy, direct-selling firms do little advertising. Hence, there is little public awareness of most direct-selling firms. In addition, the majority of direct-selling firms are small, privately owned firms created and operated by entrepreneurs, many of whom often want a low public profile.

According to the Direct Selling Association, the direct-selling industry trade association, industry sales in the United States were slightly more than $23 billion in 1998. This figure reflects an average annual growth rate of 8.7 percent during the 1990s. (Globally, direct sales were estimated to be about $82 billion, with Japan accounting for slightly more than $28 billion.)

Virtually all direct sellers (99%+) are independent contractors. Of the estimated 9.7 million direct sellers in the United States in 1998 (up from 5.1 million in 1991), 73 percent are women. Only 10 percent of direct sellers work full time in direct selling, and one source estimated that nearly half earned less than $500 annually. A survey of direct sellers conducted for the Direct Selling Association in 1997 revealed that a substantial number work only to earn money for a particular purchase (e.g., a vacation), work only because they like and use a product or service themselves, or work only because they enjoy the social aspect of direct selling.

Seventy percent of direct selling takes place in a residence. Nearly three-quarters (72 percent) takes place on a one-to-one basis. The other major form of direct selling is the "party plan." Party plan selling represents a combination of group selling and entertainment. The Tupperware party in which six to eight housewives get together at the home of a hostess is the quintessential example of party plan selling.

The most popular form of one-to-one direct selling is network or multilevel marketing. About 81 percent of all independent contractors selling one-to-one do so through a multilevel marketing program. Direct sellers in a multilevel marketing program are not only rewarded for the sales that they personally make but also rewarded for the sales of individuals they recruit and the sales of people in turn recruited by the individuals they recruited (i.e., their "downline" in multilevel marketing terms, hence the notion of multi or many levels).

The Typical Direct-Selling Customer

Of the products and services marketed through direct selling, personal care and home-related products and services are among the most popular. Cosmetics, vitamins and dietary supplements, kitchenware, long-distance telephone services, and cleaning products are currently among the best-selling products and services in the direct-selling industry. Even so, virtually any product or service seems to be amenable to this mode of marketing (in Japan, a large percentage of new automobiles are sold door-to-door).

Although estimates differ, a majority of the households in the United States have at one time or another purchased a product or service from a direct seller. This suggests that the typical direct-selling customer should have characteristics similar to people in general, or at least people who shop retail stores. More specifically, direct-selling customers tend to be affluent females 35 to 54 years of age. Relative to the overall population in the United States, the typical direct-selling customer has somewhat more education and a larger household income.

■ THE INTERNET ISSUE

For more than three years, Michael Lancellot and the other executives at Vector and ALCAS had been grappling with the issue of what role the Internet should play, if any, in Vector's marketing. During that time period, access to the Internet, and especially the World Wide Web ("Web"), had literally exploded. Although estimates vary dramatically, there is general agreement that a plurality of households in the United States currently has Web access and e-mail addresses. Initially, Web access was limited to academics and "technogeeks," but with each passing day the types of people accessing it are becoming more similar to the general population. By the end of 1999, the modal Web user in the United States was a male 35 to 54 years of age with an average income in excess of $50,000. Nearly all college students have access to the Web and an e-mail address, whether through their school or personally.

Although only a small percentage of the consumers currently accessing the Web actually purchase anything, the number of consumers shopping on the Web is predicted to increase exponentially in the next few years. Books, computer software and hardware, music, and travel seem to be the product and service categories from which consumers are most likely to make a purchase on the Web. Cutlery products can be found on the Web in a variety of sites. For example, Wusthof-Trident cutlery is marketed on sites such as Plum's Cooking Co., whereas Henckels cutlery is marketed on sites such as Knife Outlet. Interestingly, the price of Henckels cutlery on the Knife Outlet Web site is about 30 percent less than its retail or list price. In late 1999, such stalwart retailers as the Gap, Neiman Marcus, Wal-Mart, and Ethan Allen established Web sites and launched aggressive e-commerce campaigns.

Direct Selling Web Sites

Although the majority of direct-selling firms have Web sites, most are limited to providing customer service and contact information. During 1999, several large direct-selling firms experimented with marketing their products and services on the Web. For example, Avon, which claims to be the largest direct seller of cosmetics and personal care products, began marketing some of its products through several Internet retailers as well as on its own Web site. Tupperware, which markets storage containers, kitchen aids, educational materials, and toys, launched an extensive Web site to market its products, facilitate party planning by its distributors, recruit new distributors, and provide distributor locations for customers. The company attempted to create the feel of a magazine by incorporating a recipe database and recipe exchange mechanism, an information forum, and so forth on its Web site.

Amway, the largest direct seller of household, personal care, nutritional, and ancillary products, took a slightly different approach to Internet marketing. It established a new company and the independent Web site Quixtar ("Quick-Star"), through which it intends to sell not only its own products but those of many other firms as well. Additionally, the Quixtar Web site offers links to "partner stores" on the Web and a mechanism for Amway and Quixtar independent contractors to do business through the site rather than on a face-to-face basis. Thus, Amway independent contractors who subscribe to Quixtar will be able to use the Web site for recruiting and can obtain commissions from sales made through the site. Unfortunately, because many of the direct sellers' Web sites were launched late in 1999, no information was yet available to the Vector and ALCAS management teams that would allow an assessment of how successful the Web sites were.

Vector Internet Activity

For more than two years, Vector has operated a customer-oriented Web site (www.cutco.com) focusing on customer service and product information. Although Vector customer service representatives have had a number of requests from consumers wishing to order CUTCO products on-line, up to this point these consumers have been advised that they could order only from a sales representative. However, as Michael Lancellot has consistently maintained:

> We have a very important responsibility to make sure that we are meeting the needs of our customers. With a 50-year reputation of product quality and service, it is imperative that Vector meet customer expectations. One of those expectations is the ability to order CUTCO products on-line. However, while it is important that we meet the expectations of our customers, it is critically important to also protect the interests of our field sales organization.

For the last year, Vector personnel, including Brett Trent, Vector's Internet manager, have been working on a strategy to use the Internet as a vehicle to recruit college students to be sales representatives. Two different Web sites (www.workforstudents.com and www.earnparttime.com) are currently being used. To date, the number of applications received on-line has been very encouraging. As one aspect of this recruiting strategy, Vector established a special Web site to provide recently interviewed recruits and their parents with information on the company and the sales program, including the commission structure. To date, the Internet recruiting strategy appears to be reasonably successful, and plans are to expand company efforts in the coming years.

KA-BAR Web Site

In September 1999, KA-BAR launched a modest Web site (www.ka-bar.com). The Web site was intended to increase product awareness, provide dealer support, facilitate communication with customers and various constituencies, and sell knives. The development cost of the Web site was $19,000, and initial set-up costs totaled $1,000, excluding hardware costs. Ongoing development and service costs are estimated at $1,000 per month. Although sales started slowly, and most sales appeared to be to business intermediaries rather than to end users, by the end of 1999 KA-BAR management felt optimistic that the Web site would eventually generate considerable revenue (despite the fact that KA-BAR knives were simultaneously being sold on the Web sites of several of its customers).

The Meeting

Because of the importance of the Internet marketing issue, a joint meeting of the Vector and ALCAS top management teams was called. Michael Lancellot opened the meeting by reminding the executives attending of the importance of meeting customer expectations. He also reiterated his belief that any Internet activity must be complementary to—and must strengthen—the Vector sales force.

Jim Stitt immediately seconded Lancellot's belief. "As a case in point," he interjected, "I had a call this morning from one of Vector's field managers who had heard that Creed (Creed Terry, Vector vice president of marketing) was proposing some sort of Internet selling test. The manager's recommendation was that we put our Net activities on hold until we see how this whole thing shakes out or we create a Web site for only the internal arena."

John Whelpley, executive vice president and chief administrative officer of Vector, then reported the results of a financial analysis that his staff had undertaken. Whelpley estimated that the cost to launch a state-of-the-art Web site would range from $200,000, if constructed by Brett Trent's staff, to $500,000 if contracted out. Part of the difference in cost, he said, was that a Web site would take 15 to 18 months if done internally but only 6 to 8 months if contracted out. Whelpley continued:

> We also estimate that the overhead of a Web site technical support group would run about $250,000 per year and that there would be major changes in the Vector service organization. Not only would we need reps available 24 × 7, we would need a new training program and perhaps even a new business philosophy. Although fulfillment costs would be similar to those experienced with catalog operations, I don't know what we would do if an order came in from South Africa or Brazil.

He concluded his presentation by posing the question: "What revenue can we expect from a Web site, and what revenue do we need for it to be commercially viable?"

Creed Terry was the next to speak, pressing the need to determine what direction to take:

> It is clear, at least to me, that the Internet could impact our business in many positive ways. What we have to determine is how best to integrate Internet strategies with our strong direct selling capabilities to realize the revenue potential of the market while maximizing the full earning opportunities available to our managers and sales representatives. The issue seems to be whether we undertake an all-out, aggressive selling approach on the Web or whether we focus only on penetrating our existing customer base.

"Well," said Erick Laine, "we certainly do not want to do anything with the Internet that would harm our direct sales operation." He continued:

> We know that selling CUTCO products requires a personal demonstration and the hands-on opportunity to "try to test drive" that only our field sales organization can provide. I can't imagine that the Internet—or anything else, for that matter—could even come close to bringing in the half million-plus new customers that the sales organization is capable of doing.
>
> However, the Internet is already here—in a big way—whether we want it or not. It could give us a way to service our existing customers even better than our catalog has done over the past several years, and hopefully just as painlessly. So . . . let's take a systematic look at our options with and through our vice presidents of sales and see if we can at least agree on a general strategy.

CHAPTER 10

Marketing Strategy Reformulation: The Control Process

Marketing strategies are rarely, if ever, timeless. As the environment changes, so must product-market and marketing-mix plans. Moreover, as organizations strive for gains in productivity, constant attention must be given to improving the efficiency of marketing efforts.

The marketing control process serves as the mechanism for achieving strategic adaptation to environmental change and operational adaptation to productivity needs.[1] Marketing control consists of two complementary activities: strategic control, which is concerned with "doing the right things," and operations control, which focuses on "doing things right." *Strategic control* assesses the direction of the organization as evidenced by its implicit or explicit goals, objectives, strategies, and capacity to perform in the context of changing environments and competitive actions. The ever-present issue of defining the fit between an organization's capabilities and objectives and environmental threats and opportunities is at the core of strategic control. *Operations control* assesses how well the organization performs marketing activities as it seeks to achieve planned outcomes. It is implicitly assumed that the direction of the organization is correct and that only the organization's ability to perform specific tasks needs to be improved.

The distinction between strategic and operations control is important to grasp. It has been noted that a "poorly executed plan can produce undesirable results just as easily as a poorly conceived plan."[2] Though undesirable results (declining sales, eroding market share, or sagging profits) may be identical, remedial actions under the two types of control will differ. Remedial efforts drawn from an operations-control perspective focus on heightening the marketing effort or identifying ways to improve *efficiency*. Alternatively, remedial efforts based on a strategic-control orientation focus on improving the *effectiveness* of the organization in seeking opportunities and mitigating threats in its environment. Improper assessment of the need for strategic versus operations control can lead to a disastrous response in which an organization pours additional funds into an ill-conceived strategy only to realize further declines in sales, market share, and profit.

STRATEGIC CHANGE

Strategic change is defined here as change in the environment that will affect the long-run well-being of the organization. Strategic change may represent opportunities or threats to an organization, depending on the organization's competitive posture. For example, the gradual aging of the U.S. population represents a potential threat to organizations catering to children, whereas this change represents an opportunity to organizations providing products for and services to the elderly.

Sources of Strategic Change

Strategic change can arise from a multitude of sources.[3] One source is *market evolution*, which results from changes in primary demand for a product class and changes in technology. For example, increased primary demand for calcium in diets prompted the marketers of Tums antacid, Total cereal, and Minute Maid orange juice to promote the presence of calcium in their products. Technological change often prompts market evolution and changes in marketing techniques, as evidenced by the growth of the Internet as described in Chapter 9.

Market redefinition is another source of strategic change. *Market redefinition* results from changes in the offering demanded by buyers or promoted by competitors. For example, firms that provided only automated teller machines (ATMs) for banks saw the market redefined to electronic funds transfer, with total systems rather than equipment alone being the offering purchased. Firms with systems capabilities, such as IBM, thus gained a competitive advantage in the redefined market.

Change in marketing channels is a third source of strategic change. The increasing role of Internet technology, the continuing focus on reducing distribution costs, and power shifts within marketing channels represent three opportunities or threats, depending on a marketer's relative position in a market. Strategic change, along these dimensions, is apparent in the distribution of automobiles in the United States.[4] Consumers today can price-comparison shop on the Internet without visiting dealers. The erosion in industry profit margins has caused manufacturers and dealers alike to look for cost-cutting opportunities, particularly in distribution costs, which represent 25 to 30 percent of the retail price of a new car. Finally, increasing consolidation of automobile dealerships by companies such as Republic Industries, the largest holder of new-car dealerships in the United States and the owner of AutoNation USA, the used-car megastore chain, has the potential to alter the bargaining power between manufacturers and dealers.

Strategic Change: Threat or Opportunity?

Threat severity or opportunity potential is determined by the organization's business definition. In other words, does the threat or opportunity relate to the types of customers served by the organization, the needs of the customers, the means by which the organization satisfies these needs, or some combination of these factors?

The effects of strategic change are apparent in the transformation of the worldwide watchmaking industry.[5] Although Swiss watchmakers had dominated this industry for a century, market evolution, market redefinition, and marketing channel changes combined to spell disaster for the Swiss. While a technologically motivated market evolution changed the offering from jeweled watches to quartz and electronic watches, the primary marketing channel changed from select jewelry stores to mass merchandisers and supermarkets. Moreover, a redefinition of the term *watch* occurred. No longer was a watch defined solely in terms of craftsmanship or elegance as jewelry. Many people began to think of a watch as an economical and disposable timepiece. These changes, brought about by Timex and such Japanese firms as Seiko and Citizen, severely affected the Swiss watchmakers. Today, Swiss watchmakers have, for the most part, retreated to a highly specialized market niche, which can be identified as the prestige, luxury, artistry watch segment. For example, Swiss watches "tell you something about yourself" (Patek) and are "the most expensive in the world" (Piaget).

This example highlights how strategic change can affect an entire industry and its individual participants. In practice, several options exist for dealing with strategic change:

1. An organization can attempt to marshal the resources necessary to alter its technical and marketing capabilities to fit the market-success requirement. (Swiss watchmakers did not do this but, rather, devoted modest research funds to perfecting the design of mechanical watches, in which they had a distinctive competency. Only Ebauches S.A. invested in electronic technology and pursued the marketing opportunity available for an inexpensive, fashion watch—the Swatch.)
2. An organization can shift its emphasis to product markets where the match between success requirements and the firm's distinctive competency is clear and can cut back efforts in those product markets where it has been outflanked. (Many Swiss watchmakers chose this option.)
3. An organization can leave the industry. (Over 1,000 Swiss watchmakers selected this option, thereby eliminating more than 45,000 Swiss jobs.)

■ OPERATIONS CONTROL

The goal of operations control is to improve the productivity of marketing efforts. Because cost identification and allocation are central to the appraisal of marketing efforts and profitability, marketing-cost analysis is a fundamental aspect of operations control. This section provides an overview of marketing-cost analysis and selected examples of product-service mix control, sales control, and marketing-channel control.

Nature of Marketing-Cost Analysis

The purpose of *marketing-cost analysis* is to trace, assign, or allocate costs to a specified marketing activity or entity (hereafter referred to as a *segment*) in a manner that accurately displays the financial contribution of activities or entities to the organization. Marketing segments are typically defined on the basis of (1) elements of the product-service offering, (2) type or size of customers, (3) sales divisions, districts, or territories, and/or (4) marketing channels. Cost allocation is based on the principle that certain costs are directly or indirectly traceable or assignable to every marketing segment.[6]

Several issues arise in regard to the cost-allocation question:

1. *How should costs be allocated to separate marketing segments?* As a general rule, the manager should attempt to assign costs in accordance with an identifiable measure of application to an entity.
2. *What costs should be allocated?* Again, as a general rule, costs arising from the performance of a marketing activity or charged to that activity according to administrative policy are the costs that should be allocated.
3. *Should all costs be allocated to marketing segments?* The answer to this question will depend on whether the manager opts for a "whole equals the sum of parts" income statement. If so, then all costs should be fully allocated. If it

appears that certain costs have no identifiable measure of application to a segment or do not arise from one particular segment, however, these costs should not be allocated.

The manager should follow two guidelines in considering the cost-allocation question. First, when costs are allocated, fundamental distinctions between cost behavior patterns should be maintained. Second, the more joint costs there are (costs that have no identifiable basis for allocation or that arise from a variety of marketing segments), the less exact cost allocations will be. In general, greater detail in cost allocation or traceability will provide more useful information for remedial action.

Product–Service Mix Control

Proper control of the product-service mix involves two interrelated tasks. First, the manager must assess the performance of offerings in the relevant markets. Second, the manager must appraise the financial worth of product-service offerings.

Sales volume, as an index of performance, can be approached from two directions. Growth or decline in unit sales volume provides a quantitative indicator of the acceptance of offerings in their relevant markets. Equally important is the proportion of sales coming from individual offerings in the product-service mix and how this sales distribution affects profitability. Many firms experience the "80-20 rule"—80 percent of sales or profits come from 20 percent of the firm's offerings. For example, in the early 1990s, 20 percent of Kodak's products contributed more than 80 percent to the firm's sales. Such an imbalance in the mix can have a disastrous effect on overall profitability if sudden changes in competitive or market behavior threaten the viability of this 20 percent. This happened to Kodak when technological innovations such as digital imaging cameras began to redefine the photographic market. Also, Fuji proved to be an aggressive competitor in Kodak's traditional film and photographic markets.[7]

Market share complements sales volume as an indicator of performance. Market share offers a means for determining whether an organization is gaining or losing ground in comparison with competitors, provided it is used properly. Several questions must be considered when market share is used for control purposes. First, what is the market on which the market-share percentage is based, and has the market definition changed? Market share can be computed by geographic area, product type or model, customer or channel type, and so forth. In the Goodyear Tire and Rubber Company case in Chapter 7, the market share for tires was reported by geography (U.S. versus worldwide), product type (passenger car and truck), type of retail outlet (company-owned stores, discount tire stores, etc.), as well as by manufacturers' total sales. Second, is the market itself changing? For example, high market share by itself may be misleading, since overall sales in the market may be declining or growing. Finally, the unit of analysis—dollar sales or unit sales—must be considered. Because of price differentials, it is better to use unit rather than dollar volume in examining market share.

A second aspect of product-service control consists of appraising the financial contribution of market offerings. An important step in this process is to assign or trace costs to offerings in a manner that reflects their profitability. However, this step is difficult and often requires astute managerial judgment. Moreover, the definition of an offering is itself illusive. For example, a "red-eye" flight (early morning or late evening) scheduled by an airline might be viewed as an offering. The decision by McDonald's and Taco Bell to open for the breakfast trade can be viewed as a market offering, the costs of which include not only the cost of producing the menu items but also the cost of being open.

From a control perspective, the manager should examine the financial worth of market offerings using a *contribution-margin approach*, in which the relevant costs charged against an offering include direct costs and assignable overhead. The units by which these costs are broken down should be those that contribute most meaningfully to the analysis.

Consider the situation in which the owner of a chain of gasoline service stations is examining operating performance. Exhibit 10.1 shows the operating performance before and after cost allocation by department. Examination of the total yields little managerially relevant information. When costs are disaggregated and measured by department, however, it becomes apparent that gasoline operates at a net loss, whereas general merchandise and automobile service operate profitably. Fortunately, each department "contributes" to overhead; that is, each department's revenue exceeds its allocated variable costs.

This analysis serves a useful purpose in identifying potential trouble spots. Several alternatives exist for taking corrective action. If the owner decided to drop the unprofitable line and leave the selling space empty, then general merchandise and automobile service would have to cover the total fixed costs, which will continue. It is doubtful that this would occur. (Note that gasoline does contribute to the payment of fixed costs.) Another possibility is that the manager might expand the other departments to use the empty space. Estimates of market demand and forecasts of revenue would be needed for further consideration of this action. Moreover, a commitment of resources would have to occur that would in effect significantly alter the nature of the business.

Sales Control

Sales control directs a manager's attention to both the behavioral and the cost aspects of sales activity. The behavioral element consists of sales effort and allocation of selling time. The cost aspect consists of expenses arising from the performance and administration of the sales function.

Sales control is usually based on a performance analysis by sales territories or districts, size and type of customers or accounts, products, or some combination of these variables. Various measures used to assess sales performance include sales revenue, gross profit, sales call frequency, penetration of accounts in a sales territory, and selling and sales administration expenditures.

Consider a situation in which a district sales manager has requested a quarterly performance review of two sales personnel in a territory within the district. These individuals have failed to achieve their sales, gross profit, and profit quotas. Exhibit 10.2 on page 556 displays the representatives' performance according to customer-volume account categories. These categories were established by the national sales manager on the basis of industry norms, as were the following expected quarterly call frequencies:

EXHIBIT 10.1

Disaggregating Service Station Costs for Product–Service Mix Control (Thousands of Dollars)

		Department		
	Total	*Gasoline*	*General Merchandise*	*Automobile Service*
Sales	$4,000	$2,000	$1,700	$300
Cost of goods sold and variable expenses	3,000	1,600	1,220	180
Contribution margin	1,000	400	480	120
Fixed expenses	900	500	310	90
Net income	$ 100	$ (100)	$ 170	$ 30

EXHIBIT 10.2

Performance Summary for Two Sales Representatives

Account Category	*(1) Potential Accounts in Sales District*[a]	*(2) Active Accounts*[b]	*(3) Sales Volume*[c]	*(4) Gross Profit*[d]	*(5) Total Calls*[e]	*(6) Selling Expenses*[f]	*(7) Sales Administration*[g]
A	80	60	$ 48,000	$14,000	195	$18,400	
B	60	40	44,000	15,400	200	17,900	
C	40	10	25,000	12,250	50	11,250	
D	20	6	33,000	16,500	42	9,000	
Totals	200	116	$150,000	$58,550	487	$56,550	$10,000

[a] Based on marketing research data identifying potential users of company products.

[b] Current accounts.

[c] Based on invoices.

[d] Based on invoice price for full mix of products sold.

[e] Based on sales call reports cross-referenced by customer name.

[f] Direct costs of sales including allocated salaries of two sales representatives.

[g] Costs not assignable on a meaningful basis; includes office expense.

Account Definition	*Expected Frequency of Quarterly Calls*
A: $1,000 or less in sales	2
B: $1,000–$1,999 in sales	4
C: $2,000–$4,999 in sales	6
D: $5,000 or more in sales	8

Both representatives had an equal number of A, B, C, and D accounts.

Exhibit 10.3 shows various indices prepared by the district sales manager from the performance summary shown in Exhibit 10.2. Among the principal findings evident from Exhibit 10.3 are the following:

1. The representatives' account penetration varied inversely with the size of the account. Whereas representatives had penetrated 75 percent of the smaller A accounts, only 30 percent of the potentially large D accounts were listed as active buyers.
2. Part of the reason for this performance appears to lie in the call frequency of the representatives. The representatives exceeded the call norm on the A and B accounts, but fell short on call frequency on the C and D accounts. Moreover, their "effort" level appears questionable (487 calls ÷ 90 days ÷ 2 representatives = 2.7 calls per day).
3. The gross profit percentage derived from sales to smaller accounts was considerably lower than that derived from sales to the larger accounts, which in turn affected profitability.
4. When account sales volume is matched with gross profit and selling expenses, it becomes apparent that the smaller accounts actually produced a net contribution dollar loss.

The sales control process in this instance revealed that the two representatives were not actively calling on accounts (only 2.7 calls per day) and that their allocation of call activity focused on smaller-volume, less profitable accounts that were in fact contributing a *loss* to overhead. Redirection of effort is clearly called for in this situation.

EXHIBIT 10.3

Selected Operating Indices of Sales Performance

Sales Volume/ Active Account (Col. 3 ÷ Col. 4)	*Gross Profit Active Account (Col. 4 ÷ Col. 2)*	*Selling Expenses/ Active Account (Col. 6 ÷ Col. 2)*	*Contribution to Sales Administration (Gross Profit— Selling Expenses)*
A: $800	$240	$307	–$67
B: $1,100	$385	$448	–$63
C: $2,500	$1,225	$1,125	$1,375
D: $5,500	$2,750	$1,500	$1,250
Account Penetration (Col. 2 ÷ Col. 3)	***Call Frequency/ Active Account (Col. 5 ÷ Col. 2)***	***Selling Expense per Call Col. 6 ÷ Col. 5)***	***Gross Profit %/ Active Account (Col. 4 ÷ Col. 3)***
A: 75%	3.25	$94.36	30%
B: 67	5.0	$89.50	35
C: 25	5.0	$225.00	49
D: 30	7.0	214.29	50

Marketing Channel Control

Marketing channel control consists of two complementary processes. The manager must first assess environmental and organizational factors that may alter the structure, conduct, and performance of marketing channels. These considerations were highlighted in Chapter 7. Second, the manager must evaluate the profitability of marketing channels.

Profitability analysis for marketing channels follows the general format outlined for product-service control. Cost identification and allocation differ, however. Two types of costs—order-getting and order-servicing costs—must be identified and traced to different marketing channels. *Order-getting costs* include sales expenses and advertising allowances. *Order-servicing expenditures* include packing and delivery costs, warehousing expenses, and billing costs.[8]

Consider a hypothetical marketer of furniture polishes, cleaners, and assorted furniture improvement products. This firm uses its own sales force to sell its products through three marketing channels: furniture stores, hardware stores, and home improvement stores. Exhibit 10.4 on page 558 shows income statements for all three channels combined, as well as individually (general and administration costs are not allocated or included). It is apparent that when costs and revenues are traced by channel, furniture store and hardware store channels generate equal sales revenue; however furniture stores incur a sizable loss and hardware stores account for almost all of net income. Why are the returns so different?

Inspection of disaggregated costs suggests the following:

1. The gross margin percentage on the mix of products sold to hardware stores is 38 percent, whereas the gross margin percentage on products sold to furniture stores and home improvement stores is 30 percent. Thus, lower-margin products are being sold through furniture and home improvement stores on the average.
2. Order-getting costs (selling and advertising) run about 21 percent of sales for furniture stores, but only 7 percent for hardware stores and 16 percent for home improvement stores.

EXHIBIT 10.4

Disaggregated Costs of Furniture Improvement Products for Marketing Channel Control (Thousands of Dollars)

		Marketing Channel		
	Total	*Furniture Stores*	*Hardware Stores*	*Home Improvement Stores*
Sales	$12,000	$5,000	$5,000	$2,000
Cost of goods sold	8,000	3,500	3,100	1,400
Gross margin	4,000	1,500	1,900	600
Expenses				
Selling	1,000	617	216	167
Advertising	750	450	150	150
Packing and delivery	800	370	300	130
Warehousing	400	200	150	50
Billing	600	300	250	50
Total expenses	3,550	1,937	1,066	547
Net channel income (loss)	$ 450	$(437)	$ 834	$ 53

3. Order-servicing costs are 17 percent of sales for furniture stores, 14 percent for hardware stores, and about 12 percent for home improvement stores.

In short, a manager can conclude that the effort (reflected in costs) necessary to generate sales and service in the furniture store channel is much greater than that needed for hardware and home improvement stores. Moreover, furniture stores purchase products with a lower gross margin. Once these problems have been identified, efforts to remedy the situation can be explored in a more systematic fashion.

Some companies trace order-getting and order-servicing costs and revenues by individual customer in a marketing channel. The result of such analyses is often illuminating. For instance, LSI Logic, a high-tech semiconductor manufacturer, recently discovered that 90 percent of its profit arose from 10 percent of its customers. Moreover, the company was losing money on half of its customers![9]

CONSIDERATIONS IN MARKETING CONTROL

Proper implementation of strategic and operations control requires that the manager be aware of several pertinent considerations. Three of these considerations follow.

Problems versus Symptoms

Effective control, whether at the strategic or the operations level, requires that the manager recognize the difference between root problems and surface symptoms. This means that the manager must develop causal relationships between occurrences. For example, if there is evidence of a sales decline or poor profit margins, the manager must "look behind" the numbers to identify the underlying causes of such performance and then attempt to remedy them. This diagnostic role is similar to that of a physician, who must first establish patient symptoms in order to identify the ailment.

Effectiveness versus Efficiency

A second consideration is the dynamic tension that exists between effectiveness and efficiency. Effectiveness addresses the question of whether the organization is achieving its intended goals, given environmental opportunities and constraints and organizational capabilities. Efficiency relates to productivity—the levels of output, given a specified unit of input. Suppose a sales representative has a high call frequency per day and a low cost-per-call expense ratio. The individual might be viewed favorably from an efficiency perspective. If the emphasis of the organization is on customer service and problem solving, however, this person might be viewed as ineffective.

Data versus Information

A third consideration is the qualitative difference between data and information. Data are essentially *reports* of activities, events, or performance. Information, on the other hand, may be viewed as a *classification* of activities, events, or performance designed to be interpretable and useful for decision making. The distinction between data and information was illustrated in the discussion of marketing-cost analysis techniques, where data were organized into meaningful classifications and operating ratios.

NOTES

1. For a review of the marketing control literature, see Bernard J. Jaworski, "Toward a Theory of Marketing Control: Environmental Context, Control Types, and Consequences," *Journal of Marketing* (July 1988): 23-29.

2. R. Paul, N. Donavan, and J. Taylor, "The Reality Gap in Strategic Planning," *Harvard Business Review* (May-June 1978): 126. See also Thomas Bonoma, "Making Your Marketing Strategy Work," *Harvard Business Review* (March-April 1984): 68-76.

3. These concepts were drawn from D. Abell, "Strategic Windows," *Journal of Marketing* (July 1978): 21-26.

4. Evan R. Hirsh, et al., "Changing Channels in the Automotive Industry: The Future of Automotive Marketing and Distribution," *Strategy & Business* (First Quarter 1999): 42-50; and "Restructure of Dealer Networks Will Change Retailing," *Marketing News* (October 26, 1998): 10.

5. This example is adapted from D. Landes, "Time Runs Out for the Swiss," *Across the Board* (January 1984): 46-55; L. Rukeyser, "Swiss Recovery of Luxury Watch Market Provides Timely Lesson," *Dallas Times Herald* (November 12, 1989): D9; and "Buying Time," *Fortune* (September 8, 1997): 192.

6. B. Ames and J. Hlavacek, "Vital Truths about Managing Your Costs," *Harvard Business Review* (January-February 1990): 140-47; and S. L. Mintz, "Two Steps Forward, One Step Back," *CFO* (December 1998): 21-25.

7. "Film vs. Digital: Can Kodak Build a Bridge?" *Business Week* (August 2, 1999): 66-69; and "Kodak's New Focus," *Business Week* (January 30, 1995): 62-68.

8. For an example of cost identification in marketing channels, see Robin Cooper and Robert S. Kaplan, "Profit Priorities from Activity-Based Costing," *Harvard Business Review* (May-June 1991): 130-37.

9. Bob Donath, "Fire Your Big Customers? Maybe You Should," *Marketing News* (June 21, 1999): 9.

CASE

Pharmacia & Upjohn, Inc.

Rogaine Hair Regrowth Treatment

On February 9, 1996, the U.S. Food and Drug Administration (FDA) approved Rogaine Hair Regrowth Treatment for sale without a physician's prescription. Rogaine, the only medically proven hair regrowth treatment at the time for men and women with common hereditary hair loss, had been sold as a prescription drug in the United States since 1988. Cumulative sales of Rogaine in the United States since its introduction exceeded $700 million. Worldwide cumulative Rogaine sales exceeded $1 billion (see Exhibit 1).[1]

With Rogaine's patent about to expire in four days, FDA approval of Rogaine as a nonprescription, or over-the-counter (OTC), drug was welcome news to Pharmacia & Upjohn, Inc., the manufacturer of the product. According to a company official, "We are pleased with the FDA's decision switching Rogaine from prescription to OTC sales. OTC availability of Rogaine is a welcome convenience for millions of men and women who experience common hair loss. We are pursuing an aggressive timetable to make Rogaine quickly and widely accessible to consumers."[2] The launch of nonprescription Rogaine was scheduled for April 1996. At that time, prescription-only Rogaine would be discontinued, since both prescription and nonprescription Rogaine had identical formulations. The company also requested the FDA to approve a three-year period of marketing exclusivity for nonprescription Rogaine under provisions of the Waxman-Hatch Amendment to the U.S. Food, Drug and Cosmetic Act. These provisions allow pharmaceutical companies to petition the FDA for a three-year marketing exclusivity if they pay for new research that is necessary to convert a prescription drug to nonprescription use. FDA response to this petition was expected in late March or April 1996.

In anticipation of FDA approval for nonprescription Rogaine following a positive recommendation by an FDA advisory committee in November 1995 and a favorable FDA response to the petition for a three-year marketing exclusivity, company officials had already outlined the marketing program for the brand scheduled for an April 1996 launch.[3] Rogaine would be targeted at men and women aged 25 to 49. The brand would be positioned as the only product available without a prescription that

---

[1] Sales figures are based on information provided in "Rogaine Will Be Sold Over-the-Counter," *PR Newswire*, February 12, 1996; estimates made by Bear, Stearns, & Company and Prudential Securities industry analysts; and data reported in "For Rogaine, No Miracle Cure—Yet," *Business Week* (June 4, 1990), p. 100, and "Blondes, Brunettes, Redheads, and Rogaine," *American Druggist* (June 1992), pp. 39–40.

[2] "Rogaine Will Be Sold Over-the-Counter," *PR Newswire,* February 12, 1996.

[3] This description is based on "Rogaine Will Be Sold Over-the-Counter," *PR Newswire*, February 12, 1996; Michael Wilke, "New Rivals Push Rogaine to Jump-Start Its OTC Ads," *Advertising Age* (April 15, 1996), p. 45; Michael Wilke, "Rogaine, Nicorette Seek Edge from FDA," *Advertising Age* (February 19, 1996), p. 4; "OTC Rogaine Receives FDA Advisory Committee Recommendation," *PR Newswire*, November 17, 1995; Sean Mehegan, "Hair Today," *BRANDWEEK* (April 8, 1996), pp. 1, 6.

This case was prepared by Professor Roger A. Kerin, of the Edwin L. Cox School of Business, Southern Methodist University, as a basis for class discussion and is not designed to illustrate effective or ineffective handling of an administrative situation. This case is based on published sources, including The Upjohn Company and Pharmacia & Upjohn, Inc. annual reports, news releases, and interviews with individuals knowledgeable about the industry. Quotes, statistics, and published information are footnoted for reference purposes.

EXHIBIT 1

Rogaine and Regaine Dollar Sales (Sales Reported Using Manufacturer Prices)

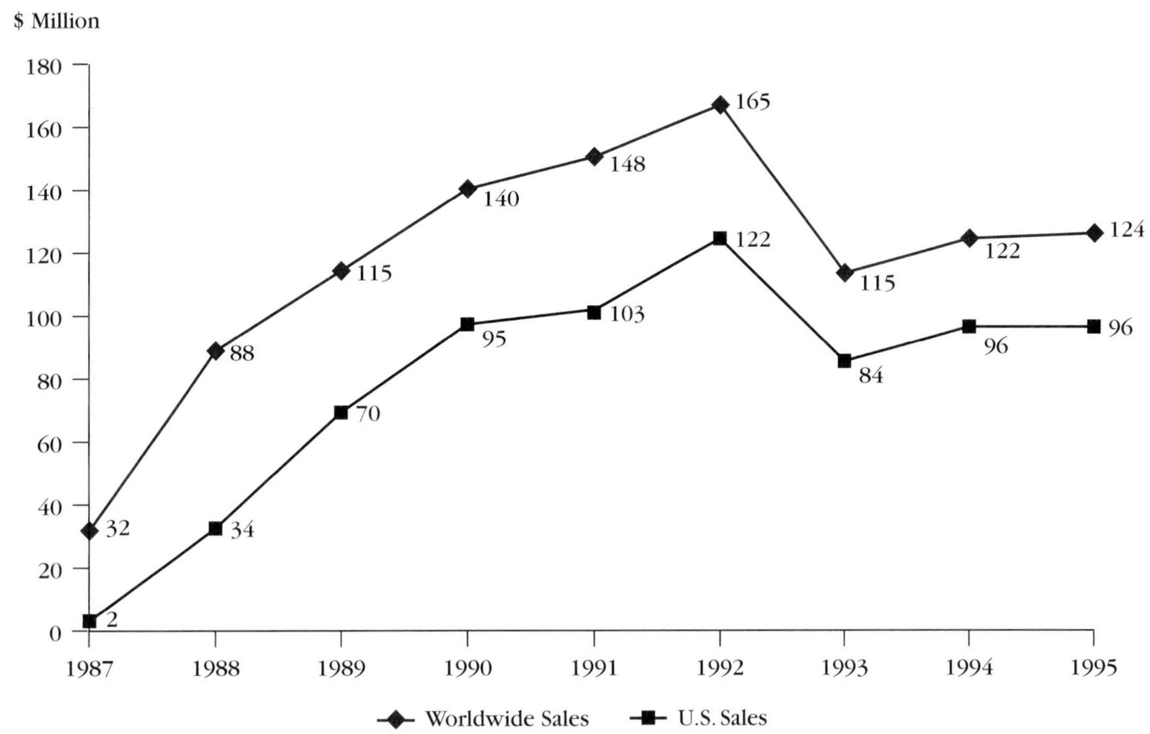

is medically proven to regrow hair. Separate packages—Rogaine for men and Rogaine for women—would be sold. Each package would feature labeling and include a brochure designed to help prospective users accurately identify themselves as Rogaine candidates. The suggested retail price for one bottle, which is equivalent to a one-month supply, would be $29.50. This price was approximately one-half the price of prescription Rogaine for a one-month supply. Distribution would be expanded to locate Rogaine in the pharmacy or hair-care section of food, drug, and mass-merchandise retail outlets. Marketing spending during the first six months of the brand introduction, estimated at $75 million, would support Rogaine and the company's relaunched nonprescription Progaine shampoo. More than half of the $75 million expenditure would be devoted to consumer advertising. The spending level represented the largest consumer and trade promotion campaign for a nonprescription product in the company's history. According to industry sources, company officials were telling retail store buyers of health and beauty aids that the brand had a retail sales potential of $250 million a year.

On April 5, 1996, the FDA notified Pharmacia & Upjohn, Inc. that its request for a three-year period of marketing exclusivity for nonprescription Rogaine had been denied.[4] In addition, by April 9, 1996, the FDA had approved three competing generic versions of Rogaine containing 2-percent solutions of minoxidil—the active chemical ingredient in Rogaine that stimulates hair regrowth—for sale without a prescrip-

[4] This discussion is based on "Generic Versions of Rogaine Ok'd," *The Dallas Morning News* (April 9, 1996), p. 4D; "Pharmacia & Upjohn Files Lawsuit Over OTC Rogaine Exclusivity," *PR Newswire*, April 12, 1996; "Rogaine Awarded Temporary Restraining Order," *PR Newswire*, April 15, 1996.

tion. Generic products, which are supposed to be medically equivalent to brand-name products, are typically priced 25 percent to 50 percent less than brand-name products and not advertised. On April 12, 1996, Pharmacia & Upjohn, Inc. filed a lawsuit against the FDA in Federal District Court in Grand Rapids, Michigan. The company asked the Court to reverse the FDA's ruling on the matter of market exclusivity for nonprescription Rogaine and to order the FDA to defer approval of competing nonprescription products containing minoxidil. On April 15, the Court issued a temporary restraining order prohibiting the FDA action. A preliminary hearing was set for April 30 to hear the Pharmacia & Upjohn, Inc. motion for a preliminary injunction which sought to extend injunctive relief until a full trial had been held.

The conversion of Rogaine from a prescription to nonprescription status and the FDA's possible denial of a three-year marketing exclusivity for Rogaine, along with approval of generic products, raised a variety of related market and marketing questions. First, what unit and dollar sales potential for the product category as a whole might be expected now that a minoxidil treatment for hair regrowth no longer required a prescription? Pharmacia & Upjohn, Inc. believed sales of $1 billion for Rogaine were possible over five years given its marketing program and assuming no competitive products. However, less optimistic views existed. One industry analyst believed "there is enough vanity out there, that a lot of people will try it, at least initially." However, another analyst noted that "those who are truly motivated have probably already tried it."[5]

Second, how might the loss of U.S. patent protection and marketing exclusivity that Rogaine had enjoyed since its introduction and competition from generic products affect sales of the Rogaine brand? There were no comparable situations to draw upon in the pharmaceutical industry to answer this question for a product like Rogaine.[6] For instance, pharmaceutical industry analysts estimate that it was common for patented prescription drugs to lose up to 60 percent of their volume within six months after their patent expired due to generic competition. However, this situation was typical of prescription drugs and not necessarily prescription drugs converting to a nonprescription status upon expiration of their patent. In another situation, Nicorette Gum, a smoking cessation product, lost its marketing exclusivity in June 1994. But with increased advertising and no direct branded or generic competition, except nicotine patches, the Nicorette brand saw dollar sales increase almost 6 percent in 1995. Unlike Nicorette Gum, if Rogaine lost its marketing exclusivity, it could face competition from generic or branded products with a 2-percent solution of minoxidil in 1996. These products were manufactured by Bausch & Lomb, Alpharma, and Lemmon Company, a division of Israeli-based Teva Pharmaceutical Industries. A Bausch & Lomb spokesperson said, "We do see a market for minoxidil as viable and would very much like to be a player." Lemmon Company manufactures generic drugs and private-label products and has announced that it intended to have a generic and private-label versions of minoxidil available by mid-1996. The company has also initiated discussions with other companies to offer a branded product. In addition, Merck was testing its prostate medicine, Proscar, for hair growth which would be in pill form. This product could be submitted for FDA approval within a year and be on the market by 1999. Finally, would the U.S. marketing strategy developed for nonprescription Rogaine prior to the FDA's recent rulings need to be modified? If so, how? Nonprescription Rogaine was already being

[5] Laurie McGinley, "Baldness Drug Cleared for Sale Over Counter," *Wall Street Journal* (February 13, 1996), p. B3; Michael Wieke, "OTC Status Might Not Be Boon to Rogaine," *Advertising Age* (January 29, 1996), p. 10.

[6] The following discussion is based on Patricia Winters, "Prescription Drug Ads Up," *Advertising Age* (January 18, 1993), pp. 10, 50; "Rogaine, Nicorette Seek Edge from FDA," *Advertising Age* (February 19, 1996), p. 4; Sean Mehegan, "Hair Today," *BRANDWEEK* (April 8, 1996), pp. 1, 6.

shipped to retailers and the consumer advertising and sales promotion program was ready to be implemented.

■ TREATMENTS FOR BALDING

There are about 300,000 hairs on the scalp of a person considered to have a "full" head of hair.[7] The exact number of hairs on a person's head depends on the number of hair follicles, which is established before birth. On average, a person will shed 100 to 150 hairs per day from the scalp and a new hair begins to emerge from the follicle. However, many people experience permanent hair loss on the scalp. Called *androgenetic alopecia*, both men and women can have this condition. With male pattern baldness, the most common form of *alopecia*, normal hair is lost initially from the temples and crown, where it is replaced by fine, downy hair. The affected area gradually becomes wider as the line of normal hair recedes. This process of hair loss is inherited and the typical progression in men is shown in Exhibit 2. Women also experience hair loss, a condition referred to as diffuse hair loss. This condition is manifested by thinning hair all over the head, rather than the progression typical of male pattern baldness, although young women and women who have passed menopause occasionally exhibit this progression.

Survey research indicates that 38.6 percent of women say they would seek treatment if they were losing their hair compared with 30.4 percent of men who say they would seek treatment.[8] However, this research also reported that at most 13.3 percent of surveyed women who were experiencing hair loss actually sought some form of treatment while at most 9.9 percent of men experiencing hair loss actually sought treatment. People with hair loss and who seek remedies have numerous options to treat this condition. The most popular treatments involve prescription and

EXHIBIT 2

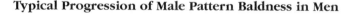

Typical Progression of Male Pattern Baldness in Men

[7] This material is based on Charles B. Clayman, ed., *The American Medical Association Encyclopedia of Medicine* (New York: Random House, 1989), pp. 88, 504; William G. Flanagan and David Stix, "The Bald Truth," *Forbes* (July 22, 1991), pp. 309–310; "Baldness: Is There Hope?," *Consumer Reports* (September 1988), pp. 533–547; Gary Belsky, "Beating Hair Loss," *MONEY* (March 1996), pp. 152–155; "Hair Loss: Does Anything Really Help?," *Consumer Reports* (August 1996), pp. 62–63.

[8] Laurie Freeman, "Upjohn Takes a Shine to Balding Women," *Advertising Age* (February 27, 1989), p. S1. These statistics are based on a Gallup Organization survey of 1,000 adults in the United States.

EXHIBIT 3

The Amount U.S. Adults Are Willing to Spend for the Treatment of Balding

Amount	*Men*	*Women*
$1,000–$10,000	11.3%	11.1%
$600–$1,000	7.1	5.3
$300–$599	13.5	9.7
$100–$299	14.2	13.5
$99 or less	27.0	28.5
Don't know	26.9	31.9
	100.0%	100.0%

Source: Gallup Organization Survey of 1,000 U.S. adults commissioned by *Advertising Age*. Reported in Laurie Freeman, "Upjohn Takes a Shine to Balding Women," *Advertising Age* (February 27, 1989), p. S1. Reproduced with the permission of *Advertising Age*.

nonprescription hair shampoos, lotions, and conditioners. These hair-thickening products are often used to treat thinning hair. It is estimated that there are 40 million balding men and 20 million women with thinning hair in the United States and they spend over $300 million annually on these kinds of products. Exhibit 3 shows the amount of money men and women say they are willing to spend per year for the treatment of balding. Hairpieces or wigs, hair transplants, and drugs, such as minoxidil, can be used when hair loss is prominent. American consumers spend about $1.3 billion annually for these treatments. Another $100 million is spent for elixirs, teas, horse-hoof ointments and the like to treat hair loss.

Hairpieces or Wigs

Hairpieces (or toupees) and wigs are worn by over two million Americans. About $400 million is spent annually for these products, including periodic cleaning and styling. Hairpieces and wigs can be made from real human hair or from synthetic material, usually nylon. Hairpieces made from human hair usually last no more than one year. Synthetic hair will last up to two years. The cost of a small filler hairpiece made from human hair for a balding man's crown can be purchased for as little as $325; a full women's wig can cost $2,000 or more. A typical man's hairpiece made of human hair costs from $1,000 to $3,500. Synthetic hairpieces for men cost between $1,800 and $2,500. Hairpieces require maintenance every six to eight weeks with the average cost for adjusting, cleaning, and styling running between $50 and $100. Spirit gum or a double-faced tape is used to hold the hairpiece or wig on the scalp.

Hair Transplants

A hair transplant consists of a surgical cosmetic operation in which hairy sections of the scalp are removed and transplanted to hairless areas. One or a combination of the following procedures may be used. "Punch grafting" is the most common procedure. With this procedure, a punch is used to remove small areas of bald scalp (about one-fourth inch across), which are replaced with areas of hairy scalp. The grafts are taped into position until the natural healing process takes effect. "Strip grafting" is a procedure whereby strips of bald skin are removed from the scalp and replaced with strips of hairy scalp which are stitched into position. "Flap grafting" is similar to strip grafting, except that flaps of hairy skin are lifted from the scalp, swiveled, and stitched to replace areas of bald skin. This procedure is typically used to form a new hairline. "Male pattern baldness reduction" consists of cutting out areas of bald scalp and then stretching surrounding areas of hairy scalp to replace the bald area. Hair transplants, no matter how successful, do not last indefinitely. As time passes, transplanted areas become bald.

About $800 million is spent each year for hair transplants in the United States. Hair transplant procedures of the grafting variety cost patients $3,500 to $15,000. Male pattern baldness reduction often costs $2,000 to $3,500 per procedure plus the transplant fee. These procedures are usually not covered by medical insurance.

Drugs

Although many topical ointments and elixirs are promoted, only one product had been approved by the FDA as a drug to restore hair growth for men and women prior to April 1996. Rogaine Hair Regrowth Treatment, produced by Pharmacia & Upjohn, Inc., received FDA approval for use by men in the United States in August 1988 and for women in August 1991. Rogaine is a 2-percent solution of minoxidil that is applied twice daily to areas of the scalp that has thinning hair or no hair. Clinical tests conducted by the company indicated that hair growth appeared to be more pronounced for men under 30 years of age and those in the early stages of the male pattern baldness progression. An estimated 35 percent of men under 30 years of age experience hair loss. The properties of minoxidil and its use as a topical ointment for hair growth are such that if not applied twice daily, hair loss results. In other words, minoxidil is a lifetime treatment if its effects on hair growth and retention are to be permanent.

Until February 1996, treatment with Rogaine required a physician's prescription. A one-month supply of the product then cost a patient $50 to $60 and up to $125 if the product was used in high concentrations, or if mixed with other drugs such as Retin-A. In addition, periodic physician office fees raised the annual patient cost for treatment. Rogaine was not typically covered by medical insurance.

In February 1996, the FDA approved Rogaine as a nonprescription drug. This decision reversed a 1994 FDA ruling that denied nonprescription status for Rogaine. At that time, FDA officials testified that the drug was most effective when applied during the early stages of baldness, but that the drug was not a cure. The group leader of the FDA's dermatology group said Rogaine was a "marginal product" in curing baldness.[9] In approving Rogaine as a nonprescription drug in 1996, the FDA reported that Rogaine resulted in "meaningful" hair growth in 25 percent of men and 20 percent of women.[10] "Meaningful" hair growth was defined by the FDA as "new individual hairs that covered some or all of the thinning areas but weren't as close together as hairs on the rest of the head." A larger percentage of users saw "minimal" hair growth in which "some new hairs were seen but not enough to cover thinning areas."

In clinical tests conducted by Pharmacia & Upjohn, Inc., 26 percent of mostly white men between the ages of 18 and 49 with moderate hair loss reported moderate to dense hair regrowth and 33 percent reported minimal regrowth after using Rogaine for four months.[11] By comparison, 11 percent of men in the 18 to 49 age group who used a placebo (a liquid without a 2-percent solution of minoxidil) reported moderate to dense hair regrowth while 31 percent reported minimal regrowth after four months of treatment. Clinical tests with mostly white women aged 18 to 45 with mild to moderate hair loss yielded different results. In these tests, 19

---

[9] "Upjohn's Rogaine Fails to Win Vote of FDA Panel in Nonprescription Bid," *Wall Street Journal* (July 28, 1994), p. A2.

[10] Laurie McGinley, "Baldness Drug Cleared for Sale Over Counter," *Wall Street Journal* (February 13, 1996), p. B3.

[11] Based on Rogaine product literature prepared by Pharmacia & Upjohn, Inc.

percent of women reported moderate hair regrowth and 40 percent reported minimal regrowth after using Rogaine for eight months. In a control group which received a placebo, 7 percent of women reported moderate regrowth and 33 percent had minimal regrowth after eight months of use.

According to a Rogaine marketing executive: "We have been very clear about what the drug delivers, that this is not a quick-fix product, that it needs the commitment to be used twice a day, every day, and it's a drug that must be used for four to six months—and for some individuals for up to a year before any results are seen."[12] Furthermore, Rogaine treated only male pattern baldness. This condition accounts for 95 percent of all hair loss cases among men and women in the United States. In addition, the drug is most likely to regrow hair on top of the head or crown, not on a receding frontal hairline.

■ PHARMACIA & UPJOHN, INC.

Pharmacia & Upjohn, Inc. was created with the merger of Pharmacia AB of Sweden and The Upjohn Company of the United States in November 1995.[13] The merger resulted in the new company becoming the world's ninth largest pharmaceutical firm. Pharmacia & Upjohn, Inc. reported net sales of $6.949 billion and net earnings of $924 million (excluding charges related to the merger) for the year ending December 31, 1995.

Pharmacia & Upjohn, Inc. is a provider of human health care products and related businesses, and operates on a global scale. Its corporate management center is located in London, England, with major research and manufacturing centers in the United States, Sweden, and Italy. Pharmaceutical products account for 90 percent of company sales; diagnostic and biotech/biosensor products produce 10 percent of company sales. Almost 70 percent of company sales are made outside of the United States.

The company's ongoing research and development effort, supported by a $1 billion annual budget, focused on developing new products and line extensions. In 1995, the company had 25 new products or line extensions expected to be submitted for regulatory approvals in the 1995–1997 period.

Human Health Care Business

With the merger, Pharmacia & Upjohn, Inc. announced its commitment to achieving and maintaining leading positions in a number of therapeutic areas. The largest of these were oncology, metabolic diseases, critical care, infectious diseases, central nervous system/neurology, women's health, and nutrition. Exhibit 4 shows the company's net sales by major therapeutic group for 1994 and 1995.

Prescription Pharmaceutical Sales. About 84 percent of company pharmaceutical sales are for prescription products. These products are marketed directly to health care providers worldwide by technically trained representatives who call on physicians, pharmacists, hospital personnel, health maintenance organizations (HMOs) and other managed health care organizations and wholesale drug outlets. Product advertising literature and sales efforts for prescription pharmaceuticals are directed mostly toward health care professionals. This practice is necessary because of long-

[12] "Rogaine: Promises, Promises, Promises," *Advertising Age* (October 3, 1993), p. S14.

[13] This company overview is based on *The Upjohn Company Annual Report: 1994* and *Pharmacia & Upjohn, Inc. Annual Report 1995*.

EXHIBIT 4

Pharmacia & Upjohn, Inc. Year-to-Year Comparison of Consolidated Net Sales by Major Therapeutic Product Groups (U.S. $ in Millions)

Product Grouping	*1995 Sales*	*% Change*	*1994 Sales*
Infectious disease	$687.1	10.3%	$622.9
Metabolic disease	635.9	(2.1)	649.4
Critical care and thrombosis	579.7	12.8	514.1
Central nervous system	571.8	.3	570.3
Oncology	566.2	6.7	530.6
Women's health	541.2	6.1	509.9
Nutrition	399.0	8.1	369.0
Ophthalmology	296.0	5.3	281.0
Other prescription pharmaceuticals	957.7	(12.8)	1,098.1
Consumer health care	441.5	(2.1)	451.2
Animal health	383.1	14.0	336.2
Chemical and contract manufacturing	199.9	17.1	170.7
Total pharmaceuticals	6,259.1	2.6	6,103.4
Biotech/Biosensor	437.0	13.5	385.0
Diagnostics	253.0	17.1	216.0
Consolidated net sales	$6,949.1	3.6%	$6,704.4

Source: Pharmacia & Upjohn, Inc. 1995 annual report, p. 37.

standing FDA regulations that require virtually all prescription drug advertising to list all product use side effects and contraindications. Complete disclosure of such information for the great majority of prescription pharmaceutical products was often cost prohibitive for television and print advertisements directed at consumers due to time and space requirements and technical language.

In 1995, sales of infectious disease products were led by the Cleocin (Dalacin outside the United States) family of antibiotic products. Sales of metabolic disease products were led by Genotropin, a growth hormone. Critical care and thrombosis product sales were led by Solu-Medrol, an injectable steroid, and other Medrol products. Sales of central nervous system agents were led by Xanax, an anti-anxiety agent; Halcion, a sleep-inducing agent; and Sermion for senile dementia. Farmorubicin, which treats solid tumors and leukemias, and Adriamycin, a cancer drug, led sales of oncology products. Sales in the women's health product category were led by Depo-Provera, an injectable contraceptive. Sales of nutrition products were led by the non-U.S. sales of Intralipid, a fat emulsion for intravenous nutrient delivery, while Healon, for cataract surgery, led sales of ophthalmology products.

Nonprescription Pharmaceutical Sales Pharmacia & Upjohn, Inc. also manufactures and distributes many other familiar products which do not require a prescription, including Motrin IB tablets and caplets, used as an analgesic; Kaopectate products, for diarrhea; Cortaid products, which are anti-inflammatory topical products containing hydrocortisone; the family of Unicap vitamin products; Dramamine products which are anti-motion sickness medicines; Mycitracin, an antibiotic ointment for treatment of minor skin infections and burns; and nonprescription laxative products, Doxidan and Surfak. The company also manufactures Nicorette Gum, a smoking cessation product, which is marketed under a license to SmithKline Beecham.

Competition in the human health care business is intense. There are at least 50 competitors in the United States that market prescription and nonprescription pharmaceutical products. Companies compete on the basis of product development and their effectiveness in introducing new or improved products for the treatment and prevention of disease. Other competitive features include product quality, pricing to and through marketing channels, and the dissemination of technical information and medical support advice to health care professionals. Advertising and sales promotions directed at consumers and trade promotions provided to retailers are important in marketing nonprescription pharmaceutical products. For this reason, these products are often referred to as "advertised remedies."

Development of Rogaine Hair Regrowth Treatment[14]

The development of Rogaine can be traced to the mid-1960s when researchers at The Upjohn Company observed that a drug, originally thought to be a possible antacid agent, lowered the blood pressure in laboratory animals. Subsequent research produced a drug, given the generic name minoxidil, which proved to be a potent agent for lowering high blood pressure in humans. Assigned the trade name Loniten, the drug was given FDA approval for marketing in 1979.

Clinical research on minoxidil as an antihypertensive drug led to an unexpected discovery in 1971 when investigators noticed unusual hair growth in some patients who were taking minoxidil orally. Then, in 1973, a patient taking minoxidil for hypertension began to grow hair on a previously bald spot on his head. Additional clinical trials of minoxidil and related studies were conducted between 1977 and 1982 with more than 4,000 patients. The primary clinical study at 27 different testing sites tracked 2,326 patients who were nearly all white men in good health, aged 18 to 49 and diagnosed as exhibiting a moderate degree of hair loss. This study concluded that a 2-percent minoxidil solution applied twice daily to the head offered the best safety and effectiveness profile for this group. The safety and effectiveness of this solution for people under 18 was not tested (Rogaine is not recommended for persons under 18 years of age). Some side effects of the drug included itching and skin irritation to the treated areas of the scalp. In terms of effectiveness, 48 percent of the patients said they had achieved moderate to dense hair growth after one year of use. Investigators at the time judged that 39 percent of the patients achieved moderate to dense hair growth after one year of use. These data were submitted to the FDA in 1985. The FDA approved the 39 percent moderate to dense hair growth claim. In 1986, The Upjohn Company began selling the 2-percent minoxidil solution outside the United States under the trade name Regaine. However, more stringent and time-consuming review procedures by the FDA slowed the approval process in the United States.

Continued study on minoxidil led company researchers to draw two basic conclusions:

> First, it was clear after four months that topical minoxidil could grow hair on some scalps. Second, efficacy seemed to be related in many cases to the age of the patient, the extent of his baldness and how long he had been bald. Younger men who were not as far into the balding process seemed to respond better to the drug. There are exceptions to this finding, however, and the correlation of age to efficacy has not been scientifically established.[15]

In 1987, the Company established the Hairgrowth Research Unit to determine the mechanism of action of minoxidil, develop new and better minoxidil analogs, and in-

---

[14] This description is based on The Upjohn Company, annual report, 1988, pp. 10–11; Steven W. Quickel, "Bald Spot," *Business Month* (November 1989), pp. 36–43; "Baldness: Is There Hope?" *Consumer Reports* (September 1988), pp. 533–547.

[15] The Upjohn Company, annual report, 1988, p. 11.

vestigate other agents that affect hair growth or loss. At the time, researchers could only theorize why minoxidil stimulated hair growth in some patients. According to the company's director of dermatology:

> The most plausible theory is that minoxidil somehow stimulates the matrix cell of the hair follicle to regrow when it is destined to turn off. It's an overcoming of the genetic propensity to shut down. But we don't know how minoxidil modifies the metabolic activity of that cell.[16]

Two noteworthy developments occurred in 1988. First, an eight-month clinical study on Rogaine use for female hair loss was completed. The study was submitted to the FDA and ultimately led to agency approval to market the minoxidil solution to women in August 1991. Pregnant women and nursing mothers were advised not to use Rogaine, however. Second, in August 1988, the FDA granted approval to market the solution to men in the United States. However, the Regaine name was replaced with the Rogaine name because an FDA official believed the Regaine name suggested that the minoxidil solution would result in complete hair growth. During this time, minoxidil had received considerable publicity in the consumer and marketing media and in the financial community as a miracle cure for baldness. For example, Wall Street financial analysts believed Rogaine's ability to reverse male pattern baldness in men would rapidly produce $400 to $500 million in annual sales.[17]

PRESCRIPTION DRUG MARKETING PROGRAM FOR ROGAINE HAIR REGROWTH TREATMENT

The initial marketing plan for prescription Rogaine for men in the United States was developed concurrently with the FDA approval process. The announced marketing objective for Rogaine was "to maximize sales of Rogaine in the new U.S. market."[18] Since Rogaine had FDA approval as a prescription drug, Upjohn's initial attention was placed on educating the members of its sales force who called on physicians, dermatologists, and other health care professionals. Rogaine was introduced to the medical community by its sales force and through advertisements in medical journals and periodicals. A company spokesperson said, "We couldn't begin marketing Rogaine to consumers until we felt the awareness level was adequate in the medical community."[19]

Consumer Advertising Program

Consumer advertising for Rogaine, targeted at 25- to 49-year-old males, began in November 1988 (see Exhibit 5 on page 570 for an age and income summary for U.S.

---

[16] "Baldness: Is There Hope?" *Consumer Reports* (September 1988), p. 544.

[17] "The Hottest Products: Baldness Treatment," *ADWEEK* (November 7, 1988), p. 6; "For Rogaine, No Miracle Cure—Yet," *Business Week* (June 4, 1990), p. 100. The Upjohn Company neither confirmed nor denied these sales projections.

[18] The Upjohn Company, annual report, 1988, p. 11. The following material is based on Stuart Elliott, "Upjohn Turns to Women to Increase Rogaine Sales," *Advertising Age* (January 2, 1992), p. 4; "Rogaine for Women Gets $20M in Support," *Advertising Age* (January 6, 1992), p. 1; "New Hope for the Hair-Impaired," *Business Week* (August 17, 1992), p. 105; "For Rogaine, No Miracle Cure—Yet," *Business Week* (June 4, 1990), p. 100; "Britain Approves Upjohn Hair Drug," *New York Times* (April 6, 1990), p. 4; Laurie Freeman, "Can Rogaine Make Gains Via Ads?" *Advertising Age* (September 11, 1989), p. 12; Stephen W. Quickel, "Bald Spot," *Business Month* (November 1989), pp. 36–37*ff*; Laurie Freeman, "Upjohn Takes a Shine to Balding Women," *Advertising Age* (February 27, 1989), p. S1; Patricia Winters and Laurie Freeman, "Nicorette, Rogaine Seek TV OK," *Advertising Age* (November 27, 1989), p. 31; "Minoxidil," *Vogue* (September 1989), p. 56; "Hair Today: Rogaine's Growing Pains," *New York* (October 30, 1990), p. 20; "Blondes, Brunettes, Redheads, and Rogaine," *American Druggist* (June 1992), pp. 39–40.

[19] Steven W. Quickel, "Bald Spot," *Business Month* (November 1989), p. 40.

EXHIBIT 5

Age and Income of Persons in the United States

Age Category	Persons (millions)	Percent Distribution by Income Level							
		Less than $2,500	*$2,500–$4,999*	*$5,000–$9,999*	*$10,000–$14,999*	*$15,000–$24,999*	*$25,000–$49,999*	*$50,000–$74,999*	*$75,000 or more*
Males									
15–24	17.4	28.1	15.1	22.0	14.9	14.8	4.9	.3	—
25–34	21.3	3.1	3.7	10.0	13.8	28.6	34.4	4.7	1.7
35–44	19.0	2.6	2.8	6.5	8.3	20.1	41.8	11.8	6.0
45–54	12.4	3.0	2.4	6.3	8.5	18.4	39.3	13.9	8.1
55–64	10.2	3.1	4.1	10.8	11.2	21.1	33.1	10.1	6.4
65 and over	12.5	1.9	5.8	24.7	20.9	24.2	16.0	3.9	2.6
Total males	92.8								
Females									
15–24	17.5	31.0	19.7	22.8	13.1	10.5	2.7	.1	—
25–34	21.6	15.7	8.8	16.5	15.3	25.0	17.2	1.2	.4
35–44	19.6	14.9	7.6	14.8	13.8	23.0	22.2	2.7	1.0
45–54	13.3	14.7	7.9	15.3	14.2	21.7	22.2	3.0	1.0
55–64	11.2	17.0	14.8	20.4	14.5	17.0	13.0	2.5	.8
65 and over	17.5	5.0	19.4	37.0	16.7	13.8	6.8	.9	.5
Total females	100.7								

Source: U.S. Bureau of the Census, *Current Population Reports.*

males and females). This start date, two months earlier than planned, was prompted by slow prescription sales due to low trial. The television campaign began on November 23, 1988. The print campaign featured advertisements in popular consumer magazines and newsstand business publications.

Television and print advertising messages emphasized a soft-sell that urged consumers to "see your doctor . . . if you're concerned about hair loss." These advertisements contained no mention of Rogaine since federal regulations at the time prohibited the use of brand names in prescription-drug advertising to consumers. However, The Upjohn Company name appeared in the advertisements. With a U.S. sales rate of $4 million per month for the first quarter of 1989, a decision was made to revamp the advertising campaign. The new campaign featured a bald man standing before his bathroom mirror. Like the earlier messages, viewers were again urged to see their doctor. Sales in the U.S. improved, reaching $70 million for 1989. A third advertising campaign was developed and launched in February 1990 with print advertisements featuring the Rogaine name for the first time with FDA approval. Advertisement copy emphasized that Rogaine was the only FDA-approved product for hair growth with the headline: "The good news is there's only one product that's proven to grow hair . . . Rogaine." Companion television advertising, however, did not mention Rogaine. Rogaine U.S. sales in 1990 totaled $95 million. This campaign continued in 1991; however, the Rogaine name now appeared in television advertisements with FDA approval. Year-end Rogaine sales totaled $103 million in 1991. Industry sources estimated that the amount spent on consumer-measured media advertising for Rogaine was $4,914,500 in 1989, $9,347,500 in 1990, and $3,443,000 in 1991.[20]

Price–Sales Promotion Program

A one-year supply of Rogaine could cost a user between $600 and $720 depending on pharmacist margins.[21] The total out-of-pocket cost to patients, including periodic physician office fees, could be as high as $800 to $900 per year, since patients were advised to visit their physicians twice per year after the initial consultation.

A variety of price incentives and sales promotion activities were also implemented to stimulate physician visits. For instance, rebates were offered to people who received a Rogaine prescription from their physician. The patient would either get a certificate worth $10 toward the purchase of the first bottle of Rogaine, or $20 for sending in the box tops from the first four bottles used. Selected barbershops and salons were also provided information packets to be given to customers worried about hair loss, including 150,000 copies of informational videos. Consumer advertising also included an 800 number to call to receive information about the product. By 1991, some one million calls had been made to The Upjohn Company. It has been estimated that The Upjohn Company spent between $40 and $50 million annually to market prescription Rogaine since its introduction through 1991. This cost included professional and consumer advertising, the price–sales promotion program, and selling expenses.

In September 1991, the price–sales promotion program for Rogaine was the subject of a day-long Congressional hearing in Washington, D.C.[22] Several members of Congress expressed criticism of the practice of using consumer rebates and cash in-

---

[20] *Measured media* refers to newspapers, consumer magazines and Sunday magazines, outdoor billboards, network, spot, syndicated and cable television, and network and spot radio. *Unmeasured media* include direct mail, co-op advertising, couponing, catalogs, and business publications.

[21] Although pharmacy margins varied, pharmacists typically obtained a gross profit margin of 10 percent based on the selling price to the consumer, based on "Blondes, Brunettes, Redheads, and Rogaine," *American Druggist* (June 1992), p. 40.

[22] Steven W. Colford and Pat Sloan, "Feds Take Aim at Rogaine Ads," *Advertising Age* (September 16, 1991), p. 47.

centives to market a prescription drug. An FDA official said, "We are concerned about this kind of tactic." Commenting on prescription drug consumer advertising in general, FDA Commissioner Dr. David Kessler commented, "We believe the public, in general, is not well-served by ads for prescription drugs." An FDA spokesperson later said the agency ". . . will let [the current Rogaine campaign] continue as it is, though we are not going to tip our hand as to what might happen in the future."

Even though the FDA and some physicians did not favor prescription drug advertising, consumer response to prescription drug advertising was generally favorable. A survey of 2,000 adult U.S. consumers reported that 40 percent said they had talked to a physician because of an advertisement they had seen, 72 percent of consumers in the survey said the advertising was an educational tool and 71 percent thought prescription drug advertising was worthwhile.[23]

Rogaine for Women[24]

FDA approval for Rogaine use by women was granted in August 1991 and the advertising and promotion program directed at women began in February 1992. The female-market entry plan mirrored the marketing program for males, including the same price and reference to the Rogaine name in advertisements. Extensive use of consumer print advertising appeared in *Cosmopolitan*, *People*, *US*, *Vogue*, and *Woman's Day*, as well as other magazines. The advertising copy for Rogaine advertising directed toward women differed from that used for men, however, because the topic of hair loss was discussed among men, but less often among women. According to an Upjohn Company official, women who suffer from hair loss "feel very much alone because no one talks about it."[25] This view materialized in the message conveyed in Rogaine print advertisements for women. For example, a woman in a Rogaine print advertisement said: "Finally I can do a lot more about my hair loss than just sit back and take it." The advertisement concluded by saying: "Take the control you've always wanted, and do it now." Television commercials also appeared in major U.S. metropolitan markets during daytime, early evening, and weekend programs on local stations and cable networks. In the television commercials, a woman portraying a news reporter says: "On this job, you cannot do a story until you get the facts. So when I heard about Rogaine with minoxidil, I wanted to get all the facts for myself."

The price-sales promotion program included a $10 incentive to visit a physician or dermatologist and an 800 number to call to receive an informational brochure about the product. Brochures were made available at drugstores and doctors' offices. An extensive professional effort evident in journal advertising, direct mail, and sales-staff support launched the product, including new print and video materials for pharmacists. The total marketing budget (including advertising) for the female market launch in 1992 was reported to be $20 million. U.S. sales of Rogaine in 1992 rose to $122 million due to the expanded customer base for the product. Total consumer advertising for Rogaine was $12,569,600 in 1992 according to industry sources.

---

[23] "Upswing Seen in R_X Drug Ads Aimed Directly At Consumer," *American Medical News* (June 1, 1990), pp. 13, 15.

[24] This discussion is based on "Blondes, Brunettes, Redheads, and Rogaine," *American Druggist* (June 1992), pp. 39–40; Steven W. Colford and Pat Sloan, "Feds Take Aim at Rogaine Ads," *Advertising Age* (September 16, 1991), p. 47; Stuart Elliott, "Upjohn Turns to Women to Increase Rogaine Sales," *Advertising Age* (January 2, 1992), p. 4.

[25] Stuart Elliott, "Upjohn Turns to Women to Increase Rogaine Sales," *Advertising Age* (January 2, 1992), p. 4.

Rogaine was marketed to both women and men as a prescription drug through 1995.[26] Two additional advertising campaigns directed at women appeared during this period and a new advertising campaign for men was launched. Advertising expenditures also increased. According to a company spokesperson, aggressive advertising that urged consumers to initiate a dialogue about hair loss with their physician was essential to maintaining sales of Rogaine. The spokesperson said: "A lot of physicians won't bring up the subject of hair loss in front of a patient."[27] Advertising in measured media was $34,579,800 in 1993, $32,404,000 in 1994, and $40 million in 1995 according to industry sources. With over $21 million spent on cable television alone in 1995, Rogaine was ranked as the fifth most-advertised brand in this medium in the United States. In addition, the company created the first-ever infomercial for a prescription drug in 1995. The 30-minute infomercial was targeted toward women and hosted by actress Cindy Williams, who interviewed a licensed dermatologist, a hair designer and stylist, and a company marketing executive. The company also established a World Wide Web site for the product, which was another industry first.

During this three-year period, company attention also was placed on building a Rogaine prospect and user database to support a relationship marketing program. This program proved to be useful for targeting prospects and users for direct mail and telemarketing. A result of this effort was that people who started the Rogaine treatment tended to stay with it for a longer period of time. Also, Rogaine's price-sales promotion program continued. Rogaine sales in the United States declined to $84 million in 1993, then rose and plateaued at $96 million in 1994 and 1995.

Product and Market Development

The company continued its product and market development efforts on Rogaine since its introduction in 1988. For example, a different concentration of minoxidil had been examined which would require only one application per day rather than two. This development could improve the product's convenience of use because, as one former company executive conceded, "It's hard to use something twice a day, come hell or high water."[28] Also, an easier-to-use gel was introduced to Europe. In early 1989, the nonprescription Progaine hair-thickener shampoo product line was introduced for use by men and women. These products did not promote hair growth, but served as a treatment for thinning hair. It was believed these products would benefit from the sound-alike name and be considered a companion to Rogaine. In December 1995, the company submitted a new drug application to the FDA for a Rogaine 5-percent minoxidil formulation to treat common hair loss. Marketing clearance for this prescription-only hair regrowth treatment was expected in late 1996.

Market development on a global scale also continued. By April 1996, Rogaine (Regaine in non-U.S. markets) was marketed in more than 80 countries and more than 3 million people had used the product. FDA approval of nonprescription Rogaine meant that the product was approved for sale without a prescription in 13 countries, including Denmark, the Netherlands, New Zealand, Spain, the United King-

---

[26] This discussion is based on Emily DeNitto, "Rogaine Raises Women's Interest," *Advertising Age* (February 28, 1994), p. 12; "Rogaine: Promises, Promises, Promises," *Advertising Age* (October 3, 1993), p. S14; Emily DeNitto, "Rogaine Fashions New Ads for Women," *Advertising Age* (February 28, 1994), p. 12; Jeffrey D. Zbar, "Upjohn Database Rallies Rogaine," *Advertising Age* (January 23, 1995), p. 42; Joshua Levine, "Scalped," *Forbes* (November 6, 1995), p. 128; "Rogaine Opens New Category for Infomercials: Pharmaceuticals," *Advertising Age* (March 11, 1996), p. 10A; "Top 80 Brands on Cable TV," *Advertising Age* (March 25, 1996), p. 34.

[27] Yumiko Ono, "Prescription-Drug Makers Heighten Hard-Sell Tactics," *Wall Street Journal* (August 29, 1994), pp. B1, B7.

[28] "For Rogaine, No Miracle Cure—Yet," *Business Week* (June 4, 1990), p. 100.

dom, and the United States. Rogaine (Regaine) sales outside the U.S. were $30 million in 1995 in the face of competition from generic brands and substitute products in non-U.S. markets.

■ OVER-THE-COUNTER MARKETING PROGRAM FOR ROGAINE HAIR REGROWTH TREATMENT

The nonprescription drug marketing plan for Rogaine called for the prescription drug marketing program to be phased out by April 1996. Production, distribution, advertising, and promotion for prescription Rogaine had stopped by April 3, 1996.

Marketing Program for Nonprescription Rogaine

The marketing program planning process for nonprescription Rogaine had begun in late 1995. Its mission was to create a new product category called the "hair regrowth category." The reported expenditure for the marketing program was $75 million. More than half of this amount would be designated for consumer advertising to create awareness and trial of the product. Principal elements of the program are outlined below.[29]

Rogaine Targeting, Product Positioning, and Packaging Like the prescription drug marketing program, the target market for Rogaine would be men and women aged 25 to 49. Rogaine would be positioned as the only product medically proven to regrow hair.

Separate packaging for men and women would be prepared even though the product was identical. Rogaine For Men would be packaged in a light blue carton. Rogaine For Women would be packaged in a salmon-pink carton. Each carton would contain a brochure with gender-based instructions for use and address possible consumer questions. Single-packs with one 60-milliliter Rogaine bottle, twin-packs with two bottles, and triple-packs with three bottles would be sold. One bottle contained sufficient solution for one month's use. The bottles would be tamper-evident and child-resistant. Rogaine For Men would come with dropper and sprayer applicators. Rogaine For Women would have an extended sprayer for ease of application with longer hair.

Rogaine Advertising and Promotion A multipronged advertising and promotion program was designed for Rogaine. The advertising objectives for Rogaine were to raise consumer awareness of the brand's recently approved nonprescription status, encourage product trial, and communicate user expectations. Initially, one new 30-second television advertisement for Rogaine For Men and one 30-second television advertisement for Rogaine For Women would be created. According to a company spokesperson, "Men and women experience the physical and psychological effects of hair loss differently. Also, men and women respond differently to Rogaine. So Rogaine advertising, like Rogaine packaging, will address the gender-specific concerns of Rogaine users."[30] The brand manager for Rogaine added that advertising will take an educational slant, emphasizing the fact that "this is the only product medically proven to regrow hair."[31] The Rogaine For Men television commercial would air dur-

---

[29] This discussion is based on "Rogaine Will Be Sold Over-the-Counter," *PR Newswire* (February 12, 1996); "OTC Rogaine Introduced," PR Newswire (April 8, 1996); "New Rogaine TV Commercials Begin," *PR Newswire* (April 22, 1996); Sean Mehegan, "Hair Today," *BRANDWEEK* (April 8, 1996), pp. 1, 6; Sean Mehegan, "Rogaine/Progaine," *MEDIAWEEK* (April 8, 1996), p. 38; Michael Wilkie, "New Rivals Push Rogaine to Jumpstart Its OTC Ads," *Advertising Age* (April 15, 1996), p. 45.

[30] "New Rogaine TV Commercials Begin," *PR Newswire* (April 22, 1996).

[31] Sean Mehegan, "Hair Today," *BRANDWEEK* (April 8, 1996), p. 6.

ing evening prime time, sports, cable sports, late-night, and syndicated programs. The Rogaine For Women television commercial would air during evening prime time and day schedules on network, cable, and syndicated programs.

The planned media schedule for Rogaine was designed so that 92 percent of the target market would see Rogaine television advertisements seven times in a four-week period following the brand's introduction as a nonprescription drug. Print advertisements were scheduled to reach 77 percent of the target audience. The advertising agency executive responsible for Rogaine said, "If there still are consumers who don't know about Rogaine, how to apply it, how it works, and the fact that it is available without a prescription, this new ad campaign will take care of that."[32]

The advertising program for Rogaine would be complemented by an extensive consumer and trade promotion campaign. An estimated 40,000 physicians would receive a mailing announcing Rogaine's nonprescription status. More than 20,000 pharmacists would be mailed a Rogaine Pharmacy Kit. Items in the kit would include an educational brochure and video for pharmacists, consumer education brochures, and an announcement easel for the pharmacy counter. Free-standing inserts (FSIs), in-store circular ads, and coupons would comprise the consumer promotion program.

Direct marketing efforts would be employed with the objective of encouraging product compliance and repeat usage, and to reinforce user expectations. Planned periodic mailings to users would include money-saving coupons, a newsletter with hair care and styling suggestions, and comments from users, dermatologists, and other authorities. Consumers could join the direct marketing program by returning an enrollment card from the Rogaine package or by calling a Rogaine toll-free number.

Rogaine Distribution and Pricing Planned distribution for Rogaine would include pharmacy or hair care sections of food, drug, and mass-merchandise retail outlets. This placement was based on Pharmacia & Upjohn, Inc. marketing research which indicated that consumers would look for and expect to find Rogaine in these sections.

Nonprescription Rogaine would be priced at about one-half of prescription Rogaine. A single-pack suggested retail price for Rogaine would be $29.50. Twin-packs would be priced at $55.00 and triple-packs would be available in some stores with a suggested retail price of $75.00. The retailer margin on Rogaine would be about 20 percent of the suggested retail price. Commenting on the expanded distribution and pricing, a senior company executive said: "The availability of OTC Rogaine is welcome news for the millions of men and women in this country who experience common hereditary hair loss. Instead of going to a doctor's office, they can simply walk into a food store, drug store, or mass merchandiser outlet and purchase Rogaine without a prescription at its full prescription strength. It's much more convenient and because the price is now lower, it's much more affordable."[33]

Hair Regrowth Category Development: Rogaine and Progaine

The launch of nonprescription Rogaine focused on creating a brand with $250 million-a-year in retail sales at the suggested retail prices in what Pharmacia & Upjohn, Inc. officials coined as the "hair regrowth category" of products. In this regard, the concurrent relaunch of Progaine shampoo represented an effort to synergize the Rogaine/Progaine brand names into a system of hair care. The Progaine relaunch in-

---

[32] "New Rogaine TV Commercials Begin," *PR Newswire* (April 22, 1996).

[33] "OTC Rogaine Introduced," *PR Newswire* (April 8, 1996).

volved a package redesign and a new formula with added proteins, conditioners, and hair-thickening agents. To bolster the linkage between Rogaine and Progaine, coupons for Progaine would be inserted in Rogaine cartons. The two products also would be located side-by-side in the hair-care aisle in retail stores. Progaine retail shampoo sales in 1995 were about $2 million. Total U.S. retail sales of shampoos in 1995 approached $1.5 billion.[34]

■ APRIL 30, 1996: THE FEDERAL DISTRICT COURT RULING

On April 30, 1996 the Federal District Court ruled in favor of the FDA.[35] This meant that Rogaine would not have a three-year marketing exclusivity and three competing generic products had approval for sale without a prescription in the United States.

This development raised a variety of issues related to the marketing opportunity for FDA-approved nonprescription hair regrowth products containing a 2-percent minoxidil solution, and the Rogaine brand in particular. For example, how might the unit and dollar sales potential of the hair regrowth category be affected? Pharmacia & Upjohn, Inc. believed sales of $1 billion were possible over five years for Rogaine when it was the only hair regrowth product containing a 2-percent minoxidil solution. Might this sales figure for the category as a whole need revision and by how much? A useful starting point might be to revisit the sales history of prescription Rogaine. This would involve simulating the trial and repeat purchase patterns for prescription Rogaine and determining how these patterns might have contributed to sales growth.

Relatedly, the absence of marketing exclusivity and the presence of generic products changed the competitive landscape for Rogaine. No longer would Rogaine hold a monopoly position as the sole supplier of a hair regrowth product with a 2-percent minoxidil solution. Rather, prospective users of this product could now try a competitive product and current Rogaine users could switch to another product. The effect on Rogaine sales required further attention.

Nonprescription hair regrowth product category sales and Rogaine's share of these sales would depend, in large measure, on the marketing program for nonprescription Rogaine. Developed in anticipation of a favorable FDA response to its petition for a three-year marketing exclusivity, this program was being currently executed. At issue at this time was how the marketing plan should be modified, if at all.

---

[34] Pat Sloan, "Brand Scorecard: Premium Products Lather Up Sales," *Advertising Age* (July 24, 1995), p. 24.

[35] "Court Allows Sale of Generic Forms of Rogaine," *New York Times* (May 1, 1996), p. 40.

CASE

3M Telecom Systems Division

Fibrlok™ Splice

It was early 1996. Dr. Dennis W. (Denny) Hamill sat back in his chair and stared at the stacks of documents in front of him on his desk. "Okay," he thought to himself, "I need to start someplace, so I might as well begin by reviewing the Fibrlok™ Splice history."

Hamill held the title of Business Director in the Telecom Systems Division of 3M Corporation, and it was his responsibility to review the performance of one of the division's most vaunted products, the Fibrlok™ Splice, a device used by telecommunications firms ("telecoms") to splice optical fibers when providing telephone service to households. Although the splice had initially exceeded the company's sales expectations, in recent years sales had leveled off, and it was Hamill's responsibility to determine if, and how, sales could be stimulated.

THE COMPANY

Minnesota Mining and Manufacturing Company, or 3M as it prefers to be called, is one of the best-known and most respected corporations in the world. 3M, whose stock price forms part of the Dow Jones Industrial Average, routinely makes the annual *Fortune* top-ten listing of the most admired U.S. companies, and recently it was rated as one of the best companies to work for. In 1995 3M received the National Medal of Technology® from President Clinton in recognition of its technological achievements over the past 90 years. It is, without question, a world-class corporation, one that employs 71,000 individuals in nearly 200 countries. Ranked 62nd in the *Fortune* 500 listing of the largest U.S. corporations in 1995, 3M's net revenue was nearly $13.5 billion. Exhibit 1 on page 578 contains selected financial and operating data for the company for the period 1993-1995. More than half (54 percent) of the company's revenue stream in 1995 was derived from international operations.

3M consists of 50 product divisions, subsidiaries, and departments organized into two major business sectors: Industrial and Consumer, and Life Sciences. About 62 percent of firm revenues are derived from the Industrial and Consumer sector. It is primarily a manufacturing company that produces in excess of 60,000 different products. These products range from adhesives, roofing granules, pharmaceuticals, overhead projectors, heart-lung machines, and coated abrasives to surgical drapery. 3M is unique among large corporations in that it does not focus on a single strategic core competency. Rather, 3M builds on some 30 core technologies in which it has acquired unique competencies. As such, the company follows a very decentralized management philosophy. In fact, the company can perhaps best be viewed as a com-

This case was prepared by Professor Robert A. Peterson, The University of Texas at Austin, as a basis for class discussion and is not designed to illustrate effective or ineffective handling of an administrative situation. Certain information is disguised. Consequently, the case is not useful for research purposes.

EXHIBIT 1

Selected 3M Operating Results, 1993–1995 (Millions of Dollars)

	1993	*1994*	*1995*
Net sales (millions)	$11,053	$12,148	$13,460
Cost of goods sold	6,344	6,839	7,713
Gross profit	4,709	5,309	5,747
Operating expenses			
Selling, general, and administrative expenses	2,918	3,219	3,446
Research and development	794	828	883
Other expenses (income)	(266)	(60)	442
Net income	1,263	1,322	976

Source: Annual reports of company.

munity of smaller business units that tend to focus on niche markets with niche products. The emphasis on "smallness" and "community" is illustrated by the fact that the average 3M factory has only 400 employees.

Company Beginning

Minnesota Mining and Manufacturing was founded in 1902 by a physician, an attorney, a merchant, and two railroad executives in Two Harbors, Minnesota, a small community on the north shore of Lake Superior. Its charter was to mine a very hard mineral, corundum, that was used in grinding wheels. When that business foundered, the company headquarters was moved to Duluth, Minnesota, with the intent of manufacturing sandpaper and abrasive wheels. In 1910, the company moved to St. Paul, Minnesota, where today it occupies a 425-acre campus with some two dozen buildings.

In 1907, William McKnight joined the company as bookkeeper. Less than seven years later he was named general manager. McKnight became the spiritual leader of the company and eventually served as chairman for more than 40 years. When he died at age 90 in 1976, McKnight was still serving on the 3M board of directors. In a 1944 speech, McKnight set forth what was to become the guiding principle of 3M: "Management that is destructively critical when mistakes are made kills initiative, and it's essential that we have many people with initiative if we are to continue to grow." This principle has been steadfastly adhered to and is embraced by the 3M corporate culture that emphasizes risk taking, teamwork, innovation, and entrepreneurship.

3M Products

One of the enduring characteristics of 3M is its continual focus on new and useful products. Consequently, 3M is legendary for the products it has pioneered. Perhaps the best-known 3M consumer products are its Scotch™-brand tapes, of which there are now hundreds of varieties. 3M also developed the first commercially viable magnetic recording tape. Other well-known 3M brands include Scotchgard™ Fabric Protector, Scotchlike™ Reflective Sheetings (for highway signs and clothing), O-Cel-O™ Stay Fresh™ Sponges, and Thinsulate™ Insulation for winter clothing. Exhibit 2 shows a breakdown of 3M's sales by general product grouping.

Bootlegging Time and Venture Teams

One of 3M's financial goals is to obtain at least 30 percent of sales every year from products less than four years old at every level in the company. Needless to say, this

EXHIBIT 2

3M Revenue by General Product Grouping (Millions of Dollars)

	Year		
Product Line	*1993*	*1994*	*1995*
Tape products	$1,617	$1,801	$2,042
Abrasive products	1,002	1,117	1,220
Automotive and chemical products	1,176	1,195	1,328
Connecting and insulating products	1,252	1,362	1,470
Consumer and office products	1,844	2,069	2,272
Health care products	1,876	2,002	2,221
Safety and personal care products	974	1,067	1,220
All other	1,312	1,535	1,687

Source: Annual reports.

goal has fostered innovation and entrepreneurship throughout the company, from top managers to rank-and-file employees. In fact, to encourage innovation, the company has a formal policy that allows technical and engineering staff members to spend up to 15 percent of their time (termed "bootlegging time") on projects of their own choosing. One of the most celebrated consequences of bootlegging is the Post-it® Note Pad. The note pad was developed by Art Fry, a company scientist who was searching for a solution to stop book marks from falling out of his hymnal during church services. Working on his bootlegging time, Fry found an adhesive that another 3M scientist, Spence Silver, had created but abandoned because it was not very sticky. Fry brushed the adhesive on some paper and created a product line that now annually generates sales in the hundreds of millions of dollars. Post-it® Notes currently come in 18 colors, 27 sizes, 56 standard shapes, and 20 fragrances.

In addition to providing bootlegging time, 3M fosters innovation by allowing the formation of both formal and informal new venture teams. A new venture team is essentially a task force with very special characteristics. Team members are volunteers on full-time, indefinite assignment from their normal task. They come from disciplines that include manufacturing, engineering, and marketing, and have the ability to stay together if a product proves to be successful. In such instances the product may form the nucleus of a new business unit. In keeping with the corporate spirit of entrepreneurship, venture teams are encouraged to "make a little, sell a little," which is interpreted at 3M to mean start small, learn how a business works, and then expand.

■ TELECOM SYSTEMS DIVISION

The Telecom Systems Division is a typical division at 3M. It has a 30-year history of selling products, first to telephone companies and now communication companies, all over the world. About 60 percent of the division's sales originate outside of the United States. The division has grown by concentrating first on products that help technicians and craft people (the "craft") in telephone companies splice copper cable and then protect those splices from the elements using closures and various kinds of cabinets. Over time the division built on these competencies by first adding testing equipment for copper wire and then by adding new technologies as the craft moved into fiber optics, coaxial cable, and wireless communications. Telecom Systems Division is part of the Electrical and Communications Markets Group, which in turn is part of the Industrial and Consumer Sector.

Since a large percentage of the Telecom Systems Division's sales are direct to large customers, it does not depend heavily on advertising for communicating its product offerings. Instead, the communication budget is focused on direct communication with customers, on trade shows, on press releases and success stories, and on technical articles emphasizing the benefits of the division's products. Advertising that is done (see Exhibit 3) is in very specific industry-focused trade publications.

Scotchlok™ Connector

In 1959, 3M introduced the Scotchlok™ Connector, a device for splicing copper wires used in telephone lines. This device allowed telecom technicians to splice two wires together by just inserting the wires into a connector (without stripping the insulation) and, through the use of a simple tool, snapping the connector together to make a connection between the wires that protects them from the environment. The Scotchlok™ Connector was an instant success and literally millions have been sold since its introduction. Indeed, it ultimately became the industry standard.

About 1969 3M introduced modular splicing, called MS^2, for splicing copper wire. MS^2 was a major innovation in that it allowed the telecom technician to splice 25 pairs of copper wires at a time in a single connector. Indeed, modular splicing was so popular that it has been credited with helping the telecommunications industry grow significantly over the last 20 years. At the present time 3M sells a two-wire Scotchlok™ Connector for about 5 cents; MS^2 sells for about \$2, but it allows splicing 50 wires together very quickly, thereby improving craft productivity substantially. Presently, there are about 10 billion copper splices produced per year globally by 3M and its competitors.

By the mid-1980s, however, fiber optic cable was replacing copper wire in telephone lines at an increasingly rapid pace. There was a concerted effort by telecoms to replace coaxial copper wire with fiber optic cable for the "backbone" of telephone networks, that is, the "long haul" or major lines that were used to transmit long-distance telephone calls from one major point to another. Copper wire trunk lines, telephone lines that originate from a backbone and lead into a particular limited geographic location (such as a neighborhood), were also being replaced by fiber optic cable. There was considerable speculation that the major telecoms or RBOCs, as they are called (i.e., the regional operating companies resulting from the breakup of AT&T, such as Pacific Telesys and U.S. West), would soon be replacing the copper loops—the telephone lines linking a neighborhood location to a single home—with fiber optic cable.

3M's Telecom Systems Division estimated that about eight times more optical fiber would be required to replace the copper loops than was used for the backbone and trunk telephone lines. Moreover, the division estimated that the number of splices required to bring fiber optic cable into homes would be approximately 20 times greater on a per mile basis than that necessary for the backbone and trunk lines. In particular, it was expected that there would be between five and ten splices (spliced points) between a central telephone office and a home. Realizing the enormity of the task of bringing optical fiber into individual homes, telecom companies began to search for ways to minimize the expenditures required for installing, testing, and maintaining fiber optic cables to the home. These companies were joined in this quest by cable television operators, one of which estimated that the cost of running fiber to homes could be as high as \$2,000 per home.

EXHIBIT 3

Typical Telecom Systems Division Trade Advertisement

From copper to fiber, you can count on 3M.

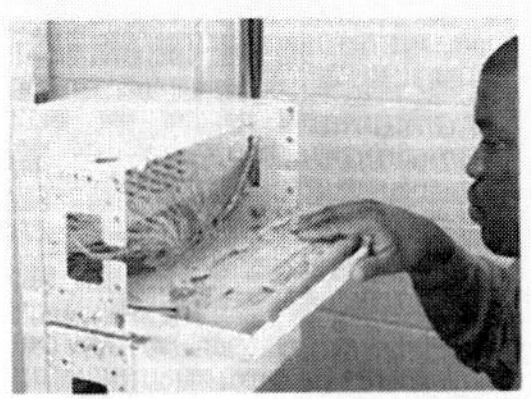

For more than 25 years, people requiring innovative solutions to their telephony or network problems have turned to 3M for answers.

3M Telecom Systems Division is a global leader in the supply of materials, components, products and services that ensure signal integrity while helping you effectively maintain the outside plant network and achieve your goals of fewer service interruptions and minimal downtime.

Copper or fiber, you can count on 3M for connections with tapes, jumpers, cable assemblies, fault finders, test sets, closures, cabinets and terminals. In fact, 3M offers thousands of products to keep your network operating day and night. And by offering this innovative blend of knowledge, hardware and skill, 3M is working to be your First Choice In Outside Plant.™

To learn more, contact your local 3M representative, fax us at 512-984-5811, or visit our Web site at www.mmm.com/telecom

3M Telecommunications

©3M

Source: 3M.

OPTICAL FIBER

Optical fibers are hair-thin strands of ultra-pure glass (often referred to as "light pipes") that digitally transmit voice, video, and computer data at the speed of light. A single fiber can transport up to 48 broadcast-quality video channels, whereas a 144-fiber cable can handle millions of simultaneous two-way telephone calls. Transmission is accomplished by means of light pulses through a glass fiber that has a diameter less than that of a human hair. In general, a fiber optic link consists of a light source (transmitter), fiber optic cables with connectors and/or splices, and a detector (receiver). More specifically, a fiber optic communication system consists of a transmitter that takes an electric signal, typically digital, and changes it into photons of light that are transmitted through the fiber. At various distances along the fiber are devices that amplify the light pulse. When the light pulse reaches its destination, it is detected and changed back into an electrical signal for reception. Light pulses are transmitted by total internal reflection. Consequently, the optical fibers are coated with a low refractive-index transparent material such as glass or plastic of a different type than that used in the fiber. This coating not only protects the internal reflecting surface of the fiber but also insulates adjacent fibers in a bundle.

Optical fiber was perfected in 1970 by scientists at Corning Glass Works (renamed Corning, Inc. in 1989). However, it was not until 1982 that the demand for fiber optic cable took off, spurred in part by the deregulation of the telecommunications industry. As of 1995, more than 60 million miles of optical fiber had been installed worldwide. In 1995, Corning alone produced more than 5.2 million miles of optical fiber.

There are more than 1,000 suppliers of fiber optic equipment in the world. Corning, Inc. with a global market share of 32 percent, and AT&T Network Cable Systems dominate worldwide production of optical fiber. In general, the fiber optic equipment market is fiercely competitive, with firms from all over the globe competing.

Fusion versus Mechanical Splices

Properly splicing fiber optic cables is a very exacting task that requires great precision. If the splice does not result in the fiber optic cable being exactly aligned, the performance of the cable will be degraded substantially. Oversimplifying somewhat, there are two types of splicing, construction splicing and restoration splicing. The primary requirements for splices used in constructing fiber optic networks are that they be permanent and provide high performance. Cost is of secondary importance. The primary requirements for splices used in restoring (repairing) fiber optic networks are that they are easy and fast to install so that service can be restored as soon as possible.

There are essentially two methods for joining optical fiber: fusion and mechanical. Both methods of splicing accomplish the same goal in that they bring together two optical fibers and hold them in such a fashion that a light pulse can pass through the splice unhindered. Fusion splicers are a type of equipment that brings two or more optical fibers together and melts them to form a single strand. Mechanical splicers are devices that join optical fibers by aligning them and then maintaining them in alignment through the use of adhesives or epoxies or what is called elastomeric material. This material deforms under compression and can accommodate minor differences in the outside diameters of spliced fibers.

The instrument used for fusion splicing can be relatively expensive. Typical prices vary from $5,000 to $30,000 or more, and the instrument can be somewhat cumbersome when used in constrained quarters (e.g., in tunnels or false ceilings in buildings). Although a mechanical splicer does not require the large capital outlay of a fusion splicer, on average the total cost of each splice is between $7 and $20 because of the physical connector required (there is no physical connector in fusion splicing). Hence, from a cost perspective, if only a few splices are required, a mechanical splicer may be preferred. However, if many splices are to be made, a fusion splicer may be more cost effective. Moreover, fusion splicing requires highly trained technicians, whereas technicians can be easily trained to make mechanical splices. According to industry sources, the fusion splice has been widely accepted in applications requiring high volume (continuous) splicing. The mechanical splice is widely used in installations requiring relatively few splices at a time.

■ THE FIBRLOK™ SPLICE

In early 1987, Dick Patterson, a research scientist in the Telecom Systems Division, was using his bootleg time to develop a better way to splice fiber optic cable. Because he had worked on Scotchlok™ connectors, Patterson was convinced that a huge market existed for a mechanical fiber optic splice that was reasonably priced, easy to install, and resulted in high performance.

By April 1987, Patterson had formed a new venture team. The team consisted of himself as leader and Don Larson, an engineering specialist, Wes Raider, a senior design engineer, Jim Carpenter, a senior engineer, Barbara Birrell, an advanced physicist, and Al Lindh, a sales and marketing manager. As Patterson later noted, "We had a cross-functional team without knowing it." In November 1987, the team successfully tested a working optical fiber lock splice design.

The team worked literally day and night testing the mechanical splice, modifying the design, testing the modified mechanical splice, and so on. A working prototype was constructed and subjected to a myriad of engineering tests at the same time that reactions were obtained from potential customers in attempts to judge market responsiveness.

In August 1988, the Fibrlok™ Splice was introduced at a trade show in Chicago; all of the telecoms sent representatives. The splice was an inch and a half long, a quarter-inch high, and one-sixth of an inch wide. It contained a grooved aluminum element inside a plastic body with a plastic cap in the middle. A technician connecting two optical fibers would cleave and slide the ends of the fibers to be spliced into the device until they met in the center. By pressing down on the cap, the fibers would be locked into a perfectly aligned permanent splice. While the technology was complex (partly because of the high quality standards required), using the splice was easy, and telecom construction and repair workers could be taught how to use it in a short period of time. In fact, splicing could be accomplished in 30 seconds using only a simple hand-operated tool once the two ends of the fiber had been properly prepared (i.e., cleaned and cleaved), a task that would take an experienced technician one to two minutes.

Exhibit 4 on page 584 contains two diagrams of the fiber optic splice. One diagram shows the size of the splice, whereas the other shows an "exploded" schematic view of the splice. Technically, the Fibrlok™ Splice was developed to facilitate permanent splicing of standard single and multi-mode optical fibers that have 125-, 250-, or 900-micron diameters. Because any failure of the splice could have enormous loss potential for the telecom (revenue streams in the hundreds of thousands of dollars per minute can pass through a fiber optic cable) as well as 3M, great caution was observed in manufacturing and testing the Fibrlok™ Splice.

Initially, the Fibrlok™ Splice was packaged in units of five in individually sealed compartments in thermal-formed packages. Three different (color-coded) splices were available, depending on the size of the two optical fibers to be joined. To use

EXHIBIT 4

Fibrlok™ Splice Schematics

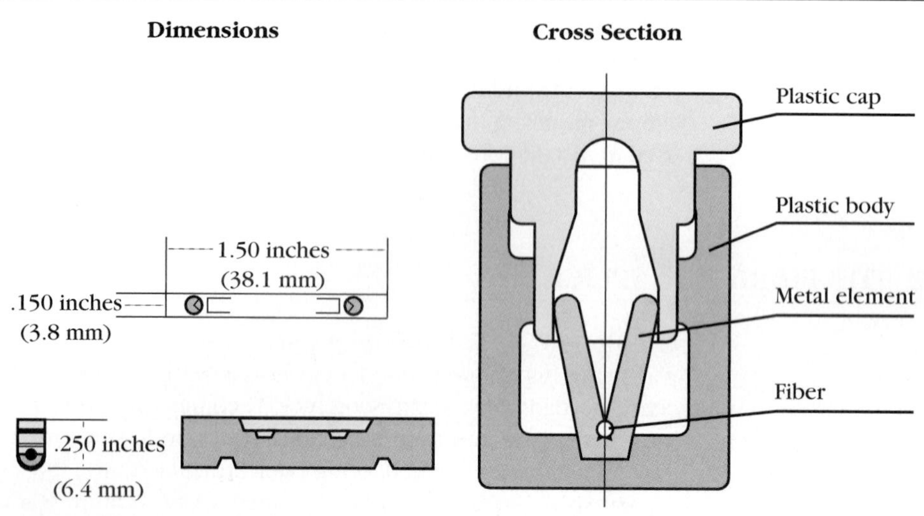

Source: Company documents.

the Fibrlok™ Splice required an assembly tool. Plans were made to market a Fibrlok™ Splice kit that included an assembly tool and 55 splices.

Similar to other Telecom Systems Division products, it was expected that the division's largest customers, such as Bell South, would buy Fibrlok™ Splices directly from 3M on a contracted price that would be negotiated. This meant that about 80 companies in the United States would buy Fibrlok™ Splices directly from 3M. The rest of the industry, literally thousands of companies, was expected to purchase Fibrlok™ Splices from 3M distributors including Anixter, Graybar, GTE Supply, and North Supply. 3M decided to price the Fibrlok™ Splice about the same regardless of whether it was sold to a distributor or to a large customer directly. Exhibit 5 contains selected information about the initial Fibrlok™ Splice offering.

The Fibrlok™ market introduction was extremely successful, with sales far exceeding projections. In October 1988, only six weeks after its introduction, sales

EXHIBIT 5

Initial Order Information and Pricing for the Fibrlok™ Splice

		Price $	
	Units/Case	*Trade*	*Distributor*
Fibrlok™ Optical Fiber Splice 250 × 250	50	16	12
Fibrlok™ Optical Fiber Splice 250 × 900	50	16	12
Fibrlok™ Optical Fiber Splice 900 × 900	50	16	12
Fibrlok™ Optical Fiber Splice Kit 250 × 250	1 each	975	755
Fibrlok™ Optical Fiber Splice Kit 250 × 900	1 each	975	755
Fibrlok™ Optical Fiber Splice Kit 900 × 900	1 each	975	755
Fibrlok™ Splice Assembly Tool	1 each	125	96.16

Source: Company records.

EXHIBIT 6

Advertisement for Fibrlok™ Splice

Take a closer look at the future of mass fiber splicing.

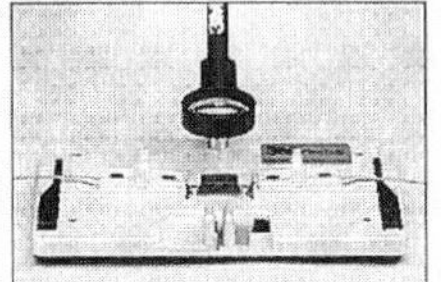

Fibrlok Multi-Fiber Splicing Assembly Tool

Mass fiber splicing will never be the same. With our Fibrlok Multi-Fiber Optical Splicing System, it's strip, cleave and splice – up to twelve fibers at a time. A completed splice can be assembled in less than five minutes, making the Fibrlok Multi-Fiber Splice ideal for both new construction and cable restoration applications.

Splice performance is comparable to our original Fibrlok Splice, delivering low insertion loss, low reflectance and superior thermal stability. Splicing is fast, efficient and permanent.

The Fibrlok Multi-Fiber Splice is easy to use and accommodates single-mode or multimode 125 micron fibers (individual and ribbon). The splice is available in 4-, 6-, 8-, 10- and 12-fiber configurations.

The low cost assembly tool is lightweight and portable, perfect for most real world applications.

To learn more, talk to an authorized 3M Telecom Systems distributor or your 3M representative. Or contact 3M Telecom Systems Division at 800/745 7459 or via fax at 512/984 5811.

3M *Innovation*

Source: 3M.

forecasts were revised. Sales were initially estimated to be approximately 85,000 units in 1989, but the early success led 3M to increase the forecast to 240,000 units. Because of the labor-intensive nature of the initial manufacturing process, a factory cost of about 50 percent of the price of each Fibrlok™ Splice was anticipated. However, it was also anticipated that significant per unit cost reductions would be achieved once manufacturing was appropriately ramped up to handle the increased demand. Exhibit 6 contains an advertisement for the Fibrlok™ Splice.

In 1995, Telecom Systems Division introduced a multi-fiber Fibrlok™ Splice. Although not much larger than the original single-fiber Fibrlok™ Splice, this new splice allowed technicians to connect up to twelve fibers at a time in a single splice. This improved craft productivity considerably. However, because taking a single fiber to the home does not necessarily require multi-fiber splicing (multi-fiber splicing occurs at points farther back in the network, such as in trunk lines where multiple fibers are in the same cable), sales of Fibrlok™ Splices did not increase substantially following the introduction of the multi-fiber Fibrlok™ Splice. Consequently, there have not been significant improvements in factory costs, and the price per fiber splice has remained fairly constant over time.

At the beginning of 1996, about 5 million single-fiber mechanical splices were being sold globally per year, with 3M's Fibrlok™ Splice holding about a 30 percent market share. Although the market for mechanical splices grew rapidly for the first three years after the Fibrlok™ Splice was introduced, in the last seven years or so it has been relatively flat. Fusion splices still outnumber mechanical splices by about 8 to 1.

■ JANUARY 1996

With a doctorate in physics, Hamill was known for his keen analytical ability, and his tenure in the company had provided him with considerable expertise in many areas. Even so, Hamill enjoyed working with marketing-related issues because of their generally challenging nature.

As Hamill finished going through the piles of reports in front of him, he leaned back in his chair and rested his hands on his head. He thought about the division's forecast for the Fibrlok™ Splice nearly 10 years ago. Back in 1987, expectations were that within 5 to 10 years every household, at least in the United States, would either be served with fiber optic cable or have fiber "right to the curb." "Strange," he muttered to himself, "that same forecast holds today. Nothing seems to have changed. The same forecast, but it just seems to move out a year every year." Hamill was intimately familiar with the history of the Fibrlok™ Splice since one of the original venture team members, Al Lindh, indirectly reported to him.

At the beginning of 1996, there were in excess of 600 million identifiable telephone lines in the world, of which roughly one quarter were in the United States. Only a negligible proportion of these telephone lines incorporated fiber optic cable. Of the households that did have fiber optic cable, virtually all were in Japan, where the giant telecom NTT operated.

From the market research reports that he had read, Hamill calculated that new construction of telephone lines globally was running about eight percent a year (using as a base the 600 million existing telephone lines). For planning purposes Hamill assumed that three annual copper wire-to-optical fiber conversion or change-out rates were possible over the next few years—2 percent, 6 percent, and 10 percent. He assigned a .65 probability of occurrence to the two percent rate, a .25 probability to the 6 percent rate, and a .10 probability to the 10 percent rate.

Three Scenarios

Just as Hamill was finishing his musings, Steve Webster walked into his office. Hamill decided to bounce a couple of ideas off of Webster. "Steve, I have been thinking about the Fibrlok™ marketing strategy for 1996 and 1997, and there are three possibilities that occur to me. The first is that the market will grow very slowly. If this is the case, are we properly positioned with our existing splices, pricing, and communications to maintain the market share that we currently have without changing our current strategy?"

"But, what if we see significantly higher growth in penetration of fiber to the home? If this happens, are we still properly positioned with respect to product, price, and market support to keep our share and to be able to grow with the growing market?" Hamill paused and thought for a moment. "Finally, is it possible that we could, through significant product redesign, different pricing and cost structures, and different marketing communications or other kinds of market support, position ourselves to actually drive market growth by offering improved productivity in fiber optic mechanical splicing? What do you think, Steve?"

Webster paced the room for a few minutes before returning to his seat. "Denny," he began, "you know as well as I do that a part of the uncertainty in predicting the rate of penetration of fiber to the home is the constant change in the preferences of consumers regarding services that they want and are willing to pay for. At the same time, since copper is already installed, telephone and cable companies are increasingly finding new ways to add electronic enhancements such as ISDN, ADSL, and so on to upgrade the copper line. These enhancements allow the lines to handle more data faster. Remember, much of what is going on in the home is being driven by the Internet, fax machines, and even e-mail. Telecoms are trading off installing fiber against the cost of electronics to enhance the capability of in-place copper."

"If the last kilometer of the network remains copper to the home, enhanced by electronics, then the present model of fiber to the neighborhood will provide continued growth for fiber splicing. This growth, though, will not be the explosive growth that would occur if we can improve installation productivity by driving down the cost of splicing. Remember, telecom technicians operate at a loaded labor rate of $60 per hour. You know, Denny, without a real breakthrough in fiber splicing costs, say to under 50¢ per splice, even wireless local loop, fed by fiber to the last kilometer, moves ahead of fiber to the home."

"Well, Steve," responded Hamill, "how can we cover all options in this uncertain market? Should we invest in major cost reduction and design strategies and attempt to drive the market? Should we partner with a major end user of fiber like NTT to reduce our risk? Or should we be satisfied with a small but profitable market?"

CASE

The Circle K Corporation

The Circle K Corporation is one of the leading specialty retailers in the United States and is the nation's second largest operator and franchiser of convenience stores. From fiscal 1984 (year-end April 30), when it embarked on a significant growth strategy, to fiscal 1990, the company acquired 3,326 stores and built another 983 stores while closing 899 units. During this period, sales increased from $1 billion in fiscal 1984 to almost $3.7 billion in fiscal 1990.

On May 15, 1990, the company and its principal subsidiaries filed for protection under Chapter 11 of the United States Bankruptcy Code. This action was taken because of the company's deteriorating financial condition, due in part to increased competition, a heavy debt burden from the expansion program, and the negative effect of merchandise and price policies instituted in 1989. Shortly after the bankruptcy filing, Circle K president Robert A. Dearth, Jr., announced that he was determined to reposition the company so that it could return to profitability and pay its debt in fiscal 1991.[1] Key elements of the plan to revitalize Circle K included a change in merchandising practices, increased promotional efforts, and an aggressive pricing program, all of which were designed to improve customer service and increase sales. In addition, opportunities to close or sell unprofitable stores would be pursued. Circle K's planned turnaround strategy was scheduled for implementation in the summer of 1990. Of critical concern to Circle K management was consumer and competitive response and the profitability of the announced strategy.

THE COMPANY

The Circle K Corporation, which is headquartered in Phoenix, Arizona, is the 30th largest retailer in the United States according to *Fortune* magazine. The company's convenience store business was begun by Circle K Convenience Stores, Inc. in 1951. In 1980, this company became a subsidiary of the Circle K Corporation. The Circle K Corporation is a holding company, which, through wholly owned subsidiaries, operates 4,631 convenience stores in the United States and related facilities. In addition, the Circle K Corporation has approximately 1,400 licensed or joint-venture stores in 13 foreign countries.

Circle K recorded an average annual increase in sales of 25 percent since fiscal 1984. The number of stores operated by Circle K increased by 14 percent per year during the period 1984 through fiscal 1990. Most of the increase in stores came from acquisitions. In the four years prior to fiscal 1989, when Circle K incurred an operat-

[1] "Circle K Squares Off with Its Creditors," *Wall Street Journal* (May 17, 1990):A4.

This case was prepared by Professor Roger A. Kerin, of the Edwin L. Cox School of Business, Southern Methodist University, as a basis for class discussion and is not designed to illustrate appropriate or inappropriate handling of administrative situations, or to be used for research purposes. The case is based on published sources, including the Circle K Corporation annual reports and 10-K Forms. The assistance of Angela Bullard and Deborah Ovitt, graduate students, in the preparation of this case is gratefully acknowledged.

ing loss of $3.8 million, the company had recorded an average annual increase in operating profit of 25 percent. Exhibit 1 and Exhibit 2 (page 590) show the Circle K Corporation's consolidated financial statements for fiscal 1988 through fiscal 1990.

Stores and Unit Expansion

Circle K stores typically have 2,600 square feet of retail selling space. Most units are located on corner sites, have parking space on one or more sides, and are equipped with modern equipment, fixtures, and refrigeration. Nearly all the stores are open seven days a week, 24 hours a day. The 4,631 stores operated by Circle K are located in 32 states. However, about 84 percent of the stores are situated in Sun Belt states ranging from California to Florida. The primary concentration of stores is in Florida

EXHIBIT 1

The Circle K Corporation's Consolidated Statement of Earnings (Thousands of Dollars)

	For the Year Ending April 30		
	1990	*1989*	*1988*
Revenues:			
Sales	$3,686,314	$3,441,384	$2,613,843
Other	50,238	53,507	42,879
Gross revenues	3,736,552	3,494,891	2,656,722
Cost of sales and expenses:			
Cost of sales	2,796,559	2,580,398	1,893,058
Operating and administrative	865,602	729,306	561,894
Reorganization and restructuring charge[a]	639,310	—	—
Depreciation and amortization	127,652	93,033	65,659
Interest and debt expense	126,799	95,912	56,608
Total cost of sales and expenses	4,555,922	3,498,649	2,577,219
Operating profit (Loss)	(819,370)	(3,758)	79,503
Gain on sale of assets[b]	—	32,323	8,198
Equity loss on foreign joint ventures	(15,064)	(1,784)	—
Earnings (loss) before federal and state income taxes and cumulative effect of accounting change	(834,434)	26,781	87,701
Federal and state income tax (expense) benefit	61,565	(11,367)	(32,790)
Net earnings (loss) before cumulative effect of accounting change	(772,869)	15,414	54,911
Cumulative effect on prior years of change in accounting for income taxes	—	—	5,500
Net earnings (Loss)	($ 772,869)	$ 15,414	$ 60,411

[a] The company had been attempting a financial restructuring since October 1989. A review and assessment of operations by the Board of Directors resulted in a reorganization and restructuring charge of $639.3 million as of April 30, 1990. The charge includes (1) excess costs over acquired net assets and foreign investment; (2) abandonment, rejection, and reserves for fixed assets in nonperforming leased stores; (3) write-downs of real estate and other projects no longer under development, and (4) debt issuance and other costs.

[b] On October 31, 1988, the company sold all of its assets in connection with its manufacturing and distribution of fragmentary and block ice, sandwiches, and other fast foods. On October 27, 1987, the company sold a 50 percent interest in its wholly owned United Kingdom subsidiary.

Source: The Circle K Corporation, Form 10-K. Fiscal Year Ended April 30, 1990; The Circle K Corporation 1989 annual report. The statement of earnings information is accompanied by extensive explanations, which are an integral part of these consolidated financial statements.

EXHIBIT 2

The Circle K Corporation's Consolidated Balance Sheet, Abridged (Thousands of Dollars)

	April 30, 1990	*April 30, 1989*	*April 30, 1988*
Current assets:			
Cash and short-term investments	$ 50,205	$ 38,488	$ 44,216
Receivables	38,138	36,265	34,446
Inventories	175,308	239,916	191,000
Other current assets	39,865	94,341	109,851
Total current assets	303,516	409,010	379,513
Property, plant, and equipment (less accumulated depreciation and amortization)	836,123	1,068,489	708,314
Other assets	134,651	567,441	447,957
Total assets	$1,274,290	$2,044,940	$1,535,784
Current liabilities:			
Due to banks	$ —	$ 91,000	$ 60,000
Accounts payable	112,111	134,944	112,144
Other current liabilities	101,504	124,501	108,463
Total current liabilities	213,615	350,445	280,607
Liabilities subject to compromise	1,206,395	—	—
Long-term debt	54,651	1,158,563	844,065
Deferred income taxes	40,496	93,045	38,133
Other liabilities	130,915	45,359	17,191
Deferred revenue	32,285	19,632	24,767
Mandatory redeemable preferred stock	42,500	47,500	47,500
Stockholders' equity	(451,567)	330,396	283,521
Total liabilities and stockholders' equity	$1,274,290	$2,044,940	$1,535,784

Source: The Circle K Corporation, Form 10-K, Fiscal Year Ended April 30, 1990; Circle K Corporation 1989 annual report. Balance sheet information is accompanied by extensive explanations, which are an integral part of these consolidated financial statements.

(846 stores), Texas (735 stores), Arizona (679 stores), California (604 stores), and Louisiana (301 stores).

The present complement of stores was an outgrowth of an aggressive acquisition program begun in December 1983 with the purchase of the nearly 1,000-store UToteM chain. This acquisition was followed in October 1984 with the purchase of Little General Stores, consisting of 435 units. In February 1985, Circle K bought 21 Day-n-Nite stores, and in September 1985, it acquired the 449-unit Stop & Go chain. The company purchased 189 units from National Convenience Stores in March 1987 and three months later bought 63 franchised 7-Eleven units from the Southland Corporation. In late 1987, Circle K's director of public relations announced that the company intended to have 5,000 stores by 1990.[2]

[2] "Mergers of Convenience," *Progressive Grocer* (December 1987): 50–51; "Karl Eller's Big Thirst for Convenience Stores," *Business Week* (June 13, 1988): 86, 88; Circle K Corporation 1990 10-K Form.

In April 1988, Circle K purchased the assets of 473 convenience stores, 90 closed stores, convenience store sites, stores under construction, and related facilities from the Southland Corporation. The company's last major acquisition occurred on September 30, 1988, with the purchase of the Charter Marketing Group. This transaction resulted in the addition of 538 gasoline and convenience stores. Circle K did not acquire any stores in fiscal 1990 because of its deteriorating financial condition, which led to the company's Chapter 11 bankruptcy filings. However, negotiations concerning the sale of 375 stores in Hawaii and the Pacific Northwest were initiated.

Product–Service Mix

Circle K stores sell over 3,800 different products and services. Food items include groceries, dairy products, candies, bakery items, produce, meat, eggs, ice cream, frozen foods, soft drinks, and alcoholic beverages (beer, wine, and liquor) where permitted. Fast food items, including fountain drinks, doughnuts, sandwiches, and coffee, are also sold. Non-food items sold by Circle K include tobacco products, health and beauty aids, magazines, books, newspapers, household goods, giftware, and toys. Food and nonfood merchandise categories accounted for 50 percent of company revenue in fiscal 1990.

Circle K sells gasoline at 77.5 percent of its stores. Gasoline accounted for 48.6 percent of company revenue in fiscal 1990. In addition, the company provides a variety of consumer services. Consumer services include money orders, lottery tickets, game machines, and video cassette rentals. These services combined with interest income and royalty and licensing fees accounted for the remainder of company revenue.

Circle K had followed a program of continual testing and introduction of new products and services designed to appeal to a broader customer base and stimulate store traffic. According to the company's chairman of the board, Karl Eller, "We're a massive distribution system. Whatever we can push through that store, we will."[3] The addition of automated teller machines (ATMs) or debit card programs at 1,146 stores and leased space at certain locations for Federal Express drop-off package service are recent innovations indicative of this strategy.

Efforts to sell and promote high-profit-margin products while cutting back on popular, though less profitable, merchandise proved costly for Circle K in the summer of 1989. While the gross profit margin for merchandise sales increased, dollar sales decreased (see Exhibit 3 on page 592, which details sales and gross margins for merchandise and gasoline). Traditional customers did not want these products, according to Dearth, the company's president. An integral part of his merchandising plan for fiscal 1991 included tailoring product and service offerings to the particular ethnic or socioeconomic character of each store's clientele.[4] National Convenience Stores, Inc., with its Stop & Go stores, has adopted a similar program, matching its merchandise with the demographics of surrounding neighborhoods. Early results from this merchandise program indicate that dollar sales will increase 4 to 5 percent.[5]

Advertising and Promotion Program

Circle K has historically used media advertising and special promotions to attract customers. In fiscal 1989, the company spent $4 million on advertising. This figure was down 41.2 percent from the fiscal 1988 advertising expenditures. For compari-

[3] Lisa Gubernick, "Stores for Our Times," *Forbes* (November 3, 1986): 40–42.

[4] "Circle K Squares Off with Its Creditors," p. A4.

[5] "Convenience Chains Pump for New Life," *Advertising Age* (April 23, 1990): 80.

EXHIBIT 3

The Circle K Corporation's Merchandise and Gasoline Sales and Gross Profit Percentage, Fiscal Years 1988–1990

	1990		*1989*		*1988*	
Revenue Source	*Sales (Millions)*	*Gross Profit (Percentage)*	*Sales (Millions)*	*Gross Profit (Percentage)*	*Sales (Millions)*	*Gross Profit (Percentage)*
Merchandise	$1,869.4	37.2%	$1,962.4	36.0%	$1,649.2	37.5%
Gasoline	1,817.0	10.8	1,479.0	10.5	964.6	10.6
Other*	50.2		53.5		42.9	
Total	$3,736.6		$3,494.9		$2,656.7	

*Other revenues consist of commissions on game machines and lottery tickets, money order fees, interest income, royalty and licensing fees, and other items.

Source: The Circle K Corporation, 1990 10-K Form, pp. 30–31.

son, National Convenience Stores, Inc. (with 1,100 Stop & Go stores), spends about $12 million annually on advertising. Advertising as a percent-of-sales for the convenience store industry as a whole was 0.6 percent in 1989 and 0.3 percent in 1988 and 1987.

Circle K curtailed advertising in late fiscal 1990. "Circle K is not advertising and has not been," the company's national advertising manager said in April 1990. "We're going through bad times."[6] The company's most recent promotion was a "price-buster" campaign in Florida and Arizona. This campaign came to an end in the second quarter of fiscal 1990.

More aggressive advertising and promotion efforts were the second part of the turnaround strategy planned by Circle K. The company announced that a $100 million promotion would be launched in the summer of 1990.[7] The eight-week promotion would be centered on a "We're Driving Down Prices" game, which included some 180 million instant-winner, scratch-off tickets distributed to customers who made purchases at over 3,700 Circle K stores. Game tickets would feature instant-win merchandise discounts, theme park discounts, and grand prizes such as Jeep Wranglers, round-trip Continental Airline tickets, and Bayliner Capri 17-foot speedboats.

The game would be publicized by in-store window banners, ceiling danglers, and tent cards located near checkout counters. Outdoor signage near gasoline pumps was also planned. In addition, the promotion would be supported by radio and outdoor advertising. The objective of the promotion was to communicate a change in store prices by providing Circle K customers "more value for their dollar," according to a company press release.

This new promotional program planned for the summer of 1990 would compete directly against a similar initiative launched by 7-Eleven in April 1990.[8] 7-Eleven's program involved giving away six-ounce samples of coffee, fountain drinks, and Slurpees. The company was also giving away a coupon book, valued at $250, with discounts on 7-Eleven products as well as merchandise from Sears, Roebuck and Company, Radio Shack, and Children's Palace. 7-Eleven was promoting its program through television and radio advertising.

[6] *Ibid.*

[7] "Circle K Unveils $100 Million Promotion," *Convenience Store News* (August 27–September 23, 1990): 12.

[8] "Convenience Chains Pump for New Life," p. 80.

Pricing Policy

The third leg in the Circle K strategy involved an overall price cut of 10 percent to be implemented concurrently with the $100 million promotion and the change in merchandising practices. "Before, we had the attitude of gouging the customer for what we could get," said Dearth.[9] Historically, Circle K was able to charge premium prices for food and nonfood items because of convenience of location, longer hours, accessibility, and fast service without long checkout lines. Promotional pricing of high-traffic items such as cigarettes, beer, bread, soft drinks, milk, and gasoline also was used periodically. These pricing practices had provided Circle K with the highest gross-profit-margin percentages in the convenience store industry. However, due to increased competitive pressures and rising costs during fiscal 1989, the company's gross-profit-margin percentage slipped to 25 percent for the first time since fiscal 1984. In addition, the Circle K Corporation incurred its first operating loss since its incorporation in 1980.

At the beginning of the 1990 fiscal year, Circle K boosted store merchandise prices by about 6 to 7 percent. According to industry analysts, store merchandise sales volume declined 8 to 10 percent. Gasoline sales volume dropped between 1 and 6 percent.[10] In February 1990, Circle K reversed the price increases. Merchandise dollar sales for Circle K in fiscal 1990 were 4.7 percent below fiscal 1989 levels, and company gross profit dropped 3.3 percent.

■ THE CONVENIENCE STORE INDUSTRY

The convenience store industry has been one of the fastest-growing sectors of retailing over the past 20 years. Since 1977, the number of convenience stores has grown at an average annual rate of 6.5 percent. Sales volume grew at an average annual rate of 17 percent. However, sales and store growth declined in the latter half of the 1980s. In 1989, the convenience store industry generated sales of $67.7 billion through an estimated 70,200 stores nationwide.

Convenience store industry profitability has fluctuated during the past five years. The industry gross profit margin fell to its lowest level in 1989 as a result of narrowing margins on store merchandise. The industry net profit margin before income taxes decreased in each of the past five years reaching a low of 0.4 percent in 1989. Rising costs of leasing, building, equipping, insuring, and operating stores coupled with financing costs attributed to store expansion contributed to this decline, according to industry analysts. A summary of industry sales, unit growth, and profitability is shown in Exhibit 4 on page 594.

Competitors

The convenience store industry is highly fragmented. In 1989, 1,353 companies were listed as belonging to the National Association of Convenience Stores. According to Alex Brown and Sons, Inc., an investment banking firm, about 42 percent of total stores and 31 percent of industry sales were accounted for by convenience store chains with fewer than 50 stores.[11] The largest single convenience store chain is the Southland Corporation (7-Eleven). The largest U.S. convenience store operators in terms of sales and units are listed in Exhibit 5 on page 595.

---

[9] "Circle K Squares Off with Its Creditors," p. A4.

[10] *Ibid.*

[11] *The Convenience Store Industry* (Baltimore: Alex Brown & Sons, 1988).

EXHIBIT 4

Convenience Store Industry Summary: 1980–1989

	Year									
	1980	*1981*	*1982*	*1983*	*1984*	*1985*	*1986*	*1987*	*1988*	*1989*
Sales, Including Gasoline										
Total sales (billions of dollars)	24.5	31.2	35.9	41.6	45.6	51.4	53.9	59.6	61.2	67.7
Year-to-year change (%)	31.0	27.3	15.1	15.9	9.6	12.7	4.9	10.5	2.7	10.6
Sales, Excluding Gasoline										
Sales (billions of dollars)	17.7	21.6	23.7	25.8	29.3	33.3	36.0	39.1	39.2	40.6
Year-to-year change (%)	22.9	22.0	15.7	8.9	13.6	13.3	8.4	8.6	—	3.6
Store Data										
Total number of stores (thousands)	44.1	47.9	51.2	54.4	58.0	61.0	64.0	67.5	69.2	70.2
Year-to-year change (%)	10.0	8.6	6.9	6.3	6.6	5.2	4.9	5.5	2.5	1.4
Sales per store (thousands of dollars) (excluding gas)	394.0	450.0	463.0	474.0	511.0	544.0	564.0	579.2	567.0	578.0
Year-to-year change (%)	11.0	14.2	2.9	2.4	7.8	6.5	3.7	2.7	2.1	1.9
Profitability Data										
Gross profit margin (%)										
Merchandise						32.5	35.5	35.9	36.4	32.1
Gasoline						7.3	11.2	10.6	11.5	11.7
Total						22.8	25.1	24.4	26.2	21.8
Net profit margin before income taxes (%)						2.7	2.6	2.2	1.9	.4

Source: Based on *The Convenience Store Industry* (Baltimore: Alex Brown & Sons, 1988): 3; *The State of the Convenience Store Industry 1990* (Alexandria, VA: National Association of Convenience Stores, 1990).

Convenience store executives believe that their principal competitors are other convenience store chains, gas stations that sell food (g-stores), supermarkets, and fast food outlets. S. R. "Dick" Dole, an executive at the Southland Corporation, believed that competition for convenience stores depends on the product category:

> If you're talking about post-mix, coffee, and sandwiches, then our competition is the "fast feeders," like McDonald's and Burger King, and other convenience stores. If you're talking about beer and soft drinks, then our competition would be supermarkets, other convenience stores, and some g-stores, or a major oil company that operates a small convenience store with major emphasis on gasoline.[12]

Oil companies that operate g-stores engage in the most direct competition with convenience stores. Texaco, Chevron Corporation, Amoco Corporation, Atlantic Richfield Company, Coastal Corporation, Mobil Corporation, BP America, and Diamond Shamrock operate more than 600 g-stores each.[13] These well-capitalized companies, with the advantage of prime locations and newer stores, have become very aggressive in the creation of convenience-type stores. Although smaller than convenience stores in terms of retail selling space and number of items stocked (convenience stores stock 33 percent more items than g-stores), g-stores have focused on items traditionally viewed as convenience store staples—tobacco products, soft drinks, and beer.

[12] "A Conversation with S. R. 'Dick' Dole," *The Southland Family* (August 1986): 9.

[13] "Convenience Chains Pump for New Life," p. 80.

EXHIBIT 5

Largest U.S. Convenience Store Operators

Company	*Key Chain(s)*	*Sales Volume (Millions of Dollars)*	*Number of Store Units (Approx.)*
The Southland Corporation	7-Eleven, High's Dairy Stores, Quick Marts, Super 7	$7,950.3	7,200
The Circle K Corporation	Circle K	3,441.4	4,631
Emro Marketing Co.	Speedway, Gastown, Starvin Marvin, Bonded	1,250.0	1,673
National Convenience Stores, Inc.	Stop N Go	1,072.5	1,147
Convenient Food Mart, Inc.	Convenient Food Mart	875.0	1,258
Cumberland Farms, Inc.	Cumberland Farms	800.0	1,150

Source: Company annual reports and 10-K forms; *Convenience Store News Industry Report 1989* (New York: BMT Publications, 1989).

Supermarkets have also been aggressive in trying to attract the convenience shopper. In particular, supermarkets have targeted the "fill-in" shoppers who typically populate the "eight items and under" express counters by offering extended store hours and prepackaged foods. This segment represents about $45 billion in annual sales. Supermarkets also cater to consumers who desire prepared foods for off-premises consumption. Prepared foods sold by supermarkets now account for more than $2.4 billion in sales annually. Furthermore, industry research shows that supermarkets enjoy a better reputation among consumers for lower prices and higher-quality food than convenience stores.[14]

Convenience Store Customer and Purchase Behavior

About 90 percent of American adults (18 years or older) visit a convenience store at least once a year. Almost two-thirds of these shoppers visit a convenience store two to three times per month. The typical convenience store customer is a white male between the ages of 18 and 34 with a high school education who is employed in a blue-collar occupation. A profile of the convenience store customer is given in Exhibit 6 on page 596.

Convenience store executives are sensitive to the fact that a stereotypic convenience store customer exists. They also recognize that opportunities for future sales growth exist in attracting women generally and particularly employed women, older consumers of both sexes, and professional and white-collar workers. According to a 7-Eleven executive:

> Two important demographic groups for 7-Eleven are the increased numbers of older people and working women. The elderly, the fastest-growing segment of the population, generally are not convenience store customers. Also, working women now rep-

[14] "Convenience Store/Supermarket Market Segment Report," *Restaurant Business* (February 10, 1990): 125.

EXHIBIT 6

Profile of Convenience Store Customers on a Given Day

	Convenience Store Customers (Percentage)	*United States Population (Percentage)*
Sex		
Male	57%	48%
Female	43	52
Age		
18 to 24	21	15
25 to 34	31	24
35 to 49	25	25
50 and over	23	35
Education		
Did not finish high school	19	18
Graduated from high school	62	60
Attended college	19	22
Annual Household Income		
Less than $10,000	14	13
$10,000 to $14,999	11	10
$15,000 to $19,999	12	10
$20,000 and over	48	48
Unknown	15	19
Race		
White	83	87
Nonwhite	17	13

Source: The Gallup Organization. Used with permission.

> resent 45 percent of the work force. By 1995, 80 percent of all women between the ages of 25 and 44 will be working. Right now, women represent less than one-third of our business. We must do a better job of attracting potential customers to our stores by developing programs that fit their needs.
>
> The 24–45 age group is experiencing a tremendous growth in disposable income, which increases our need to upgrade our stores to meet their demands and tastes.[15]

Similarly, a Circle K executive said, "We feel we can appeal to other groups than the traditional blue-collar customer of the past. We'd like to skew more toward office workers and white-collar workers."[16]

Industry analysts also believe that a broadened customer base will be necessary if the convenience store industry is to prosper in the 1990s. They note that the U.S. population between the ages of 18 and 34 will actually shrink in the early 1990s. They also point out that the industry must expand its customer base to include more older, married, dual-income customers and women shoppers.

The principal purchases by the 643 customers who visit an average convenience store daily are gasoline, tobacco products, alcoholic beverages, prepared foods, and soft drinks. These five product categories account for almost 80 percent

[15] "A Conversation with S. R. 'Dick' Dole," pp. 9–10.

[16] "Convenience Store/Supermarket Market Segment Report," p. 134.

of convenience store sales. The average merchandise sale per customer visit was $2.29 in 1989.

Industry Trends and Concerns

Industry observers have identified several trends that are likely to affect convenience store industry growth and profitability prospects for the foreseeable future. These trends and their implications are outlined below.

The first trend relates to industry maturity and store saturation. Industry analysts cite several developments, some of which are documented in Exhibit 4.

1. Industry sales growth has slowed in recent years compared with growth rates in the 1970s and early 1980s. Similarly, the number of new stores being opened has leveled off, and consolidation is occurring as firms have elected to grow through acquisition.
2. Industry profitability has declined in recent years. The downward spiral in net profit margins has hampered the ability of firms to reinvest in their operations.
3. Store saturation is present in many geographic markets. Potentially overstored areas include the southwestern, southeastern, and western United States. Industry forecasters predict that the demand for convenience stores is such that the market can only support 400 to 500 new stores per year in the period 1990–1995.

A second concern is the lack of differentiation among convenience store competitors. According to a 7-Eleven executive, "The thing to overcome is the battle of sameness."[17] The lack of differentiation has often produced costly price competition in selected markets, most notably in Florida and Texas. Efforts at differentiation reflected in new products and services have often been met with an immediate response. "We are the worst thieves around," said a Circle K executive. "As soon as one of us finds something that works, the copycats go to work."[18]

A third trend is the changing sales mix between merchandise and gasoline. In the late 1970s, roughly 82 percent of convenience store sales were merchandise. By 1989, 60 percent of sales were merchandise. The increase in gasoline sales as a percentage of total revenue has affected industry profitability because of gasoline's lower gross profit margin and often higher equipment cost. Moreover, some industry watchers believe that oil company g-stores are better equipped to deal with the lower margins. These "low-price, high-volume" g-stores, with about 80 percent of their sales coming from gasoline, and supermarkets, with a growing commitment to serving the convenience-oriented consumer, have left convenience stores "stuck in the middle," say industry analysts.[19]

STRATEGY CONSIDERATIONS FOR FISCAL 1991

One week prior to the announced bankruptcy filing, Karl Eller resigned as chairman, chief executive officer, and board director of the Circle K Corporation. He did so to pursue personal business opportunities and to give the company's board of directors "the latitude to establish new objectives for the future."[20]

[17] "Convenience Chains Pump for New Life," p. 80.

[18] "Stores for Our Times," p. 41.

[19] "Recent Events Show Plight of C-Store Chains," *National Petroleum News* (May 1990): 10.

[20] "Karl Eller Resigns as Circle K Chairman, CEO," *Wall Street Journal and Dow Jones News Wire* (May 7, 1990).

The principal elements of the announced strategy to revitalize the Circle K Corporation included (1) an overall price reduction of 10 percent, (2) a change in merchandise practices so that individual stores could stock items reflective of the socioeconomic characteristics of their trade areas, and (3) a $100 million advertising and promotion program. As the architect of the strategy, Dearth, Circle K's president, expressed no intention of downsizing the company or laying off any of the company's 27,000 employees when the bankruptcy filing was announced.

The initial reaction to the announced strategy was mixed. According to one of Circle K's bank creditors, "We would encourage any plan that generates income. We believe this [marketing] plan probably will."[21] However, industry analysts were skeptical. Some believed that the company's troubles would force it to sell about 10 percent of its stores. By August 1990, Circle K had terminated 400 leases on stores that had been shut down. These 400 leases were estimated to cost Circle K $1 million to $1.5 million per month. Furthermore, 201 unprofitable stores were scheduled to close in August 1990. In addition, the company had deals to sell 375 stores in Hawaii and the Pacific Northwest before its bankruptcy filing. These deals were delayed pending approval by the bankruptcy court. Savings from store closings, costs associated with terminating leases, and the potential gain on the sale of stores had yet to be determined.[22]

Industry analysts also expressed doubts about the financial viability of specific elements of Circle K's turnaround strategy. Lower prices might attract customers and increase store traffic. However, gross profit margins would suffer. Furthermore, efforts to modify the merchandise mix would involve a substantial change in inventories, and the advertising and promotion program was expensive. According to a convenience store analyst, "I don't know where they will get the money."[23]

In affidavits filed with the Securities and Exchange Commission, Circle K management stated that it "believes, but has no assurances, that this plan will succeed in improving operating results." Moreover, the company "expects to continue to incur operating losses until the business plan is fully implemented and refined."[24] The question yet to be answered was "Could the announced strategy return Circle K to profitability as envisioned by its president?"

---

[21] "Circle K Squares Off with Its Creditors," p. A4.

[22] "Circle K Begins Closing 201 Unprofitable Stores," *Wall Street Journal and Dow Jones News Wire* (August 21, 1990).

[23] "Circle K Squares Off with Its Creditors," p. A4.

[24] The Circle K Corporation, Form 10-K, for the fiscal year ended April 1990, "Management's Discussion and Analysis of Financial Condition and Results of Operations," pp. 26, 30.

CASE

Marshall Museum of Art

In early 2000, Ashley Mercer, Director of Development and Community Affairs, and Donald Pate, Director of Finance and Administration, of the Marshall Museum of Art, met to discuss what had transpired at a meeting the previous afternoon. The meeting, attended by the senior staff of the museum and several members of the Board of Trustees, had focused on the financial status of the museum. The Marshall Museum recorded its third consecutive annual loss in 1999, and Mercer and Pate were assigned responsibility for making recommendations that would reverse the situation.

MARSHALL MUSEUM OF ART

The Marshall Museum of Art (MMA) is a not-for-profit corporation located in Universal City, a large metropolitan area in the western United States. Founded at the turn of the century, the museum was originally chartered as the Fannel County Museum of Fine Arts and funded by an annual appropriation from Fannel County. In the early 1990s, the name was changed to the Jonathon A. Marshall Museum of Art to recognize the museum's major benefactor, Jonathon A. Marshall. Marshall, a wealthy local landowner and philanthropist, had provided the museum with a sizable endowment. According to the terms of a $25 million gift given to the museum upon his death, the museum's charter was revised and its name changed. The charter of the museum stated that its purpose was

> To provide an inviting setting for the appreciation of art in its historical and cultural contexts for the benefit of this and successive generations of Fannel County citizens and visitors.

Randall Brent III, the Museum Director, noted that this charter differentiated the MMA from other art museums. He said:

> Our charter gives us both an opportunity and a challenge. By spanning both art and history, the museum offers a unique perspective on both. On the other hand, a person can only truly appreciate what we have here if they are willing to become historically literate—that is our challenge.

In 1992, the MMA benefited from a $28 million county bond election, which led to the construction of a new and expanded facility in the central business district of Universal City, the county seat of Fannel County. The location, six blocks from the museum's previous site, had extensive parking availability and access through public

---

This case was prepared by Professor Roger A. Kerin, of the Edwin L. Cox School of Business, Southern Methodist University, as a basis for class discussion and is not designed to illustrate effective or ineffective handling of an administrative situation. The museum name and certain operating data are disguised and not useful for research purposes.

transportation. The site was made available for $1.00 from Jonathon Marshall's real estate holdings. At the dedication of the MMA in January 1995, Brent said:

> I will always believe that the greatest strength of our new museum is that it was publicly mandated. The citizens of Fannel County and the vision and generosity of Jonathon Marshall have provided the setting for the appreciation of art and its historical and cultural contexts. As stewards of this public trust, the Marshall Museum can now focus on collecting significant works of art, encouraging scholarship and education, and decoding the history and culture of art.

MUSEUM COLLECTION AND DISPLAY

The MMA has over 15,000 works of art in its permanent collection. However, as with most museums, MMA does not display all of its collection at the same time because of space limitations. Artworks in the collection are rotated, with some periodically loaned to other museums.

The MMA collection includes pre-Columbian, African, and Depression-era art, as well as European and American decorative arts. The art is displayed in different portions of the museum, where the building architecture accents the display. For example, Depression-era art is displayed in an Art Deco setting of the 1920s and 1930s; decorative and architectural art of the late nineteenth century is displayed in the Art Nouveau wing. In addition, museum docents provide a historical context for the artworks during tours.

The MMA collection is open for viewing Monday through Saturday from 10:00 A.M. to 6:00 P.M. and Thursday evenings until 8:00 P.M. Sunday hours are from 12:00 noon to 6:00 P.M. There is no charge for viewing the permanent collection; however, a modest fee of $3.00 to $5.00 is charged for special exhibitions. The MMA is also available for private showings and is often used for corporate, foundation, and various fund-raising events during weekday and weekend evenings. Exhibit 1 shows museum attendance for the period 1991–1999.

EXHIBIT 1

Museum Attendance

Year	Total Museum Attendance	Special Exhibitions[a]	
		Attendance	Proportion of Total Attendance
1991	269,786	N/A	N/A
1992	247,799	N/A	N/A
1993	303,456	N/A	N/A
1994	247,379	N/A	N/A
1995	667,949	220,867	0.33
1996	486,009	140,425	0.29
1997	527,091	227,770	0.43
1998	468,100	203,800	0.44
1999	628,472	284,865	0.45

[a] Special exhibitions attendance includes attendance at private corporation, foundation, and fund-raising events held at the museum.

Museum Organization

The MMA is organized by function: (1) Collections and Exhibitions, (2) Development and Community Affairs, and (3) Finance and Administration. Each function is headed by a director who reports to the Museum Director, Randall Brent III. The museum has a staff of 185 employees. In addition, 475 volunteers work at the museum in a variety of capacities.

The Collections and Exhibitions staff, headed by Thomas Crane, oversees the MMA's art collections, arranges special exhibits, is responsible for educational programming, and provides personnel and administrative support for museum operations that directly involve the artwork. The Finance and Administration staff, headed by Donald Pate, is responsible for the daily operation of the museum. The MMA's profit centers (the Skyline Buffet restaurant, parking, gift shop, and special exhibitions events) are also managed by this function. The Development and Community Affairs staff, under the direction of Ashley Mercer, is responsible for marketing, public relations, membership, and grants. This function engages in fund raising for the museum, which provides supplemental funds for general operating support, endowment, and acquisitions. This function also handles all applications for foundation, federal, state, and local grants.

Museum Finances

Exhibit 2 on page 602 shows the financial condition of the MMA for the period 1997–1999. Total revenues and expenses during this period are shown below:

	1999	*1998*	*1997*
Total revenue	$10,794,110	$7,783,712	$8,694,121
Total expenses	11,177,825	7,967,530	8,920,674
Net income (loss)	($ 383,715)	($ 183,818)	($ 226,533)

The three consecutive years of losses followed seven consecutive years of either break-even or profitable status. The cumulative loss of $794,066 had depleted the MMA's financial reserves.

During a recent Board of Trustees meeting, several observations and projections were made that indicated that the MMA's financial condition needed attention:

1. The appropriation from Fannel County would decline. Whereas the county appropriated about $2 million annually to the MMA in the mid- and late-1990s, the museum could expect no more than $1.6 million in county appropriations in 2000 and for the foreseeable future.
2. Low interest rates in 1999 and 2000 indicated that earnings from the MMA endowment and investments would probably remain flat or decline.
3. Income from grants and other contributions in 1999 were extraordinary, and it was unlikely that the same amounts would be forthcoming in 2000.
4. Membership revenues were down for the fifth consecutive year. Membership represented the single largest source of revenue for the museum.
5. Income from auxiliary activities—those that were intended to produce a profit—continued to show a positive contribution to museum operations.

Special exhibitions and events were very profitable. Nevertheless, limited availability of special exhibitions in 2000, a declining number of scheduled events, and rising costs (for insurance as an example) indicated that the revenues from such activities would probably decline and costs increase in 2000. The Skyline Buffet restaurant, gift shop and parking, and the Museum Association were operating at about break-even.

EXHIBIT 2

Summary of Income and Expenses, 1997–1999

	Year Ending December 31		
Operations	*1999*	*1998*	*1997*
Income			
Appropriations by Fannel County	$1,786,929	$1,699,882	$1,971,999
Memberships	2,917,325	2,956,746	3,134,082
Contributions	338,664	221,282	42,244
Grants	763,581	281,164	645,853
Investment income	27,878	28,537	32,205
Earnings from endowment	673,805	693,625	583,612
Other	149,462	128,628	196,195
Total revenue	$6,657,644	$6,009,864	$6,606,190
Expenses			
Personnel	$1,973,218	$1,086,177	$1,681,653
Memberships	854,461	869,043	906,314
Publications/public information	594,067	404,364	441,710
Education	616,828	519,805	542,076
Administration*	3,777,042	3,345,153	3,389,124
Total expenses	$7,815,616	$6,224,542	$6,960,877
Operating income	($1,157,972)	($ 214,678)	($ 354,687)
Auxiliary Activities			
Revenue from auxiliary			
Special exhibitions	$1,655,200	$ 510,415	$ 451,347
Museum gift shop	1,596,775	606,503	810,123
Skyline Buffet	515,843	305,952	418,960
Museum parking	131,512	45,068	64,651
Museum Association	337,136	305,910	342,850
Revenue from auxiliary	4,236,466	1,773,848	2,087,931
Expenses from auxiliary			
Special exhibitions	814,741	313,057	137,680
Museum gift shop	1,679,294	662,685	990,090
Skyline Buffet	592,051	457,841	462,475
Museum parking	31,168	16,528	16,536
Museum Association	344,955	292,877	353,016
Expenses from auxiliary	3,462,209	1,742,988	1,959,797
Profit from auxiliary activities	$ 774,257	$ 30,860	$ 128,134
Net income	($ 383,715)	($ 183,818)	($ 226,553)

*Administration expenses included mostly overhead costs, such as insurance, maintenance, utilities, equipment lease agreements, and so forth.

■ MUSEUM MARKETING

As Director of Development and Community Affairs, Ashley Mercer was responsible for marketing at the MMA. Her specific responsibilities related to enhancing the image of the museum, increasing museum visitation, and building museum memberships. Reflecting on her responsibilities, she said:

> In reality, museum image, visitation, and membership are intermingled. Image influences visitation and membership. Visitation is driven somewhat by membership, but membership seems to also drive visitation and, in a subtle way, affects the image of the museum.

Museum Image

Interest in the public image of the MMA began soon after the new facility was dedicated. The new four-story building, situated downtown adjacent to skyscrapers, was occasionally referred to as the "marble box" by its critics, since the building facade contained Italian marble. When asked about the image of the MMA, Brent commented:

> It is basically correct to say that, in the mind of the public, the MMA has no image. There is nothing about this [building] that says, "I'm a museum," or "Come in." There are a lot of people that are not interested in high culture and think this is a drive-in bank or an office building.
>
> Most art museums in America have a problem with image. One of the things that makes me mad is that people think there is something wrong with the museum. The MMA is the most public in the country, and more heavily dependent on the membership contribution than any other [museum]. Like most, it is underendowed and underfunded from reliable public funds. This institution has chosen to be public, with free access, and this is very noble. It is wonderful that the museum has decided not to belong to an agglomeration of very rich people.
>
> This museum has more character than it thinks it has. It has the best balanced collection between Western and non-Western art of any museum in the country. We have not chosen to sell or promote the unique aspects of this collection or the museum's emphasis on historical context. What we have are the makings of an institution that is very different from other museums, and we ought to be able to make that into an advantage rather than apologize for it.

Other staff members believed either that an image existed but was different for the various publics the museum served or that the MMA had not made a sufficient effort to create an image for itself. According to Ashley Mercer:

> Based on our marketing research, I think there are two distinctly different images. One is a non-image. People don't know what the museum is. They also don't know what we have to offer in the way of lunch, dinner, brunch, shopping, movies, etc. They are not familiar with our collections. They are probably proud, however, that their community has a beautiful art museum.
>
> The other image is that we are only for specific people. This image is probably based on our membership. About 85 percent of members are college-educated (compared to 70 percent of the county population of 2.5 million), 60 percent have household incomes in excess of $60,000 (compared to 25 percent of the county population), half are over 40 years old (compared to 25 percent of the county population), and 98 percent are white (compared to 75 percent of the county population).

Janet Blake, Staff Assistant in charge of membership, noted:

> Among our membership, the MMA is viewed as a community organization that has a cachet of class. It is exciting, educational, convenient, and inviting. It is a great place to bring visitors to our city for an afternoon of lunch and browsing.

A critic of the MMA said:

> The MMA has a definite image in my opinion. It's a great place to have lunch or brunch, buy an art or history book for the coffee table, and see a few things if time permits. Its parking facility is strategically located to allow its members to park conveniently for downtown shopping, particularly during the Christmas holidays.

Museum Visitation

Because there is a general belief that increased numbers of visitors lead to increased membership, Mercer's staff has historically focused its efforts on increasing the traffic through the museum. "Social, cultural, and educational activity in the museum is a major goal, and is not exclusive to the viewing of art," said Mercer. These efforts can be separated into general and outreach programs and programs involving special exhibitions and events.

Press Relations The MMA continually promotes its special exhibitions and activities by sending out press releases, and it maintains a close relationship with the local media. Stories about art and history, public programs, and human interest issues are often featured in the local media. A five-year anniversary party was held at the museum in early 1999, designed as a free special event aimed to involve the general public with the Museum.

Education and Outreach The MMA has many programs directed toward educating the public. Among these are public programs such as adult tours, school tours, lectures, art films, and feature films. The MMA engages in programming to create community involvement and lends performing space to local performing arts organizations.

Special Exhibitions Public service announcements written by the museum are aired on local radio stations to promote special exhibitions. Advertisements are run in local newspapers in a five-county area for special exhibitions. For major special exhibitions, advertising is usually sponsored by a local corporation.

Ashley Mercer believed that these efforts increased museum attendance. For example, periodic visitor surveys indicate that on a typical day when only the permanent collection was available for viewing, 85 percent of visitors were non-MMA members. She added that even though less than 1 percent of nonmembers actually applied for membership during a visit, this exposure helped in the annual membership solicitation.

Museum Membership

According to Mercer:

> Museum membership and the revenue earned from membership play significant roles in the success and daily operations of the MMA. The museum and its members have a symbiotic relationship. Members provide the museum with a volunteer base, without which our cost of operation would be astronomical. Member volunteers provide tours, assist at the information desk, help in the gift shop and the Skyline Buffet, and are invaluable in recruiting new members and renewing existing members.
>
> The Museum Association was created to encourage membership involvement in the MMA. The Association, with some 1,000 members, makes our volunteer effort possible—95 percent of our 475 volunteers are Association members. The Association's assistance in fund raising is critical, and we appreciate what its members have done for the MMA. Last year alone, the Association was directly responsible for raising almost $350,000. In return, the MMA sponsors social events for Association members, offers them lectures by authorities on art and history, and provides various other privileges not available to the general membership.

Member Categories, Benefits, and Costs The MMA has two distinct memberships: (1) personal and (2) corporate. These two memberships are further divided into categories based on dollar contributions and benefits received. There are six categories of personal membership ranging from $50 per year to $5,000 per year. Corporate memberships are divided into four categories ranging from $1,000 per year to $10,000 per year. These categories and participation levels were created in 1995 with the move to the new building. In 1999, there were 17,429 personal memberships and 205 corporate memberships.

Exhibit 3 shows the benefits received by each personal membership category. Exhibit 4 on page 606 provides a breakdown of personal memberships by category and the revenue generated by each category over the past five years. In 1999, personal memberships accounted for almost 80 percent of membership revenue.

Corporate memberships provide many of the same benefits as the $500 or higher personal memberships. In addition, corporate members are given "Employee Memberships" depending on their category. For example, corporate members that fall into the $1,000 category are given 25 "Employee Memberships"; those in the $10,000 category are given 250 such memberships.

The direct cost of benefits provided by the MMA to personal and corporate members was estimated by the museum's accounting firm. The MMA was required to do this because of income tax laws that limited the deductibility of membership to the difference between the direct cost of membership and the value of the benefits received. The estimated total cost of member benefits provided exceeded $1 million each year since 1995.[1] An itemized summary of benefit costs by category in 1999 is shown on page 606.

EXHIBIT 3

Membership Benefits by Membership Categories

	Membership Category					
Benefits	*$50*	*$100*	*$250*	*$500*	*$1,500*	*$5,000*
Invitations to special previews/events	*	*	*	*	*	*
Free limited parking	*	*	*	*	*	*
Free admission to special exhibits	*	*	*	*	*	*
15% discount at Skyline Buffet and gift shop	*	*	*	*	*	*
Monthly calender	*	*	*	*	*	*
Discounts on films/lectures	*	*	*	*	*	*
Reciprocal membership in other museums		*	*	*	*	*
Invitations to distinguished lectures			*	*	*	*
Listing in annual report			*	*	*	*
Personal tours of exhibition areas				*	*	*
Invitations to exclusive previews/events					*	*
Free unlimited parking					*	*
Unique travel opportunities					*	*
Recognition on plaques in the museum					*	*
First views of new acquisitions					*	*
Priority on all museum trips						*
Dinner with the Director						*

[1] The estimated cost of benefits exceeds the membership expense shown in Exhibit 2 because the cost of publications and other items is included in this estimate. These costs are allocated across several different items in Exhibit 2.

EXHIBIT 4

Personal Membership Categories and Revenues by Year, 1995–1999

		Number of Members				
Membership Category	***Amount***	*1999*	*1998*	*1997*	*1996*	*1995*
Regular	$50	13,672	12,248	13,483	16,353	17,758
Associate	$100	2,596	2,433	2,548	2,576	2,465
Collector	$250	364	325	397	461	454
Patron	$500	102	85	65	0	0
Partner	$1,500	604	638	679	741	882
Director's Club	$5,000	91	86	98	0	0
Total membership		17,429	15,815	17,370	20,131	21,559
		Membership Revenue[a]				
		1999	*1998*	*1997*	*1996*	*1995*
Regular	$50	$639,664	$556,120	$611,864	$600,188	$662,631
Associate	$100	234,871	232,398	249,317	244,961	242,981
Collector	$250	81,415	76,987	97,474	108,432	105,840
Patron	$500	48,100	44,293	35,500	0	0
Partner	$1,500	815,666	958,419	968,239	1,187,728	1,041,898
Director's Club	$5,000	406,673	405,016	458,938	282,219	0
Total membership revenue[b]		$2,298,449	$2,334,583	$2,485,352	$2,451,638	$2,079,330

[a] The number of memberships times the dollar value does not equal the amounts given as the membership revenue, since some memberships are given gratis.

[b] The inconsistency between these figures and the figures shown on the income and expense statement is due to memberships given gratis.

Category	*Benefit Cost*
Regular ($50)	$ 631,016
Associate ($100)	81,903
Collector ($250)	64,135
Patron ($500)	39,628
Partner ($1,500)	99,567
Director's Club ($5,000)	15,975
Corporate (all categories)	125,576
Total cost	$1,057,800

The principal cost items in each category were (1) free admissions to exhibits, (2) parking, (3) the monthly calendar of museum activities, exhibits, and events, and (4) discounts at the Skyline Buffet restaurant and gift shop.

Member Recruiting and Renewals "Recruiting new members and renewing existing members is a major undertaking," said Mercer. While some recruiting and renewals occur at the museum during visitation, the recruitment effort mostly revolves around mail, telephone, and personal solicitations. Mail and telephone solicitations focus primarily on recruiting and renewing personal memberships in the $50 to $250 categories. Personal solicitations by the Museum Association and Friends of the MMA are used to recruit and renew personal memberships in the $500 to $5,000 categories and corporate memberships.

The MMA uses mailing and telephone lists obtained from other cultural organizations and list agencies. These lists are culled to target zip codes and telephone prefix numbers. Mail solicitations include a letter from the Museum Director, a brochure describing the museum, and a membership application form. Telephone solicitations include a follow-up brochure and application form.

The economics of direct mail solicitation are illustrated below, based on an August 1999 mailing considered typical by Mercer.

Total mail solicitations	148,530
Total memberships obtained	1,532
Response rate	1.03%
Total membership revenue	$84,280.00
Total direct mail costs	$66,488.80

Two direct mail solicitations of this magnitude are conducted each year.

The solicitation process for personal memberships in larger dollar categories and corporate memberships relies on personal contact by MMA volunteers and corporate member executives. Prospective members are identified on the basis of personal contacts and from the lapsed membership roster, the society page, other organizations' membership lists, and lower-membership-level lists. Once identified, these prospects are approached on a one-to-one basis. An initial letter is sent introducing the prospect to the museum. This first letter is followed by a personal telephone call or another letter inviting the prospect to an informal gathering at the museum. At the gathering, the prospect is introduced to other members and is asked directly to become a member.

Renewal efforts also include mail and telephone solicitation. In addition, membership parties, special previews, and special inserts in the monthly calendar of MMA activities are used.

Museum records indicate that 70 percent of the $50 members do not renew their membership after the first year. Among those that do, 50 percent renew in each successive year. Members in the $100 to $500 categories have a renewal rate of 60 percent, and members in the $1,500 and $5,000 categories have a renewal rate of 85 percent. Mercer believed that less than 10 percent of personal members who do renew their membership increase the dollar value of their membership. Renewal rates among corporate members is about 75 percent, regardless of category.

■ CONSIDERATIONS FOR 2000

Ashley Mercer and Donald Pate met to discuss measures they might recommend to the Board of Trustees to reverse the deteriorating financial condition of the MMA. Pate noted that at an earlier meeting with his staff, personnel reductions were discussed. Specifically, he felt that a 10 percent reduction in personnel and administration costs was possible. Furthermore, his staff estimated that the appropriation from Fannel County, contributions, grants, investment income, endowment earnings, and other income would be 15 percent below 1999 levels. A "best guess" estimate from the Director of Collections and Exhibitions indicated that special exhibitions and events would generate revenues of $1.2 million and cost $675,000 in 2000. Parking revenues and expenses resulting from nonmember visitors would remain unchanged from 1999. Rough budgets for education programs indicated that an expenditure of $500,000 for 2000 was realistic, given planned efforts. Pate said that changes in other auxiliary activities for which he was responsible, namely, the Skyline Buffet restaurant and gift shop, were not planned.

Mercer was impressed with the attention Pate had already given to the museum's situation. She too had given consideration to matters of museum image, visitation, and membership prior to the meeting. Unfortunately, an earlier meeting with her staff had raised more issues than hard-and-fast recommendations. Staff suggestions ranged from implementing an admission fee of $1.00 per adult (with no charge for children under 12 years old) to instituting student (ages 13 to 22) and senior citizen (60 and older) memberships at $30. The need for institutional advertising was raised, since the MMA had only been promoting special exhibitions and events. Other staff members said that the benefits given to members needed to be enhanced. For example, raising discounts at the Skyline Buffet and gift shop to 20 percent was suggested. Another possibility raised was commissioning a "coffee table" book featuring major artwork at the MMA to be given with personal memberships of $500 or more.

Mercer listened to these suggestions, knowing that some were unlikely to receive Board of Trustee approval. These included any proposal to increase expenses for Publications/Public Information (for example, new books and paid institutional advertising). She had already been informed that expenses for such activities could not exceed the 1999 expenditure. Improving the member benefit package seemed like a good idea. Increasing restaurant and gift shop discounts, even though 65 percent of the business for both was already on discount, seemed like a good idea, at least at the margin. Pate said that he would give this suggestion consideration, but asked that Mercer think further about it in the context of the overall member-benefit package. Charging a nominal admission fee for nonmembers also seemed reasonable. Visitor surveys had shown that 50 percent of nonmember visitors said that they would be willing to pay a $1.00 admission fee for viewing the permanent collection (access to special exhibitions would continue to have admission fees). Furthermore, members could then be given an additional benefit, that is, free admission. However, Pate noted that the MMA had always prided itself on free access, and he wondered how the Board of Trustees would view this suggestion. Additional membership categories below $50 and for students and senior citizens also seemed to provide new opportunities to attract segments of the population that had not typically yielded members.

Mercer and Pate believed that their initial meeting had produced some good ideas, but both thought that they had to give these matters further thought. They agreed to meet again and begin to prepare an integrated plan of action and a pro forma income statement for 2000.

CHAPTER 11

Comprehensive Marketing Programs

An organization's comprehensive marketing program integrates the choice of which product or service markets to pursue with the choice of which marketing mix to use to reach target markets and, ultimately, create value for customers. The process of formulating and implementing a comprehensive marketing program encompasses all the concepts, tools, and perspectives described in previous chapters.

The challenge facing the manager responsible for formulating and implementing a comprehensive marketing program divides into three related decisions and actions.[1] First, the manager must decide *where to compete*. Product-market choice determines the organization's customers and competitors. This decision is often based on the organization's business definition and opportunity and target market analysis. In this regard, the manager has multiple options ranging from concentrated marketing with a focus on a single product market to differentiated marketing whereby multiple product markets are pursued simultaneously. Second, the manager must decide *how to compete*. The means a manager has available reside in the marketing-mix elements or activities. Multiple options again exist. In a simple situation with two alternatives for each of the four marketing-mix elements, 16 different marketing-mix combinations are possible. Third, the manager must determine *when to compete*. This decision relates to timing. For example, some organizations adopt a "first-to-market" posture, while others take a "wait-and-see" stance concerning market-entry decisions. Four issues are central to the design and execution of comprehensive marketing programs. First, a marketing manager must consider issues of *fit* with the market, the organization, and competition. Second, marketing-mix *sensitivities* and *interactions* must be considered as they relate to target markets. Third, issues of *implementation* must be addressed. Fourth, *organizational* issues must be taken into account. Each of these topics is discussed in this chapter.

■ MARKETING PROGRAM FIT

A successful comprehensive marketing program must effectively stimulate target markets to buy, must be consistent with organizational capabilities, and must outmaneuver competitors.[2] The fit of a program to a market is determined by the extent to which the marketing mix satisfies the unique needs and buyer requirements of a chosen target market. The fit of a program to an organization depends on the match between an organization's marketing skills and financial position, on the one hand, and the marketing mix being considered, on the other. Finally, the fit of a program to the competition relates to the strengths, weaknesses, and marketing mixes of competitors who are serving the target markets under consideration.

Establishing a program-market fit can be a daunting task. For over 20 years, DuPont explored applications for Kevlar, a synthetic fiber with five times the tensile strength of steel on an equal-weight basis. The chosen target market for Kevlar was tire makers that produced steel-belted radials. Despite Kevlar's unique qualities and $600 million of development and marketing costs, DuPont's marketing program did not persuade tire makers that Kevlar adequately satisfied their needs. Recently, DuPont's CEO announced that the company should focus "more intensely on customer needs."[3]

A comprehensive marketing program must be symbiotic with the organization implementing the program. Successful marketing programs build on an organization's strengths and distinctive competencies and avoid stressing organizational weaknesses. Failure to do this can have serious consequences. For example, Continental Airlines launched a comprehensive marketing program dubbed "Continental Lite," which centered on replicating Southwest Airlines' successful low-fare, short-flight, and point-to-point route system. However, Continental's higher operating costs and its inability to manage a short-flight, point-to-point route system produced a financial loss of almost $600 million over 15 months. The "Continental Lite" initiative was abandoned largely because it stressed organizational shortcomings rather than strengths and competencies.[4]

Finally, a successful marketing program fits the competitive realities of the marketplace. As described in chapter 10, marketing strategies are rarely timeless. As the competitive environment changes, so must marketing programs. This was the case in the recently deregulated U.S. telecommunications industry. The Telecommunications Act of 1996 allowed long-distance telephone companies (e.g., AT&T, MCI, Sprint) to compete for local telephone service with regional telephone companies such as Bell Atlantic, U.S. West, and Nynex. It also paved the way for the merging of telephone, cellular, paging, and Internet communication technologies and services and the formation of new competitor alliances, each vying to satisfy the complete communication needs of businesses and households. These developments made obsolete marketing programs created in a near monopoly environment. Marketing programs, which focused on a single communication technology (e.g., cellular) and service and high prices made possible by regulation, were replaced with marketing programs that focused on bundling communication technologies and services with lower prices.[5]

■ MARKETING-MIX SENSITIVITIES AND INTERACTIONS

Many of the case analyses thus far have implicitly or explicitly focused on target-market sensitivity to one or more elements of the marketing mix. The Jones • Blair Company case in Chapter 4 is an example. When company management embarked on a planning effort, several views on how best to stimulate sales were voiced. One executive favored an increase of $350,000 in corporate brand advertising. Another argued for a 20 percent price reduction, and still another recommended hiring additional salespeople. Each of these executives implicitly suggested that the target market was most sensitive to the marketing-mix element he recommended.

In reality, however, the options are generally broader, and interaction effects between two or more marketing-mix elements must be considered. For instance, what would be the effect on sales of increasing corporate brand advertising *and* introducing a 20 percent price reduction? Would this action be more or less effective in stimulating sales than changing only one element of the marketing mix?

Although simultaneous consideration of marketing-mix sensitivities and interactions is a complex process, it is a necessity for the marketing manager. Consider the situation faced by John Murray, the marketing manager for DuPont's Sontara, a polyester fabric used for disposable surgical gowns and drapes used in hospital operating rooms.[6] Murray's charge was to prepare a comprehensive marketing program that would meet two objectives for Sontara: (1) maintain market share and (2) persuade garment makers that DuPont could support them in promoting Sontara to end users and would remain a strong force in the disposable fabric business.

Murray thought that if sales-force/maintenance expenditures were raised from the proposed level of $450,000 to a maximum reasonable level of $550,000 while other spending was held to proposed levels, market share could reach 35 percent of the total market. Similarly, if the other mix elements were increased to their maximum reasonable levels while the remaining expenditures were held at their proposed levels, market-share increases would be likely as well, although they would not be as dramatic. Specifically, he thought:

- If instead of spending nothing on sales-force/missionary expenses, management spent $200,000, market share would increase to 33 percent.
- If trade support/maintenance expenses were increased to $100,000, a 33 percent market share would result.
- If $100,000 were spent on trade support/missionary expenses, market share would be 33 percent.
- If advertising to intermediate users were increased to $50,000, the net effect would be a 1 percent increase in market share.
- An increase to $300,000 in advertising to end users would also result in a 1 percent share gain.

Reductions in spending were thought to have the opposite effect. Reducing sales-force/maintenance expenditures to zero while holding other spending at the proposed level was thought likely to reduce Sontara's share to 22 percent of the total market during the next 12 months. Similarly, reductions to zero spending for sales-force/missionary expenditures, trade support/maintenance, trade support/missionary, advertising to intermediaries, or advertising to end users were thought likely to reduce expected market share to 32, 27, 32, 31, or 28 percent, respectively.

As a validity check on the above estimates, Murray described what he thought would happen if all mix elements were raised simultaneously to their maximum reasonable expenditure levels or if all support was withdrawn from the product. He thought that with maximum effort a 39 percent share could be realized, although he was not sure how viable such an aggressive strategy would be for the long run. If all support was withdrawn, he estimated that market share would drop to 22 percent in the next 12 months and then decline further.

This example demonstrates the complex relationships that exist among marketing-mix elements. It also illustrates the role of assumptions and judgment in considering marketing-mix sensitivities and interactions.

Increasingly, marketing managers are turning to carefully designed market tests designed to measure marketing-mix sensitivities and interactions. By experimentally manipulating the amount and type of advertising and promotion and price levels in test markets, quantitative estimates of marketing-mix elasticities and relationships can be determined for individual products and services. For example, one consistent finding from these tests is that television advertising intensity has a far greater effect on sales volume growth for new consumer products than for products already established in the marketplace.[7] Market tests help to qualify assumptions made by marketing managers; however, they are not a substitute for judgment acquired through experience.

MARKETING IMPLEMENTATION

Implementation is the third leg in developing a comprehensive marketing program. Marketing managers have come to realize that poor implementation can hamper the success of an otherwise brilliantly conceived program. More succinctly, "The best strategy for any company is a strategy it can implement."[8]

Among the wide variety of subtle factors that can make or break a marketing program is timing. Failure to execute a marketing program when a window of opportunity opens can lead to failure or reduce the likelihood of success. For example, some industry observers believe that the failure of Matilda Bay Wine Cooler, introduced by the Miller Brewing Company, was due to poor timing on two counts. First, the popularity of wine coolers was declining. Second, the product was launched in the fall, typically a slow selling season.[9]

A second factor that can hamper implementation is not considering logistical aspects of a marketing program. When Holly Farms test-marketed a roasted chicken for distribution through supermarkets, consumer response was favorable. Holly Farms soon realized, however, that the roasted chicken was edible for only 18 days and it took 9 days to get the chicken from the production plant to supermarkets. As supermarkets could not be expected to sell the chicken within 9 days, Holly Farms had to halt its planned national introduction of roasted chicken.[10]

Poor implementation is often marked by a failure to synchronize marketing mix activities. The experience of Iridium LLC is an example.[11] The company's $5 billion global satellite telephone system was intended to revolutionize telecommunications by allowing phone calls anytime, anywhere. Iridium's $100 million international marketing plan, anchored by a worldwide advertising campaign, generated over one million inquiries from potential customers. However, with no marketing channels and few salespeople in place, and a short supply of phones for demonstration, orders failed to materialize. The company filed for bankruptcy in 1999.

Formulating a comprehensive marketing program is a formidable task that demands rigorous analysis and judgment, often without the benefit of complete information. At the same time, program planning and design cannot be separated from implementation issues. "What should we do?" cannot be separated from "How do we do it?" By assigning equal attention to program formulation and program implementation, marketing managers increase the likelihood that their comprehensive marketing programs will succeed.[12]

MARKETING ORGANIZATION

Emphasis on marketing implementation focuses attention on organizational structure. It is often said that strategy determines structure and that organizational structure, in turn, determines whether a marketing strategy is effective and efficiently designed and implemented.[13]

A central issue in creating an effective and efficient marketing organization is finding the proper balance between centralization and decentralization of marketing activities, including strategy formulation and implementation. The strategy of regional marketing, whereby firms attempt to satisfy unique customer needs and meet competitive demands in limited geographical areas, has prompted increased decentralization of strategic marketing decisions and practices. For example, regional marketing groups at Frito-Lay design and implement region-specific marketing programs, including pricing practices and sales promotion activities. They also manage 30 percent of the company's advertising and promotion budget.[14] Efforts to "glocalize" marketing programs in the international arena have created elastic organizational structures that simultaneously strive for efficiencies through scale economies in product development and manufacturing, and for effectiveness through customization of advertising, promotion, pricing, and distribution in separate countries. As an example, Coca-Cola's concentrate formula and advertising theme are standardized worldwide, but the artificial sweetener and packaging differ across countries as do sales and distribution programs.[15] The relative emphasis on standardization versus customization in marketing strategy planning and execution ultimately manifests itself in organizational structure. For Frito-Lay and Coca-Cola, and an increasingly large number of other firms, the notion of "coordinated centralization" has produced domestic and global organizational structures that seek to foster adaptability to local conditions while preserving centralized direction in the pursuit of market opportunities and implementation of comprehensive marketing programs.

NOTES

1. This discussion is based on Subhash C. Jain, *Marketing Planning and Strategy*, 6th ed. (Cincinnati, OH: Southwestern Publishing Co., 2000): 24.

2. Benson P. Shapiro, "Rejuvenating the Marketing Mix," *Harvard Business Review* (September-October 1985): 28-34.

3. Scott McMurry, "Changing a Culture: DuPont Tries to Make Its Research Wizardry Serve the Bottom Line," *Wall Street Journal* (March 27, 1992): A1, A4.

4. Bridget O'Brien, "Continental's CALite Hits Some Turbulence in Battling Southwest," *Wall Street Journal* (January 10, 1995): A1, A5; "Familiar Flight Plan," *Dallas Morning News* (August 10, 1996): 1F, 11F.

5. "Telecommunications," *Wall Street Journal* (September 16, 1996): R1-R26.

6. *E. I. DuPont de NeMours & Co.: Marketing Planning for Sontara and Tyvek* (Charlottesville, VA: University of Virginia, Darden School of Business Administration).

7. For a description of this research and additional research, see Demetrios Vakratsas and Tim Ambler, "How advertising Works: What Do We Really Know," *Journal of Marketing* (January 1999): 26-43.

8. Claudio Aspesi and Dev Vardan, "Brilliant Strategy, But Can You Execute?" *The McKinsey Quarterly* (Number 1, 1999): 88-99.

9. "Miller Jumps into a Cooler Cooler Market," *Business Week* (October 26, 1987): 36-38.

10. "Holly Farms' Marketing Error: The Chicken That Laid an Egg," *Wall Street Journal* (February 9, 1988): 36.

11. "Iridium's Downfall: The Marketing Took a Back Seat to Science," *Wall Street Journal* (August 18, 1999): A2, A6.

12. For a recent discussion on marketing strategy implementation, see Charles H. Noble and Michael P. Mokwa, "Implementing Marketing Strategies: Developing and Testing a Managerial Theory," *Journal of Marketing* (October 1999): 57-73.

13. Frank V. Cespedes, *Organizing and Implementing the Marketing Effort: Text and Cases* (Reading, MA: Addison-Wesley, 1991).

14. S. McKenna, *The Complete Guide to Regional Marketing* (Homewood, IL: Richard D. Irwin, 1992).

15. John A. Quelch and Edward J. Hoff, "Customizing Global Marketing," *Harvard Business Review* (May-June 1986): 59-68; John Huey, "The World's Best Brand," *Fortune* (May 31, 1993): 44-54.

CASE

Frito-Lay, Inc.

Sun Chips™ Multigrain Snacks

In mid-1990, Dr. Dwight R. Riskey, Vice President of Marketing Research and New Business at Frito-Lay, Inc., assembled the product management team responsible for Sun Chips™ Multigrain Snacks. The purpose of the all-day meeting was to prepare a presentation to senior Frito-Lay executives on future action pertaining to the brand.

Sun Chips™ Multigrain Snacks is a crispy textured snack chip consisting of a special blend of whole wheat, corn, rice, and oat flours with a lightly salty multigrain taste and a slightly sweet aftertaste. The product contains less sodium than most snack chips and is made with canola or sunflower oil. The chip is approximately 50 percent lower in saturated fats than chips made with other cooking oils and is cholesterol-free. According to a Frito-Lay executive, it is "a thoughtful, upscale classy chip."

The product had been in test market for 10 months in the Minneapolis-St. Paul, Minnesota, metropolitan area. Even though it appeared consumer response was extremely favorable, Riskey and his associates knew their presentation to senior Frito-Lay executives would have to be persuasive. In addition to presenting a thorough assessment of test-market data, Riskey added:

> We will have to do heavy-duty selling [to top executives] because Sun Chips™ Multigrain Snacks required a new manufacturing process, carried a new brand name, and pioneered a new snack chip category. There is a huge capital investment and a huge marketing investment that could be financially justified only with a product that could be sustainable for an extended time period.

■ FRITO-LAY, INC.

Frito-Lay, Inc. is a division of PepsiCo, Inc., a New York-based diversified consumer goods and services firm. Other PepsiCo, Inc. divisions include Pizza Hut, Inc., Taco Bell Corporation, Pepsi-Cola Company, Kentucky Fried Chicken, and PepsiCo Foods International. PepsiCo, Inc. recorded net income of $1.077 billion on net sales of $17.8 billion in 1990.

Company Background

Frito-Lay, Inc. is a worldwide leader in the manufacturing and marketing of snack chips. Well-known brands include Lay's® brand and Ruffles® brand potato chips, Fritos® brand corn chips, Doritos® brand, Tostitos® brand, and Santitas® brand tortilla chips, Chee•tos® brand cheese-flavored snacks, and Rold Gold® brand pretzels.

The cooperation of Frito-Lay, Inc. in the preparation of this case is gratefully acknowledged. This case was prepared by Professor Roger A. Kerin, of the Edwin L. Cox School of Business, Southern Methodist University, and Kenneth R. Lukaska, Product Manager, Frito-Lay, Inc., as a basis for class discussion and is not designed to illustrate effective or ineffective handling of an administrative situation. Certain company information is disguised and not useful for research purposes.

EXHIBIT 1

Frito-Lay, Inc.: Major Brands

Source: 1990 PepsiCo, Inc., annual report.

The company's major brands are shown in Exhibit 1 along with estimated worldwide retail sales. Other well-known Frito-Lay products include Baken-Ets® brand fried pork skins, Munchos® brand potato crisps, and Funyuns® brand onion-flavored snacks. In addition, the company markets a line of dips, nuts, peanut butter crackers, processed beef sticks, Smartfood® brand ready-to-eat popcorn, and Grandma's® brand cookies.

Frito-Lay, Inc. accounts for 13 percent of sales in the United States snack-food industry, which includes candy, cookies, crackers, nuts, snack chips, and assorted other items. The company is the leading manufacturer of snack chips in the United States, capturing nearly one-half of the retail sales in this category. Eight of Frito-Lay's snack chips are among the top ten best-selling snack chip items in U.S. supermarkets (see Exhibit 2, page 616). Doritos® brand tortilla chips and Ruffles® brand potato chips have the distinction of being the only snack chips with $1 billion in retail sales in the world.

Frito-Lay's snack-food business spans every aspect of snack-food production, from agriculture to stacking supermarket shelves. During 1990 in the United States alone, Frito-Lay used 1.6 billion pounds of potatoes, 600 million pounds of corn, and 55 million pounds of seasonings. The company has 39 manufacturing plants, more than 1,600 distribution facilities, and a 10,000-person route-sales team that calls on

EXHIBIT 2

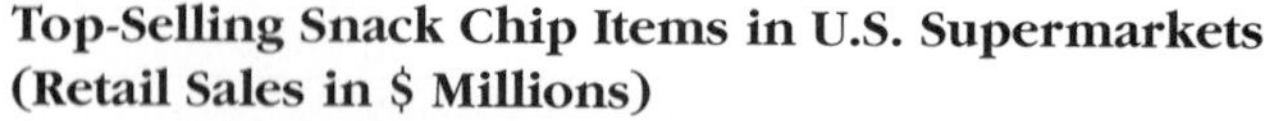

Top-Selling Snack Chip Items in U.S. Supermarkets (Retail Sales in $ Millions)

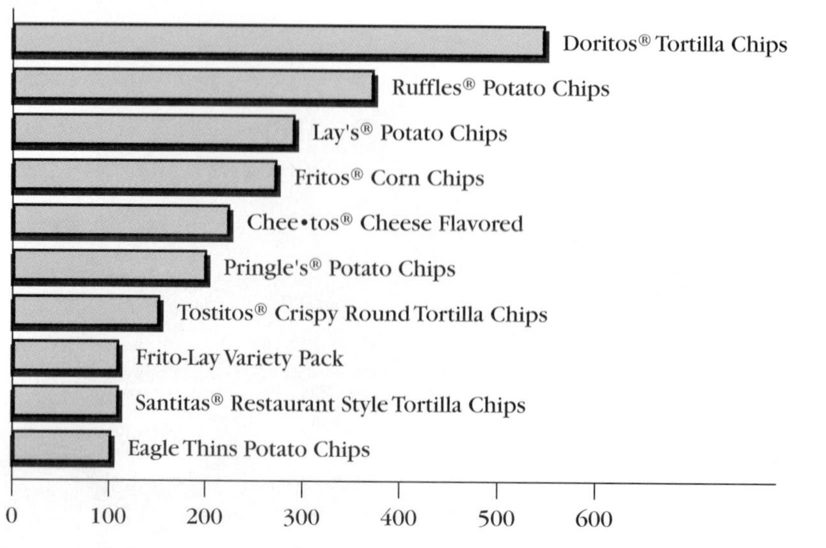

Source: 1990 PepsiCo, Inc., annual report.

more than 400,000 retail store customers each week in the United States. Frito-Lay, Inc., recorded U.S. sales of $3.5 billion in 1990.

Product-Marketing Strategies

Frito-Lay pursues growth opportunities through four product-marketing strategies.

1. *Grow established Frito-Lay brands through line extension*. Recognizing that consumers seek variety in snack tastes and sizes without compromising quality, Frito-Lay marketing executives use line extensions to satisfy these wants. Recent examples of line extension include Tostitos® brand bite-sized tortilla chips and Chee•tos® brand Flamin' Hot Cheese Flavored Snacks.
2. *Create new products to meet changing consumer preferences and needs*. Continuous marketing research at Frito-Lay is designed to uncover changing snacking needs of customers. A recent result of these efforts is evident in the launch of a low-oil light line of snack chips.
3. *Develop products for fast-growing snack-food categories*. Recognizing that snack-food categories experience different growth rates, Frito-Lay marketing executives continually monitor consumption patterns to identify new opportunities. For example, Frito-Lay acquired Smartfood® brand popcorn in 1989. In 1990, this brand became the number one ready-to-eat popcorn brand in the United States.
4. *Reproduce Frito-Lay successes in the international market*. Initiatives pursued in the United States often produce opportunities in the international arena. Primary emphasis has been placed in large, well-developed snack markets such as Mexico, Canada, Spain, and the United Kingdom. Innovative marketing coupled with product development efforts produced $1.6 billion in international snack-food sales in 1990.

THE SNACK CHIP CATEGORY

The United States snack-food industry recorded retail sales of $37 billion in 1990, representing a 5 percent increase over 1989. Dollar retail sales of snack chips consisting of potato, corn, and tortilla chips, pretzels, and ready-to-eat popcorn were estimated to be $9.8 billion—a 5 percent increase over 1989. A major source of growth in the snack chip category results from increased per capita consumption. In 1990, consumers in the United States bought 3.5 billion pounds of snack chips, or nearly 14 pounds per person; in 1986, snack chip per capita consumption was slightly less than 12 pounds.

Competitors

Three types of competitors serve the snack chip category: (1) national brand firms, (2) regional brand firms, and (3) private brand firms. National brand firms, which distribute products nationwide, include Frito-Lay, Borden (Guys brand potato and corn chips, and Wise brand potato chips, cheese puffs, and pretzels), Procter and Gamble (Pringles® brand potato chips), RJR Nabisco (several products sold under the Nabisco name as well as Planter's brand pretzels, cheese puffs, and corn and tortilla chips), Keebler Company (O'Boisies brand potato chips), and Eagle Snacks (a division of Anheuser-Busch Companies, Inc., which sells Eagle brand pretzels and potato and corn chips). A second category of competitors consists of regional brand firms, which distribute products in only certain parts of the United States. Representative firms include Snyder's, Mike Sells, and Charles Chips. Private brands are produced by regional or local manufacturers on a contractual basis for major supermarket chains (for example, Kroger and Safeway).

Competition

The snack chip category is very competitive. As many as 650 snack chip products are introduced each year by national and regional brand companies. Most of the products are new flavors for existing snack chips. The new-product failure rate for snack chips is high, and industry sources report that fewer than 1 percent of new products generate more than $25 million in first-year sales.

Snack chip competitors rely heavily on electronic and print media advertising, consumer promotions, and trade allowances to stimulate sales and retain shelf space in supermarkets. Pricing is very competitive, and snack chip manufacturers often rely on price deals to attract customers. The nature of the technology used to produce snack chips allows snack chip manufacturers to react swiftly to new product (flavor) introductions by competitors. Extensive sales and distribution systems employed by national brand competitors, in particular, allow them to monitor new product and promotion activities and place competing products quickly in supermarkets.

DEVELOPMENT OF SUN CHIPS™ MULTIGRAIN SNACKS

Sun Chips™ Multigrain Snacks resulted from Frito-Lay's ongoing marketing research and product development program. However, its taste and name heritage can be traced to the early 1970s.

Product Heritage

Frito-Lay product development personnel first explored the possibility of a multigrain product in the early 1970s when corporate marketing research studies indicated consumers were looking for nutritious snacks. A multigrain snack chip called

Prontos® was introduced in 1974 with the following positioning statement: "The different, delicious new snack made from nature's own corn, oats, and whole grain wheat all rolled into one special recipe, together in a snack for the first time from Frito-Lay." The product was only mildly successful despite advertising and merchandising support. The product was subsequently withdrawn from national distribution in 1978 due to declining sales and manufacturing difficulties. According to Frito-Lay executives, the demise of Prontos® in 1978 was driven by "noncommittal" copy, a confusing name, and a product that generated appeal among too narrow a target market. Reflecting on this experience, Riskey added, "I'm not sure there were dramatic things wrong with the product design so much as difficulty with the manufacturing process. It may have been invented and introduced before its time."

The brand name for the product had an equally arduous past. The Sun Chips™ name was originally assigned to a line of corn chips, potato chips, and puffed corn snacks in the early 1970s. In 1976, the brand name was given to a line of corn chips, but by 1985, this line was also withdrawn from distribution due to poor sales performance.

Product Development: The "Harvest" Project

Early 1980s Interest in a multigrain snack was revisited in the early 1980s when Frito-Lay marketing executives began to worry whether the aging baby boomers (people born between 1946 and 1964) would continue to eat salty snacks such as potato, corn, and tortilla chips. According to Riskey:

> The aging baby boomers were a significant factor [in our thinking]. We were looking for new products that would allow them to snack. But we were looking for "better-for-you" aspects in products and pushing against that demographic shift.

In 1981, Frito-Lay marketing research and product development personnel instituted the "Harvest" project with an objective of coming up with a multigrain snack that would have consumer appeal. After several product concept tests and in-home product use tests failed to generate any consumer excitement, it was concluded that the market for wholesome snacks was not yet fully developed to accept such products. Other evidence seemed to support this view. In 1983, Frito-Lay test marketed O'Grady's™ brand potato chips. The results had been phenomenal. Projections based on test market performance indicated the brand would produce $100 million in annual sales, which it did in 1984 and 1985.

Mid-1980s The "Harvest" project continued in the mid-1980s, albeit at a slower pace due to staff changes and other responsibilities of project team members. At about this time, a change in top management and corporate objectives focused product development efforts on traditional snacks with an emphasis on flavor line extensions for established Frito-Lay brands (for example, Cool Ranch Doritos® brand tortilla chips) and low-fat versions of its potato, corn, and tortilla chips. In addition, attention was placed on cost-containment measures coupled with continuous quality-improvement initiatives using existing manufacturing facilities and existing product and process snack chip technology.

Late 1980s Development efforts on a multigrain product were renewed in early 1988. Over the following 13 months, different product formulations (for example, low oil vs. regular oil; salt content; chip shape), alternative positionings, and branding options (extension of an existing Frito-Lay brand vs. a new brand name) were extensively studied using consumer taste tests and product concept tests. The combined results of these tests yielded a multigrain rectangular chip with ridges and an exceptional taste. Further testing of brand names and flavors revealed consumer prefer-

EXHIBIT 3

Consumer Expectations and Perceptions of Snack Chips and Multigrain Snacks

PRETRIAL PRODUCT EXPECTATIONS

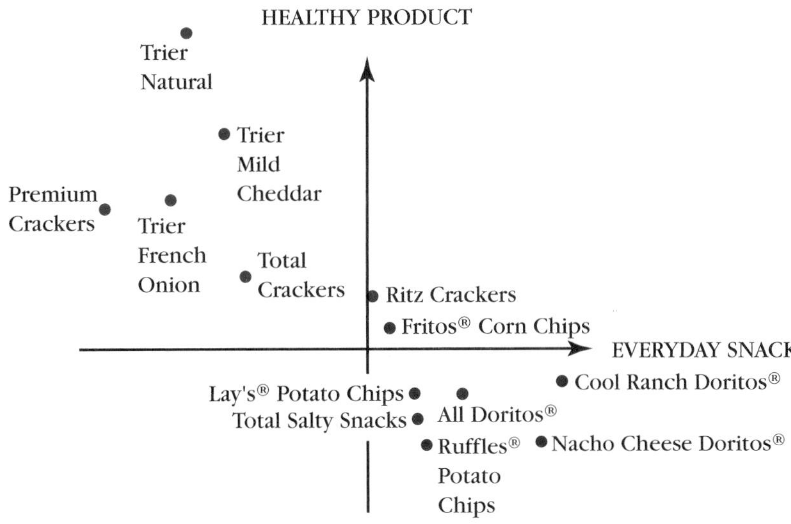

POSTUSE PERCEPTIONS: TRIER REPEATERS VS. TRIER NONREPEATERS

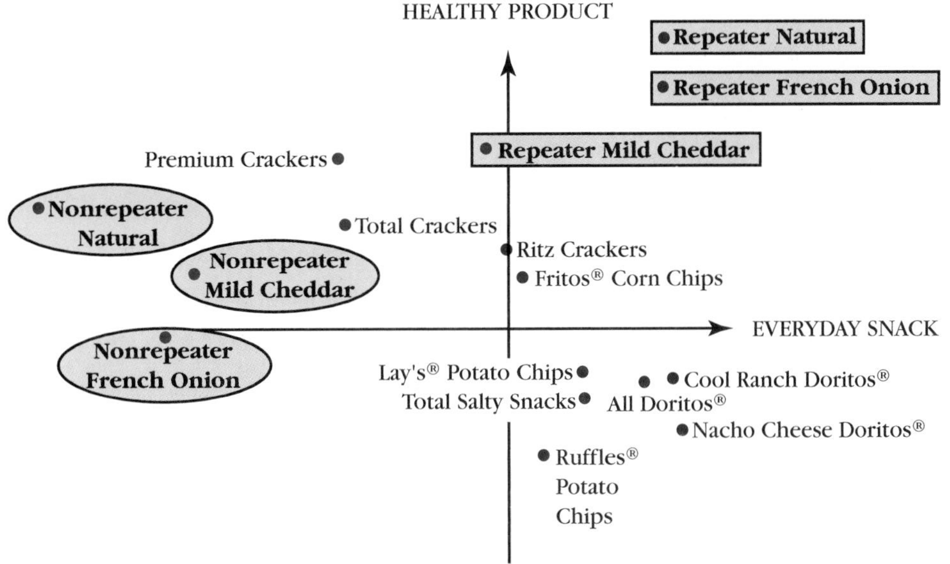

ences for two names (one of which was Sun Chips™) and three flavors (original/natural, French onion, and mild cheddar).

Further consumer research revealed that the multigrain product concept and assorted flavors were perceived as a "healthier product." This research also indicated that consumer expectations prior to use (that is, before initial trial of the product) were that the product would not be an "everyday snack" item. Consumers who tried the product, however, perceived the multigrain product to be an "everyday snack," at least for the natural and French onion flavors. Exhibit 3 shows a plot of pretrial consumer expectations and postuse perceptions of different flavors and representative

EXHIBIT 4

Concept Board for the Premarket Test

The great tasting snack chip for people who care about what they eat.

More and more people care about what they eat because they know that eating habits affect overall health and fitness. SUN CHIPS™ are a special blend of whole wheat, golden corn and other natural great tasting grains. These wholesome grains combined make a uniquely delicious chip with the golden goodness of corn and the nut-like flavor of wheat. They're cooked 'till lightly crisp and crunchy. Then they're lightly salted to let all that naturally good flavor come through. SUN CHIPS™ are a unique combination of great taste, great crunch, and natural goodness, all rolled into one remarkable chip.

So, try new SUN CHIPS™, the chip with the uniquely delicious taste for people who care about what they eat.

Available in these two delicious flavors:

• Natural • French Onion

snack chip brands and crackers. Concurrent research on brand names indicated a decided preference for the Sun Chips™ name. The name evoked positive consumer imagery and attributes of "wholesomeness, great taste, light and distinctive, and fun," according to a Frito-Lay executive.

Premarket Test

Positive consumer response to the product concept and brand name prompted an initial assessment of the commercial potential of Sun Chips™ Multigrain Snacks. A simulated test market or premarket test (PMT) was commissioned in April 1989 and conducted by an independent marketing research firm.

A PMT involves interviewing consumers about attitudes and usage behavior concerning a product category (for example, snack chips). Consumers would be exposed to a product concept using product descriptions or mock-ups of advertisements, and their responses would be assessed (see Exhibit 4). These consumers would then be given an opportunity to receive the product if interested. After an in-home usage period of several weeks, they would be contacted by telephone and asked about their attitude toward the product, use of the product, and intention to repurchase. These data would be incorporated into computer models that would include elements of the product's marketing plan (price, advertising, distribution coverage). The output provided by the PMT would include estimates of household trial rates, repeat rates, average number of units purchased on the initial trial and subsequent repeats in the first year, product cannibalism, and first-year sales volume.[1]

The product concept tested in the PMT was priced at parity with Doritos® brand tortilla chips. Planned distribution coverage was set at levels comparable for Frito-Lay potato, corn, and tortilla chips. Two-flavor combinations (natural and French onion and natural and mild cheddar) and three advertising and merchandising expenditure levels ($11 million, $17 million, and $22 million) were tested.[2]

Results from the PMT indicated that Sun Chips™ Multigrain Snacks would produce a most likely first-year sales volume of $113 million at manufacturer's prices given the marketing plan set for the product, including a $22 million advertising and merchandising expenditure. The estimated first-year sales volume exceeded the $100 million Frito-Lay sales goal for new products. The natural and French onion flavor combination produced the lowest cannibalization (42 percent) of other Frito-Lay brands. Summary statistics for the simulated test market are shown in Exhibit 5 on page 622.

■ TEST MARKET

Positive results from consumer research and the simulated test market led to a recommendation to proceed with Sun Chips™ Multigrain Snacks and implement a test market under Dwight Riskey's direction. The Minneapolis–St. Paul, Minnesota metropolitan area was chosen as the test site because Frito-Lay executives were confident it had a social and economic profile representative of the United States. Furthermore, Minneapolis–St. Paul, in general, represented a typical competitive environment in which to test consumer acceptance and competitive behavior. The Minneapolis–St. Paul metropolitan area contained 1.98 million households that were identified as users of snack chips, or 2.2 percent of the 90 million snack chip user households in the United States. Discussion among Frito-Lay marketing, sales, distribution, and manufacturing executives and the company's advertising agency indicated that the test market could begin October 9, 1989. Accordingly, a test-market plan and budget were finalized. The test market was scheduled to run for 12 months, with periodic reviews scheduled throughout the test.

Snack-food industry analysts became aware of Frito-Lay's development efforts on a multigrain snack chip soon after the company began preparation for the test market. According to one industry analyst:

---

[1] Published validation data on premarket test models indicate that 75 percent of the time they are plus or minus 10 percent of actual performance when a product was introduced (see, for example, A. Shocker and W. Hall, "Pretest Market Models: A Critical Evaluation," *Journal of Product Innovation Management* 3, (1986): 86–107.

[2] Advertising and merchandising expenditures included electronic and print media advertising, consumer promotions, and trade allowances.

EXHIBIT 5

Simulated Test-Market Results (Selected Statistics)

	Product and Promotion Strategy [a]			
	Natural & Mild Cheddar Combination		*Natural & French Onion Combination*	
	A&M Budget $17 million	*A&M Budget $22 million*	*A&M Budget $17 million*	*A&M Budget $22 million*
Purchase Dynamics				
Brand awareness (% of households)	40	48	40	48
Cumulative first-year trial rate (%)[b]	23	27	21	25
Cumulative first year repeat rate (%)[c]	61		57	
Number of purchases in first-year per repeating household	5.9		6.2	
Volume Projections ($ millions)				
Pessimistic	87	102	86	102
Most likely	96	113	95	113
Optimistic	106	125	106	125
Incremental annual volume (%)	50		58	
Cannibalized pound volume (%) (from Frito-Lay products)	50		42	

[a] The $11 million advertising and merchandising (A&M) budget for the two flavor combinations produced lower figures than those shown. For example, brand awareness was 35 percent and the cumulative first-year trial rate was 19 percent regardless of flavor combination.

[b] *Cumulative first-year trial* refers to the percentage of households that would try the product.

[c] *Cumulative first-year repeat* refers to the percentage of trier households that repurchased the product.

> This is a departure from corn or potatoes. Wheat is different. Remember they departed from corn and potatoes a few years ago with Rumbles®, Stuffers®, and Toppels®, and it was a distasteful business. I'm sure they will take their time and really test it. It's not like they don't have other products, so there's no hurry.[3]

Test-Market Plan

Product Strategy Frito-Lay executives decided to introduce both the natural and French onion flavors given consumer research and simulated test-market results. Sun Chips™ Multigrain Snacks would be packaged in two sizes: a 7-ounce package and an 11-ounce package. These package sizes were identical to Doritos® brand tortilla chips. A 2½-ounce trial package would be used as well.

[3] "New Multigrain Chip Being Readied for Test," *Advertising Age* (June 26, 1989): 4. The products referred to were Stuffers® cheese-filled snacks, Rumbles® granola nuggets, and Toppels® cheese-topped crackers. These products were introduced in the mid-1980s, failed to meet sales expectations, and were subsequently withdrawn from the market.

EXHIBIT 6

Sun Chips™ Multigrain Snacks Packaging

EXHIBIT 6 ***(continued)***

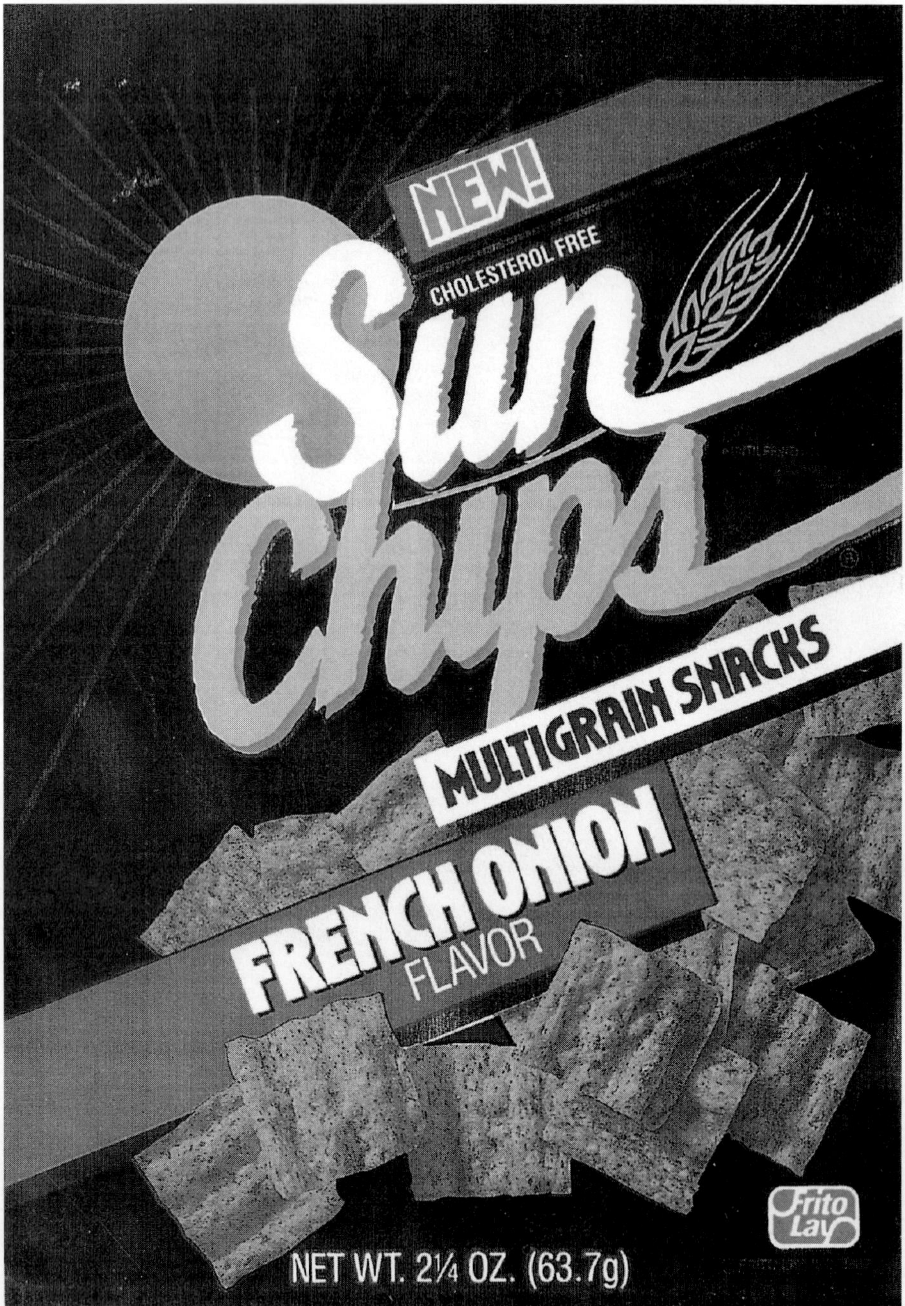

Package design was considered to be extremely important. According to a Frito-Lay executive, "We wanted distinctive, contemporary graphics which would communicate new, different and fun amidst positive images—sun and a sprig of wheat." This view materialized in a metalized flex bag with primary colors of black (natural flavor) and green (French onion flavor). Exhibit 6 shows the packages used in the test market.

Pricing Strategy Sun Chips™ Multigrain Snacks would have the same suggested retail prices as Doritos® brand tortilla chips. Research indicated these price points were consistent with consumer reference prices for snack chips and represented a

EXHIBIT 7

Sun Chips™ Multigrain Snacks Price List

Package Size	*Suggested Retail Price*	*Frito-Lay Selling Price to Retailer*
2¼ ounce	$0.69	$0.385
7 ounce	$1.69	$1.240
11 ounce	$2.39	$1.732

good value. Suggested retail prices and Frito-Lay's selling prices to retailers are shown in Exhibit 7.

Advertising and Merchandising Strategy The primary audience for Sun Chips™ Multigrain Snacks television advertising was adults between the ages of 18 and 34, since this target audience is the principal purchasers and heavy users of snack chips. A secondary audience expanded the age bracket to 49 years of age, since 34- to 49-year-olds appeared to be receptive to healthier snacks. Household members under 18 years of age would be exposed to the product through in-home usage. The advertising message would convey subtle messages, including wholesomeness, fun, and simplicity. One of the television commercials to be shown in the test market is reproduced in Exhibit 8 on page 626. In addition to television advertising, the brand would be supported by in-store displays and free-standing inserts (FSIs) in newspapers (see Exhibit 9 on page 627).

Coupons placed in newspaper FSIs were to be used during the test market to stimulate trial and repeat sales. In addition, free samples would be distributed in supermarkets. Trade allowances were provided to retailers as well.

Distribution and Sales Strategy Distribution and sales of Sun Chips™ Multigrain Snacks would be handled through Frito-Lay's store-door delivery system, in which the duties of a delivery person and a salesperson are combined. Under this system, a delivery/salesperson solicits orders, stocks shelves, and introduces merchandising programs to retail store personnel. Sun Chips™ Multigrain Snacks would be sold through supermarkets, grocery stores, convenience stores, and other retail accounts that already stocked Frito-Lay's snack products.

Manufacturing Considerations Frito-Lay manufacturing personnel worked concurrently with marketing personnel on matters related to mass production of a multigrain product. While prototypes were easily developed in limited quantities, large-scale manufacturing would require a production line capable of delivering an adequate product for a market test. Since a multigrain product required different product and process technology than corn or potato products, an investment in one new production line would be necessary. Approval was granted to create a production line to produce and package 1 million pounds of the multigrain snack per year at full theoretical capacity. The production line could be in operation to ship the product in two flavors and three package sizes for the test market in September 1989.

Test-Market Budget

The advertising and merchandising budget for the test market was equivalent to a $22 million expenditure on a nationwide distribution basis. Approximately 70 percent of the budget would be spent during the first six months of the test market.

EXHIBIT 8

Sun Chips™ Multigrain Snacks Television Commercial

LEVINE, HUNTLEY, SCHMIDT
& BEAVER, INC.
CLIENT: FRITO-LAY, INC.
PRODUCT: SUNCHIPS

TITLE: "POLLY"
LENGTH: 30 Seconds
COMM'L NO.: PESU-9013

(Music under) GUY: Polly want one?

AVO: It seems everyone who tries new SUNCHIPS feels smarter eating them.

POLLY: Polly wants another one.

AVO: Smarter because they're multigrain.

POLLY: Polly wants you to fill her water cup.

AVO: Smarter because of the taste.

POLLY: Polly thinks you should paint this room and this time pick a better color.

AVO: Smarter because they're naturally delicious.

POLLY: Polly wants to know why one species feels it's OK to imprison another

purely for its own entertainment.

AVO: New SUNCHIPS.

You'll feel smarter eating them.

Test-Market Results

Consumer response was monitored by an independent research firm from the beginning of the test market. Data gathered by the research firm were submitted to Frito-Lay monthly and consisted of the types of purchases, the incidence of trial and repeat-purchase behavior, and product cannibalization in the test market.

Type of Purchase Data supplied by the research firm indicated that the coupon program had a major impact on trial activity and approximately 90 percent of purchases were made in supermarkets and convenience stores. After 10 months in test market,

EXHIBIT 9

Sun Chips™ Multigrain Snacks Free-Standing Insert (FSI)

EXHIBIT 10

Household Trial and Repeat Rates for Sun Chips™ Multigrain Snacks

	Tracking (4-week Period)									
	1	*2*	*3*	*4*	*5*	*6*	*7*	*8*	*9*	*10*
Cumulative trial[a] (%)	4.7	8.2	9.8	11.3	14.1	15.7	16.5	17.4	19.5	19.9
Cumulative repeat[b] (%)	8.0	22.5	27.1	31.0	32.7	36.5	39.0	39.7	41.8	41.8

[a] Trial refers to the percentage of households that tried the product.

[b] Repeat refers to the percentage of trier households that repurchased the product.

the 2¹/₄-ounce package accounted for 15 percent of purchases, the 7-ounce package accounted for 47 percent of purchases, and the 11-ounce package accounted for 38 percent of purchases. Fifty-five percent of purchases were for the French onion flavor; 45 percent of purchases were for the natural flavor.

Trial and Repeat Rates Of critical concern to Frito-Lay executives were the incidences of household trial and repeat-purchase behavior for Sun Chips™ Multigrain Snacks. Exhibit 10 shows the cumulative trial and repeat rates for both flavors combined during the first 10 months of the test market. Almost one in five households in the test market had tried the product, and 41.8 percent of these trier households had repurchased the product at least once over the 10-month period.

Equally important to Frito-Lay executives were the "depth of repeat" data supplied by the research firm. *Depth of repeat* is the number of times a repeat purchaser buys a product after an initial repeat purchase. Repeater purchasers of Sun Chips™ Multigrain Snacks purchased the product an average of 2.9 times. An estimated average purchase amount for triers was 6 ounces. Repeat and repeater households purchased an average of 13 ounces per purchase occasion.

Product Cannibalization The independent research firm also identified the incidence of product cannibalization. The research firm's tracking data indicated that 30 percent of Sun Chips™ Multigrain Snack pound volume resulted from consumers switching from Frito-Lay's potato, tortilla, and corn snack chips. About one-third of the cannibalized volume from Frito-Lay's products came from Doritos® brand tortilla chips.

The 30 percent cannibalism rate was not uncommon in new product introductions in the snack food industry. For example, when Frito-Lay introduced O'Grady's™ brand potato chips, one-third of its pound volume came from its Ruffles® brand and Lay's® brand potato chips. Even though cannibalization was an issue to be considered in evaluating test-market performance, Frito-Lay executives noted that the gross profit for Sun Chips™ Multigrain Snacks was higher than that for its other snack chips.[4] (*Case writer note*: Footnote 4 contains important information for case analysis purposes.)

[4] Frito-Lay, Inc. does not divulge profitability data on individual products and product lines. However, for case analysis and class discussion purposes, a multigrain snack chip can be assumed to have a gross profit of $1.30 per pound, while other snack chips (potato, tortilla, and corn) can be assumed to have a gross profit of $1.05 per pound. Gross profit is the difference between selling price and the cost of materials and manufacturing (ingredients, packaging/cartons, direct labor, other assignable manufacturing expenses, and equipment depreciation).

■ TEST-MARKET REVIEW

Riskey's presentation to senior Frito-Lay executives would conclude with his recommendation for the future marketing of Sun Chips™ Multigrain Snacks. He could recommend that the test be continued for another six months, or be expanded to other geographical areas with the same introductory strategy or some modification. Alternatively, he could recommend that Sun Chips™ Multigrain Snacks be readied for a national introduction with the strategy used in the test market or some modification in the strategy.

Planning Considerations

Numerous topics were raised in his meeting with the product management team responsible for Sun Chips™ Multigrain Snacks. Timing and competitive reaction were important issues. Riskey believed that national and regional competitors were monitoring Frito-Lay's test market. There was also a high probability that these competitors were examining the chip with the intention of developing their own version. Timing was a concern for a variety of reasons. First, if Riskey continued testing the product, a competitor might launch a similar product nationally or regionally and upstage Frito-Lay. The opportunity to be first-to-market would be lost. Second, if an expanded test market or a national introduction was considered, a decision would be needed quickly to assure adequate manufacturing capacity was in place and operating efficiently. Manufacturing capacity expansion would require a significant capital investment. Although preliminary figures represented rough estimates, manufacturing capacity capable of serving 25 percent and 50 percent of snack chip households in the United States would involve a capital expenditure recommendation of $5 million and $10 million, respectively. A full-scale national introduction would require a capital expenditure of $20 million.

Recommendations related to manufacturing capacity expansion would require a justification of the magnitude and sustainability of Sun Chips™ Multigrain Snacks sales over time. Accordingly, Riskey requested marketing research personnel to supply him with comparative brand awareness and cumulative household trial and repeat rate data for O'Grady's™ brand potato chips, since this brand was the most recent Frito-Lay product introduction to achieve $100 million in first-year sales.

Brand-awareness studies on the two brands indicated that O'Grady's™ brand potato chips achieved brand awareness among 28 percent of snack chip households during its market test compared with 33 percent for Sun Chips™ Multigrain Snacks. Exhibit 11 on page 630 charts trial and repeat data for comparable test-market periods for Sun Chips™ Multigrain Snacks and O'Grady's™ brand potato chips. His interest in the sustainability of sales over time prompted a request for additional data on depth of repeat statistics for the two brands. The depth of repeat, or "repeats per repeater" for O'Grady's™ brand potato chips was 1.9 times, or about twice on an annual basis, compared with 2.9 times for Sun Chips™ Multigrain Snacks, or about three times on an annual basis.

Strategy Considerations

Several strategy options were also discussed. Some product management team members advocated increased advertising and merchandising spending if the brand was tested further or launched nationally. They believed that brand awareness would increase with additional spending and felt that spending the national introduction equivalent of $30 million could stimulate brand trial as well. Others interpreted the purchase data to mean that additional volume was possible by introducing a larger package size (for example, a 15-ounce package). They believed that a fourth, larger

EXHIBIT 11

Cumulative Trial and Repeat Rates for O'Grady's™ Potato Chips and Sun Chips™ Multigrain Snacks: 40-Week Test Market

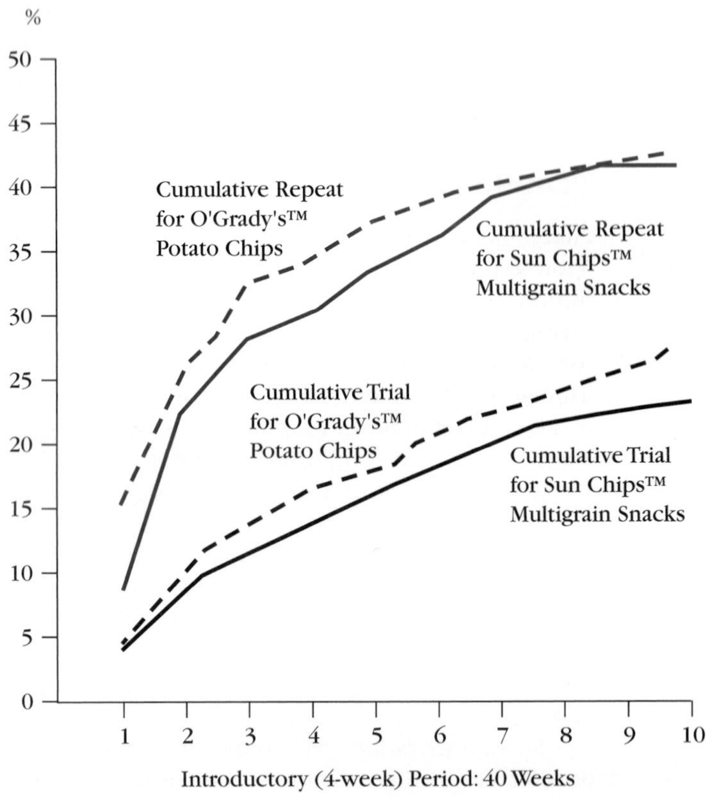

package could add about one-half ounce to the average annual purchase amount per repeat (and repeater) purchase occasion. Priced at the same price per ounce as the 11-ounce size, this action would not have a material effect on the brand's gross profit per pound. Others believed that another package size made more sense after the brand was established in the marketplace. Furthermore, the manufacturing and marketing of four sizes could stretch the production capacity, increase inventory, and challenge Frito-Lay sales personnel to get retailer shelf and display space.

Some discussion was also directed toward building the household repeat and depth of repeat business. For example, a flavor extension (for example, mild cheddar) was proposed. An advocate of this approach suggested that a flavor extension could increase the "repeats per repeater" to an average of $3^{1}/_{2}$ times per year given greater variety for consumers. However, the addition of another flavor could increase the cannibalization rate to 35 percent, some thought. Also, the mild cheddar flavor still needed to be perfected in large-scale production. Others noted that if a larger package and a flavor extension were simultaneously pursued, the number of stock-keeping units would double from six (2 flavors × 3 sizes) to twelve (3 flavors × 4 sizes). It was agreed by everyone that this action would cause severe manufacturing difficulties, since the multigrain snack process technology was still untested.

CASE

United States Census Bureau

Marketing Services Office

Jack Campbell, chief of the Marketing Services Office (MSO) in the U.S. Census Bureau, shuffled the reports sitting on the left side of his desk. "Tomorrow," he said to no one in particular. "Tomorrow we absolutely must focus on the long-range MSO marketing strategy. We simply cannot wait any longer." It was late 1999, and Campbell had scheduled a meeting with the four managers of the MSO work units. Although Campbell believed that a major part of the discussion would most likely revolve around the 2000 population census and its multimillion-dollar marketing campaign, he was determined to focus on a marketing strategy for MSO.

■ HISTORY OF THE CENSUS BUREAU

Article I, Section 2, of the United States Constitution specifies that a complete enumeration of the population of the United States must be conducted every 10 years. The original purpose of the enumeration was to obtain information to be used in determining the number of seats each state was to have in the House of Representatives as well as each state's respective share of taxes to pay for the Revolutionary War. The first census was carried out in 1790 under the supervision of United States marshals, who reported the results to President George Washington. It respectively counted the number of free white males 16 years of age and under (to determine how many men might be available for military service), the number of free white females, all other free people (including Indians who paid taxes), and the number of slaves.

United States marshals continued to supervise the next seven censuses, although they reported the results to either the Secretary of State (1800–1840) or the Secretary of the Interior (1850–1870) rather than the President. For the 1890 census, an office was established in the Interior Department, and census supervisors were appointed by the President and confirmed by the Senate. This office coordinated census efforts in 1890 and 1900. In 1902, Congress authorized a permanent census office in the Interior Department, but a year later the office was transferred to the new Department of Commerce and Labor. The Department of Commerce and Labor was divided into two separate departments in 1913, and the census office was formally named the Census Bureau and housed in the Department of Commerce, where it remains today.

The Census Bureau, headed by a director appointed by the President, is generally organized along the lines shown in Exhibit 1 on page 632. The permanent workforce of

This case was prepared by Professor Robert A. Peterson, The University of Texas at Austin, as a basis for class discussion and is not designed to illustrate effective or ineffective handling of an administrative situation. Certain case information, including the names of participants, is disguised. Consequently, the case is not useful for research purposes.

EXHIBIT 1

Organizational Structure U.S. Department of Commerce Bureau of the Census

Director

Deputy Director

PRINCIPAL ASSOCIATE DIRECTOR AND CHIEF FINANCIAL OFFICER

PRINCIPAL ASSOCIATE DIRECTOR FOR PROGRAMS

Associate Director for Finance and Administration

Associate Director for Information Technology

Associate Director for Field Operations

Associate Director for Communications

Associate Director for Economic Programs

Associate Director for Decennial Census

Associate Director for Demographic Programs

Associate Director for Methodology and Standards

Source: Census Bureau records.

the Census Bureau consists of approximately 12,165 employees. In fiscal 1998, the Bureau's budget was $703 million, nearly double that of fiscal 1997 because of preparations required for the 2000 population census. Presently, the Census Bureau is headquartered in Suitland, Maryland, a suburb of Washington, D.C. In addition to the Suitland location, there are 12 permanent regional offices; processing and support facilities in Jeffersonville, Indiana; and telephone calling centers in Tucson, Arizona, and Hagerstown, Maryland. When the decennial census is conducted in 2000, the Census Bureau will also operate 520 temporary local census offices and three additional processing facilities.

Although many people believe that the Census Bureau conducts only the decennial population census, it in fact conducts literally dozens of censuses and surveys. In addition to the population census, the Census Bureau conducts censuses of such sectors as agriculture, construction, governments, housing, irrigation, manufactures, mineral industries, transportation, and various businesses (e.g., wholesalers, retailers, and service firms). One of its most ambitious surveys is the recently created American Community Survey, a large-scale survey that was authorized in 1994. The Census Bureau also conducts numerous surveys for federal, state, and local government agencies and other organizations for which it is reimbursed. Indeed, nearly one-third of the Census Bureau's funding is derived from the reimbursable services that it provides.

The Census Bureau produces data used not only for apportionment (i.e., determining the number of congressional representatives each state will have) but also for determining federal, state, and local district voting boundaries; allocating federal funds (currently almost $200 billion per year); capturing the economic condition of the country; and providing a basis for various public and private sector decisions. Exhibit 2 presents recently released CD-ROM products that illustrate the hundreds of

EXHIBIT 2

New Census Bureau CD-ROM Releases, April–September 1999

Statistical Compendia and Reference Releases

USA Counties, 1998

State and Metropolitan Area Data Book, 1997–1998

Economic Census and Survey Releases

1996 ZIP Code Business Patterns

1997 Economic Census, Volume 1A

County Business Patterns, 1997

Foreign Trade Releases

U.S. Exports of Merchandise, February 1999–July 1999

U.S. Imports of Merchandise, February 1999–July 1999

U.S. Exports History, 1994–1998

U.S. Imports History, 1994–1998

Demographic and Decennial Census Releases

Census 2000 Dress Rehearsal Redistricting Data and Geographic Files

100 Percent Summary File

Geographic Releases

TIGER/Census Tract Street Index, Version 3

TIGER/LINE Files 1998

Source: Census Bureau records.

data products resulting from the various censuses and surveys that the Census Bureau conducts. The Census Bureau is required to make these data products available at cost to interested organizations and individuals.

THE 2000 POPULATION CENSUS

In late 1999, the eyes of the nation were focused on the upcoming 2000 population census. The Census Bureau had actually begun planning for this census before the 1990 census, and its programming and pretesting activities during the last half of the decade had consumed a large share of the Bureau's resources and attention. For example, the creation of a master address file containing all households in the United States had been in process for several years, and in 1998 the Census Bureau conducted and evaluated extensive "dress rehearsals" for the 2000 census in Sacramento, California; Menominee County, Wisconsin; and the 11 counties in and around Columbia, South Carolina.

As Dr. Kenneth Prewitt, Director of the Census Bureau, frequently points out, the 2000 census represents the largest peacetime mobilization in the country's history, with a budget of $4.5 billion and nearly 860,000 staff positions at peak employment (the entire Bureau budget is $4.6 billion). Some 426 million printed forms will be required, including questionnaires printed in six languages (Chinese, English, Korean, Spanish, Tagalog, and Vietnamese) and questionnaire assistance guides printed in at least 49 languages, ranging from Albanian to Yiddish.

To enumerate and characterize an estimated 275 million-plus people in some 124 million households in the United States in a cost-effective manner, the Census Bureau plans to use a mailout/mailback questionnaire. Virtually all households in the United States are scheduled to receive an advance notification letter in mid-March 2000, followed by a questionnaire shortly thereafter and a reminder postcard in April.[1] Each household will be requested to complete its questionnaire on April 1, 2000 ("Census Day") and return it as soon as possible to the Census Bureau. Approximately 83 percent of the households will receive a short version of the questionnaire—one asking for information on seven topics, including name, gender, Hispanic origin, race, and ownership of residence. The remaining households will receive a long version of the questionnaire, one that in addition to asking for information on the seven short-version topics will also inquire about selected social, economic, and physical characteristics of household members. Personal interviewers (enumerators) will contact households that do not mail back their questionnaires.

By December 31, 2000, the Census Bureau must deliver to the President the results of the census that will be used for apportionment. By April 1, 2001, it must deliver to the states the population counts that will be used for redistricting. Detailed demographic information on the population is scheduled to be available for public dissemination beginning in January 2001 through a new, interactive data retrieval system termed *American FactFinder*, accessible through the Internet. Nearly 1,800 State Data Centers and their affiliates (state, regional, and local agencies, libraries, chambers of commerce, planning groups, and so forth), 1,400 Federal Depository Libraries, universities, and a variety of other public and private organizations will also make census data available to the public.

During the last three population censuses, the return rate of mailed questionnaires declined precipitously. In 1970, the return rate was 78 percent. A decade later, 75 percent of the households returned questionnaires. In 1990, the return rate was only 65 percent. A National Academy of Sciences study predicted that, without any

[1] The questionnaire mailout/mailback approach will not be followed in all instances. Housing units without street names and house numbers, or in sparsely populated areas, will have questionnaires delivered by census enumerators.

changes in the manner in which the population census is conducted, the questionnaire return rate would be 55 percent in 2000. After extensive analysis, the Census Bureau projected that, with a marketing campaign and various methodological changes (e.g., increasing the readability of the questionnaires, mailing an advance notification letter), the questionnaire mailback rate would be 61 percent. The Census Bureau also estimated that each 1-percent increase in the questionnaire mailback rate above 61 percent would result in saving $25 million in personal interviewing costs.

Interest is high in the 2000 census for a variety of reasons. One reason is that the research methodology the Census Bureau intended to use had been challenged in the courts. In January 1999, the United States Supreme Court ruled that the Census Bureau must conduct a complete enumeration of the population for purposes of apportionment, but that sampling estimates could be used for other purposes, such as allocating federal funds to the states. A second reason relates to the Census Bureau's decision to implement a full-fledged marketing campaign to communicate the importance of the 2000 census and encourage people to participate.

The Marketing Campaign

The mandate of the 2000 census is to enumerate the largest, most diverse, most mobile, and, to some extent, the most skeptical population in the nation's history. Because of this mandate, and the declining questionnaire mailback rate, the Census Bureau decided to undertake an extensive and comprehensive marketing campaign. The general objectives of the marketing campaign are to increase awareness levels for the 2000 census, increase the questionnaire mailback or return rate, and facilitate the task of the personal interviewers contacting those households that do not mail back their questionnaires.

To accomplish these objectives, the Census Bureau undertook a program of research that identified a variety of demographically and attitudinally defined target segments. Using historical data, segments were defined demographically in terms of the likelihood of members being undercounted. Four segments scheduled to receive special emphasis are African Americans, Hispanics, Native Americans/Alaska Natives, and Asians. These segments have been further subdivided into subsegments or niches (e.g., Asians were divided into Asian Indians, Cambodians, Chinese [Mandarin and Cantonese], Filipinos, Hmong, Koreans, Japanese, Laotians, Thais, and Vietnamese). Members in each subsegment or niche were further classified attitudinally according to their likelihood of participating in the census ("least likely to respond," "undecided/passive," "most likely to respond").

Given the segmentation scheme, the marketing campaign is to consist of five interrelated activities:

- Partnerships between the Census Bureau and more than 32,000 government agencies, nonprofit organizations (including churches), and businesses to personally get the word out and encourage participation in the census
- Media public relations to cultivate press contacts, coordinate media inquiries and partnership activities, and obtain as much publicity as possible
- A "census in schools" program involving the distribution of teaching kits to more than 300,000 elementary and secondary school teachers in traditionally hard-to-enumerate areas
- A variety of special promotions and events, such as parades and public service documentaries
- An advertising program

Of the five campaign strategies, the advertising program is likely to be the most visible. Nearly $167 million is budgeted for advertising, of which $111 million has been allocated to media purchases. The advertising program will consist of three phases. The first phase, which focuses on creating awareness and educating the public about the census, began in November 1999 and is set to conclude in January 2000. The second phase, which begins in January 2000 and ends in the following April, focuses on motivating people to return their questionnaires. The final phase is scheduled to begin in April 2000 and conclude in July; its goal is to encourage the public to cooperate with the personal interviewers visiting those households not mailing back their questionnaires. Because of the extensiveness of the planned advertising, it is believed that the Census Bureau will be one of the largest advertisers in the United States during the first quarter of 2000.

The two-pronged advertising program will employ television, radio, newspapers and magazines, posters, outdoor and transit media, and the Internet. "Diverse America," the first component of the program, is considered the foundation: It seeks to reach 99 percent of all English-speaking people over the age of 18 in the United States an average of three dozen times. The second component targets the previously defined demographic and attitudinal segments through advertisements in 17 different languages. The Census Bureau's primary advertising agency, Young & Rubicam, estimates that a minimum of 92 percent of targeted segment members will be reached through the advertising and that, for example, the typical African American will be exposed to the advertising 122 times. Media expenditures are expected to be divided about equally between the two components.

The theme or unifying tagline of the advertising program, around which all creative efforts are organized, is "This Is Your Future, Don't Leave It Blank." This theme was selected because it draws attention to both the personal and community benefits of completing and returning a census questionnaire. Interestingly enough, this theme was slightly modified for the four major demographic target segments to increase its power:

African Americans	"This is our future. Don't leave it blank."
Asians/Pacific Islanders	"For you and future generations. Don't leave it blank."
Hispanics	"It's our future. Make yourself count."
Native Americans/ Alaskan Natives	"Generations are counting on this. Don't leave it blank."

■ THE MARKETING SERVICES OFFICE

Exhibit 3 contains a brief history of the Marketing Services Office. As noted in the exhibit, the MSO recently began reporting to the Assistant Director for Marketing and Customer Liaison. There are 49 full-time employees (and three contract workers) in the MSO. These employees are organized into four work units:

- Customer Service Center (CSC)
- Research, Planning, and Evaluation (RP&E)
- American Community Survey (ACS)
- Promotions

The work units provide marketing support services for more than 30 program areas in the Census Bureau. For example, one of the units was involved in a three-year effort that culminated in early 1999 in a new "look and feel" identity for the Census Bureau. This "look and feel" consists of a new corporate tagline ("Helping You Make Informed Decisions"), a new Census Bureau wordmark (i.e., the multi-color emblem "USCENSUSBUREAU"), a report cover design system, a standard typeface, and specified colors and graphics to use on all Census Bureau documents.

EXHIBIT 3

Background and History of the Marketing Services Office

1971	The Census Bureau establishes the Data Services Division to assist the public in obtaining and using Census Bureau information. Various offices, including Central User Services, are merged into the new division. The Central User Services Office becomes the Customer Services Branch.
1978	The Census Bureau establishes the State Data Center Program to increase dissemination and usage of data products, particularly data products from the 1980 Census. The program is housed in the Data User Services Division.
1990	The User Training Branch within the Data User Services Division becomes the Training, Education, and Marketing Staff, with the new title reflecting increased responsibilities for promoting Census Bureau data products.
1993	An interdivisional team recommends the establishment of a Census Bureau marketing office with the responsibility for marketing the Census Bureau, its programs (especially large-scale surveys for the other federal agencies), and data products.
1994	The Data User Services Division is abolished. Most of its functions are transferred to the Administrative area. Communication functions are transferred to the Public Information Office. The State Data Center program becomes a separate office, the Customer Liaison Office, with increased intergovernmental responsibilities. The marketing functions and staff of the Training, Education, and Marketing Staff are combined into a separate office known as the Customer and Product Development Office, which reports directly to the Principal Associate Director for Programs.
1995	The Customer and Product Development Office is restructured and renamed the Marketing Services Office.
1998	The Customer Services Branch is transferred to the Marketing Services Office.
1999	The Marketing Services Office and the Customer Liaison Office organizationally report to a new position, the Assistant Director for Marketing and Customer Liaison. The Assistant Director for Marketing and Customer Liaison in turn reports to the Principal Associate Director for Programs.

Source: Census Bureau records.

The CSC, managed by Harrison Leslie, processes off-the-shelf data product orders received by mail, the Internet, facsimile, and telephone. In addition, the unit's information specialists answer questions and respond to inquiries on a wide range of topics, including product specifications, software, purchasing options, shipping costs, and product content. Most often, the CSC is the first point of contact for customers external to the Census Bureau, regardless of the purpose of their inquiry.

The RP&E work unit, under the direction of manager Carol Ford, maintains and manages MSO's in-house customer database and conducts sales analyses on a regular basis. It also makes recommendations on target markets and corresponding product offerings, tracks results of promotional efforts, coordinates focus group research, and takes the lead in fostering Census Bureau–wide customer service.

Maureen Chalsonte manages the ACS work unit that is the marketing arm for the American Community Survey, the Census Bureau's recently developed survey of economic, demographic, social, housing, and population characteristics. Once implemented nationwide, the ACS will produce decennial-like population census data annually rather than once every 10 years (and replace the decennial population census long-version questionnaire). Through publications, an annual CD-ROM (10,000 copies distributed free), and other critical marketing tools, the ACS marketing staff promotes the ACS mission, stressing its importance to individuals, organizations, and planners and decision makers at all levels of government. The major challenge facing the ACS work unit is how to facilitate the distribution and acceptance of this new Census Bureau product as a primary data resource in years to come. Uncertain funding for the ACS operation through 2003, the year slated for national implementation of the survey, compounds this challenge.

The Promotions work unit, managed by Ralph Brown, plans and executes targeted direct mail campaigns, develops and places advertising and "advertorial" publicity, coordinates traveling Census Bureau exhibits and displays, and manages Census Bureau-sponsored conferences. Promotions work unit staff members perform all copywriting activities when Census Bureau catalogs, brochures, Web sites, and other publications are created. In addition, the Promotions staff is very involved with publication management and distribution, graphic design, product development and testing, and special events.

Marketing Census Bureau Data Products

One of the responsibilities of the MSO is marketing various Census Bureau data products and services. Although revenues from data products and services are minor compared to revenues obtained from reimbursable services, they are directly linked to the Census Bureau's ultimate constituency, the American public. For this reason alone, the role of the MSO is an important one in the Census Bureau.

Sales of Census Bureau data products and services are very cyclical and are in large part determined by the demand for decennial population census data. In fiscal year 1999, MSO revenues totaled approximately $1.2 million, down from $1.3 million in fiscal year 1998. In fiscal year 1997, they were about $1.6 million. More specifically, in the fiscal year just ended, the MSO processed 10,434 product orders and shipped 11,009 products. In addition, the MSO handled 17,886 telephone calls from customers and had 4,954 other (e.g., face-to-face) contacts with customers. MSO's marketing efforts have traditionally focused on person-to-person demonstrations in trade shows and conferences and some direct-mail marketing.

Recently, about 60 percent of the Census Bureau's data-products revenues have come from the sale of CD-ROMs, partly because many of the Census Bureau's printed publications are sold through and by the Government Printing Office (GPO), an organization distinct from the Census Bureau. In July 1999, the MSO started marketing data products and services through the Census Bureau's Web site. Since then, approximately 25 percent of the orders handled by the MSO have originated from the Web site. Interestingly enough, 40 percent of the Web site orders come in during nonbusiness hours, and 60 percent of the orders are from new customers.

The single-largest category of customers consists of financial institutions (e.g., banks), partially because government regulations require that financial institutions report their lending activities by census tract. Many of the largest individual customers, however, are resellers of Census Bureau data products. Resellers purchase data products from the Census Bureau and repackage and offer them in a different form or format, or in conjunction with other products. For example, most of the geographic information systems sold by firms are either directly based on or incorporate Census Bureau data.

Although most Census Bureau data products and services are sold domestically, sales are also made to customers in nearly 50 other countries. Among the nondomestic customers served, revenues from Canadian customers have consistently ranked first over the years; Mexican and Japanese customers rank second and third, respectively.

■ THE MSO MEETING

Jack Campbell began the MSO staff meeting by thanking the work unit managers for attending. He then set forth some ground rules. "I want this meeting to be a free-form exchange. At this point I don't think we should be critiquing any ideas or comments. And, just so we never lose sight of our overriding purpose today, I'd like to start by reiterating the Census Bureau's offical mission statement: 'To be the preeminent collector and provider of timely, relevant, and quality data about the people and economy of the United States.' "

Campbell continued by saying, "I believe the Census Bureau has actually and historically accomplished this mission, but 'the times are a-changing.' For the Bureau to maintain its position as the preeminent collector and provider of timely, relevant, and quality data, we need to accommodate and plan for the changing times. Based on your personal, firsthand experience in the Bureau and your knowledge of the Bureau's mission, what are some of the changes and related issues that will be affecting your work unit operations in the next couple of years?"

Carol Ford was the first to respond. "Well, the Census Bureau, similar to other federal government agencies, has been given a mandate to be more entrepreneurial. This mandate has been interpreted as recovering costs of product development and dissemination wherever and whenever logical and possible. Obviously, this mandate does not make many data users and Census Bureau data-product resellers happy since it potentially increases their costs."

Harrison Leslie cleared his throat. "I think what these changes mean to CSC is that we need to provide more useful and customized information to data users, and deliver data products and services faster, cheaper, and better. It also means providing superior customer service 100 percent of the time and keeping current customers satisfied and coming back for more of our data products and services."

The next to speak was Maureen Chalsonte. "What I think these changes mean for MSO is that it needs to be more effective in getting the word out about what the Census Bureau is doing to keep up with the demands of an electronic information society for more timely data, including surveys such as ACS."

"We need to resolve general issues such as whether we should give away all our information free through the Internet—as might be expected by the taxpaying public—and the necessity of charging for customized product development," remarked Ralph Brown. "Why should taxpayers foot the bill for filling the needs of a relatively small number of data-product customers? What exactly should be free, if anything? What data should people have to pay for? Should the government be in the business of selling at all, or should it simply leave selling to commercial entities? Why can't we sell data products and services at market value and plow any surpluses back into new product development?"

"I have a question," interjected Chalsonte. "Who exactly *is* entitled to receive products or services from the Census Bureau at no charge?"

"I can answer that," responded Ford. "The White House, members of Congress or their staffs, and most federal agencies are entitled to Census Bureau data products and services at no cost. Also, we provide free data products to our dissemination partners—state and local agencies, and public and university libraries, for example—for distribution as a public good. Furthermore, the media are not charged, provided that the benefits of the coverage outweigh the cost of providing the products and services."

"Let me shift the discussion a bit," said Campbell. "How do we overcome the lack of control over product development timetables? Pre-release product publicity has often been disseminated only to be followed by inordinate, months-long delays in the actual delivery of a finished product. What internal MSO policies need to be instituted to overcome this gap? How do we hold the program divisions' and product devlopers' feet to the fire?"

"That's a good point, Jack," added Leslie, "especially in the context of the 2000 census. What shifts in MSO tasks and activities will result when the 2000 census is finished? How do we accommodate the lag time in the dissemination of data from the decennial census? It may be close to a year before any data products are ready to be distributed from the 2000 census. And, once available, what is the most efficient and effective way to promote their availability?"

"Excellent considerations," said Campbell. "Here's another. We currently have a standard policy of offering up to 50 percent off list price, depending on volume. Since it appears we are in true cost-recovery mode only, can we actually afford to provide such discounts? Should we explore other pricing options? What might some of these options be?"

"Jack, your point gets back to my earlier comment," remarked Ralph Brown. "How do we overcome issues of non-copyrightable or public domain materials? Virtually everything the Bureau produces can be easily reproduced by outside organizations that are then free to sell its data products at whatever the market will bear."

"Further to this point, Ralph, one of our problems is that our best-selling and most popular data products are available to data users and researchers for free through Federal Depository Libraries in colleges and universities across the country." Campbell continued: "This is due to the legislated mandate of allowing the GPO to ride our production contracts and provide free copies of any materials we develop to the colleges and universities participating in the Federal Depository Library program. Further, the GPO sells some of these same materials in its own bookstores."

Carol Ford entered the discussion. "Should we make free information available solely through the Internet, and for-sale products available on CD-ROM and/or preprinted on paper or in other formats such as facsimile, photocopies of existing materials, certified copies, custom or semi-custom products, magnetic tape or cartridge, DVD, or even something we currently do not know about? How does 'print on demand' fit in with any attendant savings on related overhead costs?"

"Just what or who is really our competition? I think we need to give this issue serious thought before we move forward on any plan," remarked Chalsonte.

"And relatedly," added Leslie, "what are the demographics of our own customers? Are they institutional or individual buyers? What percentage are repackagers or resellers?"

"Whoa . . . slow down a bit." Jack Campbell leaned back in his chair and put his hands behind his head. "Back to the competition for a second. What added value can we bring to our product offerings to overcome the problem of data repackagers and resellers?"

"And," Brown intoned, "what are our top-selling data products and services?"

At that point, Carol Ford stood up and started handing out a folder of documents to each person in the meeting. "RP&E anticipated some of these questions, and I believe it has the answers to many of them. Here are the results of a relatively recent report detailing some very interesting information. These results show selected customer, product, and revenue breakdowns for a couple of time periods." (See Exhibits 4 and 5.)

After the group finished examining the documents, Ralph Brown spoke up. "We also need to look at how we can open new markets as well as expand existing ones. Only a small fraction of our sales, less than 3 percent, result from international purchases. We ought to be able to substantially increase our international sales. Unfortunately, in our first and last attempt at breaking into this market two years ago, we got a dismal response to a costly direct-mail campaign. If you will recall, our direct-mail plan had been endorsed by the Census Bureau Advisory Committee of the American Marketing Association. However, despite this initial failure, the Advisory Committee specifically recommended that we *not* give up on this potential market."

"Unfortunately, Ralph, as you pointed out, it is a costly proposition to reach the international customer group," Jack Campbell continued. "Furthermore, once the decennial census is over, the budget is likely to become very tight for the Bureau in general and the MSO in particular."

"Speaking of the decennial census," said Harrison Leslie, "come 2000, there are certain mundane logistics that will impact all of us. For example, across the country

EXHIBIT 4

Product Line Percentage Revenues

Product Line	*Percent of Revenues* 1990–1997	1999
TIGER[a]	18	12
Foreign Trade[b]	15	28
STF3[c]	13	8
CTSI[d]	12	6
Maps	10	13
All other lines	32	33

[a] The Census Bureau's TIGER (Topologically Integrated Geographic Encoding and Referencing) is a geographic database that links each household address in the United States to a spatial location, and each location to a specific geographic area.

[b] Foreign trade statistics (both import and export statistics) are available on both a product basis and a subscription basis.

[c] Summary Tape Files from 1990 decennial census.

[d] Census Tract Street Index.

Source: Census Bureau records.

a short-term workforce of hundreds of thousands of census enumerators will hit the streets. Parking at headquarters in particular will be a nightmare. People will be expected to work longer than normal hours as the census is implemented and the pressure builds. None of this bodes well for customer service in general, and especially for the Customer Service Center."

Ralph Brown immediately responded to Leslie's observation. "Harrison, you're absolutely correct. I've already answered more than one call from an irate citizen whose dinner has been interrupted by an overly zealous enumerator during the dress rehearsal. Census 2000 will impact us all in ways that we have not even thought about yet."

"Here's a consideration for all of us, although it most directly affects CSC." Leslie slowly ran his finger down one of the documents that Ford had provided. "Several program areas and divisions have their own customer service staff. What this means is that not all customer service units are on the same order entry system, customers are hearing differing instructions and policies for placing and fulfilling orders, and they may or may not be hearing accurate product descriptions. Although we are im-

EXHIBIT 5

Customer Segment Percentage Revenues

Customer Segment	*Percent of Revenues* 1990–1997
Financial institutions	14.8
Research, development, and testing services	8.3
Colleges and universities	8.0
State and local governments	5.6
Federal government	5.5
Other	57.8

Source: Census Bureau records.

plementing a unified Oracle database system, it is going to take quite a while for all the disparate areas and divisions to start using the system. How should we take this into account when planning our strategy?"

"For the purposes of this discussion," Maureen Chalsonte said, "I think we also need to look at the possible impact of *American FactFinder* on all MSO activities. Many people, I believe, are looking at this system as the ultimate tool to obtain virtually any and all census data, and this especially appears to be the thinking of some members of the Bureau's executive management team. We need to market *American FactFinder* more effectively, but whose responsibility should it be?"

Ralph Brown was the next to speak. "We have a unique opportunity coming up soon—2002 to be exact—to flaunt the wonderful work and products available from the Census Bureau. 2002 will mark the centennial anniversary of the founding of the Census Bureau in 1902. Members of my staff are already at work developing commemorative materials. Everyone in the Bureau should be encouraged to participate in what will be a year-long celebration and promotional opportunity."

Brown's comments were followed by those of Harrison Leslie. "The Internet already plays a huge role in disseminating data, services, and products in general. This role is only likely to increase over time. Catalog companies, nonprofit organizations, government agencies, and businesses across the country already report major transformations in how their customers or clients do business with them. How can the Census Bureau better position itself to deliver its data products and services via the Internet? And, again, what will be the level of customer service provided? The Internet has brought in a large community of census data users who are increasingly sophisticated. While the Internet is supposed to reduce our workload, in some sense it will likely increase our workload. The telephone staff reports that the amount of time required to service recent customers is increasing because of the complexity and breadth of technical information requested as a consequence of what we now offer on the Bureau's Web site."

"Speaking of customer service, Harrison, what about setting up a toll-free 800 number for our customers to use?" Brown appeared to wax philosophically. "In this day and age, it's almost a requirement for any substantial organization to have such a number. I know we've talked about this before. If we succeed in obtaining one, though, live operators must be standing by during business hours on both the east and west coasts of the country, and no doubt our costs would increase considerably."

"As an aside," added Ford, "recently we spent roughly $250,000 on developing a new look and feel identity for the Census Bureau. Has it been successfully implemented? I have seen only a couple of publications reflecting this new look and feel. How can we gauge whether or not it has been properly put into effect?"

"In fact," Ford noted as she rolled a pencil between her fingers, "we need to better market our own products and services to internal customers; otherwise, MSO will become obsolete. I do think we have been making inroads along these lines, but as a relatively new office, we are not out of the woods yet."

"I should have brought this up earlier, but better late than never. This year the exhibits program was transferred to MSO, and to my work unit in particular. While we were used to handling perhaps 45 to 50 exhibits in a year, Promotions is now in the midst of coordinating nearly that many conference exhibits *each month*. This situation is expected to continue for at least another 15 months due to major census 2000 partnership commitments." Brown concluded by mentioning that his work unit had been scrambling for new staff for months and could still use two or three additional full-time employees.

Leslie glanced at Campbell. "I see that Jack is starting to fidget. Before we move on, I want to mention one last thing. Because of the Internet we face more public inquiries than ever before. In fact, you are all aware that the Bureau Web site [www.census.gov] currently receives more than one million hits per day. We too are short-staffed in CSC, and to handle the expected number of inquiries that will result from the 2000 census will require even more human resources. When data products from the 1990 census were released in 1992, the demand for our services skyrocketed. In 1991, for instance, we took orders for less than 800 maps. In 1992, we processed 10,800 map orders, but in 1993 we processed less than 1,500 map orders. If the same cyclical order pattern occurs following the 2000 census that we experienced after the 1990 census, together with the natural increase in the number of orders, CSC will have to process in excess of 60,000 total orders in 2002."

"Harrison is very perceptive," Campbell said as he nodded at Leslie. "We certainly have a full plate in front of us. Let's start putting together our plan of action, and let's do so by first focusing on what seem to be the fundamental strategic marketing issues in front of us. What markets, products, and services should MSO focus on, and how?"

CASE

Biopure Corporation

It was February 5, 1998, as Carl Rausch, president and CEO of Biopure Corporation, opened his Boston Globe and read about the U.S. government's final approval of Oxyglobin (see Exhibit 1). Oxyglobin was the first of two new "blood substitutes" on which Biopure's future depended—Oxyglobin for the veterinary market and Hemopure for the human market. While Oxyglobin was ready for launch, Hemopure was still two years away from final government approval. This timing was the source of an ongoing debate within Biopure.

Ted Jacobs, vice president for Human Clinical Trials at Biopure, argued that the release of Oxyglobin should be delayed until *after* Hemopure was approved and had established itself in the marketplace (see Exhibit 2 on page 646 for an organizational chart of Biopure). Given that the two products were almost identical in physical properties and appearance, he felt that Oxyglobin would create an unrealistic price expectation for Hemopure if released first. As he made clear in a recent management meeting,

> . . . [T]he veterinary market is small and price sensitive. We'll be lucky to get $150 per unit. The human market, on the other hand, is many times larger and we can realistically achieve price points of $600 to $800 per unit. But as soon as we come out with Oxyglobin at $150, we jeopardize our ability to price Hemopure at $800. Hospitals and insurance firms will be all over us to justify a 500% price difference for what they see as the same product. That's a headache we just don't need. We've spent $200 million developing Hemopure—to risk it at this point is crazy. We should just shelve Oxyglobin for now.

At the same time, Andy Wright, vice president for Veterinary Products, had his sales organization in place and was eager to begin selling Oxyglobin. He argued that the benefits of immediately releasing Oxyglobin outweighed the risks:

> Oxyglobin would generate our first revenues ever—revenues we could use to launch Hemopure. And while the animal market is smaller than the human market, it is still attractive. Finally, I can't stress enough the value of Oxyglobin in learning how to "go to market." Would you rather make the mistakes now, with Oxyglobin, or in two years, with Hemopure?

While Carl Rausch listened to this debate, he also considered his colleagues' growing desire to take Biopure public in the near future. He wondered whether a proven success with Oxyglobin might not have a greater impact on an initial public offering (IPO) than the promise of success with Hemopure.

Professor John Gourville prepared this case as the basis for class discussion rather than to illustrate either effective or ineffective handling of an administrative situation. Some nonpublic data have been disguised and some business details have been simplified to aid in classroom discussion.

EXHIBIT 1

Excerpts from *The Boston Globe* Article, February 5, 1998

Biopure's Blood Substitute for Dogs OK'd

Veterinarians scrambling to find blood for badly injured dogs now have a blood substitute. Biopure Corp. of Cambridge said yesterday it received federal regulatory approval to market oxygen-carrying blood derived from the blood of cows.

Tested in over 250 dogs, the company's blood substitute, called Oxyglobin, is initially aimed at the [canine blood transfusion market], according to Andrew W. Wright, vice president of Biopure's veterinary products.

The US Food and Drug Administration approval makes Oxyglobin the first blood substitutes for dogs, designed for dogs needing blood transfusions because of blood loss from accidents, surgeries, parasite infections, or rare anemia cases.

"This is a breakthrough development because it quickly gets oxygen into tissue and organs and buys time for the dog's own regenerative red blood cells to come back," said Dr. Robert Murtaugh, professor of veterinary medicine and section head for emergency and critical care services at the Tufts University School of Veterinary Medicine.

The canine version is designed to largely replace drawing blood from donor dogs some veterinarians use in emergency situations.

Unlike blood that contains red blood cells, Biopure's technology uses a highly purified bovine hemoglobin that does not require blood typing or cross-matching. [Oxyglobin] can be stored in a veterinarian's storage area at room temperature for up to two years. A single bag—equivalent to a pint of whole blood—is sufficient for small to medium-sized dogs; two bags might be needed for larger dogs.

AN OVERVIEW OF BIOPURE

Biopure Corporation was founded in 1984 by entrepreneurs Carl Rausch and David Judelson as a privately owned biopharmaceutical firm specializing in the ultrapurification of proteins for human and veterinary use. By 1998, this mission had taken Biopure to the point where it was one of three legitimate contenders in the emerging field of "blood substitutes."[1] Blood substitutes were designed to replicate the oxygen-carrying function of actual blood, while eliminating the shortcomings associated with the transfusion of donated blood. Through the end of 1997, no blood substitute had received approval for use anywhere in the world.

Biopure's entries into this field were Hemopure, for the human market, and Oxyglobin, for the animal market. Both products consisted of the oxygen-carrying protein "hemoglobin" which had been removed from red blood cells, purified to eliminate infectious agents, and chemically modified to increase its safety and effectiveness. What distinguished Hemopure and Oxyglobin from other "hemoglobin-based" blood substitutes under development was the fact that they were "bovine-sourced" as opposed to "human-sourced"—they were derived from the blood of cattle. To date, Biopure had spent over $200 million in the development of Oxyglobin and Hemopure and in the construction of a state-of-the-art manufacturing facility.

[1] While the term *blood substitute* has historically been used to describe this class of product, Biopure and the medical community increasingly have used the term *oxygen therapeutic* to describe the latest generation of product. For simplicity, however, we will continue to use the term *blood substitute* in this case.

EXHIBIT 2

The Organizational Structure at Biopure Corporation

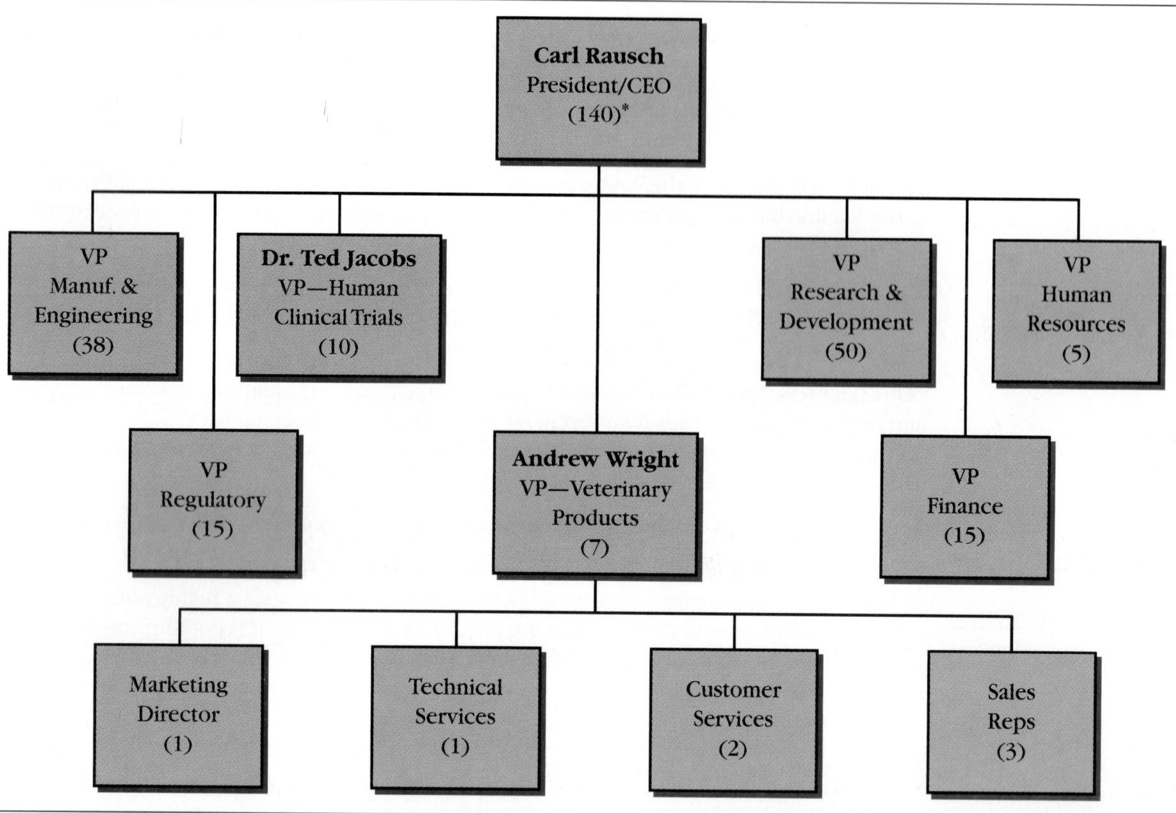

* Numbers in parentheses represents the total number of employees that fall under a particular position's span of control. Thus, 140 employees either directly or indirectly report to Carl Rausch.

Source: Biopure company records.

Both of Biopure's products fell under the approval process of the United States government's Food and Drug Administration (FDA), which required that each product be proven safe and effective for medical use (see Exhibit 3 for an overview of the FDA approval process). In this regard, Oxyglobin had just received final FDA approval for commercial release as a veterinary blood substitute, while Hemopure would soon enter Phase 3 clinical trials and was optimistically expected to see final FDA approval for release as a human blood substitute sometime in 1999.

This recent FDA approval of Oxyglobin brought to a peak a long-simmering debate within Biopure. With its primary goal being the development of a human blood substitute, Biopure's entry into the animal market had been somewhat opportunistic. During preclinical trials for Hemopure, the benefits of a blood substitute for small animals became apparent. In response, Biopure began a parallel product development process that resulted in Oxyglobin. However, there was little question within Biopure that Oxyglobin was an ancillary product to Hemopure.

As it became apparent that Oxyglobin would gain FDA approval prior to Hemopure, Carl Rausch and his management team discussed how best to manage Oxyglobin. As the first "blood substitute" of any type to receive full government approval, Rausch was eager to get the news out. With this in mind, Andy Wright and a small marketing team had been assembled to bring Oxyglobin to market. However, Ted Jacobs and others questioned whether the immediate release of Oxyglobin might not

EXHIBIT 3

The United States FDA Approval Process

Phase	*Goals*	*Characteristics*
Preclinical trials	Safety in animals	Typical length = 5–10 years Need to show safety Hope to show efficacy Testing animals include mice, rats, dogs, sheep, etc.
Phase 1 Clinical Trials	Safety in healthy human subjects	Typical length = 2–3 years 20–100 individuals Single-site testing location
Phase 2A & 2B Clinical Trials	2A - Safety in human patients 2B - Safety and efficacy in human patients	Typical length = 1–2 years 100–200 individuals Single-site or multi-site testing locations
Phase 3 Clinical Trials	Large-scale safety and efficacy in use	Typical length = 1–2 years 100–500 individuals Multisite testing locations Double-blind testing (i.e., neither patient nor doctor aware of specific product or brand)

Source: Biopure company records.

impinge on Biopure's ability to optimally price Hemopure. After months of debate, it was time to decide on the fate of Oxyglobin.

■ THE HUMAN BLOOD MARKET

Blood is essential for life. It performs many functions, the most acutely critical of which is the transportation of oxygen to the organs and tissues of the human body. Without oxygen, these organs and tissues will die within minutes.

That portion of blood responsible for oxygen transportation are the red blood cells (RBCs). RBCs capture inhaled oxygen from the lungs, carry that oxygen to the cells of the body, release it for use where needed, capture expended carbon dioxide from those cells, and carry that carbon dioxide back to the lungs, where it is released. The key to this process is "hemoglobin," the iron-containing protein found within each RBC to which oxygen and carbon dioxide molecules bind.

The adult human body contains 5,000 milliliters (ml) or about 10 pints of blood. An individual can naturally compensate for the loss of up to 30 percent of this volume through some combination of increased oxygen intake (i.e., faster breathing), increased flow of the remaining blood (i.e., faster heart rate), and the prioritization of blood delivery to vital organs. In cases of blood loss of greater than 30 percent, however, outside intervention is typically required—generally in the form of a "blood transfusion."

Human Blood Transfusions

A blood transfusion entails the direct injection of blood into a patient's bloodstream. As of 1998, the most common form of blood transfusion was the intravenous transfusion of donated RBCs.[2] Typically, a healthy individual would donate 1 unit or 500 ml of "whole" blood, which would be tested for various infectious diseases, sorted by blood type, and separated into its usable components (e.g., plasma, platelets, and RBCs). This process would yield 1 unit or 250 ml of RBCs, which then would be stored until needed by a patient.[3]

While potentially lifesaving, the transfusion of donated RBCs has limitations. These include:

- *The need for exact blood typing and cross-matching between donor and recipient.* The RBCs of each human may contain specific blood sugars, or antigens. The existence or absence of these antigens creates a complex set of allowable transfusions between donor and recipient, as shown in Exhibit 4. Transfusions outside of those outlined can be fatal to the recipient.
- *The reduced oxygen-carrying efficiency of stored RBCs.* RBCs stored for 10 days or more are only about 50 percent efficient at transporting oxygen in the first 8 to 12 hours after transfusion.
- *The limited shelf-life for stored RBCs.* RBCs can be safely stored for only about 6 weeks, after which time they are typically discarded.
- *The need for refrigeration.* For optimal shelf-life, RBCs must be stored at 4° Celsius (~40° F).
- *The risk of disease transmission.* While donated blood is tested for infectious agents, there still exists the risk of disease transmission. For example, the risk of AIDS is 1:500,000, the risk of hepatitis B is 1:200,000, and the risk of hepatitis C is 1:100,000.

Autologous Transfusions In an attempt to overcome some of these limitations, the use of "autologous" or self-donated RBCs has become increasingly common. In an autologous RBC transfusion, a medically stable patient who anticipates the need for RBCs would have his or her own blood drawn weeks in advance, separated into its components, and saved until needed. Research has shown this process to significantly

EXHIBIT 4

Human Blood Typing and Allowable Transfusions[a]

Donor Blood Type	*Percentage of Population*	*Acceptable Recipients*
AB	4%	AB[b]
A	40%	A, AB
B	11%	B, AB
O[c]	45%	O, A, B, AB

[a] In addition to ABO blood typing, RBCs are either Rh+ or Rh−, further complicating allowable transfusions.

[b] AB is often referred to as the "universal recipient."

[c] O is often referred to as the "universal donor."

Source: The American Red Cross.

---

[2] Historically, whole blood transfusions were the norm. Since the 1970s, however, whole blood increasingly had been separated into RBCs, platelets, and plasma, allowing for (1) several patients to benefit from a single unit of donated blood and (2) a reduced likelihood of negative reaction for any given patient.

[3] In blood medicine, 1 unit is defined in terms of its therapeutic value. Therefore, "1 unit" or 250 ml of RBCs provides the oxygen-carrying capacity of "1 unit" or 500 ml of whole blood. Similarly, "1 unit" of a blood substitute (i.e., typically 125 ml) provides the same oxygen-carrying capacity of "1 unit" of RBCs or whole blood.

reduce a patient's rate of complication and postoperative infection, thereby hastening recovery and shortening his or her stay in the hospital.

Human Blood Supply and Demand

Human Blood Supply Fourteen million units of RBCs were donated by 8 million people in 1995 in the United States. Approximately 12.9 million of these units came from individuals who voluntarily donated to one of over 1,000 nonprofit blood collection organizations. By far, the largest of these organizations was the American Red Cross, which collected half of all the blood donated in the United States in 1995 through a network of 44 regional blood collection centers. Typically, the Red Cross and the other blood collection organizations supported "blood mobiles," which traveled to high schools, colleges, and places of employment to reach potential donors. The remaining 1.1 million units of RBCs were autologous donations made directly to a hospital blood center.

Increasingly, blood collection was a struggle. While 75 percent of all adults qualified as a donor, fewer than 5 percent actually donated in a given year. Historically, reasons for donating included altruism and peer pressure, while reasons for not donating included fear of needles and lack of time. Since the mid-1980s, an additional reason for not donating involved the misconception that donating put one at risk for contracting AIDS. Public education had failed to counteract this misconception.

Given the low rate of donation and the relatively short shelf-life of RBCs, it was not uncommon for medical facilities and blood banks to experience periodic shortages of RBCs. This was especially true during the winter holidays and the summer months, periods which routinely displayed both increased demand and decreased rates of donation.

Human Blood Demand Of the 14 million units of RBCs donated in 1995, 2.7 million were discarded due to contamination or expiration (i.e., units older than 6 weeks). Another 3.2 million units were transfused into 1.5 million patients who suffered from chronic anemia, an ongoing deficiency in the oxygen-carrying ability of the blood. The remaining 8.1 million units were transfused into 2.5 million patients who suffered from acute blood loss brought on by elective surgeries, emergency surgeries, or trauma. Exhibit 5 on page 650 offers a breakdown of RBC transfusions in 1995.

In elective and emergency surgeries, RBCs were routinely transfused in situations where blood loss was greater than two units, as was typical in heart bypass and organ transplant surgeries. In surgeries with blood loss of one to two units, however, RBCs typically were not transfused in spite of their potential benefit. In these "borderline" transfusion surgeries, doctors typically avoided transfusions for fear of disease transmission or negative reaction caused by the transfused RBCs. There were approximately 1 million "borderline transfusion" surgeries in the United States each year.

RBC transfusions were also required in the approximate 500,000 trauma cases which occurred every year in the United States. These cases were characterized by the massive loss of blood due to automobile accidents, gunshot wounds, etc. However, due to the resources required to store, type, and administer RBCs, only 10 percent of trauma victims received RBCs "in the field" or at the site of the accident. Blood transfusions for the remaining 90 percent of victims were delayed until the victim arrived at a hospital emergency room. This delay was often cited as a contributing factor to the 30 percent fatality rate seen in these trauma cases, as evidenced by the 20,000 trauma victims who bled to death each year prior to reaching the hospital. As one doctor put it,

> . . . [T]hose first few minutes after a trauma are known as the "Golden Hour." Life and death often depends on how fast the lost blood is replaced in this period.

EXHIBIT 5

Red Blood Cell Donations and Transfusions in the United States in 1995

Use of Red Blood Cells		*Units (in Thousands)*
Acute blood loss:		
Elective surgery:		
Anonymous donations		5,800
Autologous donations[a,b]		1,100
Emergency surgery (in hospital)		1,000
Trauma (in field administration)		200
Acute blood loss subtotal		**8,100**
Chronic anemia		**3,200**
Not transfused		
Due to rejection		1,200
Due to expiration		1,500
Not transfused subtotal		**2,700**
	Total:	**14,000**

[a] Autologous donations are in elective surgery only. All other uses of RBCs represent anonymous donations.
[b] Autologous donations include both those units transfused and those unused units discarded.
Source: Stover & Associates, LLC.

Looking forward, while the demand for RBCs to treat chronic anemia was expected to remain stable, the demand for RBCs to treat acute blood loss was expected to rise with the aging U.S. population. Individuals over 65 years of age comprised 15 percent of the adult population in 1995 and received over 40 percent of all "acute blood loss" transfusions. By the year 2030, this over-65 segment was expected to double in absolute numbers and to grow to 25 percent of the adult population.

Human Blood Pricing Since the AIDS crisis, it has been illegal for an individual to sell his or her blood in the United States. As such, all blood donations are unpaid. In turn, to cover their expense of collection and administration, blood collection organizations sell this donated blood to hospitals and medical centers. Once obtained, hospitals incur additional costs to store, handle, transport, screen, type, cross-match, and

EXHIBIT 6

Cost to Patient of Donated Human Blood

	Low Estimate (per Unit)	*High Estimate (per Unit)*
Anonymous donations:		
Hospital acquisition cost	$ 75	$150
Screening/Typing/Crossmatching	25	40
Transportation/Administration	25	35
Final Price of Anonymous	**$125**	**$225**
Autologous donations:		
Added administration and handling	$150	$200
Final price of autologous	**$275**	**$425**

Source: Stover & Associates, LLC.

document the blood. Estimates for these costs are outlined in Exhibit 6. Typically, these costs are passed on to the patient or to the patient's insurance provider.

THE VETERINARY BLOOD MARKET

The role of RBCs for animals is biologically identical to its role for humans: RBCs transport oxygen to an animal's tissues and organs. In practice, however, the availability and transfusion of blood was considerably more constrained in the veterinary market than it was in the human market.

Veterinary Market Structure There were approximately 15,000 small-animal veterinary practices in the United States in 1995. Of these, about 95 percent were "primary care" practices which provided preventative care (e.g., shots, checkups), routine treatment of illness (e.g., infections, chronic anemia), and limited emergency care (e.g., simple surgery and trauma). The remaining 5 percent of practices were "emergency care" or "specialty care" practices. Approximately 75 percent of primary care practices referred some or all of their major surgery and severe trauma cases to these emergency care practices. Across both the primary care and emergency care practices, patient volume was concentrated in dogs (~50 percent of patient volume) and cats (~35 percent of volume). Exhibit 7 provides a staffing and patient profile of small-animal veterinary clinics in the United States.

Veterinary Blood Demand In practice, blood transfusions in the veterinary market were infrequent. In 1995, for example, the average veterinary practice was presented with 800 dogs suffering from acute blood loss. About 30 percent of these dogs would have benefited significantly from a transfusion of blood, but only about 2.5 percent were deemed "critical cases" and received a transfusion.

The incidence of these acute blood loss cases was relatively concentrated, with 15 percent of veterinary practices handling 65 percent of all canine surgeries and 10 percent of practices handling 55 percent of all canine trauma cases. Not surprisingly, these "high incident" practices tended to be the larger primary care practices and the emergency care practices. This concentration was also evident in blood transfusions. In 1995, an average of 17 units of canine blood were transfused by each primary care practice, while an average of 150 units were transfused by each emergency care practice.

EXHIBIT 7

Profile of the 15,000 Veterinary Practices in the United States (1995)

Class of Practice	*Average No. of Doctors*	*Relative Frequency*	*Average Monthly Case Load*			*Average Gross Revenues*
			Dogs	*Cats*	*Other*	
Primary care:						
1 Doctor practices	1	25%	200	125	80	$265,000
2 Doctor practices	2	30%	300	200	120	$460,000
3+ Doctor practices	4.6	40%	450	300	160	$800,000
Average primary care	**2.7**	**95%**	**412**	**265**	**140**	**$570,000**
Emergency care:						
Average emergency care	**4.0**	**5%**	**400**	**240**	**130**	**$770,000**

Source: Biopure company records.

Veterinary Blood Supply[4] Historically, the biggest constraint to veterinary transfusions was the lack of an adequate blood supply. In contrast to the human market, there existed few animal blood banks. As a result, the sole source of blood for most veterinary practices were donor animals which were housed at the practice for the express purpose of donating blood. When a dog or cat was in need of blood, blood was drawn from a donor dog or cat and then transfused into the animal in need. For primary care practices, donor animals provided 93 percent of all transfused blood, while blood banks provided the remaining 7 percent. In emergency practices, these proportions were 78 percent and 22 percent.

About 15 percent of veterinary practices found the "donor animal" system to be administratively or financially prohibitive and did not offer it as a service. Of the 85 percent of practices that did use a donor system, few had a good sense of its cost. In particular, few practices explicitly tracked the cost of housing the donor animal or the time required to draw the blood. As a proxy for these costs, practices typically looked to the price of a unit of blood from an animal blood bank. In 1995, that cost was $50 to $100. In turn, a typical primary care practice charged a pet owner $80 to $120 per unit and a typical emergency care practice charged a pet owner $130 to $170 per unit.

Finally, most practices that conducted transfusions lacked the time and resources to properly type both the donor and recipient blood. According to one estimate, only one-tenth of practices reported always typing the blood of both the donor and recipient animal. While complications due to incompatible blood types were not nearly as severe for dogs as they are for humans, this lack of blood typing and cross-matching was shown to prolong the recovery of a patient animal.

These factors resulted in many veterinarians viewing the transfusion of animal blood as the treatment of last resort, with 84 percent of veterinary doctors reporting overall dissatisfaction with the blood transfusion alternatives currently available in the marketplace.

HUMAN BLOOD SUBSTITUTES

Originally conceived as a vehicle to treat wounded soldiers in battlefield settings, the potential for a human blood substitute for nonmilitary use became increasingly apparent since the 1950s. This period saw a significant rise in auto accidents, the advent of open heart and organ transplant surgeries, and the AIDS crisis, which called into question the safety of the blood supply.

By 1998, several companies appeared to be on the verge of a viable blood substitute with a class of product called "hemoglobin-based blood substitutes." These products attempted to exploit the natural oxygen-carrying capabilities of hemoglobin while eliminating the limitations associated with donated RBCs. Each of these companies was attempting to (1) extract the hemoglobin found within human or animal RBCs, (2) purify that hemoglobin to eliminate infectious agents, and (3) modify the otherwise unstable free hemoglobin molecule to prevent it from breaking down. These purification and modification processes were nontrivial and represented the bulk of blood substitute research conducted over the past 20 years.

[4] Unlike the human market, transfusions in the animal market still tended to be "whole blood" transfusions.

Product Benefits

In theory, these hemoglobin-based blood substitutes eliminated many of the limitations associated with donated RBCs. In particular, they were:

- "Universal" blood substitutes, eliminating the need for blood typing and cross-matching.
- Free of infectious agents and contamination.
- Increased shelf life. These blood substitutes could be safely stored for up to 2 years.
- Immediately 100 percent efficient at transporting oxygen. Unlike whole RBCs, modified hemoglobin did not require a period of time to achieve peak oxygen-carrying efficiency.

In addition to these "anticipated" benefits, hemoglobin-based blood substitutes were displaying several "unanticipated" benefits which companies were only just beginning to investigate. In particular, given that hemoglobin molecules were significantly smaller than RBCs, they were able to flow to regions of the body that RBCs might not be able to reach. It was believed that this could lead to improved treatments in cases of stroke and heart attack—cases where RBCs often were slowed or restricted from reaching vital organs either due to artery blockages or decreased blood pressure.

Product Shortcomings At the same time, these "hemoglobin-based" blood substitutes did have some shortcomings, including:

- *A short half-life.* While donated RBCs remained in the body for up to two months after transfusion, these blood substitutes were excreted from the body within 2 to 7 days.
- *The potential for higher toxicity.* While the human body could tolerate the limitless and continuous replacement of one's blood with donated blood, the safety of these blood substitutes had been demonstrated only up to transfusion levels of 5 to 10 units.

In spite of these shortcomings, Dr. C. Everett Koop, the former Surgeon General of the United States, proclaimed:

> When the history of 20th-century medicine is written, the development of blood substitutes will be listed among the top ten advances in medicine. . . . [B]ecause of its purity, efficacy and convenience, this product class has the potential to revolutionize the practice of medicine, especially in critical-care situations. . . . [T]he next generation will not know how tough it was for those of us in medical practice before this technology became available.[5]

Others were less optimistic. One industry analyst presented a less attractive scenario for hemoglobin-based blood substitutes:

> . . . [W]e feel that there is no urgent need for blood substitutes since donated human blood is, for the most part, safe and effective. The expectation that blood substitutes will command vast markets and high price premiums is based on the assumptions that blood substitutes will prove safer and more effective than donated blood. While only time will tell if this is true, it will be an uphill battle given the widespread acceptance of donated blood.

---

[5] Biopure company Web site.

The FDA Approval Process

Human blood substitutes fell under the strict regulation of the U.S. government's Food and Drug Administration (FDA), which required that a product be proven safe and effective for medical use before being approved for commercial release (refer back to Exhibit 3). By early 1998, three companies had products that were in the final stages of this process. These products differed in their source of raw hemoglobin and in the process by which that hemoglobin was purified and modified. The FDA approval process was sensitive to these differences. Short of beginning the FDA approval process anew, each company was limited in its ability to substantially alter either the source of their hemoglobin or the process by which that hemoglobin was purified and modified. In addition, given that most of the companies had patented their purification and modification processes, there was little opportunity for a new entrant to quickly gain FDA approval.

Competitors for a Human Blood Substitute

As of 1998, Baxter International and Northfield Laboratories were the only other companies in late-stage development of a hemoglobin-based blood substitute. All other competitors were either several years behind in their development of a hemoglobin-based product or were pursuing a less promising technology.

In contrast to Biopure's use of cattle as its source of hemoglobin, both Baxter and Northfield relied on human blood as their source of hemoglobin. In particular, both companies had developed a technology to extract raw hemoglobin from "outdated" human RBCs (i.e., RBCs intended for transfusion, but which had been stored for more than 6 weeks). While their production processes and their pending FDA approval did not preclude them from using fresh RBCs, it was the stated intention of both companies to initially rely on outdated human RBCs. Through 1998, Baxter had an agreement with the American Red Cross to obtain outdated RBCs at a cost of $8 per unit. Until recently, Northfield had a similar $8 per unit agreement with Blood Centers of America, another national blood collection agency. However, in early 1997, Blood Centers of America raised its price to Northfield to $26 per unit for outdated RBCs.

In addition to their reliance on human blood, the products of Baxter and Northfield also differed from Biopure's in that they needed to be frozen or refrigerated until used. Biopure's Hemopure was shelf-stable at room temperature.

Baxter International With over $5.4 billion in sales and $670 million in net income in 1996, Baxter was an acknowledged leader in the development, manufacture, and sale of blood-related medical products, ranging from artificial heart valves to blood-collection equipment. In addition, Baxter had a long history of product breakthroughs, having developed the first sterile blood collection device in 1939, the first commercially available artificial kidney machine in 1956, and the first Factor VIII blood-clotting factor for the treatment of hemophilia in 1966.

"HemAssist," Baxter's patented blood substitute, was expected to add to this string of breakthroughs. Representing 30 years and $250 million in effort, HemAssist was the first human blood substitute to proceed to Phase 3 clinical trials in June 1996. Initially, these trials were expected to lead to full FDA approval by late 1998. However, in October 1997, Baxter revised its estimate to late 1999 or early 2000—an announcement that was followed by a 10 percent dip in Baxter's stock price.

Despite this delay, Baxter recently constructed a $100 million facility with a production capacity of 1 million units of HemAssist per year. Aside from its variable cost of source material, Baxter was expected to incur production costs of approximately $50 million per year, independent of production volume. While still just industry speculation, it was anticipated that Baxter would price HemAssist between $600 and $800 per unit.

Northfield Laboratories Northfield Laboratories of Illinois also had recently entered Phase 3 trials with a hemoglobin-based blood substitute. Northfield's product, "PolyHeme," was very similar to Baxter's HemAssist in its production and usage profile. Based on early positive results from its Phase 3 trials, Northfield anticipated full FDA approval in late 1999.

In contrast to Baxter, Northfield was a small, 45-person firm that was founded in 1985 for the sole purpose of developing a human blood substitute. As such, PolyHeme represented its only product. Analysts expected PolyHeme to be priced comparably to HemAssist upon release.

By early 1998, Northfield had spent $70 million in its development of PolyHeme and in the construction of a pilot production facility with an output capacity of 10,000 units per year. While this facility was sufficient to satisfy demand during clinical trials, Northfield management recognized the need for a full-scale production facility. With this in mind, they hoped to construct a $45 million facility with a capacity of 300,000 units per year. With this factory in place, aside from the cost of raw material, production costs were expected to be about $30 million per year, independent of production volume. By early 1998, selection of a factory site and plant construction had not yet begun.

■ ANIMAL BLOOD SUBSTITUTES

Through early 1998, Biopure was the only company that was actively engaged in the development of a blood substitute for the small-animal veterinary market. And while there was little to prevent Baxter or Northfield (or anyone else) from attempting to enter the veterinary market, any company wishing to do so would have to initiate an FDA-approval process specific to the veterinary market. By one estimate, assuming a company immediately began such a process, it would take two to five years to bring a product to market.

■ BIOPURE AND ITS BLOOD SUBSTITUTES

Hemopure and Oxyglobin were nearly identical in terms of physical characteristics and production processes. The only difference between the two products was in the size of the hemoglobin "clusters" that were contained in the final products. In the production of Oxyglobin, both large and small clusters of hemoglobin molecules were naturally formed. However, the small clusters tended to cause minor gastrointestinal problems and discoloration of urine. While considered acceptable in the animal market, these side effects were undesirable in the human market. As a result, Hemopure followed the same production process as used to make Oxyglobin, with a final step added to remove the small hemoglobin clusters.

Biopure had a single manufacturing facility, with an output capacity varying by the production mix of Oxyglobin and Hemopure. The same equipment was used to produce either product, but only one product could be produced at a time. This resulted in an annual capacity of 300,000 units of Oxyglobin or 150,000 units of Hemopure or some linear combination in between. The lower output for Hemopure reflected the facts that (1) the added step to remove the small hemoglobin clusters decreased the rate of production, and (2) the removal of the small hemoglobin clusters decreased yield.

To support these levels of output, aside from the cost of raw material, Biopure anticipated overall production costs of $15 million per year, independent of volume. For raw material, it anticipated a ready supply of bovine blood priced at $1.50 per unit. Biopure paid this money to cattle slaughterhouses to collect and transport the blood of cattle that were being processed for their meat—blood that otherwise would have been discarded. It was estimated that 10,000 cattle could supply enough raw material to support full production in Biopure's existing manufacturing facility.

Status of Hemopure

As of early 1998, Hemopure was in Phase 3 clinical trials in Europe, with FDA approval for Phase 3 trials in the United States appearing imminent. In anticipation of this approval, Biopure had established sites for Phase 3 trials and was ready to proceed immediately upon approval. While acknowledging the potential pitfalls of any clinical trials, Biopure was confident that the Phase 3 trials would be successful and that the FDA would grant full approval sometime in 1999. Biopure expected to commercially release Hemopure sometime in late 1999 or early 2000.

In line with the anticipated price of Baxter's HemAssist, Biopure planned to price Hemopure at $600 to $800 per unit. However, little systematic testing had been done by Biopure to determine the acceptability of these prices. In particular, little was known of the price sensitivity of medical personnel, insurance providers, or patients when it came to human blood substitutes.

Status of Oxyglobin

In 1997, Biopure established the Veterinary Products Division and hired Andy Wright to oversee the marketing and sale of Oxyglobin. Working under the assumption that Biopure would begin selling Oxyglobin immediately upon approval, Wright faced a host of decisions, including how to price and how to distribute Oxyglobin. Supporting him in these decisions was a team of seven employees—one director of marketing, one technical service representative (to answer technical questions and complaints), two customer service representatives (to support ordering and billing), and three sales representatives (to make sales calls and generate orders).

The Pricing of Oxyglobin Some members of Wright's sales team argued for Oxyglobin to be priced at $80 to $100 per unit. These team members pointed to the price sensitivity of the vet market, arguing that few pet owners carried health insurance on their animals. They also noted that the average cost of a visit to the vet was only about $60, with few procedures costing more than $100 (see Exhibit 8, page 657). Finally, they noted that vets tended to use a simple "doubling rule" when pricing a medical product to the pet owners, bringing the end-user price of Oxyglobin to $160 to $200 per unit.

Other members of Andy Wright's sales team felt that Oxyglobin should carry a premium price of up to $200 per unit, reflecting the many advantages of Oxyglobin relative to donated animal blood. These team members pointed out that while the average cost of a visit to a primary care practice might be only $60, the cost of a visit to an emergency care practice could easily run from $200 to over $1,000. They also questioned whether veterinary doctors would just blindly double the price of Oxyglobin without regard for its high dollar contribution. Finally, they noted that at a low price, Biopure could never hope to recoup the massive cost of product development.

To better understand the channel's willingness to pay for an animal blood substitute, Biopure conducted two surveys in 1997—one survey of 285 veterinarians and another of 200 dog owners. Exhibit 9 on page 657 offers results of the veterinarian survey and Exhibit 10 on page 658 offers results of the owner survey.

EXHIBIT 8

Small-Animal Veterinary Fees for Typical Procedures in Primary Care Practices in 1995

Procedure	*Average Fee*
Average Charge per Visit	**$58**
Office call—average minimum charge	$25
Boarding	$10
Hospitalization	$19
Anesthesia	$45
X-rays	$40
Blood transfusion	$100
Hysterectomy	$80
Heartworm treatment	$250
Annual vaccinations	$27
Rabies vaccination	$12
Lab tests—average	$23
Dental cleaning	$75
Deworming	$15

Source: *Veterinary Economics,* October 1996, p. 45.

In reviewing these surveys, Wright reminded himself that veterinarians often played the role of gatekeeper when it came to potential treatments, recommending less expensive over more expensive treatments in an effort to save their clients' money. At the same time, 90 percent of pet owners reported that they wanted to be made fully aware of all the alternatives available to treat their pets.

The Distribution of Oxyglobin Andy Wright also had to decide how best to sell and distribute Oxyglobin and how to educate veterinarians on its use. In approaching this question, he looked to the current distribution practices for medical products in the veterinary market.

In 1997, $1.2 billion worth of product was sold to veterinary practices through a network of 200 independent distributors—each of whom sold and distributed the products of many manufacturers. Two of these independent distributors were national in scope, 18 were regional (e.g., New England), and 180 were local (e.g., metropolitan Boston). Exhibit 11 on page 658 provides a sales and staffing profile for these distributors. A manufacturer might contract with one national distributor,

EXHIBIT 9

Veterinarians' Reported Willingness to Trial Oxyglobin

	Percentage of Veterinarians Who Would Trial Product	
Price to Veterinarian	*Noncritical Cases*	*Critical Cases*
$50 per unit	95%	100%
$100 per unit	70%	95%
$150 per unit	25%	80%
$200 per unit	5%	60%

Source: Biopure company records.

EXHIBIT 10

Pet Owners' Willingness to Trial Oxyglobin

Price to Pet Owner	*Percentage of Pet Owners Who Would Trial Product*	
	Noncritical Cases	*Critical Cases*
$100 per unit	60%	90%
$200 per unit	40%	85%
$300 per unit	35%	75%
$400 per unit	30%	65%

Source: Biopure company records.

several nonoverlapping regional distributors, and many nonoverlapping local distributors. In return for their selling and distribution efforts, a distributor would receive 20 percent of the manufacturer selling price on a more established product and 30 percent of the selling price on a less established or new product.

A veterinary practice could expect one 15-minute visit per week from the sales representatives of its primary distributor. These 15-minute visits would entail a focused discussion of current promotions on existing products and a more limited discussion of products new to the market. Typically, a sales rep might introduce 100 new products in a given year. To educate a particular distributor's sales reps on a new product, a manufacturer might set up a series of training sessions. These training sessions would be conducted for groups of about 10 sales representatives each and last anywhere from 1 to 4 hours, depending on the complexity of the new product.

Another $300 million worth of products were sold directly to veterinary practices through manufacturer salesforces. Termed "manufacturer direct," this type of distribution often was used by manufacturers with either high-volume, well-established products or products which required a very sophisticated sales pitch. If Biopure chose this route, in addition to the cost of maintaining a salesforce, Andy estimated the cost to physically distribute Oxyglobin to be $10 to $15 per unit.

Andy Wright also considered trade publications and trade shows as another means by which to educate veterinarians about the existence and benefits of Oxyglobin. A quick investigation revealed that five journals had almost universal coverage across veterinarians and tended to be well-read. In addition, six large veterinary trade shows held in the United States each year attracted 2,000 to 10,000 veterinarians each. Typically, these trade shows were taken seriously by attendees and were a valued source of information. Andy wondered if either of these avenues made sense for Biopure.

EXHIBIT 11

Profile of Independent Distributors of Veterinary Medicines

Type of Distributor	*Number*	*Percentage of Total Sales*	*Avg. Number of Sales Reps*
National	2	25%	100
Regional	18	60%	40
Local	180	15%	1.5

Source: Biopure company records.

■ BIOPURE'S DECISIONS

While Andy dealt with the question of how best to market Oxyglobin, Carl Rausch wrestled with the larger question of whether and when to launch Oxyglobin. Should he listen to Ted Jacobs and postpone the launch of Oxyglobin until *after* Hemopure had established itself in the marketplace? Or should he listen to Andy and immediately launch Oxyglobin and reap the near-term benefits?

Not lost on Carl was the potential impact of Oxyglobin on a possible initial public offering of Biopure stock. To this point, Biopure had remained a privately held firm with very little debt. And while it currently had no revenues, a recent round of capital venture financing had provided the firm with $50 million—enough money to support operations for another two years. Nevertheless, many stakeholders in Biopure were anxious to take the company public. In this regard, Carl wondered whether a veterinary product with small but steady sales might not prove more attractive to investors than a human product still under development. He was especially sensitive to this issue in light of some recent, high-profile product failures in the Massachusetts biotechnology community.

With all of this in mind, as president and CEO of Biopure, Carl Rausch pondered how best to leverage the opportunity offered by Oxyglobin without jeopardizing the potential of Hemopure.

CASE

Cima Mountaineering, Inc.

"What a great hike," exclaimed Anthony Simon as he tossed his Summit HX 350 hiking boots into his car. He had just finished hiking the challenging Cascade Canyon Trail in the Tetons north of Jackson, Wyoming. Anthony hiked often because it was a great way to test the hiking boots made by Cima Mountaineering, Inc., the business he inherited from his parents and owned with his sister, Margaret. As he drove back to Jackson, he began thinking about next week's meeting with Margaret, the President of Cima. During the past month they had been discussing marketing strategies for increasing the sales and profits of the company. No decisions had been made, but the preferences of each owner were becoming clear.

As illustrated in Table 1, sales and profits had grown steadily for Cima and by most measures the company was successful. However, growth was beginning to slow as a result of foreign competition and a changing market. Margaret observed that the market had shifted to a more casual, stylish hiking boot that appealed to hikers interested in a boot for a variety of uses. She favored a strategy of diversifying the company by marketing a new line of boots for the less experienced, weekend hiker. Anthony also recognized that the market had changed, but he supported expanding the existing lines of boots for mountaineers and hikers. The company had been successful with these boots, and Anthony had some ideas about how to extend the lines and expand distribution. "This is a better way to grow," he thought. "I'm concerned about the risk in Margaret's recommendation. If we move to a more casual boot, then we have to resolve a new set of marketing and competitive issues and finance a new line. I'm not sure we can do it."

When he returned to Jackson that evening, Anthony stopped by his office to check his messages. The financial statements shown in Table 2 and in Table 3 (page 662) were on his desk along with a marketing study from a Denver consulting firm. Harris Fleming, Vice President of Marketing, had commissioned a study of the hiking boot market several months earlier to help the company plan for the future. As Anthony paged

Table 1
Cima Mountaineering, Inc. Revenues and Net Income, 1990–1995

Year	*Revenues*	*Net Income*	*Profit Margin (%)*
1995	$20,091,450	$857,134	4.27
1994	18,738,529	809,505	4.32
1993	17,281,683	838,162	4.85
1992	15,614,803	776,056	4.97
1991	14,221,132	602,976	4.24
1990	13,034,562	522,606	4.01

Lawrence M. Lamont is Professor of Management at Washington and Lee University. Eva Cid and Wade Drew Hammond were seniors in the class of 1995 at Washington and Lee, majoring in Management and Accounting, respectively.

Table 2
Cima Mountaineering, Inc. Income Statement (Years Ended December 31, 1995 and December 31, 1994)

	1995	*1994*
Net sales	$20,091,450	$18,738,529
Cost of goods sold	14,381,460	13,426,156
Gross margin	5,709,990	5,312,373
Selling and admin. expenses	4,285,730	3,973,419
Operating income	1,424,260	1,338,954
Other income (expenses)		
Interest expense	(160,733)	(131,170)
Interest income	35,161	18,739
Total other income (net)	(125,572)	(112,431)
Earnings before income taxes	1,298,688	1,226,523
Income taxes	441,554	417,018
Net income	$ 857,134	$ 809,505

through the report, two figures caught his eye. One was a segmentation of the hiking boot market (see Exhibit 1 on page 663) and the other was a summary of market competition (see Exhibit 2 on page 664). "This is interesting," he mused. "I hope Margaret reads it before our meeting."

HISTORY OF CIMA MOUNTAINEERING

As children, Anthony and Margaret Simon watched their parents make western boots at the Hoback Boot Company, a small business they owned in Jackson, Wyoming. They learned the craft as they grew up and joined the company after college.

In the late 1960s, the demand for western boots began to decline and the Hoback Boot Company struggled to survive. By 1975, the parents were close to retirement and they seemed content to close the business, but Margaret and Anthony decided to try to salvage the company. Margaret, the older, became president and Anthony became the executive vice president. By the end of 1976, sales had declined to $1.5 million and the company earned profits of only $45,000. It became clear that to survive, the business would have to be refocused on products with a more promising future.

Refocusing the Business

As a college student, Anthony attended a mountaineering school north of Jackson in Teton National Park. As he learned to climb and hike, he became aware of the growing popularity of the sport and the boots being used. Because of his experience with western boots, he also noticed their limitations. Although the boots had good traction, they were heavy, uncomfortable, and had little resistance to the snow and water always present in the mountains. He convinced Margaret that Hoback should explore the possibility of developing boots for mountaineering and hiking.

In 1977, Anthony and Margaret began 12 months of marketing research. They investigated the market, the competition, and the extent to which Hoback's existing equipment could be used to produce the new boots. By the summer of 1978, Hoback had developed a mountaineering and a hiking boot that were ready for testing. Several instructors from the mountaineering school tested the boots and gave them excellent reviews.

Table 3
Cima Mountaineering, Inc. Balance Sheet (Years Ending December 31, 1995 and December 31, 1994)

	1995	*1994*
Assets		
Current assets		
Cash and equivalents	$1,571,441	$1,228,296
Accounts receivable	4,696,260	3,976,608
Inventory	6,195,450	5,327,733
Other	270,938	276,367
Total	12,734,089	10,809,004
Fixed assets		
Property, plant and equipment	3,899,568	2,961,667
Less: accumulated depreciation	(1,117,937)	(858,210)
Total fixed assets (net)	2,781,631	2,103,457
Other assets		
Intangibles	379,313	568,087
Other long-term assets	2,167,504	1,873,151
Total fixed assets (net)	$18,062,537	$15,353,699
Liabilities and shareholder equity		
Current liabilities:		
Accounts payable	$4,280,821	$4,097,595
Notes payable	1,083,752	951,929
Current maturities of long-term debt	496,720	303,236
Accrued liabilities		
Expenses	2,754,537	2,360,631
Salaries and wages	1,408,878	1,259,003
Other	1,137,940	991,235
Total current liabilities	11,162,648	9,963,629
Long-term liabilities		
Long-term debt	3,070,631	2,303,055
Lease obligations	90,313	31,629
Total long-term liabilities	3,702,820	2,334,684
Other liabilities		
Deferred taxes	36,125	92,122
Other noncurrent liabilities	312,326	429,904
Total liabilities	14,672,043	12,820,339
Owner's equity		
Retained earnings	3,390,494	2,533,360
Total liabilities and owner's equity	$18,062,537	$15,353,699

The Transition

By 1981, Hoback was ready to enter the market with two styles of boots: one for the mountaineer who wanted a boot for all-weather climbing, and the other for men and women who were advanced hikers. Both styles were made of water-repellent leather uppers and cleated soles for superior traction. Distribution was secured through mountaineering shops in Wyoming and Colorado.

Hoback continued to manufacture western boots for its loyal customers, but Margaret planned to phase them out as the hiking boot business developed. How-

EXHIBIT 1

Segmentation of the Hiking Boot Market

	Mountaineers	***Serious Hikers***	***Weekenders***	***Practical Users***	***Children***	***Fashion Seekers***
Benefits	Durability/Ruggedness Stability/Support Dryness/Warmth Grip/Traction	Stability Durability Traction Comfort/Protection	Lightweight Comfort Durability Versatility	Lightweight Durability Good value Versatility	Durability Protection Lightweight Traction	Fashion/Style Appearance Lightweight Inexpensive
Demographics	Young Primarily male Shops in specialty stores and specialized catalogs	Young, middle aged Male and female Shops in specialty stores and outdoor catalogs	Young, middle aged Male and female Shops in shoe retailers, sporting goods stores, and mail-order catalogs	Young, middle aged Primarily male Shops in shoe retailers and department stores	Young marrieds Male and female Shops in department stores and outdoor catalogs	Young Male and female Shops in shoe retailers, department stores and catalogs
Lifestyle	Adventuresome Independent Risk taker Enjoys challenge	Nature lover Outdoorsman Sportsman Backpacker	Recreational hiker Social, spends time with family and friends Enjoys the outdoors	Practical Sociable Outdoors for work and recreation	Enjoys family activities Enjoys outdoors and hiking Children are active and play outdoors Parents are value conscious	Materialistic Trendy Socially conscious Nonhikers Brand name shoppers Price conscious
Examples of brands	Asolo Cliff Raichle Mt. Blanc Salomon Adventure 9	Raichle Explorer Vasque Clarion Tecnica Pegasus Dry Hi-Tec Piramide	Reebok R-Evolution Timberland Topozoic Merrell Acadia Nike Air Mada, Zion Vasque Alpha	Merrell Eagle Nike Air Khyber Tecnica Volcano	Vasque Kids Klimber Nike Merrell Caribou	Nike Espirit Reebok Telos Hi-Tec Magnum
Estimated market share	5% Slow growth	17% Moderate growth	25% High growth	20% Stable growth	5% Slow growth	28% At peak of rapid growth cycle
Price range	\$210–\$450	\$120–\$215	\$70–\$125	\$40–\$80	Will pay up to \$40	\$65–\$100

EXHIBIT 2

Summary of Competitors

Company	*Location*	*Mountaineering (Styles)*	*Hiking (Styles)*	*Men's*	*Women's*	*Children's*	*Price Range*
Raichle	Switzerland	Yes (7)	Yes (16)	Yes	Yes	Yes	High
Salomon	France	Yes (1)	Yes (9)	Yes	Yes	No	Mid
Asolo	Italy	Yes (4)	Yes (26)	Yes	Yes	No	High
Tecnica	Italy	Yes (3)	Yes (9)	Yes	Yes	No	Mid/High
Hi-Tec	U.K.	Yes (2)	Yes (29)	Yes	Yes	Yes	Mid/Low
Vasque	Minnesota	Yes (4)	Yes (18)	Yes	Yes	Yes	Mid/High
Merrell	Vermont	Yes (5)	Yes (31)	Yes	Yes	Yes	Mid
Timberland	New Hampshire	No	Yes (4)	Yes	No	No	Mid
Nike	Oregon	No	Yes (5)	Yes	Yes	Yes	Low
Reebok	Massachusetts	No	Yes (3)	Yes	Yes	Yes	Low
Cima	Wyoming	Yes (3)	Yes (5)	Yes	Yes	No	High

Source: Published literature and company product brochures, 1995.

ever, because they did not completely understand the needs of the market, they hired Harris Fleming, a mountaineering instructor to help them with product design and marketing.

A New Company

During the 1980s, Hoback prospered as the market expanded along with the popularity of outdoor recreation. The company slowly increased its product line and achieved success by focusing on classic boots that were relatively insensitive to fashion trends. By 1986, sales of Hoback Boots had reached $3.5 million.

Over the next several years, distribution was steadily expanded. In 1987, Hoback employed independent sales representatives to handle the sales and service. Before long, Hoback boots were sold throughout Wyoming, Colorado, and Montana by retailers specializing in mountaineering and hiking equipment. Margaret decided to discontinue western boots to make room for the growing hiking boot business. To reflect the new direction of the company, the name was changed to Cima Mountaineering, Inc.

Cima Boots "Take Off"

The late 1980s were a period of exceptional growth. Demand for Cima boots grew quickly as consumers caught the trend toward healthy, active lifestyles. The company expanded its line for advanced hikers and improved the performance of its boots. By 1990, sales had reached $13 million and the company earned profits of $522,606. Margaret was satisfied with the growth, but she was concerned about low profitability as a result of foreign competition. She challenged the company to find new ways to design and manufacture boots at lower cost.

Growth and Innovation

The next five years were marked by growth, innovation, and increasing foreign and domestic competition. Market growth continued as hiking boots became popular for casual wear in addition to hiking in mountains and on trails. Cima and its competitors began to make boots with molded footbeds and utilize materials that reduced weight.[1] Fashion also became a factor, and companies like Nike and Reebok marketed lightweight boots in a variety of materials and colors to meet the demand for styling in addition to performance. Cima implemented a computer-aided design (CAD) system in 1993 to shorten product development and devote more attention to design. Late in 1994, Cima restructured its facilities and implemented a modular approach to manufacturing. The company switched from a production line to a system in which a work team applied multiple processes to each pair of boots. Significant cost savings were achieved as the new approach improved the profit and quality of the company's boots.

The Situation in 1995

As the company ended 1995, sales had grown to $20.0 million, up 7.2 percent from the previous year. Employment was at 425, and the facility was operating at 85 percent of capacity, producing several styles of mountaineering and hiking boots. Timesaving innovations and cost reduction had also worked, and profits reached an all-time high. Margaret, now 57, was still president, and Anthony remained executive vice president.

■ CIMA MARKETING STRATEGY

According to estimates, 1994 was a record year for sales of hiking and mountaineering boots in the United States. Retail sales exceeded $600 million, and about 15 million pairs of boots were sold. Consumers wore the boots for activities ranging from mountaineering to casual social events. In recent years, changes were beginning to occur in the market. Inexpensive, lightweight hiking boots were becoming increasingly popular for day hikes and trail walking and a new category of comfortable, light "trekking" shoes were being marketed by the manufacturers of athletic shoes.

Only a part of the market was targeted by Cima. Most of its customers were serious outdoor enthusiasts. They included mountaineers who climbed in rugged terrain and advanced hikers who used the boots on challenging trails and extended backpacking trips. The demand for Cima boots was seasonal, and most of the purchases were made during the summer months when the mountains and trails were most accessible.

Positioning

Cima boots were positioned as the best available for their intended purpose. Consumers saw them as durable and comfortable with exceptional performance. Retailers viewed the company as quick to adopt innovative construction techniques but conservative in styling. Cima intentionally used traditional styling to avoid fashion obsolescence and the need for frequent design changes. Some of the most popular styles had been in the market for several years without any significant modifications. The Glacier MX 350 shown in Exhibit 3 on page 666 and the Summit HX 350 boot shown in Exhibit 4, also on page 666, are good examples. The MX 350, priced at $219.00, was positioned as a classic boot for men with a unique tread design for be-

[1] Two processes are used to attach the uppers to the soles of boots. In classic welt construction, the uppers and soles are stitched. In the more contemporary method, a molded polyurethane footbed (including a one-piece heel and sole) is cemented to the upper with a waterproof adhesive. Many mountaineering boots use classic welt construction because it provides outstanding stability, while the contemporary method is often used with hiking boots to achieve lightweight construction. Cima used the classic method of construction for mountaineering boots and the contemporary method for hiking boots.

EXHIBIT 3

The Glacier MX 350 Mountaineering Boot

ginning mountaineers. The Summit HX 350 was priced at $159.00 and was a boot for men and women hiking rough trails. Exhibit 5 describes the items in the mountaineering and hiking boot lines, and Table 4 provides a sales history for Cima boots.

Product Lines

Corporate branding was used and "Cima" was embossed into the leather on the side of the boot to enhance consumer recognition. Product lines were also branded, and

EXHIBIT 4

The Summit HX 350 Hiking Boot

EXHIBIT 5

Cima Mountaineering, Inc. Mountaineering and Hiking Boot Lines

Product Line	***Description***
Glacier	
MX 550	For expert mountaineers climbing challenging mountains. Made for use on rocks, ice, and snow. Features welt construction, superior stability and support, reinforced heel and toe, padded ankle and tongue, step-in crampon insert, thermal insulation, and waterproof inner liner. Retails for $299.
MX 450	For proficient mountaineers engaging in rigorous, high-altitude hiking. Offers long-term comfort and stability on rough terrain. Features welt construction, deep cleated soles and heels, reinforced heel and toe, padded ankle and tongue, step-in crampon insert, and waterproof inner liner. Retails for $249.
MX 350	For beginning mountaineers climbing in moderate terrain and temperate climates. Features welt construction, unique tread design for traction, padded ankle and tongue, good stability and support, and a quick-dry lining. Retails for $219.
Summit	
HX 550	For experienced hikers who require uncompromising performance. Features nylon shank for stability and rigidity, waterproof inner liner, cushioned midsole, high-traction outsole, and padded ankle and tongue. Retails for $197.
HX 450	For backpackers who carry heavy loads on extended trips. Features thermal insulation, cushioned midsole, waterproof inner liner, excellent foot protection, and high-traction outsole. Retails for $179.
HX 350	For hikers who travel rough trails and a variety of backcountry terrain. Features extra cushioning, good stability and support, waterproof inner liner, and high-traction outsole for good grip in muddy and sloping surfaces. Retails for $159.
HX 250	For hikers who hike developed trails. Made with only the necessary technical features, including cushioning, foot and ankle support, waterproof inner liner, and high-traction outsole. Retails for $139.
HX 150	For individuals taking more than day and weekend hikes. Versatile boot for all kinds of excursions. Features cushioning, good support, waterproof inner liner, and high-traction outsoles for use on a variety of surfaces. Retails for $129.

alphabetic letters and numbers were used to differentiate items in the line. Each line had different styles and features to cover many of the important uses in the market. However, all boots had features that the company believed were essential to positioning. Standard features included water-repellent leather uppers and high-traction soles and heels. The hardware for the boots was plated steel, and the laces were tough, durable nylon. Quality was emphasized throughout the product lines.

Table 4
Cima Mountaineering, Inc. Product Line Sales

	Unit Sales (%)		***Sales Revenue (%)***	
Year	*Mountaineering*	*Hiking*	*Mountaineering*	*Hiking*
1995	15.00	85.00	21.74	78.26
1994	15.90	84.10	22.93	77.07
1993	17.20	82.80	24.64	75.36
1992	18.00	82.00	25.68	74.32
1991	18.80	81.20	26.71	73.29
1990	19.70	80.30	27.86	72.14

Glacier Boots for Mountaineering

The Glacier line featured three boots for men. The MX 550 was designed for expert all-weather climbers looking for the ultimate in traction, protection, and warmth. The MX 450 was for experienced climbers taking extended excursions, while the MX 350 met the needs of less-skilled individuals beginning climbing in moderate terrain and climates.

Summit Boots for Hiking

The Summit line featured five styles for men and women. The HX 550 was preferred by experienced hikers who demanded the best possible performance. The boot featured water-repellent leather uppers, a waterproof inner liner, a cushioned midsole, a nylon shank for rigidity, and a sole designed for high traction. It was available in gray and brown with different types of leather.[2] The Summit HX 150 was the least expensive boot in the line, designed for individuals who were beginning to hike more than the occasional "weekend hike." It was a versatile boot for all kinds of excursions and featured a water-repellent leather upper, a cushioned midsole, and excellent traction. The HX 150 was popular as an entry-level boot for outdoor enthusiasts.

Distribution

Cima boots were distributed in Arizona, California, Colorado, Idaho, Montana, Nevada, New Mexico, Oregon, Washington, Wyoming, and western Canada through specialty retailers selling mountaineering, backpacking, and hiking equipment. Occasionally, Cima was approached by mail-order catalog companies and chain sporting goods stores offering to sell their boots. The company considered the proposals, but had not used these channels.

Promotion

The Cima sales and marketing office was located in Jackson. It was managed by Harris Fleming and staffed with several marketing personnel. Promotion was an important aspect of the marketing strategy, and advertising, personal selling, and sales promotion were used to gain exposure for Cima branded boots. Promotion was directed to consumers and to the retailers that stocked Cima mountaineering and hiking boots.

Personal Selling

Cima used 10 independent sales representatives to sell its boots in the western states and Canada. Representatives did not sell competing boots, but they sold complementary products such as outdoor apparel and equipment for mountaineering, hiking, and backpacking. They were paid a commission and handled customer service in addition to sales. Management was also involved in personal selling. Harris Fleming trained the independent sales representatives and often accompanied them on sales calls.

---

[2] Different types of leather are used to make hiking boots. *Full Grain*: High-quality, durable, upper layer of the hide. It has a natural finish, and is strong and breatheable. *Split Grain*: Underside of the hide after the full-grain leather has been removed from the top. Lightweight and comfort are the primary characteristics. *Suede*: A very fine split-grain leather. *Nubuk*: Brushed full-grain leather. *Waxed*: A process in which leather is coated with wax to help shed water. Most Cima boots were available in two or more types of leather.

Mountaineering and hiking boots are made water repellent by treating the uppers with wax or chemical coatings. To make the boots waterproof, a fabric inner liner is built into the boot to provide waterproof protection and breatheability. All Cima boots were water repellent, but only those styles with an inner liner were waterproof.

Advertising and Sales Promotion

Advertising and sales promotion were also important promotional methods. Print advertising was used to increase brand awareness and assist retailers with promotion. Advertising was placed in leading magazines such as *Summit*, *Outside*, and *Backpacker* to reach mountaineers and hikers with the message that Cima boots were functional and durable with classic styling. In addition, cooperative advertising was offered to encourage retailers to advertise Cima boots and identify their locations.

Sales promotion was an important part of the promotion program. Along with the focus on brand name recognition, Cima provided product literature and point-of-sale display materials to assist retailers in promoting the boots. In addition, the company regularly exhibited at industry trade shows. The exhibits, staffed by marketing personnel and the company's independent sales representatives, were effective for maintaining relationships with retailers and presenting the company's products.

Pricing

Cima selling prices to retailers ranged from $64.50 to $149.50 a pair depending on the style. Mountaineering boots were more expensive because of their construction and features, while hiking boots were priced lower. Retailers were encouraged to take a 50 percent margin on the retail selling price, so retail prices shown in Exhibit 5 should be divided by two to get the Cima selling price. Cima priced its boots higher than competitors, supporting the positioning of the boots as the top quality product at each price point. Payment terms were net 30 days (similar to competitors), and boots were shipped to retailers from a warehouse located in Jackson, Wyoming.

■ SEGMENTATION OF THE HIKING BOOT MARKET

As Anthony reviewed the marketing study commissioned by Harris Fleming, his attention focused on the market segmentation shown in Exhibit 1. It was interesting, because management had never seriously thought about the segmentation in the market. Of course, Anthony was aware that not everyone was a potential customer for Cima boots, but he was surprised to see how well the product lines met the needs of mountaineers and serious hikers. As he reviewed the market segmentation, he read the descriptions for mountaineers, serious hikers, and weekenders carefully because Cima was trying to decide which of these segments to target for expansion.

Mountaineers

Mountain climbers and high-altitude hikers are in this segment. They are serious about climbing and enjoy risk and adventure. Because mountaineers' safety may often depend on their boots, they need maximum stability and support, traction for a variety of climbing conditions, and protection from wet and cold weather.

Serious Hikers

Outdoorsmen, who love nature and have a strong interest in health and fitness, comprise the serious hikers. They hike rough trails and take extended backpacking or hiking excursions. Serious hikers are brand conscious and look for durable, high-performance boots with good support, comfortable fit, and good traction.

Weekenders

Consumers in this segment are recreational hikers who enjoy casual weekend and day hikes with family and friends. They are interested in light, comfortable boots that provide good fit, protection, and traction on a variety of surfaces. Weekenders prefer versatile boots that can be worn for a variety of activities.

■ FOREIGN AND DOMESTIC COMPETITION

The second part of the marketing study that caught Anthony's attention was the analysis of competition. Although Anthony and Margaret were aware that competition had increased, they had overlooked the extent to which foreign bootmakers had entered the market. Apparently, foreign competitors had noticed the market growth and they were aggressively exporting their boots into the United States. They had established sales offices and independent sales agents to compete for the customers served by Cima. The leading foreign brands such as Asolo, Hi-Tec, Salomon, and Raichle were marketed on performance and reputation, usually to the mountaineering, serious hiker, and weekender segments of the market.

The study also summarized the most important domestic competitors. Vasque and Merrell marketed boots that competed with Cima, but others were offering products for segments of the market where the prospects for growth were better. As Anthony examined Exhibit 2, he realized that the entry of Reebok and Nike into the hiking boot market was quite logical. They had entered the market as consumer preference shifted from wearing athletic shoes for casual outdoor activities to a more rugged shoe. Each was marketing footwear that combined the appearance and durability of hiking boots with the lightness and fit of athletic shoes. The result was a line of fashionable hiking boots that appealed to brand- and style-conscious teens and young adults. Both firms were expanding their product lines and moving into segments of the market that demanded lower levels of performance.

■ MARGARET AND ANTHONY DISCUSS MARKETING STRATEGY

A few days after hiking in Cascade Canyon, Anthony met with Margaret and Harris Fleming to discuss marketing strategy. Each had read the consultant's report and studied the market segmentation and competitive summary. As the meeting opened, the conversation developed as follows:

MARGARET: It looks like we will have another record year. The economy is growing, and consumers seem confident and eager to buy. Yet, I'm concerned about the future. The foreign bootmakers are providing some stiff competition. Their boots have outstanding performance and attractive prices. The improvements we made in manufacturing helped to control costs and maintain margins, but it looks like the competition and slow growth in our markets will make it difficult to improve profits. We need to be thinking about new opportunities.

HARRIS: I agree, Margaret. Just this past week we lost Rocky Mountain Sports in Boulder, Colorado. John Kline, the sales manager, decided to drop us and pick up Asolo. We were doing $70,000 a year with them and they carried our entire line. We also lost Great Western Outfitters in Colorado Springs. They replaced us with Merrell. The sales manager said that the college students there had been asking for the lower-priced Merrell boots. They bought $60,000 last year.

ANTHONY: Rocky Mountain and Great Western were good customers. I guess I'm not surprised though. Our Glacier line needs another boot, and the Summit line is just not deep enough to cover the price points. We need to have some styles at lower prices to compete with Merrell and Asolo. I'm in favor of extending our existing lines to broaden their market appeal. It seems to me that the best way to compete is to stick with what we do best, making boots for mountaineers and serious hikers.

MARGARET: Not so fast, Anthony. The problem is that our markets are small and not growing fast enough to support the foreign competitors who have entered with excellent products. We can probably hold our own, but I doubt if we can do much better. I think the future of this company is to move with the market. Consumers are demanding more style, lower prices, and a lightweight hiking boot that can be worn for a variety of uses. Look at the segmentation again. The "Weekender" segment is large and it's growing. That's where we need to go with some stylish new boots that depart from our classic leather lines.

ANTHONY: Maybe so, but we don't have much experience working with the leather and nylon combinations that are being used in these lighter boots. Besides, I'm not sure we can finance the product development and marketing for a new market that already has plenty of competition. And I'm concerned about the brand image that we have worked so hard to establish over the past 20 years. A line of inexpensive, casual boots just doesn't seem to fit with the perception consumers have of our products.

HARRIS: I can see advantages to each strategy. I do know that we don't have the time and resources to do both, so we had better make a thoughtful choice. Also, I think we should reconsider selling to the mail-order catalog companies that specialize in mountaineering and hiking equipment. Last week, I received another call from REI requesting us to sell them some of the boots in our Summit line for the 1997 season. This might be a good source of revenue and a way of expanding our geographic market.

MARGARET: You're right, Harris. We need to rethink our position on the mail-order companies. Most of them have good market penetration in the East where we don't have distribution. I noticed that Gander Mountain is carrying some of the Timberland line and that L.L. Bean is carrying some Vasque styles along with its own line of branded boots.

ANTHONY: I agree. Why don't we each put together a proposal that summarizes our recommendations and then we can get back together to continue the discussion.

HARRIS: Good idea. Eventually we will need a sales forecast and some cost data. Send me your proposals and I'll call the consulting firm and have them prepare some forecasts. I think we already have some cost information. Give me a few days and then we can get together again.

THE MEETING TO REVIEW THE PROPOSALS

The following week, the discussion continued. Margaret presented her proposal, which is summarized in Exhibit 6 on page 672. She proposed moving Cima into the "Weekender" segment by marketing two new hiking boots. Anthony countered with the proposal summarized in Exhibit 7 on pages 673 and 674. He favored extending the existing lines by adding a new mountaineering boot and two new Summit hiking boots at lower price points. Harris presented sales forecasts for each proposal and after some discussion and modification, they were finalized as shown in Table 5 on page 674. Cost information was gathered by Harris from the Vice President of Manufacturing and is presented in Table 6 on page 675. Following a lengthy discussion, in which Margaret and Anthony were unable to agree on a course of action, Harris Fleming suggested that each proposal be explored further by conducting marketing research. He proposed the formation of teams from the Cima marketing staff to research each proposal and present it to Margaret and Anthony at a later date. Harris presented his directions to the teams in the memorandum shown in Exhibit 8 on pages 675 through 677. The discussion between Margaret and Anthony continued as follows:

EXHIBIT 6

Margaret's Marketing Proposal

MEMORANDUM

TO: Anthony Simon, Executive Vice President
Harris Fleming, Vice President of Marketing

FROM: Margaret Simon, President

RE: Marketing Proposal

I believe we have an excellent opportunity to expand the sales and profits of Cima by entering the "Weekender" segment of the hiking boot market. The segment's estimated share of the market is 25 percent and according to the consultant's report it is growing quite rapidly. I propose that we begin immediately to develop two new products and prepare a marketing strategy as discussed below.

Target Market and Positioning

Male and female recreational hikers looking for a comfortable, lightweight boot that is attractively priced and acceptable for short hikes and casual wear. Weekenders enjoy the outdoors and a day or weekend hike with family and friends.

The new boots would be positioned with magazine advertising as hiking boots that deliver performance and style for the demands of light hiking and casual outdoor wear.

Product

Two boots in men's and women's sizes. The boots would be constructed of leather and nylon uppers with a molded rubber outsole. A new branded line would be created to meet the needs of the market segment. The boots (designated WX 550 and WX 450) would have the following features:

	WX 550	*WX 450*
Leather and nylon uppers	X	X
Molded rubber outsole	X	X
Cushioned midsole	X	X
Padded collar and tongue	X	X
Durable hardware and laces	X	X
Waterproof inner liner	X	

Uppers: To be designed. Options include brown full-grain, split-grain, or suede leather combined with durable nylon in two of the following colors: beige, black, blue, gray, green, and slate.

Boot design and brand name: To be decided.

Retail Outlets

Specialty shoe retailers carrying hiking boots and casual shoes and sporting goods stores. Eventually mail order catalogs carrying outdoor apparel and hiking, backpacking, and camping equipment.

Promotion

Independent sales representatives
Magazine advertising
Co-op advertising
Point-of-sale display materials
Product brochures
Trade shows

Suggested Retail Pricing

WX 550: $89.00

WX 450: $69.00

Competitors

Timberland, Hi-Tec, Vasque, Merrell, Asolo, Nike, and Reebok.

Product Development and Required Investment

We should allow about one year for the necessary product development and testing. I estimate these costs to be $350,000. Additionally, we will need to make a capital expenditure of $150,000 for new equipment.

EXHIBIT 7

Anthony's Marketing Proposal

MEMORANDUM

TO: Margaret Simon, President
Harris Fleming, Vice President of Marketing

FROM: Anthony Simon, Executive Vice President

RE: Marketing Proposal

We have been successful with boots for mountaineers and serious hikers for years, and this is where our strengths seem to be. I recommend extending our Glacier and Summit lines instead of venturing into a new, unfamiliar market. My recommendations are summarized below:

Product Development

Introduce two new boots in the Summit line (designated HX 100 and HX 50) and market the Glacier MX 350 in a style for women with the same features as the boot for men. The new women's Glacier boot would have a suggested retail price of $219.99, while the suggested retail prices for the HX 100 and the HX 50 would be $119.00 and $89.00 respectively to provide price points at the low end of the line. The new Summit boots for men and women would be the first in the line to have leather and nylon uppers as well as the following features:

	HX 100	***HX 50***
Leather and nylon uppers	X	X
Molded rubber outsole	X	X
Cushioned midsole	X	X
Padded collar and tongue	X	X
Quick-dry lining	X	X
Waterproof inner liner	X	

The leather used in the uppers will have to be determined. We should consider full-grain, suede and nubuck since they are all popular with users in this segment. We need to select one for the initial introduction. The nylon fabric for the uppers should be available in two colors, selected from among the following: beige, brown, green, slate, maroon, and navy blue. Additional colors can be offered as sales develop and we gain a better understanding of consumer preferences.

Product Development and Required Investment

Product design and development costs of $400,000 for the MX 350, HX 100 and HX 50 styles and a capital investment of $150,000 to acquire equipment to cut and stitch the nylon/leather uppers. One year will be needed for product development and testing.

Positioning

The additions to the Summit line will be positioned as boots for serious hikers who want a quality hiking boot at a reasonable price. The boots will also be attractive to casual hikers who are looking to move up to a better boot as they gain experience in hiking and outdoor activity.

Retail Outlets

We can use our existing retail outlets. Additionally, the lower price points on the new styles will make these boots attractive to catalog shoppers. I recommend that we consider making the Summit boots available to consumers through mail order catalog companies.

Promotion

We will need to revise our product brochures and develop new advertising for the additions to the Summit line. The balance of the promotion program should remain as it exists since it is working quite well. I believe the sales representatives and retailers selling our lines will welcome the new boots since they broaden the consumer appeal of our lines.

EXHIBIT 7 *(continued)*

Suggested Retail Pricing

MX 350 for women:	$219.00
HX 100:	$119.00
HX 50:	$89.00

Competitors

Asolo, Hi-Tec, Merrell, Raichle, Salomon, Tecnica, Vasque

MARGARET: Once the marketing research is completed and we can read the reports and listen to the presentations, we should have a better idea of which strategy makes the best sense. Hopefully, a clear direction will emerge and we can move ahead with one of the proposals. In either case, I'm still intrigued with the possibility of moving into the mail order catalogs, since we really haven't developed these companies as customers. I just wish we knew how much business we could expect from them.

ANTHONY: We should seriously consider them, Margaret. Companies like L.L. Bean, Gander Mountain, and REI have been carrying a selection of hiking boots for several years. However, there may be a problem for us. Eventually the catalog companies expect their boot suppliers to make them a private brand. I'm not sure this is something we want to do since we built the company on a strategy of marketing our own brands that are made in the U.S.A. Also, I'm concerned about the reaction of our retailers when they discover we are selling to the catalog companies. It could create some problems.

HARRIS: That is a strategy issue we will have to address. However, I'm not even sure what percentage of sales the typical footwear company makes through the mail-order catalogs. If we were to solicit the catalog business, we would need an answer to this question to avoid exceeding our capacity. In the proposals, I asked

Table 5
Cima Mountaineering, Inc. Sales Forecasts for Proposed New Products (Pairs of Boots)

	Project 1		*Project 2*		
Year	*WX 550*	*WX 450*	*MX 350*	*HX 100*	*HX 50*
2001–02	16,420	24,590	2,249	15,420	12,897
2000–01	14,104	21,115	1,778	13,285	11,733
1999–00	8,420	12,605	897	10,078	9,169
1998–99	5,590	8,430	538	5,470	5,049
1997–98	4,050	6,160	414	4,049	3,813

Note: Sales forecasts are expected values derived from minimum and maximum estimates.

Some cannibalization of existing boots will occur when the new styles are introduced. The sales forecasts provided above have taken into account the impact of sales losses on existing boots. No additional adjustments need to be made.

Forecasts for WX 550, WX 450, HX 100, and HX 50 include sales of both men's and women's boots.

Table 6
Cima Mountaineering, Inc. Cost Information for Mountaineering and Hiking Boots

	Inner Liner	*No Inner Liner*
Retail margin	50%	50%
Marketing and Manufacturing Costs		
Sales commissions	10	10
Advertising and sales promotion	5	5
Materials	42	35
Labor, overhead, and transportation	28	35

Cost information for 1997-1998 only. Sales commissions, advertising and sales promotion, materials, labor, overhead, and transportation costs are based on Cima selling prices. After 1997-1998, annual increases of 3.0 percent apply to marketing and manufacturing costs and 4.0 percent apply to Cima selling prices.

each of the teams to provide an estimate for us. I have to catch an early flight to Denver in the morning. It's 6:30; why don't we call it a day.

The meeting was adjourned at 6:35 P.M. Soon thereafter, the marketing teams were formed with a leader assigned to each team.

EXHIBIT 8

Harris Fleming's Memorandum to the Marketing Staff

MEMORANDUM

TO: Marketing Staff
CC: Margaret Simon, President
Anthony Simon, Executive Vice President
FROM: Harris Fleming, Vice President of Marketing
SUBJECT: Marketing Research Projects

Attached to this memorandum are two marketing proposals (see case Exhibits 6 and 7) under consideration by our company. Each proposal is a guide for additional marketing research. You have been selected to serve on a project team to investigate one of the proposals and report your conclusions and recommendations to management. At your earliest convenience, please complete the following.

Project Team 1: Proposal to enter the "Weekender" segment of the hiking boot market.

Review the market segmentation and summary of competition in Exhibits 1 and 2. Identify consumers that would match the profile described in the market segment and conduct field research using a focus group, a survey, or both. You may also visit retailers carrying hiking boots to examine displays and product brochures. Using the information in the proposal, supplemented with your research, prepare the following:

1. A design for the hiking boots (WX 550 and WX 450). Please prepare a sketch that shows the styling for the uppers. We propose to use the same design for each boot, the only difference being the waterproof inner liner on the WX 550 boot. On your design, list the features that your proposed boot would have, considering additions or deletions to those listed in the proposal.
2. Recommend a type of leather (from among those proposed) and two colors for the nylon to be used in the panels of the uppers. We plan to make two styles, one in each color for each boot.

EXHIBIT 8 *(continued)*

3. Recommend a brand name for the product line. Include a rationale for your choice.
4. Verify the acceptability of the suggested retail pricing.
5. Prepare a magazine advertisement for the hiking boot. Provide a rationale for the advertisement in the report.
6. Convert the suggested retail prices *in the proposal* to the Cima selling price and use the sales forecasts and costs (shown in Tables 5 and 6) to prepare an estimate of before-tax profits for the new product line covering a five-year period starting in 1997–98. Assume annual cost increases of 3.0 percent and price increases of 4.0 percent beginning in 1998–99. Discount the future profits to present value using a cost of capital of 15.0 percent. Use 1996–97 as the base year for all discounting.
7. Determine the payback period for the proposal. Assume product development and investment occurs in 1996–97.
8. Provide your conclusions on the attractiveness of these styles to mail order catalog companies and their customers. You may wish to review current mail order catalogs to observe the hiking boots featured. Assuming Cima is successful selling to mail order catalog companies, estimate the percentage of our sales that could be expected from these customers.
9. Prepare a report that summarizes the recommendations of your project team, including the advantages and disadvantages of the proposal. Be prepared to present your product design, branding, pro-forma projections, payback period and recommendations to management shortly after completion of this assignment.
10. Summarize your research and list the sources of information used to prepare the report.

Project Team 2: Proposal to extend the existing lines of boots for mountaineers and hikers.

Review the market segmentation and summary of competition in Exhibits 1 and 2. Identify consumers that match the profile described in the market segment and conduct field research using a focus group, a survey, or both. You may also visit retailers carrying hiking boots to examine displays and product brochures. Using the information in the proposal, supplemented with your research, prepare the following.

1. Designs for the hiking boots (HX 100 and HX 50). Please prepare sketches showing the styling for the uppers. We propose to use a different design for each boot, so you should provide a sketch for each. On each sketch, list the features that your proposed boots would have, considering additions or deletions to those listed in the proposal. No sketch is necessary for the mountaineering boot, MX 350, since we will use the same design as the men's boot and build it on a women's last.
2. Recommend one type of leather (from among those proposed) and two colors for the nylon to be used in the panels of the uppers. We plan to make two styles, one in each color for each boot.
3. Verify the market acceptability of the suggested retail pricing.
4. Prepare a magazine advertisement for your hiking boots. Include a rationale for the advertisement in the report.
5. Using the suggested retail prices *in the proposal*, convert them to the Cima selling prices and use the sales forecasts and costs (shown in Tables 5 and 6) to prepare an estimate of before-tax profits for the new products covering a five-year period starting in 1997–98. Assume annual cost increases of 3.0 percent and price increases of 4.0 percent beginning in 1998–99. Discount the profits to present value using a cost of capital of 15.0 percent. Use 1996–97 as the base year for all discounting.
6. Determine the payback period for the proposal. Assume product development and investment occurs in 1996–97.
7. Provide your conclusions on the attractiveness of these styles to mail order catalog companies and their customers. You may wish to review current mail order catalogs to observe the hiking boots featured. Assuming Cima is successful selling to mail order catalog companies, estimate the percentage of our sales that could be expected from these customers.

EXHIBIT 8 *(continued)*

8. Prepare a report that summarizes the recommendations of your project team, including the advantages and disadvantages of the proposal. Be prepared to present your product design, pro-forma projections, payback period and recommendations to management shortly after completion of this assignment.
9. Summarize your research and list the sources of information used to prepare the report.

CASE

Blair Water Purifiers India

"A pity I couldn't have stayed for Diwali," thought Rahul Chatterjee. "But anyway it was great to be back home in Calcutta." The Diwali holiday and its festivities would begin in early November 1996, some two weeks after Chatterjee had returned to the United States. Chatterjee worked as an international market liaison for Blair Company, Inc. This was his eighth year with Blair Company and easily his favorite. "Your challenge will be in moving us from just dabbling in less developed countries (LDCs) to our thriving in them," his boss had said when Chatterjee was promoted to the job last January. Chatterjee had agreed and was thrilled when asked to visit Bombay and New Delhi in April. His purpose on that trip was to gather background data on the possibility of Blair Company entering the Indian market for home water purification devices. Initial results were encouraging and prompted the second trip.

Chatterjee had used his second trip primarily to study Indian consumers in Calcutta and Bangalore and to gather information on possible competitors. The two cities represented quite different metropolitan areas in terms of location, size, language, and infrastructure—yet both suffered from similar problems in terms of water supplied to their residents. These problems could be found in many LDCs and were favorable to home water purification.

Information gathered on both visits would be used to make a recommendation on market entry and on elements of an entry strategy. Executives at Blair Company would compare Chatterjee's recommendation to those from two other Blair Company liaisons who were focusing their efforts on Argentina, Brazil, and Indonesia.

■ INDIAN MARKET FOR HOME WATER FILTRATION AND PURIFICATION

Like most aspects of India, the market for home water filtration and purification took a good deal of effort to understand. Yet despite expending this effort, Chatterjee realized that much remained either unknown or in conflict. For example, the market seemed clearly a mature one, with four or five established Indian competitors fighting for market share. Or was it? Another view portrayed the market as a fragmented one, with no large competitor having a national presence and perhaps 100 small, regional manufacturers, each competing in just one or two of India's 25 states. Indeed, the market could be in its early growth stages, as reflected by the large number of product designs, materials, and performances. Perhaps with a next generation product and a world-class marketing effort, Blair Company could consolidate the market and stimulate tremendous growth—much like the situation in the Indian market for automobiles.

This case was written by Professor James E. Nelson, University of Colorado at Boulder. He thanks students in the Class of 1996 (Batch 31), Indian Institute of Management, Calcutta, for their invaluable help in collecting all data needed to write this case. He also thanks Professor Roger Kerin, Southern Methodist University, for his helpful comments in writing this case. The case is intended for educational purposes rather than to illustrate either effective or ineffective decision making. Some data as well as the identity of the company are disguised.

Such uncertainty made it difficult to estimate market potential. However, Chatterjee had collected unit sales estimates for a 10-year period for three similar product categories—vacuum cleaners, sewing machines, and color televisions. In addition, a Delhi-based research firm had provided him with estimates of unit sales for Aquaguard, the largest selling water purifier in several Indian states. Chatterjee had used the data in two forecasting models available at Blair Company along with three subjective scenarios—realistic, optimistic, and pessimistic—to arrive at the estimates and forecasts for water purifiers shown in Exhibit 1. "If anything," Chatterjee had explained to his boss, "my forecasts are conservative because they describe only first-time sales, not any replacement sales over the 10-year forecast horizon." He also pointed out that his forecasts applied only to industry sales in larger urban areas, which was the present industry focus.

One thing that seemed certain was that many Indians felt the need for improved water quality. Folklore, newspapers, consumer activists, and government officials regularly reinforced this need by describing the poor quality of Indian water. Quality suffered particularly during the monsoons because of highly polluted water entering treatment plants and because of numerous leaks and unauthorized withdrawals from water systems. Such leaks and withdrawals often polluted clean water after it had left the plants. Politicians running for national, state, and local government offices also reinforced the need for improved water quality through election campaign promises. Governments at these levels set standards for water quality, took measurements at thousands of locations throughout the nation, and advised consumers when water became unsafe.

During periods of poor water quality, many Indian consumers had little choice but to consume the water as they found it. However, better educated, wealthier, and more health-conscious consumers took steps to safeguard their family's health and often continued these steps year around. A good estimate of the number of such

EXHIBIT 1

Industry Sales Estimates and Forecasts for Water Purifiers in India 1990–2005 (Thousands of Units)

	Unit Sales	*Unit Sales Forecast Under . . .*		
Year	*Estimates*	*Realistic Scenario*	*Optimistic Scenario*	*Pessimistic Scenario*
1990	60			
1991	90			
1992	150			
1993	200			
1994	220			
1995	240			
1996		250	250	250
1997		320	370	300
1998		430	540	400
1999		570	800	550
2000		800	1,200	750
2001		1,000	1,500	850
2002		1,300	1,900	900
2003		1,500	2,100	750
2004		1,600	2,100	580
2005		1,500	1,900	420

households, Chatterjee thought, would be around 40 million. These consumers were similar in many respects to consumers in middle- and upper-middle-class households in the United States and the European Union. They valued comfort and product choice. They saw consumption of material goods as a means to a higher quality of life. They liked foreign brands and would pay a higher price for such brands, as long as purchased products outperformed competing Indian products. Chatterjee had identified as his target market these 40 million households plus those in another four million households who had similar values and lifestyles, but as yet took little effort to improve water quality in their homes.

Traditional Method for Home Water Purification

The traditional method of water purification in the target market relied not on any commercially supplied product but instead on boiling. Each day or several times a day, a cook, maid, or family member would boil two to five liters of water for 10 minutes, allow it to cool, and then transfer it to containers for storage (often in a refrigerator). Chatterjee estimated that about 50 percent of the target market used this procedure. Boiling was seen by consumers as inexpensive, effective in terms of eliminating dangerous bacteria, and entrenched in a traditional sense. Many consumers who used this method considered it more effective than any product on the market. However, boiling affected the palatability of water, leaving the purified product somewhat "flat" to the taste. Boiling also was cumbersome, time consuming, and ineffective in removing physical impurities and unpleasant odors. Consequently, about 10 percent of the target market took a second step by filtering their boiled water through "candle filters" before storage. Many consumers who took this action did so despite knowing that water could become recontaminated during handling and storage.

Mechanical Methods for Home Water Filtration and Purification

About 40 percent of the target market used a mechanical device to improve their water quality. Half of this group used candle filters, primarily because of their low price and ease of use. The typical candle filter comprised two containers, one resting on top of the other. The upper container held one or more porous ceramic cylinders (candles) which strained the water as gravity drew it into the lower container. Containers were made of either plastic, porcelain, or stainless steel and typically stored between 15 and 25 liters of filtered water. Purchase costs depended on materials and capacities, ranging from Rs.350 for a small plastic model to Rs.1,100 for a large stainless steel model.[1] Candle filters were slow, producing 15 liters (one candle) to 45 liters (3 candles) of filtered water each 24 hours. To maintain this productivity, candles regularly needed to be removed, cleaned, and boiled for 20 minutes. Most manufacturers recommended that consumers replace candles (Rs.40 each) either once a year or more frequently, depending on sediment levels.

The other half of this group used "water purifiers," devices that were considerably more sophisticated than candle filters. Water purifiers typically employed three water processing stages. The first removed sediments, the second objectionable odors and colors, and the third harmful bacteria and viruses. Engineers at Blair Company were skeptical that most purifiers claiming the latter benefit actually could deliver on their promise. However, all purifiers did a better job here than candle filters.

[1] In 1996, 35 Indian Rupees (Rs.) were equivalent to U.S.$1.00.

Candle filters were totally ineffective in eliminating bacteria and viruses (and might even increase this type of contamination), despite advertising claims to the contrary. Water purifiers generally used stainless steel containers and sold at prices ranging from Rs.2,000 to Rs.7,000, depending on manufacturers, features, and capacities. Common flow rates were one to two liters of purified water per minute. Simple service activities could be performed on water purifiers by consumers as needed. However, more complicated service required units to be taken to a nearby dealer or an in-home visit from a skilled technician.

The remaining 10 percent of the target market owned neither a filter nor a purifier and seldom boiled their water. Many consumers in this group were unaware of water problems and thought their water quality acceptable. However, a few consumers in this group refused to pay for products that they believed were mostly ineffective. Overall, Chatterjee believed that only a few consumers in this group could be induced to change their habits and become customers. The most attractive segments consisted of the 90 percent of households in the target market who either boiled, boiled and filtered, only filtered, or purified their water.

All segments in the target market showed a good deal of similarity in terms of what they thought important in the purchase of a water purifier. According to Chatterjee's research, the most important factor was product performance in terms of sediment removal, bacteria and virus removal, capacity (either in the form of storage or flow rate), safety, and "footprint" space. Purchase price also was an important concern among consumers who boiled, boiled and filtered, or only filtered their water. The next most important factor was ease of intallation and service, with style and appearance rated almost as important. The least important factor was warranty and availability of financing for purchase. Finally, all segments expected a water purifier to be warranted against defective operation for 18 to 24 months and to perform trouble free for five to ten years.

■ FOREIGN INVESTMENT IN INDIA

India appeared attractive to many foreign investors because of government actions begun in the 1980s during the administration of Prime Minister Rajiv Gandhi. The broad label applied to these actions was "liberalization." Liberalization had opened the Indian economy to foreign investors, stemming from recognition that protectionist policies had not worked very well and that western economies and technologies—seen against the collapse of the Soviet Union—did. Liberalization had meant major changes in approval requirements for new commercial projects, investment policies, taxation procedures, and, most importantly, attitudes of government officials. These changes had stayed in place through the two national governments that followed Gandhi's assassination in 1991.

If Blair Company entered the Indian market, it would do so in one of three ways: (1) joint working arrangement, (2) joint venture company, or (3) acquisition. In a joint working arrangement, Blair Company would supply key purifier components to an Indian company which would manufacture and market the assembled product. License fees would be remitted to Blair Company on a per unit basis over the term of the agreement (typically five years, with an option to renew for three more). A joint venture agreement would have Blair Company partnering with an existing Indian company expressly for the purpose of manufacturing and marketing water purifiers. Profits from the joint venture operation would be split between the two parties per the agreement, which usually contained a clause describing buy/sell procedures available to the two parties after a minimum time period. An acquisition entry would have Blair Company purchasing an existing Indian company whose operations then would be expanded to include the water purifier. Profits from the acquisition would belong to Blair Company.

Beyond understanding these basic entry possibilities, Chatterjee acknowledged that he was no expert in legal aspects attending the project. However, two days spent with a Calcutta consulting firm had produced the following information. Blair Company must apply for market entry to the Foreign Investment Promotion Board, Secretariat for Industrial Approvals, Ministry of Industries. The proposal would go before the Board for an assessment of the relevant technology and India's need for the technology. If approved by the Board, the proposal then would go to the Reserve Bank of India, Ministry of Finance, for approvals of any royalties and fees, remittances of dividends and interest (if any), repatriations of profits and invested capital, and repayment of foreign loans. While the process sounded cumbersome and time consuming, the consultant assured Chatterjee that the government usually would complete its deliberations in less than six months and that his consulting firm could "virtually guarantee" final approval.

Trademarks and patents were protected by law in India. Trademarks were protected for seven years and could be renewed on payment of a prescribed fee. Patents lasted for 14 years. On balance, Chatterjee had told his boss that Blair Company would have "no more problem protecting its intellectual property rights in India than in the United States—as long as we stay out of court." Chatterjee went on to explain that litigation in India was expensive and protracted. Litigation problems were compounded by an appeal process that could extend a case for easily a generation. Consequently, many foreign companies preferred arbitration, as India was a party to the Geneva Convention covering Foreign Arbitral Awards.

Foreign companies were taxed on income arising from Indian operations. They also paid taxes on any interest, dividends, and royalties received, and on any capital gains received from a sale of assets. The government offered a wide range of tax concessions to foreign investors, including liberal depreciation allowances and generous deductions. The government offered even more favorable tax treatment if foreign investors would locate in one of India's six Free Trade Zones. Overall, Chatterjee thought that corporate tax rates in India probably were somewhat higher than in the United States. However, so were profits—the average return on assets for all Indian corporations in recent years was almost 18 percent, compared to about 11 percent for United States corporations.

Approval by the Reserve Bank of India was needed for repatriation of ordinary profits. However, approval should be obtained easily if Blair Company could show that repatriated profits were being paid out of export earnings of hard currencies. Chatterjee thought that export earnings would not be difficult to realize, given India's extremely low wage rates and its central location to wealthier South Asian countries. "Profit repatriation was really not much of an issue, anyway," he thought. Three years might pass before profits of any magnitude could be realized; at least five years would pass before substantial profits would be available for repatriation. Approval of repatriation by the Reserve Bank might not be required at this time, given liberalization trends. Finally, if repatriation remained difficult, Blair Company could undertake crosstrading or other actions to unblock profits.

Overall, investment and trade regulations in India in 1996 meant that business could be conducted much easier than ever before. Hundreds of companies from the European Union, Japan, Korea, and the United States were entering India in all sectors of the country's economy. In the home appliance market, Chatterjee could identify 11 such firms—Carrier, Electrolux, General Electric, Goldstar, Matsushita, Singer, Samsung, Sanyo, Sharp, Toshiba, and Whirlpool. Many of these firms had yet to realize substantial profits, but all saw the promise of a huge market developing over the next few years.

■ BLAIR COMPANY, INC.

Blair Company was founded in 1975 by Eugene Blair, after he left his position in research and development at Culligan International Company. Blair Company's first product was a desalinator used by mobile home parks in Florida to remove salts from brackish well water supplied to residents. The product was a huge success, and markets quickly expanded to include nearby municipalities, smaller businesses, hospitals, and bottlers of water for sale to consumers. Geographic markets also expanded, first to other coastal regions near the company's headquarters in Tampa, Florida, and then to desert areas in the southwestern United States. New products were added rapidly as well and, by 1996, the product line included desalinators, particle filters, ozonators, ion exchange resins, and purifiers. Industry experts generally regarded the product line as superior in terms of performance and quality, with prices higher than those of many competitors.

Blair Company sales revenues for 1996 would be almost $400 million, with an expected profit close to $50 million. Annual growth in sales revenues averaged 12 percent for the past five years. Blair Company employed over 4,000 people, with 380 having technical backgrounds and responsibilities.

Export sales of desalinators and related products began at Blair Company in 1980. Units were sold first to resorts in Mexico and Belize and later to water bottlers in Germany. Export sales grew rapidly, and Blair Company found it necessary to organize its International Division in 1985. Sales in the International Division also grew rapidly and would reach almost $140 million in 1996. About $70 million would come from countries in Latin and South America, $30 million from Europe (including shipments to Africa), and $40 million from South Asia and Australia. The International Division had sales offices, small assembly areas, and distribution facilities in Frankfurt, Germany; Tokyo, Japan; and Singapore.

The Frankfurt office had been the impetus in 1990 for development and marketing of Blair Company's first product targeted exclusively to consumer households—a home water filter. Sales engineers at the Frankfurt office began receiving consumer and distributor requests for a home water filter soon after the fall of the Berlin wall in 1989. By late 1991, two models had been designed in the United States and introduced in Germany (particularly to the eastern regions), Poland, Hungary, Romania, the Czech Republic, and Slovakia.

Blair Company executives watched the success of the two water filters with great interest. The market for clean water in LDCs was huge, profitable, and attractive in a socially responsible sense. However, the quality of water in many LDCs was such that a water filter usually would not be satisfactory. Consequently, in late 1994, executives had directed the development of a water purifier that could be added to the product line. Engineers had given the final design in the project the brand name "Delight." For the time being, Chatterjee and the other market analysts had accepted the name, not knowing if it might infringe on any existing brand in India or in the other countries under study.

■ DELIGHT PURIFIER

The Delight purifier used a combination of technologies to remove four types of contaminants found in potable water—sediments, organic and inorganic chemicals, microbials, or cysts, and objectionable tastes and odors. The technologies were effective as long as contaminants in the water were present at "reasonable" levels. Engineers at Blair Company had interpreted "reasonable" as levels described in several

World Health Organization (WHO) reports on potable water and had combined the technologies to purify water to a level beyond WHO standards. Engineers had repeatedly assured Chatterjee that Delight's design in terms of technologies should not be a concern. Ten units operating in the company's testing laboratory showed no signs of failure or performance deterioration after some 5,000 hours of continuous use. "Still," Chatterjee thought, "we will undertake a good bit of field testing in India before entering. The risks of failure are too large to ignore. And, besides, results of our testing would be useful in convincing consumers and retailers to buy."

Chatterjee and the other market analysts still faced major design issues in configuring technologies into physical products. For example, a "point of entry" design would place the product immediately after water entry to the home, treating all water before it flowed to all water outlets. In contrast, a "point of use" design would place the product on a countertop, wall, or at the end of a faucet and treat only water arriving at that location. Based on cost estimates, designs of competing products, and his understanding of Indian consumers, Chatterjee would direct engineers to proceed only with "point of use" designs for the market.

Other technical details were yet to be worked out. For example, Chatterjee had to provide engineers with suggestions for filter flow rates, storage capacities (if any), unit layout and overall dimensions, plus a number of special features. One such feature was the possibility of a small battery to operate the filter for several hours in case of a power failure (a common occurrence in India and many other LDCs). Another might be one or two "bells or whistles" to tell cooks, maids, and family members that the unit indeed was working properly. Yet another might be an "additive" feature, permitting users to add fluoride, vitamins, or even flavorings to their water.

Chatterjee knew that the Indian market would eventually require a number of models. However, at the outset of market entry, he probably could get by with just two—one with a larger capacity for houses and bungalows and the other a smaller capacity model for flats. He thought that model styling and specific appearances should reflect a western, high-technology school of design in order to distinguish the Delight purifier from competitors' products. To that end, he had instructed a graphics artist to develop two ideas that he had used to gauge consumer reactions on his last visit (see Exhibit 2). Consumers liked both models but preferred the countertop design over the wallmount design.

■ COMPETITORS

Upwards of 100 companies competed in the Indian market for home water filters and purifiers. While information on most of these companies was difficult to obtain, Chatterjee and the Indian research agencies were able to develop descriptions of three major competitors and brief profiles of several others.

Eureka Forbes

The most established competitor in the water purifier market was Eureka Forbes, a joint venture company established in 1982 between Electrolux (Sweden) and Forbes Campbell (India). The company marketed a broad line of "modern lifestyle products" including water purifiers, vacuum cleaners, and mixers/grinders. The brand name used for its water purifiers was "Aquaguard," a name so well established that many consumers mistakenly used it to refer to other water purifiers or to the entire product category. Aquaguard, with its 10-year market history, was clearly the market leader and came close to being India's only national brand. However, Eureka Forbes

EXHIBIT 2

Delight Water Purifier Wallmount and Countertop Designs

Wallmount Design	*Countertop Design*

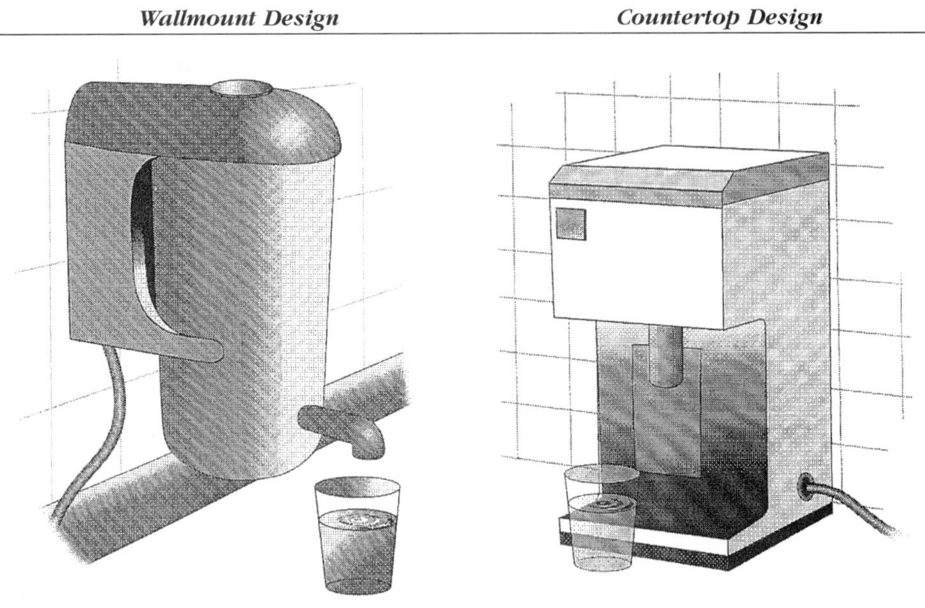

had recently introduced a second brand of water purifier called "PureSip." The PureSip model was similar to Aquaguard except for its third stage process, which used a polyiodide resin instead of ultraviolet rays to kill bacteria and viruses. This meant that water from a PureSip purifier could be stored safely for later usage. Also in contrast to Aquaguard, the PureSip model needed no electricity for its operation.

However, the biggest difference between the two products was how they were sold. Aquaguard was sold exclusively by a 2,500 person salesforce that called directly on households. In contrast, PureSip was sold by independent dealers of smaller home appliances. Unit prices to consumers for Aquaguard and PureSip in 1996 were approximately Rs.5,500 and Rs.2,000, respectively. Chatterjee believed that unit sales of PureSip were much smaller than unit sales for Aquaguard but growing at a much faster rate.

An Aquaguard unit typically was mounted on a kitchen wall, with plumbing required to bring water to the purifier's inlet. A two-meter-long power cord was connected to a 230-volt AC electrical outlet—the Indian standard. If the power supply were to drop to 190 volts or lower, the unit would stop functioning. Other limits of the product included a smallish amount of activated carbon that could eliminate only weak organic odors. It could not remove strong odors or inorganic solutes like nitrates and iron compounds. The unit had no storage capacity and its flow rate of one liter per minute seemed slow to some consumers. Removing water for storage or connecting the unit to a reservoir tank could affect water quality, like a candle filter.

Aquaguard's promotion strategy emphasized personal selling. Each salesman was assigned to a specific neighborhood and was monitored by a group leader who, in turn, was monitored by a supervisor. Each salesman was expected to canvass his neighborhood, select prospective households (e.g., those with annual incomes exceeding Rs.70,000), demonstrate the product, and make an intensive effort to sell the product. Repeated sales calls helped to educate consumers about their water quality and to reassure them that Aquaguard service was readily available. Television commercials and advertisements in magazines and newspapers (see Exhibit 3 on page 686)

EXHIBIT 3

Aquaguard Newspaper Advertisement

DON'T JUST GUARD YOUR FAMILY THIS MONSOON.

AQUAGUARD IT.

The monsoons bring a welcome relief from the long hot summer. But they also bring along some of the most dangerous water-borne diseases. Like cholera, dysentry, gastro-enteritis and jaundice. Which is why you need an Aquaguard Water Purifier, to safeguard your family.

Today, Aquaguard is synonymous with clean, pure and safe drinking water.

Aquaguard is a 3 stage water purification system using the latest Ultra Violet technology, which destroys disease causing bacteria and virus in the water. It also has a unique **Electronic Monitoring System** which stops water flow automatically if the purification level falls below pre-determined standards.

In addition, with Aquaguard you have the Eureka Forbes guarantee of After-Sales-Service at your doorstep.

So install an Aquaguard today. And help your family enjoy the monsoons better.

For a free demonstration at your home call the friendly man from Eureka Forbes or write to us at the addresses given below

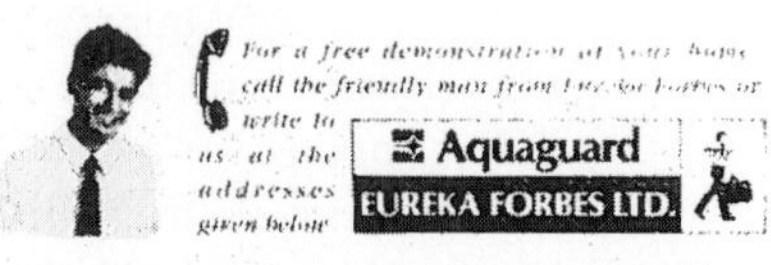

Calcutta: Mani Tower, Block Uttara, 1st Flr., 31/41 Vinoba Bhave Rd., Calcutta - 700 038. Tel: 4786845/5444. * 27 A, Lal Mohan Bhattacharjee Rd., 2nd Flr., Calcutta - 700 014. Tel: 2451548/2325. * 12 D, Chakraberia Rd. (North), Calcutta - 700 020. Tel: 746411/5326. * 177, Raja Dinendra Street, Opp. Desbandhu Park, Shyam Bazar, Calcutta - 700 004. Tel: 5545729/7248. * 21 G, Deodar Street, Calcutta - 700 019. * **Guwahati:** G.N.B.Rd., Silpukhuri, Above Jungle Travels, Near Goswami Service Station, Guwahati - 781 003. Tel: 31574. * **Howrah:** 105/106 A Panchsheel Apt., 1st Flr., 493, B.G.T. Road (South), Howrah - 711 102. Tel: 6606042. * **Siliguri:** 521 Swamiji Sarani, 1st Flr., Hakimpara P.O. Siliguri, Dist. Darjeeling. Tel: 26332.

supported the personal selling efforts. Chatterjee estimated that Eureka Forbes would spend about Rs.120 million on all sales activities in 1996 or roughly 11 percent of its sales revenues. He estimated that about Rs.100 million of the Rs.120 million would be spent in the form of sales commissions. Chatterjee thought the company's total advertising expenditures for the year would be only about Rs.1 million.

Eureka Forbes was a formidable competitor. The salesforce was huge, highly motivated, and well managed. Moreover, Aquaguard was the first product to enter the water purifier market and the name had tremendous brand equity. The product itself was probably the weakest strategic component—but it would take much to convince consumers of this. And, while the salesforce offered a huge competitive advantage, it represented an enormous fixed cost and essentially limited sales efforts to large urban areas. More than 80 percent of India's population lived in rural areas, where water quality was even lower.

Ion Exchange

Ion Exchange was the premier water treatment company in India, specializing in treatments of water, processed liquids, and waste water in industrial markets. The company began operations in 1964 as a wholly owned subsidiary of British Permutit. Permutit divested its holdings in 1985 and Ion Exchange became a wholly owned Indian company. The company presently served customers in a diverse group of industries, including nuclear and thermal power stations, fertilizers, petrochemical refineries, textiles, automobiles, and home water purifiers. Its home water purifiers carried the family brand name, ZERO-B (Zero-Bacteria).

ZERO-B purifiers used a halogenated resin technology as part of a three-stage purification process. The first stage removed suspended impurities via filter pads, the second eliminated bad odors and taste with activated carbon, and the third killed bacteria using trace quantities of polyiodide (iodine). The latter feature was attractive because it helped prevent iodine deficiency diseases and permitted purified water to be stored up to eight hours without fear of recontamination.

The basic purifier product for the home carried the name "Puristore." A Puristore unit typically sat on a kitchen counter near the tap, with no electricity or plumbing hookup needed for its operation. The unit stored 20 liters of purified water. It sold to consumers for Rs.2,000. Each year the user must replace the halogenated resin at a cost of Rs.200.

Chatterjee estimated that ZERO-B captured about 7 percent of the Indian water purifier market. Probably the biggest reason for the small share was a lack of consumer awareness. ZERO-B purifiers had been on the market for less than three years. They were not advertised heavily nor did they enjoy the sales effort intensity of Aquaguard. Distribution, too, was limited. During Chatterjee's visit, he could find only five dealers in Calcutta carrying ZERO-B products and none in Bangalore. Dealers that he contacted were of the opinion that ZERO-B's marketing efforts soon would intensify—two had heard rumors that a door-to-door salesforce was planned and that consumer advertising was about to begin.

Chatterjee had confirmed the latter point with a visit to a Calcutta advertising agency. A modest number of 10-second TV commercials soon would be aired on Zee TV and DD metro channels. The advertisements would focus on educating consumers with the position, "It is not a filter." Instead, ZERO-B is a water purifier and much more effective than a candle filter in preventing health problems. Apart from this advertising effort, the only other form of promotion used was a point of sale brochure that dealers could give to prospective customers (see Exhibit 4 on page 688).

On balance, Chatterjee thought that Ion Exchange could be a major player in the market. The company had over 30 years' experience in the field of water purification and devoted upwards of Rs.10 million each year to corporate research and development. "In fact," he thought, "all Ion Exchange really needs to do is to recognize the market's potential and to make it a priority within the company." However, this might be difficult to do, given the company's prominent emphasis on industrial markets. Chatterjee estimated that ZERO-B products would account for less than two

EXHIBIT 4

ZERO-B Sales Brochure

percent of Ion Exchange's 1996 total sales, estimated at Rs.1,000 million. He thought the total marketing expenditures for ZERO-B would be around Rs.3 million.

Singer

The newest competitor to enter the Indian water purifier market was Singer India Ltd. Originally, Singer India was a subsidiary of The Singer Company, located in the United States, but a minority share (49 percent) was sold to Indian investors in 1982. The change in ownership had led to construction of manufacturing facilities in India for sewing machines in 1983. The facilities were expanded in 1991 to produce a broad line of home appliances. Sales revenues for 1996 for the entire product line—sewing machines, food processors, irons, mixers, toaster, water heaters, ceiling fans, cooking ranges, and color televisions—would be about Rs.900 million.

During Chatterjee's time in Calcutta, he had visited a Singer Company showroom on Park Street. Initially he had hoped that Singer might be a suitable partner to manufacture and distribute the Delight purifier. However, much to his surprise, he was told that Singer now had its own brand on the market, "Aquarius." The product was not yet available in Calcutta but was being sold in Bombay and Delhi.

A marketing research agency in Delhi was able to gather some information on the Singer purifier. The product contained nine stages (!) and sold to consumers for Rs.4,000. It removed sediments, heavy metals, bad tastes, odors, and colors. It also killed bacteria and viruses, fungi, and nematodes. The purifier required water pressure (8 PSI minimum) to operate but needed no electricity. It came in a single countertop model that could be moved from one room to another. Life of the device at a flow rate of 3.8 liters per minute was listed as 40,000 liters—about four to six years of use in the typical Indian household. The product's life could be extended to 70,000 liters at a somewhat slower flow rate. However, at 70,000 liters, the product must be discarded. The agency reported a heavy advertising blitz accompanying the introduction in Delhi—emphasizing TV and newspaper advertising, plus outdoor and transit advertising as support. All 10 Singer showrooms in Delhi offered vivid demonstrations of the product's operation.

Chatterjee had to admit that photos of the Aquarius purifier shown in the Calcutta showroom looked appealing. And a trade article he found had described the product as "state of the art" in comparison to the "primitive" products now on the market. Chatterjee and Blair Company engineers tended to agree—the disinfecting resin used in Aquarius had been developed by the United States government's National Aeronautics and Space Administration (NASA) and was proven to be 100 percent effective against bacteria and viruses. "If only I could have brought a unit back with me," he thought. "We could have some test results and see just how good it is." The trade article also mentioned that Singer hoped to sell 40,000 units over the next two years.

Chatterjee knew that Singer was a well-known and respected brand name in India. Further, Singer's distribution channels were superior to those of any competitor in the market, including those of Eureka Forbes. Most prominent of Singer's three distribution channels were the 210 company-owned showrooms located in major urban areas around the country. Each sold and serviced the entire line of Singer products. Each was very well kept and staffed by knowledgeable personnel. Singer products also were sold throughout India by over 3,000 independent dealers, who received inventory from an estimated 70 Singer-appointed distributors. According to the marketing research agency in Delhi, distributors earned margins of 12 percent of the retail price for Aquarius while dealers earned margins of five percent. Finally, Singer employed over 400 salesmen who sold sewing machines and food processors door-to-door. Like Eureka Forbes, the direct salesforce sold products primarily in large urban markets.

■ OTHER COMPETITORS

Chatterjee was aware of several other water purifiers on the Indian market. The Delta brand from S & S Industries in Madras seemed a carbon copy of Aquaguard, except for a more eye-pleasing, countertop design. According to promotion literature, Delta offered a line of water-related products—purifiers, water softeners, iron removers, desalinators, and ozonators. Another competitor was Alfa Water Purifiers, Bombay. The company offered four purifier models at prices from Rs.4,300 to Rs.6,500, depending on capacity. Symphony's Spectrum brand sold well around Bombay at Rs.4,000 each but removed only suspended sediments, not heavy metals or bacteria. The Sam Group in Coimbatore recently had launched its "Water Doctor" purifier at Rs.5,200. The device used a third stage ozonator to kill bacteria and viruses and came in two attractive countertop models, 6- and 12-liter storage. Batliboi was mentioned by the Delhi research agency as yet another competitor, although Chatterjee knew nothing else about the brand. Taken all together, unit sales of all purifiers at these companies plus ZERO-B and Singer probably would account for around 60,000 units in 1996. The remaining 190,000 units would be Aquaguards and PureSips.

At least 100 Indian companies made and marketed candle filters. The largest of these probably was Bajaj Electrical Division, whose product line also included water heaters, irons, electric light bulbs, toasters, mixers, and grillers. Bajaj's candle filters were sold by a large number of dealers who carried the entire product line. Candle filters produced by other manufacturers were sold mostly through dealers who specialized in small household appliances and general hardware. Probably no single manufacturer of candle filters had more than 5 percent of any regional market in the country. No manufacturer attempted to satisfy a national market. Still, the candle filters market deserved serious consideration—perhaps Delight's entry strategy would attempt to "trade-up" users of candle filters to a better, safer product.

Finally, Chatterjee knew that sales of almost all purifiers in 1996 in India came from large urban areas. No manufacturer targeted rural or smaller urban areas and at best, Chatterjee had calculated, existing manufacturers were reaching only ten to fifteen percent of the entire Indian population. An explosion in sales would come if the right product could be sold outside metropolitan areas.

■ RECOMMENDATIONS

Chatterjee decided that an Indian market entry for Blair Company was subject to three "givens," as he called them. First, he thought that a strategic focus on rural or smaller urban areas would not be wise, at least at the start. The lack of adequate distribution and communication infrastructure in rural India meant that any market entry would begin with larger Indian cities, most likely on the west coast.

Second, market entry would require manufacturing units in India. Because the cost of skilled labor in India was around Rs.20 to Rs.25 per hour (compared to $20 to $25 per hour in the United States), importing complete units was out of the question. However, importing a few key components would be necessary at the start of operation.

Third, Blair Company should find an Indian partner. Chatterjee's visits had produced a number of promising partners: Polar Industries, Calcutta; Milton Plastics, Bombay; Videocon Appliances, Aurangabad; BPL Sanyo Utilities and Appliances, Bangalore; Onida Savak, Delhi; Hawkins India, Bombay; and Voltas, Bombay. All companies manufactured and marketed a line of high-quality household appliances, possessed one or more strong brand names, and had established dealer networks (minimum of 10,000 dealers). All were involved to greater or lesser degrees with international partners. All were medium-sized firms—not too large that a partnership with Blair Company would be one-sided, not too small that they would lack managerial talent and other resources. Finally, all were profitable (15 to 27 percent return on assets in 1995) and looking to grow. However, Chatterjee had no idea if any company would find the Delight purifier and Blair Company attractive or if they might be persuaded to sell part or all of their operations as an acquisition.

Field Testing and Product Recommendations

The most immediate decision Chatterjee faced was whether or not he should recommend a field test. The test would cost about $25,000, placing 20 units in Indian homes in three cities and monitoring their performance for three to six months. The decision to test really was more than it seemed—Chatterjee's boss had explained that a decision to test was really a decision to enter. It made no sense to spend this kind of time and money if India were not an attractive opportunity. The testing period also would give Blair Company representatives time to identify a suitable Indian company as either a licensee, joint venture partner, or acquisition.

Fundamental to market entry was product design. Engineers at Blair Company had taken the position that purification technologies planned for Delight could be "packaged in almost any fashion as long as we have electricity." Electricity was needed to operate the product's ozonator as well as to indicate to users that the unit was functioning properly (or improperly, as the case might be). Beyond this requirement, anything was possible.

Chatterjee thought that a modular approach would be best. The basic module would be a countertop unit much like that shown in Exhibit 2. The module would outperform anything now on the market in terms of flow rate, palatability, durability, and reliability, and would store two liters of purified water. Two additional modules would remove iron, calcium, and other metallic contaminants that were peculiar to particular regions. For example, Calcutta and much of the surrounding area suffered from iron contamination, which no filter or purifier now on the Indian market could remove to a satisfactory level. Water supplies in other areas in the country were known to contain objectionable concentrations of calcium, salt, arsenic, lead, or sulfur. Most Indian consumers would need neither of the additional modules, some would need one or the other, but very few would need both.

Market Entry and Marketing Planning Recommendations

Assuming that Chatterjee recommended proceeding with the field test, he would need to make a recommendation concerning mode of market entry. In addition, his recommendation should include an outline of a marketing plan.

Licensee Considerations If market entry were in the form of a joint working arrangement with a licensee, Blair Company financial investment would be minimal. Chatterjee thought that Blair Company might risk as little as \$30,000 in capital for production facilities and equipment, plus another \$5,000 for office facilities and equipment. These investments would be completely offset by the licensee's payment to Blair Company for technology transfer and personnel training. Annual fixed costs to Blair Company should not exceed \$40,000 at the outset and would decrease to \$15,000 as soon as an Indian national could be hired, trained, and left in charge. Duties of this individual would be to work with Blair Company personnel in the United States and with management at the licensee to see that units were produced per Blair Company's specifications. Apart from this activity, Blair Company would have no control over the licensee's operations. Chatterjee expected that the licensee would pay royalties to Blair Company of about Rs.280 for each unit sold in the domestic market and Rs.450 for each unit that was exported. The average royalty probably would be around Rs.300.

Joint Venture/Acquisition Considerations If entry were in the form of either a joint venture or an acquisition, financial investment and annual fixed costs would be much higher and depend greatly on the scope of operations. Chatterjee had roughed out some estimates for a joint venture entry, based on three levels of scope (see Exhibit 5 on page 692). His estimates reflected what he thought were reasonable assumptions for all needed investments plus annual fixed expenses for sales activities, general administrative overhead, research and development, insurance, and depreciation. His estimates allowed for the Delight purifier to be sold either through dealers or through a direct, door-to-door salesforce. Chatterjee thought that estimates of annual fixed expenses for market entry via acquisition would be identical to those for a joint venture. However, estimates for the investment (purchase) might be considerably higher, the same, or lower. It depended on what was purchased.

Chatterjee's estimates of Delight's unit contribution margins reflected a number of assumptions—expected economies of scale, experience curve effects, costs of Indian labor and raw materials, and competitors' pricing strategies. However, the most

EXHIBIT 5

Investments and Fixed Costs for a Joint Venture Market Entry

	Operational Scope		
	Two Regions	*Four Regions*	*National Market*
1998 Market potential (units)	55,000	110,000	430,000
Initial investment (Rs.000)	4,000	8,000	30,000
Annual fixed overhead expenses (Rs.000)			
Using dealer channels	4,000	7,000	40,000
Using direct salesforce	7,200	14,000	88,000

important assumption was Delight's pricing strategy. If a skimming strategy were used and the product sold through a dealer channel, the basic module would be priced to dealers at Rs.5,500 and to consumers at Rs.5,900. "This would give us about a Rs.650 unit contribution, once we got production flowing smoothly," he thought. In contrast, if a penetration strategy were used and the product sold through a dealer channel, the basic module would be priced to dealers at Rs.4,100, to consumers at Rs.4,400, and yield a unit contribution of Rs.300. For simplicity's sake, Chatterjee assumed that the two additional modules would be priced to dealers at Rs.800, to consumers at Rs.1,000, and would yield a unit contribution of Rs.100. Finally, he assumed that all products sold to dealers would go directly from Blair Company to the dealers (no distributors would be used).

If a direct salesforce were employed instead of dealers, Chatterjee thought that prices charged to consumers would not change from those listed above. However, sales commissions would have to be paid in addition to the fixed costs necessary to maintain and manage the salesforce. Under a skimming price strategy, the sales commission would be Rs.550 per unit and the unit contribution would be Rs.500. Under a penetration price strategy, the sales commission would be Rs.400 per unit and the unit contribution would be Rs.200. These financial estimates, he would explain in his report, would apply to 1998 or 1999, the expected first year of operation.

Skimming versus penetration was more than just a pricing strategy. Product design for the skimming strategy would be noticeably superior, with higher performance and quality, a longer warranty period, more features, and a more attractive appearance than the design for the penetration strategy. Positioning, too, most likely would be different. Chatterjee recognized several positioning possibilities: performance and taste, value for the money/low price, safety, health, convenience, attractive styling, avoiding diseases and health-related bills, and superior American technology. The only position he considered "taken" in the market was that occupied by Aquaguard—protect family health and service at your doorstep. While other competitors had claimed certain positions for their products, none had devoted financial resources of a degree that Delight could not dislodge them. Chatterjee believed that considerable advertising and promotion expenditures would be necessary to communicate Delight's positioning. He would need estimates of these expenditures in his recommendation.

"If we go ahead with Delight, we'll have to move quickly," thought Chatterjee. "The window of opportunity is open but if Singer's product is as good as they claim, we'll be in for a fight. Still, Aquarius seems vulnerable on the water pressure requirement and on price. We'll need a product category 'killer' to win."

APPENDIX

Preparing a Written Case Analysis

Chapter 3 outlined an approach to marketing decision making and case analysis. The purpose of this appendix is to provide a more detailed description of what is involved in a thorough written case analysis through the use of an example. The following case—Republic National Bank of Dallas: NOW Accounts—describes an actual problem encountered by bank executives. The case is accompanied by a student analysis in the format described in Chapter 3. The student analysis shows how to organize a written case and the nature and scope of the analysis, which includes both qualitative and quantitative analyses. You should read and analyze the case before examining the student analysis.

CASE

Republic National Bank of Dallas

NOW Accounts

■ INTRODUCTION

In early 1977, Ruth Krusen, marketing officer for Republic National Bank of Dallas (RNB), was asked to assess the impact on Republic Bank of offering NOW (negotiable order of withdrawal) accounts if they became legal nationwide. Specifically, she was asked to:

The cooperation of Republic National Bank of Dallas in the preparation of this case is gratefully acknowledged. This case was prepared by Professor Roger A. Kerin, of the Edwin L. Cox School of Business, Southern Methodist University, as a basis for class discussion and is not designed to illustrate effective or ineffective handling of an administrative situation. Certain data have been disguised.

1. Determine the impact on profits that Republic National Bank could anticipate from NOW accounts
2. Recommend a NOW account marketing strategy

NOW accounts, which are effectively interest-bearing checking accounts, have been in use since 1972 in New England. In early 1977, however, a bill was introduced into Congress that would allow commercial banks and thrift institutions in all 50 states to provide this service.[1] Despite some opposition in Congress, observers were of the opinion that legislation enabling NOW accounts would be passed by the first quarter of 1978 and would become effective January 1979.

■ BANKING IN TEXAS

Texas is a "unit banking" state. This means that individual banks cannot operate branch banks. The regulation that limits a bank to a single location was specified in the state constitution of 1876. In 1971, however, amendments to the Bank Holding Act allowed individual banks to acquire smaller institutions if the identity of the acquired bank was maintained. Since 1971, large banks in Texas have formed holding companies to improve their lending capability in order to better serve large commercial accounts. By 1977, 33 bank holding companies were operating in Texas. Holding companies owned 250 of the state's 1,360 banks and held about 55 percent of the state's total bank deposits in 1977.

Three of the largest bank holding companies in Texas are based in Dallas. Each operates its largest bank in downtown Dallas. First International Bancshares, which operates First National Bank, is the largest bank holding company in Texas. Republic of Texas Corporation operates the Republic National Bank of Dallas and is the second-largest holding company. Mercantile Texas Corporation operates Mercantile National Bank and is the fifth-largest bank holding company in terms of total assets.

Banking activity in Texas generally corresponds to pockets of urban and commercial growth. Accordingly, banking activity is concentrated in the Dallas–Fort Worth and Houston metropolitan areas. The San Antonio metropolitan area has shown a dramatic increase in banking activity due in part to population growth and increased economic growth.

■ COMPETITIVE SITUATION IN DALLAS

The Dallas banking market consists of 57 banks in the city of Dallas and an additional 43 banks in Dallas County. At the end of 1976, the 57 banks in the city of Dallas recorded total deposits of $13.27 billion. The 43 banks in Dallas County recorded deposits of about $1.25 billion.

Three large downtown banks dominate the Dallas banking market. At the end of 1976, Republic National Bank, First National Bank, and the Mercantile National Bank accounted for approximately 78 percent of total bank deposits in the city of Dallas and 71 percent of Dallas County bank deposits. Republic National Bank was the leader with approximately $4.6 billion in deposits, followed closely by First National Bank with $4.4 billion. Mercantile National Bank recorded total deposits of about

[1] Thrift institutions include mutual savings banks, cooperative banks, credit unions, and savings and loan associations. Thrift institutions differ from commercial banks in that only banks have the authority to accept demand deposits or checking accounts or offer commercial loans.

$1.3 billion at the end of 1976. These three banks are located within walking distance of one another, as well as of some 12 other banks.

Competitive activities of Dallas banks have historically focused on retail (consumer) or wholesale (business) bank account development. Banks located in suburban areas typically emphasized the retail business, whereas downtown banks emphasized the wholesale business. Nevertheless, the Dallas competitive environment in recent years has been characterized by aggressive bank marketing efforts on both fronts. According to one observer of the Dallas banking scene:

> The competitive marketing furor is fierce, and it's not just the catchy advertising themes. . . . There's a scramble going on to repackage consumer services, put forth new services, cross-sell services, and woo corporate customers. There's Saturday banking, extended hours banking, 24-hour tellers, foreign currency sales, cash machines, no-charge checking package deals, automatic payroll deposits, pension fund management services, computer billing services, specially arranged travel tours, traveler's checks to spend on travel tours, equipment leasing, credit card loans, loan syndications, lock boxes, and on and on. First National Bank in Dallas alone lists more than 400 different bank "products" in its inventory of services.[2]

Krusen confirmed the observation that the Dallas banking market was competitive. She noted that RNB continues to be competitive in banking services, but "the question of how aggressive we should be has not been resolved at least as regards retail account marketing." RNB has at least as many bank services for customers as competitors do, if not more services than are offered by the vast majority of commercial banks in Dallas.

In addition to commercial banks, savings and loan associations (S&Ls) also compete for passbook savings accounts among Dallas County residents. At the end of 1976, deposits of the 22 Dallas County-based savings and loan associations were $2.85 billion. Dallas Federal Savings was the largest savings and loan association with about $909.6 million in deposits, or about 32 percent of total deposits. Texas Federal Savings and First Texas Savings combined accounted for approximately $992 million in deposits, or 35 percent of total deposits. Dallas-based savings and loan associations operated approximately 150 offices in Dallas County. Savings and loan associations based outside Dallas County also operated about 50 offices in the county.

Savings and loan associations have aggressively sought deposits in recent years. Dallas-based associations have historically outpaced the national average for savings and loan deposit volume growth. Savings associations have emphasized two competitive advantages in their passbook savings marketing programs. First, they could pay $5^1/_4$ percent on passbook savings, whereas commercial banks were limited by law to 5 percent on passbook savings. Second, they could develop branch operations with a common name, whereas commercial banks were limited to a single location in Texas.

Savings and loan associations have placed greater emphasis on consumer, or installment, loans in recent years. Texas is unique among states in that it allows savings associations to provide installment loans, and some associations have used this opportunity to attract deposit volume. According to an industry observer, "S&Ls have historically attracted older customers. Installment loans are a useful service to bring in younger customers, introduce them to S&Ls, and get them to open a passbook savings account."

Credit unions also represent a competitive force in the Dallas market. By the end of 1976, 218 credit unions were located in the city of Dallas and its immediate

[2] Dave Clark, "A Big Pitch for Bucks," *Dallas-Fort Worth Business Quarterly* 1, no. 2.

environs. These credit unions operated 232 offices. Combined, credit unions held over $666 million in assets and served almost one-half million members.

Credit unions compete effectively in the Dallas market in three ways. First, they offer consumer, or installment, loans to their members at competitive interest rates. They hold a significant share of the automobile loans in the Dallas market. Second, credit unions hold substantial funds in member savings accounts. Third, credit unions provide share drafts to their members. A *share draft* is a withdrawal document that permits credit union members to make payments from interest-bearing savings accounts. These drafts resemble checks but are actually drafts drawn on a credit union and payable through a bank.

REPUBLIC NATIONAL BANK

Republic National Bank was founded in 1920. At that time, the bank was called Guaranty Bank and Trust, and it held a state banking charter. After several name changes, the present name was adopted in 1937, and RNB obtained a national bank charter. Today, RNB is the largest member of the Republic of Texas Corporation bank holding-company system. By the end of 1977, RNB would be ranked twenty-first in the United States in total assets and deposits and would be the largest bank in Texas and the South in terms of total assets, deposits, loans, and equity capital. Also by the end of 1977, RNB would be ranked 150th among the 500 largest banks in the non-Communist world, according to *American Banker* magazine. RNB had total assets exceeding $6 billion and a net income of approximately $36.3 million by that time.

Retail Account Marketing

Although figures are not available for competing banks, RNB is considered to have one of the largest, if not the largest, retail account bases in the Dallas area. According

EXHIBIT 1

Estimated Distribution of Personal Checking Account Balances in Early 1977

Account Size	*Percentage of Accounts*	*Percentage of Total Checking Account Deposits*
Under $200	32%	3%
$200–$499	23	3
$500–$999	14	4
$1,000–$4,999	18	13
$5,000–$9,999	7	11
$10,000–$24,999	3	13
$25,000–$100,000	2	20
Over $100,000	1	33
	100%	100%

Number of personal checking accounts: 45,000

Personal checking account deposits: $150 million

Note: Figures reported in this exhibit reflect approximations drawn from *1977 District Bank Averages: Functional Cost Analysis* (Dallas: Federal Reserve Bank of Dallas, 1977).

to Krusen, this occurred as a result of RNB's historic position of "taking chances on the little guy and community service." It was estimated that about 55 percent of RNB's retail checking accounts in 1977 were under $500. Exhibit 1 shows the distribution of accounts by account size.

This philosophy is communicated in RNB advertising. Beginning in the late 1960s with its "Silver Star Service" campaign and continuing with the "Star Treatment" advertising campaign, RNB communicated to present and potential customers that they were special and that RNB had a number of special services to provide them. In early 1977 the "Republic National Bank *Is* Dallas" campaign was launched, with Orson Welles narrating television and radio advertising spots and the Dallas Symphony playing the theme music. This campaign was designed to reflect the mutual traditions of RNB and Dallas residents as progressive and growth-oriented, as well as emphasize the interdependence of banking leadership and service with the prosperity and quality of Dallas life. Marketing research has shown that RNB has had the highest "top-of-mind awareness" of any bank in the Dallas area since 1975.

Retail Account Services

RNB retail account marketing efforts have resulted in a variety of traditional as well as innovative bank services for its customers. For example, RNB provides its Teller 24® Service, which is an automatic bank teller/cash machine. This service operates 24 hours a day at 26 locations around the city of Dallas and in six other Texas cities. Another innovation, the *Starpak* Account, is a complete package of banking services provided to customers for a fixed monthly fee of $3. Exhibit 2 on page 698 gives a description of this service. RNB personal checking is highly competitive in the Dallas market, with no service charge for accounts that maintain a minimum monthly balance of $400. A $1 charge accrues to accounts with a minimum monthly balance of $300, a $2 charge with a minimum monthly balance of $200, and a $3 charge with no minimum balance requirement.

Retail Checking Account Revenue and Cost Estimates

In the course of preparing her report, Krusen contacted the RNB Controllers Division to obtain revenue and cost data on retail checking accounts. The Controllers Division report, based largely on Federal Reserve statistics, indicated that approximately 85 percent of retail checking account deposits were investable. In other words, about 15 percent of checking account deposits must be held in reserve. Ninety-six percent of savings account balances were investable.

The Controllers Division also indicated that RNB would realize an average yield on loans and securities of about 7.5 percent in 1977. Krusen noted that this figure was the lowest experienced by RNB in recent years. In 1974 RNB had realized an average yield of 10.59 percent. Other figures obtained directly from Federal Reserve statistical averages for commercial banks with total deposits of over $200 million were as follows:

Service and handling charge revenue per account per month:	$1.56
Account cost per month (including checks, deposits, and other assignable overhead):	$5.24

EXHIBIT 2

Components of Republic National Bank's Starpak Account

1. *Unlimited Checking*—There's no minimum balance requirement, no per check charge, and no limit on the number of checks you write when you have a Starpak personal checking account.
2. *Free Personal Checks*—They're prenumbered and personalized with your name, address, and phone number, and you can order as many as you need any time you need them.
3. *Reduced Loan Rates*—With this feature alone, many people make Starpak pay for itself. At the end of the loan period, we'll refund 10 percent of the total interest you paid on installment loans of $1,000 or more, when the loan has been repaid as agreed. Of course, your loan is subject to normal credit approval.
4. *No Bank Charge for Traveler's Checks*—Or for Money Orders or Cashier's Checks when you show us your Starpak Account Card.
5. *Free Safe Deposit Box*—We'll give you the $5 size free. Or take $5 off the rent for a larger size.
6. *Combined Monthly Statement*—Your monthly statement can include status reports on any or all of the accounts you and your spouse have at Republic. You select the accounts you want the Combined Statement to cover. We can include your checking, savings, personal certificates of deposit, and even personal loans. Yes, you'll also receive separate regular statements on each of your Republic accounts you include in the Combined Statement.
7. *Numerical Check Listing*—Your monthly statement will report each check in the order written. That makes it much easier to reconcile your statement each month.
8. *Automatic Overdraft Protection*—This optional service gives you additional peace of mind and the opportunity to take advantage of an exceptional bargain. It works this way. If the checks you write exceed your balance, we'll cover the overdrafts up to the limit of your Republic Master Charge or VISA Credit. Finance charges for deferred payment will apply at the normal rate. Repayment will be through your monthly Master Charge or VISA account payment.
9. *Teller 24® Service*—You can get cash from your Starpak Checking Account, or your Republic Master Charge or VISA Card, at any of 26 Teller 24 machines located in Dallas and six other Texas cities, and at 12,000 banks nationwide. With Teller 24 your money is available 24 hours a day, 7 days a week.
10. *Automatic Loan Repayment*—If you have an installment loan at Republic, we will, at your request, withdraw your monthly loan payment from your Starpak Checking Account. It's a good way to make sure you can take advantage of the 10 percent interest refund.
11. *Automatic Savings Account Deposits*—If you've never been able to save before, this plan solves the problem. Just tell us how much and on what day of the month. On the date you specify, we'll automatically transfer the amount you select from your checking to your savings account. Then, to help your savings grow even faster, we'll pay the highest interest rates allowable.
12. *Starpak Account Card*—It identifies you as a preferred customer of Republic National Bank, entitled to the privileges and special savings available with your Starpak Account.
13. *No Separate Charges*—All these Starpak services are available for the flat monthly fee of $3. There's no separate charge.

Plus these other services available to all Republic National Bank customers—We pay postage both ways when you bank by mail. We'll validate your in-bank parking stub when you bank. And you'll have a personal banker assigned to your accounts so that you can call for advice or assistance with any banking need.

Source: Bank brochure.

NOW ACCOUNTS

NOW accounts came into being as the result of the attempt of a Massachusetts mutual savings bank to circumvent the prohibition against thrift institutions' offering checking accounts. After a two-year regulatory and legal battle, Consumer Savings Bank of Worcester, Massachusetts, won its case and in June 1972 began to offer a savings account on which checklike instruments called negotiable orders of withdrawal could be written. Other mutuals in Massachusetts and New Hampshire soon followed suit.

Although regulatory authorities persist in regarding the NOW account as a savings account on which checks can be written, from a consumer point of view (and from an operational point of view) it is a checking account that pays interest. As consumers gradually became educated about NOWs, commercial banks began to lose customers to this attractive type of account, with which they were unable to compete. In response, federal and state laws were passed permitting commercial banks as well as mutuals and S&Ls in Massachusetts and New Hampshire to offer NOW accounts starting in January 1974. As of March 1976, financial institutions in the other New England states were granted the same powers. In two of the states (Connecticut and Maine), state-chartered thrifts had been empowered to offer checking accounts a few months earlier.

In New England, NOW accounts may be offered to individuals and to nonprofit organizations (except that in Connecticut, thrifts can offer NOWs only to individuals).[3] A uniform rate ceiling of 5 percent applies to all institutions. Excerpts from a report prepared by the RNB Marketing Division on the development of NOW accounts in New England are presented in the appendix at the end of this case.

NOW ACCOUNT MARKETING STRATEGY

The task facing Krusen was difficult for a number of reasons. First, the only NOW account information available pertained to the New England experience. Although this information would be useful in gauging the rate of adoption of NOW accounts, it was not entirely clear how the Dallas-area banks and thrift institutions would react. Second, several contingency plans would have to be charted. If NOW accounts were not deemed appropriate for RNB by top management, then Krusen would have to recommend a strategy to maintain the RNB customer base. This strategy would depend on whether a "free" NOW account program became popular in the Dallas area or a more conservative approach was adopted by competitors. If the NOW account was adopted by RNB, she realized, the NOW account package (separate account or part of an existing bank service) and the price (service charges, if any) would have to be defined. The package and price would be, in part, determined by the competitive environment that developed and the cost of NOW accounts.

Timing was a third consideration. Should RNB be a leader and set the competitive tenor in the market or take a "wait and see" stance? Finally, if RNB decided to adopt the NOW account, then a question of communications would arise. For example, should RNB quietly inform present customers of NOW account availability or actively communicate availability to the Dallas market as a whole via an advertising program?

---

[3] At the time of this case and for analysis purposes, only retail (personal and nonprofit) checking accounts were affected by NOW accounts in the Dallas area.

APPENDIX: NOW ACCOUNTS IN NEW ENGLAND, A REPORT PREPARED BY THE MARKETING DIVISION OF REPUBLIC NATIONAL BANK OF DALLAS

The objectives of this investigation of NOW accounts in New England were

1. To learn the speed and magnitude of NOW account impact as a basis for estimating the impact on RNB
2. To identify and evaluate various marketing strategies and their possible relevance to our own market

Penetration of NOWs

Reaction of New England financial institutions given the power to offer NOWs is shown in Exhibit A.1. It indicates the percentages of thrifts and commercial banks that were offering NOWs by August 1976 and the market shares of commercial banks. By August 1976 mutual savings banks in Massachusetts and New Hampshire had been able to offer NOWs for 50 months, commercial banks for 30 months. In the other states, all institutions had been able to offer them for only 6 months.

Despite the resistance of commercial banks in Massachusetts and New Hampshire to offering NOWs, Exhibit A.1 shows that a substantial majority are now providing them. In the other New England states, commercial banks have moved more quickly to adopt NOW accounts. This is one of the reasons that they have a larger share of NOW accounts and balances than do commercial banks in Massachusetts and New Hampshire. Nevertheless, even in the latter states, commercial banks have captured more of the total NOW balances than have thrifts.

One conclusion supported by the data is that the competitiveness of financial institutions is directly related to the degree to which the state's population is concentrated in large urban markets.

The additional data on Massachusetts and New Hampshire shown in Exhibit A.2 indicate the substantial impact of NOWs in the personal payment account market. Exhibit A.2 shows that after four years, 72 percent of checking account balances in New Hampshire have been converted to NOWs and 44 percent have been converted in Massachusetts. Thrifts have captured 27 percent of this market in New Hampshire and 21 percent in Massachusetts.

EXHIBIT A.1

NOW Account Adoption in New England as of August 1976

	Percentage of Institutions Offering		*Commercial Banks' Share of NOW Market*	
	Thrifts	*Commercial Banks*	*Percentage of Accounts*	*Percentage of Balances*
Massachusetts	94[a]	72	32	52
New Hampshire	81[a]	64	43	62
Connecticut	69	53	35	74
Maine	32	40	68	81
Vermont	23	29	89	93
Rhode Island[b]	25	75	83	85

[a] Mutual savings banks only; in each state two-thirds of the savings and loans also offer NOWs.

[b] Rhode Island has a unique situation of affiliated mutual savings banks and commercial banks. Figures in exhibit refer only to unaffiliated thrifts and commercial banks. NOWs are offered by 66 percent of the affiliated group.

EXHIBIT A.2

Personal Payment Accounts, August 1976

	Personal Payment Balances	
	Percentage in NOWs	*Percentage in Thrifts*
New Hampshire	72%	27%
Massachusetts	44	21

Note: Personal payment accounts consist of all checking balances plus 80 percent of NOW balances. The 20 percent of NOW balances estimated to have come from savings accounts have been deducted.

Marketing Strategies

Massachusetts and New Hampshire As simple as the concept of an interest-bearing checking account appears to be, NOW account introduction in New England produced an initial confusion of positioning, pricing, and marketing strategies.

Positioning. For a variety of reasons, thrifts initially positioned NOWs as savings accounts with a special convenience feature in getting access to funds. Consumers who opened them did not regard them as checking accounts and there was relatively low account activity. Adding to the confusion, when banks began to offer NOWs, some of them were very negative in their presentations. They told customers, in effect, "We have NOW accounts, but you don't really want to spend your savings, do you?"

In time, thrifts and then banks became more daring in presenting NOWs as accounts that were identical in function to checking accounts but paid interest. NOWs are by now recognized as a substitute for checking accounts, are opened instead of checking accounts (or an existing checking account is closed when it is realized that it is no longer needed), and have virtually the same level of activity as checking accounts.

Pricing. Pricing was initially fairly conservative. In New Hampshire, NOWs were usually offered at a lower rate of interest than a savings account, while in Massachusetts per-item charges were prevalent. Then a price war began and increasing numbers of institutions offered free NOWs—that is, maximum rate of interest, no service or item charges, and no minimum balance requirements.

The proportion of institutions offering free NOWs increased until mid-1975, but since then the trend has been reversed, largely because late entrants into the field have offered less generous terms. It has also been true that some institutions that previously offered free NOWs have imposed charges or minimum balance requirements.

The free NOW resulted from a variety of causes and motives:

1. At the time of introduction, money market rates were so high that the cost of NOW funds might still allow a margin of profit.
2. Thrifts were inexperienced in the costs involved in servicing checking accounts.
3. Some thrifts were determined to establish a good market share early, regardless of short-run lack of profitability.
4. In the major market areas, there was a free checking environment.

Price and service package. Pricing structures on NOWs in New England are as varied as checking account charges have historically been. The possibility of competing through the interest rate paid is the only new element. When NOW accounts are not free, some variant of the following occurs:

1. *Interest rates*. Initially, some institutions paid less than the maximum rate on savings accounts. However, under competitive pressure, rates rose to the 5 percent ceiling in all major markets. However, some institutions do not pay on a day-of-deposit to day-of-withdrawal basis. While very few now pay only on collected balances, several large banks are contemplating going in that direction. A few banks pay only on minimum balances.
2. *Balance requirements*. Balances above which the NOW account is "free" range from $200 to $1,000. In most cases, this is the minimum balance, although one large bank, Shawmut, has an average balance requirement.
   What happens when the balance that goes below the minimum varies?
   In some cases, no interest is paid; in others, a transaction or service fee is imposed; and in some cases, both. In some isolated markets, fees are imposed on all accounts, but in competitive major markets, NOWs become free at some balance level.
3. *Transaction charges*. Charges per check range from 10 to 25 cents. Usually, the charge is levied on all checks if the balance is below the required level. In some cases, a certain number of checks are free (5 to 15 per month), and in some other cases the number of free checks is related to balances (for example, 5 checks per $100 of average balance).
4. *Service charge*. Some banks charge flat fees rather than per-transaction charges. Fees generally are $1 or $2.

Other New England States By the time NOW accounts were authorized in the other New England states, both thrifts and commercials had had the opportunity to assess the cost and competitive impact of NOWs in the two original states, and money market conditions had changed. These facts are reflected in the response of financial institutions in offering NOWs. Commercial banks have moved more rapidly than they did in Massachusetts and New Hampshire. At the same time, both thrifts and commercial banks have been more conservative in pricing.

Connecticut. Thrifts have moved aggressively to offer both checking accounts and NOWs. Although free checking prevails in major Connecticut markets and although about one-third of the thrifts offer free NOWs, large Connecticut banks have offered NOWs on conservative terms (high minimum balances with transaction charges for lower-balance accounts). The effect of this strategy is reflected in the high average balances of commercial bank NOWs—over $4,000.

Rhode Island. The financial market is highly concentrated in a very few institutions. Six months after NOWs became legal, six of the nine commercial banks affiliated with thrift institutions, six of the eight unaffiliated banks, and one of the four unaffiliated thrifts were offering NOWs. None of them offered free NOWs. As in the checking account market in this state, relatively high minimum balances are required. It should be noted that because of the thrift-commercial bank affiliations, a majority of thrifts have in effect been able to offer checking accounts to their customers.

Maine. Thrifts have concentrated harder on selling checking accounts than on offering NOWs. Neither thrifts nor commercial banks have moved very fast to offer NOWs. Few offer them free.

Vermont. This state shows the slowest gain in institutions offering NOWs. None offers them free.

STUDENT ANALYSIS

Republic National Bank of Dallas

NOW Accounts

STRATEGIC ISSUES AND PROBLEMS

Ruth Krusen, marketing officer for RNB, has been given responsibility for (1) determining the profit impact RNB could anticipate from NOW accounts and (2) recommending a contingency plan for a NOW account marketing strategy. Her task involves a number of important factors. She must assess the likelihood that the Dallas competitive environment will be liberal or conservative in its marketing of NOW accounts. An important consideration is RNB's role in affecting this environment, given its dominant position in the Dallas market and its posture regarding aggressiveness in retail account marketing. Ultimately, she must make a "go-no go" decision. A "go" decision requires a recommendation on the form of the service, its target market, its price reflected in service charges, and promotion. A "no go" decision must take into consideration RNB's competitive position without NOW accounts and measures to minimize their impact. The problem facing RNB is how to retain its dominant competitive position given an environmental threat (NOW accounts) while at the same time preserving profitability and its customer base.

INSIGHTS FROM THE NEW ENGLAND EXPERIENCE

The NOW account experience, based on the data in the report of the marketing division, reveals the following:

1. The faster commercial banks move to adopt NOW accounts, the larger their share of NOW accounts and NOW account balances.
2. Cannibalization of checking accounts occurs when NOW accounts are available; 72 percent of checking account balances in New Hampshire have been converted to NOW accounts, and 44 percent of checking accounts in Massachusetts have been converted to NOWs. These figures developed over 50 months (four years) after the NOW introduction (see Exhibit A.2).
3. Exhibit 1 in the case provides some evidence that NOW account balances are high. This could mean that those individuals with high checking account balances are more likely to switch to NOWs. Alternatively, the Connecticut experience would indicate that minimum balance requirements increase NOW account balances. Data for Massachusetts and New Hampshire—both of which experienced "free NOWs"—would tend to support the point that individuals with high account balances convert to NOWs.
4. NOW account usage activity approaches checking account activity; hence checking account costs are merely transferred to managing NOW accounts.

5. Competitive activity, reflected in the NOW package provided, reveals that "free NOWs" were initially provided. Financial institutions subsequently offered less generous terms, however.
6. NOW account packages differ greatly with respect to minimum balances, service charges, and positioning against checking and savings accounts.

Results from the New England experience suggest that three scenarios are possible in the Dallas market.

Environment	*Environment Description*
No NOW adoption:	Financial institutions refrain from adoption.
Liberal NOW adoption:	NOWs are adopted with no minimum balance, service charges, 5 percent interest, an active promotion/communication program.
Conservative NOW adoption:	NOWs are adopted with some form of minimum service charges, less than 5 percent interest, little promotion or communication.

Numerous factors will affect the likelihood of each environment's developing in the Dallas market.

Factors in favor of a no-NOW environment:

1. The New England experience suggests that a no-win possibility exists for all financial institutions. For example, banks will have to pay interest on previously interest-free funds, and S&Ls and credit unions will incur costs not previously encountered.
2. Money market rates are quite low at present, suggesting little spread to make an adequate profit margin.

Factors in favor of a NOW environment:

1. The New England experience suggests that where NOWs are legalized, they are adopted in some form, by someone.
2. If the Dallas market is competitive *and* various financial institutions are vying for deposits, then NOWs offer a means to attract deposits. Moreover, the New England experience suggests that "getting in first" is crucial. "Followership" is not rewarded.
3. S&Ls are poised to take some advantage of NOWs in that their interest rate paid on deposits will fall from $5^1/4$ percent to 5 percent, assuming a 5 percent ceiling level.

Factors in favor of a liberal NOW environment:

1. Thrifts might view NOWs as a way of gaining deposits quickly.
2. S&Ls will benefit from NOWs even if 5 percent interest is offered on NOW accounts, since they are currently paying $5^1/4$ percent on savings.
3. Share drafts provided by credit unions have characteristics similar to those of NOWs; NOW accounts would seem like a logical extension.

Factors in favor of a conservative NOW environment:

1. This appears to be the trend in New England states.
2. Dallas banks do not generally offer free checking.
3. Money market rates are low.

It would seem that a potential determinant of how the NOW environment evolves will be the decision of RNB, given its dominance in the Dallas banking market. RNB's dominant position would seem to affect the environment *only* if RNB acts immediately with a well thought out NOW account program. NOWs are probably inevitable—that is, the no-NOW environment seems unlikely. The question, then, is whether a liberal or a conservative NOW environment will develop. The environment could be influenced by RNB.

■ REPUBLIC NATIONAL BANK

RNB dominates the Dallas financial market. Its assets alone ($6 billion) are almost ten times *total* assets of all credit unions ($666 million). RNB's deposits ($4.6 billion) exceed the total for *all* S&Ls ($2.85 billion). RNB has the largest deposit base of all Dallas banks *and* the largest retail account deposit base in Dallas.

Nevertheless, RNB management apparently has not resolved how aggressive the bank should be in retail account marketing efforts. The aggressiveness issue would seem to be related to the bank's emphasis on the wholesale rather than the retail business.

Exhibit 1 in the case indicates that about 55 percent of RNB's checking accounts are under $500. However, 96 percent of total checking account balances are accounted for by accounts of $500 and up, and 53 percent of total deposits are accounted for by accounts of over $25,000. The average account size is $3,333 ($150 million in deposits divided by 45,000 accounts). A profitability analysis of checking account sizes reveals that RNB loses money on accounts that are less than $500 on an annual basis (see Exhibit 1 in this analysis). This profitability analysis indicates that accounts below $500 produce a *loss* of $519,210 annually:

Accounts under $200:	14,400 accounts × ($24.24)	=	($349,056)
Accounts $200–$499:	10,350 accounts × ($16.44)	=	($170,154)
Loss		=	($519,210)

EXHIBIT 1

RNB Retail Account Profit Analysis (Based on Exhibit 1 in the Case)

Account Size	*Average Interest Revenue per Account*[a]	+	*Average Service/ Handling Revenue per Account*[b]	=	*Average Revenue per Account*	–	*Account Cost*[b]	=	*Profit/ (Loss)*
Less than $200	$19.92		$18.72		$38.64		$62.88		$(24.24)
$200–$499	27.72		18.72		46.44		62.88		(16.44)
$500–$999	60.71		18.72		79.43		62.88		16.55
$1,000–$4,999	153.47		18.72		172.19		62.88		109.31
$5,000–$9,999	333.93		18.72		352.65		62.88		289.77
$10,000–$24,999	920.83		18.72		939.55		62.88		876.67
$25,000–100,000	2,125.00		18.72		2,143.72		62.88		2,080.84
Greater than $100,000	7,083.00		18.72		7,101.72		62.88		7,038.84

[a] Computed as follows: $\frac{\text{Account size deposit volume}}{\text{Number of accounts in category}} \times 85\% \times 0.075.$

For an account size of $200, using Exhibit 1 data: $\frac{\$4.5 \text{ million}}{14{,}400} \times 0.85 \times 0.075 = \$19.92$

[b] Annualized average account revenue and cost given in the case where service/handling charge revenue per account per month = $1.56; account cost per month = $5.24.

More important, this analysis provides important data on the pricing of NOW accounts and the form of the service, as will be discussed later.

■ PLAN OF ACTION

There are two primary alternatives open to RNB: to offer NOWs or not to offer NOWs. If NOWs are considered, then the form, price, and promotion must be determined. The alternatives are:

1. Do not offer NOW accounts.
2. Offer NOW accounts with no conditions and promote them heavily or modestly.
3. Offer NOW accounts with conditions and promote them heavily or modestly.

The advantages and disadvantages of the options available to RNB can be outlined as follows:

1. Not offering NOW accounts:

   Advantages

   - RNB is dominant and has the resources to wait and see what will happen.
   - The impact on revenue of offering NOWs would be too severe. Assuming that *all accounts* are cannibalized by NOWs and the interest yield drops from $7^1/_2$ percent to $2^1/_2$ percent because of 5 percent interest on NOWs, the interest revenue lost will be about $6.0 million.

Checking Deposits		*Percent Investable*		*Investable Deposits*
$150 million	×	85%	=	$127.5 million
				Interest Revenue
$127.5 million	×	0.075	=	$9,562,500
$144 million	×	0.025	=	−3,600,000
Interest revenue lost				$5,962,500

   Note that NOW accounts are viewed as savings accounts, and 96 percent of deposits are investable.

   Disadvantages

   - RNB will lose an opportunity to be an innovator or the "first to market," which has been shown in New England to be advantageous.
   - Erosion of accounts may occur, as individuals switch to institutions offering NOW accounts. This factor is particularly important if *large* accounts switch, and they are most likely to do so, since they stand to benefit most from NOW accounts.

2. Offering NOW accounts with no conditions:

   Advantages

   - Nonconditional NOWs will have a dramatic impact on the Dallas banking market. Banks offering them will most likely attract deposits and accounts in great numbers, particularly since they are a better deal than checking accounts with minimum balances or service charges, *plus* they give interest!
   - Nonconditional NOW accounts will set the competitive tenor of the market; retail banks not offering them may be unable to compete.

- By offering nonconditional NOWs, RNB will keep current accounts from being attracted to competitors (preemptive cannibalism).

Disadvantages

- This strategy could be very expensive. As noted earlier, in addition to the account costs, a loss of interest of $6 million is possible.
- This strategy will cannibalize checking accounts almost totally.

3. Offering NOW accounts with conditions:

Advantages

- A minimum-balance condition would allow RNB to accept only those accounts on which it can make money.
- A service/handling charge condition would also result in greater account selectivity.
- A break-even analysis shows how RNB can determine a minimum balance given current service charge and account costs per year. The break-even point is the point at which total revenues (interest plus handling/service charges) minus total costs (account cost per month) equals zero. Since RNB will net 2.5 percent in account interest revenue, has an $18.72 handling and service revenue per account per year ($1.56 × 12 months), and has an annual account cost of $62.88 ($5.24 × 12 months), solving for the minimum account balance reveals the following:

$$\text{Profit} = \begin{matrix}\text{acct. interest}\\ \text{revenue}\end{matrix} + \begin{matrix}\text{handling/}\\ \text{service charge}\end{matrix} - \begin{matrix}\text{acct.}\\ \text{cost}\end{matrix}$$

$$0 = 0.025X \quad + \$18.72 \quad - \$62.88$$

$$\$44.16 = 0.025X$$

$$\$1{,}766.40 = X$$

Thus, RNB breaks even at an account balance of $1,766.40, given existing handling/service revenue per account and account maintenance costs. This minimum balance level would be a condition that from 80 percent to 90 percent of RNB's accounts could meet (see Exhibit 1 in the case).

Disadvantages

- This strategy leaves RNB open to being undercut by competitors if conditions are too stringent.
- Overly complex conditions and the likelihood of customers' being unexpectedly hit with service charges could hurt goodwill, particularly among larger balance account holders.

■ RECOMMENDED NOW ACCOUNT MARKETING STRATEGY

The previous analysis indicates that RNB can shape the NOW account environment in Dallas. The following NOW account marketing strategy will ensure that this will happen.

Goals and Objectives

1. RNB should pioneer NOW accounts in the Dallas market to set the competitive tone and create a "rational" NOW environment.

2. RNB should focus on achieving 85% customer retention.
3. RNB should break even on NOW accounts.

Target Market

The target market for NOW accounts should be current customers with large account balances. Specifically, current customers with a minimum account size of $1,800.00 is the primary target market. This market represents almost all of RNB's current accounts. There is little to gain from attracting new customers for NOW accounts.

Marketing Mix

Product Strategy NOW accounts will be included with an existing service bundle—the Starpak Account. It is expected that NOW accounts will cannibalize existing accounts. RNB's focus on current customers is a form of preemptive cannibalism necessary to retain existing customers.

Price Strategy NOW accounts should carry a service charge. The recommended charge is $18.75 per account. This service charge, given the account cost, account interest revenue, and an account interest revenue, will allow RNB to break even on estimated annual minimum account balance of $1,766.40.

Distribution and Sales NOW accounts will be provided at all locations by the New Account staff. Training for the New Account RNB staff should begin immediately. Documentation for the Starpak Account should be immediately modified to incorporate NOW accounts.

Advertising and Promotion A modest advertising and promotion (A&P) program is recommended for NOW accounts. The A&P program should focus on current customers via a direct mail program and specifically inserts in monthly statements. Starpak print and TV advertising should incorporate reference to NOW accounts.

GLOSSARY OF SELECTED MARKETING TERMS AND CONCEPTS

Advertising opportunity. Conditions suggesting that a product or service would benefit from advertising. They are (1) favorable primary demand for the product or service category, (2) the product or service to be advertised can be significantly differentiated from its competitors, (3) the product or service has hidden qualities or benefits that can be portrayed effectively through advertising, and (4) there are strong emotional buying motives for the product or service.

Brand equity. The added value a brand name bestows on a product or service beyond the functional benefits provided.

Brand extension strategy. The practice of using a current brand name to enter a completely different product class.

Break-even analysis. The unit or dollar sales volume at which an organization neither makes a profit nor incurs a loss. The formula for determining the number of units required to break even is: unit break-even = total dollar fixed costs ÷ (unit selling price – unit variable costs).

Bundling. The practice of marketing two or more product or service items in a single "package" with one price.

Business mission. Describes the organization's purpose with reference to its customers, products or services, markets, philosophy, and technology.

Cannibalism. The process whereby the sales of a new product or service come at the expense of existing products (services) already marketed by the firm.

Chain ratio method. A technique for estimating market sales potential that involves multiplying a base number by several adjusting factors that are believed to influence market sales potential.

Channel captain. A member of a marketing channel with the power to influence the behavior of other channel members.

Channel conflict. A situation that arises when one channel member believes another channel member is engaged in behavior that is preventing it from achieving its goals.

Co-branding. The pairing of two brand names of two manufacturers on a single product.

Contribution. The difference between total sales revenue and total variable costs, or, on a per-unit basis, the difference between unit selling price and unit variable cost. Contribution can be expressed in percentage terms (contribution margin) or dollar terms (contribution per unit).

Cost of goods sold. Material, labor, and factory overhead applied directly to production.

Cross-elasticity of demand. The percentage responsiveness of the quantity demanded of one product or service to a percentage price change in another product or service.

Discounted cash flows. Future cash flows expressed in terms of their present value.

Disintermediation. The elimination of traditional intermediaries and direct distribution, often through electronic marketing channels.

Distinctive competency. An organization's unique strengths or qualities, including skills, technologies, or resources that distinguish it from other organizations. These competencies are imperfectly imitable by competitors and provide superior customer value.

Diversification. A product-market strategy that involves the development or acquisition of offerings new to the organization and the introduction of those offerings to publics (markets) not previously served by the organization.

Dual distribution. The practice of distributing products or services through two or more different marketing channels that may or may not compete for similar buyers.

Effective demand. The situation when prospective buyers have both the willingness and ability to purchase an organization's offerings.

Electronic commerce. Any activity that uses some form of electronic communication in the inventory, exchange, advertisement, distribution, and payment of goods and services.

Electronic marketing channels. Marketing channels that employ some form of electronic communication, including the Internet to make products and services available for consumption or use by consumers and industrial users.

Exclusive distribution. A distribution strategy whereby a producer sells its products or services in only one retail outlet in a specific geographical area.

Fighting brand strategy. The practice of adding a new brand whose sole purpose is to confront competitive brands in a product class being served by an organization.

Fixed cost. Expenses that do not fluctuate with output volume within a relevant time period (usually defined as a budget year), but become progressively smaller per unit of output as volume increases. Fixed costs divide into programmed costs, which result from attempts to generate sales volume, and committed costs, which are those required to maintain the organization.

Flanker brand strategy. The practice of adding new brands on the high or low end of a product line based on a price-quality continuum.

Full-cost price strategies. Those that consider both variable and fixed cost (total cost) in the pricing of a product or service.

Gross margin (or gross profit). The difference between total sales revenue and total cost of goods sold, or, on a per-unit basis, the difference between unit selling price and unit cost of goods sold. Gross margin can be expressed in dollar or percentage terms.

Harvesting. The practice of reducing the investment in a business entity (division, product) to cut costs or improve cash flow.

Integrated marketing communications. The practice of blending different elements of the communication mix in mutually reinforcing ways.

Intensive distribution. A distribution strategy whereby a producer sells its products or services in as many retail outlets as possible in a geographical area.

Life cycle. The plot of sales of a single product or brand or service or a class of products or services over time.

Market. Prospective buyers (individuals or organizations) who are willing and able to purchase the existing or potential offering (product or service) of an organization.

Market-development strategy. A product-market strategy whereby an organization introduces its offerings to markets other than those it is currently serving. In global marketing, this strategy can be implemented through exportation, licensing, joint ventures, or direct investment.

Market evolution. Changes in primary demand for a product class and changes in technology.

Market-penetration strategy. A product-market strategy whereby an organization seeks to gain greater dominance in a market in which it already has an offering. This strategy often means capturing a larger share of an existing market.

Market redefinition. Changes in the offering demanded by buyers or promoted by competitors.

Market sales potential. The maximum level of sales that might be available to all organizations serving a defined market in a specific time period given (1) the marketing-mix activities and effort of all organizations, and (2) a set of environmental conditions.

Market segmentation. The breaking down or building up of potential buyers into groups on the basis of some sort of homogeneous characteristic(s) (e.g., age, income, geography) relating to purchase or consumption behavior.

Market share. Sales of a firm, product, or brand divided by the sales of the served "market."

Market targeting (or target marketing). The specification of the particular market segment(s) the organization wishes to pursue. Differentiated marketing means that an organization simultaneously pursues several different market segments, usually with a different strategy for each. Concentrated marketing means that only a single market segment is pursued.

Marketing audit. A comprehensive, systematic, independent, and periodic examination of a company's or business unit's marketing environment, objectives, strategies, and activities with a view of determining problem areas and opportunities and recommending a plan of action to improve the company's marketing performance.

Marketing channel. Individuals and firms involved in the process of making a product or service available for consumption or use by consumers and industrial users.

Marketing-cost analysis. The practice of assigning or allocating costs to a specified marketing activity or entity in a manner that accurately displays the financial contribution of activities or entities to the organization.

Marketing mix. Those activities controllable by the organization that include the product, service, or idea offered, the manner in which the offering will be communicated to customers, the method for distributing or delivering the offering, and the price to be charged for the offering.

Mass customization. Tailoring products and services to the tastes and preferences of individual buyers in high volumes and at a relatively low cost.

New-brand strategy. The development of a new brand and often a new offering for a product class that has not been previously served by the organization.

Net profit margin (before taxes). The remainder after cost of goods sold, other variable costs, and fixed costs have been subtracted from sales revenue, or simply, total revenue minus total cost. Net profit margin can be expressed in dollar or percentage terms.

Offering. The sum total of benefits or satisfaction provided to target markets by an organization. An offering consists of a tangible product or service plus related services, warranties or guarantees, packaging, etc.

Offering mix or portfolio. The totality of an organization's offerings (products and services).

Operating leverage. The extent to which fixed costs and variable costs are used in the production and marketing of products and services.

Operations control. The practice of assessing how well an organization performs marketing activities as it seeks to achieve planned outcomes.

Opportunity analysis. The process of identifying opportunities, matching the opportunity to the organization, and evaluating the opportunity.

Opportunity cost. Alternative uses of resources that are given up when pursuing one alternative rather than another. Sometimes referred to as the benefits not obtained from not choosing an alternative.

Payback period. The number of years required for an organization to recapture its initial investment in an offering.

Penetration pricing strategy. Setting a relatively low initial price for a new product or service.

Positioning. The act of designing an organization's offering and image so that it occupies a distinct and valued place in the target customer's mind relative to competitive offerings. A product or service can be positioned by (1) attribute or benefit, (2) use or application, (3) product or service user, (4) product or service class, (5) competitors, and (6) price and quality.

Price elasticity of demand. The percentage change in quantity demanded relative to a percentage change in price for a product or service.

Product-development strategy. A product-market strategy whereby an organization creates new offerings for existing markets through product innovation, product augmentation, or product line extensions.

Pro forma income statement. An income statement containing projected revenues, budgeted (variable and fixed) expenses, and estimated net profit for an organization, product, or service during a specific planning period, usually a year.

Product-line pricing. The setting of prices for all items in a product line. It involves determining (1) the lowest-priced product price, (2) the highest-priced product, and (3) price differentials for all other products in the line.

Pull communication strategy. The practice of creating initial interest for an offering among potential buyers, who in turn demand the offering from intermediaries, ultimately "pulling" the offering through the channel. The principal emphasis is on consumer advertising and consumer promotions.

Push communication strategy. The practice of "pushing" an offering through a marketing channel in a sequential fashion, with each channel representing a distinct target market. The principal emphasis is on personal selling and trade promotions directed toward wholesalers and retailers.

Regional marketing. The practice of using different marketing mixes to accommodate unique preferences and competitive conditions in different geographical areas.

Relevant cost. Expenditures that (1) are expected to occur in the future as a result of some marketing action and (2) differ among marketing alternatives being considered.

Sales forecast. The level of sales a single organization expects to achieve based on a chosen marketing strategy and an assumed competitive environment.

Scrambled merchandising. The practice of wholesalers and retailers carrying a wider assortment of merchandise than they did in the past.

Selective distribution. A distribution strategy whereby a producer sells its products or services in a few retail outlets in a specific geographical area.

Situation analysis. The appraisal of operations to determine the reasons for the gap between what was or is expected and what has happened or will happen.

Skimming pricing strategy. Setting a relatively high initial price for a new product or service.

Strategic change. Environmental change that will affect the long-run well-being of the organization.

Strategic control. The practice of assessing the direction of the organization as evidenced by its implicit or explicit goals, objectives, strategies, and capacity to perform in the context of changing environments and competitive actions.

Strategic marketing management. The analytical process of (1) defining the organization's business, mission, and goals; (2) identifying and framing organizational opportunities; (3) formulating product-market strategies; (4) budgeting marketing, financial, and production resources; and (5) developing reformulation and recovery strategies.

Sub-branding. The practice of combining a family brand with a new brand when introducing new product or service offerings.

Success requirements. The basic tasks that must be performed by an organization in a market or industry to compete successfully. These are sometimes "key success factors," or simply KSFs.

Sunk cost. Past expenditures for a given activity that are typically irrelevant in whole or in part to future decisions. The "sunk cost fallacy" is an attempt to recoup spent dollars by spending still more dollars in the future.

SWOT analysis. A formal framework for identifying and framing organizational growth opportunities. SWOT is an acronym for an organization's *S*trengths and *W*eaknesses and external *O*pportunities and *T*hreats.

Trade margin. The difference between unit sales price and unit cost at each level of a marketing channel. Trade margin is usually expressed in percentage terms.

Trading down. The process of reducing the number of features or quality of an offering and lowering the purchase price.

Trading up. The practice of improving an offering by adding new features and higher quality materials or augmenting products with services and raising the purchase price.

Value. The ratio of perceived benefits to price for a product or service.

Variable cost. Expenses that are uniform per unit of output within a relevant time period (usually defined as a budget year); total variable costs fluctuate in direct proportion to the output volume of units produced. Variable cost includes cost of goods sold and other variable costs such as sales commissions.

Variable-cost price strategies. Those that consider only direct (variable) costs associated with the offering in pricing a product or service.

Working capital. The dollar value of an organization's current assets (such as cash, accounts receivable, prepaid expenses, inventory) *minus* the dollar value of current liabilities (such as short-term accounts payable for goods and services, income taxes).

Subject Index

Company Index

Brand Index